June 22–27, 2013
New York, New York, USA

Association for Computing Machinery

Advancing Computing as a Science & Profession

PODS'13

Proceedings of the 32nd Symposium on

Principles of Database Systems

Sponsored by:

ACM SIGACT, ACM SIGART, ACM SIGMOD

Supported by:

SAP, Goldman Sachs, Microsoft, ORACLE, Facebook, Google, IBM Research, Linked in, VMware, EMC^2, CISCO, kx, NEC, AT&T, Yahoo!, TURN, Morgan & Claypool Publishers, ELSEVIER, Morgan Kaufmann, and Cambridge University Press

Association for
Computing Machinery

Advancing Computing as a Science & Profession

The Association for Computing Machinery
2 Penn Plaza, Suite 701
New York, New York 10121-0701

ISBN: 978-1-4503-2066-5

Additional copies may be ordered prepaid from:

ACM Order Department
PO Box 30777
New York, NY 10087-0777, USA

Phone: 1-800-342-6626 (USA and Canada)
+1-212-626-0500 (Global)
Fax: +1-212-944-1318
E-mail: acmhelp@acm.org
Hours of Operation: 8:30 am – 4:30 pm ET

Printed in the USA

PODS'13 General Chair's Welcome Message

It is our great pleasure to welcome you to the *2013 ACM Symposium on Principles of Database Systems – PODS'13*, held in New York City, USA, on June 23–26, 2013, in conjunction with the 2013 ACM SIGMOD International Conference on Management of Data.

This year's symposium continues its tradition of being the premier international conference on the theoretical aspects of data management. Since the first edition of the symposium in 1982, the PODS papers are distinguished by a rigorous approach to widely diverse problems in data management, often bringing to bear techniques from a variety of different areas, including computational logic, finite model theory, computational complexity, algorithm design and analysis, programming languages, and artificial intelligence. The interested reader is referred to the PODS web pages at: http://www.sigmod.org/the-pods-pages for information on the history of this conference series.

The PODS symposia study data management challenges in a variety of application contexts, including more recently streaming data, graph data, information retrieval, ontology and semantic web, and data-driven processes and systems. This year the program includes a Symposium on Theory Challenges in Big Data, organized by Christopher Ré and Dan Suciu, which will help to inform the PODS community about a highly relevant emerging topic area.

Creating PODS'13 was a team effort. We are particularly grateful to the Program Chair, Wenfei Fan, who did an outstanding job in selecting and coordinating the program committee members, and to the whole program committee, who worked very hard in reviewing papers and providing feedback for authors. We are also grateful to the SIGMOD 2013 General Chairs, Kenneth Ross and Divesh Srivastava, for their excellent coordination of the overall SIGMOD/PODS 2013 conference, and their collaboration and support in all the issues requiring coordination between SIGMOD and PODS. Finally, we thank Floris Geerts, the PODS'13 Proceedings and Publicity Chair; Wim Martens, for maintaining the PODS web pages; and all our sponsors, in particular the ACM Special Interest Groups on Theoretical Computer Science, on Management of Data, and on Artificial Intelligence, for their invaluable support.

We wish you a profitable and enjoyable stay in New York, and we hope that you will find the PODS'13 program informative, exciting, and thought provoking, in the best tradition of the PODS Symposium.

Richard Hull
PODS'13 General Chair

PODS'13 Program Chair's Welcome Message

This volume contains the proceedings of the thirty-second ACM SIGMOD-SIGACT-SIGART Symposium on Principles of Database Systems (PODS 2013), held in New York City, USA, on June 23–26, 2013, in conjunction with the 2013 ACM SIGMOD International Conference on Management of Data.

The proceedings include papers based on the keynote address by Diego Calvanese (co-authored with Giuseppe De Giacomo and Marco Montali), and two invited tutorials by Piotr Indyk and Pablo Barceló, and 24 contributed papers that were selected by the Program Committee from 97 submissions. Submissions were unusually strong this year and the conference was very competitive. The program committee worked hard to select the best from the submissions, but many papers with high scores and good reviews could not make it into the final program. Most of the 24 accepted papers are extended abstracts.

While the submissions have been read by program committee members, they have not been formally refereed. It is anticipated that many of these papers will appear in more polished and detailed form in scientific journals.

The program committee selected the paper *Verification of Database-Driven Systems via Amalgamation* by Mikołaj Bojańczyk, Luc Segoufin and Szymon Toruńczyk for the PODS 2013 Best Paper Award. In addition, the *ACM PODS Alberto O. Mendelzon Test-of-Time Award 2013* appears in the proceedings. This year, the award is given to *Revealing Information while Preserving Privacy* by Irit Dinur and Kobbi Nissim. The paper originally appeared in the proceedings of PODS 2003. Warmest congratulations to the authors of these papers!

I thank all authors who submitted papers to the symposium. I would also like to thank all members of the core Program Committee, the External Review Committee, and many external referees for the enormous amount of work they have done. The program committee did not meet in person, but carried out extensive discussions during the electronic PC meeting. I thank Andrei Voronkov for his EasyChair system, which made it easy to manage and coordinate the discussion.

I thank Maurizio Lenzerini and Richard Hull, the former and current PODS General Chair, respectively, for their unfailing support. The PODS Executive committee helped to select the Program Committee and External Review Committee, and is instrumental in advising on issues of policy during the conference. I am particularly grateful to Michael Benedikt, Leonid Libkin, Maurizio Lenzerini and Thomas Schwentick, previous PODS Program Chairs, for their advice. Special thanks also go to Floris Geerts, the Proceedings and Publicity Chairs of PODS 2013.

I thank many colleagues involved in the organization of the conference for fruitful collaboration, in particular Kenneth Ross and Divesh Srivastava (SIGMOD General Chairs), Hila Becker (SIGMOD Web/Information Chair), and Lisa Tolles (Sheridan Communications). Finally, I thank the SIGMOD/PODS sponsors for their support.

Wenfei Fan
PODS'13 Program Chair

Table of Contents

Session 4: Indexing/Query Answering

Session Chair: Benny Kimelfeld *(IBM Almaden Research Center, USA)*

Session 5: Query processing/Verification

Session Chair: Daniel Deutch *(Ben-Gurion University, Israel)*,

Session 6 &Tutorial 2

Session Chair: Wenfei Fan *(University of Edinburgh, UK)*

Session 7: RDF and Ontologies

Session Chair: Diego Calvanese *(Free University of Bozen-Bolzano, Italy)*

Session 8: Graph and XML Querying

Session Chair: Wim Martens *(University of Bayreuth, Germany)*

Session 9: Query Languages

Session Chair: Marcelo Arenas *(Pontifical Catholic University of Chile, Chile)*

PODS 2013 Symposium Organization

General Chair: Richard Hull *(IBM T.J. Watson Research Center, USA)*

Program Chair: Wenfei Fan *(University of Edinburgh, UK)*

Proceedings & Publicity Chair: Floris Geerts *(University of Antwerp, Belgium)*

Program Committee:
Marcelo Arenas *(Pontifical Catholic University of Chile, Chile)*
Leo Bertossi *(Carleton University, Canada)*
Diego Calvanese *(Free University of Bozen-Bolzano, Italy)*
Daniel Deutch *(Ben-Gurion University, Israel)*
Alin Deutsch *(University of California San Diego, USA)*
Wenfei Fan *(University of Edinburgh, UK)*
Floris Geerts *(University of Antwerp, Belgium)*
Benny Kimelfeld *(IBM Almaden Research Center, USA)*
Maurizio Lenzerini *(Sapienza University of Rome, Italy)*
Wim Martens *(University of Bayreuth, Germany)*
Andrew McGregor *(University of Massachusetts, USA)*
Frank McSherry *(Microsoft Research, USA)*
Frank Neven *(Hasselt University, Belgium)*
Jorge Perez *(University of Chile, Chile)*
Reinhard Pichler *(Vienna University of Technology, Austria)*
Francesco Scarcello *(University of Calabria, Italy)*
Nicole Schweikardt *(Goethe University Frankfurt, Germany)*
Thomas Schwentick *(TU Dortmund University, Germany)*
Peter Widmayer *(ETH Zurich, Switzerland)*
Ryan Williams *(Stanford University, USA)*
David Woodruff *(IBM Almaden Research Center, USA)*

External Review Committee:

Cloud Computing and Next-generation Distributed Query Processing
Pierre Fraigniaud *(Université Paris Diderot, France)*
Jignesh M. Patel *(University of Wisconsin, USA)*
Sergei Vassilvitskii *(Google Research, USA)*
Milan Vojnovic *(Microsoft Research, Cambridge, UK)*

Privacy
Michael Hay *(Cornell University, USA)*
Nina Mishra *(Microsoft Research, USA)*
Kobbi Nissim *(Ben-Gurion University, Israel)*
Aaron Roth *(University of Pennsylvania, USA)*
Adam Smith *(Penn State University, USA)*
Mukund Sundararajan *(Google Research, USA)*

External Review Committee (continued):

Mining and Learning of Data Models and Queries
Pauli Miettinen *(Max-Planck Institute for Informatics, Germany)*
Evimaria Terzi *(Boston University, USA)*
Panayiotis Tsaparas *(University of Ioannina, Greece)*

Recommendation Systems and Social Networks
Gautam Das *(University of Texas at Arlington, USA)*
Joseph A. Konstan *(University of Minnesota, USA)*

Semantic, Linked, Networked, and Crowdsourced Data
Pascal Hitzler *(Wright State University, USA)*
David R. Karger *(MIT, USA)*
Boris Motik *(University of Oxford, UK)*
Axel Polleres *(Siemens, Austria)*
Neoklis (Alkis) Polyzotis *(University of California Santa Cruz, USA)*

Additional reviewers:

Peyman Afshani
Kook Jin Ahn
Tom Ameloot
Alexandr Andoni
Fabrizio Angiulli
Alessandro Artale
Babak Bagheri-Hariri
Andrey Balmin
Jeremy Barbay
Pablo Barceló
Ilaria Bartolini
Djamal Belazzougui
Michael Benedikt
Vincenzo Bonifaci
Joachim Bremer
Joshua Brody
Andrea Calì
Michael Crouch
Wojciech Czerwiński
Adnan Darwiche
Giuseppe De Giacomo
Michel De Rougemont
Camil Demetrescu
Arnaud Durand
Dora Erdos
Fabio Fassetti
Ingo Feinerer
Alan Fekete
Diego Figueira
Sergio Flesca
Gaelle Fontaine
Dominik D. Freydenberger
Filippo Furfaro
Behzad Golshan
Georg Gottlob
Gianluigi Greco
Sergio Greco
Moritz Hardt
Herman Haverkort
Tomas Hruz
Daniel Kane
Ahmet Kara
Phokion Kolaitis
Christian Konrad
Eyal Kushilevitz
Martin Lackner
Theodoros Lappas
Domenico Lembo
Chao Li
Katja Losemann
Bertram Ludaescher
James F. Lynch
Frédéric Magniez
Tomas Masopust
Matus Mihalak
Marco Montali

Additional reviewers (continued):

S Muthukrishnan
Rolf Niedermeier
Matthias Niewerth
Robert Nowak
Dan Olteanu
Rasmus Pagh
Luigi Palopoli
Paolo Penna
Jeff Phillips
Rami Puzis
Ananth Raghunathan
Matthias Renz
Juan L. Reutter
Cristian Riveros
Miguel Romero
Riccardo Rosati
Sudeepa Roy
Stefan Rümmele
Domenico Saccà
Vadim Savenkov
Georg Schnitger
Frédéric Servais
Mantas Simkus
Cristina Sirangelo
Matthew Skala
Sebastian Skritek
Daniel Stubbs
Dan Suciu
Tony Tan
Yufei Tao
Evgenia Ternovska
Laura Toma
Szymon Toruńczyk
Charalampos Tsourakakis
Denis Turdakov
Jonathan Ullman
Jan Van den Bussche
Dirk Van Gucht
Virginia Vassilevska Williams
Cong Wang
Fang Wei-Kleiner
Jef Wijsen
Bryan T. Wilkinson
Peter Wood
Ke Yi
Thomas Zeume

Alberto O. Mendelzon Test-of-Time Award Committee:

Michael Benedikt *(University of Oxford, UK)*
Tova Milo *(Tel Aviv University, Israel)*
Dirk Van Gucht (Chair) *(Indiana University, USA)*

PODS 2013 Sponsors and Supporters

ACM Sponsors:

SIGACT — SIGART

ACM SIGMOD

Diamond Supporter:

SAP

Platinum Supporters:

Goldman Sachs — Microsoft

ORACLE

Gold Supporters:

facebook — Google

IBM Research — LinkedIn

vmware — EMC²

Silver Supporters:

CISCO — kx

NEC — at&t

YAHOO! — TURN

Platinum Publisher:

MORGAN & CLAYPOOL PUBLISHERS

Silver Publishers:

ELSEVIER

MORGAN KAUFMANN

CAMBRIDGE UNIVERSITY PRESS

Foundations of Data-Aware Process Analysis: A Database Theory Perspective

Diego Calvanese, Marco Montali
Free University of Bozen/Bolzano
lastname@inf.unibz.it

Giuseppe De Giacomo
Sapienza Università di Roma
degiacomo@dis.uniroma1.it

ABSTRACT

In this work we survey the research on foundations of data-aware (business) processes that has been carried out in the database theory community. We show that this community has indeed developed over the years a multi-faceted culture of merging data and processes. We argue that it is this community that should lay the foundations to solve, at least from the point of view of formal analysis, the dichotomy between data and processes still persisting in business process management.

Categories and Subject Descriptors

D.2.4 [**Software Engineering**]: Software/Program Verification

General Terms

Verification

Keywords

Business artifacts, data-centric processes, first-order temporal logics.

1. INTRODUCTION

When it comes to manage the assets of an organization, data and processes should be considered as two sides of the same coin [105]. A 2009 survey by Forrester[1] [90], whose outcome is also reported in [108], has addressed the important question of which of the two aspects should be given priority from the point of view of IT management. Unsurprisingly, the role played by an individual within IT strongly affects the perception of the relative importance of processes and data within an organization: Professionals concerned with the management of business processes downplay the importance of data, and view it as subsidiary to the processes that manage them; as a consequence, they do not pay attention to the quality of data and on how the business processes can ensure that data assets can be maintained clean. On the contrary, data management experts consider data as the driver of the processes in an organization, and assume that guaranteeing data quality is sufficient to ensure proper consideration of business relevant data so as to impact process improvement efforts.

An immediate consequence of this dichotomy, is that there is very limited collaboration and cost sharing between the teams on the one hand running the (master) data management (MDM) initiatives and on the other hand managing the business process. This is also confirmed by Forrester's survey, where for 83% of the respondents there was no interaction, and only in 8% of the cases the master data management and business process modeling efforts were fully coordinated. A further consequence is that there is little attention also on the side of tool vendors to address in their products the requirements coming from a combined treatment of processes and data. On the one hand, data management tool vendors consider processes only insofar as they affect the direct management of the data within the tools, but they do not pay attention to the processes that actually make use of the data. On the other hand, business process modeling suites do not allow for the connection of data to the processes. Service oriented architectures (SOA), which make it possible to divide the functionality of large systems into component services, are advocated as a solution to the data-process dichotomy. However, while favoring component reuse, they do not address the need of connecting the data to the organizational processes so as to facilitate their improvement, and in fact data continues to be "hidden" inside systems [100]. In addition to SOA, [100] identifies two key areas in which an explicit representation of data in process models is crucial. The first is the *modeling of the core assets* of an organization, due to the fact that the data stored in different IT systems is crucial for the execution of the business processes that create the value of the organization itself. Hence, the business processes depend on such data, and in order to keep the organization operational, the former need access to the latter. This dependency should be accounted for explicitly. The second is *business process controlling*, due to the fact that both the key performance indicators, and the business goals of the organization on which they depend, are defined in terms of data. To evaluate and control these indicators, the activities contributing to the goals need to be identified, and this is done by considering the appropriate data objects on which these activities operate. In order to support this task, process models need to shift the emphasis from control flow to the data [120, 85].

It follows that there is a strong need to incorporate data modeling features in (business) process modeling languages, and to enrich business process analysis tools to deal with data [100]. This demands for suitable modeling languages, methodologies and systems supporting the integrated management of processes and data, and, possibly above all, it calls for a more foundational approach,

[1] `http://www.forrester.com/`

PODS'13, June 22–27, 2013, New York, New York, USA.

to provide a clear semantics for (data-aware) process models, and to consequently enable their analysis.

Analysis is attracting a lot of interest based on the momentum that verification of software and hardware systems has had in the last 15 years, also recognized by the 2007 A.M. Turing Award, given to Edmund M. Clarke, E. Allen Emerson, and Joseph Sifakis, for their role in developing Model-Checking into a highly effective verification technology that is widely adopted in the hardware and software industries. Model checking, see [122] for an introduction oriented to database theoreticians, is based on the idea of formulating dynamic properties of interest in some temporal logic like LTL, CTL, μ-calculus [79, 117] (whose temporal component is intrinsically non-first order, since based implicitly or explicitly on forms of fixpoints) and check such formulas over the transition system (explicitly or implicitly represented) mathematically capturing the dynamics of the system of interest. A key element for current model checking techniques is that states can be modelled propositionally, giving rise to a finite-state transition system.

When data are relevant, states need to be model relationally rather than propositionally [122]. That is, we associate to the state of the process the state of the data, possibly seen as a relational database. These transition systems are typically *infinite-state* since there is no bound on the number of tuples that can be added to database relations as the computation goes on. The presence of data also calls for query languages for process analysis that combine two dimensions: a *temporal dimension* to query the process execution flow, and a *first-order dimension* to query the data present in the relational structures maintained by the states of the system, and to relate objects across different states. In other words, first-order variants of temporal logics are required [122, 126, 69].

The resulting verification problem is much harder than in the pure finite-state control-flow setting, and deeply challenges the possibility of employing off-the-shelf, conventional finite-state model checkers. In particular, a data-aware process that combines a finite control-flow with the manipulation of a full-fledged database, can easily encode the behavior of a Turing machine, causing the model checking problem to become immediately undecidable even for simple propositional CTL/LTL properties.

The fundamental question is then: how can we mediate between the expressiveness of the temporal property language, and the identification of classes of data-aware processes, for which analysis becomes decidable, but at the same time still applicable to notable, real-world data-aware processes? Research in verification has tacked verification of infinite-state systems (e.g., see [50] for a survey). However, in much of this work the emphasis is on studying recursive control rather than data, which is either ignored or propositionally abstracted. If data are included they are of a very specific form, like recursive procedures with integer parameters [48], rewriting systems with data [47], or Petri nets with data associated to tokens [95].

Processes and data has been a continuously present stream of research in database theory. Over the years, a lot of work has been done on database evolution and transaction (see Section 3.1), on temporal query languages and data management (see Section 3.2), on active databases (see Section 3.3), on workflow systems (see Section 3.4), and on temporal integrity constraints (see Section 3.5). Most of this work looks at dynamics of a database system, however starting from the work on relational transducers (see Section 4.1), business processes, i.e., processes at a higher level of abstraction, have started attracting attention. Then a first call-to-arms was issued in early 2000 by Rick Hull in [86] concerning the need of modeling and analyzing business processes in the context of e- or web-services. The interest in web-services gave rise to a beautiful stream of work on verifying database-centric dynamic services (see Section 4.2). A second call-to-arms was issued again by Rick Hull in the late 2000, about the modeling and the formal analysis of "artifact-centric business processes" [85]. It is this call that has generated the latest work on data-aware process analysis that has been flourishing in the last years (see Sections 4.3 and 4.4).

In this work we present an overview of the research on foundations of data-aware (business) processes that has been carried out in the database theory community in the last three decades. We show that this community has indeed developed over the years a multi-faceted culture of combining static and dynamic aspects of data management, which has recently culminated in a series of significant lines of research addressing the foundations of data-aware process analysis. We argue that it is this community that should pursue further the investigation of the fundamental issues underlying the dichotomy between data and processes, which still persists in business process management and calls for a unifying, well-founded framework.

This survey complements four key companion surveys in the area: the ones by Rick Hull [86, 85], which single out problems and challenges on data-aware service oriented and artifact-centric computing; the one by Moshe Vardi [122], which presents the body of work on model checking, including challenges arising due to the presence of data; the one by Victor Vianu [126], which surveys the line of work developed starting from mid 2000 on verification of data-centric dynamic services; and the one by Tova Milo [69], which surveys how fundamental data management techniques can be applied to the challenging problem of managing control flows characterizing business processes.

2. THE BPM PERSPECTIVE

Process analysis is a central research theme in business process management (BPM). In a recent survey [118], Wil van der Aalst pointed out that *process model analysis* has been the second most influential topic in a decade of BPM conferences (following *process modeling languages*). However, in BPM process analysis has been mainly tackled, so far, by following a *divide et impera* approach. This has led to the development of sophisticated, effective techniques dealing with the process, control-flow dimension but abstracting away from the data. In particular, a plethora of verification techniques has been developed to verify whether the control-flow of a process meets specific, pre-defined properties (such as absence of deadlocks, boundedness, and soundness), or domain-dependent properties. Virtually all these techniques rely on the fact that the dynamics induced by a process control-flow can be captured by means of a (possibly infinite-state) propositional *labeled transition system*, whose labels represent the process tasks/activities, and where concurrency is represented by interleaving, as typically done in formal verification [27]. Usually, such a transition system is not explicitly represented, but it is instead implicitly "folded" into a Petri net, which provides a compact representation of the process control-flow thanks to its native capability of accommodating concurrency.

Beside verification of pre-defined properties, also the verification of arbitrary, domain-dependent properties has been tackled in BPM, relying on standard temporal logics such as CTL and LTL. In particular, such temporal logics are exploited to specify properties about the dynamics of the (Petri net representing the) system by either focusing on place configurations (i.e., the amount of tokens present in a given place), or on task execution [77]. In spite of the undecidability results for verification of general Petri nets [76, 77], decidability holds for safe/bounded nets, whose reachability graph consists of a finite-state labeled transition system. This, in turn, makes it possible to rely on conventional finite-state model checking techniques, lifting the focus from decidability to complexity issues [127, 109, 110, 23].

When it comes to formal specification and analysis of data-aware processes, no satisfactory solution has been provided so far within BPM. The main approach that captures data-aware extensions of Petri nets is the one of colored Petri nets. However, in the instantiation used in BPM [119] they are not suited to represent a full-fledged database. They introduce data as variables associated to tokens, and manipulate them by means of a sort of *procedural attachment*, i.e., by attaching procedures/functions to the transitions of the net. These procedures/functions can be implemented as an arbitrary program (typically written in a functional language), and hence are completely unconstrained. This lifts the system towards executability[2], but sacrifices its analyzability and verifiability.

High-level, business process modeling languages such as the OMG standard BPMN[3], and the OASIS standard BPEL[4] service orchestration language suffer from similar limitations when the data dimension is taken into account. All these languages largely leave the connection between the process dimension and the data dimension underspecified. For example, they do not conceptually capture the behavior of atomic tasks, consequently abstracting away from how they progress data. To obtain a fully-specified model, one therefore needs again to attach an arbitrary program to every BPMN atomic task or service invoked by the BPEL process [102].

3. DYNAMICS IN DATABASE THEORY

We overview here how the database theory community has been contributing to the analysis of data-aware processes. We do so by first looking at some key lines of research that have considered the interaction of both static and dynamic aspects of data management. Specifically, we consider below the following lines of research:

1. database evolution and transactions;
2. temporal data management;
3. active databases;
4. workflow formalisms and systems;
5. temporal integrity constraints.

For each of these areas we overview the main research objectives and achievements. Our aim here is not to be comprehensive, but rather to highlight the mainstream directions relevant to the topic of this paper that have characterized the research in databases.

3.1 Database Evolution and Transactions

The problem of evolution of data in a database by means of atomic operations and their combination inside transactions has been considered from early on as a key issue to investigate in databases. Apart from the fundamental problems of concurrency control and serializability (see, e.g., [93, 112, 98, 82] for early results), updates and transactions have been considered also in view of their interaction with (static) database constraints. Equivalence and optimization of relational transactions, consisting of linear sequences of insertions, deletions, and updates, using simple selection conditions based on individual attribute values for each tuple, is investigated in [13, 17]. A formal model (called *dynamic relational model*) for evolution over time of a database, seen as a sequence of instances is presented in [123, 124]. The effects on evolution of dynamic constraints (specifically, dynamic functional dependencies), which relate one database instance to the next in the sequence are studied. Specifically, the problem of inferring static constraints from knowledge about the evolution history of the database, as expressed by the dynamic constraints, is investigated. The impact of dynamic constraints on the update of a specific form of views, in which each tuple represents an object with its properties, is considered in [125].

The connection between transactions and static constraints is further investigated in [14], which presents a model where valid database states are described using a set of admissible (parameterized) transactions, as opposed to constraints. Such *transactional database schemas* are in general incomparable with schemas described via constraints, though they are able to simulate natural types of constraints, such as those generated by the early semantic database models (ER [53], IFO [7]). Equivalence of transactional schemas is shown to be undecidable in general, but decidable cases are singled out. The work studies also preservation of constraints by transactions, showing decidability, e.g., for inclusion dependencies, but undecidability for arbitrary FOL constraints. Further decidable restrictions, investigated in [15], are obtained by limiting on the one hand the kind of allowed operations to insertions and deletions (but no updates), and on the other hand the properties to be checked to specific ones (in line with what typically done in software verification). Interestingly, when the maximum length of a transaction is bound to a fixed value, decidability can be shown for stronger properties.

In the transaction language TL introduced in [16], which features inserts, deletes, and a (non-deterministic) "while" construct, transactions may use a fixed number of temporary relations, and may be "unsafe", i.e., introduce *new* values, not in the original database. Safety is also relaxed to "weak safety", where new values are allowed only in temporary relations. Further, a notion of "update completeness", which is more natural than query completeness [52], is proposed, and it is shown that TL is update complete. [18] builds on this work, by defining a variant of TL in which "while" has a deterministic semantics, and new values may not appear in the result, but only in intermediate relations. It is shown that such language is complete for deterministic updates. The variant where new values are disallowed alltogether, is shown complete for fixpoint queries, hence strictly less expressive that PSPACE updates. Instead, on an ordered domains, one obtains exactly PSPACE. The work presents also declarative update languages, which are extensions of Datalog with negation in the body, disjunction in the head, and unsafe head variables. Derivation of a fact corresponds to insertion, whereas deletions are not foreseen. Such language is equivalent to TL without deletion, and is complete for non-deterministic updates where input and output relations are disjoint.

3.2 Temporal Data Management

A temporal database provides mechanisms to store data as it evolves, and to query its historical states using suitable extensions of standard query languages like SQL. Research on temporal database originates from the observation that temporal data management can be very difficult if one uses conventional database systems [88]. The work on temporal databases and query languages goes back to [111], which provides a Description of syntax and semantics of temporal extension of Quel (a calculus-based query language for the Ingres system) that makes use of Allen's interval relations [22].

A temporal database model, in which each tuple is timestamped with a union of time intervals, is defined [80]. The notion of "weak relation" as the equivalence class of all timestamped relations for which the snapshots at each timepoint are equal, is introduced, and an algebra over such weak relations is defined and studied. Datalog

[2] `http://cpntools.org/`

[3] `http://www.bpmn.org/`

[4] `https://www.oasis-open.org/committees/wsbpel`

extended with unary function symbols (i.e., successor), is studied in [57], and a mechanism is proposed to finitely represent infinite query answers via rules that may be returned together with explicit tuples. A framework for reasoning about infinite temporal information, based on generalized tuples with additional temporal attributes and constraints, is presented in [89]. Temporal attributes are defined by infinitely repeating points (of the form $z(n) = c + kn$) and constraints are conjunctions of linear equalities and inequalities on temporal attributes. Contrast this to constraint databases, where constraints are used to describe multiple databases, as opposed to a single database with infinite temporal information. The paper relates predicates definable by generalized relations with those definable in Presburger arithmetic. It studies the complexity of relational algebra on generalized relations, which return finite representations of possibly infinite answers. Whereas positive existential queries are in PTIME (in data complexity), arbitrary queries (with negation) are NP-hard and in 2EXPTIME.

The semantics and expressive power of Templog [1], which extends horn logic programs with temporal operators (next, always, eventually) is studied in [32, 33], showing that the declarative semantics and the operational semantics, based on a suitably defined temporal extension of SLD-resolution, coincide. The resolution-based calculus is shown to be sound and complete, but restrictions that would ensure decidability of satisfiability of Templog specifications are not considered. For the propositional variant of Templog expressiveness is investigated, and shown to be equivalent to that of *fixpoint linear time logic* (i.e., Büchi automata on infinite strings) [121] restricted so as to allow only least fixpoints applied to positive formulas, which in turn corresponds to finite-word regular languages. The temporal database formalisms proposed in [57, 32, 89] are compared in [34] with respect to their power in expressing queries (query expressiveness) and constraints on the data (data expressiveness). Also a query language, operating on temporal databases [89], with the ability to express predicates over multiple temporal attributes it defined, and sufficient conditions for finite evaluation of queries, even over infinite periodic data, are given.

Several works survey the area of temporal databases and query languages. In particular, [55] surveys temporal query languages, distinguishing between abstract and concrete languages and studying formal semantics, expressiveness, and query processing. In [88], instead, the problem of temporal data management is addressed more in general, also considering design and implementation aspects for temporal database systems.

We conclude by observing that the work on temporal query languages includes also work on logics that are first-order variants of propositional temporal logics used in verification, such as first-order LTL [54] and others that we will consider later. The formulas in such logics are *monadic* in the temporal component, in the sense that they can be seen as a combination through temporal operators of open formulas that contain only one free temporal variable. However, temporal query languages go beyond these logics, allowing also for combining formulas that are not monadic in the temporal component, so as to express sophisticated relationship among data and associated timestamps [6].

3.3 Active Databases

At the end of the 80's there was a great interest in active databases. These are processes described in terms of sets of event-condition-action rules operating on a database: such rules are triggered (under the control of a condition) by an initial external event, and successively by the internal update events caused by the execution of the rule actions. Much of the research in this area has been devoted to study the execution of such languages, by defining and implementing interpreters for them [91]. A general formal framework for active databases is introduced in [103, 104], and is used as the basis for comparing several active database prototypes with respect to their expressive power and complexity.

Substantial work has also been devoted to the analysis, especially termination and confluence of rule based trigger systems [21]. The termination problem can be formulated as follows: given a set of rules, check whether, for every initial database (and every possible triggering event), every sequence of rule activations (which are in general non-deterministic) eventually terminates. Notice that, although rules are in general assumed to *not* bring in new data into the system (but just to manipulate the objects present in the initial database), the difficulty of the problem lies in the fact that termination has to be determined for every possible initial database.

The undecidability of termination in general was immediately observed. However, special cases and restrictions that guarantee decidability have been singled out. For example, [29] shows decidability of termination of *propositional* trigger systems in which the triggered rules are managed via a stack or a set. Such decidability results turn out, however, to be rather fragile; e.g., the system studied in [29] becomes undecidable when a stack replaces the queue in the management of the triggered rules. When going beyond the propositional case and considering relations updated by the rule actions, one approach, followed by [28], is to perform the analysis by an (unfaithful, i.e., sound) abstraction of data, so as to guarantee soundness (but not necessarily completeness) of the termination check. Instead, [30] aims at sound and complete techniques, and investigates the borders of decidability for the termination problem. It is shown that in the following two cases, which impose rather severe conditions on the specification of the systems, decidability holds: *(i)* updates are restricted to have a single atom in rule bodies and to be safe (i.e., all head variables appear in the body); *(ii)* updates may be arbitrary, but only unary relations may be non-empty in the initial database. In both cases, even apparently minor relaxations of these restrictions lead to undecidability.

3.4 Workflow Formalisms and Systems

A further topic integrating static and dynamic aspects of data that has been addressed by the database community is that of systems to manage workflows. A workflow can be considered as a collection of activities designed in such a way that a group of (human or artificial) agents can carry out in a coordinated way a specific complex process. Workflow management systems provide a framework for capturing the interaction among the activities in a workflow [116].

Research in databases has contributed to this area by studying formalisms and systems that would support transactional aspects of workflows [49, 46]. Specifically, [49] considers a setting that deals both with task dependencies in a workflow, and dependencies between operations on the data by multiple interacting transactions. However, it does not consider the actual data and the changes performed on it, but only the order in which operations are executed.

Another interesting perspective on workflows is the use of typical database functionalities (persistence, transactions, complex querying, provenance, etc.) to support the activities related to managing workflows and their execution [107, 35, 36, 31, 64]. The recent survey [69] contains an in-depth treatment of this aspect.

The importance of data not only in the context of a single workflow, but to drive the integration between multiple, inter-organizational workflows, has been considered since the late nineties in the Vortex workflow management system [87]. In Vortex, data implicitly introduce additional dynamic (data-flow) constraints among activities belonging to the different interacting workflows. Verification of Vortex workflows has been studied by considering the control-flow component, but by considering the contribution of the data component only in terms of the induced data-flow constraints, without explicitly capturing the complex interplay between the two components [78].

The dichotomy between an expressive workflow modeling language able to account for data, and the language used for verification, which abstracts away data, is present also in other approaches. For example, [65] adopts transaction logic with task pre-/post-conditions to model full-fledged workflows operating over relational databases, but forbids the presence of such conditions when it comes to reasoning and verification, thus effectively loosing the link between the workflow behavior and the database.

3.5 Temporal Integrity Constraints

Temporal integrity constraints are integrity constraints that collectively constrain multiples states of a database over time. Even though they are not meant to explicitly represent a business process, they nevertheless declaratively specify which evolutions of the system and of the corresponding data are considered legal.

Early on, temporal constraints were recognized important for transactions. [96] relates dynamic integrity constraints expressed in temporal logic to transaction specifications defined by FOL pre and postconditions. The aim is to monitor the integrity constraints through transactions, and it is shown how to align the transaction specification so that it generates only state sequences that satisfy the dynamic constraints. Later, [39] investigates the properties of weakest preconditions for various transaction and specification languages, concentrating on specification languages that are relevant to integrity constraints, such as FOL.

Most of the work on checking temporal constraints in temporal databases focused on first-order variants of LTL [54], which is in general highly undecidable [83]. However, a decidability condition that was singled out early on concerns safety formulas with no quantification except for implicit universal quantification allowed outside temporal operators [58, 59]. First-order LTL that uses only temporal connectives referring to the past has been proposed as a convenient language to express integrity constraints, since such formulas can be efficiently checked, by accumulating the historical information that is necessary for the check in auxiliary relations of the current state [56].

4. BUSINESS PROCESS ANALYSIS IN DATABASE THEORY

We next turn to research that directly tackle data-aware process analysis, focusing on higher level processes than transactions, such as business processes. We recall that the presence of data on the one hand makes the system dynamics infinite-state in general and, on the other hand, requires to go beyond propositional temporal logics. Indeed, in order to properly query the state of the system by extracting data, one needs first-order quantification within and across the states of the system.

Various approaches have been proposed, that differ in:

- The structure of the process component, as well as its interaction with the data component, and with the external environment.
- The kind of analysis problem that is considered; most works focus on verification of arbitrary temporal properties expressed in the adopted formalism; other approaches fix a set of specific problems they aim to solve.
- The considered temporal formalism, and consequently the kind of properties that can be expressed; such properties are typically formulated in a variant of first-order temporal logic.
- The form of quantification that is allowed in the first-order temporal formalism, where the cases that have been considered are quantification over the initial state only, and quantification across states. The latter case takes into account also those objects that have been introduced during the evolution of the system, and in general requires suitable restrictions on the scope of the quantification so as to guarantee decidability.

4.1 Relational Transducers

One of the most significant approaches proposed by the database community to model high-level (business) processes is that of relational transducers, originally proposed to support forms of e-commerce [19, 20]. Relational transducers explicitly account for a dynamic component, reminiscent of active databases and transactional workflows, on top of full-fledged databases.

More specifically, a relational transducer is a tuple (S, σ, ω), where: *(i)* S is the relational transducer schema, constituted by pairwise disjoint relational schemas for input, state, output, and fixed (external) database, and where the log is a further relational schema used to maintain the semantically meaningful portion of an input-output exchange; *(ii)* σ is a state-update transition function mapping instances of input, state and fixed database to instances of the next state; *(iii)* ω is an output-update transition function mapping instances of input, state and fixed database to instances of the next output. The semantics of a relational transducer is based on linear time. In particular, it captures the evolution of state and output sequences, in response to a sequence of inputs representing the interaction with the external world, as stored in the log.

The problems subject to analysis range from log validity (i.e., checking whether a log sequence can be generated with some input sequence), goal reachability, containment (i.e., testing whether every valid log of one transducer is also valid for another) and compatibility (i.e., checking whether two transducers have a common log) to the verification of specific first-order temporal properties with a past-time operator. These problems are in general undecidable. However, decidability and, in particular, a NEXPTIME upper bound for the verification problem, have been obtained in [19, 20] by requiring transducers to be *semi-positive cumulative state* (Spocus). In a Spocus transducer, the state accumulates all inputs received, and the outputs are defined by a non-recursive, semi-positive set of datalog rules.

In [113, 114], a generalization of Spocus transducers, called ASM transducers, has been studied. ASM transducers do not necessarily accumulate input, and their rule application is in general guarded by arbitrary first-order formulas. In this setting, the aforementioned problems are reconsidered, and verification is addressed for a variant of first-order LTL in which temporal operators cannot appear in the scope of first-order quantifiers, except for outermost universal quantifiers. Even though verification is undecidable for general ASM transducers, two main restrictions that guarantee decidability are identified: *(i)* ASM transducers for which the fixed (external) database is explicitly known, and the set of values allowed in the input is restricted to those appearing in that database; *(ii)* ASM transducers which bound a-priori the maximum amount of input that can be received in one computation step. Complexity of verification for such restricted versions range between PSPACE-complete to EXPSPACE-complete, depending on whether the maximum arity of the employed relations is bounded a-priori or not.

4.2 Data-Driven Web Systems

Web systems provide distributed access to information stored on the web, typically powered by databases and manipulated by complex web applications/services that interact with third-party services and external users. In [72], the case of a single web service that interacts with an external user is considered, studying the trade-off between the expressiveness of the web service specification language and the feasibility of verification. Verification is tackled by relying on a formalization of such kind of system in terms of a model that extends ASM transducers. In fact, a web service is modeled by means of *(i)* a database that remains fixed during the execution, *(ii)* a set of state relations that evolve in response to user inputs, *(iii)* a set of web page schemas that query the current database and state to generate user input choice, and *(iv)* state transitions that are triggered by the input chosen by the user. The firing of a transition triggers actions to be taken for progressing the state, then leading the interaction to the next web page.

To achieve decidability of verification, [72] imposes restrictions over the web service similar to [113, 114], limiting the use of quantification in state, action, and target rule formulas to *input-bounded quantification*, and limiting formulas of input rules to be existential. The expressive power of ASM transducers is extended with the possibility of referring to the input at the previous step in the run. Verification is then tackled for the input-bounded version of the linear-time logic considered in [113, 114], extended with the possibility of referring to the previous input. In particular, decidability of verification for this logic over an input-bounded web service is decidable in EXPSPACE (in fact, PSPACE-complete when the arity of the service schema is bounded a-priori). This result is obtained by a reduction to finite satisfiability of existential first-order logic augmented with a transitive closure operator. Furthermore, it is shown that even small relaxations of the imposed restrictions lead to undecidability. Beside linear-time properties, also verification of branching-time properties is tackled, by considering variants of the logics CTL and CTL*, where first-order quantification obeys to the same restrictions as in the LTL case. In particular, it is shown that for these logics it is necessary to further restrict the web service model to guarantee decidability. Two main restrictions are studied: *(i) propositional, input bounded web services*, which forbid the use of previous input relations and pose the strong assumption that all states and actions are propositional (but inputs are still parametrized in the specification); and *(ii) input-driven search web services*, which restrict the usage of previous input relations but are still able to capture common applications involving a user-driven search. In the case of propositional web services, verification for the CTL and CTL* variants is proved to be respectively in coNEXPTIME and EXPSPACE (PSPACE by fixing the database schema). Complexity of verification respectively becomes in EXPTIME and 2EXPTIME in the case of input-driven search web services.

Notably, even though the established complexity upper bounds provide no indication about the practical feasibility of verification, an effective implementation has been carried out in the WAVE system [71], focusing on the linear-time case. In particular, the experimentation carried out in [71] has demonstrated that, by leveraging on a fruitful coupling of novel verification and database optimization techniques, complete verification is practically feasible for a reasonably broad class of applications. A system building on WAVE and dealing with aspects ranging from specification of Web applications to explanation of verification results is presented in [74].

In [75, 73], the single-service setting tackled in [72, 71] has been extended to the case of composition of web-services (also called peers), which interact by asynchronous message exchange. A service reacts to incoming messages and user input by updating its internal state through a function of the current contents of the database, state, user input, and received messages, possibly replying with outgoing messages. Decidability of verification is studied for two property specification formalisms: the variant of first-order LTL studied in prior work, and conversation protocols (that leverage on an industrial standard). In particular, various semantics for message-based communication are exploited (singleton versus set messages, lossy versus perfect communication channels, bounded versus unbounded received message queues), which provide various extensions to the notion of input-boundedness in the case of multiple interacting services. Under appropriate communication semantics, decidability of verification is established in PSPACE, showing at the same time that even slight relaxations of the imposed restrictions immediately lead to undecidability.

Related to this research line is also the work on the Colombo framework for service composition [40]. There automated composition synthesis is studied in presence of data. In particular, decidability under certain conditions that ensure reduction of relational states to propositional states is established. The restriction that along a run only finitely many new object are introduced is crucial for the technique proposed therein. Notice that this input-bounded condition guarantees that service runs are "bounded", in the sense discussed in Section 4.4.

4.3 Artifact-Centric Systems

The artifact-centric approach to business process modeling, which began at IBM Research in the late 1990's and was first presented in [101], proposes business artifacts (or simply *artifacts*) to model key business-relevant entities. Artifacts are equipped with an information model, representing the data maintained by the artifact, and they evolve over time following a so-called lifecycle. Processes organize atomic tasks or available services that are of interest into a possibly complex workflow.

The artifact-centric approach provides a simple and robust structure for business process development, which has been advocated as superior to the traditional activity-centric approach, especially when dealing with complex and large process models. While the traditional workflow approach does not lend itself to componentization in a natural way [94], the artifact-centric approach is claimed to enhance efficiency, especially when dealing with business process transformations to expand and/or streamline the process [43, 41, 97]. Fundamental notions from the artifact-centric approach have also been deployed in commercial products underlying IBM's commercial service offerings [115].

The surveys [85, 60] overviewed the research results on the artifact-centric approach to business process specification, management, deployment and analysis, tracing the roadmap of research directions and challenges. As far as verification is concerned, this triggered several lines of research aiming at decidable techniques for verification over processes and data, to be reassessed and extended towards the artifact-centric setting.

Seminal works on the analysis of artifact-centric systems is presented in [81, 42]. In [81], systems constituted by multiple interconnected artifacts are studied. The artifact information model contains the current state, and a tuple of attributes. Each attribute, in turn, may refer either to a primitive value or to some other artifact instance. Artifact lifecycles have a procedural flavor, based on finite state machines whose transitions either create a new artifact, or modify/eliminate an existing one. In this setting, first-order CTL with quantification across states is considered, showing decidability of verification for such formulas in the case of bounded domains, and in the case of unbounded domains, under the assumption that quantification only ranges over artifacts (and not values), and the number of artifacts is bounded. [42] tackles artifact systems that are similar, in spirit, to the ones of [81], but where lifecycles follow a more declarative style, based on business rules that activate services. Services are in turn described in terms of preconditions and non-deterministic effects related to the creation, manipulation and elimination of artifacts. Manipulation of attributes focuses only on whether these attributes are defined or undefined (so that values are abstracted away). A set of pre-defined reasoning tasks (successful path completion, existence of dead-end paths, attribute redundancy) is tackled, showing that all are undecidable in the general case, but become decidable if no new artifacts can be created, or by imposing various restrictions, such as monotonicity of services (i.e., each attribute is written at most once).

In [70], the artifact model proposed in [42] is extended so as to include a static read-only database, and to handle a relational state in addition to attributes, whose values are not abstracted away and can be compared by service and property specifications according to a dense linear order. Runs can receive unbounded external input from the infinite domain of values. As verification formalism, a variant of first-order LTL is considered, where statements about individual artifact instances in the run may share variables that are outermost universally quantified. Decidability of verification is obtained by restricting such logic and the system specification to be *guarded*. The guarded restriction introduces a form of bounded quantification in the properties and formulas driving the system's evolution, which resembles input-boundedness [113, 114, 72]. In particular, read-only and read-write database relations are accessed differently, querying the latter only by checking whether they contain a given tuple of constants. It is shown that this restriction is tight, and that integrity constraints cannot be added to the framework, since even a single functional dependency leads to undecidability of verification. Decidability comes with a PSPACE upper bound for fixed-arity schemas, and EXPSPACE otherwise. [61, 62, 63] extend this approach by forbidding read-write relations, but this allows the extension of the decidability result to integrity constraints expressed as embedded dependencies with terminating chase, and to any decidable arithmetic.

Another line of research building on the artifact-centric paradigm is [9, 3, 10, 11], which study the specification and verification of artifact-centric systems that rely on an active XML-based information model. *Active XML* [2] (*AXML* for short) extends XML by allowing parts of the document to be specified in an intensional way, by means of embedded calls to internal functions or external services. In the artifact-centric setting, AXML documents support the design of complex workflows, providing at the same time a description of the underlying data and of the sub-tasks (formally, internal functions) to be orchestrated by the workflow. In particular, the boundaries of decidability for the verification of systems based on multiple, interacting AXML documents are delineated. Temporal properties of runs are specified in a tree pattern-based temporal logic, called Tree-LTL, which exploits tree-like patterns to query the states of the system, and combines them through linear-time temporal operators to predicate about the evolution of a system run. Similarly to the logics considered in Section 4.2, in Tree-LTL variables are existentially quantified within a state, or universally quantified by means of an outermost quantifier. The systems considered for verification rely on *guarded AXML* (*GAXML*) documents, which control the initiation and completion of sub-tasks by means of boolean combinations of tree-patterns. Decidability of verification is achieved by disallowing recursion in GAXML systems, which leads to bound the total number of sub-tasks invoked along a run. In this setting, the complexity of verification is shown to be co2-EXPTIME-complete.

In [4, 5], the problem of comparing different data-aware workflow specification frameworks based on AXML is tackled. It is argued that comparing workflow specification formalisms is intrinsically difficult because of the diversity of data models and control-flow mechanisms, and the lack of a standard yardstick for expressiveness. For example, AXML workflows could employ automata, pre-and-post conditions, or declarative temporal logic formulas to express the dynamics of the system. A unifying approach based on views is then proposed, where views are exploited to isolate the relevant aspects to be taken into account when comparing different specification frameworks. Notably, the approach is used to show that the different control mechanisms for Active XML workflows are largely equivalent, an indication of the robustness of the model.

4.4 Data-Centric Dynamic Systems

A recent line of research has been aiming at developing a framework for the combination of data and processes that is expressive and robust with respect to the system model, general in the verification formalism, and at the same time guarantees decidability of verification:

- Expressiveness guarantees the ability to capture a wide range of concrete systems (such as web applications and artifact-centric systems, which call for full create-read-update-delete, CRUD, operations over the database), and favours the adoption of the framework in real-world scenarios.
- Robustness makes the framework apt to adjustments (e.g., allowing for inclusion of different kinds of integrity constraints), which improves usability in the modeling phase.
- Generality of the verification formalism provides the ability to capture both linear-time and branching-time properties, at the same time supporting first-order quantification across states.

These apparently incompatible requirements can be accomplished together by imposing (automatically checkable) structural conditions on the process dynamics and on how they accounts for the evolution of the data over time. We refer to this kind of framework as *Data-Centric Dynamic Systems* (*DCDS*).

From a technical point of view, research on DCDSs has drawn inspiration from the works dealing with termination of rule-based systems, and in particular from acyclicity conditions in data exchange [92]. The key idea connecting data exchange with DCDSs is that the semantics of tasks progressing the data can be related to the firing of a (set of) tuple-generating dependencies (TGDs). Also, notice that all the works discussed below assume that verification is done with respect to a system with a given initial database.

The first works literally exploiting the connection between tasks and TGSs were [51, 66]. There the transition relation itself is described in terms of TGDs that map the current state, represented as a relational database instance, to the next one. Null values are used to model the incorporation of new, unknown data into the system. The process evolution is essentially a form of chase. Under suitable weak acyclicity conditions this chase terminates, guaranteeing in turn that the system is finite-state. Decidability is then shown for a first-order μ-calculus without first-order quantification across states. This approach was extended by [24], where TGDs are replaced by actions allowing negation in the preconditions. In this revised framework, values imported from the external environment are represented by uninterpreted function terms, which play the same role as nulls in the work by [51, 66]. Since both [24] and [51, 66] rely on a purely relational setting, this choice leads to an ad-hoc interpretation of equality, where each null value/function term is considered only equal to itself.

Differently from these works, [37] considered a first-order variant of CTL with no quantification across states as verification formalism. The framework supports the incorporation of new values from the external environment as parameters of the actions; the corresponding execution semantics considers all the possible actual values, thus leading to an infinite-state transition systems. As for decidability of verification, it is shown that, under the assumption that each state of the system (constituted by the union of artifacts' relational instances) has a bounded active domain, it is possible to construct a *faithful* (i.e., sound and complete with respect to the verification logic) abstract transition system which, differently from the original one, has a finite number of states. [38] looks at quantification across in this setting. It relies on the semantic property of *genericity* [8] (called there "uniformity"), which guarantees that the transition system representing the execution of the process under study is not able to distinguish among states that have the same constants and the same patterns of data. Under the assumptions of genericity and state boundedness, decidability of verification is achieved for a richer logic, namely CTL with quantification across states, interpreted under the active domain semantics.

In [26], a comprehensive study of relational DCDSs is provided, where new information from the external world can be incorporated into the system through calls to deterministic and non-deterministic services. Verification for variants of first-order μ-calculus is investigated, where first-order quantification affects the objects across the possibly infinite states of the system. With such an expressive formalism, attention must be paid so as not to accumulate along a run an unbounded amount of information about which the formula to be verified may predicate. The accumulation of information may occur in the variables that are used as arguments of quantification, hence one needs to suitably control how these variables are quantified upon in the formula. In particular, two variants of first-order μ-calculus are singled out. The first one, called *history-preserving μ-calculus*, preserves knowledge of objects encountered along a run, by relying on an active domain semantics. In this case, decidability (in EXPTIME in the initial database) is obtained under the assumption that the data introduced along a run are bounded, though they may not be bounded in the overall system (*run-boundedness* condition). The second one, called *persistence-preserving μ-calculus*, preserves knowledge of an object only if the object is continuously present across successive states. In this case, decidability (again in EXPTIME in the initial database) is obtained even when infinitely many values are introduced along a run, as long as there is an overall bound on the number of objects accumulated in the same state (*state-boundedness* condition). Technically, decidability is shown in both cases by relying on finite-state abstractions that are faithful (i.e., sound and complete) according to suitable notions of bisimulations, tailored towards the two verification languages. The abstractions exploit an implicit form of genericity, which is enforced by the model underlying DCDSs and by the services they interact with. Even though run-boundedness and state-boundedness are semantic conditions that are undecidable to check, sufficient syntactic conditions have been singled out, respectively relying on the notion of *weak acyclicity* in data exchange [92], and on the novel notion of *generate-recall acyclicity*.

Considering the combination of the results in [38] and [26], we can observe that, for state-bounded systems, in the presence of first-order quantification over the active domain of the current state, without limiting the scope of quantification to the objects that persist across states, verification is decidable in case of CTL (i.e., with alternation-fee fixpoints), but becomes undecidable for LTL, and hence for the μ-calculus in general. The proof of undecidability in [26] is based on a reduction to LTL with freeze quantifiers [68].

5. CONCLUSIONS AND OUTLOOK

In this work, we surveyed the research on foundations of data-aware (business) processes that has been carried out in the database theory community. This community has developed rich techniques to deal with data and processes and among the various areas of computer science it is probably the one in the best position to lay the foundations of data-aware process analysis.

Several challenges are ahead of us. In particular, the work done in the last years on verification of data-aware processes shows that the analysis techniques proposed are exponential in those data that "change". So circumscribing what can be changed by a process appears to be a key issue to make verification practical. This is particularly relevant in the context of processes acting on web data like those that are the focus of [12, 84].

Notably, recent significant works on the analysis of data-aware processes, such as those in [38, 26], rely on a mix of contributions, formalisms, and techniques that have their roots in several areas of computer science, in particular database theory, formal methods, logic, process management, and knowledge representation. In particular, with respect to the latter, it is worth noting that a field where data and processes have always been considered together is that of *reasoning about actions* in Artificial Intelligence. Since the introduction of Situation Calculus in [99, 106], a first-order setting was considered for describing the states that actions could modify. An additional difficulty is the presence of incomplete information, typical of knowledge bases. Verification of processes is obviously of interest, but most decidability results are based on bounding the domain, thus reducing to a propositional case. The techniques discussed here do impact that literature as well and reflect into conditions for decidability of verification (see, e.g., [67, 25]).

We also notice that the majority of contemporary techniques for data-aware process analysis rely on the construction of faithful, finite-state abstractions starting from the infinite-state transition system representing the original model. In principle, this enables the exploitation of conventional model checkers to actually address the analysis problem, which is a promising approach. At the same time, we stress the importance of further pursuing the cross-fertilization with other research such as that of *data words* [44, 45] that have developed techniques to deal with systems whose state space is in general infinite due to the presence of data.

Acknowledgements

We would like to thank Babak Bagheri Hariri, Riccardo De Masellis, Alin Deutsch, Paolo Felli, Rick Hull, Maurizio Lenzerini, Alessio Lomuscio, Fabio Patrizi, Jianwen Su, and Moshe Vardi for stimulating ideas, inspiring discussions, and novel insights on the topics of this paper. This research has been partially supported by the EU under the ICT Collaborative Project ACSI (Artifact-Centric Service Interoperation), grant agreement n. FP7-257593. Diego Calvanese acknowledges the kind support of the Wolfgang Pauli Institute Vienna and of the Technical University Vienna for his sabbatical stay.

6. REFERENCES

[1] M. Abadi and Z. Manna. Temporal logic programming. *J. of Symbolic Computation*, 8(3):277–295, 1989.

[2] S. Abiteboul, O. Benjelloun, and T. Milo. Positive active XML. In *Proc. of the 23rd ACM SIGACT SIGMOD SIGART Symp. on Principles of Database Systems (PODS 2004)*, pages 35–45, 2004.

[3] S. Abiteboul, P. Bourhis, A. Galland, and B. Marinoiu. The AXML artifact model. In *Proc. of the 16th Int. Symp. on Temporal Representation and Reasoning (TIME 2009)*, pages 11–17, 2009.

[4] S. Abiteboul, P. Bourhis, and V. Vianu. Comparing workflow specification languages: a matter of views. In

Proc. of the 14th Int. Conf. on Database Theory (ICDT 2011), pages 78–89, 2011.
[5] S. Abiteboul, P. Bourhis, and V. Vianu. Comparing workflow specification languages: A matter of views. *ACM Trans. on Database Systems*, 37(2):10:1–10:59, 2012.
[6] S. Abiteboul, L. Herr, and J. Van den Bussche. Temporal versus first-order logic to query temporal databases. In *Proc. of the 15th ACM SIGACT SIGMOD SIGART Symp. on Principles of Database Systems (PODS'96)*, pages 49–57, 1996.
[7] S. Abiteboul and R. Hull. IFO: A formal semantic database model. *ACM Trans. on Database Systems*, 12(4):297–314, 1987.
[8] S. Abiteboul, R. Hull, and V. Vianu. *Foundations of Databases*. Addison Wesley Publ. Co., 1995.
[9] S. Abiteboul, L. Segoufin, and V. Vianu. Static analysis of Active XML systems. In *Proc. of the 27th ACM SIGACT SIGMOD SIGART Symp. on Principles of Database Systems (PODS 2008)*, pages 221–230, 2008.
[10] S. Abiteboul, L. Segoufin, and V. Vianu. Modeling and verifying Active XML artifacts. *Bull. of the IEEE Computer Society Technical Committee on Data Engineering*, 32(3):10–15, 2009.
[11] S. Abiteboul, L. Segoufin, and V. Vianu. Static analysis of Active XML systems. *ACM Trans. on Database Systems*, 34(4):23:1–23:44, 2009.
[12] S. Abiteboul, P. Senellart, and V. Vianu. The ERC webdam on foundations of web data management. In *Proc. of the 21st Int. World Wide Web Conf. (WWW 2012)*, pages 211–214, 2012.
[13] S. Abiteboul and V. Vianu. Transactions in relational databases (preliminary report). In *Proc. of the 10th Int. Conf. on Very Large Data Bases (VLDB'84)*, pages 46–56, 1984.
[14] S. Abiteboul and V. Vianu. Transactions and integrity constraints. In *Proc. of the 4th ACM SIGACT SIGMOD Symp. on Principles of Database Systems (PODS'85)*, pages 193–204, 1985.
[15] S. Abiteboul and V. Vianu. Deciding properties of transactional schemas. In *Proc. of the 5th ACM SIGACT SIGMOD Symp. on Principles of Database Systems (PODS'86)*, pages 235–239, 1986.
[16] S. Abiteboul and V. Vianu. A transcation language complete for database update and specification. In *Proc. of the 6th ACM SIGACT SIGMOD SIGART Symp. on Principles of Database Systems (PODS'87)*, pages 260–268, 1987.
[17] S. Abiteboul and V. Vianu. Equivalence and optimization of relational transactions. *J. of the ACM*, 35(1):70–120, 1988.
[18] S. Abiteboul and V. Vianu. Procedural and declarative database update languages. In *Proc. of the 7th ACM SIGACT SIGMOD SIGART Symp. on Principles of Database Systems (PODS'88)*, pages 240–250, 1988.
[19] S. Abiteboul, V. Vianu, B. Fordham, and Y. Yesha. Relational transducers for electronic commerce. In *Proc. of the 17th ACM SIGACT SIGMOD SIGART Symp. on Principles of Database Systems (PODS'98)*, pages 179–187, 1998.
[20] S. Abiteboul, V. Vianu, B. Fordham, and Y. Yesha. Relational transducers for electronic commerce. *J. of Computer and System Sciences*, 61(2):236–269, 2000.
[21] A. Aiken, J. Widom, and J. M. Hellerstein. Behavior of database production rules: Termination, confluence, and observable determinism. In *Proc. of the ACM SIGMOD Int. Conf. on Management of Data*, pages 59–68, 1992.
[22] J. F. Allen. Maintaining knowledge about temporal intervals. *Communications of the ACM*, 26(11):832–843, 1983.
[23] A. Awad, G. Decker, and M. Weske. Efficient compliance checking using bpmn-q and temporal logic. In *Proc. of the 6th Int. Conference on Business Process Management (BPM 2008)*, volume 5240 of *Lecture Notes in Computer Science*, pages 326–341. Springer, 2008.
[24] B. Bagheri Hariri, D. Calvanese, G. De Giacomo, R. De Masellis, and P. Felli. Foundations of relational artifacts verification. In *Proc. of the 9th Int. Conference on Business Process Management (BPM 2011)*, volume 6896 of *Lecture Notes in Computer Science*, pages 379–395. Springer, 2011.
[25] B. Bagheri Hariri, D. Calvanese, M. Montali, G. De Giacomo, R. De Masellis, and P. Felli. Description logic Knowledge and Action Bases. *J. of Artificial Intelligence Research*, 46, 2013.
[26] B. Bagheri Hariri, D. Calvanese, M. Montali, G. De Giacomo, and A. Deutsch. Verification of relational data-centric dynamic systems with external services. In *Proc. of the 32nd ACM SIGACT SIGMOD SIGART Symp. on Principles of Database Systems (PODS 2013)*, 2013.
[27] C. Baier and J.-P. Katoen. *Principles of Model Checking*. MIT Press, 2008.
[28] J. Bailey, L. Crnogorac, K. Ramamohanarao, and H. Søndergaard. Abstract interpretation of active rules and its use in termination analysis. In *Proc. of the 6th Int. Conf. on Database Theory (ICDT'97)*, volume 1186 of *Lecture Notes in Computer Science*, pages 188–202. Springer, 1997.
[29] J. Bailey, G. Dong, and K. Ramamohanarao. Structural issues in active rule systems. In *Proc. of the 6th Int. Conf. on Database Theory (ICDT'97)*, volume 1186 of *Lecture Notes in Computer Science*, pages 203–214. Springer, 1997.
[30] J. Bailey, G. Dong, and K. Ramamohanarao. Decidability and undecidability results for the termination problem of active database rules. In *Proc. of the 17th ACM SIGACT SIGMOD SIGART Symp. on Principles of Database Systems (PODS'98)*, pages 264–273, 1998.
[31] Z. Bao, S. B. Davidson, and T. Milo. Labeling workflow views with fine-grained dependencies. *Proc. of the VLDB Endowment*, 5(11):1208–1219, 2012.
[32] M. Baudinet. Temporal logic programming is complete and expressive. In *Proc. of the 16th ACM SIGPLAN-SIGACT Symp. on Principles of Programming Languages (POPL'89)*, pages 267–280, 1989.
[33] M. Baudinet. On the expressiveness of temporal logic programming. *Information and Computation*, 117(2):157–180, 1995.
[34] M. Baudinet, M. Niézette, and P. Wolper. On the representation of infinite temporal data and queries. In *Proc. of the 10th ACM SIGACT SIGMOD SIGART Symp. on Principles of Database Systems (PODS'91)*, pages 280–290, 1991.
[35] C. Beeri, A. Eyal, S. Kamenkovich, and T. Milo. Querying business processes. In *Proc. of the 32nd Int. Conf. on Very Large Data Bases (VLDB 2006)*, pages 343–354, 2006.

[36] C. Beeri, A. Eyal, S. Kamenkovich, and T. Milo. Querying business processes with BP-QL. *Information Systems*, 33(6):477–507, 2008.

[37] F. Belardinelli, A. Lomuscio, and F. Patrizi. Verification of deployed artifact systems via data abstraction. In *Proc. of the 9th Int. Joint Conf. on Service Oriented Computing (ICSOC 2011)*, volume 7084 of *Lecture Notes in Computer Science*, pages 142–156. Springer, 2011.

[38] F. Belardinelli, A. Lomuscio, and F. Patrizi. An abstraction technique for the verification of artifact-centric systems. In *Proc. of the 13th Int. Conf. on the Principles of Knowledge Representation and Reasoning (KR 2012)*, 2012.

[39] M. Benedikt, T. Griffin, and L. Libkin. Verifiable properties of database transactions. In *Proc. of the 15th ACM SIGACT SIGMOD SIGART Symp. on Principles of Database Systems (PODS'96)*, pages 117–127, 1996.

[40] D. Berardi, D. Calvanese, G. De Giacomo, R. Hull, and M. Mecella. Automatic composition of transition-based semantic web services with messaging. In *Proc. of the 31st Int. Conf. on Very Large Data Bases (VLDB 2005)*, pages 613–624, 2005.

[41] K. Bhattacharya, N. S. Caswell, S. Kumaran, A. Nigam, and F. Y. Wu. Artifact-centered operational modeling: Lessons from customer engagements. *IBM Systems Journal*, 46(4):703–721, 2007.

[42] K. Bhattacharya, C. E. Gerede, R. Hull, R. Liu, and J. Su. Towards formal analysis of artifact-centric business process models. In *Proc. of the 5th Int. Conference on Business Process Management (BPM 2007)*, volume 4714 of *Lecture Notes in Computer Science*, pages 288–234. Springer, 2007.

[43] K. Bhattacharya, R. Guttman, K. Lyman, F. F. Heath, S. Kumaran, P. Nandi, F. Y. Wu, P. Athma, C. Freiberg, L. Johannsen, and A. Staudt. A model-driven approach to industrializing discovery processes in pharmaceutical research. *IBM Systems Journal*, 44(1):145–162, 2005.

[44] M. Bojanczyk, C. David, A. Muscholl, T. Schwentick, and L. Segoufin. Two-variable logic on data words. *ACM Trans. on Computational Logic*, 12(4):27, 2011.

[45] M. Bojanczyk and T. Place. Toward model theory with data values. In *Proc. of the 39th Int. Coll. on Automata, Languages and Programming (ICALP 2012)*, pages 116–127, 2012.

[46] A. J. Bonner. Workflow, transactions, and datalog. In *Proc. of the 18th ACM SIGACT SIGMOD SIGART Symp. on Principles of Database Systems (PODS'99)*, pages 294–305, 1999.

[47] A. Bouajjani, P. Habermehl, Y. Jurski, and M. Sighireanu. Rewriting systems with data. In *Proc. of the 16th Int. Symp. on Fundamentals of Computation Theory (FCT 2007)*, 2007.

[48] A. Bouajjani, P. Habermehl, and R. Mayr. Automatic verification of recursive procedures with one integer parameter. *Theoretical Computer Science*, 295, 2003.

[49] Y. Breitbart, A. Deacon, H.-J. Schek, A. P. Sheth, and G. Weikum. Merging application-centric and data-centric approaches to support transaction-oriented multi-system workflows. *SIGMOD Record*, 22(3):23–30, 1993.

[50] O. Burkart, D. Caucal, F. Moller, and B. Steffen. Verification of infinite structures. In *Handbook of Process Algebra*. Elsevier, 2001.

[51] P. Cangialosi, G. De Giacomo, R. De Masellis, and R. Rosati. Conjunctive artifact-centric services. In *Proc. of the 8th Int. Joint Conf. on Service Oriented Computing (ICSOC 2010)*, volume 6470 of *Lecture Notes in Computer Science*, pages 318–333. Springer, 2010.

[52] A. K. Chandra and D. Harel. Computable queries for relational data bases. *J. of Computer and System Sciences*, 21(2):156–178, 1980.

[53] P. P. Chen. The Entity-Relationship model: Toward a unified view of data. *ACM Trans. on Database Systems*, 1(1):9–36, Mar. 1976.

[54] J. Chomicki. Temporal inegrity constraints in relational databases. *Bull. of the IEEE Computer Society Technical Committee on Data Engineering*, 17(2):33–37, 1994.

[55] J. Chomicki. Temporal query languages: a survey. In *Proc. of the 1st Int. Conf. on Temporal Logic (ICTL'94)*, volume 827 of *Lecture Notes in Computer Science*, pages 506–534. Springer, 1994.

[56] J. Chomicki. Efficient checking of temporal integrity constraints using bounded history encoding. *ACM Trans. on Database Systems*, 20(2):149–186, 1995.

[57] J. Chomicki and T. Imielinski. Temporal deductive databases and infinite objects. In *Proc. of the 7th ACM SIGACT SIGMOD SIGART Symp. on Principles of Database Systems (PODS'88)*, pages 61–73, 1988.

[58] J. Chomicki and D. Niwinski. On the feasibility of checking temporal integrity constraints. In *Proc. of the 12th ACM SIGACT SIGMOD SIGART Symp. on Principles of Database Systems (PODS'93)*, pages 202–213, 1993.

[59] J. Chomicki and D. Niwinski. On the feasibility of checking temporal integrity constraints. *J. of Computer and System Sciences*, 51(3):523–535, 1995.

[60] D. Cohn and R. Hull. Business artifacts: A data-centric approach to modeling business operations and processes. *Bull. of the IEEE Computer Society Technical Committee on Data Engineering*, 32(3):3–9, 2009.

[61] E. Damaggio, A. Deutsch, R. Hull, and V. Vianu. Automatic verification of data-centric business processes. In *Proc. of the 9th Int. Conference on Business Process Management (BPM 2011)*, volume 6896 of *Lecture Notes in Computer Science*, pages 30–16. Springer, 2011.

[62] E. Damaggio, A. Deutsch, and V. Vianu. Artifact systems with data dependencies and arithmetic. In *Proc. of the 14th Int. Conf. on Database Theory (ICDT 2011)*, pages 66–77, 2011.

[63] E. Damaggio, A. Deutsch, and V. Vianu. Artifact systems with data dependencies and arithmetic. *ACM Trans. on Database Systems*, 37(3):22, 2012.

[64] S. B. Davidson, T. Milo, and S. Roy. A propagation model for provenance views of public/private workflows. In *Proc. of the 16th Int. Conf. on Database Theory (ICDT 2013)*, pages 165–176, 2013.

[65] H. Davulcu, M. Kifer, C. R. Ramakrishnan, and I. V. Ramakrishnan. Logic based modeling and analysis of workflows. In *Proc. of the 17th ACM SIGACT SIGMOD SIGART Symp. on Principles of Database Systems (PODS'98)*, pages 25–33, 1998.

[66] G. De Giacomo, R. De Masellis, and R. Rosati. Verification of conjunctive artifact-centric services. *Int. J. of Cooperative Information Systems*, 21(2):111–139, 2012.

[67] G. De Giacomo, Y. Lesperance, and F. Patrizi. Bounded situation calculus action theories and decidable verification. In *Proc. of the 13th Int. Conf. on the Principles of*

Knowledge Representation and Reasoning (KR 2012), pages 467–477, 2012.

[68] S. Demri and R. Lazić. LTL with the Freeze quantifier and register automata. In *Proc. of the 21st IEEE Symp. on Logic in Computer Science (LICS 2006)*, pages 17–26, 1996.

[69] D. Deutch and T. Milo. A quest for beauty and wealth (or, business processes for database researchers). In *Proc. of the 30th ACM SIGACT SIGMOD SIGART Symp. on Principles of Database Systems (PODS 2011)*, pages 1–12, 2011.

[70] A. Deutsch, R. Hull, F. Patrizi, and V. Vianu. Automatic verification of data-centric business processes. In *Proc. of the 12th Int. Conf. on Database Theory (ICDT 2009)*, pages 252–267, 2009.

[71] A. Deutsch, M. Marcus, L. Sui, V. Vianu, and D. Zhou. A verifier for interactive, data-driven web applications. In *Proc. of the ACM SIGMOD Int. Conf. on Management of Data*, pages 539–550, 2005.

[72] A. Deutsch, L. Sui, and V. Vianu. Specification and verification of data-driven web services. In *Proc. of the 23rd ACM SIGACT SIGMOD SIGART Symp. on Principles of Database Systems (PODS 2004)*, pages 71–82, 2004.

[73] A. Deutsch, L. Sui, and V. Vianu. Specification and verification of data-driven web applications. *J. of Computer and System Sciences*, 73(3):442–474, 2007.

[74] A. Deutsch, L. Sui, V. Vianu, and D. Zhou. A system for specification and verification of interactive, data-driven web applications. In *Proc. of the ACM SIGMOD Int. Conf. on Management of Data*, pages 772–774, 2006.

[75] A. Deutsch, L. Sui, V. Vianu, and D. Zhou. Verification of communicating data-driven web services. In *Proc. of the 25th ACM SIGACT SIGMOD SIGART Symp. on Principles of Database Systems (PODS 2006)*, pages 90–99, 2006.

[76] J. Esparza. Decidability of model checking for infinite-state concurrent systems. *Acta Informatica*, 34(2):85–107, 1997.

[77] J. Esparza. Decidability and complexity of Petri net problems – An introduction. In *Lectures on Petri Nets I*, Lecture Notes in Computer Science, pages 374–428. Springer, 1998.

[78] X. Fu, T. Bultan, R. Hull, and J. Su. Verification of Vortex workflows. In *Proc. of the 7th Int. Conf. on Tools and Algorithms for the Construction and Analysis of Systems (TACAS 2001)*, volume 2031 of *Lecture Notes in Computer Science*, pages 143–157. Springer, 2001.

[79] D. M. Gabbay, I. Hodkinson, and M. Reynolds. *Temporal Logic: Mathematical Foundations and Computational Aspects*, volume 28 of *Oxford Logic Guides*. Oxford University Press, 1994.

[80] S. K. Gadia. Weak temporal relations. In *Proc. of the 5th ACM SIGACT SIGMOD Symp. on Principles of Database Systems (PODS'86)*, pages 70–77, 1986.

[81] C. E. Gerede and J. Su. Specification and verification of artifact behaviors in business process models. In *Proc. of the 5th Int. Conf. on Service Oriented Computing (ICSOC 2007)*, volume 4749 of *Lecture Notes in Computer Science*, pages 181–192. Springer, 2007.

[82] M. H. Graham, N. D. Griffeth, and B. Smith-Thomas. Reliable scheduling of database transactions for unreliable systems. In *Proc. of the 3rd ACM SIGACT SIGMOD Symp. on Principles of Database Systems (PODS'84)*, pages 300–310, 1984.

[83] D. Harel. Recurring dominoes: Making the highly undecidable highly understandable. *Ann. of Discrete Mathematics*, 24:51–72, 1985.

[84] J. M. Hellerstein. The declarative imperative: Experiences and conjectures in distributed logics. *SIGMOD Record*, 39(1):5–19, 2010.

[85] R. Hull. Artifact-centric business process models: Brief survey of research results and challenges. In *Proc. of the On the Move Confederated Int. Conf. (OTM 2008)*, volume 5332 of *Lecture Notes in Computer Science*, pages 1152–1163. Springer, 2008.

[86] R. Hull, M. Benedikt, V. Christophides, and J. Su. E-services: a look behind the curtain. In *Proc. of the 22nd ACM SIGACT SIGMOD SIGART Symp. on Principles of Database Systems (PODS 2003)*, pages 1–14, 2003.

[87] R. Hull and J. Su. The Vortex approach to integration and coordination of workflows. In *Proc. of the Workshop on Cross-Organisational Workflow Management and Co-ordination*, volume 17 of *CEUR Electronic Workshop Proceedings*, `http://ceur-ws.org/`, 1999.

[88] C. S. Jensen and R. T. Snodgrass. Temporal data management. *IEEE Trans. on Knowledge and Data Engineering*, 11(1):36–44, 1999.

[89] F. Kabanza, J.-M. Stévenne, and P. Wolper. Handling infinite temporal data. In *Proc. of the 9th ACM SIGACT SIGMOD SIGART Symp. on Principles of Database Systems (PODS'90)*, pages 392–403, 1990.

[90] R. Karel, C. Richardson, and C. Moore. Warning: Don't assume your business processes use master data – Synchronize your business process and master data strategies. Report, Forrester, Sept. 2009.

[91] Z. M. Kedem and A. Tuzhilin. Relational database behavior: Utilizing relational discrete event systems and models. In *Proc. of the 8th ACM SIGACT SIGMOD SIGART Symp. on Principles of Database Systems (PODS'89)*, pages 336–346, 1989.

[92] P. G. Kolaitis. Schema mappings, data exchange, and metadata management. In *Proc. of the 24th ACM SIGACT SIGMOD SIGART Symp. on Principles of Database Systems (PODS 2005)*, pages 61–75, 2005.

[93] R. Krishnamurthy and U. Dayal. Theory of serializability for a parallel model of transactions. In *Proc. of the 1st ACM SIGACT SIGMOD Symp. on Principles of Database Systems (PODS'82)*, pages 293–305, 1982.

[94] S. Kumaran, R. Liu, and F. Y. Wu. On the duality of information-centric and activity-centric models of business processes. In *Proc. of the 20th Int. Conf. on Advanced Information Systems Engineering (CAiSE 2008)*, pages 32–47, 2008.

[95] R. Lazic, T. Newcomb, J. Ouaknine, A. W. Roscoe, and J. Worrell. Nets with tokens which carry data. *Fundamenta Informaticae*, 88(3):251–274, 2008.

[96] U. W. Lipeck. Transformation of dynamic integrity constraints into transaction specifications. In *Proc. of the Int. Conf. on Database Theory (ICDT'88)*, volume 326 of *Lecture Notes in Computer Science*, pages 322–337. Springer, 1988.

[97] R. Liu, K. Bhattacharya, and F. Y. Wu. Modeling business contexture and behavior using business artifacts. In *Proc. of the 19th Int. Conf. on Advanced Information Systems Engineering (CAiSE 2007)*, volume 4495 of *Lecture Notes in Computer Science*, pages 324–339. Springer, 2007.

[98] N. A. Lynch. Concurrency control for resilient nested transactions. In *Proc. of the 2nd ACM SIGACT SIGMOD Symp. on Principles of Database Systems (PODS'83)*, pages 166–181, 1983.

[99] J. McCarthy and P. J. Hayes. Some philosophical problems from the standpoint of aritificial intelligence. *Machine Intelligence*, 4:463–502, 1969.

[100] A. Meyer, S. Smirnov, and M. Weske. Data in business processes. Technical Report 50, Hasso-Plattner-Institut for IT Systems Engineering, Universität Potsdam, 2011. Available online at `http://opus.kobv.de/ubp/volltexte/2011/5304/`.

[101] A. Nigam and N. S. Caswell. Business artifacts: An approach to operational specification. *IBM Systems Journal*, 42(3):428–445, 2003.

[102] C. Ouyang, M. Dumas, A. H. M. ter Hofstede, and W. M. P. van der Aalst. From bpmn process models to bpel web services. In *Proc. of the 4th IEEE Int. Conf. on Web Services (ICWS 2006)*, pages 285–292. IEEE Computer Society Press, 2006.

[103] P. Picouet and V. Vianu. Semantics and expressiveness issues in active databases. In *Proc. of the 14th ACM SIGACT SIGMOD SIGART Symp. on Principles of Database Systems (PODS'95)*, pages 126–138, 1995.

[104] P. Picouet and V. Vianu. Expressiveness and complexity of active databases. In *Proc. of the 6th Int. Conf. on Database Theory (ICDT'97)*, volume 1186 of *Lecture Notes in Computer Science*, pages 155–172. Springer, 1997.

[105] M. Reichert. Process and data: Two sides of the same coin? In *Proc. of the On the Move Confederated Int. Conf. (OTM 2012)*, volume 7565 of *Lecture Notes in Computer Science*, pages 2–19. Springer, 2012.

[106] R. Reiter. *Knowledge in Action: Logical Foundations for Specifying and Implementing Dynamical Systems*. The MIT Press, 2001.

[107] A. Reuter, S. Ceri, J. Gray, B. Salzberg, and G. Weikum. Databases and workflow management: What is it all about? (panel). In *Proc. of the 21st Int. Conf. on Very Large Data Bases (VLDB'95)*, page 632, 1995.

[108] C. Richardson. Warning: Don't assume your business processes use master data. In *Proc. of the 8th Int. Conference on Business Process Management (BPM 2010)*, volume 6336 of *Lecture Notes in Computer Science*, pages 11–12. Springer, 2010.

[109] K. Schmidt. LoLA: A low level analyser. In *Proc. of the 21st Int. Conf. on Application and Theory of Petri Nets (ICATPN 2000)*, Lecture Notes in Computer Science, pages 465–474. Springer, 2000.

[110] K. Schmidt. Using Petri net invariants in state space construction. In *Proc. of the 9th Int. Conf. on Tools and Algorithms for the Construction and Analysis of Systems (TACAS 2003)*, volume 2619 of *Lecture Notes in Computer Science*, pages 473–488. Springer, 2003.

[111] R. T. Snodgrass. The temporal query language TQuel. In *Proc. of the 3rd ACM SIGACT SIGMOD Symp. on Principles of Database Systems (PODS'84)*, pages 204–213, 1984.

[112] E. Soisalon-Soininen and D. Wood. An optimal algorithm for testing for safety and detecting deadlocks in locked transaction systems. In *Proc. of the 1st ACM SIGACT SIGMOD Symp. on Principles of Database Systems (PODS'82)*, pages 108–116, 1982.

[113] M. Spielmann. Verification of relational transducers for electronic commerce. In *Proc. of the 19th ACM SIGACT SIGMOD SIGART Symp. on Principles of Database Systems (PODS 2000)*, pages 92–103, 2000.

[114] M. Spielmann. Verification of relational transducers for electronic commerce. *J. of Computer and System Sciences*, 66(1):40–65, 2003.

[115] J. K. Strosnider, P. Nandi, S. Kumaran, S. P. Ghosh, and A. Arsanjani. Model-driven synthesis of SOA solutions. *IBM Systems Journal*, 47(3):415–432, 2008.

[116] J. Su. Letter from the editor of the special issue on management of data-centric business workïňĆows. *Bull. of the IEEE Computer Society Technical Committee on Data Engineering*, 32(3):2, Sept. 2009.

[117] J. van Benthem. Temporal logic. In D. Gabbay, C. Hogger, and J. Robinson, editors, *Handbook of Logic in Artificial Intelligence and Logic Programming, Volume 4*, pages 241–350. Oxford Scientific Publishers, 1996.

[118] W. M. P. van der Aalst. A decade of business process management conferences: Personal reflections on a developing discipline. In *Proc. of the 10th Int. Conference on Business Process Management (BPM 2012)*, volume 7481 of *Lecture Notes in Computer Science*, pages 1–16. Springer, 2012.

[119] W. M. P. van der Aalst and C. Stahl. *Modeling Business Processes: a Petri Net-Oriented Approach*. The MIT Press, 2011.

[120] W. M. P. van der Aalst, M. Weske, and D. Grünbauer. Case handling: A new paradigm for business process support. *Data and Knowledge Engineering*, 53(2):129–162, 2005.

[121] M. Y. Vardi. A temporal fixpoint calculus. In *Proc. of the 15th ACM SIGPLAN-SIGACT Symp. on Principles of Programming Languages (POPL'88)*, pages 250–259, 1988.

[122] M. Y. Vardi. Model checking for database theoreticians. In *Proc. of the 10th Int. Conf. on Database Theory (ICDT 2005)*, volume 3363 of *Lecture Notes in Computer Science*, pages 1–16. Springer, 2005.

[123] V. Vianu. Dynamic constraints and database evolution. In *Proc. of the 2nd ACM SIGACT SIGMOD Symp. on Principles of Database Systems (PODS'83)*, pages 389–399, 1983.

[124] V. Vianu. *Dynamic Constraints and Database Evolution*. PhD thesis, University of Southern California, 1983.

[125] V. Vianu. Object projection views in the dynamic relational model. In *Proc. of the 3rd ACM SIGACT SIGMOD Symp. on Principles of Database Systems (PODS'84)*, pages 214–220, 1984.

[126] V. Vianu. Automatic verification of database-driven systems: a new frontier. In *Proc. of the 12th Int. Conf. on Database Theory (ICDT 2009)*, pages 1–13, 2009.

[127] T. Yoneda, A. Shibayama, B.-H. Schlingloff, and E. M. Clarke. Efficient verification of parallel real-time systems. In *Proc. of the 5th Int. Conf. on Computer Aided Verification (CAV'93)*, volume 697 of *Lecture Notes in Computer Science*, pages 321–346. Springer, 1993.

The Complexity of Mining Maximal Frequent Subgraphs

Benny Kimelfeld
IBM Research – Almaden
kimelfeld@us.ibm.com

Phokion G. Kolaitis
UC Santa Cruz &
IBM Research – Almaden
kolaitis@cs.ucsc.edu

ABSTRACT

A *frequent subgraph* of a given collection of graphs is a graph that is isomorphic to a subgraph of at least as many graphs in the collection as a given threshold. Frequent subgraphs generalize frequent itemsets and arise in various contexts, from bioinformatics to the Web. Since the space of frequent subgraphs is typically extremely large, research in graph mining has focused on special types of frequent subgraphs that can be orders of magnitude smaller in number, yet encapsulate the space of all frequent subgraphs. *Maximal* frequent subgraphs (i.e., the ones not properly contained in any frequent subgraph) constitute the most useful such type.

In this paper, we embark on a comprehensive investigation of the computational complexity of mining maximal frequent subgraphs. Our study is carried out by considering the effect of three different parameters: possible restrictions on the class of graphs; a fixed bound on the threshold; and a fixed bound on the number of desired answers. We focus on specific classes of connected graphs: general graphs, planar graphs, graphs of bounded degree, and graphs of bounded tree-width (trees being a special case). Moreover, each class has two variants: the one in which the nodes are unlabeled, and the one in which they are uniquely labeled. We delineate the complexity of the enumeration problem for each of these variants by determining when it is solvable in (total or incremental) polynomial time and when it is NP-hard. Specifically, for the labeled classes, we show that bounding the threshold yields tractability but, in most cases, bounding the number of answers does not, unless P=NP; an exception is the case of labeled trees, where bounding either of these two parameters yields tractability. The state of affairs turns out to be quite different for the unlabeled classes. The main (and most challenging to prove) result concerns unlabeled trees: we show NP-hardness, even if the input consists of two trees, and both the threshold and the number of desired answers are equal to just two. In other words, we establish that the following problem is NP-complete: given two unlabeled trees, do they have more than one maximal subtree in common?

PODS'13, June 22–27, 2013, New York, New York, USA.

Categories and Subject Descriptors

H.2.8 [**Database Management**]: Database Applications—*Data mining*; G.2.2 [**Discrete Mathematics**]: Graph Theory—*Graph algorithms*

General Terms

Algorithms, Theory

Keywords

Graph mining, maximal frequent subgraphs, enumeration complexity

1. INTRODUCTION

The discovery and generation of frequent patterns has occupied a central place in the area of data mining. Much of the earlier work on this topic focused on frequent itemsets and frequent sequences. In the past decade, however, the research has expanded to include the study of more complex frequent patterns, such as trees and graphs. The need to consider more complex patterns arises in applications that span a wide spectrum; examples include mining molecular data and classification of chemical compounds in bioinformatics [4, 25], behavior and link analysis in social networks [24, 28], and workflow analysis [8, 9]. In particular, graphs form a rich data structure that can capture complicated relationships between data encountered in such applications.

Given a finite sequence $\mathbf{g} = \langle g_1, \dots, g_n \rangle$ of graphs and a positive integer τ as threshold, a *frequent subgraph* of $\mathbf{g}$ is a graph that is isomorphic to a subgraph of at least τ graphs in $\mathbf{g}$. Ideally, one would like to be able to generate all frequent subgraphs; several different algorithms for this task have been proposed, including those reported in [10, 14, 15, 20, 21, 34]. However, since the space of frequent subgraphs is typically extremely large, research in graph mining has considered special types of frequent subgraphs that provide a more compact representation of this space. Maximal frequent subgraphs are arguably the most useful such type, where a *maximal frequent subgraph* is a frequent subgraph that is not properly contained in any frequent subgraph. Maximal frequent subgraphs can be orders of magnitude smaller in number than frequent subgraphs, yet they encapsulate the entire space of frequent subgraphs, as the frequent subgraphs are precisely the subgraphs of the maximal ones. By now, several different algorithms for generating all maximal frequent subgraphs have been proposed and evaluated experimentally, including SPIN [13] and MARGIN [29]. However, with the exception of some earlier work on maximal frequent itemsets [3, 11] and on the counting complexity of maximal frequent subgraphs [36], not much is known about the computational complexity of the fundamental enumeration and decision problems concerning maximal frequent subgraphs.

In this paper, we use the lens of computational complexity to systematically investigate the problem of mining maximal frequent subgraphs. More formally, we investigate the *enumeration problem* for maximal frequent subgraphs: given a sequence $\mathbf{g} = \langle g_1, \ldots, g_n \rangle$ of graphs and a threshold τ, produce all maximal frequent subgraphs of $\mathbf{g}$, up to isomorphism and without repetitions. Our study is carried out by considering the effect of three different parameters that we now discuss. First and foremost, we focus on specific classes of connected graphs of algorithmic and combinatorial significance, namely, arbitrary connected graphs, trees, planar graphs, graphs of bounded degree, and graphs of bounded treewidth. These classes are listed in Table 1. Each such a class $\mathcal{P}$ (e.g., the class $\mathbf{T}$ of all trees) consists of *unlabeled* graphs, but also has a *labeled* variant, denoted by $\mathcal{P}_{\mathsf{L}}$ (e.g., the class $\mathbf{T}_{\mathsf{L}}$ of all labeled trees), where the nodes of each graph are uniquely labeled. Note that, for each of these classes, the input to the aforementioned enumeration problem consists of a sequence $\mathbf{g}$ of graphs and a positive integer τ as threshold. We will also consider the restriction of this problem obtained by imposing a fixed bound on the threshold τ; this is the second parameter. The third parameter is a fixed bound k on the number of desired maximal frequent subgraphs; in other words, instead of enumerating all maximal frequent subgraphs, the goal is relaxed to producing just k maximal frequent subgraphs.

Even though the number of maximal frequent subgraphs (up to isomorphism) is often much smaller than the number of frequent subgraphs, it can still be exponential in the size of the given sequence of graphs. Johnson at al. [16] introduced three different yardsticks of goodness for algorithms that solve enumeration problems where the number of answers is, in the worst case, exponential in the size of the input. The weakest one is *polynomial total time*: the running time of the algorithm is polynomial in the combined size of the input and the output. The strongest and most desirable one is *polynomial delay*: the time between every two consecutive answers is polynomial in the size of the input. In between lies the notion of *incremental polynomial time*: the time between every two consecutive answers is polynomial in the combined size of the input and output up to that point. We will use these yardsticks to gauge the complexity of mining maximal frequent subgraphs.

What tools do we have to establish lower bounds for the complexity of enumeration problems? Concretely, how can one show that, under standard complexity assumptions, a particular enumeration problem cannot be solved in polynomial total time? A simple technique is to show that the underlying *non-emptiness* decision problem is intractable. For example, assuming P $\neq$ NP, no algorithm can enumerate all satisfying assignments of a Boolean formula in polynomial total time, since, otherwise, such an algorithm could be used to decide whether a satisfying assignment exists. However, this technique is limited, as there are intractable enumeration problems whose non-emptiness problem (and even the problem of producing a single answer) is solvable in polynomial time. For this reason, a more powerful technique has been used, namely, lower bounds on the complexity of enumeration problems have been established by showing that the associated *extendibility* problem is intractable [3, 17, 19]. The extendibility problem is the decision problem in which the input consists of an instance of the enumeration problem at hand together with a set of answers, and the goal is to decide whether there is an answer that is not among the given ones. It is easy to see that if an enumeration problem is solvable in polynomial total time, then its associated extendibility problem can be solved in polynomial time.

In this paper, we will study the extendibility problem as a vehicle for establishing lower bounds on the complexity of mining maximal frequent subgraphs. Actually, in Section 2, we will introduce the property of *enumeration self-reducibility* and show that, in the presence of enumeration self-reducibility, enumeration in total polynomial time is equivalent to the polynomial-time solvability of the extendibility problem. Thus, in the presence of enumeration self-reducibility, the analysis of the complexity of the enumeration problem at hand amounts to the analysis of a standard decision problem. This will be of great interest to us, because, in Section 3, we will show that all labeled variants $\mathcal{P}_{\mathsf{L}}$ of the classes $\mathcal{P}$ in Table 1, as well as the class $\mathbf{T}$ of all (unlabeled) trees and the class $\mathbf{BDG}^2$ of all (unlabeled) graphs of degree at most 2, are enumeration self-reducible.

We can now summarize our results about mining maximal frequent subgraphs for the classes in Table 1. We first consider the labeled classes. Boros et al. [3] showed that the extendibility problem for maximal frequent itemsets is NP-complete. This implies that the extendibility problem is NP-hard for all labeled classes, except for the class $\mathbf{BDG}^2_{\mathsf{L}}$ of labeled graphs of degree at most 2; for this class, the enumeration problem can be easily solved in polynomial time. In view of this, we consider the restrictions of the enumeration problem for the labeled classes, where either the threshold τ is bounded or the number k of desired answers is bounded. We show that bounding τ yields tractability. In contrast, if we bound k, then NP-hardness persists in all cases, except for the case of labeled trees for which we give a polynomial-time algorithm for extendibility. As a special case, the latter algorithm can be used for generating, in polynomial time, any bounded number k of maximal frequent itemsets. Note that this task would be intractable had we desired to enumerate *by decreasing size*, since determining whether there is a frequent set of cardinality at least as big as a given number is NP-complete [11].

The state of affairs turns out to be quite different for the unlabeled classes. To begin with, the subgraph isomorphism problem is NP-hard for all classes of Table 1, except for the class $\mathbf{T}$ of unlabeled trees and the class $\mathbf{BDG}^2$ of unlabeled graphs of degree at most 2. The intractability of subgraph isomorphism easily implies the intractability of the enumeration problem for maximal frequent subgraphs, even if τ and k are fixed small integers. The class $\mathbf{BDG}^2$ can be dealt with in a straightforward manner; in fact, the extendibility problem is in polynomial time, even when τ and k are unbounded. The main and technically most challenging result concerns unlabeled trees. We show that the extendibility problem is NP-complete, even if the input consists of only two trees and both τ and k are equal to just 2. In other words, we establish that the following problem is NP-complete: given two unlabeled trees, do they have more than one maximal subtree in common?

Finally, we consider the associated counting problem: given a sequence $\mathbf{g}$ of graphs and a threshold τ, compute the number of maximal frequent subgraphs. Yang's work [36] establishes #P-completeness for almost all cases. We focus on the effect of bounding τ, and show that the hardness of the counting complexity is aligned with the hardness of the extendibility problem. Our main contribution in this part concerns unlabeled trees and fixed τ: we prove that our reduction for extendibility can be made parsimonious, hence counting maximal frequent subtrees is #P-complete.

2. PRELIMINARIES

2.1 Enumeration Problems

An *enumeration relation* is a (possibly infinite) set $\mathcal{R}$ of pairs (x, y) of strings x and y, such that, for all strings x, the set $\mathcal{R}(x) = \{y \mid (x, y) \in \mathcal{R}\}$ is finite. A string $y \in \mathcal{R}(x)$ is called a *witness for* x. An enumeration relation $\mathcal{R}$ is said to be an NP*-relation* if the following hold:

1. There is a polynomial p such that $|y| \leq p(|x|)$, for all pairs $(x, y) \in \mathcal{R}$;
2. There is a polynomial-time algorithm for deciding membership of a given pair (x, y) in $\mathcal{R}$.

With every enumeration relation $\mathcal{R}$, we associate three algorithmic problems.

- $\mathcal{R}$-enumerate is the following function problem: given a string x as input, enumerate the set $\mathcal{R}(x)$; that is, produce all the witnesses for x without repetition.
- $\mathcal{R}$-extend is the following function problem: given a string x and a set $Y \subseteq \mathcal{R}(x)$ as input, generate a new witness $y \in \mathcal{R}(x) \setminus Y$ or declare that none exist.
- $\mathcal{R}$-extendible is the following decision problem: given a string x and a set $Y \subseteq \mathcal{R}(x)$ as input, decide whether $\mathcal{R}(x) \setminus Y \neq \emptyset$.

We also consider variants of these problems that are parameterized by a fixed bound k on the number of witnesses. Formally, let $\mathcal{R}$ be an enumeration relation and let k be a natural number.

- The problem $\mathcal{R}$-enumerate$\langle k \rangle$ is similar to the problem $\mathcal{R}$-enumerate, except that the goal is to generate a subset (any subset) of $\mathcal{R}(x)$ of size $\min(k, |\mathcal{R}(x)|)$.
- The problems $\mathcal{R}$-extend$\langle k \rangle$ and $\mathcal{R}$-extendible$\langle k \rangle$ are similar to the problems $\mathcal{R}$-extend and $\mathcal{R}$-extendible, respectively, except that the condition $|Y| < k$ is imposed on the input.

As a special case, the problem $\mathcal{R}$-extendible$\langle 1 \rangle$ is the *non-emptiness* problem for $\mathcal{R}$: given a string x, decide whether $\mathcal{R}(x) \neq \emptyset$.

2.1.1 Enumeration Complexity

Let $\mathcal{R}$ be an NP-relation. An algorithm that solves the problem $\mathcal{R}$-enumerate is called an *enumeration algorithm*. The number of witnesses an enumeration algorithm is required to produce (i.e., $|\mathcal{R}(x)|$) can be exponential in the size of the input. In particular, *polynomial running time* in the size of the input x may be a wrong yardstick of efficiency when analyzing the execution cost of such an algorithm, because just writing the output may require exponential time. For this reason, Johnson et al. [16] introduced several different notions of efficiency for enumeration algorithms. The one most commonly used is *polynomial total time*, which means that the running time is polynomial in the combined size of the input and the output (in other words, the running time is polynomial in $|x| + |\mathcal{R}(x)|$). Two stricter notions measure the time it takes to output a new answer, after a subset Y of $\mathcal{R}(x)$ has already been produced: under *polynomial delay*, this time is polynomial in the size $|x|$ of the input; under *incremental polynomial time*, this time is polynomial in $|x| + |Y|$. The following fact is immediate from the definitions; we record it here for later reference.

FACT 2.1. *Let $\mathcal{R}$ be an* NP*-relation.*

1. $\mathcal{R}$-enumerate *is in incremental polynomial time if and only if* $\mathcal{R}$-extend *is in polynomial time.*
2. *If k is a natural number, then* $\mathcal{R}$-enumerate$\langle k \rangle$ *is in polynomial time if and only if* $\mathcal{R}$-extend$\langle k \rangle$ *is in polynomial time.*

It is well known (and easy to show) that a polynomial-total-time algorithm for $\mathcal{R}$-enumerate can be used to solve the non-emptiness problem for $\mathcal{R}$. Hence, a simple technique to prove that *no* polynomial-total-time algorithm exists (under standard complexity assumptions) is to prove hardness (e.g., NP-hardness) of the non-emptiness problem (e.g., [22,37]). A more powerful technique is to show hardness of $\mathcal{R}$-extend. This technique has been used to prove that no polynomial total time algorithm exists in cases in which the non-emptiness problem is tractable or even trivial [17,19].

Figure 1 depicts the implications among tractability yardsticks for the problems we consider. The strongest yardstick, polynomial delay, implies incremental polynomial time, and so on, until the weakest—polynomial-time non-emptiness.

2.1.2 Self Reducibility

Let $\mathcal{R}$ be an enumeration relation. Clearly (and as depicted in Figure 1), if the problem $\mathcal{R}$-extend is in polynomial time, then so is the problem $\mathcal{R}$-extendible. We say that $\mathcal{R}$ is *enumeration self-reducible* if the other direction also holds, or, more precisely, if there is a polynomial-time algorithm for $\mathcal{R}$-extend using a solver for $\mathcal{R}$-extendible as an oracle. Similarly, if k is a natural number, then $\mathcal{R}$ is k*-enumeration self-reducible* if there is a polynomial-time algorithm for $\mathcal{R}$-extend$\langle k \rangle$ that uses a solver for $\mathcal{R}$-extendible$\langle k \rangle$ as an oracle. Using Fact 2.1, it is easy to prove the following proposition.

PROPOSITION 2.2. *Let $\mathcal{R}$ be an* NP*-relation that is enumeration self-reducible. The following statements are equivalent.*

- $\mathcal{R}$-extendible *is in polynomial time.*
- $\mathcal{R}$-enumerate *is in incremental polynomial time.*
- $\mathcal{R}$-enumerate *is in polynomial total time.*

Furthermore, for every $k \in \mathbb{N}$, if $\mathcal{R}$ is k-enumeration self-reducible, then the preceding equivalence holds for the versions of the problems parameterized by k.

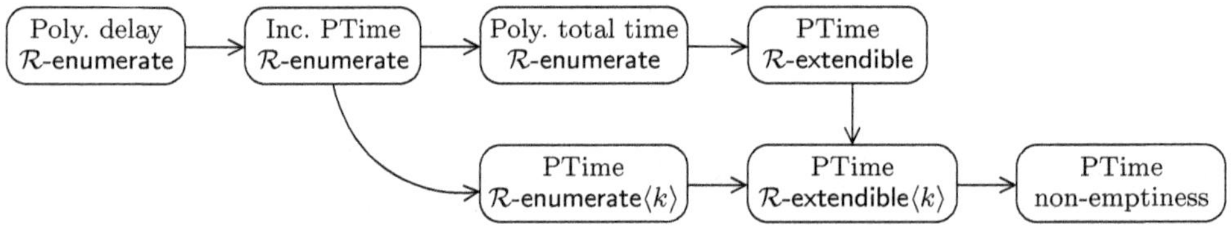

Figure 1: Levels of tractability for enumeration problems for an NP-relation $\mathcal{R}$

2.1.3 *Counting*

For an enumeration relation $\mathcal{R}$, the function $\#\mathcal{R}$ returns the number of witnesses $|\mathcal{R}(x)|$ for a given string x. We consider the following relevant concepts from computational complexity.

- FP is the class of functions that are computable in polynomial time.
- #P [31] is the class of functions $\#\mathcal{R}$, where $\mathcal{R}$ is an NP-relation. A function F is #P-*hard* if there is Turing reduction from every function in #P to F.

Recall that, with access to an oracle for a #P-hard function, one can efficiently solve every problem in the polynomial hierarchy [30]. Also, observe that if $\mathcal{R}$ is an NP-relation, then there is a straightforward polynomial-time reduction from $\mathcal{R}$-extendible to $\#\mathcal{R}$. Hence, from Proposition 2.2, we conclude that in the presence of self-reducibility, the ability to count witnesses implies the ability to enumerate them.

PROPOSITION 2.3. *Let $\mathcal{R}$ be an* NP*-relation that is enumeration self reducible. If $\#\mathcal{R} \in$ FP, then the problem $\mathcal{R}$*-enumerate *is in incremental polynomial time.*

Note that, under the assumption that FP $\neq$ #P, the other direction of Proposition 2.3 is generally false. For example, the maximal independent sets[1] of a graph can be enumerated with polynomial delay [16] (in particular, we have enumeration self reducibility), yet counting the number of such sets is a #P-hard problem [26].

2.2 Graphs and Canonized Classes

In this paper, we focus on undirected graphs to which, from now on, we refer to as, simply, graphs. If g is a graph, then the set of its nodes is denoted by nodes(g), while the set of its edges is denoted by edges(g). We assume that, for every graph g, the set nodes(g) of its nodes is a subset of some fixed countably infinite set, say, the set $\mathbb{N}$ of all natural numbers. We distinguish between two types of graphs: *unlabeled* and *labeled*. An unlabeled graph is just a graph. For the labeled graphs, we assume a countably infinite alphabet of *labels*. In a *labeled* graph g, every node v of g is associated with a *unique* label (i.e., no two nodes have the same label in g), which we denote by $\lambda_g(v)$. When the graph g is clear from the context, we may omit it from $\lambda_g(v)$ and, instead, write just $\lambda(v)$.

Let g_1 and g_2 be graphs, where we assume that either both are unlabeled or both are labeled. We say that g_1 and g_2 are *isomorphic*, denoted $g_1 \equiv g_2$, if there is a bijection μ : nodes(g_1) $\to$ nodes(g_2) that preserves edges, non-edges, and labels (when g_1 and g_2 are labeled). We write $g_1 \sqsubseteq g_2$ to denote that g_1 is isomorphic to a subgraph of g_2. We also write $g_1 \sqsubsetneq g_2$ to denote that $g_1 \sqsubseteq g_2$ and $g_1 \not\equiv g_2$.

A *class* $\mathcal{G}$ of labeled (or unlabeled) graphs is a collection of labeled (or unlabeled) graphs that is *closed under isomorphisms*; that is, if g_1 is in $\mathcal{G}$ and $g_1 \equiv g_2$, then g_2 is also in $\mathcal{G}$. We say that $\mathcal{G}$ is a *labeled* class if it consists of labeled graphs; similarly, we say that $\mathcal{G}$ is an *unlabeled* class if it consists of unlabeled graphs. Let $\mathcal{G}$ be a labeled or an unlabeled class. A *canonization for* $\mathcal{G}$ is a function $\mathcal{C} : \mathcal{G} \to \mathcal{G}$ possessing the following properties:

1. $\mathcal{C}(g) \equiv g$, for every g in $\mathcal{G}$;
2. $\mathcal{C}(g_1) = \mathcal{C}(g_2)$ for every $g_1, g_2 \in \mathcal{G}$ with $g_1 \equiv g_2$.

A *canonized class of graphs* is a pair $(\mathcal{G}, \mathcal{C})$ where $\mathcal{G}$ is a labeled class or an unlabeled class, and $\mathcal{C}$ is a canonization for $\mathcal{G}$. For a canonized class $\mathcal{P} = (\mathcal{G}, \mathcal{C})$ of graphs, we write $dom(\mathcal{P})$ to denote $\mathcal{G}$, and we write $\mathcal{C}_\mathcal{P}$ to denote $\mathcal{C}$. We say that $\mathcal{P}$ is *labeled* if $dom(\mathcal{P})$ is labeled, and *unlabeled* if $dom(\mathcal{P})$ is unlabeled. To simplify the presentation, we often abuse the notation and identify $dom(\mathcal{P})$ with $\mathcal{P}$; thus, we may write $g \in \mathcal{P}$, instead of $g \in dom(\mathcal{P})$.

In this paper, we study specific canonized classes of graphs. Table 1 lists five such unlabeled classes $\mathcal{P}$ by specifying $dom(\mathcal{P})$ in each case. Our work here is restricted to *connected* graphs; for simplicity of presentation, connectedness is implicit in the notation of the classes of Table 1. Although Table 1 does not mention the canonization of each class $\mathcal{P}$, we do assume that each class $\mathcal{P}$ comes with a fixed canonization $\mathcal{C}_\mathcal{P}$. Moreover, building on known results [2, 12, 32], we assume that if $\mathcal{P}$ is one of $\mathbf{T}$, $\mathbf{PLN}$, $\mathbf{BDG}^b$ and $\mathbf{BTW}^b$, then $\mathcal{C}_\mathcal{P}$ is computable in polynomial time. It should be pointed out that it is not known whether a polynomial-time computable canonization exists for the class $\mathbf{G}$ of all unlabeled connected graphs. Observe also that the existence of a polynomial-time computable canonization $\mathcal{C}_\mathcal{P}$ implies that $\mathcal{P}$ has polynomial-time graph isomorphism testing; thus, for a class of graphs, canonization is not easier than graph isomorphism. Note that some containment relationships hold between the domains of the classes of Table 1; for example, $\mathbf{T} \subseteq \mathbf{PLN}$ and $\mathbf{T} = \mathbf{BTW}^1$. Note also that $\mathbf{BTW}^b \subsetneq \mathbf{BTW}^{b+1}$.

For each unlabeled canonized class $\mathcal{P}$ of graphs in Table 1, we write $\mathcal{P}_\mathsf{L}$ to denote the corresponding labeled canonized class. As an example, $\mathbf{BTW}^3_\mathsf{L}$ consists of the labeled graphs of treewidth 3. For each $\mathcal{P}$ in the table, we assume that the canonization $C_{\mathcal{P}_\mathsf{L}}$ is computable in polynomial time. We can make this assumption because of the straightforward observation that there is a polynomial-time computable canonization for the class of all labeled graphs.

We now define some properties of canonized classes $\mathcal{P}$ of graphs. We say that $\mathcal{P}$ is *monotone* if $dom(P)$ is closed un-

[1]A *maximal independent set* is an independent set that is not strictly contained in any other independent set.

Table 1: Unlabeled canonized classes of graphs; each class $\mathcal{P}$ has a corresponding labeled class, which is denoted by $\mathcal{P}_L$; except for $\mathcal{P} = \mathbf{G}$, all canonizations are assumed to be computable in polynomial time.

$\mathcal{P}$	$dom(\mathcal{P})$
$\mathbf{G}$	All connected graphs
$\mathbf{T}$	All trees (acyclic connected graphs)
$\mathbf{PLN}$	All connected planar graphs
$\mathbf{BDG}^b$	All connected graphs with degree $\leq b$
$\mathbf{BTW}^b$	All connected graphs with treewidth $\leq b$

der taking subgraphs.[2] We say that $\mathcal{P}$ is *connected monotone* if $dom(P)$ is closed under taking connected subgraphs. As an example, each of the classes of Table 1 is connected monotone.

Next, we consider properties that capture different aspects of tractable behavior.

We say that a canonized class $\mathcal{P}$ of graphs has a *tractable realization* if the following two tasks can be executed in polynomial time:

- Given a graph g, determine whether $g \in \mathcal{P}$.
- Given $g \in \mathcal{P}$, compute $\mathcal{C}_{\mathcal{P}}(g)$.

We say that a canonized class $\mathcal{P}$ of graphs has *tractable subgraph isomorphism* if the subgraph isomorphism problem for $\mathcal{P}$ (i.e., given $g_1, g_2 \in \mathcal{P}$, decide whether $g_1 \sqsubseteq g_2$) can be tested in polynomial time. As an example, if $\mathcal{P}$ is labeled, then $\mathcal{P}$ has tractable subgraph isomorphism. Moreover, it is well known that $\mathbf{T}$ has tractable subgraph isomorphism, and so does $\mathbf{BDG}^2$. But, unless P = NP, none of $\mathbf{G}$, $\mathbf{PLN}$, $\mathbf{BDG}^b$ with $b > 2$ and $\mathbf{BTW}^b$ with $b > 1$ has tractable subgraph isomorphism [7, 23].

The next property of a canonized class $\mathcal{P}$ of graphs has to do with the ability to efficiently traverse the graphs of $\mathcal{P}$; we formalize it as follows. Let $g \in \mathcal{P}$ be a graph. A graph $h \in \mathcal{P}$ is an *immediate $\mathcal{P}$-extension* of g if $g \sqsubsetneq h$ and no graph $h' \in \mathcal{P}$ satisfies $g \sqsubsetneq h' \sqsubsetneq h$. Similarly, $h \in \mathcal{P}$ is an *immediate $\mathcal{P}$-reduction* of g if $h \sqsubsetneq g$ and no graph $h' \in \mathcal{P}$ satisfies $h \sqsubsetneq h' \sqsubsetneq g$. We say that $\mathcal{P}$ has *tractable progression* if there is a polynomial-time algorithm that, given a graph $g \in \mathcal{P}$, returns a set of graphs that contains all the immediate $\mathcal{P}$-extensions and immediate $\mathcal{P}$-reductions of g up to isomorphism; if $\mathcal{P}$ is labeled, then the algorithm is also given a set Σ of labels, and we require the labels of all returned graphs to have labels only from Σ. Note that, besides covering all the immediate $\mathcal{P}$-extensions and immediate $\mathcal{P}$-reductions of g up to isomorphism, the algorithm for realizing tractable progression is allowed to produce any other additional graph.

The following proposition is fairly straightforward.

Proposition 2.4. *Let $\mathcal{P}$ be a canonized class of graphs. If $\mathcal{P}$ is monotone or connected monotone, then $\mathcal{P}$ has tractable progression. Hence, all classes in Table 1 have tractable progression.*

[2]There are multiple, different definitions of monotone classes of graphs in the literature; here we follow the definition of Alon and Shapira [1] (which is different from, e.g., that of Friedgut and Kalai [6]).

3. MAXIMAL FREQUENT SUBGRAPHS

In this section, we formalize the enumeration problem of finding the maximal frequent subgraphs. We also provide some initial insights on the complexity of this problem and its variants.

Definition 3.1. Let $\mathbf{g} = \langle g_1, \ldots, g_n \rangle$ be a sequence of graphs and let h be a graph.

- The *support of h in* $\mathbf{g}$, denoted $supp(h|\mathbf{g})$, is the cardinality $|\{i \mid h \sqsubseteq g_i\}|$.
- Let τ be a natural number, which is viewed as a threshold. A *τ-frequent subgraph of* $\mathbf{g}$ is a graph h such that $supp(h|\mathbf{g}) \geq \tau$.

When $\mathbf{g}$ and τ are clear from the context, we will often use the term "frequent subgraph", instead of "τ-frequent subgraph of $\mathbf{g}$". □

Definition 3.2. Let $\mathcal{P}$ be a canonized class of graphs.

- Let τ be a natural number and let $h, g_1, \ldots, g_n$ be (not necessarily distinct) graphs in $\mathcal{P}$. We say that h is a *$\mathcal{P}$-maximal* τ-frequent subgraph of $\mathbf{g} = \langle g_1, \ldots, g_n \rangle$ if h is a frequent subgraph, and there is no frequent subgraph $h' \in \mathcal{P}$ such that $h \sqsubsetneq h'$. If $\mathbf{g}$, τ and $\mathcal{P}$ are all clear from the context, then we will often say that h is a *maximal frequent subgraph*.
- The enumeration relation $\mathsf{MaxFS}[\mathcal{P}]$ consists of all pairs (x, y) such that
  - $x = \langle \mathbf{g}, \tau \rangle$, for some sequence $\mathbf{g}$ of graphs in $\mathcal{P}$ and some threshold τ;
  - $y = \mathcal{C}_{\mathcal{P}}(h)$, for some $\mathcal{P}$-maximal τ-frequent subgraph h of $\mathbf{g}$.

Note that $\mathsf{MaxFS}[\mathcal{P}]$ is indeed an enumeration relation, since, given $\mathbf{g}$ and τ, there are only finitely many (maximal) frequent subgraphs up to isomorphism. □

In Definition 3.2, the sequence $\mathbf{g} = \langle g_1, \ldots, g_n \rangle$ is allowed to include repetitions (and isomorphic copies), since this is what may happen in data mining applications. We note that all complexity results of Sections 4–6 hold even if one requires that $g_i \not\equiv g_j$, whenever $i \neq j$. In particular, while we will use repetitions in one of the NP-hardness proofs (namely, the one of Theorem 4.11), that proof can be easily adjusted to avoid repetitions.

We will also consider the variant of this enumeration relation in which τ is a fixed parameter; specifically, $\mathsf{MaxFS}^{\tau}[\mathcal{P}]$ is defined similarly to $\mathsf{MaxFS}[\mathcal{P}]$, except that x is now just $\mathbf{g}$ (while τ is fixed). For the enumeration problems introduced in the previous section, there are actually two parameters: k (the restriction on the number of witnesses) and τ (the frequency threshold). Later in this paper, we will explore the effect of these parameters on the complexity of the enumeration problems.

3.1 Strong Tractability

Our ultimate goal is to study the complexity of the problems $\mathsf{MaxFS}[\mathcal{P}]$-enumerate, as well as their parameterized versions, for different canonized classes $\mathcal{P}$ of graphs (and with main focus on the classes of Table 1). To avoid immediate intractability hurdles, we must make some assumptions about the complexity entailed in the canonized class

$\mathcal{P}$. To begin with, we need to be able to test the validity of our input, and to produce canonical witnesses; therefore, our first requirement is that $\mathcal{P}$ should have tractable realization. However, this is not enough. Indeed, the following straightforward proposition implies that subgraph isomorphism reduces, via a trivial inspection of the output, to $\mathsf{MaxFS}[\mathcal{P}]$-enumerate, even if both τ and k are fixed small integers.

PROPOSITION 3.3. *Let $\mathcal{P}$ be a canonized class of graphs, and let g_1 and g_2 be two graphs in $\mathcal{P}$ with $|\mathsf{nodes}(g_1)| \leq |\mathsf{nodes}(g_2)|$ and $|\mathsf{edges}(g_1)| \leq |\mathsf{edges}(g_2)|$.*

- *If $\tau = 1$, then $g_1 \sqsubseteq g_2$ if and only if $\mathsf{MaxFS}^\tau[\mathcal{P}](g_1, g_2)$ is a singleton.*
- *If $\tau = 2$, then $g_1 \sqsubseteq g_2$ if and only if $\mathsf{MaxFS}^\tau[\mathcal{P}](g_1, g_2)$ is a singleton $\{h\}$, such that h has the same number of nodes and edges as g_1.*

Therefore, our second requirement is that $\mathcal{P}$ should have tractable subgraph isomorphism. The next proposition shows that tractable subgraph isomorphism is also a necessary condition, if one desires the underlying enumeration relation to be an NP-relation.

PROPOSITION 3.4. *Let $\mathcal{P}$ be a canonized class of graphs with tractable realization, but where subgraph isomorphism is* NP*-hard. The following problem is both* NP*-hard and* coNP*-hard: given h and $\mathbf{g}$, decide whether $(\mathbf{g}, h) \in \mathsf{MaxFS}^2[\mathcal{P}]$. In particular, neither $\mathsf{MaxFS}^2[\mathcal{P}]$, nor $\mathsf{MaxFS}[\mathcal{P}]$ is an* NP*-relation, unless* P = NP.

Finally, as our goal is to have algorithms for producing maximal frequent subgraphs, we need the property of tractable progression in order to create new graphs from existing ones. The property of *strong tractability* is the conjunction of the three tractability properties we introduced thus far.

DEFINITION 3.5. A canonized class $\mathcal{P}$ of graphs is *strongly tractable* if $\mathcal{P}$ has tractable realization, tractable subgraph isomorphism, and tractable progression. □

The following proposition lists the classes of Table 1 that are strongly tractable. Note that these are exactly the classes in the table that have tractable subgraph isomorphism (assuming P ≠ NP). Therefore, in view of Proposition 3.3, these are the only classes in the table for which we can hope to obtain tractability results.

PROPOSITION 3.6. *If $\mathcal{P}$ is one of the labeled variants of the classes in Table 1, or one of $\mathbf{T}$ and $\mathbf{BDG}^2$, then $\mathcal{P}$ is strongly tractable.*

The proof of the preceding Proposition 3.6 is by a straightforward combination of Proposition 2.4 and the aforementioned known results on canonization and subgraph isomorphism.

The following result states that, in the case in which $\mathcal{P}$ is strongly tractable, $\mathsf{MaxFS}[\mathcal{P}]$ and $\mathsf{MaxFS}^\tau[\mathcal{P}]$ are NP-relations.

PROPOSITION 3.7. *If $\mathcal{P}$ is a strongly tractable canonized class of graphs and τ is a natural number, then both $\mathsf{MaxFS}[\mathcal{P}]$ and $\mathsf{MaxFS}^\tau[\mathcal{P}]$ are* NP*-relations.*

3.2 Self Reducibility

We complete this section with the following theorem, stating that strong tractability of $\mathcal{P}$ also implies enumeration self-reducibility. The proof describes a polynomial-time algorithm for the problem $\mathsf{MaxFS}[\mathcal{P}]$-extend, using an oracle for $\mathcal{R}$-extendible. The algorithm consists of two main steps. In the first step, we construct a frequent subgraph $g \in \mathcal{P}$ that is not necessarily maximal, but is not isomorphic to any subgraph of any of the provided maximal subgraphs. In the second step, we extend g to a maximal frequent subgraph h and return $\mathcal{C}_\mathcal{P}(h)$. Both steps apply incremental and greedy constructions, invoking the algorithms for progression and testing subgraph isomorphism; the first step also invokes the oracle for $\mathcal{R}$-extendible. The complete proof will be given in the full version of the paper.

THEOREM 3.8. *If $\mathcal{P}$ is a strongly tractable canonized class of graphs, then $\mathsf{MaxFS}[\mathcal{P}]$ and $\mathsf{MaxFS}^\tau[\mathcal{P}]$ are both enumeration self-reducible and k-enumeration self-reducible, for all $\tau, k \in \mathbb{N}$.*

Combining Theorem 3.8 with Propositions 3.6 and 3.7, we obtain the following corollary.

COROLLARY 3.9. *Let $\mathcal{P}$ be one of the labeled variants of the classes in Table 1, or one of the classes $\mathbf{T}$ and $\mathbf{BDG}^2$. For every τ and for every k, both $\mathsf{MaxFS}[\mathcal{P}]$ and $\mathsf{MaxFS}^\tau[\mathcal{P}]$ are* NP*-relations, enumeration self-reducible and k-enumeration self-reducible.*

4. LABELED GRAPH CLASSES

In this section, we study the complexity of enumerating the maximal subgraphs for the labeled classes of Table 1. Recall from Proposition 3.6 that each of these classes is strongly tractable. We begin with the case in which both τ and k are unbounded.

4.1 The Unbounded Case

The *frequent-itemset* problem is one of the most extensively studied data mining problems. In the context of the framework described in Section 2.1, the frequent-itemset problem amounts to the enumeration problem associated with the enumeration relation MaxFIS of all pairs (x, y) such that

- $x = \langle \mathbf{s}, \tau \rangle$, for some finite sequence $\mathbf{s}$ of finite sets and some threshold τ.
- $y = s$, for some *maximal frequent subset* s.

Here, a set s is a *frequent subset* of $x = \langle \mathbf{s}, \tau \rangle$ if s is a subset of at least τ elements of $\mathbf{s}$; furthermore, s is a *maximal frequent subset* if it is a frequent subset that is not properly contained in any other frequent subset.

The following result by Boros et al. [3] will be of interest to us.

THEOREM 4.1. [3] MaxFIS-extendible *is* NP*-complete.*

One of the consequences of this result is that essentially all labeled classes of Table 1 have intractable enumeration.

COROLLARY 4.2. *Let $\mathcal{P}$ be one of the classes $\mathbf{G}_\mathsf{L}$, $\mathbf{T}_\mathsf{L}$, $\mathbf{PLN}_\mathsf{L}$, $\mathbf{BDG}^b_\mathsf{L}$ with $b \geq 3$, or $\mathbf{BTW}^w_\mathsf{L}$ with $w \geq 1$. Then the problem $\mathsf{MaxFS}[\mathcal{P}]$-extendible is* NP*-complete.*

The proof of Corollary 4.2 reduces MaxFIS-extendible to MaxFS[$\mathcal{P}$]-extendible, so that each of the associated graphs in the construction belongs to every class among those mentioned in the corollary. The complete proof will be given in the full version of the paper.

The only remaining case is MaxFS[$\mathbf{BDG}^b_{\mathsf{L}}$] with $b \leq 2$. The case of $b = 1$ is trivial, so we consider the case of $b = 2$. Let $\mathbf{g}$ and τ be an input to MaxFS[$\mathbf{BDG}^2_{\mathsf{L}}$]-enumerate. Observe that a graph of degree bounded by 2 is either a path or a simple cycle. Therefore, each of the graphs of $\mathbf{g}$, as well as any (maximal) frequent subgraph, is either a path or simple cycle. Moreover, every graph in $\mathbf{BDG}^2_{\mathsf{L}}$ has only a polynomial number of connected subgraphs. It follows that we can solve MaxFS[$\mathbf{BDG}^2_{\mathsf{L}}$]-enumerate in polynomial time via the following brute force algorithm: enumerate all subgraphs of the graphs in $\mathbf{g}$, filter out those that are not frequent, and then select the maximal among the remaining ones. Consequently, we obtain the following proposition.

PROPOSITION 4.3. MaxFS[$\mathbf{BDG}^b_{\mathsf{L}}$]-enumerate *is solvable in polynomial time if* $b \leq 2$.

4.2 Bounded Threshold

In this section, we show that, once τ is fixed, all labeled variants in Table 1 have tractable enumeration.

LEMMA 4.4. *Let $\mathcal{P}$ be a canonized class of labeled connected graphs that is connected monotonic and has tractable realization. For every integer τ,* MaxFS$^\tau$[$\mathcal{P}$]-enumerate *is solvable in polynomial time.*

The proof of Lemma 4.4 shows how to obtain in polynomial time the set of all maximal frequent graphs, by applying a form of *intersection* over each subsequence of length τ from the input sequence of graphs. The complete proof will be given in the full version of the paper. Combining the lemma with Proposition 3.6, we get following result.

THEOREM 4.5. *Let $\mathcal{P}$ be the labeled variant of one of the classes in Table 1. For every integer τ,* MaxFS$^\tau$[$\mathcal{P}$]-enumerate *is solvable in polynomial time.*

4.3 Bounded Number of Witnesses

In this section, we consider the effect of bounding the number of witnesses of interest. As we shall see, the state of affairs turns out to be more involved than the case of bounding the threshold.

4.3.1 Labeled Trees

We begin by showing that, in the case of trees, bounding the number of witnesses yields tractability.

THEOREM 4.6. MaxFS[$\mathbf{T}_{\mathsf{L}}$]-extendible$\langle k\rangle$ *is solvable in polynomial time for every fixed k.*

In what follows, we prove Theorem 4.6 by describing an algorithm for solving MaxFS[$\mathbf{T}_{\mathsf{L}}$]-extendible$\langle k\rangle$.

Let t be a labeled tree. Recall that $\lambda(v)$ denotes the label of a node v of t. For an edge $e = \{v_1, v_2\}$ of t, we write $\lambda(e)$ to denote the set $\{\lambda(v_1), \lambda(v_2)\}$. We also write $\lambda\mathsf{edges}(t)$ to denote the set $\{\lambda(e) \mid e \in \mathsf{edges}(t)\}$.

To describe our algorithm, we need the following simple observation. If t and t' are labeled trees and t has two or more nodes, then $t \sqsubseteq t'$ is equivalent to $\lambda\mathsf{edges}(t) \subseteq \lambda\mathsf{edges}(t')$. We then obtain the following lemma.

Algorithm LTEXT$\langle k\rangle(\mathbf{g}, \tau, Y)$

if there is a label that occurs at least τ times in $\mathbf{g}$ and does not occur in Y **then**
  return true
let $\mathbf{g} = \langle t_1, \dots, t_n\rangle$
for all subsets $F \subseteq \cup_{i=1}^{n} \lambda\mathsf{edges}(t_i)$ with $|F| \leq k$ **do**
  if $F \not\subseteq \lambda\mathsf{edges}(p)$ for all $p \in Y$ **then**
    for all $p' \in \mathbf{g}[F]$ **do**
      if $supp(p'|\mathbf{g}) \geq \tau$ **then**
        return true
return false

Figure 2: MaxFS[$\mathbf{T}_{\mathsf{L}}$]-extendible$\langle k\rangle$ **solver** LTEXT$\langle k\rangle$

LEMMA 4.7. *If $p', p_1, \dots, p_k$ are labeled trees and p' has two or more nodes, then the following statements are equivalent.*

1. *$p' \not\sqsubseteq p_i$, for every $i \in \{1, \dots, k\}$.*
2. *There is a set $F \subseteq \lambda\mathsf{edges}(p')$ with $|F| \leq k$, such that $F \not\subseteq \lambda\mathsf{edges}(p_i)$, for every $i \in \{1, \dots, k\}$.*

Let t be a labeled tree and F a subset of $\lambda\mathsf{edges}(t)$. Another straightforward observation is that, among the subtrees t' of t, there is exactly one tree f that is minimal among all those t' that contain F:

$$\forall t' \ [F \subseteq \lambda\mathsf{edges}(t') \Rightarrow f \sqsubseteq t']$$

We denote that subtree f by $t[F]$. The notion of $t[F]$ is similar to that of a *reduced subtree* [18]. If $\mathbf{t} = t_1, \dots, t_n$ is a sequence of labeled trees, then $\mathbf{t}[F]$ denotes the sequence that is obtained from $\mathbf{t}$ in two steps:

1. Remove every tree t_i such that $F \not\subseteq \lambda\mathsf{edges}(t_i)$.
2. Replace every remaining tree t_i with $t_i[F]$.

The algorithm LTEXT$\langle k\rangle$, depicted in Figure 2, solves the problem MaxFS[$\mathbf{T}_{\mathsf{L}}$]-extendible$\langle k\rangle$. As expected, the algorithm takes as input a sequence $\mathbf{g}$ of labeled trees, a threshold τ, and a set Y of maximal frequent subtrees. The idea behind this algorithm is as follows. The case where Y can be extended by a single-node frequent subtree is detected by a straightforward traversal over the labels of $\mathbf{g}$. So, suppose that p' is a frequent tree with at least two nodes, and that p' is contained in none of the trees in Y. From Lemma 4.7, we conclude that there is a set $F \subseteq \lambda\mathsf{edges}(p')$, such that $|F| \leq k$ and, for every $p \in Y$, F is not a subset $\lambda\mathsf{edges}(p)$. Then $p'[F]$ is isomorphic to $t[F]$ for at least τ trees t in $\mathbf{g}$. On the other hand, if some set F of label pairs is such that τ trees t in $\mathbf{g}$ share an isomorphic copy of $t[F]$, then $\mathbf{g}$ is indeed extendible. So, LTEXT$\langle k\rangle$ simply considers every possible F (or more precisely, every F that consists of k or fewer edges from $\mathbf{g}$), and every possible $t[F]$ (where t is in $\mathbf{g}$) and tests whether F is a subset of none of the $\lambda\mathsf{edges}(p)$, for $p \in Y$, and that $t[F]$ is frequent. The correctness of the algorithm LTEXT$\langle k\rangle$ is obvious from the above description. Note that, since k is fixed, the number of possible candidates F is polynomial in $\mathbf{g}$.

LEMMA 4.8. LTEXT$\langle k \rangle(\mathbf{g}, \tau, Y)$ *terminates in polynomial time, and returns* **true** *if and only if there is a frequent subtree that is contained in none of the trees in* Y.

Observe that a frequent subtree that is contained in none of the trees in Y can be extended (in polynomial time) to a maximal frequent subtree that is not isomorphic to any tree in Y. Therefore, Lemma 4.8 implies that LTEXT$\langle k \rangle(\mathbf{g}, \tau, Y)$ if and only if $\mathbf{g}$, τ and Y form a positive instance of the problem MaxFS[$\mathbf{T}_{\mathsf{L}}$]-extendible$\langle k \rangle$. This completes the proof of Theorem 4.6.

4.3.2 Beyond Labeled Trees

We continue the exploration of the effect of bounding the number k of witnesses. The first result is the special case in which $k \leq 2$.

LEMMA 4.9. *Let $\mathcal{P}$ be a canonized class of labeled connected graphs. Assume that $\mathcal{P}$ is connected monotonic, and that $\mathcal{P}$ has tractable realization. For $k \leq 2$, the problem* MaxFS[$\mathcal{P}$]-extendible$\langle k \rangle$ *is solvable in polynomial time.*

PROOF. Recall that in MaxFS[$\mathcal{P}$]-extendible$\langle k \rangle$, the input consists of a sequence $\mathbf{g}$ of graphs in $\mathcal{P}$, a threshold τ, and a set Y of at most $k-1$ maximal frequent subgraphs. The goal is to determine whether there is a (maximal) frequent subgraph h that is contained in none of the graphs in Y. For $k = 1$ the answer is always "yes" (e.g., take h to be the empty graph), unless $|\mathbf{g}| < \tau$ (in which case the answer is always "no"). So, we consider the case in which $k = 2$ and Y consists of exactly one graph h_Y. In that case, the answer is "yes" if and only if there is a frequent graph g' that consists of either a single node or a single edge, among the nodes/edges of the graphs in $\mathbf{g}$, such that $g' \not\sqsubseteq h_Y$. Here we are using the fact that $\mathcal{P}$ is connected monotonic, implying that g' is also in $\mathcal{P}$. □

Lemma 4.9 and Proposition 3.6 yield the following result.

THEOREM 4.10. *Let $\mathcal{P}$ be the labeled variant of a class in Table 1. For $k \leq 2$,* MaxFS[$\mathcal{P}$]-extendible$\langle k \rangle$ *is solvable in polynomial time.*

Finally, we show that the preceding results cover all cases where we obtain tractability by fixing k. More precisely, in what follows we assert that MaxFS[$\mathcal{P}$]-extendible$\langle k \rangle$ is NP-hard, where $\mathcal{P}$ is any one of the labeled variants of the classes in Table 1, except for the classes $\mathbf{T}_{\mathsf{L}}$ (which is also $\mathbf{BTW}^1_{\mathsf{L}}$) and $\mathbf{BDG}^b_{\mathsf{L}}$ with $b \leq 2$ (which was covered in Proposition 4.3).

THEOREM 4.11. *Let $\mathcal{P}$ be one of $\mathbf{G}_{\mathsf{L}}$, $\mathbf{PLN}_{\mathsf{L}}$, $\mathbf{BDG}^b_{\mathsf{L}}$ with $b > 2$, or $\mathbf{BTW}^w_{\mathsf{L}}$ with $w > 1$. Then, for every $k > 2$, the problem* MaxFS[$\mathcal{P}$]-extendible$\langle k \rangle$ *is* NP*-complete; moreover, this problem is* $W[1]$*-hard with respect to the parameter* τ.

PROOF. We first prove NP-completeness. Membership in NP is immediate from the fact MaxFS[$\mathcal{P}$] is strongly tractable. So, we prove NP-hardness, and it is enough to do so only for $k = 3$. We will describe a polynomial-time reduction from *Maximum Independent Set*: given a graph f and a number m, determine whether f has an independent set (i.e., a set of nodes inducing an edge-free subgraph) of size m. So, let f and m be a given input to Maximum Independent Set. Without loss of generality, we may assume that f has

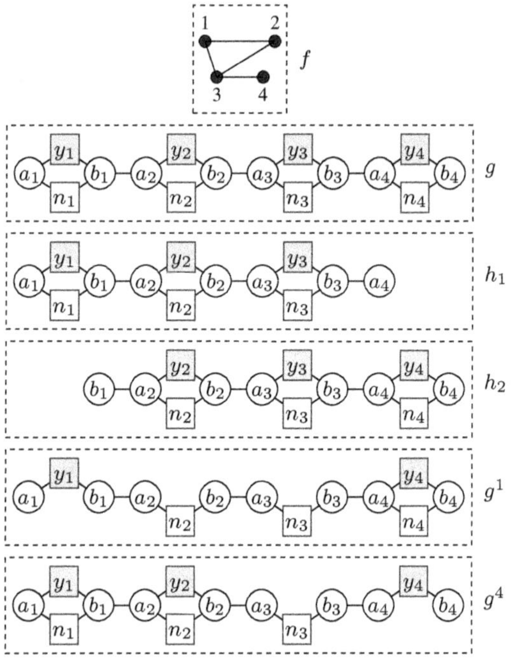

Figure 3: Reducing Maximum Independent Set to MaxFS[$\mathbf{G}_{\mathsf{L}}$]-extendible$\langle 2 \rangle$

no isolated nodes. We construct an input $\mathbf{g}$, τ, and Y to MaxFS[$\mathbf{G}_{\mathsf{L}}$]-extendible$\langle 3 \rangle$, as follows.

Suppose that $\{1, \dots, n\}$ is the node set of f. For each $i = 1, \dots, n$, we define four labels: a_i, b_i, y_i, and n_i (where y and n stand for *yes* and *no*, respectively). For simplicity, when we construct a graph over the labels we introduced, we do not distinguish between a node and its label (recall that here our graphs are uniquely labeled). We define the graph g to be the one over these $4n$ labels and with the edges $\{a_i, y_i\}$, $\{a_i, n_i\}$, $\{y_i, b_i\}$, $\{n_i, b_i\}$ for all $i = 1, \dots, n$, and $\{b_i, a_{i+1}\}$, for all $i = 1, \dots, n-1$.

Our construction is illustrated with a concrete example in Figure 3. The graphs f and g are on the top row in the figure. Note that $n = 4$ in this example.

We denote by h_1 the subgraph of g obtained by removing the nodes y_n, n_n and b_n. We also denote by h_2 the subgraph of g obtained by removing the nodes a_1, y_1 and n_1. In our example, the second top and third top rows in Figure 3 show h_1 and h_2, respectively.

Next, for $i = 1, \dots, n$, let g^i denote the subgraph of g obtained by deleting n_i and also deleting y_j, for every neighbor j of i in f. The bottom two rows of Figure 3 depict the graphs g^1 and g^4 in our example.

We are now ready to define the input $\mathbf{g}$, τ, and Y:

- $\mathbf{g} = g'_1, \dots, g'_m, g''_1, \dots, g''_m, g^1, \dots, g^n$, where each g'_i is h_1 and each g''_i is h_2.
- $\tau = m$ (i.e., the size in the given instance of Maximum Independent Set).
- $Y = \{h_1, h_2\}$.

Observe that the graphs h_1 and h_2 are indeed frequent; moreover, they are maximal since we assumed that neither 1 nor n is an isolated node. So, $(\mathbf{g}, \tau, Y)$ is a legal instance indeed.

The reduction is now complete; it remains to establish correctness, that is, some frequent graph is contained in neither h_1 nor h_2 (i.e., $(\mathbf{g}, \tau, Y)$ is a "yes" instance) if and only if f has an m-node independent set.

We say that a path p in g is a $(1,n)$-*path* if it is of the form $v_1 - b_1 - a_2 - v_2 - b_2 \cdots - b_{n-1} - a_n - v_n$, where each v_i is one of $\{y_i, n_i\}$. Observe that no graph in Y contains a $(1,n)$-path; moreover, every frequent subgraph not contained in a graph of Y must include some $(1,n)$-path. Hence, $(\mathbf{g}, \tau, Y)$ is a "yes" instance if and only if there is a frequent $(1,n)$-path. So, we will prove that there is a frequent $(1,n)$-path p if and only if f has an independent set I of size m.

For the "if" direction, suppose that I is an independent set of size m. Let p_I be the $(1,n)$-path $v_1 - b_1 - a_2 - v_2 - b_2 \cdots - b_{n-1} - a_n - v_n$, where $v_i = y_i$ if $i \in I$, and $v_i = n_i$, otherwise. For $i \in I$, the graph g^i contains the path p_I because I is an independent set. Therefore, p_I is a subgraph of m members of $\mathbf{g}$, or, equivalently, p_I is a frequent subgraph.

For the "only if" direction, suppose that $p = v_1 - b_1 - a_2 - v_2 - b_2 \cdots - b_{n-1} - a_n - v_n$ is a frequent $(1,n)$-path. Since p is a subgraph of neither h_1 nor h_2, there is a set I of m indices among $1, \ldots, n$ such that p is a subgraph of g^i, for all $i \in I$. We claim that I is an independent set of f. Indeed, if i and j are such that p is a subgraph of both g^i and g^j, then v_i and v_j must both coincide with y_i, and consequently, v_j cannot be a neighbor of v_i, since, otherwise, g^j does not have y_i as a node.

This completes the proof of correctness for the reduction. Observe that g (and, hence, every graph in $\mathbf{g}$ and Y) is in each of the classes $\mathbf{G}_\mathsf{L}$, $\mathbf{PLN}_\mathsf{L}$, $\mathbf{BDG}^b_\mathsf{L}$ with $b > 2$, or $\mathbf{BTW}^w_\mathsf{L}$ with $w > 1$.

Finally, $W[1]$-hardness with respect to the parameter τ follows immediately from our reduction, since τ is equal to m, and it is known that Maximum Independent Set is $W[1]$-hard with respect to the size of the independent set [5]. □

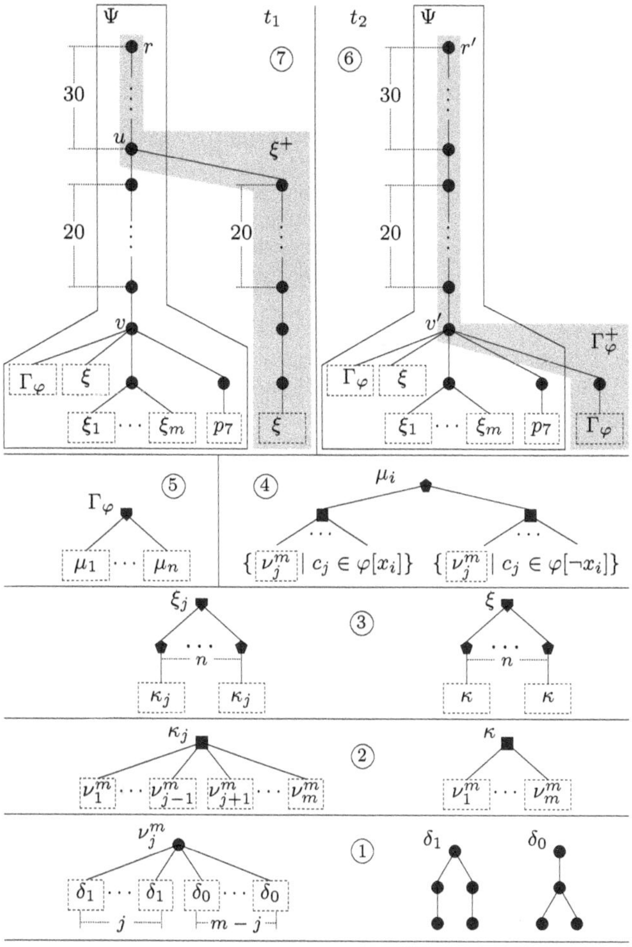

Figure 4: Constructions in the reduction

5. UNLABELED GRAPH CLASSES

In this section, we study the complexity of enumerating the maximal frequent subgraphs for the unlabeled classes in Table 1. Following Proposition 3.3 and Corollary 3.9, the classes that we can hope for tractable complexity results are $\mathbf{T}$ and $\mathbf{BDG}^2$.

We begin with the easy case, $\mathbf{BDG}^2$. By the same argument as that preceding Proposition 4.3, we obtain the following result.

PROPOSITION 5.1. $\mathsf{MaxFS}[\mathbf{BDG}^2]$-$\mathsf{enumerate}$ *is solvable in polynomial time.*

We now turn to the result with the most intricate proof in the paper. The proof itself is presented in the next section.

THEOREM 5.2. *The following is an* NP*-complete problem: Given two unlabeled trees t_1 and t_2, decide whether they have more than one maximal subtree in common (i.e., whether the set $\mathsf{MaxFS}^2[\mathbf{T}](t_1, t_2)$ has at least two members).*

Observe that obtaining one maximal frequent subgraph is in polynomial time for the class $\mathbf{T}$ (as it is for any strongly tractable canonized class of graphs). Thus, the decision problem of Theorem 5.2 reduces to $\mathsf{MaxFS}^2[\mathbf{T}]$-$\mathsf{extendible}\langle 2\rangle$. And, of course, the problem $\mathsf{MaxFS}[\mathbf{T}]$-$\mathsf{extendible}$ is in NP. Consequently, we obtain the following corollary of Theorem 5.2.

COROLLARY 5.3. *For all fixed thresholds $\tau \geq 2$, the problem $\mathsf{MaxFS}^\tau[\mathbf{T}]$-$\mathsf{extendible}\langle 2\rangle$ is* NP*-complete.*

PROOF. Theorem 5.2 gives the case $\tau = 2$. For $\tau > 2$, we still use Theorem 5.2, except that now our input $\mathbf{g}$ has $\tau - 1$ copies of t_1 (or of t_2) instead of just 1. □

By combining Corollary 5.3 with Proposition 2.2 and Corollary 3.9, we conclude that in the case of unlabeled trees and unless P = NP, it is impossible to enumerate the maximal frequent subtrees in polynomial total time, or even obtain more than one in polynomial time, even if the frequency is fixed to 2 and the input consists of just two trees.

5.1 Proof of Theorem 5.2

In this section we give the proof of Theorem 5.2. Due to space limitations, the proofs of some of the lemmas we state are omitted. The complete details will be given in the full version of the paper.

The *CNF satisfiability* problem is as follows. The input consists of a formula $\varphi = c_1 \wedge \cdots \wedge c_m$ over the free variables $x_1, \ldots, x_n$, where each c_i is a disjunction of atomic formulas (where an atomic formula is a variable or a negated variable) that we call a *clause*. The goal is to determine whether φ is satisfiable. In the remainder of this section, we prove Theorem 5.2 by giving a polynomial-time reduction from

CNF satisfiability. Specifically, we fix a formula φ as above, and show how t_1 and t_2 are constructed from φ.

We use the following notation. When there is no risk of ambiguity, we may identify φ with the set $\{c_1, \dots, c_m\}$ of its clauses. If a is an atomic formula over $x_1, \dots, x_n$ (i.e., $a = x_i$ or $a = \neg x_i$ for some $i \in \{1, \dots, n\}$), then $\varphi[a]$ denotes the set of all the clauses c_j that have a as a disjunct. A *truth assignment (for φ)* is a mapping $\alpha : \{x_1, \dots, x_n\} \to \{\mathbf{true}, \mathbf{false}\}$. If α is a truth assignment, then $\varphi[\alpha]$ denotes the set of the clauses c_j that are satisfied by α. Hence, in our notation α is *satisfying* if $\varphi[\alpha] = \varphi$, and the goal is to determine whether such an α exists.

Figure 4 shows the construction of two trees, t_1 and t_2. The construction is bottom up—each tree is built from subtrees that are defined in previous phases. We view each tree in Figure 4 as *rooted*, which means that one node is distinguished as the *root*. In the figure, the root of a tree t is always the topmost (highest) node in the corresponding figure. The figure is self explanatory, except for a few points that we explain as we go along.

- The tree ν_j^m, where $0 < j \leq m$, represents the selection of the number j out of m; in our reduction, it represents the clause c_j.
- The tree κ has every tree ν_j^m, where $j = 1, \dots, m$, placed under the root.
- The tree κ_j is obtained from κ by removing the tree ν_j^m.
- For $i = 1, \dots, n$, the tree μ_i represents the clauses satisfied by x_i and its negation: the set $\varphi[x_i]$ is represented (through the corresponding ν_j^m) under the left child, and the set $\varphi[\neg x_i]$ is represented under the right child.
- The tree p_7 is simply a path consisting of 7 nodes; it is easy to verify that p_7 is of the same height as each ξ_i.

Consider the subtree Ψ of t_1. This subtree is also a subtree of t_2. In Figure 4, both occurrences of Ψ are surrounded by polygons (with a flashlight-like shape). The following lemma states that Ψ is a maximal common subtree of t_1 and t_2.

LEMMA 5.4. *Ψ is a maximal common subtree of t_1 and t_2, that is, $\Psi \in \mathsf{MaxFS}^2[\mathbf{T}](t_1, t_2)$.*

PROOF. The proof is straightforward in view of the following two observations.

1. t_1 has exactly one subtree that is isomorphic to Ψ.
2. If t is a subtree of t_2 that is isomorphic to Ψ, then t must contain the root of t_2.

Indeed, due to the first observation, if Ψ is not maximal then the node of distance 30 from the root must have degree 3, which cannot be true due to the second observation. □

A key property in our reduction is the following simple lemma.

LEMMA 5.5. *Let j and k be two numbers in $\{1, \dots, m\}$. Then $\nu_j^m \sqsubseteq \nu_k^m$ if and only if $j = k$.*

Consider the tree Γ_φ constructed in the fifth step of the reduction (numbered 5 in Figure 4). Note that in Γ_φ, the children of the root are the trees μ_i, for $i = 1, \dots, n$. Let α be a truth assignment for φ. We denote by Γ_α the subtree of Γ_φ obtained by pruning subtrees in the following way. For all $i = 1, \dots, n$, if $\alpha(x_i) = \mathbf{true}$, then we prune away the right subtree of μ_i; otherwise (i.e., if $\alpha(x_i) = \mathbf{false}$), then we prune away the left subtree of μ_i. Observe that in Γ_α, the root has n children, as in Γ_φ, but unlike Γ_φ, in Γ_α each of these n children has precisely one child. Consider the subtree Γ_φ^+ of t_2, covered by a grey shade in Figure 4. We write Γ_α^+ to denote the subtree of Γ_φ^+ obtained by replacing Γ_φ with Γ_α. The following lemma states a key property of Γ_α^+.

LEMMA 5.6. *Let α be a truth assignment for φ. Then $\Gamma_\alpha^+ \sqsubseteq \Psi$ if and only if α is **not** a satisfying assignment.*

We can now establish the following lemma.

LEMMA 5.7. *If φ is satisfiable, then $\mathsf{MaxFS}^2[\mathbf{T}](t_1, t_2)$ contains at least two maximal frequent subgraphs.*

The proof of Lemma 5.7 is straightforward: combine Lemmas 5.4 and 5.6, and the observation that Γ_α^+ is a subtree of ξ^+ (the subtree of t_1 shaded in Figure 4), for all truth assignments α, due to the construction of ξ.

It remains to prove the other direction of Lemma 5.7, namely, $|\mathsf{MaxFS}^2[\mathbf{T}](t_1, t_2)| > 1$ implies that φ is satisfiable. We embark on this task next.

Let h be a maximal 2-frequent subtree of t_1 and t_2, such that $h \not\sqsubseteq \Psi$. We fix h for the rest of this section. We will prove that there is a satisfying assignment α such that h is isomorphic to Γ_α^+.

Fix a subtree h_1 of t_1 that is isomorphic to h, and an isomorphism $\mu_1 : \mathsf{nodes}(h) \to \mathsf{nodes}(h_1)$. Similarly, fix a subtree h_2 of t_2 that is isomorphic to h, and an isomorphism $\mu_2 : \mathsf{nodes}(h) \to \mathsf{nodes}(h_2)$.

If t and t' are two rooted trees, we write $t \sqsubseteq_{\mathsf{r}} t'$ to denote that there is an isomorphism μ from t to a subgraph of t', such that μ maps the root of t to the root of t'. Clearly, $t \sqsubseteq_{\mathsf{r}} t'$ implies $t \sqsubseteq t'$. The following lemma states that h is isomorphic to a subtree of both ξ^+ and Γ_φ^+, via root-preserving isomorphisms.

LEMMA 5.8. *$h \sqsubseteq_{\mathsf{r}} \xi^+$ and $h \sqsubseteq_{\mathsf{r}} \Gamma_\varphi^+$.*

Finally, the following lemma implies that φ is satisfiable, thereby completing the proof of Theorem 5.2.

LEMMA 5.9. *There is a satisfying assignment α such that h is isomorphic to Γ_α^+.*

PROOF. We will prove that h is isomorphic to Γ_α^+ for some truth assignment α. We will then derive that α is necessarily a satisfying assignment by using Lemma 5.6 and the assumption that $h \not\sqsubseteq \Psi$.

Lemma 5.8 states that h is isomorphic to a root subtree of both ξ^+ and Γ_α^+. Since h is maximal, h_1 consists of the path from the root all the way to the root of ξ (which corresponds to the root of Γ_φ in h_2), which we denote by r_ξ. Moreover, h being maximal implies that r_ξ has n children in h_1. Those n children correspond to the roots of the μ_i in h_2. Hence, since h is maximal, we have that each of the subtrees of μ_i in h_2 is *precisely* the one obtained by pruning away one of the two subtrees (see Step 4 in Figure 4). From the definition of Γ_α^+, it follows that h_2 is necessarily Γ_α^+ for some truth assignment α. This completes the proof because $h \equiv h_2$. □

Table 2: The complexity of MaxFS[$\mathcal{P}$]-extendible and the restricted variants MaxFS[$\mathcal{P}$]-extendible$\langle k\rangle$, MaxFS$^\tau$[$\mathcal{P}$]-extendible and MaxFS$^\tau$[$\mathcal{P}$]-extendible$\langle k\rangle$ for the strongly tractable classes of Table 1; $\surd$ stands for "polynomial time" (or "FP" when in parentheses), x stands for "NP-complete" (or "#P-complete" when in parentheses)

$\mathcal{P}$	Unrestricted (#)	$k=2$	Fix $k>2$	Fix $\tau \geq 2$ (#)	$k=2$, Fix $\tau \geq 2$
$\mathbf{T}$	x (x)	x	x	x (x)	x
$\mathbf{T}_\mathsf{L}$	x (x)	$\surd$	$\surd$	$\surd$ ($\surd$)	$\surd$
$\mathbf{BDG}^2$, $\mathbf{BDG}^2_\mathsf{L}$	$\surd$ ($\surd$)	$\surd$	$\surd$	$\surd$ ($\surd$)	$\surd$
$\mathbf{G}_\mathsf{L}$, $\mathbf{PLN}_\mathsf{L}$, $\mathbf{BDG}^{b>2}_\mathsf{L}$, $\mathbf{BTW}^{w>1}_\mathsf{L}$	x (x)	$\surd$	x	$\surd$ ($\surd$)	$\surd$

6. COUNTING COMPLEXITY

We now study the complexity of counting the number of maximal frequent subgraphs; more precisely, we study the problem $\#\mathcal{R}$ for the enumeration relations $\mathcal{R}$ considered in this paper. As a matter of fact, the problem of counting maximal frequent subgraphs has already been studied by Yang [36], who established #P-completeness for both labeled trees and unlabeled trees.

THEOREM 6.1. [36] *If $\mathcal{R}$ is* MaxFS[$\mathbf{T}$] *or* MaxFS[$\mathbf{T}_\mathsf{L}$], *then $\#\mathcal{R}$ is #P-complete. Moreover, #P-completeness holds, even if the inputs are labeled or unlabeled binary trees (equivalently, trees of degree at most 3).*

Yang's results do not cover the case of graphs of degree bounded by 2; we will consider this case next. More importantly, the threshold is part of the input in Yang's results. Thus, in what follows, we will also examine the effect of bounding the threshold. Note that, as regards counting problems, it is not meaningful to bound the number of witnesses. We begin by discussing cases for which $\#\mathcal{R}$ is in polynomial time.

PROPOSITION 6.2. *The counting problem $\#\mathcal{R}$ is in* FP *if $\mathcal{R}$ is one of* MaxFS[$\mathbf{BDG}^2$], MaxFS[$\mathbf{BDG}^2_\mathsf{L}$] *and* MaxFS$^\tau$[$\mathcal{P}_\mathsf{L}$], *where τ is a fixed threshold and $\mathcal{P}_\mathsf{L}$ is the labeled variant of a class $\mathcal{P}$ in Table 1.*

The preceding proposition is immediate from the fact that, for the enumeration relations $\mathcal{R}$ considered, $\mathcal{R}$-enumerate is solvable in polynomial time (and not just, e.g., polynomial total time); hence, one can count the witnesses in polynomial time by actually producing them first.

It remains to examine the case of unlabeled trees and fixed threshold. In the final result of this paper, we establish #P-completeness even in the case of $\tau = 2$. The proof builds on the reduction we used for proving Theorem 5.2. Although that reduction is not parsimonious, we show how it can be made so by properly changing the CNF formula. The complete proof will be given in the full version of the paper.

THEOREM 6.3. *For every fixed $\tau \geq 2$, the counting problem* #MaxFS$^\tau$[$\mathbf{T}$] *is #P-complete.*

7. CONCLUDING REMARKS

Our interest in mining maximal frequent subgraphs arose in a research project at the IBM Almaden Research Center, where we observed that a small threshold τ and a small number k of answers are often realistic assumptions in applications. In this paper, we used the lens of computational complexity to obtain a fairly comprehensive picture, shown in Table 2, for the problem of mining maximal frequent subgraphs. Furthermore, we believe that our main technical result about unlabeled trees is of independent interest as a new NP-complete problem: given two unlabeled trees, do they have more than one maximal common subtree in common?

The results presented here suggest several different directions for further research. We conclude by mentioning two such concrete directions.

In addition to maximal frequent subgraphs, a different representation of the space of all frequent subgraphs can be obtained by considering the collection of all *closed frequent subgraphs*, that is, those frequent subgraphs that no proper supergraph has the same set of containing graphs. Every maximal frequent subgraph is closed, while the converse need not be true. Thus, closed frequent subgraphs do not provide as compact a representation of the space of frequent subgraphs as the maximal ones do. On the other hand, closed frequent subgraphs can be used to compute the actual occurrences of all frequent subgraphs. Several different algorithms for enumerating all closed frequent subgraphs have been proposed [27, 33, 35, 38]. To date, no systematic investigation of the complexity of mining closed frequent subgraphs has been carried out.

Finally, note that labeled graphs and unlabeled graphs can be thought of as two extreme cases in the first of which each node has a distinct label, whereas in the second all nodes have the same label. This suggests considering an intermediate case in which every label has a bounded number of occurrences in the graph. Mining maximal frequent subgraphs in this case is a problem that remains to be explored.

Acknowledgment

The research of Phokion Kolaitis was partially supported by NSF Grant IIS-1217869.

8. REFERENCES

[1] N. Alon and A. Shapira. Every monotone graph property is testable. *SIAM J. Comput.*, 38(2):505–522, 2008.

[2] L. Babai and E. M. Luks. Canonical labeling of graphs. In *STOC*, pages 171–183. ACM, 1983.

[3] E. Boros, V. Gurvich, L. Khachiyan, and K. Makino. On maximal frequent and minimal infrequent sets in binary matrices. *Ann. Math. Artif. Intell.*, 39(3):211–221, 2003.

[4] M. Deshpande, M. Kuramochi, N. Wale, and G. Karypis. Frequent substructure-based approaches for classifying chemical compounds. *IEEE Trans. Knowl. Data Eng.*, 17(8):1036–1050, 2005.

[5] R. G. Downey and M. R. Fellows. *Parameterized Complexity*. Monographs in Computer Science. Springer, 1999.

[6] E. Friedgut and G. Kalai. Every monotone graph property has a sharp threshold. *Proc. Amer. Math. Soc.*, 124(10):2993–3002, 1996.

[7] M. R. Garey, D. S. Johnson, and R. E. Tarjan. The planar Hamiltonian circuit problem is NP-complete. *SIAM J. Comput.*, 5(4):704–714, 1976.

[8] G. Greco, A. Guzzo, G. Manco, and D. Saccà. Mining and reasoning on workflows. *IEEE Trans. Knowl. Data Eng.*, 17(4):519–534, 2005.

[9] G. Greco, A. Guzzo, G. Manco, and D. Saccà. Mining unconnected patterns in workflows. *Inf. Syst.*, 32(5):685–712, 2007.

[10] E. Gudes, S. E. Shimony, and N. Vanetik. Discovering frequent graph patterns using disjoint paths. *IEEE Trans. Knowl. Data Eng.*, 18(11):1441–1456, 2006.

[11] D. Gunopulos, R. Khardon, H. Mannila, S. Saluja, H. Toivonen, and R. S. Sharm. Discovering all most specific sentences. *ACM Trans. Database Syst.*, 28(2):140–174, 2003.

[12] J. E. Hopcroft and R. E. Tarjan. Isomorphism of planar graphs. In *Complexity of Computer Computations*, The IBM Research Symposia Series, pages 131–152. Plenum Press, New York, 1972.

[13] J. Huan, W. Wang, J. Prins, and J. Yang. SPIN: mining maximal frequent subgraphs from graph databases. In *KDD*, pages 581–586, 2004.

[14] A. Inokuchi, T. Washio, and H. Motoda. An apriori-based algorithm for mining frequent substructures from graph data. In *PKDD*, pages 13–23, 2000.

[15] A. Inokuchi, T. Washio, and H. Motoda. Complete mining of frequent patterns from graphs: Mining graph data. *Machine Learning*, 50(3):321–354, 2003.

[16] D. Johnson, M. Yannakakis, and C. Papadimitriou. On generating all maximal independent sets. *Information Processing Letters*, 27:119–123, 1988.

[17] L. Khachiyan, E. Boros, K. Borys, K. M. Elbassioni, and V. Gurvich. Generating all vertices of a polyhedron is hard. *Discrete & Computational Geometry*, 39(1-3):174–190, 2008.

[18] B. Kimelfeld and Y. Sagiv. Finding and approximating top-k answers in keyword proximity search. In *PODS*, pages 173–182. ACM, 2006.

[19] B. Kimelfeld and Y. Sagiv. Maximally joining probabilistic data. In *PODS*, pages 303–312. ACM, 2007.

[20] M. Kuramochi and G. Karypis. Frequent subgraph discovery. In *ICDM*, pages 313–320, 2001.

[21] M. Kuramochi and G. Karypis. An efficient algorithm for discovering frequent subgraphs. *IEEE Trans. Knowl. Data Eng.*, 16(9):1038–1051, 2004.

[22] K. Makino and T. Ibaraki. Interior and exterior functions of boolean functions. *Discrete Applied Mathematics*, 69(3):209–231, 1996.

[23] J. Matousek and R. Thomas. On the complexity of finding iso- and other morphisms for partial k-trees. *Discrete Mathematics*, 108(1-3):343–364, 1992.

[24] R. J. Mooney, P. Melville, L. R. Tang, J. Shavlik, I. Dutra, and D. Page. Relational data mining with inductive logic programming for link discovery. *Data Mining: Next Generation Challenges and Future Directions*, pages 239–254, 2004.

[25] S. Nijssen and J. N. Kok. Frequent graph mining and its application to molecular databases. In *SMC (5)*, pages 4571–4577. IEEE, 2004.

[26] Y. Okamoto, T. Uno, and R. Uehara. Counting the number of independent sets in chordal graphs. *J. Discrete Algorithms*, 6(2):229–242, 2008.

[27] J. Pei, J. Han, and R. Mao. CLOSET: An efficient algorithm for mining frequent closed itemsets. In *ACM SIGMOD Workshop on Research Issues in Data Mining and Knowledge Discovery*, pages 21–30, 2000.

[28] A. Stoica and C. Prieur. Structure of neighborhoods in a large social network. In *CSE (4)*, pages 26–33. IEEE Computer Society, 2009.

[29] L. T. Thomas, S. R. Valluri, and K. Karlapalem. Margin: Maximal frequent subgraph mining. *TKDD*, 4(3), 2010.

[30] S. Toda and M. Ogiwara. Counting classes are at least as hard as the polynomial-time hierarchy. *SIAM J. Comput.*, 21(2):316–328, 1992.

[31] L. G. Valiant. The complexity of computing the permanent. *Theor. Comput. Sci.*, 8:189–201, 1979.

[32] F. Wagner. Graphs of bounded treewidth can be canonized in AC^1. In *CSR*, volume 6651 of *Lecture Notes in Computer Science*, pages 209–222. Springer, 2011.

[33] J. Wang, J. Han, and J. Pei. CLOSET+: searching for the best strategies for mining frequent closed itemsets. In *KDD*, pages 236–245, 2003.

[34] X. Yan and J. Han. gSpan: Graph-based substructure pattern mining. In *ICDM*, pages 721–724, 2002.

[35] X. Yan and J. Han. CloseGraph: mining closed frequent graph patterns. In *KDD*, pages 286–295, 2003.

[36] G. Yang. The complexity of mining maximal frequent itemsets and maximal frequent patterns. In *KDD*, pages 344–353. ACM, 2004.

[37] M. Yannakakis. Algorithms for acyclic database schemes. In *VLDB*, pages 82–94. IEEE Computer Society, 1981.

[38] M. J. Zaki and C.-J. Hsiao. CHARM: An efficient algorithm for closed itemset mining. In *SDM*, 2002.

Deciding Monotone Duality and Identifying Frequent Itemsets in Quadratic Logspace*

Georg Gottlob
Department of Computer Science and Oxford Man Institute
University of Oxford
Oxford OX1 3QD, UK
georg.gottlob@cs.ox.ac.uk

ABSTRACT

The monotone duality problem is defined as follows: Given two monotone formulas f and g in irredundant DNF, decide whether f and g are dual. This problem is the same as duality testing for hypergraphs, that is, checking whether a hypergraph $\mathcal{H}$ consists of precisely all minimal transversals of a hypergraph $\mathcal{G}$. By exploiting a recent problem-decomposition method by Boros and Makino (ICALP 2009), we show that duality testing for hypergraphs, and thus for monotone DNFs, is feasible in DSPACE[$\log^2 n$], i.e., in quadratic logspace. As the monotone duality problem is equivalent to a number of problems in the areas of databases, data mining, and knowledge discovery, the results presented here yield new complexity results for those problems, too. For example, it follows from our results that whenever, for a Boolean-valued relation (whose attributes represent items), a number of maximal frequent itemsets and a number of minimal infrequent itemsets are known, then it can be decided in quadratic logspace whether there exist additional frequent or infrequent itemsets.

Categories and Subject Descriptors

F.2.2 [**Analysis of Algorithms and Problem Complexity**]: Nonnumerical Algorithms and Problems—*Computations on discrete structures*;
G.2.2 [**Discrete Mathematics**]: Graph Theory—*Graph algorithms,hypergraphs*;
H.2.8 [**Database Management**]: Database Applications—*Data mining*

*An online report version of this paper (typeset in a larger font) has been published in the Computing Research Repository (CORR) at: `http://arxiv.org/abs/1212.1881`. We plan to incorporate possible updates, corrections, and additions (if any) into future versions of this online report.

Keywords

Duality testing, frequent item set, hypergraph, transversal, data mining.

1. INTRODUCTION

This paper derives new complexity bounds for the problem DUAL of deciding whether two irredundant monotone Boolean formulas in DNF are mutually dual, or, equivalently, of deciding whether two simple hypergraphs are dual, i.e., whether each of these hypergraphs consists precisely of the minimal transversals of the other. While the exact complexity remains open, there is progress: We prove in the present paper a DSPACE[$\log^2 n$] upper bound for DUAL, and another, presumably tighter bound for the same problem, that is expressed in terms of sophisticated machine-bounded complexity classes. The DUAL problem is actually one of the most mysterious problems in theoretical computer science. It has many applications, especially in the database, data mining, and knowledge discovery areas [7, 8, 26, 27], some of which will be mentioned below. Let us first describe the DUAL problem more formally.

Duality testing for monotone DNFs and hypergraphs. A pair of Boolean formulas f and g on propositional variables $x_1, x_2, \ldots, x_n$ are *dual* if

$$f(x_1, x_2, \ldots, x_n) \equiv \neg g(\neg x_1, \neg x_2, \ldots, \neg x_n).$$

A monotone DNF is *irredundant* if the set of variables in none of its disjuncts is covered by the variable set of any other disjunct. The *duality testing problem* DUAL is the problem of testing whether two irredundant monotone DNFs f and g are dual.

A *hypergraph* $\mathcal{H}$ is a finite family of finite sets (also called *hyperedges*) defined over some set of *vertices* $V(\mathcal{H})$. $\mathcal{H}$ is simple if no hyperedge is contained in another one. By default, if $V(\mathcal{H})$ is not explicitly specified, the set of vertices of $\mathcal{H}$ is $\bigcup_{E\in\mathcal{H}} E$. A *transversal of* $\mathcal{H}$ is a subset of $V(\mathcal{H})$ that meets all hyperedges of $\mathcal{H}$, and a *minimal transversal* of $\mathcal{H}$ is a transversal of $\mathcal{H}$ that does not contain any other transversal as subset. The set of all minimal transversals of a hypergraph $\mathcal{H}$ is denoted by $tr(\mathcal{H})$. The *Hypergraph Duality Problem* is the problem of deciding for two simple hypergraphs $\mathcal{G}$ and $\mathcal{H}$ whether $\mathcal{G} = tr(\mathcal{H})$. Assume $\mathcal{G} \subseteq tr(\mathcal{H})$, then, in case $\mathcal{G} \neq tr(\mathcal{H})$, to witness this, one may want to exhibit a *new transversal of* $\mathcal{H}$ *with respect to* $\mathcal{G}$. This is a transversal of $\mathcal{H}$ that has no hyperedge of $\mathcal{G}$ as subset. Obviously, every new transversal H contains at least one *new minimal transversal of* $\mathcal{H}$ *w.r.t.* $\mathcal{G}$, but it need not be minimal itself.

It is well known that DNF duality and hypergraph duality are actually the same problem (see [7]). In fact, two irredundant monotone DNFs f and g are dual iff their hypergraphs are dual. The hypergraph associated to a monotone DNF has precisely one hyperedge for each disjunct, consisting of the set of all variables of this disjunct. Vice versa, one can trivially associate an irredundant DNF to each simple hypergraph and thus reduce hypergraph duality to DNF duality. Given that these problems essentially coincide (and can be reduced to each other via trivial reductions that are much easier than logspace reductions), we regard them as one and the same problem, which we refer to as DUAL.

The duality problem in data mining, database theory, and knowledge discovery. The DUAL problem is at the core of a number of important data mining and database problems. It is central, for example, to the determination of the maximal frequent and minimal infrequent sets in data mining. More precisely, consider a Boolean-valued data relation M over a set S of attributes called *items*, and a threshold z with $0 < z \leq |M|$. Each subset $U \subseteq S$ is called an *itemset*. For each tuple t of M, let $items(t) = \{A \in S \mid t[A] = 1\}$. The frequency $f(U)$ for an itemset U is the number of tuples t of M, such that $U \subseteq items(t)$. U is *frequent* if $f(U) > z$ and infrequent otherwise.

In data mining, one considers the *maximal frequent itemsets* and the *minimal infrequent itemsets* (under set inclusion) for M and z. Let us refer to the former as $IS^+(M,z)$ and to the latter as $IS^-(M,z)$. Clearly, both $IS^+(M,z)$ and $IS^-(M,z)$ are simple hypergraphs over S, and we abbreviate them by IS^+ and IS^-, respectively, when M and z are understood.

The maximal frequent itemsets IS^+ are of great interest in the context of data mining, but they are hard to compute. In fact, as shown in [2, 3] that for a given Boolean-valued relation M, a threshold z and a set $S \subseteq IS^+(M,z)$, deciding whether there are additional maximal frequent itemsets, i.e., whether $S \neq IS^+(M,z)$, is NP complete. It follows that, assuming NP$\neq$ P, there cannot be any algorithm for enumerating $IS^+(M,z)$ with polynomial delay, and that under the slightly weaker assumption NP$\not\subseteq$DTIME$[n^{\text{polylog } n}]$, there is no algorithm enumerating $IS^+(M,z)$ with quasipolynomial delay either. For this reason, rather than computing IS^+ only, one often computes $IS^+ \cup IS^-$, which may be exponentially larger in the worst case, but has the advantage of being computable with quasipolynomial delay [3]. As a fundamental result towards the aim of jointly computing IS^+ and IS^-, it was shown in [26] that the minimal infrequent itemsets are exactly the minimal transversals of the complements of the maximal frequent itemsets, i.e. $IS^- = tr(IS^{+c})$, and thus also $IS^+ = tr(IS^-)^c$, where for $A \subseteq 2^S$, $A^c = \{S - A | A \in S\}$. Let MAXFREQ-MININFREQ-IDENTIFICATION be the following decision problem in data mining: Given M, z, a set $\mathcal{G} \subseteq IS^-(M,z)$, and a set $\mathcal{H} \subseteq IS^+(M,z)$, decide whether $\mathcal{H} = IS^+(M,z)$ and $\mathcal{G} = IS^-(M,z)$, that is, whether there exists no additional maximal frequent or minimal infrequent itemset for M and z, that is not already in $\mathcal{G} \cup \mathcal{H}$. In [26] it was shown that that there exist no such additional itemset iff $\mathcal{G} = tr(\mathcal{H}^c)$. With regard to the computational complexity, we thus have:

PROPOSITION 1.1 ([26]). MAXFREQ-MININFREQ-IDENTIFICATION *is logspace-equivalent to* DUAL.

The results of [26] are at the base of a host of algorithms for maximal frequent itemset generation, that compute both IS^+ and IS^- incrementally. These algorithms initialize $\mathcal{G}$ and $\mathcal{H}^c$ with some easy to compute subsets of IS^- and IS^{+c}, respectively. Then, at each step they check whether for the current sets $\mathcal{G} = tr(\mathcal{H}^c)$ is true, and if not, compute one or more new transversals from which new maximal frequent itemsets or minimal infrequent itemsets can be computed easily, see, e.g. [39, 36, 25, 2, 43]. Thus, not only the decision problem DUAL is of relevance to data mining, but also the problem of effectively computing a new transversal that acts a witness that $\mathcal{G} \neq tr(\mathcal{H}^c)$. In the present paper, we will obtain results on the complexity of this latter problem, too.

Another interesting related database problem is the ADDITIONAL KEY FOR INSTANCE problem for explicitly given relational instances. Given a relational instance R over attribute set S, and a set K of minimal keys for R, determine if there exists a minimal key for R that is not already contained in K. This problem, which has been shown equivalent to $\overline{\text{DUAL}}$ in the early nineties [7], may be of renewed interest in the age of Big Data, where massive data tables arise and have to be analyzed, and where the automatic recognition of structural features such as minimal keys may be useful.

PROPOSITION 1.2 ([7]). *The* ADDITIONAL KEY FOR INSTANCE *problem is logspace equivalent to* $\overline{\text{DUAL}}$. *Moreover, enumerating the minimal keys of a relational instance* R *is equivalent to enumerating the set* $tr(\mathcal{H})$ *for some hypergraph* $\mathcal{H}$ *that is logspace-computable from* R.

Other related problems equivalent to DUAL or to $\overline{\text{DUAL}}$ deal with the construction of Armstrong relations for sets of functional dependencies [7], see also [23, 6].

We also wish to briefly mention a problem from the area of distributed databases. For quorum-based updates [35] in distributed databases, the concept of *coterie*, which is essentially a hypergraph of intersecting quorums has been introduced, and one is specifically interested in so called *non-dominated coteries* (for definitions and details, see [16, 30], and for more recent results and applications, see [37, 38, 28]). The following was proven:

PROPOSITION 1.3 ([30, 7]). *A coterie* $\mathcal{H}$ *is non-dominated iff* $tr(\mathcal{H}) = \mathcal{H}$.

There are a large number of applications of the DUAL problem and of hypergraph dualization in the areas of knowledge discovery, machine learning, and more generally in AI and knowledge representation. Just to mention a few: Learning monotone Boolean CNFs and DNFs with membership queries [26], model-based diagnosis [41, 24], computing a Horn approximation to a non-Horn theory [33, 19], and computing minimal abductive explanations to observations [10]. Surveys of these and other applications and further references can be found in [8, 7, 27].

Known complexity results. The exact complexity of DUAL has remained an open problem. Fredman and Khachiyan [15] have shown that DUAL is in DTIME[$n^{o(\log n)}$], more precisely, that it is contained in DTIME[$n^{4\chi(n)+O(1)}$], where $\chi(n)$ is defined by $\chi(n)^{\chi(n)} = n$. Eiter, Gottlob, and Makino [9], and independently, Kavvadias and Stavropoulos [34] have shown that DUAL is in the complexity class co-β_2P, which means that showing that the complement of DUAL can be solved in polynomial time with $O(\log^2 n)$ nondeterministic bits. This small amount of nondeterminism can actually be lowered to $O(\chi(n) \log n)$ which is $o(\log^2 n)$, see [9].

Research question tackled The question about the space-efficiency of DUAL, namely, whether DUAL can be solved using sub-polynomial or even polylogarithmic space was not satisfactorily answered. It was posed (explicitly or implicitly) several times since 1995, for example in [7, 44, 11]. This is the main problem we tackle. In addition, we aim at obtaining a better understanding of the DUAL problem in terms of machine-based structural complexity.

Results. We show in this paper that the decision problem DUAL is in the class DSPACE[$\log^2 n$], which is a very low class in POLYLOGSPACE. Modulo the assumption that PTIME$\not\subseteq$POLYLOGSPACE, which is widely believed, we thus obtain satisfactory evidence that DUAL is not PTIME-hard, which answers another complexity question posed in [7, 11]. Our results are based on a careful analysis of a recent problem decomposition method by Boros and Makino [4]. Their decomposition method actually yields a parallel algorithm that solves DUAL on an EREW PRAM in $O(\log^2 n)$ time using $n^{\log n}$ processors. However, it is currently not known whether such EREW PRAMS can be simulated in DSPACE[$\log^2 n$], and this is actually considered to be rather unlikely. However, Boros' and Makino's algorithm does not seem to exploit the full potential of a PRAM, and by taking into account the restricted pattern of information flow imposed by the specific self-reductions used in their algorithm, we succeeded to show that DUAL is in DSPACE[$\log^2 n$].

Complexity theorists have very good reasons to assume that the space class DSPACE[$\log^2 n$] is incomparable with respect to containment to the class co-β_2P. It is thus somewhat unsatisfactory to have two upper bounds for DUAL that are incomparable, which suggests that, most likely, there exist better bounds. This encouraged us to look for a tighter upper bound for DUAL in terms of machine-based complexity models, that would be contained in both DSPACE[$\log^2 n$] and co-β_2P, and we succeeded to find one. We can, in fact, show that $\overline{\text{DUAL}}$ belongs to the "guess and check" class GC($\log^2 n$, $[\![\text{LOGSPACE}_{\text{pol}}]\!]^{\log}$). This somewhat exotic new machine-based complexity class consists of all problems that can be solved by first guessing $O(\log^2 n)$ bits and then checking the correctness of this guess by a procedure in $[\![\text{LOGSPACE}_{\text{pol}}]\!]^{\log}$, which is a complexity class contained in PTIME we will define in the present paper. We hope that this tighter new bound will provide a better insight into the very nature of the DUAL problem, and possibly hint at the right direction for future research towards finding a matching upper bound.

Roadmap. The paper is organized as follows. In the next section we discuss decomposition methods for DUAL and give a succinct description of the method of Boros and Makino, which we consider to be the currently most advanced method. In Section 3, we define complexity classes based on iterated self-compositions of functions and prove a useful complexity-theoretic lemma. In Section 4, we use this lemma to prove our main result, namely that DUAL is in DSPACE[$\log^2 n$]. In section 5 we provide our tighter structural complexity bound for DUAL. The paper is concluded in Section 6, where we also exhibit a diagram (Fig. 1) that puts all relevant complexity classes in relation, and highlights the new upper bounds.

2. THE DECOMPOSITION METHOD BY BOROS AND MAKINO

Most algorithms for deciding DUAL rely on decompositions that start with an original DUAL instance and recursively transform it into a conjunction of smaller instances, until each instance is either seen to be a no-instance because it violates necessary conditions for duality, or until it is small and efficiently decidable. Such decompositions are also known as *self-reductions*, see, e.g., Section 5.3 of [9]. The decomposition process corresponds in the obvious way to a *decomposition tree.* Different decomposition methods give rise to decomposition trees of different shapes and depths. For example, the well-known algorithm A by Fredman and Khachiyan [15] produces a "skinny" binary decomposition tree of depth linear in the input volume $|\mathcal{G}| \times |\mathcal{H}|$, while their algorithm B produces a non-binary tree of similar depth, but with fewer nodes. Later, decomposition methods giving rise to trees of polylogarithmic depth were published. In particular, the methods of Kavvadias and Stavropoulos [34] as well as the two methods by Elbassioni in [12] give rise to decomposition trees of polylogarithmic depth. Finally, decomposition methods yielding trees of logarithmic depth were presented by Gaur [17] (see also Gaur and Krishnamurti [18]), and, more recently, by Boros and Makino [4]. As we will show, the logarithmic-depth decomposition trees generated by these methods can be used to show that DUAL is in DSPACE[$\log^2 n$]. In particular, we use the elegant decomposition method of Boros and Makino [4] to prove this, but we could have used Gaur's method [17] in a similar fashion. In the rest of this section, we give a succinct description of the method of Boros and Makino, that contains all the essentials we need for our subsequent complexity analysis. It is assumed that the input instance $I = (\mathcal{G}, \mathcal{H})$ we have $|\mathcal{H}| \leq |\mathcal{G}|$, and that $\mathcal{G} \subseteq tr(\mathcal{H})$ and $\mathcal{H} \subseteq tr(\mathcal{G})$. Clearly this can be tested in logarithmic space.

For an input instance $I = (\mathcal{G}, \mathcal{H})$ of DUAL over a vertex set V, let $T(\mathcal{G}, \mathcal{H})$ denote its decomposition tree. Let $\aleph_{\mathcal{H}} = \mathbb{N}^0 \cup \mathbb{N}^1 \cup \mathbb{N}^2 \cup \cdots \cup \mathbb{N}^{\lfloor \log |\mathcal{H}| \rfloor}$, where $\mathbb{N}$ denotes the natural numbers, and where $\mathbb{N}^0$ is defined to contain the empty sequence () only, which has length 0. Thus $\aleph_{\mathcal{H}}$ contains precisely all sequences of natural numbers of length up to $\lfloor \log |\mathcal{H}| \rfloor$.

Each node of $T(\mathcal{G}, \mathcal{H})$ has five data structures associated with it:

(i) A unique label $label(\alpha)$ consisting of a sequence in $\aleph_{\mathcal{H}}$. In particular, the root α_0 of $T(\mathcal{G}, \mathcal{H})$ is labeled by (), and the i-th child of a node labeled $(j_1, \ldots, j_k)$ is labeled $(j_1, \ldots, j_k, i)$.

(ii) A set $S_\alpha \subseteq V(\mathcal{G})$.

(iii) An instance of DUAL $inst(\alpha) = (\mathcal{G}^{S_\alpha}, \mathcal{H}_{S_\alpha})$, where $\mathcal{G}^{S_\alpha} = \{E \cap S_\alpha \mid E \in \mathcal{G}\}$ and $\mathcal{H}_{S_\alpha} = \{E \in \mathcal{H} \mid E \subseteq S_\alpha\}$,.

(iv) A marking $mark(\alpha) \in \{$DONE, FAIL, NIL$\}$, where each leaf of the final decomposition tree will be marked with DONE or FAIL, and each non-leaf will be marked with dummy value NIL. Intuitively, each leaf marked DONE identifies a branch that does not contradict $\mathcal{H} = tr(\mathcal{G})$, whereas a leaf marked FAIL identifies a branch that proves that $\mathcal{H} \neq tr(\mathcal{G})$.

(v) A set of vertices $t(\alpha) \subseteq V(\mathcal{G})$. This set will be the empty set for each node not marked FAIL, and, in case α is marked FAIL, will contain a witness for $\mathcal{H} \neq tr(\mathcal{G})$ in form of a new transversal of $\mathcal{G}$ with respect to $\mathcal{H}$.

Let us now describe the method for building $T(\mathcal{G}, \mathcal{H})$ and deciding whether $\mathcal{H} = tr(\mathcal{G})$ in detail. At each stage of the algorithm, let us denote the set of current leaf-nodes by Λ. Here is how the tree is built. The input instance $(\mathcal{G}, \mathcal{H})$ is first transformed into a initial tree consisting of the root α_0 with $label(\alpha_0) = ()$, $S_{\alpha_0} = V$, $inst(\alpha_0) = (\mathcal{G}, \mathcal{H})$, $mark(\alpha_0) =$NIL, and $t(\alpha_0) = \emptyset$. At each stage of the decomposition, first, each leaf $\alpha \in \Lambda$ where $|\mathcal{H}_{S_\alpha}| \leq 1$, will be marked by the following procedure, and will then not be further expanded and will thus be a leaf of the final tree $T(\mathcal{G}, \mathcal{H})$:

PROCEDURE MARKSMALL(α):

CASE 1. IF $|\mathcal{H}_{S_\alpha}| = 0$ and $\emptyset \notin \mathcal{G}^{S_\alpha}$, THEN $\{$ $mark(\alpha) :=$FAIL; $t(\alpha) := S_\alpha$ $\}$.

CASE 2. If $|\mathcal{H}_{S_\alpha}| = 0$ and $\emptyset \in \mathcal{G}^{S_\alpha}$, THEN $\{$ $mark(\alpha) :=$DONE; $t(\alpha) = \emptyset$ $\}$.

CASE 3. If $\mathcal{H}_{S_\alpha} = \{H\}$ and $\{\{i\} | i \in H\} \subseteq \mathcal{G}^{S_\alpha}$, THEN $\{$ $mark(\alpha) :=$DONE; $t(\alpha) = \emptyset$ $\}$.

CASE 4. OTHERWISE, let H denote the only hyperedge of $\mathcal{H}_{S_\alpha}$, and set $mark(\alpha) :=$FAIL, and $t(\alpha) := S_\alpha - \{i\}$ for some arbitrarily chosen $i \in H$ with $\{i\} \notin \mathcal{G}^{S_\alpha}$.

Then, each leaf α of Λ not yet marked is subjected to the following procedure:

PROCEDURE PROCESS(α):

1. Let I_α consist of those vertices of $\mathcal{H}_{S_\alpha}$ that occur in more than $|\mathcal{H}_{S_\alpha}|/2$ hyperedges of $\mathcal{H}_{S_\alpha}$;

2. IF I_α is a new transversal of $\mathcal{G}^{S_\alpha}$ with respect to $\mathcal{H}_{S_\alpha}$, THEN $\{$ $mark(\alpha) :=$FAIL; $t(\alpha) := I_\alpha$; EXIT PROCEDURE$\}$;

3. OTHERWISE IF there is a $G \in \mathcal{G}^{S_\alpha}$ such that $G \cap I_\alpha = \emptyset$ THEN let
$$\mathcal{C} = \{S_\alpha - (E - \{i\}) | E \in \mathcal{G}_G^{S_\alpha} \text{ and } i \in E \cap G\},$$
where $\mathcal{G}_G^{S_\alpha} = \mathcal{G}^{S_\alpha} - \{E' \in \mathcal{G}^{S_\alpha} | \ E' \subseteq S_\alpha - G\}$;

4. OTHERWISE IF there exists a $H \in \mathcal{H}_{S_\alpha}$ such that $H \subseteq I_\alpha$ THEN let
$$\mathcal{C} = \{S_\alpha - \{i\} | i \in H\} \cup \{H\};$$

5. Let $\kappa(\alpha) = |\mathcal{C}|$ and assume $\mathcal{C} = \{C_1, C_2, \ldots, C_{\kappa(\alpha)}\}$. For each C_i, $1 \leq i \leq \kappa(\alpha)$, create a new child α_i with $label(\alpha_i) = (label(\alpha), i)$, $S_{\alpha_i} = C_i$, $inst(\alpha_i) = (\mathcal{G}^{S_{\alpha_i}}, \mathcal{H}_{S_{\alpha_i}})$, $mark(\alpha_i) =$NIL, and $t(\alpha_i) = \emptyset$.

Exhaustively apply the procedures MARKSMALL (to unmarked leaves α having $|\mathcal{H}_{S_\alpha}| \leq 1$) and PROCESS (to all other unmarked leaves), until there are no unmarked leaves left in the tree. The resulting tree is then $T(\mathcal{G}, \mathcal{H})$.

Note that, due to the possible multiple choices of i in CASE 4 of the MARKSMALL procedure, and of G in Step 3 and of H in Step 4 of the PROCESS procedure, the decomposition tree $T(\mathcal{G}, \mathcal{H})$ is actually not uniquely defined. However, this is not a problem. To obtain a well-defined decomposition tree $T(\mathcal{G}, \mathcal{H})$, we may resort to any pair of deterministic versions of MARKSMALL and of PROCESS, for example, we may use the version of MARKSMALL where in CASE 4 the smallest $i \in H$ fulfilling $\{i\} \notin \mathcal{G}^{S_\alpha}$ is chosen, and the version of PROCESS where in Step 3 the lexicographically first edge $G \in \mathcal{G}^{S_\alpha}$ with $G \cap I_\alpha = \emptyset$ is chosen, and similarly for H in Step 4.

The following proposition summarizes important results by Boros and Makino [4].

PROPOSITION 2.1 (BOROS AND MAKINO [4]).

1. *$\mathcal{H} = tr(\mathcal{G})$ iff all leaves of $T(\mathcal{G}, \mathcal{H})$ are marked* DONE.
2. *The depth of $T(\mathcal{G}, \mathcal{H})$ is bounded by $\log |\mathcal{H}|$.*
3. *Each node α of $T(\mathcal{G}, \mathcal{H})$ has at most $|V| \cdot |\mathcal{G}|$ children, i.e., $\kappa(\alpha) \leq |V| \cdot |\mathcal{G}|$, where V is the set of vertices of $\mathcal{G}$ and $\mathcal{H}$.*
4. *If $\mathcal{H} \neq tr(\mathcal{G})$, then $T(\mathcal{G}, \mathcal{H})$ has at least one leaf labeled* FAIL, *and the set $t(\alpha)$ associated to each leaf α labeled* FAIL *is a new transversal of $\mathcal{G}$ w.r.t. $\mathcal{H}$.*

3. A COMPLEXITY-THEORETIC LEMMA

For a space-constructible numerical function z, we denote by DSPACE$[z(n)]$ (resp. FDSPACE$[z(n)]$), as usual, the class of all all decision problems (resp. computation problems) solvable deterministically in $O(z(n))$ space. For a function f, let $f^1 = f$ and for $i \geq 1$, let $f^{i+1} = f \circ f^i$, where $\circ$ is the usual function composition, i.e., where for each x in the domain of g, $(f \circ g)(x) = f(g(x))$. Let $Q_{\log}$ denote the set of all functions ρ from strings over some input alphabet to the non-negative natural numbers, where for each input string I, $\rho(I)$ is $O(\log |I|)$ and such that ρ is logspace-computable, i.e., $\rho(I)$ is computable in logarithmic space from I. For each function f, and for each function $\rho \in Q_{\log}$, let f^ρ denote the function that to each input I associate the output $f^\rho(I) = f^{\rho(I)}(I)$. If FC denotes a functional complexity class, then $[\![\mathrm{FC}]\!]^{\log}$ denotes the class of functions that can be built from some function f in FC via a logarithmic number $\rho(I) = O(\log n)$ of self-compositions of f for each input I of size n:

$$[\![\mathrm{FC}]\!]^{\log} = \bigcup_{f \in \mathrm{FC},\, \rho \in Q_{\log}} \{f^\rho\}.$$

For a functional complexity class FC, the subclass $\mathrm{FC}_{\mathrm{pol}}$ is defined as the set of all functions f of FC for which there exists a polynomial γ such that for each input I, and for each $i \geq 1$, $|f^i(I)| \leq \gamma(|I|)$. In general, $\mathrm{FC}_{\mathrm{pol}}$ is a proper subclass of FC. This is, in particular so for FDSPACE$[\log n]$, i.e., functional logspace, a.k.a. FLOGSPACE. To see this, let f be the function that associates to an input of size n an output consisting of n^2 zeros. Clearly, $f \in$ FDSPACE$[\log n]$, but the output sizes of the f^i are not bounded by any fixed polynomial when i grows. Thus, $f \notin [\![\mathrm{FDSPACE}[\log n]_{\mathrm{pol}}]\!]$, hence $[\![\mathrm{FDSPACE}[\log n]_{\mathrm{pol}}]\!]$ is a proper subclass of the class FDSPACE$[\log n]$.

Lemma 3.1.

$$[\![\mathrm{FDSPACE}[\log n]_{\mathrm{pol}}]\!]^{\log} \subseteq \mathrm{FDSPACE}[\log^2 n].$$

PROOF. The proof is similar the well-known proof that for any two functions $f, g \in$ FDSPACE$[\log n]$, their composition $g \circ f$ is in FDSPACE$[\log n]$, too, see, e.g. [40]). However, here, the logarithmic (rather than constant) number of compositions is responsible for the blowup of the required space by a logarithmic factor. Let f be a function from strings to strings in FDSPACE$[\log n]_{\mathrm{pol}}$, realized by a logspace Turing Machine T, and let $\rho \in Q_{\log}$. In order to prove the lemma, it is sufficient to show that one can construct a single functional Turing machine T^* with space bound $O(\log^2 n)$ that simulates the pipelined application $T^{\rho(I)}$ that outputs $f^{\rho(I)}(I)$.

T^* first computes $\rho(I)$ in logspace and then simulates an arrangement of $\rho(I)$ copies of T, say, $T_1, T_2, \ldots, T_{\rho(I)}$, such that the input string v_1 to T_1 is I, and such that for $i \geq 1$, the input string v_{i+1} to T_{i+1} is equal to the output string w_i of T_i. Given that the size of $w_i = T^i(I)$ is bounded by some fixed polynomial γ, there are numbers a and b such that each T_i requires no more than space $a + b \log n$. When simulating the pipelined computation $T_{\rho(I)}(T_{\rho(I)-1}(\cdots(T_2(T_1(I)))))$ on a single Turing machine T^*, we have to avoid the effective storage of any intermediate output w_i (or, equivalently, input v_{i+1}). To this aim, T^* simulates each T_i via a logspace procedure P_i that maintains its own space area on the worktape of T^*. Each P_i acts like T_i, except for the following modifications: For $1 < i < \rho(I)$, P_i has a single output bit which is stored on the worktape of T^*; moreover P_i takes as input a dedicated special index register d_i that specifies which output bit of T_i is to be computed, and computes only this output bit (suppressing all other output bits) and stores it in a single-bit register o_i. T_i's access to its j-th input bit is then simulated by P_i writing "j" (in binary) into the special index register d_{i-1}, starting P_{i-1}, and then waiting until P_{i-1} writes the desired output bit into o_{i-1} which corresponds to the correct value of the j-th output of T_{i-1}, and thus the j-th input bit to T_i. P_1 and $P_{\rho(I)}$ work in a similar way, except that P_1 directly accesses the input string I from the input tape of T^*, and $P_{\rho(I)}$, rather than suppressing some output bits, writes *all* output bits to the output tape of T^*.

The workspace required by each procedure P_i is easily seen to be bounded by $a' + b' \log n$ for some fixed constants a' and b' independent of n. This reflects the $a + b \log n$ bits required to execute T_i, plus the little extra space P_i may require for its index d_i, for the output bit o_i, and for a constant number of auxiliary counters and pointers (of size at most $a + b \log n$ bits each) for control and stack management for the P_i procedures. Given that $\rho(I)$ is $O(\log n)$, T^* requires $O(\log^2 n)$ space in total. □

Note that the same space bound doesn't hold for the complexity class $[\![\text{FDSPACE}[\log n]]\!]^{\log}$. In fact, with functions f in this class, intermediate outputs $f^i(I)$ may be of superpolynomial size, and in the worst case, even of exponential size $n^{\Theta(n)}$. Therefore, when omitting the "pol" restriction, $[\![\text{FDSPACE}[\log n]]\!]^{\log} \subseteq \text{FPSPACE}$ is the best space upper bound we are able to show. Since an FDSPACE$[\log^2 n]$ Turing machine has an output of size at most $n^{O(\log n)}$, it it actually holds that $[\![\text{FDSPACE}[\log n]]\!]^{\log} \not\subseteq \text{FDSPACE}[\log^2 n]$.

4. THE NEW SPACE BOUND

The main result of this section is that for a pair $(\mathcal{G}, \mathcal{H})$, the entire decomposition tree $T(\mathcal{G}, \mathcal{H})$ (with all markings and labels) produced by the decomposition method of Boros and Makino as outlined in Section 2 can be computed with quadratic logspace. The other space-complexity results follow from this as simple corollaries.

We start with a lemma that provides us with a logarithmic space bound for computing the i-th child of a node α of the decomposition tree from the fully labeled node α and from the set V of vertices of the original input instance, or for discovering that such a child does not exist. If α is a node of the decomposition tree, let us denote by $attr(\alpha)$ the attributes of α, i.e., the tuple $(label(\alpha), S_\alpha, inst(\alpha), mark(\alpha), t(\alpha))$.

Lemma 4.1. *There exists a deterministic logspace procedure* NEXT$(V, attr(\alpha), i)$, *which for each* DUAL *instance* $(\mathcal{G}, \mathcal{H})$ *over vertex set* V, *for each attribute set* $attr(\alpha)$ *of a node* α *of* $T(\mathcal{G}, \mathcal{H})$, *and for each positive integer* $i \leq |V| \cdot |\mathcal{G}|$ *outputs:*

- $attr(\alpha_i)$ *if* α_i *is the i-th child of* α *in* $T(\mathcal{G}, \mathcal{H})$*;*
- IMPOSSIBLE *otherwise (i.e., if* α *has less than* i *children).*

PROOF. First note that by simple inspection it is immediate that the procedures MARKSMALL and PROCESS given in Section 2 can be implemented by deterministic logspace transducers. In fact, these procedures only perform a fixed composition of simple cardinality checks, counting, assignments, and set theoretic operations that are all well-known to run in logspace.

A procedure NEXT, as required, can be constructed as follows. If $label(\alpha) \in \{\text{DONE}, \text{FAIL}\}$ then output IMPOSSIBLE, else perform MARKSMALL*(PROCESS*(α)), where:

- PROCESS* works like PROCESS except that it outputs only the i-th child of α, if such a child exists, rather than outputting all children, and output IMPOSSIBLE otherwise; and
- MARKSMALL* works like MARKSMALL, except that it also accepts the input IMPOSSIBLE, in which case it also outputs IMPOSSIBLE.

These minor modifications of MARKSMALL and PROCESS clearly run in deterministic logspace, therefore their composition does, and hence so does the procedure NEXT. □

A *path descriptor* for a DUAL instance $I = (\mathcal{G}, \mathcal{H})$ over a vertex set V is a list of length $\leq \lfloor \log |\mathcal{H}| \rfloor$, whose elements are integers bounded by $|V| \cdot |\mathcal{G}|$. The set of all path descriptors for I is denoted by $PD(I)$. Clearly, $PD(I) \subset \aleph_{\mathcal{H}}$, and each label $label(\alpha)$ of a node α of $T(\mathcal{G}, \mathcal{H})$ is contained in $PD(I)$. Intuitively, a path descriptor, exactly in the same way as a label, is intended to describe a sequence of child-indices, that, starting from the roof of $T(\mathcal{G}, \mathcal{H})$ lead to a specific node α of $T(\mathcal{G}, \mathcal{H})$. The root of $T(\mathcal{G}, \mathcal{H})$ is identified by the empty path descriptor. If $\pi = (i_1, i_2, \ldots, i_r)$ is a path descriptor, then $head(\pi) = i_1$ and $tail(\pi)$ is the path descriptor $(i_2, \ldots, i_r)$. Two path descriptors of the form $(i_1, \ldots, i_r)$ and $(i_1, \ldots, i_r, i_{r+1})$ are said to be *consecutive.*

Lemma 4.2. *There is a procedure* PATHNODE(I, π) *that runs in deterministic space* $O(\log^2(|I|))$, *that for each* DUAL *input instance* I *and path descriptor* $\pi \in PD(I)$ *outputs* $attr(\alpha)$ *if* π *corresponds to the label* $label(\alpha)$ *of a node* α *in* $T(\mathcal{G}, \mathcal{H})$, *and outputs* WRONGPATH *otherwise.*

PROOF. Let $I = (\mathcal{G}, \mathcal{H})$, $V = V(\mathcal{G})$, and $\pi \in PD(I)$, and let $\ell(\pi)$ denote the length of the sequence π (recall that $(\ell(\pi) \leq \log |I|)$. The procedure PATHNODE first computes in deterministic logspace $attr(\alpha_0)$ for the root α_0 of $T(\mathcal{G}, \mathcal{H})$. It then computes $f^{\ell(\pi)}(V, attr(\alpha_0), \pi)$, where f is the function corresponding to the procedure F described as follows. F accepts as input either the string WRONGPATH, or a triple $(W, attr, \gamma)$ where W is a set, $attr$ is a data structure of the same format as the attributes $attr(\beta)$ of some vertex β in a decomposition tree, and γ is a sequence of positive integers. On all other inputs, F outputs the empty string. On input WRONGPATH, F outputs WRONGPATH; otherwise F computes $F'(\text{NEXT}(W, attr, head(\gamma))$, where NEXT be as specified in Lemma 4.1, and where F' is as follows. F' outputs WRONGPATH if NEXT$(W, attr, head(\gamma)) =$ IMPOSSIBLE, and F' outputs $(W, Attr', tail(\gamma))$, whenever

$$\text{NEXT}(W, attr, head(\gamma)) = Attr'$$

for some attribute description $Attr'$. Since NEXT runs in deterministic logspace, also F' and F do, and therefore f is a logspace computable function.

By construction and by Lemma 4.1, PATHNODE precisely computes the attributes $attr(\alpha)$ if there is a node α with $label(\alpha) = \pi$ in $T(\mathcal{G}, \mathcal{H})$, whereas otherwise

PATHNODE outputs WRONGPATH. Since the function ℓ (expressing the length $\ell(\pi)$) is clearly in $Q_{\log}$, and since $f^i(V, attr(\alpha_0), \pi)$, for each i, is of size polynomially bounded in the size of the input $(V, attr(\alpha_0), \pi)$, $f^{\ell(\pi)}(V, attr(\alpha_0), \pi)$ can be computed by a procedure in $[\![\text{FDSPACE}[\log n]_{\text{pol}}]\!]^{\log}$, and therefore, by Lemma 3.1, in deterministic space $O(\log^2 n)$. The same complexity bounds obviously hold for PATHNODE. □

By using a procedure PATHNODE according to the above Lemma, we are now ready to formulate an algorithm DECOMPOSE that computes the decomposition tree $T(\mathcal{G}, \mathcal{H})$ to a DUAL instance $(\mathcal{G}, \mathcal{H})$. In particular, the algorithms first lists the vertices and then the edges of the tree $T(\mathcal{G}, \mathcal{H})$.

Algorithm DECOMPOSE:
Input: DUAL-instance $I = (\mathcal{G}, \mathcal{H})$;   Output: $T(\mathcal{G}, \mathcal{H})$.
BEGIN
OUTPUT("Vertices:");
FOR each path descriptor $\pi \in PD(I)$ DO
IF PATHNODE$(I, \pi) \neq$WRONGPATH
    THEN OUTPUT(PATHNODE(I, π));
OUTPUT("Edges:");
FOR each pair (π, π') of consecutive path descriptors in $PD(I)$ DO
    BEGIN
    $\alpha :=$ PATHNODE(I, π);
    $\alpha' :=$ PATHNODE(I, π');
    IF $\alpha' \neq$WRONGPATH THEN
        OUTPUT($\langle label(\alpha), label(\alpha')\rangle$);
    END
END.

Theorem 4.1. *The Algorithm* DECOMPOSE *computes the decomposition tree $T(\mathcal{G}, \mathcal{H})$ to a* DUAL *instance $(\mathcal{G}, \mathcal{H})$ in space $O(\log^2 n)$.*

PROOF. The correctness of the algorithm follows from the correctness of PATHNODE as shown in Lemma 4.2. For the space bound, note that each each path descriptor requires only $O(\log^2 |I|) = O(\log^2 n)$ bits, and that we can thus iterate (by re-using work-space) over all path descriptors and pairs of path descriptors in $O(\log^2 n)$ space. Given that, by Lemma 4.2, PATHNODE also runs in $O(\log^2 n)$ space, the entire DECOMPOSE algorithm needs only $O(\log^2 n)$ space. □

Corollary 4.1.

1. *Deciding* DUAL *is in* DSPACE$[\log^2 n]$.
2. *If $tr(\mathcal{G}) \neq \mathcal{H}$, then computing a new transversal of $\mathcal{G}$ with respect to $\mathcal{H}$ is in* FDSPACE$[\log^2 n]$.

PROOF. In both cases we can first compute the entire decomposition tree $T(\mathcal{G}, \mathcal{H})$ in FDSPACE$[\log^2 n]$, and then (i) for problem 1 check by a DLOGSPACE procedure whether all leaves are marked DONE, and (ii) for problem 2, use an FLOGSPACE procedure to find a node α marked FAIL in $T(\mathcal{G}, \mathcal{H})$ and output its component $t(\alpha)$. Let $\circ$ denote the composition operator for complexity classes in the obvious sense. Given that

$$\text{FDSPACE}[\log^2 n] \circ \text{DLOGSPACE} = \text{DSPACE}[\log^2 n],$$

and given that, moreover,

$$\text{FDSPACE}[\log^2 n] \circ \text{FLOGSPACE} = \text{FDSPACE}[\log^2 n],$$

the complexity bounds follow. Alternatively, we can solve the problems 1 and 2 directly by respective slight modifications of DECOMPOSE. □

Note that if $tr(\mathcal{G}) \neq \mathcal{H}$, the witness $t(\alpha)$ produced is not necessarily a *minimal* transversal of $\mathcal{G}$, but is, in general, just a transversal of $\mathcal{G}$ that contains no edge of $\mathcal{H}$ and thus witnesses that $tr(\mathcal{G}) \neq \mathcal{H}$, because $t(\alpha)$ must *contain* a missing minimal transversal of $\mathcal{G}$. From $t(\alpha)$, such a minimal transversal t can easily be computed in polynomial time by letting first $t := t(\alpha)$ and by then successively eliminating vertices v from t for which $t - \{v\}$ is still a transversal of $\mathcal{G}$. However this process requires linear space in the vertex set V to remember the eliminated vertices plus logarithmic space in the instance size $|(\mathcal{G}, \mathcal{H})|$ for checking. This is still better than polynomial space in the full instance size, but is not quite in quadratic logspace. It is currently not clear whether there exists a smarter algorithm that requires quadratic logspace only.

5. A TIGHTER BOUND FOR DUAL

By the results of the previous section, DUAL and its complement $\overline{\text{DUAL}}$ are in quadratic logspace, i.e., in the class DSPACE$[\log^2 n]$. On the other hand, as already mentioned, the complement of DUAL is in β_2P, the class of problems solvable in polynomial time with $O(\log^2 n)$ nondeterministic guesses. β_2P is identical with the complexity class GC$(\log^2 n, \text{PTIME})$ of the so called *Guess and Check* model for limited nondeterminism [5, 20], where $O(\log^2 n)$ nondeterministic bits are guessed and are appended to the input before the proper PTIME computation starts. The Guess and Check classes are, more generally, defined as follows. Let C be a complexity class and s a numerical function. Then GC$(s(n), C)$ is the class of all languages L for which there exists a language $A \in C$ such that an input string I is in L iff there is a string J of $O(s(|I|))$ bits, such that (I, J) is in A. In other words, L is in GC$(s(n), C)$ iff the membership of a string I in L can be checked in C after having guessed $O(s(n))$ nondeterministic bits that can be used as an additional input.

Given that PTIME is generally believed to be incomparable with DSPACE$[\log^2 n]$ (cf [31]), and given that obviously PTIME $\subseteq$ GC$(\log^2 n, \text{PTIME})$, it is very likely that also GC$(\log^2 n, \text{PTIME})$ and DSPACE$[\log^2 n]$ are incomparable. Since DUAL belongs to both classes, this suggests that neither well characterizes DUAL, and that DUAL is unlikely to be complete for either. This observation incited us to look out for a complexity class containing DUAL that would be contained in both classes $GC(\log^2(n), \text{PTIME})$ and $\text{DSPACE}[\log^2 n]$, that would thus constitute a tighter upper complexity bound for DUAL than all those we have seen so far. In this section, we present precisely such a complexity class. In order to describe this class, we state some definitions and prove a lemma.

The complexity class $[\![\text{LOGSPACE}_{\text{pol}}]\!]^{\log}$ is defined as the composition of $[\![\text{FDSPACE}[\log n]_{\text{pol}}]\!]^{\log}$ with LOGSPACE. Formally, $[\![\text{LOGSPACE}_{\text{pol}}]\!]^{\log}$ is equal to

$$[\![\text{FDSPACE}[\log n]_{\text{pol}}]\!]^{\log} \circ \text{LOGSPACE}.$$

Here an input I is first transformed to an output O by a procedure that runs in $[\![\text{FDSPACE}[\log n]_{\text{pol}}]\!]^{\log}$, after which O is submitted to a LOGSPACE decision procedure which will decide based on O if the original input I is accepted or rejected.

Note that $[\![\text{LOGSPACE}_{\text{pol}}]\!]^{\log}$ is by all means a complexity class defined in terms of machines and resource bounds. In addition to the classical resources such as the amount of workspace, we here involve somewhat more unusual resources such as the allowed number of self-compositions, which is here bounded by $O(\log n)$, whence the superscript log, and the allowed size of intermediate outputs in compositions, which is here polynomially bounded, whence the subscript pol.

Lemma 5.1. *Given a* DUAL *instance* $I = (\mathcal{G}, \mathcal{H})$ *and a path descriptor* $\pi \in PD(I)$, *deciding if* PATHNODE(I, π) *outputs a leaf of* $T(\mathcal{G}, \mathcal{H})$ *whose mark-component is* FAIL *is feasible with complexity* $[\![\text{LOGSPACE}_{\text{pol}}]\!]^{\log}$.

PROOF. The proof of Lemma 4.2 already shows that PATHNODE lies in in $[\![\text{FDSPACE}[\log n]_{\text{pol}}]\!]^{\log}$. Deciding whether PATHNODE(I, π) outputs a leaf of $T(\mathcal{G}, \mathcal{H})$ whose *mark*-component is FAIL can thus be implemented by first executing PATHNODE(I, π), and then checking whether the output is a node labeled FAIL. This is obviously in $[\![\text{FDSPACE}[\log n]_{\text{pol}}]\!]^{\log} \circ \text{LOGSPACE} = [\![\text{LOGSPACE}_{\text{pol}}]\!]^{\log}$ □

We next consider $GC(\log^2 n, [\![\text{LOGSPACE}_{\text{pol}}]\!]^{\log})$, the main complexity class studied in this section.

Theorem 5.1. $\overline{\text{DUAL}} \in GC(\log^2 n, [\![\text{LOGSPACE}_{\text{pol}}]\!]^{\log})$.

PROOF. In order to find a new transversal t of $\mathcal{G}$ with respect to $\mathcal{H}$ for a DUAL instance $I = (\mathcal{G}, \mathcal{H})$, rather than computing the entire decomposition tree $T(\mathcal{G}, \mathcal{H})$, it is sufficient to guess a branch of this tree that terminates in a leaf α labeled FAIL, and then compute $t(\alpha)$. Guessing such a branch amounts to guess a path descriptor π and then checking that PATHNODE(I, π) outputs a node marked FAIL. Guessing π amounts to guess $\log^2 n$ bits, and this is all our guess-and-check algorithm guesses. Checking that π is a FAIL node is, by Lemma 5.1 in $[\![\text{LOGSPACE}_{\text{pol}}]\!]^{\log}$, hence the overall computation is in $GC(\log^2 n, [\![\text{LOGSPACE}_{\text{pol}}]\!]^{\log})$. □

The last theorem of this section shows, as promised, that the class the class $GC(\log^2 n, [\![\text{LOGSPACE}_{\text{pol}}]\!]^{\log})$ is effectively a subclass of the tightest known other upper bounds that are most likely incomparable to each other: the classes $\text{DSPACE}[\log^2 n]$ and $GC(\log^2 n, \text{P}) = \beta_2\text{P}$.

Theorem 5.2. $GC(\log^2 n, [\![\text{LOGSPACE}_{\text{pol}}]\!]^{\log})$ *is contained in* $\text{DSPACE}\,[\log^2 n] \cap GC(\log^2 n, \text{PTIME})$.

PROOF. For the inclusion

$$GC(\log^2 n, [\![\text{LOGSPACE}_{\text{pol}}]\!]^{\log}) \subseteq \text{DSPACE}\,[\log^2 n],$$

note that a decision procedure in the complexity class $GC(\log^2 n, [\![\text{LOGSPACE}_{\text{pol}}]\!]^{\log})$ amounts to (i) guessing $O(\log^2 n)$ bits, which can be simulated by an exhaustive enumeration of all possible guesses (under re-use of space), which is feasible in $\text{DSPACE}\,[\log^2 n]$, and (ii) for each such simulated guess, performing a check in $[\![\text{FDSPACE}[\log n]_{\text{pol}}]\!]^{\log} \circ \text{LOGSPACE}$. Since, by Lemma 1, $[\![\text{FDSPACE}[\log n]_{\text{pol}}]\!]^{\log} \subseteq \text{DSPACE}\,[\log^2 n]$, and given that the composition of a function from the class $\text{FDSPACE}\,[\log^2 n]$ with a LOGSPACE computation yields a $\text{DSPACE}\,[\log^2 n]$ decision procedure, the overall computation is in $\text{DSPACE}\,[\log^2 n]$.

To establish the reverse inclusion

$$GC(\log^2 n, [\![\text{LOGSPACE}_{\text{pol}}]\!]^{\log}) \subseteq GC(\log^2 n, \text{PTIME}),$$

it is obviously sufficient to see that $[\![\text{LOGSPACE}_{\text{pol}}]\!]^{\log}$ is contained in PTIME. In fact, a decision procedure in $[\![\text{LOGSPACE}_{\text{pol}}]\!]^{\log}$ amounts to a pipelined execution of $O(\log n)$ instantiations of a logspace function f, where the intermediate results are guaranteed to be of polynomial size in the original input, followed by the application of a logspace Boolean procedure g. This can be replaced by the pipelined execution of $O(\log n)$ instances of a PTIME procedure equivalent to f, followed by the application of a Boolean PTIME procedure equivalent to g. In total, this latter process is in PTIME because it amounts to a logarithmic number of invocations of a PTIME procedure, where each time the input size is bounded by a polynomial in the size n of the overall input. Therefore, $[\![\text{LOGSPACE}_{\text{pol}}]\!]^{\log} \subseteq \text{PTIME}$. □

6. DISCUSSION AND CONCLUSION

In this paper we have derived new complexity bounds for the DUALproblem and its complement $\overline{\text{DUAL}}$, that show that these problems can, in principle, be implemented by space-efficient algorithms. These bounds are depicted in Figure 1 in relation to the other relevant complexity classes. Here, set-inclusion is visualized by ascending lines or paths. We believe that our results represent some progress in the long and rather tortuous battle towards a better understanding of the mysterious DUAL problem. Our results are —for the time being— mainly of theoretical interest, and we do not claim they have immediate practical consequences. In fact, it is currently not clear whether our space-efficient version of the algorithm by Boros and Makino has any *practical*

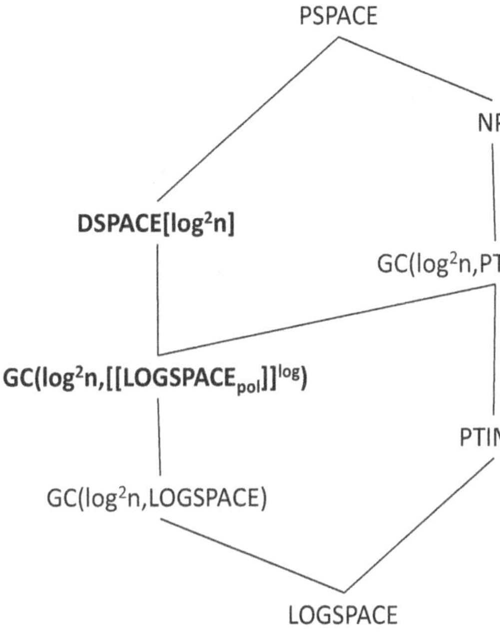

Figure 1

advantage over its original version. Future research may look at the applicability of such space-efficient techniques in presence of extremely large hypergraphs or data relations. Our bounds do prove useful for other purposes, however.

For instance, the $O(\log^2 n)$ space bound helps telling the DUAL problem apart from other problems that are candidates for completeness for intermediate classed between P and NP. For example, model-checking modal μ-calculus formulas [14], and the equivalent problem of whether a given player has a winning strategy in a parity games on graphs [13, 45], are such problems. They are not known to be tractable but lie in UP $\cap$ coUP [32], and are thus most likely not NP complete either. Given that these problems bear a certain superficial similarity to DUAL, the question arises, whether they are actually disguised versions of sub-problems of DUAL, and can thus be reduced to DUAL via simple low-level reductions (logspace or lower). By our results, this turns out not to be the case unless PTIME is in DSPACE[$\log^2 n$], which is highly unlikely. In fact, the model-checking problem for the modal μ-calculus and the equivalent parity game problem are known to be PTIME hard (see ([29]).

We hope, moreover, that our results may help steering future research towards a matching bound for the DUAL problem. We have reasons not to believe that $\overline{\mathrm{DUAL}}$ is hard for the class GC($\log^2 n$, $[\![\mathrm{LOGSPACE_{pol}}]\!]^{\log}$). This upper bound, however, gives us some intuition of where to dig further. For example, we conjecture that $\overline{\mathrm{DUAL}}$ lies in GC($\log^2 n$, LOGSPACE), and hope to be able to prove this in the near future.

Other future work will include the further analysis of hypergraph decomposition techniques to deal with the DUAL problem. It is known that DUAL is tractable for hypergraphs of bounded degeneracy, and, in particular, for acyclic hypergraphs [9]. The latter coincide with all hypergraphs of hypertree width 1 (see [22, 21, 1]). However, it was shown in [8] that for hypergraphs whose hypertree width is bounded by some constant $k \geq 2$, the DUAL problem remains as hard as in the general case. It would thus be interesting to find hypergraph decomposition methods that are more general than bounded degeneracy and still lead to tractable DUAL instances. Other research directions are to look for new parameters that lead to tractable (or even fixed-parameter tractable) instances in case they are bounded. See, for instance, [27] for some fixed-parameter tractability results, and [42] for a new parameter leading to tractability.

7. Acknowledgments

This work was supported by the EPSRC grant "Constraint Satisfaction for Configuration: Logical Fundamentals, Algorithms, and Complexity" (EP/G055114/1). The author is grateful to E. Allender, E. Boros, K. Makino, E. Malizia, P. Rossmanith, D. Saccà and H. Vollmer for help with technical questions and references, and to the reviewers for useful comments.

8. References

[1] I. Adler, G. Gottlob, and M. Grohe. Hypertree width and related hypergraph invariants. *Eur. J. Comb.*, 28(8):2167–2181, 2007.

[2] E. Boros, V. Gurvich, L. Khachiyan, and K. Makino. On the complexity of generating maximal frequent and minimal infrequent sets. In *Proceedings 19th Symposium on Theoretical Aspects of Computing (STACS'02)*, number 2285 in LNCS, pages 133–141, 2002.

[3] E. Boros, V. Gurvich, L. Khachiyan, and K. Makino. On maximal frequent and minimal infrequent sets in binary matrices. *Ann. Math. Artif. Intell.*, 39(3):211–221, 2003.

[4] E. Boros and K. Makino. A fast and simple parallel algorithm for the monotone duality problem. In S. Albers, A. Marchetti-Spaccamela, Y. Matias, S. E. Nikoletseas, and W. Thomas, editors, *ICALP (Part I)*, volume 5555 of *Lecture Notes in Computer Science*, pages 183–194. Springer, 2009.

[5] L. Cai and J. Chen. On the amount of nondeterminism and the power of verifying (extended abstract). In A. M. Borzyszkowski and S. Sokolowski, editors, *MFCS*, volume 711 of *Lecture Notes in Computer Science*, pages 311–320. Springer, 1993.

[6] J. Demetrovics and V. D. Thi. Armstrong relations, functional dependencies and strong dependencies. *Computers and Artificial Intelligence*, 14(3), 1995.

[7] T. Eiter and G. Gottlob. Identifying the minimal transversals of a hypergraph and related problems. *SIAM J. Comput.*, 24(6):1278–1304, 1995.

[8] T. Eiter and G. Gottlob. Hypergraph transversal computation and related problems in Logic and AI. In S. Flesca, S. Greco, N. Leone, and G. Ianni, editors, *JELIA*, volume 2424 of *Lecture Notes in Computer Science*, pages 549–564. Springer, 2002.

[9] T. Eiter, G. Gottlob, and K. Makino. New results on monotone dualization and generating hypergraph transversals. *SIAM J. Comput.*, 32(2):514–537, 2003.

[10] T. Eiter and K. Makino. Generating all abductive explanations for queries on propositional horn theories. In M. Baaz and J. A. Makowsky, editors, *CSL*, volume 2803 of *Lecture Notes in Computer Science*, pages 197–211. Springer, 2003.

[11] T. Eiter, K. Makino, and G. Gottlob. Computational aspects of monotone dualization: A brief survey. *Discrete Applied Mathematics*, 156(11):2035–2049, 2008.

[12] K. M. Elbassioni. On the complexity of monotone dualization and generating minimal hypergraph transversals. *Discrete Applied Mathematics*, 156(11):2109–2123, 2008.

[13] E. A. Emerson and C. S. Jutla. Tree automata, mu-calculus and determinacy (extended abstract). In *FOCS*, pages 368–377. IEEE Computer Society, 1991.

[14] E. A. Emerson, C. S. Jutla, and A. P. Sistla. On model-checking for fragments of μ-calculus. In C. Courcoubetis, editor, *CAV*, volume 697 of *Lecture Notes in Computer Science*, pages 385–396. Springer, 1993.

[15] M. Fredman and L. Khachiyan. On the Complexity of Dualization of Monotone Disjunctive Normal Forms. *Journal of Algorithms*, 21:618–628, 1996.

[16] H. Garcia-Molina and D. Barbará. How to assign votes in a distributed system. *J. ACM*, 32(4):841–860, 1985.

[17] D. Gaur. *Satisfiability and self-duality of monotone Boolean functions.* Dissertation, School of Computing Science, Simon Fraser University, January 1999.

[18] D. Gaur and R. Krishnamurti. Self-duality of bounded monotone boolean functions and related problems. In *Proceedings 11th International Conference on Algorithmic Learning Theory (ALT)*, number 1968 in LNCS, pages 209–223, 2000.

[19] G. Gogic, C. Papadimitriou, and M. Sideri. Incremental Recompilation of Knowledge. *Journal of Artificial Intelligence Research*, 8:23–37, 1998.

[20] J. Goldsmith, M. A. Levy, and M. Mundhenk. Limited nondeterminism. *SIGACT News*, 27(2):20–29, 1996.

[21] G. Gottlob, N. Leone, and F. Scarcello. Hypertree decompositions: A survey. In J. Sgall, A. Pultr, and P. Kolman, editors, *MFCS*, volume 2136 of *Lecture Notes in Computer Science*, pages 37–57. Springer, 2001.

[22] G. Gottlob, N. Leone, and F. Scarcello. Hypertree decompositions and tractable queries. *J. Comput. Syst. Sci.*, 64(3):579–627, 2002.

[23] G. Gottlob and L. Libkin. Investigations on Armstrong Relations, Dependency Inference, and Excluded Functional Dependencies. *Acta Cybernetica*, 9(4):385–402, 1990.

[24] R. Greiner, B. A. Smith, and R. W. Wilkerson. A Correction to the Algorithm in Reiter's Theory of Diagnosis. *Artificial Intelligence*, 41:79–88, 1990.

[25] D. Gunopulos, R. Khardon, H. Mannila, S. Saluja, H. Toivonen, and R. S. Sharm. Discovering all most specific sentences. *ACM Trans. Database Syst.*, 28(2):140–174, 2003.

[26] D. Gunopulos, R. Khardon, H. Mannila, and H. Toivonen. Data mining, hypergraph transversals, and machine learning. In *Proceedings of the 16th ACM SIGACT SIGMOD-SIGART Symposium on Principles of Database Systems (PODS-96)*, pages 209–216, 1993.

[27] M. Hagen. *Algorithmic and Computational Complexity Issues of MONET.* Cuvillier Verlag, 2008.

[28] T. Harada and M. Yamashita. Transversal merge operation: a nondominated coterie construction method for distributed mutual exclusion. *IEEE Transactions on Parallel and Distributed Systems*, 16(2):183–192, Feb.

[29] T. A. Henzinger, O. Kupferman, and R. Majumdar. On the universal and existential fragments of the μ-calculus. In H. Garavel and J. Hatcliff, editors, *TACAS*, volume 2619 of *Lecture Notes in Computer Science*, pages 49–64. Springer, 2003.

[30] T. Ibaraki and T. Kameda. A theory of coteries: Mutual exclusion in distributed systems. *IEEE Trans. Parallel Distrib. Syst.*, 4(7):779–794, 1993.

[31] D. S. Johnson. A Catalog of Complexity Classes. In J. van Leeuwen, editor, *Handbook of Theoretical Computer Science*, volume A, chapter 2. Elsevier Science Publishers B.V. (North-Holland), 1990.

[32] M. Jurdzinski. Deciding the winner in parity games is in up $\cap$ co-up. *Inf. Process. Lett.*, 68(3):119–124, 1998.

[33] D. Kavvadias, C. Papadimitriou, and M. Sideri. On Horn Envelopes and Hypergraph Transversals. In W. Ng, editor, *Proceedings 4th International Symposium on Algorithms and Computation (ISAAC-93)*, LNCS 762, pages 399–405, Hong Kong, December 1993. Springer.

[34] D. J. Kavvadias and E. C. Stavropoulos. Monotone Boolean Dualization is in co-NP[$\log^2$n]. *Information Processing Letters*, 85:1–6, 2003.

[35] L. Lamport. The implementation of reliable distributed multiprocess systems. *Comp. Networks*, 2:95–114, 1978.

[36] K. K. Loo, C. L. Yip, B. Kao, and D. W.-L. Cheung. Exploiting the duality of maximal frequent itemsets and minimal infrequent itemsets for i/o efficient association rule mining. In M. T. Ibrahim, J. Küng, and N. Revell, editors, *DEXA*, volume 1873 of *Lecture Notes in Computer Science*, pages 710–719. Springer, 2000.

[37] K. Makino and T. Kameda. Efficient generation of all regular non-dominated coteries. In G. Neiger, editor, *Proc. of the Nineteenth Annual ACM Symposium on Principles of Distributed Computing, July 16-19, 2000, Portland, Oregon, USA (PODC 2000)*, pages 279–288. ACM, 2000.

[38] K. Makino and T. Kameda. Transformations on regular nondominated coteries and their applications. *SIAM J. Discrete Math.*, 14(3):381–407, 2001.

[39] H. Mannila and H. Toivonen. Levelwise search and borders of theories in knowledge discovery. *Data mining and knowledge discovery*, 1(3):241–258, 1997.

[40] C. H. Papadimitriou. *Computational Complexity*. Addison-Wesley, 1994.

[41] R. Reiter. A theory of diagnosis from first principles. *Artif. Intell.*, 32(1):57–95, 1987.

[42] D. Saccà and E. Serra. Number of minimal hypergraph transversals and complexity of inverse frequent itemsets mining with infrequency constraints: they are high in theory, but often not so much in practice! *Manuscript, currently unpublished*, 2013.

[43] K. Satoh and T. Uno. Enumerating maximal frequent sets using irredundant dualization. In G. Grieser, Y. Tanaka, and A. Yamamoto, editors, *Discovery Science*, volume 2843 of *Lecture Notes in Computer Science*, pages 256–268. Springer, 2003.

[44] H. Tamaki. Space-efficient enumeration of minimal transversals of a hypergraph. *IPSJ-AL*, 75:29–36, 2000.

[45] W. Zielonka. Infinite games on finitely coloured graphs with applications to automata on infinite trees. *Theor. Comput. Sci.*, 200(1-2):135–183, 1998.

Spanners: A Formal Framework for Information Extraction

Ronald Fagin
IBM Research – Almaden
San Jose, CA, USA

Benny Kimelfeld
IBM Research – Almaden
San Jose, CA, USA

Frederick Reiss
IBM Research – Almaden
San Jose, CA, USA

Stijn Vansummeren
Université Libre de Bruxelles (ULB)
Bruxelles, Belgium

ABSTRACT

An intrinsic part of information extraction is the creation and manipulation of relations extracted from text. In this paper, we develop a foundational framework where the central construct is what we call a *spanner*. A spanner maps an input string into relations over the spans (intervals specified by bounding indices) of the string. The focus of this paper is on the representation of spanners. Conceptually, there are two kinds of such representations. Spanners defined in a *primitive* representation extract relations directly from the input string; those defined in an *algebra* apply algebraic operations to the primitively represented spanners. This framework is driven by SystemT, an IBM commercial product for text analysis, where the primitive representation is that of regular expressions with capture variables.

We define additional types of primitive spanner representations by means of two kinds of automata that assign spans to variables. We prove that the first kind has the same expressive power as regular expressions with capture variables; the second kind expresses precisely the algebra of the *regular* spanners—the closure of the first kind under standard relational operators. The *core* spanners extend the regular ones by string-equality selection (an extension used in SystemT). We give some fundamental results on the expressiveness of regular and core spanners. As an example, we prove that regular spanners are closed under difference (and complement), but core spanners are not. Finally, we establish connections with related notions in the literature.

Categories and Subject Descriptors

H.2.1 [**Database Management**]: Logical Design—*Data models*; H.2.4 [**Database Management**]: Systems—*Textual databases, Relational databases, Rule-based databases*; I.5.4 [**Pattern Recognition**]: Applications—*Text processing*; F.4.3 [**Mathematical Logic and Formal Languages**]: Formal Languages—*Algebraic language theory, Classes defined by grammars or automata, Operations on languages*; [[**F**]: .1.1]Computation by Abstract DevicesModels of Computation[Automata, Relations between models]

PODS'13, June 22–27, 2013, New York, New York, USA.

General Terms

Theory

Keywords

Information extraction, spanners, regular expressions, finite-state automata

1. INTRODUCTION

Automatically extracting structured information from text is a task that has been pursued for decades. As a discipline, Information Extraction (IE) had its start with the DARPA Message Understanding Conference in 1987 [27]. While early work in the area focused largely on military applications, recent changes have made information extraction increasingly important to an increasingly broad audience. Trends such as the rise of social media have produced huge amounts of text data, while analytics platforms like Hadoop have at the same time made the analysis of this data more accessible to a broad range of users. Since most analytics over text involves the extraction of information items (at least as a first step), IE is nowadays an important part of data analysis in the enterprise.

Broadly speaking, there are two main schools of thought on the realization of IE: the *statistical* (machine-learning) methodology and the *rule-based* approach. The first started with simple models such as AutoSlog [41], CRYSTAL [42] and SRV [22], then progressed to approaches based on probabilistic graph models [32, 33, 36]. Within the rule-based approach, most of the solutions (e.g., GATE/JAPE [18]) build upon *cascaded finite-state transducers* [3]. Most systems in both categories were built for academic settings, where most users are highly-trained computational linguists, where workloads cover only a small number of very well-defined tasks and data sets, and where extraction throughput is far less important than the accuracy of results.

When IBM researchers, driven by the increasing importance of text data in the enterprise, attempted to use these existing tools to solve customers' analytics problems, they encountered a number of practical challenges. Users needed to have an intuitive understanding of machine learning or the ability to build and understand complex and highly interdependent rules. Determining why an extractor produced a given incorrect result was extremely difficult, which made impractical the reuse of extractors across different data sets and applications. Moreover, high CPU and memory requirements made extractors cost-prohibitive in deployment over large-scale data sets.

In 2005, researchers at the IBM Almaden Research Center began the design and development of a new system, specifically geared for practical information extraction in the enterprise. This effort led to SystemT, a rule-based IE system with an SQL-like declarative language named *AQL* (Annotation Query Language) [15,31,40]. The declarative nature of AQL enables new kinds of tools for extractor development [35], and a cost-based optimizer for performance [40]. In 2010, SystemT was released as a commercial IBM product.[1] An intensive study by Chiticariu et al. [15] shows the value of SystemT, in particular the high extent to which it overcomes the difficulties mentioned earlier.

Conceptually, AQL can be viewed as built upon two main operations that were supported already in the original research prototype of SystemT [40]. The first operation (expressed as "extract" statements) is the extraction of relations from the underlying text through simple mechanisms. The most commonly used of these mechanisms is that of regular expressions with capture variables. An important special case of that mechanism is the extraction of dictionary (*gazetteer*) matches that are distinguished from general regular expressions by their syntax and underlying implementation. The second operation (expressed as "select" statements) is the manipulation of the relations (from the first operation) through algebraic operators. There are three types of algebraic operators: standard relational operators (e.g., union, projection, join), text-centric operators (e.g., string equality and containment), and conflict resolution (mainly, resolving cases of overlapping spans when those are undesired). In the actual (productized) AQL syntax, these operators are expressed as clauses of a Select-From-Where flavor.[2] In time, SystemT evolved to support additional facilities, like part-of-speech tagging, shallow parsing of XML tags, sorting and additional aggregate functions.

In this paper, we embark on an investigation of the principles underlying AQL. Our ultimate goal is to establish a formal model that is robust enough to capture the principal capabilities of systems featuring AQL's principles, and yet, that is abstract enough to yield useful insights, and solutions with provable guarantees. Towards that, we develop here a framework that captures the core functionality of SystemT, and establish some fundamental results on expressiveness and on the relationship with existing literature. We believe that this work will be the basis of further investigation of tools for text analytics. We further believe that this work and its followups will shed light on the interplay between the textual and the relational querying models (in contrast to their traditional separation as distinct steps). In the remainder of this section, we give a more technical and detailed description of our framework and results.

A *span* of a string $\mathbf{s}$ (where $\mathbf{s}$ represents the text) represents the range of a substring of $\mathbf{s}$, and is given by two indices that specify where the range begins and ends within $\mathbf{s}$. For example, if $\mathbf{s}$ is `ACM_PODS_2013`, then the span $[5,9\rangle$ refers to the part of $\mathbf{s}$ from the fifth to the eighth symbols inclusive, spanning the substring `PODS`. In this paper we introduce *spanners*, the central concept in our framework. Intuitively, a spanner extracts from a string $\mathbf{s}$ a relation over the spans of $\mathbf{s}$. It is formally defined as follows. An $\mathbf{s}$-*tuple* is associated with a finite domain V of *span variables*, and assigns a span of $\mathbf{s}$ to each variable in V. A *span relation* (*over* $\mathbf{s}$) is a set of $\mathbf{s}$-tuples, all over the same domain V of span variables. That set is naturally viewed as a relation, with the span variables playing the roles of the attribute names and the spans themselves used as attribute values. A *spanner* is a function that maps each string $\mathbf{s}$ into a span relation over $\mathbf{s}$.

For illustration, consider Figure 1, that is used for our running example in this paper. The figure shows two strings $\mathbf{s}$ and $\mathbf{t}$, and considers two spanners P_1 and P_2. The tables in the figure show the four span relations obtained by applying P_1 and P_2 to $\mathbf{s}$ and $\mathbf{t}$. For instance, the top row in the table of $P_1(\mathbf{s})$ shows the $\mathbf{s}$-tuple that assigns the spans $[1,4\rangle$, $[5,8\rangle$ and $[1,8\rangle$ to the variables x, y and z, respectively.

This paper focuses on the representation of spanners. Conceptually, we distinguish between two types of spanner representations. The first type is that of a *primitive* representation, which is a mechanism that extracts the relation directly from the input string $\mathbf{s}$. An example is a regular expression with span variables embedded as capture variables, as in AQL; here, we call such an expression a *regex formula*. The second type of a spanner representation is that of an *algebra*, which is the closure of primitive representations (of some specific class) under some algebraic operators.

Aside from regex formulas, we define two additional primitive spanner representations that are based on two corresponding types of automata. An automaton of each type is an ordinary nondeterministic finite automaton (NFA), except that it is associated with a finite set V of variables, and along a run on a string it can decide to open (i.e., begin the assigned span for) or close (i.e., end the assigned span for) a variable. In an accepting run, each variable in V must be opened and closed exactly once. The difference between the two types is in the data structures that maintain the variables. In a *variable-stack automaton* (*vstk-automaton* for short), that data structure is a stack, and hence, the closed variable is always the most recently opened one. In a *variable-set automaton* (*vset-automaton* for short), that data structure is a set, and the automaton specifies the specific (previously opened) variable to close.

We begin by showing that regex formulas, vstk-automata and vset-automata are tightly related to each other. In particular, regex formulas and vstk-automata have the same expressive power. The vset-automata can express spanners that are not expressible by vstk-automata, since a spanner representable by the latter is necessarily *hierarchical*—the spans of every output $\mathbf{s}$-tuple are nested like balanced parentheses. We prove that the spanners expressible by regex formulas are precisely the hierarchical spanners representable by vset-automata. Moreover, we prove that the expressive power of vset-automata is precisely that of the algebra that closes regex formulas under union, projection and natural join on spans. Finally, we prove that these algebraic operators *do not* increase the expressive power of vset-automata. We call the spanners expressible by vset-automata *regular spanners*. The name arises from the fact that, in the Boolean case, the languages recognizable by vset-automata are the regular ones.

An algebraic operator of AQL that was not mentioned in the previous paragraph is *string-equality* selection, which selects the $\mathbf{s}$-tuples such that the spans for two specified variables x and y correspond to equal substrings of $\mathbf{s}$ (although x and y need not be the same span). The *core* spanners, which we view as capturing the core of AQL, are the ones expressible by regex formulas along with the operators union, projection, natural join on spans, and string-equality selection. In this language, one can also simulate selection operators for other common string relationships such as containment, prefix and suffix. Standard inexpressiveness results for regular expressions easily imply that core spanners are more expressive than regular spanners. We prove a key lemma for core spanners, the "core-simplification lemma," which states that every core spanner can be represented as a *single* vset-automaton, followed by string selections and then by a projection. This lemma is a crucial ingredient for our later proofs of inexpressiveness results.

Focusing on regular and core spanners, we also look at the ability to *simulate* selection operators based on string relations (relations whose entries are strings, not spans). More formally, for a

[1]SystemT is included in IBM InfoSphere BigInsights. http://www.ibm.com/software/data/infosphere/biginsights/.

[2]See http://publib.boulder.ibm.com/infocenter/bigins/v2r0/ for the complete reference of the AQL syntax.

String s

A	a	a	_	A	b	b	_	a	a	_	B	a	a	_	B	b	b	_	b	_	A	b	a	a	_	A	b	b
1	2	3	4	5	6	7	8	9	10	11	12	13	14	15	16	17	18	19	20	21	22	23	24	25	26	27	28	29

$P_1(\mathbf{s})$

	x	y	z
μ_1	$[1,4\rangle$	$[5,8\rangle$	$[1,8\rangle$
μ_2	$[12,15\rangle$	$[16,19\rangle$	$[12,19\rangle$
μ_3	$[22,26\rangle$	$[27,30\rangle$	$[22,30\rangle$

$P_2(\mathbf{s})$

	x_1	x_2
μ_4	$[1,4\rangle$	$[22,26\rangle$

String t

A	a	a	_	A	b	b	_	A	b	b
1	2	3	4	5	6	7	8	9	10	11

$P_1(\mathbf{t})$

	x	y	z
μ_5	$[1,4\rangle$	$[5,8\rangle$	$[1,8\rangle$
μ_6	$[5,8\rangle$	$[9,12\rangle$	$[5,12\rangle$

$P_2(\mathbf{t})$

	x_1	x_2
μ_7	$[1,4\rangle$	$[5,8\rangle$

Figure 1: Running example: strings s and t, and the string relations obtained by applying two spanners P_1 and P_2

string relation R, the corresponding selection operator selects all the s-tuples such that the substrings corresponding to a specified sequence of variables (of the same arity as R) is in R. We say that R is *selectable* by a class of spanners (e.g., the regular or core) if that class is closed under the selection operator for R. Like Barceló et al. [5], we look at three classes of string relations: the *recognizable relations* [8,20], which are contained in the *regular relations* [7,20], which are contained in the *rational relations* [8, 39]. We show that every recognizable relation is selectable by the core spanners. We also show the existence of a regular (hence rational) relation that is not selectable by the core spanners, and the existence of a relation that is selectable by the core spanners but is not rational (hence not regular). As for regular spanners, it turns out that their selectable string relations are *precisely* the recognizable ones.

In Section 5 we investigate the incorporation of the *difference* operator in our setting. We prove that core spanners are *not* closed under difference. By analogy to the relational model, this may sound straightforward because all the other operators are monotonic. But this argument is invalid here, because regex formulas have the ability to simulate non-monotonic functionality. As evidence, it turns out that regular spanners *are* closed under difference. Moreover, as further evidence, some relations of a non-monotonic flavor are selectable by the core spanners, like inequality, non-prefix and non-suffix. In contrast, we prove with the core-simplification lemma that non-substring is *not* selectable by the core spanners; with that, non-closure under difference is a simple corollary.

Due to space limitations, this paper does not include proofs; those will appear in the full version of this paper.

Related Work

There is a large body of work on designing query languages for string databases (i.e., databases in which the atomic data values are strings) [7, 9, 25, 26]. There are two important differences of these works with ours. First and foremost, the atomic data values within relations in a string database are strings, whereas the atomic data values within span relations are spans. This distinction is important because it yields a different semantics for natural join: in a string database two tuples will join if they contain the same string in the shared attributes, whereas in span relations two tuples will join if they contain the same span. As we show in Section 5, it is exactly the capability of testing for equality on strings that causes loss of closure under difference. A second important difference is that query languages for string databases not only support pattern-matching for the purpose of extracting relevant information from strings, but also support powerful operations for the purpose of transforming strings. Typically, these transformation operations even make the query language Turing-complete in the class of string-to-string functions that can be expressed. In contrast, we focus on pattern matching that has low complexity.

A database query language that is closely related to regular spanners is the language of *Conjunctive Regular Path Queries* (CRPQs for short) [10, 11, 16, 19, 21]. We analyze in depth the relationship between CRPQs and our spanners in Section 6.

There is also a large body of work in extending finite state automata (or regular expressions) with mechanisms such as variables or registers. For example, Grumbach et al. [28] study variable automata. These are simple extensions to finite state automata in which the finite alphabet consists not only of letters, but also of variables that range over an infinite additional alphabet in order to be able to accept strings formed over an infinite alphabet. In contrast, the automata we consider accept only strings over a finite alphabet, and assign to each variable a span. Neven and Schwentick [38] study the expressive power of *query automata* on strings and trees. These automata define mappings from input strings or trees to sets (i.e., unary relations) of positions in the input. Spanners, in contrast, define mappings from input strings to relations of arbitrary arity over the spans of the input. Barceló et al. [6] study the extension of regular expressions with variables. In this extension, a variable can be substituted for a single alphabet letter only. In contrast, our variables bind to spans. A different extension of regular expressions with variables is given by the so called *extended regular expressions* [1, 12, 14, 23, 24]. Here, variables can not only bind to a substring during matching, but can also be used to repeat a previously matched substring. We analyze in depth the relationship between extended regular expressions and spanners in Section 6.

Classic rule-based information extraction systems build upon the *Common Pattern Specification Language* [3] (or CPSL for short), where information extraction rules are specified based on *cascaded finite-state transducers*. The idea behind these transducers is similar to the notion of *attribute grammars* [29, 30]: rules are used to parse (parts of) the input, and each rule can be assigned an action defining the values of attributes to be associated to the matched part of the input. (These attributes are considered to be the "extracted information".) While Neven and Van den Bussche [37] have investigated the expressive power of attribute grammars in querying derivation trees generated by a fixed context-free grammar, we are not aware of any formal investigation of the expressive power of the cascaded finite-state string transducers employed by CPSL. This is probably due to the fact that CPSL does not have a formal semantics. Instead, it explicitly leaves important details to the discretion of the implementation system designer. In addition, CPSL provides many extensions to standard finite state transducers, most notably a complex disambiguation policy and the ability to write rule actions in a Turing complete language through calls to arbitrary user-defined functions. For these reasons, we do not directly compare our framework against CPSL.

Finally, there is a body of research rooted in Allen's seminal paper on interval algebra [2]. In particular, while spans can be viewed as intervals, and spanners can hence be viewed as defining relations over intervals, Allen's interval algebra focuses on reasoning over relationships between intervals, but is not concerned with strings or string matching.

2. SPANNERS

At its core, our focus system (SystemT) implements a textual query language (AQL) that translates the input string into a collection of relations; in turn, those relations are manipulated in a relational-database manner [15]. The values in those relations are spans of the input string. Here we model the creation of those relations by the notion of a *spanner*, which we formally define in this section. In the following section we discuss the representation of spanners, as well as extensions by relational operators. We begin with some preliminary concepts and terminology.

2.1 String Basics

Strings and spans. We fix a finite alphabet Σ of *symbols*. We denote by Σ^* the set of all finite strings over Σ, and by Σ^+ the set of all finite strings of length at least one over Σ. A *language over* Σ is a subset of Σ^*. Let $\mathbf{s} = \sigma_1 \cdots \sigma_n \in \Sigma^*$ be a string. The length n of $\mathbf{s}$ is denoted by $|\mathbf{s}|$. A *span* identifies a substring of $\mathbf{s}$ by specifying its bounding indices. Formally, a span of $\mathbf{s}$ has the form $[i, j\rangle$, where $1 \leq i \leq j \leq n+1$. If $[i, j\rangle$ is a span of $\mathbf{s}$, then $\mathbf{s}_{[i,j\rangle}$ denotes the substring $\sigma_i \cdots \sigma_{j-1}$. Note that $\mathbf{s}_{[i,i\rangle}$ is the empty string, and that $\mathbf{s}_{[1,n+1\rangle}$ is $\mathbf{s}$. We note that the more standard notation would be $[i, j)$, but we use $[i, j\rangle$ to distinguish spans from intervals. For example, $[1, 1)$ and $[2, 2)$ are both the empty interval, hence equal, but in the case of spans we have $[i, j\rangle = [i', j'\rangle$ if and only if $i = i'$ and $j = j'$ (and in particular, $[1, 1\rangle \neq [2, 2\rangle$). We denote by $\mathsf{Spans}(\mathbf{s})$ the set of all the spans of $\mathbf{s}$. Two spans $[i, j\rangle$ and $[i', j'\rangle$ of $\mathbf{s}$ *overlap* if $i \leq i' < j$ or $i' \leq i < j'$, and are *disjoint* otherwise. Finally, $[i, j\rangle$ *contains* $[i', j'\rangle$ if $i \leq i' \leq j' \leq j$.

EXAMPLE 2.1. In a running example that we will use throughout the paper, we fix the alphabet $\Sigma = \{\mathtt{A}, \mathtt{a}, \mathtt{B}, \mathtt{b}, \_\}$ where we think of _ as representing a space between words. Figure 1 shows two strings $\mathbf{s}$ and $\mathbf{t}$ in Σ^*. Later we discuss the tables in this figure. To clarify the meaning of the spans we mention, we write the index under each character of the strings. The span $[22, 26\rangle$ is a span of $\mathbf{s}$ (but not of $\mathbf{t}$, since $22 > |\mathbf{t}| + 1 = 12$) and we have $\mathbf{s}_{[22,26\rangle} = \mathtt{Abaa}$. Also, $\mathbf{s}_{[1,4\rangle}$ and $\mathbf{t}_{[1,4\rangle}$ are both $\mathtt{Aaa}$. □

Regular expressions. Regular expressions over Σ are defined by the language

$$\gamma := \emptyset \mid \epsilon \mid \sigma \mid \gamma \vee \gamma \mid \gamma \cdot \gamma \mid \gamma^*$$

where $\emptyset$ is the empty set, ϵ is the empty string, and $\sigma \in \Sigma$. Note that "$\vee$" is the disjunction operator, "$\cdot$" is the concatenation operator, and "$*$" is the Kleene-star operator. We use γ^+ as an abbreviation of $\gamma \cdot \gamma^*$, and $\gamma?$ as an abbreviation for $\gamma \vee \epsilon$. The language recognized by a regular expression γ (i.e., the set of strings $\mathbf{s} \in \Sigma^*$ that γ matches) is denoted by $\mathcal{L}(\gamma)$. A language L over Σ is *regular* if $L = \mathcal{L}(\gamma)$ for some regular expression γ.

String relations. An *n-ary string relation* is a (possibly infinite) subset of $(\Sigma^*)^n$. We will refer to the following well-known classes of string relations: recognizable relations, regular relations (sometimes also called synchronized relations), and rational relations (see Barceló et al. [5] for concise definitions of these classes, as well as a discussion on the relationships between these classes). We denote by REC the class of all recognizable string relations, and by REC_k the class of all recognizable relations of arity k. Similarly, we denote by REG (REG_k) the class of all (k-ary) regular relations, and by RAT (RAT_k) the class of all (k-ary) rational relations. It is known that $\mathrm{REC}_1 = \mathrm{REG}_1 = \mathrm{RAT}_1$ (they all give the regular languages), and that $\mathrm{REC}_k \subsetneq \mathrm{REG}_k \subsetneq \mathrm{RAT}_k$ for all $k > 1$.

Span relations. We fix an infinite set SVars of *span variables*, which may be assigned spans. The sets Σ^* and SVars are disjoint. For a finite set $V \subseteq \mathsf{SVars}$ of variables and a string $\mathbf{s} \in \Sigma^*$, a *$(V, \mathbf{s})$-tuple* is a mapping $\mu \colon V \to \mathsf{Spans}(\mathbf{s})$ that assigns a span of $\mathbf{s}$ to each variable in V. If V is clear from the context, or V is irrelevant, we may write just "$\mathbf{s}$-tuple" instead of "$(V, \mathbf{s})$-tuple.' A set of $(V, \mathbf{s})$-tuples is called a *$(V, \mathbf{s})$-relation*. A $(V, \mathbf{s})$-relation is also called a *span relation (over* $\mathbf{s}$). Note that a span relation is always finite, since there are only finitely many $(V, \mathbf{s})$-tuples (given that V and $\mathbf{s}$ are both finite).

2.2 Spanners

A *spanner* is an operator that transforms a given string into a span relation over that string. More formally, a spanner P is a function that is associated with a finite set V of variables, and that maps every string $\mathbf{s}$ to a $(V, \mathbf{s})$-relation $P(\mathbf{s})$. We denote the set V by $\mathsf{SVars}(P)$. We say that a spanner P is *n-ary* if $|\mathsf{SVars}(P)| = n$.

EXAMPLE 2.2. In our running example (started in Example 2.1) we use two spanners: a ternary spanner P_1 and a binary spanner P_2. Later we will specify what exactly each spanner extracts from a given string. For now, the span relations (tables) in Figure 1 show the results of applying the two spanners to the strings $\mathbf{s}$ and $\mathbf{t}$ (also in the figure). □

Following are some special types of spanners that we use throughout this paper.

Boolean Spanners. A spanner P is *Boolean* if $\mathsf{SVars}(P) = \emptyset$. In that case, $P(\mathbf{s}) = \mathbf{true}$ denotes that $P(\mathbf{s})$ consists of the empty $\mathbf{s}$-tuple, and $P(\mathbf{s}) = \mathbf{false}$ denotes that $P(\mathbf{s}) = \emptyset$. If P is Boolean, then we say that P *recognizes* the language of strings that evaluate to $\mathbf{true}$.

Hierarchical spanners. Let P be a spanner. Let $\mathbf{s} \in \Sigma^*$ be a string, and let $\mu \in P(\mathbf{s})$ be an $\mathbf{s}$-tuple. We say that μ is *hierarchical* if for all variables $x, y \in \mathsf{SVars}(P)$ one of the following holds: *(1)* the span $\mu(x)$ contains $\mu(y)$, *(2)* the span $\mu(y)$ contains $\mu(x)$, *or (3)* the spans $\mu(x)$ and $\mu(y)$ are disjoint. As an example, the reader can verify that all the tuples in Figure 1 are hierarchical. We say that P is *hierarchical* if μ is hierarchical for all $\mathbf{s} \in \Sigma^*$ and $\mu \in P(\mathbf{s})$. We denote by $\mathbf{HS}$ the class of all hierarchical spanners.

Universal spanners. Let P be a spanner. We say that P is *total on* $\mathbf{s}$ if $P(\mathbf{s})$ consists of all the $\mathbf{s}$-tuples over $\mathsf{SVars}(P)$. (Note that over a finite set of variables, there are only finitely many $\mathbf{s}$-tuples.) We say that P is *hierarchically total on* $\mathbf{s}$ if $P(\mathbf{s})$ consists of (exactly) all the hierarchical $\mathbf{s}$-tuples. Let $Y \subseteq \mathsf{SVars}$ be a finite set of variables. The *universal spanner over* Y, denoted Υ_Y, is the unique spanner P such that $\mathsf{SVars}(P) = Y$ and P is total on every $\mathbf{s} \in \Sigma^*$. The *universal hierarchical spanner over* Y, denoted $\Upsilon^{\mathbf{H}}_Y$, is the unique spanner P such that $\mathsf{SVars}(P) = Y$ and P is hierarchically total on every $\mathbf{s} \in \Sigma^*$.

3. SPANNER REPRESENTATION

In our system of focus (SystemT), querying an input string $\mathbf{s}$ entails two steps (conceptually) [15]. In the first step, span relations over $\mathbf{s}$ are extracted by standard string-oriented tools like regular expressions with capture variables or dictionary matchers. In the second step, the final result is obtained by applying algebraic operators to the relations of the first step. We model these two steps by two corresponding types of representations for spanners. The first type is that of *primitive spanner representations*. The second type extends the first type by including operators of a relational algebra.

3.1 Primitive Spanner Representations

We introduce here three types of primitive spanner representations. The first is that of *regular-expression formulas* that extend regular expressions by including variables. The second and third are special automata that we call *variable-stack* and *variable-set* automata.

3.1.1 Regex Formulas

A *regular-expression formula*, or *regex formula* for short, is a regular expression with capture variables. The syntax of such formulas is almost the same as that of regular expressions:

$$\gamma := \emptyset \mid \epsilon \mid \sigma \mid \gamma \vee \gamma \mid \gamma \cdot \gamma \mid \gamma^* \mid x\{\gamma\} \qquad (1)$$

The added alternative is $x\{\gamma\}$, where $x \in \mathsf{SVars}$. We denote by $\mathsf{SVars}(\gamma)$ the set of variables that occur in γ. Before we formally define the spanner represented by a regex formula, we give an example.

EXAMPLE 3.1. We continue with our running example. Consider the formula γ_1 that is defined by

$$(\Sigma^* \cdot \_)^* \cdot z\Big\{x\{\gamma_{\mathsf{1stCap}}\} \cdot \_ \cdot y\{\gamma_{\mathsf{1stCap}}\}\Big\} \cdot (\_ \cdot \Sigma^*)^* \qquad (2)$$

where γ_{1stCap} is the regular expression $(\mathtt{A} \vee \mathtt{B}) \cdot (\mathtt{a} \vee \mathtt{b})^*$. After we define the spanner represented by a regex formula, it will turn out that γ_1 has the result of P_1 in Figure 1 on the strings $\mathbf{s}$ and $\mathbf{t}$. Note that $\mathsf{SVars}(\gamma_1) = \{x, y, z\}$. □

We now formally define the spanner that a regex formula represents. This definition is based on the notion of a *parse tree*. In general, a *tree* is associated with an alphabet Λ of labels, and is recursively defined as follows: if $t_1, \dots, t_n$ are trees (where $n \geq 0$) and $\lambda \in \Lambda$, then $\lambda(t_1 \cdots t_n)$ is a tree.

Let Λ be the alphabet $\Sigma \cup \mathsf{SVars} \cup \{\epsilon, \vee, \cdot, {}^*\}$. Let γ be a regex formula, and let $\mathbf{s}$ be a string. We use the following inductive definition. A tree t over the alphabet Λ is a *γ-parse for* $\mathbf{s}$ if one of the following holds.

- $\gamma = \epsilon$, $\mathbf{s} = \epsilon$, and $t = \epsilon()$.
- $\gamma = \sigma \in \Sigma$, $\mathbf{s} = \sigma$, and $t = \sigma()$.
- $\gamma = \gamma_1 \vee \gamma_2$, and $t = \vee(t')$ where t' is either a γ_1-parse or a γ_2-parse for $\mathbf{s}$.
- $\gamma = \gamma_1 \cdot \gamma_2$, and $t = \cdot(t_1 t_2)$ where t_i is a γ_i-parse for $\mathbf{s}_i$ ($i = 1, 2$) for some strings $\mathbf{s}_1$ and $\mathbf{s}_2$ such that $\mathbf{s} = \mathbf{s}_1\mathbf{s}_2$.
- $\gamma = \delta^*$ and there are strings $\mathbf{s}_1, \dots, \mathbf{s}_n$ such that $\mathbf{s} = \mathbf{s}_1 \cdots \mathbf{s}_n$, $t = {}^*(t_1 \cdots t_n)$, and each t_i is a δ-parse for $\mathbf{s}_i$ ($i = 1, \dots, n$).
- $\gamma = x\{\delta\}$ and $t = x(t_\delta)$ where t_δ is δ-parse for $\mathbf{s}$.

EXAMPLE 3.2. We continue with our running example. Figure 2(a) shows a γ_1-parse for $\mathbf{t}$ for the regex formula γ_1 of Example 3.1 and the string $\mathbf{t}$ of Figure 1. As we did with Figure 1, we write the index under each character. □

Note that there is no parse tree for the regex formula $\emptyset$. Clearly, a string $\mathbf{s}$ matches the regex formula γ, when variables are ignored, if and only if there exists a γ-parse for $\mathbf{s}$. In principle, a γ-parse t for $\mathbf{s}$ should determine one assignment for $\mathsf{SVars}(\gamma)$, as we later define. But for that, we need t to have *exactly* one occurrence of each variable in $\mathsf{SVars}(\gamma)$. So we restrict our regex formulas to those that guarantee such a behavior of t, a property we call *functional*.

DEFINITION 3.3. A regex formula γ is *functional* if for every string $\mathbf{s} \in \Sigma^*$ and γ-parse t for $\mathbf{s}$, each variable in $\mathsf{SVars}(\gamma)$ has precisely one occurrence in t. □

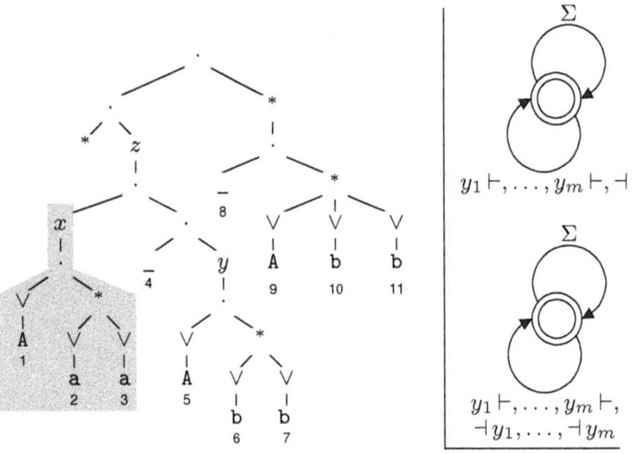

(a) (b)

Figure 2: (a) A γ_1-parse for t for the regex formula γ_1 of (2) (Example 3.1) and the string t of Figure 1 (b) A vstk-automaton A with $[\![A]\!] = \Upsilon^{\mathrm{H}}_Y$ (top) and a vset-automaton B with $[\![B]\!] = \Upsilon_Y$ (bottom) for $Y = \{y_1, \dots, y_m\}$

Note that a regex formula can be functional even though it contains multiple occurrences of a variable. An example is the regex formula γ given by $x\{\mathtt{a}\} \vee x\{\mathtt{b}\}$, which has two occurrences of the variable x, although each γ-parse has only one occurrence of x.

EXAMPLE 3.4. Consider again the regex formula γ_1 of Example 3.1. Recall that $\mathsf{SVars}(\gamma_1) = \{x, y, z\}$. Observe that in the γ_1-parse of Figure 2(a), each variable in $\mathsf{SVars}(\gamma_1)$ has indeed exactly one occurrence. In fact, it can be easily verified that this is the case for every γ_1-parse. Consequently, γ_1 is functional. □

Although Definition 3.3 is non-constructive, functionality is a property that can be tested in polynomial time.

PROPOSITION 3.5. *Whether a given formula γ is functional can be tested in polynomial time.*

In the remainder of this paper we implicitly assume that every involved regex formula is functional.

Let γ be a regex formula, and let p be a γ-parse for a string $\mathbf{s}$. If v is a node of p, then the subtree that is rooted at v naturally maps to a span p_v of $\mathbf{s}$. By μ^p we denote the assignment that maps each variable x to the span $\mu^p(x) = p_v$, where v is the unique node of t that is labeled by x. Note that v indeed exists, and is indeed unique, since we assume that γ is functional.

EXAMPLE 3.6. Let p be the γ_1-parse of $\mathbf{t}$ depicted in Figure 2(a), where γ_1 is defined in Example 3.1 and $\mathbf{t}$ is shown in Figure 1. The subtree of p rooted at the node labeled x is shaded grey. We have $\mu^p(x) = [1, 4\rangle$, $\mu^p(y) = [5, 8\rangle$, and $\mu^p(z) = [1, 8\rangle$. Hence, μ^p is the $\mathbf{t}$-tuple μ_5 of Figure 1. □

The spanner $[\![\gamma]\!]$ that is represented by the regex formula γ is the one where $\mathsf{SVars}([\![\gamma]\!])$ is the set $\mathsf{SVars}(\gamma)$, and where $[\![\gamma]\!](\mathbf{s})$ is the span relation $\{\mu^p \mid p \text{ is a } \gamma\text{-parse for } \mathbf{s}\}$.

EXAMPLE 3.7. Consider again the regex formula γ_1 of Example 3.1, the strings $\mathbf{s}$ and $\mathbf{t}$ of Figure 1, and the spanner P_1 mentioned in that figure. The reader can verify that $[\![\gamma_1]\!](\mathbf{s}) = P_1(\mathbf{s})$ and that $[\![\gamma_1]\!](\mathbf{t}) = P_1(\mathbf{t})$. □

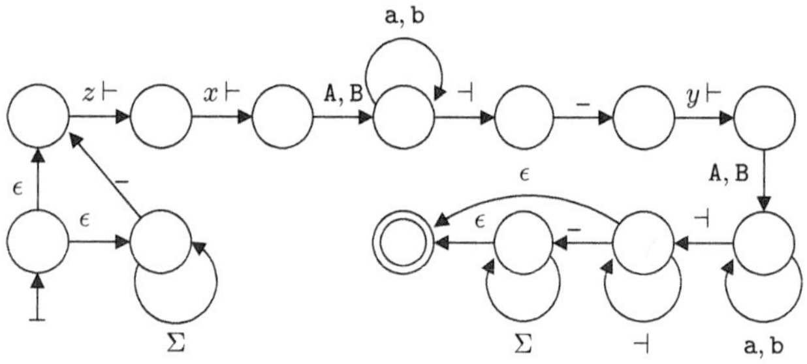

Figure 3: A vstk-automaton A with $[\![A]\!] = [\![\gamma_1]\!]$ for the regex formula γ_1 of (2) (Example 3.1)

3.1.2 Variable-Stack Automata

In this section, we define an automaton representation of a spanner. We call this automaton a *variable-stack automaton*, or just *vstk-automaton* for short. Later we will show that vstk-automata capture precisely the expressive power of regex formulas (that is, the two classes of spanner representation can express the same set of spanners).

Formally, a vstk-automaton is a tuple (Q, q_0, q_f, δ), where: Q is a finite set of *states*, $q_0 \in Q$ is an *initial state*, $q_f \in Q$ is an *accepting state*, and δ is a finite transition relation consisting of triples, each having one of the forms (q, σ, q'), (q, ϵ, q'), $(q, x\vdash, q')$ or $(q, \dashv, q')$, where $q, q' \in Q$, $\sigma \in \Sigma$, $x \in \mathsf{SVars}$, and $\dashv$ is a special *pop* symbol.

EXAMPLE 3.8. Figure 3 is a representation of a vstk-automaton A. Each circle represents a state, the double circle represents an acceping state, and a label a on an edge from q to q' represents the transition (q, a, q'). Conventionally, as a shorthand notation we write the sequence $a_1, \dots, a_k$ of labels on the edge from q to q' instead of the k edges $(q, a_1, q'), \dots, (q, a_k, q')$. Moreover, if $\Sigma = \{\sigma_1, \dots, \sigma_m\}$ then we write the label Σ instead of $\sigma_1, \dots, \sigma_m$. Later we will link the vstk-automaton A to our running example. □

Let A be a vstk-automaton. We denote by $\mathsf{SVars}(A)$ the set of variables that occur in the transitions of A. A *configuration* of a vstk-automaton A is a tuple $c = (q, \vec{v}, Y, i)$, where $q \in Q$ is the *current state*, $\vec{v}$ is a finite sequence of variables called the *current variable stack*, $Y \subseteq \mathsf{SVars}(A)$ is the set of *available variables*, and i is an index in $\{1, \dots, n+1\}$ (pointing to the next character to be read from $\mathbf{s}$).

Let $\mathbf{s} = \sigma_1 \cdots \sigma_n$ be a string and let A be a vstk-automaton. A *run* ρ of A on $\mathbf{s}$ is a sequence $c_0, \dots, c_m$ of configurations, such that $c_0 = (q_0, \epsilon, \mathsf{SVars}(A), 1)$, and for all $j = 0, \dots, m-1$ one of the following holds for $c_j = (q_j, \vec{v}_j, Y_j, i_j)$ and $c_{j+1} = (q_{j+1}, \vec{v}_{j+1}, Y_{j+1}, i_{j+1})$:

1. $\vec{v}_{j+1} = \vec{v}_j$, $Y_{j+1} = Y_j$, and either (a) $i_{j+1} = i_j + 1$ and $(q_j, s_{i_j}, q_{j+1}) \in \delta$ (ordinary transition), or (b) $i_{j+1} = i_j$ and $(q_j, \epsilon, q_{j+1}) \in \delta$ (epsilon transition).
2. $i_{j+1} = i_j$, and for some $x \in \mathsf{SVars}(A)$, either (a) $\vec{v}_{j+1} = \vec{v}_j \cdot x$, $x \in Y_j$, $Y_{j+1} = Y_j \setminus \{x\}$ and $(q_j, x\vdash, q_{j+1}) \in \delta$ (variable push), or (b) $\vec{v}_j = \vec{v}_{j+1} \cdot x$, $Y_{j+1} = Y_j$ and $(q_j, \dashv, q_{j+1}) \in \delta$ (variable pop).

An easy observation is that every configuration $(q, \vec{v}, Y, i)$ in a run is such that $\vec{v}$ and Y do not share any common variable.

The run $\rho = c_0, \dots, c_m$ is *accepting* if $c_m = (q_f, \epsilon, \emptyset, n+1)$. We let $\mathsf{ARuns}(A, \mathbf{s})$ denote the set of all accepting runs of A on $\mathbf{s}$.

If $\rho \in \mathsf{ARuns}(A, \mathbf{s})$, then for each $x \in \mathsf{SVars}(A)$ the run ρ has a unique configuration $c_b = (q_b, \vec{v}_b, Y_b, i_b)$ where x occurs in the current version of $\vec{v}$ (i.e., $\vec{v}_b$) for the first time; and later than that ρ has a unique configuration $c_e = (q_e, \vec{v}_e, Y_e, i_e)$ where x is occurs in the current version of $\vec{v}$ (i.e., $\vec{v}_e$) for the last time; the span $[i_b, i_e\rangle$ is denoted by $\rho(x)$. By μ^ρ we denote the $\mathbf{s}$-tuple that maps each variable $x \in \mathsf{SVars}(A)$ to the span $\rho(x)$. The spanner $[\![A]\!]$ that is represented by A is the one where $\mathsf{SVars}([\![A]\!])$ is the set $\mathsf{SVars}(A)$, and where $[\![A]\!](\mathbf{s})$ is the span relation $\{\mu^\rho \mid \rho \in \mathsf{ARuns}(A, \mathbf{s})\}$.

EXAMPLE 3.9. Consider the vstk-automaton A of Figure 3, described in Example 3.8. Observe that $\mathsf{SVars}(A) = \{x, y, z\}$. Note that in a run ρ, when reaching the final transition $(q, \dashv, q')$ (the leftmost occurrence of $\dashv$ in the bottom row), there is only one variable that is open, namely z. Hence, that transition can take place at most once. Moreover, if ρ is accepting then ρ must take that transition *exactly* once, since otherwise z would not be closed.

Continuing with our running example, now consider again the regex-formula γ_1 of (2), introduced in Example 3.1. The reader can verify that A and γ_1 define the same spanner, that is, $[\![\gamma_1]\!] = [\![A]\!]$. □

EXAMPLE 3.10. The top part of Figure 2(b) depicts a single-state vstk-automaton A where we have $\mathsf{SVars}(A) = Y$, with $Y = \{y_1, \dots, y_m\}$. The reader can verify that $[\![A]\!]$ is the universal hierarchical spanner $\Upsilon^{\mathbf{H}}_Y$. In particular, this example shows that the universal hierarchical spanners are expressible by vstk-automata. □

3.1.3 Variable-Set Automata

A *variable-set automaton* (or *vset-automaton*) is defined to be a tuple (Q, q_0, q_f, δ) like a vstk-automaton, except δ does not have triples $(q, \dashv, q')$; instead, δ has triples $(q, \dashv x, q')$ where $x \in \mathsf{SVars}$. We denote by $\mathsf{SVars}(A)$ the set of variables that occur in the transitions of A.

The difference between the two types of automata is also in the definition of a *configuration* and a *run*. In a vset-automaton, a *set* of variables is used rather than a *stack*. More precisely, a configuration of a vset-automaton A is a tuple $c = (q, V, Y, i)$, where $q \in Q$ is the *current state*, $V \subseteq \mathsf{SVars}(A)$ is the *active variable set*, $Y \subseteq \mathsf{SVars}(A)$ is the set of *available variables*, and i is an index in $\{1, \dots, n+1\}$.

For a string $\mathbf{s} = s_1, \dots, s_n$, a *run* ρ of A on $\mathbf{s}$ is a sequence $c_0, \dots, c_m$ of configurations, where $c_0 = (q_0, \emptyset, \mathsf{SVars}(A), 1)$, and for $j = 0, \dots, m-1$ one of the following holds for $c_j = (q_j, V_j, Y_j, i_j)$ and $c_{j+1} = (q_{j+1}, V_{j+1}, Y_{j+1}, i_{j+1})$:

1. $V_{j+1} = V_j$, $Y_{j+1} = Y_j$, and either (a) $i_{j+1} = i_j + 1$ and $(q_j, s_{i_j}, q_{j+1}) \in \delta$ (ordinary transition), or (b) $i_{j+1} = i_j$ and $(q_j, \epsilon, q_{j+1}) \in \delta$ (epsilon transition).
2. $i_{j+1} = i_j$ and for some $x \in \mathsf{SVars}(A)$, either (a) $x \in Y_j$, $V_{j+1} = V_j \cup \{x\}$, $Y_{j+1} = Y_j \setminus \{x\}$, and $(q_j, x\vdash, q_{j+1}) \in \delta$, (variable insert), or (b) $x \in V_j$, $V_{j+1} = V_j \setminus \{x\}$, $Y_{j+1} = Y_j$ and $(q_j, \dashv x, q_{j+1}) \in \delta$ (variable remove).

Note that in a run, each configuration (q, V, Y, i) is such that V and Y are disjoint. The run $\rho = c_0, \dots, c_m$ is *accepting* if $c_m = (q_f, \emptyset, \emptyset, n+1)$. The definitions of $\mathsf{ARuns}(A, \mathbf{s})$ and $[\![A]\!]$ are similar to those for a vstk-automaton (except that we replace the stack $\vec{v}$ with the set V).

EXAMPLE 3.11. Consider again Figure 2(b). The bottom part depicts a single-state vset-automaton B with $\mathsf{SVars}(B) = Y$, where $Y = \{y_1, \dots, y_m\}$. The reader can verify that $[\![B]\!] = \Upsilon_Y$. In particular, this example shows that the universal spanners are expressible by vset-automata. This example also shows that vset-automata can express spanners that regex formulas and vstk-automata cannot. In particular, an easy observation is that the spanner defined by a regex formula, or a vstk-automaton, is necessarily hierarchical. But $[\![B]\!]$ is certainly not hierarchical. □

3.1.4 Primitive Spanner Representations

We have defined three types of spanner representations. By RGX we denote the class of (functional) regex formulas, by $\mathsf{VA}_{\mathsf{stk}}$ we denote the class of vstk-automata, and by $\mathsf{VA}_{\mathsf{set}}$ we denote the class of vset-automata. We will refer to these three as our *primitive spanner representations* (to contrast with algebraic extensions of these representations).

If SR is any class spanner representations, like the primitive classes RGX, $\mathsf{VA}_{\mathsf{stk}}$ or $\mathsf{VA}_{\mathsf{set}}$, then $[\![SR]\!]$ represents the set of all the spanners representable by SR; that is, $[\![SR]\!] = \{[\![r]\!] \mid r \in SR\}$. For example, $[\![\mathsf{RGX}]\!]$ is the set of all the spanners $[\![\gamma]\!]$, where γ is a regex formula.

As mentioned in Example 3.11, every spanner defined by a regex formula or vstk-automaton is hierarchical. In our terminology it is stated as $[\![\mathsf{RGX}]\!] \subseteq \mathbf{HS}$ and $[\![\mathsf{VA}_{\mathsf{stk}}]\!] \subseteq \mathbf{HS}$. In Example 3.11 we also mentioned that $[\![\mathsf{VA}_{\mathsf{set}}]\!] \not\subseteq \mathbf{HS}$. Later, we will show that $[\![\mathsf{RGX}]\!] = [\![\mathsf{VA}_{\mathsf{stk}}]\!]$. In fact, we will show that the class of spanners definable by a vstk-automaton is *precisely* the class of hierarchical spanners definable by a vset-automaton, or in our notation, $[\![\mathsf{VA}_{\mathsf{stk}}]\!] = [\![\mathsf{VA}_{\mathsf{set}}]\!] \cap \mathbf{HS}$.

3.2 Spanner Algebras

Consider a class SR of spanner representations (e.g., one of our primitive representations). We extend SR with *algebraic operator symbols* to form a *spanner algebra*. More formally, each operator symbol corresponds to a *spanner operator*, which is a function that takes as input a fixed-length sequence of spanners (usually one or two, depending on whether the operator is unary or binary), and outputs a single spanner. We now define the spanner operators we focus on in this paper. Let P, P_1 and P_2 be spanners, and let $\mathbf{s}$ be a string.

- **Union.** The union $P_1 \cup P_2$ is defined when P_1 and P_2 are *union compatible*, that is, $\mathsf{SVars}(P_1) = \mathsf{SVars}(P_2)$. In that case, $\mathsf{SVars}(P_1 \cup P_2) = \mathsf{SVars}(P_1)$ and $(P_1 \cup P_2)(\mathbf{s}) = P_1(\mathbf{s}) \cup P_2(\mathbf{s})$.

- **Projection.** If $Y \subseteq \mathsf{SVars}(P)$, then $\pi_Y P$ is the spanner with $\mathsf{SVars}(\pi_Y P) = Y$, where $\pi_Y P(\mathbf{s})$ is obtained from $P(\mathbf{s})$ by restricting the domain of each $\mathbf{s}$-tuple to Y.

- **Natural join.** The spanner $P_1 \bowtie P_2$ is defined as follows. We have $\mathsf{SVars}(P_1 \bowtie P_2) = \mathsf{SVars}(P_1) \cup \mathsf{SVars}(P_2)$, and $(P_1 \bowtie P_2)(\mathbf{s})$ consists of all $\mathbf{s}$-tuples μ that agree with some $\mu_1 \in P_1(\mathbf{s})$ and $\mu_2 \in P_2(\mathbf{s})$; note that the existence of μ implies that μ_1 and μ_2 agree on the common variables of P_1 and P_2, that is, $\mu_1(x) = \mu_2(x)$ for all $x \in \mathsf{SVars}(P_1) \cap \mathsf{SVars}(P_2)$.

- **String selection.** Let R be a k-ary string relation. The string-selection operator ς^R is parameterized by k variables $x_1, \dots, x_k$ in $\mathsf{SVars}(P)$, and may then be written as $\varsigma^R_{x_1,\dots,x_k}$. If P' is $\varsigma^R_{x_1,\dots,x_k} P$, then the span relation $P'(\mathbf{s})$ is taken to be the restriction of $P(\mathbf{s})$ to those $\mathbf{s}$-tuples μ such that $(\mathbf{s}_{\mu(x_1)}, \dots, \mathbf{s}_{\mu(x_k)}) \in R$.

Regarding the natural join, observe that here pairs of tuples are joined based on having equal *spans* in shared variables. This is distinct from the natural join in query languages for string databases [7, 9, 25, 26], where tuples are joined if they have the equal *substrings* in shared attributes. Also observe that in the special case where P_1 and P_2 are union compatible, the spanner $P_1 \bowtie P_2$ produces the intersection $P_1(\mathbf{s}) \cap P_2(\mathbf{s})$ for the given string $\mathbf{s}$; in that case, we denote $P_1 \bowtie P_2$ also as $P_1 \cap P_2$. As another special case, if $\mathsf{SVars}(P_1)$ and $\mathsf{SVars}(P_2)$ are disjoint, then $P_1 \bowtie P_2$ produces the Cartesian product of $P_1(\mathbf{s})$ and $P_2(\mathbf{s})$; in that case, we denote $P_1 \bowtie P_2$ also as $P_1 \times P_2$.

In this work we focus mainly on one particular string-selection operator, namely the binary $\varsigma^=$. As defined above, $\varsigma^=_{x,y} P(\mathbf{s})$ restricts $P(\mathbf{s})$ to those $\mathbf{s}$-tuples μ with $\mathbf{s}_{\mu(x)} = \mathbf{s}_{\mu(y)}$. Later, we also consider other string selections (featuring other binary string relations). We do not include the *difference* operator yet, but rather dedicate to it a separate discussion in Section 5.

For clarity of presentation, we will abuse notation by using the operator symbol itself to represent the spanner operator. As an example, if γ_1 and γ_2 are regex formulas, then the expression $\gamma_1 \bowtie \gamma_2$ is well formed, and it represents the spanner $[\![\gamma_1]\!] \bowtie [\![\gamma_2]\!]$. Similarly, if A_1 and A_2 are vstk-automata then $A_1 \cup A_2$ is well formed assuming union compatibility, that is, $\mathsf{SVars}(A_1) = \mathsf{SVars}(A_2)$. Similarly, if A is a vset-automaton then $\pi_Y A$ is well formed assuming $Y \subseteq \mathsf{SVars}(A)$, and similarly $\varsigma^=_{x,y} A$ is well formed assuming $x, y \in \mathsf{SVars}(A)$.

EXAMPLE 3.12. We continue with our running example. Let γ_{12} be the regex formula that captures all spans x_1 and x_2 such that x_1 ends before x_2 begins; that is:

$$\gamma_{12}(x_1, x_2) \stackrel{\text{def}}{=} \Sigma^* \cdot x_1\{\Sigma^*\} \cdot \Sigma^* \cdot x_2\{\Sigma^*\} \cdot \Sigma^*$$

The following algebraic expression is denoted as γ_2.

$$\pi_{x_1,x_2}\Big(\varsigma^=_{y_1,y_2}\big(\gamma_1(x_1,y_1,z_1) \bowtie \gamma_1(x_2,y_2,z_2) \bowtie \gamma_{12}(x_1,x_2)\big)\Big),$$

where we use $\gamma_1(x_i, y_i, z_i)$ as the regex-formula that is obtained from γ_1 of (2) (Example 3.1) by replacing x, y and z with x_i, y_i and z_i, respectively. Observe that γ_2 selects all the spans x_1 and x_2 that occur in tuples of γ_1, such that the corresponding y_1 and y_2 span the same substrings (though y_1 and y_2 themselves are not required to be equal as spans), and moreover, x_1 ends before x_2 begins. Consider the strings $\mathbf{s}$ and $\mathbf{t}$ in Figure 1. The reader can verify that $[\![\gamma_2]\!]$ has the output of P_2 (also shown in the figure) for these two strings. □

A *spanner algebra* is a finite set of spanner operators. If SR is a class of spanner representations and O is a spanner algebra, then SR^O denotes the class of all the spanner representations defined by applying (compositions of) the operators in O to the representations in SR. In other words, S^O is the closure of SR under O (when O is taken as a set of operator symbols); consequently, $[\![SR^O]\!]$ is the closure of $[\![SR]\!]$ under O (when O is now taken as a set of spanner operators). For example, one of the algebras we later explore is $\mathsf{VA}_{\mathsf{set}}^{\{\cup,\pi,\bowtie,\varsigma^=\}}$. As another example, the expression γ_2 of Example 3.12 is in $\mathsf{RGX}^{\{\pi,\bowtie,\varsigma^=\}}$.

4. REGULAR AND CORE SPANNERS

In this section we define the classes of regular and core spanners, and study their relative expressive power.

4.1 Regular Spanners

We call a spanner *hierarchical regular* if it is definable by a vstk-automaton. We call a spanner *regular* if it is definable by a vset-automaton. In this section, we explore expressiveness aspects of hierarchical regular and regular spanners.

Observe that vstk-automata, vset-automata and NFAs are basically the same objects in the Boolean case. In particular, a language $L \subseteq \Sigma^*$ is recognized by some Boolean hierarchical regular spanner if and only if L is recognized by some Boolean regular spanner if and only if L is regular. Hence, the results of this section are of interest only in the non-Boolean case.

Key constructs that we later utilize for establishing our results here are those of a *transition graph* and the special case of a *path union*, both introduced in the next section.

4.1.1 Transition Graphs and Path Unions

We define two types of transition graphs, which function similarly to vstk-automata and vset-automata, respectively, except that in a single transition a whole substring (matching a specified regular expression) can be read, and moreover, every transition to a non-accepting state involves a single operation of opening or closing a variable. Those graphs are similar to the extended automata obtained by the known *state-removal* technique, that is used to convert an automaton into a regular expression [34]. Recall that throughout this paper we fix the alphabet Σ for the input string language.

A *variable-stack transition graph*, or *vstk-graph* for short, is a tuple $G = (Q, q_0, q_f, \delta)$ defined similarly to a vstk-automaton, except that now δ consists of edges of three forms: $(q, \gamma, x\vdash, q')$, $(q, \gamma, \dashv, q')$ and (q, γ, q_f); here, $q, q' \in Q$, γ is a regular expression over Σ, and $x \in \mathsf{SVars}$. We require the accepting state q_f to have only incoming transitions. As usual, $\mathsf{SVars}(G)$ denotes the set of variables that occur in G. A *configuration* $c = (q, \vec{v}, Y, i)$ is defined exactly as in the case of a vstk-automaton, but the definition of a run changes: a run ρ of G on a string $\mathbf{s}$ is a sequence $c_0, \dots, c_m$ of configurations, such that for all $j = 0, \dots, m-1$, the configurations $c_j = (q_j, \vec{v}_j, Y_j, i_j)$ and $c_{j+1} = (q_{j+1}, \vec{v}_{j+1}, Y_{j+1}, i_{j+1})$ satisfy the following. First, $i_j \leq i_{j+1}$. Second, δ contains a tuple $(q, \gamma, x\vdash, q')$ or a tuple $(q, \gamma, \dashv, q')$, such that $q = q_j$, the string $\mathbf{s}_{[i_j, i_{j+1}\rangle}$ is in $\mathcal{L}(\gamma)$, and $q' = q_{j+1}$; moreover, in the case of $x\vdash$ we have $x \in Y_j$, $\vec{v}_{j+1} = \vec{v}_j \cdot x$ and $Y_{j+1} = Y_j \setminus \{x\}$; and in the case of $\dashv$ we have $\vec{v}_j = \vec{v}_{j+1} \cdot x$ and $Y_{j+1} = Y_j$. The definition of an *accepting configuration* is similar to that for vstk-automata. Moreover, the definitions of $\mathsf{ARuns}(G, \mathbf{s})$ and $[\![G]\!]$ are similar to those of $\mathsf{ARuns}(A, \mathbf{s})$ and $[\![A]\!]$ in the case of a vstk-automaton A.

A vstk-graph $G = (Q, q_0, q_f, \delta)$ is a *vstk-path* if we can write Q as $\{q_0, q_1, \dots, q_k = q_f\}$ where δ contains exactly k edges: from q_0 to q_1, from q_1 to q_2, and so on, until q_k. A vstk-path is *consistent* if the variables open and close in a balanced manner (which we define in the natural way like grammatical parentheses). We say that G is a *vstk-path union* if G is the union of consistent vstk-paths, such that: *(1)* every two vstk-paths have the same set of variables, namely $\mathsf{SVars}(G)$, and *(2)* every two vstk-paths share precisely the states q_0 and q_f, as illustrated in Figure 4 (where we omit the opening and closing of variables).

Similarly to the vstk case, we define a *vset-graph* to be a variation of a vset-automaton. In particular, $\mathsf{ARuns}(G, \mathbf{s})$ and $[\![G]\!]$ are now defined when G is a vset-graph. Also similarly we define a *vset-path*, a *consistent vset-path* (where parenthetical balance is not required, but every variable needs to be opened and later closed exactly once), and a *vset-path union*.

We use $\mathsf{PU}_{\mathsf{stk}}$ and $\mathsf{PU}_{\mathsf{set}}$ to denote the class of vstk-path unions and the class of vset-path unions, respectively.

4.1.2 Relative Expressive Power

We can now give some results on the (relative) expressive power of the regular spanners. A key lemma is the following.

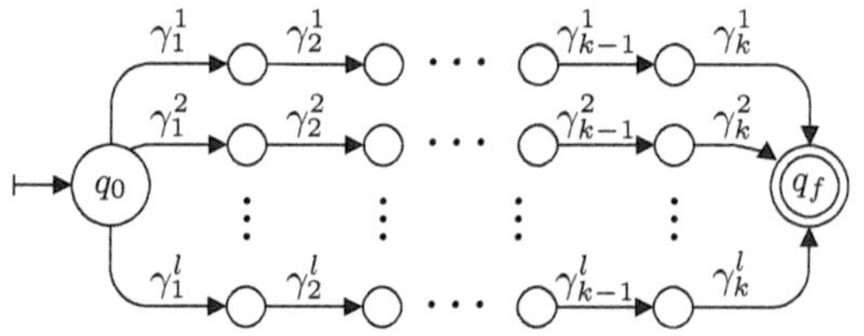

Figure 4: An illustration of a vstk-path union or a vset-path union

LEMMA 4.1. *The following hold.*

1. *Every hierarchical regular spanner is definable by a vstk-path union and vice versa; that is,* $[\![\mathsf{VA}_{\mathsf{stk}}]\!] = [\![\mathsf{PU}_{\mathsf{stk}}]\!]$.
2. *Every regular spanner is definable by a vset-path union and vice versa; that is,* $[\![\mathsf{VA}_{\mathsf{set}}]\!] = [\![\mathsf{PU}_{\mathsf{set}}]\!]$.

In the proof of Lemma 4.1, translating a vstk-path union into a vstk-automaton (resp., a vset-path union into a vset-automaton) is fairly straightforward. The translation of a vstk-automaton to a vstk-path union entails two main steps. (And similar steps are taken in the vset case.) First, the vstk-automaton is converted into a vstk-graph by an adaptation of the well known *state-removal* procedure [34] for translating an automaton into a regular expression. Second, the vstk-graph is converted into a vstk-path union through the observation that only a finite number of paths in the vstk-graph are of relevance.

Our first theorem states that the spanners definable by regex formulas are precisely the hierarchical regular ones.

THEOREM 4.2. *A spanner is hierarchical regular if and only if it is definable by a regex formula; that is,* $[\![\mathsf{VA}_{\mathsf{stk}}]\!] = [\![\mathsf{RGX}]\!]$.

The proof is as follows. We convert a regex formula into a vstk-automaton by an adaptation of the standard construction by Thompson (see, e.g., [34]), namely, incremental construction of an automaton from a regular expression through a bottom-up traversal of the parse of a regular expression. The other direction is an immediate consequence of Lemma 4.1, since the conversion of a vstk-path union into a regex formula is straightforward.

The next theorem states that the hierarchical regular spanners are precisely the spanners that are both regular and hierarchical. Again, the proof uses Lemma 4.1.

THEOREM 4.3. *A spanner is hierarchical regular if and only if it is both regular and hierarchical; that is,* $[\![\mathsf{VA}_{\mathsf{stk}}]\!] = [\![\mathsf{VA}_{\mathsf{set}}]\!] \cap \mathbf{HS}$.

The following theorem states that the union, projection and natural-join operators *do not* increase the expressive power of vset-automata.

THEOREM 4.4. *The class of regular spanners is closed under union, projection and natural join; that is,* $[\![\mathsf{VA}_{\mathsf{set}}^{\{\cup,\pi,\bowtie\}}]\!] = [\![\mathsf{VA}_{\mathsf{set}}]\!]$.

Our proof of Theorem 4.4 is by separately considering each of the operators union, projection, and natural join, and showing closure of $\mathsf{VA}_{\mathsf{set}}$ thereunder. While the first two closures are easy to prove, showing closure under natural join involves subtleties. The expected approach is similar to intersecting two NFAs: a vset-automaton for $A_1 \bowtie A_2$ runs on A_1 and A_2 in parallel; when a variable x is common to both automata, the two parallel runs must open and close x together (as x must be the same span in both runs in taking the join). This approach, however, fails, for a subtle reason. As an example, A_1 and A_2 of Figure 5 are such that

$[\![A_1]\!] = [\![A_2]\!] = [\![A_1 \bowtie A_2]\!]$. However, our construction for A_1 and A_2 will result in the empty spanner, since A_1 requires x to open *before* y (with an epsilon transition in between), and A_2 requires x to open *after* y. We solve this problem by converting A_1 and A_2 into a *normalized form* where common tuples necessarily correspond to "similar" runs (and again we are using Lemma 4.1 for that).

Finally, the next theorem implies that to express all regular spanners, it suffices to enrich the vstk-automata with union, projection and join. Our proof shows how to simulate a given vset-automaton by composing vstk-automata using the three operators.

THEOREM 4.5. $[\![\mathsf{VA}_{\mathsf{stk}}^{\{\cup,\pi,\bowtie\}}]\!] = [\![\mathsf{VA}_{\mathsf{set}}^{\{\cup,\pi,\bowtie\}}]\!] = [\![\mathsf{VA}_{\mathsf{set}}]\!]$.

4.1.3 Simulation of String Relations

Let R be a k-ary string relation, and let $\mathcal{C}$ be a class of spanners. We say that R is *selectable by* $\mathcal{C}$ if for every spanner $P \in \mathcal{C}$ and sequence $\vec{x} = x_1, \dots, x_k$ of variables in $\mathsf{SVars}(P)$, the spanner $\varsigma_{\vec{x}}^R P$ is also in $\mathcal{C}$. Let $\vec{x} = x_1, \dots, x_k$ be a sequence of span variables, and let $X = \{x_1, \dots, x_k\}$. The *R-restricted universal spanner over* $\vec{x}$, denoted $\Upsilon_{\vec{x}}^R$, is the spanner $\varsigma_{\vec{x}}^R \Upsilon_X$. (Recall that Υ_X is the universal spanner over X.) The following (straightforward) proposition states that under some assumptions (that hold in all the spanner classes of our interest), selectability of R is equivalent to the ability to define the R-restricted universal spanners. We will later use this proposition as a tool to decide whether or not a relation R is selectable by a class of spanners at hand.

PROPOSITION 4.6. *Let R be a string relation, and let $\mathcal{C}$ be a class of spanners. Assume that $\mathcal{C}$ contains all the universal spanners, and that $\mathcal{C}$ is closed under natural join. R is selectable by $\mathcal{C}$ if and only if $\Upsilon_{\vec{x}}^R \in \mathcal{C}$ for all $\vec{x} \in \mathsf{SVars}^k$.*

Let REC_k be as defined in Section 2.1. It is well known (see [8, 20]) that a k-ary string relation R is in REC_k if and only if it is a finite union of Cartesian products $L_1 \times \cdots \times L_k$, where each L_i is a regular language over Σ. That, combined with Proposition 4.6, easily implies that every recognizable relation is selectable by the regular spanners. Interestingly, the other direction is also true.

THEOREM 4.7. *A string relation is selectable by the regular spanners if and only if it is recognizable. That is,* REC *is precisely the class of string relations selectable by* $[\![\mathsf{VA}_{\mathsf{set}}]\!]$.

4.2 Core Spanners

As the core of AQL we identify the algebra $\mathsf{RGX}^{\{\cup,\pi,\bowtie,\varsigma^=\}}$. Henceforth, we call a spanner in $[\![\mathsf{RGX}^{\{\cup,\pi,\bowtie,\varsigma^=\}}]\!]$ a *core spanner*. A consequence of Theorems 4.2 and 4.5 is that the algebra $\mathsf{RGX}^{\{\cup,\pi,\bowtie,\varsigma^=\}}$ has the same expressive power as $\mathsf{VA}_{\mathsf{stk}}^{\{\cup,\pi,\bowtie,\varsigma^=\}}$ and $\mathsf{VA}_{\mathsf{set}}^{\{\cup,\pi,\bowtie,\varsigma^=\}}$. Therefore, the core spanners are obtained from the regular spanners by extending the algebra with the selection operator $\varsigma^=$.

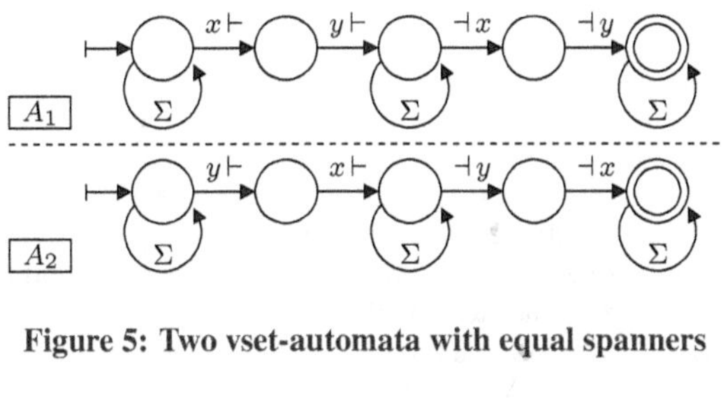

Figure 5: Two vset-automata with equal spanners

The following lemma is a key tool for reasoning about the expressiveness of core spanners. This lemma, which we call the *core-simplification lemma*, states that every core spanner can be defined by a very simple expression: a single vset-automaton, on top of which we apply string-equality selections, and finally a single projection. The proofs of the inexpressibility results we later give for core spanners are inherently based on this result.

LEMMA 4.8 (CORE-SIMPLIFICATION LEMMA). *Every core spanner is definable by an expression of the form $\pi_V SA$, where A is a vset-automaton, $V \subseteq \mathsf{SVars}(A)$, and S is a sequence of selections $\varsigma_{x,y}^=$ for $x, y \in \mathsf{SVars}(A)$.*

Next, we discuss selectable relations. Observe that string equality, which is obviously selectable by the core spanners, is not selectable by the regular spanners, because string equality is not in REC (and because of Theorem 4.7). Another way of seeing that is as follows: if string equality were selectable by the regular spanners, then a Boolean regular spanner (which can be represented as an NFA) could recognize the non-regular language $\{\mathbf{s}\cdot\mathbf{s} \mid \mathbf{s} \in \Sigma^*\}$ by $\pi_\emptyset\, \varsigma_{x,y}^=(x\{\Sigma^*\} \cdot y\{\Sigma^*\})$.

Let $\mathbf{s}$ and $\mathbf{t}$ be two strings. By $\mathbf{s} \sqsubseteq \mathbf{t}$ we denote that $\mathbf{s}$ is a (consecutive) substring of $\mathbf{t}$ (i.e, $\mathbf{s}$ is equal to some $\mathbf{t}_{[i,j\rangle}$). By $\mathbf{s} \sqsubseteq_{\mathsf{prf}} \mathbf{t}$ we denote that $\mathbf{s}$ is a prefix of $\mathbf{t}$ (i.e, $\mathbf{s}$ is equal to some $\mathbf{t}_{[1,j\rangle}$). By $\mathbf{s} \sqsubseteq_{\mathsf{sfx}} \mathbf{t}$ we denote that $\mathbf{s}$ is a suffix of $\mathbf{t}$ (i.e, $\mathbf{s}$ is equal to some $\mathbf{t}_{[i,|\mathbf{t}|+1\rangle}$).

Next, we will use Proposition 4.6 to show that the binary substring relation $\sqsubseteq$ is selectable by the core spanners. Due to Proposition 4.6, it suffices to show that the spanner $\Upsilon_{x,y}^{\sqsubseteq}$ is definable in $[\![\mathsf{RGX}^{\{\cup,\pi,\bowtie,\varsigma^=\}}]\!]$. Let $\gamma(x',y)$ be the spanner that captures the property that x' is a sub-span of y. We can define $\gamma(x',y)$ by $\Sigma^* \cdot y\{\Sigma^* \cdot x'\{\Sigma^*\} \cdot \Sigma^*\} \cdot \Sigma^*$. Then $\Upsilon_{x,y}^{\sqsubseteq}$ is defined by

$$\pi_{\{x,y\}}\, \varsigma_{x,x'}^= \left(\Upsilon_{\{x,x',y\}} \bowtie \gamma(x',y)\right) .$$

Similar constructions show that the relations $\sqsubseteq_{\mathsf{prf}}$ and $\sqsubseteq_{\mathsf{sfx}}$ are also selectable by the core spanners. We record this as a proposition, for later use. We also include in the proposition the fact that every relation in REC is also selectable by the core spanners; the proof is by the same argument that precedes Theorem 4.7.

PROPOSITION 4.9. *Every string relation in* REC, *as well as each of the string relations $\sqsubseteq$, $\sqsubseteq_{\mathsf{prf}}$ and $\sqsubseteq_{\mathsf{sfx}}$, is selectable by the core spanners.*

The next theorem shows that the classes of regular and rational relations are incomparable with the class of relations selectable by the core spanners.

THEOREM 4.10. *There is a string relation that is selectable by the core spanners but is non-rational (and hence nonregular), and there is a regular (and hence rational) relation that is not selectable by the core spanners.*

The existence of a regular relation that is not selectable by the core spanners is due to the following theorem.

THEOREM 4.11. *Assume that the alphabet Σ contains at least two symbols. The string relation $\{(\mathbf{s},\mathbf{t}) \mid |\mathbf{s}| = |\mathbf{t}|\}$ is not selectable by the core spanners.*

Theorem 4.11 is a fairly direct consequence of the following theorem.

THEOREM 4.12. *The language $\{0^m1^m \mid m \in \mathbb{N}\}$ is not recognizable by any Boolean core spanner.*

5. DIFFERENCE

In this section, we discuss the difference operator. Let P_1 and P_2 be spanners that are union compatible (that is, $\mathsf{SVars}(P_1) = \mathsf{SVars}(P_2)$). The difference $P_1 \setminus P_2$ is defined as follows. First, $\mathsf{SVars}(P_1 \setminus P_2) = \mathsf{SVars}(P_1)$. Second, if $\mathbf{s}$ is a string, then $(P_1 \setminus P_2)(\mathbf{s}) = P_1(\mathbf{s}) \setminus P_2(\mathbf{s})$.

The result with the most involved proof in this section states that core spanners are *not* closed under difference. Recall that the core spanners are those spanners that are expressible in $\mathsf{RGX}^{\{\cup,\pi,\bowtie,\varsigma^=\}}$. One may be tempted to think that non-closure of core spanners under difference should be trivial to prove due to some monotonicity properties, as in the case of ordinary relational algebra. But this is not the case, because our algebra does not involve ordinary relations, but rather spanners; and the primitive representation of spanners (e.g., regex formulas or vset-automata) can simulate non-monotonic behavior (e.g., regular expressions are closed under complement). In fact, we later show that core spanners can simulate string relations of a non-monotonic flavor. Moreover, *regular* (but not *core*) spanners are actually closed under difference.

THEOREM 5.1. *Regular spanners are closed under difference; that is,* $[\![\mathsf{VA}_{\mathsf{set}}^{\{\setminus\}}]\!] = [\![\mathsf{VA}_{\mathsf{set}}]\!]$.

In an attempt to prove that core spanners are not closed under difference (or, equivalently, complement), we tried to prove that the language $\{\mathbf{s}\#\mathbf{t} \mid \mathbf{s} \neq \mathbf{t}\}$, where $\mathbf{s}$ and $\mathbf{t}$ are over the alphabet $\{0,1\}$, and $\#$ is a new symbol, is not recognizable by any Boolean core spanner. After multiple failing attempts, we were surprised to discover that our candidate language L is a wrong candidate, since it actually *is* recognizable by a Boolean core spanner, for the following reason.

PROPOSITION 5.2. *The binary string relation* $\neq$ *is selectable by the core spanners.*

We remark that a proof similar to that of Proposition 5.2 shows that the string relations $\not\sqsubseteq_{\mathsf{prf}}$ and $\not\sqsubseteq_{\mathsf{sfx}}$ are also selectable by the core spanners. Eventually, we were able to prove non-closure of the core spanners under difference through the (complement of) the substring relation.

THEOREM 5.3. *Assume that the alphabet* Σ *contains at least two symbols. The string relation* $\not\sqsubseteq$ *is not selectable by the core spanners.*

Building on the core-simplification lemma (Lemma 4.8) and on Proposition 4.6, our proof of Theorem 5.3 obtains a contradiction by assuming that an expression E given by $\pi_V SA$, as in Lemma 4.8, is such that $[\![E]\!] = \Upsilon^{\not\sqsubseteq}_{x,y}$.

Recall from Proposition 4.9 that the string relation $\sqsubseteq$ is selectable by the core spanners. Theorem 5.3, on the other hand, states that $\not\sqsubseteq$ is not selectable by the core spanners. By combining these two we get the following.

THEOREM 5.4. *Assume that the alphabet* Σ *contains at least two symbols. Core spanners are* not *closed under difference; that is,* $[\![\mathsf{RGX}^{\{\cup,\pi,\bowtie,\varsigma^=\}}]\!] \subsetneq [\![\mathsf{RGX}^{\{\cup,\pi,\bowtie,\varsigma^=,\setminus\}}]\!]$.

Theorems 5.1 and 5.4 show an interesting contrast between regular and core spanners with respect to difference.

6. SPANNERS VS. OTHER FORMALISMS

We now discuss the relationship between (core and regular) spanners and two related formalisms in the literature.

6.1 Extended Regular Expressions

We first relate core spanners to *extended regular expressions* [1, 12, 14, 23] (xregex for short), which extend the classic regular expressions with *backreferences* (a.k.a. *variable references*) that specify repetitions of a previously matched substring. Their expressive power goes strictly beyond the class of regular languages and, due to their usefulness in practice, most modern regular expression matching engines actually support extended regular expressions [24]. From a theoretical perspective, the extended regular expressions were formalized by Aho [1], and investigated with respect to the complexity of their membership problem [1], their expressiveness and closure properties [12–14], and their conciseness and decidability [23], among other properties.

Syntactically, an xregex can be viewed as a regex formula, but with two major differences. First, there is no restriction on the number of bindings of a variable to a span. Second, in addition to the variable-binding expressions $x\{\gamma\}$ an xregex also allows variable *backreferences* of the form $\&x$. For example, if δ_1 is $x\{(0 \vee 1)^*\} \cdot \&x$, and δ_2 is $x\{(0 \vee 1)^*\} \cdot \&x \cdot x\{(0 \vee 1)^*\} \cdot \&x$, then δ_1 and δ_2 are xregexes. An xregex is interpreted from left to right as follows when parsing an input string $\mathbf{s}$ (cf., e.g., [12, 23]). As before, a binding subexpression $x\{\gamma\}$ matches a substring if γ matches the substring, in which case x is bound to the corresponding span. A backreference $\&x$ matches a substring $\mathbf{s}'$ if $\mathbf{s}' = \mathbf{s}_{[i,j\rangle}$ with $[i,j\rangle$ the span previously bound to x. If x has been bound multiple times, then the last binding prior to the backreference is taken; and if x has not been bound before, $\&x$ matches the empty string. As an example, the above xregex δ_1 matches precisely the strings $\mathbf{ss}$ with $\mathbf{s} \in \{0,1\}^*$, and δ_2 matches precisely the strings $\mathbf{sss's'}$ with $\mathbf{s}, \mathbf{s}' \in \{0,1\}^*$. Observe that neither of these languages is regular.

The evaluation of an xregex over a string is not (naturally) mapped to an $\mathbf{s}$-tuple, since a variable can be assigned multiple spans. Therefore, we restrict our discussion to the comparison of xregexes with *Boolean* core spanners. An important part of the expressive power of xregexes stems from the fact that both variable binders and backreferences can occur under the scope of a Kleene star (or plus). For example, $(x\{(0 \vee 1)^*\} \cdot \&x)^+$ matches all strings $\mathbf{s_1 s_1} \cdots \mathbf{s_n s_n}$ with $n \geq 1$ and every $\mathbf{s_i} \in \{0,1\}^*$. Moreover,

$$1^+ \cdot x\{0^*\} \cdot (1^+ \cdot \&x)^* \cdot 1^+$$

matches all strings $\mathbf{s}_1\mathbf{t}\mathbf{s}_2\mathbf{t} \cdots \mathbf{s}_{n-1}\mathbf{t}\mathbf{s}_n$, where $\mathbf{t} \in 0^*$ and every $\mathbf{s}_i$ is in 1^+. In other words, it accepts the language of strings over $\{0,1\}^*$ that start and end with 1, and where all maximal chunks of consecutive 0's are of equal length. We refer to this language as the *uniform-0-chunk* language. As the following theorem states, this language is beyond the expressive power of core spanners.

THEOREM 6.1. *The uniform-0-chunk language is recognizable by an xregex but is not recognizable by any Boolean core spanner.*

It is currently still open whether every language recognized by a Boolean core spanner can also be recognized by an xregex. We do note the following. Consider a core spanner represented by $\pi_Y SA$, as in the core-simplification lemma (Lemma 4.8). If the variables of the vset-automaton A cover disjoint spans, then it is easy to prove that such a simulating xregex must exist. To illustrate, consider the regex formula $\gamma := x\,\{\gamma_1\} \cdot \gamma_2 \cdot y\{\gamma_3\}$, where x and y are variables, and γ_1, γ_2, and γ_3 are regular expressions. Then the core spanner $\pi_\emptyset \varsigma^=_{x,y}(\gamma)$ is specified by the xregex $x\{\delta\} \cdot \gamma_2 \cdot \&x$, where δ is the regular expression that recognizes the intersection of the regular expressions γ_1 and γ_3. The problem in finding an xregex that corresponds to a Boolean core spanner arises when the variables in the core spanner have overlapping spans.

6.2 CRPQs on Marked Paths

Regular expressions have been extensively used and studied in database theory as a means to express reachability queries in semi-structured and graph databases since the late 1980s. Arguably, the simplest form of such queries are the *regular path query* (*RPQ* for short) on directed graphs with labeled edges [16, 17]. RPQs search for the existence of a path, such that the word formed by the edge labels belongs to a specified regular language. A *conjunctive regular path queries* (*CRPQ* for short) applies conjunction and existential quantification (over nodes) to RPQs; this concept has been the subject of much investigation [10, 11, 16, 19, 21].

Superficially speaking, spanners and CRPQs are inherently different concepts: spanners operate on *strings* while CRPQs operate on *graphs* (directed, edge-labeled graphs); and the variables in the spanner world represent *spans*, while those in the CRPQ world represent *nodes*. However, we can adjust CRPQs to represent spanners, as follows.

In terms of the data model, a string can be viewed as a special case of a graph, namely a simple path. Formally, given a string $\mathbf{s} = \sigma_1 \cdots \sigma_n$, we denote by $p(\mathbf{s})$ the simple path $1 \rightarrow 2 \rightarrow \cdots \rightarrow n+1$ (with the natural numbers $1, \dots, n+1$ as nodes), where for $i = 1, \dots, n$ the label of the edge $i \rightarrow i+1$ is σ_i. Now, the span $[i, j\rangle$ of $\mathbf{s}$ can be naturally represented by the pair i, j of nodes from $p(\mathbf{s})$. A CRPQ Q is evaluated over $p(\mathbf{s})$ by means of assignments α from Q's variables to the node set $\{1, \dots, n+1\}$. Restricted to the simple paths $p(\mathbf{s})$, casting a CRPQ as a spanner representation entails the following.

- The node variables of a CRPQ are set to be of two kinds: $x^{\vdash}$, where $x \in \mathsf{SVars}$, represents the left border of a span, and $x^{\dashv}$ represents the right border of the span. Hence, a span variable x is represented by $[x^{\vdash}, x^{\dashv}\rangle$.
- The valid assignments α are now required to be *consistent*: $\alpha(x^{\vdash}) \leq \alpha(x^{\dashv})$ for all relevant $x \in \mathsf{SVars}$.

It is not difficult to see that in our adjustment so far, a CRPQ Q can represent only spanners that are monotonic w.r.t. substrings: if $\mathbf{s} \sqsubseteq \mathbf{t}$, then the assignments for Q on $p(\mathbf{s})$ are, up to needed re-alignment, among the assignments for Q on $p(\mathbf{t})$. The reason is that CRPQs cannot recognize the endpoints of the input path. To go beyond monotonic spanners, we need to make those endpoints recognizable. Interestingly, it is not clear how to do so without significantly complicating the model. The cleanest way we found is to extend $p(\mathbf{s})$ with the two loops $0 \rightarrow 0$ and $(n+1) \rightarrow (n+1)$, labeled with new labels $\triangleright$ and $\triangleleft$ (not in the alphabet Σ), respectively. We call the resulting graph a *marked* path. As an example, the marked path for $\mathbf{s} = \mathtt{Aba}$ is the following.

$$\overset{\triangleright}{\circlearrowleft} 1 \xrightarrow{\mathtt{A}} 2 \xrightarrow{\mathtt{b}} 3 \xrightarrow{\mathtt{a}} 4 \overset{\triangleleft}{\circlearrowright}$$

With this adjustment, we can show that every regular spanner can be simulated by a union of CRPQs over marked paths. Quite interestingly, we can also show the reverse direction: every union of CRPQs over marked paths simulates some regular spanner. So within our adjustment, unions of CRPQs over marked paths capture precisely the regular spanners. A formal, detailed discussion will appear in the extended version of this paper.

7. SUMMARY AND DISCUSSION

We introduced the concept of a spanner, and investigated three primitive spanner representations: regex formulas, vstk-automata and vset-automata. As we showed, the classes of regex formulas and vstk-automata have the same expressive power, and vset-automata (defining the regular spanners) have the same expressive power as the closure of regex formulas under the relational operators union, natural join and projection. By adding the string-equality operator, one gets the core spanners. We gave some basic results on core spanners, like the core-simplification lemma. We discussed selectable string relations, and showed, among other things, that REC is precisely the class of relations selectable by the regular spanners. We showed that regular spanners are closed under difference, but core spanners are not (which we proved using the core-simplification lemma). Finally, we discussed the connection between core spanners and xregexes, and showed a tight connection between regular spanners and CRPQs.

This work is our first step in embarking on the investigation of spanners. Indeed, many aspects remain to be considered, and many problems remain to be solved. One major aspect is that of complexity. For example, what is the complexity of the translations among spanner representations that were applied in this paper? What is the (data and combined) complexity that query evaluation entails in each representation? Regarding the difference operator, an intriguing question is whether we can find a simple form, in the spirit of the core-simplification lemma, when adding difference to the representation of core spanners (i.e., the class $\mathsf{VA}_{\mathsf{set}}^{\{\cup,\pi,\bowtie,\varsigma^{=},\setminus\}}$); as illustrated here, such a result would be highly useful for reasoning about the expressive power of that class. As another open problem, we repeat the one we mentioned in Section 6: can extended regular expressions express every Boolean core spanner? We conclude by discussing the major issue of *conflict resolvers*.

Conflict Resolvers

Resolution of conflicting tuples has an important role in the practice of rule-based information extraction [15]. As a simple example, on the string `John_Fitzgerald_Kennedy`, one component of an extraction program may identify the span of `John_Fitzgerald` as that of a person name, another may do so for `Fitzgerald_Kennedy`, and a third may do so for `John_Fitzgerald_Kennedy`. As only one of these is the mentioning of a person name, a cleanup resolution filters out two of the three annotations. In CPSL [3], for instance, this resolution takes place implicitly at every stage (cascade). A significant differentiator of AQL is that it exposes conflict resolution as an explicit relational operator, similarly to selection, and moreover, supports multiple resolution semantics. Yet, this operator is different from a standard selection, as it is not applied in a tuple-by-tuple basis, but rather in an aggregate manner. In this section, we discuss the semantics of such an operator, which we shall investigate more deeply in a future paper.

How should a conflict resolver be defined? At the high level, it is a unary spanner operator cr_x parameterized by a variable $x \in \mathsf{SVars}$. This operator takes as input a spanner P with $x \in \mathsf{SVars}(P)$ and outputs a spanner P', such that $\mathsf{SVars}(P') = \mathsf{SVars}(P)$ and $P' \subseteq P$ (i.e., for all strings $\mathbf{s} \in \Sigma^*$ we have $P'(\mathbf{s}) \subseteq P(\mathbf{s})$). The operator cr_x filters out $\mathbf{s}$-tuples whenever conflicts are involved in the spans assigned to x by different $\mathbf{s}$-tuples. The output is a conflict-free subset of $P(\mathbf{s})$.

For concreteness, let us focus on the simple (yet practical) case where cr_x is specified by a *conflict condition* stating when two spans $\mu_1(x)$ and $\mu_2(x)$ are in conflict, and a *resolution rule* stating which of $\mu_1(x)$ and $\mu_2(x)$ prevails. Still, how should resolution be defined for a given conflict condition and resolution rule? Eliminating tuples sequentially does not seem to be the right way, since the result may be sensitive to the order in which conflicts are considered. For example, a standard conflict condition says that $\mu_1(x)$ and $\mu_2(x)$ overlap but are not equal, and the resolution rule is *left-to-right winner*: $\mu_1(x)$ prevails over $\mu_2(x)$ if $\mu_1(x)$ starts before $\mu_2(x)$; and if they start at the same position, then $\mu_1(x)$ is longer.

Now, take the three spans $\mu_1(x) = [1,3\rangle$, $\mu_2(x) = [2,4\rangle$, and $\mu_3(x) = [3,5\rangle$. Resolving conflicts from left to right gives a different result than the right-to-left resolution. Indeed, from left to right, we take $[1,3\rangle$, discard $[2,4\rangle$, then keep $[3,5\rangle$; and from right to left we take $[3,5\rangle$, then discard $[3,5\rangle$ in favor of the span $[2,4\rangle$, then discard $[2,4\rangle$ in favor of the span $[1,3\rangle$.

In accommodating the above, an approach we are exploring is adopting the concept of *inconsistent databases* [4] to our setting. Specifically, we can think of our span relation as an inconsistent relation, and every maximal non-conflicting subset of tuples as a *possible world*. But the traditional theory of inconsistent databases does not allow for different priority among tuples, and we treat such priorities as first-class citizens (and specify them with our resolution rule). Nevertheless, recent work of Staworko et al. [43] proposes and studies various concepts of inconsistent databases with *prioritized repairing*, and we are currently studying the application of prioritized repairing to conflict resolution within spanners.

Acknowledgments

We are grateful to Pablo Barceló, Kenneth Clarkson, and Leonid Libkin for helpful discussions. We also thank the SystemT group their intensive work in establishing the system, and for useful input.

8. REFERENCES

[1] A. V. Aho. Algorithms for finding patterns in strings. In *Handbook of Theoretical Computer Science, Volume A: Algorithms and Complexity (A)*, pages 255–300. North Holland, 1990.

[2] J. F. Allen. Maintaining knowledge about temporal intervals. *Commun. ACM*, 26(11):832–843, Nov. 1983.

[3] D. E. Appelt and B. Onyshkevych. The common pattern specification language. In *Proceedings of the TIPSTER Text Program: Phase III*, pages 23–30, Baltimore, Maryland, USA, 1998. Association for Computational Linguistics.

[4] M. Arenas, L. E. Bertossi, and J. Chomicki. Consistent query answers in inconsistent databases. In *PODS*, pages 68–79. ACM, 1999.

[5] P. Barceló, D. Figueira, and L. Libkin. Graph logics with rational relations and the generalized intersection problem. In *LICS*, pages 115–124. IEEE, 2012.

[6] P. Barceló, J. L. Reutter, and L. Libkin. Parameterized regular expressions and their languages. *Theor. Comput. Sci.*, 474:21–45, 2013.

[7] M. Benedikt, L. Libkin, T. Schwentick, and L. Segoufin. Definable relations and first-order query languages over strings. *J. ACM*, 50(5):694–751, 2003.

[8] J. Berstel. *Transductions and Context-Free Languages*. Teubner Studienbücher, Stuttgart, 1979.

[9] A. J. Bonner and G. Mecca. Sequences, datalog, and transducers. *J. Comput. Syst. Sci.*, 57(3):234–259, 1998.

[10] D. Calvanese, G. D. Giacomo, M. Lenzerini, and M. Y. Vardi. Containment of conjunctive regular path queries with inverse. In *KR 2000*, pages 176–185, 2000.

[11] D. Calvanese, G. D. Giacomo, M. Lenzerini, and M. Y. Vardi. View-based query processing and constraint satisfaction. In *LICS*, pages 361–371, 2000.

[12] C. Câmpeanu, K. Salomaa, and S. Yu. A formal study of practical regular expressions. *Int. J. Found. Comput. Sci.*, 14(6):1007–1018, 2003.

[13] C. Câmpeanu and N. Santean. On the intersection of regex languages with regular languages. *Theor. Comput. Sci.*, 410(24-25):2336–2344, 2009.

[14] B. Carle and P. Narendran. On extended regular expressions. In *LATA 2009*, volume 5457 of *Lecture Notes in Computer Science*, pages 279–289, 2009.

[15] L. Chiticariu, R. Krishnamurthy, Y. Li, S. Raghavan, F. Reiss, and S. Vaithyanathan. SystemT: An algebraic approach to declarative information extraction. In *ACL*, pages 128–137. The Association for Computer Linguistics, 2010.

[16] M. P. Consens and A. O. Mendelzon. Graphlog: a visual formalism for real life recursion. In *PODS*, pages 404–416. ACM, 1990.

[17] I. F. Cruz, A. O. Mendelzon, and P. T. Wood. A graphical query language supporting recursion. In *SIGMOD Conference*, pages 323–330. ACM, 1987.

[18] H. Cunningham. Gate, a general architecture for text engineering. *Computers and the Humanities*, 36(2):223–254, 2002.

[19] A. Deutsch and V. Tannen. Optimization properties for classes of conjunctive regular path queries. In *DBPL*, pages 21–39, 2001.

[20] C. C. Elgot and J. E. Mezei. On relations defined by generalized finite automata. *IBM Journal of Research and Development*, 9:47–68, 1965.

[21] D. Florescu, A. Y. Levy, and D. Suciu. Query containment for conjunctive queries with regular expressions. In *PODS*, pages 139–148, 1998.

[22] D. Freitag. Toward general-purpose learning for information extraction. In *COLING-ACL*, pages 404–408, 1998.

[23] D. D. Freydenberger. Extended regular expressions: Succinctness and decidability. In *STACS 2011*, volume 9 of *LIPIcs*, pages 507–518. Schloss Dagstuhl - Leibniz-Zentrum fuer Informatik, 2011.

[24] J. Friedl. *Mastering Regular Expressions*. O'Reilly Media, 2006.

[25] S. Ginsburg and X. S. Wang. Regular sequence operations and their use in database queries. *J. Comput. Syst. Sci.*, 56(1):1–26, 1998.

[26] G. Grahne, M. Nykänen, and E. Ukkonen. Reasoning about strings in databases. *J. Comput. Syst. Sci.*, 59(1):116–162, 1999.

[27] R. Grishman and B. Sundheim. Message understanding conference-6: A brief history. In *COLING*, pages 466–471, 1996.

[28] O. Grumberg, O. Kupferman, and S. Sheinvald. Variable automata over infinite alphabets. In A. H. Dediu, H. Fernau, and C. Martín-Vide, editors, *LATA*, volume 6031 of *Lecture Notes in Computer Science*, pages 561–572. Springer, 2010.

[29] D. E. Knuth. Semantics of context-free languages. *Mathematical Systems Theory*, 2(2):127–145, 1968.

[30] D. E. Knuth. Correction: Semantics of context-free languages. *Mathematical Systems Theory*, 5(1):95–96, 1971.

[31] R. Krishnamurthy, Y. Li, S. Raghavan, F. Reiss, S. Vaithyanathan, and H. Zhu. SystemT: a system for declarative information extraction. *SIGMOD Record*, 37(4):7–13, 2008.

[32] J. D. Lafferty, A. McCallum, and F. C. N. Pereira. Conditional random fields: Probabilistic models for segmenting and labeling sequence data. In *ICML*, pages 282–289. Morgan Kaufmann, 2001.

[33] T. R. Leek. Information extraction using hidden markov models. Master's thesis, UC San Diego, 1997.

[34] P. Linz. *An introduction to formal languages and automata*. Jones and Bartlett Publishers, Inc., Sudbury, Mass. [N.A.], third edition, 2001.

[35] B. Liu, L. Chiticariu, V. Chu, H. Jagadish, and F. Reiss. Automatic rule refinement for information extraction. *Proceedings of the VLDB Endowment*, 3(1-2):588–597, 2010.

[36] A. McCallum, D. Freitag, and F. C. N. Pereira. Maximum entropy markov models for information extraction and segmentation. In *ICML*, pages 591–598. Morgan Kaufmann, 2000.

[37] F. Neven and J. V. den Bussche. Expressiveness of structured document query languages based on attribute grammars. *J. ACM*, 49(1):56–100, 2002.

[38] F. Neven and T. Schwentick. Query automata over finite trees. *Theoretical Computer Science*, 275(2):633 – 674, 2002.

[39] M. Nivat. Transduction des langages de Chomsky. *Ann. Inst. Fourier*, 18:339–455, 1968.

[40] F. Reiss, S. Raghavan, R. Krishnamurthy, H. Zhu, and S. Vaithyanathan. An algebraic approach to rule-based information extraction. In *ICDE*, pages 933–942. IEEE, 2008.

[41] E. Riloff. Automatically constructing a dictionary for information extraction tasks. In *AAAI*, pages 811–816. AAAI Press / The MIT Press, 1993.

[42] S. Soderland, D. Fisher, J. Aseltine, and W. G. Lehnert. CRYSTAL: Inducing a conceptual dictionary. In *IJCAI*, pages 1314–1321. Morgan Kaufmann, 1995.

[43] S. Staworko, J. Chomicki, and J. Marcinkowski. Prioritized repairing and consistent query answering in relational databases. *Ann. Math. Artif. Intell.*, 64(2-3):209–246, 2012.

Learning and Verifying Quantified Boolean Queries by Example

Azza Abouzied*, Dana Angluin*, Christos Papadimitriou**,
Joseph M. Hellerstein**, Avi Silberschatz*
*Yale University, ** University of California, Berkeley
azza@cs.yale.edu, angluin@cs.yale.edu, christos@cs.berkeley.edu,
hellerstein@cs.berkeley.edu, avi@cs.yale.edu

ABSTRACT

To help a user specify and verify quantified queries — a class of database queries known to be very challenging for all but the most expert users — one can question the user on whether certain data objects are *answers* or *non-answers* to her intended query. In this paper, we analyze the number of questions needed to learn or verify *qhorn* queries, a special class of Boolean quantified queries whose underlying form is *conjunctions of quantified Horn expressions*. We provide optimal *polynomial-question* and *polynomial-time* learning and verification algorithms for two subclasses of the class qhorn with upper constant limits on a query's *causal density*.

Categories and Subject Descriptors

H.2.3 [**Database Management**]: Languages—*query languages*; I.2.2 [**Artificial Intelligence**]: Automatic Programming—*program synthesis, program verification*; I.2.6 [**Artificial Intelligence**]: Learning—*concept learning*

Keywords

quantified boolean queries, qhorn, query learning, query verification, example-driven synthesis

1. INTRODUCTION

It's a lovely morning, and you want to buy a box of chocolates for your research group. You walk into a chocolate store and ask for "a box with dark chocolates — some sugar-free with nuts or filling". However, your server is a pedantic logician who expects first-order logic statements. In response to your informal query he places in front of you a hundred boxes! Despite your frustration, you are intrigued: you open the first box only to find one dark, sugar-free chocolate with nuts and many other varieties of white chocolates that you didn't order. You push it aside, indicating your disapproval, and proceed to the second. Inside, you are wondering: Is there hope that I can communicate to this person my needs through a sequence of such interactions?

Everyday, we request things from each other using informal and incomplete query specifications. Our casual interactions facilitate such under-specified requests because we have developed questioning skills that help us clarify such requests. A typical interlocutor might ask you about corner cases, such as the presence of white chocolates in the box, to get to a precise query specification by example. As requesters, we prefer to begin with an outline of our query — the key properties of the chocolates — and then make our query precise using a few examples. As responders, we can build a precise query from the query outline and a few positive or negative examples — acceptable or unacceptable chocolate boxes.

Typical database query interfaces behave like our logician. SQL interfaces, for example, force us to formulate precise quantified queries from the get go. Users find quantified query specification extremely challenging [2, 13]. Such queries evaluate propositions over *sets of tuples* rather than individual tuples, to determine whether a set as a whole satisfies the query. Inherent in these queries are (i) the grouping of tuples into sets, and (ii) the binding of query expressions with either existential or universal quantifiers. Existential quantifiers ensure that some tuple in the set satisfies the expression, while universal quantifiers ensure that all tuples in the set satisfy the expression.

To simplify the specification of quantified queries, we built DataPlay [2]. DataPlay tries to mimic casual human interactions: users first specify the simple propositions of a query. DataPlay then generates a simple quantified query that contains all the propositions. Since, this query may be incorrect, users can label query results as *answers* or *non-answers* to their intended query. DataPlay uses this feedback on example tuple-sets to fix the incorrect query. Our evaluation of DataPlay shows that users prefer example-driven query specification techniques for specifying complex quantified queries [2]. Motivated by these findings, we set out to answer the question: *How far can we push the example-driven query specification paradigm?* This paper studies the theoretical limits of using examples to *learn* and to *verify* a special subclass of quantified queries, which we call *qhorn*, in the hope of eventually making query interfaces more human-like.

1.1 Our contributions

We formalize a query learning model (§2) where users specify propositions that form the building blocks of a Boolean quantified query. A learning algorithm then asks the users *membership questions*: each question is an example data object, which the user classifies as either an *answer* or a *non-answer*. After a few questions, the learning algorithm terminates with the unique query that satisfies the user's

PODS'13, June 22–27, 2013, New York, New York, USA.
Copyright 2013 ACM 978-1-4503-2066-5/13/06 ...$15.00.

responses to the membership questions. The key challenge we address in this paper is how to design a learning algorithm that runs in polynomial time, asks as few questions as possible and exactly identifies the intended query.

We prove the following:

1. Learning quantified Boolean queries is intractable: A doubly exponential number of questions is required (§2). Within a special class of quantified Boolean queries known as *qhorn* (§2.1), we prove two subclasses are exactly and efficiently learnable: *qhorn-1* (§2.1.3) and its superset *role-preserving qhorn* (§2.1.4) with constant limits on *causal density* (Def. 2.6).
2. We design an optimal algorithm to learn qhorn-1 queries using $O(n \lg n)$ questions where n is the number of propositions in a query (§3.1).
3. We design an efficient algorithm to learn role-preserving qhorn queries using $O(kn \lg n + n^{\theta+1})$ questions where k is *query size* (Def. 2.5), and θ is causal density (§3.2).

We also formalize a query verification model where the user specifies an entire query within the role-preserving qhorn query class. A verification algorithm then asks the user a set of membership questions known as the *verification set*. Each query has a unique verification set. The verification algorithm classifies some questions in the set as answers and others as non-answers. The query is incorrect if the user disagrees with any of the query's classification of questions in the verification set. We design a verification algorithm that asks $O(k)$ membership questions (§4).

2. PRELIMINARIES

Before we describe our query learning and verification algorithms, we first describe our data model — *nested relations* — and the qhorn query class.

DEFINITION 2.1. *Given the sets $D_1, D_2, ..., D_m$, $\mathcal{R}$ is a* ***relation*** *on these m sets if it is a set of m-tuples $(d_1, d_2, ..., d_m)$ such that $d_i \in D_i$ for $i = 1, ..., m$. $D_1, ..., D_m$ are the the domains of $\mathcal{R}$.*

DEFINITION 2.2. *A* ***nested relation*** *$\mathcal{R}$ has at least one domain D_i that is a set of subsets (powerset) of another relation $\mathcal{R}_i$. This $\mathcal{R}_i$ is said to be an embedded relation of $\mathcal{R}$.*

DEFINITION 2.3. *A relation $\mathcal{R}$ is a* ***flat relation*** *if all its domains $D_1, ..., D_m$ are not powersets of another relation.*

For example, a flat relation of chocolates can have the following schema:

```
Chocolate(isDark, hasFilling, isSugarFree,
  hasNuts, origin)
```

A nested relation of boxes of chocolates can have the following schema:

```
Box(name, Chocolate(isDark, hasFilling,
  isSugarFree, hasNuts, origin))
```

In this paper, we analyze queries over a nested relation with single-level nesting, i.e. the embedded relation is flat. The `Box` relation satisfies single-level nesting as the `Chocolate` relation embedded in it is flat. To avoid confusion, we refer to elements of the nested relation as *objects* and elements of the embedded flat relation as *tuples*. So the boxes are objects and the individual chocolates are tuples.

DEFINITION 2.4. *A* ***Boolean query*** *maps objects into either* answers *or* non-answers.

The atoms of a query are Boolean propositions such as:

$$p_1 : c.\texttt{isDark},\ p_2 : c.\texttt{hasFilling},$$
$$p_3 : c.\texttt{origin = Madagascar}$$

A complete query statement assigns quantifiers to expressions on propositions over attributes of the embedded relation. For example:

$$\forall c \in \texttt{Box.Chocolates}\ (p_1) \wedge$$
$$\exists c \in \texttt{Box.Chocolates}\ (p_2 \wedge p_3) \quad (1)$$

A box of chocolates is an answer to this query if every chocolate in the box is dark and there is at least one chocolate in the box that has filling and comes from Madagascar.

Given a collection of propositions, we can construct an abstract Boolean representation for the tuples of the nested relation. For example, given propositions p_1, p_2, p_3, we can transform the chocolates from the data domain to the Boolean domain as seen in Figure 1.

Box	origin	isSugar Free	is Dark	has Filling	has Nuts
Global Ground	Madagascar	1	1	1	0
	Belgium	1	0	0	1
	Germany	1	1	1	1
Europe's Finest	Belgium	1	1	0	0
	Belgium	0	1	0	1
	Sweden	0	1	1	1

Box (S)	p_1:is Dark	p_2: has Filling	p_3: origin = Madagascar
	x_1	x_2	x_3
S_1	1	1	1
	0	0	0
	1	1	0
S_2	1	0	0
	1	1	0

Figure 1: Transforming data from its domain into a Boolean domain.

Thus, each proposition p_i is replaced with a Boolean variable x_i. We rewrite the Boolean query (1) as follows:

$$\forall t \in S\ (x_1) \wedge$$
$$\exists t \in S\ (x_2 \wedge x_3)$$

where S is the set of Boolean tuples for an object. This Boolean representation allows us to create learning and verification algorithms independent of the data domain or of the actual propositions that the user writes.

To support this Boolean representation of tuples, however, we assume that (i) it is relatively efficient to construct an actual data tuple from a Boolean tuple and that (ii) the true/false assignment to one proposition does not interfere with the true/false assignments to other propositions. The propositions p_m : $c.$`origin = Madagascar` and p_b : $c.$`origin = Belgium` interfere with each other as a chocolate cannot be both from Madagascar and Belgium: $p_m \rightarrow \neg p_b$ and $p_b \rightarrow \neg p_m$.

With three propositions, we can construct 2^3 possible Boolean tuples, corresponding to the 2^3 possible true or false assignments to the individual propositions, i.e. we can construct 8 different chocolate classes. With n propositions, we can construct 2^n Boolean tuples.

There are 2^{2^n} possible sets of Boolean tuples or unique objects. With our three chocolate propositions, we can construct 256 boxes of distinct mixes of the 8 chocolate classes.

Since, a Boolean query maps each possible object into an answer or a non-answer, it follows that there are $2^{2^{2^n}}$ distinguishable Boolean queries (for $n = 3$, about 10^{77}). If our goal is to learn *any* query from n simple propositions by asking users to label objects as answers or non-answers, i.e. asking *membership questions*, then we would have to distinguish between $2^{2^{2^n}}$ queries using $\Omega(\lg(2^{2^{2^n}}))$ or 2^{2^n} questions.

Since this ambitious goal of learning any query with few membership questions is doomed to fail, we have to constrain the query space. We study the learnability of a special space of queries, which we refer to as *qhorn*.

2.1 Qhorn

Qhorn has the following properties:

1. It supports if-then query semantics via quantified *Horn* expressions: $\forall t \in S\ (x_1 \wedge x_2 \rightarrow x_3)$. A Horn expression has a conjunction of body variables that imply a single head variable. The degenerate *headless* Horn expression is simply a quantified conjunction of body variables ($\exists t \in S(x_1 \wedge x_2)$) and the degenerate *bodyless* Horn expression is simply a single quantified variable ($\forall t \in S(\mathbf{T} \rightarrow x_1) \equiv \forall t \in S(x_1)$).
2. It requires at least one positive instance for each Horn expression via a *guarantee clause*. Thus, we add the existential clause $\exists t \in S\ (x_1 \wedge x_2 \wedge x_3)$ to the expression $\forall t \in S\ (x_1 \wedge x_2 \rightarrow x_3)$ to get a complete query. Note that the expression $\exists t \in S\ (x_1 \wedge x_2 \rightarrow x_3)$ is implied by its guarantee clause $\exists t \in S\ (x_1 \wedge x_2 \wedge x_3)$.

   We justify the naturalness of guarantee clauses with the following example: consider a user looking for a box of only sugar-free chocolates. Without the guarantee clause, an empty box satisfies the user's query. While such a result is logical, we contend that most users would not consider the result as representative of sugar-free chocolate boxes.
3. It represents queries in a normalized form: *conjunctions of quantified (Horn) expressions.*

We use a shorthand notation for queries in qhorn. We drop the implicit '$t \in S$', the '$\wedge$' symbol and the guarantee clause. Thus, we write the query

$$\begin{array}{l}\forall t \in S\ (x_1 \wedge x_2 \rightarrow x_3)\ \wedge\ \exists t \in S\ (x_1 \wedge x_2 \wedge x_3) \wedge \\ \forall t \in S\ (x_4)\ \wedge\ \exists t \in S\ (x_4)\ \wedge\ \exists t \in S\ (x_5)\end{array}$$

as $\forall x_1 x_2 \rightarrow x_3\ \forall x_4\ \exists x_5$.

2.1.1 Qhorn's Equivalence Rules

R1 The query representation $\exists x_1 x_2 x_3\ \exists x_1 x_2\ \exists x_2 x_3$ is equivalent to $\exists x_1 x_2 x_3$. This is because if a set contains a tuple that satisfies $\exists x_1 x_2 x_3$, that tuple will also satisfy $\exists x_1 x_2$ and $\exists x_2 x_3$. An existential conjunction over a set of variables **dominates** any conjunction over a subset of those variables.

R2 The query representation $\forall x_1 x_2 x_3 \rightarrow h\ \forall x_1 x_2 \rightarrow h\ \forall x_1 \rightarrow h$ is equivalent to $\forall x_1 \rightarrow h\ \exists x_1 x_2 x_3 \rightarrow h$. This is because h has to be true whenever x_1 is true regardless of the true/false assignment of x_2, x_3. Thus a universal Horn expression with body variables B and head variable h **dominates** any universal Horn expression with body variables B' and head variable h where $B' \supseteq B$.

R3 The query representation $\forall x_1 \rightarrow h\ \exists x_1 x_3$ is equivalent to $\forall x_1 \rightarrow h\ \exists x_1 x_3 h$. Again, this equivalence is because h has to be true whenever x_1 is true.

2.1.2 Learning with Membership Questions

A **membership question** is simply an object along with its nested data tuples. The user responds to such a question by classifying the object as an answer or a non-answer for their intended query.

Given a collection of n propositions on the nested relation, the learning algorithm constructs a membership question in the Boolean domain: a set of Boolean tuples on n Boolean variables $x_1, ..., x_n$ — a variable for each proposition. Such a set is transformed into an object in the data domain before presentation to the user.

For brevity, we describe a membership question in the Boolean domain only. As a notational shorthand, we use 1^n to denote a Boolean tuple where all variables are true. We use lowercase letters for variables and uppercase letters for sets of variables.

The following definitions describe two structural properties of qhorn queries that influence its learnability:

DEFINITION 2.5. ***Query size**, k, is the number of expressions in the query.*

DEFINITION 2.6. ***Causal Density**, θ, is the maximum number of distinct non-dominated universal Horn expressions for a given head variable h.*

Conceptually, universal Horn expressions represent causation: whenever the body variables are true, the head variable has to be true. If a head variable has many universal Horn expressions, it has many causes for it to be true and thus has a high causal density.

The following inequality between causal density, θ and query size k holds: $0 \leq \theta \leq k$. We would expect users' queries to be small in size $k = O(n)$ and to have low causal density θ.

A query class is *efficiently* learnable if (i) the number of membership questions that a learning algorithm asks the user is polynomial in the number of propositions n and query size k and (ii) the learning algorithm runs in time polynomial in n and k. Question generation needs to be in polynomial time to ensure interactive performance. This requirement entails that the number of Boolean tuples per question is polynomial in n and k. A query class is *exactly* learnable if we can learn the exact target query that satisfies the user's responses to the membership questions.

Due to the following theorem, qhorn cannot be efficiently and exactly learned with a tractable number of questions (even when query size is polynomially bounded in the number of propositions ($k = n$) and causal density has an upper bound of one ($\theta = 1$)).

THEOREM 2.1. *Learning qhorn queries where variables can repeat $r \geq 2$ times requires $\Omega(2^n)$ questions.*

Proof: See full version of this paper [1].

Qhorn's intractability does not mean that we cannot construct efficiently and exactly learnable qhorn subclasses. We describe two such sub-classes:

2.1.3 Qhorn-1

Qhorn-1 defines certain syntactic restrictions on qhorn. Not counting guarantee clauses, if a query has k distinct expressions ($1 \leq k \leq n$) and each expression i has body variables B_i and a head variable h_i, such that $B = B_1 \cup ... \cup B_k$ is the collection of all body variables and $H = \{h_1, ...h_m\}$ is the set of all head variables then the following restrictions hold in qhorn-1:

1. $B_i \cap B_j = \emptyset \vee B_i = B_j$ if $i \neq j$
2. $h_i \neq h_j$ if $i \neq j$
3. $B \cap H = \emptyset$

The first restriction ensures that different head variables can either share the exact same set of body variables or have disjoint bodies. The second restriction ensures that a head variable has only one body. Finally, the third restriction ensures that a head variable does not reappear as a body variable. Effectively, qhorn-1 has *no variable repetition*: a variable can appear **once** either in a set of body variables or as a head variable. The following diagram labels the different components of a qhorn-1 query.

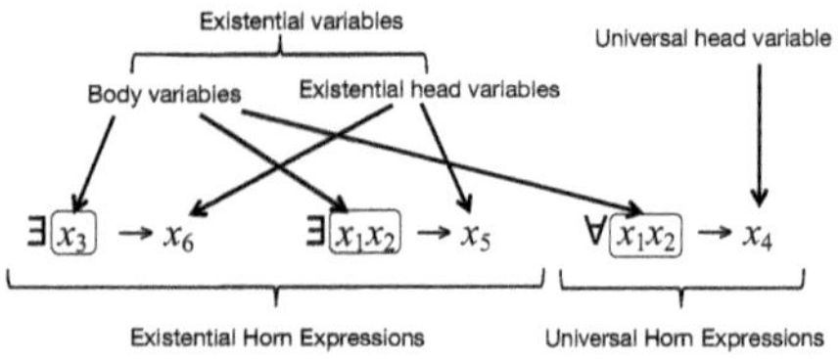

Figure 2: The different components of a qhorn-1 query.

Note that qhorn-1 queries have a maximum query size k of n and have a causal density θ of at most one. From an information-theoretic perspective, $\Omega(n \lg n)$ membership questions are required to learn a target query in qhorn-1 [1].

2.1.4 Role-preserving qhorn

In role-preserving qhorn queries, variables can repeat many times, but across universal Horn expressions head variables can only repeat as head variables and body variables can only repeat as body variables. For example, the following query is in role-preserving qhorn

$$\forall x_1 x_4 \rightarrow x_5 \; \forall x_3 x_4 \rightarrow x_5 \; \forall x_2 x_4 \rightarrow x_6 \; \exists x_1 x_2 x_3 \; \exists x_1 x_2 x_5 x_6$$

while the following query is not in role-preserving qhorn

$$\forall x_1 x_4 \rightarrow x_5 \; \forall x_2 x_3 x_5 \rightarrow x_6$$

because x_5 appears both as a head variable and a body variable in two universally quantified Horn expressions. Existential Horn expressions in role-preserving qhorn are rewritten as existential conjunctions and variables do not have *roles* in these conjunctions. Thus, existential conjunctions can contain one or more head variables (e.g. $\exists x_1 x_2 x_5 x_6$ in the first query). The following diagram labels the different components of a role-preserving qhorn query.

Both query size and causal density play a role in the behavior of learning and verification algorithms. Once we remove the syntactic restriction of variables appearing at most once, the size of a target query instance is no longer polynomially bounded in n. Thus, the complexity of learning and verification algorithms for role-preserving qhorn queries is parameterized by k, θ and n. We would expect user queries

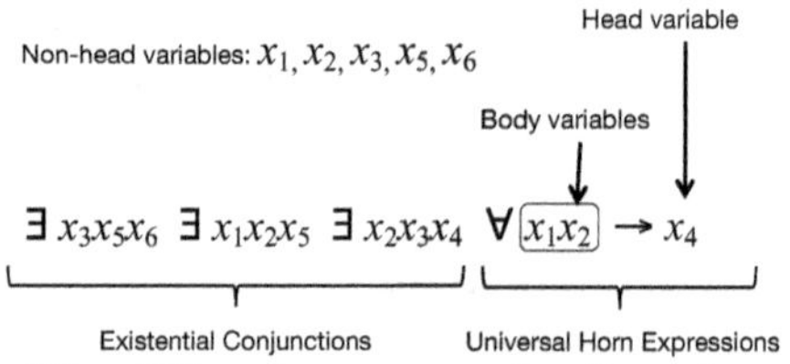

Figure 3: The different components of a role-preserving qhorn query.

to have low causal densities and to be small in size. Provided that θ has a constant upper bound, then we can efficiently learn role-preserving queries.

3. QUERY LEARNING

3.1 Learning qhorn-1

THEOREM 3.1. *$O(n \lg n)$ questions are sufficient to learn qhorn-1 queries in polynomial time.*

Proof: The learning algorithm breaks down query learning into a series of small tasks. First, it classifies all variables into either *universal head* variables or *existential* variables (Fig. 2 describes qhorn-1 terminology). Second, it learns the body variables (if any) for each universal head variable. Finally, it learns existential Horn expressions. We show that each task requires at most $O(n \lg n)$ membership questions (Section 3.1.1, Lemmas 3.2 and 3.3), thus proving that the learning algorithm asks $O(n \lg n)$ questions. □

3.1.1 Learning universal head variables

The simplest learning task is to determine whether a variable is a universal head variable. Suppose we have three variables: x_1, x_2, x_3. To determine if x_1 is the head of a universal Horn expression, we ask the user if the set $\{111, 011\}$ is an answer. By setting the other variables (x_2, x_3) to be always true, we are setting all potential body variables of x_1 to true. We are also neutralizing the effect of other unknown head variables on the outcome of a membership question. If the set $\{111, 011\}$ is an answer, then we are sure that x_1 is not a universal head variable because it can exist with a false value as long as at least one tuple has a true value for it. If the set is a non-answer, then we learn that x_1 is a universal head variable.

We need one question to determine whether a variable is a universal head variable and we need $O(n)$ time to generate each question — the time to construct a set with two tuples of size n. Thus, we learn which variables are universal head variables, U, and which variables are existential variables, E, in polynomial time.

3.1.2 Learning body variables of universal Horn expressions

DEFINITION 3.1. *Given a universal head variable h and a subset of existential variables $V \subseteq E$, a* ***universal dependence question*** *on h and V is a membership question with two tuples: 1^n and a tuple where h and V are false and all other variables are true.*

If a universal dependence question on h and V is an answer, then we learn that a subset of h's body variables is in V. This is because when the conjunction of body variables is not satisfied, the head variable can be false. We say that

h *depends* on some variables in V. If the question is a non-answer, then we learn that h's body variables are a subset of $E - V$; h has no body variables in V because in qhorn-1, h can have at most one body.

The most straightforward way to learn the body variables, B, of one universal variable is with $O(|E|) = O(n)$ universal dependence questions: we serially test if h depends on each variable $e \in E$. This means we use $O(n^2)$ questions to determine the body variables for all universal variables. We can do better.

We perform a binary search for h's body variables in E. If h has B body variables, we ask $O(|B| \lg n)$ instead of $O(n)$ questions to determine B. Suppose we have four variables x_1, x_2, x_3, x_4 such that x_1 is a universal head variable and all other variables are existential variables. x_2, x_3, x_4 are potential body variables for x_1. If the set $\{1^n, 0^n\}$ is a non-answer then x_1 is independent of all other variables and it has no body. If the set is an answer, we divide and conquer the variables. We ask if x_1 universally depends on half the variables, $\{x_2, x_3\}$, with the set $\{1^n, 0001\}$. If the set is a non-answer then we eliminate half the variables, $\{x_2, x_3\}$, from further consideration as body variables. We know that a body variable has to exist in the remaining half and since, x_4 is the last remaining variable, we learn the expression $\forall x_4 \rightarrow x_1$. If the set $\{1^n, 0001\}$ is an answer, then we know at least one body variable exists in $\{x_2, x_3\}$ and we continue the search for body variables in $\{x_2, x_3\}$, making sure that we also search the other half $\{x_4\}$ for body variables.

LEMMA 3.2. *$O(n \lg n)$ universal dependence questions are sufficient to learn the body variables of all universal head variables.*

Proof: Suppose we partition all variables into m non-overlapping parts of sizes $k_1, k_2, ..., k_m$ such that $\sum_{i=1}^{m} k_i = n$. Each part has at least one body variable and at least one universal head variable. Such a query class is in qhorn-1 as all body variables are disjoint across parts and head variables cannot reappear as head variables for other bodies or in the bodies of other head variables.

Given a head variable h_i, we can determine its body variables B_i using the binary search strategy above: we ask $O(|B_i| \lg n)$ questions (it takes $O(\lg n)$ questions to determine one body variable). For each additional head variable, h_i', that shares B_i, we require at most $1 \lg n$ questions: we only need to determine that h_i' has one body variable in the set B_i. Thus to determine all variables and their roles in a part of size k_i with $|B_i|$ body variables and $|H_i|$ head variables we need $O(|B_i| \lg n + |H_i| \times 1 \lg n) = O(k_i \lg n)$ questions. Since there are m parts, we ask a total of $O(\sum_{i=1}^{m} k_i \lg n) = O(n \lg n)$ questions. □

Since universal dependence questions consist of two tuples we only need $O(n)$ time to generate each question. Thus, the overall running time of this subtask is in polynomial time.

3.1.3 Learning existential Horn expressions

After learning universal Horn expressions, we have established some non-overlapping distinct bodies and their universal head variables. Each variable in the remaining set of existential variables, can either be (i) an existential head variable of one of the existing bodies or (ii) an existential head variable of a new body or (i) a body variable in the new body. We use *existential independence* questions to differentiate between these cases.

DEFINITION 3.2. *Given two disjoint subsets of existential variables $X \subset E, Y \subset E, X \cap Y = \emptyset$, an **existential independence question** is a membership question with two tuples: (i) a tuple where all variables $x \in X$ are false and all other variables are true and (ii) a tuple where all variables $y \in Y$ are false and all other variables are true.*

If an independence question between two existential variables x and y is an answer then either:

1. x and y are existential head variables of the same body
2. or x and y are not in the same Horn expression.

We say that x and y are *independent* of each other. Two sets X and Y are independent of each other if all variables $x \in X$ are independent of all variables $y \in Y$. Conversely, if an independence question between x and y is a non-answer then either:

1. x and y are body variables in the same body or
2. y is an existential head variable and x is in its body or
3. x is an existential head variable and y is in its body

We say that x and y *depend* on each other. If sets X and Y depend on each other then at least one variable $x \in X$ depends on one variable $y \in Y$.

Given an existential variable e, if we discover that e depends on a body variable b of a known set of body variables B, then we learn that e is an existential head variable in the Horn expression: $\exists B \rightarrow e$.

Otherwise, we find all existential variables D that e depends on. We can find all such variables with $O(|D| \lg n)$ existential independence questions using the binary search strategy of Section 3.1.2.

Knowing that D depends on e only tell us that one of the following holds: (i) A subset H of D are existential head variables for the body of $e \cup (D - H)$ or (ii) e is a head variable and D is a body. To differentiate between the two possibilities we make use of the following rule: *If two variables x, y depend on z but x and y are independent then z is a body variable and x, y are head variables.* If we find a pair of independent variables h_1, h_2 in D, we learn that x must be a body variable. If we do not find a pair of independent variables in D then we may assume that x is an existential head variable and all variables in D are body variables.

After finding head variables in D, we can determine the roles of the remaining variables in D with $|D| = O(n)$ independence questions between h_1 and each variable $d \in D - h_1$. If h_1 and d are independent then d is an existential head variable, otherwise d is a body variable.

Our goal, therefore, is to locate a definitive existential head variable in D by searching for an independent pair of variables.

DEFINITION 3.3. *An **independence matrix question** on D variables consists of $|D|$ tuples. For each variable $d \in D$, there is one tuple in the question where d is false and all other variables are true.*

Suppose we have four variables $x_1, ..., x_4$; $D = \{x_2, x_3, x_4\}$ and D depends on x_1. $\{\mathbf{1011}, \mathbf{1101}, \mathbf{1110}\}$ is a matrix question on D. If such a question is an answer then there is *at least a pair* of head variables in D: the question will always contain a pair of tuples that ensure that each head and the body is true. For example if x_2, x_4 are head variables then tuples $\{\mathbf{1011}, \mathbf{1110}\}$ in the question satisfy the Horn expressions: $\exists x_1 x_3 \rightarrow x_2, \exists x_1 x_3 \rightarrow x_4$. If *at most one* variable in D is a head variable, then there is no tuple in the matrix question where all body variables are true and the head variable is true and the question is a non-answer. For example, if only x_4 is a head variable, then the tuple, 1111 that satisfies the Horn expression $\exists x_1 x_2 x_3 \rightarrow x_4$ is absent from the question.

LEMMA 3.3. *Given an existential variable x and its dependents D, we can find an existential head variable in D with $O(|D| \lg |D|)$ independence matrix questions of $O(|D|)$ tuples each if at least two head variables exist in D.*

Algorithm 1 Get Head

x: an existential variable
D: the dependents of x, $|D| \geq 1$
$D_1 \leftarrow D, D_2 \leftarrow \emptyset, D_3 \leftarrow \emptyset$
while $D_1 \neq \emptyset$ **do**
  if isAnswer(Ask(MatrixQuestion(x, D_1))) **then**
    if $|D_1| = 2 \wedge D_2 = \emptyset$ **then return** D_1
    else if $|D_1| > 2 \wedge D_2 = \emptyset$ **then**
      Split D_1 into D_1 (1st half) and D_3 (2nd half)
    else if $|D_2| = 1$ **then return** D_2
    else
      Split D_2 into D_2 (1st half) and D_3 (2nd half)
      $D_1 \leftarrow D_1 - D_3$
    end if
  else
    if $D_3 = \emptyset$ **then return** $\emptyset$
    else if $|D_3| = 1$ **then return** D_3
    else
      Split D_3 into D_2 (1st half) and D_3 (2nd half)
      $D_1 \leftarrow D_1 \cup D_2$
    end if
  end if
end while

Proof. Consider the 'GetHead' procedure in Alg. 1 that finds an existential head variable in the set D of dependents of variable x. The central idea behind the 'GetHead' procedure is if the user responds that a matrix question on D_1 ($D_1 \subseteq D$) is an answer, then a pair of head variables must exist in D_1 and we can eliminate the remaining variables $D - D_1$ from further consideration. Otherwise, we know that at most one head variable exists in D_1 and another exists in $D - D_1$ so we can eliminate D_1 from further consideration and focus on finding the head variable in $D - D_1$.

Each membership question eliminates half the variables from further consideration as head variables. Thus, we require only $O(\lg |D|) = O(\lg n)$ questions to pinpoint one head variable.

Then, we ask $O(|D|)$ questions to differentiate head from body variables in D. If we do not find head variables in $|D|$ then we may assume that x is a head variable and all variables in D are body variables. Once we learn one existential Horn expression, we process the remaining existential variables in E. If a variable depends on any one of the body variables, B, of a learned existential Horn expression, it is a head variable to all body variables in B.

Suppose a query has m distinct existential expressions with $k_1, ..., k_m$ variables each, then $\sum_{i=1}^{m} k_i < n$. The size of each set of dependent variables for each expression i is $k_i - 1$. So the total number of questions we ask is $\sum_{i=1}^{m} (O(k_i \lg n) + O(\lg k_i) + O(k_i)) = O(n \lg n)$

Note, however, that each matrix question has $O(|D|) = O(n)$ tuples of n variables each and therefore requires $O(n^2)$ time to generate. If we limit the number of tuples per question to a constant number, then we increase the number of questions asked to $\Omega(n^2)$ [1].

3.2 Learning role-preserving qhorn

Since some queries are more complex than others within the role-preserving qhorn query class it is natural to allow our learning algorithm more time, more questions and more tuples per question to learn the more complex target queries. One can argue that such a powerful learning algorithm may not be practical or usable as it may ask many questions with many tuples each. If we assume that user queries tend to be simple (i.e they are small in size k (Def. 2.5) and have low causal densities θ (Def. 2.6)), then such an algorithm can be effective in the general case.

Role-preserving qhorn queries contain two types of expressions: universal Horn expressions ($\forall x_1 x_2 ... \rightarrow h$) and existential conjunctions ($\exists x_1 x_2 ...$) (Fig. 3 describes role-preserving qhorn terminology). In this section, we show that we can learn all universal Horn expressions with $O(n^{\theta+1})$ questions and all existential conjunctions with $O(kn \lg n)$ questions[1]. Since run-time is polynomial in the number of questions asked, our run-time is *poly*(nk) and *poly*(n^{θ}) respectively. By setting a constant upper limit on the causal density of a head variable we can learn role-preserving qhorn queries in *poly*(nk) time.

We employ a Boolean lattice on the n variables of a query to learn the query's expressions. Fig. 4 illustrates the Boolean lattice and its key properties. Each point in the lattice is a tuple of true or false assignments to the variables. A lattice has $n + 1$ levels. Each level l starting from level 0 consists of tuples where exactly l variables are false. A tuple's children are generated by setting exactly one of the true variables to false. Tuples at l have out-degree of $n - l$, i.e. they have $n - l$ children and in-degree of l or l parents. A tuple has an *upset* and a *downset*. These are visually illustrated in Fig. 4. If a tuple is not in the upset or downset of another tuple, then these two tuples are *incomparable*.

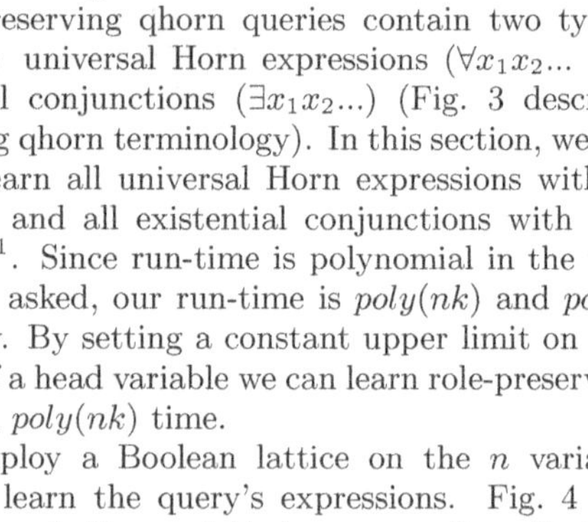

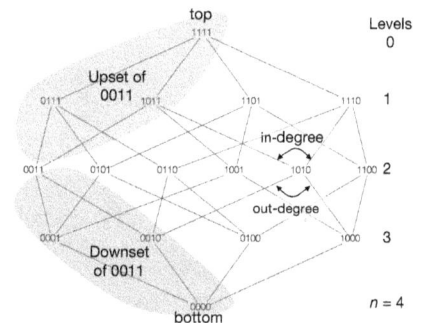

Figure 4: The Boolean lattice on four variables.

The gist of our lattice-based learning algorithms is as follows:

1. We map each tuple in the lattice to a distinct expression. This mapping respects a certain *generality* ordering of expressions. For example, the lattice we use to learn existential conjunctions maps the top tuple in the lattice

[1]We show lower bounds of $\Omega(\frac{n}{\theta}^{\theta-1})$ for learning universal Horn expressions and $\Omega(nk)$ for learning existential conjunctions in [1]

to the most specific conjunction $\exists x_1 x_2 ... x_n$; tuples in the level above the bottom of the lattice map to the more general conjunctions $\exists x_1$, $\exists x_2$, ..., $\exists x_n$ (§3.2.2). The exact details of this mapping for learning universal Horn expressions and learning existential conjunctions are described in the following section.

2. We search the lattice in a *top-to-bottom* fashion for the tuple that *distinguishes* or maps to the target query expression. The learning algorithm generates membership questions from the tuples of the lattice and the user's responses to these questions either *prune* the lattice or *guide* the search.

3.2.1 Learning universal Horn expressions

We first determine head variables of universal Horn expressions. We use the same algorithm of (§3.1.1). The algorithm uses $O(n)$ questions. We then determine *bodyless* head variables. To determine if h is bodyless, we construct a question with two tuples: 1^n and a tuple where h and all existential variables are false and all other variables are true. If the question is a non-answer then h is bodyless. If h is not bodyless then we utilize a special lattice (Fig. 5) to learn h's different bodies. In this lattice, we neutralize the effect of other head variables by fixing their value to true and we fix the value of h to false.

DEFINITION 3.4. *A universal Horn expression for a given head variable h is* ***distinguished*** *by a tuple if the true variables of the tuple represent a complete body for h.*

Thus, each tuple in the lattice distinguishes a unique universal Horn expression. For example, consider the target query:

$$\forall x_1 x_4 \rightarrow x_5 \; \forall x_3 x_4 \rightarrow x_5 \; \forall x_1 x_2 \rightarrow x_6$$
$$\exists x_1 x_2 x_3 \; \exists x_2 x_3 x_4 \; \exists x_1 x_2 x_5 \; \exists x_2 x_3 x_5 x_6$$

In the target query, the head variable x_5 has two universal Horn expressions:

$$\forall x_1 x_4 \rightarrow x_5 \; \forall x_3 x_4 \rightarrow x_5$$

In Fig. 5, we marked the two tuples that *distinguish* x_5's universal Horn expressions: 100101 and 001101. Notice that the universal Horn expressions are ordered from most to least specific. For example the top tuple of the lattice in Fig. 5 is the distinguishing tuple for the expression $\forall x_1 x_2 x_3 x_4 \rightarrow x_5$. While the bottom tuple is the distinguishing tuple for the expression $\forall x_5$. Our learning algorithm searches for distinguishing tuples of only *dominant* universal Horn expressions.

A membership question with a distinguishing tuple and the all-true tuple (a tuple where all variables are true) is a non-answer for one reason only: *it violates the universal Horn expression it distinguishes.* This is because the all-true tuple satisfies all the other expressions in the target query and the distinguishing tuple sets a complete set of body variables to true but the head to false. More importantly, all such membership questions constructed from tuples in the upset of the distinguishing tuple are non-answers and all questions constructed from tuples in the downset of the distinguishing tuple are answers. Thus, the key idea behind the learning algorithm is to efficiently search the lattice to find a tuple where questions constructed from tuples in the upset are non-answers and questions constructed from tuples in the downset are answers.

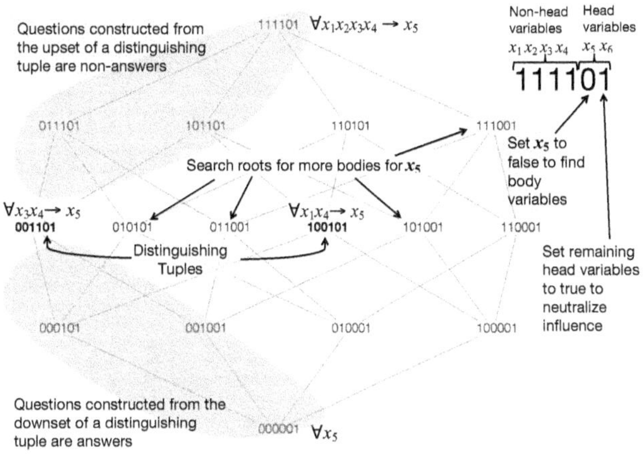

Figure 5: Learning bodies for a given head variable

Given a head variable h and n (non-head) variables, we use a Boolean lattice on n variables (with $h = 0$ and all other head variables set to true). We construct a membership question with a tuple t from the lattice and the all-true tuple — a tuple where all variables, including the head variable, are true. We begin by describing how we can use the lattice to find just one set of body variables that determine h with $O(n)$ questions. We start at the top of the lattice, we construct a question from the top tuple and proceed as follows:

1. If the question is an answer, then it does not contain an entire set of body variables that determine h. We prune its *downset*. We move to the next tuple on the same level of the lattice.

2. If the question is a non-answer then some of the true variables in t form a body and we move down the lattice (skipping previously pruned tuples). If all of t's children are answers, then t is a *universal distinguishing tuple* for the head variable h.

Once we find a body, we can safely eliminate its *upset*. Any body in the upset is *dominated* (Rule 2) by the discovered distinguishing tuple. Looking at Fig. 5, we notice that the upset simply contains all tuples where all body variables of the distinguishing tuple are true. The remaining lattice structure is rooted at tuples where one of the body variables is false. Since two incomparable bodies need to differ on at least one body variable, we set one body variable to false and search the resulting sub-lattices for bodies.

THEOREM 3.4. *$O(n^\theta)$ membership questions, where θ is the causal density of the given head variable h, are sufficient to the learn the θ universal Horn expressions of h.*

Proof: Let b_i denote the number of body variables for each distinguishing tuple t_i found. Initially we set b_0 to n and we search the entire lattice or the n sub-lattices rooted at the tuples where exactly one Boolean variable is false. In Fig. 5 those are the tuples at level 1: {0111*01*, 1011*01*, 1101*01*, 1110*01*}.

If the first distinguishing tuple found has $|B_1|$ true variables, then we need to search $|B_1|$ sub-lattices for bodies. For example, after finding the distinguishing tuple 0011*01*, we continue searching for more distinguishing tuples from $|B_1| = 2$ roots: $\{1101\mathit{01}, 1110\mathit{01}\}$.

Suppose we find a second distinguishing tuple: 1001*01* with B_2 body variables; then we need to search for more bodies in the sub-lattices rooted at tuples where one of each body variable from the distinct bodies are set to false. Our new $|B_1| \times |B_2|$ roots are: {0101*01*, 0110*01*, 1010*01*, 1110*01*}. These *search roots* are illustrated in Fig. 5.

In the worst case, we ask $O(n)$ questions to find a body. Thus to determine all θ expressions for a universal head variable, an upper bound on the number of questions, Q, is:

$$Q \leq \begin{array}{l}(n) + (|B_1| + n) + (|B_1| \times |B_2| + n) + ... + \\ (|B_1| \times |B_2| \times ... \times |B_\theta|)\end{array}$$

$$Q \leq n\theta + \sum_{b=1}^{\theta}(\prod_{i=1}^{b}|B_i|) \leq n\theta + \sum_{i=1}^{\theta}(n^i) = O(n^\theta) \quad \square$$

Since there are $O(n)$ head variables and for each head variable we ask $O(n^\theta)$ questions to determine its universal Horn expressions, we learn all universal Horn expression with $O(n \times n^\theta) = O(n^{\theta+1})$ questions.

3.2.2 Learning existential conjunctions

To learn existential conjunctions of a query we use the full Boolean lattice on all n variables of a query (including head variables).

DEFINITION 3.5. *An existential conjunction C is* ***distinguished*** *by a tuple if the true variables of the tuple are the variables of the conjunction.*

Thus, each tuple in the lattice distinguishes a unique existential conjunction. For example, consider the target query:

$$\begin{array}{c}\forall x_1x_4 \rightarrow x_5 \; \forall x_3x_4 \rightarrow x_5 \; \forall x_1x_2 \rightarrow x_6 \\ \exists x_1x_2x_3 \; \exists x_2x_3x_4 \; \exists x_1x_2x_5 \; \exists x_2x_3x_5x_6\end{array}$$

The conjunction $\exists x_2x_3x_5x_6$ is distinguished by the tuple 011011 in a six-variable Boolean lattice.

Existential conjunctions are ordered from most to least specific on the lattice. For example, the top tuple 111111 of a six-variable lattice is the distinguishing tuple for the expression $\exists x_1x_2x_3x_4x_5x_6$; the tuples $\{00001, 000010, 000100, 001000, 010000, 100000\}$ at level five of the lattice are the distinguishing tuples for the expressions $\exists x_6$, $\exists x_5$, $\exists x_4$, $\exists x_3$, $\exists x_2$, $\exists x_1$ respectively.

Our learning algorithm searches for distinguishing tuples of a *normalized* target query. For example, the target query above is normalized to the following semantically equivalent query using (Rule 3):

$$\begin{array}{c}\forall x_1x_4 \rightarrow x_5 \; \forall x_3x_4 \rightarrow x_5 \; \forall x_1x_2 \rightarrow x_6 \\ \exists x_1x_2x_3x_6 \; \exists x_2x_3x_4x_5 \; \exists x_1x_2x_5x_6 \; \exists x_2x_3x_5x_6\end{array} \qquad (2)$$

This query has the following *dominant* conjunctions (which include guarantee clauses):

$$\exists x_1x_4x_5 \; \exists x_1x_2x_3x_6 \; \exists x_2x_3x_4x_5 \; \exists x_1x_2x_5x_6 \; \exists x_2x_3x_5x_6$$

A membership question with **all dominant** distinguishing tuples of a query is an answer: all existential conjunctions (including guarantee clauses) are satisfied. For example, a question with the tuples: $\{100110, 111001, 011110, 110011, 011011\}$ is an answer for the target query above (2).

Replacing a distinguishing tuple with its children results in a non-answer: the existential conjunction of that tuple is no longer satisfied. For example replacing 011011 with its children $\{001011, 010011, 011001, 011010\}$ results in a membership question where none of the tuples satisfy the expression $\exists x_2x_3x_5x_6$.

Replacing a distinguishing tuple with any tuple in its upset *that does not violate a universal Horn expression* still results in an answer.

Thus, the learning algorithm searches level-by-level from top-to-bottom for distinguishing tuples by detecting a change in the user's response to a membership question from answer to non-answer. The efficiency of the learning algorithm stems from *pruning*: when we replace a tuple with its children, we prune those down to a minimal set of tuples that still dominate all the distinguishing tuples.

We describe the learning algorithm (Alg. 2) with an example and then prove that the learning algorithm runs in $O(kn \lg n)$ time (Theorem. 3.5)[2].

Algorithm 2 Find Existential Distinguishing Tuples

```
T ← {1^n}                                          ▷ The top tuple.
D ← {}        ▷ D is the set of discovered distinguishing tuples.
while T ≠ ∅ do
    T' ← {}
    for t ∈ T do
        C ← Children(t)
        C ← RemoveUniversalHornViolations(C)
        T ← T − {t}
        if isAnswer(Ask(D ∪ T ∪ C ∪ T')) then
            T' ← T' ∪ Prune(C, T ∪ D)
        else
            D ← D ∪ {t}
        end if
    end for
    T ← T'
end while
return D
```

Algorithm 3 Prune

```
T: the tuples to prune
O: other tuples
K ← {}                           ▷ K is the set of tuples to keep.
Split T into T1 (1st half) and T2 (2nd half).
while T1 ∪ T2 ≠ ∅ do
    if isAnswer(Ask(T1 ∪ K ∪ O)) then
        Split T1 into T1 (1st half) and T2 (2nd half).
    else
        if |T2| = 1 then
            K ← K ∪ T2
        else
            Add 1st half of T2 to T1. Set T2 to 2nd half of T2.
        end if
    end if
end while
return K
```

Suppose we wish to learn the existential conjunctions of the target query listed in (2). We use the six-variable Boolean lattice with the following modification: we remove all tuples that violate a universal Horn expression. These are tuples where the body variables of a universal Horn expression are true and the head variable is false. For example, the tuple 111110 violates $\forall x_1x_2 \rightarrow x_6$ is therefore removed from the lattice.

[2] In [1], we prove the algorithm's correctness and provide a lower bound of $O(nk)$ for learning existential conjunctions.

Level 1: We start at the top of the lattice. Since the tuple 111111 will satisfy any query, we skip to level one. We now construct a membership question with all the tuples of level 1 (after removing the tuples that violate universal Horn expressions: 111110, 111101): 111011, 110111, 101111, 011111. If such a question is a non-answer, then the distinguishing tuple is one level above and the target query has one dominant existential conjunction: $\exists x_1 x_2 x_3 x_4 x_5 x_6$.

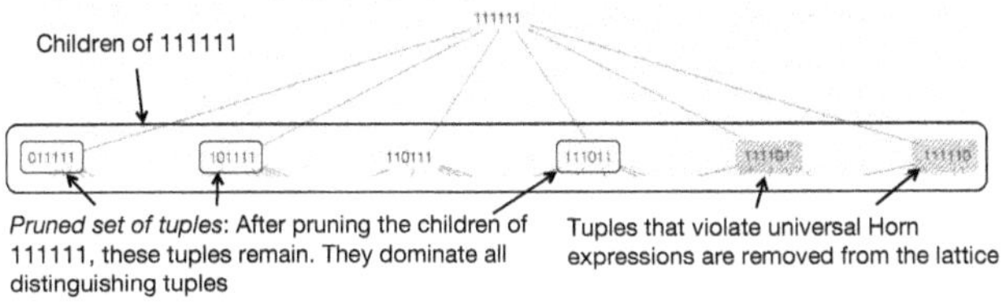

If the question is an answer, we need to search for tuples we can safely *prune*. So we remove one tuple from the question set and test its membership. Suppose we prune the tuple 110111, the question is still an answer since all conjunctions of the target query are still satisfied: the remaining set of tuples still dominate the distinguishing tuples of the target query.

We then prune 011111. This question is a non-answer since no tuple satisfies the clause $\exists x_2 x_3 x_4 x_5$. We put 011111 back in and continue searching at level one for tuples to prune. We are left with the tuples: 111011, 101111 and 011111. Note that we asked $O(n)$ questions to determine which tuples to safely prune. We can do better. In particular, we only need $O(\lg n)$ questions for each tuple we need to keep if we use a binary search strategy.

Level 2: We replace one of the tuples, 111011, with its children on level 2: {011011, 101011, 110011, 111001}. Note, that we removed 111010 because it violates $\forall x_1 x_2 \rightarrow x_6$. As before we determine which tuples we can safely prune. We are left with {110011, 111001}.

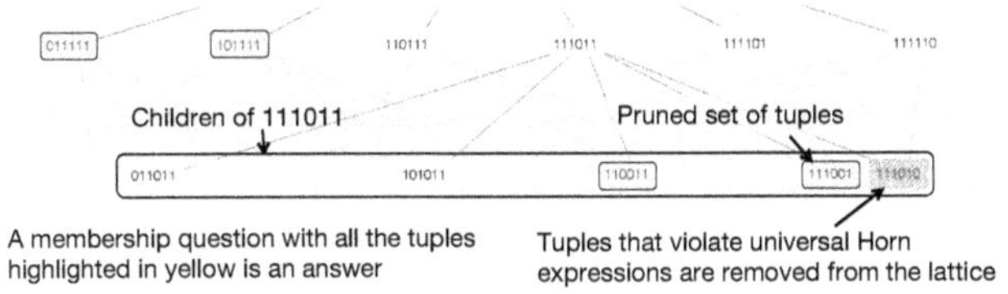

Similarly we replace 101111 with its children on level 2: {001111, 100111, 101011, 101110}. We did not consider 101101 because it violates $\forall x_3 x_4 \rightarrow x_5$. We can safely prune the children down to one tuple: 101110. We then replace 011111 with its children on level 2 and prune those down to {011011, 011110}. At the end of processing level 2, we are left with the tuples: {110011, 111001, 101110, 011011, 011110}. We repeat this process again now replacing each tuple, with tuples from level 3.

Level 3: When we replace 011110 with its children {010110, 011010, 001110}, we can no longer satisfy $\exists x_2 x_3 x_4 x_5$. The question is a non-answer and we learn that 011110 is a distinguishing tuple and that $\exists x_2 x_3 x_4 x_5$ is a conjunction in the target query. Note that we did not consider the child tuple 011100 because it violates the universal Horn expression $\forall x_3 x_4 \rightarrow x_5$. We fix 011110 in all subsequent membership questions.

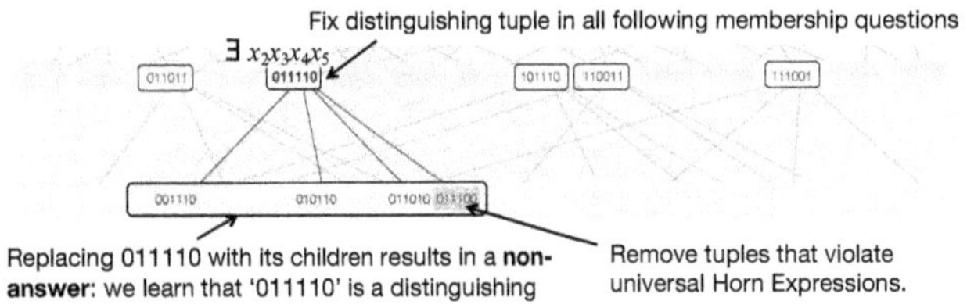

When we replace 011011 with its children {001011, 010011, 011001, 011010}, we can no longer satisfy $\exists x_2 x_3 x_5 x_6$. The question is a non-answer and we learn that 011011 is a distinguishing tuple and that $\exists x_2 x_3 x_5 x_6$ is a conjunction in the target query. We fix 011011 in all subsequent membership questions.

When we replace 111001 with its children {011001, 101001, 110001}, the question is a non-answer, and we learn that 111001 is distinguishing tuple and that $\exists x_1 x_2 x_3 x_6$ is a conjunction in the target query. Note that we did not consider the tuple 111000 because it violates $\forall x_1 x_2 \rightarrow x_6$. We fix 111001 in all subsequent membership questions.

We can replace 101110 with the children {001110, 100110, 101010}. Note that the child 101100 is removed because it violates $\forall x_1 x_4 \rightarrow x_5$. We can safely prune the children down to one tuple 100110.

When we replace 110011 with its children {010011, 100011, 110001}, we can no longer satisfy $\exists x_1 x_2 x_5 x_6$. Thus, the question is a non-answer and we learn that 110011 is a distinguishing tuple. Note that we did not consider the tuple 110010 because it violates $\forall x_1 x_2 \rightarrow x_6$.

At this stage, we are left with the following tuples: {**110011**, 100110, **111001**, **011011**, **011110**}. At this point, we can continue searching for conjunctions in the downset of 100110 which is the distinguishing tuple for a known guarantee clause for the universal Horn expression: $\forall x_1 x_4 \rightarrow x_5$. As an optimization to the algorithm, we do not search the downset because all tuples in the downset are dominated by 100110[3].

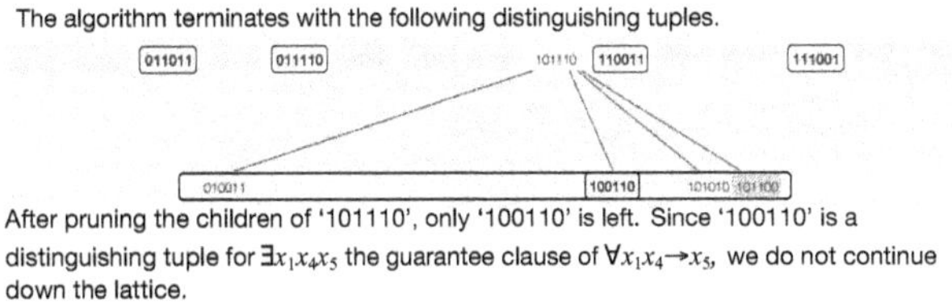

The learning algorithm terminates with the following distinguishing tuples {110011, 100110, 111001, 011011, 011110} which represent the expressions:

$$\exists x_1 x_2 x_5 x_6 \; \exists x_1 x_4 x_5 \; \exists x_1 x_2 x_3 x_6 \; \exists x_2 x_3 x_5 x_6 \; \exists x_2 x_3 x_4 x_5$$

THEOREM 3.5. *The lattice-based learning algorithm asks $O(kn \lg n)$ membership questions where k is the number of existential conjunctions.*

Proof: Consider the cost of learning one distinguishing tuple t_l at level l. From the top of the Boolean lattice to t_l, there is at least one tuple t_i at each level i ($0 < i < l$) that we did not prune and we traversed down from to get to t_l.

[3]We can relax the requirement of guarantee clauses for universal Horn expressions and our learning algorithms will still function correctly if they are allowed to ask about the membership of an empty set.

Let N_i be the set of t_i's siblings. At each level i, we asked at most $\lg |N_i|$ questions. $|N_i| = n - (i - 1)$ or the out-degree of N_i's parent. In the worst-case, $l = n$, and the cost of learning t_l is $\sum_{i=1}^{n} \lg(n - (i - 1)) \leq \sum_{i=1}^{n} \lg n = O(n \lg n)$. With k distinguishing tuples we ask at most $O(kn \lg n)$ questions. □

4. QUERY VERIFICATION

A query verifier constructs a set of membership questions to determine whether a given query is correct. The verifier will not find an alternate query if the query is incorrect. Thus, while query learning is a *search problem* — a learner searches for the one correct query that satisfies the user's responses to membership questions; query verification is the *decision problem* — a verifier decides if a given query is correct or incorrect given the user's responses to membership questions.

Our approach to query verification is straightforward: for a given role-preserving qhorn[4] query q_g, we generate a *verification set* of $O(k)$ membership questions, where k is the number of expressions in q_g. Note that our learning algorithm for role-preserving qhorn queries asks $O(n^{\theta+1} + kn \lg n)$ questions. If the user's intended query q_i is semantically different from the given query q_g, then for at least one of the membership questions M in the verification set $q_g(M) \neq q_i(M)$.

PROPOSITION 4.1. *A user's intended query q_i is semantically different from a given query q_g iff q_i and q_g have distinct sets of existential (Def. 3.5) and universal (Def. 3.4) distinguishing tuples.*

Suppose we try to learn the two role-preserving qhorn queries q_i and q_g. If q_i and q_g are semantically different, then our learning algorithm will terminate with distinct sets of existential(Def. 3.5) and universal(Def. 3.4) distinguishing tuples for each query. The verification set consists of membership questions that detect semantic differences between two queries by detecting differences in their respective sets of distinguishing tuples[5]. Fig. 6 lists six types of membership questions from which the verification algorithm constructs a verification set for a given query.

THEOREM 4.2. *A verification set with all membership questions of Fig. 6 surfaces semantic differences between the given query q_g and the intended query q_i by surfacing differences between the sets of distinguishing tuples of q_g and q_i.*

Proof: Case 1: q_i and q_g have different sets of dominant existential distinguishing tuples then by Lemma 4.3, questions A1 and N1 surface differences in the sets of dominant existential distinguishing tuples of q_g and q_i.

Case 2: q_i and q_g have different sets of dominant universal distinguishing tuples then

1. Both q_i and q_g classify h as a head variable. q_i has a dominant universal Horn expression $C_i : \forall B_i \rightarrow h$ (B is a set of body variables) and q_g has dominant universal Horn expressions of the form $\forall B_g \rightarrow h$.
   (a) If for *any* B_g in q_g, $B_i \subset B_g$ or $B_i \supset B_g$ then by Lemmas 4.4 and 4.5 questions A2 and N2 will surface this difference.
   (b) If for *all* B_g in q_g, B_i and B_g are incomparable then either (i) C_i's guarantee clause dominates q_g's existential expressions and q_g's set of existential distinguishing tuples does not have the distinguishing tuple for C_i's guarantee clause (See Case 1) or (ii) C_i's guarantee clause is dominated by an existential expression in q_g and by Lemma 4.6 question A3 surfaces the difference.
2. h is a head variable in q_i but is a non-head variable in q_g then by Lemma 4.7 question A4 surfaces the difference. □

LEMMA 4.3. *Let D_i be the set of q_i's dominant existential distinguishing tuples and let D_g be the set of q_g's dominant existential distinguishing tuples; membership questions A1 and N1 surface $D_i \neq D_g$.*

Proof: An existential distinguishing tuple represents an inflection point: all questions constructed with tuples in the distinguishing tuple's upset are answers and all questions constructed with only tuples in the rest of the lattice are non-answers. We use this feature to detect if $D_i \neq D_g$.

First, we define the following order relations over D_i and D_g:

1. $D_g \leq D_i$ if for every tuple $t_i \in D_i$, there exists a tuple $t_g \in D_g$ such that t_g is in the upset of t_i.
2. $D_g \geq D_i$ if all tuples in D_g are in the downset of D_i.
3. $D_g || D_i$, otherwise, i.e. they are incomparable.

Since $D_g \neq D_i$ only the following cases are possible:

Case 1: $D_g || D_i$ or $D_g > D_i$: D_g or membership question A1 is a non-answer to the user's intended query q_i. The user will detect the discrepancy as D_g is presented as an answer in q_g's verification set.

Case 2: $D_g < D_i$. Suppose all tuples in D_g are in the upset of one of D_i's tuples. Let $D_g(t)$ be the set of distinguishing tuples where we replace $t \in D_g$ with its children. There are $|D_g| = O(k)$ such sets. These sets form membership questions N1. For any $t \in D_g$, $D_g(t)$ is always a non-answer to q_g. However, for at least one tuple t, $D_g(t)$ is an answer to q_i. This is because if $D_g < D_i$ then at least one of D_i's tuples is a descendant of one of D_g's tuples, in which case $D_g(t)$ is still in the upset of that tuple and thus an answer. The user will detect the discrepancy as $D_g(t)$ is presented as a non-answer in q_g's verification set. □

Like existential distinguishing tuples, universal distinguishing tuples represent an inflection point. All tuples in the upset of the universal distinguishing tuple are non-answers (as all of h's body variables are true but h is false). All descendants of the universal distinguishing tuple are answers (as no complete set of h's body variables is true).

Let t_i be q_i's universal distinguishing tuple for an expression on the head variable h. Let t_g be one of q_g's universal distinguishing tuples for expressions on the head variable h. We define the following order relations between t_i and t_g:

1. $t_i \leq t_g$ if t_i is in the upset of t_g.
2. $t_i \geq t_g$ if t_i is in the downset of t_g.
3. $t_i || t_g$ if t_i and t_g are incomparable.

Consider two distinct (dominant) tuples t_{g_1} and t_{g_2} of the given query. By qhorn's equivalence rules(§2.1.1) queries t_{g_1}

[4]Since qhorn-1 is a sub-class of role-preserving qhorn, our verification approach works for both query classes.

[5]In [1], we describe how we normalize a given query and extract dominant distinguishing tuples from its expressions.

Answers				Non-Answers			
	Membership Questions	*# of Questions*	*Tuples / Question*		*Membership Questions*	*# of Questions*	*Tuples / Question*
A1	Distinguishing tuples for all dominant existential expressions (including guarantee clauses and existential Horn expressions)[1]	$O(1)$	$O(k)$	**N1**	For each distinguishing tuple in A1 that is not due to a guarantee clause: (i) Children of the distinguishing tuple[1] (ii) All other tuples from A1	$O(k)$	$O(n+k)$
A2	For each dominant universal Horn expression: (i) a tuple where all variables are true (ii) Children of the distinguishing tuple	$O(k)$	$O(n)$	**N2**	For each dominant universal Horn expression: (i) a tuple where all variables are true (ii) The distinguishing tuple	$O(k)$	$O(1)$
A3	For each dominant existential expression on C variables such that there are one or more universal Horn expressions $\forall B_1 \rightarrow h \ldots \forall B_\theta \rightarrow h$ where $B_i \subset C$ for $i = 1 \ldots \theta$: (i) a tuple where all variables are true (ii) Search roots: a tuple where one body variable from each body $B_1 \ldots B_\theta$ is false and all other variables in C are true and h is false	$O(k)$	$O(n^\theta)$				
A4	(i) A tuple where all variables are true (ii) A tuple for each non-head variable x such that x is false and all other variables are true	$O(1)$	$O(n)$				

[1]In constructing these questions, we do not violate universal Horn expressions: i.e. we set a head variable to true if the existential expression contains a body for the head variable

Figure 6: Membership questions of a verification set.

and t_{g_2} are incomparable ($t_{g_1}||t_{g_2}$). Consequently, for any two distinct tuples both $t_i < t_{g_1}$ and $t_i > t_{g_2}$ cannot hold.

LEMMA 4.4. *Membership question A2 detects $t_i > t_g$.*

Proof: Suppose, q_g has one universal distinguishing tuple t_g such that $t_i > t_g$. Then the membership question A2 that consists of the all-true tuple and t_g's children is an answer for q_g as none of t_g's children have all the body variables set to true, so the head variable can be false. If $t_i > t_g$ then q_i's universal Horn expression on h has a strict subset of the body variables represented by t_g. Therefore, in at least one of t_g's children, all of t_i's body variables are set to true and h is still false. Thus, A2 is a non-answer to q_i. For all other universal distinguishing tuples t_g of q_g, either $t_i > t_g$ or $t_i||t_g$. If $t_i||t_g$ then A2 is still an answer. □

LEMMA 4.5. *Membership question N2 detects $t_i < t_g$.*

Proof: Suppose, q_g has one universal distinguishing tuple t_g such that $t_i < t_g$. Then the membership question N2 that consists of the all-true tuple and t_g is a non-answer for q_g as t_g has all body variables set to true but the head variable h is false. If $t_i < t_g$ then q_i's universal Horn expression on h has a strict superset of the body variables represented by t_g. Therefore, t_g does not have all body variables set to true and h can be false. Thus, N2 is an answer to q_i.

For all other universal distinguishing tuples t_g of q_g, either $t_i < t_g$ or $t_i||t_g$. If $t_i||t_g$ then N2 is still a non-answer. □

LEMMA 4.6. *If*

- *h is a head variable in q_i and q_g.*
- *q_i has a dominant universal Horn expression $\forall M \rightarrow h$ which q_g does not have.*
- *q_g has universal Horn expressions $\forall B_1 \rightarrow h \ldots \forall B_\theta \rightarrow h$.*
- *$B_i||M$ for $i = 1 \ldots \theta$*
- *q_g has an existential expression on C variables ($\exists$ C) such that $C \supseteq M$ and $C \supset B_i$ for $i = 1 \ldots \theta$*

then A3 surfaces a missing universal Horn expression ($\forall M \rightarrow h$) from q_g.

Proof: Consider q_g's universal Horn expressions whose guarantee clauses are dominated by $\exists$ C:

$$\forall B_1 \rightarrow h, \forall B_2 \rightarrow h, \ldots \forall B_\theta \rightarrow h$$

such that $B_i \subset C$ for $i = 1 \ldots \theta$. To build A3, we set one body variable from each of $B_1, \ldots, B_\theta$ to false, the remaining variables in C to true and h to false. There are $|B_1| \times |B_2| \times \ldots \times |B_\theta| = O(n^\theta)$ such tuples. A3 now consists of all such tuples and the all-true tuple.

A3 acts like the search phase of the learning algorithm that looks for new universal Horn expressions(§3.2.1). A3 is a non-answer for q_i as at least one of the tuples has all variables in M set to true (because $M||B_i$ for $i = 1 \ldots \theta$) and h to false, thus violating $\forall M \rightarrow h$. □

LEMMA 4.7. *If h is a head variable in q_i but not in q_g then question A4 surfaces the difference.*

Proof: The all-true tuple satisfies all existential expressions in q_g. For each body variable x in q_g, A4 has a tuple where x is false and all other variables are true. If x is a head variable in q_i, then A4 should be a non-answer. □

This concludes the proof of Theorem. 4.2

5. RELATED WORK

Learning & Verifying Boolean Formula: Our work is influenced by the field of computational learning theory. Using membership questions to learn Boolean formulas was introduced in 1988 [3]. Angluin et al. demonstrated the polynomial learnability of conjunctions of (non-quantified) Horn clauses using membership questions and a more powerful class of questions known as equivalence questions [4]. The learning algorithm runs in time $O(k^2n^2)$ where n is the number of variables and k is the number of clauses. Interestingly, Angluin proved that there is no PTIME algorithm for learning conjunctions of Horn clauses that only uses membership questions. Angluin et al.'s algorithm for learning conjunctions of Horn formula was extended to learn first-order Horn expressions [12, 10]. First-order Horn expressions contain quantifiers. We differ from this prior work in that in qhorn we quantify over tuples of an object's nested relation; we do not quantify over the values of variables. Our syntactic restrictions on qhorn have counterparts in Boolean formulas. Both qhorn-1 and *read-once* Boolean formulas [5] allow variables to occur at most once. Both role-preserving qhorn queries and *depth-1 acyclic Horn formulas* [9] do not allow variables to be both head and body variables.

Verification sets are analogous to the *teaching sequences* of Goldman and Kearns [8]. A teaching sequence is the smallest sequence of classified examples a teacher must reveal to a learner to help it uniquely identify a target concept from a concept class. Prior work provides algorithms to determine the teaching sequences for several classes of Boolean formula [6, 8, 14] but not for our class of qhorn queries.

Learning in the Database Domain: Two recent works on example-driven database query learning techniques — Query by Output (QBO) [17] and Synthesizing View Definitions (SVD) [7] — focus on the problem of learning a query Q from a given input database D, and an output view V. There are several key differences between this body of work and ours. First, QBO and SVD perform as decision trees; they infer a query's propositions so as to split D into tuples in V and tuples not in V. We assume that users can provide with us the propositions, so we focus on learning the structure of the query instead. Second, we work on a different subset of queries: QBO infers select-project-join queries and SVD infers unions of conjunctive queries. Learning unions of conjunctive queries is equivalent to learning k-term Disjunctive Normal Form (DNF) Boolean formulae [11]. We learn conjunctions of *quantified* Horn formulae. Since our target queries operate over objects with nested-sets of tuples instead of flat tuples, we learn queries in an exponentially larger query and data space. Finally, QBO and SVD work with a complete mapping from input tuples to output tuples. Our goal, however, is to learn queries from the smallest possible mapping of input to output objects, as it is generally impractical for users to label an entire database of objects as answers or non-answers. We point out that we synthesize our input when constructing membership questions, thus we can learn queries independent of the peculiarities of a particular input database D.

Using membership (and more powerful) questions to learn concepts within the database domain is not novel. For example, Cate, Dalmau and Kolaitis use membership and equivalence questions to learn schema mappings [16]. Staworko and Wieczorek use example XML documents given by the user to infer XML queries [15]. In both these works, the concept class learned is quite different from the qhorn query class.

6. CONCLUSION & FUTURE WORK

In this paper, we have studied the learnability of a special class of Boolean database queries — qhorn. We believe that other quantified-query classes (other than conjunctions of quantified Horn expressions) may exhibit different learnability properties. Mapping out the properties of different query classes will help us better understand the limits of example-driven querying. In our learning/verification model, we made the following assumptions: (i) the user's intended query is either in qhorn-1 or role-preserving qhorn, (ii) the data has at most one level nesting. We plan to design algorithms to verify that the user's query is indeed in qhorn-1 or role-preserving qhorn. We have yet to analyze the complexity of learning queries over data with multiple-levels of nesting. In such queries, a single expression can have several quantifiers.

We plan to investigate *Probably Approximately Correct* learning: we use randomly-generated membership questions to learn a query with a certain probability of error [18]. We note that membership questions provide only one bit of information — a response to membership question is either 'answer' (1) or 'non-answer' (0). We plan to examine the plausibility of constructing other types of questions that provide more information bits but still maintain interface usability. One possibility is to ask questions to directly determine how propositions interact[6] such as: "do you think p_1 and p_2 both have to be satisfied by at least one tuple?" or "when does p_1 have to be satisfied?"

Finally, we see an opportunity to create efficient *query revision* algorithms. Given a query which is *close* to the user's intended query, our goal is to determine the intended query through few membership questions — polynomial in the distance between the given query and the intended query. Efficient revision algorithms exist for (non-quantified) role-preserving Horn formula [9]. The Boolean-lattice provides us with a natural way to measure how close two queries are: the distance between the distinguishing tuples of the given and intended queries.

7. ACKNOWLEDGMENTS

Partial funding provided by NSF Grants CCF-0963922, CCF-0916389, CC-0964033 and a Google University Research Award.

8. REFERENCES

[1] A. Abouzied et al. Learning and verifying quantified boolean queries by example. arXiv:1304.4303 [cs.DB].

[2] A. Abouzied, J. Hellerstein, and A. Silberschatz. Dataplay: interactive tweaking and example-driven correction of graphical database queries. In *UIST*, 2012.

[3] D. Angluin. Queries and concept learning. *Mach. Learn.*, 2(4):319–342, 1988.

[4] D. Angluin, M. Frazier, and L. Pitt. Learning conjunctions of horn clauses. In *COLT*, 1990.

[5] D. Angluin, L. Hellerstein, and M. Karpinski. Learning read-once formulas with queries. *J. ACM*, 40(1):185–210, 1993.

[6] M. Anthony et al. On exact specification by examples. In *COLT*, 1992.

[7] A. Das Sarma et al. Synthesizing view definitions from data. In *ICDT*, 2010.

[8] S. A. Goldman and M. J. Kearns. On the complexity of teaching. In *COLT*, 1991.

[9] J. Goldsmith and R. H. Sloan. New horn revision algorithms. *J. Mach. Learn. Res.*, 6:1919–1938, Dec. 2005.

[10] D. Haussler. Learning conjunctive concepts in structural domains. *Mach. Learn.*, 4(1):7–40, 1989.

[11] M. J. Kearns and U. V. Vazirani. *An introduction to computational learning theory.* MIT Press, Cambridge, MA, USA, 1994.

[12] R. Khardon. Learning first order universal horn expressions. In *COLT*, 1998.

[13] P. Reisner. Use of psychological experimentation as an aid to development of a query language. *IEEE Trans. on Soft. Eng.*, SE-3(3):218–229, 1977.

[14] A. Shinohara and S. Miyano. Teachability in computational learning. *New Gen. Comput.*, 8(4):337–347, 1991.

[15] S. Staworko and P. Wieczorek. Learning twig and path queries. In *ICDT*, 2012.

[16] B. ten Cate, V. Dalmau, and P. G. Kolaitis. Learning schema mappings. In *ICDT*, 2012.

[17] Q. T. Tran, C. Chan, and S. Parthasarathy. Query by output. In *SIGMOD*, 2009.

[18] L. G. Valiant. A theory of the learnable. *CACM*, 27(11):1134–1142, 1984.

[6]We thank our anonymous reviewer for this suggestion.

The ACM PODS Alberto O. Mendelzon Test-of-Time Award 2013

In 2007, the PODS Executive Committee decided to establish a Test-of-Time Award, named after the late Alberto O. Mendelzon, in recognition of his scientific legacy, and his service and dedication to the database community. Mendelzon was an international leader in database theory, whose pioneering and fundamental work has inspired and influenced both database theoreticians and practitioners, and continues to be applied in a variety of advanced settings. He served the database community in many ways; in particular, he served as the General Chair of the PODS conference, and was instrumental in bringing together the PODS and SIGMOD conferences. He also was an outstanding educator, who guided the research of numerous doctoral students and postdoctoral fellows. The Award is to be awarded each year to a paper or a small number of papers published in the PODS proceedings ten years prior, that had the most impact (in terms of research, methodology, or transfer of practice) over the intervening decade. The decision was approved by SIGMOD and ACM. The funds for the Award were contributed by IBM Toronto.

The PODS Executive Chair has appointed us to serve as the Award Committee for 2013. After careful consideration, we have decided to select the following paper as the award winner for 2013:

Revealing Information while Preserving Privacy
by Irit Dinur and Kobbi Nissim

This paper dealt with the following fundamental question: given a system holding a database with sensitive data, how many queries can it permit to be answered, and with what accuracy, while preserving the privacy of the data?

A database is modelled by an n-bitstring $d_1, \cdots, d_n$ with a query being a subset q of $\{1, \ldots, n\}$. The answer to q is defined as the sum of all database entries specified by q, i.e., $\sum_{i \in q} d_i$. When q is issued, the system itself will return this answer perturbed by some random noise. Relative to this setting, Dinur and Nissim established the following fundamental, but negative, result: *If, for each query, the system's added noise is bounded by $o(\sqrt{n})$, then an adversary can almost entirely reconstruct the database from the answers of just $O(n \log^2 n)$ randomly selected queries.* Furthermore, the reconstruction can be done in polynomial time.

Fortunately, for very large n, obtaining answers to $O(nlog^2n)$ queries may be prohibitively expensive. What would happen if only a sublinear number of queries is allowed? This problem was addressed in the second part of the paper. This led to positive results for a very strong notion of privacy, which would, through the work of additional researchers, evolve into what is now known as "differential privacy."

The Dinur-Nissim paper has received hundreds of citations. It has had a fundamental impact on the theory and practice of private data analysis. Furthermore, it was the seed for the development of differential privacy.

Michael Benedikt	**Tova Milo**	**Dirk Van Gucht** (Chair)
University of Oxford, UK	Tel Aviv University, Israel	Indiana University, USA

The Alberto O. Mendelzon Test-of-Time Award Committee for 2013.

Verification of Database-driven Systems via Amalgamation

Mikołaj Bojańczyk*
Univ. of Warsaw

Luc Segoufin
INRIA and ENS Cachan

Szymon Toruńczyk*
Univ. of Warsaw

ABSTRACT

We describe a general framework for static verification of systems that base their decisions upon queries to databases. The database is specified using constraints, typically a schema, and is not modified during a run of the system. The system is equipped with a finite number of registers for storing intermediate information from the database and the specification consists of a transition table described using quantifier-free formulas that can query either the database or the registers.

Our main result concerns systems querying XML databases – modeled as data trees – using quantifier-free formulas with predicates such as the descendant axis or comparison of data values. In this scenario we show an EXPSPACE algorithm for deciding reachability.

Our technique is based on the notion of amalgamation and is quite general. For instance it also applies to relational databases (with an optimal PSPACE algorithm).

We also show that minor extensions of the model lead to undecidability.

Categories and Subject Descriptors

F.4.1 [**Mathematical Logic and Formal Languages**]: Mathematical Logic

Keywords

Database-driven Systems, Register Automata, Amalgamation, Fraïssé classes

1. INTRODUCTION

In this paper we describe a general framework for static verification of *database-driven* systems. Such a system bases its decisions upon queries to databases. Typical examples are web services, web applications, or data-centric business processes. These systems can be complex and error prone. Computer-aided static analysis can improve their robustness and correctness.

*Authors supported by ERC Starting Grant "Sosna"

In order to perform static analysis, the behavior of the database-driven system is specified in a suitable formalism; the desired properties of its executions are also specified in a suitable formalism. The computer then automatically checks whether all runs of the system verify these properties.

As advocated in [10], classical software verification techniques have serious limitations when applied to such systems – the main reason is that they abstract away data values, resulting in serious loss of semantics for both the system and the properties being verified.

For this reason, several specific formalisms have been designed allowing meaningful specification of relational database-driven systems. See for instance [8, 6, 4, 5, 9]. As demonstrated in [9], for these scenarios, the system can be described using a register automaton whose transition rules are quantifier-free first-order formulas querying the database and the registers. The correctness criterion for executions of the system is specified using a language mixing queries to the database and temporal behavior that can easily be translated into the same register automata model. Altogether the static analysis problem boils down to testing the existence of a database such that the register automaton has an accepting run driven by that database.

In this paper we develop general techniques for testing reachability of such automata models. These techniques encompass the examples cited above concerning relational databases, but also apply to XML databases and – in general – to any kind of structures having "good" model properties.

Following [9], we specify database-driven systems using transition rules controlling their workflow. Each such rule may be based on the result of quantifier-free queries to the database. The database is not fixed and may vary from run to run. It is however restricted to range over a certain class of databases typically specified using a schema and possibly several other constraints. Moreover the system has only read access to the database and the database does not change during a run.

To give an idea of the setting we are dealing with, let us describe a toy example of a database-driven system $\mathcal{S}$ that fits into our framework. The system $\mathcal{S}$ is equipped with one register capable of storing nodes of XML documents. We specify the transitions of $\mathcal{S}$ as follows:

> *The node stored in the register after the transition is a descendant of the node stored in the register before the transition and the attribute* a *of both nodes (before and after) contains the same data value.*

Furthermore, we specify that in the initial configuration of the system, the register stores the root of the tree, and in an accepting configuration, it must store some leaf of the tree. Observe that the transitions do not modify the database.

We are interested in the following question: is there some XML document t such that the described system has an accepting run driven by t? We may ask more detailed questions: is there some XML document t satisfying a certain XML schema such that the described system has an accepting run driven by t?

In general our goal is to give an algorithm for the following problem, parametrized by a class $\mathcal{C}$ of databases.

> **Input:** A database-driven system.
>
> **Output:** Does the system have some finite accepting run driven by some database in $\mathcal{C}$?

We show that if the class $\mathcal{C}$ of databases satisfies a certain model-theoretic assumption – namely, it is a computable *Fraïssé class* – then there exists an algorithm for the described problem.

Our main technical result shows that many natural classes of databases are Fraïssé. Examples include: all databases over a given relational schema, three-colorable graphs (more generally, any property of databases expressed as a Constraint Satisfaction Problem), XML documents viewed as data trees satisfying a given XML schema (more generally, any property of trees recognized by a tree automaton).

The most interesting and most difficult result is the XML case. In this scenario the database is an XML document that must verify a certain XML schema. The system can query the XML document using the descendant axis, the document order and the closest common ancestor relation. It can also test equality or inequality between attribute values. Our generic technique shows that in this setting the above problem is decidable in ExpSpace.

In the setting of relational databases, we derive from our generic technique an optimal PSpace decision procedure.

We also show how extending slightly the expressive power of these systems quickly leads to undecidability. For instance, in the XML setting, allowing the system to use the sibling or child axis in its queries leads to undecidability.

Comparison with previous work. The model described in this paper generalizes the previous existing models of automata introduced for relational database-driven systems [8, 6, 4, 5, 9]. In particular, the domain can be linearly ordered and the specification of the database-driven system may use this order within the quantifier-free formulas. In this paper we notice that the key is the Fraïssé property, which holds for linear orders, and show that the XML setting is also Fraïssé.

This paper considers only finite runs and generalizes all the previous known results concerning the existence of finite runs. As shown in several of the above cited papers, considering infinite runs leads to additional challenges. However, in all the practical cases mentioned here, the existence of infinite runs can be reduced to the existence of finite runs using a Ramsey argument as described in [9].

2. DATABASE-DRIVEN SYSTEMS

We model databases as finite structures over finite schemas containing relation and function symbols. We use standard terminology from model theory (see [7] for a reference); we now briefly recall the relevant notions.

Basic notions.

A *schema* Σ is a finite set of relation symbols and function symbols, each with a given arity (0-ary function symbols are *constant* symbols). A *model*, or *structure*, $\mathbb{A}$ over a schema Σ is a set $\text{dom}(\mathbb{A})$ – the *domain* of $\mathbb{A}$ – together with an interpretation $s^{\mathbb{A}}$ for each symbol $s \in \Sigma$ as a relation or function over the domain of an appropriate arity, as described by the schema. A structure is said to be *finite* if its domain is finite. A *database* is a finite structure over a given schema.

By *substructure* we always mean in this paper an *induced substructure*, i.e. a restriction of the initial structure to a subset of its domain, which is closed under the function symbols from the schema.

A *homomorphism* from a structure $\mathbb{A}$ to a structure $\mathbb{B}$, is a mapping $h : \text{dom}(\mathbb{A}) \to \text{dom}(\mathbb{B})$ that preserves the relations and functions from Σ, i.e. $(a_1, \ldots, a_k) \in R^{\mathbb{A}}$ implies $h(a_1, \ldots, a_k) \in R^{\mathbb{B}}$, and $h(f^{\mathbb{A}}(a_1, \ldots, a_k)) = f^{\mathbb{B}}(h(a_1, \ldots, a_k))$, for all tuples $a_1, \ldots, a_k$ of elements of $\text{dom}(\mathbb{A})$ and function/relation symbols of arity k. An *isomorphism* is a bijective homomorphism whose inverse mapping is also a homomorphism. An *automorphism* is an isomorphism from $\mathbb{A}$ to itself. Finally an *embedding* is a mapping h that is an isomorphism onto the substructure induced by the image of h.

We assume familiarity with first-order logic. We write $\mathbb{A} \models_{\text{val}} \varphi$ to express the fact that a first-order formula φ holds in the structure $\mathbb{A}$ with the valuation val for its free variables.

Database-driven systems.

A *database-driven system* over a schema Σ is described by the following components.

- A finite set of *control states* $Q = \{p, q, \ldots\}$
- A finite set of *registers* $X = \{x, y, \ldots\}$
- A subset of *initial* states $I \subseteq Q$
- A subset of *accepting* states $F \subseteq Q$
- Finitely many *transition rules* of the form:

  $$p \xrightarrow{\delta} q$$

  where p, q are control states and δ is a quantifier-free first-order formula over the schema Σ with free variables in the set $X \times \{\text{new}, \text{old}\}$. The formula δ is called the *guard* of the transition and relates the values of the registers before and after the transition.

Fix a database-driven system as described above. A *configuration* is a triple $(\mathbb{D}, q, \text{val})$, where:

- $\mathbb{D}$ is a database over the schema Σ;
- q is a control state;
- $\text{val} : X \to \mathbb{D}$ is a valuation, which maps the registers to elements in the domain of $\mathbb{D}$.

We say that there is a *transition* between configurations $(\mathbb{D}_{\text{old}}, q_{\text{old}}, \text{val}_{\text{old}})$ and $(\mathbb{D}_{\text{new}}, q_{\text{new}}, \text{val}_{\text{new}})$, if

- $\mathbb{D}_{\text{old}} = \mathbb{D}_{\text{new}}$ (*transitions do not modify the database*)
- There is a transition rule $q_{\text{old}} \xrightarrow{\delta} q_{\text{new}}$ such that

  $$\mathbb{D}_{\text{old}} \models_{\text{val}} \delta$$

  where $\text{val}(x, i) = \text{val}_i(x)$ for $x \in X, i \in \{\text{old}, \text{new}\}$.

A *run* of the system is a sequence of configurations that begins in a configuration with an initial state, and where two consecutive configurations are connected by a transition. In this paper, we are interested in finite runs. A run is *accepting* if the control state in its last configuration is accepting. It follows from the definition that for each run, there is some database $\mathbb{D}$ that is shared by all configurations in the run. We say that the run is *driven by* $\mathbb{D}$. Note that different runs of the same system may be driven by different databases.

Example 1. Consider directed graphs, where some of the nodes are colored red, and the remaining nodes are white. This corresponds to a schema with one binary edge predicate E and one unary predicate *red*.

We describe a database-driven system whose accepting runs trace odd-length cycles of red nodes. The system has the following components.

- The control states are $\{start, q_0, q_1, end\}$. The initial state is *start* and the accepting state is *end*.
- The registers are x, y.
- There is a transition rule $q_0 \xrightarrow{\delta} q_1$, where the guard δ is

  $$(x_{\text{old}} = x_{\text{new}}) \wedge E(y_{\text{old}}, y_{\text{new}}) \wedge red(y_{\text{new}}).$$

  There is also a transition rule $q_1 \xrightarrow{\delta} q_0$, with the same guard. This means that the system alternates between the states q_0 and q_1, each time moving the content of register y along an edge to some red node (the content of register x stays in place).

  There is a transition rule $start \xrightarrow{\alpha} q_0$, where the guard α is

  $$x_{\text{old}} = x_{\text{new}} = y_{\text{old}} = y_{\text{new}}$$

  There is also a transition $q_1 \xrightarrow{\alpha} end$, with the same guard. This means that, in order to exit the initial state, both registers need to point to the same vertex; likewise, in order to enter the accepting state, both registers need to point to the same vertex.

Here is an example run of the system. The run is driven by the database that is the graph $\mathbb{G}$ depicted below. The nodes of the graph are colored red or white; the numbers are not part of the database, they are used to identify the nodes.

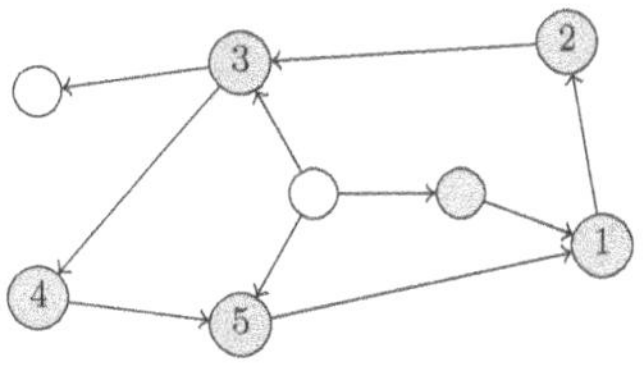

An accepting run of the system, driven by $\mathbb{G}$ is:

$$(\mathbb{G}, start, [1,1]) \to (\mathbb{G}, q_0, [1,1]) \to (\mathbb{G}, q_1, [1,2]) \to (\mathbb{G}, q_0, [1,3]) \to$$
$$\to (\mathbb{G}, q_1, [1,4]) \to (\mathbb{G}, q_0, [1,5]) \to (\mathbb{G}, q_1, [1,1]) \to (\mathbb{G}, end, [1,1]),$$

where $[i, j]$ denotes the valuation that maps x to the node marked with i and y to the node marked with j.

In general, the described system has an accepting run driven by a graph $\mathbb{G}$ if and only if there is a cycle in $\mathbb{G}$ of odd length, consisting only of red nodes.

The emptiness problem. In this paper, we study the following decision problem, which is parametrized by a class $\mathcal{C}$ of databases over a common schema Σ, and called *emptiness of database-driven systems over* $\mathcal{C}$.

> **Input:** A database-driven system over Σ.
>
> **Output:** Does the system have some finite accepting run driven by some database in $\mathcal{C}$?

Actually, in some of our results also a finite description of the class $\mathcal{C}$ will be given on input. The following observation shows that the problem is PSPACE-hard for almost any choice of parameter $\mathcal{C}$.

LEMMA 1. *The emptiness problem for database-driven systems over $\mathcal{C}$ is* PSPACE*-hard if $\mathcal{C}$ contains at least one database with at least two elements.*

Existential guards. Before describing our results in more detail, we point out that replacing quantifier-free formulas by existential formulas in the guards when specifying the system does not affect the expressive power nor the decidability results, as quantified variables can be simulated by using extra registers and nondeterminism.

FACT 2. *For every database-driven system with existential guards one can compute in linear time a database-driven system with quantifier-free guards accepting the same runs driven by the same databases.*

However, as we shall show later on, further extensions of the guards, such as boolean combinations of existential formulas, break decidability.

3. DECIDABILITY RESULTS

In this section, we present the main results of the paper, which show that emptiness of database-driven systems is decidable over certain classes of databases.

3.1 XML documents and regular tree languages

This class is motivated by XML databases. We work with vertex-labeled, unranked and sibling-ordered trees. We use the standard terminology for trees: root, leaf, descendant, ancestor, child, parent, sibling. The *next sibling* of a node x is the first (and therefore unique) sibling after x in document order, which might not exist if x is a rightmost sibling. The *following sibling* is the transitive (but not reflexive) closure of the next sibling relation. Likewise, each node has at most one *previous sibling*, but possibly many *preceding siblings*. We use the standard notion of regular languages for unranked trees. The automaton model is presented in Section 5.3.

It is easy to see that in the presence of a successor relation database-driven systems can simulate counters and are therefore undecidable. See also Section 6.1. For this reason we disallow in our model the use of the child, parent, next sibling and previous sibling relations and only allow relations such as ancestor, descendant, following and preceding sibling. As a matter of fact we can also include the document order and the closest common ancestor function that maps x, y to the node that is a descendant of all common ancestors of both x and y.

We model a tree t as a database, denoted by Treedb(t), whose domain is the nodes of the tree, and which is equipped with the following predicates and functions:

- A unary predicate for every possible node label (there are finitely many labels);
- Binary predicates for document order (denoted by $\leq_{doc}$) and descendant order (denoted by $\preceq_v$);
- A binary function for closest common ancestor, which is denoted by $x \wedge y$. Observe that the descendant relation is defined in terms of this function by a quantifier-free formula:

$$x \preceq_v y \qquad \text{iff} \qquad x = x \wedge y$$

If the set of node labels is A, then the schema above is denoted by TreeSchema(A).

Our main result on trees is that emptiness of database-driven systems is decidable over any regular tree language, even when the description of the regular language is also part of the input.

THEOREM 3. *The following problem is decidable:*

> **Input:** *A tree automaton defining a language L of trees labeled by an alphabet A, and a database-driven system over* TreeSchema(A).
>
> **Output:** *Is there a tree $t \in L$ and an accepting run of the system driven by* Treedb(t)*?*

For a fixed tree automaton, the problem is PSPACE*-complete. When both the tree automaton and the system are given on input, the problem is in* EXPSPACE.

The database-driven systems are only allowed to access the trees through quantifier-free formulas that use the predicates included in TreeSchema(A). By Fact 2, we could also allow the systems to use existential formulas defined in terms of the predicates in TreeSchema(A). Some navigation predicates for trees, such as child, next sibling, or even simply sibling are not definable this way. We will later show (Section 6) that adding any one of the above three predicates leads to undecidability.

The proof of Theorem 3 will be given in Sections 4 and 5.

Adding data values. We show in Section 4.4 a composition method implying that our results extend to databases storing data values allowing equality tests. In particular, the result of Theorem 3 remains valid if each node of the tree also carries a data value in $\mathbb{N}$ and the query can test these values using equalities or inequalities. The complexity bound is not affected by this extension.

3.2 Homomorphims

In this section, we consider schemas with relations only, and no functions. Suppose that $\mathbb{G}$ and $\mathbb{H}$ are two databases over the same schema. Suppose that $\mathbb{H}$ is some database. By $\mathcal{HOM}(\mathbb{H})$ we denote the class of all databases over the schema of $\mathbb{H}$ that map homomorphically to $\mathbb{H}$. In other words, $\mathbb{G} \in \mathcal{HOM}(\mathbb{H})$ if and only if there is a homomorphism $f : \mathbb{G} \to \mathbb{H}$.

The database $\mathbb{H}$ is called the *template* for the class $\mathcal{HOM}(\mathbb{H})$. Examples of $\mathcal{HOM}(\mathbb{H})$ include n-colorable graphs for every n (when $\mathbb{H}$ is an n-clique).

We show that if a class of databases can be defined as $\mathcal{HOM}(\mathbb{H})$ for some $\mathbb{H}$, then it admits an algorithm for emptiness of database-driven systems. As for Theorem 3, we actually prove a stronger result where the template is also part of the input.

THEOREM 4. *The following problem is* PSPACE*-complete.*

> **Input:** *A template database $\mathbb{H}$ and a database-driven system over the schema of $\mathbb{H}$*
>
> **Output:** *Does the system have an accepting run driven by some database in $\mathcal{HOM}(\mathbb{H})$?*

Example 2. Let $\mathbb{H}$ be the graph below, with nodes colored red or white.

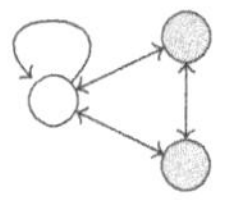

Then a graph $\mathbb{G}$ maps homomorphically to $\mathbb{H}$ if and only if there is no red cycle of odd length in $\mathbb{G}$. On the other hand, the system from Example 1 has a $\mathbb{G}$-driven run if and only if there is some red cycle of odd length in $\mathbb{G}$. Therefore, there is no database $\mathbb{G} \in \mathcal{HOM}(\mathbb{H})$ such that the system has an accepting run driven by $\mathbb{G}$.

The proof of Theorem 4 will be given in Section 4.

Adding data values. As for the previous case, the result of Theorem 4 remains valid if each node of the tree also carries a data value in $\mathbb{N}$ and the query can test these values using equalities or inequalities.

4. THE METHOD

Both decidability results stated in the previous section, namely Theorems 3 and 4, are proved using the same method. The method is presented in this section. The general idea is to add some more predicates or functions to the databases, so that the resulting class of databases has good closure properties, of which the most important is closure under amalgamation.

4.1 Fraïssé classes and amalgamation

An *instance of amalgamation* consists of two embeddings of the same database $\mathbb{C}$ into two other databases:

$$\alpha_1 : \mathbb{C} \to \mathbb{A}_1 \qquad \alpha_2 : \mathbb{C} \to \mathbb{A}_2.$$

A *solution* to the instance is a database $\mathbb{D}$, together with embeddings

$$\beta_1 : \mathbb{A}_1 \to \mathbb{D} \qquad \beta_2 : \mathbb{A}_2 \to \mathbb{D}.$$

such that the diagram below commutes, i.e. $\beta_1 \circ \alpha_1 = \beta_2 \circ \alpha_2$.

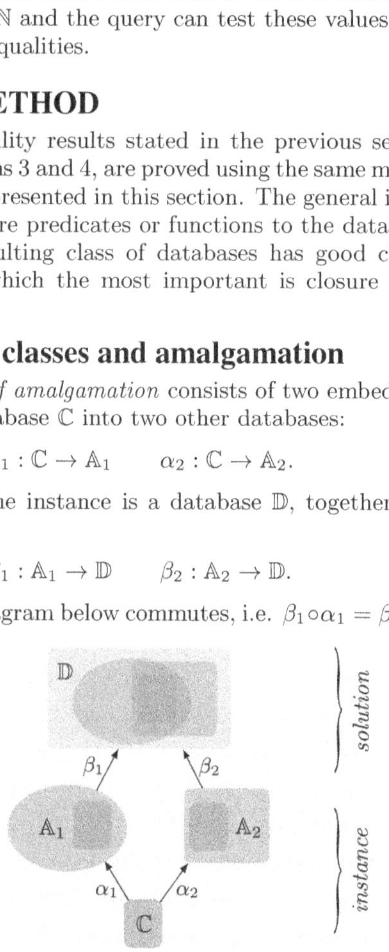

Following [7, Chapter 6, Section 6.1] a *Fraïssé class* is a class $\mathcal{C}$ of databases over a common schema such that:

- $\mathcal{C}$ is *closed under embeddings*: if $\mathbb{C}$ is a database in $\mathcal{C}$ and $\mathbb{D}$ is any database over the same schema that embeds into $\mathbb{C}$, then $\mathbb{D} \in \mathcal{C}$;
- $\mathcal{C}$ is *closed under amalgamation*: every instance of amalgamation, where the databases $\mathbb{A}_1, \mathbb{A}_2, \mathbb{C}$ all belong to $\mathcal{C}$, has a solution $\mathbb{D}$ that belongs to $\mathcal{C}$; and
- $\mathcal{C}$ has the *joint embedding property*: every two databases from $\mathcal{C}$ can be embedded into a single database from $\mathcal{C}$.

Example 3. Consider a schema with one binary relation. The reader can verify that Fraïssé classes over this schema include: all finite linear orders, all finite directed graphs, and all equivalence relations over finite sets. The class of forests (understood as directed graphs) is not closed under amalgamation: the instance depicted below does not have a solution which is a forest.

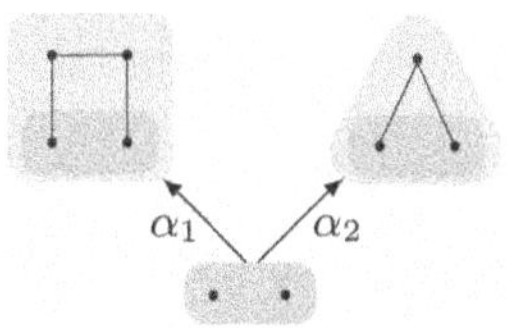

We will show that, under weak assumptions, emptiness for database-driven systems is decidable over Fraïssé classes. The weak assumptions are that membership in the Fraïssé class is decidable, and that if the schema contains function symbols, then sets of elements of bounded size cannot generate databases of unbounded size via images of functions.

Let $\mathbb{C}$ be a database and S a subset of its domain. We say that S *generates* $\mathbb{C}$ if there is no proper substructure $\mathbb{C}' \subsetneq \mathbb{C}$ that contains S. A database is called *n-generated* if its domain has a subset of size n that generates it. The *blowup function* of a Fraïssé class $\mathcal{C}$ is the function

$$\text{blowup}_{\mathcal{C}} : \mathbb{N} \to \mathbb{N} \cup \{\infty\}$$

that maps $n \in \mathbb{N}$ to the least upper bound on the size of n-generated databases in $\mathcal{C}$. Note that in the absence of function symbols in the schema, any n-generated database has size n and therefore $\text{blowup}_{\mathcal{C}}(n) = n$.

THEOREM 5. *Let $\mathcal{C}$ be a Fraïssé class with membership in* PSPACE. *Emptiness of database-driven systems is decidable for $\mathcal{C}$ in space*

$$\log(n) \cdot \textit{poly}(\text{blowup}_{\mathcal{C}}(2k))$$

where n is the number of control states and k is the number of registers in the database-driven system.

PROOF. We describe a nondeterministic algorithm for the emptiness problem. A configuration $(\mathbb{A}, q, \text{val})$ of the system is called *small* if the database $\mathbb{A}$ belongs to $\mathcal{C}$ and is generated by the contents of the registers as described by val. Note that the size of $\mathbb{A}$ is bounded by $\text{blowup}_{\mathcal{C}}(k)$ and by our assumption on membership in $\mathcal{C}$, testing $\mathbb{A} \in \mathcal{C}$ requires space polynomial in $\text{blowup}_{\mathcal{C}}(k)$. Consider two small configurations

$$(\mathbb{A}_{\text{old}}, q_{\text{old}}, \text{val}_{\text{old}}) \qquad (\mathbb{A}_{\text{new}}, q_{\text{new}}, \text{val}_{\text{new}}).$$

We say that there is a *sub-transition* between them if there is a database $\mathbb{A} \in \mathcal{C}$ and two embeddings

$$f_{\text{old}} : \mathbb{A}_{\text{old}} \to \mathbb{A} \qquad f_{\text{new}} : \mathbb{A}_{\text{new}} \to \mathbb{A}$$

such that

$$(\mathbb{A}, q_{\text{old}}, f_{\text{old}} \circ \text{val}_{\text{old}}) \qquad (\mathbb{A}, q_{\text{new}}, f_{\text{new}} \circ \text{val}_{\text{new}})$$

is a transition of the system. Checking if there is a sub-transition requires space polynomial in $\text{blowup}_{\mathcal{C}}(2k)$ because the class is closed under embeddings and we can therefore assume that the database $\mathbb{A}$ is generated by the images of the valuations $f_{\text{old}} \circ \text{val}_{\text{old}}$ and $f_{\text{new}} \circ \text{val}_{\text{new}}$. This leads to the following nondeterministic algorithm.

1. Nondeterministically guess a small configuration where the state is initial.

2. If the state of the current configuration is final, then terminate and accept. Otherwise, nondeterministically guess a new small configuration accessible from the previous one by a sub-transition. Repeat step 2.

The space consumption of the algorithm is as required by the theorem. The proof of its correctness is based on the fact that the class $\mathcal{C}$ is closed under embeddings and under amalgamation. In particular, from a run of our algorithm we construct a run of the system by amalgamating the databases that appear in the small configurations.

Completeness. Consider an accepting run of the system, driven by some database $\mathbb{A} \in \mathcal{C}$:

$$(\mathbb{A}, q_0, \text{val}_0)(\mathbb{A}, q_1, \text{val}_1) \cdots (\mathbb{A}, q_n, \text{val}_n)$$

Let $\mathbb{B}_i$ be the substructure of $\mathbb{A}$ generated by the content of the registers at step i. By closure under embedding, $\mathbb{B}_i \in \mathcal{C}$ for all i. Moreover $\mathbb{A}$ witnesses the fact that there is a sub-transition from $(\mathbb{B}_i, q_i, \text{val}_i)$ to $(\mathbb{B}_{i+1}, q_{i+1}, \text{val}_{i+1})$. Hence our algorithm has an accepting run.

Soundness. Assume that our algorithm has a run:

$$(\mathbb{B}_0, q_0, \text{val}_0)(\mathbb{B}_1, q_1, \text{val}_1) \cdots (\mathbb{B}_n, q_n, \text{val}_n)$$

By induction on n we exhibit a database $\mathbb{B}$ and embeddings $f_i : \mathbb{B}_i \to \mathbb{B}$ such that

$$(\mathbb{B}, q_0, f_0 \circ \text{val}_0)(\mathbb{B}, q_1, f_1 \circ \text{val}_1) \cdots (\mathbb{B}, q_i, f_n \circ \text{val}_n)$$

is a valid run of the database-driven system. For $n = 0$ we take $\mathbb{B} = \mathbb{B}_0$ and f_0 the identity.

Assume we have $\mathbb{B}$ for the run until step $(n-1)$ and consider $(\mathbb{B}_n, q_n, \text{val}_n)$. By definition there is a database $\mathbb{A}$ and embeddings $g_{n-1} : \mathbb{B}_{n-1} \to \mathbb{A}$ and $g_n : \mathbb{B}_n \to \mathbb{A}$ such that there is a transition from $(\mathbb{A}, q_{n-1}, g_{n-1} \circ \text{val}_{n-1})$ to $(\mathbb{A}, q_n, g_n \circ \text{val}_n)$. But we also have an embedding $f_{n-1} : \mathbb{B}_{n-1} \to \mathbb{B}$. By closure under amalgamation, we get a database $\mathbb{A}'$ and embeddings $f : \mathbb{A} \to \mathbb{A}'$ and $g : \mathbb{B} \to \mathbb{A}'$ with good commuting properties. It is now easy to verify that $\mathbb{A}'$ is the database we where looking for with embeddings $g \circ f_i$ for $i < n$ and $f \circ g_n$ for $i = n$.

This proves the correctness of the algorithm. □

Observe that the algorithm does not use the joint embedding property. There are two (related) reasons why we use the joint embedding property: first, it is part of the classical definition of a Fraïssé class; second it is necessary for the Fraenkel-Mostowski approach described in the Section 4.5.

4.2 Semi-Fraïssé classes

For some of the classes we are interested in, Theorem 5 will not work, because the classes are not closed under amalgamation.

Example 4. Consider graphs that are 2-colorable or, equivalently, have no odd-length cycle. This class is $\mathcal{HOM}(\mathbb{H})$ where $\mathbb{H}$ is a 2-clique, over the schema Σ consisting of one binary relation.

This class is not closed under amalgamation. Indeed, there is an odd-length cycle in every solution of the instance of amalgamation depicted in Example 3.

A solution to the problem is to consider not 2-colorable graphs, but 2-*colored* graphs, i.e. graphs with a 2-coloring. This corresponds to considering an extended schema Γ, with the original binary edge relation, and two unary predicates denoting the colors. The 2-clique $\mathbb{H}$ lifts to a canonical graph $\tilde{\mathbb{H}}$ over this schema, where each node gets a different color. The class $\mathcal{HOM}(\tilde{\mathbb{H}})$ is now closed under amalgamation, and is Fraïssé.

In the example above, we added some structure to the databases in order to recover amalgamation. We formalize this strategy below. Let $\mathbb{G}$ be a database over a schema Γ and let Σ be a subset of the schema Γ. The Σ-*projection* $\Sigma(\mathbb{G})$ *of* $\mathbb{G}$ is the same as $\mathbb{G}$, only the interpretation is restricted to the smaller schema. The Σ-projection of a class $\mathcal{C}$ of databases over Γ, denoted by $\Sigma(\mathcal{C})$, is defined pointwise.

The proof of the following lemma is fairly simple as quantifier-free formulas are invariant under extending the domain or the schema. For a class of databases $\mathcal{C}$, by substructures($\mathcal{C}$) we denote the smallest class of databases containing $\mathcal{C}$ that is closed under embeddings.

LEMMA 6. *Let $\mathcal{C}$ be a class of finite databases over a schema Σ. Suppose that $\mathcal{D}$ is a Fraïssé class over a schema $\Gamma \supseteq \Sigma$, such that*

$$\mathcal{C} \subseteq \Sigma(\mathcal{D}) \subseteq \text{substructures}(\mathcal{C}).$$

Then emptiness of database-driven systems over $\mathcal{C}$ is decidable with the same complexity bounds as over $\mathcal{D}$.

A class $\mathcal{C}$ for which there exists a Fraïssé class $\mathcal{D}$ that satisfies the assumptions of the above lemma will be called a *semi-Fraïssé* class. In Example 4, the class $\mathcal{HOM}(\mathbb{H})$ is semi-Fraïssé, as witnessed by $\mathcal{HOM}(\tilde{\mathbb{H}})$.

4.3 HOMs are Semi-Fraïssé

As a simple application of the method, we prove Theorem 4. By Theorem 5 and Lemma 6 it is a consequence of the following lemma:

LEMMA 7. *If $\mathbb{H}$ is a finite database, then $\mathcal{HOM}(\mathbb{H})$ is a semi-Fraïssé class.*

PROOF. The schema Γ is the schema Σ extended by a family $\{h\}_{h \in \mathbb{H}}$ of unary predicates, one for each element of the domain of $\mathbb{H}$. We may view the database $\mathbb{H}$ as a database $\tilde{\mathbb{H}}$ over the extended schema Γ, where a node $h \in \mathbb{H}$ gets the color h. It is easy to see that $\mathcal{HOM}(\mathbb{H})$ is the Σ-projection of $\mathcal{HOM}(\tilde{\mathbb{H}})$. To complete the lemma, we prove that $\mathcal{HOM}(\tilde{\mathbb{H}})$ is Fraïssé.

We only show here amalgamation, the other two properties being trivial. Consider an instance $\mathbb{A}_1, \mathbb{A}_2, \mathbb{C}$ of amalgamation. The desired structure $\mathbb{D}$ is simply constructed from the disjoint union of $\mathbb{A}_1$ and $\mathbb{A}_2$ by identifying the images of $\mathbb{C}$. It remains to show that $\mathbb{D} \in \mathcal{HOM}(\tilde{\mathbb{H}})$. This is witnessed by the mapping sending each node of $\mathbb{D}$ to its color. The reader can verify that this mapping is a homomorphism. □

Note that the schema of $\tilde{\mathbb{H}}$ in the proof of Lemma 7 contains no function symbols, hence we have $\text{blowup}_{\mathcal{HOM}(\tilde{\mathbb{H}})}(n) = n$, and the complexity is PSPACE as desired.

4.4 Data values

In this section we show how Theorems 3 and 4 extend to databases whose nodes are additionally equipped with data values, and where the transition systems may test equality and inequality of data values. The method is again very general – the data values themselves may carry some structure; we only require that the data values come from a homogeneous relational structure. After introducing some preliminary notions, we describe this general setting.

Homogeneous structures. The notion of homogeneity comes from model theory. An infinite structure $\mathbb{F}$ over a schema Σ is called *homogeneous* if every isomorphism $f : \mathbb{F}_1 \to \mathbb{F}_2$ between two finite substructures $\mathbb{F}_1, \mathbb{F}_2$ of $\mathbb{F}$ can be extended to an automorphism $\tilde{f}$ of $\mathbb{F}$.

Homogeneous structures abound; important examples include:

- The set of natural numbers, with the equality relation denoted $\sim$, denoted $\langle \mathbb{N}, \sim \rangle$;
- The rational numbers, with the linear ordering, denoted $\langle \mathbb{Q}, < \rangle$.

A theorem of Fraïssé (see [7, Chapter 6] and also Section 4.5) says that we can associate to every Fraïssé class an infinite countable structure, called the *Fraïssé limit of the Fraïssé class* which is a homogeneous structure.

Data values. Fix a homogeneous structure $\mathbb{F}$, whose elements will model *data values.* We assume that the schema of $\mathbb{F}$ is purely relational, i.e. does not contain function symbols. For instance $\mathbb{F}$ could be the structure $\langle \mathbb{N}, \sim \rangle$ or $\langle \mathbb{Q}, < \rangle$.

Consider a finite database $\mathbb{A}$ over a schema Σ. Let $\lambda : \mathbb{A} \to \mathbb{F}$ be any labeling of the nodes of $\mathbb{A}$ by elements of $\mathbb{F}$. We denote by $\mathbb{A} \otimes \lambda$ the (finite) database extending $\mathbb{A}$ by symbols from the schema of $\mathbb{F}$, which are interpreted in $\mathbb{A} \otimes \lambda$ via the mapping λ: if R is a relation symbol in $\mathbb{F}$, then

$$(\mathbb{A} \otimes \lambda) \models R(x_1, \ldots, x_k) \iff \mathbb{F} \models R(\lambda(x_1), \ldots, \lambda(x_k)).$$

The schema of $\mathbb{A} \otimes \lambda$ is therefore the union of the schema of $\mathbb{A}$ and the schema of $\mathbb{F}$. The database $\mathbb{A} \otimes \lambda$ can be seen as a database whose nodes are additionally labeled by data values, and the database contains relation symbols from $\mathbb{F}$ allowing to compare the data values. If $\mathcal{C}$ is a class of finite databases, then by $\mathcal{C} \otimes \mathbb{F}$ we denote the class of databases of the form $\mathbb{A} \otimes \lambda$, where $\mathbb{A} \in \mathcal{C}$ and λ is a mapping from $\mathbb{A}$ to $\mathbb{F}$. By $\mathcal{C} \odot \mathbb{F}$ we denote subset of $\mathcal{C} \otimes \mathbb{F}$ consisting of those databases $\mathbb{A} \otimes \lambda$, where the mapping λ is *injective*, i.e. each node gets a different data value[1].

[1]We consider the two variants $\otimes$ and $\odot$ because in relational databases, we want every value to be unique – to avoid redundancy – while in XML databases, attributes are used for identifying distinct nodes. See Examples 5 and 6.

Example 5. Let t be a finite tree and let Treedb(t) be the corresponding database. Let $\lambda\colon t \to \langle \mathbb{N}, \sim \rangle$ be a labeling of the nodes of t by natural numbers. Then the database Treedb(t) $\otimes \lambda$ can be seen as a tree equipped with data values (or *attributes*); two nodes x, y store the same attribute if $x \sim y$.

Example 6. Let $\mathbb{G}$ be a finite graph and let $\lambda\colon \mathbb{G} \to \langle \mathbb{N}, \sim \rangle$ be an injective labeling of $\mathbb{G}$ by natural numbers. Then the database $\mathbb{G} \otimes \lambda$ can be seen as a graph whose nodes are natural numbers: because λ is injective, we can identify a node x with the number $\lambda(x)$. If $\mathcal{G}$ denotes the class of all graphs, then the structures in $\mathcal{G} \odot \langle \mathbb{N}, \sim \rangle$ can be interpreted as graphs on natural numbers. Similarly, the structures in $\mathcal{G} \odot \langle \mathbb{Q}, < \rangle$ can be interpreted as graphs on rational numbers; in particular, their nodes are linearly ordered.

Using the theorem of Fraïssé and a construction for combining two Fraïssé classes into one class, we can obtain the following proposition whose proof is omitted here.

PROPOSITION 1. *Let $\mathbb{F}$ be a purely relational homogeneous structure, such that deciding whether a finite database embeds into $\mathbb{F}$ can be done in* PSPACE. *Then, for any Fraïssé class $\mathcal{C}$ (over any schema), the classes $\mathcal{C} \otimes \mathbb{F}$ and $\mathcal{C} \odot \mathbb{F}$ are Fraïssé classes, with the same blowup function as $\mathcal{C}$.*

As a consequence of Proposition 1 and Lemma 7 we get the following extension of Theorem 4.

COROLLARY 8. *The following problem is decidable in* PSPACE:

Input: *A relational database $\mathbb{H}$ a database-driven system over the union of the schemas of $\mathbb{H}$ and $\mathbb{F}$.*

Output: *Is there a database $(\mathbb{A} \otimes \lambda) \in \mathcal{HOM}(\mathbb{H}) \odot \mathbb{F}$ and an accepting run of the system driven by $\mathbb{A}$?*

Special cases of this result – without the condition $\mathbb{A} \in \mathcal{HOM}(\mathbb{H})$ – have been proved earlier for $\mathbb{F} = \langle \mathbb{N}, \sim \rangle$ in [5] and $\mathbb{F} = \langle \mathbb{Q}, < \rangle$ in [4].

Our abstract machinery applies also to database-driven systems, where the databases are trees with data values.

THEOREM 9. *The following problem is decidable:*

Input: *A tree automaton defining a language L of trees labeled by an alphabet A, and a database-driven system over the schema* TreeSchema(A) $\cup \{\sim\}$.

Output: *Is there a tree $t \in L$, a labeling λ of t by elements of $\mathbb{N}$, and an accepting run of the system driven by* Treedb(t) $\otimes \lambda$?

For a fixed tree automaton, the problem is PSPACE*-complete. When both the tree automaton and the system are input, the problem is in* EXPSPACE.

Remark 1. Theorem 9 works for any countable homogeneous structure $\mathbb{F}$ such that testing whether a given finite database $\mathbb{A}$ embeds into $\mathbb{F}$ can be done in PSPACE. For instance $\langle \mathbb{N}, \sim \rangle$ could be replaced by $\langle \mathbb{Q}, < \rangle$. Actually it only matters that substructures($\mathbb{F}$) is a Fraïssé class. In particular, as

$$\text{substructures}(\langle \mathbb{N}, < \rangle) = \text{substructures}(\langle \mathbb{Q}, < \rangle),$$

the result also hold for $\mathbb{F} = \langle \mathbb{N}, < \rangle$. Similarly, by considering semi-Fraïssé classes instead of Fraïssé, the result also works with $\langle \mathbb{N}, < \rangle$ augmented with constants, thus capturing the setting of [9].

4.5 Fraenkel-Mostowski sets

In this section, we comment on a bigger picture that contains Theorem 5, but also implies other results, such as emptiness of database-driven systems with pushdowns. To simplify the discussion, we only focus on decidability and not on complexity. The bigger picture is called nominal sets, or Fraenkel-Mostowski sets.

The Fraïssé limit. We begin by observing that instead of talking about a class of finite databases, we can talk about a single limit structure (which is usually infinite so it should not be called a database). The theorem of Fraïssé says that if $\mathcal{C}$ is a Fraïssé class, then there exists a single countable (but usually infinite) homogeneous structure $\mathbb{F}$ – the *Fraïssé limit* of $\mathcal{C}$ – such that the databases in $\mathcal{C}$ are exactly the finitely generated substructures of $\mathbb{F}$. Fraïssé limits have many good model-theoretic properties, for instance they are ω-categorical.

What is the connection with database-driven systems? A run of a database-driven system is finite, and therefore visits only finitely many elements of a database with its registers. It follows that a database-driven system has a run driven by some finite database in $\mathcal{C}$ if and only if it has a run driven by the Fraïssé limit of $\mathcal{C}$. Therefore, instead of studying emptiness over a class $\mathcal{C}$, we could study emptiness of a system that uses registers to store elements of the Fraïssé limit.

Fraenkel-Mostowski sets and their automata. Automata that store values from a Fraïssé limit in their registers have already been studied in [2], as part of a more general framework called *Fraenkel-Mostowski sets.* From the results in [2] it follows that emptiness for such automata is decidable, which implies the decidability result in Theorem 5. (We included a proof of Theorem 5 to make this paper self-contained, and also to get the precise complexity.) Apart from finite automata with registers, the Fraenkel-Mostowski framework contains other computational devices with decidable emptiness, which can then be used to get decidability results for extensions of database-driven systems. The results concerning these devices include:

- Emptiness is decidable for pushdown automata, which are allowed to store elements of a Fraïssé limit both in their state and on the pushdown, see [2]. This implies decidable emptiness for a natural pushdown extension of database-driven systems.
- Emptiness is decidable for tree automata, where a configuration can have more than one successor configuration. This implies decidable emptiness for a natural branching extension of database-driven systems.
- Under additional assumptions, which hold for regular tree languages but not for equivalence relations and HOMs, even certain alternating automata have decidable emptiness [1]. This implies decidable emptiness for a certain alternating extension of database-driven systems.

We would like to point out that the first two results (pushdown automata and tree automata) can be easily obtained without using the abstract framework of Fraenkel-Mostowski sets (this is no longer true for alternating automata, where the proof is quite involved and follows the lines of [3]). We believe, however, that seeing database-driven systems as a special case of automata in Fraenkel-Mostowski sets gives a uniform explanation for the decidability results. We plan to given a more detailed discussion of the Fraenkel-Mostowski connection, including a precise definition of the extended database-driven models, in the full version of this paper.

5. REGULAR TREE LANGUAGES

In this section, we prove Theorem 3, which is the main technical result of the paper. The theorem says that emptiness is decidable for database-driven systems over regular tree languages. Since the proof is quite technical, we begin by illustrating the main ideas in the case of words.

5.1 Regular Word Languages

Like in the case of trees, to a word w over an alphabet A, we associate a database Worddb(w), where the domain is the positions of the word, there are unary predicates $\{a(x)\}_{a \in A}$ for the labels, and a binary predicate $x < y$ for the natural order on word positions. Call WordSchema(A) the schema of this database.

THEOREM 10. *The following problem is* PSPACE*-complete.*

> **Input:** *A regular word language $L \subseteq A^*$, given by an nondeterministic finite automaton, and a database-driven system over the schema* WordSchema(A).
>
> **Output:** *Is there a word $w \in L$ and an accepting run of the system driven by* Worddb(w)*?*

The rest of Section 5.1 is devoted to showing the above theorem. Fix a regular word language $L \subseteq A^*$. Let Q be the states of an NFA that recognizes L. Define

$$\text{Worddb}(L) = \{\text{Worddb}(w) : w \in L\}.$$

For a class of databases $\mathcal{C}$, let $\mathcal{C}^*$ denote the closure of $\mathcal{C}$ under disjoint unions. The point of studying $\mathcal{C}^*$ is that it is guaranteed to have the joint embedding property. In the specific case of $\mathcal{C} = \text{Worddb}(L)$, the disjoint union is defined so that positions from different words are incomparable with respect to $<$.

We will prove that Worddb$(L)^*$ is a semi-Fraïssé class, and therefore has decidable emptiness for database-driven systems. The following lemma reduces emptiness from Worddb(L) to Worddb$(L)^*$.

LEMMA 11. *For every database-driven system $\mathcal{S}$, there is a database-driven system $\mathcal{S}^*$, such that emptiness of $\mathcal{S}$ over* Worddb(L) *is equivalent to emptiness of $\mathcal{S}^*$ over* Worddb$(L)^*$.

PROOF SKETCH. Define the system $\mathcal{S}^*$ as extending $\mathcal{S}$ with a new register. The idea is that this new register stores some position of the word. The new register does not change contents during the whole run, and all other registers are required to be comparable with the new register in the order $<$. Apart from this, the other registers behave as in the system $\mathcal{S}$. Even when driven by a disjoint union of words, the registers will only use positions from one of the words. □

From this point, our aim is to prove that Worddb$(L)^*$ is a semi-Fraïssé class. In particular, we do not consider database-driven systems any more.

Fix an automaton $\mathcal{A}$ recognizing the language L. We assume the automaton does not contain useless states: every state in the automaton is reachable from some initial state, and that from every state an accepting state can be reached. We also assume that for each state q of the automaton, there is a unique letter a that can be read in that state, i.e. a unique letter such that the automaton contains transitions of the form $p \xrightarrow{a} q$ (the state q is not unique, of course). This assumption can be enforced by splitting each state into one copy for each letter of the input alphabet. Denote by $\rightarrow$ the one-step reachability relation on states in the automaton, i.e. $p \rightarrow q$ holds if there is a transition $p \xrightarrow{a} q$. Let $\rightarrow^+$ be the transitive closure of this relation, i.e. reachability via nonempty words. We will be interested in strongly connected components of this relation, which we call *components*. We adopt the convention that if a state q is not reachable from itself, then it is also in a component, which contains only the state q. Thanks to this convention, the components form a partition of the states of the automaton. We denote components by Γ.

We define a *pre-run* of the automaton to be an input word, together with a labeling of positions by states, where position x gets the state after reading it. (In particular, the first state of the run, before reading any position, does not appear in the labeling.) A pre-run, call it ρ, is interpreted as a database, denoted by Rundb(ρ) as follows:

- There are the original predicates $\{a(x)\}_{a \in A}$ and $x < y$ for the input word. In other words, Rundb(ρ) extends the database Worddb(w), where w is the input word in the run.
- There are unary state predicates $\{q(x)\}_{q \in Q}$ for the states in the run.
- For each component Γ of the automaton, there is a unary function *leftmost*$_\Gamma(x)$ that maps a position x to the leftmost position before x that has a state in component Γ. If there is no such appearance, then *leftmost*$_\Gamma(x)$ is x. Likewise, we have a *rightmost*$_\Gamma(x)$ unary function[2]. We use the name *pointers* for the *leftmost* and *rightmost* functions.

Define $\mathcal{C}$ to be the closure under substructures of

$$\{\text{Rundb}(\rho) : \rho \text{ is a run.}\}.$$

PROPOSITION 2. *$\mathcal{C}$ is closed under amalgamation.*

Before showing the proposition, we show how it implies Theorem 10.

PROOF OF THEOREM 10. The theorem will follow from the items below thanks to Lemmas 6 and 11.

1. It is not difficult to see that the projection assumption (when projecting a pre-run to its input word) in Lemma 6 is satisfied:
$$\text{Worddb}(L)^* \subseteq \text{WordSchema}(\mathcal{C})^* \subseteq \\ \subseteq \textit{substructures}(\text{Worddb}(L)^*)$$
2. $\mathcal{C}^*$ is a Fraïssé class. The class $\mathcal{C}^*$ is closed under substructures by definition. It is also closed under isomorphism. The joint embedding property is easy because we can simply take disjoint unions[3]. Closure of

[2]It would seem more natural to define *leftmost*$_\Gamma$ and *rightmost*$_\Gamma$ as nullary functions, i.e. constants. We choose unary functions for two reasons: to make the tree case more similar, and to make disjoint unions of runs easier.

[3]The joint embedding property is the reason why we work with $\mathcal{C}^*$ and Worddb$(L)^*$ instead of $\mathcal{C}$ and Worddb(L).

a class under amalgamation is preserved by the operation $\mathcal{C} \mapsto \mathcal{C}^*$, and therefore $\mathcal{C}^*$ is closed under amalgamation by Proposition 2. In conclusion, $\mathcal{C}^*$ is a Fraïssé class, and so $\text{Worddb}(L)^*$ is a semi-Fraïssé class.

3. The blowup of $\mathcal{C}^*$ is small. There are at most $|Q|$ components in the automaton. Since we have two unary functions per component, the blowup function for $\mathcal{C}^*$ is at most $n \mapsto 2|Q| \cdot n$. This gives the PSPACE complexity bound.

□

We now resume the proof of Proposition 2. We will use the following characterization of $\mathcal{C}$.

LEMMA 12. *Let ρ be a pre-run, where the states are $q_1, \dots, q_n$ listed from left to right. Then* $\text{Rundb}(\rho) \in \mathcal{C}$ *if and only if*

$$q_1 \to^+ q_2 \to^+ \cdots \to^+ q_n$$

Instead of proving that $\mathcal{C}$ is closed under amalgamation, we prove that it is closed under *inclusion amalgamation.* An instance of inclusion amalgamation consists of two databases $\mathbb{A}$ and $\mathbb{B}$ that are *consistent*, i.e. the functions and predicates are defined the same way on the elements that appear in both domains. A solution of inclusion amalgamation is a database $\mathbb{C}$ that contains both $\mathbb{A}$ and $\mathbb{B}$ as substructures.

LEMMA 13. *Let $\mathcal{C}$ be a class of structures closed under isomorphism. Then $\mathcal{C}$ is closed under amalgamation if and only if it is closed under inclusion amalgamation.*

PROOF OF PROPOSITION 2. The proof is more wordy than it needs to be, because we want it to have the same structure as the proof for the more complicated case of trees.

Consider an instance of inclusion amalgamation in the class $\mathcal{C}$, i.e. two pre-runs ρ_1 and ρ_2 such that the databases $\text{Rundb}(\rho_1)$ and $\text{Rundb}(\rho_2)$ are consistent and in $\mathcal{C}$. Define $\text{Rundb}(\rho)$ to be the common part, i.e. the intersection of the two databases, which is a substructure of both, so it also belongs to $\mathcal{C}$.

We need to show a database in $\mathcal{C}$ that contains both $\text{Rundb}(\rho_1)$ and $\text{Rundb}(\rho_2)$ as substructures. The proof is by induction on the number of elements in ρ_1 not in ρ. In the induction base $\text{Rundb}(\rho_1)$ is a substructure of $\text{Rundb}(\rho_2)$, and we already have a solution to amalgamation.

For the induction step, suppose that y is in the domain of ρ_1, but not in ρ. Choose y so that its preceding position in ρ_1, call it x, is already in ρ. The situation is illustrated in the following picture:

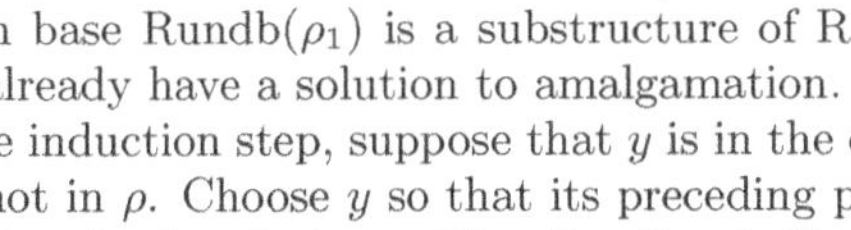

In the picture, the positions of ρ_1 are colored, the positions of ρ_2 have a black border, the positions of ρ are colored and have a black border. To advance the induction, we add y to ρ_2, as in the following picture:

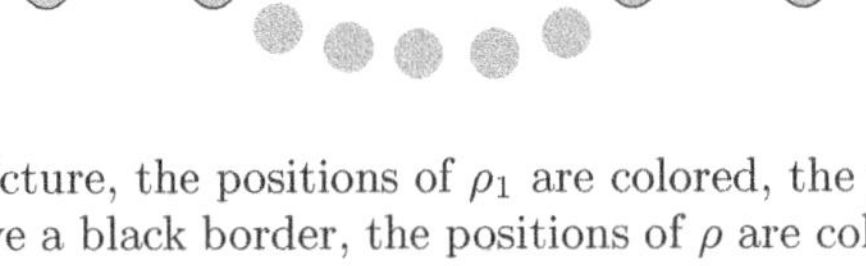

Define a pre-run ρ_2', by adding position y (with its state and input label) to ρ_2 right after x, with the same state as y. We claim that

1. $\text{Rundb}(\rho_2') \in \mathcal{C}$;
2. $\text{Rundb}(\rho_2) \subseteq \text{Rundb}(\rho_2')$;
3. $\text{Rundb}(\rho_1)$ and $\text{Rundb}(\rho_2')$ are consistent.

If we prove the claims above, then we are done. This is because $\text{Rundb}(\rho_1)$ and $\text{Rundb}(\rho_2')$ are an instance of inclusion amalgamation with a smaller induction parameter. The induction assumption says that some database in $\mathcal{C}$ contains both $\text{Rundb}(\rho_1)$ and $\text{Rundb}(\rho_2')$, and therefore it also contains $\text{Rundb}(\rho_1)$ and $\text{Rundb}(\rho_2)$.

Let Γ be the component of the state in y. Consider the values of the pointers $leftmost_\Gamma$ that are assigned to the position x in the three databases $\text{Rundb}(\rho)$, $\text{Rundb}(\rho_1)$ and $\text{Rundb}(\rho_2)$. Because the databases are consistent, these are all the same position, i.e.

$$leftmost^{\rho}_{\Gamma}(x) = leftmost^{\rho_1}_{\Gamma}(x) = leftmost^{\rho_2}_{\Gamma}(x)$$

Call the position above y_{left}, it is before y in ρ_1. Likewise, we define a position y_{right}.

To prove $\text{Rundb}(\rho_2') \in \mathcal{C}$, we use Lemma 12. By this lemma, in the run ρ_2, all positions between y_{left} and y_{right} have states in component Γ. The position y is added between these positions, so it does not violate the condition from Lemma 12.

To prove $\text{Rundb}(\rho_2) \subseteq \text{Rundb}(\rho_2')$, we only need to show that the functions in $\text{Rundb}(\rho_2')$ are defined the same way for the positions from $\text{Rundb}(\rho_2)$. This is not difficult to see, because in $\text{Rundb}(\rho_2')$ there is one new position, which is both followed and preceded by states in the same component. The same argument shows that $\text{Rundb}(\rho_1)$ and $\text{Rundb}(\rho_2')$ are consistent. □

5.2 Proof Strategy for Regular Tree Languages

We now resume the proof of Theorem 3, which says that emptiness is decidable for database-driven systems over regular tree languages. We use the same proof strategy as for words. For a tree language L, define

$$\text{Treedb}(L) = \{\text{Treedb}(t) : t \in L\}.$$

Like in the case of words, we will have a class $\mathcal{C}$ that represents substructures of runs.

5.3 Tree automata and their components

We begin by presenting the model of tree automata that we use. Out of the many equivalent models of automata on unranked trees, we choose a model where the runs are easier to pump.

A *tree automaton* consists of:

- An input alphabet A. The automaton is used to accept or reject trees labeled by A.
- A set of states Q. A *run* of the automaton over an input tree is a labeling of the tree nodes by states from Q, subject to some local consistency requirements described below.
- As in the word case, we assume that for each state q, there is a unique input letter a that can be used in that state.

- The automaton has distinguished subsets of: *leaf states*, which are the only states allowed for leaves, *root states*, which are the only states allowed for the root, and *rightmost states*, which are the only states allowed for rightmost children.
- A binary first-child relation $\rightarrow_{firstchild}$ on states. In a run, if a node has state q and its leftmost child has state p, then $p \rightarrow_{firstchild} q$ holds.
- A binary next-sibling relation $\rightarrow_{nextsibling}$ on states. In a run, if a node has state q and its next sibling has state p, then $p \rightarrow_{nextsibling} q$ holds.

A tree is accepted by the automaton if it admits some run (we do not distinguish between runs and accepting runs). Let us fix for the rest of Section 5 a tree automaton as described above, which recognizes a tree language L.

Components. Define two binary relations on states of the automaton: a relation

$$\rightarrow_h \stackrel{def}{=} \rightarrow^+_{nextsibling}$$

that corresponds to following sibling, and a relation

$$\rightarrow_v \stackrel{def}{=} \left(\rightarrow_{firstchild} \circ \rightarrow^*_{nextsibling} \right)^+$$

that corresponds to descendant. We use the name *descendant component* for strongly connected components of the relation $\rightarrow_v$, and the name *horizontal component* for strongly connected components of the relation $\rightarrow_h$. Again, we adopt the convention that when a state is not reachable from itself by $\rightarrow_v$, then it still forms a (singleton) descendant component, likewise for horizontal component. We distinguish two kinds of descendant components:

- A descendant component Γ is called *branching* if in some run, some node with state in Γ has two children with states in Γ.
- A descendant component Γ is called *linear* otherwise. This means that in every run, every node with state in Γ has at most one child with a state in Γ.

For a descendant component, define a set of states $left(\Gamma)$ as follows. Suppose that in some run, a node x has two descendants y and z, such that z is before y in document order, and is not on the path from x to y. If the states in x and y are in Γ, then we put the state in z into the set $left(\Gamma)$. The set $right(\Gamma)$ is defined similarly.

5.4 The class $\mathcal{C}$

We are now ready to define the class $\mathcal{C}$, which contains databases representing runs.

The pointers. Define a *pre-run* to be any tree where each node is labeled by a letter $a \in A$, as well as a state $q \in Q$ such that a is the unique letter that can be read in state q. A pre-run need not satisfy the consistency conditions in the definition of a tree automaton run. A node x in a pre-run is called *component maximal* if none of its children have a state in the same descendant component. For a pre-run ρ, we define $\mathrm{Rundb}(\rho)$ to be the following database.

- We have the standard database $\mathrm{Treedb}(t)$ for the input tree t: the node labels, the descendant order, the document order, and the closest common ancestor function.
- For each state q, there is a unary function $leftmost_q(x)$ defined as follows. If x is a component maximal node, then $leftmost_q(x)$ maps x to the leftmost child with a state in q. If x is not component maximal, or it has no children with state q, then the function is "undefined", which is encoded by $leftmost_q(x) = x$.
- In the same way, we define a function $rightmost_q(x)$, but for the rightmost child with a state in Γ.
- For each descendant component Γ, there is a unary function $ancestormost_\Gamma(x)$, whose value is the last node on the path from x to the root that has label q. If there is no such node, then the function is "undefined", which is encoded by $ancestormost_\Gamma(x) = x$.
- Suppose that x is a node whose state is in a linear descendant component Γ. Then $descendantmost(x)$ maps x to the unique descendant of x that has a state in Γ, and has no children with states in Γ. If the state of x is not in a linear descendant component, then the function is "undefined", which is encoded by $down(x) = x$.

The class $\mathcal{C}$. Define $\mathcal{C}$ to be the closure under substructures of the class

$$\{\mathrm{Rundb}(\rho) : \rho \text{ is a run of the automaton}\}.$$

In other words, a database belongs to $\mathcal{C}$ if it can be extracted from a run (not a pre-run) so that nodes are extracted together with the values of their pointers. Following the same proof as in Theorem 10, to prove Theorem 3, it will be sufficient to prove the following results, whose proofs are omitted here.

LEMMA 14. *The blowup function for $\mathcal{C}^*$ is $n \mapsto c{\cdot}n$, where the constant c is exponential in the state space Q.*

PROPOSITION 3. *$\mathcal{C}$ is closed under amalgamation.*

6. UNDECIDABLE MODELS

We consider in this section several ways of extending the model. In most cases, the extensions lead to undecidability. For instance, if the trees are additionally equipped with the child relation or the sibling relation, then the emptiness problem becomes undecidable, even for a fixed tree language. A more interesting question is what happens if we extend the expressive power of the logics used for describing the transitions of the system. These extensions also quickly lead to undecidability.

6.1 Child and sibling axes

Adding axes such as *next sibling* or *child* leads to undecidability. The reason is that already for unary words with the successor relation on positions, we get undecidability. More precisely, a unary word w can be viewed as a structure whose domain is the set $1, 2, \ldots, |w|$ of positions of w, and $succ(x, y)$ holds if $y - x = 1$.

FACT 15. *Let L be any infinite set of words over the unary alphabet, viewed as structures over the schema consisting of the binary symbol succ. Then, the following problem is undecidable.*

Input: *A database-driven system over the schema consisting of succ.*

Output: *Is there a word $w \in L$ and an accepting run of the system driven by the word w?*

PROOF SKETCH. Using one register, the system can simulate a counter of a counter machine: a transition can increment or decrement the counter using the relation *succ*. There are no zero tests, but this can be simulated by keeping one register z that is never changed (using $z_{\text{old}} = z_{\text{new}}$ as a conjunct in all rules); then a zero test of the counter is simulated by the formula $x = z$. Since the halting problem is undecidable for two-counter machines, the fact follows. □

It follows immediately from Fact 15 that in the presence of the *child* or *next sibling* axis it is undecidable whether a database-driven has an accepting run.

The sibling axis.

We show that even extending the set of predicates by the sibling relation also leads to undecidability. Formally, we model a tree t as a database with two predicates: the closest common ancestor $\wedge$ and the transitive, symmetric and irreflexive binary *sibling* relation (the document order nor the unary predicates are needed for this undecidability result).

FACT 16. *There exists a regular tree language L over a unary alphabet, such that the following problem is undecidable:*

Input: *A database-driven system over the schema consisting of $\wedge$ and sibling.*

Output: *Is there a tree $t \in L$ and an accepting run of the system driven by the tree t?*

PROOF SKETCH. The language L is defined as the set of trees of the form t_n, where $n \in \mathbb{N}$ and t_n is the tree depicted in the left-hand side of the figure below, of height n.

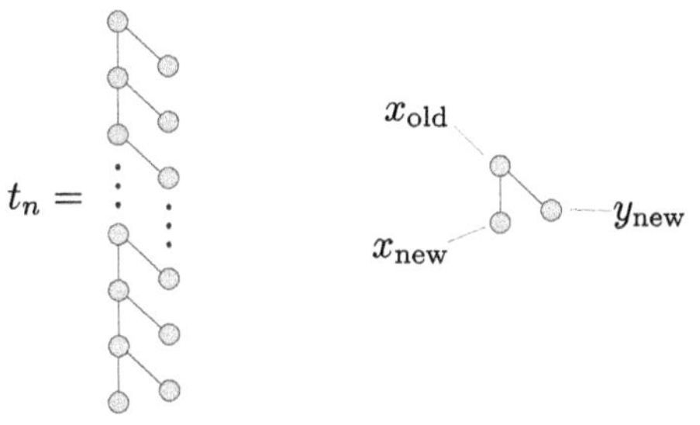

The reduction is again from counter machines. We show that a system can simulate a counter using a register x.

To simulate incrementation of the counter, the machine uses an auxiliary register y (see right-hand side of the figure above), and follows a transition whose guard is the following formula:

$$(x_{\text{old}} = (x_{\text{new}} \wedge y_{\text{new}})) \quad \wedge \quad sibling(x_{\text{new}}, y_{\text{new}})$$

These conditions guarantee that x_{new} is a child of x_{old} (they do not guarantee that x_{new} is the left child, as is the case in the figure, but this is not necessary).

Decrementation of a counter is obtained by swapping "old" with "new" in the guard. As in the proof of Fact 15, using additional counters, one can simulate zero tests. This way, a database-driven system using the predicates $\wedge$ and the successor relation can simulate a counter machine. □

Remark 2. We don't know whether emptiness is decidable for database-driven systems over the schema consisting of the sibling relation, the document order and the descendant order, but not the closest common ancestor (when both a regular language L and a system are given on input).

6.2 Rules that are not existential

A legitimate question is whether one can extend the expressivity of our model by extending the power of the formulas defining the transitions of the system, for instance by allowing first-order formulas, while preserving the decidability of the emptiness problem.

We have seen in Fact 2 that systems with transitions guarded by existential formulas can be simulated by systems where the transitions are guarded by quantifier-free formulas. However, already allowing boolean combinations of existential formulas quickly leads to undecidability. For instance, in the tree case, this is a consequence of Fact 15. Indeed, using boolean combinations of existential formulas, one can define the *child* axis:

$$child(x, y) \iff x \preceq_v y \quad \wedge \quad \neg\exists z: \quad x \prec_v z \prec_v y$$

6.3 Data tree patterns

We also considered the setting where the queries are data tree patterns. A data tree pattern selects data values within a tree, depending on the existence of nodes whose positions verify the tree pattern (we use an injective semantics for tree patterns, where each node of the tree pattern must match a different node of the tree). With our terminology, a tree pattern is a special case of an existential formula; the hope being that systems using boolean combination of tree patterns would be decidable.

To make this setting fit into our formalism, we assume the system is over DataTreeSchema(A) and has rules guarded by boolean combinations of formulas of the following form (called tree pattern formulas):

$$\delta(\bar{x}_{\text{new}}, \bar{x}_{\text{old}}) \quad : \quad \exists^{\neq} v_1, v_2, \ldots, v_l \quad \phi(v_1, \ldots, v_l),$$

where the notation $\exists^{\neq}$ implies that the nodes $v_1, \ldots, v_l$ are pairwise distinct (to reflect the injective semantics of tree patterns), and ϕ is a conjunction of conjuncts of the following three possible forms:

$$v_i \sim x_j, \qquad v_i \preceq_v v_j, \qquad \lambda(v_i).$$

Note that the restriction on ϕ implies that a formula δ cannot (directly) tell whether two registers x and y of the system point to the same node; it can only test whether they have the same datavalue.

Example 7. Consider trees labeled by $\{a, b, r\}$. The following tree pattern:

$$\exists^{\neq} v, l_a, l_b, r_a, r_b. \ \Big(a(l_a) \wedge b(l_b) \wedge a(r_a) \wedge b(r_b) \wedge r(v)\Big) \wedge$$
$$(v \preceq_v l_a \preceq_v l_b) \wedge (v \preceq_v r_a \preceq_v r_b) \wedge (u_a \sim x_{\text{old}}) \quad \wedge \quad (u_a \sim x_{\text{new}})$$

can be graphically represented as follows (dashed lines represent descendant relationships):

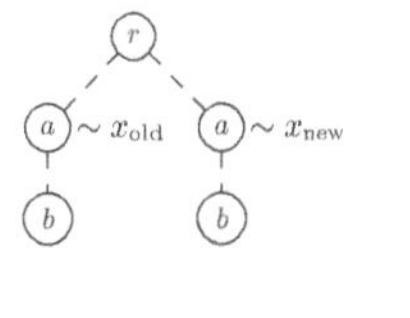

It turns out that restricting the queries to boolean combinations of tree patterns is not sufficient to regain decidability.

THEOREM 17. *There is a language of A-labeled trees L such that the following decision problem is undecidable.*

> **Input:** *A database-driven system over the schema $\{\preceq_v, \sim, \{a\}_{a\in A}\}$, where transitions are boolean combinations of tree pattern queries.*
>
> **Output:** *Is there a tree $t \in L$ and an accepting run of the system driven by the tree t?*

Having described the applications and limitations of our framework, we end this paper.

7. REFERENCES

[1] Mikołaj Bojańczyk, Laurent Braud, Bartek Klin, and Slawomir Lasota. Towards nominal computation. In *Symp. on Principles of Programming Languages (POPL)*, pages 401–412, 2012.

[2] Mikołaj Bojańczyk, Bartek Klin, and Slawomir Lasota. Automata with group actions. In *Symp. on Logic in Computer Science (LICS)*, pages 355–364, 2011.

[3] Stéphane Demri and Ranko Lazic. LTL with the freeze quantifier and register automata. In *Symp. on Logic in Computer Science (LICS)*, pages 17–26, 2006.

[4] Alin Deutsch, Richard Hull, Fabio Patrizi, and Victor Vianu. Automatic verification of data-centric business processes. In *Intl. Conf. on Database Theory (ICDT)*, 2009.

[5] Alin Deutsch, Liying Sui, and Victor Vianu. Specification and verification of data-driven web applications. *J. Comput. Syst. Sci.*, 73(3):442–474, 2007.

[6] Alin Deutsch, Liying Sui, Victor Vianu, and Dayou Zhou. A system for specification and verification of interactive, data-driven web applications. In *Intl. Conf. on Management of Data (SIGMOD)*, 2006.

[7] W. Hodges. *A shorter model theory.* Cambridge Univerity Press, 1997.

[8] Sheila A. McIlraith, Tran Cao Son, and Honglei Zeng. Semantic web services. *IEEE Intelligent Systems*, 16(2):46–53, 2001.

[9] Luc Segoufin and Szymon Toruńczyk. Automata based verification over linearly ordered data domains. In *Intl. Symp. on Theoretical Aspects of Computer Science (STACS)*, 2011.

[10] Victor Vianu. Automatic verification of database-driven systems: a new frontier. In *Intl. Conf. on Database Theory (ICDT)*, pages 1–13, 2009.

When is Naïve Evaluation Possible?

Amélie Gheerbrant
School of Informatics
University of Edinburgh
agheerbr@inf.ed.ac.uk

Leonid Libkin
School of Informatics
University of Edinburgh
libkin@inf.ed.ac.uk

Cristina Sirangelo
LSV, ENS-Cachan
INRIA & CNRS
sirangel@lsv.ens-cachan.fr

ABSTRACT

The term naïve evaluation refers to evaluating queries over incomplete databases as if nulls were usual data values, i.e., to using the standard database query evaluation engine. Since the semantics of query answering over incomplete databases is that of certain answers, we would like to know when naïve evaluation computes them: i.e., when certain answers can be found without inventing new specialized algorithms. For relational databases it is well known that unions of conjunctive queries possess this desirable property, and results on preservation of formulae under homomorphisms tell us that within relational calculus, this class cannot be extended under the open-world assumption.

Our goal here is twofold. First, we develop a general framework that allows us to determine, for a given semantics of incompleteness, classes of queries for which naïve evaluation computes certain answers. Second, we apply this approach to a variety of semantics, showing that for many classes of queries beyond unions of conjunctive queries, naïve evaluation makes perfect sense under assumptions different from open-world. Our key observations are: (1) naïve evaluation is equivalent to monotonicity of queries with respect to a semantics-induced ordering, and (2) for most reasonable semantics, such monotonicity is captured by preservation under various types of homomorphisms. Using these results we find classes of queries for which naïve evaluation works, e.g., positive first-order formulae for the closed-world semantics. Even more, we introduce a general relation-based framework for defining semantics of incompleteness, show how it can be used to capture many known semantics and to introduce new ones, and describe classes of first-order queries for which naïve evaluation works under such semantics.

Categories and Subject Descriptors. H.2.1 [**Database Management**]: Logical Design—*Data Models*; H.2.1 [**Database Management**]: Languages—*Query Languages*; H.2.4 [**Database Management**]: Systems—*Query Processing*
General Terms. Theory, Languages, Algorithms
Keywords. Incompleteness, naive tables/evaluation, certain answers, orderings, homomorphisms

1. INTRODUCTION

Database applications need to handle incomplete data; this is especially true these days due to the proliferation of data obtained as the result of integrating or exchanging data sets, or data found on the Web. At the same time, there is a huge gap between our theoretical knowledge and the handling of incompleteness in practice:

- In SQL, the design of null-related features is one of the most criticized aspects of the language [13], due to the oversimplification of the model (which even leads to paradoxical behavior: it is consistent with SQL's semantics that $|X| > |Y|$ and $X - Y = \emptyset$, if the set Y contains nulls!)
- In theory, we understand that the proper way of evaluating queries on incomplete databases is to find *certain answers* to them. Unfortunately, for many classes of queries, even within first-order logic, this is an intractable problem [2], and even when it is tractable, there is no guarantee the algorithms can be easily implementable on top of commercial DBMSs [15].

Despite this seemingly enormous gap, there is one instance when theoretical approaches and functionalities of practical systems converge nicely. For some types of queries, evaluating them on the incomplete database itself (i.e. as if nulls were the usual data values) does produce certain answers. This is usually referred to as *naïve evaluation* [1, 19]. To give an example, consider databases with *naïve nulls* (also called marked nulls), that appear most commonly in integration and exchange scenarios, and that can very easily be supported by commercial RDBMSs. Two such relations are shown below, with nulls indicated by the symbol $\bot$ with subscripts:

R:

A	B
1	$\bot_1$
$\bot_2$	$\bot_3$

S:

B	C
$\bot_1$	4
$\bot_3$	5

Suppose we have a conjunctive query $\pi_{AC}(R \bowtie S)$ or, equivalently, $\varphi(x, y) = \exists z \, (R(x, z) \wedge S(z, y))$. Naïve evaluation says: evaluate the query directly on R and S, proceed as if nulls were usual values; they are equal only if they are syntactically the same (for instance $\bot_1 = \bot_1$ but $\bot_1 \neq \bot_2$). Then evaluating the above query results in two tuples: $(1, 4)$, and $(\bot_2, 5)$. Tuples with nulls cannot be certain answers, so we only keep the tuple $(1, 4)$.

One does not need any new functionalities of the DBMS to find the result of naïve evaluation (in fact most implementations of marked nulls are such that equality tests for them are really the syntactic equality). This is good, but in general, naïve evaluation need not compute certain answers. Recall that these are answers which hold true in all possible complete databases represented by the incomplete one, under some semantics of incompleteness.

For the query above, the tuple $(1, 4)$ is however the certain answer, under the common open-world semantics (to be properly defined later). This is true because [19] showed that if Q is a union of conjunctive queries, then naïve evaluation works for it (i.e., computes certain answers). This result is not so easy to extend: for instance, [24] showed that under the open-world semantics, if naïve evaluation works for a Boolean first-order (FO) query Q, then Q must be equivalent to a union of conjunctive queries. That result crucially relied on a preservation theorem from mathematical logic [11], and in particular on its version over finite structures [30].

This observation suggests that the limits of naïve evaluation depend on the semantics of incompleteness, and that syntactic restrictions on queries admitting such evaluation may be obtained from preservation theorems in logic. This is the starting point of our investigation. In general we would like to understand how, for a given semantics of incompleteness, we can find the class of queries for which certain answers will be found naïvely.

In slightly more detail, we would like to answer the following three questions:

1. What are the most general conditions underlying naïve evaluation, under different semantics?
2. When can naïve evaluation be characterized by preservation results?
3. How can we find relevant classes of queries that admit naïve evaluation?

We answer these three questions, by clarifying the relationship between semantics, naïve evaluation, preservation, and syntactic classes. Roughly, our results can be seen as establishing the following equivalences:

Naïve evaluation works for a query Q
$\|$
Q is monotone wrt the semantic ordering
$\|$
Q is preserved under a class of homomorphisms

We now explain the key ideas behind the main equivalences and the terminology we use.

Naïve evaluation and monotonicity For the first group of results, we deal with a very abstract setting that can be applied to many data models (relational, XML, etc) under different semantics. We assume that incomplete database objects x come with a notion of semantics $[\![x]\!]$, which is the set of complete objects they describe. We define the semantic ordering in the standard way: $x \preceq y \Leftrightarrow [\![y]\!] \subseteq [\![x]\!]$ (that is, x is less informative if it describes more objects, i.e., has more incompleteness in it). In this setting we define queries, naïve evaluation, and certain answers and prove that under very mild conditions, naïve evaluation works for a query iff it is monotone with respect to the semantic ordering. In fact, under even milder conditions, naïve evaluation corresponds to a weak notion of monotonicity, that only considers going from an object x to a more informative object $y \in [\![x]\!]$.

Monotonicity and preservation We next connect monotonicity with preservation. To start, we analyze multiple semantics of incompleteness, and come up with a uniform scheme for generating them. The key observation is that each semantics is obtained in two steps. In step one, common to all interpretations, we substitute constant values for nulls. Step two, that essentially defines the semantics, is given by a relation R showing how the result of the substitution can be modified. For instance, under the open-world semantics, tuples can be added; under the strictest form of the closed-world semantics, nothing can be changed at all.

Having done that, we prove that under some very mild condition, monotonicity of a query Q corresponds to preservation under homomorphisms that respect relation R: that is, if Q is true in D (say, for a Boolean Q), and we have a homomorphism respecting R from D to D', then Q is true in D'. Instances of such homomorphisms are the usual homomorphisms, under the open-world semantics, or onto homomorphisms, under (a version of) the closed-world semantics.

Preservation and syntactic classes We have so far established that naïve evaluation is captured by preservation under a class of homomorphisms. Such preservation results are classical in mathematical logic [11], and thus we would like to use them to find syntactic classes of queries for which naïve evaluation works.

One immediate difficulty is that classical logic results are proved for infinite structures, and they tend to fail in the finite [4, 32], or are notoriously hard to establish (a well-known example is Rossman's theorem [30], which answered a question opened for many years). Thus, we are in general happy with good sufficient conditions for preservation, especially if they are given by nice syntactic classes corresponding to meaningful classes of database queries. The key ideas behind the classes we use are restrictions to positive formulae (admitting $\forall$ but disallowing $\neg$) or existential positive formulae (i.e., unions of conjunctive queries), and extending some of them with universally quantified *guarded* formulae.

This gives us a good understanding of what is required to make naïve evaluation work. In Sections 3–5 we carry out the program outlined above and obtain classes of FO queries for which naïve evaluation works under standard relational semantics. Also, to keep notations simple initially, in these early sections we deal with Boolean queries (all results extend to arbitrary queries easily, as we show in Section 8).

In Sections 6, 7, and 9 we offer a more detailed study of other relational semantics of incompleteness. We take a closer look at semantic orderings, explain their justification via updates that incrementally improve informativeness of a database, and compare them with known orderings on Codd databases, that model SQL's null features. We show that capturing one of such well known orderings on Codd databases leads to a new class of *powerset* semantics, and we provide preservation results for that class, using the general methodology established earlier. We then look at *minimal* semantics that find their justification in the study of various forms of the closed world assumption. For them, the notion of a core of an instance [17] plays a crucial role: for example, naïve evaluation for previously considered classes of queries is only guaranteed over cores.

Organization In Section 2, we give the main definitions. In Section 3, we explain the connection between naïve evaluation and monotonicity, and in Section 4 we relate monotonicity to preservation. In Section 5 we deal with Boolean FO queries and provide sufficient conditions for naïve evaluation. In Section 6, we study semantic orderings on incomplete databases, and in Section 7 we study naïve evaluation for the resulting new class of semantics. Section 8 shows how to lift all the results for Boolean queries to queries with free variables. In Section 9, we carry out a similar program for minimal semantics.

2. PRELIMINARIES

Incomplete databases We begin with some standard definitions. In incomplete databases there are two types of values: constants and nulls. The set of constants is denoted by Const and the set of nulls by Null. These are countably infinite sets. Nulls will normally be denoted by $\bot$, sometimes with sub- or superscripts.

A relational schema (vocabulary) is a set of relation names with associated arities. An incomplete relational instance D assigns to each k-ary relation symbol S from the vocabulary a k-ary relation over $\mathsf{Const} \cup \mathsf{Null}$, i.e., a finite subset of $(\mathsf{Const} \cup \mathsf{Null})^k$. Such incomplete relational instances are referred to as *naïve* databases [1, 19]; note that a null $\bot \in \mathsf{Null}$ can appear multiple times in such an instance. If each null $\bot \in \mathsf{Null}$ appears at most once, we speak of *Codd* databases [1, 19]. If we talk about single relations, it is common to refer to them as naïve tables and Codd tables.

We write $\mathsf{Const}(D)$ and $\mathsf{Null}(D)$ for the sets of constants and nulls that occur in a database D. The *active domain* of D is $\mathrm{adom}(D) = \mathsf{Const}(D) \cup \mathsf{Null}(D)$. A *complete* database D has no nulls, i.e., $\mathrm{adom}(D) \subseteq \mathsf{Const}$.

Homomorphisms They are crucial for us in two contexts: to define the semantics of incomplete databases, and to define the notion of preservation of logical formulae as a condition for naïve evaluation to work.

Given two relational structures D and D', a homomorphism $h : D \to D'$ is a map from the active domain of D to the active domain of D' so that for every relation symbol S, if a tuple $\bar{u}$ is in relation S in D, then the tuple $h(\bar{u})$ is in the relation S in D'.

In database literature, it is common to require that homomorphisms preserve elements of Const, i.e., the map h is also required to satisfy $h(c) = c$ for every $c \in \mathsf{Const}$. Of course this can easily be cast as a special instance of the general notion, simply by extending the vocabulary with a constant symbol for each $c \in \mathsf{Const}$. To make clear what our assumptions are, whenever there is any ambiguity, we shall talk about *database homomorphisms* if they are the identity on Const.

Given a homomorphism h and a database D, by $h(D)$ we mean the image of D, i.e., the set of all tuples $S(h(\bar{u}))$ where $S(\bar{u})$ is in D. If $h : D \to D'$ is a homomorphism, then $h(D)$ is a subinstance of D'.

Semantics and valuations We shall see many possible semantics for incomplete information, but first we review two common ones: open-world and closed-world semantics. We need the notion of a *valuation*, which assigns a constant to each null. That is, a valuation is a database homomorphism whose image contains only values in Const.

In general, the semantics $[\![D]\!]$ of an incomplete database is a set of *complete* databases D'. The semantics under the closed-world assumption (or CWA *semantics*) is defined as

$$[\![D]\!]_{\text{CWA}} = \{h(D) \mid h \text{ is a valuation}\}.$$

The semantics under the open-world assumption (or OWA *semantics*) is defined as

$$[\![D]\!]_{\text{OWA}} = \left\{ D' \;\middle|\; \begin{array}{l} D' \text{ is complete and} \\ \text{there is a valuation } h : D \to D' \end{array} \right\}.$$

Alternatively, $D' \in [\![D]\!]_{\text{OWA}}$ iff D' is complete and contains a database $D'' \in [\![D]\!]_{\text{CWA}}$ as a subinstance.

As an example, consider $D_0 = \{(\bot, \bot'), (\bot', \bot)\}$. Then $[\![D_0]\!]_{\text{CWA}}$ consists of all instances $\{(c, c'), (c', c)\}$ with $c, c' \in \mathsf{Const}$ (and possibly $c = c'$), and $[\![D_0]\!]_{\text{OWA}}$ has all complete instances containing $\{(c, c'), (c', c)\}$, for $c, c' \in \mathsf{Const}$.

Certain answers and naïve evaluation Given an incomplete database D, a semantics of incompleteness $[\![\,]\!]$, and a query Q, one normally computes *certain answers under the* $[\![\,]\!]$ *semantics*:

$$\mathsf{certain}(Q, D) = \bigcap \{Q(R) \mid R \in [\![D]\!]\},$$

i.e., answers that are true regardless of the interpretation of nulls under the given semantics. Even for first-order queries, the standard semantics are problematic in general: finding certain answers under the OWA semantics may be undecidable, and finding them under the CWA semantics may be coNP-hard [2].

Naïve evaluation of a query Q refers to a two-step procedure: first, evaluate Q on the incomplete database itself, as if nulls were values (i.e., equal iff they are syntactically the same: e.g., $\bot_1 = \bot_1$, $\bot_1 \neq \bot_2$, $\bot_1 \neq c$ for every $c \in \mathsf{Const}$), and then eliminate tuples with nulls from the result. Note that if Q is a Boolean query, the second step is unnecessary.

We say that *naïve evaluation works for* Q (under semantics $[\![\,]\!]$) if its result is exactly the certain answers under $[\![\,]\!]$, for every D.

Fact 1. (see [19, 24]) *Let Q be a union of conjunctive queries. Then naïve evaluation works for Q under both* OWA *and* CWA. *Moreover, if Q is a Boolean FO query and naïve evaluation works for Q under* OWA, *then Q is equivalent to a union of conjunctive queries.*

The last equivalence result only works under the OWA semantics. Consider again the instance D_0 and a query $\exists x, y\ D(x, y) \wedge D(y, x)$. The certain answer to this query is true under both OWA and CWA, and indeed it evaluates to true naïvely over D_0. On the other hand, a query Q given by $\forall x \exists y\ D(x, y)$ (not equivalent to a union of conjunctive queries) evaluated naïvely, returns true on D_0, but under OWA its certain answer is false. However, under CWA, its certain answer is true. This is not an isolated phenomenon: we will later see that Q belongs to a class, extending unions of conjunctive queries, for which naïve evaluation works under CWA on all databases.

Note that in this paper we assume the active domain semantics for relational first-order queries.

3. NAÏVE EVALUATION AND MONOTONICITY

The goal of this section is twofold. First we present a very general setting for talking about incompleteness and its semantics, as well as orderings representing the notion of "having more information". We formulate the notion of naïve evaluation in this setting, and show that it guarantees to compute certain answers for monotone queries.

Database domains, semantics, and ordering We now define a simple abstract setting for handling incompleteness. We operate with just four basic concepts: the set of instances, the set of complete instances, their isomorphism, and their semantics.

A *database domain* is a structure $\mathbb{D} = \langle \mathcal{D}, \mathcal{C}, [\![\cdot]\!], \approx \rangle$, where $\mathcal{D}$ is a set, $\mathcal{C}$ is a subset of $\mathcal{D}$, the function $[\![\cdot]\!]$ is from $\mathcal{D}$ to nonempty subsets of $\mathcal{C}$, and $\approx$ is an equivalence relation on $\mathcal{D}$. The interpretation is as follows:

- $\mathcal{D}$ is a set of database objects (e.g., incomplete relational databases over the same schema),
- $\mathcal{C}$ is the set of complete objects (e.g., databases without nulls);
- $[\![x]\!] \subseteq \mathcal{C}$ is the semantics of an incomplete database x, i.e., the set of all complete databases that x can represent; and
- $\approx$ is the structural equivalence relation, that we need to describe the notion of generic queries; for instance, for relational databases, $D \approx D'$ means that they are isomorphic as objects, i.e., $\pi(D) = D'$ for some 1-1 mapping on data values in D.

The semantic function of a database domain lets us describe the degree of incompleteness via an ordering defined as $x \preceq y$ iff $[\![y]\!] \subseteq [\![x]\!]$. Indeed, the less we know about an object, the more other objects it can potentially describe. This setting is reminiscent of the ideas in programming semantics, where partial functions are similarly ordered [16], and such orderings have been used to provide semantics of incompleteness in the past [9, 23, 24, 26, 31]. Note that $\preceq$ is a *preorder*.

Queries and certain answers For now we look at Boolean queries in the most abstract setting (we will generalize them later). Given a database domain $\mathbb{D} = \langle \mathcal{D}, \mathcal{C}, [\![\cdot]\!], \approx \rangle$, a *query* is a mapping $Q : \mathcal{D} \to \{0, 1\}$. We use 0 to represent *false* and 1 to represent *true*, as usual. A query is *generic* if $Q(x) = Q(y)$ whenever $x \approx y$.

For each $x \in \mathcal{D}$, the certain answer (under $[\![\,]\!]$) is

$$\mathsf{certain}(Q, x) = \bigwedge \{Q(c) \mid c \in [\![x]\!]\}$$

We say that *naïve evaluation works* for Q if $Q(x) = \mathsf{certain}(Q, x)$ for every x.

Saturation property We now impose an additional property on database domains saying, essentially, that there are enough complete objects. A database domain $\mathbb{D} = \langle \mathcal{D}, \mathcal{C}, [\![\cdot]\!], \approx \rangle$ is *saturated* if every object has a complete object in its semantics that is isomorphic to it: that is, for each $x \in \mathcal{D}$ there is $y \in [\![x]\!]$ such that $x \approx y$.

In the case of the usual semantics of incompleteness, this property trivially holds: if we have an instance D

with nulls $\bot_1, \ldots, \bot_n$, we simply replace them with distinct constants $c_1, \ldots, c_n$ that do not occur elsewhere in D, to obtain a complete database isomorphic to D.

Naïve evaluation and monotonicity We say that a query Q is *weakly monotone* if

$$y \in [\![x]\!] \Rightarrow Q(x) \preccurlyeq Q(y).$$

That is, if y is a complete object representing x, and Q is already true on x, then Q must be true on y. This property characterizes naïve evaluation over saturated database domains.

Theorem 1. *Let $\mathbb{D}$ be a database domain with the saturation property, and Q a generic Boolean query. Then naïve evaluation works for Q iff Q is weakly monotone.*

Of course one can also look at the natural definition of monotonicity: a query Q is *monotone* if $x \preceq y$ implies $Q(x) \preccurlyeq Q(y)$. Recall that $x \preceq y$ means that $[\![y]\!] \subseteq [\![x]\!]$. This condition turns out to be equivalent to weak monotonicity in database domains that satisfy one additional property. To state it, note that there is a natural duality between preorders and semantics: each semantics $[\![\,]\!]$ gives rise to the ordering $x \preceq y \Leftrightarrow [\![y]\!] \subseteq [\![x]\!]$, and conversely any preorder $\preccurlyeq$ on $\mathcal{D}$ gives a semantics $[\![x]\!]_{\preccurlyeq} = \{y \in \mathcal{C} \mid x \preccurlyeq y\}$. We say that a database domain is *fair* if $[\![\,]\!]$ and its ordering $\preceq$ agree: that is, the semantics that the ordering $\preceq$ gives rise to is $[\![\,]\!]$ itself. Fair domains can be easily characterized:

Proposition 1. *A database domain $\mathbb{D}$ is fair iff the following conditions hold:*

1. *$c \in [\![c]\!]$ for each $c \in \mathcal{C}$;*
2. *if $c \in [\![x]\!]$, then $[\![c]\!] \subseteq [\![x]\!]$.*

The standard semantics – including all those seen in the previous section – satisfy these conditions. The first condition says that the semantics of a complete object should contain at least that object. The second says that by removing incompleteness from an object, we cannot get one that denotes more objects. Note also that in a fair domain, $y \in [\![x]\!]$ implies $x \preceq y$, so weak monotonicity is indeed weaker than monotonicity.

In fair database domains, we can extend Theorem 1:

Proposition 2. *Let $\mathbb{D}$ be a fair database domain with the saturation property, and Q a generic Boolean query. Then the following are equivalent:*

1. *Naïve evaluation works for Q;*
2. *Q is monotone;*
3. *Q is weakly monotone.*

Theorem 1 and Proposition 2 establish the promised connection between monotonicity and naïve evaluation. Extension to non-Boolean queries is given in Section 8.

4. SEMANTICS, RELATIONS, AND HOMOMORPHISMS

We have seen that getting naïve evaluation to work (at least for Boolean queries), is equivalent to their (weak) monotonicity. To apply this to concrete semantics, we need to understand how different semantics can be defined. We explain that most of them are obtained by composing two types of relations: one corresponds to applying valuations to nulls, and the other to specific semantic assumptions such as open or closed-world. After that, we show a connection between naïve evaluation and preservation under a class of homomorphisms.

Semantics via relations

We have already seen two concrete relational semantics: the OWA semantics $[\![D]\!]_{\text{OWA}}$ and the CWA semantics $[\![D]\!]_{\text{CWA}}$. What is common to them is that they are all defined in two steps. First, valuations are applied to nulls (i.e., nulls are replaced by values). Second, the resulting database may be modified in some way (left as it was for CWA, or expanded arbitrarily for OWA). Our idea is then to capture this via two relations. We now define them in the setting of database domains and then show how they behave in concrete cases.

Given a database domain $\mathbb{D} = \langle \mathcal{D}, \mathcal{C}, [\![\,]\!], \approx \rangle$, we consider a pair $\mathcal{R} = (\mathcal{R}_{\text{val}}, \mathcal{R}_{\text{sem}})$ of relations:

The *valuation* relation $\mathcal{R}_{\text{val}} \subseteq \mathcal{D} \times \mathcal{C}$ between arbitrary databases and complete databases. Intuitively, a pair (x, c) is in $\mathcal{R}_{\text{val}}$ if c is obtained from x by replacing nulls by constants. The restriction of $\mathcal{R}_{\text{val}}$ to $\mathcal{C}$ is the identity: $\mathcal{R}_{\text{val}} \cap (\mathcal{C} \times \mathcal{C}) = \{(c, c) \mid c \in \mathcal{C}\}$ (if there are no nulls, there is no substitution). And since for every object there is some way to replace nulls by constants, $\mathcal{R}_{\text{val}}$ is total.

The *semantic* relation $\mathcal{R}_{\text{sem}}$ is a reflexive binary relation on $\mathcal{C}$ (i.e., $\mathcal{R}_{\text{sem}} \subseteq \mathcal{C} \times \mathcal{C}$). Intuitively, this corresponds to the modification step such as extending complete relations by new tuples. Since, at the very least, one can do nothing with the result of the substitution of nulls by constants, such a relation must be reflexive.

We say that $[\![\,]\!]$ *is given by* $\mathcal{R}$ if $\mathcal{R}$ satisfies the above conditions, and $y \in [\![x]\!]$ iff $(x, y) \in \mathcal{R}_{\text{val}} \circ \mathcal{R}_{\text{sem}}$.

Proposition 3. *Let $\mathbb{D}$ be a database domain whose semantics $[\![\,]\!]$ is given by a pair $\mathcal{R} = (\mathcal{R}_{\text{val}}, \mathcal{R}_{\text{sem}})$. Then $\mathbb{D}$ is fair iff $\mathcal{R}_{\text{sem}}$ is transitive.*

Relational databases When we deal with relational databases, the most natural valuation relation is $\mathcal{R}^{\text{rdb}}_{\text{val}}$ defined as follows:

$$(D, D') \in \mathcal{R}^{\text{rdb}}_{\text{val}} \Leftrightarrow D' = v(D) \text{ for some valuation } v.$$

So we assume, for now, that in relational semantics of incompleteness, the valuation relation is $\mathcal{R}_{\text{val}}^{\text{rdb}}$, and thus such semantics are defined by relation $\mathcal{R}_{\text{sem}}$. For OWA and CWA, these are particularly easy:

- For CWA, $\mathcal{R}_{\text{sem}}$ is the identity (i.e., $=$);
- For OWA, $\mathcal{R}_{\text{sem}}$ is the subset relation (i.e., $\subseteq$).

The special form of relation $\mathcal{R}_{\text{val}}^{\text{rdb}}$ implies the saturation property. Therefore we have:

Proposition 4. *For an arbitrary relational semantics given by relation $\mathcal{R}_{\text{sem}}$, and an arbitrary generic Boolean query Q, naïve evaluation works for Q iff Q is weakly monotone.*

Naïve evaluation via homomorphism preservation

We shall now relate weak monotonicity and preservation under homomorphisms (at least for relational semantics).

Consider relational databases over constants. Given two such databases D and D', a mapping h defined on the active domain $\text{adom}(D)$ of D is an $\mathcal{R}_{\text{sem}}$-*homomorphism* from D to D' if $(h(D), D') \in \mathcal{R}_{\text{sem}}$.

A query Q is *preserved* under $\mathcal{R}_{\text{sem}}$-homomorphisms if for every database D and every $\mathcal{R}_{\text{sem}}$-homomorphism h from D to D', if Q is true in D, then Q is true in D'.

Proposition 5. *If a relational semantics is given by a relation $\mathcal{R}_{\text{sem}}$ and Q is a generic Boolean query, then Q is weakly monotone iff it is preserved under $\mathcal{R}_{\text{sem}}$-homomorphisms.*

Putting everything together, we have our first key result for naïve evaluation over incomplete databases.

Theorem 2. *For a relational incompleteness semantics given by a semantic relation $\mathcal{R}_{\text{sem}}$, and a generic Boolean query Q, naïve evaluation works for Q iff Q is preserved under $\mathcal{R}_{\text{sem}}$-homomorphisms.*

Homomorphisms for relational semantics Theorem 2 connects naïve evaluation with homomorphism preservation. We now investigate what these $\mathcal{R}_{\text{sem}}$-homomorphisms are.

CWA **semantics** In this case $\mathcal{R}_{\text{sem}}$ is the identity, and the definition states that h is an $\mathcal{R}_{\text{sem}}$-homomorphism from D to D' if $D' = h(D)$. That is, under CWA, $\mathcal{R}_{\text{sem}}$-homomorphisms are the *strong onto* homomorphisms, i.e., homomorphisms from D to $h(D)$.

OWA **semantics** In this case $\mathcal{R}_{\text{sem}}$ is $\subseteq$, and the definition states that h is an $\mathcal{R}_{\text{sem}}$-homomorphism from D to D' if $h(D) \subseteq D'$. That is, under OWA, $\mathcal{R}_{\text{sem}}$-homomorphisms are just the usual homomorphisms.

Another well known notion of homomorphisms is that of *onto* homomorphisms. When used in the database context, an onto homomorphism h from D to D' is a homomorphism between D and D' so that $h(\text{adom}(D)) = \text{adom}(D')$. For instance, if $D = \{(1,2)\}$, and $h(1) = 3, h(2) = 4$, then h is a strong onto homomorphism from D to $D' = \{(3,4)\}$, and an onto homomorphism to $D'' = \{(3,4),(4,3)\}$. Note that while D'' contains more than $h(D)$, all the tuples in D'' only use elements that occur in $h(D)$.

A semantics of incompleteness that corresponds to this notion, that we refer to as *weak* CWA, or WCWA semantics, was actually previously studied [27] (in a slightly different, deductive-database context). We define it as follows:

$$[\![D]\!]_{\text{WCWA}} = \left\{ D' \;\middle|\; \begin{array}{l} D' \text{ is complete and} \\ \text{there is a valuation } h : D \to D' \\ \text{so that } \text{adom}(D') = \text{adom}(h(D)) \end{array} \right\}.$$

For this semantics, $\mathcal{R}_{\text{sem}}$ contains all pairs (D, D') so that $D \subseteq D'$ and $\text{adom}(D) = \text{adom}(D')$. That is, D can be expanded only within its active domain. Thus, $\mathcal{R}_{\text{sem}}$-homomorphisms are exactly onto homomorphisms.

For this relation $\mathcal{R}_{\text{sem}}$, the notion of preservation under $\mathcal{R}_{\text{sem}}$-homomorphisms is exactly the notion of preservation under onto homomorphisms. Thus, the WCWA semantics, defined long time ago, also corresponds to a very natural logical notion of preservation.

Note that $[\![D]\!]_{\text{CWA}} \subseteq [\![D]\!]_{\text{WCWA}} \subseteq [\![D]\!]_{\text{OWA}}$, and in general inclusions can be strict.

Naïve evaluation and relational semantics

We can finally state the equivalence of naïve evaluation and homomorphism preservation for three concrete semantics of incomplete relational databases:

Corollary 1. *Let Q be a Boolean generic query. Then:*

- *Under* OWA, *naïve evaluation works for Q iff Q is preserved under homomorphisms.*
- *Under* CWA, *naïve evaluation works for Q iff Q is preserved under strong onto homomorphisms.*
- *Under* WCWA, *naïve evaluation works for Q iff Q is preserved under onto homomorphisms.*

5. NAÏVE EVALUATION AND PRESERVATION FOR FO QUERIES

Corollary 1 reduces the problem of checking whether naïve evaluation works to preservation under homomorphisms. Thus, for FO queries, we deal with a very well known notion in logic [11]. However, what we need is preservation on *finite* structures, and those notions are well known to behave differently from their infinite counterpart. In fact, it was only proved recently by

Rossman that for FO sentences, preservation under arbitrary homomorphisms in the finite is equivalent to being an existential positive formula [30]. In database language, this means being a union of conjunctive queries, which led to an observation [24] that naïve evaluation works for a Boolean FO query Q iff Q is equivalent to a union of conjunctive queries.

The difficulty in establishing preservation results in the finite is due to losing access to classical logical tools such as compactness. Rossman's theorem, for instance, was a major open problem for many years. To make matters worse, even some existing infinite preservation results [21] have holes in their proofs.

Thus, it is unrealistic for a single paper to settle several very hard problems concerning preservation results in the finite (sometimes even without infinite analogs!). What we shall do instead is settle for classes of queries that *imply* preservation, and at the same time are easy to describe syntactically.

Positive and existential positive formulae Recall that the class Pos of *positive* formulae is defined inductively as follows:

- *true* and *false* are in Pos;
- every positive atomic formula (i.e., $R(\bar{x})$ or $x = y$) is in Pos;
- if $\varphi, \psi \in \mathsf{Pos}$, then $\varphi \vee \psi$ and $\varphi \wedge \psi$ are in Pos;
- if φ is in Pos, then $\exists x\varphi$ and $\forall x\psi$ are in Pos.

If only $\exists x\varphi$ remains in the class, we obtain the class $\exists\mathsf{Pos}$ of *existential positive formulae.* Formulae from $\exists\mathsf{Pos}$ are also known as unions of conjunctive queries.

Rossman's theorem [30] says that an FO sentence φ is preserved under homomorphisms over finite structures iff φ is equivalent to a sentence from $\exists\mathsf{Pos}$. Lyndon's theorem [11] says that an FO sentence φ is preserved under onto homomorphisms (over arbitrary structures) iff φ is equivalent to a sentence from Pos. Lyndon's theorem fails in the finite [4, 32] but the implication from being positive to preservation is still valid.

A characterization of preservation under strong onto homomorphisms was stated in [20, 21], but the syntactic class had a rather messy definition and was limited to a single binary relation. Even worse, we discovered a gap in one of the key lemmas in [21]. So instead we propose a simple extension of positive formulae that gives preservation under strong onto homomorphisms.

Extensions with universal guards The fragment $\mathsf{Pos} + \forall\mathsf{G}$, whose definition is inspired by [12], extends Pos with universal guards. It is defined as a fragment closed under all the formation rules for Pos and, in addition, the following rule:

- for a $\mathsf{Pos} + \forall\mathsf{G}$ formula φ, a tuple of distinct variables $\bar{x}$, and a relation symbol R (possibly the equality relation), the formula $\forall\bar{x}(R(\bar{x}) \rightarrow \varphi)$ is in $\mathsf{Pos} + \forall\mathsf{G}$.

Clearly we have $\exists\mathsf{Pos} \subsetneq \mathsf{Pos} \subsetneq \mathsf{Pos} + \forall\mathsf{G}$.

Proposition 6. *Sentences in* $\mathsf{Pos} + \forall\mathsf{G}$ *are preserved under strong onto homomorphisms.*

We now combine all the previous implications (preservation $\rightarrow$ monotonicity $\rightarrow$ naïve evaluation) to show that naïve evaluation can work beyond unions of conjunctive queries under realistic semantic assumptions.

Theorem 3. *Let Q be a Boolean FO query. Then:*

- *If Q is in* $\exists\mathsf{Pos}$, *then naïve evaluation works for Q under* OWA.
- *If Q is in* Pos, *then naïve evaluation works for Q under* WCWA.
- *If Q is in* $\mathsf{Pos} + \forall\mathsf{G}$, *then naïve evaluation works for Q under* CWA.

Contrast this with the result of [24] saying that under OWA, the first statement is 'if and only if', i.e., one cannot go beyond $\exists\mathsf{Pos}$. Now we see that, under other semantics, one can indeed go well beyond that class, essentially limiting only unrestricted negation, and still use naïve evaluation.

One immediate question is what happens with non-Boolean queries. There is a simple answer: *all results extend to non-Boolean queries.* We explain how this is done in Section 8, once we have looked at other semantics (as the lifting will apply to all of them).

6. SEMANTIC ORDERINGS

In this section we study semantic orderings arising from the usual relational semantics of incompleteness. We recall known results about the study of such orderings in the context of Codd databases [9, 23, 26, 31]. Such results are of two kinds: they connect orderings based on incompleteness with well-known orderings from the field of programming semantics, and they describe those via elementary *updates* that increase the information content of an instance.

Codd databases

SQL uses a single value `null` for missing information. As comparisons of a null with other values in SQL do not evaluate to true (technically, they evaluate to *unknown*, as SQL uses three-valued logic), this is properly modeled by a special kind of naïve databases, called *Codd databases*, in which nulls do not repeat.

For tuples $t = (a_1, \ldots, a_n)$ and $t' = (a'_1, \ldots, a'_n)$ over $\mathsf{Const} \cup \mathsf{Null}$ in which nulls do not repeat, we write $t \sqsubseteq t'$ if $a_i \in \mathsf{Const}$ implies $a'_i = a_i$. The meaning is that t'

is at least as informative as t. There are two standard ways of lifting $\sqsubseteq$ to sets:

$$D \sqsubseteq^{\mathrm{H}} D' \quad \Leftrightarrow \quad \forall t \in D\ \exists t' \in D' : t \sqsubseteq t'$$
$$D \sqsubseteq^{\mathrm{P}} D' \quad \Leftrightarrow \quad \forall t' \in D'\ \exists t \in D : t \sqsubseteq t' \text{ and } D \sqsubseteq^{\mathrm{H}} D'$$

Superscripts H and P stand for Hoare and Plotkin, who first studied these orderings in the context of the semantics of concurrent processes, cf. [16].

These had been previously accepted as the correct orderings to represent the OWA and the CWA semantics over Codd databases [9, 23, 26, 31]. This can be justified by considering updates that affect informativeness of incomplete databases. Consider, for example, two tuples $(1,2)$ and $(2,2)$, and assume that we somehow lose the value of the first attribute. SQL has a unique null value, so both tuples become $(\texttt{null}, 2)$, which thus must represent the instance $\{(1,2),(2,2)\}$ even under CWA, since no tuples were lost, only individual values. Alternatively, one can view this as an *allowed update*, under CWA, from $(\texttt{null}, 2)$, that produces a more informative instance $\{(1,2),(2,2)\}$ by replacing the null twice. In the case of OWA, one can have updates that add arbitrary new tuples.

Let D be a database, R a relation in it, t a tuple, and i a position in that tuple that contains a null $\bot$. Then by $D[v/R(t.i)]$ we mean D in which that occurrence of $\bot$ is replaced by $v \in \mathsf{Const} \cup \mathsf{Null}$, and by $D^+[v/R(t.i)]$ we mean D to which a tuple obtained from t by replacing the occurrence of $\bot$ in the ith position with v is added (i.e., the original t is retained). Now we consider updates $D \rightarrowtail^{\mathrm{codd}} D'$ of two kinds:

- Codd CWA updates: $D \rightarrowtail^{\mathrm{codd}}_{\mathrm{CWA}} D[v/R(t.i)]$ and and $D \rightarrowtail^{\mathrm{codd}}_{\mathrm{CWA}} D^+[v/R(t.i)]$;
- OWA update: $D \rightarrowtail^{\mathrm{codd}}_{\mathrm{OWA}} D \cup R(t)$ that adds a tuple to a relation in a database.

It is known [23] that the reflexive-transitive closure

- of $\rightarrowtail^{\mathrm{codd}}_{\mathrm{CWA}} \cup \rightarrowtail^{\mathrm{codd}}_{\mathrm{OWA}}$ is exactly $\sqsubseteq^{\mathrm{H}}$; and
- of $\rightarrowtail^{\mathrm{codd}}_{\mathrm{CWA}}$ is exactly $\sqsubseteq^{\mathrm{P}}$,

over Codd databases. Our next goal is to describe orderings corresponding to OWA and CWA for naïve databases, and to give an update semantics for them.

Naïve databases

Firstly we describe the semantic orderings $\preceq_*$ given by the semantics $[\![\,]\!]_*$, where $*$ is OWA, CWA, or WCWA. They are characterized via database homomorphisms as follows (the first item was already shown in [24]).

Proposition 7. *$D \preceq_{\mathrm{OWA}} D'$ (respectively $D \preceq_{\mathrm{CWA}} D'$ or $D \preceq_{\mathrm{WCWA}} D'$) iff there is a database homomorphism (respectively, strong onto, or onto database homomorphism) from D to D'.*

Next, we provide update justification for these orderings. OWA updates just add tuples as before; we denote them by $\rightarrowtail_{\mathrm{OWA}}$. CWA updates are different, to account for repetition of nulls. In particular, once a null is replaced by some value v, *all* its occurrences must be replaced. Formally, if $\bot$ is a null that occurs in D, then $D[v/\bot]$ is D in which $v \in \mathsf{Const} \cup \mathsf{Null}$ replaces $\bot$ everywhere. The CWA update is now an update $D \rightarrowtail_{\mathrm{CWA}} D[v/\bot]$.

Let * stand for the transitive-reflexive closure of a relation (i.e., a sequence of updates). Then we have:

Theorem 4.
- $\rightarrowtail^*_{\mathrm{CWA}} \ = \ \preceq_{\mathrm{CWA}}$;
- $(\rightarrowtail_{\mathrm{CWA}} \cup \rightarrowtail_{\mathrm{OWA}})^* \ = \ \preceq_{\mathrm{OWA}}$.

In other words, D is less informative than D' iff D' is obtained from D by a sequence of

- CWA updates, under CWA;
- CWA and OWA updates, under OWA.

What are the orderings $\preceq_{\mathrm{OWA}}$ and $\preceq_{\mathrm{CWA}}$ when we restrict them to Codd databases? One would expect them to be $\sqsubseteq^{\mathrm{H}}$ and $\sqsubseteq^{\mathrm{P}}$, corresponding to OWA and CWA for the Codd semantics, but this is only partly true. In fact, [24] proved that over Codd databases,

- $\preceq_{\mathrm{OWA}}$ and $\sqsubseteq^{\mathrm{H}}$ coincide;
- $D \preceq_{\mathrm{CWA}} D'$ iff $D \sqsubseteq^{\mathrm{P}} D'$ and relation $\sqsubseteq$ has a perfect matching from D' to D.

So this leads to a question: is there is a "natural" semantic ordering over naïve databases that, when restricted to Codd databases, coincides precisely with $\sqsubseteq^{\mathrm{P}}$? In the next section, we present such an ordering, and show that it gives rise to a whole new family of semantics of incompleteness.

7. POWERSET SEMANTICS

Our search for the answer to the question at the end of the previous section leads us to consider a new class of semantics of incompleteness, in which not one, but several valuations can be applied to nulls. In other words, we produce several valuations (hence the name *powerset semantics*), and then combine them into a single one. Notationally, we distinguish them by using $(\!|\ |\!)$ brackets.

We start with a semantics defined as follows:

$$(\!|D|\!)_{\mathrm{CWA}} \ = \ \left\{ h_1(D) \cup \ldots \cup h_n(D) \ \middle| \ \begin{array}{c} h_1,\ldots,h_n \text{ are} \\ \text{valuations}, n \geqslant 1 \end{array} \right\}.$$

That is, $D' \in (\!|D|\!)_{\mathrm{CWA}}$ iff there exists a set of valuations $h_1, \ldots, h_n$ on D so that $D' = \bigcup\{h_i(D) \mid 1 \leqslant i \leqslant n\}$. We call it the CWA powerset semantic.

Next, we describe the ordering $\sqsubseteq_{\mathrm{CWA}}$ induced by this semantics: that is, $D \sqsubseteq_{\mathrm{CWA}} D'$ iff $(\!|D'|\!)_{\mathrm{CWA}} \subseteq (\!|D|\!)_{\mathrm{CWA}}$.

To updates used as the justification of orderings in the previous section, we now add a new type. A *copying* CWA *update* is of the form

$$D \rightarrowtail\!\!\!\rightarrow_{\text{CWA}} D[v/\bot] \cup D^{\text{fresh}},$$

where D^{fresh} is a copy of D in which all nulls are replaced by fresh ones. This is a relaxation of CWA: we can add tuples in an update, but only in a very limited way, if they mimic the original database.

It turns out that the ordering $\sqsubseteq_{\text{CWA}}$ can be seen as a sequence of regular and copying CWA updates, and that when restricted to Codd databases, it coincides precisely with $\sqsubseteq^{\text{P}}$. That is, we have the following.

Theorem 5. • *$D \sqsubseteq_{\text{CWA}} D'$ iff there exists a set of database homomorphisms $h_1, \ldots, h_n$ defined on D so that $D' = \bigcup\{h_i(D) \mid 1 \leqslant i \leqslant n\}$.*

- $(\rightarrowtail_{\text{CWA}} \cup \rightarrowtail\!\!\!\rightarrow_{\text{CWA}})^* \ = \ \sqsubseteq_{\text{CWA}}$.
- *Over Codd databases, $\sqsubseteq_{\text{CWA}}$ and $\sqsubseteq^{\text{P}}$ coincide.*

Preservation for powerset semantics

Our next goal is to understand how we can make naïve evaluation work under the powerset semantics. For the standard semantics of incompleteness, we related naïve evaluation to preservation of queries under homomorphisms. We shall do the same here, but the setting for homomorphisms will be a bit different.

Recall that before we looked at relational semantics defined by two relations, relation $\mathcal{R}_{\text{val}}^{\text{rdb}} = \{(D, v(D)) \mid v \text{ is a valuation}\}$ and relation $\mathcal{R}_{\text{sem}}$ between complete databases. We now replace $\mathcal{R}_{\text{val}}^{\text{rdb}}$ with

$$\boldsymbol{\mathcal{R}}_{\text{val}}^{\text{rdb}} = \{(D, \{v_1(D), \ldots, v_n(D)\}) \mid v_i\text{'s are valuations}\},$$

and consider relations $\boldsymbol{\mathcal{R}}_{\text{sem}}$ between a finite set of complete databases and a single complete database. We require that $\boldsymbol{\mathcal{R}}_{\text{sem}}$ be total and contain pairs $(\{c\}, c)$ for all complete objects c. An example is the relation $\boldsymbol{\mathcal{R}}_{\cup} = \{(\mathcal{X}, X) \mid X = \bigcup \mathcal{X}\}$, corresponding to taking the union of databases.

A powerset semantics $(\!|\ |\!)$ is *given by relation* $\boldsymbol{\mathcal{R}}_{\text{sem}}$ if

$$D' \in (\!|D|\!) \Leftrightarrow (D, D') \in \boldsymbol{\mathcal{R}}_{\text{val}}^{\text{rdb}} \circ \boldsymbol{\mathcal{R}}_{\text{sem}}.$$

For instance, the semantics $(\!|\ |\!)_{\text{CWA}}$ is given by the relation $\boldsymbol{\mathcal{R}}_{\cup}$.

Consider complete relational databases D and D'. An $\boldsymbol{\mathcal{R}}_{\text{sem}}$*-homomorphism* between D and D' is a set $\{h_1, \ldots, h_n\}$ of mappings defined on $\text{adom}(D)$ so that $\{h_1(D), \ldots, h_n(D)\}\boldsymbol{\mathcal{R}}_{\text{sem}}D'$. Note that if $n = 1$, this is exactly the notion of $\mathcal{R}_{\text{sem}}$-homomorphisms seen earlier. The connection between naïve evaluation and homomorphism preservation now extends to powerset semantics.

Proposition 8. *For every powerset semantics given by a relation $\boldsymbol{\mathcal{R}}_{\text{sem}}$, naïve evaluation works for a generic Boolean query Q iff Q is preserved under $\boldsymbol{\mathcal{R}}_{\text{sem}}$-homomorphisms.*

Let us now look at the semantics $(\!|\ |\!)_{\text{CWA}}$ given by relation $\boldsymbol{\mathcal{R}}_{\cup}$. The notion of preservation under $\boldsymbol{\mathcal{R}}_{\cup}$-homomorphisms is preservation *under union of strong onto homomorphisms*: if Q is true in D, and $h_1, \ldots, h_n$ are homomorphisms defined on D, then Q is true in $h_1(D) \cup \ldots \cup h_n(D)$.

For previous preservation results among FO queries, we looked at classes Pos and $\exists\mathsf{Pos}$ of positive and existential positive queries, and the class $\mathsf{Pos}{+}\forall\mathsf{G}$ of positive queries with universal guards. Now let $\exists\mathsf{Pos} + \forall\mathsf{G}^{\text{bool}}$ be the class of existential positive queries extended with *Boolean universal guards*, i.e., universally guarded formulae which are sentences. More precisely, if $\bar{x}$ is a tuple of distinct variables, $\varphi(\bar{y})$ is a formula in $\exists\mathsf{Pos} + \forall\mathsf{G}^{\text{bool}}$, where all $\bar{y}$ variables are contained in $\bar{x}$, and R is a relation symbol (possibly the equality relation), then $\forall\bar{x}\ (R(\bar{x}) \rightarrow \varphi(\bar{y}))$ is in $\exists\mathsf{Pos} + \forall\mathsf{G}^{\text{bool}}$.

Lemma 1. *Sentences in $\exists\mathsf{Pos}{+}\forall\mathsf{G}^{\text{bool}}$ are preserved under unions of strong onto homomorphisms.*

Combining, we get the following result.

Corollary 2. *If Q is a Boolean query from the class $\exists\mathsf{Pos} + \forall\mathsf{G}^{\text{bool}}$, then naïve evaluation works for Q under the $(\!|\ |\!)_{\text{CWA}}$ semantics.*

Semantics similar to $(\!|\ |\!)_{\text{CWA}}$ did appear in the literature. In fact, the closest comes from the study of CWA in the context of data exchange [5]. It was presented in [18] (and based in turn on a semantics from [25]), and essentially boils down to the $(\!|\ |\!)_{\text{CWA}}$ semantics, but based on a restricted notion of valuations, namely minimal valuations. We shall study those in Section 9.

8. LIFTING TO NON-BOOLEAN QUERIES

So far our results dealt with Boolean queries. Now we show how to lift them to the setting of arbitrary k-ary relational queries. The basic idea is to consider database domains where objects are pairs consisting of a database and a k-tuple of constants. This turns queries into Boolean, and we apply our results. This requires more technical development than seems to be implied by the simple idea, but it can be carried out for all the semantics. We sketch now how the extension works.

A k-ary query Q maps a database D to a subset of $\text{adom}(D)^k$. It is *generic* if, for each one-to-one map $f : \text{adom}(D) \rightarrow \mathsf{Const} \cup \mathsf{Null}$, we have $Q(f(D)) = f(Q(D))$.

Given a semantics $[\![\ ]\!]$, certain answers to Q are defined as $\mathsf{certain}(Q, D) = \bigcap\{Q(D') \mid D' \in [\![D]\!]\}$. Naïve evaluation *works* for Q if $\mathsf{certain}(Q, D)$ is precisely the set of tuples in $Q(D)$ that do not have nulls. We refer to this set (i.e., $Q(D) \cap \mathsf{Const}^k$) as $Q^{\mathsf{C}}(D)$.

As before, Q is monotone if $D \preceq D'$ implies $Q^{\mathsf{C}}(D) \subseteq Q^{\mathsf{C}}(D')$ for the semantic ordering $\preceq$, and Q is weakly monotone if the above is true whenever $D' \in [\![D]\!]$.

We will need a stronger form of saturation property. A relational database domain is *strongly saturated* if every database has "sufficiently" many complete instances in its semantics that are isomorphic to it. More precisely, for each database D, and each finite set $C \subset \mathsf{Const}$, there is an isomorphic instance $D' \in [\![D]\!]$ such that both the isomorphism from D to D' and its inverse are the identity on C.

If we deal, as before, with relational semantics given by pairs $\mathcal{R} = (\mathcal{R}_{\text{val}}^{\text{rdb}}, \mathcal{R}_{\text{sem}})$, we say that a k-ary query is *weakly preserved* under a class of $\mathcal{R}_{\text{sem}}$-homomorphisms if for every database D, a k-tuple t of constants, and an $\mathcal{R}_{\text{sem}}$-homomorphism $h : D \to D'$ from the class that is the identity on t, the condition $t \in Q(D)$ implies $t \in Q(D')$. Note that for Boolean queries this is the same as preservation under $\mathcal{R}_{\text{sem}}$-homomorphisms.

Then the main connections continue to hold.

Lemma 2. *Let $\mathbb{D}$ be a relational database domain with the strong saturation property, and Q a k-ary generic query. Then the following are equivalent:*

1. *naïve evaluation works for Q;*
2. *Q is weakly monotone; and*
3. *(if the semantics is given by a relation $\mathcal{R}_{\text{sem}}$): Q is weakly preserved under $\mathcal{R}_{\text{sem}}$-homomorphisms.*

One can then check that for all the classes of FO formulae considered here, preservation results hold when extended to formulae with free variables. In addition, one can develop similar transfer technique for powerset semantics and conclude that all the results remain true for non-Boolean queries.

Theorem 6. *Let Q be a k-ary FO query, $k \geqslant 0$. Then:*

- *If Q is in $\exists\mathsf{Pos}$, then naïve evaluation works for Q under* OWA.
- *If Q is in Pos, then naïve evaluation works for Q under* WCWA.
- *If Q is in $\mathsf{Pos} + \forall\mathsf{G}$, then naïve evaluation works for Q under* CWA.
- *If Q is in $\exists\mathsf{Pos} + \forall\mathsf{G}^{\text{bool}}$, then naïve evaluation works for Q under $(\!|\ |\!)_{\text{CWA}}$.*

9. MINIMAL VALUATIONS SEMANTICS

So far all the semantics that we saw allowed arbitrary valuations to be applied to instances with nulls. These are not the only possible semantics. In fact [18], based on earlier work in the area of logic programming [25], proposed a powerset semantics that is based on *minimal* valuations. We now introduce it in our context (as [18] defined it in the context of data exchange).

For now we deal with database homomorphisms, i.e., $h(c) = c$ for each $c \in \mathsf{Const}$. We say that a homomorphism h defined on an instance D is *D-minimal* if no proper subinstance of $h(D)$ is a homomorphic image of D; equivalently, there is no other homomorphism h' so that $h'(D) \subsetneq h(D)$. If h is a valuation, then we talk about a D-minimal valuation.

Not every valuation (or homomorphism) is minimal. Consider an incomplete table $D = \{(\bot, \bot), (\bot, \bot')\}$ and a valuation $v(\bot) = 1$, $v(\bot') = 2$. This is not minimal: take for instance $v'(\bot) = v'(\bot') = 1$ and we have $v'(D) \subsetneq v(D)$. The valuation v' is minimal.

The semantics of [18] is defined as

$$(\!|D|\!)_{\text{CWA}}^{\min} = \left\{ \bigcup_{h \in \mathcal{H}} h(D) \;\middle|\; \begin{array}{l} \mathcal{H} \text{ is a nonempty set of} \\ D\text{-minimal valuations.} \end{array} \right\}.$$

This is a powerset-based semantics, and the semantic relation it uses is the union relation $\mathcal{R}_{\cup}$, the same as in Section 7. However the valuation relation is no longer $\mathcal{R}_{\text{val}}^{\text{rdb}}$, allowing all valuations, but rather $\mathcal{R}_{\text{val}}^{\min}$ containing all pairs $(D, \{h(D) \mid h \in \mathcal{H}\})$ with $\mathcal{H}$ ranging over nonempty sets of D-minimal valuations.

The fact that we no longer allow all valuations makes the equivalence of naïve evaluation and preservation of $\mathcal{R}_{\text{sem}}$-homomorphisms invalid (we shall see an example soon). The main reason is that the saturation property does not longer hold, and therefore Theorem 1 is no longer applicable. The solution to the problem lies in establishing connections between minimal homomorphisms, naïve evaluations, and *cores* of database instances, which we do next.

Minimal homomorphisms and cores

Recall that a *core* of a structure D (in our case, a relational database of vocabulary σ) is a substructure $D' \subseteq D$ such that D' is a homomorphic image of D but no proper subinstance of D' is. In other words, there is a homomorphism $h : D \to D'$ but there is no homomorphism $g : D \to D''$ for $D'' \subsetneq D'$. It is known that a core is unique up to isomorphism, so we can talk of *the* core of D, and denote it by $\text{core}(D)$. A structure is called a core if $D = \text{core}(D)$. The cores are commonly used over graphs [17]; here we use them with the database notion of homomorphism that preserves constants (for which all results about cores remain true [14]).

Even if minimal homomorphisms are related to cores, their images cannot be described precisely in terms of cores, as shown next. We strengthen results given in several examples in [18] (where constants were used in an essential way):

Proposition 9. *If h is D-minimal, then $h(D)$ is a core and $h(D) = h(\text{core}(D))$. However, there is a core D and a homomorphism h defined on it so that $h(D)$ is a core, but h is not D-minimal. This also holds if both D and $h(D)$ contain only nulls, and if D is a graph.*

This also shows that $[\![D]\!]_{\text{CWA}}^{\min}$ need not be the same as $[\![\text{core}(D)]\!]_{\text{CWA}}$. Nevertheless, cores do play a crucial role in the study of minimal semantics. Recall that a generic Boolean query Q is weakly monotone under $(\!|\,|\!)^{\min}_{\text{CWA}}$ if $Q(D) = 1$ and $D' \in (\!|D|\!)^{\min}_{\text{CWA}}$ imply $Q(D') = 1$.

Theorem 7. *Let Q be a generic Boolean query. Then naïve evaluation works for Q under $(\!|\,|\!)^{\min}_{\text{CWA}}$ iff*

1. *Q is weakly monotone under $(\!|\,|\!)^{\min}_{\text{CWA}}$, and*
2. *$Q(D) = Q(\text{core}(D))$ for every D.*

Hence, the crucial new condition for naïve evaluation under minimal semantics is that Q cannot distinguish a database from its core.

Preservation and naïve evaluation We now relate weak monotonicity to homomorphism preservation. For this, we consider minimality for instances D over Const. For such an instance, and a homomorphism h defined on D, we let $\text{fix}(h, D) = \{c \in \mathsf{Const}(D) \mid h(c) = c\}$. Then h is called D-minimal if there is no homomorphism g with $\text{fix}(h, D) \subseteq \text{fix}(g, D)$ and $g(D) \subsetneq h(D)$. Note that database homomorphisms fix precisely the set of constants in D, so the first condition was not necessary.

Given a Boolean query Q, we say that it is *preserved under unions of minimal homomorphisms* if, whenever D is a database over Const and $\mathcal{H}$ is a nonempty set of D-minimal homomorphisms such that $\text{fix}(h, D) = \text{fix}(g, D)$ whenever $f, g \in \mathcal{H}$, we have that $Q(D) = 1$ implies $Q(\bigcup\{h(D) \mid h \in \mathcal{H}\}) = 1$.

Proposition 10. *Let Q be a generic Boolean query. Then it is weakly monotone under $(\!|\,|\!)^{\min}_{\text{CWA}}$ iff it is preserved under unions of minimal homomorphisms.*

From this, we can derive the following result. We say that naïve evaluation works for Q over D if the certain answer to Q over D coincides with $Q(D)$.

Theorem 8. *Let Q be a Boolean query from $\exists\mathsf{Pos} + \forall\mathsf{G}^{\text{bool}}$. Then, under the $(\!|\,|\!)^{\min}_{\text{CWA}}$:*

- *naïve evaluation works for Q over D if D is a core; and*
- *naïve evaluation works for Q iff $Q(D) = Q(\text{core}(D))$ for all D.*

Note that the second statement of the theorem is an immediate corollary of Proposition 10 and the fact that minimal homomorphisms are homomorphisms.

The preconditions that D be a core, or that $Q(D) = Q(\text{core}(D))$, are essential. To see this, consider an incomplete instance $D = \{(\bot, \bot), (\bot, \bot')\}$. Every D-minimal valuation h must satisfy $h(\bot) = h(\bot')$, i.e., their images are precisely the instances $\{(c, c)\}$ for $c \in \mathsf{Const}$. Hence, under $(\!|\,|\!)^{\min}_{\text{CWA}}$, the certain answer to $\forall x, y\, (D(x, y) \rightarrow x = y)$ is true, while evaluating this formula on D produces false. The reason naïve evaluation does not return certain answers (although the formula is in $\exists\mathsf{Pos} + \forall\mathsf{G}^{\text{bool}}$) is that $Q(D) \neq Q(\text{core}(D))$, since $\text{core}(D) = \{(\bot, \bot)\}$.

Non-boolean queries As before, results shown here extend to non-Boolean queries. Specifically, we can show the following, using the notion of weak preservation and techniques of Section 8.

Proposition 11. *Given a generic k-ary query Q, naïve evaluation works for Q under $(\!|\,|\!)^{\min}_{\text{CWA}}$ iff Q is weakly preserved under unions of minimal homomorphisms and $Q^{\mathsf{C}}(D) = Q^{\mathsf{C}}(\text{core}(D))$, for each database D.*

In particular, if Q is an $\exists\mathsf{Pos} + \forall\mathsf{G}^{\text{bool}}$ query, then naïve evaluation works for Q over cores; and furthermore, naïve evaluation works for Q over all databases iff $Q^{\mathsf{C}}(D) = Q^{\mathsf{C}}(\text{core}(D))$, for every D.

10. FUTURE WORK

We now present the main directions in which we would like to extend this work.

Other data models So far we looked at either a very general setting, which can subsume practically every data model, or at relational databases. We would like to extend our results to XML. At this time, we have a good understanding of the semantics of incomplete XML documents and the complexity of answering queries over them [3, 8, 15] that can serve as a good starting point.

Other languages When we dealt with relations, we studied FO as the main query language. However, our structural results are in no way limited to FO. In fact it is known that naïve evaluation works for datalog (without negation). Given the toolkit of this paper, we would like to consider queries in languages that go beyond FO and admit naïve evaluation.

Preservation results There are open questions related to preservation results in both finite and infinite model theory. We already mentioned that the results of [21] about preservation under strong onto homomorphisms are limited to a simple vocabulary, and even then appear to be problematic. We would like to establish a precise characterization in the infinite case, and see whether it holds or fails in the finite. We also want to look at preservation on restricted classes of structures, following [7] which looked at bounded treewidth (but does not capture XML with data).

The impact of constraints Constraints (e.g., keys and foreign keys) have a huge impact on the complexity of finding certain answers [10, 33], so it is thus natural to ask how they affect good classes we described in this paper. Constraints appear in another model of incompleteness – conditional tables [19] – that in general have higher complexity of query evaluation [2] but are nonetheless useful in several applications [6].

Applications In applications such as data integration and exchange, finding certain answers is the standard query answering semantics [5, 22]. In fact one of our semantics came from data exchange literature [18].

Semantics	symbol	Naïve evaluation works for
open world	$[\![\ ]\!]_{\mathrm{OWA}}$	$\exists\mathsf{Pos}$ = unions of CQs
weak closed-world	$[\![\ ]\!]_{\mathrm{WCWA}}$	Pos
closed world:	$[\![\ ]\!]_{\mathrm{CWA}}$	$\mathsf{Pos} + \forall\mathsf{G}$
powerset closed-world	$(\!\|\ \|\!)_{\mathrm{CWA}}$	$\exists\mathsf{Pos} + \forall\mathsf{G}^{\mathrm{bool}}$
minimal, powerset closed-world	$(\!\|\ \|\!)^{\min}_{\mathrm{CWA}}$	$\exists\mathsf{Pos} + \forall\mathsf{G}^{\mathrm{bool}}$, over cores

Figure 1: Summary of naïve evaluation results for FO queries

We would like to see whether our techniques help find classes of queries for which query answering becomes easy in exchange and integration scenarios.

Minimal semantics: why cores? What makes cores so special for minimal semantics? Can results of Section 9 be extended to other types of semantics, with different constructions playing the role of cores? And are there other natural semantics based on the notion of minimality?

Bringing back the infinite We have used a number of results from infinite model theory to get our syntactic classes. Another way of appealing to logic over infinite structures to handle incompleteness was advocated by Reiter [27, 29] three decades ago. In that approach, an incomplete database D is viewed as a logical theory T_D, and finding certain answers to Q amounts to checking whether T_D entails Q. This is in general an undecidable problem, and entailment in the finite is known to be more problematic than unrestricted one. This is reminiscent of the situation with homomorphism preservation results, but we saw that we can use infinite results to obtain useful sufficient conditions. Motivated by this, we would like to revisit Reiter's proof-theoretic approach and connect it with our semantic approach.

Acknowledgments Work partly supported by EPSRC grants G049165 and J015377.

11. References

[1] S. Abiteboul, R. Hull, and V. Vianu. *Foundations of Databases.* Addison-Wesley, 1995.

[2] S. Abiteboul, P Kanellakis, and G. Grahne. On the representation and querying of sets of possible worlds. *TCS*, 78(1):158–187, 1991.

[3] S. Abiteboul, L. Segoufin, and V. Vianu. Representing and querying XML with incomplete information. *ACM TODS*, 31(1):208–254, 2006.

[4] M. Ajtai, Y. Gurevich. Monotone versus positive. *J. ACM* 34(4):1004-1015 (1987).

[5] M. Arenas, P. Barceló, L. Libkin, F. Murlak. *Relational and XML Data Exchange.* Morgan & Claypool, 2010.

[6] M. Arenas, J. Pérez, J. Reutter. Data exchange beyond complete data. In *PODS'11*, pages 83–94.

[7] A. Atserias, A. Dawar, P. Kolaitis. On preservation under homomorphisms and unions of conjunctive queries. *J. ACM* 53(2):208-237 (2006).

[8] P. Barceló, L. Libkin, A. Poggi, and C. Sirangelo. XML with incomplete information. *J. ACM* 58(1): 1–62 (2010).

[9] P. Buneman, A. Jung, A. Ohori. Using powerdomains to generalize relational databases. *TCS* 91 (1991), 23–55.

[10] A. Calì, D. Lembo, and R. Rosati. On the decidability and complexity of query answering over inconsistent and incomplete databases. In *PODS'03*, pages 260–271.

[11] C.C. Chang and H.J. Keisler. *Model Theory.* North Holland, 1990.

[12] K. Compton. Some useful preservation theorems. *J. Symb. Logic* 48 (1983), 427–440.

[13] C. Date and H. Darwin. *A Guide to the SQL Standard.* Addison-Wesley, 1996.

[14] R. Fagin, P. Kolaitis, L. Popa. Data exchange: getting to the core. *ACM TODS* 30(1):174-210 (2005).

[15] A. Gheerbrant, L. Libkin, T. Tan. On the complexity of query answering over incomplete XML documents. *ICDT'12*, pages 169-181.

[16] C. Gunter. *Semantics of Programming Languages.* The MIT Press, 1992.

[17] P. Hell and J. Nešetřil. *Graphs and Homomorphisms.* Oxford University Press, 2004.

[18] A. Hernich. Answering non-monotonic queries in relational data exchange. *LMCS* 7(3) (2011).

[19] T. Imieliński and W. Lipski. Incomplete information in relational databases. *J. ACM*, 31(4):761–791, 1984.

[20] H. J. Keisler. Finite approximations of infinitely long formulas. *Symp. Theory of Models*, 1965, pages 158–169.

[21] H. J. Keisler. Some applications of infinitely long formulas. *Journal of Symbolic Logic*, 1965, pages 339–349.

[22] M. Lenzerini. Data integration: a theoretical perspective. In *PODS'02*, pages 233–246.

[23] L. Libkin. A semantics-based approach to design of query languages for partial information. In *Semantics in Databases*, LNCS 1358, 1998, pages 170–208.

[24] L. Libkin. Incomplete information and certain answers in general data models. *PODS'11*, pages 59–70.

[25] J. Minker. On indefinite databases and the closed world assumption. In *CADE'82*, pages 292–308.

[26] A. Ohori. Semantics of types for database objects. *Theoretical Computer Science* 76 (1990), 53–91.

[27] R. Reiter. On closed world data bases. In *Logic and Data Bases*, 1977, pages 55–76.

[28] R. Reiter. Equality and domain closure in first-order databases. *J. ACM* 27(2): 235-249 (1980).

[29] R. Reiter. Towards a logical reconstruction of relationál database theory. In *On Conceptual Modelling*, 1982, pages 191–233.

[30] B. Rossman. Homomorphism preservation theorems. *J. ACM* 55(3): (2008).

[31] B. Rounds. Situation-theoretic aspects of databases. In *Situation Theory and Appl.*, CSLI vol. 26, 1991, pages 229-256.

[32] A. Stolboushkin. Finitely monotone properties. In *LICS'95*, pages 324–330.

[33] M. Vardi. On the integrity of databases with incomplete information. In *PODS'86*, pages 252–266.

Sketching via Hashing: From Heavy Hitters to Compressive Sensing to Sparse Fourier Transform

Piotr Indyk
MIT
indyk@mit.edu

Categories and Subject Descriptors

F.2.1 [**Analysis of Algorithms and Problem Complexity**]: Numerical Algorithms and Problems—*Computations on matrices; Computation of transforms (e.g., fast Fourier transform)*

General Terms

Algorithms

Keywords

Dimensionality reduction, hashing, sparse Fourier transform, sparsity

1. INTRODUCTION

Sketching via hashing is a popular and useful method for processing large data sets. Its basic idea is as follows. Suppose that we have a large multi-set of elements $S = \{a_1, \ldots a_s\} \subset \{1 \ldots n\}$, and we would like to identify the elements[1] that occur "frequently" in S. The algorithm starts by selecting a hash function h that maps the elements into an array $c[1 \ldots m]$. The array entries are initialized to 0. Then, for each element $a \in S$, the algorithm increments[2] $c[h(a)]$. At the end of the process, each array entry $c[j]$ contains the count of all data elements $a \in S$ mapped to j. It can be observed that if an element a occurs frequently enough in the data set S, then the value of the counter $c[h(a)]$ must be large. That is, "frequent" elements are mapped to "heavy" buckets. By identifying the elements mapped to heavy buckets and repeating the process several times, one can efficiently recover the frequent elements, possibly together with a few extra ones (false positives).

[1]These elements are often referred to as *heavy hitters* or *elephants*.

[2]Typically, the value is incremented by 1. However, some algorithms such as Count Sketch [CCF02] or the pre-identification procedure of [GGI$^+$02b] use randomly chosen increments.

PODS'13, June 22–27, 2013, New York, New York, USA.

Variants of this method have originated in several fields, including databases [FSGM$^+$98, CM03a, CM03b], computer networks [FCAB98, EV02] (cf. [BM04]) and theoretical computer science [CCF02, GGI$^+$02b, CM04]. One of the key features of this method is that it allows to *approximate* the counts of the elements using very limited storage while making only a single pass over the data. As a result, the method has become one of the staples in the field of *data stream computing* [Mut05]. However, this was just the beginning. Over the last decade, this approach has been used to design improved algorithms for remarkably diverse tasks such as *compressive sensing, dimensionality reduction* and *sparse Fourier transforms.* In this survey we give a brief overview of how hashing is used in the aforementioned applications.

In order to apply the approach to those tasks, the first step is to view the hashing process as a linear mapping of the characteristic vector x of the set S to the vector c. Specifically, for any $j = 1 \ldots m$, $c[j] = \sum_{a:h(a)=j} x_a$. This can be written as $c = Ax$ where A is a sparse binary $m \times n$ matrix. The algorithmic benefit of using such mappings is due to the sparsity of the matrix A (which makes it easy to perform various tasks such as matrix-vector multiplication efficiently) as well as the overall simplicity of the hashing process.

2. COMPRESSED SENSING

In compressed sensing [Don06, CRT06] one is given the vector Ax and the goal is to recover an approximation x' to x that is k-sparse, i.e., that has at most k non-zero entries. The approximation should (approximately) minimize the error $\|x' - x\|_p$ for some choice of the ℓ_p norm. Note that for any value of p, the error $\|x - x'\|_p$ is minimized when the approximation x' consists of the k largest (in magnitude) coefficients of x. This problem has numerous applications in signal processing or imaging, where signals are quite sparse, possibly after applying an appropriate change-of-basis transform. In those applications compressed sensing allows one to recover a good approximation to a signal x from only few "measurements" Ax. In particular, the result of [CRT06] shows that one can recover a k-sparse approximation to x using only $m = O(k \log(n/k))$ measurements, and it is known that this bound cannot be improved [Don06, DIPW10, FPRU10]. The bound is achieved using matrices A with random i.i.d. Gaussian or Bernoulli entries. Unfortunately, any operation on such matrices takes $O(nm)$

time, which makes the recovery algorithms somewhat slow for high values of n.[3]

It was observed in [CM06] (cf. [GI10]) that the algorithm of [CCF02] yields a recovery procedure and a matrix A with $O(k \log n)$ measurements, which is not too far from the optimal bound (although the recovery procedure is only correct with high probability). At the same time, thanks to the sparsity of the matrix A, the approximation x' can be computed in only $O(n \log n)$ time. Compressive sensing via sparse matrices has attracted a considerable interest in the literature, see e.g., [SBB06, CM06, WGR07, GSTV07, XH07, SBB10, WWR10, KDXH11, Ind08, LMP+08, BGI+08, IR08, BIR08, JXHC09, GLPS10, GM11, PR12, BJCC12] or a survey [GI10]. In particular, the results of [BGI+08, IR08, BIR08, GLPS10] show that sparse matrices can match the optimal $O(k \log(n/k))$ measurement bound achieved via fully random matrices while supporting faster algorithms, albeit in some cases providing somewhat weaker approximation guarantees.

3. DIMENSIONALITY REDUCTION

A mapping from x to Ax can be also used to reduce the dimensionality of general (non-sparse) vectors x, as per the Johnson-Lindenstrauss theorem [JL84]. The original theorem used random dense matrices, which necessitated $O(nm)$ matrix-vector multiplication time. Faster dimensionality reduction is possible by using structured matrices that support much faster matrix-vector multiplication procedures [AC10, AL11, KW11, NPW12], but the reduced dimension is either sub-optimal or restricted. Moreover, the running times of those procedures do not scale with the the sparsity of the vector x. In contrast, the line of research on sparse dimensionality reduction matrices [SPD+09, WDL+09, DKS10, BOR10, KN12] has led to matrices with optimal reduced dimension bounds that are supported by algorithms with runtime $O(\epsilon km)$, where k is the number of non-zero entries in x and $\epsilon > 0$ is an approximation parameter that is arbitrarily close to 0. Using such matrices, [CW13] (see also [NN12, MM13]) recently showed almost linear time approximate algorithms for sparse regression and low-rank approximation, the key problems in numerical linear algebra.

4. SPARSE FOURIER TRANSFORM

The Discrete Fourier Transform (DFT) maps an n-dimensional signal x sampled in time domain into an n-dimensional spectrum $\hat{x}$. The widely used Fast Fourier Transform algorithm performs this task in $O(n \log n)$ time. It is not known whether this algorithm can be further improved. However, it is known that one can compute DFT significantly faster for signals whose spectrum is (approximately) sparse. Such sparsity is common for many data sets occurring in signal processing, imaging and communication. For such signals, one may hope for faster algorithms.

The first algorithms of this type were designed for the Hadamard Transform, i.e., the Fourier transform over the Boolean cube [KM91, Lev93] (cf. [GL89, Gol99]). Soon, algorithms for the complex Fourier transform were discovered as well [Man92, GGI+02a, AGS03, GMS05, Iwe10, Iwe12, Aka10, HIKP12b, HIKP12a, LWC12, BCG+12, GHI+13, HKPV13]. In particular, the algorithm given in [HIKP12a] computes the DFT of a signal with k-sparse spectrum in $O(k \log n)$ time. Note that this running time improves over the FFT as long as $k = o(n)$. In fact, for low values of k the running time is *sub-linear* in n, i.e., the algorithm does not even read its input. Instead, it infers the large Fourier coefficients by randomly sampling the signal x.

Perhaps surprisingly, most of the aforementioned algorithms (notably [Lev93, GGI+02a, GMS05, Iwe10, Iwe12, Aka10, HIKP12b, HIKP12a, LWC12, BCG+12, GHI+13, HKPV13])[4] use sketching via hashing, albeit in the frequency domain. Specifically, the algorithms utilize multiple band-pass filters which bin the spectrum coefficients into a number of "buckets". The process is randomized to ensure that each coefficient is mapped to a "random" bucket and that two large coefficients are not likely to collide. A somewhat distinctive feature of this process is that can yield "leaky" buckets, where a large coefficient affects not only the bucket it is mapped into, but also the nearby ones. Fortunately, thanks to a careful filter design, the leakage can be made negligible [HIKP12b, HIKP12a, BCG+12, HKPV13] or even be completely eliminated [Iwe10, Iwe12, LWC12, GHI+13].

For further overview of recent work on sub-linear algorithms for sparse Fourier transform as well their applications, see [GIKR13].

5. REFERENCES

[AC10] Nir Ailon and Bernard Chazelle. Faster dimension reduction. *Communications of the ACM*, 53(2):97–104, 2010.

[AGS03] A. Akavia, S. Goldwasser, and S. Safra. Proving hard-core predicates using list decoding. *FOCS*, 44:146–159, 2003.

[Aka10] A. Akavia. Deterministic sparse Fourier approximation via fooling arithmetic progressions. *COLT*, pages 381–393, 2010.

[AL11] Nir Ailon and Edo Liberty. An almost optimal unrestricted fast Johnson-Lindenstrauss transform. *SODA*, pages 185–191, 2011.

[BCG+12] P. Boufounos, V. Cevher, A. C. Gilbert, Y. Li, and M. J. Strauss. What's the frequency, kenneth?: Sublinear Fourier sampling off the grid. *RANDOM/APPROX*, 2012.

[BGI+08] R. Berinde, A. Gilbert, P. Indyk, H. Karloff, and M. Strauss. Combining geometry and combinatorics: a unified approach to sparse signal recovery. *Allerton*, 2008.

[BIR08] R. Berinde, P. Indyk, and M. Ruzic. Practical near-optimal sparse recovery in the l_1 norm. *Allerton*, 2008.

[BJCC12] Mayank Bakshi, Sidharth Jaggi, Sheng Cai, and Minghua Chen. Sho-fa: Robust compressive sensing with order-optimal complexity, measurements, and bits. *arXiv preprint arXiv:1207.2335*, 2012.

[BM04] Andrei Broder and Michael Mitzenmacher. Network applications of bloom filters: A

[3]This issue can be alleviated by using random *structured* matrices, which support matrix-vector product in $O(n \log n)$ time [CT06, RV06, CGV13, NPW12]. However, even the best construction due to [NPW12] requires the number of measurements to be $O(\log^2 n)$ times larger than optimal, at least in theory.

[4]See also [GOS+11] which applied a similar method to the related problem of testing Fourier sparsity.

survey. *Internet Mathematics*, 1(4):485–509, 2004.

[BOR10] Vladimir Braverman, Rafail Ostrovsky, and Yuval Rabani. Rademacher chaos, random eulerian graphs and the sparse Johnson-Lindenstrauss transform. *arXiv preprint arXiv:1011.2590*, 2010.

[CCF02] M. Charikar, K. Chen, and M. Farach-Colton. Finding frequent items in data streams. *ICALP*, 2002.

[CGV13] Mahdi Cheraghchi, Venkatesan Guruswami, and Ameya Velingker. Restricted isometry of Fourier matrices and list decodability of random linear codes. *SODA*, 2013.

[CM03a] Saar Cohen and Yossi Matias. Spectral bloom filters. *SIGMOD*, pages 241–252, 2003.

[CM03b] Graham Cormode and S. Muthukrishnan. What's hot and what's not: tracking most frequent items dynamically. *PODS*, pages 296–306, 2003.

[CM04] G. Cormode and S. Muthukrishnan. Improved data stream summaries: The count-min sketch and its applications. *LATIN*, 2004.

[CM06] G. Cormode and S. Muthukrishnan. Combinatorial algorithms for Compressed Sensing. *Proc. 40th Ann. Conf. Information Sciences and Systems*, Mar. 2006.

[CRT06] E. J. Candès, J. Romberg, and T. Tao. Stable signal recovery from incomplete and inaccurate measurements. *Comm. Pure Appl. Math.*, 59(8):1208–1223, 2006.

[CT06] Emmanuel J Candes and Terence Tao. Near-optimal signal recovery from random projections: Universal encoding strategies? *Information Theory, IEEE Transactions on*, 52(12):5406–5425, 2006.

[CW13] Kenneth L Clarkson and David P Woodruff. Low rank approximation and regression in input sparsity time. *STOC*, 2013.

[DIPW10] K. Do Ba, P. Indyk, E. Price, and D. Woodruff. Lower bounds for sparse recovery. *SODA*, 2010.

[DKS10] Anirban Dasgupta, Ravi Kumar, and Tamás Sarlós. A sparse Johnson-Lindenstrauss transform. *STOC*, pages 341–350, 2010.

[Don06] D. L. Donoho. Compressed Sensing. *Information Theory, IEEE Transactions on*, 52(4):1289–1306, Apr. 2006.

[EV02] Cristian Estan and George Varghese. New directions in traffic measurement and accounting. *SIGCOMM*, 2002.

[FCAB98] Li Fan, Pei Cao, Jussara M. Almeida, and Andrei Z. Broder. Summary cache: A scalable wide-area web cache sharing protocol. *SIGCOMM*, pages 254–265, 1998.

[FPRU10] S. Foucart, A. Pajor, H. Rauhut, and T. Ullrich. The gelfand widths of lp-balls for $0 < p \leq 1$. *preprint*, 2010.

[FSGM+98] Min Fang, Narayanan Shivakumar, Hector Garcia-Molina, Rajeev Motwani, and Jeffrey D Ullman. Computing iceberg queries efficiently. *VLDB*, 1998.

[GGI+02a] A. Gilbert, S. Guha, P. Indyk, M. Muthukrishnan, and M. Strauss. Near-optimal sparse Fourier representations via sampling. *STOC*, 2002.

[GGI+02b] A. C. Gilbert, S. Guha, P. Indyk, Y. Kotidis, S. Muthukrishnan, and M. J. Strauss. Fast, small-space algorithms for approximate histogram maintenance. *STOC*, 2002.

[GHI+13] Badih Ghazi, Haitham Hassanieh, Piotr Indyk, Dina Katabi, Eric Price, and Lixin Shi. Sample-optimal average-case sparse fourier transform in two dimensions. *arXiv preprint arXiv:1303.1209*, 2013.

[GI10] A. Gilbert and P. Indyk. Sparse recovery using sparse matrices. *Proceedings of IEEE*, 2010.

[GIKR13] Anna Gilbert, Piotr Indyk, Dina Katabi, and Ramesh Raskar. Workshop on sparse Fourier transform etc. *http://groups.csail.mit.edu/netmit/sFFT/workshop.html*, 2013.

[GL89] O. Goldreich and L. Levin. A hard-corepredicate for all one-way functions. *STOC*, pages 25–32, 1989.

[GLPS10] A. C. Gilbert, Y. Li, E. Porat, and M. J. Strauss. Approximate sparse recovery: optimizing time and measurements. *STOC*, pages 475–484, 2010.

[GM11] Michael T Goodrich and Michael Mitzenmacher. Invertible bloom lookup tables. In *Allerton*, pages 792–799, 2011.

[GMS05] A. Gilbert, M. Muthukrishnan, and M. Strauss. Improved time bounds for near-optimal space Fourier representations. *SPIE Conference, Wavelets*, 2005.

[Gol99] O. Goldreich. Modern cryptography, probabilistic proofs and pseudorandomness. *Algorithms and Combinatorics*, 17, 1999.

[GOS+11] Parikshit Gopalan, Ryan O'Donnell, Rocco A. Servedio, Amir Shpilka, and Karl Wimmer. Testing fourier dimensionality and sparsity. *SIAM J. Comput.*, 40(4):1075–1100, 2011.

[GSTV07] A. C. Gilbert, M. J. Strauss, J. A. Tropp, and R. Vershynin. One sketch for all: fast algorithms for compressed sensing. *STOC*, pages 237–246, 2007.

[HIKP12a] H. Hassanieh, P. Indyk, D. Katabi, and E. Price. Near-optimal algorithm for sparse Fourier transform. *STOC*, 2012.

[HIKP12b] H. Hassanieh, P. Indyk, D. Katabi, and E. Price. Simple and practical algorithm for sparse Fourier transform. *SODA*, 2012.

[HKPV13] Sabine Heider, Stefan Kunis, Daniel Potts, and Michael Veit. A sparse prony fft. 2013.

[Ind08] P. Indyk. Explicit constructions for compressed sensing of sparse signals. *SODA*, 2008.

[IR08] P. Indyk and M. Ruzic. Near-optimal sparse recovery in the l_1 norm. *FOCS*, 2008.

[Iwe10] M. A. Iwen. Combinatorial sublinear-time Fourier algorithms. *Foundations of*

Computational Mathematics, 10:303–338, 2010.

[Iwe12] M.A. Iwen. Improved approximation guarantees for sublinear-time Fourier algorithms. *Applied And Computational Harmonic Analysis*, 2012.

[JL84] W. B. Johnson and J. Lindenstrauss. Extensions of Lipschitz mapping into Hilbert space. *Conf. in modern analysis and probability*, 26:189–206, 1984.

[JXHC09] S. Jafarpour, W. Xu, B. Hassibi, and A. R. Calderbank. Efficient and robust compressed sensing using high-quality expander graphs. *Information Theory, IEEE Transactions on*, 55(9):4299–4308, 2009.

[KDXH11] M. A. Khajehnejad, A. G. Dimakis, W. Xu, and B. Hassibi. Sparse recovery of positive signals with minimal expansion. *Signal Processing, IEEE Transactions on*, 59(1):196–208, 2011.

[KM91] E. Kushilevitz and Y. Mansour. Learning decision trees using the Fourier spectrum. *STOC*, 1991.

[KN12] Daniel M Kane and Jelani Nelson. Sparser Johnson-Lindenstrauss transforms. *SODA*, pages 1195–1206, 2012.

[KW11] Felix Krahmer and Rachel Ward. New and improved Johnson-Lindenstrauss embeddings via the restricted isometry property. *SIAM Journal on Mathematical Analysis*, 43(3):1269–1281, 2011.

[Lev93] L.A. Levin. Randomness and non-determinism. *J. Symb. Logic*, 58(3):1102–1103, 1993.

[LMP+08] Y. Lu, A. Montanari, B. Prabhakar, S. Dharmapurikar, and A. Kabbani. Counter braids: A novel counter architecture for per-flow measurement. *SIGMETRICS*, 2008.

[LWC12] D. Lawlor, Y. Wang, and A. Christlieb. Adaptive sub-linear time Fourier algorithms. *arXiv:1207.6368*, 2012.

[Man92] Y. Mansour. Randomized interpolation and approximation of sparse polynomials. *ICALP*, 1992.

[MM13] Xiangrui Meng and Michael W Mahoney. Low-distortion subspace embeddings in input-sparsity time and applications to robust linear regression. *STOC*, 2013.

[Mut05] S Muthukrishnan. *Data streams: Algorithms and applications*. Now Publishers Inc, 2005.

[NN12] Jelani Nelson and Huy L Nguyên. Osnap: Faster numerical linear algebra algorithms via sparser subspace embeddings. *arXiv preprint arXiv:1211.1002*, 2012.

[NPW12] Jelani Nelson, Eric Price, and Mary Wootters. New constructions of RIP matrices with fast multiplication and fewer rows. *CoRR*, abs/1211.0986, 2012.

[PR12] Sameer Pawar and Kannan Ramchandran. A hybrid dft-ldpc framework for fast, efficient and robust compressive sensing. In *Allerton*, pages 1943–1950, 2012.

[RV06] M. Rudelson and R. Veshynin. Sparse reconstruction by convex relaxation: Fourier and Gaussian measurements. *Proc. 40th Ann. Conf. Information Sciences and Systems*, Mar. 2006.

[SBB06] S. Sarvotham, D. Baron, and R. G. Baraniuk. Sudocodes - fast measurement and reconstruction of sparse signals. *IEEE International Symposium on Information Theory*, 2006.

[SBB10] S. Sarvotham, D. Baron, and R. G. Baraniuk. Bayesian compressive sensing via belief propagation. *Signal Processing, IEEE Transactions on*, 58(1):269–280, 2010.

[SPD+09] Qinfeng Shi, James Petterson, Gideon Dror, John Langford, Alex Smola, and SVN Vishwanathan. Hash kernels for structured data. *The Journal of Machine Learning Research*, 10:2615–2637, 2009.

[WDL+09] Kilian Weinberger, Anirban Dasgupta, John Langford, Alex Smola, and Josh Attenberg. Feature hashing for large scale multitask learning. *ICML*, pages 1113–1120, 2009.

[WGR07] Wei Wang, Minos Garofalakis, and Kannan Ramchandran. Distributed sparse random projections for refinable approximation. *IPSN*, pages 331–339, 2007.

[WWR10] W. Wang, M. J. Wainwright, and K. Ramchandran. Information-theoretic limits on sparse signal recovery: Dense versus sparse measurement matrices. *Information Theory, IEEE Transactions on*, 56(6):2967–2979, 2010.

[XH07] W. Xu and B. Hassibi. Efficient compressive sensing with determinstic guarantees using expander graphs. *IEEE Information Theory Workshop*, 2007.

Collaborative Data-Driven Workflows: Think Global, Act Local*

Serge Abiteboul
INRIA Saclay & ENS Cachan
94235 CACHAN Cedex, France
serge.abiteboul@inria.fr

Victor Vianu†
UC San Diego & INRIA Saclay
La Jolla, CA 92093
vianu@cs.ucsd.edu

ABSTRACT

We introduce and study a model of *collaborative data-driven workflows*. In a local-as-view style, each peer has a partial view of a global instance that remains purely virtual. Local updates have side effects on other peers' data, defined via the global instance. We also assume that the peers provide (an abstraction of) their specifications, so that each peer can actually see and reason on the specification of the entire system.

We study the ability of a peer to carry out runtime reasoning about the global run of the system, and in particular about actions of other peers, based on its own local observations. A main contribution is to show that, under a reasonable restriction (namely, *key-visibility*), one can construct a finite symbolic representation of the infinite set of global runs consistent with given local observations. Using the symbolic representation, we show that we can evaluate in PSPACE a large class of properties over global runs, expressed in an extension of first-order logic with past linear-time temporal operators, PLTL-FO. We also provide a variant of the algorithm allowing to *incrementally* monitor a statically defined property, and then develop an extension allowing to monitor an infinite class of properties sharing the same temporal structure, defined dynamically as the run unfolds. Finally, we consider an extension of the language, that permits workflow control with PLTL-FO formulas. We prove that this does not increase the power of the workflow specification language, thereby showing that the language is closed under such introspective reasoning.

*This work has been partially funded by the European Research Council under the European Community's Seventh Framework Programme (FP7/2007-2013) / ERC grant Webdam, agreement 226513. http://webdam.inria.fr/

†This author was supported in part by the NSF under award III-0916515. Work done in part while visiting INRIA.

PODS'13, June 22–27, 2013, New York, New York, USA.

Categories and Subject Descriptors

H.4.1 [**Office Automation**]: Workflow management; H.2.3 [**Languages**]: Query languages

Keywords

Views, peers, monitoring, reasoning

1. INTRODUCTION

Process-centric workflows focus on control flow, often abstracting away data almost entirely. In contrast, recently proposed data-driven workflows treat data as first-class citizens, e.g., the *business artifact model* pioneered in [21] and deployed by IBM in commercial products. Data-driven workflows have become ubiquitous in a wide array of application domains. Their system architecture may range from totally centralized to fully distributed. While multiple-peer workflows have been extensively studied in the process-centric case using finite-state models, little formal research has been done on collaborative workflows centered around a database, which have infinitely many states (see related work). In this paper, we introduce a simple model for collaborative data-driven workflows and provide techniques that enable a peer to reason about runs of the global workflow based on its local observations.

In our model, peers modify local data using condition/update actions. The connection between the data at different peers is specified using a local-as-view approach, in which the data at each peer is an exact view of a virtual global database. We impose restrictions (using the presence of keys) to guarantee that peer updates can be propagated in an unambiguous manner to other peers. We assume that update propagation is instantaneous, i.e., we assume some underlying synchronization mechanism to support update propagation.

Our goal is to enable peers to reason, based on local observations, about the global state of the system and about actions occurring at other peers. This can serve as the basis for a wealth of runtime tools for monitoring the global run, detecting and diagnosing anomalous behavior, balancing load to improve efficiency, or analyzing the current run to derive competitive advantage over other peers.

Consider a peer p in such a system. We assume p knows the specification of all the other peers. (In fact, p is likely to only be given an *abstraction* of these specifications, hiding details and confidential behavior of the peers.) Peer p only sees a local view of the global run. Note that there are generally infinitely many global runs that are consistent with p's observations. Based on this local view, one would like to evaluate queries over the global run, specified by an extension of first-order logic (FO) with temporal operators (PLTL-FO), referring to the entire history of the run. In particular, we would like to decide whether a formula in this language is *possibly* or *certainly* true in the global runs that correspond to what p sees locally. Deciding such properties is at the heart of the paper.

More precisely, our main contributions are the following:

- developing a finite symbolic representation system for the infinite set of global runs consistent with local observations;
- using the representation system to provide a PSPACE algorithm for evaluating PLTL-FO properties of the global runs consistent with the local observations, with respect to both possible and certain world semantics;
- developing an incremental variant of the algorithm suitable for monitoring some properties specified beforehand; and extending this variant to monitor an infinite class of properties sharing the same temporal structure, so that properties can be chosen in this class while the run unfolds.

Finally, we consider the effect of integrating the reasoning previously described into the control of the workflow itself. This allows a peer to guide its actions based on properties of the global run that can be monitored, detecting some other peer actions that are not visible locally. We show, somewhat surprisingly, that adding such control features does not increase the expressiveness of the workflow specification language. Intuitively, this shows that the workflow specification language is closed under such introspective reasoning.

Related work. Although not focused explicitly on workflows, Dedalus [8, 16] and Webdamlog [4, 2] are systems supporting distributed data processing based on condition/action rules. Local-as-view approaches are considered in a number of P2P data management systems, e.g., Piazza [22] that also consider richer mappings to specify views. Update propagation between views is considered in a number of systems, e.g., based on ECA rules in Hyperion [9].

Finite-state workflows with multiple peers have been formalized and extensively studied using communicating finite-state systems (called CFSMs in [1, 10], and *e-compositions* in the context of Web services, as surveyed in [17, 18]). Formal research on infinite-state, data-driven collaborative workflows is still in an early stage. The business artifact model [21] has pioneered data-driven workflows, but formal studies have focused on the single-user scenario. Compositions of data-driven web services are studied in [12], focusing on automatic verification. Active XML [3] provides distributed data-driven workflows manipulating XML data.

A collaborative system for distributed data sharing geared towards life sciences applications is provided by the Orchestra project [15, 20]. The underlying update propagation model among peers is based on schema mappings and is similar to our local-as-view approach. However, Orchestra does not address the kind of analysis problems studied here.

Organization. After some preliminaries, we introduce the model of collaborative workflows. We then develop in Section 3 the representation system for the infinite set of global runs consistent with given peer observations. In Section 4, we show how the representation system can be used to evaluate PLTL-FO properties of global runs. We also consider incremental and preemptive evaluation, and discuss the expressiveness of introspection in workflow control.

2. THE MODEL

In this section, we introduce the model of collaborative workflows. We begin with some preliminaries, then introduce collaborative workflows.

Preliminaries. We assume an infinite data domain **dom** with one distinguished element $\perp$ (representing undefined data values). We also assume an infinite countable domain of variables **var** disjoint from **dom**. We denote variables by x, y, z, possibly with subscripts. A *relation schema* is a relation symbol together with a sequence of distinct attributes (whose length is the *arity* of the relation). We denote the set of attributes of R by $att(R)$. A *database schema* is a finite set of relation schemas. An *instance* of a database schema is a mapping I associating to each relation schema R a finite relation $I(R)$ over **dom**, of the same arity as R. An instance (or tuple) containing $\perp$ is called *partial*, and otherwise *total*.

We assume that each relation schema R is equipped with a unique key K, consisting of a non-empty subset of its attributes. We say that an instance I over R is *valid* if I satisfies the key constraint and all tuples in I are total on the key attributes.

We recall the notion of *conjunctive query with safe negation* ($\text{CQ}^\neg$ query for short). A *term* is a variable or a constant. A *literal* is of the form $R(\bar{x})$, $\neg R(\bar{x})$, $x = y$, $x \neq y$, where $\bar{x}$ is a sequence of terms of appropriate arity, x is a variable, and y a term. A $\text{CQ}^\neg$ query is an expression $A_1 \wedge ... \wedge A_n$ (for $n \geq 0$) where each A_i is a literal and each variable x occurs in a positive relational literal or in an equality $x = c$ where $c \in$ **dom** (i.e., x is *bound*).

Collaborative schema and instance. A *collaborative schema* $\mathcal{S}$ consists of:

1. A database schema $\mathcal{D}$, the *global schema*, in which each relation is equipped with a key.
2. A finite set of peer names $\{p_i \mid 1 \leq i \leq m\}$.
3. For each peer p_i, the *local schema* $\mathcal{D}_i$ consisting of a set of relation schemas $R@p_i$, where $R \in \mathcal{D}$, $att(R@p_i) \subseteq att(R)$, and $att(R@p_i)$ contains the key of R.
4. For each $R \in \mathcal{D}$, $att(R) = \cup\{att(R@p_i) \mid R@p_i \in \mathcal{D}_i, 1 \leq i \leq m\}$.

The main motivation for (4) is to guarantee that the global instance (which is purely virtual) can be computed from the peer instances. Consider for instance some relation R in the global schema. Note that R may be "invisible" from some particular p_i, i.e., $R@p_i$ is not in $\mathcal{D}_i$. However because of (4) and the key constraints, $I(R)$ can be reconstructed from its projections on the peer schemas.

Let $\mathcal{S}$ be a collaborative schema with global schema $\mathcal{D}$ and peers $\{p_i \mid 1 \leq i \leq m\}$. A *global instance* of $\mathcal{S}$ is a valid instance I over $\mathcal{D}$. The *peer view* of I at p_i, denoted $I@p_i$, is the instance over $\mathcal{D}_i$ defined by: for each $R@p_i \in \mathcal{D}_i$, $I@p_i(R@p_i) = \pi_{att(R@p_i)}(I(R))$. Observe that this introduces a constraint on the instances $I@p_i$: they are projections of the same global instance. Note also that the peer views of an instance I uniquely determine the global instance because of the key constraints and condition (4). More precisely, for each R in $\mathcal{D}$, $I(R) = \bowtie \{I@p_i(R) \mid R@p_i \in \mathcal{D}_i\}$. In particular, this induces a connection between the local instances $\{I@p_i\}_{1 \leq i \leq m}$ that can be stated without reference to the global instance I (which is purely virtual and never materialized):

$$\text{for each } j \text{ and } R@p_j \in \mathcal{D}_j, I@p_j(R@p_j) = \pi_{att(R@p_j)}(\bowtie \{I@p_i(R@p_i) \mid R@p_i \in \mathcal{D}_i, 1 \leq i \leq m\})$$

REMARK 2.1. *The views we consider are limited to simple projections. However, more complex views can be provided using actions performed by peers. For instance, consider a selection query σ over a relation R. A peer p_i that sees a relation R can maintain in another relation, say R_σ, the result of $\sigma(R)$. Then any peer p_j that sees R_σ will see the result of that selection even if p_j does not have access to R.*

Example 2.2 We use as a running example a very simplified workflow to process travel expenses in a research institute. The workflow involves the following peers: researchers, e.g., Alice, who can initiate trip requests; a travel agency that provides expense estimates; and admin services that approve or deny trip expenses. The global schema has 3 relations (each with key Id): Submitted(Id, Person, Date, Location), Processing(Id, Person, Expense, Comment, Status) and Web(Id, Person, Date, Conference, Domain). If Domain="inter", the information is published on the Internet. If Domain="intra", it is only published on the Intranet of the institute. The peers' schemas (with the obvious associated view definitions) are the following (as noted in Remark 2.1, selections in view definitions can be simulated and are used for convenience):
Alice (and similarly for all other researchers):

Submitted(Id, "Alice", Date, Location)
Processing(Id, "Alice")
Web(Id, Person, Date, Conference, Domain)

Travel agency schema:

Submitted(Id, Person, Date, Location)
Processing(Id, Person, Expense)
Web(Id, Person, Date, Conference, "inter")

Admin services schema: same as global schema. □

An update to a peer's local data can be propagated to the other peers so that the local instances remain the views of a valid global instance. We assume here that propagation of updates is instantaneous, which can be ensured by the underlying system with a protocol involving asynchronous communication. We do not address this aspect here.

Formally, we define the effect on a global instance I of performing a tuple insertion and deletion at peer p_i. The semantics will guarantee that the resulting global instance remains valid.

Consider the deletion of a tuple t from $I(R@p_i)$. The resulting global instance J is obtained by deleting from $I(R)$ the tuple whose projection on $att(R@p_i)$ equals t, if such a tuple exists (note that there is at most one such tuple per relation).

Now consider the insertion of a tuple t in $I(R@p_i)$ (the more interesting case). Let $\bar{t}$ be the tuple over $att(R)$ extending t with $\perp$ for all attributes in $att(R) - att(R@p_i)$. Let J be the result of inserting into I the tuple $\bar{t}$, then chasing with respect to the key K of R. Specifically, the chase consists of the following. If there is another tuple u agreeing with $\bar{t}$ on K, and an attribute A for which one of $u(A)$ and $\bar{t}(A)$ is defined and the other is not (i.e. equals $\perp$), replace $\perp$ by the defined value of A in the other tuple. The insertion is said to be *consistent* if J is valid (the update is rejected otherwise).

We next illustrate the semantics of updates.

Example 2.3 Suppose we have a relation R over $ABCD$ with key A, $R@p1$ is over ABD and $R@p_2$ over ACD. The insertion of $(0,0,0)$ and $(1,1,1)$ in $R@p1$ propagates to the insertion of $(0,\perp,0)$ and $(1,\perp,1)$ in $R@p_2$. Then the deletion of $(0,\perp,0)$ from $R@p_2$ propagates to the deletion of $(0,0,0)$ from $R@p1$. And the insertion of $(1,2,2)$ in $R@p_2$ is refused. A subtlety is that we cannot consistently *modify* attributes of tuples with a given key across peers without losing information. For instance, suppose we wish to modify the D column of the tuple $(1,\perp,1)$ in $R@p_2$ from 1 to 2. This is done by deleting $(1,\perp,1)$ and inserting $(1,\perp,2)$. However, this does not propagate to a modification of D from 1 to 2 in $R@p_1$. Indeed, the previous deletion and insertion first delete $(1,1,1)$ from $R@p_1$, then insert the tuple $(1,\perp,2)$. Thus, the B column was lost as a side effect. It is not hard to extend the model with explicit modifications circumventing this problem. □

Collaborative workflow. A *collaborative workflow specification* (in short *workflow spec*) $\mathcal{W}$ consists of a collaborative schema $\mathcal{S}$ and a finite set of actions for each peer p_i of $\mathcal{W}$. An *action* at peer p_i is an expression
Update :- *Condition* where:

- *Condition* is a $CQ^\neg$ query over $\mathcal{D}_i$.
- *Update* is a non-empty sequence of positive and negative relational literals over $\mathcal{D}_i$ such that each variable occurring in a negative literal also occurs in *Condition*.

Intuitively, positive literals in the update are interpreted as insertions, and negative literals as deletions. Note that positive literals may use variables that do not occur in the condition. As we shall see, these are assigned new values, not in the current active domain.

Example 2.4 Continuing with Example 2.2, we next show some of the actions of the travel expense processing workflow. For readability, we use attribute names for variables, and underline those occurring only in insertions of actions, generating new values. The workflow proceeds as follows.

1. *Alice initiates a new trip request*
   Submitted(<u>Id</u>, "Alice", <u>Date</u>, <u>Location</u>) :-
2. *Alice publishes the trip on the Intranet*
   Web(Id, "Alice", Date, <u>Conference</u>, "intra") :-
   Submitted(Id, "Alice", Date, Location)
3. *Travel agency inserts an estimate of the cost*
   Processing(Id, Person, <u>Expense</u>) :-
   Submitted(Id, Person, Date, Location)

4. *Admin inserts comments*

   ¬ Processing(Id, Person, Expense, Comment, ⊥),
   Processing(Id, Person, Expense, Comment, ⊥) :-
   Processing(Id, Person, Expense, Comment, ⊥)

5. *Admin approves or rejects*

   Processing(Id, Person, Expense, Comment, "approve")
   :- Processing(Id, Person, Expense, Comment, ⊥)
   Processing(Id, Person, Expense, Comment, "reject") :-
   Processing(Id, Person, Expense, Comment, ⊥)

6. *Admin deletes rejected trip from the Intranet*

   ¬ Web(Id, Person, Date, Conference, "intra") :-
   Web(Id, Person, Date, Conference, "intra"),
   Processing(Id, Person, Expense, Comment, "reject")

7. *Admin publishes approved trip on the Internet*

   ¬ Web(Id, Person, Date, Conference, "intra"),
   Web(Id, Person, Date, Conference, "inter") :-
   Web(Id, Person, Date, Conference, "intra"),
   Processing(Id, Person, Expense, Comment, "approve")

Note that the workflow imposes a number of constraints on the actions of participants. For instance, an admin can modify a comment as many times as wished before a decision is made, but once a trip has been approved or rejected, the comment cannot be modified, because the condition of Rule (4) requires the status to be undefined (⊥). Rules (6,7) are internal computations of peer *Admin*: deletion of a rejected trip from the Intranet, and posting of an approved trip on the Internet. We may prefer that rules such as these be triggered automatically once a decision is made, and we could easily extend the model with immediate triggers. Observe the underlined variables in Rules (1-4), not bound in the body. Such unbound values have to be supplied either by the user or by the system; in which case, we will assume the system chooses new values outside the active domain. To simplify the presentation, we will ignore in the paper the differences between user and system actions, and assume that unbound variables are always assigned values outside the active domain. This assumption can be easily relaxed and does not affect our results. □

Workflow runs. Intuitively, the semantics of a workflow spec consists of runs of consecutive global instances. (Clearly, one could also consider trees of runs.) Note that this also determines the runs of the corresponding peer views. Each transition is caused by one application of one instantiation of one action at one peer.

A run starts at an *initial global instance* of $\mathcal{W}$, i.e. a valid instance over $\mathcal{D}$. In practice, one may wish to impose some conditions on initial global instances. For instance, it may make sense to require that some relations be initially total, or initially empty (for relations recording tasks to be performed). To simplify, we ignore here this aspect, which does not affect the results.

The transition relation $\vdash$ is defined using the auxiliary notion of *instantiation* of an action at peer p_i for a global instance I. We use the notion of *active domain*. First, the active domain of $\mathcal{W}$, denoted $adom(\mathcal{W})$, consists of the constants used in $\mathcal{W}$, and $\bot$. The active domain of an instance I, denoted $adom(I)$, is the set of constants occurring in I together with $adom(\mathcal{W})$. Let $\alpha = Update(\bar{x}, \bar{y})$:- $Condition(\bar{x})$ be an action at p_i where $\bar{x}$ are the variables occurring in *Condition* and $\bar{y}$ are the variables in *Update* other than $\bar{x}$. Let ν be a valuation of $\bar{x}$ in **dom** such that $I@p_i \models Condition(\nu(\bar{x}))$. Let $\bar{\nu}$ be an extension of ν mapping variables in $\bar{y}$ to distinct values in **dom** outside the active domain of I. Then $\bar{\nu}\alpha$ is an instantiation of this action at peer p_i for the global instance I.

For two global instances I and J over $\mathcal{D}$, $I \vdash_e J$ if the following holds:

> (†) There is a peer p_i, an instantiation $\bar{\nu}\alpha$ of an action at peer p_i for I such that J is obtained from I by applying the sequence of insertions and deletions in $Update(\bar{\nu}(\bar{x}, \bar{y}))$, in the specified order, and all insertions are consistent.

The label e, referred to as the *event* causing the transition, consists of the triple $(peer(e), action(e), val(e))$ where $peer(e) = p_i$, $action(e) = \alpha$ and $val(e) = \bar{\nu}$. We denote by a special symbol *init* the vacuous event creating the initial instance in a run, needed for technical reasons. From the definition, it follows that if I is valid and $I \vdash_e J$, then J is valid.

Note a subtlety in the active domain semantics we use. In the definition, the active domain refers to the current snapshot I. However, in some applications, it is desirable for new values to be outside the active domain of the *entire run* leading to I. For instance, new values may represent task IDs, and we may wish for them to be unique in each run. Such a semantics can be easily simulated with the one adopted here, simply by keeping in a designated relation the values that may not be reused.

We next define runs of workflow specs.

A *run* of $\mathcal{W}$ is a finite sequence $\{(I_i, e_i)\}_{0 \le i \le n}$, such that:

- $e_0 = init$ and I_0 is a valid instance over $\mathcal{D}$,
- for each $0 < i \le n$, $I_{i-1} \vdash_{e_i} I_i$

Note that the sequence $\{I_i\}_{0 \le i \le n}$ of instances in a run does *not* generally determine the events causing each transition. However, if desired, the actions of $\mathcal{W}$ can be modified so that events are explicitly recorded in designated relations. When this is the case, the sequence of instances is sufficient to uniquely identify the events.

REMARK 2.5. *Although left implicit, it is easy to see that our collaborative workflows provide an expressive model that can simulate the execution of sets of tasks and can capture hierarchical tasks of arbitrary depth, making use of keys and invented values. In particular, our collaborative workflows subsume the popular business artifact model [21]. This can be formalized using the framework developed in [5] for comparing the expressiveness of workflow languages.*

3. SYMBOLIC RUNS

We next develop a symbolic representation for the set of global runs consistent with given local observations at a peer. This will be used in the next section to carry out reasoning about the global runs, given such local observations. As we will see, it will be necessary to impose some simple restrictions on workflow specifications in order to render such reasoning feasible.

Consider a global run of a workflow spec $\mathcal{W}$. Let p be a peer of $\mathcal{W}$. The information about the run as observed by p is captured by the notion of *p-trace*, defined next. Intuitively, a p-trace retains only transitions caused by actions of p, or by actions of other peers that have visible side effects at p. In this latter case, p does not know which action actually took place. We use the symbol $\star$ to denote such an unknown action. Also, some transitions are completely invisible to p, so do not participate to the p-trace. Formally:

DEFINITION 3.1. *Let $\rho = \{(I_i, e_i)\}_{0 \leq i \leq n}$ be a run of some workflow spec $\mathcal{W}$, and let p be a peer of $\mathcal{W}$. Let $\rho@p = \{(I_i@p, f_i)\}_{0 \leq i \leq n}$ where $f_i = e_i$ if $\text{peer}(e_i) = p$ and $f_i = \star$ otherwise, where $\star$ is a new symbol. The* p-trace *of ρ, denoted $\nu_p(\rho)$, is the sequence obtained from $\rho@p$ by recursively deleting all $(I_j@p, f_j)$ such that $I_j@p = I_{j-1}@p$ and $f_j = \star$.*

Suppose that p observes a p-trace τ in the course of the run of $\mathcal{W}$. We would like to describe and reason about the set of all runs ρ of $\mathcal{W}$ that are consistent with τ, i.e., such that $\nu_p(\rho) = \tau$. We denote this set by $\nu_p^{-1}(\tau)$. Note that, because of silent transitions, the set $\nu_p^{-1}(\tau)$ may contain runs of unbounded length and is generally infinite. Unfortunately, even basic properties of such runs are generally undecidable. To illustrate, we mention a few such properties.

THEOREM 3.2. *The following are undecidable, for a workflow spec $\mathcal{W}$ and a p-trace τ:*

current *Is it possible/certain that the current local instance at some peer satisfies some first-order (FO) property φ?*

past *Is it possible/certain that some local instance at a peer satisfied some FO property φ during the run?*

event *Is it possible/certain that some peer q performed some particular action α during the run?*

validation *Is a sequence $\{(I_i@p, f_i)\}_{0 \leq i \leq n}$ that is syntactically a p-trace an actual p-trace of a global run?*

The proofs are by reduction from the undecidability of FO satisfiability (see [6]), using the fact that workflow computations can compute the answer to an FO query.

The above undecidability results are not surprising. A main contribution of the paper is to demonstrate decidability of a wide range of properties (including the previous ones) for a large class of workflow specs. The restriction we impose, called *key visibility*, is often reasonable in practice and is an acceptable price to pay for the ability to perform useful reasoning tasks. Key visibility requires that peer p sees at least *some* projection view of *each* global relation (which by definition includes its key). Formally (with $\mathcal{D}_p$ denoting the schema of peer p):

DEFINITION 3.3. *A workflow spec $\mathcal{W}$ with schema $\mathcal{D}$ is* key-visible *at p if $R@p \in \mathcal{D}_p$ for each relation $R \in \mathcal{D}$.*

For instance, the workflow of Example 2.2 is key-visible at all peers. While key visibility is a strong restriction for arbitrary specifications, it is reasonable in the likely event that the specification available to p is an *abstraction* of the actual specification, provided to p as a surrogate (or explanation) for it. In actual specifications, peers q will generally use relations not revealed to p, that determine their precise behavior. The abstraction available to p can be expected to provide an approximation of the actual behavior of other peers on relations they share, in some sense a contract between p and such peers. This enables reasoning by p while ignoring the full details of other peers' specification.

Even for a workflow that is key-visible at p, the set of global runs consistent with a given p-trace may be infinite. However, we are able to provide a symbolic representation for runs of key-visible workflows given a trace. We do this next. The representation is based on a variant of the classic conditional tables, a formalism introduced to capture incomplete information [19]. Intuitively, we capture a set of possible global instances of the system using a table. We then consider "transitions" between such tables to represent possible moves. So the set of global runs consistent with a p-trace can be described by a transition system over a set of tables.

Incomplete instances. We use the following auxiliary notions. An *atomic constraint* is an expression $x = (\neq)\, t$ where $x \in \mathbf{var}$ and $t \in \mathbf{var} \cup \mathbf{dom}$. An atomic constraint is *trivial* if it is $x = x$ for some $x \in \mathbf{var}$. A *constraint* is a Boolean combination of atomic constraints and a *conjunctive constraint* is a conjunction of atomic constraints, with no repetition of the same atom. As a shorthand, if $\bar{x}$ and $\bar{y}$ are tuples of the same arity, we denote by $\bar{x} = \bar{y}$ the conjunction of the componentwise equalities, and by $\bar{x} \neq \bar{y}$ the disjunction of the componentwise inequalities. The *closure* φ_V^* of a conjunctive constraint φ on a subset V of its variables is the conjunction of all non-trivial atomic constraints implied by φ, whose variables are in V. If V consists of all variables in φ, we simply write φ^* instead of φ_V^*.

We can now define the notion of *incomplete instance*, *I-instance* for short. Intuitively, it includes some unknown values (not to be confused with the $\perp$ values) denoted by variables, and a global constraint on these variables.

An *I-instance* over $\mathcal{D}$ is a pair $(\mathcal{I}, \varphi)$, where:

- $\mathcal{I}$ is a mapping associating to each $R \in \mathcal{D}$ a finite relation over R using values in $\mathbf{dom} \cup \mathbf{var}$.
- φ is a satisfiable conjunctive constraint using variables in $\mathcal{I}$ and a finite set of constants.
- $\varphi \models \varphi_{key}$ where φ_{key} is a constraint stating that no distinct tuples in $\mathcal{I}(R)$ agree on the key attributes of R, for every $R \in \mathcal{D}$.

An I-instance represents a set of possible instances as follows. For an I-instance $(\mathcal{I}, \varphi)$, we denote by $var(\mathcal{I})$ the set of variables occurring in tuples of $\mathcal{I}$. Given an I-instance $(\mathcal{I}, \varphi)$ over $\mathcal{D}$, the set of instances over $\mathcal{D}$ represented by $(\mathcal{I}, \varphi)$ is

$$rep(\mathcal{I}, \varphi) = \{v(\mathcal{I}) \mid v \text{ is a valuation of } var(\mathcal{I}) \text{ into } \mathbf{dom} \text{ satisfying } \varphi\}$$

It is clear that, by definition, every $I \in rep(\mathcal{I}, \varphi)$ is a valid instance. Note also that (because of the completeness of the keys) the number of rows in $\mathcal{I}(R)$ is the same as the number of rows in $I(R)$ for each $I \in rep(\mathcal{I}, \varphi)$ and $R \in \mathcal{D}$.

Symbolic transitions. As noted earlier, given a p-trace, there are infinitely many corresponding runs, which renders the analysis nontrivial. However, we will see that we can represent such runs by "symbolic runs", essentially by considering I-instances and abstract actions on such I-instances. Intuitively, when applying an abstract action to an I-instance, we obtain another I-instance by applying symbolically the peer action to the original I-instance. Such a transition from one I-instance to another generates additional constraints on the original I-instance, akin to preconditions, and transitions are labeled by these constraints. We next describe these transitions.

Intuitively, a symbolic transition (S-transition) $(\mathcal{I},\varphi) \vdash_{f,\gamma} (\mathcal{J},\psi)$ captures how an action f updates instances in $rep(\mathcal{I},\varphi)$ to instances in $rep(\mathcal{J},\psi)$ assuming that the *transition constraint* γ (to be defined) is satisfied. We will define S-transitions and prove that they provide a complete representation for actual transitions (Lemma 3.4).

We first describe symbolic transitions informally, then provide more details. It will be useful to consider a normal form for actions $Update(\bar{x},\bar{y})$:- $Condition(\bar{x})$. The normal form requires that each variable occurs at most once in the relational atoms of the rule. It is easy to see that all specifications can be rewritten in normal form by introducing additional variables and equalities between variables resulting from repeated occurrences. In the following, we assume the actions are all in normal form.

Consider an I-instance $(\mathcal{I},\varphi)$. Let q be a peer. We define the local I-instance at peer q by $(\mathcal{I},\varphi)@q = (\mathcal{I}@q, \varphi@q)$ where $\mathcal{I}@q$ is the projection view of $\mathcal{I}$ at peer q, and $\varphi@q$ is the closure of φ on the variables in $\mathcal{I}@q$.

Consider an action $Update(\bar{x},\bar{y})$:- $Condition(\bar{x})$ at peer q (assumed to be in normal form). Intuitively, the action is applied to a local I-instance in two stages: first find a valuation v of $\bar{x}$ into the I-instance. The valuation transfers the constraints from $Condition(\bar{x})$ to $v(\bar{x})$, and imposes "new value" constraints on $\bar{y}$. These become part of the transition constraints. Next, the updates in $Update(v(\bar{x}),v(\bar{y}))$ are applied for the valuation v. When a tuple is inserted, this may yield several transitions, depending on agreement with already existing tuples on the key. In each case, the resulting I-instance is obtained by chasing with the key. When a tuple is deleted, the result depends once again on the possible equalities of the deleted tuple with existing tuples in the instance. Each such equality is captured by a constraint and generates a separate transition. If the final transition constraint is γ, the resulting I-instance is $(\mathcal{J},\psi)$ where $\mathcal{J}$ is obtained by applying a sequence of updates to $\mathcal{I}$ corresponding to $Update(v(\bar{x}),v(\bar{y}))$, and ψ is the closure of $\varphi \wedge \gamma$ on the variables of $\mathcal{J}$. The transition constraint γ involves variables from both $\mathcal{I}$ and $\mathcal{J}$, so cannot be absorbed into the static I-instance constraints.

We next present the construction of S-transitions in more detail. For convenience, we first define transition constraints that are *not* necessarily conjunctive. Subsequently, each such transition is replaced with a set of transitions, one for each disjunct in the disjunctive normal form (DNF) of the constraint, yielding conjunctive transition constraints.

We will need the notion of *active domain* of $(\mathcal{I},\varphi)$, denoted $adom(\mathcal{I},\varphi)$. This consists of the set of constants c in **dom** that

- occur explicitly in some tuple of $\mathcal{I}$; or
- occur in a conjunct $x = c$ of φ; or
- occur in $\mathcal{W}$ or $\{\perp\}$.

Consider, as above, an I-instance $(\mathcal{I},\varphi)$, a peer q and an action $Update(\bar{x},\bar{y})$:- $Condition(\bar{x})$ at peer q. A *valuation* for the variables of the action into $\mathcal{I}@q$ is a mapping v from $\bar{x} \cup \bar{y}$ (extended with the identity on constants) such that:

- v maps $\bar{x}$ to variables and constants in $\mathcal{I}@q$, and $\bar{y}$ to the first $|\bar{y}|$ distinct variables in **var** $- \, var(\mathcal{I})$ with the smallest index[1].
- for each $R@q(\bar{z})$ of $Condition(\bar{x})$, $R@q(v(\bar{z}))$ is a tuple in $\mathcal{I}@q$.

[1]This is done to use variables economically, which is needed for technical reasons explained further.

The transition constraint γ_v induced by v is the conjunction of the following:

- $v(x) = (\neq)\ v(y)$ where $x = (\neq)\ y$ is an (in)equality in $Condition(\bar{x})$
- for each $\neg R@q(\bar{z})$ in $Condition(\bar{x})$ and tuple $R@q(\bar{w})$ in $\mathcal{I}@q$, the constraint $v(\bar{z}) \neq \bar{w}$.
- $v(y) \neq t$ where $y \in \bar{y}$ and t is a variable in $\mathcal{I}$ or a constant in the active domain of $(\mathcal{I},\varphi)$.

Note that the above is *not* a conjunctive constraint because of the tuple inequality in the second item. Next, fix a valuation v as above and consider $Update(v(\bar{x}),v(\bar{y}))$. We describe the effect of tuple insertions and deletions, with the associated transition constraints. Consider first a tuple insertion $R@q(v(\bar{z}))$. Let $R(v(\bar{z})\ \perp^*)$ be the extension of $R@q(v(\bar{z}))$ to $att(R)$ obtained by padding the missing attributes with $\perp$. For each tuple $R(\bar{w})$, denote by $\bar{w}_K$ the subsequence of $\bar{w}$ corresponding to the key K of R. Similarly, let $\bar{z}_K$ consist of the subsequence of $\bar{z}$ correponding to K. If $\bar{z}_K$ contains some variable in $\bar{y}$ then the result of the insertion consists of adding $R(v(\bar{z})\ \perp^*)$ to R. Otherwise, the result depends on whether $R(v(\bar{z})\ \perp^*)$ agrees with an existing tuple on the key. More precisely, the transitions generated by the insertion are as follows:

- For each tuple $R(\bar{w})$ in $\mathcal{I}$, the result of the insertion under the transition constraint $v(\bar{z}_K) = \bar{w}_K$ is obtained by chasing $R(\bar{w})$ as follows. Let A be an non-key attribute of R and z_A, w_A be the values of $R(v(\bar{z})\ \perp^*)$ and $R(\bar{w})$ for attribute A. If $z_A, w_A \in \textbf{dom} - \{\perp\}$, the chase fails and there is no transition. If $w_A = \perp$ then it is replaced by z_A. If w_A and z_A are both variables, then $w_A = z_A$ is added to the transition constraint.
- Finally, one transition occurs for each disjunct in the DNF of the constraint consisting of the conjunction of $\bar{w}_K \neq v(\bar{z}_K)$ for all tuples $R(\bar{w})$ in $\mathcal{I}$, yielding the instance obtained by inserting the tuple $R(v(\bar{z})\ \perp^*)$ into $\mathcal{I}$.

Consider now a tuple deletion $\neg R@q(v(\bar{z}))$. The result depends again on agreement with existing tuples on the key attributes. Recall that deleted tuples contain no "new" variables among $\bar{y}$. There is one possible transition for each tuple $R(\bar{w})$ in $\mathcal{I}$, consisting of deleting the tuple under the transition constraint $\bar{w}_K = \bar{z}_K$. In addition there are transitions leaving $\mathcal{I}$ unchanged, for the constraint consisting of the conjunction of all inequalities $\bar{z}_K \neq \bar{w}_K$ for all tuples $R(\bar{w})$ in $\mathcal{I}$. As earlier, each disjunct in the DNF of the constraint generates a separate transition.

Finally, the transitions caused by the sequence of updates in $Update(\bar{x},\bar{y})$ are the compositions of the transitions for each update. Each transition constraint is the conjunction of the constraints for the composed transitions. Note that, by construction, these are conjunctive constraints. The local constraint ψ for each resulting I-instance $(\mathcal{J},\psi)$ consists of the closure of $\varphi \wedge \gamma$ on the variables of $\mathcal{J}$, where γ is the corresponding transition constraint. Note that this again yields a conjunctive constraint.

If $(\mathcal{J},\psi)$ is obtained from $(\mathcal{I},\varphi)$ by an S-transition with transition constraint γ, action α at peer q and valuation v, we say that $e = (q,\alpha,v)$ is the *event* of the transition. If furthermore $\psi \wedge \gamma$ is satisfiable, we write $(\mathcal{I},\varphi) \vdash_{e,\gamma} (\mathcal{J},\psi)$. It is easy to see that, by construction, $\psi \models \varphi_{key}$, so $(\mathcal{J},\psi)$ is an I-instance. This defines the S-transition relation among I-instances over $\mathcal{D}$.

Similarly to I-instances, the purpose of S-transitions is to represent a set of actual transitions among global instances. Let $(\mathcal{I}, \varphi) \vdash_{e,\gamma} (\mathcal{J}, \psi)$ be an S-transition, where e is the event (q, α, v). The set of transitions represented by the above S-transition is

$rep((\mathcal{I}, \varphi) \vdash_{e,\gamma} (\mathcal{J}, \psi)) = \{(\nu(\mathcal{I}) \vdash_{\nu(e)} \nu(\mathcal{J})) \mid \nu$ is a valuation of the variables in $\mathcal{I} \cup \mathcal{J}$ into **dom** satisfying $\varphi \wedge \gamma \wedge \psi$ and $\nu(e) = (q, \alpha, v \circ \nu)\}$

The following key lemma says that, starting from some I-instance, the S-transitions capture all possible actual transitions from instances represented by the I-instance. Thus, S-transitions are a complete representation of actual transitions.

LEMMA 3.4. *For each I-instance* $(\mathcal{I}, \varphi)$,

$$\begin{aligned}\{(I \vdash_e J) \mid\ & I \in rep(\mathcal{I}, \varphi), e \text{ is an event}\} = \\ \{(I \vdash_e J) \mid\ & \text{there exists } (\mathcal{I}, \varphi) \vdash_{f,\gamma} (\mathcal{J}, \psi) \text{ such that} \\ & (I \vdash_e J) \in rep((\mathcal{I}, \varphi) \vdash_{f,\gamma} (\mathcal{J}, \psi))\}\end{aligned}$$

Lemma 3.4 follows from the construction of S-transitions. The fact that I-instances satisfy φ_{key} is critical, because it guarantees that no distinct tuples in $(\mathcal{I}, \varphi)$ may represent the same tuple in some $I \in rep(\mathcal{I}, \varphi)$. The construction would not be correct otherwise.

Symbolic runs. We now turn to the notion of symbolic run, and to the connection between symbolic runs and actual runs. A *symbolic run* (S-run) of $\mathcal{W}$ is a sequence

$$\{((\mathcal{I}_i, \varphi_i), (e_i, \gamma_i))\}_{0 \le i \le n}$$

such that

- $e_0 = init$ and $\gamma_0 = true$
- for each $0 < i \le n$, $(\mathcal{I}_{i-1}, \varphi_{i-1}) \vdash_{e_i,\gamma_i} (\mathcal{I}_i, \varphi_i)$

Thus, an S-run is a finite sequence of consecutive symbolic transitions. Let **s** be an S-run $\{((\mathcal{I}_i, \varphi_i), (e_i, \gamma_i))\}_{0 \le i \le n}$. The set of actual runs represented by **s**, denoted $rep(\mathbf{s})$, consists of all runs $\{(I_i, g_i)\}_{0 \le i \le n}$ for which $(I_{i-1} \vdash_{g_i} I_i) \in rep((\mathcal{I}_{i-1}, \varphi_{i-1}) \vdash_{e_i,\gamma_i} (\mathcal{I}_i, \varphi_i))$ for all $0 < i \le n$.

As a consequence of Lemma 3.4, S-runs provide a complete representation of actual runs.

Symbolic runs constrained by traces. Next, consider a p-trace τ. We wish to use S-runs to represent *precisely* the global runs in $\nu^{-1}(\tau)$. To this end, we need to constrain symbolic runs by p's observations as given by τ. Since all relations in $\mathcal{D}$ are key-visible at p, we need to only consider I-instances that are fully instantiated on the attributes visible at p (which include all key attributes). Therefore, we need to compute specializations of transitions limited to such instances.

Let I_p be an instance over $\mathcal{D}_p$ (at peer p). We say that an I-instance $(\mathcal{I}, \varphi)$ is I_p-instantiated if $I@p = I_p$ for every $I \in rep(\mathcal{I}, \varphi)$. Now consider an I_p-instantiated I-instance $(\mathcal{I}, \varphi)$ and let J_p be another instance of $\mathcal{D}_p$ (which may equal I_p, as allowed in a p-trace). We wish to find representations of transitions from $(\mathcal{I}, \varphi)$ constrained to produce J_p-instantiated instances. Such constrained transitions define a new relation among I-instances, that we call J_p-constrained transition relation, denoted $\vdash^{J_p}$. The relation $\vdash^{J_p}$ is obtained by specializing the unrestricted transition relation $\vdash$ as follows. Consider an I-transition $(\mathcal{I}, \varphi) \vdash_{e,\gamma} (\mathcal{J}, \psi)$. Let $\mathcal{V}$ be the set of valuations ν mapping variables in $\mathcal{J}@p$ into values in J_p such that ν satisfies ψ and $\nu(\mathcal{J}@p) = J_p$. Let θ_ν be the constraint consisting of the conjunction of all equalities $x = \nu(x)$. The set of J_p-constrained transitions generated by $(\mathcal{I}, \varphi) \vdash_{e,\gamma} (\mathcal{J}, \psi)$ consists of all expressions $(\mathcal{I}, \varphi) \vdash^{J_p}_{e,(\gamma \wedge \theta_\nu)} (\mathcal{J}, \psi \wedge \theta_\nu)$ for $\nu \in \mathcal{V}$. The semantics of J_p-constrained transitions is the same as for unconstrained transitions. More precisely, $rep((\mathcal{I}, \varphi) \vdash^{J_p}_{e,\pi} (\mathcal{J}, \xi)) = \{\nu(\mathcal{I}) \vdash_{\nu(e)} \nu(\mathcal{J}) \mid \nu$ is a valuation from the variables of $\mathcal{I} \cup \mathcal{J}$ into **dom** satisfying $\varphi \wedge \pi \wedge \xi\}$.

The next result follows easily by construction.

LEMMA 3.5. *There is a* PTIME *nondeterministic algorithm that, given* $(\mathcal{I}, \varphi)$ *and* J_p, *outputs each* J_p*-constrained transition from* $(\mathcal{I}, \varphi)$.

Next, consider a p-trace $\tau = \{(P_i, f_i)\}_{0 \le i \le k}$. Let us first ignore the order of the local instances and the operations f_i. So, let $\mathcal{P}_\tau = \{P_i \mid 0 \le i \le k\}$. Recall that each instance in $\nu^{-1}(\tau)$ is P_j-instantiated for some $P_j \in \mathcal{P}_\tau$. We are therefore interested in runs in which each transition is P_j-constrained for some $P_j \in \mathcal{P}_\tau$. We call such runs $\mathcal{P}_\tau$-constrained.

DEFINITION 3.6. *A* $\mathcal{P}_\tau$*-constrained run is a finite sequence* $\{((\mathcal{I}_i, \varphi_i), (e_i, \gamma_i, P_{j_i}))\}_{0 \le i \le n}$ *such that*

(i) $e_0 = $ init, $\tau_0 = $ true, $\mathcal{J}_0@p = P_{j_0}$, *and* $var(\mathcal{J}_0) = \{x_1, \ldots, x_m\}$ *for some* $m \ge 0$.

(ii) for each $0 < i \le n$, $(\mathcal{I}_{i-1}, \varphi_{i-1}) \vdash^{P_{j_i}}_{e_i,\gamma_i} (\mathcal{I}_i, \varphi_i)$

Note that, in the initial instance of a $\mathcal{P}_\tau$-constrained run, there are no variables occurring in the attributes visible at p. Moreover, the variables occurring in $\mathcal{J}_0$ are picked among those of smallest index. This is a harmless assumption useful for technical reasons. In particular, we can show the following.

LEMMA 3.7. *For each finite* $\mathcal{P}_\tau$, *the set of I-instances reachable by* $\mathcal{P}_\tau$*-constrained runs is finite.*

PROOF. First note that there exists $M > 0$ so that for every $\mathcal{P}_\tau$-constrained run $\{((\mathcal{I}_i, \varphi_i), (e_i, \gamma_i, P_{j_i}))\}_{0 \le i \le n}$, the set of variables occurring in $\mathcal{I}_j$ is included in $\{x_1, \ldots, x_M\}$ for each j. This is due to the following:

- there is a fixed bound on the number of tuples (and therefore variables) in a P-instantiated I-instance for $P \in \mathcal{P}_\tau$,
- the variables in $\mathcal{J}_0$ are $\{x_1, \ldots, x_m\}$ for some $m \ge 0$, and
- by construction of S-transitions, new variables introduced by transitions are picked among those of smallest index that are currently unused.

Finally, there are finitely many conjunctive constraints using the variables $\{x_1, \ldots, x_M\}$ and constants occurring in $\mathcal{P}_\tau$, $\mathcal{W}$, or $\{\perp\}$. □

We are close to our goal. The $\mathcal{P}_\tau$-constrained runs we defined produce p-traces using only instances in the p-trace $\tau = \{(P_i, f_i)\}_{0 \le i \le k}$, but not necessarily in the correct order nor with proper f_i. In order to define precisely $\nu^{-1}(\tau)$ we need to further constrain the runs. We do this using a nondeterministic finite-state automaton A_τ defined as follows:

the set of states of A_τ is $\{p_0\} \cup \{q_i \mid 0 \le i \le k\}$, with initial state p_0 and final state q_k.

the alphabet consists of the finite set of all $((\mathcal{I},\varphi),(e,\gamma,P))$ occurring in $\mathcal{P}_\tau$-constrained runs of $\mathcal{W}$.

the transition mapping δ is defined as follows:

start $\delta(p_0,((\mathcal{I},\varphi),(e,\gamma,P))) = q_0$ if $((\mathcal{I},\varphi),(e,\gamma,P))$ is the initial instance of a $\mathcal{P}_\tau$-constrained run and $P = P_0$,

visible for $0 \leq i < k$, $\delta(q_i,((\mathcal{I},\varphi),(e,\gamma,P))) = q_{i+1}$ if $P = P_{i+1}$, and (nonlocal) $f_{i+1} = \star$ and $peer(e) \neq p$, or (local) $f_{i+1} = p$ and $peer(e) = p$.

silent for $0 \leq i \leq k$, $\delta(q_i,((\mathcal{I},\varphi),(e,\gamma,P))) = q_i$ if $P = P_i$ and $peer(e) \neq p$,

Let $A_\tau(\mathcal{P}_\tau)$ denote the set of $\mathcal{P}_\tau$-constrained runs accepted by A_τ. We have the following.

THEOREM 3.8. *Let τ be a p-trace for a peer p of $\mathcal{W}$. Then* $\nu^{-1}(\tau) = \cup\{rep(\mathbf{s}) \mid \mathbf{s} \in A_\tau(\mathcal{P}_\tau)\}$.

PROOF. We use the following property, that considers partial instantiations of S-transitions. Let $(\mathcal{I},\varphi) \vdash_{e,\gamma} (\mathcal{J},\psi)$ be an S-transition and ν a partial valuation of the variables of $\mathcal{I}\cup\mathcal{J}$ into **dom**. For a constraint β, let $\nu(\beta)$ denote the constraint obtained by replacing in β each variable $x \in dom(\nu)$ by $\nu(x)$. For an event $e = (p,\alpha,v)$, we denote by $\nu(e)$ the event $(p,\alpha,v\circ\nu)$. The following is shown similarly to Lemma 3.4.

(†) Let $(\mathcal{I},\varphi) \vdash_{e,\gamma} (\mathcal{J},\psi)$ be an S-transition and ν a partial valuation of the variables of $\mathcal{I}\cup\mathcal{J}$ into **dom** such that $\nu(\varphi \wedge \gamma \wedge \psi)$ is satisfiable. Then $(\nu(\mathcal{I}),\nu(\varphi)) \vdash_{\nu(e),\nu(\gamma)} (\nu(\mathcal{J}),\nu(\psi))$ is also an S-transition.

Lemma 3.4 together with (†) shows the following completeness result.

(‡) For each I-instance $(\mathcal{I},\varphi)$ and instance J_p at peer p,

$$\{(I \vdash_e J) \mid I \in rep(\mathcal{I},\varphi), e \text{ is an event}, , J@p = J_p\} = \{(I \vdash_e J) \mid \text{there exists } (\mathcal{I},\varphi) \vdash^{J_p}_{e,\gamma} (\mathcal{J},\psi) \text{ such that } (I \vdash_e J) \in rep((\mathcal{I},\varphi) \vdash^{J_p}_{e,\gamma} (\mathcal{J},\psi))\}$$

Theorem 3.8 now follows from (‡) and the construction of A_τ. □

Thus, A_τ together with our transition system on $\mathcal{P}_\tau$-constrained instances provide a finite representation of the infinite set of runs in $\nu^{-1}(\tau)$.

REMARK 3.9. *It is easy to see that the size of $A_\tau(\mathcal{P}_\tau)$ is exponential in τ. However, the evaluation algorithm of the next section never materializes the full $A_\tau(\mathcal{P}_\tau)$. Instead, the S-runs in $A_\tau(\mathcal{P}_\tau)$ are explored lazily, one transition at a time. As we shall see, this yields an algorithm of complexity* PSPACE *in τ.*

4. PEER REASONING

We next formalize the properties of global runs that we focus on, and show how they can be evaluated using the representation system developed in the previous section.

Temporal properties of runs. Recall that we are interested in verifying and monitoring properties of global runs based on local observations at a given peer. We specify the properties of interest in an extension of Past Linear-Time Temporal Logic (PLTL). The language, denoted PLTL-FO, is obtained from propositional PLTL with past operators (e.g., see [13]) by interpreting each proposition as an FO formula.

We first recall the language PLTL that is obtained by augmenting propositional logic with: past temporal operators Z (initially), X^{-1} (previously), S (since) and G^{-1} (always previously) as follows. If ϕ and ϕ' are formulas, then so are $Z\phi$, $X^{-1}\phi$, $\phi\ S\ \phi'$ and $G^{-1}\phi$. A *PLTL formula* is evaluated on finite sequences $\sigma_0 \ldots \sigma_n$ of truth assignments to its propositions. The semantics is defined as follows (we omit the standard definition of $\wedge$ and $\neg$).

- $\sigma_0 \ldots \sigma_n \models r$ for a proposition r if $\sigma_n(r) = 1$.
- $\sigma_0 \ldots \sigma_n \models Z\phi$ if $n = 0$ and $\sigma_0 \models \phi$.
- $\sigma_0 \ldots \sigma_n \models X^{-1}\phi$ iff $n > 0$ and $\sigma_0 \ldots \sigma_{n-1} \models \phi$.
- $\sigma_0 \ldots \sigma_n \models \phi\ S\ \phi'$ iff $\sigma_0 \ldots \sigma_j \models \phi'$ for some $j \leq n$ and $\sigma_0 \ldots \sigma_k \models \phi$ for every h, $j < h \leq n$.
- $\sigma_0 \ldots \sigma_n \models G^{-1}\phi$ iff $\sigma_0 \ldots \sigma_j \models \phi$ for each $j \in [0,n]$.

Consider a PLTL formula ϕ, the set P of propositions occurring in ϕ and the set of sequences of truth assignments over P satisfying ϕ. It is straightforward to construct a finite-state alternating automaton with alphabet 2^P that accepts precisely this set of sequences, with a number of states linear in ϕ. This alternating automaton can then be converted to a nondeterministic automaton A_ϕ with a number of states exponential in ϕ. Moreover, there is a nondeterministic PSPACE algorithm (w.r.t. ϕ) that, given a state q of A_ϕ and a truth assignment σ, outputs the successors of q under input σ (see [23, 11]).

We next define the extension PLTL-FO. A *PLTL-FO formula* over $\mathcal{W}$ is an expression $\phi_f = (\phi, f)$ where ϕ is a propositional PLTL formula and f maps each proposition r of ϕ to an FO formula $f(r)$. Each FO formula $f(r)$ is called an FO *component* of ϕ_f. FO components are formulas over the global schema $\mathcal{D}$, extended as follows: for each action $\alpha = Update(\bar{x},\bar{y})$:-$Condition(\bar{x})$ at peer q, we add to $\mathcal{D}$ an action-relation α_q of arity $|\bar{x}| + |\bar{y}|$ (with the semantics that $\alpha_q(\bar{a},\bar{b})$ holds at some step if the corresponding action is taken with valuation $\nu(\bar{x}) = \bar{a}$ and $\nu(\bar{y}) = \bar{b}$). Note that FO components may contain free variables. In particular, the same free variable may appear in different FO components, allowing to refer to the same value across different instances in the run.

In addition, FO components may use constants in $adom(\mathcal{W})$. (It is always possible, if desired, to introduce any fixed set of constants considered significant to the active domain).

In a run $\{(I_i,e_i)\}_{0\leq i\leq n}$, an FO component $f(r)$ with no free variables holds in (I_i,e_i), denoted $(I_i,e_i) \models f(r)$, if $f(r)$ is true in the structure I_i extended to the action relations as above.

The semantics of ϕ_f is defined as follows. Consider a run $\rho = \{(I_i,e_i)\}_{0\leq i\leq n}$ of $\mathcal{W}$. For each i, let σ_i be the truth assignment to propositions in ϕ defined by $\sigma_i(r) = 1$ iff $(I_i,e_i) \models f(r)$. The run ρ satisfies ϕ_f iff $\sigma_0 \ldots \sigma_n \models \phi$. Clearly, checking that $\rho \models \phi_f$ can be done in PSPACE by nondeterministically running the automaton A_ϕ on the sequence of truth assignments $\sigma_0 \ldots \sigma_n$ computed on ρ.

In the presence of incomplete information on runs, we are interested in giving possible and certain world semantics to PLTL-FO formulas. Let $\phi_f(\bar{x})$ be a PLTL-FO formula and $\mathcal{R}$ a set of runs of $\mathcal{W}$. We say that $poss(\phi_f(\bar{x}))$ holds in $\mathcal{R}$ if there exists a run $\rho \in \mathcal{R}$ and there exists a valuation ν for $\bar{x}$ in the active domain of ρ, such that ρ satisfies $\phi_f(\nu(\bar{x}))$.

Likewise, $cert(\phi_f(\bar{x}))$ holds in $\mathcal{R}$ if $\phi_f(\nu(\bar{x})$ holds for each run $\rho \in \mathcal{R}$ and each valuation ν of $\bar{x}$ into the active domain of ρ. Thus, the free variables are quantified existentially in possible world semantics and universally in certain world semantics. Note that certain world semantics is analogous to that of the modal operator $K_i\phi$ (agent i knows ϕ) in the context of reasoning about the knowledge of multiple agents [14].

Example 4.1 Consider the rules in Example 2.4. Suppose that a researcher, say Bob, would like to know if Alice's trip Id455 has been rejected. Bob does not have direct access to this information. However, he does see the trips that are inserted and deleted from the Intranet and Internet. Based on these local observations, he can *infer*, once Alice's trip is posted on the Internet, that the trip has been approved; and, if the trip is first posted on the Intranet and then deleted, Bob can infer that it has been rejected. On the other hand, if the trip is posted on the Intranet but not (yet) deleted, the trip may or may not have been rejected. Clearly, the acceptance/rejection of Alice's trip can be expressed in PLTL-FO (with certain or possible semantics). We will see next how such properties can be evaluated using the local observations. □

Evaluating PLTL-FO properties. Given a p-trace τ, we are interested in evaluating $poss(\phi_f(\bar{x}))$ and $cert(\phi_f(\bar{x}))$ on the set of global runs of $\mathcal{W}$ compatible with τ, that is, $\nu^{-1}(\tau)$. We now show how this can be done using the framework developed earlier. To simplify the presentation, we assume without loss of generality that FO components of PLTL-FO formulas are over the schema $\mathcal{D}$, without the extension to action relations defined above. (Intuitively, one can simulate the reasoning in the extended global schema by considering a schema with additional "normal" relations carrying the extra information.)

We next show how to use this to evaluate and monitor temporal properties of runs in $\nu^{-1}(\tau)$.

Let us fix a PLTL-FO property ϕ_f we wish to evaluate under possible and certain semantics on $\nu^{-1}(\tau)$. Suppose for the moment that ϕ_f has no free variables. In order to evaluate FO components of ϕ_f we will use I-instances in which the equality type of all variables and constants is completely specified. More precisely, let $(\mathcal{I}, \varphi)$ be an I-instance. We call $(\mathcal{I}, \varphi)$ *complete* if for each $x \in var(\mathcal{I})$ and $t \in var(\mathcal{I}) \cup adom(\mathcal{I}, \varphi)$, $\varphi \models x = t$ or $\varphi \models x \neq t$. A $\mathcal{P}_\tau$-constrained run is *complete* if each of its I-instances is complete.

Observe the following.

LEMMA 4.2. *(i) Let $(\mathcal{I}, \varphi)$ be a complete I-instance and $f(r)$ an FO component of ϕ_f. Then $f(r)$ has the same truth value in every $I \in \text{rep}(\mathcal{I}, \varphi)$. (ii) If*

$$\{((\mathcal{I}_i, \varphi_i), (e_i, \gamma_i, P_{j_i}))\}_{0 \leq i \leq n}$$

is a $\mathcal{P}_\tau$-constrained run and $(\mathcal{I}_0, \varphi_0)$ is a complete I-instance, then $(\mathcal{I}_i, \varphi_i)$ is a complete I-instance for every $i > 0$.

PROOF. (i) Consider $J_i \in rep(\mathcal{I}, \varphi)$, such that $J_i = \nu_i(\mathcal{I})$, $i = 1, 2$. Define the mapping h from J_1 to J_2 by $h(\nu_1(t)) = \nu_2(t)$ for $t \in var(\mathcal{I}) \cup adom(\mathcal{I}, \varphi)$. It is easy to see that, because of completeness of $(\mathcal{I}, \varphi)$, h is well defined and an isomorphism from J_1 to J_2 fixing $adom(\mathcal{W})$. Since $f(r)$ uses only constants in $adom(\mathcal{W})$, it has the same truth value on J_1 and J_2. (ii) The preservation of completeness by transitions is due to the fact that all newly introduced variables in a transition are constrained to differ from all variables and constants in the active domain of the current I-instance. □

Because of (i), complete runs are convenient in order to evaluate ϕ_f, because the truth value of each FO component is well defined on each I-instance of the run. More precisely, given a complete $\mathcal{P}_\tau$-constrained run

$$\mathbf{s} = \{((\mathcal{I}_i, \varphi_i), (e_i, \gamma_i, P_{j_i}))\}_{0 \leq i \leq n},$$

the truth value of an FO component $f(r)$ at $(\mathcal{I}_i, \varphi_i)$ can be defined as its truth value on *any* instance $I_i \in rep(\mathcal{I}_i, \varphi_i)$, and can clearly be computed in PSPACE.

We are now ready to show the following main result.

THEOREM 4.3. *Let $\mathcal{W}$ be a workflow spec, p a peer of $\mathcal{W}$, τ a p-trace of $\mathcal{W}$ and $\phi_f(\bar{x})$ a PLTL-FO property over $\mathcal{W}$. Then* poss$(\phi_f(\bar{x}))$ *and* cert$(\phi_f(\bar{x}))$ *can be evaluated in* PSPACE *with respect to ϕ_f and τ.*

PROOF. Since $cert(\phi_f(\bar{x}))$ is equivalent to $\neg poss(\neg\phi_f(\bar{x}))$, it is enough to consider the possible world semantics. We outline a nondeterministic algorithm for evaluating $poss(\phi_f(\bar{x}))$ given a p-trace τ, of complexity PSPACE w.r.t. ϕ_f and τ. Consider first the case when ϕ_f has no free variables $\bar{x}$. We need to check whether there exists a run $\rho \in \nu^{-1}(\tau)$ such that $\rho \models \phi_f$. The algorithm consists of nondeterministically generating a complete $\mathcal{P}_\tau$-constrained run together with computations of $A_\tau(\mathcal{P}_\tau)$ and A_ϕ on the run. The algorithm outputs YES if both automata accept. To make sure the $\mathcal{P}_\tau$-constrained run is complete, it is enough, as noted in Lemma 4.2, that its initial I-instance be complete. Note that the size of each generated I-instance in the run is polynomial in the number of constants occurring in previous I-instances in the run or in $\mathcal{W}$. By Lemma 3.5, the $\mathcal{P}_\tau$-constrained transitions from an I-instance $(\mathcal{I}, \varphi)$ can be computed nondeterministically in PTIME w.r.t. $(\mathcal{I}, \varphi)$ and $\mathcal{P}_\tau$. Also recall that each transition of A_ϕ can be computed nondeterministically in PSPACE w.r.t. ϕ, and each transition of $A_\tau(\mathcal{P}_\tau)$ can clearly be computed in PTIME with respect to τ. Thus, the algorithm has complexity PSPACE w.r.t. ϕ_f and τ, for fixed $\mathcal{W}$. If $\mathcal{W}$ is not fixed, then the algorithm is EXPSPACE (with the maximum arity of relations in $\mathcal{D}$ in the exponent). The correctness of the algorithm follows from Theorem 3.8 and Lemma 4.2.

Now consider the case when ϕ_f has free variables $\bar{x}$. We need to check whether there exists a run $\rho \in \nu^{-1}(\tau)$ *and* a valuation v of $\bar{x}$ into the active domain of ρ such that $\rho \models \phi_f(v(\bar{x}))$. To verify this, we augment the previous algorithm generating a complete $\mathcal{P}_\tau$-constrained run accepted by A_ϕ and $A_\tau(\mathcal{P}_\tau)$ by *guessing* a consistent connection between the variables in $\bar{x}$ and the variables or constants in the I-instances in the run, and evaluating the FO components of $\phi_f(\bar{x})$ according to that guess. More precisely, this is done as follows. Let $\mathbf{s} = \{((\mathcal{I}_i, \varphi_i), (e_i, \gamma_i, P_{j_i}))\}_{0 \leq i \leq n}$ be a complete $\mathcal{P}_\tau$-constrained run generated as in the earlier algorithm. As the run is generated, an additional conjunctive constraint $\psi_i(\bar{x})$ over $\bar{x}$ is computed nondeterministically for every i. The formula $\psi_i(\bar{x})$ is of the form $\beta_i(\bar{x}) \wedge \gamma_i(\bar{x})$. Intuitively, $\beta_i(\bar{x})$ guesses the connection of $\bar{x}$ with variables and constants in the current I-instance, and $\gamma_i(\bar{x})$ consists of the constraints on $\bar{x}$ inherited from previous guesses. Specifically, $\psi_i(\bar{x}) = \beta_i(\bar{x}) \wedge \gamma_i(\bar{x})$ is defined inductively as follows.

For $i = 0$, $\beta_0(\bar{x})$ consists, for each $z \in \bar{x}$, of an equality $z = t$ for some $t \in var(\mathcal{I}_0) \cup adom(\mathcal{I}_0, \varphi_0)$, or the conjunction of all inequalities $z \neq t$ for all such t. The constraint $\gamma_0(\bar{x}) = true$. For $i > 0$, $\gamma_i(\bar{x}) = (\varphi_{i-1} \wedge \psi_{i-1}(\bar{x}))^*_{\bar{x}}$ and $\beta_i(\bar{x})$ consists, as for the base case, of a nondeterministically chosen conjunction consisting, for each $z \in \bar{x}$, of an equality $z = t$ for some $t \in var(\mathcal{I}_i) \cup adom(\mathcal{I}_i, \varphi_i)$, or the conjunction of all inequalities $z \neq t$ for all such t, such that $\varphi_i \wedge \psi_i(\bar{x})$ is satisfiable.

We can show the following:

> (†) Let $\mathbf{s} = \{((\mathcal{I}_i, \varphi_i), (e_i, \gamma_i, P_{j_i}))\}_{0 \leq i \leq n}$ be a $\mathcal{P}_\tau$-constrained run. There exists a sequence $\{\psi_i(\bar{x})\}_{0 \leq i \leq n}$ computed as above for $\mathbf{s}$ iff there exists a run $\rho = \{(I_i, g_i)\}_{0 \leq i \leq n}$ in $rep(\mathbf{s})$, and a valuation v of $\bar{x}$ into $adom(\rho)$ such that the following holds for every i ($0 \leq i \leq n$), $z \in \bar{x}$, $t \in var(\mathcal{I}_i) \cup adom(\mathcal{I}_i, \varphi_i)$, and the unique valuation v_i such that $I_i = v_i(\mathcal{I}_i)$: $\beta_i(\bar{x}) \models z = t$ iff $v(z) = v_i(t)$.

Intuitively, (†) says that each equality type induced by $\beta_i(\bar{x})$ w.r.t. the constants and variables in $\mathcal{I}_i$ is realizable in a run $\rho \in rep(\mathbf{s})$ for some *fixed* valuation of $\bar{x}$ in the $adom(\rho)$. Furthemore, the sequence of formulas $\{\psi_i(\bar{x})\}_{0 \leq i \leq n}$ can be computed successfully for $\mathbf{s}$ iff such a run ρ and valuation v exists. We define the following extension of our notion of $\mathcal{P}_\tau$-constrained run. A *parameterized* $\mathcal{P}_\tau$-constrained run is a sequence $\mathbf{s}(\bar{x}) = \{((\mathcal{I}_i, \varphi_i, \psi_i(\bar{x})), (e_i, \gamma_i, P_{j_i}))\}_{0 \leq i \leq n}$ where $\{((\mathcal{I}_i, \varphi_i), (e_i, \gamma_i, P_{j_i}))\}_{0 \leq i \leq n}$ is a $\mathcal{P}_\tau$-constrained run and the sequence $\{\psi_i(\bar{x})\}_{0 \leq i \leq n}$ is computed as above. Also, we refer to each $(\mathcal{I}_i, \varphi_i, \psi_i(\bar{x}))$ as a *parameterized* I-instance.

We will use the following notion of isomorphic parameterized I-instances. Given $(\mathcal{I}, \varphi, \psi(\bar{x}))$, let $\sim$ be the equivalence relation on variables and constants in $var(\mathcal{I}) \cup \{\bar{x}\} \cup adom(\mathcal{I}, \varphi)$ defined by $z \sim t$ iff $\varphi \wedge \psi(\bar{x}) \models z = t$, and let $[z]$ be the equivalence class of z w.r.t. $\sim$. Let $\mathcal{I}/_\sim$ be obtained by replacing in $\mathcal{I}$ each variable z by the unique constant in $[z]$, if it exists, or otherwise by the variable of smallest index in $[z]$. We say that $(\mathcal{I}_1, \varphi_1, \psi_1(\bar{x}))$ and $(\mathcal{I}_2, \varphi_2, \psi_2(\bar{x}))$ are isomorphic if $\mathcal{I}_1/_\sim$ and $\mathcal{I}_2/_\sim$ are isomorphic when variables are frozen as distinct constants. The *isomorphism type* of $h = (\mathcal{I}, \varphi, \psi(\bar{x}))$ is its equivalence class under isomorphism, denoted $\hat{h}$.

Let $\mathbf{s}(\bar{x}) = \{((\mathcal{I}_i, \varphi_i, \psi_i(\bar{x})), (e_i, \gamma_i, P_{j_i}))\}_{0 \leq i \leq n}$ be a $\mathcal{P}_\tau$-constrained parameterized run. Consider the evaluation of $\phi_f(\bar{x})$. Clearly, for each $i \geq 0$, $\varphi_i \wedge \psi_i(\bar{x})$ completely determines the isomorphism type of $(\mathcal{I}_i, \varphi_i, \psi_i(\bar{x}))$. Thus, the truth value of each FO component $f(r)(\bar{x})$ of $\phi_f(\bar{x})$ is well defined and can be evaluated at each $(\mathcal{I}_i, \varphi_i, \psi_i(\bar{x}))$. As before, the algorithm outputs YES if a $\mathcal{P}_\tau$-constrained parameterized run $\mathbf{s}(\bar{x})$ can be generated that is accepted by both A_ϕ and $A(\mathcal{P}_\tau)$. The complexity remains PSPACE w.r.t. $\phi_f(\bar{x})$ and τ. □

REMARK 4.4. *As stated in Theorem 4.3, the algorithm described above has complexity* PSPACE *w.r.t.* $\phi_f(\bar{x})$ *and* τ. *It is of interest to note the impact of the* length *of* τ *on complexity. It is easy to see that, if* adom(τ) *and* $\varphi_f(\bar{x})$ *are fixed, the algorithm is in NL (nondeterministic logarithmic space) in the length of* τ.

REMARK 4.5. *Theorem 3.2 provided examples of useful properties that are undecidable without the key-visible restriction. As a consequence of Theorem 4.3, all questions of Theorem 3.2 become decidable for key-visible specs.*

Incremental monitoring. We next adapt the algorithm described in the proof of Theorem 4.3 in order to incrementally monitor PLTL-FO properties. The goal is to avoid re-evaluating the formula after each move. We will present an incremental algorithm that avoids computations that depend on the entire trace. However, as we will see, this is at the cost of maintaining a possibly very large auxiliary structure.

Consider a PLTL-FO property $\phi_f(\bar{x})$ to be monitored. An incremental algorithm for evaluating $poss(\phi_f(\bar{x}))$ on a p-trace τ uses two functions, aux and inc_{aux}. As we shall see, $aux(\tau)$ provides enough information to answer $poss(\phi_f(\bar{x}))$, and provides additional information needed to incrementally maintain its own value using the second function inc_{aux}. More precisely, for a new observation (J, f) at peer p, $aux(\tau \cdot (J, f)) = inc_{aux}(aux(\tau), (J, f))$.

The functions aux and inc_{aux} are defined as follows. Consider first aux. Intuitively, $aux(\tau)$ consists of all I-instances $(\mathcal{I}, \varphi)$ with associated formula $\psi(\bar{x})$ reachable by complete runs in $\nu^{-1}(\tau)$, together with the set of states of A_ϕ reachable on such runs. More precisely, $aux(\tau)$ consists of the set of tuples $(\mathcal{I}, \varphi, \psi(\bar{x}), Q)$ where:

- there exists a complete $\mathcal{P}_\tau$-constrained parameterized run $\mathbf{s}(\bar{x}) = \{((\mathcal{I}_i, \varphi_i, \psi_i(\bar{x})), (e_i, \gamma_i, P_{j_i}))\}_{0 \leq i \leq n}$ accepted by A_τ, defined as in the proof of Theorem 4.3, for which $(\mathcal{I}, \varphi) = (\mathcal{I}_n, \varphi_n)$, and $\psi(\bar{x}) = \psi_n(\bar{x})$,
- Q is the set of states of A_ϕ reachable from the initial state on some run $\mathbf{s}$ as above.

Clearly, $poss(\phi_f(\bar{x}))$ is true on τ iff there exists $(\mathcal{I}, \varphi, \psi(\bar{x}), Q)$ in $aux(\tau)$ for which Q contains an accepting state of A_ϕ.

Next, consider the function inc_{aux}. Given $aux(\tau)$ as above, and a new observation (J, f) at peer p, $inc_{aux}(aux(\tau), (J, f))$ consists of all $(\mathcal{I}', \varphi', \psi'(\bar{x}), Q')$ such that, for some $(\mathcal{I}, \varphi, \psi(\bar{x}), Q)$ in $aux(\tau)$:

- there exists a J-constrained parameterized run suffix $\mathbf{s}(\bar{x}) = \{((\mathcal{I}_i, \varphi_i, \psi_i(\bar{x})), (e_i, \gamma_i, J))\}_{0 \leq i \leq n}$, where:
  - (i) $(\mathcal{I}', \varphi') = (\mathcal{I}_n, \varphi_n)$ and $\psi'(\bar{x}) = \psi_n(\bar{x})$,
  - (ii) $(\mathcal{I}, \varphi) \vdash^J_{e_0, \gamma_0} (\mathcal{I}_0, \varphi_0)$, $peer(e_0) = p$ if $f = p$ and $peer(e_0) \neq p$ if $f = \star$, and $peer(e_i) \neq p$ for $i > 0$,
  - (iii) $\psi_0(\bar{x})$ is computed from $\psi(\bar{x})$ and the initial transition $(\mathcal{I}, \varphi) \vdash^J_{e_0, \gamma_0} (\mathcal{I}_0, \varphi_0)$
- Q' is the set of states of A_ϕ reachable from some $q \in Q$ on runs $\mathbf{s}$ as above.

Clearly, $inc_{aux}(aux(\tau), (J, f)) = aux(\tau \cdot (J, f))$, as desired.

Since $cert(\phi_f(\bar{x})) = \neg poss(\neg \phi_f(\bar{x}))$, the incremental evaluation algorithm for $poss(\neg \phi_f(\bar{x}))$ also provides an incremental evaluation algorithm for $cert(\phi_f(\bar{x}))$.

Clearly, the size of $aux(\tau)$ is exponential in $adom(\tau)$ and ϕ (for $\mathcal{W}$ fixed). The function inc_{aux} can be computed in EXPTIME w.r.t. $adom(\tau)$ and ϕ. In terms of complexity, the main advantage of incremental evaluation over re-evaluation on the entire run is that the complexity w.r.t. τ depends only on the size $adom(\tau)$ and not on the length of τ. However, this has to be balanced against the need to create intermediate results of exponential size w.r.t. $adom(\tau)$ and ϕ.

Pre-emptive monitoring. We have so far considered the incremental monitoring of statically specified properties. Suppose that the properties to be monitored are not known ahead of time but instead may be specified dynamically as the run unfolds. Is some form of incremental evaluation still possible? We provide here a partially affirmative answer. Indeed, we show that large classes of properties can be preemptively monitored, as long as partial information is available on the *type* of temporal property they specify. More precisely, the *temporal type* of a PLTL-FO property $\phi_f(\bar{x})$ is the propositional formula ϕ. For example, commonly arising types include $G^{-1}r$, or $F^{-1}r$, or $G^{-1}(r_1 \rightarrow F^{-1}r_2)$. In addition to the temporal type, we also need to know the maximum number of free variables $|\bar{x}|$.

DEFINITION 4.6. *A PLTL-FO property type is a pair* (Φ, m), *where* Φ *is a finite set of PLTL formulas and* $m \geq 0$. *A PLTL-FO formula* $\phi_f(\bar{x})$ *for* $\mathcal{W}$ *is of type* (Φ, m) *if* $\phi \in \Phi$ *and* $|\bar{x}| \leq m$.

For example, $(\{G^{-1}r,\ F^{-1}r,\ G^{-1}(r_1 \rightarrow F^{-1}r_2)\},\ 10)$ is a PLTL-FO type.

We next outline an incremental algorithm that allows to evaluate *all* formulas of a given type (Φ, m). Note that there are infinitely many such formulas. Let P_Φ be the set of propositions occuring in Φ. The main idea of the algorithm is to modify the incremental algorithm for monitoring $\phi_f(\bar{x})$ described in the previous section as follows. Recall that the algorithm generates constrained parameterized runs and produces the tuples $(\mathcal{I}, \varphi, \psi(\bar{x}), Q)$ of reachable I-instances, constraint $\psi(\bar{x})$ on the free variables $\bar{x}$, and the set Q of corresponding states reachable in the automaton A_ϕ. The input of A_ϕ at each transition consists of the truth value to the propositions of ϕ induced by the FO components $f(r)$. In our case, the FO components are unknown. Instead of evaluating each $f(r)$, the new algorithm simply *guesses* the truth assignments σ for the propositions in ϕ, for the isomorphism types of all reachable I-instances and free variables $\bar{x}$.

Let τ be a p-trace. Let $\mathcal{S}(\tau)$ be the set of all isomorphism types[2] of $(\mathcal{I}, \varphi, \psi(\bar{x}))$ such that there is a $\mathcal{P}_\tau$-constrained parameterized run $\mathbf{s}(\bar{x}) = \{((\mathcal{I}_i, \varphi_i, \psi_i(\bar{x})), (e_i, \gamma_i, P_{j_i}))\}_{0 \leq i \leq n}$ accepted by A_τ, with $\mathcal{I} = \mathcal{I}_j, \varphi = \varphi_j, \psi(\bar{x}) = \psi_j(\bar{x})$ for some $j \in [0, n]$. A truth assignment mapping for $\mathcal{S}(\tau)$ is a mapping Σ from $\mathcal{S}(\tau)$ to truth assignments of P_Φ.

The auxiliary information $aux(\tau)$ computed by the incremental algorithm now consists of the set of all pairs $(\Sigma, \mathcal{H})$ where Σ is a truth assignment mapping for $\mathcal{S}(\tau)$ and $\mathcal{H}$ is the set of tuples $(\mathcal{I}, \varphi, \psi(\bar{x}), \{Q_\pi \mid \pi \in \Phi\})$ where:

- there exists a complete $\mathcal{P}_\tau$-constrained parameterized run $\mathbf{s}(\bar{x}) = \{((\mathcal{I}_i, \varphi_i, \psi_i(\bar{x})), (e_i, \gamma_i, P_{j_i}))\}_{0 \leq i \leq n}$ accepted by A_τ, for which $(\mathcal{I}, \varphi) = (\mathcal{I}_n, \varphi_n)$, and $\psi(\bar{x}) = \psi_n(\bar{x})$,
- for each $\pi \in \Phi$, Q_π is the set of states of A_π reachable from the initial state on some run $\mathbf{s}(\bar{x})$ as above, where the truth assignment for P_Φ at the i-th transition is $\Sigma(\hat{h})$, for $h = (\mathcal{I}_i, \varphi_i, \psi_i(\bar{x}))$.

The function $aux(\tau)$ can be maintained incrementally by a function inc_{aux} similar to the previous section. The set Σ of truth assignment mappings is maintained by augmenting it with truth assignments for isomorphism types of newly reached instances in the run suffixes generated when a new observation (J, f) is added (we ommit the straightforward details).

Now suppose that we wish evaluate $poss(\phi_f(\bar{x}))$ for a PLTL-FO formula $\phi_f(\bar{x})$ of type (Φ, m), for the p-trace τ. Let $aux(\tau)$ be as defined above. Let Σ be such that for each proposition r of ϕ and every $\hat{h} \in \mathcal{S}(\tau)$, $f(r)$ holds in $\hat{h}$ iff $\Sigma(\hat{h})(r) = 1$. Let $\mathcal{H}$ be such that $(\Sigma, \mathcal{H}) \in aux(\tau)$. Then $poss(\phi_f(\bar{x}))$ holds iff there exists $(\mathcal{I}, \varphi, \psi(\bar{x}), \{Q_\pi \mid \pi \in \Phi\}) \in \mathcal{H}$ such that Q_ϕ contains an accepting state of A_ϕ.

To evaluate the size of $aux(\tau)$, note that the number of isomorphism types in $\mathcal{S}(\tau)$ is exponential in the maximum size of an I-instance in τ (and independent of its active domain). Thus, the number of truth assignment mappings Σ is double exponential in the same (single exponential for fixed type (Φ, m)). For each Σ, the size of $\mathcal{H}$ is exponential in (Φ, m) and $adom(\tau)$. Finally, the evaluation of a PLTL-FO property $\phi_f(\bar{x})$ of type (Φ, m) on $aux(\tau)$ is in PSPACE.

Clearly, the use of preemptive incremental monitoring becomes beneficial compared to direct evaluation over the entire p-trace τ only under certain conditions, including the following: (i) $adom(\tau)$ is small relative to the length of τ, (ii) the number of isomorphism types of parameterized I-instances in runs of $A_\tau(\mathcal{P}_\tau)$ is small relative to $adom(\tau)$, and (iii) the number of formulas of type (Φ, m) to be evaluated is large.

Introspective closure. We showed how a peer can reason about temporal properties of global runs based on its local observations. In many cases, it would be desirable for a peer to be able to use the information gained by such reasoning to make decisions on the actions it takes in the workflow. A natural question is whether the specification language we defined would need to be extended or whether it is already closed under such introspective reasoning. We next show that it is closed under introspective reasoning, for a natural definition of simulation.

We can straightforwardly define an extension of workflow specs allowing the use in conditions of atoms of the form $poss(\phi_f(\bar{x}))$ and $cert(\phi_f(\bar{x}))$, that we refer to as *introspective atoms*. The semantics of these atoms (that refer to the global run) is as previously defined. Specifically, $poss(\phi_f(\bar{x}))$ is evaluated on the p-trace of the run leading to the current application of the action. We refer to specs that allow introspective atoms in the actions of peers p for which the spec is key-visible, as *introspective* specs.

In order to compare the expressiveness of introspective and regular specs, we define a natural notion of simulation. Intuitively, a spec simulating $\mathcal{W}$ is allowed to use additional relations and actions, but its restriction to the relations and actions of $\mathcal{W}$ must yield exactly the runs of $\mathcal{W}$. We make this more precise. First, consider a spec $\mathcal{W}$, let $\mathcal{D}_0$ be a subset of its schema and $\mathcal{A}_0$ a subset of its actions. For each run ρ of $\mathcal{W}$, the projection of $\rho = \{(I_i, e_i)\}_{0 \leq i \leq n}$ on $\mathcal{D}_0$ and $\mathcal{A}_0$, denoted $\pi_{\mathcal{D}_0, \mathcal{A}_0}(\rho)$, is the sequence obtained by removing from ρ all terms (I_i, e_i) for which $action(e_i) \notin \mathcal{A}_0$ and restricting each instance in the remaining sequence to $\mathcal{D}_0$.

Let $\mathcal{W}_1$ and $\mathcal{W}_2$ be specs with the same set of peers, both key-visible at p. We denote by $\mathcal{D}_i$ the schema of $\mathcal{W}_i$. We say that $\mathcal{W}_2$ *simulates* $\mathcal{W}_1$ if: (i) $\mathcal{D}_1 \subseteq \mathcal{D}_2$, (ii) each action α of $\mathcal{W}_1$ has a corresponding action $\bar{\alpha}$ in $\mathcal{W}_2$ at the same peer (we denote $\bar{\mathcal{A}}_1 = \{\bar{\alpha} \mid \alpha \in \mathcal{A}_1\}$), and

(*iii*) $\{\pi_{\mathcal{D}_1, \bar{\mathcal{A}}_1}(\rho_2) \mid \rho_2$ is a run of $\mathcal{W}_2\} =$
$\{\{(I_i, \bar{e}_i)\}_{0 \leq i \leq n} \mid \{(I_i, e_i)\}_{0 \leq i \leq n}$ is a run of $\mathcal{W}_1$,
$peer(e_i) = peer(\bar{e}_i)$, $action(\bar{e}_i) = \overline{action}(e_i)$,
$val(\bar{e}_i) = val(e_i), i \in [0, n]\}$

We can show the following.

[2] Recall the definition in the proof of Theorem 4.3.

THEOREM 4.7. *For every introspective workflow spec $\mathcal{W}_1$ there exists a workflow spec $\mathcal{W}_2$ that simulates $\mathcal{W}_1$.*

PROOF. Let $\mathcal{W}_1$ be an introspective workflow. Let p be a peer such as $\mathcal{W}_1$ is key-visible at p. The simulation by $\mathcal{W}_2$ of introspective atoms used in actions of p has two main aspects. First, $\mathcal{W}_2$ uses additional relations to store the p-trace of the current run. This is done by copying, at each transition caused by p or with side-effects at p, the corresponding observation in the p-trace. Moreover, each copy is timestamped by a new value created using a variable occurring only in the updates of an action, and the timestamps are ordered. Doing this at each transition requires additional control, which is enforced using additonal propositions. Second, peer p must evaluate introspective atoms $poss(\phi_f(\bar{x}))$ or $cert(\phi_f(\bar{x}))$ on the currently stored p-trace. This can be done because sets of actions at p, with appropriate control provided by propositions, are computationally complete. Once again, this is due to the ability to create new values using variables occurring only in the updates of actions. The proof is similar to the query completeness of nondeterministic Datalog$^\neg$ with value invention (using variables occurring only in heads of rules), see [7]. □

5. CONCLUSIONS

We conclude with several directions for future work. It is clearly of interest to relax some of the restrictions imposed to obtain our positive results. This includes the key-visibility condition as well as the limitation to projection views. Another issue requiring further investigation is the assumption that each peer has available a specification of the entire collaborative workflow. We argued that this is reasonable because peers are likely to be provided with an abstraction of the actual specification in order to understand the global workflow, while hiding private or irrelevant information. It remains open how such abstractions can be obtained, what faithfulness conditions they should satisfy with respect to the full specification, and whether such conditions can be statically checked. Finally, our model assumes an underlying synchronization mechanism ensuring instantaneous propagation of local updates to all peers. It is of interest to consider a model allowing for asynchronous communication among peers, and efficient protocols to ensure consistency of runs.

6. ACKNOWLEDGEMENTS

We thank Val Tannen for useful discussions on the update propagation model of collaborative workflows, inspired by the Orchestra approach to data sharing.

7. REFERENCES

[1] P. A. Abdulla and B. Jonsson. Verifying programs with unreliable channels. *Inf. and Comp.*, 127(2), 1996.

[2] S. Abiteboul, E. Antoine, and J. Stoyanovich. Viewing the web as a distributed knowledge base. In *ICDE*, 2012.

[3] S. Abiteboul, O. Benjelloun, and T. Milo. The Active XML project: an overview. *VLDB J.*, 17(5), 2008.

[4] S. Abiteboul, M. Bienvenu, A. Galland, and E. Antoine. A rule-based language for web data management. In *PODS*, pages 293–304, 2011.

[5] S. Abiteboul, P. Bourhis, and V. Vianu. Comparing workflow specification languages: A matter of views. *TODS*, 37(2), 2012.

[6] S. Abiteboul, R. Hull, and V. Vianu. *Foundations of Databases.* Addison Wesley, 1995.

[7] S. Abiteboul and V. Vianu. Datalog extensions for database queries and updates. *JCSS*, 43(1), 1991.

[8] P. Alvaro, W. R. Marczak, N. Conway, J. M. Hellerstein, D. Maier, and R. Sears. Dedalus: Datalog in time and space. In *Datalog*, pages 262–281, 2010.

[9] M. Arenas, V. Kantere, A. Kementsietsidis, I. Kiringa, R. J. Miller, and J. Mylopoulos. The hyperion project: from data integration to data coordination. *SIGMOD Record*, 32(3):53–58, 2003.

[10] D. Brand and P. Zafiropulo. On communicating finite-state machines. *JACM*, 30(2), 1983.

[11] J. Brzozwski and E. Leiss. Finite automata and sequential networks. *Theoretical Computer Science*, 10, 1980.

[12] A. Deutsch, L. Sui, V. Vianu, and D. Zhou. Verification of communicating data-driven web services. In *PODS*, 2006.

[13] E. A. Emerson. Temporal and modal logic. In J. V. Leeuwen, editor, *Handbook of Theoretical Computer Science, Volume B: Formal Models and Sematics.* North-Holland Pub. Co./MIT Press, 1990.

[14] R. Fagin, J. Y. Halpern, Y. Moses, and M. Y. Vardi. *Reasoning about Knowledge.* MIT Press, 1995.

[15] T. J. Green, G. Karvounarakis, N. E. Taylor, O. Biton, Z. G. Ives, and V. Tannen. Orchestra: facilitating collaborative data sharing. In *SIGMOD*, 2007.

[16] J. M. Hellerstein. The declarative imperative: experiences and conjectures in distributed logic. *SIGMOD Record*, 39(1), 2010.

[17] R. Hull. Web services composition: A story of models, automata, and logics. In *ICSOC*, 2005.

[18] R. Hull and J. Su. Tools for composite web services: a short overview. *SIGMOD Record*, 34(2):86–95, 2005.

[19] T. Imieliński and W. Lipski. Incomplete information in relational databases. *JACM*, 31(4), 1984.

[20] Z. G. Ives, T. J. Green, G. Karvounarakis, N. E. Taylor, V. Tannen, P. P. Talukdar, M. Jacob, and F. Pereira. The orchestra collaborative data sharing system. *SIGMOD Record*, 37(3), 2008.

[21] A. Nigam and N. S. Caswell. Business artifacts: An approach to operational specification. *IBM Systems Journal*, 42(3):428–445, 2003.

[22] I. Tatarinov, Z. G. Ives, J. Madhavan, A. Y. Halevy, D. Suciu, N. N. Dalvi, X. Dong, Y. Kadiyska, G. Miklau, and P. Mork. The piazza peer data management project. *SIGMOD Record*, 32(3):47–52, 2003.

[23] M. Vardi. An automata-theoretic approach to linear temporal logic. In *Banff Higher Order Workshop*, 1995.

I/O-Efficient Planar Range Skyline and Attrition Priority Queues*

Casper Kejlberg-Rasmussen[1] Yufei Tao[2,3] Konstantinos Tsakalidis[4]
Kostas Tsichlas[5] Jeonghun Yoon[3]

[1]MADALGO[†] Aarhus University
[2]Chinese University of Hong Kong
[3]Korea Advanced Institute of Science and Technology
[4]Hong Kong University of Science and Technology
[5]Aristotle University of Thessaloniki

ABSTRACT

We study the static and dynamic *planar range skyline reporting problem* in the external memory model with block size B, under a linear space budget. The problem asks for an $O(n/B)$ space data structure that stores n points in the plane, and supports reporting the k maximal input points (a.k.a. *skyline*) among the points that lie within a given query rectangle $Q = [\alpha_1, \alpha_2] \times [\beta_1, \beta_2]$. When Q is *3-sided*, i.e. one of its edges is grounded, two variants arise: *top-open* for $\beta_2 = \infty$ and *left-open* for $\alpha_1 = -\infty$ (symmetrically *bottom-open* and *right-open*) queries.

We present optimal static data structures for *top-open* queries, for the cases where the universe is $\mathbb{R}^2$, a $U \times U$ grid, and rank space $[\mathcal{O}(n)]^2$. We also show that *left-open* queries are harder, as they require $\Omega((n/B)^\epsilon + k/B)$ I/Os for $\epsilon > 0$, when only linear space is allowed. We show that the lower bound is tight, by a structure that supports 4-sided queries in matching complexities. Interestingly, these lower and upper bounds coincide with those of the *planar orthogonal range reporting problem*, i.e., the skyline requirement does not alter the problem difficulty at all!

Finally, we present the first dynamic linear space data structure that supports top-open queries in $O(\log_{2B^\epsilon} n + k/B^{1-\epsilon})$ and updates in $O(\log_{2B^\epsilon} n)$ worst case I/Os, for $\epsilon \in [0, 1]$. This also yields a linear space data structure for 4-sided queries with optimal query I/Os and $\mathcal{O}(\log(n/B))$ amortized update I/Os. We consider of independent interest the main component of our dynamic structures, a new real-time I/O-efficient and catenable variant of the fundamental structure *priority queue with attrition* by Sundar.

*The full version is found on http://arxiv.org under the same title.

†MADALGO (Center for Massive Data Algorithmics – a Center of the Danish National Research Foundation)

PODS'13, June 22–27, 2013, New York, New York, USA.

Categories and Subject Descriptors

F.2.2 [**Analysis of algorithms and problem complexity**]: Nonnumerical Algorithms and Problems—*computations on discrete structures*; H.3.1 [**Information storage and retrieval**]: Content analysis and indexing—*indexing methods*

Keywords

Skyline, range reporting, priority queues, external memory, data structures

1. INTRODUCTION

Given two different points $p = (x_p, y_p)$ and $q = (x_q, y_q)$ in $\mathbb{R}^2$, where $\mathbb{R}$ denotes the real domain, we say that p *dominates* q if $x_p \geq x_q$ and $y_p \geq y_q$. Let P be a set of n points in $\mathbb{R}^2$. A point $p \in P$ is *maximal* if it is not dominated by any other point in P. The *skyline* of P consists of all maximal points of P. Notice that the skyline naturally forms an orthogonal staircase where increasing x-coordinates imply decreasing y-coordinates. Figure 1a shows an example where the maximal points are in black.

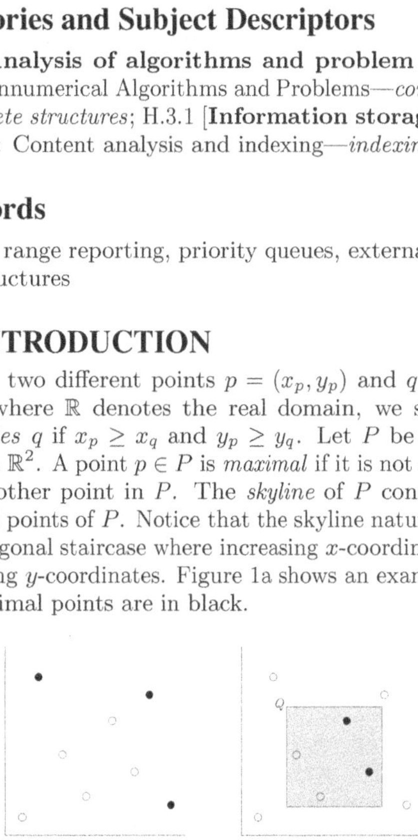

(a) Skyline (b) Range skyline

Figure 1: Range skyline queries.

Given an axis-parallel rectangle Q, a *range skyline query* (also known as a *range maxima query*) reports the skyline of $P \cap Q$. In Figure 1b, for instance, Q is the shaded rectangle, and the two black points constitute the query result. When Q is a 3-sided rectangle, a range skyline query becomes a *top-open*, *right-open*, *bottom-open* or *left-open* query, as shown in Figures 2a-2d respectively. A *dominance* (resp. *anti-dominance*) query Q is a 2-sided rectangle with both the top and right (resp. the bottom and left) edges grounded, as shown in Figure 2e (resp. 2f). Another well-studied variation is the *contour* query, where Q is a 1-sided rectangle that is the half-plane to the left of a vertical line (Figure 2g).

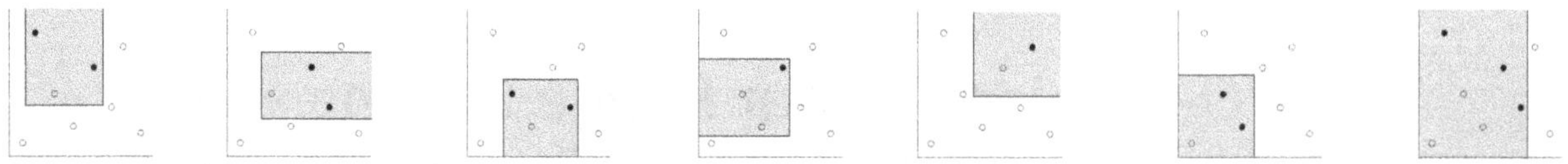

(a) Top-open (b) Right-open (c) Bottom-open (d) Left-open (e) Dominance (f) Anti-dominance (g) Contour

Figure 2: Variations of range skyline queries (black points represent the query results).

This paper studies linear-size data structures that can answer range skyline queries efficiently, in both the static and dynamic settings. Our analysis focuses on the *external memory* (EM) model [1], which has become the dominant computation model for studying I/O-efficient algorithms. In this model, a machine has M words of memory, and a disk of an unbounded size. The disk is divided into disjoint *blocks*, each of which is formed by B consecutive words. An *I/O* loads a block of data from the disk to memory, or conversely, writes B words from memory to a disk block. The space of a structure equals the number of blocks it occupies, while the cost of an algorithm equals the number of I/Os it performs. CPU time is for free.

By default, the data universe is $\mathbb{R}^2$. Given an integer $U > 0$, $[U]$ represents the set $\{0, 1, \ldots, U-1\}$. All the above queries remain well defined in the universe $[U]^2$. Particularly, when $U = \mathcal{O}(n)$, the universe is called *rank space*. In general, for a smaller universe, it may be possible to achieve better query cost under the same space budget. We consider that P is in general position, i.e., no two points in P have the same x- or y-coordinate (datasets not in general position can be supported by standard tie breaking). When the universe is $[U]^2$, we make the standard assumption that a machine word has at least $\log_2 U$ bits.

1.1 Motivation of 2D Range Skyline

Skylines have drawn very significant attention (see [4,6,7, 10–12,15,20,21,23,24,26–31] and the references therein) from the research community due to their crucial importance to multi-criteria optimization, which in turn is vital to numerous applications. In particular, the rectangle of a range skyline query represents range predicates specified by a user. An effective index is essential for maximizing the efficiency of these queries in database systems [24,28].

This paper concentrates on 2D data for several reasons. First, *planar range skyline reporting* (i.e., our problem) is a classic topic that has been extensively studied in theory [7,11,12,15,20,21,23,27]. However, nearly all the existing results apply to internal memory (as reviewed in the next subsection), while currently there is little understanding about the characteristics of the problem in I/O environments.

The second, more practical, reason is that many skyline applications are *inherently* 2D. In fact, the special importance of 2D arises from the fact that one often faces the situation of having to strike a balance between a pair of naturally contradicting factors. A prominent example is *price* vs. *quality* in product selection. A range skyline query can be used to find the products that are not dominated by others in both aspects, when the price and quality need to fall in specific ranges. Other pairs of naturally contradicting factors include *space* vs. *query time* (in choosing data structures), *privacy protection* vs. *disclosed information* (the perpetual dilemma in privacy preservation [9]), and so on.

The last reason, and maybe the most important, is that clearly range skyline reporting cannot become easier as the dimensionality increases, whereas even for two dimensions, we will prove a hardness result showing that the problem (unfortunately) is already difficult enough to forbid sub-polynomial query cost under the linear space budget! In other words, the "easiest" dimensionality of 2 is not so easy after all, which also points to the absence of query-efficient structures in any higher dimension when only linear space is permitted.

1.2 Previous Results

Range Skyline in Internal Memory. We first review the existing results when the dataset P fits in main memory. Early research focused on dominance and contour queries, both of which can be solved in $\mathcal{O}(\log n + k)$ time using a structure of $\mathcal{O}(n)$ size, where k is the number of points reported [11,15,20,23,27]. Brodal and Tsakalidis [7] were the first to discover an optimal dynamic structure for top-open queries, which capture both dominance and contour queries as special cases. Their structure occupies $\mathcal{O}(n)$ space, answers queries in $\mathcal{O}(\log n + k)$ time, and supports updates in $\mathcal{O}(\log n)$ time. The above structures belong to the *pointer machine* model. Utilizing features of the RAM model, Brodal and Tsakalidis [7] also presented an alternative structure in universe $[U]^2$, which uses $\mathcal{O}(n)$ space, answers queries in $\mathcal{O}(\frac{\log n}{\log \log n} + k)$ time, and can be updated in $\mathcal{O}(\frac{\log n}{\log \log n})$ time. In RAM, the static top-open problem can be easily settled using an RMQ (*range minimum queries*) structure (see, e.g., [36]), which occupies $\mathcal{O}(n)$ space and answers queries in $\mathcal{O}(1 + k)$ time.

For general range skyline queries (i.e., 4-sided), all the known structures demand super-linear space. Specifically, Brodal and Tsakalidis [7] gave a pointer-machine structure of $\mathcal{O}(n \log n)$ size, $\mathcal{O}(\log^2 n + k)$ query time, and $\mathcal{O}(\log^2 n)$ update time. Kalavagattu et al. [21] designed a static RAM-structure that occupies $O(n \log n)$ space and achieves query time $\mathcal{O}(\log n + k)$. In rank space, Das et al. [12] proposed a static RAM-structure with $\mathcal{O}(n \frac{\log n}{\log \log n})$ space and $\mathcal{O}(\frac{\log n}{\log \log n} + k)$ query time.

The above results also hold directly in external memory, but they are far from being satisfactory. In particular, all of them incur $\Omega(k)$ I/Os to report k points. An I/O-efficient structure ought to achieve $\mathcal{O}(k/B)$ I/Os for this purpose.

Range Skyline in External Memory. In contrast to internal memory where there exist a large number of results, range skyline queries have not been well studied in external memory. As a naive solution, we can first scan the entire point set P to eliminate the points falling outside the query rectangle Q, and then find the skyline of the remaining points by the fastest skyline algorithm [31] on non-preprocessed input sets. This expensive solution can incur $\mathcal{O}((n/B) \log_{M/B}(n/B))$ I/Os.

Papadias et al. [28] described a branch-and-bound algorithm when the dataset is indexed by an R-tree [17]. The algorithm is heuristic and cannot guarantee better worst

	space	query	insertion	deletion	remark
top-open in $\mathbb{R}^2$	$\mathcal{O}(n/B)$	$\mathcal{O}(\log_B n + k/B)$	-	-	optimal
top-open in U^2	$\mathcal{O}(n/B)$	$\mathcal{O}(\log\log_B U + k/B)$	-	-	optimal
top-open in $[\mathcal{O}(n)]^2$	$\mathcal{O}(n/B)$	$\mathcal{O}(1 + k/B)$	-	-	optimal
anti-dominance in $\mathbb{R}^2$	$\mathcal{O}(n/B)$	$\Omega((n/B)^\epsilon + k/B)$	-	-	lower bound (indexability)
4-sided in $\mathbb{R}^2$	$\mathcal{O}(n/B)$	$\mathcal{O}((n/B)^\epsilon + k/B)$	-	-	optimal (indexability)
top-open in $\mathbb{R}^2$	$\mathcal{O}(n/B)$	$\mathcal{O}(\log_{2B^\epsilon} n + k/B^{1-\epsilon})$	$\mathcal{O}(\log_{2B^\epsilon} n)$	$\mathcal{O}(\log_{2B^\epsilon} n)$	for any constant $\epsilon \in [0, 1]$
4-sided in $\mathbb{R}^2$	$\mathcal{O}(n/B)$	$\mathcal{O}((n/B)^\epsilon + k/B)$	$\mathcal{O}(\log(n/B))$	$\mathcal{O}(\log(n/B))$	update cost is amortized

Table 1: Summary of our range skyline results (all complexities are in the worst case by default).

case query I/Os than the naive solution mentioned earlier. Different approaches have been proposed for skyline maintenance in external memory under various assumptions on the updates [19, 28, 33, 35]. The performance of those methods, however, was again evaluated only experimentally on certain "representative" datasets. No I/O-efficient structure exists for answering range skyline queries even in sublinear I/Os under arbitrary updates.

Priority Queues with Attrition (PQAs). Let S be a set of elements drawn from an ordered domain, and let $\min(S)$ be the smallest element in S. A PQA on S is a data structure that supports the following operations:

- FINDMIN: Return $\min(S)$.
- DELETEMIN: Remove and return $\min(S)$.
- INSERTANDATTRITE: Add a new element e to S and remove from S all the elements at least e. After the operation, the new content is $S' = \{e' \in S \mid e' < e\} \cup \{e\}$. The elements $\{e' \in S \mid e' \geq e\}$ are *attrited.*

In internal memory, Sundar [32] described how to implement a PQA that supports all operations in $\mathcal{O}(1)$ worst case time, and occupies $\mathcal{O}(n - m)$ space after n INSERTANDATTRITE and m DELETEMIN operations.

1.3 Our Results

This paper presents external memory structures for solving the planar range skyline reporting problem using only linear space. At the core of one of these structures is a new PQA that supports the extra functionality of catenation. This PQA is a non-trivial extension of Sundar's version [32]. It can be implemented I/O-efficiently, and is of independent interest due to its fundamental nature. Next, we provide an overview of our results.

Static Range Skyline. When P is static, we describe several linear-size structures with the optimal query cost. Our structures also separate the hard variants of the problem from the easy ones.

For top-open queries, we present a structure that answers queries in optimal $\mathcal{O}(\log_B n + k/B)$ I/Os (Theorem 1) when the universe is $\mathbb{R}^2$. To obtain the result, we give an elegant reduction of the problem to *segment intersection*, which can be settled by a *partially persistent B-tree* (PPB-tree) [5]. Furthermore, we show that this PPB-tree is (what we call) *sort-aware build-efficient* (SABE), namely, it can be constructed in linear I/Os, provided that P is already sorted by x-coordinate (Theorem 1). The construction algorithm exploits several intrinsic properties of top-open queries, whereas none of the known approaches [2, 14, 34] for bulkloading a PPB-tree is SABE.

The above structure is *indivisible*, namely, it treats each coordinate as an atom by always storing it using an entire word. As the second step, we improve the top-open query overhead beyond the logarithmic bound when the data universe is small. Specifically, when the universe is $[U]^2$ where U is an integer, we give a *divisible* structure with optimal $\mathcal{O}(\log\log_B U + k/B)$ query I/Os (Corollary 1). In the rank space, we further reduce the query cost again optimally to $\mathcal{O}(1 + k/B)$ (Theorem 2).

Clearly, top-open queries are equivalent to right-open queries by symmetry, and capture dominance and contour queries as special cases, so the results aforementioned are applicable to those variants immediately.

Unfortunately, fast query cost with linear space is impossible for the remaining variants under the well-known *indexability model* of [18] (all the structures in this paper belong to this model). Specifically, for anti-dominance queries, we establish a lower bound showing that every linear-size structure must incur $\Omega((n/B)^\epsilon + k/B)$ I/Os in the worst case (Theorem 5), where $\epsilon > 0$ can be an arbitrarily small constant. Furthermore, we prove that this is tight, by giving a structure to answer a 4-sided query in $\mathcal{O}((n/B)^\epsilon + k/B)$ I/Os (Theorem 6). Since 4-sided is more general than anti-dominance, these matching lower and upper bounds imply that they, as well as left- and bottom-open queries, have exactly the same difficulty.

The above 4-sided results also reveal a somewhat unexpected fact: planar range skyline reporting has precisely the same hardness as *planar range reporting* (where, given an axis-parallel rectangle Q, we want to find all the points in $P \cap Q$, instead of just the maxima; see [3, 18] for the matching lower and upper bounds on planar range reporting). In other words, the extra skyline requirement does not alter the difficulty at all.

Dynamic Range Skyline. The aforementioned static structures cannot be updated efficiently when insertions and deletions occur in P. For top-open queries, we provide an alternative structure with fast worst case update overhead, at a minor expense of query efficiency. Specifically, our structure occupies linear space, is SABE, answers queries in $\mathcal{O}(\log_{2B^\epsilon}(n/B) + k/B^{1-\epsilon})$ I/Os, and supports updates in $\mathcal{O}(\log_{2B^\epsilon}(n/B))$ I/Os, where ϵ can be any parameter satisfying $0 \leq \epsilon \leq 1$ (Theorem 4). Note that setting $\epsilon = 0$ gives a structure with query cost $\mathcal{O}(\log(n/B) + k/B)$ and update cost $\mathcal{O}(\log(n/B))$.

The combination of this structure and our (static) 4-sided structure leads to a dynamic 4-sided structure that uses linear space, answers queries optimally in $\mathcal{O}((n/B)^\epsilon + k/B)$ I/Os, and supports updates in $\mathcal{O}(\log(n/B))$ I/Os amortized (Theorem 6). Table 1 summarizes our structures.

Catenable Priority Queues with Attrition. A central ingredient of our dynamic structures is a new PQA that is more powerful than the traditional version of Sundar [32].

Specifically, besides FINDMIN, DELETEMIN and INSERTANDATTRITE (already reviewed in Section 1.2), it also supports:

- CATENATEANDATTRITE: Given two PQAs on sets S_1 and S_2 respectively, the operation returns a single PQA on $S = \{e \in S_1 \mid e < \min(S_2)\} \cup S_2$. In other words, the elements in $\{e \in S_1 \mid e \geq \min(S_2)\}$ are attrited.

We are not aware of any previous work that addressed the above operation, which turns out to be rather challenging even in internal memory.

Our structure, named *I/O-efficient catenable priority queue with attrition* (I/O-CPQA), supports all operations in $\mathcal{O}(1)$ worst case and $\mathcal{O}(1/B)$ amortized I/Os (the amortized bound requires that a constant number of blocks be pinned in main memory, which is a standard and compulsory assumption to achieve $o(1)$ amortized update cost of most, if not all, known structures, e.g., the linked list). The space cost is $\mathcal{O}((n-m)/B)$ after n INSERTANDATTRITE and CATENATEANDATTRITE operations, and after m DELETEMIN operations.

All the missing proofs of theorems, lemmata and corollaries can be found in the full version.

2. SABE TOP-OPEN STRUCTURE

In this section, we describe a structure of linear size to answer a top-open query in $\mathcal{O}(\log_B n + k/B)$ I/Os. The structure is SABE, namely, it can be constructed in linear I/Os provided that the input set P is sorted by x-coordinate.

2.1 Reduction to Segment Intersection

We first describe a simple structure by converting top-open range skyline reporting to the *segment intersection problem*: the input is a set S of horizontal segments in $\mathbb{R}^2$; given a vertical segment q, a query reports all the segments of S intersecting q.

Given a point p in P, denote by *leftdom*(p) the leftmost point among all the points in P dominating p. If such a point does not exist, *leftdom*$(p) = nil$. We convert p to a horizontal segment $\sigma(p)$ as follows. Let $q =$ *leftdom*(p). If $q = nil$, then $\sigma(p) = [x_p, \infty[\times y_p$; otherwise, $\sigma(p) = [x_p, x_q[\times y_p$. Define $\Sigma(P) = \{\sigma(p) \mid p \in P\}$, i.e., the set of segments converted from the points of P. See Figure 3a for an example.

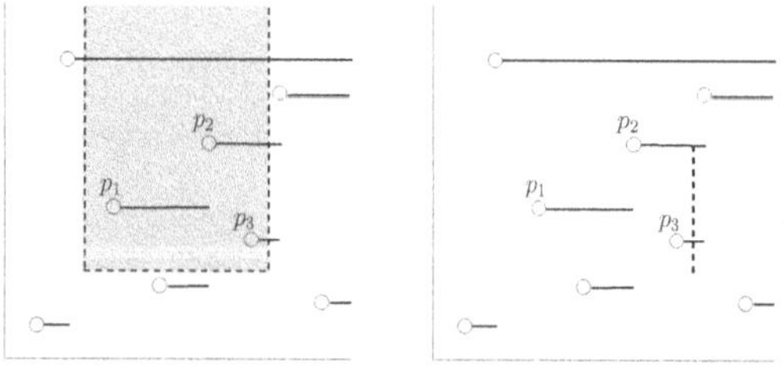

(a) Data conversion (b) Converted query

Figure 3: Reduction.

Now, consider a top-open query with rectangle $Q = [\alpha_1, \alpha_2] \times [\beta, \infty[$. We answer it by performing segment intersection on $\Sigma(P)$. First, obtain β' as the highest y-coordinate of the points in $P \cap Q$. Then, report all segments in $\Sigma(P)$ that intersect the vertical segment $\alpha_2 \times [\beta, \beta']$. An example is shown in Figure 3b. A proof of the correctness of the algorithm can be found in the full version.

We can find β' in $\mathcal{O}(\log_B n)$ I/Os with a *range-max query* on a B-tree indexing the x-coordinates in P. For retrieving the segments intersecting $\alpha_2 \times [\beta, \beta']$, we store $\Sigma(P)$ in a partially persistent B-tree (PPB-tree) [5]. As $\Sigma(P)$ has n segments, the PPB-tree occupies $\mathcal{O}(n/B)$ space and answers a segment intersection query in $\mathcal{O}(\log_B n + k/B)$ I/Os. We thus have obtained a linear-size top-open structure with $\mathcal{O}(\log_B n + k/B)$ query I/Os.

More effort, however, is needed to make the structure SABE. In particular, two challenges are to be overcome. First, we must generate $\Sigma(P)$ in linear I/Os. Second, the PPB-tree on $\Sigma(P)$ must be built with asymptotically the same cost (note that the range-max B-tree is already SABE). We will tackle these challenges in the rest of the section.

2.2 Computing $\Sigma(P)$

$\Sigma(P)$ is not an arbitrary set of segments. We observe:

LEMMA 1. *$\Sigma(P)$ has the following properties:*

- **(Nesting)** *for any two segments s_1 and s_2 in $\Sigma(P)$, their x-intervals are either disjoint, or such that one x-interval contains the other.*
- **(Monotonic)** *let ℓ be any vertical line, and $S(\ell)$ the set of segments in $\Sigma(P)$ intersected by ℓ. If we sort the segments of $S(\ell)$ in ascending order of their y-coordinates, the lengths of their x-intervals are non-decreasing.*

We are ready to present our algorithm for computing $\Sigma(P)$, after P has been sorted by x-coordinates. Conceptually, we sweep a vertical line ℓ from $x = -\infty$ to ∞. At any time, the algorithm (essentially) stores the set $S(\ell)$ of segments in a stack, which are en-stacked in descending order of y-coordinates. Whenever a segment is popped out of the stack, its right endpoint is decided, and the segment is output. In general, the segments of $\Sigma(P)$ are output in non-descending order of their right endpoints' x-coordinates.

Specifically, the algorithm starts by pushing the leftmost point of P onto the stack. Iteratively, let p be the next point fetched from P, and q the point currently at the top of the stack. If $y_q < y_p$, we know that $p =$ *leftdom*(q). Hence, the algorithm pops q off the stack, and outputs segment $\sigma(q) = [x_q, x_p[\times y_q$. Then, letting q be the point that tops the stack currently, the algorithm checks again whether $y_q < y_p$, and if so, repeats the above steps. This continues until either the stack is empty or $y_q > y_p$. In either case, the iteration finishes by pushing p onto the stack. It is clear that the algorithm generates $\Sigma(P)$ in $\mathcal{O}(n/B)$ I/Os.

2.3 Constructing the PPB-tree

Remember that we need a PPB-tree T on $\Sigma(P)$. The known algorithms for PPB-tree construction require super-linear I/Os even after sorting [2, 5, 14, 34]. Next, we show that the two properties of $\Sigma(P)$ in Lemma 1 allow building T in linear I/Os. Let us number the leaf level as *level 0*. In general, the parent of a level-i ($i \geq 0$) node is at level $i + 1$. We will build T in a bottom-up manner, i.e., starting from the leaf level, then level 1, and so on.

Leaf Level. To create the leaf nodes, we need to first sort the left and right endpoints of the segments in $\Sigma(P)$ together by x-coordinate. This can be done in $\mathcal{O}(n/B)$ I/Os as follows. First, P, which is sorted by x-coordinates, gives a sorted list of the left endpoints. On the other hand, our algorithm of the previous subsection generates $\Sigma(P)$ in non-descending order of the right endpoints' x-coordinates (breaking ties by favoring lower points). By merging the two lists, we obtain the desired sorted list of left and right endpoints combined.

Let us briefly review the algorithm proposed in [5] to build a PPB-tree. The algorithm conceptually moves a vertical line ℓ from $x = -\infty$ to ∞. At any moment, it maintains a B-tree $T(\ell)$ on the y-coordinates of the segments in $S(\ell)$. We call $T(\ell)$ a *snapshot B-tree*. To do so, whenever ℓ hits the left (resp. right) endpoint of a segment s, it inserts (resp. deletes) the y-coordinate of s in $T(\ell)$. The PPB-tree can be regarded as a space-efficient union of all the snapshot B-trees. The algorithm incurs $\mathcal{O}(n \log_B n)$ I/Os because (i) there are $2n$ updates, and (ii) for each update, $\mathcal{O}(\log_B n)$ I/Os are needed to locate the leaf node affected.

When $\Sigma(P)$ is nesting and monotonic, the construction can be significantly accelerated. A crucial observation is that any update to $S(\ell)$ happens only *at the bottom* of ℓ. Specifically, whenever ℓ hits the left/right endpoint of a segment $s \in \Sigma(P)$, s must be the lowest segment in $S(\ell)$. This implies that the leaf node of $T(\ell)$ to be altered must be the leftmost[1] one in $T(\ell)$. Hence, we can find this leaf without any I/Os by buffering it in memory, in contrast to the $\mathcal{O}(\log_B n)$ cost originally needed.

The other details are standard, and are sketched below assuming the knowledge of the classic algorithm in [5]. Whenever the leftmost leaf u of $T(\ell)$ is full, we version copy it to u', and possibly perform a split or merge, if u' strong-version overflows or underflows, respectively[2]. A version copy, split, and merge can all be handled in $\mathcal{O}(1)$ I/Os, and can happen only $\mathcal{O}(n/B)$ times. Therefore, the cost of building the leaf level is $\mathcal{O}(n/B)$.

Internal Levels. The level-1 nodes can be built by exactly the same algorithm, but on a different set of segments Σ_1 which are generated from the leaf nodes of the PPB-tree. To explain, let us first review an intuitive way [13] to visualize a node in a PPB-tree. A node u can be viewed as a rectangle $r(u) = [x_1, x_2[\times[y_1, y_2[$ in $\mathbb{R}^2$, where x_1 (resp. x_2) is the position of ℓ when u is created (resp. version copied), and $[y_1, y_2[$ represents the y-range of u in all the snapshot B-trees where u belongs. See Figure 4.

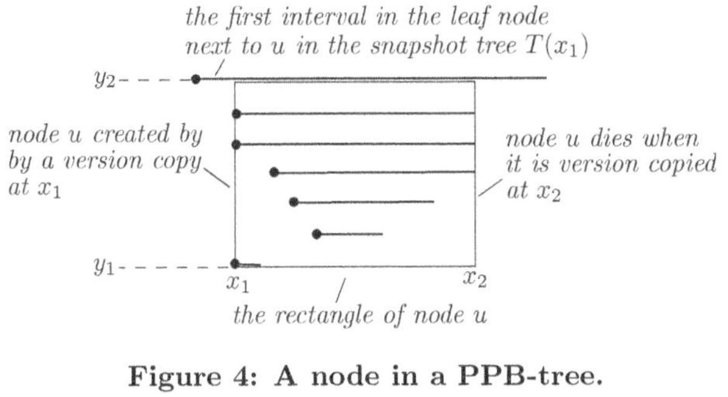

Figure 4: A node in a PPB-tree.

For each leaf node u (already created), we add its the bottom edge of $r(u)$, namely $[x_1, x_2[\times y_1$, into Σ_1. The next lemma points out a crucial fact.

LEMMA 2. *Σ_1 is both nesting and monotonic.*

[1]We adopt the convention that the leaf elements of a B-tree are ordered from left to right in ascending order.

[2]Version copy, strong-version overflow and strong-version underflow are concepts from the terminology of [5].

Our algorithm (for building the leaf nodes) writes the left and right endpoints of the segments in Σ_1 in non-descending order of their x-coordinates (breaking ties by favoring lower endpoints). This, together with Lemma 2, permits us to create the level-1 nodes using the same algorithm in $\mathcal{O}(n/B^2)$ I/Os (as $|\Sigma_1| = \mathcal{O}(n/B)$). We repeat the above process to construct the nodes of higher levels. The cost decreases by a factor of B each level up. The overall construction cost is therefore $\mathcal{O}(n/B)$. Leaving the other details to the full version, we now conclude with the first main result:

THEOREM 1. *There is an indivisible linear-size structure on n points in $\mathbb{R}^2$, such that top-open range skyline queries can be answered in $\mathcal{O}(\log_B n + k/B)$ I/Os, where k is the number of reported points. If all points have been sorted by x-coordinates, the structure can be built in linear I/Os. The query cost is optimal (even without assuming indivisibility).*

3. DIVISIBLE TOP-OPEN STRUCTURE

Theorem 1 holds under the external memory model with the indivisibility assumption. This section eliminates the assumption, and unleashes the power endowed by bit manipulation. As we will see, when the universe is small, it admits linear-size structures with lower query cost.

In Section 3.1, we study a different problem called ray-dragging. Then, in Section 3.2, our ray-dragging structure is deployed to develop a "few-point structure" for answering top-open queries on a small point set. Finally, in Section 3.3, we combine our few-point structure with an existing structure [7] to obtain the final optimal top-open structure.

3.1 Ray Dragging

In the *ray dragging problem*, the input is a set S of m points in $[U]^2$ where $U \geq m$ is an integer. Given a vertical ray $\rho = \alpha \times [\beta, U]$ where $\alpha, \beta \in [U]$, a ray dragging query reports the first point in S to be hit by ρ when ρ moves left. The rest of the subsection serves as the proof for:

LEMMA 3. *For $m = (B \log U)^{\mathcal{O}(1)}$, we can store S in a structure of size $\mathcal{O}(1 + m/B)$ that can answer ray dragging queries in $\mathcal{O}(1)$ I/Os.*

Minute Structure. Set $b = B \log_2 U$. We first consider the scenario where S has very few points: $m \leq b^{1/3}$. Let us convert S to a set S' of points in an $m \times m$ grid. Specifically, map a point $p \in S$ to $p' \in S'$ such that $x_{p'}$ (resp. $y_{p'}$) is the *rank* of x_p (resp. y_p) among the x- (y-) coordinates in S.

Given a ray $\rho = \alpha \times [\beta, \infty[$, we instead answer a query in $[m]^2$ using a ray $\rho' = \alpha' \times [\beta', \infty[$, where α' (resp. β') is the rank of the predecessor of α (resp. β) among the x- (resp. y-) coordinates in S. Create a *fusion tree* [16, 25] on the x- (resp. y-) coordinates in S so that the predecessor of α (resp. β) can be found in $\mathcal{O}(\log_b m) = \mathcal{O}(1)$ I/Os, which is thus also the cost of turning ρ into ρ'. The fusion tree uses $\mathcal{O}(1 + m/B)$ blocks.

We will ensure that the query with ρ' (in $[m]^2$) returns an id from 1 to m that uniquely identifies a point p in S, if the result is non-empty. To convert the id into the coordinates of p, we store S in an array of $\mathcal{O}(1 + m/B)$ blocks such that any point can be retrieved in one I/O by id.

The benefit of working with S' is that each coordinate in $[m]^2$ requires fewer bits to represent (than in $[U]^2$), that is, $\log_2 m$ bits. In particular, we need $3 \log_2 m$ bits in total to represent a point's x-, y-coordinates, and id. Since $|S'| = m$, the storage of the entire S' demands $3m \log m = \mathcal{O}(b^{1/3} \log_2 b)$ bits. If $B \geq \log_2 U$, then $b^{1/3} \log_2 b = \mathcal{O}((B^2)^{1/3} \log_2(B^2)) = \mathcal{O}(B)$. On the other hand, if $B < \log_2 U$, then $b^{1/3} \log_2 b = \mathcal{O}((\log_2^2 U)^{1/3} \log_2(\log_2^2 U)) = \mathcal{O}(\log_2 U)$. In other words, we can always store the entire set S' in a single block! Given a query with ρ', we simply load this block into memory, and answer the query in memory with no more I/O.

We have completed the description of a structure that uses $\mathcal{O}(1 + m/B)$ blocks, and answers queries in constant I/Os when $m \leq b^{1/3}$. We refer to it as a *minute structure*.

Proof of Lemma 3. We store S in a B-tree that indexes the x-coordinates of the points in S. We set the B-tree's leaf capacity to B and internal fanout to $f = b^{1/3}$. Note that the tree has a constant height.

Given a node u in the tree, define $Y_{max}(u)$ as the highest point whose x-coordinate is stored in the subtree of u. Now, consider u to be an internal node with child nodes $v_1, ..., v_f$. Define $Y^*_{max}(u) = \{Y_{max}(v_i) \mid 1 \leq i \leq f\}$. We store $Y^*_{max}(u)$ in a minute structure. Also, for each point $p \in Y^*_{max}(u)$, we store an index indicating the child node whose subtree contains the x-coordinate of p. A child index requires $\log_2 b^{1/3} = \mathcal{O}(\log_2 m) = \mathcal{O}(\log U)$ bits, which is no more than the length of a coordinate. Hence, we can store the index along with p in the minute structure without increasing its space by more than a constant factor. For a leaf node z, define $Y^*_{max}(z)$ to be the set of points whose x-coordinates are stored in z.

Since there are $\mathcal{O}(1 + m/(b^{1/3}B))$ internal nodes and each minute structure demands $\mathcal{O}(1+b^{1/3}/B)$ space, all the minute structures occupy $\mathcal{O}((1 + \frac{m}{b^{1/3}B})(\frac{b^{1/3}}{B} + 1)) = \mathcal{O}(1 + m/B)$ blocks in total. Therefore, the overall structure consumes linear space.

We answer a ray-dragging query with ray $\rho = \alpha \times [\beta, U]$ as follows. First, descend a root-to-leaf path π to the leaf node containing the predecessor of α among the x-coordinates in S. Let u be the *lowest* node on π such that $Y^*_{max}(u)$ has a point that can be hit by ρ when ρ moves left. For each node $v \in \pi$, whether $Y^*_{max}(v)$ has such a point can be checked in $\mathcal{O}(1)$ I/Os by querying the minute structure over $Y^*_{max}(v)$. Hence, u can be identified in $\mathcal{O}(h)$ I/Os where h is the height of the B-tree. If u does not exist, we return an empty result (i.e., ρ does not hit any point no matter how far it moves).

If u exists, let p be the first point in $Y^*_{max}(u)$ hit by ρ when it moves left. Suppose that the x-coordinate of p is in the subtree of v, where v is a child node of u. The query result must be in the subtree of v, although it may not necessarily be p. To find out, we descend another path from v to a leaf. Specifically, we set u to v, and find the first point p in $Y^*_{max}(u)$ ($= Y^*_{max}(v)$) that is hit by ρ when it moves left (notice that p has changed). Now, letting v be the child node of u whose subtree p is from, we repeat the above steps. This continues until u becomes a leaf, in which case the algorithm returns p as the final answer. The query cost is $\mathcal{O}(h) = \mathcal{O}(1)$. This completes the proof of Lemma 3. We will refer to the above structure as a *ray-drag tree*.

3.2 Top-Open Structure on Few Points

Next, we present a structure for answering top-open queries on small P, called henceforth the *few-point structure*. Remember that P is a set of n points in $[U]^2$ for some integer $U \geq n$, and a query is a rectangle $Q = [\alpha_1, \alpha_2] \times [\beta, U]$ where $\alpha_1, \alpha_2, \beta \in [U]$.

LEMMA 4. *For $n \leq (B \log U)^{\mathcal{O}(1)}$, we can store P in a structure of $\mathcal{O}(1 + n/B)$ space that answers top-open range skyline queries with output size k in $\mathcal{O}(1 + k/B)$ I/Os.*

PROOF. Consider a query with $Q = [\alpha_1, \alpha_2] \times [\beta, U]$. Let p be the first point hit by the ray $\rho = \alpha_2 \times [\beta, U]$ when ρ moves left. If p does not exist or is out of Q (i.e., $x_p < \alpha_1$), the top-open query has an empty result. Otherwise, p must be the lowest point in the skyline of $P \cap Q$.

The subsequent discussion focuses on the scenario where $p \in Q$. We index $\Sigma(P)$ with a PPB-tree T, as in Theorem 1. Recall that the top-open query can be solved by retrieving the set S of segments in $\Sigma(P)$ intersecting the vertical segment $\psi = \alpha_2 \times [\beta, \beta']$, where β' is the highest y-coordinate of the points in $P \cap Q$. To do so in $\mathcal{O}(1 + k/B)$ I/Os, we utilize the next two observations. (see the full version for their proofs):

OBSERVATION 1. All segments of S intersect $\psi' = x_p \times [y_p, \beta']$.

OBSERVATION 2. Let $T(\ell)$ be the snapshot B-tree in T when ℓ is at the position $x = x_p$. Once we have obtained the leaf node in $T(\ell)$ containing y_p, we can retrieve S in $\mathcal{O}(1 + k/B)$ I/Os without knowing the value of β'.

We now elaborate on the structure of Lemma 4. Besides T, also create a structure of Lemma 3 on P. Moreover, for every point $p \in P$, keep a pointer to the leaf node of T that (i) is in the snapshot B-tree $T(\ell)$ when ℓ is at $x = x_p$, and (ii) contains y_p. Call the leaf node the *host leaf* of p. Store the pointers in an array of size n to permit retrieving the pointer of any point in one I/O.

The query algorithm should have become straightforward from the above two observations. We first find in $O(1)$ I/Os the first point p hit by ρ when ρ moves left. Then, using p, we jump to the host leaf of p. Next, by Observation 2, we retrieve S in $O(1 + k/B)$ I/Os. The total query cost is $\mathcal{O}(1 + k/B)$. □

3.3 Final Top-Open Structure

We are ready to describe our top-open structure that achieves sub-logarithmic query I/Os for arbitrary n. For this purpose, we externalize an internal-memory structure of [7]. The structure of [7], however, has logarithmic query overhead, which we improve with new ideas based on the few-point structure in Lemma 4. Delegating the details to the full version, we now state our main results in rank space and universe $[U]^2$:

THEOREM 2. *There is a linear-size structure on n points in rank space such that top-open range skyline queries can be answered optimally in $\mathcal{O}(1 + k/B)$ I/Os, where k is the number of reported points.*

COROLLARY 1. *There is a linear-size structure on a set of n points in $[U]^2$ (where $U \geq n$ is an integer) such that a top-open range skyline query can be answered optimally in $\mathcal{O}(\log \log_B U + k/B)$ I/Os, when k points are reported.*

4. DYNAMIC TOP-OPEN STRUCTURE

In this section, we present a dynamic data structure, which is SABE, that uses linear space, and supports top-open queries in $\mathcal{O}(\log_{2B^\epsilon}(n/B) + k/B^{1-\epsilon})$ I/Os and updates in $\mathcal{O}(\log_{2B^\epsilon}(n/B))$ I/Os, for any parameter $0 \leq \epsilon \leq 1$. We are inspired by the approach of Overmars and van Leeuwen [27] for maintaining the planar skyline in the pointer machine. As a brief review, a dynamic binary base tree indexes the x-coordinates of P, and every internal node stores the skyline of the points in its subtree using a secondary search tree. More specifically, the skyline of an internal node is $(L \backslash L') \cup R$, where L (resp. R) is the skyline of its left (resp. right) child node, and L' is the set of points in L dominated by the leftmost (and thus also highest) point of R.

Our approach is based on I/O-CPQAs, which are described in Section 4.1. We observe that attrition can be utilized to maintain the internal node skylines in [27], after mirroring the y-axis. To explain this, let us first map the input set P to its mirrored counterpart $\widetilde{P} = \{(x_p, -y_p) \mid (x_p, y_p) \in P\}$. In the context of PQAs, we will interpret each point $(\widetilde{x}_p, \widetilde{y}_p) \in \widetilde{P}$ as an *element* with "key" value $\widetilde{y}_p$ that is inserted at "time" $\widetilde{x}_p$. To formalize the notion of time, we define the $<_x$-ordering of two elements $\widetilde{p}, \widetilde{q} \in \widetilde{P}$ to be $\widetilde{p} <_x \widetilde{q}$, if and only if $\widetilde{x}_p < \widetilde{x}_q$ holds. It is easy to see that element $\widetilde{p} \in \widetilde{P}$ is attrited by element $\widetilde{q} \in \widetilde{P}$, if and only if point $p \in P$ is dominated by point $q \in P$. See Figure 5 for a geometric illustration of the mirroring transformation and the effects of attrition.

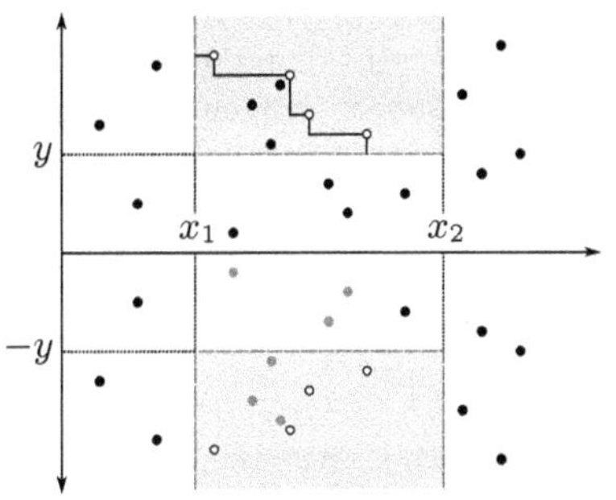

Figure 5: The skyline problem (above) mirrored to the attrition problem (below). White points are reported for the gray query area $[x_1, x_2] \times [y, \infty[$, while gray elements are attrited within $[x_1, x_2]$.

Thus, we index the $<_x$-ordering of $\widetilde{P}$ in a $(2B^\epsilon, 4B^\epsilon)$-tree, for a parameter $0 \leq \epsilon \leq 1$, and employ I/O-CPQAs as secondary structures, such that the I/O-CPQA at an internal node is simply the concatenation of its children's I/O-CPQAs. To obtain logarithmic query and update I/Os, this sequence of consecutive CATENATEANDATTRITE operations at an internal node must be performed in $\mathcal{O}(1)$ I/Os (Lemma 5). The presented I/O-CPQAs are *ephemeral* (not persistent), and thus the supported operations are *destructive*, as they destroy the initial configuration of the structure. This only allows operating on the I/O-CPQA that is the final result of all concatenations and resides at the root of the base tree. However, in order to support top-open queries efficiently, accessing I/O-CPQAs at the internal nodes is required. This is made possible by non-destructive operations. Therefore, we render the I/O-CPQAs confluently persistent by merely replacing the catenable deques, which are used as black boxes in our ephemeral construction, with real-time purely functional catenable deques [22]. Since the imposed overhead is $\mathcal{O}(1)$ worst case I/Os, confluently persistent I/O-CPQAs ensure the same I/O bounds as their ephemeral counterparts. Section 4.2 describes our dynamic data structure in detail.

4.1 I/O-Efficient Catenable Attrition Priority Queues

Here we present ephemeral *I/O-efficient catenable priority queues with attrition (I/O-CPQAs)* that store a set of elements from a total order and support all operations in $\mathcal{O}(1)$ I/Os. Also the operations take $\mathcal{O}(1/b)$ amortized I/Os, when a constant number of blocks are already loaded into main memory for every root I/O-CPQA, for any parameter $1 \leq b \leq B$. We call these preloaded records *critical records*. For the sake of simplicity, we identify an element with its value. Denote by Q an I/O-CPQA and by $\min(Q)$ the smallest element stored in Q. We denote by Q also the set of elements in I/O-CPQA Q. Next, we re-state the supported operations in the context of I/O-CPQAs:

- FINDMIN(Q) returns $\min(Q)$.
- DELETEMIN(Q) returns $\min(Q)$ and removes it from Q. The resulting I/O-CPQA is $Q' = Q \backslash \{\min(Q)\}$, and Q is discarded.
- CATENATEANDATTRITE(Q_1, Q_2)[3] catenates I/O-CPQA Q_2 to the end of another I/O-CPQA Q_1, removes all elements in Q_1 that are larger than or equal to $\min(Q_2)$ (attrition), and returns the result as a combined I/O-CPQA $Q_1' = \{e \in Q_1 \mid e < \min(Q_2)\} \cup Q_2$. The old I/O-CPQAs Q_1 and Q_2 are discarded.

An I/O-CPQA Q consists of two sorted buffers, called the first buffer $F(Q)$ with $[b, 4b]$ elements and the last buffer $L(Q)$ with $[0, 4b]$ elements, and $k_Q + 2$ deques of records, called the *clean* deque $C(Q)$, the *buffer* deque $B(Q)$ and the *dirty* deques $D_1(Q), \ldots, D_{k_Q}(Q)$, where $k_Q \geq 0$. A *record* $r = (l, p)$ consists of a buffer l of $[b, 4b]$ sorted elements and a pointer p to an I/O-CPQA. A record is *simple* when its pointer p is *nil*. The definition of I/O-CPQAs implies an underlying tree structure when pointers are considered as edges and I/O-CPQAs as subtrees. We define the ordering of the elements in a record r to be all elements of its buffer l followed by all elements in the I/O-CPQA referenced by pointer p. We define the queue order of I/O-CPQA Q to be F, $C(Q)$, $B(Q)$ and $D_1(Q), \ldots, D_{k_Q}(Q)$ and L. It corresponds to an Euler tour over the tree structure. See Figure 6 for an overview of the structure.

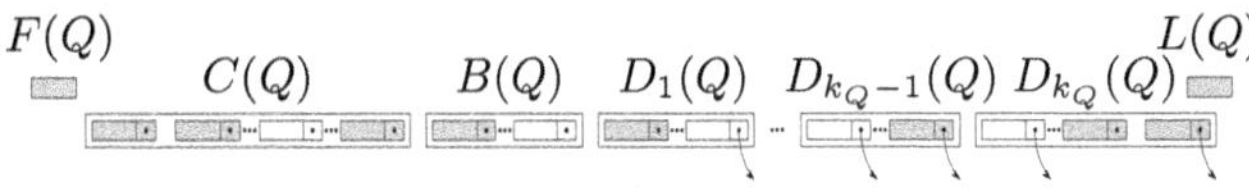

Figure 6: I/O-CPQA Q. Critical records are shown in gray.

Given a record $r = (l, p)$, the minimum and maximum elements in the buffers of r, are denoted by $\min(r) = \min(l)$ and $\max(r) = \max(l)$, respectively. They appear respectively first and last in the queue order of l, since the buffer of r is sorted by value. Given a deque q, the first and the last records are denoted by first(q) and last(q), respectively. Also, rest(q) denotes all records of the deque q excluding the record first(q). Similarly, front(q) denotes all records of the deque q excluding the record last(q). The size $|F|$ ($|L|$) of the buffer F (L) is defined to be the number of elements in F (L). The size $|r|$ of a record r is defined to be the number of elements in its buffer. The size $|q|$ of a deque q is defined to be the

[3] INSERTANDATTRITE(Q, e) corresponds to CATENATEANDATTRITE(Q_1, Q_2), where Q_2 contains only element e.

number of records it contains. The size $|Q|$ of the I/O-CPQA Q is defined to be the number of elements (both attrited and non-attrited) that Q contains. For an I/O-CPQA Q we denote by first(Q) and last(Q), respectively the first and last records out of all the records of all the deques $C(Q), B(Q), D_1(Q), \ldots, D_{k_Q}(Q)$ that exist in Q. For an I/O-CPQA Q we maintain the following invariants:

I.1) For every record $r = (l, p)$ where pointer p references I/O-CPQA Q', $\max(l) < \min(Q')$ holds.

I.2) In all deques of Q where record $r_1 = (l_1, p_1)$ precedes record $r_2 = (l_2, p_2)$: $\max(l_1) < \min(l_2)$ holds.

I.3) For the buffer $F(Q)$ and deques $C(Q), B(Q), D_1(Q)$: $\max(F(Q)) < \min(\text{first}(C(Q))) < \max(\text{last}(C(Q))) < \min(\text{first}(B(Q))) < \min(\text{first}(D_1(Q)))$ holds.

I.4) Element $\min(\text{first}(D_1(Q)))$ is the smallest element in the dirty deques $D_1(Q), \ldots, D_k(Q)$.

I.5) $\min(\text{first}(D_1(Q))) < \min(L(Q))$.

I.6) All records in the deques $C(Q)$ and $B(Q)$ are simple.

I.7) $|C(Q)| \geq \sum_{i=1}^{k_Q} |D_i(Q)| + k_Q$.

I.8) $|F(Q)| < b$ holds iff $|Q| < b$ holds.

I.9) If Q is a child of another I/O-CPQA then $F(Q) = \emptyset$ and $L(Q) = \emptyset$ holds.

From Invariants I.2, I.3, I.4 and I.5, we have that $\min(Q) = \min(F(Q))$. We say that an operation *improves* or *aggravates* the inequality of Invariant I.7 by a parameter c for I/O-CPQA Q, when the operation, respectively, increases or decreases by c the *state* of Q:

$$\Delta(Q) = |C(Q)| - \sum_{i=1}^{k_Q} |D_i(Q)| - k_Q$$

To argue about the $\mathcal{O}(1/b)$ amortized I/O bounds we need more definitions. The *critical records* of I/O-CPQA Q are first($C(Q)$), first(rest($C(Q)$)), last($C(Q)$), first($B(Q)$), first($D_1(Q)$), last($D_{k_Q}(Q)$) and last(front($D_{k_Q}(Q)$)), if it exists. Otherwise last($D_{k_Q-1}(Q)$) is critical. By records(Q) we denote all records in Q and the records in the I/O-CPQAs pointed to by Q and its descendants. We call an I/O-CPQA Q *large* if $|Q| \geq b$ and *small* otherwise. We define the following potential functions for large and small I/O-CPQAs. In particular, for large I/O-CPQAs Q the potential $\Phi(Q)$ is defined as

$$\Phi(Q) = \Phi_F(|F(Q)|) + |\text{records}(Q)| + \Phi_L(|L(Q)|),$$

where

$$\Phi_F(x) = \begin{cases} 5 - \frac{2x}{b}, & b \leq x < 2b \\ 1, & 2b \leq x < 3b \\ \frac{2x}{b} - 5, & 3b \leq x \leq 4b \end{cases}$$

and

$$\Phi_L(x) = \begin{cases} \frac{x}{b}, & 0 \leq x < b \\ 1, & b \leq x \leq 3b \\ \frac{2x}{b} - 5, & 3b < x \leq 4b \end{cases}$$

For small I/O-CPQAs Q, the potential $\Phi(Q)$ is defined as

$$\Phi(Q) = \frac{3|Q|}{b}$$

The total potential Φ_T is defined as

$$\Phi_T = \sum_Q \Phi(Q) + \sum_{Q, b \leq |Q|} 1,$$

where the first sum is the total potential of all I/O-CPQAs Q and the second sum counts the number of large I/O-CPQAs Q.

Operations. In the following, we describe the algorithms that implement the operations supported by the I/O-CPQA Q. Most of the operations call the auxiliary operations BIAS(Q) and FILL(Q), which we describe last. BIAS improves the inequality of I.7 for Q by at least 1 if Q contains any records. FILL(Q) ensures I.8.

<u>FINDMIN(Q)</u> returns the value $\min(F(Q))$.

<u>DELETEMIN(Q)</u> removes element $e = \min(F(Q))$ from the first buffer $F(Q)$, calls FILL(Q) and returns e.

<u>CATENATEANDATTRITE(Q_1, Q_2)</u> creates a new I/O-CPQA Q_1' by modifying Q_1 and Q_2, and by calling BIAS(Q_1'), BIAS(Q_2), FILL(Q_1') and FILL(Q_2).

If $|Q_1| < b$ holds, then Q_1 consists only of the first buffer $F(Q_1)$. Let $F'(Q_1)$ be the non-attrited elements of $F(Q_1)$, under attrition by $\min(F(Q_2))$. Prepend $F'(Q_1)$ onto the first buffer $F(Q_2)$ of Q_2. If this prepend causes $F(Q_2) > 4b$, then we take the last $2b$ elements out of $F(Q_2)$, make a new record out of them and we prepend it onto the deque $C(Q_2)$.

If $|Q_2| < b$ holds, then Q_2 only consists of $F(Q_2)$. If $|Q_1| < b$ then we delete attrited elements in $F(Q_1)$ and append $F(Q_2)$ to $F(Q_1)$. We now assume that $|Q_1| \geq b$. We have three cases, depending on how much of Q_1 is attrited by Q_2. Let $r = (l, \cdot) = \text{last}(Q_1)$ and let $e = \min(Q_2)$.

1. $e \leq \min(r)$: Delete r. We now have four cases:
   1) If $e \leq \min(F(Q_1))$ holds, we discard I/O-CPQA Q_1 and set $Q_1' = Q_2$.
   2) Else if $e \leq \max(\text{last}(C(Q_1)))$ holds, we prepend $F(Q_1)$ onto $C(Q_1)$, set $F(Q_1') = \emptyset$, $C(Q_1') = \emptyset$, $B(Q_1') = C(Q_1)$, $k_{Q_1'} = 0$ and $L(Q_1') = F(Q_2)$. We call BIAS(Q_1') once to restore I.7 and then call FILL(Q_1') once to restore Invariant I.8.
   3) Else if $e \leq \min(\text{first}(B(Q_1)))$ or $e \leq \min(\text{first}(D_1(Q_1)))$ holds, we set $Q_1' = Q_1$ and $k_{Q_1'} = 0$ and set $L(Q_1') = F(Q_2)$. If $e \leq \min(\text{first}(B(Q_1)))$ holds, we set $B(Q_1') = \emptyset$, else we set $B(Q_1') = B(Q_1)$.
   4) Else, let $L'(Q_1)$ be the non-attrited elements under attrition by $\min(F(Q_2))$. If $|L'(Q_1)| + |F(Q_2| \leq 4b$ then append $F(Q_2)$ to $L'(Q_1)$, else $|L'(Q_1)| + |F(Q_2| > 4b$ so take the first $4b$ elements of $L'(Q_1)$ and $F(Q_2)$ and make into a new record in a new last dirty queue of Q_1', leave the rest in $L(Q_1')$, set $k_{Q_1'} = k_{Q_1} + 1$ and call BIAS(Q_1') twice to restore I.7.

2. Else if $e \leq \min(L(Q_1))$, we set $Q_1' = Q_1$ and $L(Q_1') = F(Q_2)$.

3. Else $\min(L(Q_1)) < e$: Let l' be the non-attrited elements of l, under attrition by $\min(L(Q_1))$, and $L'(Q_1)$ be the non-attrited elements, under attrition by e. If

$|L'(Q_1)| + |F(Q_2)| > 4b$ holds, we do the following: if $|l'| < |l|$ holds, we put the first $4b - |l'|$ elements of $L'(Q_1)$ and $F(Q_2)$ into l along with l'. Moreover, if we still have more than $3b$ elements left in $L'(Q_1)$ and $F(Q_2)$, we put the first $3b$ elements into a new last record of $D_{k_{Q_1}}(Q_1)$. Finally, we leave the remaining elements in $L(Q_1)$. If we added a new last record to $D_{k_{Q_1}}(Q_1)$, we also call BIAS(Q) once.

We have now entirely dealt with the cases where $|Q_1| < b$ or $|Q_2| < b$ holds, so in the following we assume that $|Q_1| \geq b$ and $|Q_2| \geq b$ hold, i.e. any I/Os incurred in the cases (1–4) below are already paid for, since the total number of large I/O-CPQAs decreases by one. Let $e = \min(Q_2)$.

1) If $e \leq \min(F(Q_1))$ holds, we discard I/O-CPQA Q_1 and set $Q_1' = Q_2$.

2) Else if $e \leq \max(\text{last}(C(Q_1)))$ holds, we prepend $F(Q_1)$ onto $C(Q_1)$ and $F(Q_2)$ onto $C(Q_2)$. We remove the simple record $(l, \cdot) = \text{first}(C(Q_2))$ from $C(Q_2)$, set $Q_1' = Q_1$, $F(Q_1') = \emptyset$, $C(Q_1') = \emptyset$, $B(Q_1') = C(Q_1)$, $D_1(Q_1') = (l, p)$, $k_{Q_1'} = 1$, $L(Q_1') = L(Q_2)$ and $L(Q_2') = \emptyset$, where p points to Q_2' if it exists. This gives $\Delta(Q_1') = -2$, thus we call BIAS(Q_1') twice and FILL(Q_1') once.

3) Else if $e \leq \min(\text{first}(B(Q_1)))$ or $e \leq \min(\text{first}(D_1(Q_1)))$ holds, we prepend $F(Q_2)$ onto $C(Q_2)$ and remove the simple record $(l, \cdot) = \text{first}(C(Q_2))$ from $C(Q_2)$, set $Q_1' = Q_1$, $D_1(Q_1') = (l, p)$, $k_{Q_1'} = 1$, $L(Q_1') = L(Q_2)$, $L(Q_2') = \emptyset$ and set p to point to Q_2', if it exists. If $e \leq \min(\text{first}(B(Q_1)))$ holds, we set $B(Q_1') = \emptyset$, else we set $B(Q_1') = B(Q_1)$. This gives $\Delta(Q_1') = -2$ in the worst case, thus we call BIAS(Q_1') twice.

4) Else let $L'(Q_1)$ be the non-attrited elements of $L(Q_1)$, under attrition by $F(Q_2)$. If $|L'(Q_1)| + |F(Q_2)| \leq 4b$ holds, then we make $L'(Q_1)$ and $F(Q_2)$ into the first record of $C(Q_2)$. Else we make them into the first two records of $C(Q_2)$ of size $\lfloor(|L'(Q_1)| + |F(Q_2)|)/2\rfloor$ and $\lceil(|L(Q_1)| + |F(Q_2)|)/2\rceil$ each. We set $Q_1' = Q_1$, $F(Q_2') = \emptyset$, $L(Q_1') = L(Q_2)$, $L(Q_2') = \emptyset$, remove $(l_2, \cdot) = \text{first}(C(Q_2))$ from $C(Q_2)$. Moreover, we add (l_2, p) as a new record in $D_{k_{Q_1}+1}(Q_1')$, where p points to the rest of Q_2', if it exists, and set $k_{Q_1'} = k_{Q_1} + 1$. All this aggravates the inequality of I.7 for Q_1' by at most 2, so we call BIAS(Q_1') twice.

FILL(Q) restores Invariant I.8, if it is violated. In particular, if $|F(Q)| < b$ and $|Q| \geq b$, let $r = (l, \cdot) = \text{first}(C(Q))$. If $|l| \geq 2b$ holds, then we take the b first elements of l and append them to $F(Q)$. Else $|l| < 2b$ holds, so we append l to $F(Q)$, discard r and call BIAS(Q) once.

BIAS(Q) improves the inequality of I.7 for Q by at least 1 if Q contains any records. It also ensures that Invariant I.8 is maintained. We distinguish two basic cases with respect to $|B(Q)|$, namely $|B(Q)| = 0$ and $|B(Q)| > 0$.

1) $|B(Q)| > 0$: We have two cases depending on if $k_Q \geq 1$ or $k_Q = 0$.

   1) $k_Q = 0$: Let $e = \min(L(Q))$, if it exists. We remove the first record $r_1 = (l_1, \cdot) = \text{first}(B(Q))$ from $B(Q)$. Let l_1' be the non-attrited elements of l_1, under attrition by element e. If $|l_1'| = |l_1|$ holds nothing is attrited, so we just add $r_1 = (l_1, \cdot)$ at the end of $C(Q)$.
   Else $|l_1'| < |l_1|$ holds, so we set $B(Q) = \emptyset$. If $|l_1'| \geq b$ holds, then we make record r_1 with buffer l_1' into the new last record of $C(Q)$. Else $|l_1'| < b$ holds, so if $|l_1'| + |L(Q)| \leq 3b$ also holds, we add l_1' to $L(Q)$ and discard r_1. Else $|l_1'| + |L(Q)| > 3b$ also holds, so we take the $2b$ first elements of l_1' and $L(Q)$ and put them into r_1, making it the new last record of $C(Q)$.

   2) $k_Q \geq 1$: Let $e = \min(\text{first}(D_1(Q)))$. We remove the first record $r_1 = (l_1, \cdot) = \text{first}(B(Q))$ from $B(Q)$. Let l_1' be the non-attrited elements of l_1, under attrition by element e.
   If $|l_1'| = |l_1|$ or $b \leq |l_1'| < |l_1|$ holds, we just add $r_1 = (l_1', \cdot)$ at the end of $C(Q)$. Else $|l_1'| < b$ and $|l_1'| < |l_1|$ hold. We set $B(Q) = \emptyset$. Let $r_2 = (l_2, p_2) = \text{first}(D_1(Q))$. If $|l_1'| + |l_2| \leq 4b$ holds, we discard r_1 and prepend l_1' onto l_2 of r_2. Else $|l_1'| + |l_2| > 4b$ holds, so we take the first $2b$ elements of l_1' and l_2 and put them in r_1, making it the new last record of $C(Q)$. If this causes $\min(L(Q)) \leq \min(\text{first}(D_1(Q)))$, we discard all dirty queues.

   If r_1 was discarded, then we have that $|B(Q)| = 0$ and we call BIAS recursively, which will not invoke this case again. In all cases the inequality of I.7 for Q is improved by 1.

2) $|B(Q)| = 0$: we have three cases depending on the number of dirty queues, namely cases $k_Q > 1$, $k_Q = 1$ and $k_Q = 0$.

   1) $k_Q > 1$: If $\min(L(Q)) \leq \min(\text{first}(D_{k_Q}(Q)))$ holds, we set $k_Q = k_Q - 1$ and discard $D_{k_Q}(Q)$. This improves the inequality of I.7 for Q by at least 2. Else let $e = \min(\text{first}(D_{k_Q}(Q)))$.
   If $e \leq \min(\text{last}(D_{k_Q-1}(Q)))$ holds, we remove the record $\text{last}(D_{k_Q-1}(Q))$ from $D_{k_Q-1}(Q)$. This improves the inequality of I.7 for Q by 1.
   If $\min(\text{last}(D_{k_Q-1}(Q))) < e \leq \max(\text{last}(D_{k_Q-1}(Q)))$ holds, we remove record $r_1 = (l_1, p_1) = \text{last}(D_{k_Q-1}(Q))$ from $D_{k_Q-1}(Q)$, and let $r_2 = (l_2, p_2) = \text{first}(D_{k_Q}(Q))$. We delete any elements in l_1 that are attrited by e, and let l_1' denote the set of non-attrited elements. If $|l_1'| + |l_2| \leq 4b$ holds, we prepend l_1' onto l_2 of r_2 and discard r_1. Else we take the first $\lfloor(|l_1'| + |l_2|)/2\rfloor$ elements of l_1' and l_2 and replace r_1 of $D_{k_Q-1}(Q)$ with them. Finally, we concatenate $D_{k_Q-1}(Q)$ and $D_{k_Q}(Q)$ into a single deque. This improves the inequality of I.7 for Q by at least 1.
   Else $\max(\text{last}(D_{k_Q-1}(Q))) < e$ holds and we just concatenate the deques $D_{k_Q-1}(Q)$ and $D_{k_Q}(Q)$, which improves the inequality of I.7 for Q by 1.

   2) $k_Q = 1$: In this case Q contains only deques $C(Q)$ and $D_1(Q)$. Let $r = (l, p) = \text{first}(D_1(Q))$. If $\min(L(Q)) \leq \min(\text{first}(\text{rest}(D_1(Q))))$ holds, we discard all dirty queues, except for record r of $D_1(Q)$.
   If $\min(L(Q)) \leq \max(l)$ holds, we discard all the dirty deques and let l' be the non-attrited elements of l. If $|l'| + |L(Q)| \leq 3b$ holds, we prepend l' onto $L(Q)$. Else $|l'| + |L(Q)| > 3b$ holds, so we take the first $2b$ elements of l' and $L(Q)$ and make them the new last record of $C(Q)$ and leave the rest in $L(Q)$. This improves the inequality of I.7 for Q by 1.

Else $\max(\ell) < \min(L(Q))$ holds, so we remove r and insert buffer l into a new record at the end of $C(Q)$. This improves the inequality of I.7 for Q by at least 1. If r is not simple, let the pointer p of r reference I/O-CPQA Q'. We restore I.6 for Q by *merging* I/O-CPQAs Q and Q' into one I/O-CPQA; see Figure 7. In particular, let $e = \min(\min(\text{first}(D_1(Q))), \min(L(Q)))$.

We proceed as follows: If $e \leq \min(Q')$ holds, we discard Q'. Else if $\min(\text{first}(C(Q'))) < e \leq \max(\text{last}(C(Q'))$ holds, we set $B(Q) = C(Q')$ and discard the rest of Q'. In both cases, the inequality of I.7 for Q remains unaffected.

Else if $\max(\text{last}(C(Q')) < e \leq \min(\text{first}(D_1(Q')))$ holds, we concatenate the deque $C(Q')$ at the end of $C(Q)$. If moreover $\min(\text{first}(B(Q'))) < e$ holds, we set $B(Q) = B(Q')$. Finally, we discard the rest of Q'. This improves the inequality of I.7 for Q by $|C(Q')|$.

Else $\min(\text{first}(D_1(Q'))) < e$ holds. We concatenate the deque $C(Q')$ at the end of $C(Q)$, we set $B(Q) = B(Q')$, we set $D_1(Q'), \ldots, D_{k_{Q'}}(Q')$ as the first $k_{Q'}$ dirty queues of Q and we set $D_1(Q)$ as the last dirty queue of Q. This improves the inequality of I.7 for Q by $\Delta(Q') \geq 0$, since Q' satisfied Invariant I.7 before the operation.

3) $k_Q = 0$: If all deques are empty, $L(Q) \neq \emptyset$ and $|F(Q)| \leq 2b$ hold, we take the first b elements of $L(Q)$ and append to $F(Q)$. The inequality of I.7 for Q remains $\Delta(Q) = 0$.

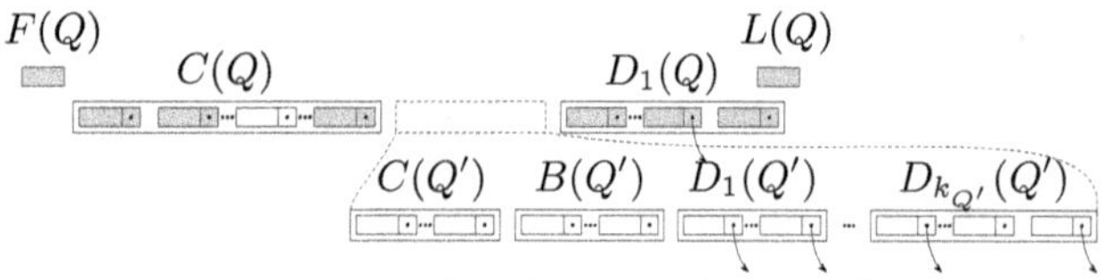

Figure 7: Merging I/O-CPQAs Q and Q'. This case can only occur when $B(Q) = \emptyset$ and $k_Q = 1$.

THEOREM 3. *An I/O-CPQA supports* FINDMIN, DELETEMIN, CATENATEANDATTRITE *and* INSERTANDATTRITE *in $\mathcal{O}(1)$ I/Os per operation. It occupies $\mathcal{O}((n-m)/B)$ blocks after calling* CATENATEANDATTRITE *and* INSERTANDATTRITE *n times and* DELETEMIN *m times, respectively.*

All operations are supported by a set of ℓ I/O-CPQAs in $\mathcal{O}(1/b)$ amortized I/Os, when $M = \Omega(\ell b)$, using $\mathcal{O}((n-m)/b)$ blocks of space, for any parameter $1 \leq b \leq B$.

PROOF. (Sketch) The correctness follows by closely noticing that we maintain Invariants I.1–I.9, which in turn imply that DELETEMIN(Q) and FINDMIN(Q) always return the minimum element of Q. The $\mathcal{O}(1)$ worst case I/O bound is trivial as every operation only accesses $\mathcal{O}(1)$ records. Although BIAS is recursive, notice that in the case where $|B(Q)| > 0$, BIAS only calls itself after making $|B(Q)| = 0$, so it will not end up in this case again. We elaborate on all the operations that modify the I/O-CPQA in order to argue for the amortized bounds:

DELETEMIN: If after the call $|F(Q)| \geq b$ holds, no I/Os are incurred and the amortized cost of $\leq \frac{3}{b}$ pays for increasing the potential. Otherwise $\Phi_F(|F(Q)|) \geq 3$ pays for any I/Os to call FILL and BIAS.

CATENATEANDATTRITE: $|Q_1| < b$: If $|F'(Q_1)| + |F(Q_2)| \leq 4b$ holds, $\Phi(|F(Q_1)|)$ pays for any increase in potential. Else the new record of $C(Q_2)$ is paid for by $\Delta(\Phi_T) > 1$.

$|Q_2| < b$: In cases (1) and (2) the potential decreases. In case (3), the potential does not change if $|L'(Q_1)| + |F(Q_2)| > 4b$. If $L'(Q_1)$ and $F(Q_2)$ still contain $> 3b$ elements, the change in potential is paid for by $\Delta(\Phi_T) > 0$.

In the following cases, both Q_1 and Q_2 are large. Since concatenating them decreases by one the number of large I/O-CPQA's, the potential decreases by at least 1, which is enough to pay for any other I/Os also incurred by BIAS and FILL. So we only need to argue that the potential does not increase in any of the cases. In fact, in cases (1 - 3) the potential only decreases. In case (4), if we make one record, it is paid for by $\Phi_F(|F(Q_2)|) \geq 1$. Otherwise the second record is paid for by $\Phi_L(|L(Q_1)|) \geq 1$ if moreover $|L'(Q_1)| + |F(Q_2)| > 4b$ holds, or by $\Phi_L(|L(Q_1)|) + \Phi_F(|F(Q_2)|) > 2$ otherwise.

All I/Os in FILL and BIAS have been paid for by a decrease in potential caused by their caller. Thus, it suffices to argue that these operations do not increase the potential.

FILL: Indeed, $\Phi_F(|F(Q)|)$ only decreases, when $|F(Q)| < b$ and $|Q| \geq b$ hold.

BIAS: Indeed, cases (1) and (2.1) do not create new records. Similarly for (2.2), unless $|l'| + |L(Q)| \leq 3b$ holds, where r pays for increasing the potential by 1. In (2.3) $\Phi_F(|F(Q)|)$ or $\Phi_L(|L(Q)|)$ decreases. □

Catenating a set of I/O-CPQAs. The following lemma is required by the dynamic structure of the next section.

LEMMA 5. *A set of I/O-CPQAs Q_i for $i \in [1, \ell]$ can be concatenated into a single I/O-CPQA without any access to external memory, by calling only* CATENATEANDATTRITE *operations, provided that for all i:*

1. *$\Delta(Q_i) \geq 2$ holds, unless Q_i contains only one record, in which case $\Delta(Q_i) \geq 1$ suffices.*
2. *The critical records of Q_i are loaded in main memory.*

4.2 Final Dynamic Top-Open Structure

The data structure consists of a base tree, implemented as a dynamic $(a, 2a)$-tree where the leaves store between k and $2k$ elements. We set $a = \lceil 2B^{\epsilon} \rceil$ and $k = B$, for a given $0 \leq \epsilon \leq 1$. The base tree indexes the $<_x$-ordering of $\widetilde{P}$, and is augmented with confluently persistent I/O-CPQAs with buffer size $b = B^{1-\epsilon}$ as secondary structures. In particular, after constructing the base tree, we augment it with secondary I/O-CPQAs in a bottom-up manner, as follows. For every leaf we make one I/O-CPQA over its elements, and execute an appropriate amount of BIAS operations, such that the state of the I/O-CPQA satisfies Lemma 5. We associate the I/O-CPQA with the leaf. In a second pass over the leaves, we gather its critical records into a *representative block* in its parent. The procedure continues one level above. For every internal node u, we access the representative blocks that contain the critical records of the children I/O-CPQAs of u, and CATENATEANDATTRITE them into a new I/O-CPQA as implied by Lemma 5. We execute BIAS on the I/O-CPQA enough times such that its state also satifies Lemma 5. We associate the I/O-CPQA with u. After the level has been processed, we create the representative blocks for I/O-CPQAs associated with the nodes of the level, in the same way as described above. The augmentation ends at the root node of the base tree. We will ensure that our algorithms access the I/O-CPQA associated with a node through the representative block stored at the parent of the node. Thus, it will suffice to explicitly store only the representative blocks in every internal node and not its associated I/O-CPQA.

Since every leaf contains $\mathcal{O}(B)$ elements, the base tree has $\mathcal{O}(n/B)$ leaves and thus also $\mathcal{O}(n/B)$ internal nodes. Every internal node has $\Theta(B^{\epsilon})$ children, each associated with an I/O-CPQA with $\mathcal{O}(1)$ critical records of size $\mathcal{O}(B^{1-\epsilon})$. Thus the representative blocks stored in the internal node occupy $\mathcal{O}(1)$ blocks of space. Thus the structure occupies $\mathcal{O}(n/B)$ blocks in total. Assume that $\widetilde{P}$ is already sorted by the $<_x$-ordering. The leaves' I/O-CPQAs are created in $\mathcal{O}(1)$ I/Os, since they contain at most $\mathcal{O}(B)$ elements. All representative blocks are created in $\mathcal{O}(n/B)$ I/Os. To create the internal nodes' I/O-CPQAs, we need only $\mathcal{O}(1)$ I/Os to access the representative blocks and to execute BIAS on the resulting I/O-CPQA. Its representative blocks residing in memory thus are written on disk in $\mathcal{O}(1)$ I/Os. Thus the total preprocessing cost is $\mathcal{O}(n/B)$; the structure is SABE.

Updates. To insert (resp. delete) a point p into (resp. from) P, we insert (resp. delete) $\widetilde{p} = (\widetilde{x}_p, \widetilde{y}_p)$ in the structure. In particular, we first find the leaf to insert (resp. delete) that contains the predecessor of $\widetilde{x}_p$ (resp. contains $\widetilde{x}_p$), by a top-down traversal of the path from the root of the base tree. For every node u on the path, we also discard the part of its representative block corresponding to the child that the search path goes into, and u's associated I/O-CPQA by executing in reverse the operations that created it. Next we insert (resp. delete) $\widetilde{p}$ into (from) the accessed leaf, and rebalance the base tree by executing the appropriate splits and merges on the nodes along the path in a bottom-up manner. Moreover, we recompute the I/O-CPQA of every accessed node on the path, as described above. The total update I/Os are $\mathcal{O}(\log_{2B^{\epsilon}}(n/B))$ in the worst case, since we spend $\mathcal{O}(1)$ I/Os to rebalance every accessed node and to recompute its secondary structures.

Queries. To report the skyline points of P that reside within a given top-open query range $[\alpha_1, \alpha_2] \times [\beta, \infty[$, we first traverse top-down the two search paths $\widetilde{\pi_1} = \pi\pi_1$ and $\widetilde{\pi_2} = \pi\pi_2$ from the root of the base tree to the leaves ℓ_1 and ℓ_2 that contain points of $\widetilde{P}$ whose $<_x$-ordering succeed and precede the query parameters α_1 and α_2, respectively. Let node u be on the path $\pi_1 \cup \pi_2$, and let $c(u)$ be the children nodes of u whose subtrees are fully contained within $[\alpha_1, \alpha_2]$. For every u, we load its representative block into memory in order to access the critical records of the I/O-CPQAs associated with $c(u)$ and to CATENATEANDATTRITE them into a temporary I/O-CPQA, as implied by Lemma 5. We consider the temporary I/O-CPQAs of nodes u and the I/O-CPQAs of the leaves ℓ_1 and ℓ_2 from right to left, and we CATENATEANDATTRITE them into one auxiliary I/O-CPQA. The I/O-CPQAs for ℓ_1 and ℓ_2 are created only on the points within the x-range $[\alpha_1, \alpha_2]$ in $\mathcal{O}(1)$ I/Os.

To report the skyline points within the query range, we call DELETEMIN on the auxiliary I/O-CPQA. The procedure stops as soon as a point with $\widetilde{y}_p > -\beta$ is returned, or when the auxiliary I/O-CPQA becomes empty.

There are $\mathcal{O}(\log_{2B^{\epsilon}}(n/B))$ nodes on $\pi_1 \cup \pi_2$ and we spend $\mathcal{O}(1)$ I/Os to access the representative block of each node. After this, the construction of the auxiliary I/O-CPQA costs $\mathcal{O}(\log_{2B^{\epsilon}}(n/B))$ I/Os. Reporting the k output points costs $\mathcal{O}(\frac{k}{B^{1-\epsilon}} + 1)$ I/Os. Therefore the query takes $\mathcal{O}(\log_{2B^{\epsilon}}(n/B) + \frac{k}{B^{1-\epsilon}})$ I/Os in total. We conclude that:

THEOREM 4. *There is an indivisible linear-size dynamic data structure on n points in $\mathbb{R}^2$ that supports top-open range skyline queries in $\mathcal{O}(\log_{2B^{\epsilon}}(n/B) + k/B^{1-\epsilon})$ I/Os when k points are reported, and updates in $\mathcal{O}(\log_{2B^{\epsilon}}(n/B))$ I/Os for any parameter $0 \le \epsilon \le 1$. The structure can be constructed in $\mathcal{O}(n/B)$ I/Os, assuming an initial sorting on the input points' x-coordinates.*

5. GENERAL RANGE SKYLINE QUERIES

We now move on to discuss the other variants of range skyline reporting that are neither symmetric to nor subsumed by top-open queries. It would be nice if they could be answered in $\mathcal{O}(\log_B n + k/B)$ I/Os by a linear-size structure. Unfortunately, we will prove its impossibility. In fact, even sub-polynomial query cost is already unachievable for anti-dominance queries, let alone left-open and 4-sided queries. In fact, anti-dominance, left-open and 4-sided are just as hard as each other. Next, we will formally establish these facts. Refer to the full version for the proofs.

5.1 A Query Lower Bound

By making a crucial observation on a variant of the low-discrepancy point set proposed by Chazelle and Liu [8], we manage to prove the next geometric fact:

LEMMA 6. *For any integer $\omega \ge 1$ and $\lambda \ge 1$, there is a set P of ω^{λ} points in $\mathbb{R}^2$ and a set G of $\lambda\omega^{\lambda-1}$ anti-dominance queries such that (i) each query in G retrieves d points of P, and (ii) at most one point in P is returned by two different queries in G simultaneously.*

We use the term (ω, λ)*-input* to refer to the point set P obtained in Lemma 6 after ω and λ have been fixed. We deploy such input sets to derive:

LEMMA 7. *Regarding anti-dominance queries on n points in $\mathbb{R}^2$, any structure (in the indexability model) of at most cn/B blocks must incur $\Omega((n/B)^{1/(25c)} + k/B)$ I/Os to answer a query in the worst case, where $c \ge 1$ is a constant and k is the result size.*

THEOREM 5. *Regarding anti-dominance queries on n points, any linear-size structure under the indexability model must incur $\Omega((n/B)^{\epsilon} + k/B)$ I/Os answering a query in the worst case, where $\epsilon > 0$ can be an arbitrarily small constant, and k is the result size.*

Remarks. In the full version, we utilize Lemma 6 to prove that any internal memory pointer-based data structure that supports anti-dominance queries in $\mathcal{O}(\log^{\mathcal{O}(1)} + k)$ time requires $\Omega(n\frac{\log n}{\log\log n})$ space. Thus, the dynamic structure of [7] for 4-sided queries occupies optimal space within a $\mathcal{O}(\log\log n)$ factor, for the attained query time.

5.2 Query-Optimal Structure

The above lower bound is tight. In fact, we are able to prove a stronger fact: a *4-sided* query can be answered in $\mathcal{O}((n/B)^{\epsilon} + k/B)$ I/Os by a linear-size dynamic structure. Deferring the details to the full version, we claim:

THEOREM 6. *There is an indivisible linear-size structure on n points in $\mathbb{R}^2$ such that, 4-sided range skyline queries can be answered in $\mathcal{O}((n/B)^\epsilon + k/B)$ I/Os, where k is the number of reported points. The query cost is optimal under the indexability model. The structure can be updated in $\mathcal{O}(\log(n/B))$ amortized I/Os.*

ACKNOWLEDGEMENTS

The work of Yufei Tao and Jeonghun Yoon was supported in part by (i) projects GRF 4166/10, 4165/11, and 4164/12 from HKRGC, and (ii) the WCU (World Class University) program under the National Research Foundation of Korea, and funded by the Ministry of Education, Science and Technology of Korea (Project No: R31-30007).

6. REFERENCES

[1] A. Aggarwal and S. Vitter, Jeffrey. The input/output complexity of sorting and related problems. *CACM*, 31(9):1116–1127, 1988.

[2] L. Arge. The buffer tree: A technique for designing batched external data structures. *Algorithmica*, 37(1):1–24, 2003.

[3] L. Arge, V. Samoladas, and J. S. Vitter. On two-dimensional indexability and optimal range search indexing. In *PODS*, pages 346–357, 1999.

[4] I. Bartolini, P. Ciaccia, and M. Patella. Efficient sort-based skyline evaluation. *TODS*, 33(4), 2008.

[5] B. Becker, S. Gschwind, T. Ohler, B. Seeger, and P. Widmayer. An asymptotically optimal multiversion B-tree. *VLDB J.*, 5(4):264–275, 1996.

[6] S. Börzsönyi, D. Kossmann, and K. Stocker. The skyline operator. In *ICDE*, pages 421–430, 2001.

[7] G. Brodal and K. Tsakalidis. Dynamic planar range maxima queries. In *ICALP*, pages 256–267, 2011.

[8] B. Chazelle and D. Liu. Lower bounds for intersection searching and fractional cascading in higher dimension. *JCSS*, 68(2):269 – 284, 2004.

[9] B.-C. Chen, R. Ramakrishnan, and K. LeFevre. Privacy skyline: Privacy with multidimensional adversarial knowledge. In *VLDB*, pages 770–781, 2007.

[10] J. Chomicki, P. Godfrey, J. Gryz, and D. Liang. Skyline with presorting: Theory and optimizations. In *Intelligent Information Systems*, pages 595–604, 2005.

[11] F. d'Amore, P. G. Franciosa, R. Giaccio, and M. Talamo. Maintaining maxima under boundary updates. In *Italian Conference on Algorithms and Complexity*, pages 100–109, 1997.

[12] A. Das, P. Gupta, A. Kalavagattu, J. Agarwal, K. Srinathan, and K. Kothapalli. Range aggregate maximal points in the plane. In *WALCOM: Algorithms and Computation*, volume 7157, pages 52–63, 2012.

[13] J. V. den Bercken and B. Seeger. Query processing techniques for multiversion access methods. In *VLDB*, pages 168–179, 1996.

[14] J. V. den Bercken, B. Seeger, and P. Widmayer. A generic approach to bulk loading multidimensional index structures. In *VLDB*, pages 406–415, 1997.

[15] G. N. Frederickson and S. Rodger. A new approach to the dynamic maintenance of maximal points in a plane. *Discrete & Computational Geometry*, 5:365–374, 1990.

[16] M. L. Fredman and D. E. Willard. Surpassing the information theoretic bound with fusion trees. *JCSS*, 47(3):424 – 436, 1993.

[17] A. Guttman. R-trees: a dynamic index structure for spatial searching. In *SIGMOD*, pages 47–57, 1984.

[18] J. M. Hellerstein, E. Koutsoupias, D. P. Miranker, C. H. Papadimitriou, and V. Samoladas. On a model of indexability and its bounds for range queries. *JACM*, 49(1):35–55, 2002.

[19] Z. Huang, H. Lu, B. C. Ooi, and A. K. H. Tung. Continuous skyline queries for moving objects. *TKDE*, 18(12):1645–1658, 2006.

[20] R. Janardan. On the dynamic maintenance of maximal points in the plane. *IPL*, 40(2):59 – 64, 1991.

[21] A. K. Kalavagattu, A. S. Das, K. Kothapalli, and K. Srinathan. On finding skyline points for range queries in plane. In *CCCG*, 2011.

[22] H. Kaplan and R. E. Tarjan. Purely functional, real-time deques with catenation. *JACM*, 46(5):577–603, 1999.

[23] S. Kapoor. Dynamic maintenance of maxima of 2-d point sets. *SIAM J. of Comp.*, 29:1858–1877, 2000.

[24] D. Kossmann, F. Ramsak, and S. Rost. Shooting stars in the sky: An online algorithm for skyline queries. In *VLDB*, pages 275–286, 2002.

[25] K. G. Larsen and R. Pagh. I/O-efficient data structures for colored range and prefix reporting. In *SODA*, pages 583–592, 2012.

[26] M. D. Morse, J. M. Patel, and H. V. Jagadish. Efficient skyline computation over low-cardinality domains. In *VLDB*, pages 267–278, 2007.

[27] M. H. Overmars and J. van Leeuwen. Maintenance of configurations in the plane. *JCSS*, 23(2):166 – 204, 1981.

[28] D. Papadias, Y. Tao, G. Fu, and B. Seeger. Progressive skyline computation in database systems. *TODS*, 30(1):41–82, 2005.

[29] A. D. Sarma, A. Lall, D. Nanongkai, and J. Xu. Randomized multi-pass streaming skyline algorithms. *PVLDB*, 2(1):85–96, 2009.

[30] M. Sharifzadeh, C. Shahabi, and L. Kazemi. Processing spatial skyline queries in both vector spaces and spatial network databases. *TODS*, 34(3), 2009.

[31] C. Sheng and Y. Tao. On finding skylines in external memory. In *PODS*, pages 107–116, 2011.

[32] R. Sundar. Worst-case data structures for the priority queue with attrition. *IPL*, 31:69–75, 1989.

[33] Y. Tao and D. Papadias. Maintaining sliding window skylines on data streams. *TKDE*, 18(3):377–391, 2006.

[34] J. S. Vitter. Algorithms and data structures for external memory. *Found. Trends Theor. Comput. Sci.*, 2(4):305–474, 2008.

[35] P. Wu, D. Agrawal, Ö. Egecioglu, and A. E. Abbadi. Deltasky: Optimal maintenance of skyline deletions without exclusive dominance region generation. In *ICDE*, pages 486–495, 2007.

[36] H. Yuan and M. J. Atallah. Data structures for range minimum queries in multidimensional arrays. In *SODA*, pages 150–160, 2010.

Nearest Neighbor Searching Under Uncertainty II

Pankaj K. Agarwal
Duke University

Boris Aronov
Polytechnic Institute of NYU

Sariel Har-Peled
University of Illinois

Jeff M. Phillips
University of Utah

Ke Yi
HKUST

Wuzhou Zhang
Duke University

ABSTRACT

Nearest-neighbor (NN) search, which returns the nearest neighbor of a query point in a set of points, is an important and widely studied problem in many fields, and it has wide range of applications. In many of them, such as sensor databases, location-based services, face recognition, and mobile data, the location of data is imprecise. We therefore study nearest neighbor queries in a probabilistic framework in which the location of each input point is specified as a probability distribution function. We present efficient algorithms for (i) computing all points that are nearest neighbors of a query point with nonzero probability; (ii) estimating, within a specified additive error, the probability of a point being the nearest neighbor of a query point; (iii) using it to return the point that maximizes the probability being the nearest neighbor, or all the points with probabilities greater than some threshold to be the NN. We also present some experimental results to demonstrate the effectiveness of our approach.

Categories and Subject Descriptors

F.2 [**Analysis of algorithms and problem complexity**]: Nonnumerical algorithms and problems; H.3.1 [**Information storage and retrieval**]: Content analysis and indexing—*indexing methods*

General Terms

Algorithms, Theory

Keywords

Indexing uncertain data, probabilistic nearest neighbor, approximate nearest neighbor, threshold queries

1. INTRODUCTION

Nearest-neighbor search is a fundamental problem in data management. It has applications in such diverse areas as spatial databases, information retrieval, data mining, pattern recognition, etc. In its simplest form, it asks for preprocessing a set S of n points in $\mathbb{R}^d$ into an index so that given any query point q, the nearest neighbor (NN) of q in S can be reported efficiently. This problem has been studied extensively in both the database and the computational geometry community, and is now relatively well understood. However, in some of the applications mentioned above, data is imprecise and is often modeled as probabilistic distributions. This has led to a flurry of research activities on query processing over probabilistic data, including the NN problem; see [7, 16] for surveys on uncertain data, and see, e.g., [15, 25] for application scenarios of NN search under uncertainty.

However, despite many efforts devoted to the probabilistic NN problem, it still lacks a theoretical foundation. Specifically, not only are we yet to understand its complexity (is the problem inherently more difficult than on precise data?), but we also lack efficient algorithms to solve it. Furthermore, existing solutions all use heuristics without nontrivial performance guarantees. This paper addresses some of these issues.

1.1 Problem definition

An *uncertain* point[1] P in $\mathbb{R}^2$ is represented as a continuous probability distribution defined by a probability density function (pdf) $f_P\colon \mathbb{R}^2 \to \mathbb{R}_{\geq 0}$; f_P may be a parametric pdf such as a uniform distribution or a Gaussian distribution, or may be a non-parametric pdf such as a histogram. The *uncertainty region* of P (or the *support* of f_P) is the set of points for which f_P is positive, i.e., $\mathrm{Sup}\, f_P = \{x \in \mathbb{R}^2 \mid f_P(x) > 0\}$. We assume P has a bounded uncertainty region: if f_P is Gaussian, we work on truncated Gaussian, as in [10, 12]. We also consider the case where P is represented as a discrete distribution defined by a finite set $P = \{p_1, \ldots, p_k\} \subset \mathbb{R}^2$ along with a set of probabilities $\{w_1, \ldots, w_k\} \subset [0,1]$, where $w_i = \Pr[P \text{ is } p_i]$ and $\sum_{i=1}^k w_i = 1$.

Let $\mathcal{P} = \{P_1, \ldots, P_n\}$ be a set of n uncertain points in $\mathbb{R}^2$, and let $d(\cdot,\cdot)$ be the Euclidean distance. For a point $q \in \mathbb{R}^2$, let $\pi_i(q) = \pi(P_i, q)$ be the probability of $P_i \in \mathcal{P}$ being the nearest neighbor of q, referred to as its *qualification probability*, defined as follows:

For a point q, and $i = 1, \ldots, n$, let $g_{q,i}$ be the pdf of the distance between q and P_i. That is, $g_{q,i}(x) = \Pr[x \leq d(q, P_i) \leq x + \mathrm{d}x]$. See Fig. 1 for an example of $g_{q,i}$. Let $G_{q,i}(x) = \int_0^x g_{q,i}(y)\mathrm{d}y$ denote the cumulative distribution function (cdf) of the distance between q and P_i. Then $\pi_i(q)$,

[1] If the location of data is precise, we call it *certain*.

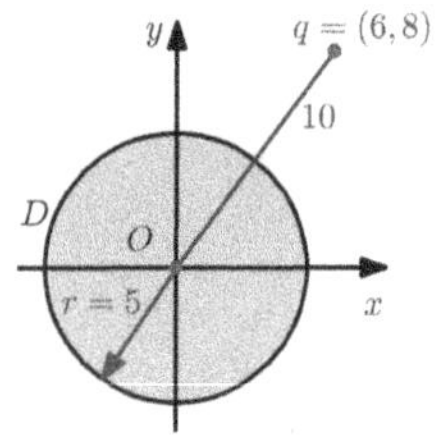

(a)

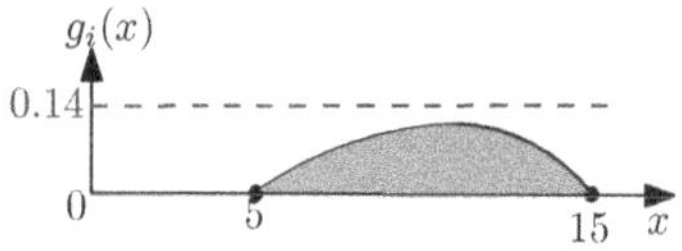

(b)

Figure 1. (a) P_i is represented by a uniform distribution defined on a disk D of radius $r = 5$ and centered at origin O, $q = (6, 8)$, and $d(\cdot, \cdot)$ is L_2 metric; (b) $g_{q,i}(x)$.

the probability that P_i is the NN of q, is

$$\pi_i(q) = \int_0^\infty g_{q,i}(r) \prod_{j \neq i} (1 - G_{q,j}(r)) \mathrm{d}r. \quad (1)$$

Given a set $\mathcal{P}$ of n uncertain points, the *probabilistic nearest neighbor* (PNN) problem is to preprocess $\mathcal{P}$ into an index so that, for any given query point q, we can efficiently return all pairs $(P_i, \pi_i(q))$ such that $\pi_i(q) > 0$.

In addition, one can consider the *most likely NN* of q, denoted NN_L, which is the P_i with the maximum $\pi_i(q)$; or the *threshold NN*, i.e., all the P_i's with $\pi_i(q)$ exceeding a given threshold τ.

Usually, the PNN problem is divided into the following two subproblems, which are often considered separately.

Nonzero NNs. The first subproblem is to find all the P_i's with $\pi_i(q) > 0$ without computing the actual qualification probabilities, i.e., to find

$$\mathsf{NN}_{\neq 0}(q, \mathcal{P}) = \{P_i \mid \pi_i(q) > 0\}.$$

If the point set $\mathcal{P}$ is obvious from the context, we drop the argument $\mathcal{P}$ from $\mathsf{NN}_{\neq 0}(q, \mathcal{P})$, and write it as $\mathsf{NN}_{\neq 0}(q)$. Note that $\mathsf{NN}_{\neq 0}(q)$ depends (besides q) only on the uncertainty regions of the uncertain points, but not on the actual pdf's.

A possible approach to compute nearest neighbors is to use Voronoi diagrams. For example, the standard Voronoi diagram of a set of points in $\mathbb{R}^2$ (without uncertainty) is the planar subdivision so that all points in the same face have the same nearest neighbor. In our case, we define the *nonzero Voronoi diagram*, denoted by $\mathcal{V}_{\neq 0}(\mathcal{P})$, to be the subdivision of $\mathbb{R}^2$ into maximal connected regions such that $\mathsf{NN}_{\neq 0}(q)$ is the same for all points q within each region. That is, for a subset $\mathcal{T} \subseteq \mathcal{P}$, let

$$\mathrm{cell}_{\neq 0}(\mathcal{T}) = \{q \in \mathbb{R}^2 \mid \mathsf{NN}_{\neq 0}(q) = \mathcal{T}\}. \quad (2)$$

Although there are 2^n subsets of $\mathcal{P}$, we will see below that only a small number of them have nonempty Voronoi cells. The planar subdivision $\mathcal{V}_{\neq 0}(\mathcal{P})$ is induced by all the nonempty $\mathrm{cell}_{\neq 0}(\mathcal{T})$'s for $\mathcal{T} \subseteq \mathcal{P}$. The (combinatorial) complexity of $\mathcal{V}_{\neq 0}(\mathcal{P})$ is the total number of vertices, edges, and faces in $\mathcal{V}_{\neq 0}(\mathcal{P})$. In this paper, we study the worst-case complexity of $\mathcal{V}_{\neq 0}(\mathcal{P})$ and how it can be efficiently constructed. The complexity of the Voronoi diagram is often regarded as a measure of the complexity of the corresponding nearest-neighbor problem. In addition, once we have $\mathcal{V}_{\neq 0}(\mathcal{P})$, a point-location structure can be built on top of it to support $\mathsf{NN}_{\neq 0}$ queries in logarithmic time.

Similarly, one can consider the *most likely Voronoi diagram* (partitioning the plane into regions having the same most likely NN) and the *threshold Voronoi diagram* (partitioning the plane into regions having the same set of points with qualification probabilities exceeding τ). However, these Voronoi diagrams tend to be more complex as they depend on the actual distributions of the uncertain points.

Computing qualification probabilities. The second subproblem is to compute the qualification probability $\pi_i(q)$ for a given q and P_i. Since exact values of these probabilities are often unstable — a far away point can affect these probabilities — and computing them requires a complex n-dimensional integration, which is often expensive, we resort to computing $\pi_i(q)$ approximately within a given error tolerance $0 < \varepsilon < 1$. More precisely, we aim at returning a value $\hat{\pi}_i(q)$ such that $|\pi_i(q) - \hat{\pi}_i(q)| \leq \varepsilon$.

Note that, having solved these two subproblems, we obtain immediate approximate solutions to the most likely NN and the threshold NN problems.

1.2 Previous work

Nonzero NNs. Sember and Evans [28] showed that the worst-case complexity of the nonzero Voronoi diagram (though they did not use this term explicitly) when the uncertainty regions of the uncertain points are disks is $O(n^4)$; they did not offer any lower bound. If one only considers those cells of $\mathcal{V}_{\neq 0}(P)$ in which $\mathsf{NN}_{\neq 0}(q)$ contains only one uncertain point P_i, they showed that the complexity of these cells is $O(n)$. Note that for such a cell, we always have $\pi_i(q) = 1$ for any q in the cell, so they are called the *guaranteed Voronoi diagram*. Probably unaware of the work by Sember and Evans [28], Cheng *et al.* [15] proved an exponential upper bound for the complexity of the nonzero Voronoi diagram, which they referred to as UV-diagram.

The nonzero Voronoi diagram is not the only way to find the nonzero NNs. Cheng *et al.* [14] designed a branch-and-prune solution based on the R-tree. Recently, Zhang *et al.* [32] proposed to combine the nonzero Voronoi diagram with R-tree-like bounding rectangles. These methods do not have any performance guarantees.

Computing qualification probabilities. Computing the qualification probabilities has attracted a lot of attention in the database community. Cheng *et al.* [14] used numerical integration, which is quite expensive. Cheng *et al.* [12] and Bernecker *et al.* [9] proposed some filter-refinement methods to give upper and lower bounds on the qualification probabilities. Kriegel *et al.* [23] took a random sample from the continuous distribution of each uncertain point to convert it to a discrete one, so that the integration becomes a sum, and they clustered each sample to further reduce the complexity of the query computation. These methods are best-effort based: they do not always give the ε-error that we aim at — how tight the bounds are depends on the data.

Other variants of the problem. The PNN problem we focus on in this paper is the most commonly studied version of the problem, but many variants and extensions have been considered.

The probabilistic model we use is often called the *locational model*, where the location of an uncertain point follows the given distribution. This is to be compared with the *existential model*, where each point has a precise location but it appears with a given probability.

Besides using the qualification probability, one can also consider the expected distance from a query point q to an uncertain point, and return the one minimizing the expected distance as the nearest neighbor; this was studied by Agarwal *et al.* [3]. This NN definition is much easier since the expected distance to each uncertain point can be computed separately, whereas the qualification probability involves the interaction among all uncertain points. However, the expected nearest neighbor is not a good indicator under large uncertainty (see [31] for details).

Finally, instead of returning only the nearest neighbor, one can ask to return the k nearest neighbors in a ranked order (the kNN problem). If we use expected distance, the ranking is straightforward. However, when qualification probabilities are considered, many different criteria for ranking the results are possible, leading to different problem variants.

Various combinations of these extensions have been studied in the literature; see, e.g., [10, 13, 22, 25, 31].

1.3 Our results

In this paper, we present efficient algorithms with proven guarantees on their performances for the nonzero NN problem as well as for computing the qualification probabilities.

Nonzero NNs. We first study (in Section 2.1) the complexity of $\mathcal{V}_{\neq 0}(\mathcal{P})$. Suppose the uncertainty region of each $P_i \in \mathcal{P}$ is a disk and $d(\cdot,\cdot)$ is the L_2 metric. We show that $\mathcal{V}_{\neq 0}(\mathcal{P})$ has $O(n^3)$ complexity, and that this bound is tight in the worst case. This significantly improves the bound in [28] and closes the problem. If the disks are pairwise disjoint and the ratio of their radii is at most λ, then the complexity of $\mathcal{V}_{\neq 0}(\mathcal{P})$ is $O(\lambda n^2)$. In either case, $\mathcal{V}_{\neq 0}(\mathcal{P})$ can be computed in $O(n^2 \log n + \mu)$ expected time, where μ is the complexity of $\mathcal{V}_{\neq 0}(\mathcal{P})$. We can build a point-location structure on top of $\mathcal{V}_{\neq 0}(\mathcal{P})$ whose size is proportional to the complexity of $\mathcal{V}_{\neq 0}(\mathcal{P})$ and answer an $\mathsf{NN}_{\neq 0}$ query in $O(\log n + t)$ time, where t is the output size.

If each point in $\mathcal{P}$ has a discrete distribution of size at most k, then we show that $\mathcal{V}_{\neq 0}(\mathcal{P})$ has $O(kn^3)$ complexity. Hence, we can answer an $\mathsf{NN}_{\neq 0}$ query in $O(\log(nk) + t)$ time using $O(kn^3)$ space.

Next, we consider (in Section 2.2) how quickly $\mathsf{NN}_{\neq 0}$ queries can be answered using less space. If the uncertainty region of each uncertain point is a disk, then an $\mathsf{NN}_{\neq 0}$ query can be answered in $O(\log n + t)$ time using $O(n^{1+\varepsilon})$ space, for any constant $\varepsilon > 0$, where t is the output size. If each uncertain point has at most k possible locations, then an $\mathsf{NN}_{\neq 0}$ query can be answered in $O(\log(nk) + t)$ time using $O((nk)^{2+\varepsilon})$ (for any $\varepsilon > 0$) space, or in $O((nk)^{1/2+\varepsilon} + t)$ time using $O(nk)$ space, where t is the output size.

Computing qualification probabilities. We present two algorithms for computing the qualification probabilities efficiently. The first (see Section 3.1) is a Monte-Carlo algorithm for estimating $\pi_i(q)$ for any P_i and q within error ε with high probability. First we argue that if each uncertain point has a discrete distribution of size poly(n), then we can estimate $\pi_i(q)$ within error ε by using $s_\varepsilon = O(\frac{1}{\varepsilon^2} \log \frac{n}{\varepsilon})$ random instantiations of $\mathcal{P}$. (Note that there are at most $1/\varepsilon$ P_i's for which $\pi_i(q) > \varepsilon$.) Consequently, we can preprocess $\mathcal{P}$ into an index of size $O(\frac{n}{\varepsilon^2} \log \frac{n}{\varepsilon})$ so that for any query point $q \in \mathbb{R}^2$, $\pi_i(q)$ for all P_i's can be estimated within error ε in $O(\frac{1}{\varepsilon^2} \log \frac{n}{\varepsilon} \log n)$ time, with probability at least $1 - 1/n$. The algorithms explicitly computes the estimates of $\pi_i(q)$'s for at most s_ε points and sets the estimate to 0 for the rest of the points. This index can also be used to find the (approximate) most likely NN and the threshold NN within the same time bound. We also show that this approach works even if the distribution of each P_i is continuous.

Next, we describe (in Section 3.2) a deterministic algorithm for computing $\pi_i(q)$ approximately provided that the distribution of each P_i is discrete. Let $P_i = \{p_{i1}, \ldots, p_{ik}\}$ and $w_{ij} = \Pr[P_i \text{ is } p_{ij}]$. We set $\rho = \frac{\max w_{ij}}{\min w_{ij}}$, where maximum and minimum are taken over all the location probabilities of points in $S = \bigcup_{i=1}^{n} P_i$. We show that $\mathcal{P}$ can be preprocessed into an index of $O(n)$ size so that for any $q \in \mathbb{R}^2$ and for any $\varepsilon > 0$, $\pi_i(q)$, for all $i \leq n$, can be computed with error at most ε in $O(\rho k \log(\rho/\varepsilon) + \log n)$ time. Our result shows that there are at most $m(\rho, \varepsilon) = \rho k \ln(\rho/\varepsilon) + k - 1$ points of $\mathcal{P}$ for which $\pi_i(q) > \varepsilon$. The algorithm explicitly estimates $\pi_i(q)$ for at most $m(\rho, \varepsilon)$ points and sets the estimate to 0 for the rest of the points. As earlier, this index can be used to solve the most likely NN and the threshold NN problem approximately within the same time bound.

Finally, we present experimental results, in Section 4, to demonstrate the efficacy of our approach for estimating quantification probabilities.

2. NONZERO PROBABILISTIC NN

In this section, we describe algorithms for answering $\mathsf{NN}_{\neq 0}$ queries. We first describe algorithms for computing $\mathcal{V}_{\neq 0}$ so that an $\mathsf{NN}_{\neq 0}$ query can be answered in logarithmic time by preprocessing $\mathcal{V}_{\neq 0}$ for point-location queries, and then describe indexing methods for answering $\mathsf{NN}_{\neq 0}$ queries using less space.

2.1 Nonzero Probabilistic Voronoi Diagram

Let $\mathcal{P}$ be a set of n uncertain points as described earlier. We analyze the combinatorial structure of $\mathcal{V}_{\neq 0}(\mathcal{P})$ and describe algorithms for constructing it. We first consider the case when the distribution of each point is continuous and then consider the discrete case.

Continuous case. For simplicity, we assume that the uncertainty region of each P_i is a circular disk D_i of radius r_i centered at c_i.

We first observe that the actual pdf of P_i is not important for computing $\mathcal{V}_{\neq 0}(\mathcal{P})$. What really matters is the uncertainty region D_i. More precisely, for each $1 \leq i \leq n$ and for $q \in \mathbb{R}^2$, let

$$\Delta_i(q) = \max_{p \in D_i} d(q, p) = d(q, c_i) + r_i,$$

$$\delta_i(q) = \min_{p \in D_i} d(x, q) = \max\{d(q, c_i) - r_i, 0\}$$

be the maximum and minimum possible distance, respectively, from q to a P_i.

The proof of the following lemma is straightforward.

LEMMA 2.1. *For a point $x \in \mathbb{R}^2$, a point $P_i \in \mathcal{P}$ belongs to $\mathsf{NN}_{\neq 0}(x, \mathcal{P})$ if and only if*

$$\delta_i(x) < \Delta_j(x) \text{ for all } 1 \leq j \neq i \leq n.$$

Let $\Delta \colon \mathbb{R}^2 \to \mathbb{R}$ denote the *lower envelope*[2] of $\Delta_1, \ldots, \Delta_n$;

[2] The lower envelope, L_F, of a set F of functions is their pointwise minimum, i.e., $L_F(x) = \min_{f \in F} f(x)$. The upper envelope, U_F, of F is the pointwise maximum, i.e., $U_F(x) = \max_{f \in F} f(x)$.

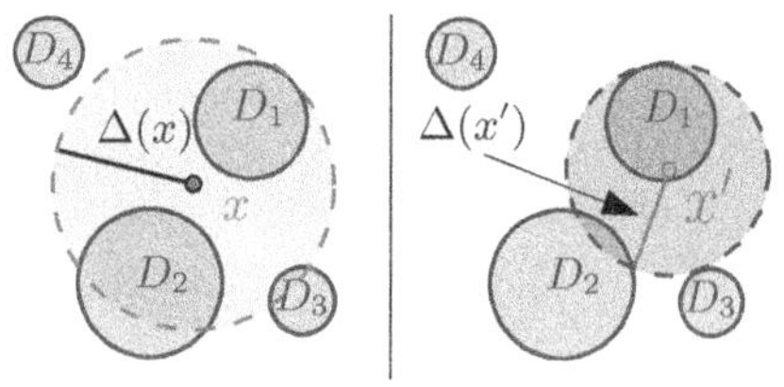

Figure 2. $\mathcal{P} = \{P_1, \ldots, P_5\}$. $\Delta(x) = \Delta_1(x)$, $\mathsf{NN}_{\neq 0}(x, \mathcal{P}) = \{P_1, P_2, P_3\}$, $\Delta(x') = \Delta_1(x')$, $\mathsf{NN}_{\neq 0}(x', \mathcal{P}) = \{P_1, P_2\}$, and x' lies on an edge of $\mathcal{V}_{\neq 0}(\mathcal{P})$.

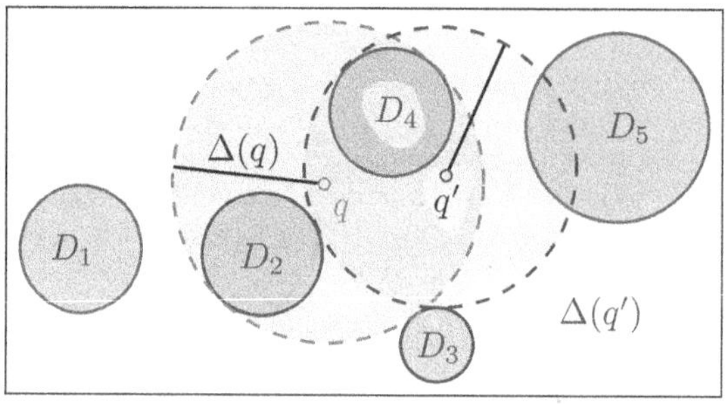

Figure 3. The point q is a breakpoint of γ_3 and q' is an intersection point of γ_2 and γ_3.

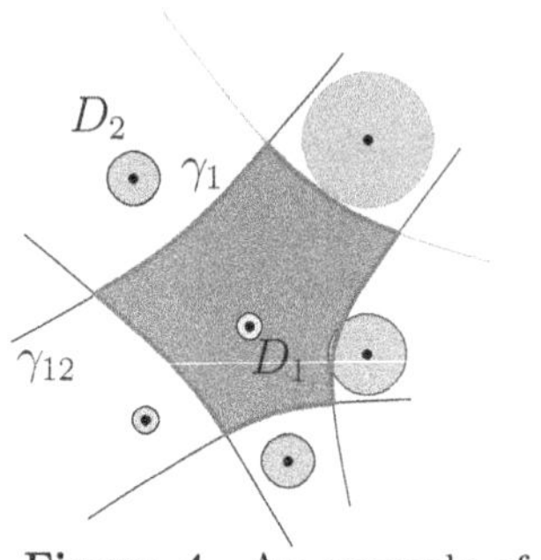

Figure 4. An example of γ_1.

that is, for any $q \in \mathbb{R}^2$,

$$\Delta(q) = \min_{1 \le i \le n} \Delta_i(q).$$

The projection of the graph of $\Delta(x)$ onto the xy-plane is the additive-weighted Voronoi diagram of the points $c_1, \ldots, c_n$, where the weight of c_i is r_i, and the weighted distance from q to c_i is $d(q, c_i) + r_i$, for $i = 1, \ldots, n$. Let $\mathbb{M}$ denote this planar subdivision. It has linear complexity and each of its edges is a hyperbolic arc; see [8]. Lemma 2.1 implies that, for any $q \in \mathbb{R}^2$,

$$\mathsf{NN}_{\neq 0}(q, \mathcal{P}) = \{P_i \mid \delta_i(q) < \Delta(q)\}. \tag{3}$$

See Fig. 2. It also implies that, as we move x continuously in $\mathbb{R}^2$, $\mathsf{NN}_{\neq 0}(x, \mathcal{P})$ remains the same until $\delta_i(x)$, for some $1 \le i \le n$, becomes equal to $\Delta(x)$ (e.g., x' in Fig. 2). The above was also observed in previous work. See, e.g. [12, 14]. Using this observation we can now characterize $\mathcal{V}_{\neq 0}(\mathcal{P})$.

For $i = 1, \ldots, n$, let $\gamma_i = \{x \in \mathbb{R}^2 \mid \delta_i(x) = \Delta(x)\}$ be the zero set of the function $\Delta(x) - \delta_i(x)$. Set $\Gamma = \{\gamma_1, \ldots, \gamma_n\}$.

The curve γ_i partitions the plane into two open regions: $\Delta(x) < \delta_i(x)$ and $\Delta(x) > \delta_i(x)$. By Eq. (3), $P_i \in \mathsf{NN}_{\neq 0}(x, \mathcal{P})$ for all points x inside the latter region and for none of the points x inside the former region. It is well known that for any fixed $j \neq i$, $\gamma_{ij} = \{x \in \mathbb{R}^2 \mid \delta_i(x) = \Delta_j(x)\}$ is a hyperbolic curve [8]. The curve γ_i is composed of pieces of γ_{ij}, for $j \neq i$. We refer to the endpoints of these pieces as *breakpoints* of γ_i. They are the intersection points of γ_i with an edge of $\mathbb{M}$ and correspond to points q such that the disk of radius $\Delta(q)$ centered at q touches (at least) two disks of $\mathcal{D}$ from inside, touches D_i from outside, and does not contain any disk of $\mathcal{D}$ in its interior. See Fig. 3. Formally, we say that a disk D_1 touches a disk D_2 from the *outside* (resp. *inside*) if $\partial D_1 \cap \partial D_2 \neq \emptyset$ and $\operatorname{int} D_1 \cap \operatorname{int} D_2 = \emptyset$ (resp. $\operatorname{int} D_2 \subseteq \operatorname{int} D_1$).

LEMMA 2.2. *The curve γ_i, $1 \le i \le n$, has at most $2n$ breakpoints, and it can be computed in $O(n \log n)$ time.*

PROOF. Let $\Gamma_i = \{\gamma_{ij} \mid j \neq i, 1 \le j \le n\}$. It can be verified that a ray emanating from c_i intersects γ_{ij}, for any $j \neq i$, in at most one point, so γ_{ij} can be viewed as the graph of a function in polar coordinates with c_i as the origin. That is, let $\gamma_{ij} \colon [0, 2\pi) \to \mathbb{R}_{\ge 0}$, where $\gamma_{ij}(\theta)$ is the distance from c_i to γ_{ij} in direction θ. Then γ_i is the lower envelope of Γ_i. Since each pair of arcs in Γ_i intersects at most twice, a well-known result on lower envelopes implies that γ_i has at most $2n$ breakpoints, and that it can be computed in $O(n \log n)$ time [29]. See Fig. 4 for an example. □

Let $\mathcal{A}(\Gamma)$ denote the planar subdivision induced by Γ: its vertices are the breakpoints of γ_i's and the intersection points of two curves in Γ, its edges are the portions of γ_i's between two consecutive vertices, and its cells are the maximal connected regions of Γ that do not intersect any curve of Γ. We refer to vertices, edges, and cells of $\mathcal{A}(\Gamma)$ as its 0-, 1-, and 2-dimensional *faces*.

For a face ϕ (of any dimension), and for any two points $x, y \in \phi$, the sets $\{P_i \mid \delta_i(x) < \Delta(x)\}$ and $\{P_j \mid \delta_j(y) < \Delta(y)\}$ are the same; we denote this set by $\mathcal{P}_\phi$.

LEMMA 2.3. *Let $x \in \mathbb{R}^2$ be a point lying in a face ϕ of $\mathcal{A}(\Gamma)$. Then $\mathsf{NN}_{\neq 0}(x, \mathcal{P}) = \mathcal{P}_\phi$.*

For a subset $\mathcal{T} \subseteq \mathcal{P}$, let $\mathrm{cell}_{\neq 0}(\mathcal{T})$ be as defined in Eq. (2). An immediate corollary of the above lemma is:

COROLLARY 2.4. *(i) For any $\mathcal{T} \subseteq \mathcal{P}$, $\mathrm{cell}_{\neq 0}(\mathcal{T}) \neq \emptyset$ if and only if there is a face ϕ of $\mathcal{A}(\Gamma)$ with $\mathcal{T} = \mathcal{P}_\phi$.*
(ii) The planar subdivision $\mathcal{A}(\Gamma)$ coincides with $\mathcal{V}_{\neq 0}(\mathcal{P})$.

We now bound the complexity of $\mathcal{A}(\Gamma)$ and thus of $\mathcal{V}_{\neq 0}(\mathcal{P})$.

THEOREM 2.5. *Let $\mathcal{P} = \{P_1, \ldots, P_n\}$ be a set of n uncertain points in $\mathbb{R}^2$ such that the uncertainty region of each point is a disk. Then $\mathcal{V}_{\neq 0}(\mathcal{P})$ has $O(n^3)$ complexity. Moreover, it can be computed in $O(n^2 \log n + \mu)$ expected time, where μ is the complexity of $\mathcal{V}_{\neq 0}(\mathcal{P})$.*

PROOF. Since $\mathcal{V}_{\neq 0}(\mathcal{P})$ is a planar subdivision, the number of edges and cells in it is proportional to the number of its vertices, so it suffices to bound the number of vertices. By Lemma 2.2, each γ_i has $O(n)$ breakpoints, so there are a total of $O(n^2)$ breakpoints. We claim that each pair of curves γ_i and γ_j intersect $O(n)$ times — each such intersection point corresponds to a point $v \in \mathbb{R}^2$ such that the disk of radius $\Delta(v)$ centered at v touches D_i and D_j from the outside and another disk D_k of $\mathcal{D}$, the one realizing the value of $\Delta(v)$, from the inside (e.g., q' in Fig. 3). For a fixed k, it can be shown that there are at most two points v such that $\delta_i(v) = \delta_j(v) = \Delta_k(v)$. Hence, the number of vertices in $\mathcal{V}_{\neq 0}(\mathcal{P})$ is $O(n^3)$, as claimed.

By Lemma 2.10, one can first compute all these curves in Γ in $O(n^2 \log n)$ time, and then compute the planar subdivision $\mathcal{A}(\Gamma)$ of Γ in $O(\mu)$ time using randomized incremental method [6], where μ is the complexity of $\mathcal{V}_{\neq 0}(\mathcal{P})$. Hence $\mathcal{V}_{\neq 0}(\mathcal{P})$ can be computed in $O(n^2 \log n + \mu)$ expected time. □

Remarks. This bound holds even if the uncertainty region of each point is a *semialgebraic* set of *constant description complexity*, i.e., each region is defined by Boolean operations (union, intersection, and complementation) of a constant number of bivariate polynomial inequalities of constant maximum degree each.

Next we show that the above upper bound is tight in the worst case.

THEOREM 2.6. *There exists a set $\mathcal{P}$ of n uncertain points for which $\mathcal{V}_{\neq 0}(\mathcal{P})$ has $\Omega(n^3)$ vertices.*

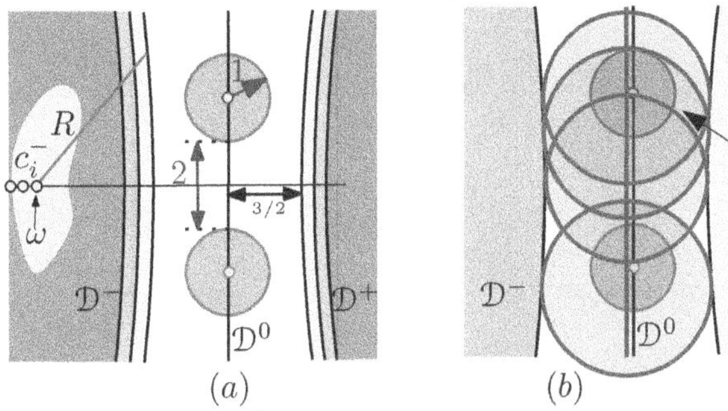

Figure 5. (a) $\Omega(n^3)$ lower bound construction with $m = 3$; only some disks are drawn. (b) Illustration of the proof.

PROOF. Assume that $n = 4m$ for some $m \in \mathbb{N}^+$. We choose two parameters $R = 8n^2$ and $\omega = 1/n^2$. We construct three families of disks: $\mathcal{D}^- = \{D_1^-, \ldots, D_m^-\}$, $\mathcal{D}^+ = \{D_1^+, \ldots, D_m^+\}$, and $\mathcal{D}^0 = \{D_1^0, \ldots, D_{2m}^0\}$. The radius of all disks in $\mathcal{D}^- \cup \mathcal{D}^+$ is R and their centers lie on the x-axis; the radius of all disks in $\mathcal{D}^0$ is 1 and their centers lie on the y-axis. More precisely, for $1 \leq i, j \leq m$, the center of D_i^- is $c_i^- = (-R - 3/2 - (i-1)\omega, 0)$ and the center of D_j^+ is $c_j^+ = (R + 3/2 + (j-1)\omega, 0)$, and for $1 \leq k \leq 2m$, the center of D_k^0 is $(0, 4(k-m) - 2)$. See Fig. 5 (a).

We claim that for every triple i, j, k with $1 \leq i, j \leq m$ and $1 \leq k \leq 2m$, there are two disks touching D_i^- and D_j^+ from the outside and D_k^0 from the inside and not containing any disk of $\mathcal{D}^- \cup \mathcal{D}^+ \cup \mathcal{D}^0$ in its interior. See Fig. 5(b).

Fix such a triple i, j, k. Since the radius of D_i^- and D_j^+ is the same, the locus b_{ij} of the centers of disks that simultaneously touch D_i^- and D_j^+ from the outside is the bisector of their centers, i.e., b_{ij} is the vertical line $x = (x(c_i^-) + x(c_j^+))/2 = (j-i)\omega/2$. Let σ_{ij} denote the intersection point of b_{ij} and the x-axis; $\sigma_{ij} = (\frac{1}{2}(j-i)\omega, 0)$. A point on b_{ij} can be represented by its y-coordinate; we will not distinguish between the two. For y-value a, let ξ_a be the disk centered at a and simultaneously touching D_i^- and D_j^+. The radius of ξ_a is

$$\begin{aligned}\|a - c_i^-\| - R &= \sqrt{a^2 + \|c_i^- - \sigma_{ij}\|^2} - R \\ &= \sqrt{a^2 + \left(R + 3/2 + \left(\frac{i+j}{2} - 1\right)\omega\right)^2} - R.\end{aligned}$$

The radius of ξ_a is thus at least $3/2$, and for $a \in [-4m, 4m]$, it is at most 2 (using the fact that $R \geq 8n^2$ and $\omega = 1/n^2$). Hence for $a \in [-4m, 4m]$, ξ_a contains at most one disk of $\mathcal{D}^0$ in its interior, and obviously ξ_a does not contain any disk of $\mathcal{D}^- \cup \mathcal{D}^+$ in its interior.

Let $a_k = 4(k-m) - 2$. Then the disk ξ_{a_k} contains D_k^0 in its interior because the distance between the centers of D_k^0 and ξ_{a_k} is at most $m\omega \leq 1/(4n)$, the radius of D_k^0 is 1, and the radius of ξ_{a_k} is at least $3/2$. On the other hand, the disk ξ_a for $a = a_k \pm 2$ does not contain D_k^0 in its interior because the radius of ξ_a is at most 2 and the distance between the center of D_k^0 and ξ_a is at least 2. Therefore, by a continuity argument, there is a value $a^+ \in [a_k, a_k + 2]$ at which ξ_{a^+} touches D_k^0 from the inside. Similarly, there is a value $a^- \in [a_k - 2, a_k]$ at which ξ_{a^-} touches D_k^0 from the inside.

This proves the claim that there are two disks touching D_i^- and D_j^+ from the outside and D_k^0 from the inside and not containing any disk of $\mathcal{D}^- \cup \mathcal{D}^+ \cup \mathcal{D}^0$ in its interior. In other words, each triple i, j, k contributes two vertices to $\mathcal{V}_{\neq 0}(\mathcal{P})$. Hence $\mathcal{V}_{\neq 0}(\mathcal{P})$ has $\Omega(n^3)$ vertices. □

Remarks. A more careful construction gives an $\Omega(n^3)$ lower bound on the complexity of $\mathcal{V}_{\neq 0}(\mathcal{P})$ even if all disks in $\mathcal{D}$ have the same radius.

Next, if the disks in $\mathcal{D}$ are pairwise disjoint and the ratio of the radii of the largest to the smallest disk is bounded by λ, then we prove a refined bound on the complexity of $\mathcal{V}_{\neq 0}(\mathcal{P})$ that depends on λ.

LEMMA 2.7. *If $\mathcal{P} = \{P_1, \ldots, P_n\}$ is a set of n uncertain points in $\mathbb{R}^2$ such that their uncertainty regions are pairwise-disjoint disks with radii in the range $[1, \lambda]$, a pair of curves in Γ intersects in $O(\lambda)$ points.*

PROOF. Fix a pair of curves γ_1 and γ_2, let D_1 and D_2 be the corresponding disks, and let c_1 and c_2 be their centers, respectively. By applying rotation and translation to the plane, we can assume D_1 and D_2 are centered on the x-axis, with D_1 to the left of D_2.

For a parameter t, $1 \leq t \leq \lambda$, let $\mathcal{D}$ denote the set of all the disks associated with $\mathcal{P}$, excluding D_1 and D_2, with radii between t and $2t$. An intersection point $q \in \gamma_1 \cap \gamma_2$ corresponds to a *witness* disk W centered at q that touches both D_1 and D_2 from the outside, touches exactly one other disk $E \in \mathcal{D}$ from the inside, and properly contains no disks of $\mathcal{D}$. The family of disks that touch both D_1 and D_2 from the outside is a *pencil*, which sweeps over portion of the plane as the tangency points with D_1 and D_2 move continuously (see Fig. 5(b)). A disk of $\mathcal{D}$ can contribute at most two intersection points to $\gamma_1 \cap \gamma_2$, as its boundary gets swept over at most twice by the circles of the pencil.

For a disk $E \in \mathcal{D}$, if its tangency point with its witness disk W is on the top portion of W (i.e., we break ∂W into two curves, *top* and *bottom*, at W's tangency points with D_1 and D_2) then it is a *top tangency event*, otherwise it is a *bottom tangency event*. Let $\mathcal{D}_1$ (resp. $\mathcal{D}_2$) be the set of disks in $\mathcal{D}$ that are closer to D_1 (resp. D_2). See Fig. 6(a).

Below we bound the number of top tangency events involving disks in $\mathcal{D}_2$. Other tangency events are handled by a symmetric argument.

We remove from $\mathcal{D}_2$ all the disks at distance at most $T = \xi t$ from D_2, where ξ is a sufficiently large constant. The ring with outer radius $\mathsf{r}(D_2) + 4T$ and inner radius $\mathsf{r}(D_2)$ has area $\alpha = \pi\left((\mathsf{r}(D_2) + 4T)^2 - (\mathsf{r}(D_2))^2\right) = O(T\mathsf{r}(D_2) + T^2)$. Disks removed from $\mathcal{D}_2$ have the following properties:

(i) they are interior-disjoint,
(ii) their radius is $\in [t, 2t]$,
(iii) they are contained in the aforementioned ring, and
(iv) the area of each such disk is at least πt^2.

Hence the number of removed disks is

$$O((T\mathsf{r}(D_2) + T^2)/t^2) = O(\lambda/t),$$

as $\mathsf{r}(D_2) \leq \lambda$.

Consider the circle σ_2 of radius $\mathsf{r}(D_2) + T/2$ centered at c_2. Consider any disk $E \in \mathcal{D}_2$ and its witness disk W touching both D_1 and D_2 from the outside. Let $W_{\ominus T}$ be

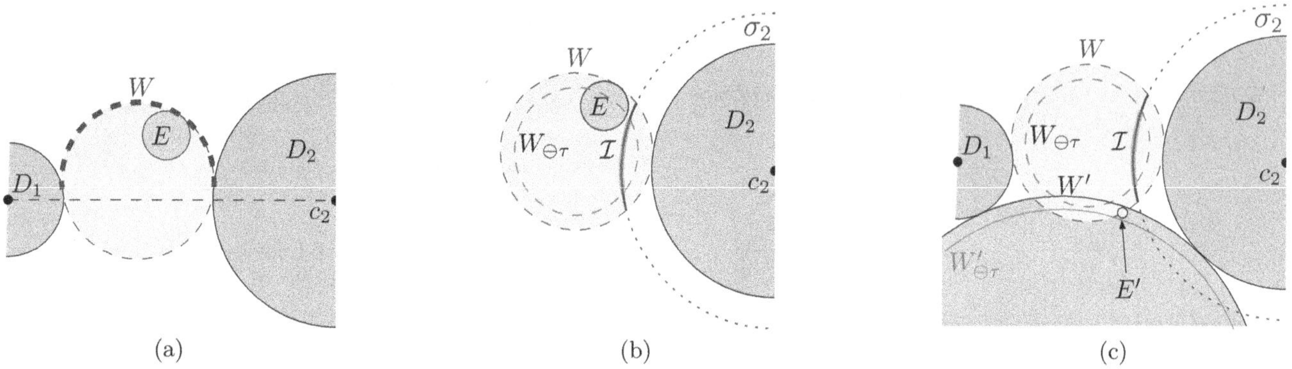

Figure 6. An illustration for the proof of Lemma 2.7.

the disk concentric with W with radius $\mathsf{r}(W) - \tau$, where $\tau = 4t$. (Note that since E has not been removed from $\mathcal{D}_2$, $\mathsf{r}(W) \geq (T + 2t)/2$; in particular it is larger than $T/2$.) The disk $W_{\ominus\tau}$ is interior-disjoint from all disks in $\mathcal{D}_2$, as E touches W from inside and W cannot fully contain any other disks from $\mathcal{D}_2$.

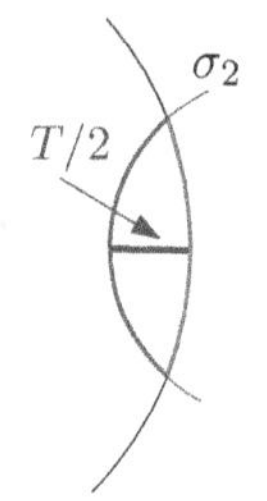

The witness disk W covers an arc of length at least $T/2$ on σ_2. Indeed, neither of these two disks covers the center of the other, and the inner distance between the two intersection arcs is $T/2$, see figure on the right. Similarly, let $\mathcal{I}(E)$ be the arc $W_{\ominus\tau} \cap \sigma_2$. By the same argument, we have that $\mathcal{I}(E)$ is of length at least $T/2 - \tau = \Omega(t)$.

The perimeter of σ_2 is $2\pi(\mathsf{r}(D_2) + T/2) = O(\lambda)$, so if the arcs $\mathcal{I}(E)$, for $E \in \mathcal{D}_2$, are pairwise disjoint, we are done, as this implies that there could be at most $\lambda/(T/2 - \tau) = O(\lambda/t)$ such arcs and thus the size of the original $\mathcal{D}_2$ is $O(\lambda/t)$. See Fig. 6(b). We will therefore proceed to prove that any two such arcs are disjoint.

So, consider two disks $E, E' \in \mathcal{D}_2$, both realizing a top tangency event. Let W (resp. W') be the witness disk that is tangent to D_1, D_2 and E (resp. E'). Assume that the tangency of W with D_2 is clockwise to the tangency of W' with D_2 (i.e., E is "above" E'). If $W_{\ominus\tau}$ and $W'_{\ominus\tau}$ are disjoint then their corresponding arcs are disjoint. Otherwise, as we already observed, E' and $W_{\ominus\tau}$ are disjoint. Furthermore, it is easy to verify that E' must lie in the region "between" σ_2, $W_{\ominus\tau}$, and $W'_{\ominus\tau}$, and therefore the arcs $\mathcal{I}(E)$ and $\mathcal{I}(E')$ are disjoint, as claimed; refer to Fig. 6(c).

We now repeat the above counting argument, for $t = 1, 2, 4, \ldots, 2^m$, where $m = \lceil \log_2 \lambda \rceil$. We get that the number of intersection points between γ_1 and γ_2 is bounded by $\sum_{i=1}^{m} O(\lambda/2^i) = O(\lambda)$, as claimed. □

THEOREM 2.8. *Let $\mathcal{P} = \{P_1, \ldots, P_n\}$ be a set of n uncertain points in $\mathbb{R}^2$ such that their uncertainty regions are pairwise-disjoint disks and that the ratio of the largest and the smallest radii of the disks is at most λ. Then the complexity of $\mathcal{V}_{\neq 0}(\mathcal{P})$ is $O(\lambda n^2)$, and it can be computed in $O(n^2 \log n + \mu)$ expected time, where μ is the complexity of $\mathcal{V}_{\neq 0}(\mathcal{P})$. Furthermore, there exists such a set $\mathcal{P}$ of uncertain points for which $\mathcal{V}_{\neq 0}(\mathcal{P})$ has $\Omega(n^2)$ complexity.*

PROOF. The upper bound on the complexity of $\mathcal{V}_{\neq 0}(\mathcal{P})$ follows from Lemma 2.7. By the same argument as in the proof of Theorem 2.5, $\mathcal{V}_{\neq 0}(\mathcal{P})$ can be computed in $O(n^2 \log n + \mu)$ time, where μ is the number of vertices in $\mathcal{V}_{\neq 0}(\mathcal{P})$. The lower-bound construction is omitted from this abstract due to lack of space. □

We store the index i of each uncertain point P_i instead of P_i itself. If we store $\mathcal{P}_\phi$ for each cell ϕ of $\mathcal{V}_{\neq 0}(\mathcal{P})$ explicitly, the size increases by a factor of n. However, we observe that for two adjacent cells ϕ, ϕ' of $\mathcal{V}_{\neq 0}(\mathcal{P})$, i.e., two cells that share a common edge, $|\mathcal{P}_\phi \oplus \mathcal{P}_{\phi'}| = 1$, where $\oplus$ denotes the symmetric difference of two sets. Therefore, using a persistent data structure [18], we can store $\mathcal{P}_\phi$ for all cells of $\mathcal{V}_{\neq 0}(\mathcal{P})$ in $O(\mu)$ space, where μ is the complexity of $\mathcal{V}_{\neq 0}(\mathcal{P})$, so that for any cell ϕ, $\mathcal{P}_\phi$ can be retrieved in $O(\log n + |\mathcal{P}_\phi|)$ time. By combining this with the planar point-location indexing schemes [17], we obtain the following:

THEOREM 2.9. *Let $\mathcal{P}$ be a set of n uncertain points in $\mathbb{R}^2$, and let μ be the complexity of $\mathcal{V}_{\neq 0}(\mathcal{P})$. Then $\mathcal{V}_{\neq 0}(\mathcal{P})$ can be preprocessed in $O(\mu \log \mu)$ time into an index of size $O(\mu)$ so that for a query point $q \in \mathbb{R}^2$, $\mathsf{NN}_{\neq 0}(q, \mathcal{P})$ can be computed in $O(\log n + t)$ time, where t is the output size.*

Remarks. This bound can be extended to the case when each uncertainty region is an α-fat semialgebraic set of constant description complexity. A set C is called α-fat, if there exist two concentric disks, $D \subseteq C \subseteq D'$, such that the ratio between the radii of D' and D is at most α. The constant of proportionality also depends on α and the number and maximum degree of polynomials defining the uncertainty regions.

Discrete case. We now analyze the complexity of $\mathcal{V}_{\neq 0}(\mathcal{P})$ when the distribution of each point P_i in $\mathcal{P}$ is discrete. Let $P_i = \{p_{i1}, \ldots, p_{ik}\}$. For $1 \leq j \leq k$, let $w_{ij} = \Pr[P_i \text{ is } p_{ij}]$. As in the previous section, for a point x, let $\Delta_i(x) = \max_{1 \leq j \leq k} d(x, p_{ij})$ and $\delta_i(x) = \min_{1 \leq j \leq k} d(x, p_{ij})$. Note that the projection of the graph of Δ_i (resp. δ_i) onto the xy-plane is the farthest-point (resp. nearest-point) Voronoi diagram of P_i. Let $\Delta(x) = \min_{1 \leq i \leq n} \Delta_i(x)$. For each i, let $\gamma_i = \{x \in \mathbb{R}^2 \mid \delta_i(x) = \Delta(x)\}$, and set $\Gamma = \{\gamma_1, \ldots, \gamma_n\}$. Then $\mathcal{V}_{\neq 0}(\mathcal{P})$ is the planar subdivision induced by Γ, as defined above. We need the following lemma to bound the complexity of $\mathcal{V}_{\neq 0}(\mathcal{P})$.

LEMMA 2.10. *For any pair i, j, $1 \leq i \neq j \leq n$, let $\gamma_{ij} = \{x \in \mathbb{R}^2 \mid \delta_i(x) = \Delta_j(x)\}$, then γ_{ij} is a convex polygonal curve with $O(k)$ vertices.*

PROOF. Let $p \in \mathbb{R}^2$ be a fixed point. Then we define a linear function $g: \mathbb{R}^2 \to \mathbb{R}$ as

$$g(x) = d^2(x, p) - \|x\|^2 = \|p\|^2 - 2\langle x, p\rangle.$$

For $1 \le i \le n$, define $\varphi_i(x) = \min_{1\le j\le k} g(x, p_{ij})$ and $\Phi_i(x) = \max_{1\le j\le k} g(x, p_{ij})$. Then for any pair i, j, $\delta_i(x) = \Delta_j(x)$ if and only if $\varphi_i(x) = \Phi_j(x)$. Hence, γ_{ij} is also the zero set of the function $\Phi_j(x) - \varphi_i(x)$.

Note that Φ_j is the upper envelope of k linear functions, and that it is a piecewise-linear concave function, and that φ_i, the lower envelope of k linear functions, is a piecewise-linear convex function. Hence $\Phi_j(x) - \varphi_i(x)$ is a piecewise-linear concave function, which implies that $\gamma_{ij} = \{x \in \mathbb{R}^2 \mid \Phi_j(x) = \varphi_i(x)\}$ is a convex polygonal curve. Since γ_{ij} is the projection of the intersection curve of the graphs of Φ_j and φ_i, each of which is a convex polyhedron with at most k faces, γ_{ij} has $O(k)$ vertices. □

THEOREM 2.11. *Let $\mathcal{P} = \{P_1, \ldots, P_n\}$ be a set of n uncertain points in $\mathbb{R}^2$, where each P_i has a discrete distribution of size at most k. The complexity of $\mathcal{V}_{\neq 0}(\mathcal{P})$ is $\mu = O(kn^3)$ in the worst case, and it can be computed in expected time $O(n^2 \log n + \mu)$. Furthermore, it can be preprocessed into an index of size $O(\mu)$ so that an $\mathsf{NN}_{\neq 0}(q)$ query can be answered in $O(\log \mu + t)$, where t is the output size.*

PROOF. We follow the same argument as in the proof of Theorem 2.5. We need to bound the number of intersection points between a pair of curves γ_i and γ_j. Fix an index u. Let $\gamma_{iu} = \{x \in \mathbb{R}^2 \mid \delta_i(x) = \Delta_u(x)\}$ and $\gamma_{ju} = \{x \in \mathbb{R}^2 \mid \delta_j(x) = \Delta_u(x)\}$. By Lemma 2.10, each of γ_{iu} and γ_{ju} is a convex polygonal curve in $\mathbb{R}^2$ with $O(k)$ vertices. Since two convex polygonal curves in general position with n_1 and n_2 vertices intersect in at most $2(n_1 + n_2)$ points, γ_{iu} and γ_{ju} intersect at $O(k)$ points. Hence γ_i and γ_j intersect at $O(nk)$ points, implying that $\mathcal{V}_{\neq 0}(\mathcal{P})$ has $O(kn^3)$ vertices. The running time follows from the proof of Theorem 2.5. □

2.2 Indexing schemes for $\mathsf{NN}_{\neq 0}$ queries

Despite the maximum size of $\mathcal{V}_{\neq 0}$ being $\Theta(n^3)$ or $\Theta(n^2)$, we can obtain indexing schemes with less space such that $\mathsf{NN}_{\neq 0}$ queries can be answered in poly-logarithmic or sublinear time. We consider both continuous and discrete cases.

An $\mathsf{NN}_{\neq 0}(q)$ query is answered in two stages. The first stage computes $\Delta(q)$, and the second stage computes all points $P_i \in \mathcal{P}$ for which $\delta_i(q) < \Delta(q)$. We build a separate index for each stage.

Continuous case. We assume that the uncertainty region of each point P_i is a disk D_i of radius r_i centered at c_i. Recall from Section 2.1 that the projection of the graph of the function Δ onto the xy-plane, a planar subdivision $\mathbb{M}$, is the weighted Voronoi diagram of the point set $c_1, \ldots, c_n$, and it has linear complexity. Hence $\mathbb{M}$ can be preprocessed in $O(n \log n)$ time into an index of size $O(n)$ so that for a query point $q \in \mathbb{R}^2$, $\Delta(q)$ can be computed in $O(\log n)$ time.

Next, the problem of reporting $\mathsf{NN}_{\neq 0}(q)$ reduces to reporting all disks of $D_1, \ldots, D_n$ that intersect the disk of radius $\Delta(q)$ centered at q. Using the approach described in [4], $D_1, \ldots, D_n$ can be preprocessed into an index of size $O(n^{1+\varepsilon})$, for any constant $\varepsilon > 0$, so that all t disks intersecting a query disk can be reported in $O(\log n + t)$ time. We thus obtain the following:

THEOREM 2.12. *Let $\mathcal{P} = \{P_1, \ldots, P_n\}$ be a set of n uncertain points in $\mathbb{R}^2$ so that the uncertainty region of each P_i is a disk. Then $\mathcal{P}$ can be preprocessed into an index of size $O(n^{1+\varepsilon})$, for any $\varepsilon > 0$, so that an $\mathsf{NN}_{\neq 0}(q)$ query can be answered in $O(\log n + t)$ time, where t is the output size.*

Remarks. (i) Note that Theorem 2.12 gives a better result than Theorem 2.9 if the uncertainty regions of $\mathcal{P}$ are allowed to intersect, but the Voronoi–diagram-based index is much simpler and practical.

(ii) If we use L_1 or L_∞ metric to compute the distance between points and use disks in L_1 or L_∞ metric (i.e., a diamond or a square), then an $\mathsf{NN}_{\neq 0}(q)$ query can be answered in $O(\log^2 n + t)$ time using $O(n \log^2 n)$ space.

Discrete case. If the distribution of each P_i is discrete, then the functions Δ_i and δ_i are complex and thus the index for $\mathsf{NN}_{\neq 0}(q)$ queries is more involved. First we observe that the problem of reporting all points $\mathcal{P}_i \in \mathcal{P}$ such that $\delta_i(q) \le R$ for a query point $q \in \mathbb{R}^2$ and $R > 0$, can be formulated as a colored disk range reporting. Namely, we color all k points of P_i with color i. Let $S = \bigcup_{i=1}^n P_i$. Then given a disk D of radius R centered at q, we wish to report the colors of all points in S that lie inside D — each color should be reported only once. Following the same approach as in [19], this can be done with $O(\log^2(nk) + t)$ query time using $O((nk)^{2+\varepsilon})$ space (for any $\varepsilon > 0$), or with $O((nk)^{1/2+\varepsilon} + t)$ query time using $O((nk)\log^2(nk))$ space.

Alternatively, using standard reduction from reporting to emptiness, this can be solved using, space $O(nk \log n)$, preprocessing $O(nk \log^2 n)$, and $O((1 + t)\log^2 n)$ query time. Indeed, build a balanced tree over the colors, and for each internal node, build a standard emptiness range searching data-structure for all the disks having the colors stored in this subtree. Here, the emptiness data-structure is a point-location data-structure in a weighted additive Voronoi diagram. Now, given a query disk, traverse this color tree, recursing into a subtree if the emptiness data-structure reports that a disk in this subtree intersects the query. An emptiness query takes $O(\log n)$ time, and $O(t \log n)$ nodes in the tree are visited by the query process.

It thus suffices to describe how we compute $\Delta(q)$ for a query point $q \in \mathbb{R}^2$. Recall that the projection of Δ_i onto the xy-plane, for $1 \le i \le n$, is the farthest-point Voronoi diagram of P_i, and that Δ is the lower envelope of $\Delta_1, \ldots, \Delta_n$. Following the same argument as by Huttenlocher *et al.* [21], we can prove the following.

LEMMA 2.13. *The xy-projection of the graph of the function Δ is a planar subdivision with $O(n^2 k\alpha(n^2 k))$ vertices, and it can be computed in $O(n^2 k \log(nk))$ time, where $\alpha(\cdot)$ is the inverse Ackerman function.*

If the convex hulls of the point clouds are disjoint, the problem is significantly easier, see [11].

Hence by preprocessing the projection of Δ for point-location queries, $\Delta(q)$ can be computed in $O(\log(nk))$ time, for any query point q.

If we wish to construct a linear-size index, we rely on multi-level partition–tree-based [5] indexing schemes. We sketch the main idea and omit the details. Let $S = \bigcup_{i=1}^n P_i$, which is a set of nk (certain) points in $\mathbb{R}^2$. For a point $q \in \mathbb{R}^2$, let $S(q) = \{p_1, \ldots, p_n\}$ where p_i is the farthest neighbor of q in P_i. We build a partition tree $\mathcal{T}$ on S and the farthest-point Voronoi diagrams of $P_1, \ldots, P_n$ of size $O(nk)$, which basically constructs a family $\mathcal{F} = \{e_1, \ldots, e_m\}$ of "canonical" subsets of S such that:

(i) $\sum_i |e_i| = O(nk)$;

(ii) for any query point $q \in \mathbb{R}^2$, $S(q)$ can be represented as the union of $O((nk)^{1/2+\varepsilon})$ (for any $\varepsilon > 0$) canonical subsets of $\mathcal{F}$, denoted by $\mathcal{F}(q)$.

$\mathcal{T}$ can be constructed in $O(nk\log(nk))$ time, and using the hierarchical structure of $\mathcal{T}$, $\mathcal{F}(q)$ for a query point q can be computed in $O((nk)^{1/2+\varepsilon})$ time. Next, we build a linear-size index on each e_i for answering NN queries in $O(\log n)$ time. Putting everything together, the overall size of the index is $O(nk)$ and it can be constructed in $O(nk\log(nk))$ time. See [5, 26] for details.

Given a query point $q \in \mathbb{R}^2$, we first compute $\mathcal{F}(q)$, then for each $e \in \mathcal{F}(q)$, we compute the nearest neighbor of q in e, and finally choose the nearest one among them. The total query time is $O((nk)^{1/2+\varepsilon}\log n) = O((nk)^{1/2+\varepsilon'})$ for any $\varepsilon' > \varepsilon$.

Hence, we obtain the following:

THEOREM 2.14. *Let $\mathcal{P}$ be a set of n uncertain points in $\mathbb{R}^2$, each of size at most k. $\mathcal{P}$ can be preprocessed into an index of size $O((nk)^{2+\varepsilon})$, for any $\varepsilon > 0$, so that an $\mathsf{NN}_{\neq 0}(q)$ query can be answered in $O(\log(nk) + t)$ time, or into an index of size $O(nk)$ with $O((nk)^{1/2+\varepsilon} + t)$ query time, where t is the output size. The preprocessing times are $O((nk)^{2+\varepsilon})$ and $O(nk\log(nk))$ time, respectively.*

3. QUANTIFICATION PROBABILITIES

We begin with exact algorithms for uncertain point sets, in which each uncertain point has k possible locations. We can build a structure called the *probabilistic Voronoi diagram* $\mathcal{V}_{\Pr}(\mathcal{P})$ that decomposes $\mathbb{R}^2$ into a set of cells, so that any point q in a cell has the same $\pi_i(q)$ value for all $P_i \in \mathcal{P}$; that is, for any point q in this cell, we know exactly the probability of each point $P \in \mathcal{P}$ being the NN of q.

LEMMA 3.1. *Let $\mathcal{P}$ be a set of n uncertain points in $\mathbb{R}^2$, each with at most k possible locations, then the complexity of $\mathcal{V}_{\Pr}(\mathcal{P})$ is $O(n^4k^4)$.*

PROOF. There are nk possible locations. Each pair of possible locations determines a bisector, resulting in $O(n^2k^2)$ bisectors. These bisectors partition the plane into $O(n^4k^4)$ convex cells so the order of all distances to each of the nk possible locations, and thus also all the qualification probabilities, are preserved within each cell. Therefore the resulting planar subdivision is a refinement of $\mathcal{V}_{\Pr}(\mathcal{P})$, and thus $O(n^4k^4)$ is an upper bound on the complexity of $\mathcal{V}_{\Pr}(\mathcal{P})$. □

Note, that the related notion of most likely NN is not stable in the sense that a single possible location of point that is possibly far from a query can affect which point is the most likely NN. Since the $\mathcal{V}_{\Pr}(\mathcal{P})$ is too large to be efficient in practice, we explore how to approximate $\pi_i(q)$.

3.1 Monte Carlo Algorithm

In this section we describe a simple Monte Carlo approach to build an index for quickly computing $\hat{\pi}_i(q)$ for all P_i for any query point q, which approximates the quantification probability $\pi_i(q)$. For a fixed value s, to be specified later, the preprocessing step has s rounds. In the jth round the algorithm creates a sample $R_j = \{r_{j1}, r_{j2}, \ldots, r_{jn}\} \subseteq \mathbb{R}^2$ by choosing each r_{ji} using the distribution of P_i. For each $j \leq s$, we construct the Voronoi diagram $\mathsf{Vor}(R_j)$ in $O(n\log n)$ time and preprocess it for point-location queries in additional $O(n\log n)$ time.

To estimate quantification probabilities of a query q, we initialize a counter $c_i = 0$ for each point P_i. For each R_j, we find the point r_{ji} whose cell in $\mathsf{Vor}(R_j)$ contains the query point q, and increment c_i by 1. Finally we estimate $\hat{\pi}_i(q) = c_i/s$. Note that at most s distinct c_i's have nonzero values, so we can implicitly set the others to 0.

Discrete case. If each $P_i \in \mathcal{P}$ has a discrete distribution of size k, then this algorithm can be implemented very efficiently. Each r_i can be selected in $O(\log k)$ time after preprocessing each P_i, in $O(k)$ time, into a balanced binary tree with total weight calculated for each subtree [27]. Thus total preprocessing takes $O(s(n(\log n + \log k)) + nk) = O(nk + sn\log(nk))$ time and $O(sn)$ space, and each query takes $O(s\log n)$ time.

It remains to determine the value of s so that $|\pi_i(q) - \hat{\pi}_i(q)| \leq \varepsilon$ for all P_i and all queries q, with probability at least $1 - \delta$. For fixed q, P_i, and instantiation R_j, let X_i be the random indicator variable, which is 1 if r_i is the NN of q and 0 otherwise. Since $\mathsf{E}[\mathrm{X}_i] = \pi_i(q)$ and $\mathrm{X}_i \in \{0, 1\}$, applying a Chernoff-Hoeffding bound to

$$\hat{\pi}_i(q) = \frac{c_i}{s} = \frac{1}{s}\sum_i \mathrm{X}_i,$$

we observe that

$$\Pr\left[|\hat{\pi}_i(q) - \pi_i(q)| \geq \varepsilon\right] \leq 2\exp(-2\varepsilon^2 s). \tag{4}$$

For each cell of $\mathcal{V}_{\Pr}(\mathcal{P})$, we choose one point, and let Q be the resulting set of points. If $|\hat{\pi}_i(q) - \pi_i(q)| \leq \varepsilon$ for every point $q \in Q$, then $|\hat{\pi}_i(q) - \pi_i(q)| \leq \varepsilon$ for every point $q \in \mathbb{R}^2$. Since there are n different values of i, by applying the union bound to (4), the probability that there exist a point $q \in \mathbb{R}^2$ and an index $i \leq n$ with $|\hat{\pi}_i(q) - \pi_i(q)| \geq \varepsilon$ is at most $2n|Q|\exp(-2\varepsilon^2 s)$. Hence, by setting

$$s = \frac{1}{2\varepsilon^2}\ln\frac{2n|Q|}{\delta},$$

$|\hat{\pi}_i(q) - \pi_i(q)| \leq \varepsilon$ for all $q \in \mathbb{R}^2$ and for all $i \leq n$, with probability at least $1 - \delta$. By Lemma 3.1, $|Q| = O(n^4k^4)$, so we obtain the following result.

THEOREM 3.2. *Let $\mathcal{P}$ be a set of n uncertain points in $\mathbb{R}^2$, each with a discrete distribution of size k, and let $\varepsilon, \delta \in (0, 1)$ be two parameters. $\mathcal{P}$ can be preprocessed, in*

$$O(nk + (n/\varepsilon^2)\log(nk)\log(nk/\delta))$$

time, into an index of size $O((n/\varepsilon^2)\log(nk/\delta))$, which computes, for any query point $q \in \mathbb{R}^2$, in $O((1/\varepsilon^2)\log(nk/\delta)\log n)$ time, a value $\hat{\pi}_i(q)$ for every P_i such that $|\pi_i(q) - \hat{\pi}_i(q)| \leq \varepsilon$ for all i with probability at least $1 - \delta$.

Continuous case. There are two technical issues in extending this technique and analysis to continuous distributions. First, we instantiate a certain point r_i from each P_i. Herein we assume the representation of the pdf is such that this can be done in constant time for each P_i.

Second, we need to bound the number of distinct queries that need to be considered to apply the union bound as we did above. Since $\pi_i(q)$ may vary continuously with the query location, unlike the discrete case, we cannot hope for a bounded number of distinct results. However, we just need to define a finite set $\bar{Q}$ of query points so that any query $q \in \mathbb{R}^2$ has $\max_i |\pi_i(q) - \pi_i(q')| \le \varepsilon/2$ for some $q' \in \bar{Q}$. Then we can choose s large enough so that it permits at most $\varepsilon/2$ error on each query in $\bar{Q}$. Specifically, choosing $s = O((1/\varepsilon^2)\log(n|\bar{Q}|/\delta))$ is sufficient, so all that remains is to bound $|\bar{Q}|$.

To choose $\bar{Q}$, we show that each pdf of P_i can be approximated with a discrete distribution of size $O((n^2/\varepsilon^2)\log(n/\delta))$, and then reduce the problem to the discrete case.

For parameters $\alpha > 0$ and $\delta' \in (0,1)$, set

$$k(\alpha) = \frac{c}{\alpha^2}\log\frac{1}{\delta'},$$

where c is a constant. For each $i \le n$, we choose a random sample $\bar{P}_i \subset P_i$ of size $k(\alpha)$, according to the distribution defined by the location pdf f_i of P_i. We regard $\bar{P}_i$ as an uncertain point with uniform location probability. Set $\bar{\mathcal{P}} = \{\bar{P}_1, \ldots, \bar{P}_n\}$.

For a point $q \in \mathbb{R}^2$, let $\bar{G}_{q,i}$ denote the cdf of the distance between q and $\bar{P}_i$, i.e., $\bar{G}_{q,i}(r) = \Pr[d(q,\bar{P}_i) \le r]$, or equivalently, it is the probability of $\bar{P}_i$ lying in the disk of radius r centered at q. A well-known result in the theory of random sampling [24, 30] implies that for all $r \ge 0$,

$$\left|G_{q,i}(r) - \bar{G}_{q,i}(r)\right| \le \alpha, \qquad (5)$$

with probability at least $1-\delta'$, provided that the constant c in $k(\alpha)$ is chosen sufficiently large.

Let $\bar{\pi}_i(q)$ denote the probability of $\bar{P}_i$ being the NN of q in $\bar{\mathcal{P}}$. We prove the following:

Lemma 3.3. *For any $q \in \mathbb{R}^2$, and for any fixed $i \le n$,*

$$|\pi_i(q) - \bar{\pi}_i(q)| \le \alpha n,$$

with probability at least $1-\delta'$.

Proof. Recall that by (1),

$$\pi_i(q) = \int_0^\infty g_{q,i}(r)\prod_{j\ne i}(1 - G_{q,j}(r))\mathrm{d}r.$$

Using (5), and the fact that $G_{q,j}(r), \bar{G}_{q,j}(r) \in [0,1]$ for all j, we obtain

$$\pi_i(q) \le \int_0^\infty g_{q,i}(r)\prod_{j\ne i}(1-\bar{G}_{q,j}(r))\mathrm{d}r + (n-1)\alpha.$$

Note that $\prod_{j\ne i}(1-\bar{G}_{q,j}(r))$ is the probability that the closest point of q in $\bar{\mathcal{P}}\setminus\{\bar{P}_i\}$ is at least distance r away from q. Let $h_{q,i}$ be the pdf of the distance between q and its closest point in $\bar{\mathcal{P}}\setminus\{\bar{P}_i\}$. Then

$$\prod_{j\ne i}(1-\bar{G}_{q,j}(r)) = \int_r^\infty h_{q,i}(\theta)\mathrm{d}\theta.$$

Therefore

$$\pi_i(q) \le \int_0^\infty\int_r^\infty g_{q,i}(r)h_{q,i}(\theta)\mathrm{d}\theta\mathrm{d}r + (n-1)\alpha.$$

By reversing the order of integration, we obtain

$$\begin{aligned}\pi_i(q) &\le \int_0^\infty\int_0^\theta h_{q,i}(\theta)g_{q,i}(r)\mathrm{d}r\mathrm{d}\theta + (n-1)\alpha\\ &= \int_0^\infty h_{q,i}(\theta)G_{q,i}(\theta)\mathrm{d}\theta + (n-1)\alpha\\ &\le \int_0^\infty h_{q,i}(\theta)(\bar{G}_{q,i}(\theta)+\alpha)\mathrm{d}\theta + (n-1)\alpha\\ &\quad\text{(using (5))}\\ &= \int_0^\infty h_{q,i}(\theta)\bar{G}_{q,i}(\theta)\mathrm{d}\theta + n\alpha\\ &= \bar{\pi}_i(q) + n\alpha.\end{aligned}$$

A similar argument shows that $\pi_i(q) \ge \bar{\pi}_i(q) - n\alpha$. This completes the proof of the lemma. □

Thus by setting $\alpha = \varepsilon/2n$, a random sample $\bar{P}_i$ of size $O((n^2/\varepsilon^2)\log(n/\delta))$ from each P_i ensures that

$$|\pi_i(q) - \bar{\pi}_i(q)| \le \varepsilon/2 \qquad (6)$$

for all queries. By choosing $\delta' = \delta/2n$, (6) holds for all $i \le n$ with probability at least $1-\delta/2$.

We consider $\mathcal{V}_{\Pr}(\bar{\mathcal{P}})$, choose one point from each of its cells, and set $\bar{Q}$ to be the resulting set of points. For a point $q \in \mathbb{R}^2$, let $\bar{q} \in \bar{Q}$ be the representative point of the cell of $\mathcal{V}_{\Pr}(\bar{\mathcal{P}})$ that contains q. Then $|\pi_i(q) - \bar{\pi}_i(\bar{q})| < \varepsilon/2$ for all points $q \in \mathbb{R}^2$ and $i \le n$, with probability at least $1-\delta/2$.

Now applying the analysis for the discrete case on the point set $\bar{\mathcal{P}}$, if we choose

$$s = O\Big(\frac{1}{\varepsilon^2}\log\frac{n|\bar{Q}|}{\delta}\Big),$$

then $|\bar{\pi}_i(q) - \hat{\pi}_i(q)| < \varepsilon$ for all points $q \in \mathbb{R}^2$ and for all $i \le n$ with probability at least $1-\delta/2$. Since

$$|\bar{P}_i| = k\Big(\frac{\varepsilon}{2n}\Big) = O\Big(\frac{n^2}{\varepsilon^2}\log\frac{n}{\delta}\Big),$$

by Lemma 3.1,

$$|\bar{Q}| = O\Big(n^4\Big(k\Big(\frac{\varepsilon}{2n}\Big)\Big)^4\Big) = O\Big(\frac{n^{12}}{\varepsilon^8}\log^4\frac{n}{\delta}\Big).$$

Putting everything together, we obtain the following.

Theorem 3.4. *Let $\mathcal{P} = \{P_1, \ldots, P_n\}$ be a set of n uncertain points in $\mathbb{R}^2$ so a random instantiation of P_i can be performed in $O(1)$ time, let $0 < \varepsilon, \delta < 1$. $\mathcal{P}$ can be preprocessed in $O((n/\varepsilon^2)\log(n/\varepsilon\delta)\log n)$ time into an index of size $O((n/\varepsilon^2)\log(n/\varepsilon\delta))$, which computes for any query point $q \in \mathbb{R}^2$, in $O((1/\varepsilon^2)\log(n/\varepsilon\delta)\log n)$ time, a value $\hat{\pi}_i(q)$ for every P_i such that $|\pi_i(q) - \hat{\pi}_i(q)| \le \varepsilon$ for all i with probability at least $1-\delta$.*

3.2 Spiral Search Algorithm

If the distribution of each point in $\mathcal{P}$ is discrete, then there is an alternative approach to approximate the quantification probabilities for a given query q: set a parameter $m > 1$, choose m points of $S = \bigcup_{i=1}^n P_i$ that are closest to q, and use only these m points to estimate $\pi_i(q)$ for each P_i. We show this works for a small value of m when, for each P_i, each location is approximately equally likely, but is not efficient if we have no bounds on the weights of these locations.

Let $P_i = \{p_{i1}, \ldots, p_{ik}\}$ and $w_{ij} = \Pr[P_i = p_{ij}]$. Set $S = \bigcup_{i=1}^n P_i$. We refer to the quantity

$$\rho = \frac{\max w_{ij}}{\min w_{ij}} \qquad (7)$$

as the *spread* of location probabilities. Set

$$m(\rho,\varepsilon) = \rho k\ln(\rho/\varepsilon) + k - 1.$$

Fix a query point $q \in \mathbb{R}^2$, and let $\bar{S} \subseteq S$ be the $m(\rho, \varepsilon)$ nearest neighbors of q in S. Let $\bar{P}_i = \bar{S} \cap P_i$, and $\bar{\mathcal{P}} = \{\bar{P}_1, \dots, \bar{P}_n\}$. Note that $\sum_{p_{i,a} \in \bar{P}_i} w_{i,a}$ is not necessarily equal to 1, so we cannot regard $\bar{P}_i$ as an uncertain point, but still it will be useful to think of $\bar{P}_i$ as an uncertain point.

For a set Y of points and another point $\xi \in \mathbb{R}^2$, let

$$Y[\xi] = \{p \in Y \mid d(q,p) \leq d(q,\xi)\}.$$

Then for a point $p := p_{i,a} \in P_i$, $\pi_p(q)$, the probability that p is the nearest neighbor of q in $\mathcal{P}$ is

$$\pi_p(q) = w_{i,a} \prod_{j \neq i} \Big(1 - \sum_{p_{j,\ell} \in P_j[p]} w_{j,\ell}\Big). \tag{8}$$

Moreover,

$$\pi_i(q) = \sum_{p_{i,a} \in P_i} \pi_{p_{i,a}}(q). \tag{9}$$

For each $i \leq n$, we analogously define a quantity $\hat{\pi}_i(q)$ using (8) and (9) but replacing P_j with $\bar{P}_j$ for every $j \leq n$. Intuitively, if $\bar{\mathcal{P}}$ were a family of uncertain points, then $\hat{\pi}_i(q)$ would be the probability of $\bar{P}_i$ being the NN of q in $\bar{\mathcal{P}}$.

Lemma 3.5. *For all $i \leq n$,*

$$|\pi_i(q) - \hat{\pi}_i(q)| \leq \varepsilon.$$

Proof. Fix a point $p \in P_i$. Set $x_j = |P_j[p]|$ and $m = \sum_{j \neq i} x_j$. Note that each $w_{j,a}$ satisfies

$$1/\rho k \leq w_{j,a} \leq \rho/k.$$

Then for a point $p := p_{i,a} \in P_i$, we obtain using (8)

$$\begin{aligned}\pi_p(q) &= w_{i,a} \prod_{j \neq i} \Big(1 - \sum_{p_\ell \in P_j[p]} w_{j,\ell}\Big) \\ &\leq \frac{\rho}{k} \prod_{j \neq i} \Big(1 - \frac{x_j}{\rho k}\Big) \\ &\leq \frac{\rho}{k} \prod_{j \neq i} \exp\left(-x_j/\rho k\right) = \frac{\rho}{k} \exp\left(-m/\rho k\right).\end{aligned}$$

Thus any point $p \in P_i$ that has $m \geq \rho k \ln(\rho/\varepsilon)$ points in $\mathcal{P} \setminus \{P_i\}$ closer to q than itself, has probability at most ε/k of being the closest point to q. Since each $P_i \in \mathcal{P}$ consists of at most k points, the combined effect of all of these far points cannot contribute more than ε to the total probability that P_i is the nearest neighbor. Also $k-1$ points from P_i may also be closer to q than p. Thus if p is not an $m(\rho, \varepsilon)$-nearest neighbor of q in S, i.e., $p \notin \bar{P}_i$, then $\pi_p(q) < \varepsilon/k$. Hence,

$$\pi_i(q) \leq \sum_{p \in \bar{P}_i} \pi_p(q) + \varepsilon = \sum_{p \in \bar{P}_i} \hat{\pi}_p(q) + \varepsilon = \hat{\pi}_i(q) + \varepsilon.$$

This completes the proof of the lemma. □

For any i, if $P_i \cap \bar{S}(q) = \emptyset$, then we can implicitly set $\hat{\pi}_i(q)$ to 0. Finally, the following result shows that the m nearest neighbors of q in S can be chosen efficiently in $\mathbb{R}^2$.

Lemma 3.6 (Afshani and Chan [1]). *Given a set of N points in $\mathbb{R}^2$, with $O(N \log N)$ expected preprocessing time and $O(N)$ space, we can return the closest m points to q in $O(m + \log N)$ time, for any query point $q \in \mathbb{R}^2$.*

We thus obtain the following result:

Theorem 3.7. *Let $\mathcal{P}$ be a set of n uncertain points in $\mathbb{R}^2$, let ρ be the spread of location probabilities, and let $\varepsilon > 0$ be a parameter. $\mathcal{P}$ can be preprocessed in $O(nk \log(nk))$ expected time into an index of $O(nk)$ size, so that for a query point $q \in \mathbb{R}^2$ and a parameter $\varepsilon > 0$, it can compute, in time $O(\rho k \log(\rho/\varepsilon) + \log(nk))$, values $\hat{\pi}_i(q)$ for all $P_i \in \mathcal{P}$ such that $|\pi_i(q) - \hat{\pi}_i(q)| \leq \varepsilon$ for all $i \leq n$.*

Remarks. (i) Unfortunately, this approach is not efficient when the spread of location probabilities is unbounded. In this case, one may have to retrieve $\Omega(n)$ points. Another approach may be to ignore points with weight smaller than ε/k, since even k such weights from a single uncertain point P_i cannot contribute more than ε to $\pi_i(q)$. However, the union of all such points may distort other probabilities.

Consider the following example. Let $p_1 \in P_1 \in \mathcal{P}$ be the closest point to the query point q. Let $w(p_1) = 3\varepsilon$. Let the next $n/2$ closest points $p_3, \dots, p_{n/2+2}$ be from different uncertain points $P_3, \dots, P_{n/2+2}$ and each have weights $w(p) = 2/(n+2) \ll \varepsilon/k$. Let the next closest point $p_2 \in P_2 \in \mathcal{P}$ have weight $w(p_2) = 5\varepsilon$. With probability $\pi_{p_1}(q) = 3\varepsilon$ the nearest neighbor is p_1. The probability that p_2 is the nearest neighbor is $\pi_{p_2}(q) = (5\varepsilon)(1-3\varepsilon)(1-2/n)^{n/2} < (5\varepsilon)(1-3\varepsilon)(1/e) < 2\varepsilon$. Thus p_1 is more likely to be the nearest neighbor than p_2. However, if we ignore points $p_3, \dots, p_{n/2+2}$ because they have small weights, then we calculate p_2 has probability $\hat{\pi}_{p_2}(q) = (1-3\varepsilon)(5\varepsilon) > 4\varepsilon$ for being the nearest neighbor. So $\pi_2(q)$ will be off by more than 2ε and it would incorrectly appear that p_2 is more likely to be the nearest neighbor than p_1.

(ii) Though Lemma 3.6 is optimal theoretically, it is too complex to be implemented. Instead, one may use order-m Voronoi diagram to retrieve the m closest points (in unsorted order) to q. This would yield an index with $O(m(nk-m))$ space and $O(m(nk-m)\log(nk) + nk\log^3(nk))$ expected preprocessing time [2], while preserving the query time $(\log(nk) + m)$, where $m = O(\rho k \log(\rho/\varepsilon))$. Alternatively, one may use quad-trees and a branch-and-bound algorithm to retrieve m points of S closest to q [20].

4. EXPERIMENTAL RESULTS

We have conducted experiments on synthetic datasets to demonstrate the efficacy of our methods for estimating qualification probabilities.

Experimental setup. We assume each uncertain point has a discrete distribution of size k. We set $r = \frac{c}{\sqrt{n}}$, where $c > 0$ is a parameter. The value of c indicates the level of uncertainty: the bigger value c is, the larger uncertainty each uncertain point has. We synthetically generated n uncertain points in two steps as follows: (1) For each uncertain point, we first generate a disk of radius r whose center is randomly chosen inside the unit square $[0,1]^2$. (2) We then choose k possible locations within the disk of each uncertain point. We chose k possible locations uniformly inside the disk (we also tried Gaussian distribution and got similar results). In our experiments, we set $n = 1000, k = 5$, and $c \in \{0.5, 1.0\}$.

Measuring the effectiveness. We test how effective the Monte Carlo method and the spiral-search methods are in computing the most likely nearest neighbor, NN_L, and the estimates of qualification probabilities. In the experiments, 1000 queries were issued for each input, and we measured the following three quantities:

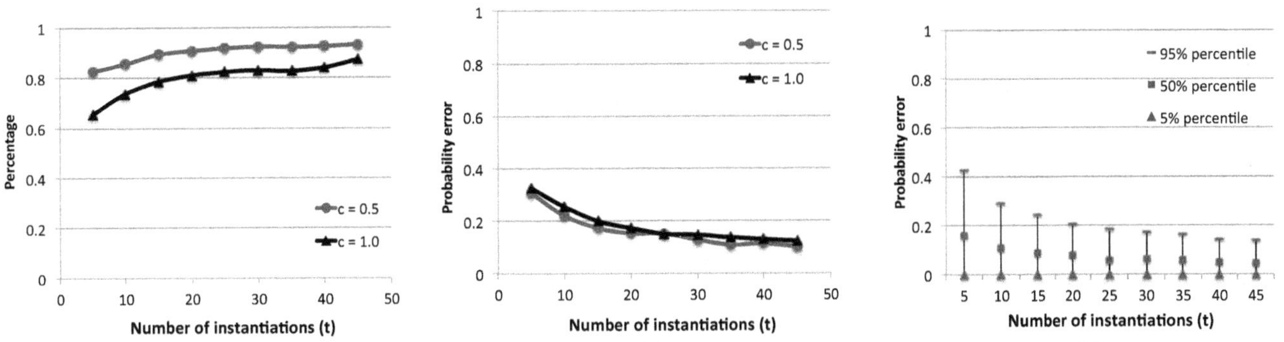

(a) (b) (c)

Figure 7. Monte Carlo method: (a) percentage of NN_L; (b) probability error of NN_L; (c) probability error of all points.

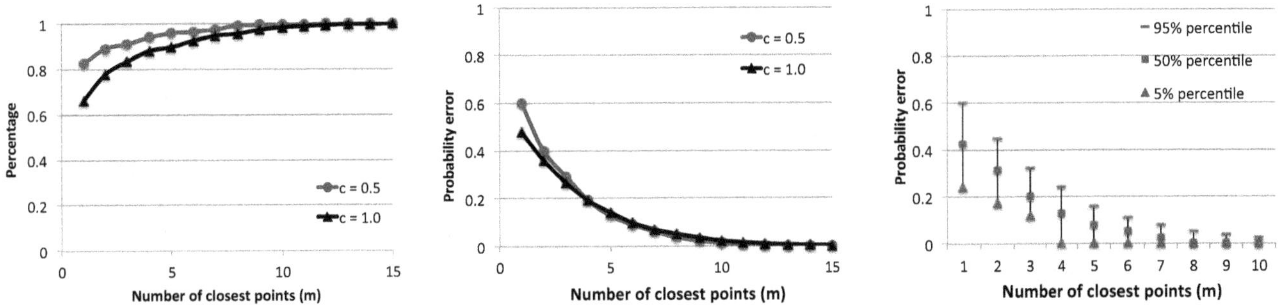

(a) (b) (c)

Figure 8. Spiral search method: (a) percentage of NN_L; (b) probability error of NN_L; (c) probability error of all points.

(i) The percentage of trials in which the algorithm returns the correct NN_L.
(ii) The error in estimated qualification probability of NN_L. Specifically for each query, suppose P_i is the true NN_L, then the *NN_L probability error* is $|\pi_i - \hat{\pi}_i|$; we report the 90% percentile of these errors.
(iii) For each query q, we compute $\max_i |\pi_i(q) - \hat{\pi}_i(q)|$, the maximum error in probability. Among all 1000 trials, we report the 5%, 50%, and 95% percentiles of these errors. We only used $c = 0.5$ for quantity (iii).

Monte Carlo method. We tested how quantities (i)-(iii) changed as we varied t, the number of instantiations t. Fig. 7(a)–(c) show these quantities as t varies from 5 to 45. Not surprisingly, as t increases, the percentage of correct NN_L increases, and the probability errors decrease. The smaller uncertainty (as denoted by c) we have, the better performance. For both $c = 0.5$ and $c = 1.0$, the NN_L is returned correctly at least 80% of the times if $t \geq 20$, and this also generally provides probability error less than 0.15.

Spiral search method. We also tested how (i) – (iii) changed as we varied m, the number of closest points retrieved to estimate the qualification probabilities. Fig. 8(a)–(c) show these quantities as m varies from 1 to 15 (or 10 in Fig. 8(c)). Compared to the Monte Carlo approach, the spiral search method accuracy seems to converge much faster (although t versus m is not directly comparable). After only $m = 9$ closest points are retrieved, the NN_L is found more than 95% of the time, and the probability error goes to practically 0. Recall $k = 5$ so from these experiments it appears retrieving only $2k$ points to be effective. This method also seems less affected by the scale of uncertainty (parameter c). Since many practical k-nearest-neighbor algorithms exist, we believe this has the potential for practical use.

5. CONCLUSION

In this paper, we investigated NN queries in a probabilistic framework in which the location of each input point is specified as a probability distribution function. We presented efficient methods for returning all the non-zero probability points, estimating the quantification probabilities and using it for threshold NN queries. We also conducted some preliminary experiments to demonstrate the effectiveness of our methods. We conclude by mentioning two open problems:

(i) What is the complexity of the probabilistic Voronoi diagram? The bound proved in Lemma 3.1 is not tight, and it does not work for continuous distributions.

(ii) Extend the spiral search method to continuous distributions (at least for some simple, well-behaved distributions such as Gaussian), so that the query time is always sublinear.

Acknowledgments. P. Agarwal and W. Zhang are supported by NSF under grants CCF-09-40671, CCF-10-12254, and CCF-11-61359, by ARO grants W911NF-07-1-0376 and W911NF-08-1-0452, and by an ERDC contract W9132V-11-C-0003. B. Aronov is supported by NSF grants CCF-08-30691, CCF-11-17336, and CCF-12-18791, and by NSA MSP Grant H98230-10-1-0210. S. Har-Peled is supported by NSF grants CCF-09-15984 and CCF-12-17462.

6. REFERENCES

[1] P. Afshani and T. M. Chan. Optimal halfspace range reporting in three dimensions. In *Proc. 20th ACM-SIAM Sympos. Discrete Algs.*, pages 180–186, 2009.

[2] P. K. Agarwal, M. de Berg, J. Matoušek, and O. Schwarzkopf. Constructing levels in arrangements and higher order Voronoi diagrams. *SIAM J. Comput.*, 27:654–667, 1998.

[3] P. K. Agarwal, A. Efrat, S. Sankararaman, and W. Zhang. Nearest-neighbor searching under uncertainty. In *Proc. 31st ACM Sympos. Principles Database Syst.*, pages 225–236, 2012.

[4] P. K. Agarwal, A. Efrat, and M. Sharir. Vertical decomposition of shallow levels in 3-dimensional arrangements and its applications. *SIAM J. Comput.*, 29:912–953, 1999.

[5] P. K. Agarwal and J. Erickson. Geometric range searching and its relatives. In B. Chazelle, J. E. Goodman, and R. Pollack, editors, *Advances in Discrete and Computational Geometry*, pages 1–56. Amer. Math. Soc., 1999.

[6] P. K. Agarwal and M. Sharir. Arrangements and their applications. In J.-R. Sack and J. Urrutia, editors, *Handbook of Computational Geometry*, pages 49–119. Elsevier, 2000.

[7] C. Aggarwal. *Managing and Mining Uncertain Data.* Springer-Verlag, 2009.

[8] P. F. Ash and E. D. Bolker. Generalized Dirichlet tessellations. *Geometriae Dedicata*, 20:209–243, 1986.

[9] T. Bernecker, T. Emrich, H.-P. Kriegel, N. Mamoulis, M. Renz, and A. Zuefle. A novel probabilistic pruning approach to speed up similarity queries in uncertain databases. In *Proc. 27th IEEE Int. Conf. Data Eng.*, pages 339–350, 2011.

[10] G. Beskales, M. A. Soliman, and I. F. Ilyas. Efficient search for the top-k probable nearest neighbors in uncertain databases. *Proc. Int. Conf. Very Large Data.*, pages 326–339, 2008.

[11] P. Cheilaris, E. Khramtcova, and E. Papadopoulou. Randomized incremental construction of the Hausdorff Voronoi diagram of non-crossing clusters. Technical Report 2012/03, University of Lugano, 2012.

[12] R. Cheng, J. Chen, M. Mokbel, and C. Chow. Probabilistic verifiers: Evaluating constrained nearest-neighbor queries over uncertain data. In *Proc. 24th IEEE Int. Conf. Data Eng.*, pages 973–982, 2008.

[13] R. Cheng, L. Chen, J. Chen, and X. Xie. Evaluating probability threshold k-nearest-neighbor queries over uncertain data. In *Proc. 12th Int. Conf. Ext. Database Tech.*, pages 672–683, 2009.

[14] R. Cheng, D. V. Kalashnikov, and S. Prabhakar. Querying imprecise data in moving object environments. *IEEE Trans. Know. Data Eng.*, 16(9):1112–1127, 2004.

[15] R. Cheng, X. Xie, M. L. Yiu, J. Chen, and L. Sun. UV-diagram: A Voronoi diagram for uncertain data. In *Proc. 26th IEEE Int. Conf. Data Eng.*, pages 796–807, 2010.

[16] N. N. Dalvi, C. Ré, and D. Suciu. Probabilistic databases: Diamonds in the dirt. *Commun. ACM*, 52(7):86–94, 2009.

[17] M. de Berg, O. Cheong, M. van Kreveld, and M. H. Overmars. *Computational Geometry: Algorithms and Applications.* Springer-Verlag, 3rd edition, 2008.

[18] J. R. Driscoll, N. Sarnak, D. D. Sleator, and R. E. Tarjan. Making data structures persistent. *J. Comput. Syst. Sci.*, 38:86–124, 1989.

[19] P. Gupta, R. Janardan, and M. Smid. Algorithms for generalized halfspace range searching and other intersection searching problems. *Comput. Geom. Theory Appl.*, 5:321–340, 1996.

[20] S. Har-Peled. *Geometric Approximation Algorithms.* Mathematical Surveys and Monographs. American Mathematical Society, 2011.

[21] D. P. Huttenlocher, K. Kedem, and M. Sharir. The upper envelope of Voronoi surfaces and its applications. In *Proc. 7th Annu. ACM Sympos. Comput. Geom.*, pages 194–203, 1991.

[22] P. Kamousi, T. M. Chan, and S. Suri. Closest pair and the post office problem for stochastic points. In *Proc. 12th Workshop Algorithms Data Struct.*, pages 548–559, 2011.

[23] H.-P. Kriegel, P. Kunath, and M. Renz. Probabilistic nearest-neighbor query on uncertain objects. In *Proc. 12th Int. Conf. Database Sys. Adv. App.*, pages 337–348, 2007.

[24] Y. Li, P. M. Long, and A. Srinivasan. Improved bounds on the sample complexity of learning. *J. Comput. Syst. Sci.*, 62(3):516–527, 2001.

[25] V. Ljosa and A. K. Singh. APLA: Indexing arbitrary probability distributions. In *Proc. 23rd IEEE Int. Conf. Data Eng.*, pages 946–955, 2007.

[26] J. Matoušek. Range searching with efficient hierarchical cuttings. *Discrete Comput. Geom.*, 10(2):157–182, 1993.

[27] R. Motwani and P. Raghavan. *Randomized Algorithms.* Cambridge University Press, 1995.

[28] J. Sember and W. Evans. Guaranteed Voronoi diagrams of uncertain sites. In *Proc. 20th Canad. Conf. Comput. Geom.*, 2008.

[29] M. Sharir and P. K. Agarwal. *Davenport-Schinzel Sequences and Their Geometric Applications.* Cambridge University Press, 1995.

[30] V. N. Vapnik and A. Y. Chervonenkis. On the uniform convergence of relative frequencies of events to their probabilities. *Theory Probab. Appl.*, 16:264–280, 1971.

[31] S. M. Yuen, Y. Tao, X. Xiao, J. Pei, and D. Zhang. Superseding nearest neighbor search on uncertain spatial databases. *IEEE Trans. Know. Data Eng.*, 22(7):1041–1055, 2010.

[32] P. Zhang, R. Cheng, N. Mamoulis, M. Renz, A. Zufile, Y. Tang, and T. Emrich. Voronoi-based nearest neighbor search for multi-dimensional uncertain databases. In *Proc. 29th IEEE Int. Conf. Data Eng.*, 2013. to appear.

On the BDD/FC Conjecture *

[Extended Abstract]

Tomasz Gogacz
Institute of Computer Science
University of Wrocław
Poland
gogo@cs.uni.wroc.pl

Jerzy Marcinkowski
Institute of Computer Science
University of Wrocław
Poland
jma@cs.uni.wroc.pl

ABSTRACT

Bounded Derivation Depth property (BDD) and Finite Controllability (FC) are two properties of sets of datalog rules and tuple generating dependencies (known as Datalog$^\exists$ programs), which recently attracted some attention. We conjecture that the first of these properties implies the second, and support this conjecture by some evidence proving, among other results, that it holds true for all theories over binary signature.

Categories and Subject Descriptors

F.4.1 [**Theory of Computation**]: Mathematical Logic and Formal Languages:Mathematical Logic; H.2.4 [**Database Management**]: Systems - Relational databasesrule-based databases, query processing

Keywords

Bounded Derivation Depth, Tuple Generating Dependencies, Finite Controllability

1. INTRODUCTION

Tuple generating dependencies (TGDs), recently known also as Datalog$^\exists$ rules, are studied in various areas, from database theory to description logics, and in various contexts. The context we are interested in here, is computing certain answers to queries in the situation when some semantical information about the database is known, and represented by some theory $\mathcal{T}$ (or a Datalog$^\exists$ program), consisting of existential TGDs and plain datalog rules, but it is assumed that our knowledge of the database facts is incomplete (this is known as the open-world assumption).

In this paradigm, for a database instance D (understood here as a set of facts – atomic formulas), the semantics of D, in presence of $\mathcal{T}$ is defined as the (*) set of all the database instances $\bar{D}$ which are supersets of D and satisfy $\mathcal{T}$. In other words, we are interested whether, for a given query[1] Φ, it holds that $\mathcal{T}, D \models \Phi$.

The problem is of course undecidable in general, so some restricted classes of theories are being studied. For example Linear Datalog$^\exists$ programs, which consist of TGDs which, as the body, have a single atomic formula, were studied in [R06], Guarded Datalog$^\exists$, being an extension of Linear (see Section 5.6 for more details) was analyzed in [BGO10] and Sticky Datalog$^\exists$ programs were introduced (in two flavors) in [CGP10] and [CGP10'].

As it turns out, decidability of query answering is not that hard to prove for theories from these classes. But there are good reasons why we would like to have more than just decidability. The desired properties of $\mathcal{T}$ are (among others) Bounded Derivation Depth property (BDD) and Finite Controllability (FC).

The theory $\mathcal{T}$ has the Finite Controllability property (for short: "$\mathcal{T}$ is FC"), if the expression "the set of all database instances" in the definition (*) above can be equivalently replaced by, more natural from the database point of view, "the set of all finite database instances". To be more precise:

Definition 1. $\mathcal{T}$ is FC if for each database instance D and each query Φ, if $\mathcal{T}, D \not\models \Phi$ then there exists a database instance $\mathcal{M}$ such that $\mathcal{M} \models D, \mathcal{T}$ but $\mathcal{M} \not\models \Phi$.

The difficult technical results in [R06] (solving an old problem stated in [JK84]) and in [BGO10] concern Finite Controllability of, respectively, Linear and Guarded Datalog$^\exists$. (Actually, the result in [R06] is stated in terms of Inclusion Dependencies rather than TGDs, which, in this context, is another language to talk about the same thing.) The question if the Sticky Datalog$^\exists$ programs are FC was left as an open problem in [CGP10] and was solved, positively, in [GM12].

The theory $\mathcal{T}$ has the Bounded Derivation Depth property (or just: "$\mathcal{T}$ is BDD") if it admits positive first order query rewriting. In other words:

Definition 2. $\mathcal{T}$ is BDD if for each query Φ there exists a union of conjunctive queries Φ' such that for every database instance D the equivalence : $\mathcal{T}, D \models \Phi$ if and only if $D \models \Phi'$ holds. (This is the definition we actually need here, but not the standard one. See Section 1.1 for an equivalent, more standard definition.)

*Supported by Polish Ministry of Science and Higher Education NCN grant N N206 371339.

[1]Whenever we say "query" in this paper we mean a conjunctive query without negation. Whenever we say "TGD" we mean a single-head tuple generating dependency.

This means that instead of computing the answer to Φ over the infinite set of databases having D as their subset (or instead of computing the answer to Φ over the infinite database $Chase(D, \mathcal{T})$ – see Section 1.1) it is enough to compute the answer to Φ' over the known finite database D. There is no need to explain how desirable in the database context BDD is, so many of the good classes of Datalog$^{\exists}$ programs (including Linear Datalog$^{\exists}$ and Sticky Datalog$^{\exists}$) are tailored to have this property. It is worth mentioning that, while of course BDD is an undecidable property of $\mathcal{T}$, still in all practical situations we know about, proving the statement "all the programs from class $\mathcal{C}$ are BDD" is an easy exercise (if it is true). This is in sharp contrast to Finite Controllability which is, as we mentioned above, typically quite hard to prove.

BDD is typically easy to prove. FC is hard to prove. But each time we had a class of BDD theories, finally we were able to show that this class is also FC. This leads to a conjecture we would like to state here:

CONJECTURE 1 (THE BDD/FC CONJECTURE). *If some theory $\mathcal{T}$, being a set of existential TGDs and plain datalog rules, is BDD then it is also FC.*

The evidence we support our conjecture with is:

THEOREM 1 (THE MAIN RESULT OF THIS PAPER). *Conjecture 1 is true for programs over binary signature.*

The proof of Theorem 1 is the main technical contribution of this paper and is, as we believe, quite difficult. It is presented in Section 3 but relies on a system of tools developed in Sections 2 and 4.

Finally, in Section 5 we discuss the possible applications of our tools and their limitations, In subsection 5.1 we show that Theorem 1 can be extended also to quite a wide class of non-binary theories (see Theorem 3). In subsection 5.4 we explain however, why our techniques do not seem to extend to the proof of Conjecture 1 in general. In subsection 5.6 we show how Guarded Datalog$^{\exists}$ programs can be seen as binary programs, and how our techniques can be easily applied in this context.

1.1 TGDs and Chase – preliminaries

Let us remind the reader that a TGD is a formula of the form $\forall \bar{x}\ (\Phi(\bar{x}) \Rightarrow \exists y\ Q(y, \bar{y}))$ where Φ is a conjunctive query, Q is a relation symbol, $\bar{x}, \bar{y}$ are tuples of variables and $\bar{y} \subseteq \bar{x}$ (see Section 5.3 for a comment on the multi-head TGDs). The universal quantifier in front of the formula is usually omitted.

Finite sets consisting of existential TGDs and plain datalog rules will be called theories.

For a theory $\mathcal{T}$ and a database instance D we denote by $Chase^1(D, \mathcal{T})$ the result of the following operation. For each tuple $\bar{x}$ in D satisfying a body of an rule $t_i = \forall \bar{x}\ (\Phi(\bar{x}) \Rightarrow \exists y\ Q(y, \bar{y}))$ form $\mathcal{T}$, such that there is no $y \in D$ satisfying $D \models Q(y, \bar{y})$), we simultaneously add new constant $c_{t_i, \bar{x}}$ into database and an atom $Q(c_{t_i, \bar{x}}, \bar{y})$.

Then define $Chase^{i+1}(D, \mathcal{T})$ as $Chase^1(Chase^i(D, \mathcal{T}), \mathcal{T})$ and by Chase denote $\bigcup_i Chase^i(D, \mathcal{T})$, which is the least fixpoint of the $Chase^1$ operator.

Clearly, we have $Chase(D, \mathcal{T}) \models D, \mathcal{T}$, but there is no reason to think that $Chase^i(D, \mathcal{T}) \models \mathcal{T}$ for any $i \in \mathbb{N}$. Note that the chase we consider in this paper is the non-oblivious one – new elements are only created if needed, as opposed to the blind Chase, which creates a new witness each time it is demanded.

Since $Chase(D, \mathcal{T})$ is a "free structure", it is very easy to see that for any query Φ (being a UCQ – a union of positive conjunctive queries) $D, \mathcal{T} \models \Phi$ (which reads as "Φ is certainly true in D, in presence of $\mathcal{T}$"), if and only if $Chase(D, \mathcal{T}) \models \Phi$.

A set $\mathcal{T}$ of TGDs is usually said to have Bounded Derivation Depth property if for each query Ψ, there is a constant $k_\Psi \in \mathbb{N}$, such that for each database instance D if $Chase(D, \mathcal{T}) \models \Psi$ then $Chase^{k_\Psi}(D, \mathcal{T}) \models \Psi$. It is easy to see ([CGT09]) that this definition of the BDD property is equivalent to Definition 2.

Notations. When we say that $\mathcal{C}$ is a structure we may mean both, the set of elements and the set of atoms of $\mathcal{C}$. If we feel this may cause confusion we write Dom($\mathcal{C}$) for the set of elements of $\mathcal{C}$. By $\mathcal{C} \models R$ (or $\mathcal{C} \models \psi$) we mean that an atom R (or a formula ψ) is true in $\mathcal{C}$. By $\mathcal{C}_1 \models \mathcal{C}_2$ we mean that each atom of $\mathcal{C}_2$ is an atom of $\mathcal{C}_1$. For a structure $\mathcal{C}$ and a set A (or a signature Σ) by $\mathcal{C} \restriction A$ (resp. by $\mathcal{C} \restriction \Sigma$) we mean the structure consisting of such atoms $R(\bar{a})$ that $\mathcal{C} \models R(\bar{a})$ and $\bar{a} \subseteq A$ (resp. $R \in \Sigma$). For a structure $\mathcal{C}$ over some signature Σ by $\mathcal{C}_{con}$ we mean, depending on context, the set of elements of $\mathcal{C}$ which are interpretations of constants from Σ or the structure $\mathcal{C} \restriction \mathcal{C}_{con}$. Similarly, by $\mathcal{C}_{non}$ we mean the set of elements of $\mathcal{C}$ which are not incarnations of constants from Σ or the structure $\mathcal{C} \restriction \mathcal{C}_{non}$.

In paper we consider only Boolean conjunctive queries. Sometimes free variables are omitted to keep the notation light. In such cases one should treat them as existentially quantified. (For example, for a query $\Phi(\bar{x})$ the term $M \models \Phi$ should be read as $M \models \exists \bar{x}\ \Phi(\bar{x})$).

2. TYPES AND PROJECTIONS

2.1 The main ideas and the structure of the proof

In order to prove Theorem 1 we need to construct, for a given BDD theory $\mathcal{T}$ over a binary signature, for a conjunctive query $Q(\bar{x})$ and for a finite structure D, such that $Chase(D, \mathcal{T}) \not\models \exists \bar{x}\ Q(\bar{x})$, a new finite structure M, such that $M \models D, \mathcal{T}$ but $M \not\models \exists \bar{x}\ Q(\bar{x})$.

Such M will always contain a substructure M' being a homomorphic image of $Chase(D, \mathcal{T})$. This M' is easy to construct inside M (if we had M): start from D, which is a substructure of both M and $Chase(D, \mathcal{T})$, and then mimic, inside M, all the applications of rules that led to the construction of $Chase(D, \mathcal{T})$.

Isn't M' itself always the finite model we are looking for? No, because it may very well happen that by identifying elements of $Chase(D, \mathcal{T})$ the homomorphism (call it q) created new instances of the bodies of the rules of $\mathcal{T}$ in M', leading to the situation when applications of rules is possible that were not applied in $Chase(D, \mathcal{T})$. For example suppose that $E(x, y), R(y, z) \Rightarrow U(y)$ is a rule of $\mathcal{T}$ and $Chase(D, \mathcal{T}) \models E(a, b), R(b', c)$, but $Chase(D, \mathcal{T}) \not\models U(b)$ and $Chase(D, \mathcal{T}) \not\models U(b')$. Suppose also that $q(b) = q(b')$. Then the fact $U(q(b))$, which may not be homomorphic image of any fact in $Chase(D, \mathcal{T})$, is provable in M. This can lead to a process in which an answer to Q is built in M, something we need to avoid. This can also lead to infinite chase, while we want M to be a finite structure. Let us illustrate this problem with one more example:

Example 1. Let $\mathcal{T}$ be a theory consisting of three rules:
$E(x,y) \Rightarrow \exists z\ E(y,z)$
$E(x,y), E(y,z), E(z,x) \Rightarrow \exists t\ U(x,t)$
$U(x,y) \Rightarrow \exists z\ U(y,z)$
and a database instance $D = \{E(a,b)\}$.

Then $Chase(D,\mathcal{T})$ is an infinite $E-chain$, beginning with a and b. Consider M' consisting of elements a, b and c and atoms $E(a,b)$, $E(b,c)$ and $E(c,a)$. Then M' is a homomorphic image of $Chase(D,\mathcal{T})$, but is not itself a model of $\mathcal{T}$ - the last rule, which was never triggered when $Chase(D,\mathcal{T})$ was built, can be used in M'. Moreover, it is easy to see that $Chase(M',\mathcal{T})$ is an infinite structure.

The idea of the construction we present in this paper is to make sure that some sort of first order type of each a in $Chase(D,\mathcal{T})$ is always the same as the type of its image $q(a)$ in the homomorphic image of $Chase(D,\mathcal{T})$. The definition of the type should be tailored in such a way that such preservation of types implies that no harmful new applications of rules from $\mathcal{T}$ for $q(a)$ exist in M.

In Section 2 we develop a sort of theory of positive types and their preservation. We built a framework in which the Main Lemma (Lemma 2) can be expressed. In Section 3 this Main Lemma is used to prove Theorem 1. In Section 4 we prove the Main Lemma. Sections 3 and 4 are independent and can be read in any order.

The two most important technical tricks of the paper can be found in proofs of Lemma 5 (in Section 3) and Lemma 11 (in Section 4). In the proof of Lemma 5 we show how the assumption that the theory $\mathcal{T}$ is BDD can be used. The trick in the proof of Lemma 11 relies on the construction, presented already in Section 2.3, where we construct not just one finite structure, but an infinite sequence of finite structures M_n that in some sense converge to $Chase(D,\mathcal{T})$. Then the idea is that if some query Ψ is true in M_{n+1} (which we do not like, as we do not want too many queries to be true in the finite structures we construct) then a query Φ, being a "one-step normalized" version of Ψ may not be true in M_{n+1} but it will be true in M_n. This then implies that if Ψ is true in all M_n then its "normal form" also is. This "converging to the Chase" trick is also used in our another paper [GM13] and we believe it can have further applications.

2.2 Positive types

Definition 3. Let $\mathcal{C}$ be a relational structure over signature Θ. Let $e \in \mathcal{C}$ and let n be a natural number. We define $ptp_n(\mathcal{C}, e, \Theta)$ (which reads "positive n-type of e in $\mathcal{C}$ over Θ") as the set of all such conjunctive queries $\Psi(\bar{x}, y)$ that:

- $|\bar{x}| < n$,
- all relations (and constants) used in Ψ are in Θ
- $\mathcal{C} \models \Psi(\bar{x}, e)$.

We assume that equality belongs to each Θ, which means that atoms of the form $x = c$ (but not of the form $x \neq c$), where x is a variable and c is a constant from Θ, are allowed in the queries.

Example 2. Let $\mathcal{T}$, D and M' be like in Example 1, and let Θ consist of E and U. Then $ptp_2(Chase(D,\mathcal{T})), a, \Theta)$ equals $ptp_2(M', a, \Theta)$, and each of them consists of the same two queries: $E(x,y)$ and $E(y,x)$. But $ptp_3(Chase(D,\mathcal{T})), a, \Theta)$ does not equal $ptp_3(M', a, \Theta)$: the query $E(y,x_1) \wedge E(x_1,x_2)$ $\wedge E(x_2,y)$ belongs to the second of those two types but not to the first one.

Remark 1. Notice that if c is a constant[2] from Θ, and if $a \neq c$ is any other element of $\mathcal{C}$, then $ptp_n(\mathcal{C}, c, \Theta) \neq ptp_n(\mathcal{C}, a, \Theta)$ for each $n \geq 1$. This is because we allowed a query of the form $y = c$, which belongs to $ptp_1(\mathcal{C}, c, \Theta)$, but not to $ptp_1(\mathcal{C}, a, \Theta)$.

All the signatures under consideration are finite, so the number of possible conjunctive queries with at most n variables is finite. In consequence the number of positive n-types is finite, for a given n.

Let us remark here that our positive n-types carry much less information than the standard first order types (in the sense of Geifman or Hanf). Take for example a structure $\mathcal{C}$, over the signature $\Theta = \{R, E\}$, consisting of elements a,b,c,d,e, and atoms $R(a,b)$, $R(a,c)$, $E(a,c)$, $E(d,e)$, $R(d,e)$. Then $ptp_2(\mathcal{C}, a, \Theta) = ptp_2(\mathcal{C}, e, \Theta)$. But the first order 2-types of a and e differ: consider for example the formula: $\psi(x) = \exists z, y\ R(x,y) \wedge E(x,z) \wedge y \neq z$. Then $\mathcal{C} \models \psi(a)$ but $\mathcal{C} \not\models \psi(d)$.

2.3 How the finite structures are born

Definition 4. Let d and e be two elements of $\mathcal{C}$. We define $d \equiv_n e$ if and only if $ptp_n(\mathcal{C}, d, \Theta) = ptp_n(\mathcal{C}, e, \Theta)$.

Notice that both the relation $\equiv_n$ and the structures $M_n(\mathcal{C})$ (as defined below) depend on Θ, and the signature should be added as a parameter in Definitions 4 and 5. We will try to avoid confusion while keeping the notation light, but when really needed we will include the parameter, writing $M_n^\Theta(\mathcal{C})$ instead of $M_n(\mathcal{C})$.

Definition 5. For a relational structure $\mathcal{C}$ define $M_n(\mathcal{C})$ as a relational structure whose set of elements is $\mathcal{C}/\equiv_n$, and such that $M_n(\mathcal{C}) \models R(< [a_i]_{\equiv_n} >_i)$ iff $\forall i\ \exists b_i \in [a_i]_{\equiv_n}$ such that $\mathcal{C} \models R(< b_i >_i)$.

In other words, the relations in $M_n(\mathcal{C})$ are defined in the natural way, as minimal (with respect to inclusion) relations such that the quotient mapping $q_n : \mathcal{C} \longrightarrow M_n(\mathcal{C})$ is a homomorphism.

We usually imagine q_n as a projection[3], so that the atoms in $M_n(\mathcal{C})$ are projections of atoms in $\mathcal{C}$.

Clearly each $M_n(\mathcal{C})$ is a finite structure.

LEMMA 1. *If $q_n(d) = q_n(e)$ then $q_{n-1}(d) = q_{n-1}(e)$. The structure $M_{n-1}(\mathcal{C})$ is a homomorphic image of $M_n(\mathcal{C})$.*

For the proof of the first claim notice that it follows from Definition 3 that if the positive n-types of two elements are equal then their positive $(n-1)$-types are also equal. The second is an easy exercise in basic universal algebra.

(♠ 1.) The function q_n, as defined above, has $\mathcal{C}$ as its domain. It will however be convenient to be able to write $q_n(a)$

[2]Strictly speaking, we mean a value of this constant in $\mathcal{C}$, but we are not always going to make this distinction.
[3]"Projection" in the geometric sense not the database sense.

also for $a \in M_{n+1}(\mathcal{C})$. In such a case $q_n(a)$ will be defined as $q_n(b)$, where $b \in \mathcal{C}$ is any element such that $q_{n+1}(b) = a$. It follows from Lemma 1 that the value of $q_n(a)$ does not depend on the choice of b.

We defined a canonical way of building finite structures. But is there any chance that they really resemble the original infinite structure? What we are particularly interested in is what happens to the positive m-types of elements of $\mathcal{C}$. Are they preserved by q_n? It is easy to see that we always have $ptp_m(\mathcal{C}, e, \Theta) \subseteq ptp_m(M_n(\mathcal{C}), q_n(e), \Theta)$. But can the inclusion be replaced with equality? Is the positive m-type of $e \in \mathcal{C}$ always the same as the positive m-type of $q_n(e)$?[4] Unfortunately this is not yet the case:

Example 3. Let $\Sigma = \{E\}$ and let $\mathcal{C}$ be the set $\{a_0, a_1, a_2 \ldots\}$ with $E(a_i, a_{i+1})$ for each i. Notice that the names of the elements a_i are not part of Σ, so they are invisible for the inhabitants of the structure, and the positive n-types of elements a_i and a_j, with $i \neq j$, are equal if and only if $i, j \geq n$. (Actually, not only the positive types of a_i and a_j are equal, but even their n-Gaifman neighborhood are isomorphic.) So $M_n^{\Sigma}(\mathcal{C})$ is a structure with elements $\{b_0, b_1, b_2, \ldots b_n\}$, with $E(b_i, b_{i+1})$ for each $i < n$ and with $E(b_n, b_n)$. Clearly, $q_n(a_n) = b_n$. But the positive 1-type of b_n in $M_n(\mathcal{C})$ contains the query $\exists y R(y, y)$, which is not in the positive 1-type of a_n in $\mathcal{C}$.

2.4 Colored structures

We are not quite happy with the quotient structure we got in Example 3. Too many elements of $\mathcal{C}$ are identified, and even a very small conjunctive query can easily see the difference between $\mathcal{C}$ and $M_n(\mathcal{C})$. But consider another example:

Example 4. Let Σ and $\mathcal{C}$ be like in Example 3. Let $\bar{\Sigma} = \Sigma \cup \{K_0, K_1, \ldots K_m\}$, where $K_0, K_1, \ldots K_m$ are unary predicates (colors) and let $\bar{\mathcal{C}}$ be like $\mathcal{C}$, but with each a_i satisfying also $K_{i \bmod (m+1)}$.

Let $n > m$. Then the positive n-types of elements a_i and a_j, with $i \neq j$, are equal if and only if $i, j \geq n$ and $i = j \mod m + 1$. So $M_n^{\bar{\Sigma}}(\bar{\mathcal{C}})$ will be a structure with elements $\{b_0, b_1, b_2, \ldots b_{n+m}\}$, with $E(b_i, b_{i+1})$ for each $i < n + m$ and with $E(b_{n+m}, b_n)$. It is not hard to see that now $ptp_m(\bar{\mathcal{C}}, a, \Sigma) = ptp_m(M_n^{\bar{\Sigma}}(\bar{\mathcal{C}}), q_n(a), \Sigma)$ for each element $a \in \bar{\mathcal{C}}$. The positive m-types of the elements of $\mathcal{C}$ are preserved by the quotient operation.

Notice however that the positive $(m+1)$-types are not preserved. This is because, unlike $\mathcal{C}$, the structure $M_n^{\bar{\Sigma}}(\bar{\mathcal{C}})$ contains a cycle of length $m+1$, which is easy to detect with a query with $m+1$ variables. If we want to preserve positive m-types for bigger numbers m we need to use more colors.

Notice also that if we took $n < m$ then we would get $ptp_m(\bar{\mathcal{C}}, a_n, \Sigma) \neq ptp_m(M_n^{\bar{\Sigma}}(\bar{\mathcal{C}}), q_n(a_n), \Sigma)$. This is because a_n would then be identified with all the elements a_{n+km+1} for $k \in \mathbb{N}$, and therefore the query

$$\exists x_1 \ldots x_{m-1} E(x_1, x_2) \wedge E(x_2, x_3) \wedge \ldots \wedge E(x_{m-1}, q_n(a_n))$$

would be satisfied in $M_n^{\bar{\Sigma}}(\bar{\mathcal{C}})$, while the query

$$\exists x_1 \ldots x_{m-1} E(x_1, x_2) \wedge E(x_2, x_3) \wedge \ldots \wedge E(x_{m-1}, a_n)$$

is not satisfied in $\bar{\mathcal{C}}$.

[4]Notice that we use two natural numbers here: n, which we imagine is big – the bigger it is the more similar $M_n(\mathcal{C})$ and $\mathcal{C}$ are, and m – the smaller it is the easier it is preserve the positive m-types.

The last example motivates the following definitions:

Definition 6. Each of the unary predicates K_h^l for some $h, l \in \mathbb{N}$ will be called a color, with the number h being called the hue of the color and the number l being called its lightness. The set of all colors will be denoted as $\mathcal{K}$.

So far we just defined an infinite set of unary predicates (with strange names, that we will need much later). Now a definition of coloring. A natural one:

Definition 7. For a structure $\mathcal{C}$ over a signature Σ by a coloring of $\mathcal{C}$ we will mean a structure $\bar{\mathcal{C}}$ over some finite signature $\bar{\Sigma}$ such that:

1. $\Sigma \subset \bar{\Sigma} \subset \Sigma \cup \mathcal{K}$
2. $\bar{\mathcal{C}} \upharpoonright \Sigma = \mathcal{C}$
3. for each $a \in \bar{\mathcal{C}}$ there is exactly one color $K \in \mathcal{K}$ such that $\bar{\mathcal{C}} \models K(a)$.

where $\bar{\mathcal{C}} \upharpoonright \Sigma$ is the structure $\bar{\mathcal{C}}$ restricted to the signature Σ.

2.5 Conservative structures

Definition 8. Let $\mathcal{C}$ be a structure and let $m, n \in \mathbb{N}$. We will say that a coloring $\bar{\mathcal{C}}$ of $\mathcal{C}$ is n-conservative up to size m if:

(♠ 2.) *$ptp_m(\mathcal{C}, e, \Sigma) = ptp_m(M_n^{\bar{\Sigma}}(\bar{\mathcal{C}}), q_n(e), \Sigma)$ for each $e \in \mathcal{C}$, where Σ and $\bar{\Sigma}$ are like in Definition 7.*

Being n-conservative up to size m means that the positive m-types (**with respect to the signature** Σ) of elements of $\bar{\mathcal{C}}$ are preserved by the quotient mapping q_n leading to the structure $M_n^{\bar{\Sigma}}(\bar{\mathcal{C}})$. So, for example, the coloring $\bar{\mathcal{C}}$ from Example 4 is n-conservative up to size m, if only $n > m$, but is not n-conservative up to size $m+1$ for any n.

Definition 9. A structure $\mathcal{C}$ is ptp-conservative if for each $m \in \mathbb{N}$ there exist $n \in \mathbb{N}$ and a coloring $\bar{\mathcal{C}}$ of $\mathcal{C}$, such that $\bar{\mathcal{C}}$ is n-conservative up to size m.

The following remark will be useful in Section 4

Remark 2. Consider a coloring $\bar{\mathcal{C}}$ of $\mathcal{C}$ and a number m. Suppose there is no such n that $\bar{\mathcal{C}}$ is n-conservative up to size m. This means that for each $n \in \mathbb{N}$ there is a query $\exists \bar{x} \Psi_n(\bar{x}, y)$, with at most m variables, and an element $e \in \mathcal{C}$ such that $M_n(\bar{\mathcal{C}}) \models \exists \bar{x} \Psi_n(\bar{x}, q_n(e))$ but $\mathcal{C} \not\models \exists \bar{x} \Psi_n(\bar{x}, e)$.

But since there are only finitely many queries of at most m variables, this implies that there is a query Ψ which is Ψ_n for infinitely many numbers n.

Notice also that if $n' < n$ and $M_n(\bar{\mathcal{C}}) \models \exists \bar{x} \Psi(\bar{x}, q_n(e))$ then $M_{n'}(\bar{\mathcal{C}}) \models \exists \bar{x} \Psi(\bar{x}, q_{n'}(e))$.

So, if there is no such n that $\bar{\mathcal{C}}$ is n-conservative up to size m then it must exist a single query $\Psi(\bar{x}, y)$, with $|x| < m$, such that for every n there is an element e of $\mathcal{C}$ such that $M_n(\bar{\mathcal{C}}) \models \exists \bar{x} \Psi(\bar{x}, q_n(e))$ but $\mathcal{C} \not\models \exists \bar{x} \Psi(\bar{x}, e)$.

2.6 Further examples and remarks

Example 5. It is very easy to see that the structure $\mathcal{C}$ from Examples 3 and 4 is ptp-conservative. Given m one just needs to define the coloring $\bar{\mathcal{C}}$ using $m+1$ colors, like in Example 4, and take $n = m+2$. Then $\bar{\mathcal{C}}$ will be n-conservative up to size m.

Example 6. Let $\mathcal{C}$ be any infinite set with a total (irreflexive) order E. Then it is easy to see that $\mathcal{C}$ is not ptp-conservative. Actually, it is impossible to find a coloring $\bar{\mathcal{C}}$ of $\mathcal{C}$ and a number n such that $\bar{\mathcal{C}}$ is n-conservative up to size 1: whatever the coloring, there would be an element e in $\mathcal{C}$ such that $M_n^{\Sigma}(\bar{\mathcal{C}}) \models E(q_n(e), q_n(e))$.

Remark 3. It is very important to see the role of the element e in Definition 8. Condition (♠ 2.), which says that each element of $\mathcal{C}$ keeps its positive type after the quotient operation, is **strictly** stronger than:

(♠ 3.) *for each conjunctive query Ψ over Σ, with at most m variables, $\mathcal{C} \models \Psi$ if and only if $M_n^{\Sigma}(\bar{\mathcal{C}}) \models \Psi$.*

which says that no new positive m-types appear in $M_n^{\Sigma}\bar{\mathcal{C}}$.

To see that, consider a theory $\mathcal{T}$ consisting of the rules:
$E(x,y) \Rightarrow \exists z\; E(y,z)$
$E(x,y), E(y,z) \Rightarrow E(x,z)$
and a database instance $D = \{E(a,a), E(b,c)\}$.

Let $\mathcal{C} = Chase(D, \mathcal{T})$. Then $\mathcal{C}$ satisfies condition (♠ 3.) (since, due to the presence of the atom $E(a,a)$, all possible queries are true in $\mathcal{C}$), but is not ptp-conservative as it contains an infinite irreflexive total order (see Example 6).

Next remark explains what Definition 9 is good for:

Remark 4. Imagine that we have some theory $\mathcal{T}$ over a binary signature Σ, and there is a existential TGD Ψ in $\mathcal{T}$ of the form $\psi(\bar{x}, y) \Rightarrow \exists z\; R(y,z)$, where m is the number of variables in x. Let $\mathcal{C} = Chase(D, \mathcal{T})$. Clearly $\mathcal{C} \models \Psi$, so if for some $e \in \mathcal{C}$ it holds that $\exists \bar{x} \psi(\bar{x}, y) \in ptp_m(\mathcal{C}, e, \Sigma)$, then there exists $d \in \mathcal{C}$ such that $\mathcal{C} \models R(e,d)$.

Suppose we now color $\mathcal{C}$ and project it, using q_n, creating some finite structure $M_n(\bar{\mathcal{C}})$. We would like to be sure that $M_n(\mathcal{C})$ is still a model (or at least some sort of pre-model) of $\mathcal{T}$. So in particular we would like to be sure that $M_n(\mathcal{C}) \models \Psi$.

But if $\bar{\mathcal{C}}$ was n-conservative up to size m, then we can be sure that whenever we have an element $a = q_n(e)$ in $M_n(\bar{\mathcal{C}})$, such that $M_n(\bar{\mathcal{C}}) \models \exists \bar{x} \psi(\bar{x}, a)$ then also $\mathcal{C} \models \exists \bar{x} \psi(\bar{x}, e)$, which implies that $\mathcal{C} \models \exists z\; R(e,z)$, which implies that $M_n(\bar{\mathcal{C}}) \models \exists z\; R(a,z)$ (notice that what we use here is really Condition (♠ 2.) and that Condition (♠ 3.) would not be strong enough)

So, if $\bar{\mathcal{C}}$ was n-conservative up to size m, then $M_n(\bar{\mathcal{C}})$ is a model of Ψ, and if $\mathcal{C}$ is ptp-conservative then we can choose m greater than the maximal size of the body of a existential TGD rule in $\mathcal{T}$ and be sure that there exists a coloring, and number n, leading to $M_n(\bar{\mathcal{C}})$ in which all the existential TGDs of $\mathcal{T}$ are satisfied.

We now know how to turn a ptp-conservative Chase $\mathcal{C}$ of $\mathcal{T}$ into a finite structure $M_n(\bar{\mathcal{C}})$ satisfying all the existential TGDs in $\mathcal{T}$. But does it mean that $M_n(\bar{\mathcal{C}}) \models \mathcal{T}$ then? As the following example shows, not necessarily, even if $\mathcal{T}$ is BDD:

Example 7. Consider the following BDD theory $\mathcal{T}$:
$E(x,y) \Rightarrow \exists z\; E(y,z)$
$E(x,y), E(x',y) \Rightarrow R(x,x')$
and a database instance $D = \{E(a,b)\}$.

Let $\mathcal{C} = Chase(D, \mathcal{T})$. Clearly, $\mathcal{C}$ is an infinite E-chain, with an atom $R(e,e)$ true for each $e \in \mathcal{C}$. Whatever coloring we now use, the only R atoms in $M_n(\bar{\mathcal{C}})$ will be the ones of the form $R(e,e)$. And whatever the coloring, there must be a triple of elements a, b, c in $M_n(\bar{\mathcal{C}})$ such that $a \neq b$ and $M_n(\bar{\mathcal{C}}) \models E(a,c), E(b,c)$, which shows that $M_n(\bar{\mathcal{C}})$ is not a model of the plain datalog rule from $\mathcal{T}$.

Of course all the above definitions – of types, of $\equiv_n$, of M_n and of conservativity, make sense also when we consider any signatures, not just binary. But Remark 4 is not valid any more for such signatures, which means that it is very hard to make sure that M_n will actually resemble a model of $\mathcal{T}$. We will be back to this point in Section 5.4.

2.7 Very Treelike DAGs and the Main Lemma

Most of the notions we defined so far apply to structures over any signature. But what we are really interested in in this paper are binary signatures. They consist of some binary relations, some unary relations and constants. Structures over such signatures can be in a natural way seen as directed graphs with edges, and vertices, labeled with some finite number of labels (i.e. the names of the relations). Thanks to that we can use the language of graphs – for example our infinite structures are usually (directed) trees or DAGs.

We will concentrate on Very Treelike DAGs:

Definition 10. For an element $e \in \mathcal{C}$ we define $\mathcal{P}(e) = \{e\}$ if $e \in \mathcal{C}_{con}$ and $\mathcal{P}(e) = \{e\} \cup \{x \in \mathcal{C}_{non} : \mathcal{C} \models R(x,e)$ for some $R \in \Sigma\,\}$ if $e \in \mathcal{C}_{non}$

Definition 11. A structure $\mathcal{C}$ is called a Very Treelike DAG (VTDAG) if $\mathcal{C}_{non}$ is a DAG and:

- for each binary relation R and each $e \in \mathcal{C}_{non}$ there is at most one $d \in \mathcal{C}_{non}$ such that $R(d,e)$;
- for each $e \in \mathcal{C}_{non}$ if $d, d' \in \mathcal{P}(e)$ then $d \in \mathcal{P}(d')$ or $d' \in \mathcal{P}(d)$.

The first condition says that each non-constant e has at most one non-constant "direct predecessor" in each binary relation. The second says that the set of "direct predecessors" of e is a (directed) clique.

Each tree is trivially a VTDAG. In order to prove Theorem 1 it is enough to restrict the attention to trees only. VTDAGs which are not trees will not be considered before Section 5.

The main tool in the proof of Theorem 1 is:

LEMMA 2. *[The Main Lemma]*
Each VTDAG is ptp-conservative.

In Section 3 we use Lemma 2 to prove Theorem 1. Then, in Section 4, we present a proof of Lemma 2. Sections 3 and 4 are independent and can be read in any order.

3. FROM THE MAIN LEMMA TO THEOREM 2

3.1 Hiding the query inside the theory

Nothing complicated happens in this subsection. We are just making some simplifying (although without loss of generality) assumptions about the BDD theory under consideration. This will help us to keep the notations simpler in the rest of Section 3

For a binary BDD theory $\mathcal{T}_0$ and a conjunctive query $Q(\bar{x}, y)$ define a new theory $\mathcal{T}$ as $\mathcal{T}_0$ enriched with a new TGD:

(♠ 4.) $Q(\bar{x}, y) \Rightarrow \exists z\ F(y, z)$

where F is a new predicate symbol. It is now easy to see that, for any database instance D such that F does not occur in D, a finite structure $\mathcal{M}$ such that $\mathcal{M} \models \mathcal{T}_0, D, \neg Q$ exists if and only if a finite structure $\mathcal{M}$ such that $\mathcal{M} \models \mathcal{T}, D, \neg F$ exists. This means that, in order to prove Theorem 1 it is enough to show:

THEOREM 2. *For a binary BDD theory $\mathcal{T}$, containing a rule of the form (♠ 4.), with predicate F not occurring anywhere else in $\mathcal{T}$, and for each database instance D, if F does not occur in $Chase(D, \mathcal{T})$ then there exists a finite structure $\mathcal{M}$ such that $\mathcal{M} \models D, \mathcal{T}$, without any atom of predicate F occurring in $\mathcal{M}$.*

From now on we assume that $\mathcal{T}$ is like in the assumptions of the above Theorem. We also assume, in order to keep the notations simple, that:

(♠ 5.)

- *the head of each existential TGD in $\mathcal{T}$ is of the form $\exists z\ R(y, z)$, which means that the witness, whose existence is demanded by the TGD, is the second argument of the predicate in the head;*
- *if the predicate R occurs as the head of some existential TGD in $\mathcal{T}$ then it does not occur as the head of any datalog rule in $\mathcal{T}$. We call such predicates TGPs – tuple generating predicates.*

We leave it for the readers as an exercise to see that every $\mathcal{T}$ can be easily modified to satisfy (♠ 5.), for the cost of some additional predicates and datalog rules, and this modification neither changes the BDD status of the theory nor its FC status.

Hint: For each predicate R in the signature introduce two new predicates R' and R''. Add to theory datalog rules $R'(x, y) \to R(x, y)$ and $R''(x, y) \to R(y, x)$. Replace each head of an existential TGD which is of the form $\exists z\ R(y, z)$ by $\exists z\ R'(y, z)$ and each head of the form $\exists z\ R(z, y)$ by $\exists z\ R''(y, z)$.

3.2 The structure $\mathcal{S}(D, \mathcal{T})$

Let now D be a database instance without atoms of F and let Θ be the signature of D and $\mathcal{T}$. Define $\Sigma \supseteq \Theta$ as a new signature which contains, apart from the relations and constants from Θ, a name for each element in D. Why do we prefer the elements of D to be named? Because we want to be sure that their positive types in $Chase(D, \mathcal{T})$ differ, and, in consequence, that they remain distinct after a quotient operation (see Remark 1).

Now we are going to define the structure to which the techniques of Section 2 will be applied. Since we want to make use of Lemma 2, this structure must be a tree (or at least a VTDAG). And of course we cannot expect $Chase(D, \mathcal{T})$ to be a VTDAG.

Definition 12. By $\mathcal{S}(D, \mathcal{T})$ (or just $\mathcal{S}$, as the context is always clear) we mean the substructure of $Chase(D, \mathcal{T})$ consisting of all the elements of $Chase(D, \mathcal{T})$, all the atoms in D and all the atoms of the TGPs. We understand that $\mathcal{S}$ is a structure over the signature Σ.

We will call the atoms in $\mathcal{S}$ *skeleton atoms*, as we imagine $\mathcal{S}$ as a sort of a skeleton of $Chase(D, \mathcal{T})$. The atoms of $Chase(D, \mathcal{T})$ which are not in $\mathcal{S}$ will be called *flesh atoms.* So the flesh atoms are the ones created in the process of chase by the datalog rules.

It follows easily from (♠ 5.) that:

LEMMA 3. *(i) The graph $\mathcal{S}_{non}$ is acyclic;*

(ii) the in-degree of any element of $\mathcal{S}_{non}$ is 1;

(iii) $\mathcal{S}_{non}$ is a forest;

(iv) the degree of the elements of $\mathcal{S}_{non}$ is bounded by $|\Sigma|+1$;

Remember that all the elements of D are constants from Σ, so they are not in $\mathcal{C}_{non}$.

PROOF. For the proof of (i) and (ii) notice that the only way a TGP atom $R(a, b)$ can be created is to be created together with a new element b. Acyclicity follows from the fact that b is always a "younger" element of $Chase(D, \mathcal{T})$ than a. The claim (iii) follows from (i) and (ii). Finally, (iv) follows from the fact, that the chase we consider is a non-oblivious one, so for any fixed $a \in \mathcal{S}$ and for any TGP R from Σ at most one $b \in \mathcal{S}$ can exist such that $\mathcal{S} \models R(a, b)$. □

Let us now think of $\mathcal{S}$ as of a new database instance:

LEMMA 4. *$Chase(D, \mathcal{T}) \models Chase(\mathcal{S}, \mathcal{T})$. In particular,* $\mathrm{Dom}(Chase(\mathcal{S}, \mathcal{T})) = \mathrm{Dom}(Chase(D, \mathcal{T})) = \mathrm{Dom}(\mathcal{S})$

For the (easy) proof of Lemma 5 see the full version. It is very easy to see that also $Chase(\mathcal{S}, \mathcal{T}) \models Chase(D, \mathcal{T})$, so we get that $Chase(D, \mathcal{T}) = Chase(\mathcal{S}, \mathcal{T})$.

The idea behind the Lemma is that while $\mathcal{S}$ is a simple structure – simple enough to be ptp-conservative – still not only it contains all elements of $Chase(D, \mathcal{T})$ but also the complete information about the relations between elements of $Chase(D, \mathcal{T})$ that need a witness and the needed witnesses. Thanks to that $Chase(D, \mathcal{T})$ can be rebuilt, starting from the skeleton $\mathcal{S}$, in a process of a (non-oblivious) chase that only triggers datalog rules, but never the existential TGDs. Notice that this would no longer be true if a single atom $R(a, a')$ was removed from $\mathcal{S}$ (even if the elements a,a' were kept, as arguments of some other atoms). This is because at some point a TGD with the head $\exists x\ R(a, x)$ would be triggered, and a **new** element a'' would be created.

3.3 Proof of Theorem 2

Recall that for a BDD theory $\mathcal{T}$ and query Ψ by Ψ' we mean the positive first order rewriting of Ψ, which means that Ψ' is such a query (a union of conjunctive queries), that for each database instance D it holds that $Chase(D, \mathcal{T}) \models \Psi \Leftrightarrow D \models \Psi'$.

Let $\kappa = \max\{|Var(\Psi')| : \Psi \Rightarrow \psi$ is a rule in $\mathcal{T}\}$. In other words, κ is the maximal number of variables in a query being a positive first order rewriting of a body of some rule of the theory $\mathcal{T}$. By Lemma 2 there exists a coloring $\bar{\mathcal{S}}$ of $\mathcal{S}$ and $\eta \in \mathbb{N}$ such that $\bar{\mathcal{S}}$ is η-ptp conservative up to the size κ, which means that the elements of $M_\eta^{\bar{\Sigma}}(\bar{\mathcal{S}})$ have the same positive κ-types over Σ as their counter-images in $\mathcal{S}$.

Now there are five structures one should imagine:

(i) $\mathcal{S}$

(ii) Chase$(D, \mathcal{T}) = Chase(\mathcal{S}, \mathcal{T})$

(iii) $M_\eta^{\bar{\Sigma}}(\bar{\mathcal{S}})$

(iv) Chase$(M_\eta^{\bar{\Sigma}}(\bar{\mathcal{S}}), \mathcal{T})$

(v) q_η(Chase$(D, \mathcal{T})$)

The first two of them were already introduced in this Section. The third is the result of the quotient operation applied to $\bar{\mathcal{S}}$ – something we discussed in Section 2. Since $\bar{\mathcal{S}}$ is η-ptp conservative up to the size κ, we know that $M_\eta^{\bar{\Sigma}}(\bar{\mathcal{S}})$ is a model for all existential TGDs in $\mathcal{T}$ (see Remark 4). But, as we saw in Example 7, we cannot be sure that $M_\eta^{\bar{\Sigma}}(\bar{\mathcal{S}}) \models \mathcal{T}$, as some datalog rules from $\mathcal{T}$ may be false in $M_\eta^{\bar{\Sigma}}(\bar{\mathcal{S}})$. So to get a model of $\mathcal{T}$ we apply chase to $M_\eta^{\bar{\Sigma}}(\bar{\mathcal{S}})$, which leads to our fourth structure, Chase$(M_\eta^{\bar{\Sigma}}(\bar{\mathcal{S}}), \mathcal{T})$. So far we know nothing about this structure, in particular we do not even know whether Chase$(M_\eta^{\bar{\Sigma}}(\bar{\mathcal{S}}), \mathcal{T})$ is finite.

The fifth structure, q_η(Chase$(D, \mathcal{T})$) is only needed in example 8 which we hope explains some issues concerning Chase$(M_\eta^{\bar{\Sigma}}(\bar{\mathcal{S}}), \mathcal{T})$. **If** you feel you not need more explanations **go directly to Lemma 5**. q_η(Chase$(D, \mathcal{T})$) is defined as:

- Dom(q_η(Chase$(D, \mathcal{T})$)) = Dom$(M_\eta^{\bar{\Sigma}}(\bar{\mathcal{S}}))$;
- relations are defined in q_η(Chase$(D, \mathcal{T})$) as the minimal relations such that q_η, understood as a mapping from Chase$(D, \mathcal{T})$ to q_η(Chase$(D, \mathcal{T})$), is a homomorphism.

So while the relations $M_\eta^{\bar{\Sigma}}(\bar{\mathcal{S}})$ are defined as projections of the skeleton relations, the relations q_η(Chase$(D, \mathcal{T})$) are projections of both, the skeleton and the flesh atoms.

One can see that Chase$(M_\eta^{\bar{\Sigma}}(\bar{\mathcal{S}}), \mathcal{T}) \models q_\eta$(Chase$(D, \mathcal{T})$). Indeed, any atom in q_η(Chase$(D, \mathcal{T})$) which is not in $M_\eta^{\bar{\Sigma}}(\bar{\mathcal{S}})$ is a projection of some flesh atom in Chase$(D, \mathcal{T})$. This last atom must have been proved by some derivation in Chase$(D, \mathcal{T})$. But a projection of a valid derivation from Chase$(D, \mathcal{T})$ is a valid derivation in Chase$(M_\eta^{\bar{\Sigma}}(\bar{\mathcal{S}}), \mathcal{T})$.

At this point it would be reasonable to conjecture that maybe q_η(Chase$(D, \mathcal{T})$) = Chase$(M_\eta^{\bar{\Sigma}}(\bar{\mathcal{S}}), \mathcal{T})$. But this is not always the case, as the following example shows:

Example 8. Let $\mathcal{T}$ and D be like in Example 7. Let $\mathcal{C} = Chase(\mathcal{T}, D)$. Now $\mathcal{S}$ is the structure $\mathcal{C}$ from Example 4. Let m be the number of colors, $n > m$ and let $\bar{\mathcal{S}}$ be a coloring of $\mathcal{S}$, like in Example 4. Now, the only R atoms in $q_n(M_n^{\bar{\Sigma}}(\bar{\mathcal{S}}))$ are atoms of the form $R(a, a)$ for some $a \in M_n^{\bar{\Sigma}}$. But it is easy to see that Chase$(M_n^{\bar{\Sigma}}, T) \models R(b_{n-1}, b_{n+m})$ (where b_{n-1}, b_{n+m} are again like in Example 4).

In the last example an atom was derived in Chase$(M_\eta^{\bar{\Sigma}}(\bar{\mathcal{S}}), \mathcal{T})$, which was not a projection of any flesh atom. The meaning of the next lemma is that while, in the process on chase on $M_\eta^{\bar{\Sigma}}(\bar{\mathcal{S}})$, some datalog derivations can arise not being projections of datalog derivations in chase on $\mathcal{S}$, still (like in Lemma 4) no existential TGDs will be used, and no new elements will be created. To be more precise:

LEMMA 5. Dom($Chase(M_\eta(\bar{\mathcal{S}}), \mathcal{T})$) = Dom$(M_\eta(\bar{\mathcal{S}}))$

For the proof of Lemma 5 see the full version. This proof is not very long but we believe it is quite tricky. It is here where things really happen: Lemma 2 meets the assumption that $\mathcal{T}$ is BDD.

As we show in Section 5.4, there is no hope to have anything similar to Lemma 5 in the general (non-binary) case.

We are ready to present the **proof of Theorem 2:**

In order to prove Theorem 2 (and, in consequence, Theorem 1) we need to show a finite model of D and $\mathcal{T}$ without any atom of the predicate symbol F. The structure $Chase(M_\eta(\bar{\mathcal{S}}), \mathcal{T})$ is clearly a model of $D, \mathcal{T}$. It follows from the Lemma 5 that its domain is exactly the domain of $M_\eta(\bar{\mathcal{S}})$, so it is finite.

Since no atom of the relation F occurs in $\mathcal{S}$ there is also no such atom in $M_\eta(\bar{\mathcal{S}})$. So the only way any such atom could appear in $Chase(M_\eta(\bar{\mathcal{S}}), \mathcal{T})$ would be to derive it in the process of chase. But the only rule that derives F is a existential TGD which demands a new element, and no such rule could have been used, due to Lemma 5. □

4. PROOF OF THE MAIN LEMMA

Fix a VTDAG $\mathcal{C}$ and a natural number m. Let Σ be the signature of $\mathcal{C}$. To prove Lemma 2 we need to find $n \in \mathbb{N}$ and a coloring $\bar{\mathcal{C}}$ of $\mathcal{C}$ such that $\bar{\mathcal{C}}$ is n-conservative up to the size m.

First let us define the coloring:

Definition 13. For $e \in \mathcal{C}$ let $\mathcal{P}(e)$ be like in Definition 10.

- For $e \in \mathcal{C}_{non}$ let $\mathcal{P}_0(e) = \mathcal{P}(e)$.
- For $e \in \mathcal{C}_{non}$ let $\mathcal{P}_k(e) = \bigcup_{a \in \mathcal{P}_{k-1}(e)} P(a)$

Definition 14. A coloring $\bar{\mathcal{C}}$ of $\mathcal{C}$ will be called natural if it satisfies the following conditions:

- if $e, e' \in \mathcal{C}$ are such that $e' \in \mathcal{P}_m(e)$ and if $\bar{\mathcal{C}} \models K_h^l(e), K_{h'}^{l'}(e')$ then $h \neq h'$;
- if $e, e' \in \mathcal{C}$ are such that $\bar{\mathcal{C}} \models K_h^l(e), K_{h'}^l(e')$ then $\mathcal{C} \upharpoonright (\mathcal{P}(e) \cup \mathcal{C}_{con})$ and $\mathcal{C} \upharpoonright (\mathcal{P}(e') \cup \mathcal{C}_{con})$ are isomorphic.

It is easy to see that for each VTDAG $\mathcal{C}$ there exists a natural coloring $\bar{\mathcal{C}}$. From now on by $\bar{\mathcal{C}}$ we will mean a fixed natural coloring of $\mathcal{C}$.

By Remark 2 the proof of Lemma 2 will be finished when we show:

LEMMA 6. *For each query $\Phi(\bar{x}, y)$ over Σ, with $|\bar{x}| < m$, there exists $n \in \mathbb{N}$ such that for each element $e \in \mathcal{C}$:*
$M_n(\bar{\mathcal{C}}) \models \exists \bar{x} \Phi(\bar{x}, q_n(e))$ if and only if $\mathcal{C} \models \exists \bar{x} \Phi(\bar{x}, e)$

Proof of Lemma 6 begins here.
It will take till the end of Section 4 to finish.

First of all notice that if the Lemma 6 was false, then there would exists a **counterexample** – a conjunctive query $\Phi(\bar{x}, y)$ such that:

(♣) for each $n \in \mathbb{N}$ there exists an element e_n^Φ of $\mathcal{C}$ and a valuation $\sigma_n^\Phi : Var(\Phi) \to M_n(\bar{\mathcal{C}})$, with $\sigma_n^\Phi(y) = q_n(e_n^\Phi)$, such that $M_n(\bar{\mathcal{C}}) \models \sigma_n^\Phi(\Phi)$ and $\mathcal{C} \not\models \exists\bar{x}\Phi(\bar{x}, e_n^\Phi)$.

Each time we will say that query Φ is a counterexample we will think that is satisfies condition (♣).

By a colors statement we will mean a query of the form:

$$\bigwedge_{z \in Var(\Phi)} K_{h_z}^{l_z}$$

where $K_{h_z}^{l_z}$ is any of the possible colors from $\mathcal{K}$. By a color closure of Φ we will mean any query of the form $\Phi \wedge \Upsilon$, where Υ is a colors statement. Of course there are finitely many colors statements, and so there are finitely many possible color closures of Φ. A query which is a color closure of some other query will be called color closed.

LEMMA 7. *(i) Let Φ be a counterexample. Then for each n there is a query Φ_c, being a color closure of Φ, such that $M_n(\bar{\mathcal{C}}) \models \sigma_n^\Phi(\Phi_c)$ and $\bar{\mathcal{C}} \not\models \exists\bar{x}\Phi_c(\bar{x}, e_n^\Phi)$.*

(ii) For each counterexample Φ there exists a color closure $\bar{\Phi}$ of Φ, which also is a counterexample.

(iii) If there exists a query Φ being a color closed counterexample, then there also exists another color closed counterexample Ψ such that for each constant c from Σ, for each variable $z \in Var(\Psi)$ and for each $n \in \mathbb{N}$ there is $\sigma_n^\Psi(z) \neq c$, where σ_n^Ψ is as (♣). We will say that counterexample Ψ avoids constants.

PROOF. (i) The elements $\sigma_n^\Phi(z)$, where $z \in Var(\Phi)$ have some colors. Adding to Φ a statement asserting that they have the colors they really have will not make the new query $\sigma_n(\Phi_C)$ less true in $M_n(\bar{\mathcal{C}})$ than $\sigma_n^\Phi(\Phi)$ was.

On the other hand, $\exists\bar{x}\Phi(\bar{x}, e_n)$ was false in $\mathcal{C}$ already before the color statement was added and adding more constraints never makes a query more true.

(ii) Use (i) and an argument like in Remark 2.

(iii) Suppose Φ is a color closed counterexample and $\sigma_n^\Phi(z) = c$ for some constant $c \in \Sigma$, some variable $z \in Var(\Psi)$ and some $n \in \mathbb{N}$. By the definition of natural coloring, the color of c is unique in $\mathcal{C}_{con}$ and thus the equality $\sigma_n^\Phi(z) = c$ must hold for each n, and thus Ψ being the result of replacing each occurrence of z in Φ by c is also a counterexample. □

We are now going to view queries as graphs. What we mean here is a sort of Gaifman graphs, where vertices are the variables in the query and the edges are the atoms of the query. As we only have binary and unary atoms, we can in a natural way see each query as a directed (labeled) graph. Concerning the constants in the query, they are not understood to be vertices in the graph, and it is good to think that an atom of the form $R(a, x)$ in a query, where a is a constant and x is a variable, is just a unary predicate, telling us something about x alone. Notice that atoms of the form $R(a, b)$ in a query, where both a and b are constants, are irrelevant from the point of view of Lemma 6, as the part of $\mathcal{C}$ consisting of the constants remains unchanged after our projections.

Now our plan of the proof of Lemma 6 is as follows. We want to show that no query is an avoiding constants color closed counterexample. So first we will notice (Lemma 8 and Lemma 9) that neither a query being an undirected tree, nor a query containing a directed cycle can ever be a counterexample. At this point we will know that if there is any avoiding constants color closed counterexample Φ then Φ must contain an undirected cycle (but not a directed one). But then, in Lemma 10 we show that if such a Φ existed, then also another counterexample would exist, being a tree or containing a directed cycle. That would however contradict Lemma 8 and Lemma 9.

Proofs of Lemma 8 and Lemma 9 are easy. Proof of Lemma 10, where we deal with queries containing an undirected cycle, is much more complicated. A technique of normalization of queries is used there, which we find to be the deepest idea of this paper (we also employ this technique, in different context, in [GM12], where it is called *second little trick*). Why are the undirected cycles in the query so much harder to deal with than directed ones? The answer is in:

Example 9. Let a theory $\mathcal{T}$ consist of the rules:

$F(x, y) \Rightarrow \exists z\ F(y, z)$ $\qquad$ $F(x, y) \Rightarrow \exists z\ G(y, z)$
$G(x, y) \Rightarrow \exists z\ F(y, z)$ $\qquad$ $G(x, y) \Rightarrow \exists z\ G(y, z)$

Let $D = \{F(a, b)\}$ and let $\mathcal{C}$ be $Chase(D, \mathcal{T})$, which means that $\mathcal{C}$ is an infinite tree, where each element has exactly two successors. Or, in other words, $\mathcal{C}$ consists, except from a and b, of all the elements $w(b)$, where $w \in \{f, g\}^*$. Let $\bar{\mathcal{C}}$ be a natural coloring of $\mathcal{C}$.

Let e_1, e_2 be two elements of $\mathcal{C}$ of the form $e_1 = vfw(b)$, $e_2 = vgw(b)$, where $v, w \in \{f, g\}^*$ and where $|v| = n - 1$.

Then $a_1 = q_n(e_1) \neq q_n(e_2) = a_2$ are two distinct elements of $M_n(\bar{\mathcal{C}})$ – the length of v is not big enough to hide the slight difference in the positive types of e_1 and e_2. Of course also $a_3 = q_n(f(e_1)) \neq q_n(g(e_1)) = a_4$ are two distinct elements (each of them distinct than a_1 and a_2). But $a_3 = q_n(f(e_2))$ and $a_4 = q_n(g(e_2))$. This means that the atoms $F(a_1, a_3), F(a_2, a_3), G(a_2, a_4), G(a_1, a_4)$ are all true in $M_n(\bar{\mathcal{C}})$, and so there is an undirected cycle in $M_n(\bar{\mathcal{C}})$ consisting of 4 distinct elements.

As we saw in Example 4, by using coloring we can easily make sure that there are no small directed cycles in $M_n(\bar{\mathcal{C}})$. But we cannot rule out small undirected new (not present in $\bar{\mathcal{C}}$) cycles in $M_n(\bar{\mathcal{C}})$. So we need to prove that, while the new cycles exist, no small query can actually notice them.

LEMMA 8. *Let $n \geq m$. Then for each element $e \in \mathcal{C}$ and each query $\Psi(\bar{x}, y)$, which is an undirected tree: $\Psi \in ptp_m(\bar{\mathcal{C}}, e, \Sigma)$ if and only if $\Psi \in ptp_m(M_n(\bar{\mathcal{C}}), q_n(e), \Sigma)$.*

It of course follows from the lemma that no query being an undirected tree can be a counterexample.

LEMMA 9. *Let $n \geq m$. Suppose Φ is a query containing a directed cycle, by which we mean a sub-query of the form: $R_1(x_1, x_2), R_2(x_2, x_3), \ldots R_{k-1}(x_{k-1}, x_k), R_k(x_k, x_1)$ where $k < m$ and R_i are relation symbols from Σ. Then $M_n(\bar{\mathcal{C}}) \not\models \Phi$.*

Clearly, as being a counterexample means, among other conditions, being true in $M_n(\bar{\mathcal{C}})$, the lemma implies that Φ, containing a directed cycle, never is a counterexample.

For the proofs of Lemma 8 and 9 see the full version. Now, Lemma 6 follows from Lemma 7, Lemma 8, Lemma 9 and from the following:

LEMMA 10. *If there exists a color closed counterexample Φ which avoids constants and which contains an undirected cycle then there exists also a counterexample being a tree or a counterexample containing a directed cycle.*

4.1 Proof of Lemma 10

Consider a query $\Psi(\bar{x}, y)$ which contains an undirected cycle, which is not a directed cycle. Then Ψ must be of the form:

($\heartsuit$) $R_1(z', z) \wedge R_2(z'', z) \wedge \psi(\bar{x}, y)$

for some relations $R_1, R_2 \in \Sigma$ and some $z, z', z'' \in Var(\Psi)$.

LEMMA 11 (NORMALIZATION OF QUERIES). *If any color closed, avoiding constants, query $\Psi(\bar{x}, y)$ of the form ($\heartsuit$) is a counterexample, then there is a binary relation $P \in \Sigma$ such that one of the following queries is also a color closed, avoiding constants, counterexample:*

- $\psi(\bar{x}, y) \wedge R_1(z', z) \wedge z' = z''$
- $\psi(\bar{x}, y) \wedge R_1(z', z) \wedge P(z'', z')$
- $\psi(\bar{x}, y) \wedge R_2(z'', z) \wedge P(z', z'')$

To see how Lemma 11 implies Lemma 10, **while** Ψ is a counterexample of the form ($\heartsuit$) **do** replace it with another counterexample, the one whose existence is assured by Lemma 11. The only way to leave the while-loop is to produce a counterexample which is a tree or contains a directed cycle. So it is enough to prove that the while-loop indeed terminates.

If the first possibility from the Lemma is used as the replacement, then the new query has less variables than the old one (since adding an equivalence of variables is the same as unifying the variables). But the last two possibilities do not decrease the number of variables. So aren't they going to be applied forever? Consider the following measure of the size of a query:

$$\text{Measure}(\Phi) = \Sigma_{x \in Var(\Psi)}\, occ(x) smaller(x)$$

where $occ(x)$ is the number of the occurrences of variable x in Ψ and $smaller(x)$ is the number of variables from which x is reachable by a directed path in the graph of the query. It is easy to see that Measure(Ψ) is a natural number which decreases each time Lemma 11 is applied.

Before we prove Lemma 11 notice that the first condition in Definition 11 implies:

LEMMA 12. *Suppose a, b, c, d are non-constant elements of $\bar{\mathcal{C}}$, such that $\bar{\mathcal{C}} \models R(a, b), R(c, d)$ for some relation $R \in \Sigma$. Then $b \equiv_n d$ implies $a \equiv_{n-1} c$.*

PROOF. Suppose there was a query $\psi(\bar{x}, y)$, with $|\bar{x}| < n - 1$, such that $\bar{\mathcal{C}} \models \exists \bar{x} \psi(\bar{x}, a)$ but $\bar{\mathcal{C}} \not\models \exists \bar{x} \psi(\bar{x}, c)$. Then $\bar{\mathcal{C}} \models \exists \bar{x} x' \psi(\bar{x}, x') \wedge R(x', b)$ but $\bar{\mathcal{C}} \not\models \psi(\bar{x}, x') \wedge R(x', d)$. But this would mean that $b \not\equiv_n d$. Notice that the assumption that $\mathcal{C}$ is a VTDAG was used here. □

Proof of Lemma 11 Suppose Ψ is a color closed counterexample of the form ($\heartsuit$). Consider the color of z (call it color(z)). More precisely, color(z) is the color that is enforced by Ψ on any valuation of z that satisfies Ψ . What we are interested in is not really the full information about color(z), but its lightness – the information about the isomorphic type of $\mathcal{P}(e)$ for any $e \in \bar{\mathcal{C}}$ having the color that Ψ enforces on z.

Now please be ready for the most complicated argument of this paper. Let e be like in the previous paragraph. The set $\mathcal{P}(e)$ contains some elements e' and e'' such that $R_1(e', e) \wedge R_2(e'', e)$ are true in $\bar{\mathcal{C}}$. It follows from Definition 11 that in such case there must be an atom $Q(e', e'')$ true in $\bar{\mathcal{C}}$, where $Q(e', e'')$ is either $P(e', e'')$ or $P(e'', e')$ for some relation $P \in \Sigma$, or $e' = e''$ (this happens when $R_1 = R_2$). Notice that the atom Q only depends on the color of z not on the choice of e. Suppose Q is $P(e', e'')$, the other two possibilities are analogous. Now, we claim that $\Phi = \psi(\bar{x}, y) \wedge R_2(z'', z) \wedge P(z', z'')$ is also a counterexample, with $\sigma_n^\Phi = q_n \circ \sigma_{n+1}^\Psi$, $e_n^\Phi = e_{n+1}^\Psi$ and σ_n.

Notice that we use the notation q_n here in the sense defined in (♠ 1.): σ_{n+1}^Ψ, for an argument being a variable of Ψ (or Φ – they have the same set of variables) returns an element of $M_{n+1}(\bar{\mathcal{C}})$ and q_n for an argument from $M_{n+1}(\bar{\mathcal{C}})$ returns an element of $M_n(\bar{\mathcal{C}})$.

We need to show that the conditions from (♣) are now satisfied. It is easy to see that $\sigma_n^\Phi(y) = q_n \circ \sigma_{n+1}^\Psi(y) = q_n(e_{n+1}^\Psi) = q_n(e_n^\Phi)$.

What remains to be shown is that for each $n \in \mathbb{N}$:

(*) $M_n(\bar{\mathcal{C}}) \models \sigma_n^\Phi(\Phi)$ and (**) $\bar{\mathcal{C}} \not\models \exists \bar{x} \Phi(\bar{x}, e_n^\Phi)$.

Let us begin with (**), which is easier. Suppose $\bar{\mathcal{C}} \models \Phi(\bar{x}, e_n^\Phi)$. So there exists a valuation $\gamma : Var(\Phi) \to \bar{\mathcal{C}}$, with $\gamma(y) = e_n^\Phi$, such that $\bar{\mathcal{C}} \models \gamma(\Phi)$. Notice that $\gamma(y) = e_{n+1}^\Psi$. We claim that $\bar{\mathcal{C}} \models \gamma(\Psi)$ and this will be in contradiction with what we assumed about Ψ and e_{n+1}^Ψ.

For the proof of the last claim it is enough to show that $\bar{\mathcal{C}} \models R_1(\gamma(z'), \gamma(z))$, as this is the only atom of Ψ missing in Φ. But this follows from what we know about the isomorphic type of $\gamma(z)$, from the fact that $\bar{\mathcal{C}} \models P(\gamma(z'), \gamma(z'')) \wedge R_2(\gamma(z''), \gamma(z))$ and from the assumption that the in-degree of each of the relations in $\bar{\mathcal{C}}$ is at most 1 (first condition in Definition 11).

Now we are going to prove (*). We know that $M_{n+1}(\bar{\mathcal{C}}) \models \sigma_{n+1}^\Psi(\Psi)$, so also $M_n(\bar{\mathcal{C}}) \models q_n \circ \sigma_{n+1}^\Psi(\Psi)$. What remains to be proved is that

(*) $M_n(\bar{\mathcal{C}}) \models P(q_n \sigma_{n+1}^\Psi(z'), q_n \sigma_{n+1}^\Psi(z''))$.

We know that $M_n(\bar{\mathcal{C}}) \models R_1(\sigma_{n+1}^\Psi(z'), \sigma_{n+1}^\Psi(z))$ and that $M_n(\bar{\mathcal{C}}) \models R_2(\sigma_{n+1}^\Psi(z''), \sigma_{n+1}^\Psi(z))$. This means that there are elements a', a, b'', b of $\bar{\mathcal{C}}$ such that: $q_{n+1}(a) = q_{n+1}(b) = \sigma_{n+1}^\Psi(z)$, $q_{n+1}(a') = \sigma_{n+1}^\Psi(z')$, $q_{n+1}(a'') = \sigma_{n+1}^\Psi(z'')$ and $\bar{\mathcal{C}} \models R_1(a', a) \wedge R_2(b'', b)$. The color of a and of b is the color of z, so the isomorphic type of $\mathcal{P}(a)$ is the same as the isomorphic type of $\mathcal{P}(b)$, and the same as the isomorphic type of $\mathcal{P}(e)$, where e is as in the beginning of Lemma 11. This means that there is an element $a'' \in \bar{\mathcal{C}}$ such that $\bar{\mathcal{C}} \models R_2(a'', a)$ and $\bar{\mathcal{C}} \models P(a'', a')$. There is no reason to think that $a'' \equiv_{n+1} b''$. But from Lemma 12 we get that $a'' \equiv_n b''$. So a'' and a are two elements of $\bar{\mathcal{C}}$ such that $\bar{\mathcal{C}} \models R_2(a'', a)$, that $q_n(a) = q_n \sigma_{n+1}^\Psi(z)$ and that $q_n(a'') = q_n \sigma_{n+1}^\Psi(z'')$. □

This ends the proofs of Lemmas 10,11 , 6 and 2.

5. DISCUSSION

5.1 Beyond the binary case (slightly)

As a careful reader might already have noticed, our proof of Theorem 2 can also be read as a proof of:

THEOREM 3. *Let $\mathcal{T}$ be a set of existential TGDs and plain datalog rules, with each of its existential TGDs of the form: $\Psi(\bar{x}, y) \Rightarrow \exists \bar{z}\ \Phi(y, \bar{z})$. Then, if $\mathcal{T}$ is BDD, then it is also FC.*

It is because in the proof of Theorem 2 we only used the binarity assumption for heads of existential TGDs.

Notice that we can rewrite existential TGDs from Theorem 3 into conjunction of existential TGDs with binary heads and some arbitrary datalog rules. Hence the whole proof of Theorem 2 survives.

Hint: For each TGD $\Psi(\bar{x}, y) \Rightarrow \exists \bar{z}\ \Phi(y, \bar{z})$ we add new relational symbols $R^1_\Phi(y, z_1) \dots R^n_\Phi(y, z_n)$ where $n = |\bar{z}|$. We add to the theory rules $\Psi(\bar{x}, y) \Rightarrow \exists \bar{z}\ R^i_\Phi(y, z_i)$ and datalog rules $R^1_\Phi(y, z_1) \wedge \dots \wedge R^n_\Phi(y, z_n) \to \Phi(y, \bar{z})$.

5.2 The ternary case

Usually, once we know that some property holds for binary signatures, it is easy to prove, by some sort of reduction, that it remains true in the general case. This rule does not seem to be valid for the BDD/FC conjecture. What we can however easily show is:

THEOREM 4. *If the BDD/FC conjecture for ternary signatures is true then it is true in the general case.*

Instead of presenting a detailed proof of the theorem, which would be boring, let us show an example of how the reduction works. Suppose we have a theory $\mathcal{T}$ with a rule like:

(*) $P(x, y, z, x) \Rightarrow \exists t\ R(x, y, z, t)$

then rewrite it into the following three rules:

$P(x, y, z, x) \Rightarrow \exists w_1\ R_1(x, y, w_1)$

$P(x, y, z, x) \wedge R_1(x, y, w_1) \Rightarrow \exists w_2\ R_2(w_1, z, w_2)$

$P(x, y, z, x) \wedge R_1(x, y, r) \wedge R_2(r, z, s) \Rightarrow \exists t\ R'(s, t)$

The idea is here that using ternary predicates we can give names to lists of variables, in the good old Prolog way. We appear to still have non-ternary predicates in the bodies of the rules. But just don't think of them as of predicates any more! The P in the body of (*) is just a view over the real predicates P_1, P_2 and P' now, which relate to P in the same was as R_1, R_2 and R' relate to R.

In this way we constructed a new, ternary theory, call it $\mathcal{T}'$. What we would now need to show (if it was a real detailed proof) would be that (i) if $\mathcal{T}$ is BDD then $\mathcal{T}'$ also is, and (ii) if $\mathcal{T}'$ is FC then $\mathcal{T}$ also is. To see how (ii) works take a database instance D and query Q. Rewrite D and Q into D' and Q' in the new ternary language (possibly adding some new elements to denote lists of elements of D). Of course if $Chase(\mathcal{T}, D) \not\models Q$ then also $Chase(D', \mathcal{T}') \not\models Q'$. So, if $\mathcal{T}'$ is FC, there exists a finite $\mathcal{M}'$ being a model of $\mathcal{T}'$ and D' such that $\mathcal{M}' \not\models Q'$. Now, to finish the proof of (i), define the relations of $\mathcal{M}$ as views over respective relations in $\mathcal{M}'$.

Showing (i) is not really hard either.

5.3 Multi-head TGDs

The TGDs we consider in this paper are assumed to be single-head. Of course if the arity is not restricted, then the validity of the BDD/FC conjecture does not depend on this assumption, as every multi-head TGD Ψ can be replaced by a single-head TGD having, as its head, the join of all the atoms in the head of Ψ, and by some datalog rules splitting this join back into smaller atoms. But such a simple transformation is not possible for binary signatures. It is actually easy to see that the BDD/FC conjecture for multi-head TGDs over binary signatures is already equivalent to the full conjecture, as any ternary Datalog$^\exists$ program can be encoded in this format. For example the rule:

$P_1(x, y, z) \wedge P_2(x, y, z') \Rightarrow \exists w\ P(x, z, w)$

can be encoded as (read $A^i(t, x)$ as "x is the i'th argument in the atom t"):

$A^1_{P_1}(t_1, x) \wedge A^2_{P_1}(t_1, y) \wedge A^3_{P_1}(t_1, z) \wedge A^1_{P_2}(t_2, x) \wedge A^2_{P_2}(t_2, y) \wedge A^3_{P_2}(t_2, z') \Rightarrow \exists t\ A^1_P(t, x) \wedge A^2_P(t, y)$

and $A^1_P(t, x) \wedge A^2_P(t, y) \Rightarrow \exists w\ A^3_P(t, w)$.

5.4 Why M_n are too poor to be models (in the non-binary case)

The main idea of our proof of Theorem 1 was first to find, for a BDD theory $\mathcal{T}$ and a database instance D the skeleton $\mathcal{S}$ which is a substructure of $Chase(D, \mathcal{T})$ on one hand being simple enough to be ptp-conservative, but on the other hand not only containing all the elements of $Chase(D, \mathcal{T})$, but also sufficient information about the relations between elements which require a witness and the witnesses. Then the idea was to prove (Lemma 5) that the finite model M_n constructed from this simple structure by a quotient operation can be saturated, using the datalog rules from $\mathcal{T}$, to a model of $\mathcal{T}$, without adding any new elements being necessary.

The first reason this line of reasoning cannot be used in the general (non-binary) case is that the distinction between existential TGDs and plain datalog rules makes then no sense any more: each datalog rule can be turned into a TGD by adding a new (existentially quantified) dummy variable to the atom on the right hand side of the query. But what we view as an even more serious obstacle is that, as the following example shows, it is hard to imagine how anything analogous to Lemma 5 could be true in the general case:

Let the rules of $\mathcal{T}$ be: $R(x, x', y, z) \Rightarrow E(y, z)$

and $E(x, y), E(t, y) \Rightarrow \exists z\ R(x, t, y, z)$

and let a database instance D be $\{E(a, b)\}$.

Clearly, $\mathcal{T}$ is BDD. And $\mathcal{C} = Chase(D, \mathcal{T})$ is a very simple structure: an infinite E-chain, with additional atom $R(x, x, y, z)$ for each three consecutive elements x, y, z of this chain. But whenever any two elements of $\mathcal{C}$ are identified by a quotient operation, a new tuple satisfying the body of the (only) TGD form $\mathcal{T}$ emerges (something we have already seen in Example 7), and a new witness z is required for this tuple. Since the new witness is a function of the whole tuple, not just of (the element substituted for) y, the (already existing) element t of $M_n(\bar{\mathcal{C}})$ such that $E(y, t)$ cannot be used now, and a new one must be created. If there was just one element this would be something we could live with – our main goal is just to keep the structure finite. But notice that once the new witness z, with $E(y, z)$ is created, it enforces a new infinite E-chain to be built.

5.5 Beyond BDD. The dead end of the ordering conjecture

Anyone asked to give some examples of theories which are not FC will begin from the most natural one – the infinite total ordering from Remark 3.

And it is not immediately clear how to come out with something really different. For quite some time, we believed that the following conjecture could be true:

CONJECTURE 2 (FALSE). *$\mathcal{T}$ is not FC if and only if $\mathcal{T}$ defines an ordering, by which we mean that there exists a database instance D, an infinite set $A \subseteq Chase(D, \mathcal{T})$ and a query $\Phi(x, y)$, which is a conjunctive query with projections,* *with two free variables, such that $Chase(D, \mathcal{T}) \not\models \exists \bar{x} \Phi(x, x)$ and Φ defines a strict total ordering on A.*

Notice how beautiful it would be. Even if our BDD/FC conjecture is true (which we believe it is) it does not give a full explanation of the phenomenon of Finite Controllability, as they are many theories (for example guarded) which are FC but not BDD. Had Conjecture 2 be true, it would have given a sort of such explanation, and a very elegant one, since the above property of "defining an ordering" is very close to (the negation of) the standard, and very important, model-theoretic notion of stability [S69]. Besides, it could give the BDD/FC conjecture as a corollary, if we only could prove that a BDD theory never defines an ordering, which we believe should not be very hard.

Clearly, the "if" implication of the conjecture holds true: if D, A and Φ like in the conjecture existed, then $\exists x \Phi(x, x)$ would be a query false in $Chase(D, \mathcal{T})$ but true in each finite model of $\mathcal{T}, D$ (as each such finite model must contain a homomorphic image of $Chase(D, \mathcal{T})$, and some two elements of A must be mapped, by this homomorphism, to the same element of the finite structure)

However, as the following notorious example shows, the opposite implication is not true. Let $\mathcal{T}$ be:

$E(x, y) \Rightarrow \exists z \; E(y, z)$

$R(x, y), E(x, x'), E(y, z), E(z, y') \Rightarrow R(x', y')$

It is not hard to see that $\mathcal{T}$ does not define an ordering. We are going to show that $\mathcal{T}$ is not FC. Let D consist of the atoms $E(a_0, a_1)$ and $R(a_0, a_0)$.

Then $\mathcal{C} = Chase(D, \mathcal{T})$ is an infinite E-chain like in Example 3, but with additional atoms $R(a_i, a_{2i})$ for each i. Let $\Phi(x, y) = E(x, y) \wedge R(y, y)$. Clearly, $\mathcal{C} \not\models \Phi$ – the only element a_0 of $\mathcal{C}$ which satisfies $R(y, y)$ has no E-predecessor. But, as we are going to prove, if $\mathcal{M}$ is any finite model of $\mathcal{T}, D$ then $\mathcal{M} \models \Phi$.

Indeed, whatever the structure $\mathcal{M}$ is, it must contain a sequence $a_0, a_1, \ldots a_m \ldots a_{m+n}$ of elements such that $a_m = a_{m+n}$ and $\mathcal{M} \models E(a_i, a_{i+1})$ for each $i < m+n$. The datalog rule form $\mathcal{T}$ can then prove that $\mathcal{M} \models R(a_m, a_{m+(m \bmod n)})$, and then that $\mathcal{M} \models R(a_{m+l \bmod n}, a_{m+(m+2l \bmod n)})$. Let $l = -m \bmod n$. Now take $y = a_{m+l \bmod n}$ and $x = a_{m+l-1 \bmod n}$ to get $R(y, y)$.

It is worth mentioning that the structure $\mathcal{C}$ from the above example is ptp-conservative. As the degree of the elements of $\mathcal{C}$ is bounded by 4, this follows from:

LEMMA 13. *Each binary structure of bounded degree is ptp-conservative.*

Proof (hint): For a given number m, color the structure in such a way, that each neighborhood of radius m consists of elements whose colors are pairwise different. Then mimic the reasoning from Section 4. □

This shows ptp-conservativity of *Chase*, which – as explained in Remark 4 – guarantees that, if only n is big enough, $M_n(\overline{Chase})$ will be a model for all the existential TGDs from the theory, does not buy us much more: the devil can very well be in the plain datalog rules. Notice however, that not all datalog rules are troublemakers:

Remark 5. Suppose $\bar{\mathcal{C}}$ is n-conservative up to the size m. Let $\Psi \Rightarrow Q(x)$ be a datalog rule with at most m variables and with a unary predicate in the head. If this true in $\bar{\mathcal{C}}$ then it is also true in $M_n(\bar{\mathcal{C}})$. Proof: positive m-types of x and of $q_n(x)$ are the same.

5.6 Guarded TGDs

Guarded Datalog$^\exists$ programs, proved to be FC in [BGO10], consist of guarded rules (datalog rules and TGDs) which have an atom in the body, called the guard, containing all the variables that occur in the body of this rule. There is no restriction on the arity, in particular on the arity of the predicates in the heads of TGDs.

The witness generated by a guarded TGD appears to depend on all the variables in the head of the rule, and in consequence such a rule seems to be inherently non-binary, not even in the broad sense of Section 5.1. But, as it turns out, Guarded Datalog$^\exists$ programs are binary in disguise. And, while they are not BDD, still nothing beyond the techniques developed in Sections 2 and 4 is needed to prove they are FC.

To be more precise, suppose there exists a Guarded Program $\mathcal{T}$, a database instance D and a query Φ which are a counterexample for FC. Of course D can be also hardwired into $\mathcal{T}$ so we can assume it is empty.

Now we will show how to rewrite $\mathcal{T}$ and Φ into a binary signature, without changing their status of a counterexample. Then we will use the toolkit from Sections 2 and 4 to show very easily that the resulting binary program is FC.

(i) First step is similar to the one in the end of Section 3.1 – we want the predicates which are in the heads of TGDs (the TGPs) to be distinct that the ones in the heads of datalog rules. We also want the rules to respect the order of variables in atoms – if x is left of y in some atom in the rule then x never can be right of y in any atom of the same rule. This can be done by remembering the order of arguments as a part of the name of each predicate. Of course Φ must be rewritten – each new predicate is now a disjunction of the old predicates. Notice that guardedness implies that if $\mathcal{T}$ respects the order of variables, if $Chase(\mathcal{T}) \models R(\bar{a}, c)$ for some TGP R and if $Chase(\mathcal{T}) \models P(\bar{b}, c)$ then $\bar{b} \subseteq \bar{a}$. The elements in $\bar{a}$ are "parents of c", who were present in the atom R when c was born, and no rule can add anything else left of c in any atom.

Rename the variables in each rule in such a way, that the rightmost variable of the guard of each rule is y. Call this y the leading variable of the rule.

(ii) We want the elements to know their parents by name. If $R(x_1, \ldots x_k, y)$ is a TGP in $\mathcal{T}$ we add to T new rules:

$$R(x_1, \ldots x_k, y) \Rightarrow F_i(x_i, y)$$

for each $i \leq k$, where F_i are new binary predicates.

(iii) Replace each TGD of the form $\Psi \Rightarrow \phi$, with the leading variable y, with all possible rules of the form:

(♠ 6.) $\quad \Psi \wedge F_{i_1}(x_1, y) \wedge \ldots \wedge F_{i_k}(x_k, y) \Rightarrow \phi$

where $x_1, \ldots x_k$ are all the non-leading variables in Ψ and $i_1, \ldots i_k \leq K$, where K is the maximal arity of the predicates in $\mathcal{T}$. This changes nothing, as the elements to be substituted for x_i must have been some parents of y anyway.

(iv) Now, again in the manner of Section 3.1 rewrite the current $\mathcal{T}$ and Φ in such a way, that each TGP only occurs in one rule head (this can be easily done for the cost of some renaming datalog rules).

(v) Now perform step **(iii)** for the datalog rules of the current program.

At some point in Section 5.1 we wrote: *All we need in the proof in Section 3 is that (...) the witness generated by the rule only depends on one element in the body (the*

y), *while the additional elements in the body are just needed to make sure that y has a positive type which allows it to demand a witness.* Notice that this is exactly the case with our program now: all rules are in the form (♠ 6.) and the elements of $Chase(\mathcal{T})$ that can possibly be substituted for elements of $\bar{x}$ in the body of such rule are themselves functions of y. So t is just a function of y, not of all the elements of $\bar{x}$! The only reason why non-binary predicates could be necessary does not exist any more. Let us get rid of them.

Since the original $\mathcal{T}$ was guarded, each atom $P(\bar{a})$ in $Chase(\mathcal{T})$ was contained in some TGP atom $R(\bar{b}, c)$. Our idea is that full information about $P(\bar{a})$ will be remembered, **without materializing** $P(\bar{a})$, in a monadic way, by the element c. It will need to remember which of its parents are involved in each predicate. Of course it also needs to remember the links to its parents – this is why the relations F_i were introduced.

(vi) Replace each TGD of the form: $\Psi \Rightarrow \exists z\ R(x_1, \ldots x_k, z)$ (x_k may, or may not, by equal to y) by the following rules: $\Psi \Rightarrow \exists z\ E^R(y, z)$ and $\Psi \wedge E^R(y, z) \Rightarrow R^m(z)$ where E^R is a new binary predicate. $E^R(y, z)$ means something like "the (unique) rule which derives R was applied to a tuple led by y and a witness z was created". The newly created element z must also learn who its parents are. For each $i \in \{1, \ldots k\}$, if $F_j(x_i, y)$ was an atom in Ψ, add to the current $\mathcal{T}$ the rule:

(♢) $$F_j(x_i, y) \wedge E^R(y, z) \Rightarrow F_i(x_i, z)$$

and replace each TGP atom $R(x_1, \ldots x_k, z)$ in the body of any rule by:

$$F_1(x_1, z) \wedge \ldots F_k(x_k, z) \wedge R^m(z)$$

Now the program does not have TGPs of arity higher than 2 any more. Notice that for each variable $x \neq y$ in any rule, there exists i such that the atom $F_i(x, y)$ is in the body of this rule. We are ready to get rid also of the non-TGPs:

(vii) In each rule, with the atoms $F_{i_1}(w_1, y), \ldots F_{i_1}(w_l, y)$ in its body, replace each occurrence of a non-TGP atom $Q(w_1, \ldots w_l)$ with $Q_{i_1 i_2 \ldots i_l}(y)$, where $Q_{i_1 i_2 \ldots i_l}(y)$ is a new monadic predicate (in which y remembers what his parents with numbers $i_1, i_2, \ldots i_l$ are involved in). For each two monadic predicates of the form $Q_{i_1 i_2 \ldots i_l}(y)$ and $Q_{j_1 j_2 \ldots j_l}$ add to the program all possible rules of the form:

$$F_{i_1}(x_1, y) \ldots \wedge F_{i_l}(x_l, y) \wedge F_{j_1}(x_1, z) \ldots \wedge F_{j_l}(x_l, z) \wedge$$
$$\wedge Q_{i_1 i_2 \ldots i_l}(y) \Rightarrow Q_{j_1 j_2 \ldots j_l}(z)$$

The role of the last rule is to make sure that, once an atom of the predicate Q, involving $x_1 \ldots x_l$ is derived, all the elements that have $x_1 \ldots x_l$ among their parents are aware of that and ready to use this fact in further derivations.

We now have a new program over a binary signature, call it $\mathcal{T}'$. It follows from the construction that $\mathcal{C} = Chase(\mathcal{T}')$ is almost the same structure as $Chase(\mathcal{T})$ (where $\mathcal{T}$ is the original guarded program). They both have the same elements, and the predicates of each of them can be seen as views over the predicates of the other one. But notice that $Chase(\mathcal{T}')$ is a binary structure satisfying the assumptions of of Lemma 2. So it is ptp-conservative. This means that if n is big enough then $M_n(\bar{\mathcal{C}})$ is a model for all the existential TGDs in $\mathcal{T}'$ and that $M_n(\bar{\mathcal{C}}) \not\models \Phi'$ (where Φ' is the original query Φ after all the rewritings). To finish the proof of FC for Guarded Datalog$^\exists$ programs we only need to show that $M_n(\bar{\mathcal{C}})$ is also a model of all the datalog rules in $\mathcal{T}'$. All the datalog rules except from the rules of the form (♢) have a unary atom in the head, so (by Remark 5) we do not need to bother about them at all. What remains to be seen is that the rules of the form (♢) also remain true in $M_n(\bar{\mathcal{C}})$. So suppose $M_n(\bar{\mathcal{C}}) \models F_j(a, b) \wedge E^R(b, c)$ for some a, b, c. This means that there exist a', b', b'', c'' in $\bar{\mathcal{C}}$ such that $\bar{\mathcal{C}} \models F_j(a', b')$, $\bar{\mathcal{C}} \models E^R(b'', c'')$, $q_n(a') = a$, $q_n(b') = q_n(b'') = b$ and $q_n(c') = c$. But $\bar{\mathcal{C}}$ can be seen as a Chase of the guarded theory $\mathcal{T}$ with the natural coloring, so the types of successors of an element only depend on the type of this element, and it is easy to see that if $b' \equiv_n b''$ and $\bar{\mathcal{C}} \models E^R(b'', c'')$ then there must exist $c' \equiv_n c''$ such that $\bar{\mathcal{C}} \models E^R(b', c')$. Since the rule (♢) was true in $\bar{\mathcal{C}}$ we get that $\bar{\mathcal{C}} \models F_i(a', c')$ which implies that $M_n(\bar{\mathcal{C}}) \models F_i(a, c)$. We proved that ♢ remains true in $M_n(\bar{\mathcal{C}})$.

6. REFERENCES

BGO10 V. Barany, G. Gottlob, and M. Otto. *Querying the guarded fragment*; Proc. of the 25th IEEE Symposium on Logic in Computer Science, LICS 2010, Edinburgh, UK, pp. 1-10, 2010;

CGT09 A. Cali, G. Gottlob, and T. Lukasiewicz; *A general datalog-based framework for tractable query answering over ontologies*; in Proc. of PODS, 2009;

CGT12 A. Cali, G. Gottlob, and T. Lukasiewicz; *A general datalog-based framework for tractable query answering over ontologies*; J. Web Sem. 14, 2012, 57-83

CGP10 A. Cali, G. Gottlob, and A. Pieris; *Advanced processing for ontological queries*; Proc. VLDB-10, 3(1):554-565, 2010;

CGP10' A. Cali, G. Gottlob, and A. Pieris; *Query Answering under Non-guarded Rules in Datalog+/-* ; Web Reasoning and Rule Systems Lecture Notes in Computer Science, 2010, Volume 6333, pp 1-17;

GM12 T. Gogacz, J. Marcinkowski; *Converging to the Chase and Some Finite. Controllability Results*; Proc. of the 28th IEEE Symposium on Logic in Computer Science, LICS 2013, New Orleans, USA, to appear;

JK84 D. S. Johnson and A. C. Klug. *Testing containment of conjunctive queries under functional and inclusion dependencies*; JCSS 28(1):167-189, 1984;

R06 R. Rosati; *On the decidability and finite controllability of query processing in databases with incomplete information*; in Proc. PODS 2006, pp. 356–365;

R11 R. Rosati; *On the decidability and finite controllability of query processing in databases with incomplete information*; J. Comput. Syst. Sci. 77(3),2011, pp. 572-594

S69 S. Shelah; (1969), *Stable theories*; Israel J. Math. 7 (3): 187-202.

On the Expressive Power of Update Primitives

Tom J. Ameloot*
Hasselt University &
Transnational University of Limburg
Hasselt, Belgium
tom.ameloot@uhasselt.be

Jan Van den Bussche
Hasselt University &
Transnational University of Limburg
Hasselt, Belgium
jan.vandenbussche@uhasselt.be

Emmanuel Waller
Université Paris-Sud 11
Orsay, France
emmanuel.waller@lri.fr

ABSTRACT

The SQL standard offers three primitive operations (insert, delete, and update which is here called modify) to update a relation based on a generic query. This paper compares the expressiveness of programs composed of these three operations, with the general notion of update that simply replaces the content of the relation by the result of a query. It turns out that replacing cannot be expressed in terms of insertions, deletions, and modifications, and neither can modifications be expressed in terms of insertions and deletions. The expressive power gained by if-then-else control flow in programs is investigated as well. Different ways to perform replacing are discussed: using a temporary variable; using the new SQL merge operation; using SQL's data change delta tables; or using queries involving object creation or arithmetic. Finally the paper investigates the power of alternating the different primitives. For example, an insertion followed by a modification cannot always be expressed as a modification followed by an insertion.

Categories and Subject Descriptors

H.2.3 [**Database Management**]: Languages—Data manipulation languages (DML)

General Terms

Languages; theory

Keywords

Updates; expressive power; relational databases

*PhD Fellow of the Fund for Scientific Research, Flanders (FWO).

PODS'13, June 22–27, 2013, New York, New York, USA.

1. INTRODUCTION

The three basic update primitives for relational databases are the insertion of a tuple in a relation; the deletion of a tuple from a relation; and the modification of the components of a tuple in a relation. These three primitives are so simple, so natural and so commonplace that they are hardly ever questioned, apart perhaps from the folk wisdom that instead of modifying t to t', one can equivalently insert t' and delete t.

Much more powerful versions of the three basic update operations, however, are provided by the database query language SQL. An SQL insert operation allows to insert an entire set of tuples, given by a query applied to the current instance. Likewise an SQL delete operation allows to delete an entire set of tuples, again determined by a condition that can be an arbitrarily complex boolean query. For example, acting on a relation R(A,B) in SQL we can write delete from R R0 where exists (select R1.B from R R1 where R1.B=R0.A).

Also an SQL update operation allows to modify a set of tuples determined by a query condition, and moreover, the new values of the modified tuples can again be determined by queries as well, which are applied to the instance before the update. These queries must return single values (the so-called "scalar subqueries"). A classical example is to modify the salary of some employee to the current average salary, but scalar subqueries are not restricted to aggregate functions. For example, in SQL we can write update R R0 set R0.B = (select R1.B from R R1 where R1.A=R0.B). This will succeed on any instance satisfying the constraint that for every tuple (a_0, b_0) in R there exists exactly one tuple (a_1, b_1) in R with $a_1 = b_0$. By using a more complicated query, we can make the update succeed on any instance, leaving tuples (a_0, b_0) that violate the constraint unchanged.

The goal of the present paper is to understand better the expressive power of these query-based insertions, deletions and modifications. For instance, can we still express a modification by an insert followed by a delete? At first this may appear to be the case. For a simplistic example, consider again a relation R(A,B), and a typical modification like update R set B=0 where A=5. Assuming we are satisfied with relations as sets, as opposed to SQL's relations as bags, we can express this modification by insert into R (select A,0 from R where A=5) followed by delete from R where A=5 and not B=0. However, this is not always so easy; the reader is invited to try to express update R set A=B, B=A, which simply swaps the two columns, by a sequence of insertions and deletions acting solely on R.

The last qualification is important: if we can use a temporary relation S as scratch space, then quite trivially we can express *any* update using only insertions and deletions. More specifically, for any query $Q(R)$ that maps instances of R to instances of R, we may consider the *replacement* update that replaces the content of R by $Q(R)$.[1] Any such replacement can be expressed by the following crude procedure: erase S; insert $Q(R)$ in S; erase R; and insert all of S in R. Interestingly, we will see that this procedure can also be mimicked using SQL:2011's new "data change delta tables" [29, 33]. Furthermore, the procedure can also be mimicked when the query language is powerful enough and allows the introduction of new data elements; or when the data elements in the relation are numbers and the query language can do arithmetic.

Nevertheless, achieving a desired update "in place" may be preferred over ways that copy information around, for instance for reasons of efficiency. So we should better understand the *intrinsic* expressive power of the basic update primitives, in the absence of temporary relations. The ideal framework for such a study is given by the *generic queries* from the classical theory of database query languages [2, 5, 7, 14, 22]. Such queries do not interpret data elements as numbers, and neither do they introduce new data elements, but apart from that they cover exactly all data manipulations on the level of the logical structure of the relations in the database. In this framework every update to a relation can be modeled as a replacement update, defined by some generic query Q.

We consider a simple update language, called $\mathcal{UL}$, where programs are built from insertions, deletions and modifications using sequential composition and if-then-else statements. We will show that modification is primitive in $\mathcal{UL}$: there exist modifications that are not expressible by any program not using modification. An example is the modification that swaps the two columns of R, already mentioned above. (Insertion and deletion are likewise primitive, but this is obvious.) Moreover, $\mathcal{UL}$ is not update-complete: there exist simple updates that are not expressible by any program. This result holds even though arbitrary queries can be used in the update operations. An example of an inexpressible update is the replacement of R by its complement (with respect to its active domain).

Interestingly, the latest SQL:2011 standard [29, 33] has a *merge* operation that allows to combine insertions and deletions (and modifications as well) in a single operation.[2] We will provide a formalization of this operation and will show that any replacement can be expressed by a single merge. In this sense, our results show that the addition of merge has strictly increased the power of SQL's repertoire of update operations.

We also investigate how the if-then-else construct influences the expressive power of update programs. We show that in general it does, not only in the full language, but also in every fragment (obtained by omitting one or two update primitives). These results hold even though if-then-else may well be expressible by the queries used inside the individual update operations.

[1]This general notion of replacement should not be confused with MySQL's 'replace' operation [28], which behaves like an "upsert": an insert that behaves like a modify for insertions that violate some declared key constraint.

[2]Earlier editions of SQL already had a version of merge, but did not allow to combine insertions and deletions.

Finally we investigate the expressive power of alternating the update primitives. For database queries expressed in first-order logic, it is well known that using more alternations between existential and universal quantifiers allows the expression of more queries [15]. In our setting, we show that an insertion followed by a modification is not always expressible by a modification followed by an insertion. The converse separation holds as well, and we have similar separations for combinations of insertions and deletions, and of deletions and modifications. These results can be likened to the separation of the levels Σ_1 and Π_1 in the above-mentioned quantifier alternation hierarchy; but this analogy should not be taken too literally. Indeed, as in all our results, the generic queries used inside the update operations can be arbitrarily powerful. Since we have solved only the first level, the hierarchy for higher levels of alternation of update primitives remains to be further explored.

Most of the inexpressibility proofs amount to showing that, when trying to express some update by an unsuitable program, some loss of information cannot be prevented. This points at the fundamental weakness of in-place updating. The property that generic queries do not distinguish between isomorphic instances, or subinstances, plays an essential role in our arguments.

To conclude this introduction we would like to remark that efficiency, mentioned above as a potential motivation, is not our only motivation, as indeed we do not give any concrete results regarding efficiency. We mainly believe that the simplicity of the question of in-place updates calls for a thorough foundational understanding. Moreover, update operations are ubiquitous and, as mentioned above, as late as 2011 the SQL standard has made two fundamental additions to SQL's update features. This shows that there is a still current interest in powerful in-place updating in practice. We hope our work may serve in part as some theoretical justification of these additions to the standard.

This paper is organized as follows. Section 2 discusses related work. Section 3 defines the update language $\mathcal{UL}$ formally. Section 4 presents the results on the expressive power of the language and its fragments. Section 5 presents the results on alternation. Section 6 discusses the different ways in which one can express general replacement updates. Section 7 concludes with a discussion of open problems and topics for further research.

2. RELATED WORK

The authoritative reference on the expressive power of update languages is still Abiteboul and Vianu's work on the language TL and its variants [5, 6]. The present paper is complementary in scope to that work. Indeed, in TL, temporary relations are taken for granted, so the questions investigated in the present paper were not considered. For instance, in TL, modifications are superfluous. Abiteboul and Vianu also invented a technique of versioning using value invention (the introduction of new data elements). By this technique, in a setting with temporary relations and where input relations need not be preserved (altogether different from our setting), even deletions can become superfluous [6]. In Section 6 we will show a different application of the value invention technique, to simulate replacement updates using just in-place insertions and deletions.

An even earlier seminal paper by Abiteboul and Vianu is that on relational transactions [4]. In that work, programs that are sequential compositions of insertions, deletions and modifications are considered, very much as in the present paper. However, the queries inside the update operations in a relational transaction are limited to selections expressed by conjunctions of equalities and nonequalities between attributes and constants. In the present paper, formalizing the update operations of SQL, we allow at least first-order queries, or even arbitrary generic queries inside update operations.

In the present paper we work in the relational data model and are inspired by SQL, but it should be noted that over the past decade there has also been much interest in providing facilities to update XML data in the context of XQuery [30, 10, 32]. It should be interesting to extend our work to that context; indeed some work on the expressive power of the XQuery-based update primitives has already been reported by the Antwerp school [21].

In general there is a large literature concerned with updates, investigating topics such as equivalence [23], order-independence [25, 8], commutativity [17, 19], type checking [11] and independence [26, 12]; we can only give a few references. The recent work cited above is mostly in the setting of XML [13]; updates in the relational model are the topic in Abiteboul's 1988 invited paper [1]. We also recall the rather large interest in declarative specification of updates that existed in the 1990s; we only cite two reference volumes [27, 18]. Finally we mention the challenging and ever ongoing topic of belief revision and knowledge update in the field of Artificial Intelligence.

3. UPDATES

In this section we formalize the three basic update primitives (insertion, deletion, and modification) and also introduce the general primitive of replacement. We then define the simple update language considered in this paper.

3.1 Preliminaries

We recall some basic notions and terminology from the theory of relational databases. From the outset we assume a countably infinite universe **dom** of data elements. For a natural number k, a k-ary *relation* is a finite subset of $\mathbf{dom}\times\cdots\times\mathbf{dom}$ (k times), or, in other words, a finite set of k-tuples of data elements. The set of all k-ary relations is denoted by $Rel(k)$. A *database schema* is a finite set $\mathbf{S}$ of *relation names* where every relation name has an associated arity (a natural number). An *instance* I of $\mathbf{S}$ is an assignment of a relation $I(R)$ to every relation name $R \in \mathbf{S}$, so that if R has arity k then $I(R)$ is k-ary. The set of all instances of $\mathbf{S}$ is denoted by $inst(\mathbf{S})$.

Generic queries and updates.

We next define queries and updates as two special kinds of database transformations as defined in general by Abiteboul and Vianu [5]. Recall that a *permutation* of **dom** is a bijection from **dom** to **dom**. A permutation can also be applied to a relation or to an instance, simply by applying the permutation to all appearances of data elements in the relation or instance.[3] When a permutation ρ is the identity on some given subset $C \subseteq \mathbf{dom}$, then ρ is also called a C-permutation.

Let k be a natural number and let $\mathbf{S}$ be a database schema.

- A k-ary *query* over $\mathbf{S}$ is a mapping $q : inst(\mathbf{S}) \to Rel(k)$ for which there exists a finite set $C \subseteq \mathbf{dom}$ such that for every C-permutation ρ of **dom**, we have $q(\rho(I)) = \rho(q(I))$ for all instances I. We say that q is C*-generic.*

- An *update* over $\mathbf{S}$ is a partial mapping $u : inst(\mathbf{S}) \to inst(\mathbf{S})$ that is again C-generic for some finite set $C \subseteq \mathbf{dom}$, i.e., for every C-permutation ρ and every instance I, we have $u(I)$ is defined iff $u(\rho(I))$ is defined, and if so then $u(\rho(I)) = \rho(u(I))$.

The intuition behind C-genericity is that the query or update may interpret the constants in C specially, but otherwise treats all data elements generically, in the typical database fashion of set-oriented bulk data processing [2, 7, 14, 22]. For example, the SQL query `select * from R where A=5` is $\{5\}$-generic, and the SQL update `update R set B=0 where A=5` is $\{0, 5\}$-generic.

We assume familiarity with first-order logic, relational algebra, and relational calculus as basic languages for expressing queries [2].

We also recall that a nullary query can be likened to a logic formula without free variables, thus merely returning a boolean value true (the nonempty nullary relation) or false (the empty nullary relation) on every instance. Hence nullary queries are also called *boolean* queries. We will use boolean queries as the conditions in the if-then-else statements of our update language.

Remark 1. We allow updates to be partial mappings because in general, modification updates may be undefined on some instances as we will see in the next section. We assume queries to be total for simplicity; our results do not depend on this assumption. Also, one normally requires queries and updates to be computable. We omit this requirement simply because we do not need it. We assure the reader that none of our results relies on the use of noncomputable queries.

3.2 Update operations

Replace.

The most general update operation is replace, defined as follows. Let $\mathbf{S}$ be a database schema and $R \in \mathbf{S}$ a relation name of arity k. Let q be a k-ary query over $\mathbf{S}$. Then $\mathsf{replace}_R(q)$ is the update over $\mathbf{S}$ defined as follows. For any instance I of $\mathbf{S}$, we have $\mathsf{replace}_R(q)(I)(R) = q(I)$, and $\mathsf{replace}_R(q)(I)(S) = I(S)$ for each $S \neq R$. So, the content of relation R is simply replaced by the result of the query q.

Insert.

The update $\mathsf{insert}_R(q)$ can now be defined as $\mathsf{replace}_R(q')$, where q' is the query defined by $q'(I) = I(R) \cup q(I)$.

Delete.

The update $\mathsf{delete}_R(q)$ can now be defined as $\mathsf{replace}_R(q')$, where q' is the query defined by $q'(I) = I(R) - q(I)$ (set difference).

[3]Formally, if $t = (a_1, \ldots, a_k)$ is a tuple and ρ is a permutation, then $\rho(t)$ equals the tuple $(\rho(a_1), \ldots, \rho(a_k))$. If r is a relation then $\rho(r)$ equals the relation $\{\rho(t) \mid t \in r\}$. Finally, if I is an instance then $\rho(I)$ equals the instance given by $\rho(I)(R) = \rho(I(R))$ for each relation name R.

Modify.

For a modification of a relation R of arity k, we need a query q of arity $2k$ rather than just k. The intuition is that q returns pairs of tuples (t, t') where t' is the modified version of t. To avoid ambiguity we require q to return a $2k$-ary relation that is a *function* on k-tuples, i.e., that does not contain two tuples of the form (t, t') and (t, t'') where t, t' and t'' are k-tuples and $t' \neq t''$. This formalizes the requirement in SQL that only scalar subqueries can be used in the assignment clause of an SQL update statement.

Formally, we define the update $\mathsf{modify}_R(q)$ to be defined on an instance I only if $q(I)$ is a function. In that case $\mathsf{modify}_R(q)(I)$ is defined to be equal to $\mathsf{replace}_R(q')(I)$, where q' is the query defined by

$$q'(I) = \{t \in I(R) \mid \neg\exists t' : (t, t') \in q(I)\} \cup \{t' \mid \exists t \in I(R) : (t, t') \in q(I)\}.$$

So, the tuples from relation R that are not mentioned in the result of q are left untouched, and the other tuples are modified. We feel this definition most elegantly formalizes the use of queries in an SQL update statement, by bundling the query in the where-clause together with the queries used in the assignment clause, all in a single $2k$-ary query.

Example 1. For a relation $R(A, B)$, the SQL statement update R set B=0 where A=5 can be modeled as $\mathsf{modify}_R(q)$, where q is the query $\{(5, y, 5, 0) \mid R(5, y)\}$ (expressed in first-order logic). Likewise, the SQL statement update R set B=A, A=B is modeled as $\mathsf{modify}_R(q)$, where q is the query $\{(x, y, y, x) \mid R(x, y)\}$. Now recall the SQL update from the Introduction, update R R0 set R0.B = (select R1.B from R R1 where R1.A=R0.B). It would not be quite correct to model this as $\mathsf{modify}_R(q)$ where q is the query $\{(x, y, x, z) \mid R(x, y) \wedge R(y, z)\}$. Indeed, by our above-defined semantics, that update leaves any tuples in $q_{\text{undef}} := \{(x, y) \mid R(x, y) \wedge \neg\exists z\, R(y, z)\}$ untouched, whereas the SQL update is well defined only if q_{undef} is empty. Hence the strictly correct way to model the SQL update is to use for q the query $\{(x, y, x, z) \mid q_{\text{undef}} = \emptyset \rightarrow (R(x, y) \wedge R(y, z))\}$, which makes that q does not return a function (and thus the modification undefined) whenever q_{undef} is nonempty. Note furthermore that the update is also undefined if $q^{(2)}_{\text{undef}} := \{(x, y) \mid R(x, y) \wedge \exists^{\geq 2} z\, R(y, z)\}$ is nonempty (here $\exists^{\geq 2} z$ is an abbreviation for "there exist at least two distinct z"). In summary, we can write a "safe" version of the update by using for q the query

$$\{(x, y, x, z) \mid R(x, y) \wedge (q^{(2)}_{\text{undef}}(x, y) \rightarrow z = y) \wedge (\neg q^{(2)}_{\text{undef}}(x, y) \rightarrow R(y, z))\}.$$

Since this query returns a function on all instances, the corresponding modification update is always defined. Tuples in $q_{\text{undef}} \cup q^{(2)}_{\text{undef}}$ are left untouched.

Remark 2. One may wonder how it can be guaranteed that a $2k$-ary query q returns a function on all inputs, or on all inputs that satisfy a given set Σ of integrity constraints. For a $2k$-ary relation r, requiring that r is a function on k-tuples amounts to the constraint on r that the first k columns form a superkey, which is a special kind of functional dependency (FD). Given a conjunctive query q, a set Σ of FDs, and an FD σ, the implied constraint problem that $q(I)$ satisfies σ for every I that satisfies Σ, can be solved by the chase algorithm [2, 24]. For first-order queries, the property of always returning a function is undecidable. It is an interesting research topic to see if there exists a syntactic fragment of the first-order queries that would be expressively complete for the first-order function-returning queries in the presence of FDs. □

That queries must return functions poses a serious limitation on the expressive power of modifications. The following technical lemma shows that if there are too many symmetries in the instance, it is very difficult for a query to return a function. Recall that an *automorphism* of an instance I is a permutation ρ such that $\rho(I) = I$. When an automorphism ρ is the identity on $C \subseteq \mathbf{dom}$, then ρ is also called a C-automorphism. We say that ρ *fixes* a tuple t simply when $\rho(t) = t$.

LEMMA 3.1. *Let $\mathbf{S}$ be a database schema, let q be a C-generic, $2k$-ary query over $\mathbf{S}$, and let I be an instance of $\mathbf{S}$. If $q(I)$ is a function, then for every pair of k-tuples $(t, t') \in q(I)$, the tuple t' is C-*fixed *with respect to (I, t), meaning that every C-automorphism of I that fixes t also fixes t'.*

PROOF. For the sake of contradiction, suppose ρ is a C-automorphism of I that fixes t but not t', so $\rho(t') \neq t'$. We have $\rho(t, t') = (t, \rho(t')) \in \rho(q(I)) = q(\rho(I)) = q(I)$, whence $q(I)$ is not a function, a contradiction. □

Example 2. Let $\mathbf{S}$ consist of a single unary relation name S and let I be an instance of $\mathbf{S}$ where $I(S) = \{a, b, c, d\}$. Using a and b as constants, we can easily modify a in S to b, by using the modification $\mathsf{modify}_S(\{(a, b)\})$. Here, $\{(a, b)\}$ denotes the constant query q that always outputs $\{(a, b)\}$; note that this query is $\{a, b\}$-generic. In SQL, we would write (using attribute name A for the single column of S) the statement update S set A=b where A=a.

But no modification $\mathsf{modify}_S(q)$, with q any $\{a, b\}$-generic query, is able to modify a to c. Indeed, c is not $\{a, b\}$-fixed with respect to (I, a), as witnessed by the permutation that swaps c and d but leaves a and b fixed. Hence, by the above Lemma, (a, c) cannot be in $q(I)$.

3.3 The update languages $\mathcal{UL}$ and $\mathcal{UL}^{\text{while}}$

Let $\mathbf{S}$ be a database schema. We define the *update programs* over $\mathbf{S}$ as follows.

- If $R \in \mathbf{S}$ is a relation name of arity k and q is a k-ary query over $\mathbf{S}$, then '$\mathsf{insert}_R(q)$' and '$\mathsf{delete}_R(q)$' are programs.
- If $R \in \mathbf{S}$ is a relation name of arity k and q is a $2k$-ary query over $\mathbf{S}$, then '$\mathsf{modify}_R(q)$' is a program.
- If P_1 and P_2 are programs, then $P_1; P_2$ is also a program.
- If q is a boolean query over $\mathbf{S}$ and P_1 and P_2 are programs, then 'if q then P_1 else P_2 endif' is a program.
- If q is a boolean query over $\mathbf{S}$ and P is a program, then 'while q do P enddo' is a program.

The language $\mathcal{UL}$ is formed by all programs that do not use while-loops; the extended language allowing while-loops is denoted by $\mathcal{UL}^{\text{while}}$.

Every program denotes an update in the obvious manner. The construct $P_1; P_2$ signifies sequential composition, and if-then-else statements and while-loops have the familiar meaning. A program that contains modifications may not be well defined on every input. Indeed we agree that when a program running on an instance I encounters a modification step that is not defined on the current instance, the entire program is undefined on I. Furthermore, programs may be undefined on some instances due to nonterminating while-loops.

Note that every program P is indeed C-generic for some C. Specifically, let $\mathcal{Q}$ be the set of all queries used in P. This set is finite. Each q in $\mathcal{Q}$ is C_q-generic for some finite set C_q. Then take the union $C = \bigcup_{q \in \mathcal{Q}} C_q$.

FO-programs.

Most of our inexpressibility results concern arbitrary programs, which may use arbitrary queries inside the update operations. But when writing down a program, we need a query language to express the queries. In all our positive results (results where we have to give a specific program) we will be sufficient with first-order logic (FO) as the query language; programs using first-order queries are called *FO-programs*. In writing FO-programs we will often use a mix of relational algebra and relational calculus whenever convenient.

Example 3. A simple example of an FO-program over a database schema with relations R, S and T, where R and T have the same arity, is the following:

$$\text{if } S \neq \emptyset \text{ then } \mathsf{insert}_T(R) \text{ else } \mathsf{delete}_T(R) \text{ endif.}$$

This program inserts all of R in T if S is nonempty, and deletes all of R from T otherwise. Note that this program can be equivalently written without an if-then-else construct as follows:

$\mathsf{insert}_T(\{x \mid R(x) \wedge S \neq \emptyset\})$;
$\mathsf{delete}_T(\{x \mid R(x) \wedge S = \emptyset\})$.

Clearly this works because conditionals can be expressed in queries, but also because this example program has a simple behavior. In particular, the first statement does not change the relation S, so that the condition in the second statement is not influenced by the execution of the first statement. We will see later that, in general, if-then-else constructs cannot be eliminated from the language.

For an example of a program in $\mathcal{UL}^{\text{while}}$, the following FO-program closes off binary relation R transitively:

while $\exists x, y, z(R(x,y) \wedge R(y,z) \wedge \neg R(x,z))$ do
  $\mathsf{insert}_R(\{(x,z) \mid \exists y(R(x,y) \wedge R(y,z))\})$
enddo

4. EXPRESSIVENESS OF UPDATE PRIMITIVES

The update language from the previous section features the three ubiquitous update primitives, which can be combined using sequential composition, if-then-else, and while-loops. Two natural questions arise as to the expressive power of this language.

The first question concerns replacement. Earlier we have defined replacement as the most general update primitive, which simply replaces a relation with a prescribed new content, given by a query. Is every replacement operation expressible by a program in our language?

The second question concerns the minimality of the language. Is every feature of the language really primitive? It is quite obvious that deletions cannot be eliminated, as they are the only construct that allow a relation to be erased. Likewise it is obvious that insertions cannot be eliminated, as they are the only construct that allow the cardinality of a relation to increase. While-loops are obviously primitive in FO-programs, but when more powerful queries can be used in programs, their primitivity remains open. In the following, the question of minimality will be focused on modifications and the if-then-else construct.

4.1 Inexpressibility of replacement

Recall that the *active domain* of an instance I, denoted by $adom(I)$, is the set of all data elements appearing in the relations of I. Now fix the database schema $\mathbf{S}_{\text{graph}}$ consisting of a single relation name R of arity 2. Each instance I of $\mathbf{S}_{\text{graph}}$ can be viewed as a directed graph (V, E) where $V = adom(I)$ and $E = I(R)$. Consider the *complementation* query, denoted by R^c, over $\mathbf{S}_{\text{graph}}$, defined by $R^c(I) = adom(I)^2 - I(R)$. This query is $\emptyset$-generic.

We now show that complementing the set of edges of a directed graph is not possible by any update program.

Theorem 4.1. *No update program in $\mathcal{UL}^{\text{while}}$ over $\mathbf{S}_{\text{graph}}$ can express the update* $\mathsf{replace}_R(R^c)$.

Proof. Let us denote $\mathsf{replace}_R(R^c)$ by u. Consider an instance I where $I(R)$ is of the form $\{(a,c),(c,a),(b,d),(d,b),(a,a),(b,b),(c,c),(d,d)\}$, for four distinct data elements a, b, c and d. We can view I as a graph G with undirected (symmetric) edges and a loop at each node. Similarly, $u(I)$ then equals the graph G_5:

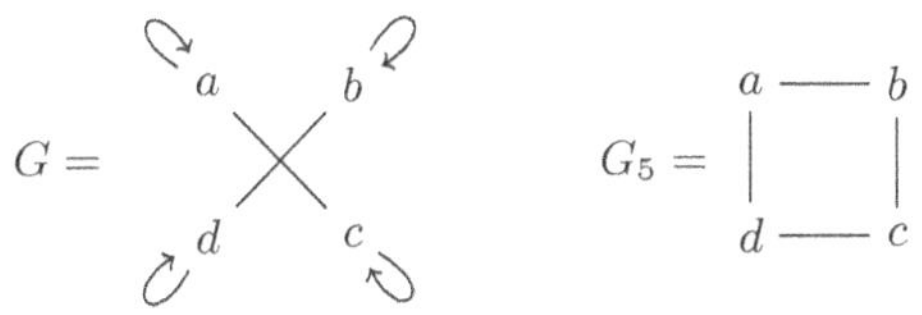

We also consider the following graphs:

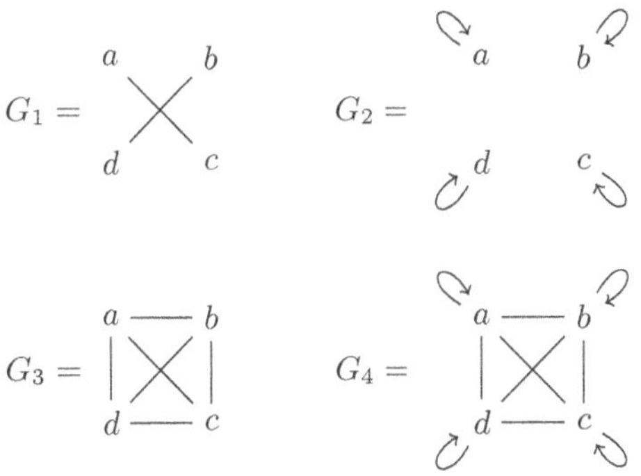

The empty instance over $\mathbf{S}_{\text{graph}}$ will be denoted by G_0.

We also need a notion of "adornment", that we define as follows. Let C be a finite set of data elements, disjoint from $\{a, b, c, d\}$. For any fixed $z \in C$, we call the sets $\{(a,z),(b,z),(c,z),(d,z)\}$ and $\{(z,a),(z,b),(z,c),(z,d)\}$ C-*adornments*. Edges belonging to such adornments are called *adornment edges*. Also any subset of $C \times C$ is called a C-adornment. Edges belonging to such adornments are called *constant edges*. Finally a union of C-adornments is also called a C-adornment. Now for any graph G' on the nodes $\{a, b, c, d\}$ and any C-adornment Z, we call $G' \cup Z$ a *C-adorned version* of G'.

We can now make the following claim: *Let P be a sequence of C-generic insertions, deletions, and modifications, where C is disjoint from $\{a, b, c, d\}$. Let G' be a C-adorned version of G or G_1. Then $P(G')$ equals a C-adorned version of G or of one of G_0–G_4.* Assuming this claim, the theorem follows readily. Indeed, take any program P. We know that P is C-generic for some C. Choose a, b, c and d not in C. The execution of P on I traces out a sequence of C-generic insertions, deletions, and modifications. Hence, by the claim, the result of P on I is a C-adorned version of G or of one of G_0–G_4, and not the desired result G_5.

We prove the claim by induction on the length of the sequence P. For the empty sequence the claim holds trivially. Now consider a sequence $u; P$; there are three possible cases for the first update u.

The first case is that u is $\mathsf{modify}_R(q)$ for some C-generic, 4-ary query q. We will take G' to be a C-adorned version of G; the argument for G_1 is similar but simpler. By C-genericity of q, we know that every C-automorphism of G' is also an automorphism of $q(G')$. When we make use of this fact below, we will simply write "by symmetry". Note that the C-automorphisms of G' are the symmetries of the square, which form the dihedral group of order 4. Specifically, they are the eight permutations of $\{a, b, c, d\}$ generated by the rotation $(a\ b\ c\ d)$ and the reflection $(a\ b)(c\ d)$.

Consider the possibilities for the modification made by u to edge (a, c) in G'. By Lemma 3.1, the new tuple must be fixed by every C-automorphism of G' that fixes (a, c). Thus there are four possibilities:[4]

1. $(a, c, a, c) \in q(G')$ or $(a, c, c, a) \in q(G')$, i.e., u modifies (a, c) to itself, or to its reversal.

2. $(a, c, a, a) \in q(G')$ or $(a, c, c, c) \in q(G')$, i.e., u modifies (a, c) to a loop at its tail, or at its head.[5]

3. $(a, c, a, x) \in q(G')$, or $(a, c, c, x) \in q(G')$, or $(a, c, x, a) \in q(G')$, or $(a, c, x, c) \in q(G')$ for some $x \in C$, i.e., u modifies (a, c) to an adornment edge between its head or tail and a constant in C.

4. $(a, c, x, x') \in q(G')$ for some $x, x' \in C$, i.e., u modifies (a, c) to a constant edge.

By symmetry, u has the same behavior on the three other edges (c, a), (b, d) and (d, b) as it has on (a, c). So, exactly one of the above four cases applies for all these four edges uniformly.

Always using Lemma 3.1, we can similarly list the possibilities for the modification made by u to the loops in G', and to the adornment edges. Constant edges, by symmetry, can only be modified to constant edges. By going through all combinations of possibilities one then verifies that $u(G')$ must be of one of the desired forms. These details are omitted. □

[4]There is also the possibility that (a, c) is not present in $\pi_{1,2}(q(G'))$, but this possibility has the same consequences as possibility 1.

[5]For a directed edge $e = (x, y)$, the node x is called the *tail* of e and y is called the *head* [9].

4.2 Primitivity of modify

The five constructs of the language $\mathcal{UL}^{\text{while}}$ are insertion, deletion, modification, if-then-else, and while-loops. In general, we say that a construct is *redundant* if for every database schema $\mathbf{S}$ and every program P over $\mathbf{S}$ that uses the construct, P is equivalent to a program over $\mathbf{S}$ that does not use the construct. We say that a construct is *primitive* if it is not redundant. We now show that modifications are primitive in this sense. Consider again the database schema $\mathbf{S}_{\text{graph}}$ of directed graphs and the FO query $q_{\text{rev}} \equiv \{(x, y, y, x) \mid R(x, y)\}$ over $\mathbf{S}_{\text{graph}}$. Query q_{rev} is $\emptyset$-generic. Note, $\mathsf{modify}_R(q_{\text{rev}})$ is the update that reverses all edges of the graph. This update is total.

THEOREM 4.2. *No update program in $\mathcal{UL}^{\text{while}}$ over $\mathbf{S}_{\text{graph}}$, that does not use modifications, can express $\mathsf{modify}_R(q_{\text{rev}})$.*

The theorem is proved like Theorem 4.1 by a nonreachability argument, based on symmetry and Lemma 3.1. We omit the details.

4.3 Primitivity of if-then-else

That if-then-else is primitive is not entirely trivial, because queries used in update operations can be arbitrarily powerful and express conditionals. This was already illustrated in Examples 1 and 3. We will show that if-then-else is primitive in $\mathcal{UL}$ and in all its fragments, with the caveat that some of our results assume programs without constants.[6]

Formally, for each nonempty subset $\mathcal{F}$ of $\{\mathsf{insert}, \mathsf{delete}, \mathsf{modify}\}$, we define the fragment $\mathcal{UL}(\mathcal{F})$ consisting of all $\mathcal{UL}$ programs that can use if-then-else in addition to only the update primitives in $\mathcal{F}$. A program not using if-then-else is called a *straight-line* program. It will be convenient to also allow the empty straight-line program and agree it expresses the identity update.

4.3.1 Inexpressibility by straight-line programs

The following useful lemma, which may be interesting in its own right, brings out a limitation of straight-line programs.

LEMMA 4.3. *If a straight-line program P expresses a total and injective update, then P is equivalent to the subsequence of P consisting of all the modifications of P.*

The proof of this lemma, that we omit for brevity, is based on another lemma:

LEMMA 4.4. *Every total, injective update is also surjective.*

By Lemma 4.3, in order to find an update not expressible by any straight-line program, it suffices to find an update that is total, injective, and not expressible by modifications only. Over the by now familiar database schema $\mathbf{S}_{\text{graph}}$, we can define such an update, which, moreover, is expressible by an FO-program in $\mathcal{UL}(\{\mathsf{insert}, \mathsf{delete}\})$ as well as in $\mathcal{UL}(\{\mathsf{insert}, \mathsf{modify}\})$. We omit the details of this update, but we conclude:

[6]However, if-then-else is not primitive in the presence of temporary relations (cf. Section 6), since temporary relations can store the result of boolean conditions.

THEOREM 4.5. *There exists a total update over* $\mathbf{S}_{\text{graph}}$ *that is expressible by an FO-program in* $\mathcal{UL}(\{\mathsf{insert}, \mathsf{delete}\})$ *and by an FO-program in* $\mathcal{UL}(\{\mathsf{insert}, \mathsf{modify}\})$*, but not expressible by any straight-line program.*

It immediately follows that if-then-else is primitive in the two mentioned fragments, as well as in $\mathcal{UL}$ in its entirety.

4.3.2 The fragment $\{\mathsf{delete}, \mathsf{modify}\}$

For the fragment $\{\mathsf{delete}, \mathsf{modify}\}$ a result as sharp as Theorem 4.5 remains open. We still can show, however, that if-then-else is primitive in this fragment, except that we have not proven this for programs with constants. Programs with constants can make various markings in a graph, so that it becomes trickier to prove that they are unable to achieve a certain task.

Formally, a program *without constants* is a program in which all queries used in update operations are C-generic with $C = \emptyset$. We say that if-then-else is *primitive without constants* if there exists a program without constants but using if-then-else, that is not equivalent to a straight-line program without constants.

PROPOSITION 4.6. *Over the schema* $\mathbf{S}_{\text{graph}}$*, if-then-else is primitive without constants in* $\mathcal{UL}(\mathsf{delete}, \mathsf{modify})$.

PROOF. Let u be the update over $\mathbf{S}_{\text{graph}}$ expressed by the following FO-program:

if $\exists x\, R(x, x)$ then
  $\mathsf{delete}_R(\{(x, x) \mid R(x, x)\})$;
  $\mathsf{modify}_R(\{(x, y, x, x) \mid R(x, y)\})$
else *(do nothing)* endif

Here, *(do nothing)* can be expressed by, say, $\mathsf{delete}_R(\emptyset)$.

Suppose, for the sake of contradiction, that u is expressed by an $\emptyset$-generic straight-line program P in $\mathcal{UL}(\mathsf{delete}, \mathsf{modify})$. Choose nine data elements a, b, ..., h, i and consider the following graph:

$G =$ 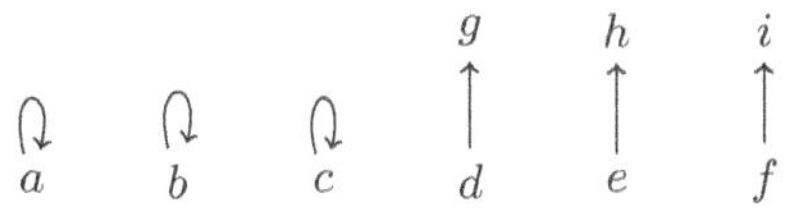

We have

$u(G) =$ 

We cannot use an unreachability argument as in the proofs of Theorems 4.1 and 4.2, as indeed, $u(G)$ is reachable from G by deletions and modifications. Instead, we use a fooling argument. The idea is that at some point in the execution of P, the program is confused whether it is working on input G or on the subset of G without the loops. These details are omitted. $\square$

4.3.3 The single-primitive fragments

What about the fragments $\mathcal{UL}(\mathsf{insert})$, $\mathcal{UL}(\mathsf{delete})$, and $\mathcal{UL}(\mathsf{modify})$? We can show that if-then-else is still primitive in these fragments, but no longer over the schema $\mathbf{S}_{\text{graph}}$, by the following easy proposition:

PROPOSITION 4.7. *Over any database schema that consists of a single relation name, if-then-else is redundant in the fragments* $\mathcal{UL}(\mathsf{insert})$, $\mathcal{UL}(\mathsf{delete})$, *and* $\mathcal{UL}(\mathsf{modify})$.

The proof of this proposition, that we omit for brevity, is based on the following lemma:

LEMMA 4.8. *Let* $\mathbf{S}$ *be a single-relation database schema and let* $m \in \{\mathsf{insert}, \mathsf{delete}, \mathsf{modify}\}$*. Then every straight-line program* P *over* $\mathbf{S}$ *that uses only operations of kind* m*, is equivalent to a single operation of kind* m.

So we must go to multiple-relation database schemas. It turns out that unary relations are already sufficient now. For the fragment $\mathcal{UL}(\mathsf{modify})$, our result is again without constants only. We omit the proof details.

PROPOSITION 4.9. *Let* R*,* S *and* T *be unary relations.*

- *Over the schema* $\{R, S\}$*, if-then-else is primitive in* $\mathcal{UL}(\mathsf{insert})$.
- *Over the schema* $\{R, S, T\}$*, if-then-else is primitive in* $\mathcal{UL}(\mathsf{delete})$.
- *Over the schema* $\{R, S, T\}$*, if-then-else is primitive without constants in* $\mathcal{UL}(\mathsf{modify})$.

Remark 3. Proving the above proposition requires some creativity in coming up with the inexpressible updates, but is otherwise quite straightforward, because each update operation can act on a single relation only. It may be interesting to consider update operations that can change multiple relations in parallel. Such operations are not provided in SQL.

5. ALTERNATION

In this section we present some initial results on the expressive power of alternating different update primitives. Everything else in this direction remains to be further explored. We work over the database schema $\mathbf{S}_{\text{graph}}$ of directed graphs; an analogous investigation could be performed over other schemas as well. Another caveat is that we restrict attention to updates without constants (formally, C-generic updates with $C = \emptyset$).

For $m, m' \in \{\mathsf{insert}, \mathsf{delete}, \mathsf{modify}\}$, an *update of the form* $m; m'$ is a composition of two update operations $\mathrm{op}_1; \mathrm{op}_2$ where op_1 is of kind m and op_2 is of kind m'.

THEOREM 5.1. *Let* $m, m' \in \{\mathsf{insert}, \mathsf{delete}, \mathsf{modify}\}$ *be two different update primitives. Then there exists a first-order update over* $\mathbf{S}_{\text{graph}}$*, without constants, of the form* $m; m'$*, that is not equivalent to any update, without constants, of the form* $m'; m$.

The lengthy proof, that we will omit here, gives in each of the six cases an inexpressible update. The essential idea is always that information loss cannot be prevented when we have to start with an unsuitable operation. More specifically, for each update, we choose an input with some symmetries. Then after the first step, these symmetries cause generic queries to be confused how to proceed on an intermediate result that may correspond to different inputs with different outputs.

The above theorem shows that between any two primitives, the two different forms of one alternation (starting with either of the two primitives) can be separated. Much more generally one would expect a hierarchy in analogy (but not more than an analogy) to the quantifier alternation hierarchy for first-order queries on relational databases [15].

The question remains to be explored. We can only offer an example in the fragment $\mathcal{UL}$(insert, delete) of a straight-line program with two alternations that cannot be expressed using only one alternation.

Example 4. Over the schema $\mathbf{S}_{\text{graph}}$ consider the update $u \equiv \text{replace}_R(R \circ R)$, where $R \circ R \equiv \{(x, z) \mid \exists y(R(x, y) \wedge R(y, z))\}$. We conjecture that this update is not expressible in $\mathcal{UL}^{\text{while}}$ at all. At least we can show that u is not expressible by any straight-line program in $\mathcal{UL}$(insert, delete) that is without constants and uses only one alternation. Since $\mathbf{S}_{\text{graph}}$ has only a single relation name, by Lemma 4.8, such a program is of the form insert; delete or delete; insert. Consider the following instance I and its updated version $u(I)$:

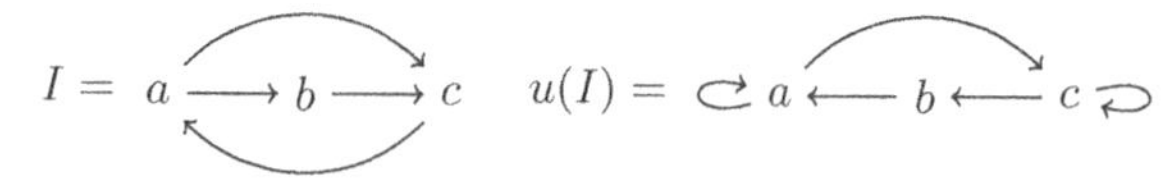

First, consider any program P, without constants, of the form insert; delete. For P to compute $u(I)$ on input I, the insertion step must insert all edges of $u(I)$ that are not in I, yielding an instance that has the transposition $(a\ c)$ as an automorphism. Since $u(I)$ does not have this transposition as an automorphism, we cannot go from the intermediate result to $u(I)$ by an $\emptyset$-generic update. By a similar argument we can see that no program of the form delete; insert can compute $u(I)$ on input I.

Nevertheless, the following ad-hoc program does compute $u(I)$ from I using two alternations: delete (c, a); insert (a, a), (b, a), (c, b), and (c, c); delete (a, b) and (b, c). Here, a, b and c are *not* used as constants but can be distinguished on the relevant intermediate results by generic queries.

We conclude that the update "if the input J is isomorphic to I, output $u(J)$; otherwise, do nothing" is expressible using two alternations but not using only one.

6. EXPRESSING REPLACE

As already mentioned in the Introduction, the limitations in expressive power of the language $\mathcal{UL}^{\text{while}}$ as illustrated by Theorems 4.1 and 4.2 vanish in the presence of temporary relations. Temporary relations can be elegantly formalized as follows [5]. Let u be an update over some database schema $\mathbf{S}$. To express u by a program P, we allow P to be a program over a larger schema $\mathbf{S}' \supseteq \mathbf{S}$. When given an instance of $\mathbf{S}$ as input to P, the relations outside $\mathbf{S}$ are initialized to the empty set. The final result of P, an instance of $\mathbf{S}'$, is restricted to the relations from $\mathbf{S}$. In the presence of temporary relations, there is not that much difference anymore between an update language and a general query language. At any rate, the expressive power of $\mathcal{UL}^{\text{while}}$ with temporary relations is quite large and well-understood. When the queries used inside programs are first-order, the expressible queries (or updates) are known as the *while*-queries, or the queries expressible in FO(PFP), the extension of first-order logic with partial fixpoints [2].

In SQL practice, however, the use of temporary relations can be cumbersome, perhaps harder to optimize, and in-place update operations seem to be preferred by SQL programmers. To wit, the SQL community has standardized two extensions of the basic insert–delete–modify update repertoire in the recent SQL:2011 standard: the merge statement and *data change delta tables* [29]. We will show that these two extensions both allow to express the general replace primitive.

6.1 Merge

The SQL:2011 merge statement is a quite complex instruction that involves a combination of insertions, deletions, and modifications, performed on a target relation by processing a source relation [33]. We refer to the DB2 documentation for a detailed description [16]. We offer the following formalization.

Let R be a relation name of arity k and let q_{source} be a query of arity l. Furthermore, let q_{match} be a query of arity $k + l$; let q_{update} be a query of arity $2k + l$; and let q_{delete} and q_{insert} be queries of arity $k + l$. Then

$$\text{merge}_R(q_{\text{source}}, q_{\text{match}}, q_{\text{update}}, q_{\text{delete}}, q_{\text{insert}})$$

is the update u defined as follows. Let I be an instance. We define the following relations:

- $r_{\text{source}} = q_{\text{source}}(I)$. This formalizes the source relation of the SQL merge statement.
- $r_{\text{match}} = \{(t, s) \in q_{\text{match}}(I) \mid t \in I(R) \wedge s \in r_{\text{source}}\}$. This formalizes that target tuple t and source tuple s match.
- $r_{\text{update}} = \{(t, s, t') \in q_{\text{update}}(I) \mid (t, s) \in r_{\text{match}}\}$. This represents that the matching pair (t, s) qualifies the conditions to do an update ('update' in the SQL sense); t' is the modified tuple.
- $r_{\text{delete}} = q_{\text{delete}}(I) \cap r_{\text{match}}$. This returns the matching pairs that qualify to do a delete.
- $r_{\text{nomatch}} = r_{\text{source}} - \pi_{k+1,\dots,k+l}(r_{\text{match}})$. This returns the source tuples that do not match.
- $r_{\text{insert}} = \{(s, t) \in q_{\text{insert}}(I) \mid s \in r_{\text{nomatch}}\}$. This represents the insert action specified for source tuples that do not match any target tuple.

For u to be defined on I, a number of requirements must be satisfied:

- The first k columns should be a superkey for r_{match}, i.e., each target tuple can match with at most one source tuple.
- The first $k + l$ columns should be a key for r_{update}, similar to the well-definedness requirement for modifications;
- Relation r_{delete} must be disjoint from $\pi_{1,\dots,k+l}(r_{\text{update}})$;
- The first l columns should be a key for r_{insert}, i.e., each nonmatched source tuple can insert at most one tuple.

If these requirements are satisfied by I, then $u(I)$ replaces the contents of relation R by the relation

$$\begin{aligned}&\big(I(R) - (\pi_{1,\dots,k}(r_{\text{update}}) \cup \pi_{1,\dots,k}(r_{\text{delete}}))\big)\\ &\qquad \cup \pi_{k+l+1,\dots,2k+l}(r_{\text{update}}) \cup \pi_{l+1,\dots,l+k}(r_{\text{insert}})\end{aligned}$$

It is now clear that an arbitrary replacement $\text{replace}_R(q)$ can be expressed by merge using the following queries: q_{source} is $(R - q) \cup (q - R)$; q_{update} is $\emptyset$; and q_{match}, q_{delete}, and q_{insert} are the equality query $\{(x_1, \dots, x_k, y_1, \dots, y_k) \mid x_1 =$

$y_1 \wedge \cdots \wedge x_k = y_k\}$. Quite simply, all tuples in $R - q$ match for equality and are deleted; all tuples in $q - R$ do not match for equality and are inserted. So, we need only a very simple application of the merge statement. Yet, the crucial feature that was added to SQL:2011 in comparison to earlier standards is that deletions as well as insertions can be used in one merge statement, and it is exactly that feature that allows our replacement procedure to work.

Example 5. In SQL syntax, over a binary relation R(A,B), the following statement replaces R by $R \circ R$ (compare Example 4):

```
merge into R
using (
  ((select A,B from R)
   except
   (select R1.A,R2.B from R R1, R R2
    where R1.B=R2.A))
  union
  ((select R1.A,R2.B from R R1, R R2
    where R1.B=R2.A)
   except
   (select A,B from R)))
  as S(A,B)
on R.A=S.A and R.B=S.B
when matched then delete
when not matched then insert values (S.A,S.B)
```

6.2 Data change delta tables

Data change delta tables are a feature of SQL:2011 that allow update operations to be put inside queries. The table before the update, as well as the table after the update, can be accessed by the query.[7] This is also called "pipelined DML" [33]. Data change delta tables can be used to perform arbitrary in-place replacement updates, when used in conjunction with the with clause of select statements. The with clause allows intermediate queries to be given a temporary name inside a larger query, and is better known as the way to specify recursion in SQL; here we do not use recursion.

Specifically, remember the procedure to perform a replacement $\mathsf{replace}_R(q)$ using a scratch relation S: insert q into S; erase R; and insert S into R. This procedure can be almost literally programmed as follows:

```
with S as (q),
     Dummy as (select * from old table (delete from R))
select *
from new table (insert into R (select * from S))
```

The specifications old table and new table are not actually important for the above to work. So, we need only a very limited application of data change delta tables; the only feature we really need is the ability to put updates in queries, and the ability to simulate temporary relations using the with clause.

6.3 Value invention

The classical definitions of C-generic query and update imply that the active domain of the output $q(I)$ is a subset of the active domain of the input I (plus the constants in C). One can extend the notion of generic query and update, however, to allow for *value invention*: the introduction of new data elements in the result [5, 3, 31, 2].

We now describe an, admittedly artificial, technique to perform $\mathsf{replace}_R(q)$, with q a classical C-generic query, using only in-place insertions and deletions on R, if the queries allowed inside insertions can do value invention. So, value invention is used as an auxiliary mechanism only. We assume the query language inside insertions is sufficiently powerful to do counting and iteration. Although the combination of iteration and value invention in general leads to Turing completeness, our technique has only polynomial complexity. It remains open if replacement can still be simulated if only first-order logic, extended with value invention, is permitted inside the queries.

THEOREM 6.1. *Operation* $\mathsf{replace}_R(q)$*, with q a classical C-generic query, can be expressed by a $\mathcal{UL}$ program over $\{R\}$ if the queries allowed inside insertions can do value invention, counting, and iteration.*

In the proof sketch below, we concretely assume that R is binary, but the method can be adapted to higher arities. We proceed in four steps, using only insertions and deletions.

Encoding: Let n be the cardinality of $adom(R) \cup C$. Then for every edge $e = (a, b) \in R$ we insert in R a chain of $n+2$ new data elements $(e_0, e_1), (e_1, e_2), \ldots, (e_n, e_{n+1})$, along with edges (e_n, b) and (e_0, a) and a final loop (e_{n+1}, e_{n+1}). Note that after this insertion, the newly introduced data elements are indistinguishable from the original data elements except by their structural properties. And indeed, they can still be structurally distinguished as follows. In the instance after the insertion, call a *sl-chain* any chain of distinct data elements starting in a source node (node without entering edges) and ending in a loop. The *length* of a chain is the number of elements on it. Let m be the maximum length of an sl-chain. Chains of distinct nodes in the original graph can be at most n long. The start node of such a chain is linked from its new e_0 element, making a total length of $n + 1$. Since the new elements form sl-chains of length $n + 2$, they can be distinguished by their lying on an sl-chain of maximum length m.

Remove original edges: After the encoding step, the original graph is still definable. Indeed, it consists of all pairs (a, b) such that there is an sl-chain $e_0 \ldots e_m$ and edges (e_0, a) and (e_m, b). Note that a can be distinguished from e_1 by the maximum length of the chain as explained above. Hence, we can delete the original edges without loss of information.

Insert q: We can now determine the result of query q on the original instance, since the original relation R is still encoded in the current relation R. The result is inserted into R. Note that, since q is a classical C-generic query, this inserts only edges between original elements of R. In particular, as before, this insertion cannot introduce sl-chains of length longer than $n + 1$.

Remove encoding: We can finally remove all elements lying on a maximal-length sl-chain, and we are left with the desired value of the replacement.

[7] Our presentation of delta tables will be kept informal, because they are so tightly integrated in SQL select-statements that their formalization would require a full formalization of SQL select-statements, which is outside the scope of this paper.

6.4 Arithmetic

Also when interpreting the data elements in relations as numbers on which arithmetic can be performed, we leave the framework of generic queries. Queries again no longer need to be domain-preserving, as witnessed by the simple SQL query select A+B from R.

In this context we can simulate replacement in a way similar to the simulation using value invention, but simpler, since no iteration over long chains is needed anymore. In fact, the whole procedure can now be programmed in SQL as a sequence of insert and delete statements using normal query expressions, i.e., without using the programming facilities of SQL/PSM. The arithmetical operators needed below are order comparisons, addition, and the aggregate functions max and count. It would be interesting to understand better exactly how much (or how little) arithmetic is really needed.

The encoding step is now much simpler. Let M be the maximum number appearing in both relations R and $q(R)$. Also, for any edge $e = (a, b)$ in R, let n_e be its rank in a lexicographic ordering of the tuples of R. Then we encode e by inserting the edges (e_0, e_1), (e_1, b), (e_0, a), where now e_0 and e_1 are no longer abstract new data elements, but the numbers $e_0 = M + 2(n_e - 1) + 1$ and $e_1 = e_0 + 1$.

After inserting these edge encodings, the original edges can still be distinguished. The source nodes are exactly all elements e_0. The two edges leaving a source node e_0 are (e_0, a) and (e_0, e_1), and a can be distinguished from e_1 simply by $a < e_1$. Then b can be retrieved as the only node pointed to by e_1.

7. CONCLUSION

Theoretical computer science has a rich tradition of investigating its computational models to the bone, with the goal of understanding the power and complexity of each individual feature. In database theory we have certainly followed this tradition in the investigation of high-level logical query languages. Computational models for updating deserve the same attention, because of their practical interest as witnessed by additions to recent SQL standards.

In this paper we have scratched the surface of much that remains to be explored. Throughout the text we have identified open problems, mostly of a technical or theoretical nature. One theory-oriented question we have not yet mentioned is the arity required of temporary relations, similarly to questions investigated about the arity required of auxiliary relations in first-order incremental evaluation systems (see the recent paper [20] and references therein).

Here we conclude with some directions for further research. In Section 2 we have already mentioned the obvious direction of working with other data models than the relational model.

We have focused on updating a single relation, possibly part of a multi-relation database. As such, replacement of a single relation by a query applied to the database was the natural upper bound on expressive power for our investigation. However, in general one wants to perform multi-relation updates and much of our study needs to be reconsidered for that context.

In this paper we have also focused on sequential composition as a natural way of executing programs. Database servers in practice also process sequences of SQL statements. Yet it seems interesting to also study parallel composition of updates. Also, in practice, updates often happen through cursors. It would be interesting to model this by a formally defined programming language, so that again the possibilities and limitations of cursor-based SQL programming can be investigated on the theoretical level.

Finally, we have not investigated the efficiency, performance, and optimization aspects of updating. It would be interesting to compare the efficiency of using temporary relations versus other ways of performing complicated updates. Also, it would be interesting to rigorously test the thesis that in-place updates are more efficient than general replacement updates.

8. ACKNOWLEDGEMENTS

We thank the PODS reviewers for their comments.

9. REFERENCES

[1] S. Abiteboul. Updates, a new frontier. In M. Gyssens, J. Paredaens, and D. Van Gucht, editors, *ICDT'88*, volume 326 of *Lecture Notes in Computer Science*, pages 1–18. Springer-Verlag, 1988.

[2] S. Abiteboul, R. Hull, and V. Vianu. *Foundations of Databases*. Addison-Wesley, 1995.

[3] S. Abiteboul and P. Kanellakis. Object identity as a query language primitive. *J. ACM*, 45(5):798–842, 1998.

[4] S. Abiteboul and V. Vianu. Equivalence and optimization of relational transactions. *J. ACM*, 35:70–120, 1988.

[5] S. Abiteboul and V. Vianu. Procedural languages for database queries and updates. *J. Comput. Syst. Sci.*, 41(2):181–229, 1990.

[6] S. Abiteboul and V. Vianu. Datalog extensions for database queries and updates. *J. Comput. Syst. Sci.*, 43(1):62–124, 1991.

[7] A. Aho and J. Ullman. Universality of data retrieval languages. In *Conference Record, 6th ACM Symposium on Principles of Programming Languages*, pages 110–120, 1979.

[8] M. Andries, L. Cabibbo, J. Paredaens, and J. Van den Bussche. Applying an update method to a set of receivers. *ACM Trans. Database Syst.*, 25(1):1–40, 2001.

[9] J. Bang-Jensen and G. Gutin. *Digraphs*. Springer, second edition, 2009.

[10] M. Benedikt, A. Bonifati, S. Flesca, and A. Vyas. Verification of tree updates for optimization. In K. Etessami and S. Rajamani, editors, *Computer Aided Verification, 17th International Conference*, volume 3576 of *Lecture Notes in Computer Science*, pages 379–393. Springer, 2005.

[11] M. Benedikt and J. Cheney. Semantics, types and effects for XML updates. In P. Gardner and F. Geerts, editors, *Proceedings 12th International Symposium on Database Programming Languages*, volume 5708 of *Lecture Notes in Computer Science*, pages 1–17. Springer, 2009.

[12] M. Benedikt and J. Cheney. Destabilizers and independence of XML updates. *Proceedings VLDB*, 3(1):906–917, 2010.

[13] M. Benedikt, D. Florescu, P. Gardner, G. Guerrini, M. Mesiti, and E. Waller. Report on the EDBT/ICDT

2010 workshop on updates in XML. *SIGMOD Record*, 39(1):54–57, 2010.

[14] A. Chandra and D. Harel. Computable queries for relational data bases. *J. Comput. Syst. Sci.*, 21(2):156–178, 1980.

[15] A. Chandra and D. Harel. Structure and complexity of relational queries. *J. Comput. Syst. Sci.*, 25:99–128, 1982.

[16] Database reference–SQL–statements–MERGE. IBM DB2 10.1 Information Center for Linux, UNIX, and Windows, `http://pic.dhe.ibm.com/infocenter/db2luw/v10r1/`, 15 November 2012.

[17] S. Dekeyser, J. Hidders, and J. Paredaens. A transaction model for XML databases. *World Wide Web: Internet and Web Information Systems*, 7:29–57, 2004.

[18] B. Freitag, H. Decker, M. Kifer, and A. Voronkov, editors. *Transactions and Change in Logic Databases*, volume 1472 of *Lecture Notes in Computer Science*. Springer, 1998.

[19] G. Ghelli, K. Høgsbro Rose, and J. Siméon. Commutativity analysis for XML updates. *ACM Trans. Database Syst.*, 33(4):article 29, 2008.

[20] E. Grädel and S. Siebertz. Dynamic definability. In *Proceedings 15th International Conference on Database Theory*, 2012.

[21] J. Hidders, J. Paredaens, and R. Vercammen. On the expressive power of XQuery-based update languages. In *Database and XML Technologies, Proceedings 4th XSym*, volume 4156 of *Lecture Notes in Computer Science*, pages 92–106. Springer, 2006.

[22] R. Hull and C. Yap. The format model, a theory of database organization. *J. ACM*, 31(3):518–537, 1984.

[23] D. Karabeg and V. Vianu. Simplification rules and complete axiomatization for relational update transactions. *ACM Trans. Database Syst.*, 16(3):439–475, 1991.

[24] A. Klug. Calculating constraints on relational expressions. *ACM Trans. Database Syst.*, 5(3):260–290, 1980.

[25] C. Laasch and M. Scholl. Deterministic semantics of set-oriented update sequences. In *Proceedings, 9th International Conference on Data Engineering*, pages 4–13. IEEE Computer Society Press, 1993.

[26] A. Levy and Y. Sagiv. Queries independent of updates. In R. Agrawal, S. Baker, and D. Bell, editors, *Proceedings 19th International Conference on Very Large Data Bases*, pages 171–181. Morgan Kaufmann, 1993.

[27] U. W. Lipeck and B. Thalheim, editors. *Modelling Database Dynamics*. Workshops in Computing. Springer-Verlag, 1992.

[28] MySQL reference manuals. `http://dev.mysql.com/doc/`.

[29] Information technology — database languages — SQL — part 2: Foundations. International Standard ISO/IEC 9075, 2012.

[30] I. Tatarinov, Z. Ives, A. Halevy, and D. Weld. Updating XML. In *Proceedings 2001 ACM SIGMOD International Conference on Management of Data*, pages 413–424. ACM Press, 2001.

[31] J. Van den Bussche, D. Van Gucht, M. Andries, and M. Gyssens. On the completeness of object-creating database transformation languages. *J. ACM*, 44(2):272–319, 1997.

[32] XQuery update facility 1.0. W3C Recommendation 17 March 2011.

[33] F. Zemke. What's new in SQL:2011. *SIGMOD Record*, 41(1):67–73, 2012.

Flag & Check: Data Access with Monadically Defined Queries

Sebastian Rudolph
Fakultät Informatik
Technische Universität Dresden, DE
sebastian.rudolph@tu-dresden.de

Markus Krötzsch
Department of Computer Science
University of Oxford, UK
markus.kroetzsch@cs.ox.ac.uk

ABSTRACT

We introduce *monadically defined queries* (MODEQs) and *nested monadically defined queries* (NEMODEQs), two querying formalisms that extend conjunctive queries, conjunctive two-way regular path queries, and monadic Datalog queries. Both can be expressed as Datalog queries and in monadic second-order logic, yet they have a decidable query containment problem and favorable query answering complexities: a data complexity of P, and a combined complexity of NP (MODEQs) and PSPACE (NEMODEQs).

We show that (NE)MODEQ answering remains decidable in the presence of a well-known generic class of tuple-generating dependencies. In addition, techniques to rewrite queries under dependencies into (NE)MODEQs are introduced. Rewriting can be applied partially, and (NE)MODEQ answering is still decidable if the non-rewritable part of the TGDs permits decidable (NE)MODEQ answering on other grounds.

Categories and Subject Descriptors

H.2.3 [**Database Management**]: Languages—*query languages*; F.4.1 [**Mathematical Logic and Formal Languages**]: Mathematical Logic—*computational logic*

Keywords

query containment; tuple-generating dependencies; Datalog

1. INTRODUCTION

Query languages are fundamental to the design of database systems. A good query language should be able to express a wide range of common information needs, and allow queries to be answered efficiently with limited computational resources. Moreover, databases are often considered in combination with dependencies, e.g., in the form of *tuple-generating dependencies* (TGDs), which are also playing an important role in data exchange, information integration, and database integrity checking [1]. While query answering under dependencies is undecidable in general, there are many decidable cases, and a query language should be robustly applicable to such extensions [39]. Another important task in database management and optimization is to check *query containment*, that is, to determine whether the answers of one query are contained in the answers of another query over arbitrary databases, possibly under the additional assumption that certain constraints are satisfied. A query language should therefore allow for such checks.

Unfortunately, these basic requirements are in conflict. Very simple query languages like *conjunctive queries* (CQs, [17]) allow for efficient query answering (NP combined/AC_0 data[1]) and containment checking, but have very limited expressivity. First-order logic (FOL) queries extend expressivity, but are still restricted to "local" queries, excluding, e.g., the transitive closure of a relation. Query containment is undecidable for FOL, and query answering becomes PSPACE-complete for combined complexity [44], but remains AC_0 for data [31]. Another extension of CQs is *Datalog*, which introduces rule-based recursion. The price are higher complexities (EXPTIME combined/P data), and undecidability of query containment [23, 43]. FOL and Datalog are incomparable; both are subsumed by second-order logic (SO), which is more expressive but also more complex (EXPSPACE combined/PH data) [31, 45].

To find more tractable query languages, various smaller fragments of Datalog have been considered. *Linear Datalog* allows only one inferred predicate per rule body, which significantly reduces query complexity (PSPACE combined/ NLOGSPACE data) [29]. Still, query containment remains undecidable. Two query languages for which containment is decidable are *monadic Datalog* and *conjunctive 2-way regular path queries* (C2RPQs) [27, 15]. The query complexity of C2RPQs (NP combined/NLOGSPACE data) is slightly lower than that of monadic Datalog (NP combined/P data), but the expressivity of the languages is incomparable. In particular, monadic Datalog cannot express transitive closure. Two well-known query languages subsuming monadic Datalog and C2RPQs are Datalog and *monadic second-order logic* (MSO) [36]. Query containment is decidable for neither of these. Both languages are incomparable, even regarding query complexities (MSO has PSPACE combined/PH data [44, 46, 36]), their common upper bound being SO.

This reveals a glaring gap in the landscape of known query languages: no formalism that captures monadic Datalog and C2RPQs ensures tractable data complexity and decidable query containment. To address this, we propose *monadically defined queries* (MODEQs) and *nested monadically defined queries* NEMODEQs as novel query formalisms that combine these desirable properties. Their relationship to the aforementioned languages is also illustrated in Fig. 1.

The contribution of this paper can be split in two parts. In the first part, we introduce the new querying formalism and clarify its relations to established query notions and the complexity for query answering. More precisely:

- We define MODEQs, discuss the underlying intuition, and provide examples demonstrating their expressivity.

[1]As usual, query complexities refer to the problem of deciding whether a query has a particular certain answer. *Combined complexity* is the complexity for arbitrary queries and databases; *data complexity* is the complexity if the query is fixed or bounded.

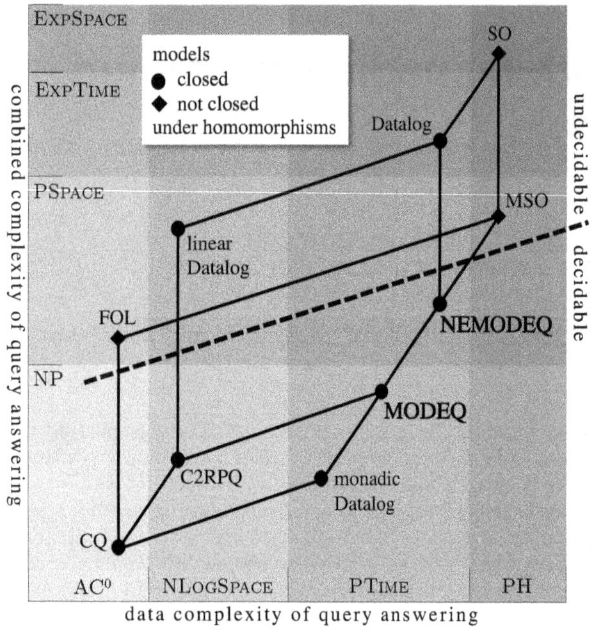

Figure 1: Overview of complexities and relations of monadically defined queries to other query formalisms as established in this paper; information indicated for conjunctive queries (CQ) and conjunctive 2-way regular path queries (C2RPQ) also hold when allowing unions (UCQ and UC2RPQ); all other formalisms are closed under unions

- We show that MODEQs capture (unions of) CQs, C2RPQs, and monadic Datalog queries.
- We prove MODEQ answering to be NP-complete for combined complexity (i.e., on par with CQs) and P-complete for data complexity, ensuring data-tractability as one of the central desiderata for querying large data sets.

We then extend MODEQs with nested subqueries, leading to a broader class of NEMODEQs that generalize MODEQs.

- We show that NEMODEQs (thus MODEQs) are expressible by both Datalog queries and MSO formulae.
- We prove NEMODEQ answering to be PSpace-complete for combined complexity (on par with FOL-based query languages like SQL) and P-complete for data complexity.
- We show that, unlike for Datalog and MSO queries, query containment for (NE)MODEQs is decidable.

In the second part of the paper, we study (NE)MODEQs in the context of dependencies and ontology-based data access. To this end, an important tool are (finite or infinite) *universal models*, which represent solutions to data exchange and constraint repair problems in the presence of TGDs [24]. As models of (NE)MODEQ are closed under homomorphisms, we find that universal models can be used to answer such queries, making them very robust to a wide class of TGDs.

- We immediately obtain decidability of query answering under all TGDs that admit a finite universal model. This property of TGDs is undecidable, but can be approximated by various notions of *acyclicity* [25, 26, 24, 38, 30, 34].
- More generally, we show that MODEQ answering is decidable in the presence of rules giving rise to (possibly infinite) universal models of *bounded treewidth*. This applies to many lightweight ontology languages as well as guarded TGDs and generalizations thereof [9, 4, 34, 5].
- In analogy to the popular notion of first-order rewritability, we introduce (NE)MODEQ rewritability, and we identify basic criteria for rewriting Datalog rules.
- Finally, we show that query answering is decidable under any set of TGDs that can be decomposed into one that is (NE)MODEQ-rewritable and one with the bounded-treewidth-model property.

Proofs omitted in the main paper are given in the accompanying technical report [42].

2. PRELIMINARIES

We consider a standard language of first-order predicate logic, based on an infinite set $\mathbf{C}$ of *constant symbols*, an infinite set $\mathbf{P}$ of *predicate symbols*, and an infinite set $\mathbf{V}$ of first-order *variables*. Each predicate $p \in \mathbf{P}$ is associated with a natural number $\mathsf{ar}(p)$ called the *arity* of p. The list of predicates and constants forms the language's *signature* $\mathscr{S} = \langle \mathbf{P}, \mathbf{C} \rangle$. We generally assume $\mathscr{S} = \langle \mathbf{P}, \mathbf{C} \rangle$ to be fixed, and only refer to it explicitly if needed.

Databases, Rules, and Queries. A *term* is a variable $x \in \mathbf{V}$ or a constant $c \in \mathbf{C}$. We use symbols s, t to denote terms, x, y, z, v, w to denote variables, a, b, c to denote constants. Expressions like $\boldsymbol{t}$, $\boldsymbol{x}$, $\boldsymbol{c}$ denote finite lists of such entities. We use the standard predicate logic definitions of *atom* and *formula*, using symbols φ, ψ for the latter. A formula is *ground* if it contains no variables. A *database*, usually denoted by D, is a finite set of ground atoms. We write $\varphi[\boldsymbol{x}]$ to emphasize that a formula φ has free variables $\boldsymbol{x}$; we write $\varphi[\boldsymbol{c}/\boldsymbol{x}]$ for the formula obtained from φ by replacing each variable in $\boldsymbol{x}$ by the respective constant in $\boldsymbol{c}$ (both lists must have the same length). A formula without free variables is a *sentence*.

A *conjunctive query* (CQ) is a formula $Q[\boldsymbol{x}] = \exists \boldsymbol{y}.\psi[\boldsymbol{x}, \boldsymbol{y}]$ where $\psi[\boldsymbol{x}, \boldsymbol{y}]$ is a conjunction of atoms. A *tuple-generating dependency* (TGD) is a formula of the form $\forall \boldsymbol{x}, \boldsymbol{y}.\varphi[\boldsymbol{x}, \boldsymbol{y}] \to \exists \boldsymbol{z}.\psi[\boldsymbol{x}, \boldsymbol{z}]$ where φ and ψ are conjunctions of atoms, called the *body* and *head* of the TGD, respectively. TGDs never have free variables, so we usually omit the universal quantifier when writing them. We use the symbol Σ, possibly with subscripts, to denote sets of TGDs. A *Datalog rule* is a TGD without existentially quantified variables; sets of Datalog rules will be denoted by symbols $\mathbb{P}, \mathbb{R}, \mathbb{S}$.

We use the standard semantics of first-order logic (FOL). An *interpretation* $\mathcal{I}$ consists of a (possibly infinite) set $\Delta^{\mathcal{I}}$ called *domain* and a function $\cdot^{\mathcal{I}}$ that maps constants c to domain elements $c^{\mathcal{I}} \in \Delta^{\mathcal{I}}$ and predicate symbols p to relations $p^{\mathcal{I}} \subseteq (\Delta^{\mathcal{I}})^{\mathsf{ar}(p)}$, thereby $p^{\mathcal{I}}$ is called the *extension* of p. A *variable assignment* for $\mathcal{I}$ is a function $\mathcal{Z} : \mathbf{V} \to \Delta^{\mathcal{I}}$. Conditions for $\mathcal{I}$ and $\mathcal{Z}$ to satisfy a FOL formula φ (i.e., to be a *model* of φ, written $\mathcal{I}, \mathcal{Z} \models \varphi$) are defined as usual. If φ is a sentence, then $\mathcal{Z}$ is irrelevant for satisfaction and can be omitted. An *answer* to a CQ $Q[\boldsymbol{x}]$ over a database D and set Σ of TGDs is a list of constants $\boldsymbol{c}$ for which $D \cup \Sigma \models Q[\boldsymbol{c}/\boldsymbol{x}]$.

Given an interpretation $\mathcal{I}$ and a formula $\varphi[\boldsymbol{x}]$ with free variables $\boldsymbol{x} = \langle x_1, \ldots, x_m \rangle$, the *extension* of $\varphi[\boldsymbol{x}]$ is the subset of $(\Delta^{\mathcal{I}})^m$ containing all those tuples $\langle \delta_1, \ldots, \delta_m \rangle$ for which $\mathcal{I}, \{x_i \mapsto \delta_i \mid 1 \le i \le m\} \models \varphi[\boldsymbol{x}]$. Two formulae $\varphi[\boldsymbol{x}]$ and $\psi[\boldsymbol{x}]$ with the same free variables $\boldsymbol{x}$ are called *equivalent* if their extensions coincide for every interpretation $\mathcal{I}$.

Homomorphisms and Universal Models. Given interpretations $\mathcal{I}$, $\mathcal{J}$, a *homomorphism* π from $\mathcal{I}$ to $\mathcal{J}$ is a function $\pi : \Delta^{\mathcal{I}} \to \Delta^{\mathcal{J}}$ such that: (i) for all constants c, we have $\pi(c^{\mathcal{I}}) = c^{\mathcal{J}}$, and (ii) for all predicate symbols p and list of domain elements $\boldsymbol{\delta}$, we have $\boldsymbol{\delta} \in p^{\mathcal{I}}$ implies $\pi(\boldsymbol{\delta}) \in p^{\mathcal{J}}$.

Finding query answers is facilitated in practice since one may focus on universal models. A *universal model* of a set of sentences Ψ is an interpretation $\mathcal{I}$ such that (i) $\mathcal{I} \models \Psi$, and (ii) for every interpretation $\mathcal{J}$ with $\mathcal{J} \models \Psi$, there is a homomorphism from $\mathcal{I}$ to $\mathcal{J}$. For TGDs (and for plain databases), there is always a universal model if there is any model at all. It can be defined by a (possibly infinite) construction process called the *chase*. In particular, we let $\mathcal{I}(D \cup \Sigma)$ denote the universal model, for which every homomorphism into any other model of $D \cup \Sigma$ is injective. $\mathcal{I}(D \cup \Sigma)$ always exists for satisfiable $D \cup \Sigma$, and it is unique up to isomorphism [24].

For a wide range of queries, entailment of query answers can be reduced to model checking in the universal model:

FACT 1 (ENTAILMENT VIA MODEL CHECKING). *If $Q[\mathbf{x}]$ is a query for which the set of models of $\exists\mathbf{x}.Q[\mathbf{x}]$ is closed under homomorphisms, then, for every database D and set Σ of TGDs, $D \cup \Sigma \models Q[\mathbf{c}/\mathbf{x}]$ if and only if either $D \cup \Sigma$ is inconsistent or $\mathcal{I}(D \cup \Sigma) \models Q[\mathbf{c}/\mathbf{x}]$.*

This applies to CQs and to all other query languages studied herein. The case $\Sigma = \emptyset$ shows that one can equivalently represent databases using models $\mathcal{I}(D)$ instead of sets of facts D. Our perspective is more natural when using TGDs.

3. MONADICALLY DEFINED QUERIES

We now introduce a new query formalism, called *monadically defined queries (MODEQs)*, and state complexity results on query answering in this language. To deepen our understanding for the expressivity of MODEQs, we show that they strictly generalize the well-known query formalisms of *conjunctive 2-way regular path queries* (Section 3.1) and *monadic Datalog queries* (Section 3.2).

The heart of our query formalism is a mechanism for defining new predicates based on existing ones. This mechanism – which we refer to as *"flag & check"* – specifies new predicates by providing a procedure for testing if a particular tuple $\boldsymbol{\delta}=\langle\delta_1,\ldots,\delta_m\rangle \in (\Delta^{\mathcal{I}})^m$ is in the predicate's extension or not. To this end, the candidate tuple is first "flagged" by associating each δ_i with an auxiliary constant name λ_i that represents this element. The "check" is performed by running a Datalog program with this fixed interpretation of the constants λ_i. The check succeeds if a special fact `hit` is derived.

EXAMPLE 1. *To illustrate the idea, we consider a typical transitive closure query. Suppose that the binary predicate certifiedBy represents the direct certification of one entity by another, e.g., in a security application. We are interested in certification chains, which could be expressed in Datalog as follows:*

$$\mathit{certifiedBy}(x,y) \to \mathit{certChain}(x,y) \quad (1)$$

$$\mathit{certChain}(x,y) \wedge \mathit{certifiedBy}(y,z) \to \mathit{certChain}(x,z) \quad (2)$$

Corresponding Datalog rules $\mathbb{P}_1$ for "flag & check" are:

$$\mathit{certifiedBy}(\lambda_1,y) \to \mathtt{U}_1(y) \quad (3)$$

$$\mathtt{U}_1(y) \wedge \mathit{certifiedBy}(y,z) \to \mathtt{U}_1(z) \quad (4)$$

$$\mathtt{U}_1(\lambda_2) \to \mathtt{hit} \quad (5)$$

We define certChain to contain all pairs $\langle\delta_1,\delta_2\rangle$ for which $\mathbb{P}_1$ entails `hit` when interpreting λ_1 as δ_1 and λ_2 as δ_2.

As in Example 1, the Datalog rules that we consider for the checking phase only use `hit` or new, unary predicates $\mathtt{U}_i$ in rule heads. Such unary predicates can be imagined as "colors" that are assigned to elements of the domain, and the check thus is a deterministic, recursive procedure of coloring the domain, starting from the flagged candidate elements. This idea is defined formally as follows.

DEFINITION 1 (MODEQ SYNTAX AND SEMANTICS). *Given a signature $\mathscr{S}$, a* monadically defined predicate (MODEP) *of arity m is based on a signature $\mathscr{S}'$ that extends $\mathscr{S}$ with m fresh constant symbols $\lambda_1,\ldots,\lambda_m$, a fresh nullary predicate `hit`, and $k \geq 0$ fresh unary predicates $\mathtt{U}_1,\ldots,\mathtt{U}_k$. A MODEP is a set $\mathbb{P}$ of Datalog rules over $\mathscr{S}'$ where only $\mathtt{U}_1,\ldots,\mathtt{U}_k$, and `hit` occur in rule heads.*

Let $\mathcal{I}$ be an interpretation over $\mathscr{S}$. The extension $\mathbb{P}^{\mathcal{I}}$ of $\mathbb{P}$ is the set of all tuples $\langle\delta_1,\ldots,\delta_m\rangle \in (\Delta^{\mathcal{I}})^m$ for which $\mathcal{I}' \models \mathbb{P}$ implies $\mathcal{I}' \models$ `hit`, for all interpretations $\mathcal{I}'$ that extend $\mathcal{I}$ to the symbols in $\mathscr{S}'$ such that $\langle\lambda_1^{\mathcal{I}'},\ldots,\lambda_m^{\mathcal{I}'}\rangle = \langle\delta_1,\ldots,\delta_m\rangle$.

A monadically defined query (MODEQ) *is a conjunctive query that uses both normal predicates and monadically defined predicates in its atoms. The semantics of MODEQs is defined in the obvious way via the semantics of MODEPs.*

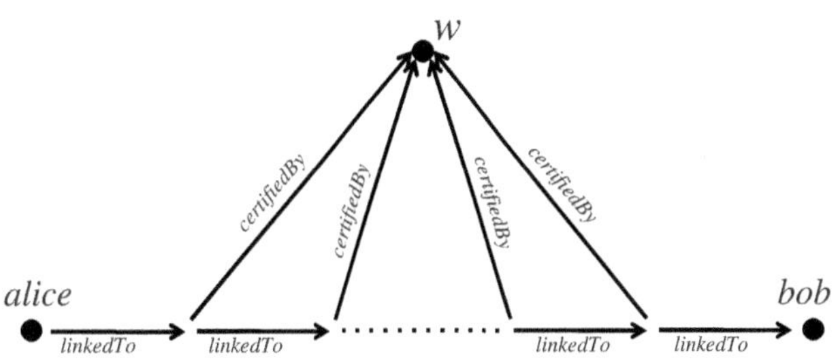

Figure 2: Structure recognized by MODEQ $\mathfrak{Q}_2$ in Example 2

EXAMPLE 2. *The rules (3)–(5) define a binary MODEP $\mathbb{P}_1$, so the query of Example 1 can be written as a MODEQ $\mathfrak{Q}_1[v,w] = \mathbb{P}_1(v,w)$. For another example, assume there are entities certifying the security of message handling in certain nodes of a network. We are interested in entities y that can (directly) certify secure treatment of the message at all nodes on some path from Alice to Bob, as illustrated in Fig. 2. This is expressed by the MODEQ $\mathfrak{Q}_2[w] = \mathbb{P}_2(w)$, where $\mathbb{P}_2$ consists of the following rules:*

$$\mathit{certifiedBy}(x,\lambda_1) \to \mathtt{U}_3(x) \quad (6)$$

$$\mathit{linkedTo}(\mathit{alice},x) \to \mathtt{U}_2(x) \quad (7)$$

$$\mathtt{U}_2(x) \wedge \mathtt{U}_3(x) \wedge \mathit{linkedTo}(x,x') \to \mathtt{U}_2(x') \quad (8)$$

$$\mathtt{U}_2(\mathit{bob}) \to \mathtt{hit} \quad (9)$$

This new query notion is rather powerful. It is easy to see that it subsumes conjunctive queries (CQs) as well as unions of CQs. Indeed, given k CQs $\exists\mathbf{y}_i.Q_i[\mathbf{x},\mathbf{y}_i]$ with $i \in \{1,\ldots,k\}$, their union is expressed as the MODEQ $\{Q_i[\boldsymbol{\lambda},\mathbf{y}_i] \to \mathtt{hit} \mid 1 \leq i \leq k\}(\mathbf{x})$. Before showing that MODEQs also capture more powerful query languages, we observe closure under homomorphism (see Fact 1) and state a basic complexity result.

THEOREM 2. *For every MODEQ $\mathfrak{Q}[\mathbf{x}]$, the set of all models of $\exists\mathbf{x}.\mathfrak{Q}[\mathbf{x}]$ is closed under homomorphisms.*

THEOREM 3 (MODEQ ANSWERING COMPLEXITY). *Testing if $\mathbf{c}$ is an answer to a MODEQ $\mathfrak{Q}[\mathbf{x}]$ over a database D is* P*-complete in the size of D, and* NP*-complete in the combined size of D and $\mathfrak{Q}$.*

Hardness follows from the fact that MODEQs subsume monadic Datalog, shown in Section 3.2 below. P membership for data complexity is a consequence of the fact that Datalog subsumes MODEQs, demonstrated in Section 4.1. Membership in NP for combined complexity is established directly by showing that every query match is witnessed by a proof that can be guessed and verified in polynomial time.

3.1 MODEQs Capture Regular Path Queries

We now show that MODEQs subsume *conjunctive two-way regular path queries (C2RPQs)*, which generalize CQs by regular expressions over binary predicates [27, 15]. Variants of this type of queries are used, e.g., by the XPath query language for querying semi-structured XML data. Recent versions of the SPARQL 1.1 query language for RDF also support some of regular expressions that can be evaluated under a similar semantics.

C2RPQs are defined like MODEQs, but with MODEPs replaced by another form of defined predicates based on regular expressions over binary predicates and their inverses:

DEFINITION 2 (C2RPQ SYNTAX AND SEMANTICS). *A* two-way regular path predicate (2RPP) *is a regular expression over the alphabet* $\Gamma = \{p, p^- \mid \mathsf{ar}(p) = 2\}$ *of normal and inverse binary predicate symbols. All 2RPPs are of arity 2. Consider an interpretation* $\mathcal{I}$. *For inverse predicates* p^-, *we define* $(p^-)^{\mathcal{I}} := \{\langle\delta_2, \delta_1\rangle \mid \langle\delta_1, \delta_2\rangle \in p^{\mathcal{I}}\}$. *For a 2RPP P, we set* $\langle\delta, \delta'\rangle \in P^{\mathcal{I}}$ *if there is a word* $\gamma_1 \ldots \gamma_n$ *matching the regular expression P, and a sequence* $\delta_0 \ldots \delta_n$ *of domain elements such that* $\delta_0 = \delta$, $\delta_n = \delta'$, *and* $\langle\delta_i, \delta_{i+1}\rangle \in \gamma_i^{\mathcal{I}}$ *for every* $i \in \{0, \ldots, n-1\}$.

A conjunctive two-way regular path query (C2RPQ) *is a conjunctive query that uses both normal predicates and 2RPPs in its atoms. The semantics of C2RPQs is defined in the obvious way based on the semantics of 2RPPs.*

EXAMPLE 3. *The query of Example 1 is expressed by the C2RPQ* $\mathit{certifiedBy}^*(x, y)$. *Another C2RPQ with inverses is*

$$\mathit{mountain}(x) \wedge \mathit{continent}(y) \wedge (\mathit{locatedIn}|\mathit{hasPart}^-)^*(x, y). \quad (10)$$

Query answering for C2RPQs is NP-complete regarding the size of the database and query, which is the same as for CQs. In terms of data complexity, C2RPQs are NLOGSPACE-complete, and thus harder than CQs (AC_0). One can show hardness via graph reachability, and membership via a translation to linear Datalog [13].

DEFINITION 3 (C2RPQ TO MODEQ TRANSLATION). *Consider a 2RPP P and a finite automaton* $\mathcal{A}_P = \langle\Gamma, S, I, F, T\rangle$ *that recognizes P. The binary MODEP* $\mathsf{modep}(P)$ *consists of the rules*

$$\begin{array}{rl} \to \mathtt{U}_s(\lambda_1) & \textit{for every initial state } s \in I, \\ \mathtt{U}_s(z) \wedge p(z, z') \to \mathtt{U}_{s'}(z') & \textit{for every transition } \langle s, p, s'\rangle \in T, \\ \mathtt{U}_s(z) \wedge p(z', z) \to \mathtt{U}_{s'}(z') & \textit{for every transition } \langle s, p^-, s'\rangle \in T, \\ \mathtt{U}_s(\lambda_2) \to \mathtt{hit} & \textit{for every final state } s \in F. \end{array}$$

Given a C2RPQ Q, a MODEQ $\mathsf{modeq}(Q)$ *is obtained by replacing every 2RPP P in Q by* $\mathsf{modep}(P)$.

The intuition behind the translation of C2RPQs to MODEQs is to find bindings for x and y in $P(x, y)$ by simulating all possible runs of the automaton corresponding to a C2RPQ. Colors $\mathtt{U}_s$ are associated to states s of the automaton to record which domain elements can be reached in which states when starting in an initial state at x. The success criterion is that y is colored by a final state. One can thus show the following:

THEOREM 4 (MODEQS CAPTURE C2RPQS). *For every C2RPQ Q, the MODEQ* $\mathsf{modeq}(Q)$ *can be constructed in linear time, and is equivalent to Q. In particular, the answers for Q and* $\mathsf{modeq}(Q)$ *coincide.*

EXAMPLE 4. *Let Q be the regular path query* (10). *The corresponding MODEQ* $\mathsf{modeq}(Q)$ *is* $\mathit{mountain}(x) \wedge \mathit{continent}(y) \wedge \mathbb{P}(x, y)$ *where* $\mathbb{P} = \mathsf{modep}((\mathit{locatedIn}|\mathit{hasPart}^-)^*)$ *consists of the rules:*

$$\to \mathtt{U}(\lambda_1) \quad (11)$$

$$\mathtt{U}(z) \wedge \mathit{locatedIn}(z, z') \to \mathtt{U}(z') \quad (12)$$

$$\mathtt{U}(z) \wedge \mathit{hasPart}(z', z) \to \mathtt{U}(z') \quad (13)$$

$$\mathtt{U}(\lambda_2) \to \mathtt{hit}. \quad (14)$$

Here we only need one "color" U *that is propagated over locatedIn and inversely over hasPart. The pairs in* $\mathbb{P}$ *are those for which this process, started at the first element, will eventually color the second argument.*

However, the expressivity of MODEQs goes well beyond that of C2RPQs, even when considering only binary predicates. This follows from the easy observation that for every C2RPQ Q there is an integer n, such that whenever Q matches into a graph G, it also matches into a graph G' where all vertices have degree $\leq n$ and from which there is a homomorphism into G. It is easy to see that the MODEQ $\mathfrak{Q}_2$ from Example 2 does not have this property.

3.2 MODEQs Capture Monadic Datalog

Monadic Datalog queries are another type of query language that enjoys favorable computational properties. They are used, e.g., for information extraction from the Web [28]. We now show that MODEQs can express monadic Datalog queries, which is another way to see that they are strictly more general than C2RPQs.

DEFINITION 4 (MONADIC DATALOG QUERY). *Given a signature* $\mathscr{S}$, *a* Datalog query *is based on a signature* $\mathscr{S}'$ *that extends* $\mathscr{S}$ *with additional predicates, called* intensional database (IDB) predicates. *A Datalog query is a pair* $\langle\mathtt{goal}, \mathbb{S}\rangle$, *where* goal *is an IDB predicate, and* $\mathbb{S}$ *is a set of Datalog rules over* $\mathscr{S}'$ *where only IDB predicates occur in rule heads and* goal *does not occur in rule bodies. A* monadic Datalog query *is a query where all IDB predicates other than* goal *have arity* 1.

Given an interpretation $\mathcal{I}$, *the* extension *of* $\langle\mathtt{goal}, \mathbb{S}\rangle$ *is the set of tuples* $\boldsymbol{\delta}$ *over* $\Delta^{\mathcal{I}}$ *for which every extension* $\mathcal{I}'$ *of* $\mathcal{I}$ *to* $\mathscr{S}'$ *which satisfies* $\mathbb{S}$ *must also satisfy* $\boldsymbol{\delta} \in \mathtt{goal}^{\mathcal{I}'}$.

Note that sometimes in the literature, the arity of goal is restricted to 1. Allowing it to be arbitrary does not affect the complexity of the formalism.

DEFINITION 5 (MONADIC DATALOG TO MODEQ). *Given a monadic Datalog query* $Q = \langle\mathtt{goal}, \mathbb{S}\rangle$, *we let* $\mathsf{modeq}(Q)$ *denote the MODEQ* $\mathbb{P}(\boldsymbol{x})$ *where* $\mathbb{P}$ *is obtained from* $\mathbb{S}$ *by*

- *replacing each rule* $\varphi[\boldsymbol{x}, \boldsymbol{y}] \to \mathtt{goal}(\boldsymbol{x})$ *by* $\varphi[\boldsymbol{\lambda}, \boldsymbol{y}] \to \mathtt{hit}$,
- *replacing each IDB predicate, uniformly and injectively, by a predicate* $\mathtt{U}_j$.

THEOREM 5 (MODEQS CAPTURE MONADIC DATALOG). *For every monadic Datalog query Q, the MODEQ* $\mathsf{modeq}(Q)$ *can be constructed in linear time, and is equivalent to Q. In particular, the answers for Q and* $\mathsf{modeq}(Q)$ *coincide.*

From the correspondence thus established it follows that the lower complexity bounds of monadic Datalog carry over and MODEQ answering on databases must thus be P-hard for data complexity and NP-hard for combined complexity [28], showing one direction of Theorem 3. MODEQs are strictly more expressive than monadic Datalog queries, shown by the fact that even a simple connectedness query like the one in Example 1 cannot be expressed in monadic Datalog.

We would like to specifically note that, although the rules used in the definitions of MODEPs are in fact monadic Datalog rules, the query evaluation schemes underlying monadic Datalog and MODEQs are fundamentally different: while in the case of monadic Datalog, all elements of the extension can be obtained at once by a forward chaining saturation process on the given interpretation (or database), the *flag & check* strategy that underlies the semantics definition of MODEPs crucially hinges on each potential extension element being verified in a *separate* saturation process. In Section 4.1, we will see that this idea can be captured by Datalog queries, but not by monadic ones.

4. NESTED MODEQS

Query nesting is the process of using an n-ary subquery instead of an n-ary predicate symbol within a query, with the obvious semantics. In this section, we use this mechanism to extend MODEQs, leading to the more general language of *nested monadically defined queries (NEMODEQs)*. We then show that queries of this type can be expressed in Datalog (Section 4.1) and monadic second-order logic (Section 4.2). These results extend to MODEQs as a special case of NEMODEPs, and help to establish some additional upper bounds for complexity.

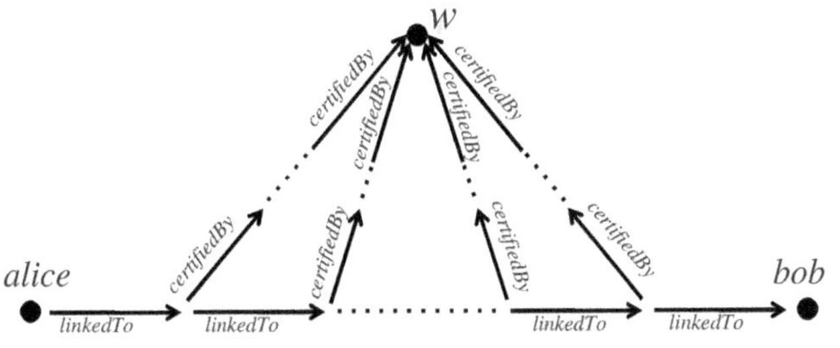

Figure 3: Structure recognized by $\mathfrak{Q}_3$ in Example 5

It is interesting to ask if nesting of queries actually leads to a new query language or not. A query language is *closed under nesting* if every query with nested subqueries can be expressed by some non-nested query. Many query languages are trivially closed under nestings as they allow nesting as part of their syntax (e.g., CQs, FOL, MSO, and SO), other languages require more or less complex reformulations to eliminate nested queries (e.g., UCQs, Datalog, and monadic Datalog), others are not closed under nestings (e.g., linear Datalog). Example 6 below shows that MODEQs are not closed under nestings, motivating the following definition.

Definition 6 (NEMODEQ syntax & semantics). *Let $\mathscr{S}$ be the underlying signature. A* nested monadically defined predicate (NEMODEP) *of degree* 1 *over $\mathscr{S}$ is a MODEP over $\mathscr{S}$. Consider a finite set $\mathbb{P}_i$ ($i = 1, \dots, k$) of NEMODEPs of degree $\leq d$ over $\mathscr{S}$. A NEMODEP of degree $d+1$ is a MODEP over a signature $\mathscr{S}'$ that extends $\mathscr{S}$ with additional predicate names $\mathbb{P}_i$ that have the same arity as the respective queries.*

The semantics of NEMODEPs of degree $d > 1$ is defined as for MODEPs, based on the (recursively defined) semantics of NEMODEPs of degree $< d$. A nested monadically defined query (NEMODEQ) *is a conjunctive query that uses both normal predicates and nested monadically defined predicates in its atoms. The semantics of NEMODEQs is defined in the obvious way.*

Note that the auxiliary symbols λ_i, $\mathtt{U}_j$, and $\mathtt{hit}$ do not need to be distinct in different subqueries, or in queries and their subqueries. This does not cause semantic interactions.

Example 5. *Consider again Example 2, and assume that we are now also interested in entities that can certify the security of a communication indirectly, i.e., through a chain of certifications, as shown in Fig. 3. This can be expressed by nesting MODEP $\mathbb{P}_1$ in $\mathfrak{Q}_2$, leading to a NEMODEQ of degree 2 $\mathfrak{Q}_3 = \mathbb{P}_3(w)$, where $\mathbb{P}_3$ coincides with $\mathbb{P}_2$ except that rule (6) is replaced by $\mathbb{P}_1(x, \lambda_1) \to \mathtt{U}_3(x)$.*

However, even if a query is more easily expressed as a NEMODEQ, it might still be expressible as a MODEQ. The next example shows that this is the case for $\mathfrak{Q}_3$ above, and presents a query that cannot be expressed by any MODEQ.

Example 6. *$\mathfrak{Q}_3$ of Example 5 can equivalently be expressed by the MODEQ $\mathfrak{Q}_4[w] = \mathbb{P}_4(w)$, where $\mathbb{P}_4$ consists of the following rules:*

$$\mathit{certifiedBy}(x, \lambda_1) \to \mathtt{U}_3(x) \quad (15)$$
$$\mathtt{U}_3(y) \wedge \mathit{certifiedBy}(x, y) \to \mathtt{U}_3(x) \quad (16)$$
$$\mathit{linkedTo}(\mathit{alice}, x) \to \mathtt{U}_2(x) \quad (17)$$
$$\mathtt{U}_2(x) \wedge \mathtt{U}_3(x) \wedge \mathit{linkedTo}(x, x') \to \mathtt{U}_2(x') \quad (18)$$
$$\mathtt{U}_2(\mathit{bob}) \to \mathtt{hit} \quad (19)$$

To define a NEMODEQ that cannot be expressed as a MODEQ, we first modify this example to ask for all pairs of persons who are connected by a communication chain that is certified by a single entity, i.e., we query for the possible pairs of "alice" and "bob." Let $\mathbb{P}_5$ be the ternary MODEP that consists of the following rules:

$$\mathit{certifiedBy}(x, \lambda_1) \to \mathtt{U}_3(x) \quad (20)$$
$$\mathtt{U}_3(y) \wedge \mathit{certifiedBy}(x, y) \to \mathtt{U}_3(x) \quad (21)$$
$$\mathit{linkedTo}(\lambda_2, x) \to \mathtt{U}_2(x) \quad (22)$$
$$\mathtt{U}_2(x) \wedge \mathtt{U}_3(x) \wedge \mathit{linkedTo}(x, x') \to \mathtt{U}_2(x') \quad (23)$$
$$\mathtt{U}_2(\lambda_3) \to \mathtt{hit} \quad (24)$$

We now form a NEMODEQ that asks for all pairs of persons who can communicate through a chain of such secure channels that goes via multiple people. Moreover, we require that all of these people are "friends," that is, trustworthy in the context of the application. Let $\mathbb{P}_6$ be the binary NEMODEP with the following rules:

$$\to \mathtt{U}_1(\lambda_1) \quad (25)$$
$$\mathtt{U}_1(y) \wedge \mathbb{P}_5(x, y, z) \wedge \mathit{friend}(z) \to \mathtt{U}_1(z) \quad (26)$$
$$\mathtt{U}_1(y) \wedge \mathbb{P}_5(x, y, \lambda_2) \to \mathtt{hit} \quad (27)$$

The NEMODEQ $\mathfrak{Q}_4 = \mathbb{P}_6(v, w)$ (see Fig. 4) cannot be expressed as a MODEQ. To show this, one assumes the existence of such a MODEQ and constructs a database where it must accept a match that is not accepted by $\mathfrak{Q}_4$. Details are given in the technical report.

4.1 Expressing NEMODEQs in Datalog

We now show that NEMODEQs of arbitrary degree can be expressed as Datalog queries. To this end, the auxiliary predicates have to be "contextualized," which increases their arity. Hence the translation usually does not lead to monadic Datalog queries.

Definition 7 (NEMODEQ to Datalog). *Given a MODEP $\mathbb{P}$ of arity m, the set* $\mathsf{datalog}(\mathbb{P})$ *of Datalog rules over an extended signature contains, for each rule in $\mathbb{P}$, a new rule obtained by replacing*

- *each constant λ_i with a variable x_{λ_i},*
- *each atom $\mathtt{U}_i(z)$ with the atom $\hat{U}_i(z, x_{\lambda_1}, \dots, x_{\lambda_m})$ where $\hat{U}_i$ is a fresh predicate of arity $m+1$,*
- *each atom $\mathtt{hit}$ with the atom $p_{\mathbb{P}}(x_{\lambda_1}, \dots, x_{\lambda_m})$ where $p_{\mathbb{P}}$ is a fresh predicate symbol of arity m.*

For a NEMODEP $\mathbb{P}$ of degree $d > 1$, let $\mathbb{P}'$ be the MODEP obtained by replacing each direct sub-NEMODEP $\mathbb{Q}$ of $\mathbb{P}$ with the predicate $p_{\mathbb{Q}}$. The Datalog translation of $\mathbb{P}$ is recursively defined as:

$$\mathsf{datalog}(\mathbb{P}) := \mathsf{datalog}(\mathbb{P}') \cup \bigcup_{\mathbb{Q} \text{ a direct sub-NEMODEP of } \mathbb{P}} \mathsf{datalog}(\mathbb{Q}).$$

Given a NEMODEQ $\mathfrak{Q}[\mathbf{x}] = \exists \mathbf{y}.\varphi[\mathbf{x}, \mathbf{y}]$, we define its translation $\mathsf{datalog}(\mathfrak{Q})$ *as* $\mathsf{datalog}(\{\varphi[\boldsymbol{\lambda}, \mathbf{y}] \to \mathtt{hit}\})$*, where the predicate used to replace* $\mathtt{hit}$ *will be denoted by $p_{\mathfrak{Q}}$.*

Note that the predicates $\hat{U}_i$ must be globally fresh, even if multiple subqueries use the same $\mathtt{U}_i$. The rules in $\mathsf{datalog}(\mathfrak{Q})$ might be unsafe, i.e., they may contain universally quantified variables in the head that do not occur in the body. This is no problem with the logical semantics we consider.

Theorem 6 (Datalog expressibility of NEMODEQs). *For any NEMODEQ $\mathfrak{Q}$,* $\mathsf{datalog}(\mathfrak{Q})$ *can be constructed in linear time. Moreover, the queries $\mathfrak{Q}[\mathbf{x}]$ and $\langle p_{\mathfrak{Q}}, \mathsf{datalog}(\mathfrak{Q})\rangle$ are equivalent, i.e., their answers coincide.*

Example 7. *The Datalog translation for the MODEQ $\mathfrak{Q}_3$ from Example 5 is as follows:*

$$
\begin{array}{|l|}
\hline
\mathsf{datalog}(\mathfrak{Q}_3) \\
\begin{array}{|l|}
\hline
\mathsf{datalog}(\mathbb{P}_3) \\
\begin{array}{|lr|}
\hline
\mathsf{datalog}(\mathbb{P}_1) & \mathit{certifiedBy}(x_{\lambda_1}, y) \rightarrow \hat{U}_1(y, x_{\lambda_1}, x_{\lambda_2}) \\
 & \hat{U}_1(y, x_{\lambda_1}, x_{\lambda_2}) \wedge \mathit{certifiedBy}(y, z) \rightarrow \hat{U}_1(z, x_{\lambda_1}, x_{\lambda_2}) \\
 & \hat{U}_1(x_{\lambda_2}, x_{\lambda_1}, x_{\lambda_2}) \rightarrow p_{\mathbb{P}_1}(x_{\lambda_1}, x_{\lambda_2}) \\
\hline
\end{array} \\
\hfill p_{\mathbb{P}_1}(x, x_{\lambda_1}) \rightarrow \hat{U}_3(x, x_{\lambda_1}) \\
\hfill \mathit{linkedTo}(\mathit{alice}, x) \rightarrow \hat{U}_2(x, x_{\lambda_1}) \\
\hat{U}_2(x, x_{\lambda_1}) \wedge \hat{U}_3(x, x_{\lambda_1}) \wedge \mathit{linkedTo}(x, x') \rightarrow \hat{U}_2(x', x_{\lambda_1}) \\
\hfill \hat{U}_2(\mathit{bob}, x_{\lambda_1}) \rightarrow p_{\mathbb{P}_3}(x_{\lambda_1}) \\
\hline
\end{array} \\
\hfill p_{\mathbb{P}_3}(x_{\lambda_1}) \rightarrow p_{\mathfrak{Q}_3}(x_{\lambda_1}) \\
\hline
\end{array}
$$

Using backward-chaining, the goal $p_{\mathfrak{Q}}(\boldsymbol{x})$ can be expanded under the rules $\mathsf{datalog}(\mathfrak{Q})$ to obtain a (possibly infinite) set of CQs that do not contain auxiliary predicates $p_{\mathfrak{Q}'}$. Thus $\mathfrak{Q}$ can be considered as a union of (possibly infinitely many) conjunctive queries.

The linear translation of NEMODEQs (and thus also MODEQs) to Datalog leads to various results. First, NEMODEQs inherit Datalog's PTIME upper bound for data complexity of query answering [23]. The results of Section 3.2 show that this bound is tight. Second, we find that the models of NEMODEQs are closed under homomorphisms, since Datalog has this property. Again, this shows that query entailment coincides with model checking (Fact 1).

THEOREM 7. *For any NEMODEQ $\mathfrak{Q}[\boldsymbol{x}]$, the set of models of $\exists \boldsymbol{x}.\mathfrak{Q}$ is closed under homomorphisms.*

4.2 Expressing NEMODEQs in MSO Logic

In this section, we show that NEMODEQs can also be expressed in *monadic second-order logic (MSO)*, the extension of first-order logic with *set variables*, used like predicates of arity 1. To distinguish them from object variables x, y, z, we denote set variables by the uppercase letter U, possibly with subscripts, hinting at their close relation to the unary coloring predicates $\mathtt{U}$. We adhere to the standard semantics of MSO that we will not repeat here.

To simplify the presentation of the next definition, we henceforth assume that every variable x, constant λ_i, or monadic predicate $\mathtt{U}_j$ is used in at most one (sub-)predicate $\mathbb{P}$ of any NEMODEQ or NEMODEP we consider. This can always be achieved by renaming variables and predicates.

DEFINITION 8 (NEMODEQ TO MSO). *For a MODEP $\mathbb{P}$ of arity m with auxiliary unary predicates $\mathtt{U}_1, \ldots, \mathtt{U}_k$, and a list of terms $\boldsymbol{t} = \langle t_1, \ldots, t_m \rangle$, we define an MSO formula*

$$\mathsf{mso}(\mathbb{P}(\boldsymbol{t})) := \forall U_1, \ldots, U_k. \neg \bigwedge_{\rho \in \mathbb{P}} \mathsf{mso}(\rho, \boldsymbol{t})$$

where $\mathsf{mso}(\rho, \boldsymbol{t})$ is the rule obtained from rule ρ by replacing each occurrence of a constant λ_i by t_i, each occurrence of `hit` by $\bot$ (the falsity atom), and each occurrence of a unary predicate $\mathtt{U}_i$ by a set variable U_i. We extend mso to NEMODEPs of higher degree by applying it recursively to NEMODEP atoms. For a NEMODEQ $\mathfrak{Q}$, we obtain $\mathsf{mso}(\mathfrak{Q})$ by replacing every NEMODEP atom $\mathbb{P}(\boldsymbol{t})$ in $\mathfrak{Q}$ by $\mathsf{mso}(\mathbb{P}(\boldsymbol{t}))$.

By replacing `hit` with $\bot$, the derivation of a query match becomes the derivation of an inconsistency. The formula $\mathsf{mso}(\mathbb{P}(\boldsymbol{t}))$ evaluates to true if this occurs for all possible interpretations of the predicates $\mathtt{U}_j$, expressed here by universal quantification over the set variables U_j. The interpretation of $\boldsymbol{t}$ corresponds to the flagged tuple $\boldsymbol{\lambda}$ that is to be checked. It is thus easy to see that the translation captures the semantic conditions of Definitions 1 and 6.

THEOREM 8 (MSO EXPRESSIBILITY OF NEMODEQs). *For every NEMODEQ $\mathfrak{Q}[\boldsymbol{x}]$, $\mathsf{mso}(\mathfrak{Q}[\boldsymbol{x}])$ can be constructed in linear time and is equivalent to $\mathfrak{Q}[\boldsymbol{x}]$.*

EXAMPLE 8. *Consider NEMODEQ $\mathfrak{Q}_3$ from Example 5. Then $\mathsf{mso}(\mathfrak{Q}_3)$ is the MSO formula*

$$
\forall U_2, U_3. \neg \left(\begin{array}{ll}
 & \forall v. \left(\boxed{ \forall U_1. \neg \left(\begin{array}{lr} & \forall y.(\mathit{certBy}(v,y) \rightarrow U_1(y)) \\ \wedge & \forall y,z.(U_1(y) \wedge \mathit{certBy}(y,z) \rightarrow U_1(z)) \\ \wedge & (U_1(w) \rightarrow \bot) \end{array} \right) } \rightarrow U_3(v) \right) \\
\wedge & \forall x.(\mathit{linkedTo}(\mathit{alice}, x) \rightarrow U_2(x)) \\
\wedge & \forall x,x'.(U_2(x) \wedge U_3(x) \wedge \mathit{linkedTo}(x, x') \rightarrow U_2(x')) \\
\wedge & (U_2(\mathit{bob}) \rightarrow \bot)
\end{array} \right)
$$

with free variable w (using certBy to abbreviate certifiedBy). The framed subformula is $\mathsf{mso}(\mathbb{P}_1(v, w))$.

Expressibility of NEMODEQs (and thus also MODEQs) in MSO is a useful feature, which we will further exploit below. For the moment, we just note the direct consequence that the PSPACE combined complexity of model checking in MSO directly gives us PSPACE-membership of query answering for NEMODEQs and MODEQs.

The following theorem closes the gap w.r.t. the combined complexity of query answering by showing PSPACE hardness for NEMODEQs by a reduction from the validity problem of quantified Boolean formulae.

THEOREM 9 (COMPLEXITY OF NEMODEQ ANSWERING). *The task of checking if $\boldsymbol{c}$ is an answer to a NEMODEQ $\mathfrak{Q}[\boldsymbol{x}]$ over a database D is P-complete in the size of D, and PSPACE-complete in the size of D and $\mathfrak{Q}$.*

Figure 1 gives an overview of the relationships established so far, regarding both expressivity and complexity. MODEQs feature the same complexities as monadic Datalog, while providing a significant extension of expressivity. The step to NEMODEQs leads to increased combined complexity. Nevertheless, combined complexity is still lower than for Datalog and data complexity is still lower than for MSO. In addition, in the next sections, we will show that NEMODEQs (and MODEQs) are also more well-behaved than these two when it comes to checking containment or interaction with rule sets that give rise to infinite structures.

5. DECIDING QUERY CONTAINMENT

Checking query containment is an essential task in database management, facilitating query optimization, information integration and exchange, and database integrity checking. The *containment* or *subsumption problem* of two queries $\mathfrak{P}$ and $\mathfrak{Q}$ is the question whether the answers of $\mathfrak{Q}$ are contained in the answers of $\mathfrak{P}$ over any database. In this section, we show that this problem is decidable for NEMODEQs. At its core, this result is based on previous work by Courcelle [20], from which we can derive the following general theorem, which is interesting in its own right:

THEOREM 10 (DECIDING DATALOG CONTAINMENT IN MSO). *There exists an algorithm that decides, given any Datalog query $\langle \mathtt{goal}, \mathbb{P} \rangle$ and any MSO query φ whose set of models is closed under homomorphisms, if the query $\langle \mathtt{goal}, \mathbb{P} \rangle$ is contained in φ.*

The underling result in [20] is formulated for queries without free variables and without constant symbols, using a variant of multi-sorted monadic second-order logic and a notion of graph grammar derived from Datalog queries. The appendix recalls the relevant notions and relates them to our setting to prove Theorem 10.

By Theorems 6, 7, and 8, NEMODEQs can be considered as Datalog queries and as MSO queries whose models are closed under homomorphisms. This shows the following:

THEOREM 11 (DECIDING NEMODEQ CONTAINMENT). *The query containment problem for NEMODEQs is decidable.*

The complexity of NEMODEQ containment remains to be determined. A lower bound is the 2EXPTIME-hardness of monadic Datalog containment shown recently [7].

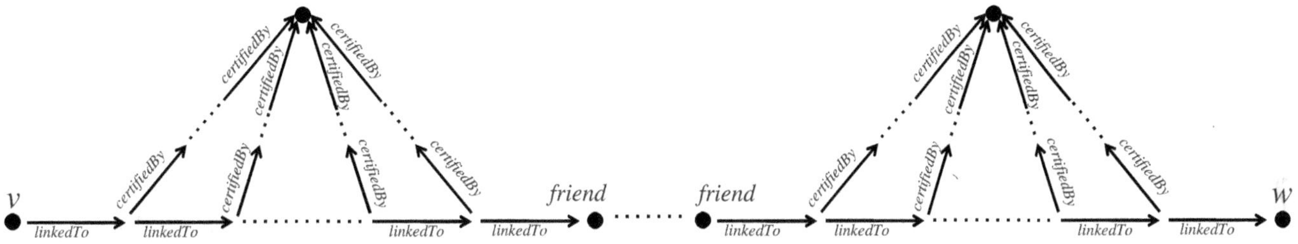

Figure 4: Structure recognized by $\mathfrak{Q}_4$ in Example 6

6. QUERYING UNDER DEPENDENCIES

Dependencies play an important role in many database applications, be it to formulate constraints, to specify views for data integration, or to define relationships in data exchange. Dependencies can be viewed as logical implications, like the TGDs introduced in Section 2, and one is generally interested in answering queries w.r.t. to their logical entailments. Universal models (Section 2) can be viewed as solutions to data exchange problems or as minimal ways of repairing constraint violations over a database. Querying under dependencies thus corresponds to finding *certain answers*, as is common, e.g., in data integration scenarios.

EXAMPLE 9. *Consider the following set of TGDs:*

$$\begin{aligned} hasAuthor(x,y) &\rightarrow publication(x) \\ cites(x,y) &\rightarrow publication(x) \wedge publication(y) \\ publication(x) &\rightarrow \exists y.hasAuthor(x,y) \end{aligned}$$

For a database $\{hasAuthor(a,c), cites(a,b)\}$, *the conjunctive query* $\exists z.(hasAuthor(x,z))$ *has* $x \mapsto a$ *as its only answer. When taking the above dependencies into account, the certain answers additionally contain* $x \mapsto b$.

The extension of TGDs with equality is known as *embedded dependencies*, a special case of which are *equality-generating dependencies* [1]. We will not focus on equality here, and state most of our results for TGDs.

The problem of computing CQ answers under TGDs is undecidable in general [16, 6]. A practical approach for computing certain answers is to compute a finite universal model, if possible. All combinations of TGDs and databases have universal models, but it is undecidable whether any such model is finite; the *core chase* is a known semi-decision procedure that computes a finite universal model whenever it exists [24]. Many other variants of the chase have been proposed to compute (finite) universal models in certain cases.

One can compute certain answers under TGDs even in cases where no finite universal model exists, as long as there is a universal model that is sufficiently "regular" to allow for a finite representation. One of the most general criteria is based on the well-known notion of *treewidth* (see, e.g., [4] for a formal definition). A rule set Σ is called *bounded treewidth set (bts)* if for every database D, there is a universal model $\mathcal{I}(D \cup \Sigma)$ of bounded treewidth. The treewidth bound in each case can depend on Σ and D. Recognizing whether a rule set has this property is undecidable in general [4], but many sufficient conditions have been identified. This includes the case of rule sets with finite models as a special case of models with bounded treewidth. TGDs without existential quantifiers, called *full dependencies* or Datalog rules [1], trivially have finite models. More elaborate are various notions of *acyclicity* based on analyzing the interaction of TGDs [25, 26, 37, 38, 4, 34].

Cases where $\mathcal{I}(D \cup \Sigma)$ may be infinite but treewidth-bounded are also manifold. A basic case are *guarded TGDs*, inspired by the guarded fragment of first-order logic [2]. These have been generalized to *weakly guarded TGDs* [9] and *frontier-guarded rules* [4], both of which are subsumed by *weakly frontier-guarded TGDs* [4]. The most expressive currently known bts fragments are *greedy bts TGDs* [5] and *glut-guarded TGDs* [34].

Another type of dependencies comes from the area of *Description Logics* (DLs). Originally conceived as ontology languages, DLs have also been applied to express database constraints [14]. DLs use a different syntax, but share a similar first-order semantics that makes them compatible with TGDs. Most DLs considered in database applications are Horn logics (that allow for universal models), and can thus be presented as rules [10].

EXAMPLE 10. *The set of TGDs in Example 9 can equivalently be expressed by the DL-Lite ontology*

$$\begin{aligned} \exists hasAuthor &\sqsubseteq publication & \exists cites &\sqsubseteq publication \\ publication &\sqsubseteq \exists hasAuthor & \exists cites^- &\sqsubseteq publication. \end{aligned}$$

Many DLs enjoy tree-model properties, but some expressive DLs are not bounded treewidth. This mainly applies to DLs that support transitivity or its generalizations [35, 40].

As mentioned before, the entailment problem $D, \Sigma \models Q$ is known to be decidable if Σ is bts and Q is a conjunctive query. Our main result of this section is that this extends to NEMODEQs provided that the following holds.

CONJECTURE 12. *Satisfiability of monadic second-order logic on countable interpretations of bounded treewidth is decidable.*

This statement is often taken for granted and proof sketches have been communicated. A similar result was shown in [19] for a different notion of *width*. A modern account of the relevant proof techniques that uses our notion of treewidth is given in [22] for finite graphs. Formulating the proof of [19] in these terms, one could show Conjecture 12 [21]. We cautiously characterize this statement as a conjecture since no full proof has been published.

THEOREM 13 (NEMODEQ ANSWERING UNDER BTS). *Let D be a database and let Σ be a set of rules for which the treewidth of $\mathcal{I}(D \cup \Sigma)$ is bounded. Let $\mathfrak{Q}[\boldsymbol{x}]$ be a NEMODEQ.*

1. $D \cup \Sigma \models \mathfrak{Q}[\boldsymbol{c}/\boldsymbol{x}]$ *if and only if* $D \cup \Sigma \cup \{\neg\mathfrak{Q}[\boldsymbol{c}/\boldsymbol{x}]\}$ *has no countable model with bounded treewidth.*
2. *If Conjecture 12 holds, then* $D \cup \Sigma \models \mathfrak{Q}[\boldsymbol{c}/\boldsymbol{x}]$ *is decidable.*

The proof of this theorem exploits universality of $\mathcal{I}(D \cup \Sigma)$ and preservation of NEMODEQ matches under homomorphisms (Theorem 7). The second claim follows from the first by applying Conjecture 12 and the observation that the MSO theory $D \cup \Sigma \cup \{\neg\mathsf{mso}(\mathfrak{Q}[\boldsymbol{c}/\boldsymbol{x}])\}$ is equivalent to $D \cup \Sigma \cup \{\neg\mathfrak{Q}[\boldsymbol{c}/\boldsymbol{x}]\}$ by Theorem 8.

7. MODEQ REWRITABILITY

Query rewriting is an important technique for answering queries under dependencies, and the main alternative to the chase. The general idea is to find "substitute queries" that can be evaluated directly over the database, without taking TGDs into account, and yet deliver the same answer. We now extend this approach to MODEQs and NEMODEQs, and we establish basic cases where Datalog queries can be rewritten to MODEQs, which we extend further in Section 8.

The most common notion is *first-order rewritability*, where a conjunctive query and a set of TGDs is rewritten into a first-order query – typically a union of conjunctive queries [1]. Importantly, the rewriting does not depend on the underlying database but only on the inital query and TGDs.

Example 11. *Given the rule set from Example 9 and the conjunctive query $\exists v, w.(hasAuthor(v, w))$, an appropriate first-order rewriting is*

$$\exists v, w.(hasAuthor(v, w)) \lor \exists v, w.(cites(v, w)) \lor \exists v.(publication(v)).$$

First-order rewritability is a desirable property as there are efficient implementations for evaluating first-order queries (that is, SQL). First-order rewritable sets of TGDs are also called *finite unification sets* [4]. It is undecidable whether a set of TGDs belongs to this class, but an iterative backward chaining algorithm can be defined that terminates on FO-rewritable rule sets and provides the rewritten FO formula [4]. Known sufficient conditions for FO-rewritability led to the definition of *atomic-hypothesis rules* and *domain restricted rules* [4], *linear Datalog+/–* [10], as well as *sticky sets of TGDs* and *sticky-join sets of TGDs* [11, 12]. These criteria were recently found to be subsumed by an efficiently checkable condition that gives rise to the class of *weakly recursive TGDs* [18]. Important FO-rewritable description logics include the DL-Lite family of logics [14]. However, many useful TGDs can not be expressed as first-order queries.

Example 12. *First-order logic cannot express transitive closure, so there is no first-order rewriting for the CQ $s(v) \land r(v, w) \land s(w)$ under the TGD $r(x, y) \land r(y, z) \to r(x, z)$.*

This motivates the consideration of more expressive query languages in query rewriting.

Example 13. *The TGD and query of Example 12 can be rewritten as a Datalog query*

$$r(x, y) \to r_{\mathrm{IDB}}(x, y) \quad (28)$$
$$r_{\mathrm{IDB}}(x, y) \land r_{\mathrm{IDB}}(y, z) \to r_{\mathrm{IDB}}(x, z) \quad (29)$$
$$s(v) \land r_{\mathrm{IDB}}(v, w) \land s(w) \to \mathtt{goal}, \quad (30)$$

but also as a conjunctive regular path query

$$\exists v, w.s(v) \land r^*(v, w) \land s(w).$$

Rewriting CQs under TGDs into Datalog queries is interesting, but the evaluation of Datalog queries remains complex. The undecidability of Datalog query containment also makes it intrinsically difficult to determine if such a query captures a set of TGDs. The use of C2RPQs is more interesting. Yet, to the best of our knowledge, rewriting of conjunctive queries into C2RPQs has been addressed only very implicitly by now [40]. Moreover, as discussed in Section 3.1, C2RPQs are still rather constrained: besides further structural restrictions, they only allow for recursion over binary predicates. We therefore consider query rewritability under MODEQs and NEMODEQs, defined as follows:

Definition 9 (NEMODEQ rewritability). *Let Σ be a set of TGDs and let $Q[\boldsymbol{x}]$ be a CQ. A (NE)MODEQ $\mathfrak{Q}_{Q,\Sigma}$ is a* rewriting *of Q under Σ if, for all databases D and potential query answers $\boldsymbol{c}$, we have $D \cup \Sigma \models Q[\boldsymbol{c}/\boldsymbol{x}]$ iff $D \models \mathfrak{Q}_{Q,\Sigma}[\boldsymbol{c}/\boldsymbol{x}]$. Σ is called* (NE)MODEQ-rewritable *if every conjunctive query Q has a (NE)MODEQ rewriting for Σ and Q.*

Rewritability of conjunctive queries entails rewritability of MODEQs, so the conditions of Definition 9 hold even when considering MODEQs instead of CQs. This is shown by replacing CQs in rule bodies with MODEQs, where care must be taken that the existentially quantified variables in the CQ are not used anywhere else in the rule body:

Lemma 14 (Replacement Lemma). *Consider a set Σ of TGDs, a conjunctive query $Q = \exists \boldsymbol{y}.\psi[\boldsymbol{x}, \boldsymbol{y}]$, and a NEMODEQ $\mathfrak{Q}[\boldsymbol{x}]$ that is a rewriting for Σ and Q. Then Q and $\mathfrak{Q}$ are equivalent in all models of Σ, i.e., $\Sigma \models \forall \boldsymbol{x}.Q[\boldsymbol{x}] \leftrightarrow \mathfrak{Q}[\boldsymbol{x}]$.*

Let $\psi[\boldsymbol{t}/\boldsymbol{x}, \boldsymbol{y}'/\boldsymbol{y}]$ be the conjunction of Q with variables $\boldsymbol{x}$ replaced by terms $\boldsymbol{t}$ and variables $\boldsymbol{y}$ replaced by variables $\boldsymbol{y}'$. We say that $\psi[\boldsymbol{t}/\boldsymbol{x}, \boldsymbol{y}'/\boldsymbol{y}]$ is a match *in a Datalog rule ρ if ρ is of the form $\psi[\boldsymbol{t}/\boldsymbol{x}, \boldsymbol{y}'/\boldsymbol{y}] \land \varphi \to \chi$ where the $\boldsymbol{y}'$ occur neither in φ nor in χ.*

Given some NEMODEQ $\mathfrak{P}[\boldsymbol{z}]$ over Σ, let $\mathfrak{P}'[\boldsymbol{z}]$ denote a NEMODEQ obtained by replacing a match $\psi[\boldsymbol{t}/\boldsymbol{x}, \boldsymbol{y}'/\boldsymbol{y}]$ of Q in some rule of $\mathfrak{P}$ by $\mathfrak{Q}[\boldsymbol{t}/\boldsymbol{x}]$, where the bound variables in $\mathfrak{Q}$ do not occur in $\mathfrak{P}$. Then $\mathfrak{P}$ and $\mathfrak{P}'$ are equivalent in all models of Σ, i.e., $\Sigma \models \forall \boldsymbol{z}.\mathfrak{P}[\boldsymbol{z}] \leftrightarrow \mathfrak{P}'[\boldsymbol{z}]$.

All known FO-rewritable classes are rewritten to unions of CQs. Since every union of CQs can be expressed as MODEQ, all such rule sets are also MODEQ-rewritable. Moreover, Section 3.2 implies that every set of monadic Datalog rules is MODEQ-rewritable. Since MODEQs are strictly more expressive than monadic Datalog queries, one would expect to find larger classes of MODEQ-rewritable TGDs. An appropriate generalization of monadic Datalog is as follows:

Definition 10 (j-oriented rule set). *We call a set of Datalog rules Σ* j-oriented *for the integer j if all head predicates have the same arity n, and $1 \le j \le n$, and we have: if a rule's body contains an atom $p(\boldsymbol{t})$ for some head predicate p and the rule's head contains an atom $q(\boldsymbol{t}')$, then $\boldsymbol{t}$ and $\boldsymbol{t}'$ agree on all positions other than possibly j.*

Intuitively speaking, recursive derivations in j-oriented rule sets can only modify the content of a single position j while keeping all other arguments fixed in all derived facts.

Example 14. *The following rule set Σ_{family} is 3-oriented. We use atoms $parentsSon(x, y, z)$ and $parentsDghtr(x, y, z)$ to denote that z is the son and daughter of x and y, respectively.*

$$parentsSon(x, y, z) \land hasBrother(z, z') \to parentsSon(x, y, z')$$
$$parentsSon(x, y, z) \land hasSister(z, z') \to parentsDghtr(x, y, z')$$
$$parentsDghtr(x, y, z) \land hasBrother(z, z') \to parentsSon(x, y, z')$$
$$parentsDghtr(x, y, z) \land hasSister(z, z') \to parentsDghtr(x, y, z')$$

Definition 11 (Single predicate rewriting). *For a j-oriented set Σ of Datalog rules and a head predicate p of Σ, a MODEP $\mathbb{P}_{p,\Sigma}$ is defined as follows. Let $\mathtt{U}_q$ be an auxiliary unary predicate for each head predicate q in Σ, let $\mathtt{V}_i$ be a auxiliary unary predicate for each $i \in \{1, \ldots, \mathsf{ar}(p)\}$ with $i \ne j$, and let $\tilde{z}_j$ be an additional variable not occurring in Σ. Then $\mathbb{P}_{p,\Sigma}$ contains the following rules:*

- *a rule $\mathtt{U}_p(\lambda_j) \to \mathtt{hit}$;*
- *for each set variable $\mathtt{V}_i$, a rule $\to \mathtt{V}_i(\lambda_i)$ with empty body;*
- *for each $\psi \to q(t_1, \ldots, t_n) \in \Sigma$, a rule $\psi' \to \mathtt{U}_q(t_j)$ where ψ' is obtained from ψ by replacing each atom $q'(t_1, \ldots, t'_j, \ldots, t_n)$ (with q' a head predicate) by $\mathtt{U}_{q'}(t'_j)$, and by adding for each term t_i with $i \ne j$ a new body atom $\mathtt{V}_i(t_i)$;*
- *a rule $q'(\lambda_1, \ldots, \tilde{z}_j, \ldots, \lambda_n) \to \mathtt{U}_{q'}(\tilde{z}_j)$ for each head predicate q'.*

For a list $\boldsymbol{z}$ of $\mathsf{ar}(p)$ variables, the MODEQ $\mathfrak{Q}_{p,\Sigma}[\boldsymbol{z}]$ is defined as $\mathbb{P}_{p,\Sigma}(\boldsymbol{z})$.

This operation allows us to express the extension of a predicate p by means of a MODEQ.

THEOREM 15 (SINGLE PREDICATE REWRITING CORRECTNESS). *If Σ is j-oriented and p is a head predicate, then $\mathfrak{Q}_{p,\Sigma}[z]$ is a rewriting for Σ and $p(z)$.*

EXAMPLE 15. *For the rule set in Example 14, we obtain the rewriting $\mathfrak{Q}_{parentsSon,\Sigma}[z_1, z_2, z_3] = \mathbb{P}_{parentsSon,\Sigma}(z_1, z_2, z_3)$ with rules*

$$\mathtt{U}_{parentsSon}(\lambda_3) \to \mathtt{hit} \qquad \to \mathtt{V}_1(\lambda_1) \qquad \to \mathtt{V}_2(\lambda_2)$$

$$\mathtt{V}_1(x) \wedge \mathtt{V}_2(y) \wedge \mathtt{U}_{parentsSon}(z) \wedge hasBrother(z, z') \to \mathtt{U}_{parentsSon}(z')$$

$$\mathtt{V}_1(x) \wedge \mathtt{V}_2(y) \wedge \mathtt{U}_{parentsSon}(z) \wedge hasSister(z, z') \to \mathtt{U}_{parentsDghtr}(z')$$

$$\mathtt{V}_1(x) \wedge \mathtt{V}_2(y) \wedge \mathtt{U}_{parentsDghtr}(z) \wedge hasBrother(z, z') \to \mathtt{U}_{parentsSon}(z')$$

$$\mathtt{V}_1(x) \wedge \mathtt{V}_2(y) \wedge \mathtt{U}_{parentsDghtr}(z) \wedge hasSister(z, z') \to \mathtt{U}_{parentsDghtr}(z')$$

$$parentsSon(\lambda_1, \lambda_2, \tilde{z}_3) \to \mathtt{U}_{parentsSon}(\tilde{z}_3)$$

$$parentsDghtr(\lambda_1, \lambda_2, \tilde{z}_3) \to \mathtt{U}_{parentsDghtr}(\tilde{z}_3).$$

The $\mathtt{V}$ *predicates are not really needed here, since rule bodies do not impose any conditions on the respective variables. If no constants from* **C** *occur, one could always replace* $\mathtt{V}$ *with the respective* λ*s, but expressions like* $\mathtt{V}_1(c)$ *would require an equality predicate to state* $\lambda_1 \approx c$*. For the semantics of NEMODEQs to be meaningful, constants* λ_i *must always be allowed to be equal to other constants, even if a unique name assumption is adopted for constants in* **C**.

Using the Replacement Lemma 14, we can extend Theorem 15 to arbitrary conjunctive queries:

THEOREM 16 (*j*-ORIENTEDNESS IMPLIES REWRITABILITY). *Every j-oriented rule set is MODEQ-rewritable.*

8. REWRITING LAYERS OF TGDS

In the previous section, we have identified a first criterion for MODEQ-rewritability, and thus decidability of query entailment. However, there are many cases where only some of the given TGDs are rewritable. On the other hand, our results from Section 6 guarantee that NEMODEQ answering is still decidable in the presence of TGDs that are in bts, based on techniques that do not require rewriting. We now show how to combine both results by applying query rewriting to a subset of TGDs that is suitably "layered above" the remaining TGDs. This allows us to define a class of *fully oriented rule sets* that generalizes *j*-oriented rule sets to cover the full expressiveness of NEMODEQs. More generally, the combination of bts and NEMODEQ-rewritability captures some of the most expressive ontology languages for which query answering is known to be decidable.

Given a set of TGDs, we first clarify which subsets of TGDs can be rewritten into queries that can be evaluated over the remaining TGDs and databases without loosing results. To this end, we consider a notion of *rule dependency*. Related notions were first described in [3], and independently in [24]. Our presentation is closely related to [4].

DEFINITION 12 (RULE DEPENDENCY, CUT). *Let $\rho_1 = B_1 \to H_1$ and $\rho_2 = B_2 \to H_2$ be two TGDs. We say that ρ_2* depends on *ρ_1, written $\rho_1 \prec \rho_2$, if there is*

- *a database D,*
- *a substitution θ of all variables in B_1 with terms in D such that $\theta(B_1) \subseteq D$, and*
- *a substitution θ' of all variables in B_2 with terms in $D \cup \theta(H_1)$ such that $\theta'(B_2) \subseteq D \cup \theta(H_1)$ but $\theta'(B_2) \nsubseteq D$.*

We say that ρ_2 strongly depends *on ρ_1, written $\rho_1 \ll \rho_2$, if H_1 contains a predicate that occurs in B_2.*

A (strong) cut *of a set of rules Σ is a partition $\Sigma_1 \cup \Sigma_2$ of Σ such that no rule in Σ_1 (strongly) depends on a rule in Σ_2. It is denoted $\Sigma_1 \triangleright \Sigma_2$ ($\Sigma_1 \mathrel{\triangleright\!\!\triangleright} \Sigma_2$).*

The notion of rule dependencies encodes which rule can possibly trigger which other rule. Checking if a rule depends on another is an NP-complete task [4]. We thus introduce the simpler notion of strong dependency that can be checked in polynomial time. Clearly, dependency implies strong dependency, but the converse might not be true.

EXAMPLE 16. *Consider the following Datalog rules:*

$$A(x) \wedge B(x) \to C(x) \tag{31}$$

$$C(x) \to \exists v.p(x, v), A(v) \tag{32}$$

Rule (32) *strongly depends on* (31) *and vice versa. Moreover,* (32) *depends on* (31)*, where the database of Definition 12 could be $D = \{A(c), B(c)\}$ using $\theta = \theta' = \{x \mapsto c\}$. However,* (31) *does not depend on* (32)*: a substitution θ' can map x to v (introduced as a new term when applying* (32)*), but the required fact $B(v)$ is not derived by* (32) *and cannot be in any initial database D (since it is not ground).*

Intuitively speaking, we can evaluate a TGD set Σ of the form $\Sigma_1 \triangleright \Sigma_2$ by first applying the rules in Σ_1, and then applying the rules of Σ_2. This is the essence of the following theorem, shown in [4].

THEOREM 17 (BAGET ET AL.). *Let Σ be a set of rules admitting a cut $\Sigma_1 \triangleright \Sigma_2$. Then, for every database D and every conjunctive query $Q[\mathbf{x}]$ we have that $D \cup \Sigma \models Q[\mathbf{x}/\mathbf{c}]$ exactly if there is a Boolean conjunctive query Q' such that $D \cup \Sigma_1 \models Q'$ and $Q', \Sigma_2 \models Q[\mathbf{x}/\mathbf{c}]$.*

We can thus rewrite queries in "layers" based on cuts:

LEMMA 18 (QUERY REWRITING WITH CUTS). *Let D be a database and let $\Sigma_1 \triangleright \Sigma_2$ be two sets of TGDs.*

1. *If $\mathfrak{Q}_{Q,\Sigma_2}[\mathbf{x}]$ is a NEMODEQ-rewriting of a conjunctive query $Q[\mathbf{x}]$, then:*
   $$D \cup \Sigma_1 \cup \Sigma_2 \models Q[\mathbf{c}/\mathbf{x}] \text{ if and only if } D \cup \Sigma_1 \models \mathfrak{Q}_{Q,\Sigma_2}[\mathbf{c}/\mathbf{x}].$$
2. *If Σ_1 and Σ_2 are NEMODEQ-rewritable, then so is $\Sigma_1 \cup \Sigma_2$.*

This observation has two useful implications. The second item outlines an approach of extending and combining rewriting procedures that we will elaborate on in the remainder of this section. The first item hints at a very general approach for constructing TGD languages for which query answering is decidable, as expressed in the next theorem.

THEOREM 19 (QUERY ANSWERING WITH CUTS). *Consider rule sets $\Sigma_1 \triangleright \Sigma_2$, such that NEMODEQ answering is decidable under Σ_1, and NEMODEQ rewriting is decidable under Σ_2. Then NEMODEQ answering is decidable under $\Sigma_1 \cup \Sigma_2$.*

Using Theorem 13, this result specifically applies in cases where Σ_1 is a bounded treewidth set. We have noted that there are a number of effectively checkable criteria for this general class of TGDs. Much less is known about NEMODEQ rewritability beyond rewritability to unions of CQs. For a more general criterion, we can extend *j*-oriented rules along the lines of Lemma 18 (2).

DEFINITION 13 (FULLY ORIENTED RULE SET). *Let $\approx_{\ll}$ be the reflexive symmetric transitive closure of $\ll$. The set Σ is* fully oriented *if, for every $\rho \in \Sigma$, the equivalence class $[\rho]_{\ll} = \{\rho' \in \Sigma \mid \rho \approx_{\ll} \rho'\}$ is j-oriented (not necessarily for the same j and predicate arity).*

Given a fully oriented rule set, we can construct NEMODEQ rewritings for individual classes $[\rho]_{\ll}$ as in Definition 11, and combine these rewritings using Lemma 14:

THEOREM 20 (FULLY ORIENTED RULE SETS ARE REWRITABLE). *For a rule set Σ, it can be detected in polynomial time if Σ is fully oriented. Every fully oriented set Σ is MODEQ-rewritable.*

The use of $\ll$ instead of $<$ is relevant for deciding full orientedness in polynomial time. Even with this restriction, fully oriented Datalog queries have the same expressivity as NEMODEQs. Moreover, every NEMODEQ-rewritable TGD set can be expressed as a set of rules that can be transformed into a MODEQ using Theorem 20.

THEOREM 21 (NEMODEQs = FULLY ORIENTED DATALOG). *For every NEMODEQ $\mathfrak{Q}$, the rule set* datalog($\mathfrak{Q}$) *of Definition 7 is fully oriented. Moreover, for every NEMODEQ-rewritable set Σ of TGDs, there is a fully oriented set of Datalog rules Σ' such that:*

- *every predicate p in Σ has a corresponding head predicate q_p in Σ' that does not occur in Σ,*
- *for every database D and conjunctive query $Q[\mathbf{x}]$ that do not contain predicates of the form q_p, and for every list of constants $\mathbf{c}$, $D \cup \Sigma \models Q[\mathbf{c}/\mathbf{x}]$ iff $D \cup \Sigma' \models Q'[\mathbf{c}/\mathbf{x}]$ where Q' is obtained from Q by replacing all predicates p by q_p.*

Another interesting criterion for NEMODEQ rewritability has been studied for Description Logics (DLs), where all predicates are of arity one or two. Expressive DL ontologies consist of two kinds of terminological axioms: concept inclusion axioms and role inclusion axioms. A role inclusion axiom is a Datalog rule of the form $R_1(x_0, x_1) \wedge \ldots \wedge R_n(x_{n-1}, x_n) \rightarrow R(x_0, x_n)$, which can be viewed as a generalized transitivity statement. Even in relatively inexpressive DLs, role inclusion axioms lead to undecidability of CQ answering [35]. To overcome this, syntactic restrictions are imposed on role inclusions, to ensure that all role inclusions can be captured using finite automata [33]. This is equivalent to rewriting role inclusions to regular path queries, and has indeed been exploited to decide CQ answering over expressive DLs [40]. This can be viewed as an implicit application of Theorem 19.[2] Many reasoning procedures for DLs are based on tree-like models, so various approaches to DL CQ answering can indeed be viewed as special combinations of bounded treewidth sets and NEMODEQ rewritable sets of TGDs [35, 40]. This supports the relevance of the general relationships observed here, and it motivates the further study of criteria for NEMODEQ rewritability. The rewriting methods used in DLs are based on regular languages, so it seems promising to consider their generalizations to graph grammars when dealing with arbitrary TGDs [22].

9. CONCLUSION

Monadically defined queries and their nested extension achieve a balance between expressivity and computability. They capture and significantly extend the query capabilities of (unions of) conjunctive queries as well as (unions of) conjunctive two-way regular path queries and monadic Datalog queries, the prevailing querying paradigms for structured and semi-structured databases. At the same time, they are conveniently expressible both in Datalog and monadic second-order logic. Yet, as opposed to these two, they ensure decidability of query containment and of query answering in the presence of depdendencies that allow for universal models with bounded treewidth – a property shared by many of the known decidable TGD classes.

[2] DL concept and role inclusion axioms are not always separated by a cut. There are well known rewriting methods to achieve this [32].

The novel notions of MODEQ-rewritability and NEMODEQ-rewritability significantly extend first-order rewritability, which has been proven useful for theoretical considerations and practical realization of query answering alike. This extension allows for capturing much larger classes of TGD sets covering features like transitivity, which are considered difficult to handle within the known decision frameworks. Moreover, (NE)MODEQ-rewritable TGD sets can smoothly be integrated with bounded treewidth TGD sets as long as certain dependency constraints are obeyed. This provides a valuable perspective on rule-based data access as a task that can be solved by combining bottom-up techniques like the *chase* with top-down techniques like query rewriting.

Our work raises a number of interesting questions for future research: How general are (NE)MODEQs? Are there larger, more expressive fragments which jointly satisfy all the established properties? Is every rewriting for a TGD set and a given CQ that is expressible in MSO logic equivalent to a NEMODEQ? What is the precise complexity of deciding query containment? Which more general syntactic criteria ensure NEMODEQ-rewritability? Can all fragments of TGDs (including those considered in description logics) for which conjunctive query answering is known to be decidable be captured as a combination of bts and NEMODEQ-rewriting? Answering these questions will not only contribute to our understanding of NEMODEQs, but also provide a more unified view on query answering under dependencies in general.

Acknowledgments. We acknowledge contributions of various people: Bruno Courcelle and Detlef Seese gave very helpful comments on their work on MSO and structures of bounded treewidth; Diego Calvanese helped clarifying complexities of C2RPQs; Pierre Bourhis provided feedback leading to our formulation of Theorem 10; various anonymous reviewers gave valuable input on earlier versions of this work.

This work was supported by the Royal Society, the Seventh Framework Program (FP7) of the European Commission under Grant Agreement 318338, 'Optique', and the EPSRC projects ExODA, Score! and MaSI3.

10. REFERENCES

[1] S. Abiteboul, R. Hull, and V. Vianu. *Foundations of Databases*. Addison Wesley, 1994.

[2] H. Andréka, I. Németi, and J. van Benthem. Modal languages and bounded fragments of predicate logic. *Journal of Philosophical Logic*, 27(3):217–274, 1998.

[3] J.-F. Baget. Improving the forward chaining algorithm for conceptual graphs rules. In D. Dubois, C. A. Welty, and M.-A. Williams, editors, *KR*, pages 407–414. AAAI Press, 2004.

[4] J.-F. Baget, M. Leclère, M.-L. Mugnier, and E. Salvat. On rules with existential variables: Walking the decidability line. *Artificial Intelligence*, 175(9–10):1620–1654, 2011.

[5] J.-F. Baget, M.-L. Mugnier, S. Rudolph, and M. Thomazo. Walking the complexity lines for generalized guarded existential rules. In Walsh [47], pages 712–717.

[6] C. Beeri and M. Y. Vardi. The implication problem for data dependencies. In *Proceedings of the 8th Colloquium on Automata, Languages and Programming*, pages 73–85. Springer, 1981.

[7] M. Benedikt, P. Bourhis, and P. Senellart. Monadic datalog containment. In A. Czumaj, K. Mehlhorn, A. M. Pitts, and R. Wattenhofer, editors, *ICALP (2)*, volume 7392 of *LNCS*, pages 79–91. Springer, 2012.

[8] G. Brewka and J. Lang, editors. *Proceedings of the 11th International Conference on Principles of Knowledge Representation and Reasoning (KR'08)*. AAAI Press, 2008.

[9] A. Calì, G. Gottlob, and M. Kifer. Taming the infinite chase: Query answering under expressive relational constraints. In Brewka and Lang [8], pages 70–80.

[10] A. Calì, G. Gottlob, and T. Lukasiewicz. A general datalog-based framework for tractable query answering over ontologies. In Paredaens and Su [41], pages 77–86.

[11] A. Calì, G. Gottlob, and A. Pieris. Advanced processing for ontological queries. *Proceedings of VLDB 2010*, 3(1):554–565, 2010.

[12] A. Calì, G. Gottlob, and A. Pieris. Query answering under non-guarded rules in Datalog+/-. In P. Hitzler and T. Lukasiewicz, editors, *Web Reasoning and Rule Systems*, volume 6333 of *LNCS*, pages 1–17. Springer, 2010.

[13] D. Calvanese. Personal communication, September 2011.

[14] D. Calvanese, G. D. Giacomo, D. Lembo, M. Lenzerini, and R. Rosati. Tractable reasoning and efficient query answering in description logics: The DL-Lite family. *Journal of Automated Reasoning*, 39(3):385–429, 2007.

[15] D. Calvanese, G. D. Giacomo, M. Lenzerini, and M. Y. Vardi. Reasoning on regular path queries. *SIGMOD Record*, 32(4):83–92, 2003.

[16] A. K. Chandra, H. R. Lewis, and J. A. Makowsky. Embedded implicational dependencies and their inference problem. In *Conference Proceedings of the 13th Annual ACM Symposium on Theory of Computation (STOC'81)*, pages 342–354. ACM, 1981.

[17] A. K. Chandra and P. M. Merlin. Optimal implementation of conjunctive queries in relational data bases. In J. E. Hopcroft, E. P. Friedman, and M. A. Harrison, editors, *Proceedings of the 9th Annual ACM Symposium on Theory of Computing (STOC'77)*, pages 77–90. ACM, 1977.

[18] C. Civili and R. Rosati. A broad class of first-order rewritable tuple-generating dependencies. In P. Barceló and R. Pichler, editors, *Proceedings of the 2nd Workshop on the Resurgence of Datalog in Academia and Industry (Datalog 2.0, 2012)*, volume 7494 of *LNCS*. Springer, 2012.

[19] B. Courcelle. The monadic second-order logic of graphs, ii: Infinite graphs of bounded width. *Mathematical Systems Theory*, 21(4):187–221, 1989.

[20] B. Courcelle. Recursive queries and context-free graph grammars. *Theoretical Computer Science*, 78(1):217–244, 1991.

[21] B. Courcelle. Personal communication, August 2011.

[22] B. Courcelle and J. Engelfriet. Graph structure and monadic second-order logic, a language theoretic approach. manuscript, to be published at Cambridge University Press; available at http://www.labri.fr/perso/courcell/Book/TheBook.pdf, April 2011.

[23] E. Dantsin, T. Eiter, G. Gottlob, and A. Voronkov. Complexity and expressive power of logic programming. *ACM Computing Surveys*, 33(3):374–425, 2001.

[24] A. Deutsch, A. Nash, and J. B. Remmel. The chase revisited. In M. Lenzerini and D. Lembo, editors, *Proc. 27th Symposium on Principles of Database Systems (PODS'08)*, pages 149–158. ACM, 2008.

[25] A. Deutsch and V. Tannen. Reformulation of XML queries and constraints. In D. Calvanese, M. Lenzerini, and R. Motwani, editors, *Proceedings of the 9th International Conference on Database Theory (ICDT 2003)*, volume 2572 of *LNCS*, pages 225–241. Springer, 2003.

[26] R. Fagin, P. G. Kolaitis, R. J. Miller, and L. Popa. Data exchange: semantics and query answering. *Theoretical Computer Science*, 336(1):89–124, 2005.

[27] D. Florescu, A. Levy, and D. Suciu. Query containment for conjunctive queries with regular expressions. In *Proceedings of the seventeenth ACM symposium on Principles of database systems*, PODS '98, pages 139–148. ACM, 1998.

[28] G. Gottlob and C. Koch. Monadic datalog and the expressive power of languages for web information extraction. *J. ACM*, 51(1):74–113, 2004.

[29] G. Gottlob and C. H. Papadimitriou. On the complexity of single-rule datalog queries. *Inf. Comput.*, 183(1):104–122, 2003.

[30] S. Greco and F. Spezzano. Chase termination: A constraints rewriting approach. *Proceedings of VLDB 2010*, 3(1):93–104, 2010.

[31] N. Immerman. Languages that capture complexity classes. *SIAM J. Comput.*, 16(4):760–778, 1987.

[32] Y. Kazakov. $\mathcal{RIQ}$ and $\mathcal{SROIQ}$ are harder than $\mathcal{SHOIQ}$. In Brewka and Lang [8], pages 274–284.

[33] Y. Kazakov. An extension of complex role inclusion axioms in the description logic $\mathcal{SROIQ}$. In *Proceedings of the 5th International Joint Conference on Automated Reasoning (IJCAR 2010)*, LNCS. Springer, 2010.

[34] M. Krötzsch and S. Rudolph. Extending decidable existential rules by joining acyclicity and guardedness. In Walsh [47], pages 963–968.

[35] M. Krötzsch, S. Rudolph, and P. Hitzler. Conjunctive queries for a tractable fragment of OWL 1.1. In K. Aberer et al., editor, *Proceedings of the 6th International Semantic Web Conference (ISWC'07)*, volume 4825 of *LNCS*, pages 310–323. Springer, 2007.

[36] L. Libkin. *Elements of Finite Model Theory*. Springer, 2004.

[37] B. Marnette. Generalized schema-mappings: from termination to tractability. In Paredaens and Su [41], pages 13–22.

[38] M. Meier, M. Schmidt, and G. Lausen. On chase termination beyond stratification. *Proceedings of VLDB 2009*, 2(1):970–981, 2009.

[39] M.-L. Mugnier. Ontological query answering with existential rules. In S. Rudolph and C. Gutierrez, editors, *Web Reasoning and Rule Systems (RR 2011)*, volume 6902 of *LNCS*, pages 2–23. Springer, 2011.

[40] M. Ortiz, S. Rudolph, and M. Simkus. Query answering in the Horn fragments of the description logics $\mathcal{SHOIQ}$ and $\mathcal{SROIQ}$. In Walsh [47], pages 1039–1044.

[41] J. Paredaens and J. Su, editors. *Proc. 28th Symposium on Principles of Database Systems (PODS'09)*. ACM, 2009.

[42] S. Rudolph and M. Krötzsch. Flag & check – data-tractable expressive queries for intelligent databases (extended technical report). Technical Report 3030, Institute AIFB, Karlsruhe Institute of Technology, 2012. http://www.aifb.kit.edu/web/Techreport3030.

[43] O. Shmueli. Equivalence of DATALOG queries is undecidable. *J. Log. Program.*, 15(3):231–241, 1993.

[44] L. J. Stockmeyer. *The Complexity of Decision Problems in Automata Theory and Logic*. PhD thesis, Massachusetts Institute of Technology, 1974.

[45] L. J. Stockmeyer. The polynomial-time hierarchy. *Theor. Comput. Sci.*, 3(1):1–22, 1976.

[46] M. Y. Vardi. The complexity of relational query languages. In H. R. Lewis, B. B. Simons, W. A. Burkhard, and L. H. Landweber, editors, *STOC*, pages 137–146. ACM, 1982.

[47] T. Walsh, editor. *Proc. 22nd Int. Joint Conf. on Artificial Intelligence (IJCAI'11)*. AAAI Press/IJCAI, 2011.

Verification of Relational Data-Centric Dynamic Systems with External Services*

Babak Bagheri Hariri
Diego Calvanese
Marco Montali
Free Univ. of Bozen/Bolzano
lastname@inf.unibz.it

Giuseppe De Giacomo
Sapienza Università di Roma
degiacomo@dis.uniroma1.it

Alin Deutsch
UC San Diego
deutsch@cs.ucsd.edu

ABSTRACT

Data-centric dynamic systems are systems where both the process controlling the dynamics and the manipulation of data are equally central. We study verification of (first-order) μ-calculus variants over *relational data-centric dynamic systems*, where data are maintained in a relational database, and the process is described in terms of atomic actions that evolve the database. Action execution may involve calls to external services, thus inserting fresh data into the system. As a result such systems are infinite-state. We show that verification is undecidable in general, and we isolate notable cases where decidability is achieved. Specifically we start by considering service calls that return values deterministically (depending only on passed parameters). We show that in a μ-calculus variant that preserves knowledge of objects appeared along a run we get decidability under the assumption that the fresh data introduced along a run are bounded, though they might not be bounded in the overall system. In fact we tie such a result to a notion related to weak acyclicity studied in data exchange. Then, we move to nondeterministic services and we investigate decidability under the assumption that knowledge of objects is preserved only if they are continuously present. We show that if infinitely many values occur in a run but do not accumulate in the same state, then we get again decidability. We give syntactic conditions to avoid this accumulation through the novel notion of "generate-recall acyclicity", which ensures that every service call activation generates new values that cannot be accumulated indefinitely.

Categories and Subject Descriptors

D.2.4 [**Software Engineering**]: Software/Program Verification
TERMS(Verification)

Keywords

Business artifacts, data-centric processes, first-order temporal logics.

*This research has been partially supported by the EU under the ICT Collaborative Project ACSI (Artifact-Centric Service Interoperation), grant agreement n. FP7-257593, and by the NSF under grant IIS-0916515.

PODS'13, June 22–27, 2013, New York, New York, USA.

1. INTRODUCTION

Business process management is central to the operation of organizations in various domains, ranging from business to governmental, scientific, and beyond. Business process specification frameworks have recently evolved from the traditional process-centric approach towards data-awareness. Process-centric formalisms focus on control flow while under-specifying the underlying data and its manipulations by the process tasks, often abstracting them away completely. In contrast, data-aware formalisms treat data as first-class citizens [37, 30, 19, 16, 40, 1]. The holistic view of data and processes together promises to avoid the notorious discrepancy between data modeling and process modeling of more traditional approaches that consider these two aspects separately [9]. In particular, this separation precludes the development of data-aware automatic tools for formal verification, i.e., static analysis and run-time monitoring. Such tools are desperately needed given the complexity of modern business processes, much of which is due to subtle interactions between business process tasks and data.

A notable exponent of the data-aware class of specification frameworks is the *artifact-centric model* pioneered in [37], deployed by IBM in commercial products and consulting services, and further studied in a line of follow-up works [8, 28, 29, 9, 32, 23, 20, 21]. Business artifacts (or simply "artifacts") model key business-relevant entities, updated by a set of business process tasks (actions). This modeling approach has been successfully deployed in practice, yielding proven savings when performing business process transformations [8] to expand and/or streamline the process.

Data-aware processes deeply challenge formal verification by requiring simultaneous attention to both data and process: on the one hand they deal with full-fledged processes and require analysis in terms of sophisticated temporal properties [18]; on the other hand, the presence of possibly unbounded data makes the usual analysis based on finite-state model checking impossible in general, since, when data is taken into account, the system becomes infinite-state.

In this work we focus on data-aware static verification, selecting the artifact-centric model as a natural vehicle for our investigation due to its practical relevance. Given the family of variations on this model found in the literature, for the sake of a uniform terminology we introduce our own pristine formalization, which captures the artifact-centric dialects in [7, 24, 25, 23, 21]. We call our business process formalism "Data-Centric Dynamic Systems" (DCDSs). The correspondence between DCDSs and the family of artifact models is discussed in Sections 6 and 7. DCDSs comprise *(i)* a *data layer*, which holds the relevant information to be manipulated by the system and technically can be seen as a *relational* database, and *(ii)* a *process layer* formed by invokable *(atomic) actions* and a process based on them. Such a process characterizes the dynamic behavior of the system. Executing an action has effects on the data manipulated by the system, on the process state, and on the information exchanged with the external world.

Our setting is in line with recent industrial artifact model proposals [19] and research papers [7, 24, 25, 23] and it subsumes particular case variations in which the artifact is a record, modeled as a single-tuple database [20]. The execution of actions may involve calls to external services, providing fresh data inserted into the system. As a result such systems are infinite-state in general.

As verification formalism, we adopt a FO variant of μ-calculus [34, 38, 26, 14]. μ-calculus is well known to be more expressive than virtually all temporal logics used in verification, including widely adopted logics such as CTL, LTL, and CTL*. Our variant of μ-calculus is based on first-order queries over data in the states of the DCDS, and allows for first-order quantification across states (within and across runs), though in a controlled way. No limitations whatsoever are instead put on the fixpoint formulae, which are the key element of the μ-calculus.

In particular we consider two FO variations of μ-calculus. The first, called $\mu\mathcal{L}_A$, requires that first-order quantification across states is always bounded to the active domain of the state where the quantification is evaluated. This quantification mechanism indirectly preserves, at any point, knowledge of objects that appeared in the history so far, even if they disappeared in the meantime. The second, called $\mu\mathcal{L}_P$, further restricts the first-order quantification in $\mu\mathcal{L}_A$ by stating that only quantified objects that are still present in the current domain remain of interest as we move from one state to the next. That is, knowledge of objects is preserved only if they are continuously present. We define novel notions of bisimulation that characterize the forms of quantification used in the two logics.

Verification of data-aware processes, including artifact systems and DCDSs, is undecidable even for very simple system specifications and propositional CTL/LTL properties [7, 25, 23, 17]. However, we isolate two notable sufficient conditions over DCDSs, which respectively guarantee decidability of full $\mu\mathcal{L}_A$ and $\mu\mathcal{L}_P$ verification under specific assumptions about the external services.

Specifically we start by considering service calls that return values deterministically (depending only on passed parameters). We show that verification of $\mu\mathcal{L}_A$ properties is decidable under the assumption that the cardinality of fresh data introduced along each run is bounded (*run-bounded* DCDSs), though it need not be bounded across runs. Decidability is not obvious, since the logic permits quantification over values occurring across (potentially infinitely many) branching run continuations. Run-boundedness is an undecidable semantic property for which we propose a sufficient syntactic condition related to the notion of weak acyclicity studied in data exchange [27]. Then, we move to nondeterministic services where same-argument calls possibly return different values at different time moments. To exploit the results on run-bounded DCDSs in this case we would have to limit the number of service calls that can be invoked during the execution, which would be a too restrictive condition on the form of DCDSs. We show that if infinitely many values occur in a run but do not accumulate in the same state (our system is then called *state-bounded*) then $\mu\mathcal{L}_P$ verification is decidable (while $\mu\mathcal{L}_A$ is not). This is remarkable, since when compared to run-boundedness, state-boundedness permits an additional kind of data unboundedness (*within* the run, as opposed to only *across* runs). State-boundedness is also an undecidable semantic property, for which we provide a novel sufficient syntactic condition called "generate-recall acyclicity".

The decidability results come with an EXPTIME upper bound on the size of the initial database of the DCDS data layer. This is in line with previously known complexity bounds on systems that can be seen as special cases of our framework [7, 24, 25, 23, 17]. While at a first sight this seems an obstacle for practical verification, we observe that when DCDSs represent artifacts, which is our main use case, verification is affected only by the specific data needed to progress the artifacts along their lifecycle (process). The size of such data is in practice small when compared to the size of the entire data layer. Verification of data aware processes according to algorithms exponential in the initial state has already been successfully implemented in systems such as [24]. This is a strong indication of feasibility potential even in the more general setting presented here.

The rest of the paper is organized as follows. Section 2 introduces DCDSs. Section 3 introduces verification of DCDSs and the two variants of μ-calculus that we consider. Section 4 focusses the analysis of DCDSs under the assumption that external service calls behave deterministically. Section 5 considers the case in which external service calls behave nondeterministically. Section 6 discusses the various notions introduced. Section 7 reports on related work. Finally, Section 8 concludes the paper.

An extended version of this paper with full proofs is available [4].

2. DATA-CENTRIC DYNAMIC SYSTEMS

We base our investigation on a model called *(relational) data-centric dynamic system*, or simply DCDS, which can be seen as a pristine version of several proposals in the literature [7, 24, 25, 23], and is in particular equivalent in expressive power to the most expressive artifact model variations, such as [21] (see Section 6).

A DCDS is a pair $\mathcal{S} = \langle \mathcal{D}, \mathcal{P} \rangle$ formed by two interacting layers: a *data layer* $\mathcal{D}$ and a *process layer* $\mathcal{P}$ over $\mathcal{D}$. Intuitively, the data layer keeps all the data of interest, while the process layer modifies and evolves such data. We keep the structure of both layers to the minimum, in particular we do not distinguish between various possible components providing the data, nor those providing the subprocesses running concurrently.

Data Layer. The data layer represents the information of interest in our application. It is constituted by a relational schema $\mathcal{R}$ equipped with equality constraints[1] $\mathcal{E}$, e.g., to state keys of relations, and an initial database instance $\mathcal{I}_0$, which conforms to the relational schema and the equality constraints. The values stored in this database belong to a countably infinite domain $\mathcal{C}$. The elements of this domain are treated as constants, interpreted as themselves, blurring the distinction between constants and values. We will use the two terms interchangeably.

Given a database instance $\mathcal{I}$, its active domain $\text{ADOM}(\mathcal{I})$ is the subset of $\mathcal{C}$ such that $c \in \text{ADOM}(\mathcal{I})$ if and only if c occurs in $\mathcal{I}$.

Formally, a *data layer* is a tuple $\mathcal{D} = \langle \mathcal{C}, \mathcal{R}, \mathcal{E}, \mathcal{I}_0 \rangle$ where:

- $\mathcal{R} = \{R_1, \dots, R_n\}$ is a database schema, constituted by a finite set of relation schemas;
- $\mathcal{E}$ is a finite set $\{\mathcal{E}_1, \dots, \mathcal{E}_m\}$ of equality constraints. Each $\mathcal{E}_i$ has the form $Q_i \rightarrow \bigwedge_{j=1,\dots,k} z_{ij} = y_{ij}$, where Q_i is a domain independent FO query over $\mathcal{R}$, possibly using constants from $\text{ADOM}(\mathcal{I}_0)$, whose free variables are $\vec{x}$, and z_{ij} and y_{ij} are either variables in $\vec{x}$ or constants in $\text{ADOM}(\mathcal{I}_0)$.[2]
- $\mathcal{I}_0$ is a database instance that represents the initial state of the data layer, which conforms to the schema $\mathcal{R}$ and *satisfies* the constraints $\mathcal{E}$: namely, for each constraint $Q_i \rightarrow \bigwedge_{j=1,\dots,k} z_{ij}{=}y_{ij}$ and for each tuple (i.e., substitution for the free variables) $\theta \in ans(Q_i, \mathcal{I})$, it holds that $z_{ij}\theta = y_{ij}\theta$.[3]

[1]Other kinds of constraints can also be included without affecting the results reported here (cf. Section 6).

[2]For convenience, and without loss of generality, we assume that all constants used inside formulae appear in $\mathcal{I}_0$.

[3]We use the notation $t\theta$ (resp., $\varphi\theta$) to denote the term (resp., the formula) obtained by applying the substitution θ to t (resp., φ).

Process Layer. The process layer constitutes the progression mechanism for the DCDS. We assume that at every time the current instance of the data layer can be arbitrarily queried, and can be updated through action executions, possibly involving external service calls to get new values from the environment. Hence, the process layer is composed of three main notions: *actions*, which are the atomic update steps on the data layer; *external services*, which can be called during the execution of actions; and *processes*, which are essentially nondeterministic programs that use actions as atomic instructions. While we require the execution of actions to be sequential, we do not impose any such constraints on processes, which in principle can be formed by several concurrent branches, including fork, join, and so on. Concurrency is to be interpreted by interleaving and hence reduced to nondeterminism, as often done in formal verification [5, 26]. There can be many ways to provide the control flow specification for processes. Here we adopt a simple rule-based mechanism, but our results can be immediately generalized to processes whose control flow is finite-state. Observe that this does not imply that the transition system associated to a process over the data layer is finite-state as well, since the data manipulated in the data layer may grow over time in an unbounded way.

Formally, a process layer $\mathcal{P}$ over a data layer $\mathcal{D} = \langle \mathcal{C}, \mathcal{R}, \mathcal{E}, \mathcal{I}_0 \rangle$, is a tuple $\mathcal{P} = \langle \mathcal{F}, \mathcal{A}, \varrho \rangle$ where:

- $\mathcal{F}$ is a finite set of *functions*, each representing the interface to an *external service*. Such services can be called, and as a result the function is activated and the answer is produced. How the result is actually computed is *unknown* to the DCDS since the services are external.
- $\mathcal{A}$ is a finite set of *actions*, whose execution updates the data layer, and may involve external service calls.
- ϱ is a finite set of *condition-action rules* that form the specification of the overall *process*, which tells at any moment which actions can be executed.

The crucial aspect of actions is how they affect the data layer. Actions query the current state of the data layer and use the results of such queries, together with the data returned from the external service calls, to instantiate the data layer in the new state. To specify the action effects, we resort to rules that resemble tuple generating dependencies (TGDs) [2], except that we allow for negation when querying the database and we use results of service calls instead of labeled nulls. Note that negation is key to capturing "if-then-else" style business rules, while service calls are used for modeling the input of new data from the external environment.

Formally, an *action* $\alpha \in \mathcal{A}$ is an expression $\alpha(p_1, \ldots, p_n)$: $\{e_1, \ldots, e_m\}$, where: *(i)* $\alpha(p_1, \ldots, p_n)$ is its *signature*, constituted by a name α and a sequence $p_1, \ldots, p_n$ of *parameters*, to be substituted with values when the action is invoked, and *(ii)* $\{e_1, \ldots, e_m\}$, also denoted as $\text{EFFECT}(\alpha)$, is a set of *specifications of effects*, which are assumed to take place simultaneously. Each e_i has the form $q_i^+ \wedge Q_i^- \rightsquigarrow E_i$, where:

- $q_i^+ \wedge Q_i^-$ is a query over $\mathcal{R}$ whose terms are variables, action parameters, and constants from $\text{ADOM}(\mathcal{I}_0)$, where q_i^+ is a union of conjunctive queries, and Q_i^- is an arbitrary FO formula whose free variables are among those of q_i^+. Intuitively, q_i^+ selects the tuples to instantiate the effect with, and Q_i^- filters away some of them[4].

Furthermore, given a FO query Q and a database instance $\mathcal{I}$, the *answer* $ans(Q, \mathcal{I})$ to Q over $\mathcal{I}$ is the set of assignments θ from the free variables of Q to $\text{ADOM}(\mathcal{I})$, such that $\mathcal{I} \models Q\theta$. We treat $Q\theta$ as a boolean query, and with some abuse of notation, we say $ans(Q\theta, \mathcal{I}) \equiv \mathsf{true}$ if and only if $\mathcal{I} \models Q\theta$.

[4]Note that while in principle we could replace $q_i^+ \wedge Q_i^-$ with any domain independent FO query, distinguishing between q_i^+ and Q_i^- gives us leverage (under the control of the designer) for singling out interesting syntactic conditions for decidability (see Sections 4.3 and 5.3).

- E_i is the effect, i.e., a set of facts for $\mathcal{R}$, which includes as terms: terms in $\text{ADOM}(\mathcal{I}_0)$, free variables of q_i^+ and Q_i^- (including action parameters), and Skolem terms formed by applying a function $f \in \mathcal{F}$ to one of the previous kinds of terms. Such Skolem terms involving functions represent external service calls and are interpreted as the returned value chosen by an external user/environment when executing the action.

The *process* ϱ is a finite set of *condition-action rules*, of the form $Q \mapsto \alpha$, where α is an action in $\mathcal{A}$ and Q is a FO query over $\mathcal{R}$ whose free variables are exactly the parameters of α, and whose other terms can be quantified variables or constants in $\text{ADOM}(\mathcal{I}_0)$.

Semantics via Transition System. The semantics of a DCDS is defined in terms of a possibly infinite transition system whose states are labeled by databases. Such a transition system represents all possible computations that the process layer can do on the data layer. A transition system Υ is a tuple $\langle \Delta, \mathcal{R}, \Sigma, s_0, db, \Rightarrow \rangle$, where:

- Δ is a countably infinite set of values;
- $\mathcal{R}$ is a database schema;
- Σ is a set of states;
- $s_0 \in \Sigma$ is the initial state;
- db is a function that, given a state $s \in \Sigma$, returns the database of s, which is made up of values in Δ and conforms to $\mathcal{R}$;
- $\Rightarrow \subseteq \Sigma \times \Sigma$ is a transition relation over states.

In order to precisely build the transition system associated to a DCDS, we need to better characterize the behavior of the external services, which are called in the effects of actions. This is done in Sections 4 and 5.

EXAMPLE 2.1. (Travel Reimbursement DCDS) We model the process of reimbursing travel expenses in a university, and the corresponding audit system, in two different subsystems. In particular, the first subsystem, called the *request system* manages the submission of reimbursement requests by an employee, and preliminary inspection and approval of the request by a *monitor* working in the accounting department. The log of accepted requests will be submitted to the second subsystem, the *audit system*, in which requests can be accumulated, and they can be checked for accuracy by calling external web services (for instance to obtain the exchange rate from foreign currency to USD on a past date, or to check that the employee actually was on the declared flight). Here we model selected parts of the request system (the full-fledged example, including the whole audit system, is developed in [4]).

A request is associated with the name of the employee and comprises information related to the corresponding flight and hotel costs. The monitor decides to accept or reject the request. In case of rejection, the employee needs to modify the information regarding hotel and flight. After the update by the employee, the monitor checks again the request, and the reject-check loop continues until the monitor accepts the request. After a request is accepted a log of the request is sent to the audit system, and the request system is ready to process the next travel request.

We model the request system by a DCDS $\mathcal{S}_R = \langle \mathcal{D}, \mathcal{P} \rangle$, where $\mathcal{D} = \langle \mathcal{C}, \mathcal{R}, \mathcal{E}, \mathcal{I}_0 \rangle$, $\mathcal{I}_0$ contains the fact Status(*'readyForRequest'*) as well as the initial state of the ApprHotel relation, and $\mathcal{R}$ is a database schema including

- $\mathsf{Status} = \langle \mathsf{status} \rangle$, a unary relation that keeps the state of the request subsystem, and can take three different values: *'readyForRequest'*, *'readyToVerify'*, and *'readyToUpdate'*,
- $\mathsf{Travel} = \langle \mathsf{eName} \rangle$, holding the name of the employee;

- $\mathsf{Hotel} = \langle \mathsf{hName}, \mathsf{date}, \mathsf{price}, \mathsf{currency}, \mathsf{priceInUSD} \rangle$, holding the hotel cost information of the employee's travel, which might have been paid in some other currency than USD,
- $\mathsf{Flight} = \langle \mathsf{date}, \mathsf{fNum}, \mathsf{price}, \mathsf{currency}, \mathsf{priceInUSD} \rangle$, holding the flight cost information,
- $\mathsf{ApprHotel} = \langle \mathsf{hName} \rangle$, holding a list of approved hotels.

The process layer is defined as $\mathcal{P} = \langle \mathcal{F}, \mathcal{A}, \varrho \rangle$, where $\mathcal{F}$ is a set of service calls, modeling an input of an external value by the employee for each attribute of the request. For instance, $\mathcal{F}$ includes INHNAME() for the hotel name, INHDATE() for the arrival date, etc. DECIDE() models the decision of the human monitor, returning *'accepted'* if the request is accepted, and *'readyToUpdate'* if the request needs to be updated by the employee.

The set $\mathcal{A}$ of actions includes *InitiateRequest*, *VerifyRequest*, *UpdateRequest*, and *AcceptRequest*. When a request is initiated (modeled by the action *InitiateRequest*), *(i)* the system changes state to "waiting for verification", *(ii)* a travel event is generated and the employee fills in his name, and *(iii)* the employee fills in hotel and flight information. Action *VerifyRequest* models the preliminary check by the monitor. Travel event, hotel, and flight information are copied unchanged to the next state, and this is necessary to preserve such information according to our semantics (see Sections 4 and 5). The system status is set as follows: if the hotel is on the approved list, then the request is automatically accepted. Otherwise, the request is handled by a human monitor, modeled by the non-deterministic service call DECIDE(). If the monitor rejects, she sets the next state to *'readyToUpdate'*, triggering the action *UpdateRequest*, which collects once again the hotel and flight information from the employee, moving the status to *'readyToVerify'*. Finally, action *AcceptRequest* returns the system in the state *'readyForRequest'*, in which it is ready to accept a new request. The condition-action rules in the set ϱ below guard the actions by the current system's state:

$$\begin{array}{rcl} \mathsf{Status}(\textit{'readyForRequest'}) & \mapsto & \textit{InitiateRequest} \\ \mathsf{Status}(\textit{'readyToVerify'}) & \mapsto & \textit{VerifyRequest} \\ \mathsf{Status}(\textit{'readyToUpdate'}) & \mapsto & \textit{UpdateRequest} \\ \mathsf{Status}(\textit{'accepted'}) & \mapsto & \textit{AcceptRequest} \end{array}$$

We conclude the example by detailing *VerifyRequest*:

$$\begin{array}{rcl} \mathsf{Hotel}(x_1,\ldots,x_5) \land \mathsf{ApprHotel}(x_1) & \rightsquigarrow & \mathsf{Status}(\textit{'accepted'}) \\ \mathsf{Hotel}(x_1,\ldots,x_5) \land \neg\mathsf{ApprHotel}(x_1) & \rightsquigarrow & \mathsf{Status}(\text{DECIDE}()) \\ \mathsf{Travel}(n) & \rightsquigarrow & \mathsf{Travel}(n) \\ \mathsf{Hotel}(x_1,\ldots,x_5) & \rightsquigarrow & \mathsf{Hotel}(x_1,\ldots,x_5) \\ \mathsf{Flight}(x_1,\ldots,x_5) & \rightsquigarrow & \mathsf{Flight}(x_1,\ldots,x_5) \\ \mathsf{ApprHotel}(x) & \rightsquigarrow & \mathsf{ApprHotel}(x) \end{array}$$ ■

3. VERIFICATION

To specify dynamic properties over a DCDS, we use μ-calculus [26, 39, 14], one of the most powerful temporal logics for which model checking has been investigated in the finite-state setting. Indeed, such a logic is able to express both linear time logics such as LTL and PSL, and branching time logics such as CTL and CTL* [18]. The main characteristic of μ-calculus is the ability of expressing directly least and greatest fixpoints of (predicate-transformer) operators formed using formulae relating the current state to the next one. By using such fixpoint constructs one can easily express sophisticated properties defined by induction or co-induction. This is the reason why virtually all logics used in verification are essentially fragments of μ-calculus. From a technical viewpoint, μ-calculus separates local properties, i.e., properties asserted on the current state or on states that are immediate successors of the current one, and properties that talk about states that are arbitrarily far away from the current one [14]. The latter are expressed using fixpoints.

In this work, we use a first-order extension of the μ-calculus [38], called $\mu\mathcal{L}$ and defined as follows:

$$\Phi ::= Q \mid \neg\Phi \mid \Phi_1 \land \Phi_2 \mid \exists x.\Phi \mid \langle - \rangle\Phi \mid Z \mid \mu Z.\Phi$$

where Q is a possibly open FO query, and Z is a second order predicate variable (of arity 0). We make use of the following abbreviations: $\forall x.\Phi = \neg(\exists x.\neg\Phi)$, $\Phi_1 \lor \Phi_2 = \neg(\neg\Phi_1 \land \neg\Phi_2)$, $[-]\Phi = \neg\langle - \rangle\neg\Phi$, and $\nu Z.\Phi = \neg\mu Z.\neg\Phi[Z/\neg Z]$.

As usual in μ-calculus, formulae of the form $\mu Z.\Phi$ (and $\nu Z.\Phi$) must obey to the *syntactic monotonicity* of Φ w.r.t. Z, which states that every occurrence of the variable Z in Φ must be within the scope of an even number of negation symbols. This ensures that both $\mu Z.\Phi$ and $\nu Z.\Phi$ always exist.

Since $\mu\mathcal{L}$ also contains formulae with both individual and predicate free variables, given a transition system Υ, we introduce an individual variable valuation v, i.e., a mapping from individual variables x to Δ, and a predicate variable valuation V, i.e., a mapping from predicate variables Z to subsets of Σ. With these three notions in place, we assign meaning to formulae by associating to Υ, v, and V an *extension function* $(\cdot)^{\Upsilon}_{v,V}$, which maps formulae to subsets of Σ. Formally, the extension function $(\cdot)^{\Upsilon}_{v,V}$ is defined inductively as shown in Figure 1. When Φ is a closed formula, $(\Phi)^{\Upsilon}_{v,V}$ depends neither on v nor on V, and we denote the extension of Φ simply by $(\Phi)^{\Upsilon}$. We say that a closed formula Φ holds in a state $s \in \Sigma$ if $s \in (\Phi)^{\Upsilon}$. In this case, we write $\Upsilon, s \models \Phi$. We say that a closed formula Φ holds in Υ, denoted by $\Upsilon \models \Phi$, if $\Upsilon, s_0 \models \Phi$, where s_0 is the initial state of Υ. We call *model checking* verifying whether $\Upsilon \models \Phi$ holds. In particular, we are interested in formally verifying properties of a DCDS. Given the transition system $\Upsilon_{\mathcal{S}}$ of a DCDS $\mathcal{S}$ and a $\mu\mathcal{L}$ dynamic property Φ,[5] we say that $\mathcal{S}$ *verifies* Φ if $\Upsilon_{\mathcal{S}} \models \Phi$.

EXAMPLE 3.1. It is easy to write $\mu\mathcal{L}$ formulae that express typical temporal properties such as:

- *liveness (on a run)*: there exists a run such that α eventually holds, i.e. $\mu Z.\alpha \lor \langle - \rangle Z$;
- *liveness (on all runs)*: eventually in the future α will hold, i.e., $\mu Z.\alpha \lor [-]Z$;
- *safety (on all runs)*: for all (future) situations α holds, i.e., $\nu Z.\alpha \land [-]Z$;
- *response (on all runs)*: always when α then eventually β, i.e., $\nu Z_1.(\alpha \rightarrow \mu Z_2.\beta \lor [-]Z_2) \land [-]Z_1$;
- *strong fairness (on a run)*: there exists a run where α is true infinitely often, i.e., $\nu X.\mu Y.(\alpha \land \langle - \rangle X) \lor \langle - \rangle Y$. ■

EXAMPLE 3.2. Consider the $\mu\mathcal{L}$ formula:

$$\exists x_1,\ldots,x_n. \bigwedge_{i \neq j} x_i \neq x_j \land \bigwedge_{i \in \{1,\ldots,n\}} \mu Z.(\textit{Stud}(x_i) \lor \langle - \rangle Z)$$

It asserts that there are at least n distinct objects/values, each of which eventually denotes a student along some execution path. The formula does not imply that all of these students will be in the same state, nor that they will all occur in a single run. It only says that in the entire transition system there are (at least) n distinct students. ■

The challenging point is that $\Upsilon_{\mathcal{S}}$ is in general infinite-state, so we would like to devise a finite-state transition system to model check, which is a faithful abstraction of $\Upsilon_{\mathcal{S}}$ in the sense that it

[5]We remind the reader that, without loss of generality, we assume that all constants used inside formulae Φ appear in the initial database instance of the DCDS.

$$
\begin{aligned}
(Q)^{\Upsilon}_{v,V} &= \{s \in \Sigma \mid ans(Qv, db(s))\}\\
(\neg\Phi)^{\Upsilon}_{v,V} &= \Sigma - (\Phi)^{\Upsilon}_{v,V}\\
(\Phi_1 \wedge \Phi_2)^{\Upsilon}_{v,V} &= (\Phi_1)^{\Upsilon}_{v,V} \cap (\Phi_2)^{\Upsilon}_{v,V}\\
(\exists x.\Phi)^{\Upsilon}_{v,V} &= \{s \in \Sigma \mid \exists t.t \in \Delta \text{ and } s \in (\Phi)^{\Upsilon}_{v[x/t],V}\}\\
(\langle - \rangle\Phi)^{\Upsilon}_{v,V} &= \{s \in \Sigma \mid \exists s'.s \Rightarrow s' \text{ and } s' \in (\Phi)^{\Upsilon}_{v,V}\}\\
(Z)^{\Upsilon}_{v,V} &= V(Z)\\
(\mu Z.\Phi)^{\Upsilon}_{v,V} &= \bigcap\{\mathcal{S} \subseteq \Sigma \mid (\Phi)^{\Upsilon}_{v,V[Z/\mathcal{S}]} \subseteq \mathcal{S}\}
\end{aligned}
$$

Figure 1: Semantics of $\mu\mathcal{L}$.

preserves the truth value of all $\mu\mathcal{L}$ formulae. Unfortunately, this program is doomed if we insist on using full $\mu\mathcal{L}$ as the verification formalism. Indeed, there are $\mu\mathcal{L}$ formulae, such as the one shown in Example 3.2, that defeat any kind of finite-state abstraction (in the precise sense of Theorem 4.5). So next we introduce two interesting sublogics of $\mu\mathcal{L}$ that better serve our objective.

3.1 History-Preserving Mu-Calculus

The first fragment of $\mu\mathcal{L}$ that we consider is $\mu\mathcal{L}_A$, which is characterized by the assumption that quantification over objects is restricted to objects that are present in the current database. To enforce such a restriction, we introduce a special predicate $\text{LIVE}(x)$, which states that x belongs to the current active domain. The logic $\mu\mathcal{L}_A$ is defined as follows:

$$\Phi ::= Q \mid \neg\Phi \mid \Phi_1 \wedge \Phi_2 \mid \exists x.\text{LIVE}(x) \wedge \Phi \mid \langle - \rangle\Phi \mid Z \mid \mu Z.\Phi$$

We make use of the usual abbreviations, including $\forall x.\text{LIVE}(x) \rightarrow \Phi = \neg(\exists x.\text{LIVE}(x) \wedge \neg\Phi)$. Formally, the extension function $(\cdot)^{\Upsilon}_{v,V}$ is defined inductively as in Figure 1, with the new special predicate $\text{LIVE}(x)$ interpreted as follows:

$$(\text{LIVE}(x))^{\Upsilon}_{v,V} = \{s \in \Sigma \mid x/d \in v \text{ implies } d \in \text{ADOM}(db(s))\}$$

EXAMPLE 3.3. $\mu\mathcal{L}_A$ requires the bindings of quantified variables to be live in the step when the quantification is evaluated. This can be done by using LIVE or simply by using any relation, such as $Stud$ and $Grad$ in the following formula:

$$\nu X.(\forall x.Stud(x) \rightarrow \mu Y.(\exists y.Grad(x,y) \vee \langle - \rangle Y) \wedge [-]X)$$

The formula states that, along every path, it is always true, for each student x, that there exists an evolution that eventually leads to the graduation of x (with some final mark y). ■

We are going to show that under suitable conditions we can get a faithful finite abstraction for a DCDS that preserves all formulae of $\mu\mathcal{L}_A$, and hence enables us to use standard model checking techniques. Towards this goal, we introduce a notion of bisimulation between two transition systems, which is suitable for the kind of transition systems we consider here. In particular, we have to take into account that the two transition systems are over different data domains, and hence we have to consider the correspondence between the data in the two transition systems and how such data evolve over time. To do so, we introduce the following notions.

Given two domains Δ_1 and Δ_2, a *partial bijection* h between Δ_1 and Δ_2 is a bijection between a subset of Δ_1 and Δ_2. Given a partial function $f : S \rightarrow S'$, we denote with $\text{DOM}(f)$ the domain of f, i.e., the set of elements in S on which f is defined, and with $\text{IM}(f)$ the image of f, i.e., the set of elements s' in S' such that $s' = f(s)$ for some $s \in S$. A partial bijection h' *extends* h if $\text{DOM}(h) \subseteq \text{DOM}(h')$ (or equivalently $\text{IM}(h) \subseteq \text{IM}(h')$) and $h'(x) = h(x)$ for all $x \in \text{DOM}(h)$ (or equivalently $h'^{-1}(y) = h^{-1}(y)$ for all $y \in \text{IM}(h)$). Let db_1 and db_2 be two databases over two domains Δ_1 and Δ_2 respectively, both conforming to the same schema $\mathcal{R}$. We say that a partial bijection h *induces an isomorphism* between db_1 and db_2 if $\text{ADOM}(db_1) \subseteq \text{DOM}(h)$, $\text{ADOM}(db_2) \subseteq \text{IM}(h)$, and h projected on $\text{ADOM}(db_1)$ is an isomorphism between db_1 and db_2.

Let $\Upsilon_1 = \langle \Delta_1, \mathcal{R}, \Sigma_1, s_{01}, db_1, \Rightarrow_1 \rangle$ and $\Upsilon_2 = \langle \Delta_2, \mathcal{R}, \Sigma_2, s_{02}, db_2, \Rightarrow_2 \rangle$ be transition systems and H the set of partial bijections between Δ_1 and Δ_2 that are the identity between $\text{ADOM}(db_1(s_{01}))$ and $\text{ADOM}(db_2(s_{02}))$. A *history preserving bisimulation* between Υ_1 and Υ_2 is a relation $\mathcal{B} \subseteq \Sigma_1 \times H \times \Sigma_2$ such that $\langle s_1, h, s_2 \rangle \in \mathcal{B}$ implies that:

1. h is a partial bijection between Δ_1 and Δ_2 that induces an isomorphism between $db_1(s_1)$ and $db_2(s_2)$;
2. for each s_1', if $s_1 \Rightarrow_1 s_1'$ then there is an s_2' with $s_2 \Rightarrow_2 s_2'$ and a bijection h' that extends h, such that $\langle s_1', h', s_2' \rangle \in \mathcal{B}$.
3. for each s_2', if $s_2 \Rightarrow_2 s_2'$ then there is an s_1' with $s_1 \Rightarrow_1 s_1'$ and a bijection h' that extends h, such that $\langle s_1', h', s_2' \rangle \in \mathcal{B}$.

A state $s_1 \in \Sigma_1$ is *history-preserving bisimilar* to $s_2 \in \Sigma_2$ *w.r.t. a partial bijection* h, written $s_1 \approx_h s_2$, if there exists a history-preserving bisimulation $\mathcal{B}$ between Υ_1 and Υ_2 such that $\langle s_1, h, s_2 \rangle \in \mathcal{B}$. A state $s_1 \in \Sigma_1$ is *history-preserving bisimilar* to $s_2 \in \Sigma_2$, written $s_1 \approx s_2$, if there exists a partial bijection h and a history-preserving bisimulation $\mathcal{B}$ between Υ_1 and Υ_2 such that $\langle s_1, h, s_2 \rangle \in \mathcal{B}$. A transition system Υ_1 is *history-preserving bisimilar* to Υ_2, written $\Upsilon_1 \approx \Upsilon_2$, if $s_{01} \approx s_{02}$. The next theorem gives us the classical invariance result of μ-calculus w.r.t. bisimulation, in our setting.

THEOREM 3.1. *Consider two transition systems Υ_1 and Υ_2 such that $\Upsilon_1 \approx \Upsilon_2$. For every $\mu\mathcal{L}_A$ closed formula Φ, we have: $\Upsilon_1 \models \Phi$ if and only if $\Upsilon_2 \models \Phi$.*

3.2 Persistence-Preserving Mu-Calculus

The second fragment of $\mu\mathcal{L}$ that we consider is $\mu\mathcal{L}_P$, which further restricts $\mu\mathcal{L}_A$ by requiring that individuals over which we quantify must continuously persist along the system evolution for the quantification to take effect. In the following, we use $\text{LIVE}(x_1, \ldots, x_n)$ as an abbreviation for $\bigwedge_{i \in \{1,\ldots,n\}} \text{LIVE}(x_i)$.

The logic $\mu\mathcal{L}_P$ is defined as follows:

$$\Phi ::= Q \mid \neg\Phi \mid \Phi_1 \wedge \Phi_2 \mid \exists x.\text{LIVE}(x) \wedge \Phi \mid \text{LIVE}(\vec{x}) \wedge \langle - \rangle\Phi \mid \text{LIVE}(\vec{x}) \wedge [-]\Phi \mid Z \mid \mu Z.\Phi$$

where the following assumption holds: in $\text{LIVE}(\vec{x}) \wedge \langle - \rangle\Phi$ and $\text{LIVE}(\vec{x}) \wedge [-]\Phi$, the variables $\vec{x}$ are exactly the free variables of Φ, once we substitute to each bounded predicate variable Z in Φ its bounding formula $\mu Z.\Phi'$. We use the usual abbreviations, including: $\text{LIVE}(\vec{x}) \rightarrow \langle - \rangle\Phi = \neg(\text{LIVE}(\vec{x}) \wedge [-]\neg\Phi)$ and $\text{LIVE}(\vec{x}) \rightarrow [-]\Phi = \neg(\text{LIVE}(\vec{x}) \wedge \langle - \rangle\neg\Phi)$. Intuitively, the use of $\text{LIVE}(\cdot)$ in $\mu\mathcal{L}_P$ ensures that individuals are only considered if they persist along the system evolution, while the evaluation of a formula with individuals that are not present in the current database trivially leads to false or true.

EXAMPLE 3.4. Consider the $\mu\mathcal{L}_A$ formula in Example 3.3. $\mu\mathcal{L}_P$ can express two variations of such a formula. The first one,

$$\nu X.(\forall x.Stud(x) \rightarrow \mu Y.(\exists y.Grad(x,y) \vee (\text{LIVE}(x) \wedge \langle - \rangle Y)) \wedge [-]X)$$

strengthens the original formula stating that, along every path, it is always true, for each student x, that there exists an evolution in which x persists in the database until she eventually graduates (with some final mark y). The second variation,

$$\nu X.(\forall x.Stud(x) \rightarrow \mu Y.(\exists y.Grad(x,y) \vee (\text{LIVE}(x) \rightarrow \langle - \rangle Y)) \wedge [-]X)$$

weakens the original formula stating that, along every path, it is always true, for each student x, that there exists an evolution in which if x persists, she eventually graduates (with final mark y). ■

The bisimulation relation that captures $\mu\mathcal{L}_P$ is as follows. Let $\Upsilon_1 = \langle \Delta_1, \mathcal{R}, \Sigma_1, s_{01}, db_1, \Rightarrow_1 \rangle$ and $\Upsilon_2 = \langle \Delta_2, \mathcal{R}, \Sigma_2, s_{02}, db_2, \Rightarrow_2 \rangle$ be transition systems, and H the set of partial bijections between Δ_1 and Δ_2, which are the identity between $\text{ADOM}(db_1(s_{01}))$ and $\text{ADOM}(db_2(s_{02}))$. A *persistence-preserving bisimulation* between Υ_1 and Υ_2 is a relation $\mathcal{B} \subseteq \Sigma_1 \times H \times \Sigma_2$ such that $\langle s_1, h, s_2 \rangle \in \mathcal{B}$ implies that:

1. h is an isomorphism between $db_1(s_1)$ and $db_2(s_2)$;[6]
2. for each s_1', if $s_1 \Rightarrow_1 s_1'$ then there exists an s_2' with $s_2 \Rightarrow_2 s_2'$ and a bijection h' that extends $h|_{\text{ADOM}(db_1(s_1)) \cap \text{ADOM}(db_1(s_1'))}$, such that $\langle s_1', h', s_2' \rangle \in \mathcal{B}$;[7]
3. for each s_2', if $s_2 \Rightarrow_2 s_2'$ then there exists an s_1' with $s_1 \Rightarrow_1 s_1'$ and a bijection h' that extends $h|_{\text{ADOM}(db_1(s_1)) \cap \text{ADOM}(db_1(s_1'))}$, such that $\langle s_1', h', s_2' \rangle \in \mathcal{B}$.

We say that a state $s_1 \in \Sigma_1$ is *persistence-preserving bisimilar* to $s_2 \in \Sigma_2$ *w.r.t. a partial bijection h*, written $s_1 \sim_h s_2$, if there exists a persistence-preserving bisimulation $\mathcal{B}$ between Υ_1 and Υ_2 such that $\langle s_1, h, s_2 \rangle \in \mathcal{B}$. A state $s_1 \in \Sigma_1$ is *persistence-preserving bisimilar* to $s_2 \in \Sigma_2$, written $s_1 \sim s_2$, if there exists a partial bijection h and a persistence-preserving bisimulation $\mathcal{B}$ between Υ_1 and Υ_2 such that $\langle s_1, h, s_2 \rangle \in \mathcal{B}$. A transition system Υ_1 is *persistence-preserving bisimilar* to Υ_2, written $\Upsilon_1 \sim \Upsilon_2$, if $s_{01} \sim s_{02}$. The next theorem shows that $\mu\mathcal{L}_P$ enjoys invariance under this notion of bisimulation.

THEOREM 3.2. *Consider two transition systems Υ_1 and Υ_2 such that $\Upsilon_1 \sim \Upsilon_2$. Then for every $\mu\mathcal{L}_P$ closed formula Φ, we have that $\Upsilon_1 \models \Phi$ if and only if $\Upsilon_2 \models \Phi$.*

EXAMPLE 3.5. We illustrate some $\mu\mathcal{L}_P$ properties pertaining to the proper operation of the request system of Example 2.1. Recall that $\mu\mathcal{L}_P$ requires the bindings of quantified variables to be continuously live between the step when the quantification was evaluated and the step when the variable is used. This can be done by using LIVE or by using any relation, in our example Travel.

A property of interest is that once initiated, a request will eventually be decided by the monitor, and the decision can only be *'readyToUpdate'* or *'accepted'* (a liveness property):

$$\begin{array}{l}\nu X.(\forall n.\mathsf{Travel}(n) \rightarrow \\ \quad \mu Y.(\mathsf{Status}(\textit{'readyToUpdate'}) \vee \mathsf{Status}(\textit{'accepted'}) \\ \qquad \vee\, \mathsf{Travel}(n) \wedge [-]Y)) \wedge [-]X\end{array}$$

Another property of interest is that if the flight cost is not specified, then the request is not accepted (a safety property):

$$\begin{array}{l}\nu X.(\neg(\exists x_1, \ldots, x_4.\mathsf{Status}(\textit{'accepted'}) \wedge \\ \qquad\qquad \mathsf{Flight}(x_1, x_2, \bot, x_3, x_4))) \wedge [-]X\end{array}$$

where the special constant $\bot$ denotes a "non-specified" value (this need not be treated specially in the semantics, any value of the domain can be reserved for this purpose). ■

4. DETERMINISTIC SERVICES

We revisit the semantics of DCDSs, and analyze them under the assumption that external services behave deterministically. This means that the evaluation of functions $f \in \mathcal{F}$, representing the services in the process layer, is independent from the moment in which the function is called: if an external service is called twice with the same parameters, it must return the same value. So, for example, if the function invocation $f(a)$ returned b at a certain time, then in all successive moments the call $f(a)$ will return b again. In particular, *stateless* services can be modeled with deterministic service calls. In Example 2.1 (and its extended version in [4]) all web services invoked by the audit system (e.g., to determine the monetary conversion rate on a given date, or to check whether the employee took a specific flight), are inherently deterministic.

4.1 Semantics

We now define the transition system of a DCDS under the assumption of deterministic services. We call such a transition system "concrete" to avoid confusion with an "abstract" transition system that we are going to introduce for our verification technique.

Let $\mathcal{S} = \langle \mathcal{D}, \mathcal{P} \rangle$ be a DCDS with data layer $\mathcal{D} = \langle \mathcal{C}, \mathcal{R}, \mathcal{E}, \mathcal{I}_0 \rangle$ and process layer $\mathcal{P} = \langle \mathcal{F}, \mathcal{A}, \varrho \rangle$.

First we focus on what is needed to characterize the states of the concrete transition system. One such state obviously needs to maintain the current instance of the data layer. This instance is a database made up of values in $\mathcal{C}$, which conforms to the schema $\mathcal{R}$ and satisfies the equality constraints in $\mathcal{E}$. Together with the current instance, however, we also need to remember all answers we had so far when calling the external services.

To meet the requirement that service calls behave deterministically, the states of the transition system keep track of all results of the service calls made so far, in the form of equalities between Skolem terms (involving functions in $\mathcal{F}$ and arguments in $\mathcal{C}$) and returned values in $\mathcal{C}$.[8] More precisely, we define the set of (Skolem terms representing) service calls as $\mathbb{SC} = \{f(v_1, \ldots, v_n) \mid f/n \in \mathcal{F} \text{ and } \{v_1, \ldots, v_n\} \subseteq \mathcal{C}\}$, where f/n stands for a function f of arity n. Then we introduce a *service call map*, which is a partial function $\mathcal{M} : \mathbb{SC} \rightarrow \mathcal{C}$. Now we are ready to formally define states of the concrete transition system. A *(concrete) state* is a pair $\langle \mathcal{I}, \mathcal{M} \rangle$, where $\mathcal{I}$ is a relational instance of $\mathcal{R}$ over $\mathcal{C}$ satisfying each equality constraint in $\mathcal{E}$, and $\mathcal{M}$ is a service call map. The *initial concrete state* is $\langle \mathcal{I}_0, \emptyset \rangle$.

Next we look at the result of executing an action in a state. Let α be an action in $\mathcal{A}$ with parameters $p_1, \ldots, p_m$, $\alpha(p_1, \ldots, p_m) : \{e_1, \ldots, e_m\}$ where $e_i = q_i^+ \wedge Q_i^- \rightsquigarrow E_i$. Let σ be a substitution for $p_1, \ldots, p_m$ with values taken from $\mathcal{C}$. We say that σ is *legal* for α in state $\langle \mathcal{I}, \mathcal{M} \rangle$ if there exists a condition-action rule $Q \mapsto \alpha$ in ϱ such that $\langle p_1, \ldots, p_m \rangle \sigma \in ans(Q, \mathcal{I})$.

We denote with $\text{DO}(\mathcal{I}, \alpha, \sigma)$ the instance obtained by evaluating the effects of action α with parameters σ on instance $\mathcal{I}$, i.e.:

$$\text{DO}(\mathcal{I}, \alpha, \sigma) = \bigcup_{q_i^+ \wedge Q_i^- \rightsquigarrow E_i \in \text{EFFECT}(\alpha)} \quad \bigcup_{\theta \in ans((q_i^+ \wedge Q_i^-)\sigma, \mathcal{I})} E_i\sigma\theta$$

Intuitively, the returned instance is the union of the results of applying the effects specifications $\text{EFFECT}(\alpha)$, where the result of each effect specification $q_i^+ \wedge Q_i^- \rightsquigarrow E_i$ is, in turn, the set of facts $E_i\sigma\theta$ obtained from $E_i\sigma$ grounded on all the assignments θ that satisfy the query $q_i^+ \wedge Q_i^-$ over $\mathcal{I}$.

[6]Notice that this implies $\text{DOM}(h) = \text{ADOM}(db_1(s_1))$ and $\text{IM}(h) = \text{ADOM}(db_2(s_2))$.

[7]Given a set D, we denote by $f|_D$ the *restriction* of f to D, i.e., $\text{DOM}(f|_D) = \text{DOM}(f) \cap D$, and $f|_D(x) = f(x)$ for every $x \in \text{DOM}(f) \cap D$.

[8]Notice that we assume no knowledge of the specific functions adopted by the external services, and we simply assume that such functions return some value from $\mathcal{C}$. Services returning values from an enumerated subset of $\mathcal{C}$, such as DECIDE() in Ex. 2.1, are syntactic sugar that we can simulate in our model. We are going to have different executions of the system corresponding to each way to assign values to the Skolem terms representing the service calls.

DO() generates an instance over values from $\mathcal{C}$ and over Skolem terms, which model service calls. For any such instance $\bar{\mathcal{I}}$, we denote with CALLS($\bar{\mathcal{I}}$) the set of calls it contains. For a given set $D \subseteq \mathcal{C}$, we denote with EVALS$_D(\mathcal{I}, \alpha, \sigma)$ the set of substitutions that replace all service calls in DO$(\mathcal{I}, \alpha, \sigma)$ with values in D,

$$\text{EVALS}_D(\mathcal{I}, \alpha, \sigma) = \{\theta \mid \theta \text{ is a total function } \theta : \text{CALLS}(\text{DO}(\mathcal{I}, \alpha, \sigma)) \rightarrow D\}.$$

Each substitution in EVALS$_D(\mathcal{I}, \alpha, \sigma)$ models the simultaneous evaluation of all service calls, which replaces the calls with results selected arbitrarily from D. In the following, we refer to these substitutions as *evaluations*.

Concrete action execution. To capture what happens when α is executed in a state using a substitution σ for its parameters, we introduce a transition relation D-EXEC$_\mathcal{S}$ between states, called *concrete execution* of $\alpha\sigma$, such that $\langle\langle\mathcal{I}, \mathcal{M}\rangle, \alpha\sigma, \langle\mathcal{I}', \mathcal{M}'\rangle\rangle \in$ D-EXEC$_\mathcal{S}$ if the following holds:

1. σ is a legal parameter assignment for α in state $\langle\mathcal{I}, \mathcal{M}\rangle$,
2. there exists $\theta \in$ EVALS$_\mathcal{C}(\mathcal{I}, \alpha, \sigma)$ that is compatible with $\mathcal{M}$ (i.e., θ and $\mathcal{M}$ agree on the common values in their domains),
3. $\mathcal{I}' =$ DO$(\mathcal{I}, \alpha, \sigma)\theta$, and $\mathcal{I}'$ satisfies $\mathcal{E}$,
4. $\mathcal{M}' = \mathcal{M} \cup \theta$.

In the above definition, the purpose of $\mathcal{M}$ is to record the history of service calls and their results, while θ contains the service calls invoked in the current transition, with their results (arbitrary values from $\mathcal{C}$). The compatibility of $\mathcal{M}$ and θ in condition (2) forces the current invocation of a call to return the same result as its past invocations, thus realizing the intended deterministic semantics.

Concrete transition system. The *concrete transition system* $\Upsilon_\mathcal{S}$ for $\mathcal{S}$ is a (possibly infinite-state) transition system $\langle\mathcal{C}, \mathcal{R}, \Sigma, s_0, db, \Rightarrow\rangle$ where: $s_0 = \langle\mathcal{I}_0, \emptyset\rangle$; db is such that $db(\langle\mathcal{I}, \mathcal{M}\rangle) = \mathcal{I}$; Σ and $\Rightarrow$ are defined by simultaneous induction as the smallest sets satisfying the following properties: *(i)* $s_0 \in \Sigma$; *(ii)* if $\langle\mathcal{I}, \mathcal{M}\rangle \in \Sigma$, then for all substitutions σ for the parameters of α and for all $\langle\mathcal{I}', \mathcal{M}'\rangle$ such that $\langle\langle\mathcal{I}, \mathcal{M}\rangle, \alpha\sigma, \langle\mathcal{I}', \mathcal{M}'\rangle\rangle \in$ D-EXEC$_\mathcal{S}$, we have $\langle\mathcal{I}', \mathcal{M}'\rangle \in \Sigma$ and $\langle\mathcal{I}, \mathcal{M}\rangle \Rightarrow \langle\mathcal{I}', \mathcal{M}'\rangle$.

Intuitively, to define the concrete transition system of the DCDS $\mathcal{S}$ we start from the initial state $s_0 = \langle\mathcal{I}_0, \emptyset\rangle$, and calculate all states s such that $\langle s_0, \alpha\sigma, s\rangle \in$ D-EXEC$_\mathcal{S}$. Then we repeat the same steps considering each s, and so on. The computation of successor states is done by: getting all legal substitutions of the action parameters according to the condition-action rule in the process; executing the instantiated actions; picking all the possible combinations of resulting values for the newly introduced service calls; and filtering away those successors that violate the equality constraints. It is worth noting that the number of successors can be countably infinite because the service call results come from $\mathcal{C}$.

4.2 Run-Bounded Systems

We now study the verification of DCDSs with deterministic services. In particular, we are interested in the following problem: given a DCDS $\mathcal{S}$ and a temporal property Φ, check whether $\Upsilon_\mathcal{S} \models \Phi$. Not surprisingly, given the expressive power of DCDS as a computation model, the verification problem is undecidable for all the μ-calculus variants introduced in Section 3. In fact, we can show an even stronger undecidability result, namely for safety properties expressible in both propositional LTL and CTL [5].

THEOREM 4.1. *There exists a DCDS $\mathcal{S}$ with deterministic services, and a propositional safety property Φ expressible in LTL $\cap$ CTL, such that checking $\Upsilon_\mathcal{S} \models \Phi$ is undecidable.*

Next, we isolate a notable class of DCDS for which verification of $\mu\mathcal{L}_A$ is not only decidable, but can also be reduced to standard finite-state model checking. Consider a transition system $\Upsilon = \langle\Delta, \mathcal{R}, \Sigma, s_0, db, \Rightarrow\rangle$. A *run* τ in Υ is a (finite or infinite) sequence of states $s_0 s_1 s_2 \cdots$ rooted at s_0, where $s_i \Rightarrow s_{i+1}$. We use $\tau(i)$ to denote s_i and $\tau[i]$ to represent the finite prefix $s_0 \cdots s_i$ of τ. A run $\tau = s_0 s_1 s_2 \cdots$ is *(data) bounded* if the total number of values occurring in its databases is bounded, i.e., there exists a finite bound $b > |\bigcup_{s \text{ state of } \tau} \text{ADOM}(db(s))|$. This is equivalent to saying that, for every finite prefix $\tau[i]$ of τ, $|\bigcup_{j \in \{0,\ldots,i\}} \text{ADOM}(db(s_j))| < b$. We say that Υ is *run-bounded* if there exists a bound b such that every run in Υ is (data) bounded by b. A DCDS $\mathcal{S}$ is run-bounded if its concrete transition system $\Upsilon_\mathcal{S}$ is run-bounded.

Intuitively, a (data) unbounded run represents an execution of the DCDS in which infinitely many distinct values occur because infinitely many different service calls are issued. Since we model deterministic services whose number is finite, this can only happen if some service is repeatedly called with arguments that are the result of previous service calls. This means that the values of the run indirectly depend on arbitrarily many states in the past.

Notice that run boundedness does not impose any restriction about the branching of the transition system; in particular, $\Upsilon_\mathcal{S}$ is typically infinite-branching because new service calls may return any possible value. We show that this restriction guarantees decidability of $\mu\mathcal{L}_A$ verification for run-bounded DCDSs with deterministic services.

THEOREM 4.2. *Verification of $\mu\mathcal{L}_A$ properties on run-bounded DCDSs with deterministic services is decidable.*

We get this result by showing that for run-bounded DCDSs we can always construct, without knowing the bound beforehand, an abstract finite-state transition system that is history-preserving bisimilar to the concrete one, and hence satisfies the same $\mu\mathcal{L}_A$ formulae as the concrete transition system.

PROPOSITION 4.3. *Let $\mathcal{S}$ be a run-bounded DCDS with deterministic services and $\Upsilon_\mathcal{S}$ its concrete transition system. Then there exists an (abstract)* finite-state *transition system $\Theta_\mathcal{S}$ such that $\Theta_\mathcal{S}$ is history-preserving bisimilar to $\Upsilon_\mathcal{S}$, i.e., $\Theta_\mathcal{S} \approx \Upsilon_\mathcal{S}$.*

Let Σ be the set of states of $\Theta_\mathcal{S}$ and $\text{ADOM}(\Theta_\mathcal{S}) = \bigcup_{s_i \in \Sigma} \text{ADOM}(db(s_i))$. If $\Theta_\mathcal{S}$ is finite-state, then there exists a bound b such that $|\text{ADOM}(\Theta_\mathcal{S})| < b$. Consequently, it is possible to transform a $\mu\mathcal{L}_A$ property Φ into an equivalent *finite* propositional μ-calculus formula PROP(Φ), where PROP(Φ) is inductively defined by recurring over the structure of Φ and substituting PROP$(\exists x.\text{LIVE}(x) \wedge \Psi(x))$ with $\bigvee_{t_i \in \text{ADOM}(\Theta_\mathcal{S})} \text{LIVE}(t_i) \wedge$ PROP$(\Psi(t_i))$. Clearly, $\Theta_\mathcal{S} \models \Phi$ if and only if $\Theta_\mathcal{S} \models$ PROP(Φ).

THEOREM 4.4. *Verification of $\mu\mathcal{L}_A$ properties for run-bounded DCDSs with deterministic services can be reduced to model checking of propositional μ-calculus over a finite transition system.*

By the above theorem, and recalling that model checking of propositional μ-calculus formulae over finite transition systems is decidable [26], we get Theorem 4.2.

We conclude the section by observing that the approach presented above for $\mu\mathcal{L}_A$ does not extend to full $\mu\mathcal{L}$.

THEOREM 4.5. *There exists a run-bounded DCDS $\mathcal{S}$ for which it is impossible to find a faithful finite-state abstraction that satisfies the same $\mu\mathcal{L}$ properties as $\mathcal{S}$.*

Theorem 4.5 is proved by exhibiting, for every n, a $\mu\mathcal{L}$ property that requires the existence of at least n objects in the transition system, such as the one in Example 3.2. While this result does not imply undecidability of model checking $\mu\mathcal{L}$ properties over run-bounded DCDSs, it dashes any hope of reducing this problem to standard, finite-state model checking.

4.3 Weakly Acyclic DCDSs

The decidability results in Section 4.2 rely on the hypothesis that the DCDS is run-bounded, which is a semantic condition. A natural question is whether it is possible to check run-boundedness of a DCDS. We provide a negative answer to this question.

THEOREM 4.6. *Checking run-boundedness of DCDSs with deterministic services is undecidable.*

To mitigate this issue, we investigate a sufficient syntactic condition that can be effectively tested over the process layer of the DCDS: if the condition is met, then the DCDS is guaranteed to be run-bounded, otherwise nothing can be said. To this end, we recast the approach of [17] and [3] in the more expressive framework here presented. To derive a sufficient condition for $\mathcal{S}$ to be run-bounded, we exploit a correspondence between (a carefully constructed approximation of) the execution of an action and a step in the chase of a set of TGDs in data exchange [2, 27]. In particular, we resort to a well-known result in data exchange, namely chase termination for *weakly acyclic* TGDs [27]. In our setting, the weak acyclicity of a process layer $\mathcal{P}$ is a property over a dataflow graph constructed from $\mathcal{P}$, where we consider only the contribution of the union of conjunctive queries q^+ in each action effect. We omit the definition of weak acyclicity and provide an intuition here (see [4] for details). The problem of non run-bounded DCDSs comes from services that are repeatedly called, every time using fresh values that are directly or indirectly obtained by manipulating previous results produced by the same service. This self-dependency can potentially lead to incorporating unboundedly many results of these service calls into the run. Weak acyclicity rules out such self dependencies, being in fact a sufficient, polynomially-checkable condition for run-boundedness.[9]

THEOREM 4.7. *Every weakly acyclic DCDS with deterministic services is run-bounded.*

This, together with Theorem 4.4, gives us an effective way to verify DCDSs by reduction to conventional model checking.

THEOREM 4.8. *Verification of $\mu\mathcal{L}_A$ properties for weakly acyclic DCDSs with deterministic services is decidable.*

5. NONDETERMINISTIC SERVICES

We now consider DCDSs under the assumption that services behave nondeterministically, i.e., two calls of a service with the same arguments may return distinct results during the same run. This case captures both services that model a truly nondeterministic process (e.g., human operators, random processes), and services that model stateful servers. In Example 2.1, all the reimbursement system services (e.g., DECIDE() and INHNAME()) are inherently nondeterministic as they model human input. In the remainder of this section, services are implicitly assumed nondeterministic.

5.1 Semantics

As in the case of deterministic services, we define the semantics of a DCDS $\mathcal{S}$ in terms of a (possibly infinite) transition system $\Upsilon_\mathcal{S}$.

Let $\mathcal{S} = \langle \mathcal{D}, \mathcal{P} \rangle$ be a DCDS with data layer $\mathcal{D} = \langle \mathcal{C}, \mathcal{R}, \mathcal{E}, \mathcal{I}_0 \rangle$ and process layer $\mathcal{P} = \langle \mathcal{F}, \mathcal{A}, \varrho \rangle$. A *state* is simply a relational instance of $\mathcal{R}$ over $\mathcal{C}$ satisfying each constraint in $\mathcal{E}$. We denote the *initial state* with $\mathcal{I}_0$.

Next, we define the semantics of action application. Let α be an action in $\mathcal{A}$ with parameters $p_1, \ldots, p_m$. Let σ be a substitution for $p_1, \ldots, p_m$ with values taken from $\mathcal{C}$, that is legal according to the process ϱ. We recall the definitions of DO() and EVALS$_D$() from Section 4.1. DO$(\mathcal{I}, \alpha, \sigma)$ denotes the instance obtained by evaluating the effects of action α with parameters σ on instance $\mathcal{I}$. For a given set $D \subseteq \mathcal{C}$, EVALS$_D(\mathcal{I}, \alpha, \sigma)$ is the set of substitutions that replace all service calls in DO$(\mathcal{I}, \alpha, \sigma)$ with values in D.

Concrete action execution. We introduce a transition relation N-EXEC$_\mathcal{S}$ between states, called *concrete execution* of $\alpha\sigma$, such that $\langle \mathcal{I}, \alpha\sigma, \mathcal{I}' \rangle \in$ N-EXEC$_\mathcal{S}$ if we have:

1. σ is a legal parameter assignment for α in state $\mathcal{I}$,
2. there exists $\theta \in$ EVALS$_\mathcal{C}(\mathcal{I}, \alpha, \sigma)$,
3. $\mathcal{I}' =$ DO$(\mathcal{I}, \alpha, \sigma)\theta$, and $\mathcal{I}'$ satisfies the constraints $\mathcal{E}$.

In contrast to the deterministic services case, the choice of evaluation θ is not subject to the requirement that it evaluates a service call to the same result *across* concrete execution steps (indeed, we no longer accumulate the successive choices of θ in the service call map $\mathcal{M}$). However, notice that *within* a concrete execution step, all occurrences of the same service call evaluate to the same result (modeling the fact that a call with given arguments is invoked only once per transition, and the returned result is copied as needed).

Concrete transition system. The *concrete transition system* $\Upsilon_\mathcal{S}$ for $\mathcal{S}$ is a transition system whose states are labeled by databases. More precisely, $\Upsilon_\mathcal{S} = \langle \mathcal{C}, \mathcal{R}, \Sigma, s_0, db, \Rightarrow \rangle$ where $s_0 = \mathcal{I}_0$ and db is such that $db(\mathcal{I}) = \mathcal{I}$. Σ and $\Rightarrow$ are defined by simultaneous induction as the smallest sets satisfying the following properties: *(i)* $\mathcal{I}_0 \in \Sigma$; *(ii)* if $\mathcal{I} \in \Sigma$, then for all α, σ and $\mathcal{I}'$ such that $\langle \mathcal{I}, \alpha\sigma, \mathcal{I}' \rangle \in$ N-EXEC$_\mathcal{S}$, we have that $\mathcal{I}' \in \Sigma$, and $\mathcal{I} \Rightarrow \mathcal{I}'$.

5.2 State-Bounded Systems

We consider the verification problem for DCDS with nondeterministic services. As in the deterministic case, an analogous undecidability result to Theorem 4.1 holds.

THEOREM 5.1. *There exists a DCDS $\mathcal{S}$ with nondeterministic services, and a propositional safety property Φ expressible in LTL $\cap$ CTL, such that checking $\Upsilon_\mathcal{S} \models \Phi$ is undecidable.*

Towards devising interesting decidable cases we start by observing that, with nondeterministic services, the run-boundedness restriction of Section 4.2 is very limiting on the form of the DCDS, as it boils down to imposing a bound on how many times each service may be called with the same arguments. Contrast this with deterministic services, where unlimited same-argument calls are allowed, as they all return the same result. We propose a less restrictive alternative. We say that DCDS $\mathcal{S}$ is *state-bounded* if there is a finite bound b such that for each state $\mathcal{I}$ of $\Upsilon_\mathcal{S}$, $|$ADOM$(\mathcal{I})| < b$. In contrast to run-boundedness, state-boundedness allows for runs in which infinitely many distinct values occur because infinitely many service calls are issued. These call results are distributed *across* states of the run, but may not accumulate *within* a single state. For example, the request system in Example 2.1 is not run-bounded, since a user can update the request information with an unbounded number of new values during a run. However, it is state-bounded, since each state contains exactly one request. $\mu\mathcal{L}_A$ can record past values in the run through quantification even if they are not present in the system anymore. The following result shows that this leads to undecidability.

THEOREM 5.2. *Verification of $\mu\mathcal{L}_A$ properties on state-bounded DCDSs with nondeterministic services is undecidable.*

We therefore focus on to the logic $\mu\mathcal{L}_P$ (presented in Section 3.2), in which this recording through quantification is disallowed.

THEOREM 5.3. *Verification of $\mu\mathcal{L}_P$ properties by state-bounded DCDS with nondeterministic services is decidable.*

[9]Notice that we can also use other variants of weak acyclicity [35].

We give the main ideas behind the proof of this theorem. Given a DCDS $\mathcal{S}$, we show that if concrete transition system $\Upsilon_\mathcal{S}$ is state-bounded, then there is a finite-state abstract transition system $\Theta_\mathcal{S}$ that is persistence-preserving bisimilar to $\Upsilon_\mathcal{S}$ (and hence satisfies the same $\mu\mathcal{L}_P$ properties, by Theorem 3.2). Since $\Theta_\mathcal{S}$ is finite-state, the verification of $\mu\mathcal{L}_P$ properties on $\Upsilon_\mathcal{S}$ reduces to finite-state model checking on $\Theta_\mathcal{S}$, and hence is decidable.

THEOREM 5.4. *Verification of $\mu\mathcal{L}_P$ properties for state-bounded DCDSs with nondeterministic services can be reduced to model checking of propositional μ-calculus over a finite transition system.*

The existence of $\Theta_\mathcal{S}$ follows from the key fact that if two states of $\Upsilon_\mathcal{S}$ are isomorphic, then they are persistence-preserving bisimilar. This implies that one can construct a finitely-branching transition system $\Theta_\mathcal{S}$ (i.e. with finite number of successors per state), such that $\Theta_\mathcal{S}$ is persistence-preserving bisimilar to $\Upsilon_\mathcal{S}$, by dropping sibling states from $\Upsilon_\mathcal{S}$ as follows: instead of listing among the successors of s one state for each possible instantiation of the service call results, just keep a *representative* state for each isomorphism type. Since the number of service calls made in each state is finite, the number of distinct isomorphism types is finite, so the finite branching follows. We call a transition system $\Theta_\mathcal{S}$ obtained as above a *pruning of* $\Upsilon_\mathcal{S}$.

Despite being finitely-branching, any pruning $\Theta_\mathcal{S}$ can still have infinitely many states, as it may contain infinitely long simple runs τ (a *simple* run is one in which no state appears more than once), along which the service calls return in each state "fresh" values, i.e., values distinct from all values appearing in the predecessors of this state on τ. This problem is solved by judiciously selecting which representatives to keep in $\Theta_\mathcal{S}$ for the successors of a state s. Namely, whenever the representatives of a given isomorphism type $\mathcal{T}$ include states generated exclusively by service calls that "recycle" values, select only such states (finitely many thereof, of course). By recycled values we mean values appearing on a path leading into s.

If $\Upsilon_\mathcal{S}$ is state-bounded, then the number of service calls per state is bounded, and due to the construction's preference for recycling, it follows that all simple runs in $\Theta_\mathcal{S}$ must have finite length. Together with the finite branching, this implies finiteness of $\Theta_\mathcal{S}$.

Notice that proving the existence of $\Theta_\mathcal{S}$ does not suffice for decidability, as the proof is non-constructive. We therefore provide an algorithm for constructing $\Theta_\mathcal{S}$ (cf. algorithm RCYCL in [4]). One of the technical problems we need to overcome in developing the algorithm is that we cannot start from the infinite-state concrete transition system, and instead need to explore a portion thereof. This means that it is not obvious how to decide whether the successors of a state are generated by recycling service calls, since these calls may recycle from paths that the algorithm has not explored yet. Therefore, the algorithm may sometimes select non-recycling service calls even when a recycling alternative exists. However, we can prove that it constructs what we call an *eventually recycling pruning*, which in essence means it may fail to detect recycling service calls, but only a bounded number of times. We note that the algorithm does not need to know a priori the bound on the state size; its mere existence guarantees that the construction terminates. This, together with Theorem 3.2, directly implies Theorem 5.3.

5.3 GR-Acyclic DCDSs

As with run-boundedness in the deterministic services case, for nondeterministic services state-boundedness is a semantic property, which in general is undecidable.

THEOREM 5.5. *Checking state-boundedness of DCDSs is undecidable.*

Consequently we propose a sufficient syntactic condition. Intuitively, for a run to have unbounded states, it must issue unboundedly many service calls. Since there are only a bounded number of effects in the process layer specification, there must exist some service-calling effect that "cyclically generates" fresh values (i.e., is invoked infinitely many times during the run). Notice that unbounded generation of fresh values does not break state-boundedness per se: these values must also accumulate in the states to do so. But by definition of the DCDS semantics, a transition drops ("forgets") all values that are not explicitly copied ("recalled") into the successor. Therefore, to accumulate, a value must be "cyclically recalled" throughout the run (copied infinitely many times).

GR-acyclicity is stated in terms of a dataflow graph constructed by analyzing the process layer. The graph identifies how service calls and value recalls can chain. In essence, GR-acyclicity requires the absence of a "generate cycle" that feeds into a "recall cycle".

GR-acyclicity. We call *dataflow graph* of a set $\mathcal{A}$ of actions the directed edge-labeled graph $\langle N, G\rangle$ whose set N of nodes is the set of relation names occurring in $\mathcal{A}$, and in which each edge in G is a 4-tuple (R_1, id, R_2, b), where R_1 and R_2 are two nodes in N, id is a (unique) edge identifier, and b is a boolean flag used to mark *special* edges. Formally, G is the minimal set satisfying the following condition: for each effect e in $\mathcal{A}$ of the form $q^+ \wedge Q^- \rightsquigarrow E$, each R in q^+, each $Q(t_1, \ldots, t_m)$ in E, and each $i \in \{1, \ldots, m\}$:

- if t_i is either an element of $\textsc{adom}(\mathcal{I}_0)$ or a free variable, then $(R, id, Q, \mathsf{false}) \in G$, where id is a fresh edge identifier.
- if t_i is a service call, then $(R, id, Q, \mathsf{true}) \in G$, where id is a fresh edge identifier.

We say that $\mathcal{A}$ is *GR-acyclic* if there is no path $\pi = \pi_1\pi_2\pi_3$ in the dataflow graph of $\mathcal{A}$, such that π_1, π_3 are simple cycles and π_2 is a path containing a special edge, and having at least some edge disjoint from the edges of π_1: $edges(\pi_2) \setminus edges(\pi_1) \neq \emptyset$. We say that a process layer $\mathcal{P} = \langle \mathcal{F}, \mathcal{A}, \varrho\rangle$ is GR-acyclic, if $\mathcal{A}$ is GR-acyclic. A DCDS GR-acyclic if its process layer is GR-acyclic.

Note that GR-acyclicity is a purely syntactic notion. It can be checked in coNP since the dataflow graph is polynomial in the size of the process layer specification, and since, if there is a violation of GR-acyclicity, then there is a polynomial-sized one as well.

THEOREM 5.6. *Any GR-acyclic DCDS is state-bounded.*

We give the main ideas behind the proof of this theorem, noting that the dataflow analysis is significantly more subtle than suggested above. First, note that ordinary edges correspond to an effect copying a value from a relation of the current state to a relation of the successor state. Special edges correspond to feeding a value of the current state to a service call and storing the result in a relation of the successor state. Note that the cycles π_1 and π_3 allow both kinds of edges, reflecting the insight that the size of the state is affected in the same way regardless of whether a value is *copied* to the successor, or it is *replaced* with a service call result. π_1, π_3 are both "recall cycles": the number of values moving around them does not decrease (this is of course a conservative statement; reality depends on the semantics of queries in the effects, which is abstracted away). Note that π_2 contains a special edge G, which means that the values moving around π_1 are cyclically fed into the service call f of G. The key insight here is that, even if the set of values moving around π_1 does not change (no special edges in π_1 replace them), and thus the service call f sees the same bounded set of distinct arguments over time, it can still generate an unbounded number of fresh values because f is nondeterministic. $\pi_1\pi_2$ constitute the "generate cycle" we mention above. The generated values are stored in the recall cycle π_3, where they accumulate and force the size of the relations of π_3 to grow unboundedly.

We observe that GR-acyclicity is not related to weak acyclicity. In particular, a DCDS may be GR-acyclic but not weakly acyclic.

GR$^+$-acyclicity. GR-acyclicity can be relaxed based on the insight that, for a cycle Υ_S in the dataflow graph to truly preserve the number of values moving in it, Υ_S's edges must not all be simultaneously inactive. We say that an edge is *active* in a step of the run when the action corresponding to it executes. By the DCDS semantics, if all edges of Υ_S are simultaneously inactive, then none of the corresponding copy/call operations are executed and all relations involved in Υ_S forget their value in the next state. Υ_S is effectively flushed. GR$^+$-acyclicity is the relaxation that does allow a path $\pi = \pi_1\pi_2\pi_3$ as in the definition of GR-acyclicity, provided that π_2 contains an edge e that cannot be active at the same time as any of the subsequent edges e' in $\pi_2\pi_3$. Formally, we associate with every edge ϵ in the dataflow graph the action $action(\epsilon)$ it corresponds to (computed via simple inspection of the process layer). Then for every $e \in \pi_2, e' \in \pi_2\pi_3$ as above, we require that $action(e) \neq action(e')$. Semantically this ensures that in order for the generate cycle $\pi_1\pi_2$ to push fresh values toward recall cycle π_3, the action corresponding to e must execute, and in the meantime all actions maintaining the values in cycle π_3 are disabled, thus flushing π_3. π_3 thus receives an unbounded number of waves of fresh values from $\pi_1\pi_2$, but it forgets each wave before the next arrives. GR$^+$-acyclicity can also be checked in coNP. Theorem 5.6 extends to GR$^+$-acyclicity.

THEOREM 5.7. *Every GR$^+$-acyclic DCDS is state-bounded.*

This, together with Theorem 5.3, implies:

THEOREM 5.8. *Verification of $\mu\mathcal{L}_P$ properties for GR$^+$-acyclic DCDS with nondeterministic services is decidable.*

EXAMPLE 5.1. The dataflow graph for the request system of Example 2.1 is depicted in Figure 2, where special edges are starred.

Notice that there can be multiple normal/special edges between the same two nodes (these are distinguished by unique edge ids; to avoid clutter in the figure we omit the ids, and show edge multiplicities in square brackets; missing brackets denote multiplicity 1). For example, the red simple edge from Hotel to Status is due to the first effect of action *VerifyRequest*, while the special edge in parallel with it is due to the DECIDE() call in the second effect. The red self-loops on Flight, Hotel, Travel and ApprHotel reflect the remaining effects of *VerifyRequest*. The five black special edges from the true node (with the obvious meaning) to the Hotel node correspond to the employee filling in the hotel information in action *UpdateRequest*, modeled by calls to such services as INHNAME(). We refer to [4] for a complete treatment of the example. An inspection of this dataflow graph reveals that the request system is not GR-acyclic, since it contains several instances of two simple cycles connected by a path that includes a special edge: for instance, the path π comprised of the normal self-loops around Hotel and Status and the special edge between them. However, the request system is GR$^+$-acyclic, confirming that the system is indeed state-bounded: all edges of cycles downstream of special edges e are due to actions (colors) disjoint from e's. ∎

6. DISCUSSION

Summary of results. We summarize our results in Table 1 where, for completeness, we add additional results that can be proven analogously to the ones in the body of the paper (see [4]). Arrows denote implications between results. We note that exhibiting a finite faithful abstraction of a concrete transition system is more

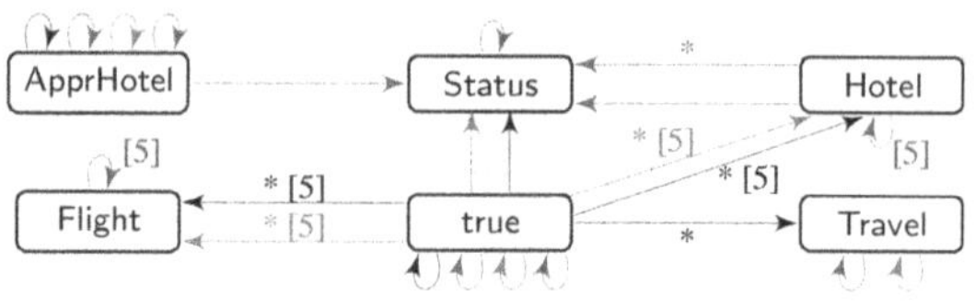

Figure 2: Dataflow graph for Example 5.1: colors black, red, green, blue correspond respectively to actions *InitiateRequest*, *VerifyRequest*, *UpdateRequest*, and *AcceptRequest*.

than a means towards showing decidability, being a desirable goal in its own right as the most promising avenue towards practical implementation. We list as open the verification of $\mu\mathcal{L}$ properties on run-bounded DCDSs, but recall from Section 4.2 that in this case there exists no faithful finite-state abstract transition system.

Complexity. Both in the case of weakly acyclic DCDSs with deterministic services and of GR$^+$-acyclic DCDSs with nondeterministic services, our construction generates a finite transition system whose number of states is exponential in the size of the initial database. Let Φ be a $\mu\mathcal{L}_A$ or $\mu\mathcal{L}_P$ formula of size ℓ with k alternating nested fixpoints. The proofs of Theorems 4.7 and 5.7 guarantee that the total number of values appearing in the abstract transition system is bounded by a polynomial $P(n)$ of the size n of the DCDS initial database. Then, considering the complexity of propositional μ-calculus model checking on finite transition systems [26], the complexity of verification of Φ is $O(2^{P(n)^a} \cdot P(n)^\ell)^k$, where a is the maximum arity of the database schema. Hence, verification is in EXPTIME in the size n of the initial database.

Mixed semantics. It is possible to integrate into a unique system both deterministic and nondeterministic services, and to extend our verification results to this case. The request and audit modules of the running example are part of such a mixed system (see [4]).

Support for arbitrary integrity constraints. Note that the definition of DCDS semantics is independent of the type of constraints used, as it simply requires their satisfaction by each state of the concrete transition system. Our decidability results hold even in the presence of integrity constraints on the database expressed as arbitrary FO sentences under the active domain semantics (see [4] for how we can model them without changes to the DCDS model).

Connection with the artifact model. In terms of expressive capabilities, our DCDS model is equivalent to the artifact-centric model [37, 21] (see Section 7). The reductions between the DCDS and artifact models are sketched in [4].

7. RELATED WORK

As mentioned in Section 6, the unrestricted artifact-centric and DCDS models have equivalent expressive capabilities. Our work is therefore most closely related to prior work on verification of

	DETERMINISTIC					NONDETERMINISTIC				
	$\mu\mathcal{L}$		$\mu\mathcal{L}_A$		$\mu\mathcal{L}_P$	$\mu\mathcal{L}$		$\mu\mathcal{L}_A$		$\mu\mathcal{L}_P$
un-restricted	**U**	←	**U**	←	**U**^{1}(Th.4.1)	**U**	←	**U**	←	**U**^{1}(Th.5.1)
	↑		↑			↑		↑		
state-bounded	**U**	←	**U** [4]		**D** [4]	**U**	←	**U** (Th.5.2)		**D**^{3}(Th.5.3)
					↓					↓
run-bounded	**?**^{2}(Th.4.5)		**D**^{3}(Th.4.2)	→	**D**	**?**^{2}(Th.4.5)		**D**^{3} [4]	→	**D**

^{1}Holds even for propositional LTL/CTL.
^{2}Decidability cannot rely on faithful finite-state abstraction.
^{3}Via reduction to finite-state model checking.

Table 1: Summary of our (un)decidability results

artifact-centric business processes. The difference lies in how each work trades off between restricting the class of business processes versus the class of properties to verify.

Artifact-centric processes with no database. Work on formal analysis of artifact-based business processes in restricted contexts has been reported in [28, 29, 9]. Properties investigated include reachability [28, 29], general temporal constraints [29], and the existence of complete execution or dead end [9]. For each considered variant, verification is generally undecidable; decidability results were obtained only under rather severe restrictions, e.g., restricting all pre-conditions to be "true" [28], restricting to bounded domains [29, 9], or restricting the pre- and post-conditions to be propositional, and thus not referring to data values [29]. [16] adopts an artifact model variation with arithmetic operations but no database. It proposes a criterion for comparing the expressiveness of specifications using the notion of *dominance*, based on the input/output pairs of business processes. Decidability relies on restricting runs to bounded length. [41] addresses the problem of the existence of a run that satisfies a temporal property, for a restricted case with no database and only propositional LTL properties. All of these works model no underlying database (and hence no integrity constraints).

Artifact-centric processes with underlying database. More recently, two lines of work have considered artifact-centric processes that also model an underlying relational database. One considers branching time, one only linear time.

Branching time. Our approach for deterministic services stems from a line of research that started with [17] and continued with [3] in the context of artifact-centric processes. These works, however, considered a limited form of deterministic services, and use as verification formalism, first-order μ-calculus without first-order quantification across states. The connection between evolution of data-centric dynamic systems and data exchange that we exploit in this paper was first devised in [17]. There the dynamic system transition relation itself is described in terms of TGDs mapping the current state to the next, and the evolution of the system is essentially a form of chase. Under suitable weak acyclicity conditions such a chase terminates, thus making the DCDS transition system finite. Notice the role of getting new objects/values from the external environment, played here by service calls, is played there by nulls. These ideas where further developed in [3], where TGDs were replaced by action rules with the same syntax as here. Semantically however the dynamic system formalism there is deeply different: what we call here service calls are treated there as uninterpreted Skolem terms. This results in an ad-hoc interpretation of equality which sees every Skolem term as equal only to itself (as in the case of nulls [17]). A form of weak acyclicity gives a sufficient condition for getting finite-state transition systems and decidability.

Differently from [3], in our framework we do interpret service calls. This decision is motivated by our goal of modeling real-life external services, for which two distinct service calls may very well return equal results, even under the deterministic semantics (for instance if the same service is called with different arguments, or if distinct services are invoked). Interpreting service calls raises a major challenge: even under the run-bounded restriction, the concrete transition system is infinite, because it is infinitely branching (a service call can be interpreted with any of the values from the infinite domain). In contrast to [3], what we show in this case is not that the concrete transition system is finite (it never is), but that it is *bisimilar* to a finite abstract transition system. This leads to a proof technique that is interesting in its own right, being based on novel notions of bisimilarity for the considered μ-calculus variants. The reason standard bisimilarity is insufficient is that our logics $\mu\mathcal{L}_P$ and $\mu\mathcal{L}_A$ allow first-order quantification across states, so bisimilarity must respect the connection between values appearing both in the current and successor state. Our decision to include first-order quantification across states was motivated by the need to express liveness properties that refer to the same data at various points in time (e.g. "if student x is enrolled now and continues to be enrolled in the future, then x will eventually graduate").

For our treatment of non-deterministic services, the most related work is [6]. Inspired by [3], [6] builds a similar framework where actions are specified via pre- and post-conditions given as FO formulae interpreted over active domains which include new values passed through action parameters. The verification logic considered is an FO variant of CTL, which precludes expressing certain desirable properties such as fairness. [6] shows that if each state has a bounded active domain, one can construct an abstract finite transition system that can be checked instead of the original concrete transition system, which is infinite-state in general. [6] develops independently an approach that is similar to ours for nondeterministic services. Indeed, the results we present here on state-boundedness apply to the setting of [6] as well. In contrast to [6], we investigate non-trivial, sufficient syntactic conditions for state-boundedness. Moreover, as opposed to [6], the bound on the state size need not be a priori known to our abstraction building algorithm. The bound's mere existence guarantees the algorithm's convergence. On the other hand, [6] presents an interesting result that applies to our setting: verifying formulas corresponding to CTL is decidable.

Linear time. [23] considers an artifact model that has the same expressive capabilities as an unrestricted class of DCDS in which the infinite domain is equipped with a dense linear order, which can be mentioned in pre-, post-conditions, and properties. Runs can receive unbounded external input from an infinite domain, and this input corresponds to nondeterministic services in a DCDS. Verification is decidable even if the input accumulates in states, and runs are neither run-bounded, nor state-bounded. However, this expressive power requires restrictions that render the result incomparable to ours. First, the property language is a first-order extension of LTL, and it is shown that extension to branching time (CTL*) leads to undecidability. Second, pre-, post-conditions and properties access read-only and read-write database relations differently, querying the latter only in limited fashion. In essence, data can arbitrarily accumulate in read-write relations, but these can be queried only by checking that they contain a given tuple of constants. It is shown that this restriction is tight, as even the ability to check emptiness of a read-write relation leads to undecidability. In addition, no integrity constraints are supported as it is shown that allowing a single functional dependency leads to undecidability. [20] disallows read-write relations entirely (only the artifact variables are writable), but this allows the extension of the decidability result to integrity constraints expressed as embedded dependencies with terminating chase, and to any decidable arithmetic. Again the result is incomparable to ours, as our modeling needs to include read-write relations and their unrestricted querying.

Infinite-state systems. DCDSs are a particular case of infinite-state systems. Research on verification of infinite-state systems has also focused on extending classical model checking techniques (e.g., see [15] for a survey). However, in much of this work the emphasis is on studying recursive control rather than data, which is either ignored or finitely abstracted. More recent work has focused specifically on data as a source of infinity. This includes augmenting recursive procedures with integer parameters [12], rewriting systems with data [11], Petri nets with data associated to tokens [33], automata and logics over infinite alphabets [36, 10, 11], and temporal logics manipulating data [13, 22, 31]. However, the restricted use of data and the particular properties verified have limited applicability to the business process setting we target with the DCDS model.

8. CONCLUSIONS

We believe that DCDSs are a natural and expressive model for business processes powered by an underlying database, and thus are an ideal vehicle for foundational research with potential to transfer to alternative models. The design space for FO extensions of propositional μ-calculus is broad, and notoriously contains bounded-state settings for which satisfiability of even modest extensions of propositional LTL is highly undecidable (e.g. LTL with freeze quantifier over infinite data words [22]). In light of this, our decidability results come as a pleasant surprise, and the two $\mu\mathcal{L}$ variants studied here, paired with the respective DCDS classes, strike a fortuitous balance between expressivity and verification feasibility.

9. REFERENCES

[1] S. Abiteboul, P. Bourhis, A. Galland, and B. Marinoiu. The AXML artifact model. In *TIME*, 2009.

[2] S. Abiteboul, R. Hull, and V. Vianu. *Foundations of Databases*. Addison Wesley, 1995.

[3] B. Bagheri Hariri, D. Calvanese, G. De Giacomo, R. De Masellis, and P. Felli. Foundations of relational artifacts verification. In *BPM*, 2011.

[4] B. Bagheri Hariri, D. Calvanese, G. De Giacomo, A. Deutsch, and M. Montali. Verification of relational data-centric dynamic systems with external services. Corr technical report, arXiv.org e-Print archive, 2012. Available at `http://arxiv.org/abs/1203.0024`.

[5] C. Baier and J.-P. Katoen. *Principles of Model Checking*. MIT Press, 2008.

[6] F. Belardinelli, A. Lomuscio, and F. Patrizi. An abstraction technique for the verification of artifact-centric systems. In *KR*, 2012.

[7] D. Berardi, D. Calvanese, G. De Giacomo, R. Hull, and M. Mecella. Automatic composition of transition-based semantic web services with messaging. In *VLDB*, 2005.

[8] K. Bhattacharya, N. S. Caswell, S. Kumaran, A. Nigam, and F. Y. Wu. Artifact-centered operational modeling: Lessons from customer engagements. *IBM Systems Journal*, 46(4):703–721, 2007.

[9] K. Bhattacharya, C. E. Gerede, R. Hull, R. Liu, and J. Su. Towards formal analysis of artifact-centric business process models. In *BPM*, 2007.

[10] M. Bojanczyk, A. Muscholl, T. Schwentick, L. Segoufin, and C. David. Two-variable logic on words with data. In *LICS*, 2006.

[11] A. Bouajjani, P. Habermehl, Y. Jurski, and M. Sighireanu. Rewriting systems with data. In *FCT*, 2007.

[12] A. Bouajjani, P. Habermehl, and R. Mayr. Automatic verification of recursive procedures with one integer parameter. *TCS*, 295, 2003.

[13] P. Bouyer, A. Petit, and D. Thérien. An algebraic approach to data languages and timed languages. *Information and Computation*, 182(2), 2003.

[14] J. Bradfield and C. Stirling. Modal mu-calculi. In *Handbook of Modal Logic*, volume 3. Elsevier, 2007.

[15] O. Burkart, D. Caucal, F. Moller, and B. Steffen. Verification of infinite structures. In *Handbook of Process Algebra*. Elsevier Science, 2001.

[16] D. Calvanese, G. De Giacomo, R. Hull, and J. Su. Artifact-centric workflow dominance. In *ICSOC*, 2009.

[17] P. Cangialosi, G. De Giacomo, R. De Masellis, and R. Rosati. Conjunctive artifact-centric services. In *ICSOC*, 2010.

[18] E. M. Clarke, O. Grumberg, and D. A. Peled. *Model checking*. The MIT Press, 1999.

[19] D. Cohn and R. Hull. Business artifacts: A data-centric approach to modeling business operations and processes. *IEEE Data Engineering Bullettin*, 32(3), 2009.

[20] E. Damaggio, A. Deutsch, and V. Vianu. Artifact systems with data dependencies and arithmetic. In *ICDT*, 2011.

[21] E. Damaggio, R. Hull, and R. Vaculín. On the equivalence of incremental and fixpoint semantics for business artifacts with guard-stage-milestone lifecycles. In *BPM*, 2011.

[22] S. Demri and R. Lazić. LTL with the freeze quantifier and register automata. *ACM TOCL*, 10(3), 2009.

[23] A. Deutsch, R. Hull, F. Patrizi, and V. Vianu. Automatic verification of data-centric business processes. In *ICDT*, 2009.

[24] A. Deutsch, M. Marcus, L. Sui, V. Vianu, and D. Zhou. A verifier for interactive, data-driven web applications. In *SIGMOD*, 2005.

[25] A. Deutsch, L. Sui, and V. Vianu. Specification and verification of data-driven web applications. *JCSS*, 73(3):442–474, 2007.

[26] E. A. Emerson. Model checking and the mu-calculus. In *Descriptive Complexity and Finite Models*, 1996.

[27] R. Fagin, P. G. Kolaitis, R. J. Miller, and L. Popa. Data exchange: semantics and query answering. *TCS*, 336(1), 2005.

[28] C. E. Gerede, K. Bhattacharya, and J. Su. Static analysis of business artifact-centric operational models. In *IEEE Int. Conf. on Service-Oriented Computing and Applications*, 2007.

[29] C. E. Gerede and J. Su. Specification and verification of artifact behaviors in business process models. In *ICSOC*, 2007.

[30] R. Hull. Artifact-centric business process models: Brief survey of research results and challenges. In *OTM Confederated Int. Conf.*, 2008.

[31] M. Jurdzinski and R. Lazić. Alternation-free modal mu-calculus for data trees. In *LICS*, 2007.

[32] J. Küster, K. Ryndina, and H. Gall. Generation of BPM for object life cycle compliance. In *BPM*, 2007.

[33] R. Lazić, T. Newcomb, J. Ouaknine, A. Roscoe, and J. Worrell. Nets with tokens which carry data. In *ICATPN*, 2007.

[34] D. C. Luckham, D. M. R. Park, and M. Paterson. On formalised computer programs. *JCSS*, 4(3), 1970.

[35] M. Meier, M. Schmidt, F. Wei, and G. Lausen. Semantic query optimization in the presence of types. In *PODS*, 2010.

[36] F. Neven, T. Schwentick, and V. Vianu. Finite state machines for strings over infinite alphabets. *ACM TOCL*, 5(3), 2004.

[37] A. Nigam and N. S. Caswell. Business artifacts: An approach to operational specification. *IBM Systems Journal*, 42(3), 2003.

[38] D. M. R. Park. Finiteness is mu-ineffable. *TCS*, 3(2), 1976.

[39] C. Stirling. *Modal and Temporal Properties of Processes*. Springer, 2001.

[40] W. M. P. van der Aalst, P. Barthelmess, C. A. Ellis, and J. Wainer. Proclets: A framework for lightweight interacting workflow processes. *Int. J. of Cooperative Information Systems*, 10(4), 2001.

[41] X. Zhao, J. Su, H. Yang, and Z. Qiu. Enforcing constraints on life cycles of business artifacts. In *TASE*, 2009.

Querying Graph Databases

Pablo Barceló
Dept. of Computer Science, University of Chile
pbarcelo@dcc.uchile.cl

ABSTRACT

Graph databases have gained renewed interest in the last years, due to their applications in areas such as the Semantic Web and Social Networks Analysis. We study the problem of querying graph databases, and, in particular, the expressiveness and complexity of evaluation for several general-purpose navigational query languages, such as the regular path queries and its extensions with conjunctions and inverses. We distinguish between two semantics for these languages. The first one, based on simple paths, easily leads to intractability in data complexity, while the second one, based on arbitrary paths, allows tractable evaluation for an expressive family of languages.

We also study two recent extensions of these languages that have been motivated by modern applications of graph databases. The first one allows to treat paths as first-class citizens, while the second one permits to express queries that combine the topology of the graph with its underlying data.

Categories and Subject Descriptors

H.2.3 [**Database Management**]: Languages—*Query Languages*

Keywords

Graph databases, conjunctive regular path queries, query evaluation, expressiveness, containment.

1. INTRODUCTION

Graph databases are crucial for many applications in which the topology of the data is as important as the data itself. While early interest in graph databases could be explained by their applications in hypertext systems [33], or their connections with semistructured data [3, 24] and object databases [54], new application domains have taken the field by storm in the last decade, including the Semantic Web [10], social networks analysis [42], biological networks [63], data provenance [7], and several others.

In their simplest form, graph databases are finite, directed, edge-labeled graphs. We study the problem of querying those graph databases. An obvious question one faces regarding this problem is whether it could be tackled applying existing relational technology; that is, by first representing each graph database $\mathcal{G}$ as a relational database $\mathcal{D}(\mathcal{G})$ (in a standard way), and then querying $\mathcal{D}(\mathcal{G})$ (using a relational language) instead of $\mathcal{G}$. The drawback of this approach is that many graph database queries are navigational (e.g., *regular path queries* [36], that check the existence of a path between two nodes whose label satisfies a regular condition), and, thus, they cannot be easily expressed by relational languages, such as SQL, which allow limited recursion.

On the other hand, several navigational languages for graph databases can be embedded into the relational language Datalog [2], which is the recursive extension of the class of unions of conjunctive queries. Nevertheless, this translation is not really fruitful: While data complexity of Datalog is PTIME-complete (and, thus, not parallelizable under widely-held complexity assumptions [51]), the data complexity of many languages we study along the paper falls into the parallelizable class NLOGSPACE. Moreover, while some basic static analysis tasks for Datalog are undecidable (e.g. containment [2]), they are decidable for several expressive languages that we study in this article.

The needs of different graph database applications have led to a variety of navigational query languages. This includes languages for querying: (a) Graph-based object databases (e.g., GraphDB [53], GOOD [54] and G-Log [73]), (b) heterogeneous and unstructured data (e.g., Lorel [3], StruQL [43], and UnQL [26]), (c) social networks (e.g., SoQL [76], BiQL [40], and SNQL [78]), etc. Our study deals only with the most basic navigational query languages, and, in particular, those that express a common set of useful features for different graph database applications. This includes the regular path queries, as introduced above, and some languages that express the existence of patterns in a graph database satisfying a set of regular constraints (e.g., the *conjunctive* regular path queries [36, 34]). These two features, which form the core of most of the languages mentioned above, have been the topic of a vast amount of research over the last 25 years [36, 34, 69, 46, 27, 13, 16, 18].

Main problems we study The languages presented in the paper are studied with respect to expressiveness, complexity of query evaluation and the containment problem, as described below:

Expressiveness We study the limits of what can be expressed in a language. Obviously, there is a trade-off between the expressive power of a query language and the cost of query evaluation, as defined next.

Complexity of evaluation Given a query language $\mathcal{L}$, we study the cost of query evaluation in $\mathcal{L}$, i.e., the complexity of the problem $\mathcal{L}$-EVAL defined as follows: Given a graph database $\mathcal{G}$, a query $Q \in \mathcal{L}$, and a tuple $\bar{t}$ of objects (e.g., nodes, symbols, paths, etc) of the right type for $\mathcal{L}$, does $\bar{t}$ belong to the evaluation $[\![Q]\!]_{\mathcal{G}}$ of Q on $\mathcal{G}$? The complexity is thus measured in terms of $|\mathcal{G}|$ and $|Q|$, the lengths of reasonable encodings of $\mathcal{G}$ and Q, respectively. Note that the input to $\mathcal{L}$-EVAL consists of a graph database and a query, and, thus, in terms of Vardi's taxonomy, it measures the *combined complexity* of the evaluation problem [80].

In databases one is also interested in the *data complexity* of the evaluation problem [80], which is measured only in terms of the size of the graph database (i.e., the query Q is assumed to be fixed). We denote by EVAL(Q) the evaluation problem for a fixed query Q. If $\mathcal{C}$ is a complexity class, we say that $\mathcal{L}$-EVAL is in $\mathcal{C}$ in data complexity, if EVAL(Q) is in $\mathcal{C}$ for each query Q in $\mathcal{L}$. Moreover, $\mathcal{L}$-EVAL is $\mathcal{C}$-hard in data complexity, if there is a query Q in $\mathcal{L}$ such that EVAL(Q) is $\mathcal{C}$-hard. Finally, $\mathcal{L}$-EVAL is $\mathcal{C}$-complete in data complexity, if it is in $\mathcal{C}$ and it is $\mathcal{C}$-hard in data complexity.

Containment problem Containment is a crucial problem in query processing and optimization [2]. We study its complexity for several query languages. Formally, if $\mathcal{L}$ is a query language, the problem $\mathcal{L}$-CONT is defined as follows: Given queries $Q, Q' \in \mathcal{L}$, is $[\![Q]\!]_\mathcal{G} \subseteq [\![Q']\!]_\mathcal{G}$ for each graph database $\mathcal{G}$?

Contents of the paper and organization Section 2 presents the basics of graph databases. The study of query languages starts in Section 3, where we present a simple pattern language for graph databases, called **G**, which was introduced in the late 80s by Cruz, Mendelzon and Wood [36]. The importance of this language is, of course, historical – it was one of the earliest graph database languages ever introduced – but also methodological – it identified for the first time a simple set of features that were common to many navigational graph query languages, and that required more detailed theoretical study. This language is also worth presentating due to its semantics based on simple paths, which has almost completely disappeared from modern query languages for graph databases due to its inherently high computational complexity.

In turn, modern navigational languages for graph databases implement a semantics based on arbitrary (as opposed to simple) paths. This semantics allows for tractable evaluation in data complexity for a family of languages that are based on **G**. This includes the regular path queries (RPQs), and their extensions with conjunction (CRPQs) [36, 34], inverses (C2RPQs) [27], and unions (UC2RPQs). Some relevant restrictions of these classes, with tractable combined complexity, can also be identified. This includes the class of acyclic C2RPQs [13, 18] and the nested regular expressions [17]. We study these languages in detail in Section 4.

In Section 5 we study some recently proposed languages for graph databases – namely, the extended CRPQs, or ECRPQs [13, 12] – that treat paths as first-class citizens. In particular, ECRPQs extend CRPQs with the ability to output and compare paths. These features are motivated by some modern applications of graph databases, such as the Semantic Web, biological networks and provenance, for which the ability to verify and output complex semantic associations between nodes is crucial [8, 62, 52, 58]. Notably, the importance of including paths in the output was already foreseen by Abiteboul et al. in the 90s, and included as a feature in the language Lorel [3].

As is to be expected, the data complexity of ECRPQ evaluation depends on the language that we allow for expressing path comparisons. We study two such languages; the *regular* and the *rational* relations [41, 49, 20]. Regular relations are a simple formalism that extends the class of regular languages to relations of arbitrary arity over words, while rational relations are a powerful formalism that properly extends the regular relations. While the evaluation problem for ECRPQs with regular relations is tractable in data complexity, it becomes undecidable, or highly intractable, for queries that combine regular relations with some practically relevant rational relations such as the subword or subsequence relations. We identify, however, an important syntactic restriction of the class of ECRPQs with rational relations that is tractable in data complexity.

Most of the existing studies of navigational languages for graph databases have centered around queries that exploit the topology of the graph. On the other hand, the study of languages that combine the topology with the underlying data has been almost completely overlooked. We present some recent developments that go in the direction of overcoming this deficiency. In particular, we study the problem of querying graph databases in which each node contains a piece of data. We concentrate on *data path* queries, which check for the existence of a path whose label together with its underlying data values satisfy a given condition. It is shown that allowing queries that freely combine these two features easily leads to intractability in data complexity, but that there is a relevant class of queries – namely, the regular expressions with memory [65] – whose evaluation problem for fixed queries is tractable.

Finally, in Section 7 we present the concluding remarks and a list of big challenges for graph databases in the future.

What is not included The sheer volume of graph database literature, plus some space constraints, have forced us not to include several query languages we would have liked to. Notable omissions are the extensions of the query languages we study in Section 4 with aggregation [35], a family of query languages based on relation algebra that has been recently studied with respect to relative expressiveness [45], the powerfuk Walk Logic, which has been proposed as an alternative to ECRPQs for expressing path properties of graph databases [57], and the deep study of view-based query answering for views specified as (C)2RPQs [28, 29]. We expect to present each one of them in full detail in a full version of the paper.

Proviso We assume familiarity with regular expressions and automata. Throughout the paper we do not distinguish between a regular expression and the regular language it defines (e.g., we write $w \in R$ to express that the word w belongs to the regular language defined by regular expression R). We also assume familiarity with usual query languages for relational databases, such as conjunctive queries (CQs), first-order logic (FO) and Datalog, and with usual complexity classes, such as NLOGSPACE, NP, PSPACE, and others.

2. GRAPH DATABASES

Different applications impose different constraints on its underlying graph data model, which has given rise to a myriad of different models for graph databases (see [5] for a survey). We study here the simplest possible such model: that of finite, directed and edge-labeled graphs. The reason is twofold; first, this model is flexible enough to express many interesting graph database scenarios, and, second, the most fundamental theoretical issues related to graph databases already appear in full force for it. We formalize this model below.

Let $\mathcal{V}$ be a countably infinite set of node ids. Given a finite alphabet Σ, a *graph database* $\mathcal{G}$ over Σ is a pair (V, E), where V is a finite set of node ids (i.e., $V \subseteq \mathcal{V}$) and $E \subseteq V \times \Sigma \times V$. Thus, each edge in $\mathcal{G}$ is a triple $(v, a, v') \in V \times \Sigma \times V$, whose interpretation is an a-labeled edge from v to v' in $\mathcal{G}$. When Σ is clear from the context, we shall speak simply of a graph database.

Notice that each graph database $\mathcal{G} = (V, E)$ over Σ can be naturally seen as a non-deterministic finite automaton (NFA) over the alphabet Σ, without initial and final states. Its states are the nodes in V and its transitions are the edges in E.

A *path* in a graph database $\mathcal{G} = (V, E)$ is a sequence

$$\rho = v_0 a_0 v_1 a_1 v_2 \cdots v_{k-1} a_{k-1} v_k, \quad (k \geq 0),$$

such that $(v_{i-1}, a_{i-1}, v_i) \in E$, for each i with $1 \leq i \leq k$. The *label* of ρ, denoted $\lambda(\rho)$, is the string $a_0 a_1 \cdots a_{k-1}$ in Σ^*. Notice that the definition of a path includes the *empty* path v, for each $v \in V$. The label of such path is the empty string ϵ. The path ρ is *simple* if it does not go through the same node twice, i.e., $v_i \neq v_j$ for each i, j with $0 \leq i < j \leq k$.

3. THE LANGUAGE G AND THE SIMPLE PATH SEMANTICS

Since the early days, graph databases and query languages were not thought as competitors of their relational counterparts, but as suitable complements for data that could be more naturally represented in the form of a graph (in particular, semistructured data). In such context, Cruz, Mendelzon and Wood designed in 1987 one of the earliest (and, also, most influential) navigational languages for edge-labeled graph-structured data, that was simply called **G** [36].

We present the syntax and semantics of **G** in the context of the graph data model studied here. We leave out some syntactic sugar and intricacies in the definition of the semantics that complicate the presentation without being essential to the query language.

The language **G** uses a semantics based on simple paths, motivated by early applications of graph databases for which simple paths were more meaningful than arbitrary ones. As we see in the present section, this causes intractability of query evaluation for the language even in data complexity.

Syntax Queries in **G** are unions of *graph patterns*, which are graph databases extended with three new features: (1) *node variables*, (2) *label variables*, and (3) regular expressions as labels for edges. Thus, a graph pattern over Σ is a graph database in which each node is either a node id in $\mathcal{V}$ or a node variable, and each edge is labeled with a regular expression over the alphabet that extends Σ with all label variables. We formalize this below.

Let $\mathcal{V}_{\text{node}}$ and $\mathcal{V}_{\text{label}}$ be two disjoint and countably infinite sets of node and label variables, respectively, which are pairwise disjoint from the set $\mathcal{V}$ of node ids. Given a (not necessarily finite) alphabet Γ, we denote by $\text{REG}(\Gamma)$ the set of regular expressions over Γ. A graph pattern π over the finite alphabet Σ is a pair (N, A), where N is a finite set of nodes ids and node variables (that is, $N \subseteq \mathcal{V} \cup \mathcal{V}_{\text{node}}$), and $A \subseteq V \times \text{REG}(\Sigma \cup \mathcal{V}_{\text{label}}) \times V$ is the set of edges labeled with regular expressions over the alphabet that extends Σ with the label variables in $\mathcal{V}_{\text{label}}$.

In order to view a graph pattern as a query, it is necessary to specify which variables in the graph pattern are projected in the output. As such, we assume that each graph pattern $\pi = (N, A)$ has an associated pair $(\bar{x}, \bar{X})$ of *free* variables, where $\bar{x}$ is an ordered tuple of node variables in N and $\bar{X}$ is an ordered tuple of label variables occuring in A. We write $\pi(\bar{x}, \bar{X})$ to specify that $(\bar{x}, \bar{X})$ are the free variables of π. If both $\bar{x}$ and $\bar{X}$ are the empty tuple, we follow usual terminology and say that π is Boolean.

DEFINITION 1 (**G** LANGUAGE [36]). *A query Π of the language* **G** *over Σ is an expression of the form $\bigcup_{1 \leq i \leq k} \pi_i$ ($k \geq 1$), where each π_i ($1 \leq i \leq k$) is a graph pattern over Σ.*

Semantics The semantics of **G** queries depends on the semantics of graph patterns, which is, in turn, based on a refined notion of *homeomorphism*. These are mappings that match node variables into node ids in V, label variables into elements of Σ, and each edge labeled by regular expression R into a *simple* path in the graph database that is labeled with a word in R.

Since variables appear both in nodes and edges of patterns, it will be convenient to define homeomorphisms as pairs of mappings. Formally, given a graph pattern $\pi = (N, A)$ and a graph database $\mathcal{G} = (V, E)$, both over Σ, a *homeomorphism* from π to $\mathcal{G}$ is a pair of mappings (ν_1, ν_2), such that:

- ν_1 maps nodes in π to node ids in V, and ν_2 maps label variables used in A to symbols in Σ; that is, $\nu_1 : N \to V$, and if $\mathcal{X}$ is the set of label variables occuring in A, then $\nu_2 : \mathcal{X} \to \Sigma$;
- ν_1 is the identitity on node ids; that is, $\nu_1(v) = v$, for each node id v in N (i.e., for each $v \in N \cap \mathcal{V}$);[1]
- each edge labeled by a regular expression R is mapped to a simple path labeled by a word in R, after label variables are replaced according to ν_2.

  Formally, for each $(p, L, q) \in A$, where $p, q \in N$ and $L \in \text{REG}(\Sigma \cup \mathcal{V}_{\text{label}})$, there is a simple path ρ from $\nu_1(p)$ to $\nu_1(q)$ in $\mathcal{G}$ such that $\lambda(\rho) \in \nu_2(L)$, where $\nu_2(L)$ is the regular language over Σ that is obtained from L by replacing each occurence of a symbol $X \in \mathcal{X}$ with $\nu_2(X)$.

The evaluation $[\![\pi]\!]^{\mathsf{s}}_{\mathcal{G}}$ of a graph pattern $\pi(\bar{x}, \bar{X})$ on $\mathcal{G}$ is the set of ordered tuples of the form $(\nu_1(\bar{x}), \nu_2(\bar{X}))$, for each homeomorphism (ν_1, ν_2) from π to G. We use the superscript s in $[\![\pi]\!]^{\mathsf{s}}_{\mathcal{G}}$ to stress the fact that we are using a semantics based on simple paths (which is not the case for the rest of the languages we study in the paper). If π is Boolean, i.e., $\bar{x}$ and $\bar{X}$ are the empty tuple, then the answer *true* is, as usual, modeled by the set containing the empty tuple, and the answer *false* by the empty set.

Finally, if $\Pi = \bigcup_{1 \leq i \leq k} \pi_i$ is a **G** query, then $[\![\Pi]\!]^{\mathsf{s}}_{\mathcal{G}} = \bigcup_{1 \leq i \leq k} [\![\pi_i]\!]^{\mathsf{s}}_{\mathcal{G}}$, for each graph database $\mathcal{G} = (V, E)$.

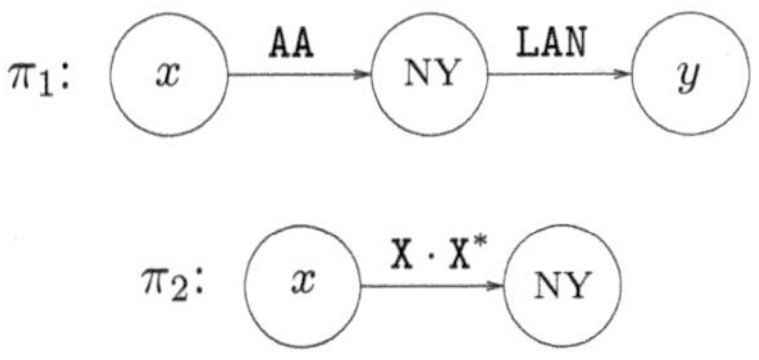

Figure 1: Patterns π_1 and π_2 used in Example 1.

EXAMPLE 1. We present a toy example based on ideas from [36]. Let Σ be the set of airlines and $\mathcal{G} = (V, E)$ be the graph database over Σ such that the node ids in V represent cities and there is an edge in E from city c to city c' labeled with airline A iff A has a direct flight from c to c'.

Figure 1 shows the graphical depiction of a **G** query Π composed by the union of two patterns $\pi_1(x, y)$ and $\pi_2(x, X)$. We assume all node and label variables to be free. Then $[\![\pi_1]\!]^{\mathsf{s}}_{\mathcal{G}}$ is the set of pairs (c, c') of cities such that there is a flight from c to NY with AA and a flight from NY to c' with LAN. On the other hand, $[\![\pi_2]\!]^{\mathsf{s}}_{\mathcal{G}}$ is the set of tuples of the form $(c, \mathtt{A})$, where c is a city and A is an airline, such that there is a (nonempty) sequence of flights from c to NY with the same airline A. Finally, $[\![\Pi]\!]^{\mathsf{s}}_{\mathcal{G}} = [\![\pi_1]\!]^{\mathsf{s}}_{\mathcal{G}} \cup [\![\pi_2]\!]^{\mathsf{s}}_{\mathcal{G}}$. □

The previous example illustrates why the simple path semantics might be useful in some cases. In fact, if we are looking for flights connecting two cities under certain regular conditions, we are only interested in those that do not stop twice in the same city. As we will see next, this choice has an important cost in the complexity of query evaluation.

[1] In the original definition of the semantics of **G**, the mapping ν_1 is also forced to be a 1-1 mapping; i.e., different node variables have to be mapped to different node ids. We have relaxed this condition to allow a uniform treatment with other query languages presented in the article. This modification is inessential to the complexity of query evaluation for the language.

3.1 Complexity of evaluation of G queries

The evaluation problem **G**-EVAL is as follows: Given a query Π in **G**, a graph database $\mathcal{G} = (V, E)$, a tuple $\bar{v}$ of node ids in V and a tuple $\bar{A}$ of symbols in Σ, determine whether $(\bar{v}, \bar{A}) \in [\![\Pi]\!]^{\mathbf{s}}_{\mathcal{G}}$. It is not hard to see that this problem can be solved in NP.

PROPOSITION 1. **G**-EVAL *is in* NP.

The intuition behind this fact is as follows. In order to check whether $(\bar{v}, \bar{A}) \in [\![\Pi]\!]^{\mathbf{s}}_{\mathcal{G}}$, we only have to guess a graph pattern $\pi(\bar{x}, \bar{X})$ in Π and a homeomorphism (ν_1, ν_2) from π to $\mathcal{G}$ such that $\nu_1(\bar{x}) = \bar{v}$ and $\nu_2(\bar{X}) = \bar{A}$. To verify that (ν_1, ν_2) is indeed a homeomorphism, we have to check that for each edge (p, L, q) there is a simple path in $\mathcal{G}$ from $\nu_1(p)$ to $\nu_1(q)$ whose label belongs to $\nu_2(L)$. But the length of each simple path in $\mathcal{G}$ is bounded by $|V|$, and hence this fact admits a polynomial size witness.

We show next that the query evaluation problem for **G** is NP-complete. Surprisingly, this holds already in data complexity for a very simple class of queries.

Finding regular simple paths In order to understand the precise complexity of query evaluation for **G**, and, in particular, the impact of the simple path semantics, Mendelzon and Wood decided to study the evaluation problem for a simple class of **G** queries, often known as *regular path queries* (RPQs) [69]. These are graph patterns that consist of a single edge of the form (x, L, y), where x and y are differerent node variables and L is a regular expression over Σ (i.e., L contains no label variables). Thus, the query evaluation problem for RPQs boils down to the problem of finding regular simple paths in a graph database, as follows:

PROBLEM:	REGULARSIMPLEPATH
INPUT:	A graph database $\mathcal{G}$, nodes v, v' in $\mathcal{G}$, a regular expression L.
QUESTION:	Is there a simple path ρ from v to v' in $\mathcal{G}$ such that $\lambda(\rho) \in L$?

When the input consists of $\mathcal{G}$ and v, v' only (i.e., when L is fixed) we refer to this problem as FIXEDREGULARSIMPLEPATH(L). We state below that for a big class of regular expressions this problem is NP-complete, which immediately implies that **G**-EVAL is NP-complete in data complexity.

THEOREM 1 ([69]). *Let Σ be a finite alphabet and w be a string in Σ^* of length at least 2. Then* FIXEDREGULARSIMPLEPATH(w^*) *is* NP*-complete.*

Consider, for instance, the simplest possible case $\Sigma = \{0\}$ and $w = 00$. Then FIXEDREGULARSIMPLEPATH($(00)^*$) checks whether there is a simple path of even length from node v to v' in a directed graph $\mathcal{G}$, which is an NP-complete problem [64].

The problem FIXEDREGULARSIMPLEPATH(L) is also NP-complete for some simple languages that do not follow the pattern in Theorem 1, such as $L = 0^*10^*$ [69]. On the other hand, FIXEDREGULARSIMPLEPATH(L) can be solved in PTIME for each L that defines a finite language (e.g., each L that does not make use of the Kleene-star $*$). However, this restriction does not lead to tractability in combined complexity:

PROPOSITION 2. REGULARSIMPLEPATH *is* NP*-complete, even if restricted to the class of regular expressions that do not use the Kleene-star.*

Tractable cases of the problem REGULARSIMPLEPATH can be found by restricting the shape of graph databases (e.g., DAGs) or the class of regular languages allowed in RPQs (e.g., closed under removal of symbols from a word) [69].

Final remarks The intractability of **G** in data complexity is bad news, as it implies that the language is impractical. In order to cope with this problem, the graph database community has opted for a different semantics, based on arbitrary paths, that allows to evaluate full-fledged recursive queries with low data complexity.

In the last few years we have witnessed a revival of the simple path semantics, due to its application in early versions of SPARQL 1.1 [56], the standard for navigational querying of the Semantic Web data model RDF. It has been shown in [11, 67] that this easily leads to intractability in data complexity.

4. BASIC LANGUAGES UNDER THE ARBITRARY PATH SEMANTICS

In this section, we study the basics of modern navigational languages for graph databases. Its building blocks are clearly rooted on **G**, but there are three important differences:

1. First, the semantics of current query languages for graph databases is based on arbitrary (instead of simple) paths. The choice of the new semantics is justified by two facts: (a) It leads to tractable combined complexity for RPQs and tractable data complexity for a family of expressive languages. (b) Several graph-based applications only care about connectivity of the data under regular constraints, and, thus, simple paths do not seem to be essential.

2. Second, label variables have mostly disappeared from modern graph query languages. We have not found an explanation for this, but provide here a plausible one: Although label variables do not increase data complexity for usual query languages, its inclusion in even the most basic language (RPQs) leads to intractability in combined complexity. As we argue in Section 4.3, this complicates the evaluation of the most basic queries with variables over modern applications of graph databases that store massive amounts of data.

3. Third, current query languages allow to traverse edges in the graph database in both directions. This allows an important increase in expressive power without having an impact on complexity.

For simplicity of presentation, we leave out constants (node ids) from queries, but they can be easily incorporated at no computational cost.

4.1 Regular path queries

RPQs (i.e., queries of the form (x, L, y), for L a regular language) are the basic navigational mechanism for graph databases. From now on, we use the shorthand L for the RPQ (x, L, y). Under the semantics we study in this section, the evaluation $[\![L]\!]_{\mathcal{G}}$ of the RPQ L on a graph database $\mathcal{G} = (V, E)$ consists of the set of pairs (v, v') of node ids in V such that there is a (not necessarily simple) path ρ in $\mathcal{G}$ from v to v' whose label $\lambda(\rho)$ belongs to L. Notice that we have removed the superscript $\mathbf{s}$ from $[\![L]\!]_{\mathcal{G}}$, as we are no longer using a simple paths semantics.

We show in this section that RPQs (and even its extension with inverses) can be evaluated efficiently under the arbitrary path semantics. However, this is no longer the case if RPQs are extended with label variables.

RPQs with inverse RPQs are often extended to traverse edges in both directions (a feature that was absent in **G**). This defines the

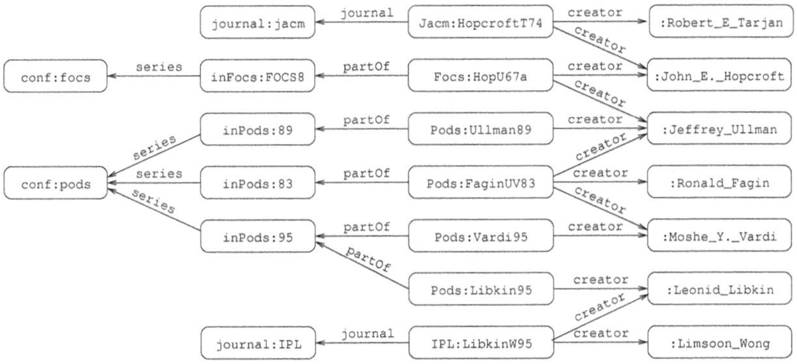

Figure 2: An abstraction of a fragment of the RDF representation of DBLP available at `http://dblp.l3s.de/d2r/`

notion of RPQs with *inverse*, or 2RPQs [27, 28]. A 2RPQ over Σ is an RPQ over the alphabet $\Sigma^{\pm}$ which extends Σ with the symbol a^{-}, for each $a \in \Sigma$. While evaluation of 2RPQs can be easily reduced to evaluation of RPQs by extending the underlying graph database with inverses of edges (something that we properly define in the next paragraph), the presence of inverses complicates the static analysis of queries, e.g., with respect to containment [30, 18].

To define the semantics of 2RPQs we use the notion of the *completion* of a graph database $\mathcal{G}$, denoted by $\mathcal{G}^{\pm}$. This is the graph database over $\Sigma^{\pm}$ that is obtained from $\mathcal{G} = (V, E)$ by adding the edge (u, a^{-}, v), for each $(v, a, u) \in E$. We define the evaluation $[\![L]\!]_{\mathcal{G}}$ of the 2RPQ L over $\mathcal{G}$ to be $[\![L]\!]_{\mathcal{G}^{\pm}}$ (the latter is well-defined since L is an RPQ over $\Sigma^{\pm}$). Notice that the 2RPQ a^{-} defines on a graph database $\mathcal{G} = (V, E)$ precisely the inverse of the RPQ a; that is, $[\![a^{-}]\!]_{\mathcal{G}} = \{(u, v) \mid (v, a, u) \in E\}$.

EXAMPLE 2. Let $\mathcal{G}$ be the graph database over $\Sigma = \{\texttt{creator}, \texttt{partOf}, \texttt{series}\}$ in Figure 2. This graph contains an abstraction of a fragment of the *RDF Linked Data* representation of DBLP [37] (and it is based on an example by Arenas and Pérez in an earlier PODS tutorial [10]). The following is a simple 2RPQ that matches all pairs (x, y) such that x is an author that published a paper in conference y:

$$L \;=\; \texttt{creator}^{-} \cdot \texttt{partOf} \cdot \texttt{series}$$

For example, the pairs $(\texttt{:Jeffrey\_D.\_Ullman}, \texttt{conf:focs})$ and $(\texttt{:Ronald\_Fagin}, \texttt{conf:pods})$ are in $[\![L]\!]_{\mathcal{G}}$. We can conclude that 2RPQs are more expressive than RPQs: For no RPQ L' over Σ it is the case that $[\![L]\!]_{\mathcal{G}} = [\![L']\!]_{\mathcal{G}}$. □

2RPQs have particularly good properties: They can be evaluated linearly in both the size of the data and the expression.

THEOREM 2 (SEE E.G., [69]). 2RPQ-EVAL *can be solved in time* $O(|\mathcal{G}| \cdot |L|)$, *for* $\mathcal{G}$ *a graph database and* L *a* 2RPQ.

Proof (Sketch): We check whether $(u, v) \in [\![L]\!]_{\mathcal{G}}$, for a pair (u, v) of node ids in $\mathcal{G}$, as follows. First, we compute $\mathcal{G}^{\pm}$ from $\mathcal{G}$ in time $O(|\mathcal{G}|)$, and then an NFA $\mathcal{A}_L$ that defines the same language than L in time $O(|L|)$. Let $\mathcal{G}^{\pm}(u, v)$ be the NFA that is obtained from $\mathcal{G}^{\pm}$ by setting its initial and final states to be u and v, respectively. Clearly, $(u, v) \in [\![L]\!]_{\mathcal{G}}$ iff $(u, v) \in [\![L]\!]_{\mathcal{G}^{\pm}}$ iff there is a word accepted by both $\mathcal{G}^{\pm}(u, v)$ and $\mathcal{A}_L$. The latter is equivalent to checking the product of $\mathcal{G}^{\pm}(u, v)$ and $\mathcal{A}_L$ for nonemptiness, which can be done in time $O(|\mathcal{G}^{\pm}| \cdot |\mathcal{A}_L|)$. The whole process takes time $O(|\mathcal{G}| + |L| + |\mathcal{G}^{\pm}| \cdot |\mathcal{A}_L|)$, that is, $O(|\mathcal{G}| \cdot |L|)$. □

It is worth contrasting Theorem 2 with Theorem 1, that states that RPQ-EVAL under the simple path semantics is intractable in data complexity. The difference is that checking the existence of an arbitrary path satisfying a regular condition can be efficiently reduced to a nonemptiness automata problem (see the proof of Theorem 2), but this is unlikely to be the case for simple paths.

In terms of data complexity, 2RPQs are in NLOGSPACE. Not only that, the whole set $[\![L]\!]_{\mathcal{G}}$ can be computed in NLOGSPACE for each fixed 2RPQ L:

PROPOSITION 3 (SEE E.G., [34]). *Let* L *be a fixed* 2RPQ. *There is an* NLOGSPACE *procedure that computes* $[\![L]\!]_{\mathcal{G}}$ *for each graph database* $\mathcal{G}$.

Proof (Sketch): For each pair (u, v) of node ids in V, we check whether it belongs to $[\![L]\!]_{\mathcal{G}}$ by following the proof of Proposition 2. Clearly, $\mathcal{G}^{\pm}$ can be constructed in LOGSPACE from $\mathcal{G}$, and $\mathcal{A}_L$ in constant time from L (since L is fixed). Nonemptiness of the product of $\mathcal{G}^{\pm}(u, v)$ and $\mathcal{A}_L$ can be checked in NLOGSPACE in $|\mathcal{G}|$ using a standard "on-the-fly" algorithm. The whole process can be carried out in NLOGSPACE (because NLOGSPACE computable functions are closed under composition). We conclude that $[\![L]\!]_{\mathcal{G}}$ can be computed in NLOGSPACE for each fixed 2RPQ L. □

It is easy to see, on the other hand, that RPQs are NLOGSPACE-complete in data complexity (under LOGSPACE reductions): If $\Sigma = \{0\}$ the RPQ 0^* checks, for each pair (u, v) of node ids in $\mathcal{G}$, if there is a directed path from u to v in $\mathcal{G}$, which is a well-known NLOGSPACE-complete problem.

RPQs with label variables As we mentioned earlier, label variables have almost disappeared from modern graph query languages. We provide a partial explanation to this fact by stating that, as opposed to the case of RPQs, evaluation of RPQVs is intractable.

RPQs *with label variables* (RPQVs) are of the form R, for $R \in \text{REG}(\Sigma \cup \mathcal{V}_{\text{label}})$. Assume $\mathcal{X}$ is the set of label variables mentioned in R. The evaluation $[\![R]\!]_{\mathcal{G}}$ of R on $\mathcal{G} = (V, E)$ is the set of pairs (u, v) of node ids in V such that there is a mapping $\nu : \mathcal{X} \to \Sigma$ and a path ρ in $\mathcal{G}$ from u to v that satisfies that $\lambda(\rho) \in \nu(R)$.

THEOREM 3 ([15]). RPQV-EVAL *is* NP-*complete.*

4.2 Conjunctive 2RPQs

Recall that patterns in **G** are graph databases such that each one of its edges is an RPQ and some variables are allowed to be projected in the output. In other words, patterns in **G** represent the closure of RPQs under joins and existential quantification. In modern graph query languages, this idea gives rise to the class of *conjunctive* 2RPQs, or C2RPQs [34, 1, 27]. We state in this section that C2RPQs (and even its extension with unions) preserve tractability in data complexity, but their combined complexity is NP-complete.

Let $\bar{x} = \{x_1, \ldots, x_n\}$ and $\bar{y} = \{y_1, \ldots, y_m\}$ be (possibly empty) disjoint sets of node variables. A C2RPQ, with free variables $\bar{x}$, over Σ is a rule $\varphi(\bar{x})$ of the form

$$Ans(\bar{x}) \leftarrow \bigwedge_{1 \leq i \leq k} (z_i, L_i, z_i') \quad (1)$$

where (a) L_i is a 2RPQ over Σ, for every i with $1 \leq i \leq k$, (b) $z_1, z_1', \ldots z_k, z_k'$ are (not necessarily distinct) variables, and (c) $\{z_1, z_1', \ldots, z_k, z_k'\} = \bar{x} \cup \bar{y}$. This C2RPQ is Boolean if $\bar{x} = \emptyset$. A CRPQ is a C2RPQ of the form (1), in which each L_i is an RPQ.

The semantics of C2RPQs is defined in terms of *homomorphisms*. Given a graph database $\mathcal{G} = (V, E)$, a homomorphism from a C2RPQ $\varphi(\bar{x})$ of the form (1) to $\mathcal{G}$ is a mapping $h : \bar{x} \cup \bar{y} \rightarrow V$ such that $(h(z_i), h(z_i')) \in [\![L_i]\!]_{\mathcal{G}}$, for each $1 \leq i \leq k$. Homomorphisms are not to be confused with the homeomorphisms introduced in Section 3, which define a simple path semantics.

The evaluation $[\![\varphi(\bar{x})]\!]_{\mathcal{G}}$ of $\varphi(\bar{x})$ on $\mathcal{G}$ is defined as the set of tuples of the form $h(\bar{x})$, for each homomorphism h from $\varphi(\bar{x})$ to $\mathcal{G}$. Boolean C2RPQs evaluate to *true* and *false*, as defined for **G**.

EXAMPLE 3. Consider the C2RPQ $\varphi(x, y)$:

$$Ans(x, y) \leftarrow (x, \texttt{creator}^-, u) \wedge (u, \texttt{partOf}, v) \wedge (v, \texttt{series}, w) \wedge (u, \texttt{creator}, y).$$

Its evaluation $[\![\varphi(x, y)]\!]_{\mathcal{G}}$ over the graph database $\mathcal{G}$ shown in Figure 2 consists of the pairs (x, y) of (not necessarily distinct) authors that have a joint conference paper, e.g., (`:Jeffrey_D._Ullman`, `:Ronald_Fagin`) and (`:Ronald_Fagin`, `:Moshe_Y._Vardi`) are in $[\![\varphi(x, y)]\!]_{\mathcal{G}}$. It is easy to see that this query cannot be expressed as a 2RPQ over $\mathcal{G}$, that is, for every 2RPQ L over Σ it is the case that $[\![L]\!]_{\mathcal{G}} \neq [\![\varphi(x, y)]\!]_{\mathcal{G}}$. □

Unions of C2RPQs The language **G** is closed under unions. Closing C2RPQs under unions gives rise to the class of UC2RPQs, which are formulas $\psi(\bar{x})$ of the form $\bigcup_{1 \leq i \leq k} \varphi_i(\bar{x})$, where $\varphi_i(\bar{x})$ is a C2RPQ for each i with $1 \leq i \leq k$. We have that $[\![\psi(\bar{x})]\!]_{\mathcal{G}} = \bigcup_{1 \leq i \leq k} [\![\varphi_i(\bar{x})]\!]_{\mathcal{G}}$, for each graph database $\mathcal{G}$.

Next proposition shows that the increase in expressiveness from 2RPQs to UC2RPQs has an important cost in the complexity of evaluation (even for CRPQs). Still, evaluating UC2RPQs is not more costly than evaluating CQs over relational databases; namely, NP-complete [32].

PROPOSITION 4 (SEE E.G., [13]). UC2RPQ-EVAL *is* NP-*complete, even if restricted to Boolean* CRPQs.

On the other hand, moving from RPQs to UC2RPQs is free in data complexity.

PROPOSITION 5 (SEE E.G., [34]). *The problem* UC2RPQ-EVAL *is in* NLOGSPACE *in data complexity.*

Proof (Sketch): It is sufficient to show that each fixed C2RPQ φ of the form (1) can be evaluated in NLOGSPACE. Let $\mathcal{G} = (V, E)$ be a graph database and $\bar{v}$ a tuple of node ids in V. To check whether $\bar{v} \in [\![\varphi]\!]_{\mathcal{G}}$, we compute the relational database $\mathcal{D}$ that contains all binary relations $R_i := [\![L_i]\!]_{\mathcal{G}}$, for $1 \leq i \leq k$. This can be done in NLOGSPACE using Proposition 3 and the fact that φ is fixed. Clearly, $\bar{v} \in [\![\varphi]\!]_{\mathcal{G}}$ iff $\bar{v}$ belongs to the evaluation of the CQ $\exists \bar{y} \bigwedge_{1 \leq i \leq k} R_i(z_i, z_i')$ over $\mathcal{D}$. But since evaluation of CQs is in LOGSPACE in data complexity [2], the whole process can be carried out in NLOGSPACE. □

Again, it is worth contrasting this result with the intractability of **G** in data complexity.

Expressive power UC2RPQs can be evaluated in NLOGSPACE in data complexity, but not every NLOGSPACE property can be expressed as a UC2RPQ. This is easy to see: While UC2RPQs are *monotone* (that is, $[\![Q]\!]_{\mathcal{G}} \subseteq [\![Q]\!]_{\mathcal{G}'}$ for every UC2RPQ Q and graph databases $\mathcal{G}, \mathcal{G}'$ such that $\mathcal{G}'$ extends $\mathcal{G}$ with new nodes and edges), there are NLOGSPACE properties that are not monotone (e.g., the property that the number of nodes in the graph database is even).

More interestingly, there are some simple monotone NLOGSPACE computable queries that are not expressible as UC2RPQs. Consider again the C2RPQ $\varphi(x, y)$ in Example 3. Imagine that we want to express the transitive closure $\varphi(x, y)^+$ of $\varphi(x, y)$; in particular, over the graph database $\mathcal{G}$ in Figure 2 the query $\varphi(x, y)^+$ defines the set of pairs (x, y) of authors that are linked by a *conference coauthorship sequence*. The syntax of UC2RPQs does not allow to express $\varphi(x, y)^+$ directly, and, even more, it can be proved (e.g., using techniques in [17]) that this query cannot be expressed as a UC2RPQ. This means that there is no UC2RPQ $\varphi'(x, y)$ such that $[\![\varphi'(x, y)]\!]_{\mathcal{G}} = [\![\varphi(x, y)^+]\!]_{\mathcal{G}}$, for each graph database $\mathcal{G}$ over $\Sigma = \{\texttt{creator}, \texttt{partOf}, \texttt{series}\}$. Notice that $\varphi(x, y)^+$ is a *monotone* query and EVAL($\varphi(x, y)^+$) can be computed in NLOGSPACE. We thus obtain the following:

PROPOSITION 6 ([17]). *There exists a monotone,* NLOGSPACE *computable query that is not expressible as a* UC2RPQ.

To overcome this lack of expressiveness, Consens and Mendelzon proposed a language, called GraphLog [34], that can be seen as a natural extension of the class of UC2RPQs that expresses all NLOGSPACE properties. Intuitively, GraphLog queries are recursive sets of UC2RPQs rules with distinguished outputs – in the style of a Datalog program – in which the body of a rule is allowed to use the head (output) $V(\bar{x})$ of another rule, its negation $\neg V(\bar{x})$, its transitive closure $V(\bar{x})^+$, and the negation of $V(\bar{x})^+$, with the expected semantics. For instance, the following simple GraphLog query defines the conference coauthorship sequence $\varphi(x, y)^+$ presented earlier: $\{V(x) \leftarrow \phi(x, y),\ Ans(x, y) \leftarrow V(x)^+\}$.

4.3 Low Complexity Queries

UC2RPQs are tractable in data complexity. However, this does not seem the right measure of complexity for several modern data-centric applications that store massive amounts of information. For instance, evaluation of a CRPQ Q over a graph database $\mathcal{G}$ is of the order $|\mathcal{G}|^{O(|Q|)}$ [81]. Although this is polynomial in data complexity, it is clearly infeasible for big $\mathcal{G}$ even if Q is small. In this scenario, we thus require query languages that are tractable in combined complexity, or, at least, *fixed-parameter tractable* [72]. Recall that the latter means that there exists a computable function $f : \mathbb{N} \rightarrow \mathbb{N}$, and a constant $c \geq 0$, such that the evaluation of each query Q in the language over a graph database $\mathcal{G}$ can be solved in time $O(|\mathcal{G}|^c \cdot f(|Q|))$.

The only query language we have seen with tractable combined complexity is the class of 2RPQs (in fact, Theorem 2 states that each 2RPQ L can be evaluated in linear time $O(|\mathcal{G}| \cdot |L|)$ over a graph database $\mathcal{G}$). The mildest extension of RPQs we know, the CRPQs, does not preserve this good property: Proposition 4 states that CRPQ-EVAL is NP-complete, and, even worst, under widely-held complexity theoretical assumptions, CRPQs are not fixed-parameter tractable [72]. We study below two ways in which the class of 2RPQs can be extended by preserving tractable combined complexity: By restricting the syntactic shape of C2RPQs, and by extending the navigational features of 2RPQs.

Acyclic C2RPQs In the case of CQs over relational databases, that are also NP-complete in combined complexity, several syntactic restrictions have been identified that lead to tractable evaluation. One of the oldest and most common such restriction is *acyclicity*. It was proved by Yannakakis that an acyclic CQ Q can be evaluated over a relational database $\mathcal{D}$ in linear time $O(|\mathcal{D}| \cdot |Q|)$ [83].

The acyclicity condition can also be applied to find tractable cases of C2RPQ-EVAL [13]. Acyclicity of a C2RPQ $\phi = Ans(\bar{x}) \leftarrow \bigwedge_{1 \leq i \leq n}(z_i, L_i, z_i')$ is often defined in terms of the acyclicity of its *underlying CQ* [13, 18], but a simpler and equivalent definition can be provided in terms of the *underlying graph of* ϕ: This is the graph U_ϕ whose nodes are the variables of ϕ and its set of edges is $\{\{z_i, z_i'\} \mid 1 \leq i \leq n,\ z_i \neq z_i'\}$. Notice that U_ϕ is simple (it contains neither loops nor multiedges) and undirected. The C2RPQ ϕ is acyclic if U_ϕ is acyclic. We denote by AC2RPQ the class of acyclic C2RPQs. It is worth noticing that acyclicity allows for cycles of length at most 2 in C2RPQs; e.g., the C2RPQ $\phi = Ans() \leftarrow (x, a, x) \wedge (x, a, y) \wedge (y, b, x)$ is acyclic (since U_ϕ consists of a unique edge linking the variables x and y).

THEOREM 4. AC2RPQ-EVAL *can be solved in time* $O(|\mathcal{G}|^2 \cdot |\phi|^2)$, *for each graph database* $\mathcal{G}$ *and acyclic* C2RPQ ϕ.

Proof (Sketch): Let $\mathcal{G} = (V, E)$ be a graph database and $\phi(\bar{x}) = Ans(\bar{x}) \leftarrow \bigwedge_{1 \leq i \leq n}(z_i, L_i, z_i')$ an acyclic C2RPQ. To check whether $\bar{v} \in [\![\phi]\!]_\mathcal{G}$, for $\bar{v}$ a tuple of node ids in V, we first compute the relational database $\mathcal{D}$ that contains all binary relations $R_i := [\![L_i]\!]_\mathcal{G}$, for $1 \leq i \leq n$. Each R_i can be computed in time $O(|\mathcal{G}|^2 \cdot |L_i|)$ using Proposition 3, and, thus, $\mathcal{D}$ can be computed in time $O(|\mathcal{G}|^2 \cdot |\phi|)$. Clearly, $\bar{v} \in [\![\phi]\!]_\mathcal{G}$ if and only if $\bar{v}$ belongs to the evaluation of the CQ $Q = \exists \bar{y} \bigwedge_{1 \leq i \leq n} R_i(z_i, z_i')$ over $\mathcal{D}$, where $\bar{y}$ is the tuple of variables in ϕ that are not mentioned in $\bar{x}$. It can be proved that Q is an acyclic CQ (since ϕ is acyclic), and hence it can be evaluated over $\mathcal{D}$ in time $O(|\mathcal{D}| \cdot |Q|)$. The whole process takes time $O(|\mathcal{G}|^2 \cdot |\phi|) + O(|\mathcal{D}| \cdot |Q|)$, and, thus, $O(|\mathcal{G}|^2 \cdot |\phi|^2)$ because $|Q|$ is $O(|\phi|)$. □

In terms of expressive power, the class of AC2RPQs lies strictly in between 2RPQs and C2RPQs: The C2RPQ $Ans(x, y) \leftarrow (x, \texttt{creator}^-, u) \wedge (u, \texttt{partOf}, v) \wedge (v, \texttt{series}, w) \wedge (u, \texttt{creator}, y)$, presented in Example 3, is acyclic but it is not expressible as a 2RPQ. On the other hand, a simple argument proves that the CRPQ $Ans(x, y, z) \leftarrow (x, a, y), (y, b, z), (z, c, x)$, over the alphabet $\Sigma = \{a, b, c\}$, is not expressible as an AC2RPQ.

The evaluation of AC2RPQs is quadratic in the size of the data, which might not be ideal for very big graph databases. The question of whether acyclic C2RPQs (or even acyclic CRPQs) can be evaluated linearly in the size of the data is related to some important open problems in the area of algorithmic graph theory. For instance, assume that $\Sigma = \{a\}$, then the acyclic CRPQ $Ans() \leftarrow (x, aaa, x)$ checks the existence of a *triangle* (i.e., a cycle of length 3) in an undirected simple graph, a problem for which no linear algorithm is known to date [6].

It is possible to obtain a class of AC2RPQs with linear time evaluation by further restricting its syntax. The only thing that we need to do is disallow loops and multiedges. Formally, let $\phi(\bar{x}) = Ans(\bar{x}) \leftarrow \bigwedge_{1 \leq i \leq k}(z_i, L_i, z_i')$ be an AC2RPQ. Then ϕ is *strongly* acyclic if (a) $z_i \neq z_i'$, for each i with $1 \leq i \leq k$ (no loops), and (b) for each i, j with $1 \leq i < j \leq k$ it is the case that $\{z_i, z_i'\} \neq \{z_j, z_j'\}$ (no multiedges). The class of strongly acyclic C2RPQs is denoted by SAC2RPQ. Using techniques in [17] one can prove the following:

PROPOSITION 7. SAC2RPQ-EVAL *can be solved in time* $O(|\mathcal{G}| \cdot |\phi|)$, *for each graph database* $\mathcal{G}$ *and* SAC2RPQ ϕ.

Nested regular expressions We can extend the expressive power of 2RPQs with an existential branching operator $\langle \cdot \rangle$ *á la* PDL [55] or XPath [38], while retaining good complexity of evaluation. This gives rise to the class of *nested regular expressions* (NREs) [17], that were originally proposed (with a slightly different syntax) for querying Semantic Web data with an RDFS vocabulary [74].

Formally, given a finite alphabet Σ, the class of NREs n over Σ is defined by the following grammar:

$$n \ := \ \varepsilon \mid a\ (a \in \Sigma) \mid a^-\ (a \in \Sigma) \mid n{+}n \mid n{\cdot}n \mid n^* \mid \langle n \rangle$$

We inductively formalize the semantics of a NRE n over a graph database $\mathcal{G} = (V, E)$ as a binary relation $[\![n]\!]_\mathcal{G}$ defined as follows, where a is a symbol in Σ and n, n_1, n_2 are arbitrary NREs over Σ:

$$\begin{aligned}
[\![\varepsilon]\!]_\mathcal{G} &= \{(u, u) \mid u \in V\} \\
[\![a]\!]_\mathcal{G} &= \{(u, v) \mid (u, a, v) \in E\} \\
[\![a^-]\!]_\mathcal{G} &= \{(u, v) \mid (v, a, u) \in E\} \\
[\![n_1 + n_2]\!]_\mathcal{G} &= [\![n_1]\!]_\mathcal{G} \cup [\![n_2]\!]_\mathcal{G} \\
[\![n_1 \cdot n_2]\!]_\mathcal{G} &= [\![n_1]\!]_\mathcal{G} \circ [\![n_2]\!]_\mathcal{G} \\
[\![n^*]\!]_\mathcal{G} &= [\![\varepsilon]\!]_\mathcal{G} \cup [\![n]\!]_\mathcal{G} \cup [\![n \cdot n]\!]_\mathcal{G} \cup [\![n \cdot n \cdot n]\!]_\mathcal{G} \cup \cdots \\
[\![\langle n \rangle]\!]_\mathcal{G} &= \{(u, u) \mid \text{there exists } v \text{ such that } (u, v) \in [\![n]\!]_\mathcal{G}\}.
\end{aligned}$$

Here, the symbol $\circ$ denotes the usual composition of binary relations, that is, $[\![n_1]\!]_\mathcal{G} \circ [\![n_2]\!]_\mathcal{G} = \{(u, v) \mid$ there exists w such that $(u, w) \in [\![n_1]\!]_\mathcal{G}$ and $(w, v) \in [\![n_2]\!]_\mathcal{G}\}$. As it is customary, we use n^+ as a shortcut for $n \cdot n^*$.

Clearly, the class of 2RPQs is contained in the class of NREs, but the opposite does not hold: We know that the acyclic C2RPQ $Ans(x, y) \leftarrow (x, \texttt{creator}^-, u) \wedge (u, \texttt{partOf}, v) \wedge (v, \texttt{series}, w) \wedge (u, \texttt{creator}, y)$, presented in Example 3, cannot be expressed as a 2RPQ, but it is equivalent to the NRE

$$n = \texttt{creator}^- \cdot \langle \texttt{partOf} \cdot \texttt{series} \rangle \cdot \texttt{creator}.$$

Although strictly more expressive, NREs retain the good properties of 2RPQs for query evaluation:

THEOREM 5 (SEE E.G., [74]). NRE-EVAL *can be solved in time* $O(|\mathcal{G}| \cdot |n|)$, *for each graph database* $\mathcal{G}$ *and* NRE n.

The expressive power of C2RPQs and NREs can only be compared in terms of binary C2RPQs (since NREs define binary relations). Interestingly enough, binary C2RPQs and NREs are incomparable in terms of their expressive power [17]:

PROPOSITION 8.

- *There exists a* C2RPQ $\varphi(x, y)$ *over a finite alphabet* Σ, *such that for no* NRE n *over* Σ *it is the case that* $[\![\varphi(x, y)]\!]_\mathcal{G} = [\![n]\!]_\mathcal{G}$, *for each graph database* $\mathcal{G}$.
- *There exists a* NRE n *over a finite alphabet* Σ, *such that for no* C2RPQ $\varphi(x, y)$ *over* Σ *it is the case that* $[\![\varphi(x, y)]\!]_\mathcal{G} = [\![n]\!]_\mathcal{G}$, *for each graph database* $\mathcal{G}$.

The proof of the first part is very simple: NREs are acyclic, and, thus, they cannot define arbitrary non-acyclic CRPQs such as $Ans(x, y) \leftarrow (x, a, y), (y, b, z), (z, c, x)$. The second part is more interesting. The proof is based on the fact that NREs allow the use of the Kleene-star $*$ over the branching operator $\langle\cdot\rangle$, a feature that cannot be codified in C2RPQs. For instance, the NRE

$$n = \left(\texttt{creator}^{-} \cdot \langle\texttt{partOf} \cdot \texttt{series}\rangle \cdot \texttt{creator}\right)^{+}$$

expresses the transitive closure of the conference coauthorship query in Example 3. This query is not expressible as a C2RPQ.

4.4 Containment

We study the containment problem for some of the languages presented in this section: 2RPQs, NREs and UC2RPQs. Recall that the containment problem $\mathcal{L}$-CONT, for query language $\mathcal{L}$, is defined as follows: Given queries Q and Q' in $\mathcal{L}$, is it the case that $[\![Q]\!]_{\mathcal{G}} \subseteq [\![Q']\!]_{\mathcal{G}}$ for every graph database $\mathcal{G}$?

We start with 2RPQs:

THEOREM 6 ([30]). 2RPQ-CONT *is* PSPACE-*complete.*

Proving PSPACE-completeness for RPQs is easy. Let L and L' be RPQs, i.e., regular expressions over Σ. It can be proved that $[\![L]\!]_{\mathcal{G}} \subseteq [\![L']\!]_{\mathcal{G}}$, for each graph database $\mathcal{G}$, iff the regular language defined by L is contained in the regular language defined by L', which is a well-known PSPACE-complete problem [79]. Extending the PSPACE upper bound to 2RPQs requires more work, as one has to reason about paths that traverse edges in both directions with two-way automata, and then check containment for them with only one exponential blow up [30].

Notably, NREs not only preserve the complexity of evaluation of 2RPQs, but also the complexity of containment (at the cost of a more involved proof):

THEOREM 7 ([75]). NRE-CONT *is* PSPACE-*complete.*

But moving towards UC2RPQs causes a jump in complexity:

THEOREM 8 ([27]). UC2RPQ-CONT *is* EXPSPACE-*complete. The problem remains hard even if restricted to Boolean acyclic* CRPQs.

The upper bound in [27] is only proved for C2RPQs, but it is easy to see that the same techniques extend to UC2RPQs. Those techniques are based on a clever codification of the problem as a containment problem for two-way automata of exponential size. An EXPSPACE upper bound for the containment of CRPQs (i.e., no inverses) had been previously obtained in [46] using different techniques. The lower bound is proved via a reduction from an EXPSPACE version of the tiling problem [27]. An inspection of the proof shows that this lower bound holds even for checking containment of Boolean acyclic CRPQs.

5. PATH QUERIES

The class of UC2RPQs falls short of expressive power for several modern applications of graph databases. In many of these applications a minimal requirement for sufficiently expressive queries are: (a) the ability to define complex semantic relationships among paths, and (b) the ability to include paths in the output of a query. None of these functionalities is provided by UC2RPQs.

There are multiple examples of queries that require these new capabilities. For instance, several important Semantic Web queries (as we will see later) can only be expressed by comparing paths [8, 9], biological sequences are often compared with respect to edit distance and path similarity [52], route-finding applications need to compare paths based on length or number of occurences of labels [19], etc. In addition, including paths in the output has applications in the Semantic Web [9, 62], provenance of data [58], semantic search over the Web [82], and others.

For the sake of simplicity, we only consider extensions with the new capabilities for CRPQs. Fix a countable set of *node* variables (typically denoted by $x, y, z, \ldots$), and a countable set of *path* variables (denoted by $\pi, \omega, \chi, \ldots$). Let $\mathcal{S}$ be a set of relations on finite words, such that each $S \in \mathcal{S}$ is a relation over some finite alphabet Σ, and assume that $\mathcal{S}$ includes all regular languages. (Examples of a set $\mathcal{S}$ of this kind are the *regular* and *rational* relations, as we define afterwards). The class of $\mathcal{S}$*-extended* CRPQs (from now on, ECRPQ($\mathcal{S}$)) over Σ consists of all rules $\theta(\bar{x}, \bar{\chi})$ of the form:

$$Ans(\bar{x}, \bar{\chi}) \leftarrow \bigwedge_{1 \leq i \leq k} (z_i, \pi_i, z_i'), \bigwedge_{1 \leq j \leq t} S_j(\bar{\omega}_j) \qquad (2)$$

such that the following holds:

- each one of the elements in $Z = \{z_1, z_1', \ldots, z_k, z_k'\}$ is a node variable, and each one of the elements in $P = \{\pi_1, \ldots, \pi_t\}$ is a path variable;
- $\bar{x}$ is a tuple of node variables among those in Z, and $\bar{\chi}$ is a tuple of path variables among those in P;
- each $\bar{\omega}_j$ $(1 \leq j \leq t)$ is a tuple of elements in P; and
- each S_j $(1 \leq j \leq t)$ is a relation in $\mathcal{S}$ over Σ, of the same arity than $\bar{\omega}_j$.

Notice that this definition meets our requirements: ECRPQ($\mathcal{S}$) queries allow for paths to be compared with respect to the relations in $\mathcal{S}$, and, in addition, path variables are admitted in the output.

The semantics of a rule $\theta(\bar{x}, \bar{\chi})$ of the form (2) is defined in terms of homomorphisms. A homomorphism from θ to a graph database $\mathcal{G} = (V, E)$ consists of a pair (σ, ν) of mappings such that $\sigma : \{z_1, z_1', \ldots, z_k, z_k'\} \to V$, the mapping ν assigns a path in $\mathcal{G}$ to each path variable π_i, $1 \leq i \leq k$, and the following holds: (1) $\nu(\pi_i)$ is a path from $\sigma(z_i)$ to $\sigma(z_i')$, for each i with $1 \leq i \leq k$, and (2) the tuple $\lambda(\nu(\bar{\omega}_j))$ – defined by the labels of the paths in the tuple $\nu(\bar{\omega}_j)$ – belongs to S_j, for each j with $1 \leq j \leq t$. We define $[\![\theta(\bar{x}, \bar{\chi})]\!]_{\mathcal{G}}$ as the set of tuples of the form $(\sigma(\bar{x}), \nu(\bar{\chi}))$, for each homomorphism (σ, ν) from $\theta(\bar{x}, \bar{\chi})$ to $\mathcal{G}$.

We can now justify why the languages are called *extended* CRPQs. Indeed, the class of CRPQs is contained in the class of ECRPQ($\mathcal{S}$) queries: the CRPQ $Ans(\bar{x}) \leftarrow \bigwedge_i (z_i, L_i, z_i')$ can be expressed as the ECRPQ($\mathcal{S}$) $Ans(\bar{x}) \leftarrow \bigwedge_i (z_i, \pi_i, z_i'), L_i(\pi_i)$ (since we assume that $\mathcal{S}$ contains all regular languages).

The expressiveness and complexity of ECRPQs depends, of course, on the class of relations on words we allow on $\mathcal{S}$. We study next two important such classes: regular and rational relations.

5.1 Regular relations

Following the idea behind CRPQs, which allow regular conditions on paths, we use *regular relations* [41, 49, 21] for path comparisons in ECRPQs [13]. As we will see next, regular relations permit a good trade-off between expressiveness and complexity for ECRPQs based on them.

Regular relations are recognized by *synchronous n-ary automata*, that have n input tapes onto which the input strings are written, followed by an infinite sequence of $\perp$ symbols. At each step the automaton simultaneously reads the next symbol on each tape, terminating when it reads $\perp$ on each tape.

Formally, let $\perp$ be a symbol not in Σ. We denote the extended alphabet $(\Sigma \cup \{\perp\})$ by $\Sigma_\perp$. Let $\bar{s} = (s_1, \ldots, s_n)$ be an n-tuple of strings over alphabet Σ. We construct a string $[\bar{s}]$ over alphabet $(\Sigma_\perp)^n$, whose length is the maximum of the s_j's, and whose i-th symbol is a tuple $(c_1, \ldots, c_n)$, where each c_k is the i-th symbol of s_k, if the length of s_k is at least i, or $\perp$ otherwise. In other words, we pad shorter strings with the symbol $\perp$, and then view the n strings as one string over the alphabet of n-tuples of letters.

An n-ary relation S on Σ^* is *regular*, if the set $\{[\bar{s}] \mid \bar{s} \in S\}$ of strings over alphabet $(\Sigma_\perp)^n$ is regular (i.e., accepted by an automaton over $(\Sigma_\perp)^n$, or given by a regular expression over $(\Sigma_\perp)^n$). We denote by Reg the set of all regular relations.

Clearly, the regular relations of arity 1 are exactly the regular languages. Examples of binary regular relations on words w_1 and w_2 are: (a) path equality: $w_1 = w_2$; (b) length comparisons: $|w_1| = |w_2|$ (and likewise for $<$ and $\leq$); (c) prefix: w_1 is a prefix of w_2; (d) small edit distance: edit distance between w_1 and w_2 is at most k, for a fixed k. On the other hand, several interesting relations on words are not regular; e.g., the binary relation $\preceq_{ss}$, that consists of all pairs (w_1, w_2) such that w_1 is a subsequence of w_2 (i.e., w_1 can be obtained by deleting some letters, perhaps none, from w_2), and the binary subword relation $\preceq_{sw}$ that contains all pairs (w_1, w_2) such that $w_3 w_1 w_4 = w_2$, for words w_3, w_4.

Thus, an ECRPQ(Reg) query over Σ is an expression of the form $Ans(\bar{x}, \bar{\chi}) \leftarrow \bigwedge_i (z_i, \pi_i, z_i'), \bigwedge_j R_j(\bar{\omega}_j)$, where each R_j is a regular relation over Σ. While ECRPQ(Reg) contains all CRPQs, it can be proved, on the contrary, that the containment is proper: Assume that el is the binary regular relation that checks whether two words have the same length. The ECRPQ(Reg) query

$$Ans(x, y) \leftarrow (x, \pi_1, z) \wedge (z, \pi_2, y) \wedge a^*(\pi_1) \wedge b^*(\pi_2) \wedge el(\pi_1, \pi_2)$$

computes all nodes in a graph database over $\Sigma = \{a, b\}$ that are linked by a path labeled in $\{a^n b^n \mid n \geq 0\}$. A pumping argument shows that this query is not expressible as a CRPQ [13, 48].

EXAMPLE 4. The ECRPQ(Reg) $Ans(x, y, z) \leftarrow (x, \pi_1, z) \wedge (y, \pi_2, z) \wedge el(\pi_1, \pi_2)$ defines the tuples (x, y, z) of nodes such that z can be reached from both x and y following paths of the same length. This query might be of interest, e.g., in route-finding applications. If we replace el with the binary relation that checks whether the edit distance between the labels of π_1 and π_2 is at most k, we have a similarity query motivated by sequence alignment in biological networks.

In a query language for RDF introduced in [8], paths can be compared based on specific *semantic associations*. Edges correspond to RDF properties and paths to property sequences. A property a can be declared to be a subproperty of property b, which we denote by $a \prec b$. Two property sequences u and v are called ρ-isomorphic iff $u = u_1 \cdots u_n$ and $v = v_1 \cdots v_n$, for some n, and $u_i \prec v_i$ or $v_i \prec u_i$ for every $i \leq n$. Nodes x and y are *ρ-isoAssociated* iff x and y are the origins of two ρ-isomorphic property sequences.

Finding nodes which are ρ-isoAssociated cannot be done in a query language supporting only conventional regular expressions, not least because doing so requires checking that two paths are of equal length. However, pairs of ρ-isomorphic sequences can be expressed using the regular relation R given by the following regular expression: $(\bigcup_{a,b \in \Sigma:\ (a \prec b \vee b \prec a)} (a, b))^*$. Then an ECRPQ(Reg) returning pairs of nodes x and y that are ρ-isoAssociated, and the respective paths, can be written as follows: $Ans(x, y, \pi_1, \pi_2) \leftarrow (x, \pi_1, z_1) \wedge (y, \pi_2, z_2) \wedge R(\pi_1, \pi_2)$. □

Complexity and containment ECRPQ(Reg) extends the class of CRPQs, but is there an associated complexity cost? Recall that ECRPQ(Reg)-EVAL is the problem of, given a graph database $\mathcal{G} = (V, E)$, an ECRPQ(Reg) query $\theta(\bar{x}, \bar{\chi})$, a tuple $\bar{v}$ of nodes in V and a tuple $\bar{\rho}$ of paths in $\mathcal{G}$, does $(\bar{v}, \bar{\rho})$ belong to $[\![\theta(\bar{x}, \bar{\chi})]\!]_{\mathcal{G}}$?

THEOREM 9 ([13]). ECRPQ(Reg)-EVAL *is* PSPACE-*complete, and* NLOGSPACE-*complete in data complexity.*

Thus, extending CRPQs with regular relations is free in data complexity, but combined complexity goes up from NP to PSPACE (which is, in any case, the same as the complexity of evaluation of FO over relational databases [2]).

Since ECRPQ(Reg) queries can return paths, the evaluation of a query might be infinite (for example, if there is a cycle in the graph database, then we have infinitely many paths). In such cases it is possible to return a compact representation of the answer. In fact, for each graph database $\mathcal{G}$, ECRPQ(Reg) query $\theta(\bar{x}, \bar{\chi})$, and tuple $\bar{v}$ of node ids, the set $\{\bar{\rho} \mid (\bar{v}, \bar{\rho}) \in [\![\theta]\!]_{\mathcal{G}}\}$ is a regular relation, and an automaton defining exactly this relation can be constructed in exponential time (and in polynomial time if θ is fixed) [13].

The precise complexity of evaluation for several extensions and restrictions of the class ECRPQ(Reg) is studied in [13]. The expressive power of the class is also by now well understood [48].

Let us consider finally the containment problem for ECRPQ(Reg). While this problem is decidable for CRPQs (Theorem 8), adding regular relations to compare paths dramatically changes the situation.

THEOREM 10 ([13]). ECRPQ(Reg)-CONT *is undecidable, even for Boolean queries over a fixed alphabet.*

The proof follows by a codification of the containment problem for *pattern languages* [77], which is undecidable [60, 47].

5.2 Rational relations

ECRPQ(Reg) queries are still short of the expressiveness needed in many applications. For instance, associations between paths used in RDF or biological networks often deal with subwords or subsequences, but these relations are not regular. They are rational [20]: they are still accepted by automata, but those whose heads move asynchronously.

Adding rational relations to a query language must be done with extreme care: simply replacing regular relations with rational in ECRPQs makes query evaluation undecidable or impractical. In fact, as we show below this happens even if the class ECRPQ(Reg) is extended with no more than the subword (or subsequence) relation to compare path labels. On the other hand, we can achieve tractable data complexity (and reasonable combined complexity) by restricting the syntactic shape of queries and disallowing rational relations of arity three or more.

Rational relations can be defined by means of *asynchronous* n-tape automata, that have n heads for the tapes and one additional control; at every step, based on the state and the letters it is reading, the automaton can enter a new state and move some (but not necessarily all) tape heads. Alternatively, n-ary rational relations can be defined as regular expressions over the alphabet $(\Sigma \cup \{\epsilon\})^n$, where ϵ denotes the empty symbol [20]. We use the notation Rat to denote the class of all rational relations.

Clearly, Reg $\subseteq$ Rat. Furthermore, Reg $=$ Rat for relations of arity 1 (both define exactly the class of regular languages). On the other hand, Rat $\not\subseteq$ Reg for relations of arity bigger than 1: The binary subsequence and subword relations – $\preceq_{ss}$ and $\preceq_{sw}$, respectively, as defined in Section 5.1 – are not regular but they can easily be proved to be rational.

An ECRPQ(Rat) query over Σ is thus an expression of the form $Ans(\bar{x}, \bar{\chi}) \leftarrow \bigwedge_i (z_i, \pi_i, z_i'), \bigwedge_j S_j(\bar{\omega}_j)$, where each S_j is a rational relation over Σ. For instance, the ECRPQ(Rat) query

$$Ans(x, y) \leftarrow (x, \pi_1, z) \wedge (y, \pi_2, w) \wedge \preceq_{ss} (\pi_1, \pi_2)$$

defines the pairs (x, y) of nodes such that x is the starting point of the path π_1, y is the starting point of the path π_2, and $\lambda(\pi_1)$ is a subsequence of $\lambda(\pi_2)$.

Complexity It follows easily from the undecidability of the intersection problem for rational relations [20] that ECRPQ(Rat)-EVAL is undecidable. However, we are not interested here in arbitrary rational relations but only on those that are useful in practice, e.g., $\preceq_{sw}$ and $\preceq_{ss}$. Unfortunately, none of these relations can be added to the class ECRPQ(Reg) without imposing further conditions:

THEOREM 11 ([12]). *1. There exists an* ECRPQ(Reg $\cup$ $\{\preceq_{sw}\}$) *query Q such that* EVAL(Q) *is undecidable.*

2. ECRPQ(Reg $\cup$ $\{\preceq_{ss}\}$)-EVAL *is decidable, but there exists an* ECRPQ(Reg $\cup$ $\{\preceq_{ss}\}$) *query Q such that* EVAL(Q) *is nonelementary.*

Theorem 11 rules out the applicability of query languages for graph databases that freely combine regular relations with some of the most common rational relations. In order to obtain acceptable complexity bounds, we thus need to further restrict the syntactic shape of queries. We study next a robust class of queries, with a simple syntactic definition, that yields tractable data complexity and reasonable combined complexity for queries defined by arbitrary rational relations of arity at most 2. The intuitive idea behind this restriction is forbidding features in ECRPQ(Rat) that allow to codify the intersection of rational relations, since it is known that this leads to undecidability of query evaluation.

Let $\mathsf{Rat}_{\leq 2}$ be the class of unary and binary rational relations. We can assume without loss of generality that an ECRPQ($\mathsf{Rat}_{\leq 2}$) query is an ECRPQ(Rat) expression of the form:

$$Ans(\bar{x}, \bar{\chi}) \leftarrow \bigwedge_{1 \leq i \leq k} (z_i, \pi_i, z_i'), S_i(\pi_i), \bigwedge_{1 \leq j \leq t} S_j'(\omega_j^1, \omega_j^2),$$

such that the S_i's are regular languages, the S_j''s are binary rational relations, and each ω_j^1 and ω_j^2 is a path variable among $\{\pi_1, \ldots, \pi_k\}$. This query is *intersection-free* if the following holds:

1. For each $1 \leq i \leq k$ it is the case that $\omega_i^1 \neq \omega_i^2$, and for each $1 \leq i < j \leq t$ it is the case that $\{\omega_i^1, \omega_i^2\} \neq \{\omega_j^1, \omega_j^2\}$. The first condition disallows the codification of the intersection of binary rational relations in an atom $S_i(\omega_i^1, \omega_i^2)$, and the second one over two different atoms $S_i'(\omega_i^1, \omega_i^2)$ and $S_j'(\omega_j^1, \omega_j^2)$.

2. Let I be the subset of $\{1, \ldots, k\} \times \{1, \ldots, k\}$ such that $(i_1, i_2) \in I$ ($1 \leq i_1, i_2 \leq k$) if and only if for some $1 \leq j \leq t$ it is the case that $\omega_j^1 = \pi_{i_1}$ and $\omega_j^2 = \pi_{i_2}$. We require that the undirected graph defined by I on $\{1, \ldots, k\}$ is acyclic. The reason is that intersection of binary rational relations can be codified in the query using cycles in I.

As an example, the following Boolean query is intersection-free (we have omitted the head predicate $Ans()$):

$$\bigwedge_{1 \leq i \leq 4} (x_i, \pi_i, y) \wedge \preceq_{ss} (\pi_1, \pi_2) \wedge \preceq_{ss} (\pi_2, \pi_3) \wedge \preceq_{sw} (\pi_2, \pi_4).$$

Intersection-free ECRPQ($\mathsf{Rat}_{\leq 2}$) queries have been studied in the literature under the name of *acyclic* queries [12]. We decided to change its name here since a different and important notion of acyclicity was already introduced in Section 4.3 for CRPQs.

Intersection-free ECRPQ($\mathsf{Rat}_{\leq 2}$) queries allow for tractable evaluation in data complexity, and its complexity coincides with that of ECRPQ(Reg) queries:

THEOREM 12 ([12]). *Let $\mathcal{F}$ be the class of intersection-free* ECRPQ($\mathsf{Rat}_{\leq 2}$) *queries. Then $\mathcal{F}$-*EVAL *is* PSPACE*-complete, and* NLOGSPACE*-complete in data complexity.*

Notably, the conditions imposed by intersection-free queries are, in a sense, optimal: Removing either condition (1) or (2) from its definition leads to undecidability [12]. The same happens if we allow relations of arity 3 or more in queries, even under strong extensions of conditions (1) and (2). On the other hand, the acyclicity condition (2) can be removed at the cost of restricting the rational relations allowed in queries. Results of this kind for several binary rational relations of interest (e.g., the subsequence or suffix relations) can be found in [12].

6. QUERIES ON GRAPHS WITH DATA

All query languages we have studied so far concentrate on the topological properties of the graph database, but do not talk much about the data itself. However, it is clear that graph databases contain data; e,g. in social networks nodes represent persons, and these persons have associated attributes such as name, age, location, etc. In addition, queries that combine topology and data are relevant in practice. Think, for instance, of the query that asks for pairs of persons of the same age that are connected via profesional links in a social network, or the query that asks for authors in DBLP that have papers in at least 3 different conferences.

We show in this section that languages that freely compare data values along a path easily become intractable in data complexity, but that there is a nice class of path queries, with tractable data complexity, that expresses relevant topological properties of the data.

Data model Let $\mathcal{D}$ be a countably infinite set of data values. A *data graph* is a graph database in which each node stores a data value from $\mathcal{D}$. Formally, given a finite alphabet Σ, a data graph $\mathfrak{G}$ over Σ is a tuple (V, E, κ), such that (V, E) is a graph database over Σ and κ is a mapping that assigns a data value in $\mathcal{D}$ to each node $v \in V$. Notice that graph databases in which nodes are labeled with more than one data value can be represented in this model: We simply add extra edges to nodes with those data values.

Query languages over data graphs talk about *data paths*, which are obtained from paths by replacing each node by its data value. Formally, let $\mathfrak{G} = (V, E, \kappa)$ be a data graph. With each path $\rho = v_0 a_0 v_1 \cdots v_{k-1} a_{k-1} v_k$ in (V, E) there is an associated data path $\rho_{\mathcal{D}} = \kappa(v_0) a_0 \kappa(v_1) \cdots \kappa(v_{k-1}) a_{k-1} \kappa(v_k)$ in $\mathfrak{G}$.

Query languages Data paths are very close to an object that has received considerable attention in the XML community: *Data words* [23], which are words over the infinite alphabet $\Sigma \times \mathcal{D}$. In fact, one can represent each data path as a data word with an extra data value in the end. The importance of this is that one can easily adapt the multiple formalisms that have been developed in the literature to query data words to express queries about data paths. These formalisms include FO extended with a binary relation $\sim$ that stores pairs of nodes with the same data value [22], pebble automata [71], register automata [61] and some versions of XPath.

Nevertheless, choosing the right formalism for querying data graphs has to be done with care. This is because checking even some simple data path properties is an intractable problem:

THEOREM 13 ([65]). *The following problem is NP-complete: Given a data graph $\mathfrak{G} = (V, E, \kappa)$ and two nodes $v, v' \in V$, determine if there is a data path $\rho_{\mathcal{D}}$ in $\mathfrak{G}$ from v to v' such that all data values in $\rho_{\mathcal{D}}$ are different.*

Thus, any query language for data graphs that expresses this simple property will be NP-complete in data complexity, and, thus, impractical. This rules out all formalisms mentioned before, except register automata. Libkin and Vrgoč studied the class of register automata as a querying formalism for data paths, and established some of its good properties [65]. But, as they argue, expressing properties of data paths with register automata is not simple. This motivated them to introduce the class of *regular expressions with memory* (REMs), that is based on register automata, but allows a more natural specification of queries over data graphs. We present this formalism below.

REMs REMs allow us to specify when data values are remembered and used. Data values are stored in k registers, represented by variables $x_1, \ldots, x_k$. At any point we can compare a data value with one previously stored in the registers. As an example, consider the REM $\downarrow x.a^+[x^=]$. It can be read as follows: Store the current data value in x, and then check that after reading a word in a^+ we see the same data value again (condition $[x^=]$). We formally define the class of REMs below.

Let $x_1, \ldots, x_k$ be variables. The set of *conditions* over $\{x_1, \ldots, x_k\}$ is recursively defined as: $c := x_i^= \mid c \wedge c \mid \neg c$, for $1 \leq i \leq k$. Satisfaction of conditions is defined with respect to a data value $d \in D$ and a tuple $\tau = (d_1, \ldots, d_k) \in \mathcal{D}^k$ as follows (we omit Boolean conditions): $(d, \tau) \models x_i^=$ iff $d = d_i$.

The class of REMs over Σ and $\{x_1, \ldots, x_k\}$ is given by the grammar:

$$e := \varepsilon \mid a \mid e \cup e \mid e \cdot e \mid e^+ \mid e[c] \mid \downarrow \bar{x}.e$$

where a ranges over symbols in Σ, c over conditions over $\{x_1, \ldots, x_k\}$, and $\bar{x}$ over tuples of elements in $\{x_1, \ldots, x_k\}$. We need to rule out some pathological cases if we want to have a clear semantics for REMs. In order to do that, we assume the following: (1) Subexpressions of the form e^+, $e[c]$ and $\downarrow \bar{x}.e$ are not allowed, for each e that *reduces* to ε. The expression e reduces to ε if $e = \epsilon$, or e is of the form $e_1 \cup e_2$ or $e_1 \cdot e_2$ or e_1^+ or $e_1[c]$ or $\downarrow \bar{x}.e_1$, where e_1 (and e_2) reduce to ε. (2) No variable appears in a condition before it has been mentioned in $\downarrow \bar{x}$.

REMs are used as analogs of RPQs for data graphs. As such, they define pairs of nodes linked by data paths satisfying the conditions expressed in the REM. To define the evaluation $[\![e]\!]_{\mathfrak{G}}$ of a REM e over a data graph $\mathfrak{G} = (V, E, \kappa)$, we use a relation $(e, \rho_{\mathcal{D}}, \lambda) \vdash \lambda'$, for e a REM, $\rho_{\mathcal{D}}$ a data path, and λ, λ' two k-tuples over $\mathcal{D} \cup \{\perp\}$ (the symbol $\perp$ represents that the variable has not been assigned a data value yet). The intuition behind the relation $(e, \rho_{\mathcal{D}}, \lambda) \vdash \lambda'$ is the following: The data path $\rho_{\mathcal{D}}$ can be parsed according to e, with λ being the initial assignment of the variables, in such a way that the final assignment is λ'. We then define $[\![e]\!]_{\mathfrak{G}}$ as the pairs (u, v) of node ids in V, such that there is a data path $\rho_{\mathcal{D}}$ in $\mathfrak{G}$ from u to v for which it is the case that $(e, \rho_{\mathcal{D}}, \perp^k) \vdash \lambda$, for some k-tuple λ over $\mathcal{D} \cup \{\perp\}$.

We inductively define the relation $(e, \rho_{\mathcal{D}}, \lambda) \vdash \lambda'$ below. But before, we need to introduce some extra terminology. We assume that $\lambda_{\bar{x}=d}$ is the tuple obtained from λ by setting all variables in $\bar{x}$ to be d. Also, the *concatenation* of two data paths of the form $d_0 a_0 d_1 \cdots d_{k-1} a_{k-1} d_k$ and $d_k a_k d_{k+1} \cdots d_{n-1} a_{n-1} d_n$ is defined as $d_0 a_0 d_1 \cdots d_{k-1} a_{k-1} d_k a_k d_{k+1} \cdots d_{n-1} a_{n-1} d_n$. If $\rho_{\mathcal{D}}$ is obtained by concatenating the data paths $\rho_{\mathcal{D}}^1, \rho_{\mathcal{D}}^2, \ldots, \rho_{\mathcal{D}}^\ell$, i.e., $\rho_{\mathcal{D}} = \rho_{\mathcal{D}}^1 \rho_{\mathcal{D}}^2 \cdots \rho_{\mathcal{D}}^\ell$, then we say that there is a *splitting* of $\rho_{\mathcal{D}}$ into $\rho_{\mathcal{D}}^1 \rho_{\mathcal{D}}^2 \cdots \rho_{\mathcal{D}}^\ell$. Then:

- $(\varepsilon, \rho_{\mathcal{D}}, \lambda) \vdash \lambda'$ iff $\rho_{\mathcal{D}} = d$, for some $d \in \mathcal{D}$, and $\lambda = \lambda'$.
- $(a, \rho_{\mathcal{D}}, \lambda) \vdash \lambda'$ iff $\rho_{\mathcal{D}} = d_1 a d_2$ and $\lambda = \lambda'$.
- $(e_1 \cup e_2, \rho_{\mathcal{D}}, \lambda) \vdash \lambda'$ iff $(e_1, \rho_{\mathcal{D}}, \lambda) \vdash \lambda'$ or $(e_2, \rho_{\mathcal{D}}, \lambda) \vdash \lambda'$.
- $(e_1 \cdot e_2, \rho_{\mathcal{D}}, \lambda) \vdash \lambda'$ iff there is a splitting $\rho_{\mathcal{D}}^1 \rho_{\mathcal{D}}^2$ of $\rho_{\mathcal{D}}$ and a k-tuple λ'' over $\mathcal{D} \cup \{\perp\}$, such that $(e_1, \rho_{\mathcal{D}}^1, \lambda) \vdash \lambda''$ and $(e_2, \rho_{\mathcal{D}}^2, \lambda'') \vdash \lambda'$.
- $(e^+, \rho_{\mathcal{D}}, \lambda) \vdash \lambda'$) iff there is a splitting $\rho_{\mathcal{D}}^1 \rho_{\mathcal{D}}^2 \cdots \rho_{\mathcal{D}}^\ell$ of $\rho_{\mathcal{D}}$ and k-tuples $\lambda = \lambda_0, \lambda_1, \ldots, \lambda_m = \lambda'$ over $\mathcal{D} \cup \{\perp\}$, such that $(e, \rho_{\mathcal{D}}^i, \lambda_{i-1}) \vdash \lambda_i$, for all i with $1 \leq i \leq \ell$.
- $(e[c], \rho_{\mathcal{D}}, \lambda) \vdash \lambda'$ iff $(e, \rho_{\mathcal{D}}, \lambda) \vdash \lambda'$ and $(d, \lambda') \models c$, where d is the last data value of $\rho_{\mathcal{D}}$.
- $(\downarrow \bar{x}.e, \rho_{\mathcal{D}}, \lambda) \vdash \lambda'$ iff $(e, \rho_{\mathcal{D}}, \lambda_{\bar{x}=d}) \vdash \lambda'$, where d is the first data value of $\rho_{\mathcal{D}}$.

EXAMPLE 5. The REM $\Sigma^* \cdot (\downarrow x.\Sigma^+[x^=]) \cdot \Sigma^*$ defines the pairs of nodes that are linked by a data path in which two data values are the same. Notice that the complement of this query defines precisely the NP-complete property in Theorem 13, which is not expressible as a REM [65] (in particular, REMs are not closed under complementation). The REM $\downarrow x.(a[\neg x^=])^+$ defines the pairs of nodes that are linked by a data path labeled in a, such that its first data value is different from all other data values. □

REMs are tractable in data complexity and have no worst combined complexity than FO over relational databases:

THEOREM 14 ([65]). *REM-*EVAL *is* PSPACE*-complete, and* NLOGSPACE*-complete in data complexity.*

It is easy to see that this behavior extends to the class of *conjunctive* REMs, that can be defined analogously to CRPQs but assuming that basic atoms are REMs. Tractable cases of REM evaluation in combined complexity can be obtained by restricting the data comparison power of the expressions [65]. Different query languages for data graphs with tractable combined complexity have been designed using XPath features [66].

Finally, containment of REMs is undecidable. This follows from undecidability of containment for register automata [71].

THEOREM 15. *REM-*CONT *is undecidable.*

7. CONCLUSIONS AND FUTURE CHALLENGES

Figure 3 summarizes the complexity of evaluation and containment for most of the query languages studied in the paper. This includes traditional query languages for graph databases, such as G, 2RPQs, and C2RPQs. For the first one, even data complexity is intractable due to the simple path semantics. Allowing a semantics based on arbitrary paths yields tractable data complexity for C2RPQs. Combined complexity of C2RPQs is intractable, which has motivated the search for expressive fragments with good evaluation properties. This includes the classes of acyclic C2RPQs and NREs, that can be evaluated in quadratic and linear time in the size of the data, respectively. The containment problem for C2RPQs is in EXPSPACE, but for 2RPQs and NREs it is in PSPACE.

We also studied expressive languages for path queries. The class ECRPQ(Reg) preserves good data complexity, but fails to retain

	Combined complexity	Data complexity	Containment
G	NP-complete	NP-complete	?
2RPQs	$O(\|\mathcal{G}\| \cdot \|L\|)$	NLOGSPACE-complete	PSPACE-complete
C2RPQs	NP-complete	NLOGSPACE-complete	EXPSPACE-complete
AC2RPQs	$O(\|\mathcal{G}\|^2 \cdot \|\phi\|^2)$	NLOGSPACE-complete	EXPSPACE-complete
NREs	$O(\|\mathcal{G}\| \cdot \|n\|)$	NLOGSPACE-complete	PSPACE-complete
ECRPQ(Reg)	PSPACE-complete	NLOGSPACE-complete	undecidable
ECRPQ(Reg $\cup \{\preceq_{sw}\}$)	undecidable	undecidable	undecidable
ECRPQ(Reg $\cup \{\preceq_{ss}\}$)	nonelementary	nonelementary	undecidable
Intersection-free ECRPQ(Rat$_{\leq 2}$)	PSPACE-complete	NLOGSPACE-complete	undecidable
REMs	PSPACE-complete	NLOGSPACE-complete	undecidable

Figure 3: Combined complexity, data complexity, and complexity of containment for several languages studied in the paper.

decidability for containment. Adding some natural non-rational relations (such as subword or subsequence) to ECRPQ(Reg) leads to either undecidability or high complexity of evaluation (even for a fixed query). However, intersection-free ECRPQ(Rat$_{\leq 2}$) queries, that allow arbitrary rational relations of arity at most 2 but restrict the syntactic shape of queries, preserve the evaluation properties of ECRPQ(Reg). Finally, we studied languages for graph databases with data values. Even some simple data path properties are intractable in data complexity, but an expressive language, that is also tractable, was identified; namely, REMs.

The study of graph databases is at an early stage of development, and many crucial questions about them remain unanswered:

Optimization: Most of the work on optimization has dealt with the containment and equivalence problem for 2RPQs and C2RPQs. Almost nothing is known about decidable cases of these problems for path or data queries. Furthermore, the study of heuristics based on optimization rules that help determining the most efficient way to execute a query has received not much attention.

Recently, a new notion of *approximate* optimization has been introduced in the context of CQ evaluation over relational databases [16], and subsequently studied for UC2RPQs over graph databases [18]. This notion is motivated by the scenarios of big graph databases, in which tractable combined complexity of evaluation is crucial. The basic idea is, given a UC2RPQ Q and a tractable class $\mathcal{C}$ of UC2RPQs (e.g. unions of AC2RPQs), find a query $Q' \in \mathcal{C}$ (the approximation) that is "as close as possible" to $\mathcal{C}$, and then run the fast query Q' over the underlying data. Approximations studied so far have several good properties, but are a bit coarse in some cases. The introduction of more informative notions of approximations in graph databases is a challenging open problem.

Constraints: Graph database constraints received a good amount of attention about 10 years ago, particularly in relationship with the containment problem [4, 50, 39, 25]. On the other hand, query optimization in the presence of constraints is almost unexplored (save for simple queries, such as RPQs [44]), and the topic of dependencies over data graphs has not been studied. Furthermore, research on general purpose languages that allow to express the kind of dependencies that modern graph database applications (e.g. social or biological networks) require is completely open.

A practical query language: Current systems for graph databases, such as Dex [68], Neo4j [70], InfiniteGraph [59], and others, lack a language with clear syntax and semantics. This difficults the accurate evaluation of the expressive power and the computational cost of the queries they permit. We believe that the time is ripe for the theoretical community to interact with the graph database vendors, and design a core query language for graph databases that allows to express a common set of queries for different domains, and that can be evaluated at a reasonable computational cost.

Acknowledgements I am very grateful to Marcelo Arenas, Gaelle Fontaine, Miguel Romero and Juan Reutter for carefully reading an earlier version of the article and providing me with comments. The author is funded by Fondecyt grant 1130104.

8. REFERENCES

[1] S. Abiteboul, P. Buneman, D. Suciu. *Data on the Web: From Relations to Semistructured Data and XML*. Morgan Kauffman, 1999.

[2] S. Abiteboul, R. Hull, V. Vianu. *Foundations of databases*. Addison-Wesley, 1995.

[3] S. Abiteboul, D. Quass, J. McHugh, J. Widom, J. L. Wiener. The Lorel query language for semistructured data. *Int. J. on Digital Libraries* 1(1), pages 68-88, 1997.

[4] S. Abiteboul, V. Vianu. Regular path queries with constraints. *JCSS* 58(3), pages 428-452, 1999.

[5] R. Angles, C. Gutiérrez. Survey of graph database models. *ACM Comput. Surv.* 40(1), 2008.

[6] N. Alon, R. Yuster, U. Zwick. Finding and counting given length cycles (Extended abstract). In *ESA* 1994, pages 354-364.

[7] M. K. Anand, S. Bowers, B. Ludäscher. Techniques for efficiently querying scientific workflow provenance graphs. In *EDBT* 2010, pages 287-298.

[8] K. Anyanwu, A. P. Sheth. ρ-queries: enabling querying for semantic associations on the semantic web. In *WWW* 2003, pages 690-699.

[9] K. Anyanwu, A. Maduko, A. P. Sheth. SPARQ2L: towards support for subgraph extraction queries in RDF databases. In *WWW* 2007, pages 797-806.

[10] M. Arenas, J. Pérez. Querying semantic web data with SPARQL. In *PODS* 2011, pages 305-316.

[11] M. Arenas, S. Conca, J. Pérez. Counting beyond a Yottabyte, or how SPARQL 1.1 property paths will prevent adoption of the standard. In *WWW* 2012, pages 629-638.

[12] P. Barceló, D. Figueira, L. Libkin. Graph-logics with rational relations and the generalized intersection problem. In *LICS* 2012, pages 115-124.

[13] P. Barceló, L. Libkin, A. W. Lin, P. T. Wood. Expressive languages for path queries over graph-structured Data. *TODS* 37(4), 2012.

[14] P. Barceló, L. Libkin, J. Reutter. Querying graph patterns. In *PODS* 2011, pages 199-210.

[15] P. Barceló, L. Libkin, J. Reutter. Parameterized regular expressions and their languages. *TCS* 474, pages 21-45, 2013.

[16] P. Barceló, L. Libkin, M. Romero. Efficient approximations of conjunctive queries. In *PODS*, pages 249-260, 2012.

[17] P. Barceló, J. Reutter, J. Pérez. Relative expressiveness of nested regular expressions. In *AMW* 2012, pages 180-195.

[18] P. Barceló, M. Romero, M. Y. Vardi. Semantic acyclicity on graph databases. In *PODS* 2013.

[19] C.L. Barrett, R. Jacob, M.V. Marathe. Formal-language-constrained path problems. *SIAM J. on Comp.*, 30(3), pages 809–837, 2000.

[20] J.M. Berstel. *Transductions and Context-Free Languages*. B. G. Teubner, 1979.

[21] A. Blumensath, E. Grädel. Automatic structures. In *LICS* 2000, pages 51-62.

[22] M. Bojanczyk, A. Muscholl, Th. Schwentick, L. Segoufin. Two-variable logic on data trees and XML reasoning. *JACM* 56(3), 2009.

[23] M. Bojanczyk. Automata for data words and data trees. In *RTA*, 2010.

[24] P. Buneman. Semistructured data. In *PODS* 1997, pages 117-121.

[25] P. Buneman, W. Fan, S. Weinstein. Path constraints in semistructured databases. *JCSS* 61(2), pages 146-193, 2000.

[26] P. Buneman, M. F. Fernandez, D. Suciu. UnQL: A query language and algebra for semistructured data based on structural recursion. *VLDB J.* 9(1), pages 76-110, 2000.

[27] D. Calvanese, G. de Giacomo, M. Lenzerini, M. Y. Vardi. Containment of conjunctive regular path queries with inverse. In *KR* 2000, pages 176-185.

[28] D. Calvanese, G. de Giacomo, M. Lenzerini, M. Y. Vardi. Rewriting of regular expressions and regular path queries. *JCSS*, 64(3), pages 443-465, 2002.

[29] D. Calvanese, G. de Giacomo, M. Lenzerini, M. Y. Vardi. View-based query containment. In *PODS* 2003, pages 56-67.

[30] D. Calvanese, G. de Giacomo, M. Lenzerini, M. Y. Vardi. Reasoning on regular path queries. *SIGMOD Record* 32(4), pages 83-92, 2003.

[31] P. Chambart, Ph. Schnoebelen. Post embedding problem is not primitive recursive, with applications to channel systems. In *FSTTCS* 2007, pages 265-276.

[32] A. Chandra and P. Merlin. Optimal implementation of conjunctive queries in relational data bases. In *STOC* 1977, pages 77–90.

[33] M. P. Consens, A. O. Mendelzon. Expressing structural hypertext queries in GraphLog. In *Hypertext* 1989, pages 269-292.

[34] M. P. Consens, A. O. Mendelzon. GraphLog: a visual formalism for real life recursion. In *PODS* 1990, pages 404-416.

[35] M. P. Consens, A. O. Mendelzon. Low complexity aggregation in graphLog and datalog. *TCS* 116(1 & 2), pages 95-116, 1993.

[36] I. Cruz, A. Mendelzon, P. Wood. A graphical query language supporting recursion. In *SIGMOD* 1987, pages 323-330.

[37] L3S dblp bibliography DB: `http://dblp.l3s.de/d2r/`.

[38] S. DeRose. J. Clark. Xml path language (xpath). W3C Recommendation, November 1999, http://www.w3.org/TR/xpath.

[39] A. Deutsch, V. Tannen. Optimization properties for classes of conjunctive regular path queries. In *DBPL* 2001, pages 21-39.

[40] A. Dries, S. Nijssen, L. De Raedt. A query language for analyzing networks. In *CIKM* 2009, pages 485-494.

[41] C. Elgot, J. Mezei. On relations defined by generalized finite automata. *IBM Journal of Research and Development*, 9(1), pages 47-68, 1965.

[42] W. Fan. Graph pattern matching revised for social network analysis. In *ICDT* 2012, pages 8-21.

[43] M. F. Fernández, D. Florescu, A. Y. Levy, D. Suciu. Declarative specification of web sites with Strudel. *VLDB J.* 9(1), pages 38-55, 2000.

[44] M. F. Fernandez, D. Suciu. Optimizing regular path expressions using graph schemas. In *ICDE* 1998, pages 14-23.

[45] G. H. L. Fletcher, M. Gyssens, D. Leinders, J. Van den Bussche, D. Van Gucht, S. Vansummeren, Y. Wu. Relative expressive power of navigational querying on graphs. In *ICDT* 2011, pages 197-207.

[46] D. Florescu, A. Y. Levy, D. Suciu. Query containment for conjunctive queries with regular expressions. In *PODS* 1998, pages 139-148.

[47] D. D. Freydenberger, D. Reidenbach. Bad news on decision problems for patterns. *Inf. Comput.* 208(1), pages 83-96, 2010.

[48] D. D. Freydenberger, N. Schweikardt. Expressiveness and static analysis of extended conjunctive regular path queries. In *AMW* 2011.

[49] Ch. Frougny, J. Sakarovitch. Rational relations with bounded delay. In *STACS* 1991, pages 50-63.

[50] G. Grahne, A. Thomo. Query containment and rewriting using views for regular path queries under constraints. In *PODS* 2003, pages 111-122.

[51] R. Greenlaw, J. Hoover, W. Ruzzo. *Limits to parallel computation: P-completeness theory*. Oxford University Press, 1995.

[52] D. Gusfield. *Algorithms on strings, trees and sequences: Computer science and computational biology*. Cambridge University Press, 1997.

[53] R. H. Güting. GraphDB: Modeling and querying graphs in databases. In *VLDB* 1994, pages 297-308.

[54] M. Gyssens, J. Paredaens, J. Van den Bussche, D. Van Gucht. A graph-oriented object database model. *IEEE Trans. Knowl. Data Eng.* 6(4), pages 572-586, 1994.

[55] D. Harel, D. Kozen, J. Tiuryn. *Dynamic Logic*. MIT Press, 2000.

[56] S. Harris, A. Seaborne. SPARQL 1.1 query language. W3C working draft. `http://www.w3.org/TR/sparql11-query/, July 2012.`

[57] J. Hellings, B. Kuijpers, J. Van den Bussche, X. Zhang. Walk logic as a framework for path query languages on graph databases. In *ICDT* 2013, pages 117-128.

[58] D.A. Holland, U. Braun, D. Maclean, K.K. Muniswamy-Reddy, M.I. Seltzer. Choosing a data model and query language for provenance. In *IPAW* 2008, pages 98-115.

[59] Infinite graph. `http://objectivity.com`

[60] T. Jiang, A. Salomaa, K. Salomaa, S. Yu. Decision problems for patterns. *JCSS* 50(1), pages 53-63, 1995.

[61] M. Kaminski, N. Francez. Finite memory automata. *TCS*, 134(2), pages 329-363, 1994.

[62] K. Kochut, M. Janik. SPARQLeR: Extended Sparql for semantic association discovery. In *ESWC* 2007, pages 145-159.

[63] Z. Lacroix, H. Murthy, F. Naumann, L. Raschid. Links and paths through life sciences data Sources. In *DILS* 2004, pages 203-211.

[64] A. LaPaugh, Ch. Papadimitriou. The even path problem for graphs and digraphs. *Networks* 14(4), pages 507-513, 1984.

[65] L. Libkin, D. Vrgoč. Regular path queries on graphs with data. In *ICDT* 2012, pages 74-85.

[66] L. Libkin, W. Martens, D. Vrgoč. Querying graph databases with XPath. In *ICDT* 2013.

[67] K. Losemann, W. Martens. The complexity of evaluating path expressions in SPARQL. In *PODS* 2012, pages 101-112.

[68] N. Martínez-Bazan, V. Muntés-Mulero, S. Gomez-Villamor, J. Nin, M. Sánchez-Martínez, J. L. Larriba-Pey. Dex: high-performance exploration on large graphs for information retrieval. In *CIKM* 2007, pages 573-582.

[69] A. Mendelzon, P. Wood. Finding regular simple paths in graph databases. *SIAM J. Comput.* 24(6), pages 1235-1258, 1995.

[70] Neo4j. `http://www.neo4j.org/`

[71] F. Neven, Th. Schwentick, V. Vianu. Finite state machines for strings over infinite alphabets. *ACM TOCL* 5(3), pages 403-435, 2004.

[72] Ch. Papadimitriou, M. Yannakakis. On the complexity of database queries. In *PODS* 1997, pages 12-19.

[73] J. Paredaens, P. Peelman, L. Tanca. G-Log: A graph-based query language. *IEEE Trans. Knowl. Data Eng.* 7(3), pages 436-453, 1995.

[74] J. Pérez, M. Arenas, C. Gutierrez. nSPARQL: A navigational language for RDF. *Journal of Web Semantics* 8(4), pages 255-270, 2010.

[75] J. Reutter. Containment of nested regular expressions. `http://arxiv.org/abs/1304.2637`

[76] R. Ronen, O. Shmueli. SoQL: A language for querying and creating data in social networks. In *ICDE* 2009, pages 1595-1602.

[77] A. Salomaa. Patterns. *Bulletin of the EATCS* 54, pages 194-206, 1994.

[78] M. San Martín, C. Gutierrez, P. T. Wood. SNQL: A social networks query and transformation language. In *AMW* 2011.

[79] L. J. Stockmeyer, A. R. Meyer. Word problems requiring exponential time: Preliminary report. In *STOC* 1973, pages 1-9.

[80] M. Y. Vardi. The complexity of relational query languages. In *STOC* 1982, pages 137-146.

[81] M.Y. Vardi. On the complexity of bounded variable queries. In *PODS* 1995, pages 266-276.

[82] G. Weikum, G. Kasneci, M. Ramanath, F. M. Suchanek. Database and information-retrieval methods for knowledge discovery. *CACM* 52(4), pages 56-64, 2009.

[83] M. Yannakakis. Algorithms for acyclic database schemes. In *VLDB* 1981, pages 82-94.

Charting the Tractability Frontier of Certain Conjunctive Query Answering

Jef Wijsen
Université de Mons (UMONS)
jef.wijsen@umons.ac.be

ABSTRACT

An uncertain database is defined as a relational database in which primary keys need not be satisfied. A repair (or possible world) of such database is obtained by selecting a maximal number of tuples without ever selecting two distinct tuples with the same primary key value. For a Boolean query q, the decision problem $\mathsf{CERTAINTY}(q)$ takes as input an uncertain database **db** and asks whether q is satisfied by every repair of **db**. Our main focus is on acyclic Boolean conjunctive queries without self-join. Previous work [24] has introduced the notion of (directed) attack graph of such queries, and has proved that $\mathsf{CERTAINTY}(q)$ is first-order expressible if and only if the attack graph of q is acyclic. The current paper investigates the boundary between tractability and intractability of $\mathsf{CERTAINTY}(q)$. We first classify cycles in attack graphs as either weak or strong, and then prove among others the following. If the attack graph of a query q contains a strong cycle, then $\mathsf{CERTAINTY}(q)$ is **coNP**-complete. If the attack graph of q contains no strong cycle and every weak cycle is terminal (i.e., no edge leads from a vertex in the cycle to a vertex outside the cycle), then $\mathsf{CERTAINTY}(q)$ is in **P**. We then partially address the only remaining open case, i.e., when the attack graph contains some nonterminal cycle and no strong cycle. Finally, we establish a relationship between the complexities of $\mathsf{CERTAINTY}(q)$ and evaluating q on probabilistic databases.

Categories and Subject Descriptors

H.2.3 [**Database Management**]: Languages—*query languages*; H.2.4 [**Database Management**]: Systems—*relational databases*

General Terms

Theory, Algorithms

PODS'13, June 22–27, 2013, New York, New York, USA.

C	conf	year	city
	PODS	2016	Rome
	PODS	2016	Paris
	KDD	2017	Rome

R	conf	rank
	PODS	A
	KDD	A
	KDD	B

Figure 1: Uncertain database.

Keywords

Conjunctive queries; consistent query answering; primary keys; probabilistic databases

1. INTRODUCTION

Primary key violations are a natural way for modeling uncertainty in the relational model. If two distinct tuples have the same primary key value, then at least one of them must be mistaken, but we do not know which one. This representation of uncertainty is also used in probabilistic databases, where each tuple is associated with a probability and distinct tuples with the same primary key value are disjoint probabilistic events [19, page 35].

In this paper, the term *uncertain database* is used for databases with primary key constraints that need not be satisfied. A repair (or possible world) of an uncertain database **db** is a maximal subset of **db** that satisfies all primary key constraints. Semantics of querying follows the conventional paradigm of *consistent query answering* [1, 3]: Given a Boolean query q, the decision problem $\mathsf{CERTAINTY}(q)$ takes as input an uncertain database **db** and asks whether q is satisfied by every repair of **db**. Notice that q is not part of the input, so the complexity of the problem is data complexity.

Primary keys are underlined in the conference planning database of Fig. 1. Maximal sets of tuples that agree on their primary key, called *blocks*, are separated by dashed lines. There is uncertainty about the city of PODS 2016, and about the rank of KDD. The database has four repairs. The query $\exists x \exists y(\mathbf{C}(\underline{x}, y, \text{'Rome'}) \wedge \mathbf{R}(\underline{x}, \text{'A'}))$ (Will Rome host some A conference?) is true in only three repairs.

The problem $\mathsf{CERTAINTY}(q)$ is in **coNP** for first-order queries q (a "no" certificate is a repair falsifying q). Its complexity for conjunctive queries has attracted the attention of several authors, also outside the database community (see, e.g., [4, 5]). A major research objective is to find an effective method that takes as input a conjunctive query q and determines to which complexity classes $\mathsf{CERTAINTY}(q)$ belongs, or does not belong. Complexity classes of interest are the class of first-order expressible problems (or $\mathbf{AC}^0$), $\mathbf{P}$, and $\mathbf{coNP}$-complete.

Unless specified otherwise, whenever we say "query" outside a theorem-like environment, we mean a Boolean conjunctive query without self-join (i.e., without repeated relation names). Such queries are called acyclic if they have a join tree [2]. Most (but not all) of our results are restricted to acyclic queries.

Prior work [22, 24] has revealed the frontier between first-order expressibility and inexpressibility of $\mathsf{CERTAINTY}(q)$ for acyclic queries q. In the current work, we study the frontier between tractability and intractability of $\mathsf{CERTAINTY}(q)$ for the same class of queries. That is, we aim at an effective method that takes as input a query q and determines whether $\mathsf{CERTAINTY}(q)$ is in $\mathbf{P}$ or $\mathbf{coNP}$-complete (or neither of the two, which is theoretically possible [15]). For queries with exactly two atoms, such a method was recently found by Kolaitis and Pema [13], but moving from two to more than two atoms is a major challenge.

Uncertain databases become probabilistic when we assume that the probabilities of all repairs are equal and sum up to 1. In probabilistic terms, distinct tuples of the same block represent disjoint (i.e., exclusive) events, while tuples of distinct blocks are independent. Such probabilistic databases have been called *block-independent-disjoint* (BID) [7]. The tractability/intractability frontier of query evaluation on BID probabilistic databases has been revealed by Dalvi et al. [8]. Here, evaluating a Boolean query is a function problem that takes as input a BID probabilistic database and asks the probability (a real number between 0 and 1) that q is true. The decision problem $\mathsf{CERTAINTY}(q)$, on the other hand, simply asks whether this probability is equal to 1.

In prior work [24], we introduced the (directed) attack graph of an acyclic query q, and showed that $\mathsf{CERTAINTY}(q)$ is first-order expressible if and only if q's attack graph is acyclic. In the current paper, we study attack graphs in more depth. We will classify cycles in attack graphs as either weak or strong. The main contributions can then be summarized as follows.

1. If the attack graph of an acyclic query q contains a strong cycle, then $\mathsf{CERTAINTY}(q)$ is $\mathbf{coNP}$-complete. This will be Theorem 2.

2. If the attack graph of an acyclic query q contains no strong cycle and all weak cycles are terminal (i.e., no edge leads from a vertex in the cycle to a vertex outside the cycle), then $\mathsf{CERTAINTY}(q)$ is in $\mathbf{P}$. This will be Theorem 3.

3. The only acyclic queries q not covered by the two preceding results have an attack graph with some non-terminal cycle and without a strong cycle. We provide evidence for the conjecture that $\mathsf{CERTAINTY}(q)$ is tractable for such queries. We show among others that $\mathsf{CERTAINTY}(q)$ is tractable for "cycle" queries q of the form $\exists^*(R_1(\underline{x_1}, x_2) \wedge R_2(\underline{x_2}, x_3) \wedge \cdots \wedge R_{k-1}(\underline{x_{k-1}}, x_k) \wedge R_k(\underline{x_k}, x_1))$. These queries arise in the work of Fuxman and Miller [10]. The case $k = 2$ was first solved in [23], but the case $k > 2$ was open and will be settled by Corollary 1.

4. Theorem 6 and its Corollary 2 will establish a relationship between the tractability frontiers of $\mathsf{CERTAINTY}(q)$ and query evaluation on probabilistic databases.

Our work significantly extends and generalizes known results in the literature.

The remainder of this paper is organized as follows. The next section further discusses related work. Section 3 defines the basic notions of certain conjunctive query answering. Section 4 defines the notion of attack graph. Sections 5 and 6 show our main intractability and tractability results respectively. Section 7 establishes a relationship between the complexities of $\mathsf{CERTAINTY}(q)$ and evaluating query q on probabilistic databases. Section 8 concludes the paper and raises challenges for future research.

2. MORE RELATED WORK

The investigation of $\mathsf{CERTAINTY}(q)$ was pioneered by Fuxman and Miller [9, 10], who defined a class of queries q for which $\mathsf{CERTAINTY}(q)$ is first-order expressible. This class has later on been extended by Wijsen [22, 24], who developed an effective method to decide whether $\mathsf{CERTAINTY}(q)$ is first-order expressible for acyclic queries q. In their conclusion, Fuxman and Miller [9, 10] stated as an open question whether there exist queries q, without self-join, such that $\mathsf{CERTAINTY}(q)$ is in $\mathbf{P}$ but not first-order expressible. The first example of such a query was identified by Wijsen [23]. The current paper identifies a large class of such queries (all acyclic queries with a cyclic attack graph in which all cycles are weak and terminal).

Kolaitis and Pema [13] recently showed that for every query q with exactly two atoms, $\mathsf{CERTAINTY}(q)$ is either in $\mathbf{P}$ or $\mathbf{coNP}$-complete, and it is decidable which of the two is the case.[1] If $\mathsf{CERTAINTY}(q)$ is in $\mathbf{P}$ and not first-order expressible, then it can be reduced in polynomial time to the problem of finding maximal (with respect to cardinality) independent sets of vertices in claw-free graphs. The latter problem can be solved in polynomial time by an ingenious algorithm of Minty [17]. Unfortunately, the proposed reduction is not applicable on queries with more than two atoms. Notice incidentally that our contributions mentioned in Section 1 cover all queries with exactly two atoms, because if q has exactly two atoms, then q is acyclic and all (there can be at most one) cycles in q's attack graph are terminal.

The counting variant of $\mathsf{CERTAINTY}(q)$, which has been denoted $\natural\mathsf{CERTAINTY}(q)$, takes as input an uncertain database $\mathbf{db}$ and asks to determine the number of repairs of $\mathbf{db}$ that satisfy query q. Maslowski and Wijsen [16] have recently showed that for every query q, the counting problem $\natural\mathsf{CERTAINTY}(q)$ is either in $\mathbf{FP}$ or $\natural\mathbf{P}$-complete, and it is decidable which of the two is the case.

As observed in Section 1, uncertain databases are a restricted case of block-independent-disjoint (BID) probabilistic databases [7, 8]. This observation will be elaborated in Section 7.

All aforementioned results assume queries without self-join. For queries q with self-joins, only fragmentary results about the complexity of $\mathsf{CERTAINTY}(q)$ are known [6, 21]. The extension to unions of conjunctive queries has been studied in [12].

[1] Recall from Section 1 that, unless specified otherwise, whenever we say "query" in the running text, we mean a Boolean conjunctive query without self-join.

3. PRELIMINARIES

We assume disjoint sets of *variables* and *constants*. If $\vec{x}$ is a sequence containing variables and constants, then $\mathsf{vars}(\vec{x})$ denotes the set of variables that occur in $\vec{x}$, and $|\vec{x}|$ denotes the length of $\vec{x}$.

Let U be a set of variables. A *valuation over* U is a total mapping θ from U to the set of constants. Such valuation θ is extended to be the identity on constants and on variables not in U.

Atoms and key-equal facts. Every *relation name* R has a fixed *signature*, which is a pair $[n, k]$ with $n \geq k \geq 1$: the integer n is the *arity* of the relation name and $\{1, 2, \ldots, k\}$ is the *primary key*. The relation name R is *all-key* if $n = k$. If R is a relation name with signature $[n, k]$, then $R(s_1, \ldots, s_n)$ is an R-*atom* (or simply atom), where each s_i is either a constant or a variable ($1 \leq i \leq n$). Such atom is commonly written as $R(\underline{\vec{x}}, \vec{y})$ where the primary key value $\vec{x} = s_1, \ldots, s_k$ is underlined and $\vec{y} = s_{k+1}, \ldots, s_n$. A *fact* is an atom in which no variable occurs. Two facts $R_1(\underline{\vec{a}_1}, \vec{b}_1), R_2(\underline{\vec{a}_2}, \vec{b}_2)$ are *key-equal* if $R_1 = R_2$ and $\vec{a}_1 = \vec{a}_2$.

We will use letters F, G, H, I for atoms, and A, B, C for facts of an uncertain database. For atom $F = R(\underline{\vec{x}}, \vec{y})$, we denote by $\mathsf{key}(F)$ the set of variables that occur in $\vec{x}$, and by $\mathsf{vars}(F)$ the set of variables that occur in F, that is, $\mathsf{key}(F) = \mathsf{vars}(\vec{x})$ and $\mathsf{vars}(F) = \mathsf{vars}(\vec{x}) \cup \mathsf{vars}(\vec{y})$.

Uncertain database, blocks, and repairs. A *database schema* is a finite set of *relation names*. All constructs that follow are defined relative to a fixed database schema.

An *uncertain database* is a finite set **db** of facts using only the relation names of the schema. A *block* of **db** is a maximal set of key-equal facts of **db**. If $A \in \mathbf{db}$, then $\mathsf{block}(A, \mathbf{db})$ denotes the block of **db** containing A. An uncertain database **db** is *consistent* if it does not contain two distinct facts that are key-equal (i.e., if every block of **db** is a singleton). A *repair* of **db** is a maximal (with respect to set containment) consistent subset of **db**.

Boolean conjunctive query. A *Boolean conjunctive query* is a finite set $q = \{R_1(\underline{\vec{x}_1}, \vec{y}_1), \ldots, R_n(\underline{\vec{x}_n}, \vec{y}_n)\}$ of atoms. By $\mathsf{vars}(q)$, we denote the set of variables that occur in q. The set q represents the first-order sentence

$$\exists u_1 \cdots \exists u_k \big(R_1(\underline{\vec{x}_1}, \vec{y}_1) \wedge \cdots \wedge R_n(\underline{\vec{x}_n}, \vec{y}_n)\big),$$

where $\{u_1, \ldots, u_k\} = \mathsf{vars}(q)$. The query q is *satisfied* by uncertain database **db**, denoted $\mathbf{db} \models q$, if there exists a valuation θ over $\mathsf{vars}(q)$ such that for each $i \in \{1, \ldots, n\}$, $R_i(\underline{\theta(\vec{x}_i)}, \theta(\vec{y}_i)) \in \mathbf{db}$. We say that q has a *self-join* if some relation name occurs more than once in q (i.e., if $R_i = R_j$ for some $1 \leq i < j \leq n$).

Since every relation name has a fixed signature, relevant primary key constraints are implicitly present in all queries; moreover, primary keys will be underlined.

Join tree and acyclic conjunctive query. The notions of join tree and acyclicity [2] are recalled next. A *join tree* for a conjunctive query q is an undirected tree whose vertices are the atoms of q such that the following condition is satisfied:

> *Connectedness Condition.* Whenever the same variable x occurs in two atoms F and G, then x occurs in each atom on the unique path linking F and G.

Commonly, an edge between atoms F and G is labeled by the (possibly empty) set $\mathsf{vars}(F) \cap \mathsf{vars}(G)$. The term *Connectedness Condition* appears in [11] and refers to the fact that the set of vertices in which x occurs induces a connected subtree. A conjunctive query q is *acyclic* if it has a join tree. The symbol τ will be used for join trees. We write $F \overset{L}{\frown} G$ to denote an edge between F and G with label L. A join tree is shown in Fig. 2 (left).

Certain query answering. Given a Boolean conjunctive query q, $\mathsf{CERTAINTY}(q)$ is (the complexity of) the following set.

$$\mathsf{CERTAINTY}(q) = \{\mathbf{db} \mid \mathbf{db} \text{ is an uncertain database such that every repair of } \mathbf{db} \text{ satisfies } q\}$$

$\mathsf{CERTAINTY}(q)$ is said to be *first-order expressible* if there exists a first-order sentence φ such that for every uncertain database **db**, $\mathbf{db} \in \mathsf{CERTAINTY}(q)$ if and only if $\mathbf{db} \models \varphi$. The formula φ, if it exists, is called a *consistent first-order rewriting of* q.

Purified uncertain databases. Let q be a Boolean conjunctive query. An uncertain database **db** is said to be *purified relative to* q if for every fact $A \in \mathbf{db}$, there exists a valuation θ over $\mathsf{vars}(q)$ such that $A \in \theta(q) \subseteq \mathbf{db}$. Intuitively, every fact in a purified uncertain database is relevant for the query. This notion of purified database is new and illustrated next.

Example 1. If $\mathbf{db} = \{R(\underline{a}, b), S(\underline{b}, a), S(\underline{b}, c)\}$, then **db** is not purified relative to the query $\{R(\underline{x}, y), S(\underline{y}, x)\}$ because **db** contains no R-fact that "joins" with $S(\underline{b}, c)$.

The following lemma implies that in the study of tractability of $\mathsf{CERTAINTY}(q)$, we can assume without loss of generality that uncertain databases are purified; this assumption will simplify the technical treatment. Notice that the query q in the lemma's statement is not required to be acyclic.

LEMMA 1. *Let q be a Boolean conjunctive query. Let $\mathbf{db}_0$ be an uncertain database. It is possible to compute in polynomial time an uncertain database* **db** *that is purified relative to q such that $\mathbf{db} \in \mathsf{CERTAINTY}(q)$ if and only if $\mathbf{db}_0 \in \mathsf{CERTAINTY}(q)$.*

4. ATTACK GRAPH

The primary key of an atom F gives rise to a functional dependency among the variables that occur in F. For example, $R(\underline{x, y}, z, u)$ gives rise to $\{x, y\} \rightarrow \{x, y, z, u\}$, which will be abbreviated as $xy \rightarrow xyzu$ (and which is equivalent to $xy \rightarrow zu$). The set $\mathcal{K}(q)$ defined next collects all functional dependencies that arise in atoms of q.

Definition 1. Let q be a Boolean conjunctive query. We define $\mathcal{K}(q)$ as the following set of functional dependencies.

$$\mathcal{K}(q) = \{\mathsf{key}(F) \rightarrow \mathsf{vars}(F) \mid F \in q\}$$

Concerning the following definition, recall from relational database theory [20, page 387] that if Σ is a set of functional dependencies over a set U of attributes and $X \subseteq U$, then the attribute closure of X (with respect to Σ) is the set $\{A \in U \mid \Sigma \models X \rightarrow A\}$.

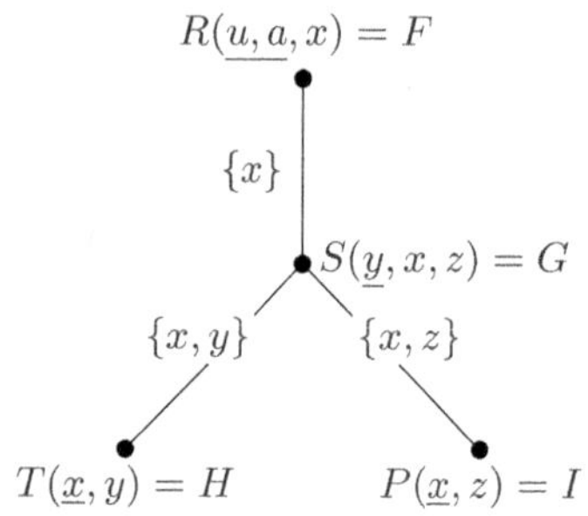

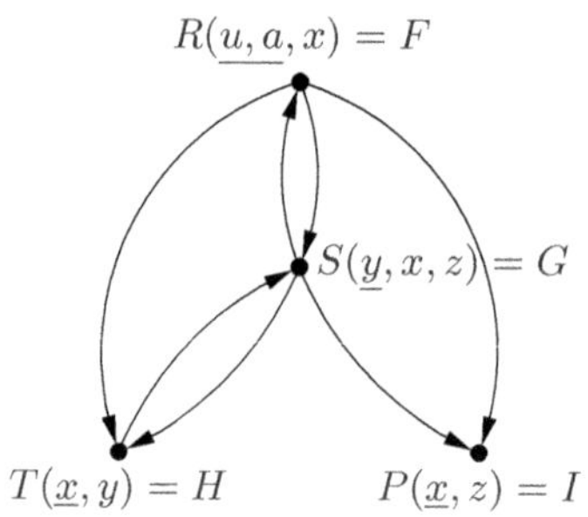

Figure 2: Join tree (left) and attack graph (right) of query q_1. The attack from G to F is strong. All other attacks are weak.

Definition 2. Let q be a Boolean conjunctive query. For every $F \in q$, we define $F^{+,q}$ as the following set of variables.

$$F^{+,q} = \{x \in \mathsf{vars}(q) \mid \mathcal{K}(q \setminus \{F\}) \models \mathsf{key}(F) \rightarrow x\}$$

In words, $F^{+,q}$ is the attribute closure of the set $\mathsf{key}(F)$ with respect to the set of functional dependencies that arise in the atoms of $q \setminus \{F\}$. Note that variables play the role of attributes in our framework.

Example 2. A join tree for the query $q_1 = \{R(\underline{u}, a, x), S(\underline{y}, x, z), T(\underline{x}, y), P(\underline{x}, z)\}$, where a is a constant, is shown in Fig. 2 (left). To shorten notation, let $F = R(\underline{u}, a, x)$, $G = S(\underline{y}, x, z)$, $H = T(\underline{x}, y)$, and $I = P(\underline{x}, z)$, as indicated in the figure. We have the following.

$$\mathcal{K}(q_1 \setminus \{F\}) = \{y \rightarrow xyz, x \rightarrow xy, x \rightarrow xz\}$$
$$\mathsf{key}(F) = \{u\} \text{ and } F^{+,q_1} = \{u\}$$

$$\mathcal{K}(q_1 \setminus \{G\}) = \{u \rightarrow ux, x \rightarrow xy, x \rightarrow xz\}$$
$$\mathsf{key}(G) = \{y\} \text{ and } G^{+,q_1} = \{y\}$$

$$\mathcal{K}(q_1 \setminus \{H\}) = \{u \rightarrow ux, y \rightarrow xyz, x \rightarrow xz\}$$
$$\mathsf{key}(H) = \{x\} \text{ and } H^{+,q_1} = \{x, z\}$$

$$\mathcal{K}(q_1 \setminus \{I\}) = \{u \rightarrow ux, y \rightarrow xyz, x \rightarrow xy\}$$
$$\mathsf{key}(I) = \{x\} \text{ and } I^{+,q_1} = \{x, y, z\}$$

Definition 3. Let q be an acyclic Boolean conjunctive query. Let τ be a join tree for q. The *attack graph* of τ is a directed graph whose vertices are the atoms of q. There is a directed edge from F to G if F, G are distinct atoms such that for every label L on the unique path that links F and G in τ, we have $L \nsubseteq F^{+,q}$.

We write $F \overset{\tau}{\rightsquigarrow} G$ if the attack graph of τ contains a directed edge from F to G. The directed edge $F \overset{\tau}{\rightsquigarrow} G$ is also called an *attack from F to G*. If $F \overset{\tau}{\rightsquigarrow} G$, we say that F *attacks* G (or that G is attacked by F).

Example 3. This is a continuation of Example 2. Figure 2 (left) shows a join tree τ_1 for query q_1. The attack graph of τ_1 is shown in Fig. 2 (right) and is computed as follows.

Let us first compute the attacks outgoing from F. The path from F to G in the join tree is $F \overset{\{x\}}{\frown} G$. Since the label $\{x\}$ is not contained in F^{+,q_1}, the attack graph contains a directed edge from F to G, i.e., $F \overset{\tau_1}{\rightsquigarrow} G$. The path from F to H in the join tree is $F \overset{\{x\}}{\frown} G \overset{\{x,y\}}{\frown} H$. Since no label on that path is contained in F^{+,q_1}, the attack graph contains a directed edge from F to H. In the same way, one finds that F attacks I.

Let us next compute the attacks outgoing from H. The path from H to G in the join tree is $H \overset{\{x,y\}}{\frown} G$. Since the label $\{x, y\}$ is not contained in G^{+,q_1}, the attack graph contains a directed edge from H to G, .i.e., $H \overset{\tau_1}{\rightsquigarrow} G$. The path from H to F in the join tree is $H \overset{\{x,y\}}{\frown} G \overset{\{x\}}{\frown} F$. Since the label $\{x\}$ is contained in H^{+,q_1}, the attack graph contains no directed edge from H to F. And so on. The complete attack graph is shown in Fig. 2 (right).

Remarkably, it was shown in [24] that if τ_1 and τ_2 are distinct join trees for the same acyclic query q, then the attack graph of τ_1 is identical to the attack graph of τ_2. This motivates the following definition.

Definition 4. Let q be an acyclic Boolean conjunctive query. The attack graph of q is the attack graph of τ for any join tree τ for q. We write $F \overset{q}{\rightsquigarrow} G$ (or simply $F \rightsquigarrow G$ if q is clear from the context) to indicate that the attack graph of q contains a directed edge from F to G. We write $F \overset{q}{\not\rightsquigarrow} G$ if it is not the case that $F \overset{q}{\rightsquigarrow} G$.

The attack graph of an acyclic query q can be computed in quadratic time in the length of q [24]. Figures 4 and 5 show attack graphs, but omit join trees. The main result in [24] is the following.

THEOREM 1 ([24]). *The following are equivalent for all acyclic Boolean conjunctive queries q without self-join:*

1. *The attack graph of q is acyclic.*
2. $\mathsf{CERTAINTY}(q)$ *is first-order expressible.*

Finally, we provide two lemmas that will be useful later on.

LEMMA 2. *Let q be an acyclic Boolean conjunctive query. Let F, G be distinct atoms of q. If $F \rightsquigarrow G$, then $\mathsf{key}(G) \nsubseteq F^{+,q}$ and $\mathsf{vars}(F) \nsubseteq F^{+,q}$.*

LEMMA 3 ([24]). *Let q be an acyclic Boolean conjunctive query. Let F, G, H be distinct atoms of q. If $F \rightsquigarrow G$ and $G \rightsquigarrow H$, then $F \rightsquigarrow H$ or $G \rightsquigarrow F$.*

5. INTRACTABILITY

The following definition classifies cycles in attack graphs as either strong or weak. The main result of this section is that CERTAINTY(q) is **coNP**-complete for acyclic queries q whose attack graph contains a strong cycle.

Definition 5. Let q be an acyclic Boolean conjunctive query. For every $F \in q$, we define $F^{\boxplus,q}$ as the following set of variables.

$$F^{\boxplus,q} = \{x \in \mathsf{vars}(q) \mid \mathcal{K}(q) \models \mathsf{key}(F) \to x\}$$

An attack $F \rightsquigarrow G$ in the attack graph of q is called *weak* if $\mathsf{key}(G) \subseteq F^{\boxplus,q}$. An attack that is not weak, is called *strong*.

A (directed) *cycle of size n* in the attack graph of q is a sequence of edges $F_0 \rightsquigarrow F_1 \rightsquigarrow F_2 \rightsquigarrow \cdots \rightsquigarrow F_{n-1} \rightsquigarrow F_0$ such that $i \neq j$ implies $F_i \neq F_j$. Thus, *cycle* means elementary cycle.

A cycle in the attack graph of q is called *strong* if at least one attack in the cycle is strong. A cycle that is not strong, is called *weak*.

It is straightforward that $F^{+,q} \subseteq F^{\boxplus,q}$.

Example 4. For the query q_1 in Fig. 2, we have the following.

$$\begin{aligned}
\mathcal{K}(q_1) &= \{u \to ux, y \to xyz, x \to xy, x \to xz\} \\
F^{\boxplus,q_1} &= \{u, x, y, z\} \\
G^{\boxplus,q_1} &= \{x, y, z\} \\
H^{\boxplus,q_1} &= \{x, y, z\} \\
I^{\boxplus,q_1} &= \{x, y, z\}
\end{aligned}$$

The attack $F \overset{q_1}{\rightsquigarrow} G$ is weak, because $\mathsf{key}(G) = \{y\} \subseteq F^{\boxplus,q_1}$. The attack $G \overset{q_1}{\rightsquigarrow} F$ is strong, because $\mathsf{key}(F) = \{u\} \not\subseteq G^{\boxplus,q_1}$. One can verify that the attack from G to F is the only strong attack in the attack graph of q_1.

The attack cycle $G \overset{q_1}{\rightsquigarrow} H \overset{q_1}{\rightsquigarrow} G$ is weak. The attack cycle $F \overset{q_1}{\rightsquigarrow} G \overset{q_1}{\rightsquigarrow} F$ is strong, because it contains the strong attack $G \overset{q_1}{\rightsquigarrow} F$. For the same reason, the attack cycle $F \overset{q_1}{\rightsquigarrow} H \overset{q_1}{\rightsquigarrow} G \overset{q_1}{\rightsquigarrow} F$ is strong.

Example 4 showed that the attack graph of q_1 has a strong cycle of length 3, and a strong cycle of length 2. This is no coincidence, as stated by the following lemma.

LEMMA 4. *Let q be an acyclic Boolean conjunctive query. If the attack graph of q contains a strong cycle, then it contains a strong cycle of length 2.*

The following proof establishes that for every acyclic query q whose attack graph contains a strong cycle, there exists a polynomial-time many-one reduction from CERTAINTY(q_0) to CERTAINTY(q), where $q_0 = \{R_0(\underline{x}, y), S_0(\underline{y, z}, x)\}$. Since CERTAINTY($q_0$) was proved **coNP**-hard by Kolaitis and Pema [13], we obtain the desired **coNP**-hard lower bound for CERTAINTY(q). As the proof is rather involved, we provide in Fig. 3 a mnemonic for the construction in the beginning of the proof. To further improve readability, some parts of the proof will be stated as sublemmas.

THEOREM 2. *Let q be an acyclic Boolean conjunctive query without self-join. If the attack graph of q contains a strong cycle, then* CERTAINTY(q) *is* **coNP**-*complete.*

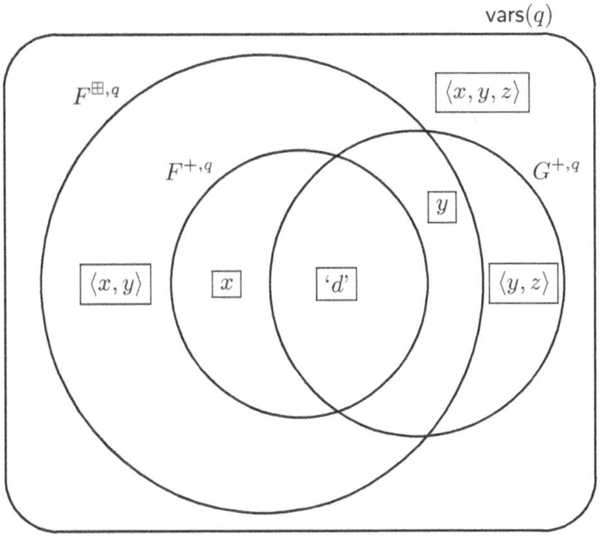

Figure 3: Help for the proof of Theorem 2.

PROOF. Since CERTAINTY(q) is obviously in **coNP**, it suffices to show that it is **coNP**-hard. Assume that the attack graph of q contains a strong cycle. By Lemma 4, we can assume $F, G \in q$ such that $F \rightsquigarrow G \rightsquigarrow F$ and the attack $F \rightsquigarrow G$ is strong. For every valuation θ over $\{x, y, z\}$, we define $\widehat{\theta}$ as the following valuation over $\mathsf{vars}(q)$.

1. If $u \in F^{+,q} \cap G^{+,q}$, then $\widehat{\theta}(u) =$ 'd' for some fixed constant d;
2. if $u \in F^{+,q} \setminus G^{+,q}$, then $\widehat{\theta}(u) = \theta(x)$;
3. if $u \in G^{+,q} \setminus F^{\boxplus,q}$, then $\widehat{\theta}(u) = \langle\theta(y), \theta(z)\rangle$;
4. if $u \in \left(G^{+,q} \cap F^{\boxplus,q}\right) \setminus F^{+,q}$, then $\widehat{\theta}(u) = \theta(y)$;
5. if $u \in F^{\boxplus,q} \setminus \left(F^{+,q} \cup G^{+,q}\right)$, then $\widehat{\theta}(u) = \langle\theta(x), \theta(y)\rangle$; and
6. if $u \notin F^{\boxplus,q} \cup G^{+,q}$, then $\widehat{\theta}(u) = \langle\theta(x), \theta(y), \theta(z)\rangle$.

Notice that $\widehat{\theta}(u)$ can be a sequence of length two or three; two sequences of the same length are equal if they contain the same elements in the same order. The Venn diagram of Fig. 3 will come in handy: every region contains a boxed label that indicates how $\widehat{\theta}(u)$ is computed for variables u in that region. For example, assume u belongs to the region with label $\langle x, y\rangle$ (i.e., $u \in F^{\boxplus,q} \setminus (F^{+,q} \cup G^{+,q})$), then $\widehat{\theta}(u) = \langle\theta(x), \theta(y)\rangle$.

We show three sublemmas that will be used later on in the proof.

SUBLEMMA 1. *Let θ_1, θ_2 be two valuations over $\{x, y, z\}$. If $H \in q$ such that $F \neq H \neq G$, then $\{\widehat{\theta_1}(H), \widehat{\theta_2}(H)\}$ is consistent.*

PROOF OF SUBLEMMA 1. Let $H \in q$ such that $F \neq H \neq G$. Assume the following.

$$\text{For every } u \in \mathsf{key}(H), \widehat{\theta_1}(u) = \widehat{\theta_2}(u). \tag{1}$$

It suffices to show the following.

$$\text{For every } u \in \mathsf{vars}(H), \widehat{\theta_1}(u) = \widehat{\theta_2}(u). \tag{2}$$

We consider four cases.

Case $\theta_1(x) = \theta_2(x)$ and $\theta_1(y) = \theta_2(y)$. If $\theta_1(z) = \theta_2(z)$, then $\theta_1 = \theta_2$, and (2) holds vacuously. Assume next $\theta_1(z) \neq \theta_2(z)$. Then it follows from (1) that no variable of $\mathsf{key}(H)$ belongs to a region of the Venn diagram (see Fig. 3) that contains z. Since z occurs in all regions outside $F^{\boxplus,q}$, we conclude $\mathsf{key}(H) \subseteq F^{\boxplus,q}$. Since $\mathcal{K}(q)$ contains $\mathsf{key}(H) \rightarrow \mathsf{vars}(H)$, it follows $\mathsf{vars}(H) \subseteq F^{\boxplus,q}$. Since z does not occur inside $F^{\boxplus,q}$ in the Venn diagram, we conclude (2).

Case $\theta_1(x) = \theta_2(x)$ and $\theta_1(y) \neq \theta_2(y)$. By (1), no variable of $\mathsf{key}(H)$ belongs to a region of the Venn diagram that contains y. It follows $\mathsf{key}(H) \subseteq F^{+,q}$. Consequently, $\mathsf{vars}(H) \subseteq F^{+,q}$. Since neither y nor z occurs inside $F^{+,q}$ in the Venn diagram, we conclude (2).

Case $\theta_1(x) \neq \theta_2(x)$ and $\theta_1(y) = \theta_2(y)$. First assume $\theta_1(z) = \theta_2(z)$. By (1), no variable of $\mathsf{key}(H)$ belongs to a region of the Venn diagram that contains x. Consequently, $\mathsf{key}(H) \subseteq G^{+,q}$. It follows $\mathsf{vars}(H) \subseteq G^{+,q}$. Since x does not occur inside $G^{+,q}$ in the Venn diagram, we conclude (2).

Next assume $\theta_1(z) \neq \theta_2(z)$. By (1), no variable of $\mathsf{key}(H)$ belongs to a region of the Venn diagram that contains x or z. Consequently, $\mathsf{key}(H) \subseteq F^{\boxplus,q} \cap G^{+,q}$. It follows $\mathsf{vars}(H) \subseteq F^{\boxplus,q} \cap G^{+,q}$. Since neither x nor z occurs inside $F^{\boxplus,q} \cap G^{+,q}$ in the Venn diagram, we conclude (2).

Case $\theta_1(x) \neq \theta_2(x)$ and $\theta_1(y) \neq \theta_2(y)$. By (1), no variable of $\mathsf{key}(H)$ belongs to a region of the Venn diagram that contains x or y. Consequently, $\mathsf{key}(H) \subseteq F^{+,q} \cap G^{+,q}$. It follows $\mathsf{vars}(H) \subseteq F^{+,q} \cap G^{+,q}$. Since none of x, y, or z occurs inside $F^{+,q} \cap G^{+,q}$ in the Venn diagram, we conclude (2). This concludes the proof of Sublemma 1. □

SUBLEMMA 2. *Let θ_1, θ_2 be two valuations over $\{x, y, z\}$.*

1. *$\widehat{\theta_1}(F)$ and $\widehat{\theta_2}(F)$ are key-equal $\iff \theta_1(x) = \theta_2(x)$.*
2. *$\widehat{\theta_1}(F) = \widehat{\theta_2}(F) \iff \theta_1(x) = \theta_2(x)$ and $\theta_1(y) = \theta_2(y)$.*

SUBLEMMA 3. *Let θ_1, θ_2 be two valuations over $\{x, y, z\}$.*

1. *$\widehat{\theta_1}(G)$ and $\widehat{\theta_2}(G)$ are key-equal $\iff \theta_1(y) = \theta_2(y)$ and $\theta_1(z) = \theta_2(z)$.*
2. *$\widehat{\theta_1}(G) = \widehat{\theta_2}(G) \iff \theta_1 = \theta_2$.*

We continue the proof of Theorem 2. Let $q_0 = \{R_0(\underline{x}, y), S_0(\underline{y, z}, x)\}$. The signatures of R_0 and S_0 are [2, 1] and [3, 2] respectively. Let $F_0 = R_0(\underline{x}, y)$ and $G_0 = S_0(\underline{y, z}, x)$. In the remainder of the proof, we establish a polynomial-time many-one reduction from $\mathsf{CERTAINTY}(q_0)$ to $\mathsf{CERTAINTY}(q)$. **coNP**-hardness of $\mathsf{CERTAINTY}(q)$ then follows from **coNP**-hardness of $\mathsf{CERTAINTY}(q_0)$, which was established in [13].

Let $\mathbf{db}_0$ be an uncertain database. By Lemma 1, we can assume that $\mathbf{db}_0$ is purified relative to q_0. Let $\mathcal{V}$ be the set of valuations θ over $\{x, y, z\}$ such that $\theta(q_0) \subseteq \mathbf{db}_0$. Since $\mathbf{db}_0$ is purified, the following holds.

$$\mathbf{db}_0 = \{\theta(F_0) \mid \theta \in \mathcal{V}\} \cup \{\theta(G_0) \mid \theta \in \mathcal{V}\}$$

Let $\mathbf{db} = \{\widehat{\theta}(H) \mid H \in q, \theta \in \mathcal{V}\}$. Since $\mathcal{V}$ can be computed in polynomial time in the size of $\mathbf{db}_0$, the reduction from $\mathbf{db}_0$ to $\mathbf{db}$ is in polynomial time. Since q contains no self-join, the set $\mathbf{db}$ is partitioned by the three disjoint subsets defined next.

$$\begin{aligned}\mathbf{db}_F &= \{\widehat{\theta}(F) \mid \theta \in \mathcal{V}\}\\ \mathbf{db}_G &= \{\widehat{\theta}(G) \mid \theta \in \mathcal{V}\}\\ \mathbf{db}_{\mathsf{rest}} &= \{\widehat{\theta}(H) \mid H \in q, F \neq H \neq G, \theta \in \mathcal{V}\}\end{aligned}$$

Since $\mathbf{db}_{\mathsf{rest}}$ is consistent by Sublemma 1, every repair of $\mathbf{db}$ is the disjoint union of $\mathbf{db}_{\mathsf{rest}}$, a repair of $\mathbf{db}_F$, and a repair of $\mathbf{db}_G$. In the next step of the proof, we establish a one-to-one relationship between repairs of $\mathbf{db}_0$ and repairs of $\mathbf{db}$.

The function map will map repairs of $\mathbf{db}_0$ to repairs of $\mathbf{db}$. For every repair $\mathbf{r}_0$ of $\mathbf{db}_0$, $\mathsf{map}(\mathbf{r}_0)$ is the disjoint union of three sets, as follows.

$$\begin{aligned}\mathsf{map}(\mathbf{r}_0) = &\quad \{\widehat{\theta}(F) \mid \theta(F_0) \in \mathbf{r}_0, \theta \in \mathcal{V}\}\\ &\cup \{\widehat{\theta}(G) \mid \theta(G_0) \in \mathbf{r}_0, \theta \in \mathcal{V}\}\\ &\cup \mathbf{db}_{\mathsf{rest}}\end{aligned}$$

Clearly, the first of these three sets is contained in $\mathbf{db}_F$, and the second in $\mathbf{db}_G$. By Sublemmas 2 and 3, for every $\theta \in \mathcal{V}$,

$$\theta(F_0) \in \mathbf{r}_0 \iff \widehat{\theta}(F) \in \mathsf{map}(\mathbf{r}_0) \tag{3}$$

$$\theta(G_0) \in \mathbf{r}_0 \iff \widehat{\theta}(G) \in \mathsf{map}(\mathbf{r}_0) \tag{4}$$

To prove the $\Longleftarrow$-direction of (3) (the other implications are straightforward), assume $A \in \mathsf{map}(\mathbf{r}_0)$ with $A = \widehat{\theta}(F)$. By the definition of map, we can assume $\theta' \in \mathcal{V}$ such that $\theta'(F_0) \in \mathbf{r}_0$ and $\widehat{\theta'}(F) = A$. From $\widehat{\theta}(F) = \widehat{\theta'}(F)$, it follows by Sublemma 2 that $\theta(F_0) = \theta'(F_0)$, hence $\theta(F_0) \in \mathbf{r}_0$.

The following sublemma states that map is a bijection from the set of repairs of $\mathbf{db}_0$ to the set of repairs of $\mathbf{db}$.

SUBLEMMA 4. 1. *If $\mathbf{r}_0$ is a repair of $\mathbf{db}_0$, then $\mathsf{map}(\mathbf{r}_0)$ is a repair of $\mathbf{db}$.*

2. *For every repair $\mathbf{r}$ of $\mathbf{db}$, there exists a repair $\mathbf{r}_0$ of $\mathbf{db}_0$ such that $\mathbf{r} = \mathsf{map}(\mathbf{r}_0)$.*
3. *If $\mathbf{r}_0, \mathbf{r}_0'$ are distinct repairs of $\mathbf{db}_0$, then $\mathsf{map}(\mathbf{r}_0) \neq \mathsf{map}(\mathbf{r}_0')$.*

To conclude the proof of Theorem 2, we show:

$$\mathbf{db}_0 \in \mathsf{CERTAINTY}(q_0) \iff \mathbf{db} \in \mathsf{CERTAINTY}(q).$$

By Sublemma 4, it is sufficient to prove that for every repair $\mathbf{r}_0$ of $\mathbf{db}_0$,

$$\mathbf{r}_0 \models q_0 \iff \mathsf{map}(\mathbf{r}_0) \models q.$$

$\boxed{\Longrightarrow}$ Assume $\mathbf{r}_0 \models q_0$. We can assume $\theta \in \mathcal{V}$ such that $\theta(q_0) \subseteq \mathbf{r}_0$. Obviously, $\widehat{\theta}(q) \subseteq \mathsf{map}(\mathbf{r}_0)$.

$\boxed{\Longleftarrow}$ Assume $\mathsf{map}(\mathbf{r}_0) \models q$. We can assume a valuation μ over $\mathsf{vars}(q)$ such that $\mu(q) \subseteq \mathsf{map}(\mathbf{r}_0)$.

Let τ be a join tree for q. Let $H_0 \overset{L_1}{\frown} H_1 \cdots \overset{L_\ell}{\frown} H_\ell$ be the unique path in τ between F and G, where $H_0 = F$ and $H_\ell = G$. For $i \in \{0, \ldots, \ell\}$, we can assume $\theta_i \in \mathcal{V}$ such that $\mu(H_i) = \widehat{\theta_i}(H_i) \in \mathsf{map}(\mathbf{r}_0)$. Let $i \in \{0, \ldots, \ell - 1\}$. We show $\theta_i(x) = \theta_{i+1}(x)$ and $\theta_i(y) = \theta_{i+1}(y)$. Since $F \rightsquigarrow G \rightsquigarrow F$, the label L_i contains a variable u_i such that $u_i \notin F^{+,q}$ and a variable w_i such that $w_i \notin G^{+,q}$ (possibly $u_i = w_i$).

Since $u_i \in \mathsf{vars}(H_i) \cap \mathsf{vars}(H_{i+1})$, it must be the case that $\widehat{\theta_i}(u_i) = \mu(u_i) = \widehat{\theta_{i+1}}(u_i)$. Since y occurs in every region

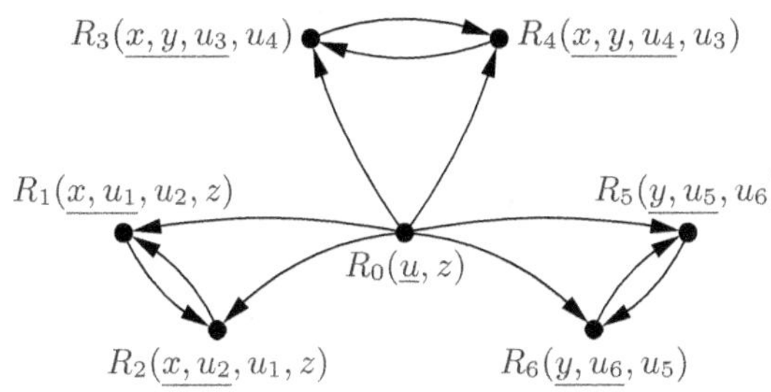

Figure 4: Attack graph. All cycles are weak and terminal.

outside $F^{+,q}$ in the Venn diagram (Fig. 3) and $u_i \notin F^{+,q}$, it is correct to conclude $\theta_i(y) = \theta_{i+1}(y)$.

Likewise, since $w_i \in \mathsf{vars}(H_i) \cap \mathsf{vars}(H_{i+1})$, it must be the case that $\widehat{\theta_i}(w_i) = \mu(w_i) = \widehat{\theta_{i+1}}(w_i)$. Since x occurs in every region outside $G^{+,q}$ in the Venn diagram and $w_i \notin G^{+,q}$, it is correct to conclude $\theta_i(x) = \theta_{i+1}(x)$.

Consequently, $\theta_0(x) = \theta_\ell(x)$ and $\theta_0(y) = \theta_\ell(y)$. From $\widehat{\theta_0}(H_0), \widehat{\theta_\ell}(H_\ell) \in \mathsf{map}(\mathbf{r}_0)$, $H_0 = F$, and $H_\ell = G$, it follows $\theta_0(F_0), \theta_\ell(G_0) \in \mathbf{r}_0$ by (3) and (4). Since θ_0 and θ_ℓ agree on each variable in $\mathsf{vars}(F_0) \cap \mathsf{vars}(G_0) = \{x, y\}$, it follows $\mathbf{r}_0 \models q_0$. This concludes the proof of Theorem 2. □

6. TRACTABILITY

We conjecture that if the attack graph of an acyclic query q contains no strong cycle, then $\mathsf{CERTAINTY}(q)$ is in **P**.

CONJECTURE 1. *Let q be an acyclic Boolean conjunctive query without self-join. If all cycles in the attack graph of q are weak, then* $\mathsf{CERTAINTY}(q)$ *is in* **P**.

Notice that by Theorem 1, we know that Conjecture 1 holds in the special case where q's attack graph contains no cycle at all. Theorem 2 and Conjecture 1 together imply that for every acyclic query q, $\mathsf{CERTAINTY}(q)$ is either in **P** or **coNP**-complete. In the following section, a somewhat weaker version of Conjecture 1 is proved (Theorem 3).

6.1 All Cycles are Weak and Terminal

We show a weaker version of Conjecture 1. In this weaker version, the premise "all cycles are weak" is strengthened into "all cycles are weak and terminal."

Definition 6. A cycle in a directed graph is called *terminal* if the graph contains no directed edge from a vertex in the cycle to a vertex outside the cycle. A cycle is *nonterminal* if it is not terminal.

Example 5. Figure 4 shows the attack graph of the acyclic query $\{R_1(\underline{x, u_1}, u_2, z),\ R_2(\underline{x, u_2}, u_1, z),\ R_3(\underline{x, y, u_3}, u_4),\ R_4(\underline{x, y, u_4}, u_3),\ R_5(\underline{y, u_5}, u_6),\ R_6(\underline{y, u_6}, u_5)\}$. All attack cycles are terminal and weak.

Example 6. In the attack graph of Fig. 5, all cycles are weak, but no cycle is terminal.

THEOREM 3. *Let q be an acyclic Boolean conjunctive query without self-join. If all cycles in the attack graph of q are weak and terminal, then* $\mathsf{CERTAINTY}(q)$ *is in* **P**.

Notice that if a query q has exactly two atoms, then q is acyclic and every cycle in q's attack graph must be terminal. Therefore Theorems 2 and 3 together imply the dichotomy theorem of Kolaitis and Pema [13].

To prove Theorem 3, we need four helping lemmas. In simple words, the first lemma states that if we replace a variable with a constant in an acyclic query, then no new attacks are generated, and weak attacks cannot become strong.

Definition 7. Let q be a Boolean conjunctive query. If $\vec{x} = \langle x_1, \ldots, x_\ell \rangle$ is a sequence of distinct variables and $\vec{a} = \langle a_1, \ldots, a_\ell \rangle$ a sequence of constants, then $q_{[\vec{x} \mapsto \vec{a}]}$ denotes the query obtained from q by replacing each occurrence of x_i with a_i, for all $i \in \{1, \ldots, \ell\}$. If θ is a valuation, then $\theta_{[\vec{x} \mapsto \vec{a}]}$ is the valuation such that $\theta_{[\vec{x} \mapsto \vec{a}]}(\vec{x}) = \vec{a}$ and $\theta_{[\vec{x} \mapsto \vec{a}]}(y) = \theta(y)$ if $y \notin \mathsf{vars}(\vec{x})$.

LEMMA 5. *Let q be an acyclic Boolean conjunctive query without self-join. Let $F, G \in q$. Let $z \in \mathsf{vars}(q)$ and let c be a constant. Let $q' = q_{[z \mapsto c]}$, $F' = F_{[z \mapsto c]}$, and $G' = G_{[z \mapsto c]}$. Then, the following hold.*

1. *q' is acyclic.*
2. *If $F' \overset{q'}{\rightsquigarrow} G'$, then $F \overset{q}{\rightsquigarrow} G$.*
3. *If $F' \overset{q'}{\rightsquigarrow} G'$ and $F \overset{q}{\rightsquigarrow} G$ is a weak attack, then $F' \overset{q'}{\rightsquigarrow} G'$ is a weak attack.*

LEMMA 6. *Let q be an acyclic Boolean conjunctive query. If each cycle in the attack graph of q is terminal, then each cycle in the attack graph has length 2.*

LEMMA 7. *Let q be an acyclic Boolean conjunctive query such that each cycle in the attack graph of q is terminal and each atom of q belongs to a cycle of the attack graph.*

1. *If the same variable x occurs in two distinct cycles of the attack graph, then for each atom F in these cycles, $x \in \mathsf{key}(F)$.*
2. *If $F \overset{q}{\rightsquigarrow} G$ is a weak attack, then $\mathsf{key}(G) \subseteq \mathsf{vars}(F)$.*

The following lemma applies to queries with an atom whose primary key contains no variables.

LEMMA 8. *Let q be a Boolean conjunctive query without self-join. Let $F \in q$ such that $\mathsf{key}(F) = \emptyset$. Let $q' = q \setminus \{F\}$. Let $\vec{y}$ be a sequence of distinct variables such that $\mathsf{vars}(\vec{y}) = \mathsf{vars}(F)$. Let* **db** *be an uncertain database that is purified relative to q, and let D be the active domain of* **db**. *Then the following are equivalent:*

1. **db** $\in \mathsf{CERTAINTY}(q)$.
2. **db** $\neq \emptyset$ *and for all $\vec{b} \in D^{|\vec{y}|}$, if $F_{[\vec{y} \mapsto \vec{b}]} \in$* **db**, *then* **db** $\in \mathsf{CERTAINTY}(q'_{[\vec{y} \mapsto \vec{b}]})$.

The proof of Theorem 3 can now be given.

PROOF OF THEOREM 3. Given uncertain database **db**, we need to show that it can be decided in polynomial time (in the size of **db**) whether **db** $\in \mathsf{CERTAINTY}(q)$. Let D be the active domain of **db**. By Lemma 1, we can assume that **db** is purified relative to q.

The proof runs by induction on the length of q. For the base of the induction, we consider the case where the attack graph of q contains no unattacked atom (i.e., no atom has zero indegree). $\mathsf{CERTAINTY}(q)$ is obviously in $\mathbf{P}$ if $q = \{\}$. Assume next that q is nonempty.

Since all cycles of q's attack graph are terminal and every atom has an incoming attack, every atom of q belongs to some cycle of the attack graph. By Lemma 6, the attack graph of q is a set of disjoint weak cycles $F_1 \rightsquigarrow G_1 \rightsquigarrow F_1, \dots, F_\ell \rightsquigarrow G_\ell \rightsquigarrow F_\ell$ for some $\ell \geq 1$. For $i \in \{1, \dots, \ell\}$, let $q_i = \{F_i, G_i\}$, and let $\vec{x}_i$ be a sequence of distinct variables that contains every variable $x \in \mathsf{vars}(q_i)$ such that for some $j \neq i$, $x \in \mathsf{vars}(q_j)$. By Lemma 7, $\mathsf{vars}(\vec{x}_i) \subseteq \mathsf{key}(F_i) \cap \mathsf{key}(G_i)$.

For $i \in \{1, \dots, \ell\}$, let $\mathbf{db}_i$ be the subset of $\mathbf{db}$ containing every fact A with the same relation name as F_i or G_i. Call a *partition* of $\mathbf{db}_i$ a maximal subset P of $\mathbf{db}_i$ such that for some $\vec{a} \in D^{|\vec{x}_i|}$, for all $A \in P$, there exists a valuation θ such that $A = \theta_{[\vec{x}_i \mapsto \vec{a}]}(F_i)$ or $A = \theta_{[\vec{x}_i \mapsto \vec{a}]}(G_i)$. The sequence $\vec{a}$ is called the *vector* of partition P.

In words, each partition of $\mathbf{db}_i$ groups facts that can be obtained from F_i or G_i by replacing the variables of $\vec{x}_i$ with the same fixed constants. For example, the attack graph in Fig. 4 contains an attack cycle involving $R_3(\underline{x, y, u_3}, u_4)$ and $R_4(\underline{x, y, u_4}, u_3)$. The sequence $\langle x, y \rangle$ contains the variables that also occur in other cycles. The facts $R_3(\underline{a, b, c}, d)$ and $R_4(\underline{a, b, e}, f)$ both belong to the partition with vector $\langle a, b \rangle$.

Clearly, two facts that belong to distinct partitions of $\mathbf{db}_i$ cannot be key-equal. It follows that each repair of $\mathbf{db}_i$ is a disjoint union of repairs, one for each partition of $\mathbf{db}_i$.

Let $\lfloor\!\lfloor \mathbf{db}_i \rfloor\!\rfloor$ be the smallest subset of $\mathbf{db}_i$ that contains every partition P satisfying $P \in \mathsf{CERTAINTY}(q_i)$. By Lemma 7 and [13, Theorem 2], $\mathsf{CERTAINTY}(q_i)$ is in $\mathbf{P}$ for $1 \leq i \leq \ell$. From the following sublemma, it follows that $\mathsf{CERTAINTY}(q)$ is in $\mathbf{P}$.

SUBLEMMA 5. *The following are equivalent:*

1. $\mathbf{db} \in \mathsf{CERTAINTY}(q)$.
2. $\bigcup_{1 \leq i \leq \ell} \lfloor\!\lfloor \mathbf{db}_i \rfloor\!\rfloor \models q$.

For the step of the induction, let F be an unattacked atom in q's attack graph. Let $\vec{x}$ be a sequence of distinct variables such that $\mathsf{vars}(\vec{x}) = \mathsf{key}(F)$. By Corollary 8.11 in [24], the following are equivalent:

1. $\mathbf{db} \in \mathsf{CERTAINTY}(q)$.
2. For some $\vec{a} \in D^{|\vec{x}|}$, $\mathbf{db} \in \mathsf{CERTAINTY}(q_{[\vec{x} \mapsto \vec{a}]})$.

Let $\vec{y}$ be a sequence of distinct variables such that $\mathsf{vars}(\vec{y}) = \mathsf{vars}(F) \setminus \mathsf{key}(F)$. Let $q' = q \setminus \{F\}$. By Lemma 1, it is possible to compute in polynomial time a database $\mathbf{db}'$ that is purified relative to $q_{[\vec{x} \mapsto \vec{a}]}$ such that $\mathbf{db} \in \mathsf{CERTAINTY}(q_{[\vec{x} \mapsto \vec{a}]})$ if and only if $\mathbf{db}' \in \mathsf{CERTAINTY}(q_{[\vec{x} \mapsto \vec{a}]})$. By Lemma 8, the following are equivalent:

1. $\mathbf{db}' \in \mathsf{CERTAINTY}(q_{[\vec{x} \mapsto \vec{a}]})$.
2. $\mathbf{db}' \neq \emptyset$ and for all $\vec{b} \in D^{|\vec{y}|}$, if $F_{[\vec{x}\vec{y} \mapsto \vec{a}\vec{b}]} \in \mathbf{db}'$, then $\mathbf{db}' \in \mathsf{CERTAINTY}(q'_{[\vec{x}\vec{y} \mapsto \vec{a}\vec{b}]})$.

By Lemma 5, all cycles in the attack graph of $q'_{[\vec{x}\vec{y} \mapsto \vec{a}\vec{b}]}$ are weak and terminal. By the induction hypothesis, it follows that $\mathsf{CERTAINTY}(q'_{[\vec{x}\vec{y} \mapsto \vec{a}\vec{b}]})$ is in $\mathbf{P}$. Since the sizes of $D^{|\vec{x}|}$ and $D^{|\vec{y}|}$ are polynomially bounded in the size of $\mathbf{db}$, it is correct to conclude that $\mathsf{CERTAINTY}(q)$ is in $\mathbf{P}$. □

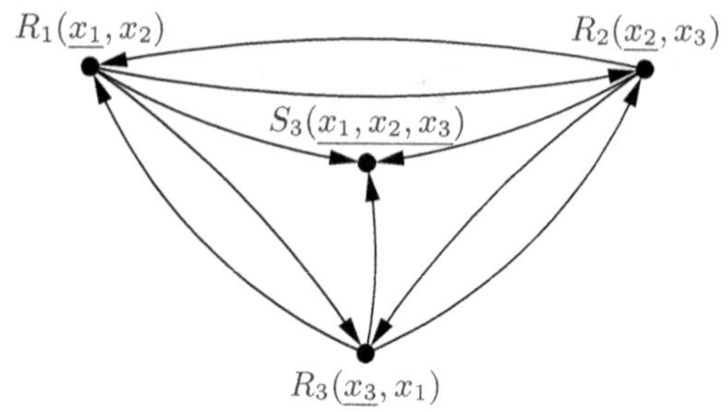

Figure 5: Attack graph of $\mathsf{AC}(3)$. All cycles are weak and nonterminal

6.2 Nonterminal Weak Cycles

Theorems 2 and 3 tell us nothing about the complexity of $\mathsf{CERTAINTY}(q)$ when the attack graph of q contains one or more nonterminal weak cycles and no strong cycle. In this section, we zoom in on acyclic queries $\mathsf{AC}(k)$, defined next for $k \in \{2, 3, \dots\}$, whose attack graph contains $\frac{k(k-1)}{2}$ nonterminal weak cycles and no strong cycle. By showing tractability of $\mathsf{CERTAINTY}(\mathsf{AC}(k))$, we obtain more supporting evidence for Conjecture 1. As a side result, we will solve a complexity issue raised by Fuxman and Miller [10].

Definition 8. For $k \geq 2$, let $\mathsf{C}(k)$ and $\mathsf{AC}(k)$ denote the following Boolean conjunctive queries without self-join.

$$\begin{aligned} \mathsf{C}(k) &= \{R_1(\underline{x_1}, x_2), R_2(\underline{x_2}, x_3), \dots, R_{k-1}(\underline{x_{k-1}}, x_k), \\ &\qquad R_k(\underline{x_k}, x_1)\}, \\ \mathsf{AC}(k) &= \{R_1(\underline{x_1}, x_2), R_2(\underline{x_2}, x_3), \dots, R_{k-1}(\underline{x_{k-1}}, x_k), \\ &\qquad R_k(\underline{x_k}, x_1), S_k(\underline{x_1, x_2, \dots, x_k})\}, \end{aligned}$$

where $x_1, \dots, x_k$ are distinct variables and $R_1, \dots, R_k, S_k$ distinct relation names. For $i \in \{1, \dots, k\}$, relation name R_i is of signature $[2, 1]$, and S_k is of signature $[k, k]$.

Obviously, a query q is acyclic if it contains an atom F such that $\mathsf{vars}(F) = \mathsf{vars}(q)$. Therefore, $\mathsf{AC}(k)$ is acyclic because the S_k-atom contains all variables that occur in the query. On the other hand, $\mathsf{C}(k)$ is acyclic if $k = 2$ and cyclic if $k \geq 3$.

For $i \in \{1, \dots, k\}$, the attack graph of $\mathsf{AC}(k)$ contains attacks from the R_i-atom to every other atom. Figure 5 shows the attack graph of $\mathsf{AC}(3)$. All attack cycles are weak, but Theorem 3 does not apply because the cycles are nonterminal.

$\mathsf{CERTAINTY}(\mathsf{C}(k))$ was claimed $\mathbf{coNP}$-hard for all $k \geq 2$ in [10]. Later, however, Wijsen [23] found a mistake in the proof of that claim and showed that $\mathsf{CERTAINTY}(\mathsf{C}(k))$ is tractable if $k = 2$. The complexity of $\mathsf{CERTAINTY}(\mathsf{C}(k))$ for $k \geq 3$ will be settled by Corollary 1.

THEOREM 4. *For $k \geq 2$, $\mathsf{CERTAINTY}(\mathsf{AC}(k))$ is in $\mathbf{P}$.*

PROOF. Let $\mathbf{db}$ be an uncertain database with schema $\{R_1, \dots, R_k, S_k\}$. By Lemma 1, we can assume without loss of generality that $\mathbf{db}$ is purified relative to $\mathsf{AC}(k)$. Let D be the active domain of $\mathbf{db}$. For every $i \in \{1, \dots, k\}$, define $\mathsf{type}(x_i)$ as the subset of D that contains a if for some

R_1	1	2
	a	b
	a	b'
	a'	b

R_2	1	2
	b	c
	b	c'
	b'	c

R_3	1	2
	c	a
	c	a'
	c'	a

S_3	1	2	3
	a	b	c'
	a	b'	c
	a'	b	c

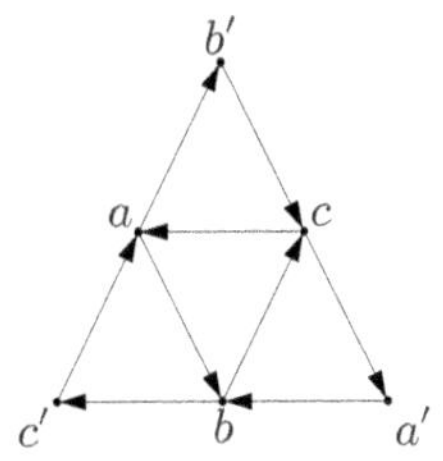

Figure 6: At the left: uncertain database that is purified relative to AC(3). At the right: graph representation of $R_1 \cup R_2 \cup R_3$. Note that the three cycles encoded in S_3 are clockwise.

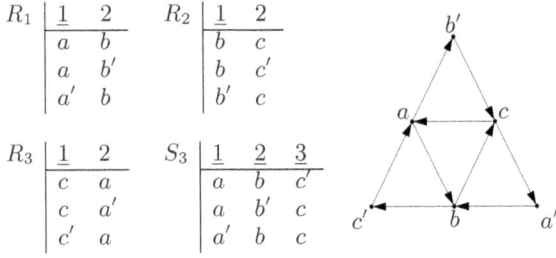

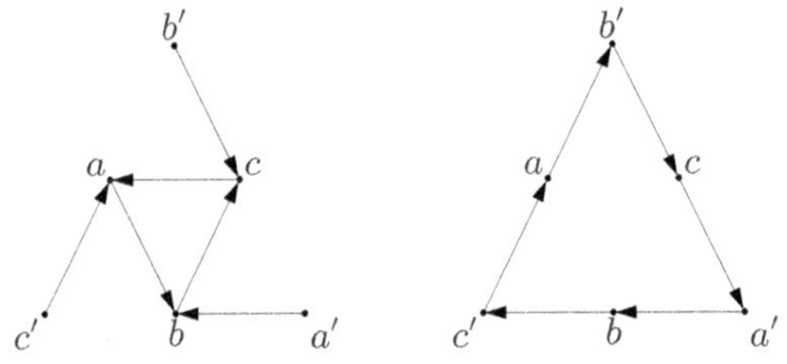

Figure 7: Graph representation of two repairs (of the uncertain database of Fig. 6) that falsify AC(3). The left cycle is anticlockwise and not encoded in S_3.

valuation μ, $\mu_{[x_i \mapsto a]}(\mathsf{AC}(k)) \subseteq \mathbf{db}$. Since $\mathsf{AC}(k)$ has no self-join, we can assume without loss of generality that $i \neq j$ implies $\mathsf{type}(x_i) \cap \mathsf{type}(x_j) = \emptyset$.

For example, assume $R_i(\underline{a}, b), R_j(\underline{c}, d) \in \mathbf{db}$ with $i < j$. Since $a \in \mathsf{type}(x_i)$, $b \in \mathsf{type}(x_{i+1})$, and $c \in \mathsf{type}(x_j)$, it follows that $b \neq a \neq c$ and that $b = c$ implies $j = i + 1$.

The R_i-facts of $\mathbf{db}$ can be viewed as edges of a directed graph ($1 \leq i \leq k$). This is illustrated in Fig. 6 for $k = 3$. Let $G = (V, E)$ be the directed graph such that $V = D$ and $E = \{(a, b) \mid R_i(\underline{a}, b) \in \mathbf{db}$ for some $i\}$. Then, G is k-partite with vertex classes $\mathsf{type}(x_1)$, ..., $\mathsf{type}(x_k)$. Furthermore, whenever $(a, b) \in E$ and $a \in \mathsf{type}(x_i)$, then $b \in \mathsf{type}(x_{i+1})$ if $i < k$ (and $b \in \mathsf{type}(x_1)$ if $i = k$). It follows that the length of every elementary cycle in G must be a multiple of k. Since $\mathbf{db}$ is purified, no vertex has zero outdegree. We define $\mathcal{C}$ as the set of cycles of length k such that if $\mathbf{db}$ contains $S_k(\underline{a_1, \ldots, a_k})$, then $\mathcal{C}$ contains the cycle $a_1, a_2, \ldots, a_k, a_1$.

Since $\mathbf{db}$ is purified, G is a vertex-disjoint union of strong components $S_1, \ldots, S_\ell$ (for some $\ell \geq 0$) such that for $i \neq j$, no edge leads from a vertex in S_i to a vertex in S_j.[2]

In what follows, some vertices and edges of G will be *marked*. It is straightforward that $\mathbf{db} \notin \mathsf{CERTAINTY}(\mathsf{AC}(k))$ is equivalent to the following.

It is possible to mark exactly one outgoing edge for each vertex of G without marking all edges of some cycle in $\mathcal{C}$. (5)

[2]A strong component of a graph G is a maximal strongly connected subgraph of G. A graph is strongly connected if there is a path from any vertex to any other.

We provide a polynomial-time algorithm for testing condition (5). Marking one outgoing edge for each vertex will create a cycle of marked edges in each strong component.

For each strong component S_i, consider the following cases successively and execute the first one that applies.

Case S_i contains a cycle of length k that does not belong to $\mathcal{C}$. Such a cycle is illustrated by Fig. 7 (left). Mark all vertices and edges of the cycle. Notice that the number of cycles of length k is at most $|V|^k$, which is polynomial in the size of $\mathbf{db}$.

Case S_i contains an elementary cycle of length (strictly) greater than k. Such a cycle is illustrated by Fig. 7 (right). Mark all vertices and edges of the cycle. To see that this step is in polynomial time, notice that the following are equivalent:

- S_i contains an elementary cycle of length greater than k.
- S_i contains a path $a_1, a_2, \ldots, a_k, a_{k+1}$ such that $a_1 \neq a_{k+1}$ and S_i contains a path from a_{k+1} to a_1 that contains no edge from $\{a_1, a_2, \ldots, a_k\} \times V$.

The latter condition can be tested in polynomial time, because there are at most $|V|^{k+1}$ distinct choices for $a_1, \ldots, a_{k+1}$ and paths can be found in polynomial time.

Case neither of the above two cases applies. Conclude that (5) is false.

If after the previous step every strong component contains a cycle of marked edges, then it is correct to conclude that (5) is true. Notice that every cycle of $\mathcal{C}$ now contains at least one unmarked edge. We can achieve (5) by marking, for each yet unmarked vertex, the vertices and edges on a shortest path to some marked vertex. This can be done without creating new cycles of marked edges. □

Since query $\mathsf{C}(k)$ is acyclic if $k \geq 3$, attack graphs are not defined for $\mathsf{C}(k)$ if $k \geq 3$. Nevertheless, the following lemma immediately implies that if $\mathsf{CERTAINTY}(\mathsf{AC}(k))$ is tractable, then so is $\mathsf{CERTAINTY}(\mathsf{C}(k))$.

LEMMA 9. *Let q be a Boolean conjunctive query without self-join. If $q' \subseteq q$ and every atom in $q \setminus q'$ is all-key, then there exists an $\mathbf{AC}^0$ many-one reduction from $\mathsf{CERTAINTY}(q')$ to $\mathsf{CERTAINTY}(q)$.*

COROLLARY 1. *For $k \geq 2$, $\mathsf{CERTAINTY}(\mathsf{C}(k))$ is in $\mathbf{P}$.*

Unsurprisingly, there exist acyclic queries $q \notin \{\mathsf{AC}(k) \mid k \geq 2\}$ whose attack graph contains some nonterminal cycle and no strong cycle. The complexity of $\mathsf{CERTAINTY}(q)$ for such queries q is open.

7. UNCERTAINTY AND PROBABILITY

In this section, we study the relationship between the complexities of $\mathsf{CERTAINTY}(q)$ and evaluating q on probabilistic databases. The motivation is that, on input of an uncertain database $\mathbf{db}$, the problem $\mathsf{CERTAINTY}(q)$ is solved if we can determine whether query q evaluates to probability 1 on the probabilistic database obtained from $\mathbf{db}$ by assuming a uniform probability distribution over the set of repairs of $\mathbf{db}$. We show, however, that this approach provides no new insights in the tractability frontier of $\mathsf{CERTAINTY}(q)$.

C	conf	year	city	Pr
	PODS	2016	Rome	0.4
	PODS	2016	Paris	0.4
	KDD	2017	Rome	1.0

R	conf	rank	Pr
	PODS	A	1.0
	KDD	A	0.7
	KDD	B	0.3

Figure 8: Compact representation of a BID probabilistic database.

7.1 Background from Probabilistic Databases

In this section, we review an important result from probabilistic database theory, which appears in [8]. The definitions of [8] naturally carry over to our framework.

Definition 9. A *possible world* $\mathbf{w}$ of an uncertain database $\mathbf{db}$ is a consistent subset of $\mathbf{db}$. The set of possible worlds of $\mathbf{db}$ is denoted $\mathsf{worlds}(\mathbf{db})$.

A *probabilistic database* is a pair $(\mathbf{db}, P)$ where $\mathbf{db}$ is an uncertain database and $P : \mathsf{worlds}(\mathbf{db}) \rightarrow [0,1]$ is a total function such that $\sum_{\mathbf{w} \in \mathsf{worlds}(\mathbf{db})} P(\mathbf{w}) = 1$. We will assume that the codomain of P is the set of rational numbers.

Notice that possible worlds, unlike repairs, need not be maximal consistent. The function *Pr* is defined relative to a probabilistic database and assigns probabilities to Boolean queries.

Definition 10. Let $(\mathbf{db}, P)$ be a probabilistic database. Let q be a Boolean first-order query. We define

$$Pr(q) = \sum_{\mathbf{w} \in \mathsf{worlds}(\mathbf{db}) : \mathbf{w} \models q} P(\mathbf{w}).$$

In words, $Pr(q)$ sums up the probabilities of the possible worlds that satisfy q.

Of special interest is the application of Definition 10 in case q is a single fact, or a conjunction/disjunction of facts. Clearly, if $(\mathbf{db}, P)$ is a probabilistic database and $A_1, \dots, A_n$ are distinct facts belonging to a same block of the uncertain database $\mathbf{db}$, then $Pr(A_1 \lor A_2 \lor \dots \lor A_n) = \sum_{i=1}^{n} Pr(A_i)$, because no possible world can contain two distinct facts that belong to a same block.

Definition 11. A probabilistic database $(\mathbf{db}, P)$ is called *block-independent-disjoint* (BID) if the following holds: whenever $A_1, \dots, A_n$ are facts of $\mathbf{db}$ taken from n distinct blocks ($n \geq 1$), then $Pr(A_1 \land A_2 \land \dots \land A_n) = \prod_{i=1}^{n} Pr(A_i)$.

Theorem 2.4 in [8] implies that every BID probabilistic database $(\mathbf{db}, P)$ is uniquely determined if $Pr(A)$ is given for every fact $A \in \mathbf{db}$. This allows for a compact representation: rather than specifying $P(\mathbf{w})$ for every $\mathbf{w} \in \mathsf{worlds}(\mathbf{db})$, it suffices to specify $Pr(A)$ for every $A \in \mathbf{db}$. In the complexity results that follow, this compact representation is assumed.

Example 7. In Fig. 8, every fact is associated with a probability. If we denote $A = \mathbf{C}(\underline{\mathrm{PODS}, 2016}, \mathrm{Rome})$ and $B = \mathbf{C}(\underline{\mathrm{PODS}, 2016}, \mathrm{Paris})$, then $Pr(A \lor B) = 0.4 + 0.4 = 0.8$, which is smaller than 1. It follows that there exist possible worlds with non-zero probability that contain neither A nor B.

The problem of query answering in BID probabilistic databases is defined next.

Function IsSafe(q) Determine whether q is safe [8]

Input: q is a Boolean conjunctive query without self-join.
Result: Boolean in $\{\mathbf{true}, \mathbf{false}\}$.
begin
R1: **if** $|q| = 1$ *and* $\mathsf{vars}(q) = \emptyset$ **then**
  return true;
R2: **if** $q = q_1 \cup q_2$ *with* $q_1 \neq \emptyset \neq q_2$, $\mathsf{vars}(q_1) \cap \mathsf{vars}(q_2) = \emptyset$ **then**
  return $IsSafe(q_1) \land IsSafe(q_2)$;
/* a is an arbitrary constant */
R3: **if** $\bigcap_{F \in q} \mathsf{key}(F) \neq \emptyset$ **then**
  select $x \in \bigcap_{F \in q} \mathsf{key}(F)$;
  return $IsSafe(q_{[x \mapsto a]})$;
R4: **if** *there exists* $F \in q$ *such that* $\mathsf{key}(F) = \emptyset \neq \mathsf{vars}(F)$ **then**
  select $F \in q$ such that $\mathsf{key}(F) = \emptyset \neq \mathsf{vars}(F)$; select $x \in \mathsf{vars}(F)$;
  return $IsSafe(q_{[x \mapsto a]})$;
if *none of the above* **then**
  return false;

Definition 12. For every Boolean first-order query q, we define $\mathsf{PROBABILITY}(q)$ as the following function problem: on input of (the compact representation of) a BID probabilistic database $(\mathbf{db}, P)$, determine the value of $Pr(q)$.

Dalvi et al. [8] have shown a complexity dichotomy for $\mathsf{PROBABILITY}(q)$ when q ranges over the set of Boolean conjunctive queries without self-join. Each such a query q is categorized as either safe or unsafe by structural recursion on the syntax of q.

Definition 13. A Boolean conjunctive query q, without self-join, is called *safe* if Algorithm IsSafe returns **true**; otherwise q is *unsafe*.

The complexity dichotomy for $\mathsf{PROBABILITY}(q)$ can now be stated.

THEOREM 5 ([8]). *Let q be a Boolean conjunctive query without self-join.*

1. *If q is safe, then* $\mathsf{PROBABILITY}(q)$ *is in* **FP**.
2. *If q is unsafe, then* $\mathsf{PROBABILITY}(q)$ *is* $\sharp$**P**-*hard.*

7.2 Comparing Complexities

The following proposition establishes a straightforward relationship between the problems $\mathsf{PROBABILITY}(q)$ and $\mathsf{CERTAINTY}(q)$. The only subtlety is that a repair contains a fact of each block, while a possible world and a block may have an empty intersection, as illustrated by Example 7. In the statement of this proposition, $\mathbf{db}'$ restricts $\mathbf{db}$ to the set of blocks whose probabilities sum up to 1.

PROPOSITION 1. *Let $(\mathbf{db}, P)$ be a BID probabilistic database. Let $\mathbf{db}'$ be the smallest subset of $\mathbf{db}$ that contains every block $\mathbf{b}$ of $\mathbf{db}$ such that $\sum_{A \in \mathbf{b}} Pr(A) = 1$. Let q be a Boolean conjunctive query. Then the following are equivalent:*

1. $\mathbf{db}' \in \mathsf{CERTAINTY}(q)$.
2. *On input $(\mathbf{db}, P)$, the answer to the function problem* $\mathsf{PROBABILITY}(q)$ *is* 1.

The following theorem establishes a nontrivial relationship between the complexities of the problems CERTAINTY(q) and PROBABILITY(q). Notice that the query q in the theorem's statement is not required to be acyclic.

THEOREM 6. *Let q be a Boolean conjunctive query without self-join. If q is safe, then* CERTAINTY(q) *is first-order expressible.*

PROOF. The proof runs by induction on the execution of Algorithm IsSafe. Since q is safe, some rule of IsSafe applies to q.

Case R1 applies. If q consists of a single fact, then CERTAINTY(q) is obviously first-order expressible.

Case R2 applies. Let $q = q_1 \cup q_2$ with $q_1 \neq \emptyset \neq q_2$ and $\mathsf{vars}(q_1) \cap \mathsf{vars}(q_2) = \emptyset$. Since q is safe, q_1 and q_2 are safe by definition of safety. By the induction hypothesis, there exists a consistent first-order rewriting φ_1 of q_1, and a consistent first-order rewriting φ_2 of q_2. Obviously, $\varphi_1 \wedge \varphi_2$ is a consistent first-order rewriting of q.

Case R3 applies. Assume variable x such that for every $F \in q$, $x \in \mathsf{key}(F)$. By definition of safety, $q_{[x \mapsto a]}$ is safe. It can be easily seen that $\mathbf{db} \in$ CERTAINTY(q) if and only if for some constant a, $\mathbf{db} \in$ CERTAINTY($q_{[x \mapsto a]}$). By the induction hypothesis, CERTAINTY($q_{[x \mapsto a]}$) is first-order expressible. Let φ be a consistent first-order rewriting of $q_{[x \mapsto c]}$, where we assume without loss of generality that c is a constant that does not occur in q. Let $\varphi(x)$ be the first order formula obtained from φ by replacing each occurrence of c with x. Then, $\exists x \varphi(x)$ is a consistent first-order rewriting of q.

Case R4 applies. Assume $F \in q$ such that $\mathsf{key}(F) = \emptyset$ and $\mathsf{vars}(F) \neq \emptyset$. Let $\vec{x}$ be a sequence of distinct variables such that $\mathsf{vars}(\vec{x}) = \mathsf{vars}(F)$. Let $\vec{a} = \langle a, a, \ldots, a \rangle$ be a sequence of length $|\vec{x}|$. By definition of safety, $q_{[\vec{x} \mapsto \vec{a}]}$ is safe. By the induction hypothesis, CERTAINTY($q_{[\vec{x} \mapsto \vec{a}]}$) is first-order expressible. From Lemma 8.6 in [24], it follows that CERTAINTY(q) is first-order expressible □

COROLLARY 2. *Let q be a Boolean conjunctive query without self-join. If* CERTAINTY(q) *is not first-order expressible, then the function problem* PROBABILITY(q) *is* ♮**P***-hard.*

For acyclic queries, the only complexities of CERTAINTY(q) left open by Theorems 1, 2, and 3 concern queries q with a cyclic attack graph (in particular, an attack graph without a strong cycle and with at least one nonterminal weak cycle). For such a query q, CERTAINTY(q) is not first-order expressible (by Theorem 1), hence PROBABILITY(q) is ♮**P**-hard (by Corollary 2). Consequently, the probabilistic database approach fails to provide further insight into the tractability frontier of CERTAINTY(q).

8. DISCUSSION

In the following, we say that a class $\mathcal{P}$ of function problems *exhibits an effective* **FP**-♮**P***-dichotomy* if all problems in $\mathcal{P}$ are either in **FP** or ♮**P**-hard and it is decidable whether a given problem in $\mathcal{P}$ is in **FP** or ♮**P**-hard. Likewise, we say that a class $\mathcal{P}$ of decision problems *exhibits an effective* **P**-**coNP***-dichotomy* if all problems in $\mathcal{P}$ are either in **P** or **coNP**-hard and it is decidable whether a given problem in $\mathcal{P}$ is in **P** or **coNP**-hard.

Recall from Section 2 that ♮CERTAINTY(q) is the counting variant of CERTAINTY(q), which takes as input an uncertain database **db** and asks how many repairs of **db** satisfy query q. For the probabilistic and counting variants of CERTAINTY(q), the following dichotomies have been established.

THEOREM 7 ([8],[16]). *The following classes exhibit an effective* **FP**-♮**P***-dichotomy:*

1. *the class containing* PROBABILITY(q) *for all Boolean conjunctive queries q without self-join; and*
2. *the class containing* ♮CERTAINTY(q) *for all Boolean conjunctive queries q without self-join.*

Theorem 2 and Conjecture 1 imply the following conjecture, which is thus weaker than Conjecture 1.

CONJECTURE 2. *The class containing* CERTAINTY(q) *for all acyclic Boolean conjunctive queries q without self-join exhibits an effective* **P**-**coNP***-dichotomy.*

From Theorems 2 and 3, it follows that in order to prove Conjecture 2, it suffices to show that an effective **P-coNP**-dichotomy is exhibited by the class containing CERTAINTY(q) for all queries q whose attack graph contains some nonterminal cycle and no strong cycle.

We confidently believe that the **P-coNP**-dichotomy of Conjecture 2 (if true) will be harder to prove than the **FP**-♮**P**-dichotomies established by Theorem 7, for the following reasons. All problems PROBABILITY(q) that are in **FP** can be solved by a single, fairly simple polynomial-time algorithm which appears in [8]. Likewise, all problems ♮CERTAINTY(q) in **FP** can be solved by a single, fairly simple polynomial-time algorithm [16]. On the other hand, CERTAINTY(q) problems in **P** seem to ask for sophisticated polynomial-time algorithms. In their proof that Conjecture 2 holds for queries with exactly two atoms, Kolaitis and Pema [13] made use of an ingenious polynomial-time algorithm of Minty [17]. Our proof of Theorem 4 uses algorithms from (directed) graph theory. Despite their sophistication, these polynomial-time algorithms only solve restricted cases of CERTAINTY(q).

Notice also that by Corollary 2 and Theorem 1, the function problem PROBABILITY(q) is intractable for all acyclic queries q with a cyclic attack graph. On the other hand, cycles in attack graphs are exactly what makes Conjecture 2 hard to prove.

9. ACKNOWLEDGMENTS

While this paper was under review, the author has learned that Theorem 2 was independently discovered by the database group at UC Santa Cruz [18], and that Corollary 1 was independently discovered by Koutris and Suciu [14].

10. REFERENCES

[1] M. Arenas, L. E. Bertossi, and J. Chomicki. Consistent query answers in inconsistent databases. In V. Vianu and C. H. Papadimitriou, editors, *PODS*, pages 68–79. ACM Press, 1999.

[2] C. Beeri, R. Fagin, D. Maier, and M. Yannakakis. On the desirability of acyclic database schemes. *J. ACM*, 30(3):479–513, 1983.

[3] L. E. Bertossi. *Database Repairing and Consistent Query Answering*. Synthesis Lectures on Data Management. Morgan & Claypool Publishers, 2011.

[4] M. Bienvenu. On the complexity of consistent query answering in the presence of simple ontologies. In J. Hoffmann and B. Selman, editors, *AAAI*. AAAI Press, 2012.

[5] D. Calvanese, G. D. Giacomo, D. Lembo, M. Lenzerini, and R. Rosati. Data complexity of query answering in description logics. *Artif. Intell.*, 195:335–360, 2013.

[6] J. Chomicki and J. Marcinkowski. Minimal-change integrity maintenance using tuple deletions. *Inf. Comput.*, 197(1-2):90–121, 2005.

[7] N. N. Dalvi, C. Ré, and D. Suciu. Probabilistic databases: diamonds in the dirt. *Commun. ACM*, 52(7):86–94, 2009.

[8] N. N. Dalvi, C. Re, and D. Suciu. Queries and materialized views on probabilistic databases. *J. Comput. Syst. Sci.*, 77(3):473–490, 2011.

[9] A. Fuxman and R. J. Miller. First-order query rewriting for inconsistent databases. In T. Eiter and L. Libkin, editors, *ICDT*, volume 3363 of *Lecture Notes in Computer Science*, pages 337–351. Springer, 2005.

[10] A. Fuxman and R. J. Miller. First-order query rewriting for inconsistent databases. *J. Comput. Syst. Sci.*, 73(4):610–635, 2007.

[11] G. Gottlob, N. Leone, and F. Scarcello. Hypertree decompositions and tractable queries. *J. Comput. Syst. Sci.*, 64(3):579–627, 2002.

[12] L. Grieco, D. Lembo, R. Rosati, and M. Ruzzi. Consistent query answering under key and exclusion dependencies: algorithms and experiments. In O. Herzog, H.-J. Schek, N. Fuhr, A. Chowdhury, and W. Teiken, editors, *CIKM*, pages 792–799. ACM, 2005.

[13] P. G. Kolaitis and E. Pema. A dichotomy in the complexity of consistent query answering for queries with two atoms. *Inf. Process. Lett.*, 112(3):77–85, 2012.

[14] P. Koutris and D. Suciu. A dichotomy on the complexity of consistent query answering for atoms with simple keys. *CoRR*, abs/1212.6636, 2012.

[15] R. E. Ladner. On the structure of polynomial time reducibility. *J. ACM*, 22(1):155–171, 1975.

[16] D. Maslowski and J. Wijsen. A dichotomy in the complexity of counting database repairs. *Journal of Computer and System Sciences*, 2013.

[17] G. J. Minty. On maximal independent sets of vertices in claw-free graphs. *J. Comb. Theory, Ser. B*, 28(3):284–304, 1980.

[18] E. Pema. Personal communication, 2013.

[19] D. Suciu, D. Olteanu, C. Ré, and C. Koch. *Probabilistic Databases*. Synthesis Lectures on Data Management. Morgan & Claypool Publishers, 2011.

[20] J. D. Ullman. *Principles of Database and Knowledge-Base Systems, Volume I*. Computer Science Press, 1988.

[21] J. Wijsen. On the consistent rewriting of conjunctive queries under primary key constraints. *Inf. Syst.*, 34(7):578–601, 2009.

[22] J. Wijsen. On the first-order expressibility of computing certain answers to conjunctive queries over uncertain databases. In J. Paredaens and D. V. Gucht, editors, *PODS*, pages 179–190. ACM, 2010.

[23] J. Wijsen. A remark on the complexity of consistent conjunctive query answering under primary key violations. *Inf. Process. Lett.*, 110(21):950–955, 2010.

[24] J. Wijsen. Certain conjunctive query answering in first-order logic. *ACM Trans. Database Syst.*, 37(2):9, 2012.

TriAL for RDF: Adapting Graph Query Languages for RDF Data

Leonid Libkin
University of Edinburgh
libkin@ed.ac.uk

Juan Reutter
University of Edinburgh and PUC Chile
juan.reutter@ed.ac.uk

Domagoj Vrgoč
University of Edinburgh
domagoj.vrgoc@ed.ac.uk

ABSTRACT

Querying RDF data is viewed as one of the main applications of graph query languages, and yet the standard model of graph databases – essentially labeled graphs – is different from the triples-based model of RDF. While encodings of RDF databases into graph data exist, we show that even the most natural ones are bound to lose some functionality when used in conjunction with graph query languages. The solution is to work directly with triples, but then many properties taken for granted in the graph database context (e.g., reachability) lose their natural meaning.

Our goal is to introduce languages that work directly over triples and are closed, i.e., they produce sets of triples, rather than graphs. Our basic language is called TriAL, or Triple Algebra: it guarantees closure properties by replacing the product with a family of join operations. We extend TriAL with recursion, and explain why such an extension is more intricate for triples than for graphs. We present a declarative language, namely a fragment of datalog, capturing the recursive algebra. For both languages, the combined complexity of query evaluation is given by low-degree polynomials. We compare our languages with relational languages, such as finite-variable logics, and previously studied graph query languages such as adaptations of XPath, regular path queries, and nested regular expressions; many of these languages are subsumed by the recursive triple algebra. We also provide examples of the usefulness of TriAL in querying graph and RDF data.

Categories and Subject Descriptors. F.4.1 [**Mathematical logic and formal languages**]: Mathematical logic; H.2.1 [**Database Management**]: Logical Design—*Data Models*; H.2.3 [**Database management**]: Languages—*Query Languages*

Keywords. RDF, Triple Algebra, Query evaluation

PODS'13, June 22–27, 2013, New York, New York, USA.

1. INTRODUCTION

Graph data management is currently one of the most active research topics in the database community, fueled by the adoption of graph models in new application domains, such as social networks, bioinformatics and astronomic databases, and projects such as the Web of Data and the Semantic Web. There are many proposals for graph query languages; we now understand many issues related to query evaluation over graphs, and there are multiple vendors offering graph database products, see [2, 3, 14, 37] for surveys.

The Semantic Web and its underlying data model, RDF, are usually cited as one of the key applications of graph databases, but there is some mismatch between them. The standard model of graph databases [2, 37] that dates back to [12, 13], is that of directed edge-labeled graphs, i.e., pairs $G = (V, E)$, where V is a set of vertices (objects), and E is a set of labeled edges. Each labeled edge is of the form (v, a, v'), where v, v' are nodes in V, and a is a label from some finite labeling alphabet Σ. As such, they are the same as labeled transition systems used as a basic model in both hardware and software verification. Graph databases of course can store data associated with their nodes (e.g., information about each person in a social network).

The model of RDF data is very similar, yet slightly different. The basic concept is a *triple* (s, p, o), that consists of the subject s, the predicate p, and the object o, drawn from a domain of uniform resource identifiers (URI's). Thus, the middle element need not come from a finite alphabet, and may in addition play the role of a subject or an object in another triple. For instance, $\{(s, p, o), (p, s, o')\}$ is a valid set of RDF triples, but in graph databases, it is impossible to have two such edges.

To understand why this mismatch is a problem, consider querying graph data. Since graph databases and RDF are represented as relations, relational queries can be applied to them. But crucially, we may also query the *topology* of a graph. For instance, many graph query languages have, as their basic building block, *regular path queries*, or RPQs [13], that find nodes reachable by a path whose label belongs to a regular language.

We take the notion of reachability for granted in graph databases, but what is the corresponding notion for triples, where the middle element can serve as the source and the target of an edge? Then there are multiple possibilities, two of which are illustrated below.

Query $\mathsf{Reach}_{\rightarrow}$ looks for pairs (x, z) connected by paths of the following shape:

and $\mathsf{Reach}_{\nearrow}$ looks for the following connection pattern:

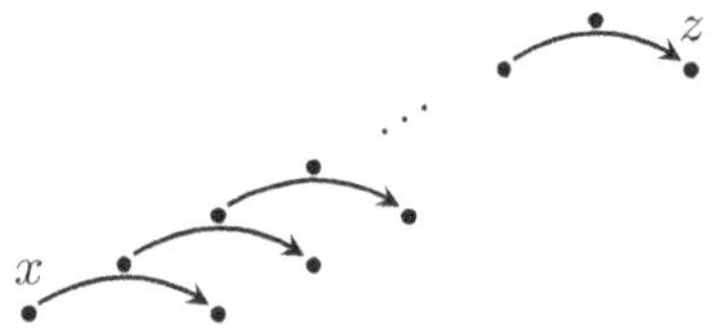

But can such patterns be defined by existing RDF query languages? Or can they be defined by existing graph query languages under some graph encoding of RDF?

To answer these, we need to understand which navigational facilities are available for RDF data. A recent survey of graph database systems [3] shows that, by and large, they either offer support for triples, or they do graphs and then can express proper reachability queries. An attempt to add navigation to RDF languages was made in [33], where a language called nSPARQL was defined by taking SPARQL [22, 32], the standard query language for RDF, and extending it with a navigational mechanism provided by *nested regular expressions*. These are essentially regular path queries with XPath-inspired node tests. The evaluation of those uses essentially a graph encoding of RDF. As the starting point of our investigation, we show that there are natural reachability patterns for triples, similar to those shown above, that *cannot* be defined in graph encodings of RDF [5] using nested regular expressions, nor in nSPARQL itself.

Thus, navigational patterns over triples are beyond reach of both RDF languages and graph query languages that work on encodings of RDF. The solution is then to design languages that work directly on RDF triples, and have both relational and navigational querying facilities, just like graph query languages. Our goal, therefore, is to adapt graph database techniques for direct RDF querying.

A crucial property of a query language is *closure*: queries should return objects of the same kind as their input. Closed languages, therefore, are compositional: their operators can be applied to results of queries. Using graph languages for RDF suffers from non-compositionality: for instance, RPQs return graphs rather than triples. So we start by defining a closed language for triples. To understand its basic operations, we first look at a language that has essentially first-order expressivity, and then add navigational features.

We take relational algebra as the basic language. Clearly projection violates closure so we throw it away. Selection and set operations, on the other hand, are fine. The problematic operation is Cartesian product: if T, T' are sets of triples, then $T \times T'$ is not a set of triples but rather a set of 6-tuples. What do we do then? We shall need reachability in the language, and for graphs, reachability is computed by iterating *composition* of relations. The composition operation for binary relations preserves closure: a pair (x, y) is in the composition $R \circ R'$ of R and R' iff $(x, z) \in R$ and $(z, y) \in R'$ for some z. So this is a join of R and R' and it seems that what we need is it analog for triples.

But queries $\mathsf{Reach}_{\rightarrow}$ and $\mathsf{Reach}_{\nearrow}$ demonstrate that there is no such thing as *the reachability* for triples. In fact, we shall see that there is not even a nice analog of composition for triples. So instead, we add *all* possible joins that keep the algebra closed. The resulting language is called *Triple Algebra*, denoted by TriAL. We then add an iteration mechanism to it, to enable it to express reachability queries based on different joins, and obtain *Recursive Triple Algebra* TriAL^*.

The algebra TriAL^* can express both reachability patterns above, as well as queries we prove to be inexpressible in nSPARQL. It has a declarative language associated with it, a fragment of Datalog. It has good query evaluation bounds: combined complexity is (low-degree) polynomial. Moreover, we exhibit a fragment with complexity of the order $O(|e| \cdot |O| \cdot |T|)$, where e is the query, O is the set of objects in the database, and T is the set of triples. This is a very natural fragment, as it restricts arbitrary recursive definitions to those essentially defining reachability properties.

The model we use is slightly more general than just triples of objects and amounts to combining triplestores as in, e.g., [24] with the representation of objects used in the Neo4j database [14, 31]. Each object participating in a triple comes associated with a set of attributes. Of course this can be modeled via more triples, but the model we use is conceptually cleaner and leads to a more natural comparison with other query languages.

The first of those comparisons is with relational querying. We show that TriAL lives between FO^3 and FO^6 (recall that FO^k refers to the fragment of First-Order Logic using only k variables). In fact it contains FO^3, is contained in FO^6, and is incomparable with FO^4 and FO^5. A similar result holds for TriAL^* and transitive closure logic.

On the graph querying side, we show that the navigational power of TriAL^* subsumes that of both regular path queries and nested regular expressions. In fact it subsumes a version of *graph XPath* recently proposed for graph databases [27]. We also compare it with conjunctive RPQs [12] and some of their extensions studied in [10, 11]. When it comes to graphs with data held in their nodes, we show that TriAL* continues to subsume some of the formalisms proposed in that context, such as graph XPath expanded with data tests and some types of regular expressions with data values [28, 27].

This shows that TriAL* is an expressive language that subsumes a number of well known relational and graph formalisms, that permits navigational queries not expressible on graph encodings of RDF or in nSPARQL, and that has good query evaluation properties.

Organization In Section 2 we review graph and RDF databases, and describe our model. We also show that some natural navigational queries over triples cannot be expressed in languages such as nSPARQL. In Section 3 we define TriAL and TriAL* and study their expressiveness. In Section 4 we give a declarative language capturing TriAL*. In Section 5 we study query evaluation, and in Sections 6.1 and 6.2 we study our languages in connection with relational and graph querying.

2. GRAPH DATABASES AND RDF

Basic Definitions

Graph databases. We now review some standard definitions (see, e.g., [2, 11, 37]). A graph database is just a finite edge-labeled graph in which each node has a data value attached. Formally, let $\mathcal{N}$ be a countably infinite set of *node ids*, Σ a finite alphabet and $\mathcal{D}$ a countably infinite set of data values. Then a *graph database* over Σ is a triple $G = (V, E, \rho)$, where $V \subset \mathcal{N}$ is a finite set of nodes, $E \subseteq V \times \Sigma \times V$ is a set of labeled edges, and $\rho : V \to \mathcal{D}$ is a function assigning a data value to each node. Each edge is a triple (u, a, v), whose interpretation is an a-labeled edge from u to v. When Σ is clear from the context, we shall simply speak of a graph database. If we work with graph databases that make no use of data values, we write $G = (V, E)$ and disregard the function ρ.

A *path* π from u_0 to u_m in G is a sequence $(u_0, a_0, u_1), (u_1, a_1, u_2), \cdots, (u_{m-1}, a_{m-1}, u_m)$, where each (u_i, a_i, u_{i+1}), for $i < m$, is an edge in E. The *label* of π, denoted by $\lambda(\pi)$, is the word $a_0 \cdots a_{m-1} \in \Sigma^*$.

Regular path queries. Typical navigational languages for graph databases use *regular path queries*, or *RPQs* [13] as the basic building block. An RPQ is an expression $x \xrightarrow{L} y$, where x and y are variables and L is a regular language over Σ. Given a graph database $G = (V, E)$ over Σ, it defines pairs of nodes (u, v) such that there is a path π from u to v with $\lambda(\pi) \in L$.

Nested regular expressions. These expressions, abbreviated as NRE, over a finite alphabet Σ, extend ordinary regular expressions with the nesting operator (essentially the node test of XPath) and inverses [8, 33]. Formally they are defined as follows:

$$e := \varepsilon \mid a \mid a^- \mid e \cdot e \mid e^* \mid e + e \mid [e], \quad a \in \Sigma.$$

An NRE defines, over a graph $G = (V, E)$, a binary relation on V. The semantics of ε is the diagonal $\{(u, u) \mid u \in V\}$; the semantics of a is the set $\{(u, v) \mid (u, a, v) \in E\}$ of a-labeled edges, and a^- defines $\{(u, v) \mid (v, a, u) \in E\}$. Operations $\cdot$, $+$, and $*$ denote composition, union, and transitive closure of binary relations. Finally, the node test $[e]$ defines pairs (u, u) so that (u, v) is in the result of e for some $v \in V$.

RDF databases. RDF databases contain triples in which, unlike in graph databases, the middle component need not come from a fixed set of labels. Formally, if $\mathbf{U}$ is a countably infinite domain of uniform resource identifiers (URI's), then an RDF triple is $(s, p, o) \in \mathbf{U} \times \mathbf{U} \times \mathbf{U}$, where s is referred to as the subject, p as the predicate, and o as the object. An RDF graph is just a collection of RDF triples. Here we deal with *ground* RDF documents [33], i.e., we do not consider blank nodes or literals in RDF documents (otherwise we need to deal with disjoint domains, which complicates the presentation).

Example 1. The RDF database D in Figure 1 contains information about cities, modes of transportation between them, and operators of those services. Each triple is represented by an arrow from the subject to the object, with the arrow itself labeled with the predicate. Examples of triples in D are (`Edinburgh`, `Train Op 1`, `London`) and (`Train Op 1`, `part_of`, `EastCoast`). For simplicity, we assume from now on that we can determine implicitly whether an object is a city or an operator. This can of course be modeled by adding an additional outgoing edge labeled `city` from each city and `operator` from each service operator.

Graph Queries for RDF

Navigational properties (e.g., reachability patterns) are among the most important functionalities of RDF query languages. However, typical RDF query languages, such as SPARQL, are in spirit relational languages. To extend them with navigation, as in [33, 4, 30], one typically uses features inspired by graph query languages, surveyed briefly earlier. Nonetheless, such approaches have their inherent limitations, as we explain here.

Looking again at the database D in Figure 1, we see the main difference between graphs and RDF: the majority of the edge labels in D are also used as subjects or objects (i.e., nodes) of other triples of D. For instance, one can travel from Edinburgh to London by using a train service Train Op 1, but in this case the label itself is viewed as a node when we express the fact that this operator is actually a part of EastCoast trains.

For RDF, one normally uses a model of *triplestores* that is different from graph databases. According to it, the database from Figure 1 is viewed as a ternary relation:

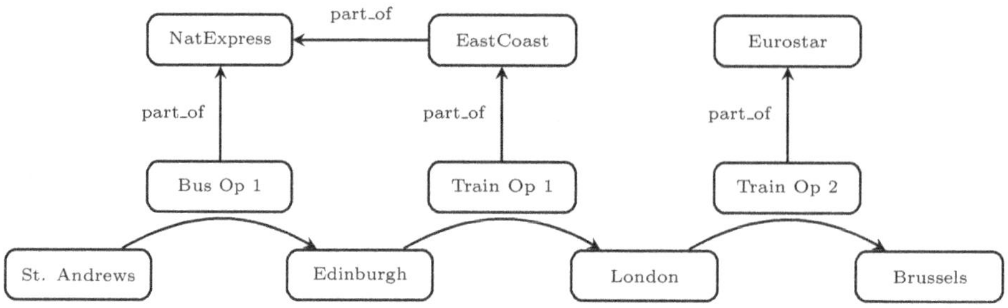

Figure 1: RDF graph storing information about cities and transport services between them

St. Andrews	Bus Op 1	Edinburgh
Edinburgh	Train Op 1	London
London	Train Op 2	Brussels
Bus Op 1	part_of	NatExpress
Train Op 1	part_of	EastCoast
Train Op 2	part_of	Eurostar
EastCoast	part_of	NatExpress

Suppose one wants to answer the following query:

Q : *Find pairs of cities (x, y) such that one can travel from x to y using services operated by the same company.*

A query like this is likely to be relevant, for instance, when integrating numerous transport services into a single ticketing interface. In our example, the pair (Edinburgh, London) belongs to $Q(D)$, and one can also check that (St. Andrews, London) is in $Q(D)$, since recursively both operators are part of NatExpress (using the transitivity of part_of). However, the pair (St. Andrews, Brussels) does not belong to $Q(D)$, since we can only travel that route if we change companies, from NatExpress to Eurostar.

To enhance SPARQL with navigational properties, [33] added nested regular expressions to it, resulting in a language called nSPARQL. The idea was to combine the usual reachability patterns of graph query languages with the XPath mechanism of node tests. However, nested regular expressions, which we saw earlier, are defined for graphs, and not for databases storing triples. Thus, they cannot be used directly over RDF databases; instead, one needs to transform an RDF database D into a graph first. An example of such transformation $D \to \sigma(D)$ was given in [5]; it is illustrated in Figure 2.

Formally, given an RDF document D, the graph $\sigma(D) = (V, E)$ is a graph database over alphabet $\Sigma = \{\text{next}, \text{node}, \text{edge}\}$, where V contains all resources from D, and for each triple (s, p, o) in D, the edge relation E contains edges (s, edge, p), (p, node, o) and (s, next, o). This transformation scheme is important in practical RDF applications (it was shown to be crucial for addressing the problem of interpreting RDFS features within SPARQL [33]). At the same time, it is not sufficient for expressing simple reachability patterns like those in query Q:

Proposition 1. *The query Q is not expressible by NREs over graph transformations $\sigma(\cdot)$ of ternary relations.*

Thus, the most common RDF navigational mechanism cannot express a very natural property, essentially due to the need to do so via a graph transformation.

One might argue that this result is due to the shortcomings of a specific transformation (however relevant to practical tasks it might be). So we ask what happens in the native RDF scenario. In particular, we would like to see what happens with the language nSPARQL [33], which is a proper RDF query language extending SPARQL with navigation based on nested regular expressions. But this language falls short too, as it fails to express the simple reachability query Q.

Theorem 1. *The query Q above cannot be expressed in nSPARQL.*

The key reason for these limitations is that the navigation mechanisms used in RDF languages are graph-based, when one really needs them to be triple-based.

Triplestore Databases

To introduce proper triple-based navigational languages, we first define a simple model of triplestores. Let $\mathcal{O}$ be a countably infinite set of objects, and $\mathcal{D}$ be a countably infinite set of data values.

Definition 1. *A* triplestore database, *or just* triplestore *over $\mathcal{D}$ is a tuple $T = (O, E_1, \ldots, E_n, \rho)$, where:*

- *$O \subset \mathcal{O}$ is a finite set of objects,*
- *each $E_i \subseteq O \times O \times O$ is a set of triples, and*
- *$\rho : O \to \mathcal{D}$ is a function that assigns a data value to each object.*

Often we have just a single ternary relation E in a triplestore database (e.g., in the previously seen examples of representing RDF databases), but all the languages and results we state here apply to multiple relations. The function ρ could also map $\mathcal{O}$ to tuples over $\mathcal{D}$, and all results remain true (one just uses $\mathcal{D}^k$ as the range of ρ, as in the example below). We use the function $\rho : O \to \mathcal{D}$ just to simplify notations.

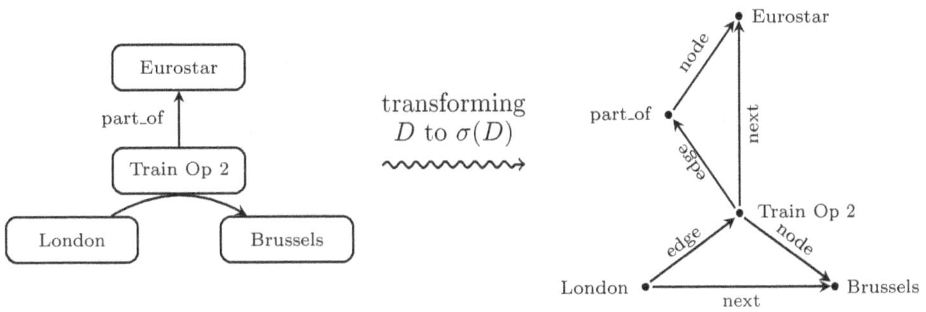

RDF graph D Transformed graph $\sigma(D)$

Figure 2: Transforming part of the RDF database from Figure 1 into a graph database

Triplestores easily model RDF, and we will see later that they model graph databases. Furthermore, they can be used to model several other applications relying on semistructured data, such as e.g. social networks.

3. AN ALGEBRA FOR RDF

We saw that problems encountered while adapting graph languages to RDF are related to the inherent limitations of the graph data model for representing RDF data. Thus, one should work directly with triples. But existing languages are either based on binary relations and fall short of the power necessary for RDF querying, or are general relational languages which are not closed when it comes to querying RDF triples. Hence, we need a language that works directly on triples, is closed, and has good query evaluation properties.

We now present such a language, based on relational algebra for triples. We start with a plain version and then add recursive primitives that provide the crucial functionality for handling reachability properties.

The operations of the usual relational algebra are selection, projection, union, difference, and cartesian product. Our language must remain *closed*, i.e., the result of each operation ought to be a valid triplestore. This clearly rules out projection. Selection and Boolean operations are fine. Cartesian product, however, would create a relation of arity six, but instead we use *joins* that only keep three positions in the result.

Triple joins. To see what kind of joins we need, let us first look at the *composition* of two relations. For binary relations S and S', their composition $S \circ S'$ has all pairs (x, y) so that $(x, z) \in S$ and $(z, y) \in S'$ for some z. Reachability with relation S is defined by recursively applying composition: $S \cup S \circ S \cup S \circ S \circ S \cup \ldots$. So we need an analog of composition for triples. To understand how it may look, we can view $S \circ S'$ as the *join* of S and S' on the condition that the 2nd component of S equals the first of S', and the output consist of the remaining components. We can write it as

$$S \underset{2=1'}{\overset{1,2'}{\bowtie}} S'$$

Here we refer to the positions in S as 1 and 2, and to the positions in S' as $1'$ and $2'$, so the join condition is $2 = 1'$ (written below the join symbol), and the output has positions 1 and $2'$. This suggests that our join operations on triples should be of the form $R \bowtie^{i,j,k}_{\text{cond}} R'$, where R and R' are tertiary relations, $i, j, k \in \{1, 2, 3, 1', 2', 3'\}$, and cond is a condition (to be defined precisely later).

But what is the most natural analog of relational composition? Note that to keep three indexes among $\{1, 2, 3, 1', 2', 3'\}$, we ought to project away three, meaning that two of them will come from one argument, and one from the other. Any such join operation on triples is bound to be *asymmetric*, and thus cannot be viewed as a full analog of relational composition.

So what do we do? Our solution is to add *all* such join operations. Formally, given two tertiary relations R and R', *join* operations are of the form

$$R \underset{\theta,\eta}{\overset{i,j,k}{\bowtie}} R',$$

where

- $i, j, k \in \{1, 1', 2, 2', 3, 3'\}$,
- θ is a set of equalities and inequalities between elements in $\{1, 1', 2, 2', 3, 3'\} \cup \mathcal{O}$,
- η is a set of equalities and inequalities between elements in $\{\rho(1), \rho(1'), \rho(2), \rho(2'), \rho(3), \rho(3')\} \cup \mathcal{D}$.

The semantics is defined as follows: (o_i, o_j, o_k) is in the result of the join iff there are triples $(o_1, o_2, o_3) \in R$ and $(o_{1'}, o_{2'}, o_{3'}) \in R'$ such that

- each condition from θ holds; that is, if $l = m$ is in θ, then $o_l = o_m$, and if $l = o$, where o is an object, is in θ, then $o_l = o$, and likewise for inequalities;
- each condition from η holds; that is, if $\rho(l) = \rho(m)$ is in η, then $\rho(o_l) = \rho(o_m)$, and if $\rho(l) = d$, where d is a data value, is in η, then $\rho(o_l) = d$, and likewise for inequalities.

Triple Algebra. We now define the expressions of the *Triple Algebra*, or TriAL for short. It is a restriction of relational algebra that guarantees closure, i.e., the result of each expression is a triplestore.

- Every relation name in a triplestore is a TriAL expression.
- If e is a TriAL expression, θ a set of equalities and inequalities over $\{1,2,3\} \cup \mathcal{O}$, and η is a set of equalities and inequalities over $\{\rho(1), \rho(2), \rho(3)\} \cup \mathcal{D}$, then $\sigma_{\theta,\eta}(e)$ is a TriAL expression.
- If e_1, e_2 are TriAL expressions, then the following are TriAL expressions:
  - $e_1 \cup e_2$;
  - $e_1 - e_2$;
  - $e_1 \bowtie^{i,j,k}_{\theta,\eta} e_2$, where i, j, k, θ, η as in the definition of the join above.

The semantics of the join operation has already been defined. The semantics of the Boolean operations is the usual one. The semantics of the selection is defined in the same way as the semantics of the join (in fact, the operator itself can be defined in terms of joins): one just chooses triples (o_1, o_2, o_3) satisfying both θ and η.

Given a triplestore database T, we write $e(T)$ for the result of expression e on T.

Note that $e(T)$ is again a triplestore, and thus TriAL defines closed operations on triplestores. This is important, for instance, when we require RDF queries to produce RDF graphs as their result (instead of arbitrary tuples of objects), as it is done in SPARQL via the CONSTRUCT operator [34].

Example 2. To get some intuition about the Triple Algebra consider the following TriAL expression:

$$e = E \underset{2=1'}{\overset{1,3',3}{\bowtie}} E$$

Indexes $(1,2,3)$ refer to positions of the first triple, and indexes $(1',2',3')$ to positions of the second triple in the join. Thus, for two triples (x_1, x_2, x_3) and $(x_{1'}, x_{2'}, x_{3'})$, such that $x_2 = x_{1'}$, expression e outputs the triple $(x_1, x_{3'}, x_3)$. E.g., in the triplestore of Fig. 1, (`London`, `Train Op 2`, `Brussels`) is joined with (`Train Op 2`, `part_of`, `Eurostar`), producing (`London`, `Eurostar`, `Brussels`); the full result is

St. Andrews	NatExpress	Edinburgh
Edinburgh	EastCoast	London
London	Eurostar	Brussels

Thus, e computes travel information for pairs of European cities together with companies one can use. It fails to take into account that `EastCoast` is a part of `NatExpress`. To add such information to query results (and produce triples such as (`Edinburgh`, `NatExpress`, `London`)), we use $e' = e \cup (e \bowtie^{1,3',3}_{2=1'} E)$.

Definable operations: intersection and complement. As usual, the intersection operation can be defined as $e_1 \cap e_2 = e_1 \bowtie^{1,2,3}_{1=1',2=2',3=3'} e_2$. Note that using join and union, we can define the set U of all triples (o_1, o_2, o_3) so that each o_i occurs in our triplestore database T. For instance, to collect all such triples so that o_1 occurs in the first position of R, and o_2, o_3 occur in the 2nd and 3rd position of R' respectively, we would use the expression $(R \bowtie^{1,2',3} R') \bowtie^{1,2,3'} R'$. Taking the union of all such expressions, gives us the relation U.

Using such U, we can define e^c, the complement of e with respect to the active domain, as $U - e$. In what follows, we regularly use intersection and complement in our examples.

Adding Recursion. One problem with Example 2 above is that it does not include triples ($\texttt{city}_1$,`service`,$\texttt{city}_2$) so that relation R contains a triple ($\texttt{city}_1$,$\texttt{service}_0$,$\texttt{city}_2$), and there is a chain, of some length, indicating that $\texttt{service}_0$ is a part of `service`. The second expression in Example 2 only accounted for such paths of length 1. To deal with paths of arbitrary length, we need reachability, which relational algebra is well known to be incapable of expressing. Thus, we need to add recursion to our language.

To do so, we expand TriAL with *right* and *left Kleene closure* of any triple join $\bowtie^{i,j,k}_{\theta,\eta}$ over an expression e, denoted as $(e \bowtie^{i,j,k}_{\theta,\eta})^*$ for right, and $(\bowtie^{i,j,k}_{\theta,\eta} e)^*$ for left. These are defined as

$$\begin{aligned}(e \bowtie)^* &= \emptyset \cup e \cup e \bowtie e \cup (e \bowtie e) \bowtie e \cup \ldots,\\ (\bowtie e)^* &= \emptyset \cup e \cup e \bowtie e \cup e \bowtie (e \bowtie e) \cup \ldots\end{aligned}$$

We refer to the resulting algebra as *Triple Algebra with Recursion* and denote it by TriAL*.

When dealing with binary relations we do not have to distinguish between left and right Kleene closures, since the composition operation for binary relations is associative. However, as the following example shows, joins over triples are not necessarily associative, which explains the need to make this distinction.

Example 3. Consider a triplestore database $T = (O, E)$, with $E = \{(a,b,c), (c,d,e), (d,e,f)\}$. The function ρ is not relevant for this example. The expression

$$e_1 = (E \underset{3=1'}{\overset{1,2,2'}{\bowtie}})^*$$

computes $e_1(T) = E \cup \{(a,b,d), (a,b,e)\}$, while

$$e_2 = (\underset{3=1'}{\overset{1,2,2'}{\bowtie}} E)^*$$

computes $e_2(T) = E \cup \{(a,b,d)\}$.

Now we present several examples of queries one can ask using the Triple Algebra.

Example 4. We refer now to reachability queries $\mathsf{Reach}_{\rightarrow}$ and $\mathsf{Reach}_{\nearrow}$ from the introduction. It can easily be checked that these are defined by

$$(E \overset{1,2,3'}{\underset{3=1'}{\bowtie}})^* \quad \text{and} \quad (\overset{1',2',3}{\underset{1=2'}{\bowtie}} E)^*$$

respectively.

Next consider the query from Theorem 1. Graphically, it can be represented as follows:

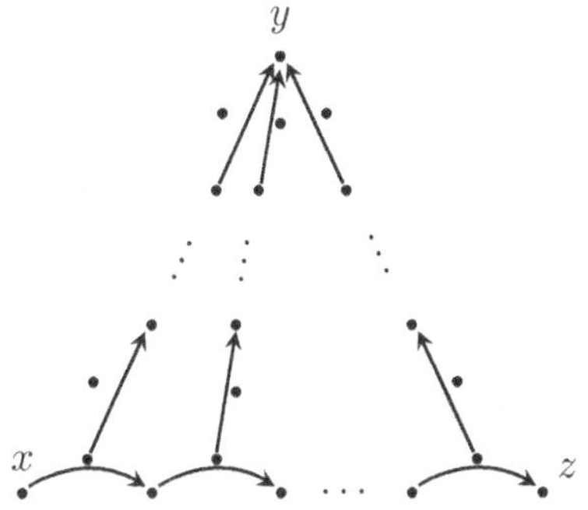

That is, we are looking for pairs of cities such that one can travel from one to the other using services operated by the same company. This query is expressed by

$$((E \overset{1,3',3}{\underset{2=1'}{\bowtie}})^* \overset{1,2,3'}{\underset{3=1',2=2'}{\bowtie}})^*.$$

Note that the interior join $(E \overset{1,3',3}{\underset{2=1'}{\bowtie}})^*$ computes all triples (x, y, z), such that $E(x, w, z)$ holds for some w, and y is reachable from w using some E-path. The outer join now simply computes the transitive closure of this relation, taking into account that the service that witnesses the connection between the cities is the same.

4. A DECLARATIVE LANGUAGE

Triple Algebra and its recursive versions are *procedural* languages. In databases, we are used to dealing with declarative languages. The most common one for expressing queries that need recursion is Datalog. It is one of the most studied database query languages, and it has reappeared recently in numerous applications. One instance of this is its well documented success in Web information extraction [19] and there are numerous others. So it seems natural to look for Datalog fragments to capture TriAL and its recursive version.

Since Datalog works over relational vocabularies, we need to explain how to represent triplestores T. The schema of these representations consists of a ternary relation symbol $E(\cdot,\cdot,\cdot)$ for each triplestore name in T, plus a binary relation symbol $\sim(\cdot,\cdot)$. Each triplestore database T can be represented as an instance I_T of this schema in the standard way: the interpretation of each relation name E in this instance corresponds to the triples in the triplestore E in T, and the interpretation of $\sim$ contains all pairs (x, y) of objects such that $\rho(x) = \rho(y)$, i.e. x and y have the same data value. If the values of ρ are tuples, we just use $\sim_i$ relations testing that the ith components of tuples are the same, for each i; this does not affect the results here at all.

We start with a Datalog fragment capturing TriAL. A TripleDatalog rule is of the form

$$\begin{aligned} S(\bar{x}) \ &\leftarrow\ S_1(\bar{x}_1), S_2(\bar{x}_2), \\ &\sim(y_1, z_1), \ldots, \sim(y_n, z_n), u_1 = v_1, \ldots, u_m = v_m \end{aligned} \quad (1)$$

where

1. S, S_1 and S_2 are (not necessarily distinct) predicate symbols of arity at most 3;
2. all variables in $\bar{x}$ and each of y_i, z_i and u_j, v_j are contained in $\bar{x}_1$ or $\bar{x}_2$.

A $\mathsf{TripleDatalog}^\neg$ rule is like the rule (1) but all equalities and predicates, except the head predicate S, can appear negated. A $\mathsf{TripleDatalog}^\neg$ *program* Π is a finite set of $\mathsf{TripleDatalog}^\neg$ rules. Such a program Π is *non-recursive* if there is an ordering $r_1, \ldots, r_k$ of the rules of Π so that the relation in the head of r_i does not occur in the body of any of the rules r_j, with $j \leq i$.

As is common with non-recursive programs, the semantics of nonrecursive $\mathsf{TripleDatalog}^\neg$ programs is given by evaluating each of the rules of Π, according to the order $r_1, \ldots, r_k$ of its rules, and taking unions whenever two rules have the same relation in their head (see [1] for the precise definition). We are now ready to present the first capturing result.

Proposition 2. TriAL *is equivalent to nonrecursive* $\mathsf{TripleDatalog}^\neg$ *programs.*

We next turn to the expressive power of recursive Triple Algebra TriAL^*. To capture it, we of course add recursion to Datalog rules, and impose a restriction that was previously used in [12]. A $\mathsf{ReachTripleDatalog}^\neg$ *program* is a $\mathsf{TripleDatalog}^\neg$ program in which each recursive predicate S is the head of exactly two rules of the form:

$$\begin{aligned} S(\bar{x}) \ &\leftarrow\ R(\bar{x}) \\ S(\bar{x}) \ &\leftarrow\ S(\bar{x}_1), R(\bar{x}_2), V(y_1, z_1), \ldots, V(y_k, z_k) \end{aligned}$$

where each $V(y_i, z_i)$ is one of the following: $y_i = z_i$, or $y_i \neq z_i$, or $\sim(y_i, z_i)$, or $\neg\sim(y_i, z_i)$, and R is a nonrecursive predicate of arity at most 3. These rules essentially mimic the standard reachability rules (for binary relation) in Datalog, and in addition one can impose equality and inequality constraints, as well as data equality and inequality constraints, along the paths.

Note that the negation in $\mathsf{ReachTripleDatalog}^\neg$ programs is *stratified.* The semantics of these programs is the standard least-fixpoint semantics [1]. A similarly defined syntactic class, but over graph databases, rather than triplestores, was shown to capture the expressive power of FO with the transitive closure operator [12]. In our case, we have a capturing result for TriAL^*.

Theorem 2. *The expressive power of* TriAL* *and* ReachTripleDatalog¬ *programs is the same.*

Next we give an example of a simple datalog program computing the query from Theorem 1.

Example 5. The following ReachTripleDatalog¬ program is equivalent to query Q from Theorem 1. Note that the answer is computed in the predicate Ans.

$$\begin{array}{rcl} S(x_1, x_2, x_3) & \leftarrow & E(x_1, x_2, x_3) \\ S(x_1, x_3', x_3) & \leftarrow & S(x_1, x_2, x_3), E(x_2, x_2', x_3') \\ \text{Ans}(x_1, x_2, x_3) & \leftarrow & S(x_1, x_2, x_3) \\ \text{Ans}(x_1, x_2, x_3') & \leftarrow & \text{Ans}(x_1, x_2, x_3), S(x_3, x_2, x_3') \end{array}$$

Recall that this query can be written in TriAL* as $Q = ((E \bowtie^{1,3',3}_{2=1'})^* \bowtie^{1,2,3'}_{3=1',2=2'})^*$. The predicate S in the program computes the inner Kleene closure of the query, while the predicate Ans computes the outer closure.

5. QUERY EVALUATION

In this section we analyze two versions of the query evaluation problems related to Triple Algebra. The *query evaluation* problem is to check if a given tuple is in the result of a query (as is standard in the study of complexity of database queries, especially when one wants to know which complexity classes they belong to). The query *computation* problem is to produce the output $e(T)$ for an expression e and a triplestore database T. We start with query evaluation.

Problem:	QUERYEVALUATION
Input:	A TriAL* expression e, a triplestore T and a tuple (x_1, x_2, x_3) of objects.
Question:	Is $(x_1, x_2, x_3) \in e(T)$?

Many graph query languages (e.g., RPQs) have PTIME upper bounds for this problem, and the data complexity (i.e., when e is assumed to be fixed) is generally in NLOGSPACE (which cannot be improved, since the simplest reachability problem over graphs is already NLOGSPACE-hard). We now show that the same upper bounds hold for our algebra, even with recursion.

Proposition 3. *The problem* QUERYEVALUATION *is* PTIME*-complete, and in* NLOGSPACE *if the algebra expression e is fixed.*

Tractable evaluation (even with respect to combined complexity) is practically a must when dealing with very large and dynamic semi-structured databases. However, in order to make a case for the practical applicability of our algebra, we need to give more precise bounds for query evaluation, rather than describe complexity classes the problem belongs to. We now show that TriAL* expressions can be evaluated in what is essentially cubic time with respect to the data. Thus, in the rest of the section we focus on the problem of actually computing the whole relation $e(T)$:

Problem:	QUERYCOMPUTATION
Input:	A TriAL* expression e and a triplestore database T.
Output:	The relation $e(T)$

We now analyze the complexity of QUERYCOMPUTATION. Following an assumption frequently made in papers on graph database query evaluation (in particular, graph pattern matching algorithms) as well as bounded variable relational languages (cf. [16, 15, 20]), we consider an *array representation* for triplestores. That is, when representing a triplestore $T = (O, E_1, \dots, E_m, \rho)$ with $O = \{o_1, \dots, o_n\}$, we assume that each relation E_l is given by a three-dimensional $n \times n \times n$ matrix, so that the ijkth entry is set to 1 iff (o_i, o_j, o_k) is in E_l. Alternatively we can have a single matrix, where entries include sets of indexes of relations E_l that triples belong to. Furthermore we have a one-dimensional array of size n whose ith entry contains $\rho(o_i)$. Using this representation we obtain the following bounds.

Theorem 3. *The problem* QUERYCOMPUTATION *can be solved in time*

- $O(|e| \cdot |T|^2)$ *for* TriAL *expressions,*
- $O(|e| \cdot |T|^3)$ *for* TriAL* *expressions.*

Note that this immediately gives the PTIME upper bound for Proposition 3.

One can examine the proofs of Proposition 2 and Theorem 2 and see that translations from Datalog into algebra are linear-time. Thus, we have the same bound for the query computation problem, when we evaluate a Datalog program Π in place of an algebra expression.

Corollary 1. *The problem* QUERYCOMPUTATION *for Datalog programs Π can be solved in time*

- $O(|\Pi| \cdot |T|^2)$ *for* TripleDatalog¬ *programs,*
- $O(|\Pi| \cdot |T|^3)$ *for* ReachTripleDatalog¬ *programs.*

Lower-complexity fragments. Even though we have acceptable combined complexity of query computation, if the size of T is very large, one may prefer to lower the it even further. We now look at fragments of TriAL* for which this is possible.

In algorithms from Theorem 3, the main difficulty arises from the presence of inequalities in join conditions. A natural restriction then is to look at a fragment TriAL$^=$ of TriAL in which all conditions θ and η used in joins can only use equalities. This fragment allows us to lower the $|T|^2$ complexity, by replacing one of the $|T|$ factors by $|O|$, the number of distinct objects.

Proposition 4. *The* QUERYCOMPUTATION *problem for* TriAL$^=$ *expressions can be solved in time $O(|e| \cdot |O| \cdot |T|)$.*

To pose navigational queries, one needs the recursive algebra, so the question is whether similar bounds can be obtained for meaningful fragments of TriAL^*. Using the ideas from the proof of Theorem 3 we immediately get an $O(|e| \cdot |O| \cdot |T|^2)$ upper bound for $\mathsf{TriAL}^=$ with recursion. However, we can improve this result for the fragment $\mathsf{reachTA}^=$ that extends $\mathsf{TriAL}^=$ with essentially *reachability* properties, such as those used in RPQs and similar query languages for graph databases.

To define it, we restrict the star operator to mimic the following graph database reachability queries:

- the query "reachable by an arbitrary path", expressed by $(R \bowtie^{1,2,3'}_{3=1'})^*$; and
- the query "reachable by a path labeled with the same element", expressed by $(R \bowtie^{1,2,3'}_{3=1',2=2'})^*$.

These are the only applications of the Kleene star permitted in $\mathsf{reachTA}^=$. For this fragment, we have the same lower complexity bound.

Proposition 5. *The problem* QUERYCOMPUTATION *for* $\mathsf{reachTA}^=$ *can be solved in time* $O(|e| \cdot |O| \cdot |T|)$.

6. TRIPLE ALGEBRA AND OTHER LANGUAGES

In this section we compare the expressive power of our algebras with relational and graph languages. As usual, we say that a language $\mathcal{L}_1$ is contained in a language $\mathcal{L}_2$ if for every query in $\mathcal{L}_1$ there is an equivalent query in $\mathcal{L}_2$. If in addition $\mathcal{L}_2$ has a query not expressible in $\mathcal{L}_1$, then $\mathcal{L}_1$ is strictly contained in $\mathcal{L}_2$. The languages are equivalent if each is contained in the other. They are incomparable if none is contained in the other.

6.1 Triple Algebra as a Relational language

To compare TriAL with relational languages, we use exactly the same relational representation of triplestores as we did when we found Datalog fragments capturing TriAL and TriAL^*. That is, we compare the expressive power of TriAL with that of First-Order Logic (FO) over vocabulary $\langle E_1, \ldots, E_n, \sim \rangle$.

Since TriAL is a restriction of relational algebra, of course it is contained in FO. We do a more detailed analysis based on the number of variables. Recall that FO^k stands for FO restricted to k variables only. To give an intuition why such restrictions are relevant for us, consider, for instance, the join operation $e = E \bowtie^{1,3',3}_{2=2'} E$. It can be expressed by the following FO^6 formula: $\varphi(x_1, x_{3'}, x_3) = \exists x_2 \exists x_{1'} \exists x_{2'} (E(x_1, x_2, x_3) \wedge E(x_{1'}, x_{2'}, x_{3'}) \wedge x_2 = x_{2'})$. This suggests that we can simulate joins using only six variables, and this extends rather easily to the whole algebra. One can furthermore show that the containment is proper in this case.

What about fragments of FO using fewer variables? Clearly we cannot go below three variables. It is not difficult to show that TriAL simulates FO^3, but the relationship with the 4 and 5 variable formalisms appears much more intricate, and its study requires more involved techniques. We can show the following.

Theorem 4.

- TriAL *is strictly contained in* FO^6.
- FO^3 *is strictly contained in* TriAL.
- TriAL *is incomparable with* FO^4 *and* FO^5.

The containment of FO^3 in TriAL is proved by induction, and we use pebble games to show that such containment is proper. For the last, more involved part of the theorem, we first show that TriAL is not contained in FO^5. Notice that the expression e given by

$$U \underset{\theta}{\overset{1,2,3}{\bowtie}} U, \text{ with } \theta = \{i \neq j \mid i, j \in \{1, 1', 2, 2', 3, 3'\}, i < j\},$$

is such that $e(T)$ is not empty if and only if T has six different objects (recall that U is the set of all triples (o_1, o_2, o_3) so that each o_i occurs in a triple in T). It then follows that TriAL is not contained in FO^5 (nor FO^4), cf. [26]. To show that FO^4 is not contained in TriAL, we devise a game that characterizes expressibility of TriAL, and use this game to show that TriAL cannot express the following FO^4 query $\varphi(x, y, z)$:

$$\exists w(\psi(x, y, w) \wedge \psi(x, w, z) \wedge \psi(w, y, z) \wedge \psi(x, y, z)),$$

where

$$\psi(x, y, z) = \exists w(E(x, w, y) \wedge E(y, w, z) \wedge E(z, w, x)).$$

The above result also shows that TriAL cannot express all conjunctive queries, since in particular the query $\varphi(x, y, z)$ is a conjunctive query. This is of course expected; the intuition is that TriAL queries have limited memory and thus cannot express queries such as the existence of a k-clique, for large values of k.

Expressivity of $\mathsf{TriAL}^=$. The TriAL queries we used to separate it from FO^5 or FO^4 make use of inequalities in the join conditions. Thus, it is natural to ask what happens when we restrict our attention to $\mathsf{TriAL}^=$, the fragment that disallows inequalities in selections and joins. We saw in Section 5 that this fragment appears to be more manageable in terms of query answering. This suggests that fewer variables may be enough, as the number of variables is often indicative of the complexity of query evaluation [23, 36]. This is indeed the case.

Theorem 5.

- FO^3 *is strictly contained in* $\mathsf{TriAL}^=$.
- $\mathsf{TriAL}^=$ *is strictly contained in* FO^4.

Next, we turn to the expressive power of TriAL^*. Since the Kleene star essentially defines the transitive closure of join operators, it seems natural for our study to compare TriAL^* with Transitive Closure Logic, or TrCl.

Formally, TrCl is defined as an extension of FO with the following operator. If $\varphi(\bar{x}, \bar{y}, \bar{z})$ is a formula, where $|\bar{x}| = |\bar{y}| = n$, and $\bar{u}, \bar{v}$ are tuples of variables of the same length n, then $[\mathbf{trcl}_{\bar{x},\bar{y}}\varphi(\bar{x}, \bar{y}, \bar{z})](\bar{u}, \bar{v})$ is a formula whose free variables are those in $\bar{z}$, $\bar{u}$ and $\bar{v}$. The semantics is as follows. For an instance I and an assignment $\bar{c}$ for variables $\bar{z}$, construct a graph G whose nodes are elements of I^n and edges contain pairs $(\bar{u}_1, \bar{u}_2)$ so that $\varphi(\bar{u}_1, \bar{u}_2, \bar{c})$ holds in I. Then $I \models [\mathbf{trcl}_{\bar{x},\bar{y}}\varphi(\bar{x}, \bar{y}, \bar{c})](\bar{a}, \bar{b})$ iff $(\bar{a}, \bar{b})$ is in the transitive closure of this graph G.

It is fairly easy to show that TriAL* is contained in TrCl; the question is whether one can find analogs of Theorem 4 for fragments of TrCl using a limited number of variables. We denote by TrCl^k the restriction of TrCl to k variables. Note that constructs of form $[\mathbf{trcl}_{\bar{x},\bar{y}}\varphi(\bar{x}, \bar{y}, \bar{z})](\bar{t}_1, \bar{t}_2)$ can be defined using $|\bar{t}_1| + |\bar{t}_2| + |\bar{z}|$ variables, by reusing $\bar{t}_1$ and $\bar{t}_2$ in φ.

Then we can show that the relationship between TriAL* and TrCl mimics the results of Theorem 4 for the case of TriAL and FO.

Theorem 6.

- TriAL* *is strictly contained in* TrCl^6.
- TrCl^3 *is strictly contained in* TriAL*.
- TriAL* *is incomparable with* TrCl^4 *and* TrCl^5.

6.2 Triple Algebra as a Graph Language

The goal of this section is to demonstrate the usefulness of TriAL* in the context of graph databases. In particular we show how to use TriAL* for querying graph databases, both with and without data values, and compare it in terms of expressiveness with several well established graph database query languages.

6.2.1 Navigational graph query languages

We compare TriAL* with a number of established formalisms for graph databases such as NREs, RPQs and *conjunctive* regular path queries (CRPQs). As our yardstick language for comparison we use a recently proposed version of XPath, adapted for graph querying [27]. Its navigational fragment, used now, is essentially Propositional Dynamic Logic (PDL) [21] with negation on paths; below we also expand it with data tests when we deal with graphs whose nodes hold data values. These languages are designed to query the topology of a graph database and specify various reachability patterns between nodes. As such, they are naturally equipped with the star operator and to make our comparison fair we will compare them with TriAL*.

The navigational language used now is called GXPath; its formulae are split into node tests, returning sets of nodes and path expressions, returning sets of pairs of nodes.

Node tests are given by the following grammar:

$$\varphi, \psi := \top \mid \neg\varphi \mid \varphi \wedge \psi \mid \varphi \vee \psi \mid \langle\alpha\rangle$$

where α is a path expression.

The path formulae of GXPath are given below. Here a ranges over the labeling alphabet Σ.

$$\alpha, \beta := \varepsilon \mid a \mid a^- \mid [\varphi] \mid \alpha \cdot \beta \mid \alpha \cup \beta \mid \overline{\alpha} \mid \alpha^*.$$

The semantics is standard, and follows the usual semantics of PDL or XPath languages. Given a graph $G = (V, E)$, $\top$ returns V, and $\langle\alpha\rangle$ returns $v \in V$ so that (v, v') is in the semantics of α for some $v' \in V$. The semantics of Boolean operators is standard. For path formulae, ε returns $\{(v, v) \mid v \in V\}$, a returns $\{(v, v') \mid (v, a, v') \in E\}$ and a^- returns $\{(v', v) \mid (v, a, v') \in E\}$. Expressions $\alpha \cdot \beta, \alpha \cup \beta, \overline{\alpha}$, and α^* denote relation composition, union, complement, and transitive closure. Finally $[\varphi]$ denotes the set of pairs (v, v) so that v is in the semantics of φ.

Since TriAL* is designed to query triplestores, we need to explain how to compare its power with that of graph query languages. Given a graph database $G = (V, E)$ over the alphabet Σ, we define a triplestore $T_G = (O, E)$, with $O = V \cup \Sigma$. Note that for now we deal with navigation; later we shall also look at data values.

To compare TriAL* with binary graph queries in a graph query language $\mathcal{L}$, we turn TriAL* ternary queries Q into binary by applying the $\pi_{1,3}(Q)$, i.e., keeping (s, o) from every triple (s, p, o) returned by Q. Under these conventions, we say that a graph query language $\mathcal{L}$ is contained in TriAL* if for every binary query $\alpha \in \mathcal{L}$ there is a TriAL* expression e_α so that $\pi_{1,3}(e_\alpha)$ and α are equivalent, and likewise, TriAL* is contained in a graph query language $\mathcal{L}$ if for every expression e in TriAL* there is a binary query $\alpha_e \in \mathcal{L}$ that is equivalent to $\pi_{1,3}(e)$. The notions of being strictly contained and incomparable extend in the same way.

Alternatively, one can do comparisons using triplestores represented as graph databases, as in Proposition 1. Since here we study the ability of TriAL* to serve as a graph query language, the comparison explained above looks more natural, but in fact all the results remain true even if we do the comparison over triplestores represented as graph databases, as described in Section 2.

We now show that all GXPath queries can be defined in TriAL*, but that there are certain properties that TriAL* can define that lie beyond the reach of GXPath.

Theorem 7. *GXPath is strictly contained in* TriAL*.

We prove this by using the equivalence of GXPath with the 3-variable fragment of reachability logic FO^* [35], shown in [27].

Note that this also implies a strict containment of languages presented in [17, 18] in TriAL*, since it is easy to show that they are subsumed by GXPath.

To compare TriAL* with common graph languages such as NREs and RPQs we observe that NREs can be thought of as path expressions of GXPath that do not use complement and where nesting is replaced with $[\langle\alpha\rangle]$. RPQs do not even have nesting. Thus:

Corollary 2.

- *NREs are strictly contained in* TriAL*.
- *RPQs are strictly contained in* TriAL*.

It is common in graph databases to consider queries that are closed under conjunction and existential quantification, such as CRPQs [13, 37], C2RPQs [10] and CNREs [9]. The latter are expressions $\varphi(\bar{x}) = \exists\bar{y} \bigwedge_{i=1}^{n}(x_i \xrightarrow{e_i} y_i)$, where all variables x_i, y_i come from $\bar{x}, \bar{y}$ and each e_i is a NRE. The semantics extends that of NREs, with each $x_i \xrightarrow{e_i} y_i$ interpreted as the existence of a path between them that is denoted by e_i. We compare TriAL* with these queries, and also with *unions* of CNREs that use bounded number of variables.

Theorem 8.

- *CNREs and* TriAL* *are incomparable in terms of expressive power.*
- *Unions of CNREs that use only three variables are strictly contained in* TriAL*.

By observing that the expressions separating CNREs from TriAL* are CRPQs, and that CNREs are more expressive than CRPQs and C2RPQS [8] we obtain:

Corollary 3.

- *CRPQs and* TriAL* *are incomparable in terms of expressive power.*
- *Unions of C2RPQs and CRPQs that use only three variables are strictly contained in* TriAL*.

There are further extensions, such as *extended* CRPQs, where paths witnessing RPQs can be named and compared for relationships between them, defined as regular or even rational relations [6, 7]. We leave the comparison with these languages as future work.

6.2.2 Query languages for graphs with data

Until now we have compared our algebra with purely navigational formalisms. Triple stores do have data values, however, and can thus model any graph database. That is, for any graph database $G = (V, E, \rho)$ we can define a triplestore $T_G = (O, E, \rho)$ with $O = V \cup \Sigma$. Note that nodes corresponding to labels have no data values assigned in our model. This is not an obstacle and can in fact be used to model graph databases that have data values on both the nodes and the edges.

We provide a comparison to an extension of GXPath with data value comparisons. The language, denoted by GXPath(∼), presented first in [27], is given by the following grammars for node and path formulae:

$$\varphi, \psi := \top | \langle\alpha = \beta\rangle \mid \langle\alpha \neq \beta\rangle \mid \neg\varphi \mid \varphi \wedge \psi \mid \varphi \vee \psi \mid \langle\alpha\rangle$$

$$\alpha, \beta := \varepsilon \mid a \mid a^{-} \mid [\varphi] \mid \alpha \cdot \beta \mid \alpha \cup \beta \mid \overline{\alpha} \mid \alpha^{*} \mid \alpha_{=} \mid \alpha_{\neq}.$$

The semantics of additional expressions is as follows: α_θ returns those pairs (v, v') returned by α for which $\rho(v)\ \theta\ \rho(v')$, for $\theta \in \{=, \neq\}$, and $\langle\alpha\ \theta\ \beta\rangle$ returns nodes v such that there are pairs (v, v_α) and (v, v_β) returned by α and β and $\rho(v_\alpha)\ \theta\ \rho(v_\beta)$. The former addition corresponds to the notion of regular expressions with equality [28], and the latter to standard XPath data-value comparisons.

To compare GXPath(∼) with TriAL*, we use the same convention as for data value-free languages. Connections of GXPath(∼) with a 3-variable reachability logic and the proof of Theorem 4 show:

Corollary 4. *GXPath(∼) is strictly contained in* TriAL*.

This also implies that TriAL* subsumes an extension of RPQs based on regular expressions with equality [28], which can test for (in)equality of data values at the beginning and the end of paths.

Another formalism proposed for querying graph databases with data values is that of *register automata* [25]. In general, these work over data words, i.e., words over both a finite alphabet and an infinite set of data values. RPQs defined by register automata find pairs of nodes connected by a path accepted by such automata. We refer to [28, 25] for precise definitions, and state the comparison result below.

Proposition 6. TriAL* *is incomparable in terms of expressive power with register automata.*

This follows since register automata can define properties not expressible with six variables, but on the other hand are not closed under complement.

7. CONCLUSIONS AND FUTURE WORK

While graph database query mechanisms have been promoted as a useful tool for querying RDF data, most of these approaches view RDF as a graph database. Although inherently similar, the two models do have significant differences. We showed that some very natural navigational queries for RDF cannot be expressed with graph-based navigational mechanisms. The solution is then to use proper triple-based models and languages.

We introduced such a model, that combines the usual idea of triplestores used in many RDF implementations, with that of graphs with data, and proposed an algebra for that model. It comes in two flavors, a non-recursive algebra TriAL and a recursive one TriAL*. We also provided Datalog-based declarative languages capturing these. We studied the query evaluation problem, as well as the expressivity of the languages, comparing them with both relational and graph query languages.

There are several future directions we would like to pursue. One relates to understanding connections with another way restriction guaranteeing closure, namely using semi-joins. Although some of the properties crucial for our goals cannot be expressed solely with semi-joins, such restrictions are closely related to the guarded fragment of FO [29], which enjoys better properties than the full FO. Another theoretical question that arises from our investigation is studying connections between languages for tuples of arbitrary arity, not just triples.

On the more practical side, we want to provide a deeper insight into the connection of our languages and nSPARQL, which seems to be the current choice for navigational RDF queries. For instance, we would like to see whether TriAL* functionalities can be included into SPARQL, resulting in a language provably more expressive than nSPARQL, that provides recursive functionalities needed to compute most navigational queries required in RDF, including property paths. Another direction is to see how possible implementations of TriAL* stack up against currently used systems. In this respect we would like to test if commercial RDBMSs can scalably implement the type of recursion we require, or whether augmenting one of the existing open-source triplestore systems will result in a more efficient evaluation when recursion is added.

Acknowledgments Work partly supported by EPSRC grants G049165 and J015377. We thank anonymous referees for their helpful suggestions.

8. References

[1] S. Abiteboul, R. Hull, and V. Vianu. *Foundations of Databases*. Addison-Wesley, 1995.

[2] R. Angles and C. Gutierrez. Survey of graph database models. *ACM Computing Surveys*, 40(1), 2008.

[3] R. Angles. A comparison of current graph database models. In *ICDE Workshops*, pages 171–177, 2012.

[4] K. Anyanwu and A. Sheth. ρ-Queries: Enabling querying for semantic associations on the Semantic Web. In *WWW'03*, pages 690–699.

[5] M. Arenas and J. Pérez. Querying semantic web data with SPARQL. In *PODS*, pages 305–316, 2011.

[6] P. Barceló, L. Libkin, A.W. Lin, and P. Wood. Expressive languages for path queries over graph-structured data. *ACM TODS* 38(4) (2012).

[7] P. Barceló, D. Figueira, and L. Libkin. Graph logics with rational relations and the generalized intersection problem. In *LICS'12*, pages 115–124.

[8] P. Barceló, J. Pérez, and J. L. Reutter. Relative expressiveness of nested regular expressions. In *AMW'12*, pages 180–195.

[9] P. Barceló, J. Pérez, and J. L. Reutter. Schema mappings and data exchange for graph databases. In *ICDT'13*.

[10] D. Calvanese, G. De Giacomo, M. Lenzerini, and M.Y. Vardi. Containment of conjunctive regular path queries with inverse. In *KR'2000*, pages 176–185.

[11] D. Calvanese, G. De Giacomo, M. Lenzerini, and M.Y. Vardi. Rewriting of regular expressions and regular path queries. *JCSS*, 64(3):443–465, 2002.

[12] M. Consens, A. Mendelzon. GraphLog: a visual formalism for real life recursion. In *PODS'90*, pages 404–416.

[13] I. Cruz, A.O. Mendelzon, and P. Wood. A graphical query language supporting recursion. In *SIGMOD'87*, pages 323–330.

[14] P. Cudré-Mauroux and S. Elnikety. Graph data management systems for new application domains. *PVLDB*, 4(12):1510–1511, 2011.

[15] W. Fan, J. Li, S. Ma, N. Tang, and Y. Wu. Adding regular expressions to graph reachability and pattern queries. In *ICDE*, pages 39–50, 2011.

[16] W. Fan, J. Li, S. Ma, N. Tang, and Y. Wu. Graph pattern matching: from intractable to polynomial time. *PVLDB*, 3(1):264–275, 2010.

[17] G. Fletcher et al. Relative expressive power of navigational querying on graphs. *ICDT 2011*, 197-207

[18] G. Fletcher et al. The impact of transitive closure on the boolean expressiveness of navigational query languages on graphs. *FoIKS 2012*, 124-143

[19] G. Gottlob and C. Koch. Monadic datalog and the expressive power of languages for web information extraction. *J. ACM*, 51(1):74–113, 2004.

[20] G. Gottlob, E. Grädel, and H. Veith. Datalog LITE: a deductive query language with linear time model checking. *ACM TOCL*, 3(1):42–79, 2002.

[21] D. Harel, D. Kozen, and J. Tiuryn. *Dynamic Logic*. MIT Press, 2000.

[22] S. Harris et al. *SPARQL 1.1 Query Language*. `http://www.w3.org/TR/sparql11-query`.

[23] N. Immerman, D. Kozen. Definability with Bounded Number of Bound Variables. *IANDC*, 83(2):121-139 (1989).

[24] The Apache Jena Manual. `http://jena.apache.org`.

[25] M. Kaminski and N. Francez. Finite memory automata. *TCS*, 134(2):329–363, 1994.

[26] L. Libkin. *Elements of Finite Model Theory*, Springer, 2004.

[27] L. Libkin, W. Martens, and D. Vrgoč. Querying graph databases with XPath. In *ICDT*, 2013.

[28] L. Libkin and D. Vrgoč. Regular path queries on graphs with data. In *ICDT'12*, pages 74–85.

[29] D. Leinders, M. Marx, J. Tyszkiewicz and J. Van den Bussche. The semijoin algebra and the guarded fragment. *Logic, Language and Information*, 14(3), 331–343, 2009.

[30] K. Losemann, W. Martens. The complexity of evaluating path expressions in SPARQL. In *PODS'12*, pages 101–112.

[31] The Neo4j Manual. `http://docs.neo4j.org`.

[32] J. Pérez, M. Arenas, and C. Gutierrez. Semantics and complexity of SPARQL. *ACM TODS*, 34(3), 2009.

[33] J. Pérez, M. Arenas, C. Gutierrez. nSPARQL: A navigational language for RDF. *J. Web Sem.*, 8(4):255–270, 2010.

[34] E. Prud'hommeaux and A. Seaborne. SPARQL query language for RDF. W3C Recommendation 15 January 2008, `http://www.w3.org/TR/rdf-sparql-query/`.

[35] B. ten Cate. The expressivity of XPath with transitive closure. In *PODS*, pages 328–337, 2006.

[36] M. Vardi. On the complexity of bounded-variable queries. In *PODS'95*, pages 266–276.

[37] P. Wood. Query languages for graph databases. *Sigmod Record*, 41(1):50–60, 2012.

Ontology-based Data Access: A Study through Disjunctive Datalog, CSP, and MMSNP

Meghyn Bienvenu
CNRS & Université Paris Sud
Orsay, France

Balder ten Cate
UC Santa Cruz
Santa Cruz, CA, USA

Carsten Lutz
University of Bremen
Bremen, Germany

Frank Wolter
University of Liverpool
Liverpool, UK

ABSTRACT

Ontology-based data access is concerned with querying incomplete data sources in the presence of domain-specific knowledge provided by an ontology. A central notion in this setting is that of an *ontology-mediated query*, which is a database query coupled with an ontology. In this paper, we study several classes of ontology-mediated queries, where the database queries are given as some form of conjunctive query and the ontologies are formulated in description logics or other relevant fragments of first-order logic, such as the guarded fragment and the unary-negation fragment. The contributions of the paper are three-fold. First, we characterize the expressive power of ontology-mediated queries in terms of fragments of disjunctive datalog. Second, we establish intimate connections between ontology-mediated queries and constraint satisfaction problems (CSPs) and their logical generalization, MMSNP formulas. Third, we exploit these connections to obtain new results regarding (i) first-order rewritability and datalog-rewritability of ontology-mediated queries, (ii) P/NP dichotomies for ontology-mediated queries, and (iii) the query containment problem for ontology-mediated queries.

Categories and Subject Descriptors

H.2.3 [**Database Management**]: Languages—*Query languages*; H.2.5 [**Database Management**]: Heterogeneous Databases

Keywords

Ontology-Based Data Access; Query Answering; Query Rewriting

1. INTRODUCTION

Ontologies are logical theories that formalize domain-specific knowledge, thereby making it available for machine processing. Recent years have seen an increasing interest in using ontologies in data-intensive applications, especially in the context of intelligent systems, the semantic web, and in data integration. A much studied scenario is that of answering queries over an incomplete database under the open world semantics, taking into account knowledge provided by an ontology [19, 18, 16]. We refer to this as *ontology-based data access (OBDA)*.

There are several important use cases for OBDA. A classical one is to enrich an incomplete data source with background knowledge, in order to obtain a more complete set of answers to a query. For example, if a medical patient database contains the facts that patient1 has finding Erythema Migrans and patient2 has finding Lyme disease, and the ontology provides the background knowledge that a finding of Erythema Migrans is sufficient for diagnosing Lyme disease, then both patient1 and patient2 can be returned when querying for patients that have the diagnosis Lyme disease. This use of ontologies is also central to query answering in the semantic web. OBDA can also be used to enrich the data schema (that is, the relation symbols used in the presentation of the data) with additional symbols to be used in a query. For example, a patient database may contain facts such as patient1 has diagnosis Lyme disease and patient2 has diagnosis Listeriosis, and an ontology could add the knowledge that Lyme disease and Listeriosis are both bacterial infections, thus enabling queries such as "return all patients with a bacterial infection" despite the fact that the data schema does not include a relation or attribute explicitly referring to bacterial infections. Especially in the bio-medical domain, applications of this kind are fueled by the availability of comprehensive professional ontologies such as SNOMED CT and FMA. A third prominent application of OBDA is in data integration, where an ontology can be used to provide a uniform view on multiple data sources [40]. This typically involves mappings from the source schemas to the schema of the ontology, which we will not explicitly consider here.

We may view the actual database query and the ontology as two components of one composite query, which we call an *ontology-mediated query*. OBDA can then be described as the problem of answering ontology-mediated queries. The database queries used in OBDA are typically unions of conjunctive queries, while the ontologies are typically specified in an ontology language that is either a description logic, or, more generally, a suitable fragment of first-order logic. For popular choices of ontology languages, the data complexity of ontology-mediated queries can be coNP-complete, which has resulted in extensive research on finding tractable classes of ontology-mediated queries, as well as on finding classes of ontology-mediated queries that are amenable to efficient query answering techniques [17, 29, 32]. In particular, relevant classes of ontology-mediated queries have been identified that admit an FO-rewriting (i.e., that are equivalent to a first-order query), or, alternatively, admit a datalog-rewriting. FO-rewritings make it possible to answer ontology-based queries using traditional database management systems. This is considered one of the most promising approaches for OBDA, and is currently the subject of significant research activity, see for example [18, 28, 30, 31, 42].

PODS'13, June 22–27, 2013, New York, New York, USA.

The main aims of this paper are (i) to characterize the expressive power of ontology-mediated queries, both in terms of more traditional database query languages and from a descriptive complexity perspective and (ii) to make progress towards complete and decidable classifications of ontology-mediated queries, with respect to their data complexity, as well as with respect to FO-rewritability and datalog-rewritability.

We take an ontology-mediated query to be a triple $(\mathbf{S}, \mathcal{O}, q)$ where $\mathbf{S}$ is a *data schema*, $\mathcal{O}$ an ontology, and q a query. Here, the data schema $\mathbf{S}$ fixes the set of relation symbols than can occur in the data and the ontology $\mathcal{O}$ is a logical theory that may use the relation symbols from $\mathbf{S}$ as well as additional symbols. The query q can use any relation symbol that occurs in $\mathbf{S}$ or $\mathcal{O}$. As ontology languages, we consider a range of standard description logics (DLs) and several fragments of first-order logic that embed ontology languages such as Datalog$^{\pm}$ [15], namely the guarded fragment (GF), the unary negation fragment (UNFO), and the guarded negation fragment (GNFO). As query languages for q, we focus on unions of conjunctive queries (UCQs) and unary atomic queries (AQs). The latter are of the form $A(x)$, with A a unary relation symbol, and correspond to what are traditionally called *instance queries* in the OBDA literature (note that A may be a relation symbol from $\mathcal{O}$ that is not part of the data schema). These two query languages are among the most used query languages in OBDA. In the following, we use $(\mathcal{L}, \mathcal{Q})$ to denote the query language that consists of all ontology-mediated queries $(\mathbf{S}, \mathcal{O}, q)$ with $\mathcal{O}$ specified in the ontology language $\mathcal{L}$ and q specified in the query language $\mathcal{Q}$. For example, (GF,UCQ) refers to ontology-mediated queries in which $\mathcal{O}$ is a GF-ontology and q is a UCQ. We refer to such query languages $(\mathcal{L}, \mathcal{Q})$ as *ontology-mediated query languages (or, OBDA languages)*.

In Section 3, we characterize the expressive power of OBDA languages in terms of natural fragments of (negation-free) disjunctive datalog. We first consider the basic description logic $\mathcal{ALC}$. We show that ($\mathcal{ALC}$,UCQ) has the same expressive power as monadic disjunctive datalog (abbreviated MDDlog) and that ($\mathcal{ALC}$,AQ) has the same expressive power as unary queries defined in a syntactic fragment of MDDlog that we call connected simple MDDlog. Similar results hold for various description logics that extend $\mathcal{ALC}$ with, for example, inverse roles, role hierarchies, and the universal role, all of which are standard operators included in the W3C-standardized ontology language OWL2 DL. Turning to other fragments of first-order logic, we then show that (UNFO,UCQ) also has the same expressive power as MDDlog, while (GF,UCQ) and (GNFO,UCQ) are strictly more expressive and coincide in expressive power with frontier-guarded disjunctive datalog, which is the DDlog fragment given by programs in which, for every atom α in the head of a rule, there is an atom β in the rule body that contains all variables from α.

In Sections 4 and 5, we study ontology-mediated queries from a *descriptive complexity* perspective. In particular, we establish an intimate connection between OBDA query languages, constraint satisfaction problems, and MMSNP. Recall that constraint satisfaction problems (CSPs) form a subclass of the complexity class NP that, although it contains NP-hard problems, is in certain ways more computationally well-behaved. The widely known Feder-Vardi conjecture [24] states that there is a dichotomy between PTIME and NP for the class of all CSPs, that is, each CSP is either in PTIME or NP-hard. In other words, the conjecture asserts that there are no CSPs which are NP-intermediate in the sense of Ladner's theorem. Monotone monadic strict NP without inequality (abbreviated MMSNP) was introduced by Feder and Vardi as a logical generalization of CSP that enjoys similar computational properties [24]. In particular, it was shown in [24, 33] that there is a dichotomy between PTIME and NP for MMSNP sentences if and only if the Feder-Vardi conjecture holds.

In Section 4, we observe that ($\mathcal{ALC}$,UCQ) and many other OBDA languages based on UCQs have the same expressive power as the query language coMMSNP, consisting of all queries whose complement is definable by an MMSNP formula with free variables. In the spirit of descriptive complexity theory, we say that ($\mathcal{ALC}$,UCQ) *captures* coMMSNP. In fact, this result is a consequence of the results in Section 3 and the observation that MDDlog has the same expressive power as coMMSNP. It has fundamental consequences regarding the data complexity of ontology-mediated queries and the containment problem for such queries, which we describe next.

First, we obtain that there is a dichotomy between PTIME and CONP for ontology-mediated queries from ($\mathcal{ALC}$,UCQ) if and only if the Feder-Vardi conjecture holds, and similarly for many other OBDA languages based on UCQs. To appreciate this result, recall that considerable effort has been directed towards identifying tractable classes of ontology-mediated queries. Ideally, one would like to classify the data complexity of every ontology-mediated query within a given OBDA language such as ($\mathcal{ALC}$,UCQ). Our aforementioned result ties this task to proving the Feder-Vardi conjecture. Significant progress has been made in understanding the complexity of CSPs and MMSNPs [14, 12, 34], and the connection established in this paper facilitates the transfer of techniques and results from CSP and MMSNP in order to analyze the data complexity of query evaluation in ($\mathcal{ALC}$,UCQ). We also consider the standard extension $\mathcal{ALCF}$ of $\mathcal{ALC}$ with functional roles and note that, for query evaluation in ($\mathcal{ALCF}$,AQ), there is no dichotomy between PTIME and CONP unless PTIME = NP.

To establish a counterpart of (GF,UCQ) and (GNFO,UCQ) in the MMSNP world, we introduce guarded monotone strict NP (abbreviated GMSNP) as a generalization of MMSNP; specifically, GMSNP is obtained from MMSNP by allowing guarded second-order quantification in the place of monadic second-order quantification, similarly as in the transition from MDDlog to frontier-guarded disjunctive datalog. The resulting query language coGMSNP has the same expressive power as frontier-guarded disjunctive datalog, and therefore, in particular, (GF,UCQ) and (GNFO,UCQ) capture coGMSNP. We observe that GMSNP has the same expressive power as the extension MMSNP_2 of MMSNP proposed in [37]. It follows from our results in Section 3 that GMSNP (and thus MMSNP_2) is strictly more expressive than MMSNP, closing an open problem from [37]. We leave it as an open problem whether GMSNP is computationally as well-behaved as MMSNP, that is, whether there is a dichotomy between PTIME and NP if the Feder-Vardi conjecture holds.

The second application of the connection between OBDA and MMSNP concerns query containment. It was shown in [24] that containment between MMSNP sentences is decidable. We use this result to prove that query containment is decidable for many OBDA languages based on UCQs, including ($\mathcal{ALC}$,UCQ) and (GF,UCQ). Note that this refers to a very general form of query containment in OBDA, as recently introduced and studied in [10]. For ($\mathcal{ALCF}$,AQ), this problem (and every other decision problem discussed below) turns out to be undecidable.

In Section 5, we consider OBDA languages based on atomic queries and establish a tight connection to (certain generalizations of) CSPs. This connection is most easily stated for *Boolean* atomic queries (BAQs): we prove that ($\mathcal{ALC}$,BAQ) captures the query language that consists of all Boolean queries definable as the complement of a CSP. Similarly ($\mathcal{ALC}$,AQ) extended with the universal role captures the query language that consists of all unary queries definable as the complement of a *generalized CSP*, which is given by a finite collection of structures enriched with a constant symbol. We then proceed to transfer results from the CSP literature to the ontology-mediated query languages ($\mathcal{ALC}$, BAQ) and ($\mathcal{ALC}$, AQ). First we immediately obtain that the existence of a PTIME/CONP dichotomy for these ontology-mediated query languages is equivalent to the Feder-Vardi conjecture. Then we show that query containment is not only decidable (as we could already conclude from the connection with coMMSNP described in Section 4), but, in fact, NEXPTIME-complete. Finally, taking advantage of recent results for CSPs [35, 26, 13], we are able to show that FO-rewritability and datalog-rewritability, as properties of ontology-mediated queries, are decidable and NEXPTIME-complete for ($\mathcal{ALC}$, AQ) and ($\mathcal{ALC}$,BAQ).

The results in Sections 4 and 5 just summarized are actually proved not only for $\mathcal{ALC}$, but also for several of its extensions. This relies on the equivalences between DL-based OBDA-languages established in Section 3.

Related Work A connection between query answering in DLs and the negation-free fragment of disjunctive datalog was first discovered and utilized in the influential [39, 29], see also [44]. This research is concerned with answer-preserving translations of ontology-mediated queries into disjunctive datalog. In contrast to the current paper, it does not consider the expressive power of ontology-mediated queries, nor their descriptive complexity. A connection between DL-based OBDA and CSPs was first found and exploited in [36], in a setup that is different from the one studied in this paper. In particular, instead of focusing on ontology-mediated queries that consist of a data schema, an ontology, and a database query, [36] concentrates on ontologies while quantifying universally over all database queries and without fixing a data schema. It establishes links to the Feder-Vardi conjecture that are incomparable to the ones found in this paper, and does not consider the expressive power and descriptive complexity of queries used in OBDA.

2. PRELIMINARIES

Schemas, Instances, and Queries. A *schema* is a finite collection $\mathbf{S} = (S_1, \dots, S_k)$ of relation symbols with associated arity. A *fact* over $\mathbf{S}$ is an expression of the form $S(a_1, \dots, a_n)$ where $S \in \mathbf{S}$ is an n-ary relation symbol, and $a_1, \dots, a_n$ are elements of some fixed, countably infinite set const of *constants*. An *instance* $\mathfrak{D}$ over $\mathbf{S}$ is a finite set of facts over $\mathbf{S}$. The *active domain* $\mathsf{adom}(\mathfrak{D})$ of $\mathfrak{D}$ is the set of all constants that occur in the facts of $\mathfrak{D}$. We will frequently use boldface notation for tuples, such as in $\mathbf{a} = (a_1, \dots, a_n)$, and we denote by () the empty tuple.

A *query over* $\mathbf{S}$ is semantically defined as a mapping q that associates with every instance $\mathfrak{D}$ over $\mathbf{S}$ a set of *answers* $q(\mathfrak{D}) \subseteq \mathsf{adom}(\mathfrak{D})^n$, where $n \geq 0$ is the *arity* of q. If $n = 0$, then we say that q is a *Boolean query*, and we write $q(\mathfrak{D}) = 1$ if $() \in q(\mathfrak{D})$ and $q(\mathfrak{D}) = 0$ otherwise.

A prominent way of specifying queries is by means of first-order logic (FO). Specifically, each schema $\mathbf{S}$ and domain-independent FO-formula $\varphi(x_1, \dots, x_n)$ that uses only relation names from $\mathbf{S}$ (and, possibly, equality) give rise to the n-ary query $q_{\varphi,\mathbf{S}}$, defined by setting for all $\mathbf{S}$-instances $\mathfrak{D}$,

$$q_{\varphi,\mathbf{S}}(\mathfrak{D}) = \{(a_1, \dots, a_n) \in \mathsf{adom}(\mathfrak{D})^n \mid \mathfrak{D} \models \varphi[a_1, \dots, a_n]\}.$$

To simplify exposition, we assume that FO-queries do not contain constants. We use FOQ to denote the set of all first-order queries, as defined above. Similarly, we use CQ and UCQ to refer to the class of conjunctive queries and unions of conjunctive queries, defined as usual and allowing the use of equality. AQ denotes the set of *atomic queries*, which are of the form $A(x)$ with A a unary relation symbol. Each of these is called a *query language*, which is defined abstractly as a set of queries. Besides FOQ, CQ, UCQ, and AQ, we consider various other query languages introduced later, including ontology-mediated ones and variants of datalog.

Two queries q_1 and q_2 over $\mathbf{S}$ are *equivalent*, written $q_1 \equiv q_2$, if for every $\mathbf{S}$-instance $\mathfrak{D}$, we have $q_1(\mathfrak{D}) = q_2(\mathfrak{D})$. We say that query language $\mathcal{Q}_2$ is *at least as expressive as* query language $\mathcal{Q}_1$, written $\mathcal{Q}_1 \preceq \mathcal{Q}_2$, if for every query $q_1 \in \mathcal{Q}_1$ over some schema $\mathbf{S}$, there is a query $q_2 \in \mathcal{Q}_2$ over $\mathbf{S}$ with $q_1 \equiv q_2$. $\mathcal{Q}_1$ and $\mathcal{Q}_2$ *have the same expressive power* if $\mathcal{Q}_1 \preceq \mathcal{Q}_2 \preceq \mathcal{Q}_1$.

Ontology-Mediated Queries. We introduce the fundamentals of ontology-based data access. An *ontology language* $\mathcal{L}$ is a fragment of first-order logic (i.e., a set of FO sentences), and an *$\mathcal{L}$-ontology* $\mathcal{O}$ is a finite set of sentences from $\mathcal{L}$. We introduce various ontology languages throughout the paper, including descriptions logics and the guarded fragment.

An *ontology-mediated query* over a schema $\mathbf{S}$ is a triple $(\mathbf{S}, \mathcal{O}, q)$, where $\mathcal{O}$ is an ontology and q a query over $\mathbf{S} \cup \mathsf{sig}(\mathcal{O})$, with $\mathsf{sig}(\mathcal{O})$ the set of relation symbols used in $\mathcal{O}$. Here, we call $\mathbf{S}$ the *data schema*. Note that the ontology can introduce symbols that are not in the data schema. As explained in the introduction, this allows the ontology to enrich the schema of the query q. Of course, we do not require that every relation of the data schema needs to occur in the ontology. We have explicitly included $\mathbf{S}$ in the specification of the ontology-mediated query to emphasize that the ontology-mediated query is interpreted as a query over $\mathbf{S}$.

The semantics of an ontology-mediated query is given in terms of *certain answers*, defined next. A *finite relational structure* over a schema $\mathbf{S}$ is a pair $\mathfrak{B} = (\mathsf{dom}, \mathfrak{D})$ where dom is a non-empty finite set called the *domain* of $\mathfrak{B}$ and $\mathfrak{D}$ is an instance over $\mathbf{S}$ with $\mathsf{adom}(\mathfrak{D}) \subseteq \mathsf{dom}$. When $\mathbf{S}$ is understood, we use $\mathsf{Mod}(\mathcal{O})$ to denote the set of all finite relational structures $\mathfrak{B}$ over $\mathbf{S} \cup \mathsf{sig}(\mathcal{O})$ such that $\mathfrak{B} \models \mathcal{O}$. Let $(\mathbf{S}, \mathcal{O}, q)$ be an ontology-mediated query with q of arity n. The *certain answers to q on an $\mathbf{S}$-instance $\mathfrak{D}$ given $\mathcal{O}$* is the set $\mathsf{cert}_{q,\mathcal{O}}(\mathfrak{D})$ of tuples $\mathbf{a} \in \mathsf{adom}(\mathfrak{D})^n$ such that for all $(\mathsf{dom}, \mathfrak{D}') \in \mathsf{Mod}(\mathcal{O})$ with $\mathfrak{D} \subseteq \mathfrak{D}'$ (that is, all models of $\mathcal{O}$ that extend $\mathfrak{D}$), we have $\mathbf{a} \in q(\mathfrak{D}')$.

Note that all ontology languages considered in this paper enjoy finite controllability, meaning that finite relational structures can be replaced with unrestricted ones without changing the certain answers to unions of conjunctive queries [6, 7].

Every ontology-mediated query $Q = (\mathbf{S}, \mathcal{O}, q)$ can be semantically interpreted as a query q_Q over $\mathbf{S}$ by setting $q_Q(\mathfrak{D}) = \mathsf{cert}_{q,\mathcal{O}}(\mathfrak{D})$ for all $\mathbf{S}$-instances $\mathfrak{D}$. Taking this view one step further, each choice of an ontology language $\mathcal{L}$ and query language $\mathcal{Q}$ gives rise to a query language, denoted $(\mathcal{L}, \mathcal{Q})$, defined as the set of queries $q_{(\mathbf{S},\mathcal{O},q)}$ with $\mathbf{S}$ a schema, $\mathcal{O}$ an $\mathcal{L}$-ontology, and $q \in \mathcal{Q}$ a query over $\mathbf{S} \cup \mathsf{sig}(\mathcal{O})$. We refer to such query languages $(\mathcal{L}, \mathcal{Q})$ as *ontology-mediated query languages* (or, *OBDA languages*).

Example 1 *The left-hand side of Table 1 shows an ontology $\mathcal{O}$ that is formulated in the guarded fragment of FO. Consider the ontology-mediated query $(\mathbf{S}, \mathcal{O}, q)$ with data schema and query*

$$\mathbf{S} = \{\mathsf{ErythemaMigrans}, \mathsf{LymeDisease}, \mathsf{HereditaryPredisposition}, \mathsf{finding}, \mathsf{diagnosis}, \mathsf{parent}\}$$
$$q(x) = \exists y(\ \mathsf{diagnosis}(x, y) \land \mathsf{BacterialInfection}(y)\ ).$$

For the instance $\mathfrak{D}$ over $\mathbf{S}$ that consists of the facts

finding(pat1, jan12find1) ErythemaMigrans(jan12find1)
diagnosis(pat2, may7diag2) Listeriosis(may7diag2)

$\forall x(\ \exists y(\mathsf{finding}(x,y) \wedge \mathsf{ErythemaMigrans}(y))$ $\rightarrow \exists y(\mathsf{diagnosis}(x,y) \wedge \mathsf{LymeDisease}(y))\ )$	$\exists\mathsf{finding}.\mathsf{ErythemaMigrans} \sqsubseteq \exists\mathsf{diagnosis}.\mathsf{LymeDisease}$
$\forall x(\ (\mathsf{LymeDisease}(x) \vee \mathsf{Listeriosis}(x)) \rightarrow \mathsf{BacterialInfection}(x)\ )$	$\mathsf{LymeDisease} \sqcup \mathsf{Listeriosis} \sqsubseteq \mathsf{BacterialInfection}$
$\forall x(\ \exists y.(\mathsf{HereditaryDisposition}(y) \wedge \mathsf{parent}(x,y)) \rightarrow \mathsf{HereditaryDisposition}(y))\ )$	$\exists\mathsf{parent}.\mathsf{HereditaryDisposition} \sqsubseteq \mathsf{HereditaryDisposition}$

Table 1: Example ontology, presented in (the guarded fragment of) first-order logic and the DL $\mathcal{ALC}$

$\top^*(x) = \top$	$(C \sqcap D)^*(x) = C^*(x) \wedge D^*(x)$
$\bot^*(x) = \bot$	$(C \sqcup D)^*(x) = C^*(x) \vee D^*(x)$
$A^*(x) = A(x)$	$(\exists R.C)^*(x) = \exists y\, R(x,y) \wedge C^*(y)$
$(\neg C)^*(x) = \neg C^*(x)$	$(\forall R.C)^*(x) = \forall y\, R(x,y) \rightarrow C^*(y)$

Table 2: First-order translation of $\mathcal{ALC}$-concepts

we have $\mathsf{cert}_{q,\mathcal{O}}(\mathfrak{D}) = \{\mathsf{pat1}, \mathsf{pat2}\}$.

Description Logics for Specifying Ontologies. In description logic, schemas are generally restricted to relations of arity one and two, called *concept names* and *role names*, respectively. For brevity, we speak of *binary schemas*. We briefly review the basic description logic $\mathcal{ALC}$. Relevant extensions of $\mathcal{ALC}$ will be introduced later on in the paper.

An $\mathcal{ALC}$-*concept* is formed according to the syntax rule

$$C, D ::= A \mid \top \mid \bot \mid \neg C \mid C \sqcap D \mid C \sqcup D \mid \exists R.C \mid \forall R.C$$

where A ranges over concept names and R over role names. An $\mathcal{ALC}$-*ontology* $\mathcal{O}$ is a finite set of *concept inclusions* $C \sqsubseteq D$, with C and D $\mathcal{ALC}$-concepts. We define the semantics of $\mathcal{ALC}$-concepts by translation to FO-formulas with one free variable, as shown in Table 2. An $\mathcal{ALC}$-ontology $\mathcal{O}$ then translates into the set of FO-sentences $\mathcal{O}^* = \{\forall x.(C^*(x) \rightarrow D^*(x)) \mid C \sqsubseteq D \in \mathcal{O}\}$. On the right-hand side of Table 1, we show the $\mathcal{ALC}$-version of the guarded fragment ontology displayed on the left-hand side. Note that, although the translation is equivalence-preserving in this case, in general, the guarded fragment is a more expressive ontology language than $\mathcal{ALC}$. Throughout the paper, we do not explicitly distinguish between a DL ontology and its translation into FO.

We remark that, from a DL perspective, the above definitions of instances and certain answers correspond to making the *standard name assumption (SNA)* in ABoxes, which in particular implies the *unique name assumption*. We make the SNA only to facilitate uniform presentation; the SNA is inessential for the results presented in this paper.

Example 2 *Let* $\mathcal{O}$ *and* $\mathbf{S}$ *be as in Example 1. For* $q_1(x) = \mathsf{BacterialInfection}(x)$, *the ontology-mediated query* $(\mathbf{S}, \mathcal{O}, q_1)$ *is equivalent to the union of conjunctive queries* $\mathsf{LymeDisease}(x) \vee \mathsf{Listeriosis}(x)$. *For* $q_2(x) = \mathsf{HereditaryDisposition}(x)$, *the ontology-mediated query* $(\mathbf{S}, \mathcal{O}, q_2)$ *is equivalent to the query defined by the datalog program*

$$P(x) \leftarrow \mathsf{HereditaryDisposition}(x) \qquad \mathsf{goal}(x) \leftarrow P(x)$$
$$P(x) \leftarrow \mathsf{parent}(y,x) \wedge P(y)$$

but not to any first-order query.

3. OBDA AND DISJUNCTIVE DATALOG

We show that for many OBDA languages, there is a natural fragment of disjunctive datalog with exactly the same expressive power.

A *disjunctive datalog rule* ρ has the form

$$S_1(\mathbf{x}_1) \vee \cdots \vee S_m(\mathbf{x}_m) \leftarrow R_1(\mathbf{y}_1) \wedge \cdots \wedge R_n(\mathbf{y}_n)$$

with $m \geq 0$ and $n > 0$. We refer to $S_1(\mathbf{x}_1) \vee \cdots \vee S_m(\mathbf{x}_m)$ as the *head* of ρ, and to $R_1(\mathbf{y}_1) \wedge \ldots \wedge R_n(\mathbf{y}_n)$ as the *body* of ρ. Every variable that occurs in the head of a rule ρ is required to also occur in the body of ρ. Empty rule heads are denoted $\bot$. A *disjunctive datalog (DDlog) program* Π is a finite set of disjunctive datalog rules with a selected *goal predicate* goal that does not occur in rule bodies and only in *goal rules* of the form $\mathsf{goal}(\mathbf{x}) \leftarrow R_1(\mathbf{x}_1) \wedge \cdots \wedge R_n(\mathbf{x}_n)$. The *arity of* Π is the arity of the goal relation. Relation symbols that occur in the head of at least one rule of Π are *intensional (IDB) predicates* of Π, and all remaining relation symbols in Π are *extensional (EDB) predicates*.

Every DDlog program Π of arity n naturally defines an n-ary query q_Π over the schema $\mathbf{S}$ that consists of the EDB predicates of Π: for every instance $\mathfrak{D}$ over $\mathbf{S}$, we have

$$q_\Pi(\mathfrak{D}) = \{\mathbf{a} \in \mathsf{adom}(\mathfrak{D})^n \mid \mathsf{goal}(\mathbf{a}) \in \mathfrak{D}' \text{ for all } \mathfrak{D}' \in \mathsf{Mod}(\Pi) \text{ with } \mathfrak{D} \subseteq \mathfrak{D}'\}.$$

Here, $\mathsf{Mod}(\Pi)$ denotes the set of all instances over $\mathbf{S}'$ that satisfy all rules in Π, with $\mathbf{S}'$ the set of all IDB and EDB predicates in Π. Note that the DDlog programs considered in this paper are negation-free. Restricted to this fragment, there is no difference between the different semantics of DDlog studied e.g. in [21].

We use $\mathsf{adom}(x)$ in rule bodies as a shorthand for "x is in the active domain of the EDB predicates". Specifically, whenever we use adom in a rule of a DDlog program Π, we assume that adom is an IDB predicate and that the program Π includes all rules of the form $\mathsf{adom}(x) \leftarrow R(\mathbf{x})$ where R is an EDB predicate of Π and $\mathbf{x}$ is a tuple of distinct variables that includes x.

A *monadic disjunctive datalog (MDDlog) program* is a DDlog program in which all IDB predicates with the possible exception of goal are monadic. We use MDDlog to denote the query language that consists of all queries defined by an MDDlog program.

3.1 Ontologies Specified in Description Logics

We show that ($\mathcal{ALC}$,UCQ) has the same expressive power as MDDlog and identify a fragment of MDDlog that has the same expressive power as ($\mathcal{ALC}$,AQ). In addition, we consider the extensions of $\mathcal{ALC}$ with inverse roles, role hierarchies, transitive roles, and the universal role, which we also relate to MDDlog and its fragments. To match the syntax of $\mathcal{ALC}$ and its extensions, we generally assume schemas to be binary throughout this section.[1]

($\mathcal{ALC}$,UCQ) and MDDlog. The first main result of this section is Theorem 1 below, which relates ($\mathcal{ALC}$,UCQ) and MDDlog.

Theorem 1 *($\mathcal{ALC}$,UCQ) and MDDlog have the same expressive power.*

[1] In fact, this assumption is inessential for Theorems 1 and 3 (which speak about UCQs), but required for Theorems 2, 4, and 5 (which speak about AQs) to hold.

Proof. (sketch) We start with giving some intuitions about answering ($\mathcal{ALC}$,UCQ) queries which guide our translation of such queries into MDDlog programs. Recall that the definition of certain answers to an ontology-mediated query on an instance $\mathfrak{D}$ involves a quantification over all models of $\mathcal{O}$ which extend $\mathfrak{D}$. It turns out that in the case of ($\mathcal{ALC}$,UCQ) queries (and, as we will see later, more generally for (UNFO,UCQ) queries), it suffices to consider a particular type of extensions of $\mathfrak{D}$ that we term *pointwise extensions*. Intuitively, such an extension of $\mathfrak{D}$ corresponds to attaching domain-disjoint structures to the elements of $\mathfrak{D}$. Formally, for instances $\mathfrak{D} \subseteq \mathfrak{D}'$, we call $\mathfrak{D}'$ a pointwise extension of $\mathfrak{D}$ if $\mathfrak{D}' \setminus \mathfrak{D}$ is the union of instances $\{\mathfrak{D}'_a \mid a \in \mathsf{adom}(\mathfrak{D})\}$ such that $\mathsf{adom}(\mathfrak{D}'_a) \cap \mathsf{adom}(\mathfrak{D}) \subseteq \{a\}$ and $\mathsf{adom}(\mathfrak{D}'_a) \cap \mathsf{adom}(\mathfrak{D}'_b) = \emptyset$ for $a \neq b$. The fact that we need only consider models of $\mathcal{O}$ which are pointwise extensions of $\mathfrak{D}$ is helpful because it constrains the ways in which a CQ can be satisfied. Specifically, every homomorphism h from q to $\mathfrak{D}'$ gives rise to a query q' obtained from q by identifying all variables that h sends to the same element, and to a decomposition of q' into a collection of components $q'_0, \ldots, q'_k$ where the 'core component' q'_0 comprises all atoms of q' whose variables h sends to elements of $\mathfrak{D}$ and for each $\mathfrak{D}'_a$ in the image of h, there is a 'non-core component' q'_i, $1 \leq i \leq k$, such that q'_i comprises all atoms of q' whose variables h sends to elements of $\mathfrak{D}'_a$. Note that the non-core components are pairwise variable-disjoint and share at most one variable with the core component.

We now detail the translation from an ontology-mediated query $(\mathbf{S}, \mathcal{O}, q) \in (\mathcal{ALC},\text{UCQ})$ into an equivalent MDDlog program. Let $\mathsf{sub}(\mathcal{O})$ be the set of subconcepts (that is, syntactic subexpressions) of concepts that occur in $\mathcal{O}$, and let $\mathsf{cl}(\mathcal{O}, q)$ denote the union of $\mathsf{sub}(\mathcal{O})$ and the set of all CQ that have at most one free variable, use only symbols from q, and whose number of atoms is bounded by the number of atoms of q. A *type* (for $\mathcal{O}$ and q) is a subset of $\mathsf{cl}(\mathcal{O}, q)$. The CQs present in $\mathsf{cl}(\mathcal{O}, q)$ include all potential 'non-core components' from the intuitive explanation above. The free variable of a CQ in $\mathsf{cl}(\mathcal{O}, q)$ (if any) represents the overlap between the core component and the non-core component.

We introduce a fresh unary relation symbol P_τ for every type τ, and we denote by $\mathbf{S}'$ the schema that extends $\mathbf{S}$ with these additional symbols. In the MDDlog program that we aim to construct, the relation symbols P_τ will be used as IDB relations, and the symbols from $\mathbf{S}$ will be the EBD relations.

We will say that a relational structure $\mathfrak{B}$ over $\mathbf{S}' \cup \mathsf{sig}(\mathcal{O})$ is *type-coherent* if $P_\tau(d) \in \mathfrak{B}$ just in the case that

$$\begin{aligned}\tau \quad = \quad & \{q' \in \mathsf{cl}(\mathcal{O}, q) \mid q' \text{ Boolean }, \mathfrak{B} \models q'\} \cup \\ & \{C \in \mathsf{cl}(\mathcal{O}, q) \mid C \text{ unary}, \mathfrak{B} \models C[d]\}.\end{aligned}$$

Set k equal to the maximum of 2 and the width of q, that is, the number of variables that occur in q. By a *diagram*, we mean a conjunction $\delta(x_1, \ldots, x_n)$ of atomic formulas over the schema $\mathbf{S}'$, with $n \leq k$ variables. A diagram $\delta(\mathbf{x})$ is *realizable* if there exists a type-coherent $\mathfrak{B} \in \mathsf{Mod}(\mathcal{O})$ that satisfies $\exists \mathbf{x} \delta(\mathbf{x})$. A diagram $\delta(\mathbf{x})$ *implies* $q(\mathbf{x}')$, with $\mathbf{x}'$ a sequence of variables from $\mathbf{x}$, if every type-coherent $\mathfrak{B} \in \mathsf{Mod}(\mathcal{O})$ that satisfies $\delta(\mathbf{x})$ under some variable assignment, satisfies $q(\mathbf{x}')$ under the same assignment.

The desired MDDlog program Π consists of the following collections of rules:

$$\begin{aligned}\bigvee_{\tau \subseteq \mathsf{cl}(\mathcal{O},q)} P_\tau(x) &\leftarrow \mathsf{adom}(x) \\ \bot &\leftarrow \delta(\mathbf{x}) \quad \text{for all non-realizable diagrams } \delta(\mathbf{x}) \\ \mathsf{goal}(\mathbf{x}') &\leftarrow \delta(\mathbf{x}) \quad \text{for all diagrams } \delta(\mathbf{x}) \text{ that imply } q(\mathbf{x}')\end{aligned}$$

Intuitively, these rules 'guess' a pointwise extension $\mathfrak{D}'$ of $\mathfrak{D}$. Specifically, the types P_τ guessed in the first line determine which subconcepts of $\mathcal{O}$ are made true at each element of $\mathfrak{D}'$. Since MDDlog does not support existential quantifiers, the $\mathfrak{D}'_a$ parts of $\mathfrak{D}'$ cannot be guessed explicitly. Instead, the CQs included in the guessed types determine those non-core component queries that matched in the $\mathfrak{D}'_a$ parts. The second line ensures coherence of the guesses and the last line guarantees that q has the required match in $\mathfrak{D}'$. It is proved in the full version of this paper that the MDDlog query q_Π is indeed equivalent to $(\mathbf{S}, \mathcal{O}, q)$.

For the converse direction, let Π be an MDDlog program. For each unary IDB relation A of Π, we introduce two fresh unary relations, denoted by A and $\bar{A}$. The ontology $\mathcal{O}$ enforces that $\bar{A}$ represents the complement of A, that is, it consists of all inclusions of the form

$$\top \sqsubseteq (A \sqcup \bar{A}) \sqcap \neg(A \sqcap \bar{A}).$$

Let q be the union of (i) all conjunctive queries that constitute the body of a goal rule, as well as (ii) all conjunctive queries obtained from a non-goal rule of the form

$$A_1(\mathbf{x}_1) \vee \cdots \vee A_m(\mathbf{x}_m) \leftarrow R_1(\mathbf{y}_1) \wedge \cdots \wedge R_n(\mathbf{y}_n)$$

by taking the conjunctive query

$$\bar{A}_1(\mathbf{x}_1) \wedge \cdots \wedge \bar{A}_m(\mathbf{x}_m) \wedge R_1(\mathbf{y}_1) \wedge \cdots \wedge R_n(\mathbf{y}_n).$$

It can be shown that the ontology-mediated query $(\mathbf{S}, \mathcal{O}, q)$, where $\mathbf{S}$ is the schema that consists of the EDB relations of Π, is equivalent to the query defined by Π. ❑

***ALC* with Atomic Queries.** We characterize ($\mathcal{ALC}$,AQ) by a fragment of MDDlog. This query language has the same expressive power as the OBDA language ($\mathcal{ALC}$,ConQ), where ConQ denotes the set of all *$\mathcal{ALC}$-concept queries*, that is, queries $C(x)$ with C a (possibly compound) $\mathcal{ALC}$-concept. Specifically, each query $(\mathbf{S}, \mathcal{O}, q) \in (\mathcal{ALC}, \text{ConQ})$ with $q = C(x)$ can be expressed as a query $(\mathbf{S}, \mathcal{O}', A(x)) \in (\mathcal{ALC}, \text{AQ})$ where A is a fresh concept name (that is, it does not occur in $\mathbf{S} \cup \mathsf{sig}(\mathcal{O})$) and $\mathcal{O}' = \mathcal{O} \cup \{C \sqsubseteq A\}$. As a consequence, ($\mathcal{ALC}$,AQ) also has the same expressive power as ($\mathcal{ALC}$, TCQ), where TCQ is the set of all CQs that take the form of a directed tree with a single answer variable at the root.

Each disjunctive datalog rule can be associated with an undirected graph whose nodes are the variables that occur in the rule and whose edges reflect co-occurrence of two variables in an atom in the rule body. We say that a rule is *connected* if its graph is connected, and that a DDlog program is connected if all its rules are connected. An MDDlog program is *simple* if each rule contains at most one atom $R(\mathbf{x})$ with R an EDB relation; additionally, we require that, in this atom, every variable occurs at most once.

Theorem 2 *($\mathcal{ALC}$,AQ) has the same expressive power as unary connected simple MDDlog.*

Proof. (sketch) The translation from ($\mathcal{ALC}$,AQ) to unary connected simple MDDlog queries is a modified version of the translation given in the proof of Theorem 1. Assume that $(\mathbf{S}, \mathcal{O}, q)$ with $q = A(x)$ is given. We now take types to be subsets of $\mathsf{sub}(\mathcal{O})$ and then define diagrams exactly as before (with $k = 2$). The MDDlog program Π consists of the following rules:

$$\begin{aligned}\bigvee_{\tau \subseteq \mathsf{sub}(\mathcal{O})} P_\tau(x) &\leftarrow \mathsf{adom}(x) \\ \bot &\leftarrow \delta(\mathbf{x}) \quad \text{for all non-realizable diagrams } \delta(\mathbf{x}) \\ & \qquad\qquad \text{of the form } P_{\tau_1}(x) \wedge P_{\tau_2}(x), \\ & \qquad\qquad P_\tau(x) \wedge A(x), \text{ or} \\ & \qquad\qquad P_{\tau_1}(x_1) \wedge S(x_1, x_2) \wedge P_{\tau_2}(x_2) \\ \mathsf{goal}(x) &\leftarrow P_\tau(x) \quad \text{for all } P_\tau \text{ with } A \in P_\tau\end{aligned}$$

Clearly, Π is unary, connected, and simple. Equivalence of the queries $(\mathbf{S}, \mathcal{O}, q)$ and q_Π is proved in the full version of this paper.

Conversely, let Π be a unary connected simple MDDlog program. It is easy to rewrite each rule of Π into an equivalent $\mathcal{ALC}$-concept inclusion, where goal is now regarded as a concept name. For example, $\mathsf{goal}(x) \leftarrow R(x,y)$ is rewritten into $\exists R.\top \sqsubseteq \mathsf{goal}$ and $P_1(x) \vee P_2(y) \leftarrow R(x,y) \wedge A(x) \wedge B(y)$ is rewritten into $A \sqcap \exists R.(B \sqcap \neg P_2) \sqsubseteq P_1$. Let $\mathcal{O}$ be the resulting ontology and let $q = \mathsf{goal}(x)$. Then the query q_Π is equivalent to the query $(\mathbf{S}, \mathcal{O}, q)$, where $\mathbf{S}$ consists of the EDB relations in Π. ❑

Note that the connectedness condition is required since one cannot express MDDlog rules such as $\mathsf{goal}(x) \leftarrow \mathsf{adom}(x) \wedge A(y)$ with $y \neq x$ in ($\mathcal{ALC}$,AQ). Multiple variable occurrences in EDB relations have to be excluded because programs such as $\mathsf{goal}(x) \leftarrow A(x)$, $\bot \leftarrow R(x,x)$ (return all elements in A if the instance contains no reflexive R-edge, and return the active domain otherwise) also cannot be expressed in ($\mathcal{ALC}$,AQ).

Extensions of $\mathcal{ALC}$. We identify several standard extensions of ($\mathcal{ALC}$,UCQ) and ($\mathcal{ALC}$,AQ) that have the same expressive power, and some that do not. We introduce the relevant extensions only briefly and refer to [4] for more details.

$\mathcal{ALCI}$ is the extension of $\mathcal{ALC}$ in which one can state that a role name R is the *inverse* of a role name S, that is, $\forall xy(R(x,y) \leftrightarrow S(y,x))$; $\mathcal{ALCH}$ is the extension in which one can state that a role name R is *included* in a role name S, that is, $\forall xy(R(x,y) \rightarrow S(x,y))$; $\mathcal{S}$ is the extension of $\mathcal{ALC}$ in which one can require some roles names to be interpreted as *transitive relations*; $\mathcal{ALCF}$ is the extension in which one can state that some role names are interpreted as *partial functions*; and $\mathcal{ALCU}$ is the extension with the *universal role* U, interpreted as $\mathsf{dom} \times \mathsf{dom}$ in any relational structure $\mathfrak{B}$ with domain dom. Note that U should be regarded as a logical symbol and is not a member of any schema. All these means of expressivity are included in the OWL2 DL profile of the W3C-standardized ontology language OWL2 [47].

We use the usual naming scheme to denote combinations of these extensions, for example $\mathcal{ALCHI}$ for the union of $\mathcal{ALCH}$ and $\mathcal{ALCI}$ and $\mathcal{SHI}$ for the union of $\mathcal{S}$ and $\mathcal{ALCHI}$. The following result summarizes the expressive power of extensions of $\mathcal{ALC}$.

Theorem 3

1. *($\mathcal{ALCHIU}$,UCQ) has the same expressive power as MDDlog and as ($\mathcal{ALC}$,UCQ).*
2. *($\mathcal{S}$,UCQ) and ($\mathcal{ALCF}$,UCQ) are strictly more expressive than ($\mathcal{ALC}$,UCQ).*

Proof. (sketch) In Point 1, we start with ($\mathcal{ALCIU}$,UCQ), for which the result follows from Theorem 6 in Section 3.2 since $\mathcal{ALCIU}$ is a fragment of UNFO. Role inclusions $\forall xy(R(x,y) \rightarrow S(x,y))$ do not add expressive power since they can be simulated by adding to the ontology the inclusions $\exists R.C \sqsubseteq \exists S.C$ for all $C \in \mathsf{sub}(\mathcal{O})$, and replacing every atom $S(x,y)$ in the UCQ by $R(x,y) \vee S(x,y)$.

For Point 2, we separate ($\mathcal{S}$,UCQ) from ($\mathcal{ALC}$,UCQ) by showing that the following ontology-mediated query $(\mathbf{S}_1, \mathcal{O}_1, q_1)$ cannot be expressed in ($\mathcal{ALC}$,UCQ): $\mathbf{S}_1$ consists of two role names R and S, $\mathcal{O}_1$ states that these role names are both transitive, and $q_1 = \exists xy(R(x,y) \wedge S(x,y))$. For ($\mathcal{ALCF}$,UCQ), we show that $(\mathbf{S}_2, \mathcal{O}_2, q_2)$ cannot be expressed in ($\mathcal{ALC}$,UCQ), where $\mathbf{S}_2$ consists of role name R and concept name A, $\mathcal{O}_2$ states that R is functional, and $q_2 = A(x)$. Detailed proofs are provided in the full version of this paper. They rely on a characterization of ($\mathcal{ALC}$,UCQ) in terms of colored forbidden patterns [38], which is a by-product of the connection between ($\mathcal{ALC}$,UCQ) and MMSNP that will be established in Section 4. ❑

The next result is interesting when contrasted with Point 2 of Theorem 3: when ($\mathcal{ALC}$,UCQ) is replaced with ($\mathcal{ALC}$,AQ), then the addition of transitive roles no longer increases the expressive power.

Theorem 4 *($\mathcal{ALC}$,AQ) has the same expressive power as ($\mathcal{SHI}$,AQ).*

Proof. (sketch) The proof of Theorem 2 given above actually shows that unary connected simple MDDlog is at least as expressive as ($\mathcal{ALCI}$,AQ). Thus, ($\mathcal{ALC}$,AQ) has the same expressive power as ($\mathcal{ALCI}$,AQ). Now it is folklore that in $\mathcal{ALCI}$ transitive roles can be replaced by certain concept inclusions without changing the certain answers to atomic queries. This can be done similarly to the elimination of role inclusions in the proof above, see [39, 45]. Thus ($\mathcal{ALCI}$,AQ) has the same expressive power as ($\mathcal{SHI}$,AQ), and the result follows. ❑

It follows from [45] that this observation can be extended to all complex role inclusions that are admitted in the description logic $\mathcal{SROIQ}$. In contrast, the addition of the universal role on the side of the OBDA query language extends the expressive power of ($\mathcal{ALC}$,AQ). Namely, it corresponds, on the MDDlog side, to dropping the requirement that rule bodies must be connected. For example, the MDDlog query $\mathsf{goal}(x) \leftarrow \mathsf{adom}(x) \wedge A(y)$ can then be expressed using the ontology $\mathcal{O} = \{\exists U.A \sqsubseteq \mathsf{goal}\}$ and the AQ $\mathsf{goal}(x)$.

Theorem 5 *($\mathcal{ALCU}$,AQ) and ($\mathcal{SHIU}$,AQ) both have the same expressive power as unary simple MDDlog.*

We close this section with a brief remark about *Boolean atomic queries* (BAQs), that is, queries of the form $\exists x.A(x)$, where A is a unary relation symbol. Such queries will be considered in Section 5. It is possible to establish modified versions of Theorems 2 to Theorem 5 above in which AQs are replaced by BAQs and unary goal predicates by 0-ary goal-predicate, respectively.

3.2 Ontologies Specified in First-Order Logic

Ontologies formulated in description logic are not able to speak about relation symbols of arity greater than two.[2] To overcome this restriction, we consider the guarded fragment of first-order logic and the unary-negation fragment of first-order logic [6, 46]. Both generalize the description logic $\mathcal{ALC}$ in different ways. We also consider their natural common generalization, the guarded negation fragment of first-order logic [7]. Our results from the previous subsection turn out to generalize to all these fragments. We start by considering the unary negation fragment.

The *unary-negation fragment of first-order logic* (UNFO) [46] is the fragment of first-order logic that consists of those formulas that are generated from atomic formulas, including equality, using conjunction, disjunction, existential quantification, and *unary negation*, that is, negation applied to a formula with at most one free variable. Thus, for example, $\neg\exists xyR(x,y)$ belongs to UNFO, whereas $\exists xy\neg R(x,y)$ does not. It is easy to show that every $\mathcal{ALC}$-TBox is equivalent to a UNFO sentence.

Theorem 6 *(UNFO,UCQ) has the same expressive power as MDDlog.*

[2] There are actually a few DLs that can handle relations of unrestricted arity, such as those presented in [19]. We do not consider such DLs in this paper, but remark that large fragments of them can be translated into UNFO.

Proof. (sketch) The translation from MDDlog to (UNFO,UCQ) is given by Theorem 1. Here, we provide the translation from (UNFO,UCQ) to MDDlog. Let $Q = (\mathbf{S}, \mathcal{O}, q) \in$ (UNFO,UCQ) be given. We assume that $\mathcal{O}$ is a single UNFO sentence that is in the normal form generated by the following grammar:

$$\varphi(x) ::= \top \mid \neg\varphi(x) \mid \exists \mathbf{y}(\psi_1(x,\mathbf{y}) \wedge \cdots \wedge \psi_n(x,\mathbf{y}))$$

where each ψ_i is either a relational atom or a formula with at most one free variable generated by the same grammar, and the free variables in ψ_i are among $x, \mathbf{y}$. Note that no equality is used and that all generated formulas have at most one free variable. Easy syntactic manipulations show that every UNFO-formula with at most one free variable is equivalent to a disjunction of formulas generated by the above grammar. In the case of $\mathcal{O}$, we may furthermore assume that it is a *single* such sentence, rather than a disjunction, because $\mathsf{cert}_{q,\mathcal{O}_1 \vee \mathcal{O}_2}(\mathfrak{D})$ is the intersection of $\mathsf{cert}_{q,\mathcal{O}_1}(\mathfrak{D})$ and $\mathsf{cert}_{q,\mathcal{O}_2}(\mathfrak{D})$, and MDDlog is closed under taking intersections of queries.

Let $\mathsf{sub}(\mathcal{O})$ be the set of all subformulas of $\mathcal{O}$ with at most one free variable z (we apply a one-to-one renaming of variables as needed to ensure that each formula in $\mathsf{sub}(\mathcal{O})$ with a free variable has the same free variable z). Let k be the maximum of the number of variables in $\mathcal{O}$ and the number of variables in q. We denote by $\mathsf{cl}_k(\mathcal{O})$ the set of all formulas $\varphi(x)$ of the form

$$\exists \mathbf{y}(\psi_1(x,\mathbf{y}) \wedge \cdots \wedge \psi_n(x,\mathbf{y}))$$

with $\mathbf{y} = (y_1, \ldots, y_m)$, $m \leq k$, where each ψ_i is either a relational atom or is of the form $\chi(x)$ or $\chi(y_i)$, for $\chi(z) \in \mathsf{sub}(\mathcal{O})$. A *type* τ is a subset of $\mathsf{cl}_k(\mathcal{O})$; the set of all types is denoted $\mathsf{type}(\mathcal{O})$.

We introduce a fresh unary relation symbol P_τ for each type τ, and we denote by $\mathbf{S}'$ the schema that extends $\mathbf{S}$ with these additional relations. As before, we call a structure $\mathfrak{B}$ over $\mathbf{S}' \cup \mathsf{sig}(\mathcal{O})$ type-coherent if for all types τ and elements d in the domain of $\mathfrak{B}$, we have $P_\tau(d) \in \mathfrak{B}$ just in the case that τ is the (unique) type realized at d in $\mathfrak{B}$. Diagrams, realizability, and "implying q" are defined as in the proof of Theorem 1. It follows from [46] that it is decidable whether a diagram implies a query, and whether a diagram is realizable. The MDDlog program Π is defined as in the proof of Theorem 1, except that now in the first rule, τ ranges over types in $\mathsf{type}(\mathcal{O})$. In the full version of this paper, we prove that the resulting MDDlog query q_Π is equivalent to Q. ❑

Next, we consider the *guarded fragment of first-order logic* (GF). It comprises all formulas built up from atomic formulas using the Boolean connectives and guarded quantification of the form $\exists \mathbf{x}(\alpha \wedge \varphi)$ and $\forall \mathbf{x}(\alpha \rightarrow \varphi)$, where, in both cases, α is an atomic formula (a "guard") that contains all free variables of φ. To simplify the presentation of the results, we consider here the equality-free version of the guarded fragment. We do allow one special case of equality, namely the use of trivial equalities of the form $x = x$ as guards, which is equivalent to allowing unguarded quantifiers applied to formulas with at most one free variable. This restricted form of equality is sufficient to translate every $\mathcal{ALC}$ TBox into an equivalent sentence of GF.

It turns out that the OBDA language (GF, UCQ) is strictly more expressive than MDDlog.

Proposition 1 *The Boolean query*

($\dagger$) *there are* $a_1, \ldots, a_n, b$, *for some* $n \geq 2$, *such that* $A(a_1)$, $B(a_n)$, *and* $P(a_i, b, a_{i+1})$ *for all* $1 \leq i < n$

is definable in (GF,UCQ) and not in MDDlog.

Proof. Let $\mathbf{S}$ consist of unary predicates A, B and a ternary predicate P, and let Q be the $\mathbf{S}$-query defined by ($\dagger$). It is easy to check that Q can be expressed by the (GF,UCQ) query $q_{\mathbf{S},\mathcal{O},\exists x U(x)}$ where

$$\begin{aligned} \mathcal{O} \;=\; & \forall xyz\,(P(x,z,y) \rightarrow (A(x) \rightarrow R(z,x))) \wedge \\ & \forall xyz\,(P(x,z,y) \rightarrow (R(z,x) \rightarrow R(z,y))) \wedge \\ & \forall xyz\,(R(x,y) \rightarrow (B(y) \rightarrow U(y))) \end{aligned}$$

We show in the full version of this paper that Q is not expressible in MDDlog using the colored forbidden patterns characterization mentioned in the proof sketch of Theorem 3. ❑

As fragments of first-order logic, the unary-negation fragment and the guarded fragment are incomparable in expressive power. They have a common generalization, which is known as the guarded-negation fragment (GNFO) [8]. This fragment is defined in the same way as UNFO, except that, besides unary negation, we allow *guarded negation* of the form $\alpha \wedge \neg\varphi$, where the guard α is an atomic formula that contains all the variables of φ. Again, for simplicity, we consider here the equality-free version of the language, except that we allow the use of trivial equalities of the form $x = x$ as guards. As we will see, for the purpose of OBDA, GNFO is no more powerful than GF. Specifically, (GF, UCQ) and (GNFO, UCQ) are expressively equivalent to a natural generalization of MDDlog, namely *frontier-guarded DDlog*. Recall that a datalog rule is *guarded* if its body includes an atom that contains all variables which occur in the rule [27]. A weaker notion of guardedness, which we call here *frontier-guardedness*, inspired by [5, 7], requires that, for each atom α in the head of the rule, there is an atom β in the rule body such that all variables that occur in α occur also in β. We define a frontier-guarded DDlog query to be a query defined by a DDlog program in which every rule is frontier-guarded. Observe that frontier-guarded DDlog subsumes MDDlog.

Theorem 7 *(GF,UCQ) and (GNFO,UCQ) have the same expressive power as frontier-guarded DDlog.*

Theorem 7 is proved in the full version of this paper via translations from (GNFO,UCQ) to frontier-guarded DDlog and back that are along the same lines as the translations from (UNFO,UCQ) to MDDlog and back. In addition, we use a result from [8] to obtain a translation from (GNFO,UCQ) to (GF,UCQ).

4. OBDA AND MMSNP

We show that MDDlog captures coMMSNP and thus, by the results obtained in the previous section, the same is true for many OBDA languages based on UCQs. We then use this connection to transfer results from MMSNP to OBDA languages with UCQs, linking the data complexity of these languages to the Feder-Vardi conjecture and establishing decidability of query containment. We also propose GMSNP, an extension of MMSNP inspired by frontier guarded DDlog, and show that (GF,UCQ) and (GNFO,UCQ) capture coGMSNP, and that GMSNP has the same expressive power as a previously proposed extension of MMSNP called MMSNP_2.

An *MMSNP formula* over schema $\mathbf{S}$ has the form $\exists X_1 \cdots \exists X_n \forall x_1 \cdots \forall x_m \varphi$ with $X_1, \ldots, X_n$ monadic second-order (SO) variables, $x_1, \ldots, x_m$ FO-variables, and φ a conjunction of quantifier-free formulas of the form

$$\psi = \alpha_1 \wedge \cdots \wedge \alpha_n \rightarrow \beta_1 \vee \cdots \vee \beta_m \text{ with } n, m \geq 0,$$

where each α_i is of the form $X_i(\mathbf{x})$, $R(\mathbf{x})$ (with $R \in \mathbf{S}$), or $x = y$, and each β_i is of the form $X_i(\mathbf{x})$. In order to use MMSNP as a query language, and in contrast to the standard definition, we admit free FO-variables and speak of *sentences* to refer to MMSNP formulas without free variables. To connect with the query languages studied thus far, we are interested in queries obtained by the complements of MMSNP formulas: each MMSNP formula Φ over schema $\mathbf{S}$ with n free variables gives rise to a query

$$q_{\Phi,\mathbf{S}}(\mathfrak{D}) = \{\mathbf{a} \in \mathsf{adom}(\mathfrak{D})^n \mid (\mathsf{adom}(\mathfrak{D}), \mathfrak{D}) \not\models \Phi[\mathbf{a}]\}$$

where we set $(\mathsf{adom}(\mathfrak{D}), \mathfrak{D}) \models \Phi$ to true when $\mathfrak{D}$ is the empty instance (that is, $\mathsf{adom}(\mathfrak{D}) = \emptyset$) and Φ is a sentence. We observe that the resulting query language *coMMSNP* has the same expressive power as MDDlog.

Proposition 2 *coMMSNP and MDDlog have the same expressive power.*

Proof. Let $\Phi = \exists X_1 \cdots \exists X_n \forall x_1 \cdots \forall x_m \varphi$ be an MMSNP formula with free variables $y_1, \dots, y_k$, and let $q_{\Phi,\mathbf{S}} \in$ coMMSNP be the corresponding query. We can assume w.l.o.g. that all implications $\psi = \alpha_1 \wedge \cdots \wedge \alpha_n \rightarrow \beta_1 \vee \cdots \vee \beta_m$ in φ satisfy the following properties: (i) $n > 0$ and, (ii) each variable that occurs in a β_i atom also occurs in an α_i atom. In fact, we can achieve both (i) and (ii) by replacing violating implications ψ with the set of implications ψ' that can be obtained from ψ by adding, for each variable x that occurs only in the head of ψ, an atom $S(\mathbf{x})$ where S is a predicate that occurs in Φ and $\mathbf{x}$ is a tuple of variables that contains x once and otherwise only fresh variables that do not occur in Φ. Define an MDDlog program Π_Φ that consists of all implications in φ whose head is not $\bot$ plus a rule

$$\mathsf{goal}(y_1, \dots, y_k) \leftarrow \vartheta \wedge \mathsf{adom}(y_1) \wedge \cdots \wedge \mathsf{adom}(y_k)$$

for each implication $\vartheta \rightarrow \bot$ in φ. It can be proved that $q_{\Phi,\mathbf{S}} = q_{\Pi_\Phi,\mathbf{S}}$ for all schemas $\mathbf{S}$. Finally, it is straightforward to remove the equalities from the rule bodies in Π_Φ.

Conversely, let Π be a k-ary MDDlog program and assume w.l.o.g. that each rule uses a disjoint set of variables. Reserve fresh variables $y_1, \dots, y_k$ as free variables for the desired MMSNP formula, and let $X_1, \dots, X_n$ be the IDB predicates in Π and $x_1, \dots, x_m$ the FO-variables in Π that do not occur in the goal predicate. Set $\Phi_\Pi = \exists X_1 \cdots \exists X_n \forall x_1 \cdots \forall x_m \varphi$ where φ is the conjunction of all non-goal rules in Π plus the implication $\vartheta' \rightarrow \bot$ for each rule $\mathsf{goal}(\mathbf{x}) \leftarrow \vartheta$ in Π. Here, ϑ' is obtained from ϑ by replacing each variable $x \in \mathbf{x}$ whose left-most occurrence in the rule head is in the i-th position with y_i, and then conjunctively adding $y_i = y_j$ whenever the i-th and j-th position in the rule head have the same variable. It can be proved that $q_{\Pi,\mathbf{S}} = q_{\Phi_\Pi,\mathbf{S}}$ for all schemas $\mathbf{S}$. ❑

Thus, the characterizations of OBDA languages in terms of MDDlog provided in Section 3 also establish the descriptive complexity of these languages by identifying them with (the complement of) MMSNP. Furthermore, Proposition 2 allow us to transfer results from MMSNP to OBDA. We start by considering the data complexity of the query evaluation problem: for a query q, the *evaluation problem* is to decide, given an instance $\mathfrak{D}$ and a tuple $\mathbf{a}$ of elements from $\mathfrak{D}$, whether $\mathbf{a} \in q(\mathfrak{D})$. Our first result is that the Feder-Vardi dichotomy conjecture for CSPs is true if and only if there is a dichotomy between PTIME and CONP for query evaluation in ($\mathcal{ALC}$,UCQ), and the same is true for several other OBDA languages. For brevity, we say that a query language *has a dichotomy between* PTIME *and* CONP, referring only implicitly to the evaluation problem.

The proof of the following theorem relies on Proposition 2 and Theorems 1, 3, and 6. It also exploits the fact that the Feder-Vardi dichotomy conjecture can equivalently be stated for MMSNP sentences [24, 33]. Some technical development is needed to deal with the presence of free variables. Details are in the full version of this paper.

Theorem 8 *($\mathcal{ALC}$,UCQ) has a dichotomy between* PTIME *and* CONP *iff the Feder-Vardi conjecture holds. The same is true for ($\mathcal{ALCHIU}$,UCQ) and (UNFO,UCQ).*

Recall that ($\mathcal{ALCF}$,UCQ) and ($\mathcal{S}$,UCQ) are two extensions of ($\mathcal{ALC}$,UCQ) that were identified in Section 3 to be more expressive than ($\mathcal{ALC}$,UCQ) itself. It was already proved in [36] (Theorem 27) that, compared to ontology-mediated queries based on $\mathcal{ALC}$, the functional roles of $\mathcal{ALCF}$ dramatically increase the computational power. This is true even for atomic queries.

Theorem 9 ([36]) *For every* NP*-Turing machine M, there is a query q in ($\mathcal{ALCF}$,AQ) such that the complement of the word problem of M has the same complexity as evaluating q, up to polynomial-time reductions. Consequently, ($\mathcal{ALCF}$,AQ) does not have a dichotomy between* PTIME *and* CONP *(unless* PTIME = NP*).*

We leave it as an open problem to analyze the computational power of ($\mathcal{S}$,UCQ).

There are other interesting results that can be transferred from MMSNP to OBDA. Here, we consider query containment. Specifically, the following general containment problem was proposed in [10] as a powerful tool for OBDA: given ontology-mediated queries $(\mathbf{S}, \mathcal{O}_i, q_i)$, $i \in \{1,2\}$, decide whether for all $\mathbf{S}$-instances $\mathfrak{D}$, we have $\mathsf{cert}_{q_1,\mathcal{O}_1}(\mathfrak{D}) \subseteq \mathsf{cert}_{q_2,\mathcal{O}_2}(\mathfrak{D})$.[3] Applications include the optimization of ontology-mediated queries and managing the effects on query answering of replacing an ontology with a new, updated version. In terms of OBDA languages such as ($\mathcal{ALC}$,UCQ), the above problem corresponds to query containment in the standard sense: an $\mathbf{S}$-query q_1 is *contained in* an $\mathbf{S}$-query q_2, written $q_1 \subseteq q_2$, if for every $\mathbf{S}$-instance $\mathfrak{D}$, we have $q_1(\mathfrak{D}) \subseteq q_2(\mathfrak{D})$. Note that there are also less general (and computationally simpler) notions of query containment in OBDA that do not fix the data schema [19].

It was proved in [24] that containment of MMSNP sentences is decidable. We thus obtain the following result for OBDA languages.

Theorem 10 *Query containment is decidable for the OBDA languages ($\mathcal{ALC}$,UCQ), ($\mathcal{ALCHIU}$,UCQ), and (UNFO,UCQ).*

Note that this result is considerably stronger than those in [10], which considered only containment of ontology-mediated queries $(\mathbf{S}, \mathcal{O}, q)$ with q an atomic query since already this basic case turned out to be technically intricate. The treatment of CQs and UCQs was left open, including all cases stated in Theorem 10.

We now consider OBDA languages based on the guarded fragment and GNFO. By Proposition 1, (GF,UCQ) and (GNFO,UCQ) are strictly more expressive than MDDlog and we cannot use Proposition 2 to relate these query languages to the Feder-Vardi conjecture. Theorem 7 suggests that it would be useful to have a generalization of MMSNP that is equivalent to frontier-guarded DDlog. Such a generalization is introduced next.

A formula of *guarded monotone strict NP (abbreviated GMSNP)* has the form $\exists X_1 \cdots \exists X_n \forall x_1 \cdots \forall x_m \varphi$ with $X_1, \dots, X_n$

[3]In fact, this definition is slightly different from the one used in [10]. There, containment is defined only over instances $\mathfrak{D}$ that are consistent w.r.t. $\mathcal{O}_1$ and $\mathcal{O}_2$, i.e., where there is at least one finite $\mathbf{S}$-structure $(\mathsf{dom}, \mathfrak{D}')$ such that $\mathfrak{D} \subseteq \mathfrak{D}'$ and $\mathfrak{D}' \in \mathsf{Mod}(\mathcal{O}_i)$.

SO variables of any arity, $x_1, \ldots, x_n$ FO-variables, and φ a conjunction of formulas

$$\psi = \alpha_1 \wedge \cdots \wedge \alpha_n \rightarrow \beta_1 \vee \cdots \vee \beta_m \text{ with } n, m \geq 0,$$

where each α_i is of the form $X_i(\mathbf{x})$, $R(\mathbf{x})$ (with $R \in \mathbf{S}$), or $x = y$, and each β_i is of the form $X_i(\mathbf{x})$. Additionally, we require that for every head atom β_i, there is a body atom α_j such that α_j contains all variables from β_i. GMSNP gives rise to a query language coGMSNP in analogy with the definition of coMMSNP. It can be shown by a straightforward syntactic transformation that every MMSNP formula is equivalent to some GMSNP formula. Together with Proposition 1 and Theorem 7, this yields the second statement of the following lemma; the first statement can be proved similarly to Proposition 2.

Theorem 11 *coGMSNP has the same expressive power as frontier-guarded DDlog and is strictly more expressive than coMMSNP.*

Although defined in a different way, GMSNP is essentially the same logic as MMSNP_2, which is studied in [37]. Specifically, MMSNP_2 is the extension of MMSNP in which monadic SO-variables range over sets of domain elements *and facts*, and where atoms of the form $X(R(\mathbf{x}))$ are allowed in place of atoms $X(x)$ with X an SO-variable and R from the data schema $\mathbf{S}$. Additionally, a guardedness condition is imposed, requiring that whenever an atom $X(R(\mathbf{x}))$ occurs in a rule head, then the atom $R(\mathbf{x})$ must occur in the rule body. Formally, the SO-variables X_i are interpreted in an instance $\mathfrak{D}$ as sets $\pi(X_i) \subseteq \mathsf{adom}(\mathfrak{D}) \cup \mathfrak{D}$ and $\mathfrak{D} \models_\pi X(R(x_1, \ldots, x_n))$ if $R(\pi(x_1), \ldots, \pi(x_n)) \in \pi(X)$. We observe the following.

Proposition 3 *GMSNP and* MMSNP_2 *have the same expressive power.*

Details for the proofs of both Theorem 11 and Lemma 3 are in the full version of this paper. In [37], it was left as an open question whether MMSNP_2 is more expressive than MMSNP, which is resolved by the results above.

We leave it as an interesting open question whether Theorem 8 can be extended to (GF,UCQ) and (GNFO,UCQ), that is, whether GMSNP (equivalently: MMSNP_2) has a dichotomy between PTIME and NP if the Feder-Vardi conjecture holds. While this question is implicit already in [37], the results established in this paper underline its significance from a different perspective.

5. OBDA AND CSP

We show that OBDA languages based on AQs capture CSPs (and generalizations thereof), and we transfer results from CSPs to OBDA languages. In comparison to the previous section, we obtain a richer set of results, and often even worst-case optimal decision procedures. Recall that each finite relational structure $\mathfrak{B}$ over a schema $\mathbf{S}$ gives rise to a *constraint satisfaction problem* which is to decide, given a finite relational structure $\mathfrak{A}$ over $\mathbf{S}$, whether there is a homomorphism from $\mathfrak{A}$ to $\mathfrak{B}$ (written $\mathfrak{A} \rightarrow \mathfrak{B}$). In this context, the relational structure $\mathfrak{B}$ is also called the *template* of the CSP.

CSPs give rise to a query language coCSP in the spirit of the query language coMMSNP introduced in the previous section. In its basic version, this language is Boolean and turns out to have exactly the same expressive power as ($\mathcal{ALC}$,BAQ), where BAQ is the class of *Boolean* atomic queries. To also cover non-Boolean AQs, we consider two natural generalizations of CSPs. First, a *generalized CSP* is defined by a finite *set $\mathcal{F}$ of templates*, rather than only a single one [25]. The problem then consists in deciding, given an input structure $\mathfrak{A}$, whether there is a template $\mathfrak{B} \in \mathcal{F}$ such that $\mathfrak{A} \rightarrow \mathfrak{B}$. Second, in a *(generalized) CSP with constant symbols*, both the template(s) and the input structure are endowed with constant symbols [23, 1]. To be more precise, let $\mathbf{S}$ be a schema and $\mathbf{c} = c_1, \ldots, c_m$ a finite sequence of distinct constant symbols. A *finite relational structure over* $\mathbf{S} \cup \mathbf{c}$ has the form $(\mathfrak{A}, d_1, \ldots, d_m)$ with $\mathfrak{A}$ a finite relational structure over $\mathfrak{A}$ that, in addition, interprets the constant symbols c_i by elements d_i of the domain dom of $\mathfrak{A}$, for $1 \leq i \leq m$. Let $(\mathfrak{A}, \mathbf{a})$ and $(\mathfrak{B}, \mathbf{b})$ be finite relational structures over $\mathbf{S} \cup \mathbf{c}$. A mapping h is a *homomorphism* from $(\mathfrak{A}, \mathbf{a})$ to $(\mathfrak{B}, \mathbf{b})$, written $(\mathfrak{A}, \mathbf{a}) \rightarrow (\mathfrak{B}, \mathbf{b})$, if it is a homomorphism from $\mathfrak{A}$ to $\mathfrak{B}$ and $h(a_i) = b_i$ for $1 \leq i \leq m$. A (generalized) CSP with constant symbols is then defined like a (generalized) CSP, based on this extended notion of homomorphism.

We now introduce the query languages obtained from the different versions of CSPs, where generalized CSPs with constant symbols constitute the most general case. Specifically, each finite set of templates $\mathcal{F}$ over $\mathbf{S} \cup \mathbf{c}$ with $\mathbf{c} = c_1, \ldots, c_m$ gives rise to an m-ary query coCSP($\mathcal{F}$) that maps every $\mathbf{S}$-instance $\mathfrak{D}$ to

$$\{\mathbf{d} \in \mathsf{adom}(\mathfrak{D})^m \mid \forall (\mathfrak{B}, \mathbf{b}) \in \mathcal{F} : (\mathfrak{D}, \mathbf{d}) \not\rightarrow (\mathfrak{B}, \mathbf{b})\},$$

where we view $(\mathfrak{D}, \mathbf{d})$ as a finite relational structure whose domain is $\mathsf{adom}(\mathfrak{D})$. The query language that consists of all such queries is called *generalized coCSP with constant symbols*. The fragment of this query language that is obtained by admitting only sets of templates $\mathcal{F}$ without constant symbols is called *generalized coCSP*, and the fragment induced by singleton sets $\mathcal{F}$ without constant symbols is called *coCSP*.

Example 3 *Selecting an illustrative fragment of Examples 1 and 2, let*

$$\mathcal{O} = \{\exists \mathsf{parent}.\mathsf{HereditaryDisposition} \sqsubseteq \mathsf{HereditaryDisposition}\}$$
$$\mathbf{S} = \{\mathsf{HereditaryDisposition}, \mathsf{parent}\}$$

Moreover, let $q_2(x) = \mathsf{HereditaryDisposition}(x)$ *be the query from Example 2. To identify a query in coCSP with constant symbols that is equivalent to the ontology-mediated query* $(\mathbf{S}, \mathcal{O}, q_2)$*, let* $\mathcal{B}$ *be the following template:*

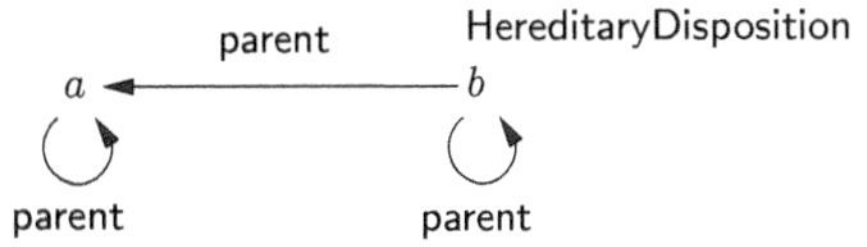

It can be shown that for all instances $\mathfrak{D}$ *over* $\mathbf{S}$ *and for all* $d \in \mathsf{adom}(\mathfrak{D})$*, we have* $d \in \mathsf{cert}_{q_2,\mathcal{O}}(\mathfrak{D})$ *iff* $(\mathfrak{D}, d) \not\rightarrow (\mathfrak{B}, a)$ *and thus the query coCSP(*$\mathfrak{B}$*) is as required.*

The following theorem summarizes the connections between OBDA languages with (Boolean) atomic queries, MDDlog, and CSPs. Note that we consider binary schemas only.

Theorem 12 *The following are lists of query languages that have the same expressive power:*

1. *($\mathcal{ALCU}$,AQ), ($\mathcal{SHIU}$,AQ), unary simple MDDlog, and generalized coCSP with one constant symbol;*
2. *($\mathcal{ALC}$,AQ), ($\mathcal{SHI}$,AQ), unary connected simple MDDlog, and generalized coCSPs with one constant symbol such that all templates are identical except for the interpretation of the constant symbol;*
3. *($\mathcal{ALCU}$,BAQ), ($\mathcal{SHIU}$,BAQ), Boolean simple MDDlog, and generalized coCSP;*

4. *($\mathcal{ALC}$,BAQ), ($\mathcal{SHI}$,BAQ), Boolean connected simple MDDlog, and coCSP.*

Moreover, given the ontology-mediated query or monadic datalog program, the correponding CSP template is of at most exponential size and can be constructed in time polynomial in the size of the template.

Proof. The equivalences between OBDA languages and fragments of MDDlog have been proved in Section 3. We give a proof of the remaining claim of Point 1, namely that ($\mathcal{ALCU}$,AQ) and generalized coCSP with one constant symbol are equally expressive. We extend the notation used in the proof of Theorem 1. For simplicity, throughout this proof we regard $\forall R.C$ as an abbreviation for $\neg\exists R.\neg C$.

Let $Q = (\mathbf{S}, \mathcal{O}, A(x))$ be an ontology-mediated query formulated in ($\mathcal{ALCU}$,AQ). A *type for* $\mathcal{O}$ is a set $\tau \subseteq \mathsf{sub}(\mathcal{O})$ and $\mathsf{tp}(\mathcal{O})$ denotes the set of all types for $\mathcal{O}$. We say that $\tau \in \mathsf{tp}(\mathcal{O})$ is *realizable* if there is an $\mathfrak{A} = (\mathsf{dom}, \mathfrak{D}) \in \mathsf{Mod}(\mathcal{O})$ and a $d \in \mathsf{dom}$ such that $C \in \tau$ iff $\mathfrak{A} \models C^*[d]$ for all $C \in \mathsf{sub}(\mathcal{O})$. A set of types $T \subseteq \mathsf{tp}(\mathcal{O})$ is *realizable in a Q-countermodel* if there is an $\mathfrak{A} \in \mathsf{Mod}(\mathcal{O})$ that realizes exactly the types in T and such that $A \notin \tau$ for at least one $\tau \in T$.

Let $\mathcal{C}$ be the set of all $T \subseteq \mathsf{tp}(\mathcal{O})$ that are realizable in a Q-countermodel and maximal with this property. Note that the number of elements of $\mathcal{C}$ is bounded by the size of $\mathcal{O}$ since for any two distinct $T_1, T_2 \in \mathcal{C}$, there must be a concept $\exists U.D \in \mathsf{sub}(\mathcal{O})$ such that $\exists U.D \in \tau$ for all $\tau \in T_1$ and $\exists U.D \notin \tau$ for all $\tau \in T_2$ or vice versa; otherwise, we can take the disjoint union of any structures $\mathfrak{A}_1, \mathfrak{A}_2$ which show that T_1, T_2 are realizable in a Q-countermodel to obtain Q-countermodel that realizes $T_1 \cup T_2$. For $R \in \mathbf{S}$, we call a pair (τ_1, τ_2) of types *R-coherent* if $\exists R.C \in \tau_1$ for every $\exists R.C \in \mathsf{sub}(\mathcal{O})$ such that $C \in \tau_2$.

With each $T \in \mathcal{C}$, we associate the *canonical* **S**-*structure* $\mathfrak{B}_T$ with domain T and the following facts:

- $B(\tau)$ for all $\tau \in T$ and $B \in \mathbf{S}$ such that $B \in \tau$;
- $R(\tau_1, \tau_2)$ for all $\tau_1, \tau_2 \in T$ and $R \in \mathbf{S}$ such that (τ_1, τ_2) is R-coherent.

Note that the construction of $\mathfrak{B}_T$ is well-known from the literature on modal and description logic. For example, $\mathfrak{B}_T$ can be viewed as a finite fragment of a canonical model of a modal logic that is constructed from maximal consistent sets of formulas [11]. Alternatively, $\mathfrak{B}_T$ can be viewed as the result of a type elimination procedure [41].

We obtain the desired set $\mathcal{F}$ of CSP templates by setting

$$\mathcal{F} = \{(\mathfrak{B}_T, \tau) \mid T \in \mathcal{C}, \tau \in T, A \notin \tau\}.$$

One can show that for every **S**-instance $\mathfrak{D}$ and $d \in \mathsf{adom}(\mathfrak{D})$, there exists $(\mathfrak{B}_T, \tau) \in \mathcal{F}$ with $(\mathfrak{D}, d) \to (\mathfrak{B}_T, \tau)$ iff $d \notin q_{\mathbf{S},\mathcal{O},A(x)}(\mathfrak{D})$. Thus, the ontology-mediated query Q is equivalent to the query defined by $\mathcal{F}$.

Conversely, assume that $\mathcal{F}$ is a finite set of **S**-structures with one constant. Take some $(\mathfrak{B}, b) \in \mathcal{F}$, and for every d in the domain $\mathsf{dom}(\mathfrak{B})$ of $\mathfrak{B}$, create some fresh concept name A_d. Let A be another fresh concept name, and set

$$\begin{aligned} \mathcal{O}_{\mathfrak{B},b} \;=\; & \{A_d \sqsubseteq \neg A_{d'} \mid d \neq d'\} \cup \\ & \{A_d \sqcap \exists R.A_{d'} \sqsubseteq \bot \mid R(d,d') \notin \mathfrak{B}, R \in \mathbf{S}\} \cup \\ & \{A_d \sqcap B \sqsubseteq \bot \mid B(d) \notin \mathfrak{B}, B \in \mathbf{S}\} \cup \\ & \{\top \sqsubseteq \bigsqcup_{d \in \mathsf{dom}(\mathfrak{B})} A_d,\ \neg A_b \sqsubseteq A\} \end{aligned}$$

Consider the ontology-mediated query $Q_{\mathfrak{B},b} = (\mathbf{S}, \mathcal{O}_{\mathfrak{B},b}, A(x))$. One can show that for every **S**-instance $\mathfrak{D}$ and $d \in \mathsf{adom}(\mathfrak{D})$, $(\mathfrak{D}, d) \to (\mathfrak{B}, b)$ iff $d \notin q_{Q_{\mathfrak{B},b}}(\mathfrak{D})$. Thus, $Q_{\mathfrak{B},b}$ is the desired query if $\mathcal{F}$ is a singleton. For the general case, let $\mathcal{O}$ be the disjunction over all $\mathcal{O}_{\mathfrak{B},b}$ with $(\mathfrak{B}, b) \in \mathcal{F}$. Note that $\mathcal{O}$ can be expressed in $\mathcal{ALCU}$: first, rewrite each $\mathcal{O}_{\mathfrak{B},b}$ into a single inclusion of the form $\top \sqsubseteq C_{\mathfrak{B},b}$ and then set

$$\mathcal{O} = \{\top \sqsubseteq \bigsqcup_{(\mathfrak{B},b)\in\mathcal{F}} \forall U.C_{\mathfrak{B},b}\}.$$

Using the above observation about the queries $Q_{\mathfrak{B},b}$, it is not hard to show that the ($\mathcal{ALCU}$,AQ)-query $Q = (\mathbf{S}, \mathcal{O}, A(x))$ is equivalent to the query coCSP($\mathcal{F}$).

This completes the proof of Point 1. The proofs of Points 2 to 4 are similar and given in the full version of this paper. ❑

Theorem 12 allows us to transfer results from the CSP world to OBDA, which, in light of recent progress on CSPs, turns out to be very fruitful. We start with data complexity.

Theorem 13 *($\mathcal{ALC}$,BAQ) has a dichotomy between* PTIME *and* CONP *iff the Feder-Vardi conjecture holds. The same is true for ($\mathcal{SHIU}$,AQ), and ($\mathcal{SHIU}$,BAQ).*

Since $\mathcal{SHIU}$-ontologies can be replaced by $\mathcal{ALCU}$-ontologies in ontology-mediated queries due to Theorem 5, the "if" direction of (all cases mentioned in) Theorem 13 actually follows from Theorem 8. The "only if" direction is a consequence of Theorem 12. We now consider further interesting applications of Theorem 12, in particular to deciding query containment, FO-rewritability, and datalog rewritability.

5.1 Query Containment

In Section 4, we have established decidability results for query containment in OBDA languages based on UCQs. For OBDA languages based on AQs and BAQs, we even obtain a tight complexity bound. It is easy to see that query containment in coCSP is characterized by homomorphisms between templates. Consequently, it is straightforward to show that query containment for generalized coCSP with constant symbols is NP-complete. Thus, Theorem 12 yields the following NEXPTIME upper bound for query containment in OBDA languages. The corresponding lower bound is proved in the full version of this paper by a non-trivial reduction of a NEXPTIME-complete tiling problem.

Theorem 14 *Query containment in ($\mathcal{SHIU}$,AQ$\cup$BQ) is in* NEXPTIME. *It is* NEXPTIME*-hard already for ($\mathcal{ALC}$,AQ) and for ($\mathcal{ALC}$,BAQ).*

It is a consequence of a result in [10] that query containment is undecidable for $\mathcal{ALCF}$. We show in the full version of this paper how the slight gap pointed out in Footnote 3 can be bridged.

5.2 FO- and Datalog-Rewritability

One prominent approach to answering ontology-mediated queries is to make use of existing relational database systems or datalog engines, eliminating the ontology by query rewriting [18, 22, 20]. Specifically, an ontology-mediated query $(\mathbf{S}, \mathcal{O}, q)$ is *FO-rewritable* if there exists an FO-query over **S** that is equivalent to it and *datalog-rewritable* if there exists a datalog program over **S** that defines it. We observe that every ontology-mediated query that is FO-rewritable is also datalog-rewritable.

Proposition 4 *If $Q = (\mathbf{S}, \mathcal{O}, q)$ is an ontology-mediated query with $\mathcal{O}$ formulated in equality-free FO and q a UCQ, then q_Q is* *preserved by homomorphisms. Consequently, it follows from [43] that if q_Q is FO-rewritable, then q_Q is rewritable into a UCQ (thus into datalog).*

Example 2 illustrates that ontology-mediated queries are not always rewritable into an FO-query, and the same holds for datalog-rewritability. It is a central problem to decide, given an ontology-mediated query, whether it is FO-rewritable and whether it is datalog-rewritable. By leveraging the CSP connection, we show that both problems are decidable and pinpoint their complexities.

On the CSP side, FO-rewritability corresponds to FO-definability, and datalog-rewritability to datalog-definability. Specifically, an $\mathbf{S}$-query coCSP($\mathcal{F}$) is *FO-definable* if there is an FO-sentence φ over $\mathbf{S}$ such that for all finite relational structures $\mathfrak{A}$ over $\mathbf{S}$, we have $\mathfrak{A} \models \varphi$ iff $\mathfrak{A} \not\rightarrow \mathfrak{B}$ for all $\mathfrak{B}$ in $\mathcal{F}$. Similarly, coCSP($\mathcal{F}$) is *datalog-definable* if there exists a datalog program Π that defines it. FO-definability and datalog-definability have been studied extensively for CSPs, culminating in the following results.

Theorem 15 *Deciding, for a given finite relational structure $\mathfrak{B}$ without constant symbols, whether coCSP($\mathfrak{B}$) is FO-definable is* NP*-complete [35]. The same is true for datalog-definability [26].*[4]

Combining the preceding theorem with Theorem 12, we obtain NEXPTIME upper bounds for deciding FO-rewritability and datalog-rewritability of queries from ($\mathcal{SHI}$,BAQ).

To capture the more important AQs rather than only BAQs, we show that Theorem 15 can be lifted, in a natural way, to generalized CSPs with constant symbols. The central step is provided by Proposition 5 below. For each finite relational structure $\mathfrak{B}$ with constant symbols $c_1, \dots, c_n$, let us denote by $\mathfrak{B}^c$ the corresponding relational structure without constant symbols over the schema that contains additional unary relations $P_1, \dots, P_n$, where each P_i denotes the singleton set that consists of the element denoted by c_i.

Proposition 5 *For every set of homomorphically incomparable structures $\mathfrak{B}_1, \dots, \mathfrak{B}_n$ with constant symbols,*

1. *coCSP($\mathfrak{B}_1, \dots, \mathfrak{B}_n$) is FO-definable iff coCSP($\mathfrak{B}_i^c$) is FO-definable for $1 \leq i \leq n$.*
2. *coCSP($\mathfrak{B}_1, \dots, \mathfrak{B}_n$) is datalog-definable iff coCSP($\mathfrak{B}_i^c$) is datalog-definable for $1 \leq i \leq n$.*

A proof of Proposition 5 is provided in the full version of this paper. It relies on the characterization of FO-definable CSPs as those CSPs that have *finite obstruction sets*; this characterization was given in [2] for structures without constant symbols and follows from results in [43] for the case of structures with constant symbols.

Note that every set of structures $\mathfrak{B}_1, \dots, \mathfrak{B}_n$ has a subset $\mathfrak{B}'_1, \dots, \mathfrak{B}'_m$ which consists of homomorphically incomparable structures such that coCSP($\mathfrak{B}_1, \dots, \mathfrak{B}_n$) is equivalent to coCSP($\mathfrak{B}'_1, \dots, \mathfrak{B}'_m$). We use this observation to establish the announced lifting of Theorem 15.

Theorem 16 *FO-definability and datalog-definability of generalized CSP with constant symbols is* NP*-complete.*

Proof. To decide whether a generalized CSP with constant symbols given as a set of templates $\mathcal{F} = \{\mathfrak{B}_1, \dots, \mathfrak{B}_n\}$ is FO-definable, it suffices to first guess a subset $\mathcal{F}' \subseteq \mathcal{F}$ and then to verify that (i) coCSP($\mathfrak{B}^c$) is FO-definable for each $\mathfrak{B} \in \mathcal{F}'$, and (ii) for each $\mathfrak{B} \in \mathcal{F}$ there is a $\mathfrak{B}' \in \mathcal{F}'$ such that $\mathfrak{B} \rightarrow \mathfrak{B}'$. By Theorem 15, this can be done in NP. Correctness follows from Proposition 5 and the fact that whenever there is a subset $\mathcal{F}'$ satisfying (i) and (ii), then by the observation above there must be a subset $\mathcal{F}'' \subseteq \mathcal{F}'$ of homomorphically incomparable structures such that coCSP($\mathcal{F}''$) is equivalent to coCSP($\mathcal{F}'$), which by (ii) is equivalent to coCSP($\mathcal{F}$). Datalog-definability can be decided analogously. ❑

From Theorems 12 and 16, we obtain a NEXPTIME upper bound for deciding FO-rewritability and datalog-rewritability of ontology-mediated queries based on DLs and (B)AQs. The corresponding lower bounds are proved in the full version of this paper using a reduction from a NEXPTIME-hard tiling problem (in fact, the same problem as in the lower bound for query containment).

Theorem 17 *It is in* NEXPTIME *to decide FO-rewritability and datalog-rewritability of queries in ($\mathcal{SHIU}$,AQ∪BAQ). Both problems are* NEXPTIME*-hard for ($\mathcal{ALC}$,AQ) and ($\mathcal{ALC}$, BAQ).*

Modulo a minor difference in the treatment of instances that are not consistent (see Footnote 3), it follows from a result in [36] that FO-rewritability is undecidable for ($\mathcal{ALCF}$,AQ). In the full version of this paper, we show how to bridge the difference and how to modify the proof so that the result also applies to datalog-rewritability.

Theorem 18 *FO-rewritability and datalog-rewritability are undecidable for ($\mathcal{ALCF}$,AQ) and ($\mathcal{ALCF}$,BAQ).*

6. CONCLUSION

Another query language frequently used in OBDA with description logics is conjunctive queries. The results in this paper imply that there is a dichotomy between PTIME and CONP for ($\mathcal{ALC}$,CQ) if and only if the Feder-Vardi conjecture holds. We leave it open whether there is a natural characterization of ($\mathcal{ALC}$,CQ) in terms of disjunctive datalog.

We mention two natural lines of future research. First, it would be interesting to understand the data complexity and query containment problem for (GF,UCQ) and (GNFO,UCQ). In particular, we would like to know whether Theorems 8 and 10 extend to (GF,UCQ) and (GNFO,UCQ). As explained in Section 4, resolving this question for Theorem 8 is equivalent to clarifying the computational status of GMSNP and MMSNP_2.

Another interesting topic for future work is to analyze FO-rewritability and datalog-rewritability of ontology-mediated queries based on UCQs (instead of AQs) as a decision problem. It follows from our results that this is equivalent to deciding FO-definability and datalog-definability of MMSNP formulas (or even GMSNP formulas).

Acknowledgements. We thank Benoit Larose and Liber Barto for discussions on datalog-definability of CSPs, and Florent Madeleine and Manuel Bodirsky for discussions on MMSNP.

Meghyn Bienvenu was supported by the ANR project PAGODA (ANR-12-JS02-007-01). Balder ten Cate was supported by NSF Grants IIS-0905276 and IIS-1217869. Carsten Lutz was supported by the DFG SFB/TR 8 "Spatial Cognition".

[4]An NP algorithm for datalog-definability is implicit in [26], based on results from [9], see also [13]. We thank Benoit Larose and Liber Barto for pointing this out.

7. REFERENCES

[1] B. Alexe, B. ten Cate, P. G. Kolaitis, and W. C. Tan. Characterizing schema mappings via data examples. *ACM Trans. Database Syst.*, 36(4), 2011.

[2] A. Atserias. On digraph coloring problems and treewidth duality. In *LICS*, 2005.

[3] F. Baader, M. Bienvenu, C. Lutz, and F. Wolter. Query and predicate emptiness in description logics. In *KR*, 2010.

[4] F. Baader, D. Calvanese, D. L. McGuiness, D. Nardi, and P. Patel-Schneider, editors. *The Description Logic Handbook*. Cambridge University Press, 2003.

[5] J.-F. Baget, M.-L. Mugnier, S. Rudolph, and M. Thomazo. Walking the complexity lines for generalized guarded existential rules. In *IJCAI*, 2011.

[6] V. Bárány, G. Gottlob, and M. Otto. Querying the guarded fragment. In *LICS*, 2010.

[7] V. Bárány, B. ten Cate, and M. Otto. Queries with guarded negation. *PVLDB*, 5(11), 2012.

[8] V. Bárány, B. ten Cate, and L. Segoufin. Guarded negation. In *ICALP*, 2011.

[9] L. Barto and M. Kozik. Constraint satisfaction problems of bounded width. In *FOCS*, 2009.

[10] M. Bienvenu, C. Lutz, and F. Wolter. Query containment in description logics reconsidered. In *KR*, 2012.

[11] P. Blackburn, M. de Rijke, and Y. Venema. Modal Logic. *Cambridge University Press*, 2001.

[12] M. Bodirsky, H. Chen, and T. Feder. On the complexity of MMSNP. *SIAM J. Discrete Math.*, 26(1):404–414, 2012.

[13] A. Bulatov. Bounded relational width. In preparation. http://www.cs.sfu.ca/ abulatov/mpapers.html.

[14] A. A. Bulatov. On the CSP dichotomy conjecture. In *CSR*, 2011.

[15] A. Calì, G. Gottlob, and T. Lukasiewicz. A general datalog-based framework for tractable query answering over ontologies. In *PODS*, 2009.

[16] A. Calì, G. Gottlob, and A. Pieris. Towards more expressive ontology languages: The query answering problem. *Artif. Intell.*, 193, 2012.

[17] D. Calvanese, G. D. Giacomo, D. Lembo, M. Lenzerini, and R. Rosati. Data complexity of query answering in description logics. In *KR*, 2006.

[18] D. Calvanese, G. D. Giacomo, D. Lembo, M. Lenzerini, and R. Rosati. Tractable reasoning and efficient query answering in description logics: The DL-Lite family. *J. Autom. Reasoning*, 39(3), 2007.

[19] D. Calvanese, G. D. Giacomo, and M. Lenzerini. On the decidability of query containment under constraints. In *PODS*, 1998.

[20] B. Cuenca Grau, M. Kaminski, and B. Motik Computing Datalog Rewritings Beyond Horn Ontologies. In *IJCAI*, 2013

[21] T. Eiter, G. Gottlob, and H. Mannila. Disjunctive datalog. *ACM Trans. Database Syst.*, 22(3), 1997.

[22] T. Eiter, M. Ortiz, M. Simkus, T.-K. Tran, and G. Xiao. Towards practical query answering for Horn-$\mathcal{SHIQ}$. In *DL*, 2012.

[23] T. Feder, F. R. Madelaine, and I. A. Stewart. Dichotomies for classes of homomorphism problems involving unary functions. *Theor. Comput. Sci.*, 314(1-2), 2004.

[24] T. Feder and M. Y. Vardi. The computational structure of monotone monadic SNP and constraint satisfaction: A study through datalog and group theory. *SIAM J. Comput.*, 28(1), 1998.

[25] J. Foniok, J. Nesetril, and C. Tardif. Generalised dualities and maximal finite antichains in the homomorphism order of relational structures. *Eur. J. Comb.*, 29(4), 2008.

[26] R. Freese, M. Kozik, A. Krokhin, M. Maróti, R. KcKenzie, and R. Willard. On Maltsev conditions associated with omitting certain types of local structures. In preparation. http://www.math.hawaii.edu/~ralph/Classes/619/OmittingTypesMaltsev.pdf

[27] G. Gottlob, E. Grädel, and H. Veith. Datalog LITE: a deductive query language with linear time model checking. *ACM Trans. Comput. Log.*, 3(1), 2002.

[28] G. Gottlob and T. Schwentick. Rewriting ontological queries into small nonrecursive datalog programs. In *KR*, 2012.

[29] U. Hustadt, B. Motik, and U. Sattler. Reasoning in description logics by a reduction to disjunctive datalog. *J. Autom. Reasoning*, 39(3), 2007.

[30] S. Kikot, R. Kontchakov, V. V. Podolskii, and M. Zakharyaschev. Exponential lower bounds and separation for query rewriting. In *ICALP*, 2012.

[31] R. Kontchakov, C. Lutz, D. Toman, F. Wolter, and M. Zakharyaschev. The combined approach to query answering in DL-Lite. In *KR*, 2010.

[32] A. Krisnadhi and C. Lutz. Data complexity in the $\mathcal{EL}$ family of DLs. In *LPAR*, 2007.

[33] G. Kun. Constraints, MMSNP, and Expander Structures. http://arxiv.org/abs/0706.1701v1, 2007.

[34] G. Kun and J. Nesetril. Forbidden lifts (NP and CSP for combinatorialists). *Eur. J. Comb.*, 29(4), 2008.

[35] B. Larose, C. Loten, and C. Tardif. A characterisation of first-order constraint satisfaction problems. *Logical Methods in Comp. Sci.*, 3(4), 2007.

[36] C. Lutz and F. Wolter. Non-uniform data complexity of query answering in description logics. In *KR*, 2012.

[37] F. R. Madelaine. Universal structures and the logic of forbidden patterns. *Logical Methods in Comp. Sci.*, 5(2), 2009.

[38] F. R. Madelaine and I. A. Stewart. Constraint satisfaction, logic and forbidden patterns. *SIAM J. Comput.*, 37(1), 2007.

[39] B. Motik. *Reasoning in description logics using resolution and deductive databases*. PhD thesis, 2006.

[40] A. Poggi, D. Lembo, D. Calvanese, G. D. Giacomo, M. Lenzerini, and R. Rosati. Linking data to ontologies. *J. Data Semantics*, 10, 2008.

[41] V. R. Pratt. Models of program logics. In *FoCS*, 1979.

[42] R. Rosati and A. Almatelli. Improving Query Answering over DL-Lite Ontologies. In *KR*, 2010.

[43] B. Rossman. Homomorphism preservation theorems. *J. ACM*, 55(3), 2008.

[44] S. Rudolph, M. Krötzsch, and P. Hitzler. Type-elimination-based reasoning for the description logic $\mathcal{SHIQ}b_s$ using decision diagrams and disjunctive datalog. *Logical Methods in Comp. Sci.*, 8(1), 2012.

[45] F. Simancik. Elimination of complex RIAs without automata. In *DL*, 2012.

[46] B. ten Cate and L. Segoufin. Unary negation. In *STACS*, 2011.

[47] W3C OWL Working Group. OWL 2 Web Ontology Language. http://www.w3.org/TR/owl2-overview/, 2012.

Well-Founded Semantics for Extended Datalog and Ontological Reasoning

André Hernich
UC Santa Cruz, USA &
Humboldt-Universität zu Berlin, Germany
hernich@informatik.hu-berlin.de

Clemens Kupke
University of Strathclyde, Glasgow, Scotland, UK
clemens.kupke@strath.ac.uk

Thomas Lukasiewicz
University of Oxford, UK
thomas.lukasiewicz@cs.ox.ac.uk

Georg Gottlob
University of Oxford, UK
georg.gottlob@cs.ox.ac.uk

ABSTRACT

The Datalog$^\pm$ family of expressive extensions of Datalog has recently been introduced as a new paradigm for query answering over ontologies, which captures and extends several common description logics. It extends plain Datalog by features such as existentially quantified rule heads and, at the same time, restricts the rule syntax so as to achieve decidability and tractability. In this paper, we continue the research on Datalog$^\pm$. More precisely, we generalize the well-founded semantics (WFS), as the standard semantics for nonmonotonic normal programs in the database context, to Datalog$^\pm$ programs with negation under the unique name assumption (UNA). We prove that for guarded Datalog$^\pm$ with negation under the standard WFS, answering normal Boolean conjunctive queries is decidable, and we provide precise complexity results for this problem, namely, in particular, completeness for PTIME (resp., 2-EXPTIME) in the data (resp., combined) complexity.

Categories and Subject Descriptors

F.2.2 [**Analysis of Algorithms and Problem Complexity**]: Nonnumerical Algorithms and Problems—*computations on discrete structures*; H.2.4 [**Database Management**]: Systems—*query processing, relational databases, rule-based databases*

Keywords

Extended Datalog with negation; well-founded semantics; ontological reasoning

1. INTRODUCTION

The recent Datalog$^\pm$ family of ontology languages [3] extends plain Datalog by the possibility of existential quantification in rule heads and other features, and simultaneously restricts the rule syntax to achieve decidability and tractability. The following example illustrates how ontological knowledge bases (encoded in a description logic (DL)) can be expressed in Datalog$^\pm$.

Example 1. (Literature) A DL knowledge base consists of a TBox and an ABox. For example, the knowledge that every conference paper is an article and that every scientist is the author of at least one paper is expressible by the two axioms *ConferencePaper* $\sqsubseteq$ *Article* and *Scientist* $\sqsubseteq \exists$*isAuthorOf* in the TBox, respectively, while the knowledge that John is a scientist is expressible by the axiom *Scientist(john)* in the ABox. In Datalog$^\pm$, the former are encoded as the rules *ConferencePaper*$(X) \rightarrow$ *Article*(X) and *Scientist*$(X) \rightarrow \exists Y$ *isAuthorOf*(X,Y), respectively, and the latter is encoded by an identical fact in the database. Moreover, the TBox axiom *ConferencePaper* $\sqsubseteq \neg$*JournalPaper*, encoding that conference papers are not journal papers, is expressible in Datalog$^\pm$ by the negative constraint *ConferencePaper* $\wedge$ *JournalPaper* $\rightarrow \bot$. A simple Boolean conjunctive query (BCQ) asking if John authors a paper is $\exists X$ *isAuthor Of*(*john*, X). ■

The Datalog$^\pm$ languages bridge an apparent gap in expressive power between database query languages and DLs as ontology languages, extending the well-known Datalog language in order to embed DLs. They also allow for transferring important concepts and proof techniques from database theory to DLs. For example, it was so far not clear how to enrich tractable DLs by the feature of nonmonotonic negation. By the results of [3], DLs can be enriched by stratified negation via mappings from DLs to Datalog$^\pm$ with stratified negation, which is defined and studied in that paper.

Given that stratified negation is quite limited, it is natural to ask whether the richer and more expressive well-founded negation could be defined for Datalog$^\pm$. The well-founded semantics (WFS) for normal (logic) programs [11] is one of the most widely used semantics for nonmonotonic normal programs, it is the standard semantics for such programs for database applications (due to its computational properties, differently from the stable model semantics), and it is thus especially under a data-oriented perspective of great importance for (dealing with very large amounts of data on) the Web (see [4] for a recent survey of Web-related applications of Datalog$^\pm$). Having many nice features, the WFS is defined for all normal programs (i.e., logic programs with the possibility of negation in rule bodies), has a polynomial data tractability, approximates the answer set semantics, and coincides with the canonical model in case of stratified normal programs.

In [6], we focus on the important problem of defining a WFS for (unrestricted) normal Datalog$^\pm$, i.e., Datalog with existentially quantified variables in rule heads and negations in rule bodies. But our research there is guided by the goal of defining a WFS for normal Datalog$^\pm$ that is close to OWL and its profiles as well as typical DLs, which all have in common that they do not make the unique name assumption (UNA). Thus, the new semantics in [6], called the *equality-friendly WFS (EFWFS)*, also does not make the UNA.

The WFS for normal Datalog$^\pm$ without the UNA, however, actually generalizes neither Datalog$^\pm$ nor standard normal (logic) programs, which make the UNA, in contrast. The UNA is also rather common in logic programming and databases in general, as well as in some important DLs, such as the *DL-Lite* family of tractable description logics [5, 9]. That is, the results in this paper (which are technically very different from those in [6]) also allow us to interpret extensions of the *DL-Lite*-family with nonmonotonic negation using the standard well-founded semantics. The following example demonstrates this for $\mathit{DL\text{-}Lite}_{\mathcal{R},\sqcap,\mathrm{not}}$ from [6].

Example 2. Consider the $\mathit{DL\text{-}Lite}_{\mathcal{R},\sqcap,\mathrm{not}}$-ontology $\mathcal{T}$:

$$\begin{aligned} \mathit{Person}, \mathit{Employed}, \mathrm{not}\exists \mathit{JobSeekerID} &\sqsubseteq \exists \mathit{EmployeeID},\\ \mathit{Person}, \mathrm{not}\mathit{Employed}, \mathrm{not}\exists \mathit{EmployeeID} &\sqsubseteq \exists \mathit{JobSeekerID},\\ \exists \mathit{EmployeeID}^- \sqcap \mathrm{not}\exists \mathit{JobSeekerID}^- &\sqsubseteq \mathit{ValidID}. \end{aligned}$$

The first rule expresses that an employed person who is not registered as a job seeker has an employee's ID, the second rule states that a person who is not employed, and does not have an employee's ID is registered as a job seeker, and the final rule expresses that IDs are only valid, if they are not an employee's and a job seeker's ID simultaneously. As pointed out in [6], it is not difficult to translate this ontology $\mathcal{T}$ into a corresponding normal guarded Datalog$^\pm$ program $P_{\mathcal{T}}$. We then have the choice of defining the semantics of $P_{\mathcal{T}}$ as either the equality-friendly WFS of $P_{\mathcal{T}}$ as in [6] or as the standard WFS of $P_{\mathcal{T}}$. The latter is possible thanks to the decidability and complexity results in this paper, and we argue that the WFS is in fact the desirable option here: If we add the set of facts

$$\{\mathit{Person}(a), \mathit{Person}(b), \mathit{Employed}(a)\},$$

it is not difficult to see that the standard WFS derives both $\mathit{EmployeeID}(a, f(a))$ and $\mathit{JobSeekerID}(b, g(b))$ and, because $f(a) \neq g(b)$, also $\mathit{ValidID}(f(a))$. In the equality-friendly WFS, however, we do not know whether or not $f(a) \neq g(b)$, and we thus cannot derive that $f(a)$ is a valid ID. ■

Moreover, there are natural examples, where one actually would like to make the UNA, and thus where the standard WFS for normal Datalog$^\pm$ more faithfully expresses the intended meaning than the equality-friendly WFS. The following is such an example.

Example 3. Consider the following set of rules Σ:

$$\begin{aligned} \mathit{Employer}(X) &\rightarrow \exists Y.\mathit{BossOf}(X,Y)\\ \mathit{BossOf}(X,Y), \mathit{Smart}(X), \neg \mathit{Bully}(X) &\rightarrow \mathit{Happy}(Y)\\ \mathit{BossOf}(X,Y), \neg \mathit{Happy}(Y) &\rightarrow \mathit{BadBoss}(X)\\ \mathit{Employer}(X), \neg \mathit{BadBoss}(X) &\rightarrow \mathit{Smart}(X) \end{aligned}$$

The rules express that each employer is someone's boss, that an employee is happy if the boss is smart and not a bully, that a boss who has an unhappy employee is a bad boss, and that an employer who is not a bad boss is smart. Here, we implicitly assume that every employee can only have one boss. Furthermore, we assume that the first rule is skolemized as $\mathit{Employer}(X) \rightarrow \mathit{BossOf}(X, f(X))$.

Consider now the database

$$D = \{\mathit{Employer}(a), \mathit{Smart}(a), \mathit{Employer}(b), \mathit{Bully}(b)\}.$$

Both the standard and the equality-friendly WFS imply the negated atom $\neg \mathit{Bully}(a)$ (no rule can possibly derive $\mathit{Bully}(a)$, as the predicate *Bully* does not occur in any rule head), $\mathit{Happy}(f(a))$ (applying the second rule), and $\neg \mathit{BadBoss}(a)$. That the latter negated atom follows is not so obvious: the reason is that the only instance of the second rule that could derive $\mathit{BadBoss}(a)$ is "blocked" by the fact that $f(a)$ — a's only subordinate — is happy. Furthermore, the (standard) WFS includes the negated atom $\neg \mathit{Happy}(f(b))$ (because all possible rule applications of the second rule that could derive $\mathit{Happy}(f(b))$ are blocked by $\mathit{Bully}(b)$), the atom $\mathit{BadBoss}(b)$ (applying the third rule), and the negated atom $\neg \mathit{Smart}(b)$ (because the instance of the fourth rule that could derive $\mathit{Smart}(b)$ is blocked by $\mathit{BadBoss}(b)$). In the equality-friendly WFS, however, the last three literals cannot be obtained, because we cannot assume that $f(a) \neq f(b)$. Therefore, it is unclear whether or not $\mathit{BossOf}(a, f(b)), \mathit{Smart}(a), \neg \mathit{Bully}(a) \rightarrow \mathit{Happy}(f(b))$ is a valid instance of the second rule. Consequently, we are left in the dark concerning the question whether or not $f(b)$ (b's employee that exists by the first rule) is happy or not — despite the fact that b is a bully, and we intended the second rule to mean that an employee can only be happy if the boss is not a bully. ■

Finally, another serious drawback of the equality-friendly WFS is that answering atomic queries is co-NP-hard in the data complexity, and thus does not have the same nice computational properties as in the standard WFS for normal logics programs, namely a polynomial data complexity. The development of a WFS for normal Datalog$^\pm$ under the UNA (with hopefully lower data complexity than the WFS without the UNA) is thus still an important open problem, which we therefore tackle in the present paper.

The central question of this paper is whether the results for guarded positive Datalog$^\pm$ from [3] can be extended to guarded normal Datalog$^\pm$ under the WFS and UNA, that is, whether there exists a finite part of a chase for normal TGDs that can be used to evaluate normal BCQs (NBCQs), which has only constant depth in the data complexity. This then implies that NBCQs to guarded normal Datalog$^\pm$ programs can be evaluated in polynomial time in the data complexity. As we will see in this paper, the answer to this central question turns out to be positive. But finding this answer is rather involved technically. Roughly speaking, this is due to the fact that compared to stratified Datalog$^\pm$ with negation [3], we now have to make sure that (i) also the derivation of negative atoms in each iteration step, which is done via greatest unfounded sets, can be done on a finite part of an infinite chase, and that (ii) we only need a finite part of the now infinite iteration for the computation of the well-founded model via its fixpoint operator (rather than a finite iteration along the finitely many different levels of a stratification).

As the main contributions of this paper, we thus obtain that answering NBCQs to guarded normal Datalog$^\pm$ under the WFS and UNA is decidable and can be done in polynomial time in the data complexity. Furthermore, we show that it is in 2-EXPTIME in the combined complexity in general and in EXPTIME in the combined complexity in the case where the arities of all predicates are bounded by a constant. Hardness for these complexity classes follows from the fact that already answering BCQs to the more restricted guarded Datalog$^\pm$ without negation is hard for them.

2. PRELIMINARIES

2.1 Databases and Queries

We assume (i) an infinite universe of *(data) constants* Δ (which constitute the "normal" domain of a database), (ii) an infinite set of *(labeled) nulls* Δ_N (used as "fresh" Skolem terms, which are placeholders for unknown values, and can thus be seen as variables), and (iii) an infinite set of variables $\mathcal{V}$ (used in queries and dependencies). Different constants represent different values (*unique name assumption*), while different nulls may represent the same value. We assume a lexicographic order on $\Delta \cup \Delta_N$, with every symbol in Δ_N following all symbols in Δ. We denote by $\mathbf{X}$ sequences of variables $X_1, \ldots, X_k$ with $k \geqslant 0$.

We assume a *relational schema* $\mathcal{R}$, which is a finite set of *relation names* (or *predicate symbols*, or simply *predicates*). A *term* t is a constant, null, or variable. An *atomic formula* (or *atom*) $\mathbf{a}$ has the form $P(t_1, ..., t_n)$, where P is an n-ary predicate, and $t_1, ..., t_n$ are terms. We denote by $pred(\mathbf{a})$ and $dom(\mathbf{a})$ its predicate and the set of all its arguments, respectively. The latter two notations are naturally extended to sets of atoms and conjunctions of atoms. A conjunction of atoms is often identified with the set of all its atoms.

A *database (instance)* D for a relational schema $\mathcal{R}$ is a (possibly infinite) set of atoms with predicates from $\mathcal{R}$ and arguments from Δ. A *conjunctive query (CQ)* over $\mathcal{R}$ has the form $Q(\mathbf{X}) = \exists \mathbf{Y}\, \Phi(\mathbf{X}, \mathbf{Y})$, where $\Phi(\mathbf{X}, \mathbf{Y})$ is a conjunction of atoms with the variables $\mathbf{X}$ and $\mathbf{Y}$, and eventually constants, but without nulls. Note that $\Phi(\mathbf{X}, \mathbf{Y})$ may also contain equalities but no inequalities. A *Boolean CQ (BCQ)* over $\mathcal{R}$ is a CQ of the form $Q()$. We often write a BCQ as the set of all its atoms, having constants and variables as arguments, and omitting the quantifiers. Answers to CQs and BCQs are defined via *homomorphisms*, which are mappings $\mu\colon \Delta \cup \Delta_N \cup \mathcal{V} \to \Delta \cup \Delta_N \cup \mathcal{V}$ such that (i) $c \in \Delta$ implies $\mu(c) = c$, (ii) $c \in \Delta_N$ implies $\mu(c) \in \Delta \cup \Delta_N$, and (iii) μ is naturally extended to atoms, sets of atoms, and conjunctions of atoms. The set of all *answers* to a CQ $Q(\mathbf{X}) = \exists \mathbf{Y}\, \Phi(\mathbf{X}, \mathbf{Y})$ over a database D, denoted $Q(D)$, is the set of all tuples $\mathbf{t}$ over Δ for which there exists a homomorphism $\mu\colon \mathbf{X} \cup \mathbf{Y} \to \Delta \cup \Delta_N$ such that $\mu(\Phi(\mathbf{X}, \mathbf{Y})) \subseteq D$ and $\mu(\mathbf{X}) = \mathbf{t}$. The *answer* to a BCQ $Q()$ over a database D is *Yes*, denoted $D \models Q$, iff $Q(D) \neq \emptyset$.

2.2 Normal Logic Programs

We now briefly recall standard normal logic programs, where no existentially quantified variables occur in rule heads. Let Ξ be a first-order vocabulary with nonempty finite sets of constant, function, and predicate symbols. Let $\mathcal{V}$ be a set of variables. A *term* is either a variable from $\mathcal{V}$, a constant symbol from Ξ, or of the form $f(t_1, \ldots, t_n)$, where f is a function symbol of arity $n \geqslant 0$ from Ξ, and $t_1, \ldots, t_n$ are terms. An *atom* is of the form $p(t_1, \ldots, t_n)$, where p is a predicate symbol of arity $n \geqslant 0$ from Ξ, and $t_1, \ldots, t_n$ are terms. A *literal* l is an atom p or a negated atom $\neg p$. A *normal rule* (or simply *rule*) r is of the form

$$\beta_1, \ldots, \beta_n, \neg\beta_{n+1}, \ldots, \neg\beta_{n+m} \to \alpha, \qquad (1)$$

where $\alpha, \beta_1, \ldots, \beta_{n+m}$ are atoms and $m, n \geqslant 0$. We call the atom α the *head* of r, denoted $H(r)$, while the conjunction $\beta_1, \ldots, \beta_n, \neg\beta_{n+1}, \ldots, \neg\beta_{n+m}$ is called its *body*. We define $B(r) = B^+(r) \cup B^-(r)$, where $B^+(r) = \{\beta_1, \ldots, \beta_n\}$ and $B^-(r) = \{\beta_{n+1}, \ldots, \beta_{n+m}\}$. A rule of the form (1) with $m = n = 0$ is also called a *fact*. A *normal program* P is a finite set of normal rules (1). We say P is *positive* iff $m = 0$ for all normal rules (1) in P. For normal programs P, we denote by P^+ the positive program obtained from P by removing all negative literals from the rule bodies.

The *Herbrand universe* of a normal program P, denoted HU_P, is the set of all terms constructed from constant and function symbols appearing in P. If there is no such constant symbol, then we take an arbitrary constant symbol from Ξ. As usual, terms, atoms, literals, rules, programs, etc. are *ground* iff they do not contain any variables. The *Herbrand base* of a normal program P, denoted HB_P, is the set of all ground atoms that can be constructed from the predicate symbols appearing in P and the ground terms in HU_P. A *ground instance* of a rule $r \in P$ is obtained from r by uniformly replacing every variable that occurs in r by a ground term from HU_P. We denote by $ground(P)$ the set of all ground instances of rules in P. For literals $\ell = a$ (resp., $\ell = \neg a$), we use $\neg.\ell$ to denote $\neg a$ (resp., a), and for sets of literals S, we define $\neg.S = \{\neg.\ell \mid \ell \in S\}$, $S^+ = \{a \in S \mid a \text{ is an atom}\}$, and $S^- = \{\neg a \mid \neg a \in S\}$. We denote by $Lit_P = HB_P \cup \neg.HB_P$ the set of all ground literals with predicate symbols from P and ground terms from HU_P. A set of ground literals $S \subseteq Lit_P$ is *consistent* iff $S \cap \neg.S = \emptyset$. A *(three-valued) interpretation* relative to P is any consistent set of ground literals $I \subseteq Lit_P$.

2.3 Normal BCQs

We add negation to BCQs as follows. A *normal Boolean conjunctive query (NBCQ)* Q is an existentially closed conjunction of atoms and negated atoms

$$\exists \mathbf{X}\, p_1(\mathbf{X}) \wedge \cdots \wedge p_m(\mathbf{X}) \wedge \neg p_{m+1}(\mathbf{X}) \wedge \cdots \wedge \neg p_{m+n}(\mathbf{X}),$$

where $m \geqslant 1$, $n \geqslant 0$, and the variables of the p_i's are among $\mathbf{X}$. We denote by Q^+ (resp., Q^-) the set of all positive (resp., negative ("$\neg$"-free)) atoms of Q. In the sequel, w.l.o.g., BCQs contain no constants. An NBCQ Q is satisfied in an interpretation $I \subseteq Lit_P$ if there is a homomorphism μ such that $\mu(a) \in I$ and $\neg\mu(b) \in I$ for all $a \in Q^+$ and $b \in Q^-$. Answers to an NBCQ over a database are then defined as in the case of BCQs.

2.4 Normal TGDs

Given a relational schema $\mathcal{R}$, a *tuple-generating dependency (TGD)* is a first-order formula of the form $\forall\mathbf{X}\forall\mathbf{Y}\, \Phi(\mathbf{X}, \mathbf{Y}) \to \exists \mathbf{Z}\, \Psi(\mathbf{X}, \mathbf{Z})$, where $\Phi(\mathbf{X}, \mathbf{Y})$ and $\Psi(\mathbf{X}, \mathbf{Z})$ are conjunctions of atoms over $\mathcal{R}$ (all these atoms without nulls). Note that TGDs can be reduced to TGDs with only single atoms in their heads. Normal TGDs are informally TGDs that may also contain (default-)negated atoms in their bodies. Given a relational schema $\mathcal{R}$, a *normal TGD (NTGD)* σ has the form $\forall\mathbf{X}\forall\mathbf{Y}\, \Phi(\mathbf{X}, \mathbf{Y}) \to \exists \mathbf{Z}\, \Psi(\mathbf{X}, \mathbf{Z})$, where $\Phi(\mathbf{X}, \mathbf{Y})$ is a conjunction of atoms and negated atoms over $\mathcal{R}$, and $\Psi(\mathbf{X}, \mathbf{Z})$ is a conjunction of atoms over $\mathcal{R}$ (all these atoms without nulls). It is also abbreviated as $\Phi(\mathbf{X}, \mathbf{Y}) \to \exists \mathbf{Z}\, \Psi(\mathbf{X}, \mathbf{Z})$. As in the case of standard TGDs, w.l.o.g., $\Psi(\mathbf{X}, \mathbf{Z})$ is a singleton atom. We denote by $head(\sigma)$ the atom in the head of σ, and by $body^+(\sigma)$ and $body^-(\sigma)$ the sets of all positive and negative ("$\neg$"-free) atoms in the body of σ, respectively.

As for the semantics, a normal TGD σ is *satisfied* in a database D for $\mathcal{R}$ iff, whenever there exists a homomorphism h for all the variables and constants in the body of σ that maps (i) all atoms of $body^+(\sigma)$ to atoms of D and (ii) no atom of $body^-(\sigma)$ to atoms of D (i.e., atoms not in D are false), then there exists an extension h' of h that maps all atoms of $head(\sigma)$ to atoms of D.

A normal TGD σ is *guarded* iff it contains a positive atom in its body, denoted $guard(\sigma)$, that contains all universally quantified variables of σ. W.l.o.g., to simplify such σ in formal proofs, constants occur only in the guards of σ (as all the other atoms with constants can be abbreviated by fresh atoms without constants, which can be defined via linear TGDs (see below)). We say σ is *linear* iff σ is guarded and has exactly one positive atom in its body.

A *guarded normal Datalog$^\pm$ program* is a finite set of guarded NTGDs, and a *linear normal Datalog$^\pm$ program* is a finite set of linear NTGDs. Guarded and linear Datalog$^\pm$ programs are defined in the same way with TGDs instead of NTGDs.

Given an NTGD $\sigma = \Phi(\mathbf{X}, \mathbf{Y}) \to \exists \mathbf{Z}\, \Psi(\mathbf{X}, \mathbf{Z})$, the *functional transformation* of σ, denoted σ^f, is the normal rule $\Phi(\mathbf{X}, \mathbf{Y}) \to \Psi(\mathbf{X}, \mathbf{f}_\sigma(\mathbf{X}, \mathbf{Y}))$, where $\mathbf{f}_\sigma$ is a vector of function symbols $f_{\sigma,Z}$

for σ, one for every variable Z in $\mathbf{Z}$. Given a set Σ of NTGDs, the *functional transformation* of Σ, denoted Σ^f, is obtained from Σ by replacing each TGD σ in Σ by σ^f. Note that the functional transformation of a guarded Datalog$^\pm$ program is a positive program.

2.5 Guarded Chase Forests

Let Σ be a guarded Datalog$^\pm$ program (without negation) over a relational schema $\mathcal{R}$, let D be a database for $\mathcal{R}$, and let $P := D \cup \Sigma^f$.

Definition 1. (Guarded chase forest). The *guarded chase forest* $\mathcal{F}(P)$ of P is the union of the following forests $\mathcal{F}_i(P)$:

- We start with a forest $\mathcal{F}_0(P)$ that contains, for each fact a in P, a unique node labeled a; there are no other nodes and no edges.
- Let $i \geq 0$. The forest $\mathcal{F}_{i+1}(P)$ is obtained from $\mathcal{F}_i(P)$ by adding new nodes and edges as follows. Let $\mathcal{A}$ be the set of all labels of nodes of $\mathcal{F}_i(P)$. For each node v in $\mathcal{F}_i(P)$ and each rule $r \in \mathit{ground}(P)$ such that guard(r) is the label of v and $B(r) \subseteq \mathcal{A}$, there is a child w of v with label $H(r)$, and the edge from v to w is labeled with r.

Given a graph G, we denote by $V(G)$ the set of nodes of G. We often write $v \in G$ instead of $v \in V(G)$. The label of a node v in $\mathcal{F}(P)$ is denoted by label(v). We extend this notation to sets $V \subseteq V(\mathcal{F}(P))$ by letting label$(V) := \bigcup_{v \in V}$ label(v), and to subforests $\mathcal{F}$ by letting label$(\mathcal{F}) :=$ label$(V(\mathcal{F}))$. The *derivation level of a node* v in $\mathcal{F}(P)$, denoted level$_P(v)$, is the smallest integer $i \geq 0$ such that $v \in \mathcal{F}_i(P)$. Observe that level$_P(v)$ is in general different from the depth of v in $\mathcal{F}(P)$. We define the *derivation level of an atom* a in $\mathcal{F}(P)$ as

$$\text{level}_P(a) := \begin{cases} \min\{\text{level}_P(v) \mid v \in \mathcal{F}(P),\ \text{label}(v) = a\}, \\ \qquad \text{if } a \in \text{label}(V(\mathcal{F}(P))), \\ \infty, \quad \text{otherwise.} \end{cases}$$

Example 4. Let Σ consist of the following guarded TGDs:

$$R(X,Y,Z) \wedge P(X) \rightarrow S(Y,Z),$$
$$S(X,Y) \rightarrow \exists Z\, R(X,Y,Z),$$
$$R(X,Y,Z) \wedge S(X,Y) \rightarrow \exists U\, T(Z,U,X),$$
$$T(X,Y,Z) \rightarrow P(Z).$$

Moreover, let $D = \{R(a,b,c), P(a)\}$. Then, up to renaming of function symbols, P is the following program:

$$R(a,b,c),$$
$$P(a),$$
$$R(X,Y,Z) \wedge P(X) \rightarrow S(Y,Z),$$
$$S(X,Y) \rightarrow R(X,Y,f(X,Y)),$$
$$R(X,Y,Z) \wedge S(X,Y) \rightarrow T(Z,g(X,Y,Z),X),$$
$$T(X,Y,Z) \rightarrow P(Z).$$

The guarded chase forest $\mathcal{F}(P)$ of P up to level 5 is shown in Figure 1. Observe that the derivation level of the node labeled $S(c,f(b,c))$ is 5, but its depth is 3. ■

Let $\mathcal{F}^d(P)$ be the guarded chase forest of P up to depth d (i.e., the subforest of $\mathcal{F}(P)$ induced by all nodes of depth up to d).

LEMMA 1 (FOLLOWS FROM [3]). *There is an algorithm that, given a relational schema $\mathcal{R}$, a guarded Datalog$^\pm$ program Σ over $\mathcal{R}$, a database D for $\mathcal{R}$, and an integer $d \geq 0$, computes $\mathcal{F}^d(D \cup \Sigma^f)$ in time $2^{\gamma \cdot d}$, where γ is exponential in $|\mathcal{R}|$ and doubly exponential in the maximum arity of a predicate in $\mathcal{R}$.*

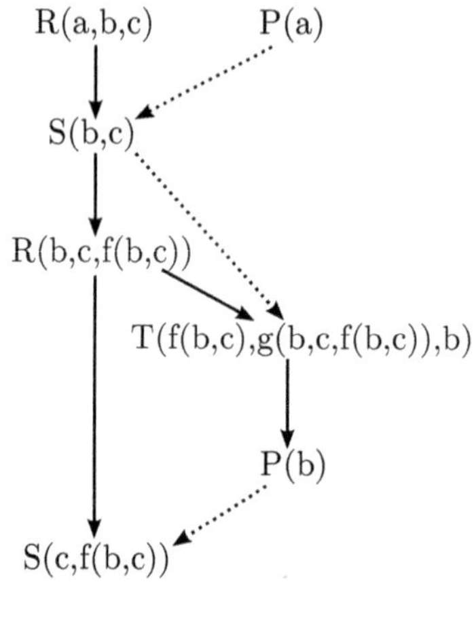

Figure 1: The guarded chase forest $\mathcal{F}(P)$ for the program P from Example 4 up to level 5. The dotted arcs do not belong to the forest; they are included in the figure merely to indicate which atoms besides the guard an atom depends on.

2.6 Well-Founded Semantics for Normal Logic Programs

The *well-founded semantics* [11] is the most widely used semantics for nonmonotonic logic programs, and it is especially under a data-oriented perspective of great importance for the Web. The well-founded semantics of normal programs P has many different equivalent definitions [11, 1]. We recall here the one based on unfounded sets, via the operators U_P, T_P, and W_P.

A set $U \subseteq HB_P$ is an *unfounded set* of P relative to $I \subseteq Lit_P$ iff for every $a \in U$ and every $r \in \mathit{ground}(P)$ with $H(r) = a$, either

(i) $\neg b \in I \cup \neg.U$ for some atom $b \in B^+(r)$, or

(ii) $b \in I$ for some atom $b \in B^-(r)$.

There exists the greatest unfounded set of P relative to I, denoted $U_P(I)$. Intuitively, if I is compatible with P, then all atoms in $U_P(I)$ can be safely switched to false and the resulting interpretation is still compatible with P. The greatest unfounded set of a partial interpretation I intuitively collects all those atoms that cannot become true when extending I with further information. An atom b is unfounded iff there is no rule with b in its head and with a body that can be made true. For example, an atom not appearing in any head is clearly unfounded. Observe that the falsity of rule bodies can be testified by unfounded atoms belonging to the same unfounded set, giving a notion of "self-supportedness".

We are now ready to define the two operators T_P and W_P on consistent $I \subseteq Lit_P$ as follows:

- $T_P(I) = \{H(r) \mid r \in \mathit{ground}(P),\ B^+(r) \cup \neg.B^-(r) \subseteq I\}$;
- $W_P(I) = T_P(I) \cup \neg.U_P(I)$.

The operator W_P is monotonic, and thus has a least fixpoint, denoted $\mathit{lfp}(W_P)$, which is the *well-founded semantics* of P, denoted $\mathit{WFS}(P)$ (a three-valued interpretation completable to a two-valued model of P). A ground atom $a \in HB_P$ is *well-founded* (resp., *unfounded*) relative to P, if a (resp., $\neg a$) is in $\mathit{lfp}(W_P)$. Intuitively, starting with $I = \emptyset$, rules are applied to obtain new positive and negated facts (via $T_P(I)$ and $\neg.U_P(I)$, respectively). This process is repeated until no longer possible. A literal $\ell \in Lit_P$ is a *consequence* of P under the well-founded semantics iff $\ell \in \mathit{WFS}(P)$.

3. WELL-FOUNDED SEMANTICS FOR GUARDED NORMAL DATALOG$^{\pm}$

This section's goal is to define and illustrate the well-founded semantics for guarded normal Datalog$^{\pm}$, and to prove some of its basic properties that are essential for the results in the next section.

3.1 Definition and Examples

The well-founded semantics for a guarded normal Datalog$^{\pm}$ program Σ relative to a given database D is defined using the well-founded semantics of the logic program obtained from taking the union of the functional transformation of Σ and D. Let us first look at a very simple concrete example.

Example 5. Consider the following normal guarded Datalog$^{\pm}$ program Σ consisting of only one rule:

$$\text{Student}(X), \neg\text{DropOut}(X) \rightarrow \exists Z.\text{hasTutor}(X, Z).$$

The rule expresses that every student (in a university database) who has not dropped out of his/her course has a tutor. The functional transformation of this rule looks as follows:

$$\text{Student}(X), \neg\text{DropOut}(X) \rightarrow \text{hasTutor}(X, f(X)).$$

Consider now the NBCQ

$$Q = \exists X \exists Y\, (\text{Student}(X) \wedge \text{hasTutor}(X, Y) \wedge \neg\text{Student}(\text{Y}))$$

and the database $D = \{\text{Student}(a)\}$. Then, the answer of the query relative to D under the well-founded semantics of the program Σ is *Yes*, as the well-founded semantics WFS($\Sigma^f \cup D$) includes the literals Student(a), $\neg$DropOut(a) (as the predicate DropOut does not occur in any rule head and so cannot be derived), and hasTutor$(a, f(a))$ (obtained by applying the functional transformation of the rule in Σ to the other two literals). Finally, the well-founded semantics also implies that $\neg$Student$(f(a))$ holds, because a is assumed to be different from $f(a)$, and because the rule cannot derive any new atoms with predicate Student. ■

The following definition gives a precise formulation of the well-founded semantics of a guarded[1] normal Datalog$^{\pm}$ program.

Definition 2. Let $\mathcal{R}$ be a relational schema, let Σ be a guarded normal Datalog$^{\pm}$ program, and let Σ^f be the functional transformation of Σ. The well-founded model of a given database D under Σ is denoted by WFS(D, Σ) and defined by WFS$(D, \Sigma) :=$ WFS$(\Sigma^f \cup D)$. An NBCQ Q is satisfied over a database D under Σ w.r.t. the well-founded semantics if WFS$(D, \Sigma) \models Q$.

Consider now a slightly more complicated example that will be used to illustrate several concepts throughout this section.

Example 6. Let Σ contain the following guarded NTGDs:

$$R(X, Y, Z) \rightarrow \exists U\, R(X, Z, U),$$
$$R(X, Y, Z) \wedge P(X, Y) \wedge \neg Q(Z) \rightarrow P(X, Z),$$
$$R(X, Y, Z) \wedge \neg P(X, Y) \rightarrow Q(Z),$$
$$R(X, Y, Z) \wedge \neg P(X, Z) \rightarrow S(X),$$
$$P(X, Y) \wedge \neg S(X) \rightarrow T(X).$$

Moreover, let $D = \{R(0, 0, 1), P(0, 0)\}$. Then, up to renaming of function symbols, the program $\Sigma^f \cup D$ is:

$$R(0, 0, 1), P(0, 0),$$
$$R(X, Y, Z) \rightarrow R(X, Z, f(X, Y, Z)),$$
$$R(X, Y, Z) \wedge P(X, Y) \wedge \neg Q(Z) \rightarrow P(X, Z),$$
$$R(X, Y, Z) \wedge \neg P(X, Y) \rightarrow Q(Z),$$
$$R(X, Y, Z) \wedge \neg P(X, Z) \rightarrow S(X),$$
$$P(X, Y) \wedge \neg S(X) \rightarrow T(X).$$

It is easy to see that WFS(D, Σ) includes the atom $R(0, 1, f(0, 0, 1))$, as we can apply the first rule in Σ^f to derive this atom from the atoms in D. Furthermore WFS(D, Σ) includes $P(0, 1)$. To see this slightly less obvious fact, note that there is no rule that can derive an atom of the form $R(*, *, 1)$, where the $*$'s could be arbitrary constants or nulls. This is due to the fact that any Skolem term of the form $f(t_1, t_2, t_3)$ is by default assumed to be different from 1. Therefore the only rule instance that could possibly derive $Q(1)$ is

$$R(0, 0, 1) \wedge \neg P(0, 0) \rightarrow Q(1),$$

but as $P(0, 0) \in D \subseteq$ WFS(D, Σ), we can conclude that $\neg Q(1)$ is in WFS(D, Σ). Now $P(0, 1) \in$ WFS(D, Σ) can be easily derived using a suitable instance of the second rule. ■

3.2 Basic Properties

When proving decidability of query answering relative to a Datalog$^{\pm}$-program, one faces the problem that query answering has to be performed relative to an infinite model that is obtained as a result of the chase algorithm. Nevertheless, as demonstrated in [3], decidability for (positive) guarded Datalog$^{\pm}$ can be achieved by showing that the guarded chase forest has the following neat "locality" property: for any node v in the guarded chase forest, the tree generated from v is determined (up-to isomorphism) by the type of the atom a by which v is labelled. Here the type of an atom is a pair consisting of a itself together with the collection of atoms b that occur in the chase such that $dom(b) \subseteq dom(a)$. As there are only finitely many non-isomorphic types relative to a given relational schema $\mathcal{R}$, the locality property ensures that any query that can be matched to atoms in the chase can be matched to atoms of bounded depth.

The main goal of this section is to demonstrate that a similar locality property holds for guarded normal Datalog$^{\pm}$ programs. To this aim, we have to consider types that contain literals rather than atoms. We then show that with respect to this more general notion of type, the guarded chase forest of the positive part of a program does satisfy a locality property that is very similar to the one for (positive) guarded Datalog$^{\pm}$: whenever two nodes v_1 and v_2 are labelled with atoms that are contained in the well-founded model and that have isomorphic types, the part of the well-founded model that is "determined" (in a sense that will be made precise) by the atoms that occur in the subtrees generated from v_1 and v_2 are isomorphic as well.

3.2.1 *Characterization via Forward Proofs*

To be able to prove the above-mentioned locality property, we first introduce the notion of a forward proof of an atom. These forward proofs are subforests of the guarded chase forest of the positive part of a guarded normal Datalog$^{\pm}$ program that witness the fact that an atom is potentially contained in the well-founded semantics (an atom without forward proof is certainly false). Forward proofs are instrumental for proving the locality property as they provide a useful link between the guarded chase forest of the positive part of the program on the one hand and the well-founded

[1]Note that guardedness is not required for the definition of the semantics, but to ensure decidability of query answering.

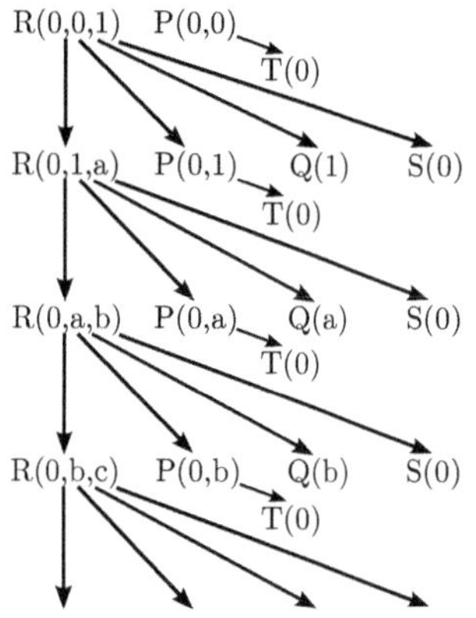

Figure 2: The forest $\mathcal{F}^+(P)$ for the program P from Example 7 up to depth 3. Here, $a := f(0,0,1)$, $b := f(0,1,a)$, and $c := f(0,a,b)$.

semantics of the program on the other hand. The characterization of the well-founded semantics for guarded normal Datalog$^\pm$ based on the concept of *forward proofs* that we are going to use is essentially the one from [10].

Let Σ be a guarded *normal* Datalog$^\pm$ program over $\mathcal{R}$, let D be a database for $\mathcal{R}$, and let $P := D \cup \Sigma^f$. Let $\mathcal{F}^+(P)$ be the forest obtained from $\mathcal{F}(P^+)$ by replacing each edge label, which is a rule $r^+ \in \mathit{ground}(P^+)$, by the rule $r \in \mathit{ground}(P)$ such that r^+ is obtained from r by dropping all negative literals (for simplicity, we assume that this rule r is unique). For every subforest $\mathcal{F}$ of $\mathcal{F}^+(P)$, let $S(\mathcal{F})$ be the set of all $b \in HB_P$ for which there is an edge in $\mathcal{F}$ from a node v to a node w labeled with a rule $r \in \mathit{ground}(P)$ such that $b \in B^+(r)$ and b is not the label of a node in $\mathcal{F}$ with smaller level than w. Furthermore, let $N(\mathcal{F})$ be the set of all $b \in HB_P$ such that $b \in B^-(r)$ for a rule r that occurs as the label of an edge in $\mathcal{F}$.

Example 7. Let Σ, D, and P be as in Example 6. Then, P^+ consists of:

$$\begin{aligned}&R(0,0,1), P(0,0),\\&R(X,Y,Z) \to R(X,Z,f(X,Y,Z)),\\&R(X,Y,Z) \wedge P(X,Y) \to P(X,Z),\\&R(X,Y,Z) \to Q(Z),\\&R(X,Y,Z) \to S(X),\\&P(X,Y) \to T(X).\end{aligned}$$

The forest $\mathcal{F}^+(P)$ up to depth three is shown in Figure 2, where the elements a, b, and c are defined as $f(0,0,1)$, $f(0,1,a)$, and $f(0,a,b)$, respectively. Edge labels are omitted, but they can easily be recovered from the information given in Figure 2. For example, the edge from $R(0,0,1)$ to $R(0,1,a)$ is labeled by $R(0,0,1) \to R(0,1,f(0,0,1))$, and the edge from $R(0,1,a)$ to $P(0,a)$ is labeled by the rule $R(0,1,a) \wedge P(0,1) \wedge \neg Q(a) \to P(0,a)$.

If $\mathcal{F}$ is the subtree containing $R(0,0,1)$, $P(0,1)$, and $T(0)$ (the child of $P(0,1)$), then $S(\mathcal{F}) = \{P(0,0)\}$ and $N(\mathcal{F}) = \{Q(1), S(0)\}$. Thus, $S(\mathcal{F})$ contains all the atoms required to fire the rules in $\mathcal{F}$ (ignoring negative literals that appear in rule bodies), while $N(\mathcal{F})$ contains all the atoms whose negation is required in order to fire all the rules in $\mathcal{F}$. ■

The following is a minor modification of the notion of *forward proof* in [10].

Definition 3. A *forward proof of an atom $a \in HB_P$ from P with negative hypotheses* (or just *forward proof* of a from P) is a finite subforest π of $\mathcal{F}^+(P)$ such that:

1. There is a distinguished node in π labeled a, called *goal node* of π.
2. For every node $v \in \pi$ that has a parent w in $\mathcal{F}^+(P)$ we have $w \in \pi$.
3. If r is the label of an edge from a node v to a node w in π, then for every $b \in B^+(r)$ there is a node $u \in \pi$ with $\mathrm{level}_P(u) < \mathrm{level}_P(w)$ and $\mathrm{label}(u) = b$.

The elements in $\neg.N(\pi)$ are the *negative hypotheses* of π.

Remark 1. We are mostly interested in inclusion-minimal forward proofs. It is not hard to see that inclusion-minimal forward proofs in the above sense and van Gelder's minimal forward proofs [10] are equivalent for guarded normal Datalog$^\pm$ programs.

Example 8. In Example 7, there is exactly one inclusion-minimal forward proof of $R(0,b,c)$ from P, namely the subtree π of $\mathcal{F}^+(P)$ induced by the nodes labeled $R(0,0,1)$, $R(0,1,a)$, $R(0,a,b)$, and $R(0,b,c)$. The proof has no negative hypotheses, i.e., $N(\pi) = \emptyset$.

The atom $P(0,a)$ has exactly one inclusion-minimal forward proof from P: the subforest π' induced by the nodes labeled $R(0,0,1)$, $R(0,1,a)$, $P(0,0)$, $P(0,1)$, and $P(0,a)$. Here, we have $N(\pi') = \{Q(1), Q(a)\}$.

However, note that there are infinitely many inclusion-minimal forward proofs of $S(0)$ from P, each corresponding to a node in $\mathcal{F}^+(P)$ labeled with $S(0)$. ■

We need the following operator from [10].[2]

Definition 4. ($\widehat{W}_P$) We define an operator $\widehat{W}_P$ on $\mathcal{P}(\mathit{Lit}_P)$ as follows. For every $I \subseteq \mathit{Lit}_P$ and every $a \in HB_P$:

- $a \in \widehat{W}_P(I)$ if there is a forward proof π of a from P with $\neg.N(\pi) \subseteq I$, and
- $\neg a \in \widehat{W}_P(I)$ if for all forward proofs of a from P there is a $b \in N(\pi)$ with $b \in I$.

It is not hard to see that $\widehat{W}_P$ is monotone, and therefore has a least fixed point. Recall that this least fixed point is defined as the union of the fixed point stages $\widehat{W}_P^0, \widehat{W}_P^1, \ldots$:

- $\widehat{W}_{P,0} := \emptyset$.
- $\widehat{W}_{P,\alpha} := \widehat{W}_P(\widehat{W}_{P,\alpha-1})$ if α is a successor ordinal.
- $\widehat{W}_{P,\alpha} := \bigcup_{\beta<\alpha} \widehat{W}_{P,\beta}$ if α is a limit ordinal.

THEOREM 2 (ESSENTIALLY [10]). *$\mathrm{WFS}(P)$ is the least fixed point of $\widehat{W}_P$. That is, $\mathrm{WFS}(P) = \bigcup_\alpha \widehat{W}_{P,\alpha}$.*

Example 9. Let us revisit Example 7. Define $t_0 := 0$, $t_1 := 1$, and $t_{i+2} := f(0, t_i, t_{i+1})$. Then, we have

$$\begin{aligned}\widehat{W}_{P,1} &= \{R(0,t_i,t_{i+1}) \mid i \geq 0\} \cup \{P(0,0)\}\\&\quad \cup \{\neg a \mid a \in HB_P,\ a \notin \mathrm{label}(\mathcal{F}^+(P))\}.\end{aligned}$$

[2]In [10], this operator is denoted by **wf**, and it is defined in terms of minimal forward proofs as defined in [10].

It is not hard to see that for every integer $i \geq 1$,

$$\widehat{W}_{P,2i} = \widehat{W}_{P,1} \cup \{P(0,t_j) \mid 0 \leq j < i\} \cup \{\neg Q(t_j) \mid 0 \leq j \leq i\},$$
$$\widehat{W}_{P,2i+1} = \widehat{W}_{P,1} \cup \{P(0,t_j) \mid 0 \leq j \leq i\} \cup \{\neg Q(t_j) \mid 0 \leq j \leq i\}.$$

Therefore,

$$\widehat{W}_{P,\omega+2} = \widehat{W}_{P,1} \cup \{P(0,t_j) \mid j \geq 0\} \cup \{\neg Q(t_j) \mid j \geq 0\} \cup \{\neg S(0), T(0)\},$$

and $\widehat{W}_{P,\omega+3} = \widehat{W}_{P,\omega+2}$, hence $\mathrm{WFS}(P) = \widehat{W}_{P,\omega+2}$.

This demonstrates that the computation of the least fixed-point of $\widehat{W}_P$ does in general not terminate after ω-many steps. The same holds true if we compute WFS(P) as least fixed point of W_P: spelling out the definitions it is not difficult to see that $W_P^{\omega}(\emptyset) = \widehat{W}_{P,\omega}$. ■

3.2.2 Locality

After having introduced the characterization of the well-founded semantics in terms of forward proofs, we are now ready to prove the locality property of the well-founded semantics that we discussed at the beginning of this section. We start by introducing the necessary technical notions: the appropriate notion of type consisting of a set of literals and the notion of an isomorphism between sets of literals.

Throughout this section, we fix a finite set Σ of guarded NTGDs over a relational schema $\mathcal{R}$, and a database D for $\mathcal{R}$. Let $P := D \cup \Sigma^f$.

The *(P-)type* of an atom $a \in HB_P$ is the pair $\mathrm{type}_P(a) := (a, S)$, where S consists of all literals $\ell \in \mathrm{WFS}(P)$ with $dom(\ell) \subseteq dom(a)$. If we speak of a P-type without mentioning the atom, we mean a P-type of some atom.

Let $I, I' \subseteq Lit_P$ and $X \subseteq dom(I) \cup dom(I')$. An *$X$-isomorphism* from I to I' is a bijective mapping f from $dom(I)$ to $dom(I')$ such that $f(I) = I'$, and for all $x \in X$,

- $x \in dom(I)$ if and only if $x \in dom(I')$, and
- if $x \in dom(I)$, then $f(x) = x$.

If there is an X-isomorphism from I to I', we say that I and I' are X-isomorphic, and denote this by $I \cong_X I'$. Given two P-types (a, S) and (a', S'), an X-isomorphism from (a, S) to (a', S') is an X-isomorphism f from $\{a\}$ to $\{a'\}$ with $f(S) = S'$. As for sets of literals, we call (a, S) and (a', S') *X-isomorphic*, and write $(a, S) \cong_X (a', S')$, if there is an X-isomorphism from (a, S) to (a', S').

Let $\mathcal{F}^*(P)$ be the subforest of $\mathcal{F}^+(P)$ induced by all the nodes in $\mathcal{F}^+(P)$ that are goal nodes of forward proofs π from P with $\neg.N(\pi) \subseteq \mathrm{WFS}(P)$. Note that $\mathcal{F}^*(P)$ contains exactly the nodes that correspond to the atoms in WFS(P). The following lemma demonstrates that the truth of any atom below some node $v \in \mathcal{F}^*(P)$ depends only on the type of label(v), the labels of the tree T generated by v and all negative literals whose arguments occur in the labels of T.

LEMMA 3. *Let $v \in \mathcal{F}^*(P)$ with $\mathrm{type}_P(\mathrm{label}(v)) = (a, S)$, let T be the subtree of $\mathcal{F}^+(P)$ rooted at v, and let I be the set of all literals $\ell \in Lit_P$ such that either $\ell \in S$, or ℓ is positive and occurs in T, or ℓ is negative and $dom(\ell) \subseteq dom(\mathrm{label}(T))$. Then, for all atoms $b \in \mathrm{label}(T)$, we have:*

1. *If there is a forward proof π of b from P with $\neg.N(\pi) \subseteq X \subseteq \mathrm{WFS}(P)$ then there exists a forward proof π' of b from $S^+ \cup \Sigma^f$ with $\neg.N(\pi') \subseteq X \cap I$ and with the property that $\mathrm{label}(\pi') \subseteq S \cup \mathrm{label}(T)$.*
2. *If there exists a forward proof π' of b from $S^+ \cup \Sigma^f$ then π' can be extended to a forward proof π of b from P with $\neg.N(\pi) \setminus \neg.N(\pi') \subseteq \mathrm{WFS}(P)$.*

PROOF. Consider first some $b \in \mathrm{label}(T)$ such that there exists a forward proof π of b from P with $\neg.N(\pi) \subseteq X \subseteq \mathrm{WFS}(P)$. We let π' be the subtree of π induced by all nodes $w \in T$ together with a set of nodes whose elements are labeled by the elements of S^+. If r is the label of an edge from a node x to a node y in π', then:

- for all $c \in B^+(r)$ for which there is not a node $u \in \pi' \cap T$ with $\mathrm{level}_P(u) < \mathrm{level}_P(y)$ and $\mathrm{label}(u) = c$, we have $c \in S^+$; and
- for all $c \in B^-(r)$ we have $\neg c \in I$, and therefore $\neg c \in X \cap I$.

Therefore π' is a forward proof of b from $S^+ \cup \Sigma^f$ with $\neg.N(\pi') \subseteq X \cap I$ and $\mathrm{label}(\pi') \subseteq S \cup \mathrm{label}(T)$ by definition as required.

For the second half of the lemma consider a $b \in \mathrm{label}(T)$ such that there exists some forward proof π' of b from $S^+ \cup \Sigma^f$.For each $c \in S^+$ there exists a forward proof π_c from P such that $\neg.N(\pi_c) \subseteq \mathrm{WFS}(P)$. The extension of π' with the union of the proofs π_c results in a forward proof π of b from P with the required property. □

Later we will also need the following lemma whose proof is based on similar ideas as for the proof of the preceding lemma.

LEMMA 4. *Let $v \in \mathcal{F}^+(P)$, let T be the subtree of $\mathcal{F}^+(P)$ rooted at v, and let b be an atom containing at least one argument that occurs in T but not in $\mathcal{F}^+(P) \setminus T$. If there is a forward proof π of b from P such that $N(\pi) \cap \mathrm{WFS}(P) = \emptyset$, then there is such a forward proof π' whose goal node is reachable from v.*

We are now able to formulate and prove the locality property of the well-founded semantics that is crucial for our decidability result.

LEMMA 5. *Let $v_1, v_2 \in \mathcal{F}^*(P)$ be two nodes with the types $\mathrm{type}_P(\mathrm{label}(v_i)) = (a_i, S_i)$ for $i = 1, 2$. Let T_i be the subtree of $\mathcal{F}^+(P)$ rooted at v_i, and let I_i be the set of all literals $\ell \in Lit_P$ such that either $\ell \in S_i$, or ℓ is positive and occurs in T_i, or ℓ is negative and $dom(\ell) \subseteq dom(\mathrm{label}(T_i))$. If f is an X-isomorphism from $\mathrm{type}_P(a_1)$ to $\mathrm{type}_P(a_2)$, then there is an X-isomorphism from $\mathrm{WFS}(P) \cap I_1$ to $\mathrm{WFS}(P) \cap I_2$ that extends f.*

PROOF. It is not difficult to extend f to an isomorphism between T_1 and T_2 and thus to a map from I_1 to I_2. We are going to show that this extension restricts to an X-isomorphism from $\mathrm{WFS}(P) \cap I_1$ to $\mathrm{WFS}(P) \cap I_2$. More concretely, we prove that for all ordinals α and for all literals b, we have that $b \in W_\alpha \cap I_1$ implies $f(b) \in \mathrm{WFS}(P) \cap I_2$ (the claim that $b \in \mathrm{WFS}(P) \cap I_2$ implies $f^{-1}(b) \in \mathrm{WFS}(P) \cap I_1$ is completely symmetric and can be proven similarly).

Let us first show the claim for atoms $b \in W_\alpha \cap I_1$. In this case, we can assume w.l.o.g. that $b \in W_\alpha \cap \mathrm{label}(T_1)$ for otherwise the claim follows trivially from the fact that the types (a_1, S_1) and (a_2, S_2) are assumed to be isomorphic. Moreover the only non-trivial case to consider is that $b \in W_\alpha \cap \mathrm{label}(T_1)$ for some successor ordinal α. By assumption on b, there exists a forward proof π of b from P such that $\neg.N(\pi) \subseteq W_{\alpha-1}$. Therefore, by Lemma 3 there exists a forward proof π' of b from $S_1^+ \cup \Sigma^f$ such that $\neg.N(\pi) \subseteq W_{\alpha-1} \cap I_1$ such that π' contains only atoms in $\text{label}(T_1) \cup S_1^+$. Using the induction hypothesis on α, it is not difficult to see that f maps π' to a forward proof $f(\pi')$ of $f(b)$ from $S_2^+ \cup \Sigma^f$ such that $\neg.N(\pi) \subseteq W_{\alpha-1} \cap I_2$, and this proof can be extended to a forward proof of $f(b)$ from P using Lemma 3 again. This shows that $f(b) \in \text{WFS}(P)$ as required.

Consider now some negative literal $\neg b \in W_\alpha \cap I_1$. W.l.o.g., we have $b \in W_\alpha \cap \text{label}(T_1)$ — in all other cases, we obviously have $\neg f(b) \in W_\alpha \cap I_2$ (here, we use that f is an iso between S_1 and S_2). We want to prove that $\neg f(b) \in \text{WFS}(P) \cap \text{label}(T_2)$.

Let π be a forward proof of $f(b)$ from P. By Lemma 3, there exists a forward proof π' of $f(b)$ from $S_2^+ \cup \Sigma^f$ such that π' is labeled with elements of $\text{label}(T_2) \cup S_2^+$. It can be easily seen that the labels in $f^{-1}(\pi')$ are contained in $\text{label}(T_1) \cup S_1^+$ and, in addition to that, that $f^{-1}(\pi')$ constitutes a forward proof of b from $S_1^+ \cup \Sigma^f$. By our assumption on b there must be some $c \in N(f^{-1}(\pi')) \cap W_{\alpha-1}$ (for otherwise - using Lemma 3 - we could extend $f^{-1}(\pi')$ to a forward proof π of b from P with $N(f^{-1}(\pi)) \cap W_{\alpha-1} = \emptyset$ contradicting the fact that $\neg b \in W_\alpha$). As the labels of $f^{-1}(\pi')$ are in $\text{label}(T_1) \cup S_1^+$ this c has to be also contained in I_1. Therefore, by the I.H., we obtain $f(c) \in N(\pi') \cap \text{WFS}(P)$ and thus $f(c) \in N(\pi) \cap \text{WFS}(P)$. As π was an arbitrary forward proof of $f(b)$ from P, this demonstrates that $\neg f(b) \in \text{WFS}(P)$ as required. □

The locality property from the previous lemma is the key for obtaining the following bound on the possible matches of a normal Boolean conjunctive query.

PROPOSITION 6. *Let $\mathcal{R}$ be a relational schema $\mathcal{R}$, and $\delta := 2 \cdot |\mathcal{R}| \cdot (2w)^w \cdot 2^{|\mathcal{R}| \cdot (2w)^w}$, where w is the maximum arity of a predicate in $\mathcal{R}$. Let D be a database for $\mathcal{R}$, Σ a set of guarded NTGDs over $\mathcal{R}$, and Q an NBCQ over $\mathcal{R}$ with n literals. If* $\text{WFS}(D \cup \Sigma^f) \models Q$, *then there is a homomorphism μ of Q into* $\text{WFS}(D \cup \Sigma^f)$ *such that:*

1. *For all $a \in Q^+$, $\mu(a)$ has depth at most $n \cdot \delta$ in $\mathcal{F}^*(P)$.*
2. *For all $a \in Q^-$, either $\mu(a)$ does not occur in $\mathcal{F}^+(P)$, or $\mu(a)$ has depth at most $n \cdot \delta$ in $\mathcal{F}^+(P)$.*

PROOF (SKETCH). We generalize the proof of Lemma 4 in [3]. Suppose that Q is satisfied in $W := \text{WFS}(D \cup \Sigma^f)$. Then there is a homomorphism μ with $\mu(Q) \subseteq W$. Recall that this means that for all atoms $a \in Q^+$ we have $\mu(a) \in W$, and for all atoms $a \in Q^-$ we have $\neg\mu(a) \in W$. Let $I_\mu^+ := \mu(Q^+)$, let I_μ^- be the set of all atoms $a \in \mu(Q^-)$ such that a occurs in $\mathcal{F}^+(P)$, and let $I_\mu := I_\mu^+ \cup I_\mu^-$. For every $a \in I_\mu^+$, let $d_a := \text{depth}_{\mathcal{F}^*(P)}(a)$, and for every $a \in I_\mu^-$, let $d_a := \text{depth}_{\mathcal{F}^+(P)}(a)$. Without loss of generality we assume that μ is chosen such that $\sum_{a \in I_\mu} d_a$ is minimized. We claim that for every $a \in I_\mu$ we have $d_a \leq n \cdot \delta$. Indeed, let $\mathcal{F}$ be an inclusion-minimal subforest of $\mathcal{F}^+(P)$ with the following properties: (1) for each atom $a \in I_\mu^+$, $\mathcal{F}$ contains a node v_a of depth d_a that is labeled a and the labels of all ancestors of v_a belong to W; (2) for each $b \in I_\mu^-$, $\mathcal{F}$ contains a node of depth d_b that is labeled b; and (3) $\mathcal{F}$ is closed under ancestors. Let V be the set of all nodes in $\mathcal{F}$ that are either labeled with an atom in I_μ or are branchings (i.e., contain at least two children in $\mathcal{F}$). Note that, by construction, none of the nodes v_a, for $a \in I_\mu^+$, can have an ancestor labeled with an atom in I_μ^-. Now, applying Lemma 5, we show—exactly as in the proof of Lemma 4 in [3]—that the length of every path between two nodes in V is bounded by the number of non-isomorphic P-types, which happens to be bounded by δ (this can be seen by a simple counting argument, which is completely analogous to the one used in Lemma 2 in [3]). Finally, notice that each path in $\mathcal{F}$ can contain at most n nodes from V, which shows that the depth of $\mathcal{F}$ is bounded by $n \cdot \delta$. □

4. MEMBERSHIP OF GROUND ATOMS IN WELL-FOUNDED MODELS

This and the following sections present our complexity bounds for evaluating NBCQs in well-founded models under guarded normal Datalog$^\pm$ programs. The present section provides the most important building block—an alternating algorithm, called *WCHECK*, that decides whether a ground atom belongs to the well-founded model of a database under a guarded normal Datalog$^\pm$ program. Subsequent sections generalize WCHECK to literals (ground and non-ground) and to NBCQs, and eventually prove the promised complexity bounds.

We start with a high-level overview of WCHECK, explaining the underlying ideas as well as problems we need to tackle, before Section 4.2 describes it in more detail.

4.1 Overview and Ideas

WCHECK's goal is to decide whether a ground atom belongs to the well-founded model of some database under a guarded normal Datalog$^\pm$ program. More precisely, its input consists of a database D, a guarded normal Datalog$^\pm$ program Σ, and a ground atom a, and its task is to decide whether $a \in \text{WFS}(P)$, where $P = D \cup \Sigma^f$.

For the case that Σ is positive (i.e., Σ contains only NTGDs without negated atoms in their bodies), the task of deciding whether a belongs to $\text{WFS}(P)$ is well-understood [2, 3]. Indeed, results in [3] imply that in this case a is in $\text{WFS}(P)$ if a belongs to a finite "initial segment" of $\text{WFS}(P)$ that is obtained by iteratively applying the W_P-operator to the empty interpretation for a finite number of times, where the number of iterations depends only on Σ.[3] In other words, it suffices to check whether a occurs in this initial segment of $\text{WFS}(P)$. However, as soon as Σ contains NTGDs with negated atoms in their bodies, this approach no longer works. Consider D and Σ from Example 6. Example 9 shows that the ground atom $T(0)$ occurs in $\text{WFS}(P)$, but "enters" $\text{WFS}(P)$ only after an infinite number of iterations of the W_P-operator. Nevertheless, it can be shown that a similar approach, based on depth-bounded forward proofs, works. This is a by-product of the WCHECK algorithm and will be made more precise in Remark 2.

Although the method for checking membership of ground atoms in well-founded models over positive guarded normal Datalog$^\pm$ programs described above does not generalize to arbitrary guarded normal Datalog$^\pm$ programs, it turns out that a different one, namely the ACHECK algorithm in [2], can be generalized. This is exactly what WCHECK does.

WCHECK is based on the idea that, if a ground atom a belongs to the well-founded model W of a database D and a guarded normal Datalog$^\pm$ program Σ, then the forest $\mathcal{F}^+(D \cup \Sigma^f)$ contains a path from some root node to a node labeled a such that all "side literals" (i.e., non-guard atoms and negated atoms in the bodies of rules applied along the path) belong to W.[4] For example, in the case of D and Σ from Example 6, the atom $T(0)$ belongs to W, and indeed $\mathcal{F}^+(D \cup \Sigma^f)$ contains a path from the root $R(0,0,1)$ to $T(0)$ whose side literals $P(0,1)$, $\neg Q(f(0,0,1))$ and $\neg S(0)$ belong to W. The idea is quite similar to ACHECK's central idea. The only difference is that in the case of ACHECK, Σ is a positive guarded normal Datalog$^\pm$ program, W is the result of the chase of D and Σ, and side literals are replaced by "side atoms" [2]. It is straightforward to verify from the definition of the well-founded model that a path as described above is a sufficient and necessary condition for a to belong to W.

[3]More precisely, it is exponential in the number of predicates in Σ, and doubly-exponential in the maximum arity of a predicate in Σ.
[4]This is actually true also for non-ground atoms.

To decide whether a path from the root of $\mathcal{F}^+(D \cup \Sigma^f)$ to a with the desired properties exists, WCHECK successively guesses atoms $a_0, a_1, a_2, \ldots$, where a_0 is the label of a root of $\mathcal{F}^+(D \cup \Sigma^f)$ and each a_{i+1} is the label of a child of (the node labeled) a_i. The idea here is to guess a path from a_0 to a. Of course, we also need to verify that all the side literals on such a path belong to W. Therefore, along with each a_i, WCHECK guesses a set S_i of literals in W all of whose arguments appear in a_i and which agree with S_{i-1} on the literals whose arguments appear in a_{i-1}, and an ordering $\preceq_i$ of the atoms (not the literals) in S_i. The idea is that S_i contains (at least) all the side literals of rules applied on the path from a_i to a that contain only arguments from a_i (this is enforced by checking that the rule generating a_{i+1} has all its side-literals in S_i), and $\preceq_i$ is the order of deriving the atoms in S_i. For example, if D and Σ are as in Example 6, a is the atom $T(0)$, and WCHECK guesses $a_0 = R(0,0,1)$, $a_1 = R(0,1,f(0,0,1))$, $a_2 = P(0, f(0,0,1))$ and $a_3 = T(0)$, then good choices for the sets S_i of literals would be $S_0 = \{P(0,1), \neg S(0)\}$, $S_1 = S_0 \cup \{\neg Q(f(0,0,1))\}$, $S_2 = \{\neg Q(f(0,0,1)), \neg S(0)\}$, and $S_3 = \{\neg S(0)\}$ (since each S_i contains at most one atom, the $\preceq_i$ are not needed in this example).

What remains is to check that all the literals in S_i belong to W. To this end, WCHECK launches subcomputations, one for each literal in an S_i. The subcomputations for positive literals $b \in S_i$, where i is assumed to be minimal, are similar to the main computation described above. For $i > 0$ (for 0, it is basically the same as above), the basic idea is to find a path from a_i to b such that all side literals along the path belong to W (where literals in S_{i-1} and literals in S_i that are $\preceq_i$-smaller than b may be assumed to belong to W). This is justified because b is in $S_i \setminus S_{i-1}$, and as such it contains at least one element that was created in a_i and must therefore occur in the subtree rooted at a_i. The case of negative literals $\neg b \in S_i$ is not so clear. The main idea is to check that every path from a_i to a node labeled b contains either a positive side literal c with $\neg c \in W$, or a negative side literal $\neg c$ with $c \in W$ (where we may assume literals in S_{i-1} belong to W). In our example above, WCHECK would find out that the only path (and thus all paths) from $a_1 = R(0,1,f(0,0,1))$ to $Q(f(0,0,1))$ in $\mathcal{F}^+(D \cup \Sigma^f)$ contains the side literal $\neg P(0,1)$, and since it knows that $P(0,1) \in W$ (since it belongs to S_0), it would conclude that $\neg Q(f(0,0,1)) \in S_1$ belongs to W. It is not obvious, though, that this test is enough to establish that $\neg b$ belongs to W. Its proof requires the machinery and results in Section 3.2.2.

4.2 Detailed Description

We now give a detailed description of WCHECK. Recall that the input to WCHECK consists of a database D for some schema $\mathcal{R}$, a guarded normal Datalog$^\pm$ program Σ over $\mathcal{R}$, and a ground atom a over $\mathcal{R}$; and that its task is to decide whether $a \in \text{WFS}(P)$, where P is the program $D \cup \Sigma^f$.

To simplify the presentation, we fix D and Σ (and $P = D \cup \Sigma^f$) throughout this section, but the reader should keep in mind that D and Σ are part of the input.

We also modify P so that the guarded chase forest of the corresponding positive program forms a tree.[5] To this end, let $c_1, \ldots, c_n$ be an enumeration of the elements in $dom(D)$, and let R^* be an n-ary predicate symbol that does not occur in $\mathcal{R}$. For each atom $a = R(c_{i_1}, \ldots, c_{i_k})$ in D, let σ_a be the guarded NTGD $R^*(x_1, \ldots, x_n) \to R(x_{i_1}, \ldots, x_{i_k})$. Finally, define the program P' by $\{R^*(c_1, \ldots, c_n)\} \cup \{\sigma_a \mid a \in D\} \cup \Sigma^f$. Thus, P' contains a single fact, $R^*(c_1, \ldots, c_n)$, rules σ_a to generate the atoms $a \in D$ from this fact, and the original rules from P. It is now straightforward to verify that a literal ℓ over $\mathcal{R}$ (note that $R^*(c_1, \ldots, c_n)$ is not such a literal) belongs to WFS(P) whenever it belongs to WFS(P'). Note also that $\mathcal{F}^+(P')$ is a tree whose root, denoted ρ, is labeled $R^*(c_1, \ldots, c_n)$, and the subtrees rooted at the children of ρ correspond to the subtrees of $\mathcal{F}^+(P)$ rooted at the root nodes of $\mathcal{F}^+(P)$.

[5] We do this without loss of generality; the algorithm could be described for inputs where the guarded chase forest is not a tree, but it would be slightly more complicated.

4.2.1 *Configurations*

WCHECK uses as basic data structures *configurations*, which are defined in the following.

Before we define configurations, we need a few definitions. For each atom $a \in HB_P$, let $Lit_P(a)$ be the set of all literals $\ell \in Lit_P$ such that $dom(\ell) \subseteq dom(a)$. That is, $Lit_P(a)$ contains all literals over the schema of P whose arguments occur as arguments of a. If, for example, $a = R(c, f(c,d))$, then $P(c)$ and $Q(f(c,d), c)$ are in $Lit_P(a)$, but $R(c,d)$ or $S(f(c,c))$ are not in $Lit_P(a)$, because d and $f(c,c)$ are not arguments of a. Let $HB_P(a) := HB_P \cap Lit_P(a)$ be the set of all atoms in $Lit_P(a)$.

Definition 5. A *configuration* $(a, S, S^+, \preceq, \ell)$ of WCHECK consists of an atom $a \in HB_P \cup \{R^*(c_1, \ldots, c_n)\}$, a set $S \subseteq Lit_P(a)$, a set $S^+ \subseteq S$, a linear order $\preceq$ on S^+, and a literal $\ell \in Lit_P$.

The components of a configuration $(a, S, S^+, \preceq, \ell)$ have the following intuitive meaning: ℓ is a literal for which we want to check if it belongs to WFS(P), a is the current atom on a possible path from the root of $\mathcal{F}^+(P')$ to ℓ (or $\neg.\ell$ if ℓ is negative), S is the set of all literals needed to fire rules on paths that start in a and lead to atoms that need to be checked later on, S^+ is the set of all those literals in S that still have to be checked for membership in WFS(P), and $\preceq$ is the derivation order of the literals in S^+.

Note that the number of configurations is in general infinite. We will later show how to obtain a finite number of configurations.

4.2.2 *Algorithm*

Let $a \in HB_P$ be an atom to be checked for membership in WFS(P) (equivalently, in WFS(P')). As explained in Section 4.1, to decide whether $a \in \text{WFS}(P)$, WCHECK decides whether there is a path in $\mathcal{F}^+(P')$ which starts at the root of $\mathcal{F}^+(P')$, leads to a node labeled with a, and has all "side literals" in WFS(P). To this end, it starts in a configuration chosen nondeterministically from among its initial configurations for a:

Definition 6. An *initial configuration* of WCHECK for a ground atom a is a configuration of the form $(a_0, S, S, \preceq, a)$, where a_0 is the label $R^*(c_1, \ldots, c_n)$ of the root of $\mathcal{F}^+(P')$, and $S \subseteq Lit_P(b)$ for a child b of a_0 in $\mathcal{F}^+(P')$.

In what follows, we describe a single step of WCHECK. To this end, let $(a, S, S^+, \preceq, \ell)$ be the current configuration.

Case 1: ℓ is positive. If $\ell = a$, then WCHECK accepts. Otherwise, it universally branches into the following subcomputations (and accepts iff all those subcomputations accept):

- The first subcomputation starts by "guessing" a rule $r \in ground(P')$ with $B^+(r) \cup \neg.B^-(r) \subseteq S$; if no such rule exists, it stops and rejects. It also guesses a set $S' \subseteq Lit_P(b)$, where $b := H(r)$, such that for all $\ell' \in HB_P(a) \cap HB_P(b)$ we have $\ell' \in S$ iff $\ell' \in S'$, and a linear order $\preceq'$ on $S' \setminus S$. It continues in configuration $(b, S' \cup \{b\}, S' \setminus (S \cup \{b\}), \preceq', \ell)$.
- For each $\ell' \in S^+$, there is a subcomputation that checks that ℓ' belongs to WFS(P). Its start configuration is $(a, S'', \emptyset,$

$\preceq'', \ell')$, where S'' is the union of $S \setminus S^+$ and the set of all literals $\ell'' \in S^+$ that are $\preceq$-smaller than ℓ', and $\preceq''$ is the (empty) linear order on $\emptyset$.

Case 2: ℓ is negative. Let $\ell = \neg b$. If $b = a$, then WCHECK rejects. Otherwise, it universally branches into the following subcomputations (and accepts iff all these subcomputations accept):

- For each rule $r \in$ *ground*(P') such that guard$(r) = a$, $\neg.B^+(r) \cap S = \emptyset$ and $B^-(r) \cap S = \emptyset$, there is a subcomputation that checks whether b cannot be reached from $c = H(r)$. Its start configuration is $(c, S', S' \setminus (S \cup \{c\}), \preceq', \ell)$, where S' and $\preceq'$ are chosen as in Case 1.
- For each $\ell' \in S^+$, there is a subcomputation that checks that ℓ' belongs to WFS(P). Its start configuration is $(a, S'', \emptyset, \preceq'', \ell')$, where S'' is the union of $S \setminus S^+$ and the set of all literals $\ell'' \in S^+$ that are $\preceq$-smaller than ℓ', and $\preceq''$ is the (empty) linear order on $\emptyset$.

This finishes the description of a single step of WCHECK.

4.2.3 Reducing the Number of Configurations

To complete the description of WCHECK, it remains to modify WCHECK so that it uses only a finite number of configurations. The idea is to *canonize* configurations, analogous to [2].

More precisely, construct an equivalence relation $\sim_X$, parameterized by a set $X \subseteq \Delta$, on the configurations as follows. Let $s_1 = (a_1, S_1, S_1^+, \preceq_1, \ell_1)$ and $s_2 = (a_2, S_2, S_2^+, \preceq_2, \ell_2)$ be configurations. We write $s_1 \sim_X s_2$ if there is an X-isomorphism f from $\{a_1, \ell_1\}$ to $\{a_2, \ell_2\}$ that maps s_1 to s_2. That is, f satisfies $f(a_1) = a_2$, $f(\ell_1) = \ell_2$, $f(S_1) = S_2$, $f(S_1^+) = S_2^+$, and for all literals $k_1, k_2 \in S_1^+$ we have $k_1 \preceq_1 k_2$ iff $f(k_1) \preceq_2 f(k_2)$. By arguing in a similar way as in the proof of Lemma 5, it is not hard to see that $s_1 \sim_X s_2$ implies that any accepting computation of WCHECK that starts in configuration s_1 can be translated into an accepting computation of WCHECK that starts in configuration s_2, and vice versa.

To obtain a finite set of configurations for WCHECK on input of a database D, a guarded normal Datalog$^\pm$ program Σ, and a ground atom a, we let $X := dom(a)$, and replace each configuration s by a (unique) representative of its equivalence class with respect to $\sim_X$. Let w be the maximum arity of a predicate in $\mathcal{R}$. By a simple counting argument, we can show that the number of different equivalence classes is bounded by a function that is exponential in $|\mathcal{R}|$, and doubly exponential in w. Indeed, we can map each configuration $s = (a, S, S^+, \preceq, \ell)$ to a canonical representation, by fixing a set C of $2w$ constants in advance, and letting the canonical representation of s be the configuration $can(s) = (\hat{a}, \hat{S}, \hat{S}^+, \hat{\preceq}, \hat{\ell})$, where $dom(\hat{a})$ and $dom(\hat{\ell})$ are subsets of C and $s \sim_X can(s)$.

Note that the length of $can(s)$ is polynomial in $|\mathcal{R}|$ and exponential in w, so the number of distinct configuration $can(s)$ is exponential in $|\mathcal{R}|$ and doubly exponential in w. It follows that WCHECK (i.e., after replacing each configuration s by $can(s)$) is an alternating algorithm with space bounded exponentially in $|\mathcal{R}|$ and doubly exponentially in w.

4.3 Correctness and Complexity

To conclude this section, we first show that WCHECK behaves as expected, and then use this to derive complexity bounds for deciding membership of ground atoms in well-founded models under guarded normal Datalog$^\pm$ programs.

LEMMA 7. *Given a database D for a schema $\mathcal{R}$, a guarded normal Datalog$^\pm$ program Σ over $\mathcal{R}$, and a ground atom a over $\mathcal{R}$, WCHECK accepts if and only if $a \in$ WFS(D, Σ).*

PROOF. In the following, let $P := D \cup \Sigma^f$. To simplify the notation, we will work with configurations $(b, S, S^+, \prec, \ell)$ instead of their canons $can\big((b, S, S^+, \prec, \ell)\big)$. The reader should substitute every occurrence of a configuration s by its canon $can(s)$.

"$\Longrightarrow$" Given a computation γ of WCHECK on input D, Σ and a, let $n(\gamma)$ be the length of the longest computation path in γ. We show by induction on $n(\gamma)$ that if γ is an accepting computation of WCHECK starting in configuration $s = (b, S, S^+, \preceq, \ell)$, and if $S \setminus S^+ \subseteq$ WFS(P), then:

1. ℓ is positive and $\ell \in$ WFS(P); or
2. ℓ is negative and there is no forward proof π of $\neg.\ell$ from P' whose goal node is reachable from the node labeled by b and which satisfies $N(\pi) \cap S = \emptyset$.

Note that this implies the "only if" direction of the lemma.

So, let γ be an accepting computation of WCHECK starting in configuration $(b, S, S^+, \preceq, \ell)$, and assume $S \setminus S^+ \subseteq$ WFS(P).

If $n(\gamma) = 0$ and ℓ is positive, then we must have $\ell = b$ because γ is accepting. This implies $\ell = b \in S \setminus S^+ \subseteq$ WFS(P). Now consider the case that $n(\gamma) = 0$ and $\ell = \neg c$. In this case, we must have $c \neq b$. Since $n(\gamma) = 0$, we also know that $(b, S, S^+, \preceq, \ell)$ does not have any successor configurations; hence $S^+ = \emptyset$ because literals in S^+ lead to successor configurations. Finally, there cannot be any rule $r \in$ *ground*(P') with guard$(r) = b$, $\neg.B^+(r) \cap S = \emptyset$ and $B^-(r) \cap S = \emptyset$. Together with $S = S \setminus S^+ \subseteq$ WFS(P), this implies condition 2 above.

Now let $n(\gamma) > 0$. Let us first consider the case that ℓ is positive. Since $n(\gamma) > 0$, we must have $\ell \neq b$. Suppose WCHECK selects rule r, set S', and the linear order $\preceq'$ on $S' \setminus S$. Since γ is accepting, we know that $B^+(r) \cup \neg.B^-(r) \subseteq S$. Let $S^+ = \{\ell_1 \preceq \ell_2 \preceq \cdots \preceq \ell_m\}$. Then, the successor configurations of $(b, S, S^+, \preceq, \ell)$ in γ are $s_0 := (H(r), S' \cup \{H(r)\}, S' \setminus (S \cup \{H(r)\}), \preceq', \ell)$ and the configurations $s_i := (b, S'', \emptyset, \emptyset, \ell_i)$, where $i \in \{1, \ldots, m\}$. Since γ is accepting, each of the subcomputations starting at a configuration s_i, $1 \leq i \leq m$, must be accepting. Hence, by the induction hypothesis, we know that conditions 1 and 2 above hold for each of the literals ℓ_i. Note that, since each of the ℓ_i contains at least one argument that was generated by the rule that created the atom b, condition 2 and the results in Section 3.2.2 (Lemma 4) actually imply that all negative literals among the ℓ_i belong to WFS(P). But this implies $S^+ \cup \{H(r)\} \subseteq$ WFS(P). Together with the induction hypothesis, this yields $S \cup \{H(r)\} \subseteq$ WFS(P). The fact that the subcomputation starting at configuration s_0 is accepting implies $\ell \in$ WFS(P).

Finally, let us consider the case that $\ell = \neg c$ is negative. Since γ is accepting, we have $c \neq b$. As above, we can now apply the induction hypothesis to obtain $S \subseteq$ WFS(P). Let $r_1, \ldots, r_k$ be all the rules in *ground*(P') such that guard$(r_i) = b$, $\neg.B^+(r_i) \cap S = \emptyset$ and $B^-(r_i) \cap S = \emptyset$. Applying the induction hypothesis as above to the subcomputations generated by the r_i shows that condition 2 holds for the literal ℓ.

"$\Longleftarrow$" It is easy to check that $a \in$ WFS(P) leads to an accepting computation of WCHECK on input D, Σ and a. Indeed, let $a \in$ WFS(P). Then there is a forward proof π of a from P' such that $\neg.N(\pi) \subseteq$ WFS(P). Let $a_0, a_1, \ldots, a_n$ be the labels along the path from the root of $\mathcal{F}^+(P')$ to the goal node of π. Then, we start WCHECK in the initial configuration $(a_0, S, S, \preceq, a)$, where $S =$

WFS(P) $\cap$ $Lit_P(a_1)$ and $\preceq$ corresponds to the order of deriving the literals in S.

It is now easy to construct an accepting computation by always choosing the "right" child of the current node, the "right" set S', and the "right" derivation order $\preceq'$. $\square$

As an immediate consequence of the lemma, we now obtain:

THEOREM 8. *Given a database D for a schema $\mathcal{R}$, a guarded normal Datalog$^\pm$ program Σ over $\mathcal{R}$, and a ground atom a over $\mathcal{R}$, deciding $a \in$ WFS(D, Σ) is:*

- *2-EXPTIME-complete in general.*
- *EXPTIME-complete in case the maximum arity w of a predicate in $\mathcal{R}$ is bounded.*
- *in PTIME in case both $|\mathcal{R}|$ and w are bounded; there are cases where the problem is PTIME-complete.*

PROOF. By Lemma 7, WCHECK is an alternating algorithm that correctly decides whether $a \in$ WFS(D, Σ). As pointed out in Section 4.2.3, its space is bounded by a function that is polynomial in $|\mathcal{R}|$ and exponential in w. So, if w is bounded, this function is polynomial, and if both $|\mathcal{R}|$ and w are bounded, it is logarithmic. The upper bounds of the lemma now follow from the fact that exponential (resp., polynomial or logarithmic) alternating space equals doubly exponential (resp., exponential, polynomial) time [8]. Hardness follows from the hardness results for answering Boolean conjunctive queries under guarded TGDs in [2]. $\square$

Remark 2. Any accepting computation γ of WCHECK on input of a database D, a guarded normal Datalog$^\pm$ program Σ and a ground atom a induces a subforest $\mathcal{F}$ of $\mathcal{F}^+(D \cup \Sigma^f)$ whose depth is exponential in the number $|\mathcal{R}|$ of the schema $\mathcal{R}$ and doubly exponential in the maximum arity w of predicate symbols in $\mathcal{R}$, and which may be seen as a certificate for $a \in$ WFS$(D \cup \Sigma^f)$. More precisely, let $C = (b, S, S^+, \preceq, \ell)$ be a configuration in γ, and let C' be its predecessor configuration in γ. If C' has the form $(R^*(c_1, \ldots, c_n), *, *, *, *)$, then $\mathcal{F}$ contains the root node v_C of $\mathcal{F}^+(P)$ that is labeled by b; otherwise it contains the child v_C of $v_{C'}$ that is labeled by b. Note that the depth of $\mathcal{F}$ is bounded by the number of distinct configurations of WCHECK on input D, Σ and a, and is thus exponential in $|\mathcal{R}|$ and doubly exponential in w. Now, a closer inspection shows that $\mathcal{F}$ includes a forward proof π of a from $D \cup \Sigma^f$. Even more, for every $b \in N(\pi)$ it contains a certificate of $\neg b$ being in WFS$(D \cup \Sigma^f)$, and this certificate contains, for every "relevant" forward proof π' of b, a certificate for an atom in $N(\pi')$ being in WFS$(D \cup \Sigma^f)$.

5. GENERALIZATION TO GROUND AND NON-GROUND LITERALS

We now show that the complexity bounds for deciding membership of grounds atoms in well-founded models under guarded normal Datalog$^\pm$ programs essentially carry over to (ground and non-ground) literals. This is the remaining piece to prove our main complexity bounds for NBCQs in the next section.

Recall the definition of the forest $\mathcal{F}^*(P)$ for a normal program P from Section 3.2.2.

LEMMA 9. *Let D be a database for a schema $\mathcal{R}$, Σ a guarded normal Datalog$^\pm$ program over $\mathcal{R}$, $P := D \cup \Sigma^f$, and ℓ a literal over $\mathcal{R}$. Let d be an upper bound on the depth of ℓ in $\mathcal{F}^*(P)$ if ℓ is positive, and on the depth of $\neg.\ell$ in $\mathcal{F}^+(P)$ if ℓ is negative. Moreover, suppose that d is exponential in $\mathcal{R}$ and doubly exponential in the maximum arity w of a predicate in $\mathcal{R}$. Then, deciding $\ell \in$ WFS(D, Σ) has the following complexity:*

- *2-EXPTIME in general.*
- *EXPTIME in case w is bounded.*
- *PTIME in case both $|\mathcal{R}|$ and w are bounded.*

PROOF (SKETCH). We extend the WCHECK algorithm from the previous section to ground and non-ground literals.

First of all, observe that by extending WCHECK slightly, we obtain an alternating algorithm that decides membership of ground negative literals $\neg a$ in WFS(D, Σ). We only have to add a universal branching at the beginning of the computation, with one subcomputation for each pair $S \subseteq Lit_P(b)$, $b \in D$, starting in configuration $(R^*(c_1, \ldots, c_n), S, S, \preceq, \neg a)$. The extended algorithm uses as much space as WCHECK (up to a constant factor), which proves the lemma for ground literals.

In the remainder of this proof, we will assume that ℓ is a non-ground literal.

We first deal with the case that $\ell = a$ for a (non-ground) atom a. In this case, we decide $a \in$ WFS(D, Σ) = WFS(P) as follows. In an initial stage we guess the labels $a_0, a_1, \ldots, a_n$ of nodes on a path in $\mathcal{F}^+(P)$ that starts at a root, leads to a, and has length at most d. Furthermore, as in WCHECK, for each a_i we guess a set $S_i \subseteq Lit_P(a_i)$ and ensure that a_{i+1} is derived by a rule r such that $B^+(r) \cup \neg.B^-(r) \subseteq S_i$. Note that, since $S_1 \subseteq Lit_P(a_1)$ and a_1 is ground, each of the literals in S_1 is ground. Since we know how to decide membership of ground literals in WFS(P), we can thus decide whether the literals in S_1 belong to WFS(P). Once $S_1 \subseteq$ WFS(P) has been established, we know that $a_2 \in$ WFS(P). In particular, the literals in S_2 are ground with respect to the database $D \cup \{a_1, a_2\}$. Thus, we can check whether each of the literals in S_2 is in WFS(P) = WFS$(P \cup \{a_1, a_2\})$. We continue this procedure until we have established that each of the S_i is a subset of WFS(P). If so, then $\ell = a$ belongs to WFS(P), and otherwise not. Note that the above extension of WCHECK increases the running time by a factor of at most $O(d)$.

It is not hard to see that the algorithm described above generalizes to non-ground negative literals ℓ.[6] $\square$

6. ANSWERING NBCQS

This section is devoted to a proof of our main complexity bounds for answering NBCQs in well-founded models under guarded normal Datalog$^\pm$ programs:

THEOREM 10. *Given a database D for a schema $\mathcal{R}$, a guarded normal Datalog$^\pm$ program Σ over $\mathcal{R}$, and an NBCQ Q over $\mathcal{R}$, the problem of deciding WFS$(D, \Sigma) \models Q$ is:*

1. *2-EXPTIME-complete in general.*
2. *EXPTIME-complete in case w is bounded.*
3. *in PTIME in case $|\mathcal{R}|$, the maximum arity w of a predicate symbol in $\mathcal{R}$, and the number of literals in Q are bounded; there are cases where the problem is PTIME-complete.*

PROOF (SKETCH). Let $P := D \cup \Sigma^f$, let $W :=$ WFS(P), and let n be the number of literals in Q. We describe an algorithm that decides $W \models Q$ with the desired resource bounds. The idea is to guess a mapping μ from the variables of Q to HU_P, and to verify that μ is a homomorphism from Q to W.

Of course, HU_P is infinite, so we need to restrict the range of μ to a suitable finite set. Specifically, let C be the set of all terms in

[6] $\neg.\ell$ does not need to occur in $\mathcal{F}^+(P)$, but if it does there must be a node labeled with $\neg.\ell$ in $\mathcal{F}^+(P)$ that has depth at most d.

HU_P of depth at most $d := n \cdot \delta$, where δ is as in Proposition 6, and the depth of a term is the nesting depth of function symbols in the term. Notice that an atom of depth at most d in $\mathcal{F}^+(P)$ or $\mathcal{F}^*(P)$ contains only arguments from C. We claim that instead of deciding the existence of a homomorphism as above, it suffices to decide whether there is a mapping μ from the variables of Q to C such that μ is a homomorphism from Q to W. Indeed, this follows from Proposition 6: If $W \models Q$, then Proposition 6 tells us that there is a homomorphism μ from Q to W satisfying:

1. For all $a \in Q^+$, $\mu(a)$ has depth at most $n \cdot \delta$ in $\mathcal{F}^*(P)$.
2. For all $a \in Q^-$, either $\mu(a)$ does not occur in $\mathcal{F}^+(P)$, or $\mu(a)$ has depth at most $n \cdot \delta$ in $\mathcal{F}^+(P)$.

This implies that all the elements in the range of μ can be assumed to be in C. In particular, μ is a mapping from the variables of Q to C and a homomorphism from Q to W, as desired. On the other hand, if there is a mapping μ from the variables of Q to C such that μ is a homomorphism from Q to W, then clearly $W \models Q$.

Now, all the algorithm has to do is to guess a mapping μ from the variables of Q to C, and to check that μ is a homomorphism from Q to W. By Lemma 9, we can check for each literal $\ell \in \mu(Q^+) \cup \neg.\mu(Q^-)$ whether or not ℓ belongs to WFS(P). Furthermore, the lemma tells us that it can be done with the following complexities: (1) 2-EXPTIME in general; (2) EXPTIME in case w is bounded; and (3) PTIME in case $|\mathcal{R}|$ and w are bounded. Altogether, this implies the upper bounds of the theorem.

The hardness results follow from the hardness results of Theorem 8. □

Remark 3. Theorem 10 (1) and (2)—the latter with an additional restriction of the query—also apply to the problem of answering (covered) NBCQs under the *equality-friendly well-founded semantics (EFWFS)* in [6]. However, [6] uses a different approach to obtain these results, namely by casting the problem of answering covered NBCQs under the EFWFS into a satisfiability problem for *guarded fixed-point logic (GFP)* [7]. The idea is to translate a database D and a guarded normal Datalog$^{\pm}$ program Σ into a GFP sentence $\varphi_{D,\Sigma}$ such that the models of $\varphi_{D,\Sigma}$ correspond to the equality-friendly well-founded models of D and Σ in such a way that a (covered) NBCQ Q is true under the EFWFS if and only if $\varphi_{D,\Sigma}$ implies a slightly modified version of Q. The complexity bounds then follow almost directly from the complexity bounds on satisfiability for GFP sentences.

A direct translation of the proof in [6] does not seem to work for the WFS due to fundamental differences between the WFS and the EFWFS. The most striking difference is that, under the EFWFS, existentially quantified variables of an NTGD may, intuitively, be assigned to constants that are not assigned to any variable in the body of the NTGD (by equating terms in the atom generated by the NTGD with other terms of the structure). In particular, this allows for building connections between the substructure "below" a certain atom in the guarded chase forest of the positive program associated with $D \cup \Sigma^f$ and the part outside that substructure, which cannot be done under the WFS. It appears that the only way to make the proof work for the WFS is to modify the GFP sentence so that it enforces existentially quantified variables to be assigned to "fresh" constants. But GFP is not expressive enough to accomplish that.

On the other hand, the present paper's approach for evaluating queries under the WFS does not work in the case of the EFWFS. For example, the WCHECK algorithm in Section 4 heavily relies on the locality property of the WFS described in Section 3.2.2, but the EFWFS does not have this property.

7. CONCLUSION

We have introduced the standard well-founded semantics (WFS) for normal Datalog$^{\pm}$ programs under the unique name assumption (UNA). We have shown that for guarded normal Datalog$^{\pm}$ under the standard WFS, answering normal Boolean conjunctive queries is decidable. Furthermore, we have shown that this problem is complete for PTIME in the data complexity, and that it is complete for 2-EXPTIME in the combined complexity in general and complete for EXPTIME in the combined complexity in the case where the arities of all predicates are bounded by a constant. A topic of future research is to explore how to add negative constraints and equality-generating dependencies (EGDs), similarly to [3].

Acknowledgments. This work was supported by the EPSRC under the grant EP/H051511/1 "ExODA: Integrating Description Logics and Database Technologies for Expressive Ontology-Based Data Access", by the European Research Council under the EU's 7th Framework Programme (FP7/2007-2013/ERC) grant 246858 – DIADEM, and by a Yahoo! Research Fellowship. Georg Gottlob is a James Martin Senior Fellow, and also gratefully acknowledges a Royal Society Wolfson Research Merit Award. The work was carried out in the context of the James Martin Institute for the Future of Computing. André Hernich was supported by a fellowship within the Postdoc-Programme of the German Academic Exchange Service (DAAD).

8. REFERENCES

[1] C. Baral and V. S. Subrahmanian. Dualities between alternative semantics for logic programming and nonmonotonic reasoning. *J. Autom. Reasoning*, 10(3):399–420, 1993.

[2] A. Calì, G. Gottlob, and M. Kifer. Taming the infinite chase: Query answering under expressive relational constraints. In *Proc. KR-2008*, pp. 70–80, 2008. Revised version: http://dbai.tuwien.ac.at/staff/gottlob/CGK.pdf.

[3] A. Calì, G. Gottlob, and T. Lukasiewicz. A general Datalog-based framework for tractable query answering over ontologies. *J. Web Sem.*, 14:57–83, 2012.

[4] A. Calì, G. Gottlob, T. Lukasiewicz, B. Marnette, and A. Pieris: Datalog+/–: A family of logical knowledge representation and query languages for new applications. In *Proc. LICS-2010*, pp. 228–242, 2010.

[5] D. Calvanese, G. De Giacomo, D. Lembo, M. Lenzerini, and R. Rosati. Tractable reasoning and efficient query answering in description logics: The *DL-Lite* family. *J. Autom. Reasoning*, 39(3):385–429, 2007.

[6] G. Gottlob, A. Hernich, C. Kupke, and T. Lukasiewicz. Equality-friendly well-founded semantics and applications to description logics. In *Proc. AAAI-2012*, pp. 757–764, 2012.

[7] E. Grädel and I. Walukiewicz. Guarded fixed point logic. In *Proc. LICS-1999*, pp. 45–54, 1999.

[8] C. H. Papadimitriou. *Computational Complexity*. Addison-Wesley, 1994.

[9] A. Poggi, D. Lembo, D. Calvanese, G. De Giacomo, M. Lenzerini, and R. Rosati. Linking data to ontologies. *J. Data Semantics*, 10:133–173, 2008.

[10] J. S. Schlipf. The expressive powers of the logic programming semantics. *J. Comput. Syst. Sci.*, 51(1):64–86, 1995.

[11] A. van Gelder, K. A. Ross, and J. S. Schlipf. The well-founded semantics for general logic programs. *J. ACM*, 38(3):620–650, 1991.

Semantic Acyclicity on Graph Databases

Pablo Barceló
Department of Computer Science, Universidad de Chile
pbarcelo@dcc.uchile.cl

Miguel Romero
Department of Computer Science, Universidad de Chile
miromero@ing.uchile.cl

Moshe Y. Vardi
Department of Computer Science, Rice University
vardi@cs.rice.edu

ABSTRACT

It is known that unions of acyclic conjunctive queries (CQs) can be evaluated in linear time, as opposed to arbitrary CQs, for which the evaluation problem is NP-complete. It follows from techniques in the area of constraint-satisfaction problems that *semantically acyclic* unions of CQs – i.e., unions of CQs that are equivalent to a union of acyclic ones – can be evaluated in polynomial time, though testing membership in the class of semantically acyclic CQs is NP-complete.

We study here the fundamental notion of semantic acyclicity in the context of graph databases and unions of conjunctive regular path queries with inverse (UC2RPQs). It is known that unions of acyclic C2RPQs can be evaluated efficiently, but it is by no means obvious whether the same holds for the class of UC2RPQs that are semantically acyclic. We prove that checking whether a UC2RPQ is semantically acyclic is decidable in 2EXPSPACE, and that it is EXPSPACE-hard even in the absence of inverses. Furthermore, we show that evaluation of semantically acyclic UC2RPQs is fixed-parameter tractable. In addition, our tools yield a strong theory of approximations for UC2RPQs when no equivalent acyclic UC2RPQ exists.

Categories and Subject Descriptors

H.2.3 [**Database Management**]: Languages—*Query Languages*

Keywords

Graph databases, conjunctive regular path queries, acyclicity, query evaluation, query approximation.

1. INTRODUCTION

Conjunctive queries (CQs) are the most fundamental class of database queries and also the most intensively studied in the database theory community. The evaluation problem for CQs is as follows: Given a CQ Q, a database $\mathcal{D}$, and a tuple $\bar{a}$ of elements in $\mathcal{D}$, does $\bar{a}$ belong to the result $Q(\mathcal{D})$ of applying Q to $\mathcal{D}$? Notice that the cost of evaluation is thus measured in terms of the size $|\mathcal{D}|$ of the database $\mathcal{D}$ and $|Q|$ of the query Q, which in database terminology corresponds to the *combined complexity* of the problem.

The evaluation problem for CQs is NP-complete [8]; this motivated a flurry of activity for finding tractable cases of the problem. One of the oldest and most important such restrictions is *acyclicity*. Yannakakis proved that acyclic CQs can in fact be evaluated in linear time in both data and query size – $O(|\mathcal{D}| \cdot |Q|)$ [31]. This good behavior extends to unions of CQs (UCQs) each one of which is acyclic (the so-called acyclic UCQs).

Acyclicity is a syntactic property of queries that is by now well-understood [19]. On the other hand, the *space* of UCQs that is defined by the notion of *semantic acyclicity*–that is, the UCQs that are *equivalent* to an acyclic one – has not received much attention. We call this the space of *semantically acyclic* UCQs. Two questions naturally arise in this context: (1) Is the evaluation problem for semantically acyclic UCQs still tractable? (2) What is the cost of verifying whether a UCQ is semantically acyclic?

The answers to these questions follow easily from known techniques in the area of *constraint satisfaction problems* (CSP), as CQ evaluation and CSP are known to have a common root – they are both equivalent to the *homomorphism problem* [24]. CSP techniques establish the following: (1) Semantically acyclic UCQs can be evaluated in polynomial time. (2) Verifying whether a UCQ is semantically acyclic is NP-complete [9, 12].

In this paper we extend the concept of semantic acyclicity from the classical setting of relational databases to the newer setting of graph databases [2], which has been the focus of much research in the last few years [3, 14, 15, 4, 17]. In fact, acyclicity has been identified as a fundamental tool for obtaining tractable – and even linear time – query evaluation in such context [23, 3, 4, 26]. It is thus of theoretical importance to understand what is the space of queries defined by the notion of acyclicity over graph databases.

Graph databases are typically modeled as edge-labeled directed graphs. In this context, query languages are *navigational*, in the sense that they allow to recursively traverse the edges of the graph while checking for some regular condition [11, 1, 7]. Navigation is often performed by traversing edges in both directions, which allows to express important properties about the inverse of the relations defined by the labels of those edges [6, 7]. When this is combined with the expressive power of CQs, it yields a powerful class of queries – the so-called *conjunctive regular path queries with inverse,*

PODS'13, June 22–27, 2013, New York, New York, USA.

or C2RPQs – that lies at the core of many query languages for graph databases (see, e.g., [11, 10, 6, 3]).

Evaluation of unions of C2RPQs (UC2RPQs) is not more expensive than evaluation of CQs, i.e. NP-complete. Recent works have studied the class of acyclic UC2RPQs – where acyclicity is defined in terms of the underlying CQ of each element of the union – and proved that queries in this class preserve the good properties of acyclic UCQs for evaluation, i.e. they can be evaluated in polynomial time, and even linearly for suitable restrictions [3, 4].

In this work we study the notion of *semantic acyclicity* for UC2RPQs, that is, we study the class of UC2RPQs that are equivalent to an acylic one, and try to answer the same questions that we posed before for the class of semantically acyclic UCQs: (1) What is the cost of evaluating queries in this class? (2) How hard is to recognize if a UC2RPQ Q is semantically acyclic, and, if so, what is the cost of computing an equivalent acyclic UC2RPQ for Q?

The first question is important since we want to understand whether semantic acyclicity leads to larger classes of UC2RPQs with good evaluation properties. The second question is relevant for static optimization of UC2RPQs, as a positive answer would allow us to construct an equivalent query in a well-behaved fragment for each semantically acyclic UC2RPQ. We present answers to both questions in the paper, in a way that our answer to the first question crucially depends on our answer to the second one.

As noted above, the evaluation problem for semantically acyclic UCQs is tractable, and this is proved by applying known techniques from CSP. Those techniques are specifically tailored for checking the existence of a homomorphism from a relational structure into another one, which fits well the semantics of CQs. On the other hand, the semantics of C2RPQs is based on a richer notion of homomorphism, which maps the atoms of a query into pairs of nodes in a graph database linked by a path satisfying some regular condition. Such notion of homomorphism does not fit well in the current landscape of CSP techniques, which means that CSP theory does not yield answers to our questions about semantically acyclic UC2RPQs.

To attack our questions about evaluation of semantically acyclic UC2RPQs, we consider first the problem of UC2RPQ *approximations*, which is motivated by recent work on approximations of UCQs [5]. In general, the evaluation of a CQ Q on a database $\mathcal{D}$ is of the order $|\mathcal{D}|^{O(|Q|)}$, which might be prohibitively expensive for a large dataset $\mathcal{D}$ even if Q is small. This led the idea of finding *approximations* of (U)CQs in tractable classes [5], in particular, in the class of acyclic (U)CQs. Intuitively, an acyclic UCQ Q' is an approximation of a UCQ Q if Q' is contained in Q and it is "as close as possible" to Q in the class of acyclic UCQs. The latter means that Q' is a maximal acyclic UCQ that is contained in Q. It follows from techniques in [5] that UCQs have good properties in terms of acyclic approximations: Each UCQ Q has a unique acyclic approximation (up to equivalence) and this approximation can be computed in single-exponential time. These good properties imply that computing and running the acyclic approximation of a UCQ Q on a database $\mathcal{D}$ takes time $O(|\mathcal{D}| \cdot 2^{p(|Q|)})$, for some polynomial $p : \mathbb{N} \to \mathbb{N}$. This is much faster than $|\mathcal{D}|^{O(|Q|)}$ on large databases. Thus, if the quality of the approximation is good, we may prefer to run this faster query instead of Q.

We show here that the good properties of UCQs in terms of acyclic approximations extend to UC2RPQs. In particular, we show that each UC2RPQ Q has a unique acyclic approximation (up to equivalence) and that an approximation of exponential size can be computed in EXPSPACE. The data complexity of evaluating this approximation is then quadratic in the size of the data, such like the data complexity of 2RPQs. This shows that acyclic approximations might be useful when evaluating the original query is infeasible, though the cost of computing the approximation is quite high. We also show that UC2RPQs behave provably worse than UCQs in terms of approximations: Verifying whether an acyclic UCQ Q' is the approximation of the UCQ Q is in the second-level of the polynomial hierarchy, but it becomes EXPSPACE-complete if Q and Q' are UC2RPQs. This is not surprising, as it is known that testing containment of UC2RPQs is EXPSPACE-complete [6].

Finally, we apply the machinery of acyclic approximation of UC2RPQs to address semantic acyclicity of this class of queries. As noted above, we can construct in EXPSPACE an exponential-sized acyclic approximation Q' of a given UC2RPQ Q. By construction, Q' is contained in Q. To check whether Q is semantically acyclic we just have to check if Q is contained in Q'. Because Q' is exponentially large, we get a 2EXPSPACE upper bound for the complexity of the last step. We also prove an EXPSPACE lower bound for the problem of checking semantic acyclicity. The precise complexity remains an open question.

Thus, we get answers to the two questions we posed above: (1) Query evaluation for semantically acyclic UC2RPQ is *fixed-parameter tractable.*[1] (2) Testing semantic acyclicity for UC2RPQs is in 2EXPSPACE and EXPSPACE-hard. The question whether semantically acyclic UC2RPQs can be evaluated in polynomial time is left as an open problem.

Organization The rest of the paper is organized as follows. In Section 2, we study semantic acyclicity for UCQs and show that the answer to the most basic questions follow from known CSP techniques. In Section 3, we introduce graph databases and UC2RPQs. In Section 4, we study acyclic approximations of UC2RPQs and show some of their good properties. Finally, in Section 5, we study semantic acyclicity of UC2RPQs. We provide upper and lower bounds for the problem of verfiying whether a UC2RPQ is semantically acyclic and show that this implies that evaluation of semantically acyclic UC2RPQs is fixed-parameter tractable. Finally, in Section 6 we provide concluding remarks and a list of open problems.

2. INTERLUDE ON UNIONS OF CONJUNCTIVE QUERIES

We start by considering semantic acyclicity in the context of traditional relational databases and unions of conjunctive queries. Although the results in this section follow from known techniques, we state them for the sake of completeness and because they will help us developing the necesssary intuitions for the more complicated case of graph databases and unions of conjunctive regular path queries.

[1]Recall that the evaluation problem for a class $\mathcal{C}$ of queries is fixed-parameter tractable if there exists a computable function $f : \mathbb{N} \to \mathbb{N}$ and a constant $k \geq 1$ such that evaluating a query $Q \in \mathcal{C}$ over a database $\mathcal{D}$ can be done in time $O(|\mathcal{D}|^k \cdot f(|Q|))$.

2.1 Basic concepts

We first provide the necessary terminology. A *schema* is a set σ of relation names $R_1, \ldots, R_\ell$, each relation R_i having an arity $n_i > 0$. A *database* of schema σ is a function $\mathcal{D}$ that maps each relation symbol R_i in σ into a finite n_i-ary relation $R_i^{\mathcal{D}}$ over a countably infinite domain dom (i.e. $R_i^{\mathcal{D}} \subseteq \mathsf{dom}^{n_i}$).

A conjunctive query (CQ) over σ is a logical formula in the $\exists, \wedge$-fragment of first-order logic, i.e., a formula of the form

$$Q(\bar{x}) \;=\; \exists \bar{y} \bigwedge_{j=1}^{m} R_{i_j}(\bar{x}_{i_j}),$$

where each R_{i_j} is a symbol from σ, and $\bar{x}_{i_j}$ is a tuple of variables among $\bar{x}, \bar{y}$ whose length is the arity of R_{i_j}. Each $R_{i_j}(\bar{x}_{i_j})$ is an *atom* of $Q(\bar{x})$.

A *union* of conjunctive queries (UCQ) is a formula of the form $Q(\bar{x}) = \bigvee_{1 \le i \le m} Q_i(\bar{x})$, where $Q_i(\bar{x})$ is a CQ for each $1 \le i \le m$. We assume familiarity with the semantics (evaluation) of (U)CQs. The set of tuples that belong to the evaluation of a UCQ Q over database $\mathcal{D}$ is denoted by $Q(\mathcal{D})$. If Q is a Boolean query (i.e. $\bar{x}$ is the empty tuple), the answer `true` is, as usual, modeled by the set containing the empty tuple, and the answer `false` by the empty set.

The evaluation problem for UCQs is as follows: Given a database $\mathcal{D}$, a UCQ $Q(\bar{x})$ and a tuple $\bar{a}$ in $\mathcal{D}$, is $\bar{a} \in Q(\mathcal{D})$? It is well-known that the evaluation of CQs is NP-complete [8]. On the other hand, tractability of (U)CQ evaluation can be obtained by restricting the syntactic shape of CQs. The oldest and most common of such restrictions is *α-acyclicity* (or, simply, acyclicity) [13], that can be defined in terms of the existence of a well-behaved *tree decomposition* of the *hypergraph* of a CQ [20]. We review such notions below.

Recall that a hypergraph is a tuple $\mathcal{H} = (V, E)$, where V is its finite set of vertices and $E \subseteq 2^V$ is its set of *hyperedges.* With each CQ we associate its hypergraph $\mathcal{H}(Q) = (V, E)$ such that V is the set of variables of Q and E consists of all sets of variables that appear in the same atom of Q. Consider for instance the CQ

$$Q(x) = \exists y \exists z \exists u \exists v \left(R(x,y,z) \wedge T(y,u,u) \wedge S(y,v)\right).$$

Then $\mathcal{H}(Q) = (V, E)$, where $V \doteq \{x, y, z, u, v\}$ and E consists of the hyperedges $\{x, y, z\}$, $\{y, u\}$ and $\{y, v\}$.

A tree decomposition of a hypergraph $\mathcal{H} = (V, E)$ is a pair (T, λ), where T is a tree and $\lambda : T \to 2^V$, that satisfies the following:

- For each $v \in V$ the set $\{t \in T \mid v \in \lambda(t)\}$ is a connected subset of T.

- Each hyperedge in E is contained in one of the sets $\lambda(t)$, for $t \in T$.

Then $\mathcal{H}$ is *acyclic* if there is a tree decomposition (T, λ) of it such that $\lambda(t)$ is a hyperedge in E, for each $t \in T$.

A CQ Q is acyclic if its hypergraph $\mathcal{H}(Q)$ is acyclic. A UCQ $\bigvee_{1 \le i \le m} Q_i(\bar{x})$ is acyclic if each $Q_i(\bar{x})$ is acyclic ($1 \le i \le m$). For instance, the CQ $Q(x) = \exists y \exists z \exists u \exists v\, R(x,y,z) \wedge T(y,u,u) \wedge S(y,v)$ presented above is acyclic, as witnessed by the following tree decomposition (T, λ) of $\mathcal{H}(Q)$: T consists of vertices $\{1,2,3\}$ and edges $\{(1,2),(1,3)\}$, and $\lambda(1) = \{x,y,z\}$, $\lambda(2) = \{y,u\}$ and $\lambda(3) = \{y,v\}$.

It follows from the seminal work of Yannakakis that the evaluation problem for acyclic UCQs can be solved in linear time $O(|\mathcal{D}| \cdot |Q|)$ [31].

2.2 Semantically acyclic UCQs

Acyclicity is a syntactic property of UCQs. On the other hand, a non-acyclic UCQ can still be equivalent to an acyclic one. Formally, a UCQ $Q(\bar{x})$ is *semantically acyclic* if there exists an acyclic UCQ $Q'(\bar{x})$ such that $Q(\mathcal{D}) = Q'(\mathcal{D})$ for each database $\mathcal{D}$. Recall that we are interested in two questions regarding semantic acyclicity: (1) Is the evaluation problem for semantically acyclic UCQs tractable? (2) What is the cost of verifying whether semantic acyclicity for UCQs?

As first pointed out in [24], there is a close connection between conjunctive query evaluation and constraint satisfaction: Both can be recasted as the problem of determining whether there is a homomorphism from one relational structure into another one. This tight connection allows us to export tools from CSP [24, 9] and prove that semantically acyclic UCQs can be evaluated in polynomial time.

THEOREM 1. *The evaluation problem for semantically acyclic UCQs can be solved in polynomial time.*

The CSP techniques that imply Theorem 1 first establish a sophisticated equivalence between the problems of query evaluation for semantically acyclic CQs and the existence of winning strategies for the duplicator in some refined version of the existential pebble game, and then prove that the required condition on games can be checked efficiently.

Notice that the class of acyclic UCQs is remarkably well-behaved for evaluation: Queries in the class are not only tractable, but also verifying whether a given UCQ belongs to the class can be done in polynomial (in fact, linear) time [30]. On the other hand, using techniques similar to those in [12], one can prove that this good behavior does not extend to the class of semantically acyclic UCQs, as the problem of verifying whether a query is semantically acyclic is computationally hard:

PROPOSITION 1. *The problem of verifying whether a UCQ $Q(\bar{x})$ is semantically acyclic is* NP*-complete. It remains* NP*-hard even if the input is restricted to Boolean CQs whose schema consists of a single binary relation (i.e. the schema of directed graphs).*

3. GRAPH DATABASES & CONJUNCTIVE REGULAR PATH QUERIES

Graph databases and C2RPQs A *graph database* [2, 7, 11] is just a finite edge-labeled graph. Let Σ be a finite alphabet, and $\mathcal{N}$ a countably infinite set of node ids. Then a graph database over Σ is a pair $\mathcal{G} = (N, E)$, where N is the set of nodes (a finite subset of $\mathcal{N}$), and E is the set of edges, i.e., $E \subseteq N \times \Sigma \times N$. That is, we view each edge as a triple (n, a, n'), whose interpretation, of course, is an a-labeled edge from n to n'. When Σ is clear from the context, we shall simply speak of a graph database.

As mentioned before, in this work we consider navigational queries that traverse edges in both directions. This defines the notion of *regular path queries with inverse* (2RPQs) [6, 7]: A 2RPQ over finite alphabet Σ is an expression R defined by the grammar:

$$R \;:=\; \varepsilon \mid a\,(a \in \Sigma) \mid a^-\;(a \in \Sigma) \mid R + R \mid R \cdot R \mid R^*$$

That is, a 2RPQ is nothing else than a regular expression over the alphabet that extends Σ with the symbol a^- for each $a \in \Sigma$. Intuitively, a^- represents the inverse of a.

The evaluation of a 2RPQ R over a graph database $\mathcal{G} = (N, E)$ is a binary relation $[\![R]\!]_\mathcal{G}$ defined as follows, where a is a symbol in Σ and R, R_1 and R_2 are arbitrary 2RPQs over Σ:

$$\begin{aligned}
[\![\varepsilon]\!]_\mathcal{G} &= \{(u,u) \mid u \in N\} \\
[\![a]\!]_\mathcal{G} &= \{(u,v) \mid (u,a,v) \in E\} \\
[\![a^-]\!]_\mathcal{G} &= \{(v,u) \mid (u,a,v) \in E\} \\
[\![R_1 + R_2]\!]_\mathcal{G} &= [\![R_1]\!]_\mathcal{G} \cup [\![R_2]\!]_\mathcal{G} \\
[\![R_1 \cdot R_2]\!]_\mathcal{G} &= [\![R_1]\!]_\mathcal{G} \circ [\![R_2]\!]_\mathcal{G} \\
[\![R^*]\!]_\mathcal{G} &= [\![\varepsilon]\!]_\mathcal{G} \cup [\![R]\!]_\mathcal{G} \cup [\![R \cdot R]\!]_\mathcal{G} \cup \cdots
\end{aligned}$$

Here, the symbol $\circ$ denotes the usual composition of binary relations, that is, $[\![R_1]\!]_\mathcal{G} \circ [\![R_2]\!]_\mathcal{G} = \{(u,v) \mid$ there exists w s.t. $(u,w) \in [\![R_1]\!]_\mathcal{G}$ and $(w,v) \in [\![R_2]\!]_\mathcal{G}\}$. As expected, the expression a^- ($a \in \Sigma$) defines the inverse of the expression a on each graph database. Intuitively, each matching of a^- in $\mathcal{G}$ represents a backward traversal of an a-labeled edge.

When the expressive power of 2RPQs is combined with the ability of CQs to express arbitrary joins and existential quantification, it yields a powerful class of queries – namely, the *conjunctive regular path queries with inverses*, or C2RPQs – that we define next.

Formally, a C2RPQ over a finite alphabet Σ is an expression of the form:

$$Q(\bar{x}) = \exists \bar{y} \bigwedge_{1 \le i \le m} (u_i, R_i, v_i), \qquad (1)$$

such that each u_i and v_i is a variable among $\bar{x}, \bar{y}$ and each R_i is a 2RPQ over Σ, for $1 \le i \le m$. A CRPQ is a C2RPQ without inverses, i.e. a C2RPQ of the form (1) in which no 2RPQ R_i ($1 \le i \le m$) mentions the inverse a^- of a symbol $a \in \Sigma$. As usual, we assume that $\bar{x}$ are the *free* variables of Q, i.e. the variables mentioned in Q that are not existentially quantified.

Intuitively, a C2RPQ $Q(\bar{x})$ of the form (1) selects tuples $\bar{x}$ for which there exist values of the remaining node variables from $\bar{y}$ such that each pair (u_i, v_i) belongs to the evaluation of the 2RPQ R_i. We formally define the semantics of C2RPQs by using a notion of homomorphism that maps atoms of Q into pairs that satisfy the corresponding 2RPQs.

Given $Q(\bar{x})$ of the form (1) and a graph database $\mathcal{G} = (N, E)$, a homomorphism from $Q(\bar{x})$ to $\mathcal{G}$ is a map $h : \bigcup_{1 \le i \le m}\{u_i, v_i\} \to N$ such that $(h(u_i), h(v_i)) \in [\![R_i]\!]_\mathcal{G}$ for every $1 \le i \le m$. Then $Q(\mathcal{G})$ is the set of all tuples $h(\bar{x})$ such that h is a homomorphism from $Q(\bar{x})$ to $\mathcal{G}$.

EXAMPLE 1. Consider a graph database $\mathcal{G} = (N, E)$ of researchers, papers, conferences and journals over the alphabet $\Sigma = \{\texttt{creator}, \texttt{inJournal}, \texttt{inConf}\}$. The set of edges E consists of the following:

- All tuples $(r, \texttt{creator}, p)$ such that r is a researcher that coauthors paper p.
- Each tuple $(p, \texttt{inJournal}, j)$ such that paper p appeared in journal j.
- All tuples $(p, \texttt{inConf}, c)$ such that paper p was published in conference c.

Consider the C2RPQ $Q(x,y)$ defined as

$$\exists z \exists w \big((x, \texttt{creator}, z) \wedge (z, \texttt{inConf}, w) \wedge (z, \texttt{creator}^-, y)\big).$$

Its evaluation over $\mathcal{G}$ consists of the set of pairs (r, r') such that researchers r and r' have a joint conference paper. The evaluation over $\mathcal{G}$ of the C2RPQ $Q'(x,y)$ defined as

$$\exists z \exists w \big((x, (\texttt{creator} \cdot \texttt{creator}^-)^*, y) \wedge (y, \texttt{creator}, z) \wedge (z, \texttt{inJournal}, w)\big)$$

consists of the set of pairs (r, r') of researchers that are linked by a coauthorhsip sequence and such that r' has at least one journal paper. □

A union of C2RPQs (UC2RPQ) is a formula of the form $\bigvee_{1 \le i \le m} Q_i(\bar{x})$, where each $Q_i(\bar{x})$ is a C2RPQ ($1 \le i \le m$). We define $Q(\mathcal{G})$ as $\bigcup_{1 \le i \le m} Q_i(\mathcal{G})$, for a graph database $\mathcal{G}$. If Q and Q' are UC2RPQs, then Q is *contained* in Q', denoted $Q \subseteq Q'$, if $Q(\mathcal{G}) \subseteq Q'(\mathcal{G})$ for each graph database $\mathcal{G}$. In addition, Q and Q' are equivalent, denoted $Q \equiv Q'$, if $Q \subseteq Q'$ and $Q' \subseteq Q$, or, equivalently, $Q(\mathcal{G}) = Q'(\mathcal{G})$ for each graph database $\mathcal{G}$.

The evaluation problem for UC2RPQs is defined in the same way as UCQs. That is, given a UC2RPQ $Q(\bar{x})$, a graph database $\mathcal{G}$, and a tuple $\bar{a}$ of node ids in $\mathcal{G}$ such that $|\bar{a}| = |\bar{x}|$, does $\bar{a}$ belong to $Q(\mathcal{G})$? It is known that evaluating UC2RPQs is not more expensive than evaluating CQs, i.e. NP-complete [3].

Acyclic C2RPQs Acyclicity of C2RPQs has been studied in several recent papers that define it in terms of the acyclicity of its *underlying conjunctive query* [3, 4]. Let $Q(\bar{x}) = \exists \bar{y} \bigwedge_{1 \le i \le m} (u_i, R_i, v_i)$ be a C2RPQ. Its underlying CQ is the query over the schema of binary relation symbols $T_1, \ldots, T_m$ defined as: $\exists \bar{y} \bigwedge_{1 \le i \le m} T_i(u_i, v_i)$. Intuitively, this underlying conjunctive query represents the structure of Q when the regular languages that label the atoms of Q are turned into relation symbols.

A C2RPQ is *acyclic* if its underlying CQ is acyclic. A UC2RPQ is acyclic if each one of its C2RPQs is acyclic. By combining techniques for UC2RPQ evaluation and polynomial time evaluation of acyclic CQs, it is possible to prove that the evaluation problem for acyclic UC2RPQs can be solved in polynomial time [31, 3].

THEOREM 2. *The problem of checking whether $\bar{a} \in Q(\mathcal{G})$, for a given graph database $\mathcal{G}$, acyclic UC2RPQ Q, and a tuple $\bar{a}$ of node ids in $\mathcal{G}$, can be solved in time $O(|\mathcal{G}|^2 \cdot |Q|^2)$.*

Recall that a CQ Q is acyclic if its hypergraph $\mathcal{H}(Q)$ admits a tree decomposition (T, λ) such that each set of the form $\lambda(t)$, for $t \in T$, is a hyperdge of $\mathcal{H}(Q)$. The fact that acyclicity of C2RPQs is defined in terms of the acyclicity of its underlying CQ – and the latter is specified in a schema of binary arity – allows us to provide a simple characterization of the class of acyclic C2RPQs that will be useful in our proofs. We explain this below.

The *simple undirected underlying graph* of a C2RPQ $Q(\bar{x})$ of the form $\exists \bar{y} \bigwedge_{1 \le i \le m} (u_i, R_i, v_i)$, which is denoted by $\mathcal{U}(Q)$, is the graph whose vertices are the variables of Q and its set of edges is $\{\{u_i, v_i\} \mid 1 \le i \le m \text{ and } u_i \neq v_i\}$. Notice that $\mathcal{U}(Q)$ is indeed simple (it contains neither loops nor multiedges) and undirected. Then:

PROPOSITION 2. *A C2RPQ Q is acyclic if and only if $\mathcal{U}(Q)$ is acyclic.*

EXAMPLE 2. Both C2RPQs $Q(x, y)$ and $Q'(x, y)$ in Example 1 are acyclic. Recall that $Q(x, y)$ is defined as

$$\exists z \exists w \big((x, \texttt{creator}, z) \wedge (z, \texttt{inConf}, w) \wedge (z, \texttt{creator}^-, y)\big),$$

and $Q'(x, y)$ is defined as

$$\exists z \exists w \big((x, (\texttt{creator} \cdot \texttt{creator}^-)^*, y) \wedge (y, \texttt{creator}, z) \wedge (z, \texttt{inJournal}, w)\big). \quad \square$$

Notice that this definition of acyclicity allows for the existence of loops and multiedges in the structure of a C2RPQ, i.e. in its underlying CQ, as shown in the following example.

EXAMPLE 3. Let L_1, L_2 and L_3 be arbitrary regular expressions over Σ. The CRPQs $Q = \exists x\,(x, L_1, x)$ and $Q' = \exists x \exists y\,\big((x, L_1, y) \wedge (y, L_2, x)\big)$ are acyclic. Notice that the underlying CQ of Q contains a loop, while the underlying CQ of Q' contains edges from x to y and from y to x. The CRPQ $Q'' = \exists x \exists y \exists z\,\big((x, L_1, y) \wedge (y, L_2, z) \wedge (z, L_3, x)\big)$ is not acyclic. $\square$

Our goal is to study the notion of semantic acyclicity for UC2RPQs. To attack the problem of evaluation for UC2RPQs that are semantically acyclic we make a necessary detour in the next section to study the problem of UC2RPQ approximation.

4. APPROXIMATIONS OF UC2RPQS

Acyclic UC2RPQs form a good class in terms of complexity of evaluation: They are tractable as opposed to arbitrary C2RPQs (and even CQs) for which the evaluation problem is NP-complete and even hard in parameterized complexity [28]. This motivates our study of approximations of UC2RPQs in the class of acyclic UC2RPQs, which is inspired by recent research on approximations of UCQs. We explain this below.

Evaluating an arbitrary CQ on a big database might be prohibitively expensive. This has led to the recent study of (U)CQ *approximations* in tractable classes [5], in particular, in the class of acyclic (U)CQs. Intuitively, an acyclic UCQ T is an approximation of a UCQ Q if the following holds: (1) T is contained in Q (i.e. T returns no false positives with respect to Q) and (2) T is "as close as possible" to Q among all acyclic UCQs.

It follows from results and techniques in [5] that approximations of UCQs have good properties.

1. First of all, they always exist, that is, each UCQ has at least one acyclic approximation, and, in addition, such approximation is unique (up to equivalence) and of at most exponential size.
2. Second, for each UCQ Q, its acyclic approximation T can be computed in single-exponential time.
3. Third, verifying whether an acyclic UCQ T is an approximation of a UCQ Q is decidable in the second-level of the polynomial hierarchy.

These good properties imply that computing and running the acyclic approximation of a UCQ Q on a database $\mathcal{D}$ takes time $O(2^{p(|Q|)} + |\mathcal{D}| \cdot 2^{r(|Q|)})$, for polynomials $p, r : \mathbb{N} \to \mathbb{N}$, which is $O(|\mathcal{D}| \cdot 2^{s(|Q|)})$, for a polynomial $s : \mathbb{N} \to \mathbb{N}$. This is much faster than $|\mathcal{D}|^{O(|Q|)}$ on large databases. Thus, if the quality of the approximation is good, we may prefer to run this faster query instead of Q.

Here we study acyclic approximations for UC2RPQs, and show that several of the good properties mentioned above for acyclic approximations of UCQs extend to UC2RPQs.

4.1 Approximations: Existence and computation

Suppose we want to approximate a UC2RPQ Q in the class AC of acyclic UC2RPQs. As explained earlier, we are interested in approximations that are guaranteed to return correct results only. Thus, we are looking for an acyclic UC2RPQ that is *maximally contained* in Q:

DEFINITION 1. **(Approximations)** *Let Q and Q' be UC2RPQs such that $Q' \in \mathsf{AC}$ and $Q' \subseteq Q$. Then Q' is an* approximation *of Q if there is no query $Q'' \in \mathsf{AC}$ with $Q'' \subseteq Q$ such that $Q' \subsetneq Q''$.*

It is worth noticing that the definition of approximations in [5] is different, but equivalent to this one.

An important property of UCQs is that each query in the class has an acyclic approximation, and that such approximation is unique. We can prove that this is also true for the class of UC2RPQs.

THEOREM 3. *Each UC2RPQ has a unique acyclic approximation (up to equivalence).*

As a corollary to the proof of Theorem 3 we get the following important result about the computation and size of approximations.

COROLLARY 1. *There exists an* EXPSPACE *algorithm that takes as input a UC2RPQ Q and computes the approximation Q' of Q. This approximation is of at most exponential size.*

Corollary 1 implies that approximations of UC2RPQs are meaningful. In fact, computing and running the acyclic approximation of a UC2RPQ Q on a graph database $\mathcal{G}$ takes time

$$O\Big(2^{2^{p(|Q|)}} + |\mathcal{G}|^2 \cdot 2^{r(|Q|)}\Big),$$

for polynomials $p, r : \mathbb{N} \to \mathbb{N}$, which is

$$O\Big(|\mathcal{G}|^2 \cdot 2^{2^{p(|Q|)}}\Big).$$

In terms of data complexity this is only $O(|\mathcal{G}|^2)$, such like the data complexity of 2RPQs. This is much faster than $|\mathcal{G}|^{O(|Q|)}$ – the order of the evaluation problem for Q on $\mathcal{G}$ – on large datasets.

We finish by proving that there is an important aspect of approximations that is harder for UC2RPQs than for UCQs: the identification problem, i.e. verifying if a query is an approximation of another. We mentioned above that checking whether an acyclic UCQ T is an approximation of a UCQ Q can be solved in the second-level of the polynomial hierarchy [5]; more precisely, it is complete for the class DP, that consists of all those languages that are the intersection of an NP and a CONP problem [27]. This problem is considerably harder for UC2RPQs:

PROPOSITION 3. *Let Q and T be UC2RPQs such that $T \in \mathsf{AC}$. The problem of verifying whether T is an acyclic approximation of Q is* EXPSPACE*-complete.*

We prove Theorem 3, Corollary 1 and Proposition 3 in the following section.

4.2 Proofs of results

All results in Section 4.1 follow from an important lemma that states that there exists an EXPSPACE algorithm that, on input a UC2RPQ Q, computes an acyclic UC2RPQ T_Q – of at most exponential size – that is a maximum of the class of acyclic UC2RPQs that are contained in Q. This lemma will also be crucial for proving decidability of the notion of semantic acyclicity for UC2RPQs in Section 5:

LEMMA 1. *There exists an* EXPSPACE *algorithm that given a UC2RPQ Q computes an acyclic UC2RPQ T_Q such that:*

1. *$T_Q \subseteq Q$.*
2. *For every acyclic UC2RPQ T such that $T \subseteq Q$ it is the case that $T \subseteq T_Q$.*
3. *The size of T_Q is at most exponential in $|Q|$.*

Before proving Lemma 1 we show how the results in Section 4.1 easily follow from it.

Proofs of Theorem 3, Corollary 1 and Proposition 3: The algorithm in Lemma 1 computes for each UC2RPQ Q a query T_Q that is the maximum of the class of acyclic UC2RPQs that are contained in Q. We conclude that T_Q is an approximation of Q. This approximation must be unique (up to equivalence) by definition.

In order to prove Corollary 1, we use the algorithm in Lemma 1 to compute the approximation T_Q of a UC2RPQ Q. The algorithm runs in EXPSPACE and its output T_Q is of at most exponential size in $|Q|$.

Finally, we prove Proposition 3. Given a UC2RPQ Q and $T \in \mathsf{AC}$, the following algorithm verifies whether T is an approximation of Q: Check whether $T \subseteq Q$ and $T_Q \subseteq T$. If this is the case $T \equiv T_Q$ and, thus, T is an approximation of Q. Using techniques in [6] both containments can be performed in EXPSPACE. The lower bound follows by an easy reduction from the containment problem of an acyclic CRPQ T in a CRPQ Q, which is EXPSPACE-complete [6]. □

We prove Lemma 1 now. We only sketch the main ideas since the complete proof is rather technical.

Proof (Sketch) of Lemma 1: The proof is based on the following claim:

CLAIM 1. *There exists a polynomial $p : \mathbb{N} \to \mathbb{N}$ such that for every UC2RPQ Q there exists a set $\mathcal{R}_Q$ of 2RPQs for which the following holds:*

1. *$\mathcal{R}_Q$ can be constructed in time $O(2^{p(|Q|)})$.*
2. *There is an acyclic UC2RPQ $T \subseteq Q$ such that each disjunct in T is of the form $\exists \bar{y} \bigwedge_{1 \leq i \leq m}(u_i, R_i, v_i)$, for $m \leq p(|Q|)$ and $R_i \in \mathcal{R}_Q$ ($1 \leq i \leq m$). Moreover, the union of all such T's is T_Q, i.e., the maximum of the class of acyclic UC2RPQs that are contained in Q.*

We show first that Claim 1 implies Lemma 1. In fact, in order to build T_Q from Q we have to do the following: Construct $\mathcal{R}_Q$ in exponential time, and then iterate through every acyclic C2RPQ T with at most $p(|Q|)$ atoms, all of them labeled with 2RPQs in $\mathcal{R}_Q$, adding as a disjunct to T_Q each such T that satisfies $T \subseteq Q$. The second item of Claim 1 implies that T_Q constructed in this way is nonempty (i.e. it contains at least one disjunct). Since each T with at most $p(|Q|)$ atoms – all of them labeled with 2RPQs in $\mathcal{R}_Q$ – is of exponential size, and checking whether $T \subseteq Q$ can be done in EXPSPACE using techniques in [6], the whole procedure can be performed in EXPSPACE. Furthermore, the size of T_Q is at most exponential in $|Q|$.

We continue with the proof of Claim 1. Let Q be a UC2RPQ. We start by explaining how the set $\mathcal{R}_Q$ of 2RPQs that label the atoms of T_Q is defined. The intuition is that we do not need more information in those labels than the *types* they describe with respect to the 2RPQs that label the atoms of Q. Formalizing such intuition requires the introduction of several concepts.

To start with, we need to define the notion of *folding*, which is very useful when dealing with 2RPQs [7]. Let $w = p_1p_2 \cdots p_k$ be a word over alphabet $\Sigma' = \Sigma \cup \{a^- \mid a \in \Sigma\}$. For $p \in \Sigma'$ we define $p^- = a^-$ if $p = a$ and $a \in \Sigma$, and $p^- = a$ if $p = a^-$ and $a \in \Sigma$. Then the word $u = q_1q_2 \cdots q_\ell$ over Σ' *folds* into w from j_1 to j_2, for $j_1, j_2 \in \{0, \ldots, k\}$, if there is a sequence $i_0, i_1, \ldots, i_\ell$ of positions in the set $\{0, \ldots, k\}$ such that:

- $i_0 = j_1$ and $i_\ell = j_2$, and
- for each $1 \leq j \leq \ell$ it is the case that $i_j = i_{j-1} + 1$ and $q_j = p_{i_j}$, or $i_j = i_{j-1} - 1$ and $q_j = p^-_{i_{j-1}}$.

Intuitively, u folds into w if u can be read in w by a two-way automaton that outputs symbol p, for $p \in \Sigma'$, each time that it is read from left-to-right, and symbol p^-, for $p \in \Sigma'$, each time that it is read from right-to-left. For instance, the word $abb^-a^-abb^-c$ folds into abb^-c from 0 to 5.

Assume that $\{R_1, \ldots, R_p\}$ is the set of 2RPQs that label the atoms of Q. With each R_i we associate an NFA $\mathcal{A}_i$ over Σ' that accepts the language defined by R_i. The *Q-type of a word w* over Σ' is the tuple

$$\Gamma = (\tau_{it}, \tau_{ti}, \tau_{ii}, \tau_{tt}),$$

such that τ_{it} corresponds to the set of triples of the form $(\mathcal{A}_i, s, t)$, for $1 \leq i \leq p$, for which the following holds: (i) s and t are states of $\mathcal{A}_i$, and (ii) there is a word u that folds into w from position 0 to $|w|$ and a run of $\mathcal{A}_i$ from state s to t over u. Correspondingly, in τ_{ti} we ask u to fold in w from $|w|$ to 0, in τ_{ii} from 0 to 0, and in τ_{tt} from $|w|$ to $|w|$.

A *Q-type* is the Q-type of some word w. Given two Q-types Γ_1 and Γ_2, we say that Γ_1 is contained in Γ_2 if each coordinate of Γ_1 is contained in the corresponding coordinate of Γ_2. For a Q-type Γ, we denote by $\mathcal{W}(\Gamma)$ the set of words w over Σ' such that Γ is contained in the Q-type of w. The next result is crucial for our proof:

LEMMA 2. *For each Q-type Γ, the language $\mathcal{W}(\Gamma)$ is regular and can be defined by a 2RPQ $\mathcal{R}_\Gamma$ of at most exponential size in $|Q|$.*

Let $\mathcal{R}^+$ be the set of all 2RPQs of the form R_Γ, for Γ a Q-type. Since the class of 2RPQs is closed under *inverse* (i.e. for each 2RPQ R there is a 2RPQ R^- such that $[\![R]\!]_\mathcal{G} = ([\![R^-]\!]_\mathcal{G})^{-1}$, for every graph database $\mathcal{G}$), we can also define the set of 2RPQs $\mathcal{R}^-$ that contains each inverse of a 2RPQ in $\mathcal{R}^+$. Finally, we define a set $\mathcal{R}^\circ$ that consists of the concatenation of at most k elements in $\mathcal{R}^+ \cup \mathcal{R}^-$, where k is polynomially bounded by $|Q|$ (precise bounds are not given in order not to complicate the presentation).

The definition of $\mathcal{R}_Q$ is rather technical, but what is important for us is that it contains the whole set of 2RPQs in $\mathcal{R}^\circ$ and can be computed in exponential time:

LEMMA 3. *A set $\mathcal{R}_Q$ that contains each 2RPQ in $\mathcal{R}^\circ$ can be constructed in exponential time in $|Q|$.*

In order to prove Claim 1 we use the following important lemma:

LEMMA 4. *For every UC2RPQ Q and acyclic UC2RPQ T that is contained in Q, there is an acyclic UC2RPQ T' with the following properties:*

1. *$T \subseteq T' \subseteq Q$,*
2. *each 2RPQ that labels an atom of a disjunct of T' belongs to $\mathcal{R}_Q$, and*
3. *the number of atoms in each disjunct of T' is polynomially bounded by $|Q|$.*

In particular, $|T'|$ is at most exponential in $|Q|$.

We show first that Lemma 4 implies Claim 1. The set $\mathcal{R}_Q$ can be constructed in exponential time, so we have to prove the following: (†) There is an acyclic UC2RPQ $T \subseteq Q$ such that each disjunct in T is of the form $\exists \bar{y} \bigwedge_{1 \leq i \leq m} (u_i, R_i, v_i)$, where $m \leq p(|Q|)$ and $R_i \in \mathcal{R}_Q$, for each $1 \leq i \leq m$. (††) The UC2RPQ T^* defined by the union of all such T's is precisely T_Q, i.e. T^* is the maximum acyclic UC2RPQ contained in Q.

Assume that $\bar{x} = (x_1, \dots, x_r)$ is the tuple of free variables of the UC2RPQ Q. It is easy to see that the CRPQ $\bigwedge_{1 \leq j \leq r-1} (x_j, \varepsilon, x_{j+1}) \wedge \bigwedge_{a \in \Sigma} (x_1, a, x_1)$ is contained in Q, and, thus, from Lemma 4 we have (†), i.e. there is an acyclic UC2RPQ T of the form $\exists \bar{y} \bigwedge_{1 \leq i \leq m} (u_i, R_i, v_i)$ such that (i) m is polynomially bounded by $|Q|$, (ii) for each $1 \leq i \leq m$ it is the case that $R_i \in \mathcal{R}_Q$, and (iii) $T \subseteq Q$. We prove (††) next, i.e. that $T^* \equiv T_Q$. Clearly, $T^* \subseteq Q$ since each disjunct of T^* is contained in Q. Let T be an arbitrary acyclic UC2RPQ that is contained in Q. Then Lemma 4 tells us that T is contained in some union of C2RPQs that is contained in T^*, and hence $T \subseteq T^*$. Thus, T^* is the maximum of the class of acyclic UC2RPQs contained in Q, and hence T^* is equivalent to T_Q.

Next we prove Lemma 4. Let T be an acyclic UC2RPQ such that $T \subseteq Q$. We make use of the following lemma to prove Lemma 4:

LEMMA 5. *Let $\mathcal{G}$ be an arbitrary graph database and $\bar{a}$ a tuple of node ids in $T(\mathcal{G})$. Then there exists an acyclic C2RPQ $T_{(\mathcal{G},\bar{a})}$ such that:*

1. *$T_{(\mathcal{G},\bar{a})} \subseteq Q$ and $\bar{a} \in T_{(\mathcal{G},\bar{a})}(\mathcal{G})$,*
2. *each 2RPQ that labels an atom of $T_{(\mathcal{G},\bar{a})}$ belongs to $\mathcal{R}_Q$, and*
3. *the number of atoms in $T_{(\mathcal{G},\bar{a})}$ is polynomially bounded by $|Q|$.*

We start by proving that Lemma 5 implies Lemma 4. In fact, we can simply define T' to be the UC2RPQ

$$\bigcup \{T_{(\mathcal{G},\bar{a})} \mid \mathcal{G} \text{ is a graph database and } \bar{a} \text{ a tuple in } T(\mathcal{G})\}.$$

From Lemma 5 each disjunct in T' is contained in Q, and, thus, $T' \subseteq Q$. Furthermore, the same lemma implies that for every graph database $\mathcal{G}$ and tuple $\bar{a} \in T(\mathcal{G})$ it is the case that $\bar{a} \in T'(\mathcal{G})$. Thus, $T \subseteq T'$. Finally, each disjunct of T' has a polynomial number of atoms and each one of its atoms is labeled by a 2RPQ in $\mathcal{R}_Q$.

The last step in the construction is proving Lemma 5, which is our technically more involved result. By known techniques we do not have to consider each graph database $\mathcal{G}$, but only those that are *canonical* for some disjunct T_1 of T [18, 6]. Intuitively, these are the graph databases $\mathcal{G}'$ that can be constructed as follows. Each variable in T_1 is added as a node id to $\mathcal{G}'$, and then for each atom of the form (u, R, v) in T_1 we build a single *semipath* (i.e. a path that traverses edges in both directions) of fresh node ids from u to v whose label satisfies R. Since a 2RPQ may accept an infinite number of strings, the space of canonical graph databases for T is potentially infinite.

Let $\mathcal{G}$ be an arbitrary canonical graph database for T and $\bar{a}$ a tuple in $T(\mathcal{G})$. Assume that $Q = \bigvee_{1 \leq i \leq l} Q_i$, where each Q_i is a C2RPQ. Since $T \subseteq Q$ we have that $\bar{a} \in Q(\mathcal{G})$, and, thus, that $\bar{a} \in Q_i(\mathcal{G})$ for some $i \leq \ell$. This implies that there is a homomorphism h from $Q_i(\bar{x})$ to $\mathcal{G}$ such that $h(\bar{x}) = \bar{a}$. Assume that $Q_i = \exists \bar{y} \bigwedge_{1 \leq i \leq m} (u_i, R_i, v_i)$. Then h satisfies that for each $1 \leq i \leq m$ the pair $(h(u_i), h(v_i)) \in [\![R_i]\!]_\mathcal{G}$, or, equivalently, that there is a semipath ρ_i in $\mathcal{G}$ from $h(u_i)$ to $h(v_i)$ whose label satisfies the 2RPQ R_i. We choose each ρ_i to be of minimal length.

Let $\mathcal{I}$ be the set of node ids in $\mathcal{G}$ that are of the form $h(u)$, for some variable u of Q, or the *least common ancestor* in $\mathcal{G}$ of two elements in $\mathcal{I}$ that are in the same connected component of $\mathcal{G}$. (This least common ancestor is well-defined since $\mathcal{G}$ "resembles" T, which is acyclic). In the search for an acyclic C2RPQ $T_{(\mathcal{G},\bar{a})}$, as defined in the statement of Lemma 5, we construct from $\mathcal{G}$ a graph database $\mathcal{G}'$ that contains as node id each element in $\mathcal{I}$. In addition, we connect $h(u_i)$ to $h(v_i)$ in $\mathcal{G}'$ by the semipath ρ_i, for each $1 \leq i \leq m$. However, since we construct $\mathcal{G}'$ in the search for the acyclic C2RPQ $T_{(\mathcal{G},\bar{a})}$, this last step has to be carried out carefully in order to avoid undesirable cycles. We explain the process below.

The idea is to avoid cycles among elements in $\mathcal{I}$. In order to do that, we first have to define a notion of adjacency between elements of $\mathcal{I}$ that defines an acylic graph, and then add semipath ρ_i from $h(u_i)$ to $h(v_i)$ in $\mathcal{G}'$, $1 \leq i \leq m$, by joining contiguous elements of $\mathcal{I}$ with respect to this adjacency relationship.

Finally, from $\mathcal{G}'$ we construct the C2RPQ $T_{(\mathcal{G},\bar{a})}$ as follows: For each pair of contiguous elements in $\mathcal{I}$ that are linked in $\mathcal{G}'$ by a semipath labeled by word $w \in \Sigma'$, we replace such semipath by the 2RPQ in $\mathcal{R}^\circ$ that completely describes w with respect to Q. Clearly, each atom in $T_{(\mathcal{G},\bar{a})}$ is labeled by a 2RPQ in $\mathcal{R}_Q$. It can also be proved that $T_{(\mathcal{G},\bar{a})}$ is acyclic, and, further, that $\bar{a} \in T_{(\mathcal{G},\bar{a})}(\mathcal{G})$. The latter is not hard to see since the identity mapping is a homomorphism from $T_{(\mathcal{G},\bar{a})}$ in $\mathcal{G}$. Furthermore, the number of atoms in $T_{(\mathcal{G},\bar{a})}$ is polynomially bounded by $|Q|$. This follows from the fact that $|\mathcal{I}|$ is polynomially bounded and the minimality of the semipaths ρ_i that have been chosen to populate $\mathcal{G}'$ (as each path ρ_i is decomposed in a polynomial number of contiguous segments in $\mathcal{G}'$).

It just rests to show that $T_{(\mathcal{G},\bar{a})}$ is contained in Q. But this can be intuitively explained using the facts that $\bar{a} \in Q(\mathcal{G})$, and the canonical databases of $T_{(\mathcal{G},\bar{a})}$ are indistinguishable from $\mathcal{G}$ by Q, i.e. for each canonical database $\mathcal{G}_1$ of $T_{(\mathcal{G},\bar{a})}$ it is the case that $\bar{a} \in Q(\mathcal{G}) \Leftrightarrow \bar{a} \in Q(\mathcal{G}_1)$. The latter holds because $T_{(\mathcal{G},\bar{a})}$ is constructed from $\mathcal{G}$ by replacing semipaths with 2RPQs that respect the Q-type of its label.

5. SEMANTIC ACYCLICITY OF UC2RPQS

We finish the paper by studying the notion of semantic acyclicity in the context of graph databases and conjunctive regular path queries. As opposed to the case of CQs, the results in this section do not follow from known results in the literature and require new techniques. We start by defining the terminology and providing some basic insights about the nature of semantic acyclicity for UC2RPQs.

5.1 Basic terminology and insights

A UC2RPQ Q is semantically acyclic if there exists an acyclic UC2RPQ Q' such that $Q \equiv Q'$. As we mentioned before, we want to answer two basic questions about semantically acyclic UC2RPQs: (1) What is the cost of evaluating queries in this class? (2) What is the cost of checking if a UC2RPQ is semantically acyclic? We will see that an answer to the second question will provide us with an answer for the first one.

Since acyclicity of C2RPQs is defined in terms of the acyclicity of its underlying CQ, one may be tempted to think that the two notions coincide. Clearly, if the underlying CQ of a C2RPQ Q is semantically acyclic then Q is also semantically acyclic. The following example shows that the opposite does not hold.

EXAMPLE 4. Consider again the non-acyclic CRPQ $Q'' = \exists x \exists y \exists z\,((x, L_1, y) \wedge (y, L_2, z) \wedge (z, L_3, x))$ in Example 3. It is not hard to prove that Q'' is equivalent to the acyclic CRPQ $\exists x\ (x, L_1L_2L_3, x)$, and, thus, it is semantically acyclic. On the other hand, the underlying CQ of Q'' is $\exists x \exists y \exists z (T_1(x, y), T_2(y, z), T_3(z, x))$, which is not semantically acyclic.

Intuitively, the query Q'' is semantically acyclic because it can be "simplified" by concatenating the regular languages that label its atoms. A more interesting example is the following Boolean CRPQ Q_{sa} over $\Sigma = \{a, \$_1, \$_2, \$_3\}$

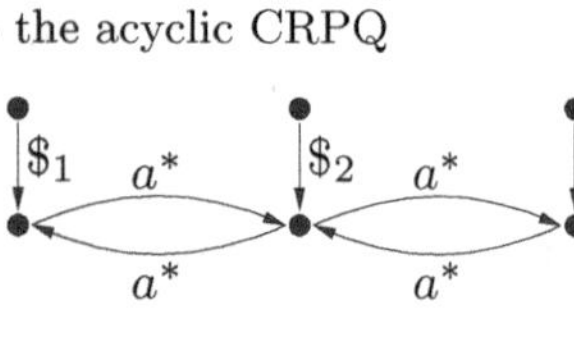

(Dots represent variables and arrows represent labeled atoms). It is easy to see that the underlying CQ of Q_{sa} is not semantically acyclic. On the other hand, it can be proved that Q_{sa} is equivalent to the acyclic CRPQ

In this case, semantic acyclicity is obtained by the way in which the regular languages that label the atoms of Q_{sa} interact with each other. □

The previous example shows that the notion of semantic acyclicity of C2RPQs is richer than the notion of acyclicity of its underlying CQs, as many queries fall in the former category but not in the latter. Not only that, the first notion is also theoretically more challenging: While the same techniques used in Section 2 can be applied to prove that the evaluation problem is tractable for UC2RPQs whose underlying CQ is semantically acyclic, it is by no means clear whether the same is true for the class of semantically acyclic UC2RPQs (and even for semantically acyclic CRPQs). We delve into this issue below.

As is mentioned in the Introduction, the CSP techniques used in Section 2 to prove that the evaluation of semantically acyclic UCQs is tractable do not yield answers to our questions about semantically acyclic UC2RPQs. The results in Section 5.2 help us proving, on the other hand, that the problem is fixed-parameter tractable (Theorem 5), which was not known to date. We leave as an open question whether the class of semantically acyclic UC2RPQs can be evaluated in polynomial time.

Before finishing the section we explore the limits of the notion of semantic acyclicity. The next example shows a simple CQ over graph databases that is not equivalent to any acyclic UC2RPQ.

EXAMPLE 5. Let $\Sigma = \{a, \$_1, \$_2, \$_3\}$ be a finite alphabet and consider the Boolean CRPQ Q_{na} over Σ that is graphically defined as:

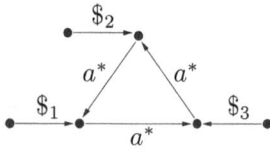

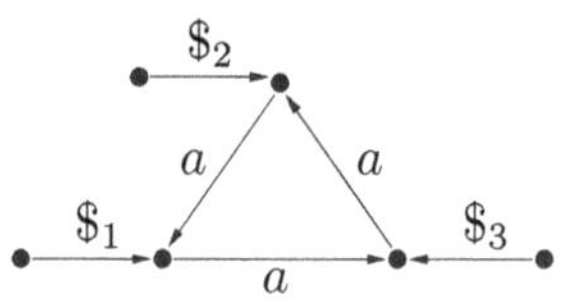

Notice that the underlying CQ of Q_{na} coincides with that of the semantically acyclic CRPQ Q_{sa} from Example 4. However, a simple case-by-case analysis shows that Q_{na} is not semantically acyclic. The reason is that Q_{na} forbids the interaction between the different RPQs that label its atoms by replacing each RPQ of the form a^* in Q_{sa} with a. □

5.2 Verification of semantic acyclicity

We start by considering our second question above: Is the notion of semantic acyclicity for UC2RPQs decidable? In this section we show that this is indeed the case and prove both upper and lower bounds for its computational cost.

We start by proving that the notion of semantic acyclicity for UC2RPQs is decidable, and provide an elementary upper bound for the problem. The algorithm also yields an equivalent UC2RPQ Q' of exponential size for a semantically acyclic UC2RPQ Q.

THEOREM 4. *There exists a* 2EXPSPACE *algorithm that on input a UC2RPQ Q does the following:*

1. *It checks whether Q is semantically acyclic.*
2. *If the latter holds, it outputs an acyclic UC2RPQ Q' of single-exponential size such that $Q \equiv Q'$.*

Proof: The algorithm in Lemma 1 computes on input Q an acyclic UC2RPQ T_Q such that T_Q is the maximum among all acyclic UC2RPQs that are contained in Q. It follows that Q is semantically acyclic iff $Q \subseteq T_Q$. Thus, in order to check semantic acyclicity of Q we only have to compute T_Q, which can be done in EXPSPACE, and then check whether $Q \subseteq T_Q$, which can be done in exponential space in $(|Q| + |T_Q|)$ [6], and hence in double-exponential space in $|Q|$ (because T_Q is of at most exponential size in $|Q|$). The whole procedure can be done in 2EXPSPACE. □

We now provide a lower bound for the problem that shows that checking semantic acyclicity of (U)C(2)RPQs is considerably harder than for UCQs:

PROPOSITION 4. *It is* EXPSPACE*-hard to check whether a UC2RPQ Q is semantically acyclic. The problem remains* EXPSPACE*-hard even if the input is restricted to Boolean CRPQs.*

Proof: Since the proof is rather tedious we only sketch it here. Checking whether a Boolean CRPQ Q_1 is contained in a Boolean CRPQ Q_2 is EXPSPACE-complete [6]. From the proof it follows that this problem remains hard even if Q_1 is acyclic and the underlying undirected graph $\mathcal{U}(Q_2)$ of Q_2 is connected, which is crucial for our construction.

The construction in [6] also yields an acyclic Q_2, but for our proof to work we require Q_2 not to be semantically acyclic. Nevertheless, this can be easily fixed: In fact, given Q_1 and Q_2 as above, we can do the following: (1) Construct in polynomial time CRPQ Q_2' by "appending" to a particular variable of Q_2 a fresh copy of the Boolean CRPQ Q_{na} in Example 5 (which is not semantically acyclic), over an alphabet Σ that is disjoint from that of Q_1 and Q_2. (2) Construct in polynomial time CRPQ Q_1' from Q_1 by "appending" to a suitable variable in Q_1 a fresh copy of the acyclic query $Q = \exists x \bigwedge_{a \in \Sigma}(x, a, x)$. It can be proved that Q_1 is contained in Q_2 iff Q_1' is contained in Q_2'. Moreover, Q_1' is acyclic (because Q is acyclic and "appending" it to Q_1 does not create cycles), $\mathcal{U}(Q_2')$ is connected, and Q_2' is not semantically acyclic (because otherwise Q_{na} would be semantically acyclic). We use this EXPSPACE-hard restriction of the containment problem to prove that our problem is also EXPSPACE-hard.

Let Q_1 and Q_2 be Boolean CRPQs such that Q_1 is acyclic, $\mathcal{U}(Q_2)$ is connected and Q_2 is not semantically acyclic. We claim that Q_1 is contained in Q_2 iff the CRPQ $Q_1 \wedge Q_2$ is semantically acyclic. Assume first that Q_1 is contained in Q_2. Then $Q_1 \wedge Q_2$ is equivalent to Q_1, which is acyclic. Assume, on the other hand, that $Q_1 \wedge Q_2 \equiv T$, where $T = \bigvee_{1 \le i \le m} T_i$ and each T_i is an acyclic C2RPQ. Since $Q_1 \wedge Q_2 \subseteq Q_2$, it follows that $T \subseteq Q_2$. Also, since $T_i \subseteq T$, it follows that $T_i \subseteq Q_2$, for each $1 \le i \le m$.

Let $T_i^1, \ldots, T_i^{k_i}$ be the C2RPQs associated with each connected component of $\mathcal{U}(T_i)$. Thus, $T_i \equiv T_i^1 \wedge \cdots \wedge T_i^{k_i}$. For each i with $1 \le i \le m$, we shall prove that $T_i^j \subseteq Q_2$ for some $1 \le j \le k_i$. Assume to the contrary. Then there exist graph databases $\mathcal{G}_1, \ldots \mathcal{G}_{k_i}$ such that $T_i^j(\mathcal{G}_j) = \mathtt{true}$ and $Q_2(\mathcal{G}_j) = \mathtt{false}$, for each $1 \le j \le k_i$. Since $\mathcal{U}(T_i^j)$ is connected, we can choose $\mathcal{G}_j$ to be connected as well (in the sense that the underlying undirected graph of $\mathcal{G}_j$ is connected), for each $1 \le j \le k_i$. Consider the disjoint union $\mathcal{G}$ of $\mathcal{G}_1, \ldots \mathcal{G}_{k_i}$. Clearly, $T_i(\mathcal{G}) = \mathtt{true}$, and since $T_i \subseteq Q_2$, it follows that $Q_2(\mathcal{G}) = \mathtt{true}$. But since $\mathcal{U}(Q_2)$ is connected it must be the case that $Q_2(\mathcal{G}_j) = \mathtt{true}$, for some $1 \le j \le k_i$, which is a contradiction.

Therefore, for each i with $1 \le i \le m$ there exists j_i with $1 \le j_i \le k_i$ such that $T_i^{j_i} \subseteq Q_2$. Consider the acyclic UC2RPQ $T' = \bigvee_{1 \le i \le m} T_i^{j_i}$. Notice that $T \subseteq T'$. Moreover, $T' \subseteq Q_2$. We shall prove that $Q_1 \subseteq T'$, which implies our desired result that $Q_1 \subseteq Q_2$. Since Q_2 is not semantically acyclic, it must be the case that $Q_2 \not\subseteq T'$. Hence there exists a graph database $\mathcal{G}^*$ such that $Q_2(\mathcal{G}^*) = \mathtt{true}$ and $T'(\mathcal{G}^*) = \mathtt{false}$. Consider an arbitrary database $\mathcal{G}$ such that $Q_1(\mathcal{G}) = \mathtt{true}$. We prove next that $T'(\mathcal{G}) = \mathtt{true}$, which implies that $Q_1 \subseteq T'$. Consider the disjoint union $\mathcal{G}'$ of $\mathcal{G}$ and $\mathcal{G}^*$. Clearly, $Q_1 \wedge Q_2(\mathcal{G}') = \mathtt{true}$, and since $Q_1 \wedge Q_2 \equiv T \subseteq T'$, it follows that $T'(\mathcal{G}') = \mathtt{true}$. Then $T_i^{j_i}(\mathcal{G}') = \mathtt{true}$, for some $1 \le i \le m$. Since $\mathcal{U}(T_i^{j_i})$ is connected, it follows that either $T_i^{j_i}(\mathcal{G}) = \mathtt{true}$ or $T_i^{j_i}(\mathcal{G}^*) = \mathtt{true}$. But $T'(\mathcal{G}^*) = \mathtt{false}$, and, thus, $T_i^{j_i}(\mathcal{G}^*) = \mathtt{false}$. We conclude that $T_i^{j_i}(\mathcal{G}) = \mathtt{true}$, and, thus, $T'(\mathcal{G}) = \mathtt{true}$. □

Evaluation of semantically acyclic UC2RPQs With the help of Theorem 4 we can provide an answer to our first question regarding semantically acyclic UC2RPQs: Its evaluation is fixed-parameter tractable.

THEOREM 5. *The problem of checking whether $\bar{a} \in Q(\mathcal{G})$, for a given graph database $\mathcal{G}$, semantically acyclic UC2RPQ Q, and tuple $\bar{a}$ of node ids in $\mathcal{G}$, is fixed-parameter tractable.*

In particular, semantically acyclic UC2RPQs can be evaluated in time $O(f(|Q|) + |\mathcal{G}|^2 \cdot 2^{p(|Q|)})$, where $p : \mathbb{N} \to \mathbb{N}$ is a polynomial and $f : \mathbb{N} \to \mathbb{N}$ is a triple-exponential function.

Features of the language: Inverses The algorithm in Theorem 4 introduces inverses in the construction of an equivalent acyclic query, even if we start from a semantically acyclic UCRPQ (i.e., a UC2RPQ without inverses). A natural question is whether this is necessary, that is, whether there are semantically acyclic UCRPQs that find an equivalent query in the class of acyclic UC2RPQs, but not in the class of acyclic UCRPQs. We prove that this is the case:

PROPOSITION 5. *There is a semantically acyclic CRPQ that is no equivalent to any acyclic UCRPQ.*

PROOF. The Boolean query Q that is graphically depicted below

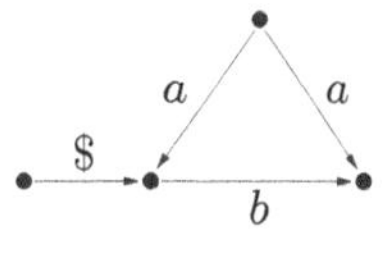

is semantically acyclic. In fact, it is equivalent to the acyclic C2RPQ $\exists x \exists y((x, \$, y) \wedge (y, ba^{-}a, y))$. A tedious case-by-case analysis proves that it is not equivalent to any acyclic UCRPQ. □

6. CONCLUSIONS AND OPEN PROBLEMS

We have studied the space of UCQs and UC2RPQs defined by the notion of acyclicity. This is relevant since acyclicity is a robust explanation for the tractability of several query languages for relational and graph databases. Furthermore, some notions of acyclicity explain the linear-time behavior of various querying mechanisms for graph databases (e.g. XPath [26], PDL [23], nested regular expressions [4], etc).

While the results about semantic acyclicity of UCQs follow from techniques in CSP, studying the notion of semantic acyclicity of UC2RPQs requires new tools and insights. We have shown that it is decidable in 2EXPSPACE whether a UC2RPQ is semantically acyclic, and that this shows that evaluation of queries in the class is fixed-parameter tractable. The techniques used to prove decidability also yield a strong theory of approximations of UC2RPQs.

As far as the notion of semantic acyclicity of UC2RPQs is concerned, in this work we have only uncovered the tip of the iceberg. Many questions remain open and we list some of them below.

Complexity We have proven that evaluation of semantically acyclic UC2RPQs is fixed-parameter tractable. But is it also polynomial? Tractability of semantically acyclic UCQs follows from a sophisticated characterization of the problem in terms of winning strategies in the existential pebble game, but we do not know whether those techniques can be extended to deal with UC2RPQs.

Also, we have left a gap in the complexity problem of identifying whether a UC2RPQ is semantically acyclic: Our current upper and lower bounds are 2EXPSPACE and EXPSPACE, respectively. The reason why we do not know how to lower the upper bound at this point, is that we need to check containment of a UC2RPQ Q into T_Q, which might be exponentially bigger than Q. The main problem with this is not that there might be an exponential number of disjuncts in T_Q, but that some of the 2RPQs that label the atoms of T_Q might be of exponential size. Proving that this containment can be checked in EXPSPACE may require of more sophisticated techniques.

Size of equivalent acyclic queries The algorithm presented in Theorem 4 computes an equivalent acyclic query of single-exponential size for a semantically acyclic UC2RPQ. Is this optimal, i.e. is there a family $(Q_n)_{n\geq 1}$ of semantically acyclic UC2RPQs such that (1) $|Q_n|$ is polynomially bounded by n, and (2) the smallest acyclic UC2RPQ that is equivalent to Q_n is of size $\Omega(2^n)$, for each $n \geq 1$?

Features of the language The algorithm that constructs an equivalent acyclic UC2RPQ T for a semantically acyclic UC2RPQ Q (Theorem 4) outputs a union of C2RPQs T even if Q is a C2RPQ. But is this necessary? That is, is there a C2RPQ Q that is semantically acyclic, but yet it is not equivalent to a *single* acyclic C2RPQ T?

Beyond acyclic queries Acyclicity is a simple syntactic criterion that ensures efficient evaluation of CQs, but it is not the only one. In the last years several criteria have been identified that extend acyclicity in different ways while retaining polynomial time evaluation for the CQs that satisfy them. Most of these criteria are based on the idea of restricting evaluation to CQs Q of bounded *(hyper)-treewidth* [21], which are also defined in terms of the existence of a tree decomposition of Q with desirable properties.

It is known that the results in Section 2 (Theorem 1 and Proposition 1) also apply to UCQs that are equivalent to unions of CQs of bounded treewidth [12, 9]. That is, such classes of UCQs can be evaluated in polynomial time, and it is NP-complete to check whether a CQ is equivalent to a CQ of treewidth at most k, for each $k \geq 1$.

On the other hand, our results for UC2RPQs are specifically designed for semantic acyclicity, and we do not know at this point how to extend them to verify whether a UC2RPQ is equivalent to a UC2RPQ of bounded hyper-treewidth. In the same way, one might be interested in extending results on approximations of UC2RPQs to classes of bounded hyper-treewidth, as it has been done for UCQs [5].

Beyond C2RPQs Instead of working with C2RPQs one could also consider the class of conjunctions of nested regular expressions (CNREs), that properly extends the former [4]. Acyclicity of CNREs also leads to tractability, and thus it makes sense to study semantic acyclicity in this extended setting. The problem is relevant since several linear-time query languages for graph databases are contained in the class of CNREs but not in the class of UC2RPQs [23, 4].

CSP for C2RPQs Our work can also be viewed as opening a new line of research in constraint satisfaction. As noted above, there is an intimate connection between conjunctive-query evaluation and constraint-satisfaction. In general this problem is NP-complete, but there is an extensive body of research studying tractable cases, either by fixing the database and focusing on expression complexity, or by studying the combined complexity of restricted classes of queries [16, 25]. The same approach, fixing the database or restricting the class of queries can also be applied to the evaluation of C2RPQs. In particular, as noted above, it is an open question whether the class of semantically acyclic C2RPQs is an "island of tractability" in the sense of [25], that is, whether its evaluation problem is tractable.

Acknowledgments Barceló is funded by Fondecyt grant 1130104. Romero is funded by CONICYT Ph.D. Scholarship. We would like to thank Gaelle Fontaine for useful conversations about the nature of semantic acyclicity.

7. REFERENCES

[1] S. Abiteboul, P. Buneman, D. Suciu. *Data on the Web: From Relations to Semistructured Data and XML*. Morgan Kauffman, 1999.

[2] R. Angles, C. Gutiérrez. Survey of graph database models. *ACM Comput. Surv.* 40(1): (2008).

[3] P. Barceló, L. Libkin, A.W. Lin, P. Wood. Expressive languages for path queries over graph-structured data. *ACM TODS* 38(4), 2012.

[4] P. Barceló, J. Perez, J. Reutter. Relative expressiveness of nested regular expressions. In *AMW* 2012, pages 180–195.

[5] P. Barceló, L. Libkin, M. Romero. Efficient approximations of conjunctive queries. In *PODS* 2012, pages 249–260.

[6] D. Calvanese, G. de Giacomo, M. Lenzerini, M. Y. Vardi. Containment of conjunctive regular path queries with inverse. In *KR'00*, pages 176–185.

[7] D. Calvanese, G. de Giacomo, M. Lenzerini, M. Y. Vardi. Rewriting of regular expressions and regular path queries. *JCSS*, 64(3):443–465, 2002.

[8] A. Chandra and P. Merlin. Optimal implementation of conjunctive queries in relational data bases. In *STOC* 1977, pages 77–90.

[9] H. Chen and V. Dalmau. Beyond hypertree width: Decomposition methods without decompositions. In *CP* 2005, pages 167–181.

[10] M. P. Consens, A. O. Mendelzon. GraphLog: a visual formalism for real life recursion. In *PODS'90*, pages 404–416.

[11] I. Cruz, A. Mendelzon, P. Wood. A graphical query language supporting recursion. In *SIGMOD'87*, pages 323-330.

[12] V. Dalmau, P. G. Kolaitis, M. Y. Vardi. Constraint satisfaction, bounded treewidth, and finite-variable logics. In *CP* 2002, pages 310–326.

[13] R. Fagin. Degrees of acyclicity for hypergraphs and relational database schemes. *JACM* 30(3), pages 514–550, 1983.

[14] W. Fan, J. Li, S. Ma, N. Tang, Y. Wu. Graph pattern matching: from intractable to polynomial time. *PVLDB* 3(1): 264-275 (2010).

[15] W. Fan, J. Li, S. Ma, N. Tang, Y. Wu. Adding regular expressions to graph reachability and pattern queries. In *ICDE 2011*, to appear.

[16] T. Feder, M. Y. Vardi. The computational structure of monotone monadic SNP and constraint satisfaction: A study through datalog and group theory. *SIAM J. Comput.* 28(1), pages 57–104, 1998.

[17] G. Fletcher, M. Gyssens, D. Leinders, J. Van den Bussche, D. Van Gucht, S. Vansummeren, Y. Wu. Relative expressive power of navigational querying on graphs. In *ICDT 2011*, pages 197–207.

[18] D. Florescu, A. Levy, D. Suciu. Query containment for conjunctive queries with regular expressions. In *PODS'98*, pages 139–148.

[19] G. Gottlob, N. Leone, F. Scarcello. The complexity of acyclic conjunctive queries. J. ACM 48(3), 2001, pages 431–498.

[20] G. Gottlob, N. Leone, F. Scarcello. Hypertree decompositions and tractable queries.*J. Comput. Syst. Sci.* 64(3), pages 579–627, 2002.

[21] G. Gottlob, N. Leone, and F. Scarcello. Hypertree decompositions and tractable queries. *JCSS*, 64 (2002), 579–627.

[22] M. Grohe. The structure of tractable constraint satisfaction problems. In *MFCS* 2006, pages 58–72.

[23] D. Harel, D. Kozen, J. Tiuryn. *Dynamic logic.* MIT Press, 2000.

[24] Ph. Kolaitis, M. Y. Vardi. Conjunctive query-containment and constraint satisfaction. *JCSS* 61(2), pages 302–332, 2000.

[25] Ph. Kolaitis, M. Y. Vardi. A Logical Approach to Constraint Satisfaction. *Complexity of Constraints*, pages 125–155, 2008.

[26] L. Libkin, W. Martens, D. Vrgoc. Querying graph databases with XPath. Accepted for publication, *ICDT* 2013.

[27] C. H. Papadimitriou and M. Yannakakis. The complexity of facets (and some facets of complexity). *JCSS*, 28 (1986), 244–259.

[28] Ch. Papadimitriou, M. Yannakakis. On the complexity of database queries. In *PODS* 1997, pages 12-19.

[29] Y. Sagiv and M. Yannakakis. Equivalences among relational expressions with the union and difference operator. *JACM* 27(4), 1980, pages 633–655.

[30] R. Tarjan and M. Yannakakis. Simple linear-time algorithms to test chordality of graphs, test selectivity of hypergraphs and selectively reduce acyclic hypergraphs. *Siam J. of Comp.*, 13, 1984, pages 566–579.

[31] M. Yannakakis. Algorithms for acyclic database schemes. In *VLDB*, 1981, pages 82–94.

On XPath with Transitive Axes and Data Tests*

Diego Figueira
University of Edinburgh
Edinburgh, UK

ABSTRACT

We study the satisfiability problem for XPath with data equality tests. XPath is a node selecting language for XML documents whose satisfiability problem is known to be undecidable, even for very simple fragments. However, we show that the satisfiability for XPath with the rightward, leftward and downward reflexive-transitive axes (namely following-sibling-or-self, preceding-sibling-or-self, descendant-or-self) is decidable. Our algorithm yields a complexity of 3EXPSPACE, and we also identify an expressive-equivalent normal form for the logic for which the satisfiability problem is in 2EXPSPACE. These results are in contrast with the undecidability of the satisfiability problem as soon as we replace the reflexive-transitive axes with just transitive (non-reflexive) ones.

Categories and Subject Descriptors

I.7.2 [**Document Preparation**]: Markup Languages; H.2.3 [**Database Management**]: Languages; H.2.3 [**Languages**]: Query Languages

General Terms

Algorithms, Languages

Keywords

XML, XPath, unranked unordered tree, reflexive transitive axes, data-tree, infinite alphabet, data values

*We acknowledge the financial support of the Future and Emerging Technologies (FET) programme within the Seventh Framework Programme for Research of the European Commission, under the FET-Open grant agreement FOX, number FP7-ICT-233599.

PODS'13, June 22–27, 2013, New York, New York, USA.

1. INTRODUCTION

The simplest way of abstracting an XML document is by seeing it as a tree over a finite alphabet of *tags* or *labels*. However, this abstraction ignores all actual data stored in the document attributes. This is why there has been an increasing interest in data trees: trees that also carry data from an infinite domain. Here, we consider an XML modeled as an unranked ordered finite tree whose every node contains a label, and a vector of data values, one for each attribute. Labels belong to some finite alphabet, and data values to some infinite domain. We call these models *multi-attribute data trees* (see Figure 1). We study logics on these models, that can express data properties, namely equality of attributes' data values.

Here, we show decidability of the satisfiability problem for XPath where navigation can be done going downwards, rightwards or leftwards in the XML document, that is, where navigation is done using the reflexive-transitive XPath axes descendant-or-self, following-sibling-or-self, and preceding-sibling-or-self.

Formalisms for trees with data values

Several formalisms have been studied lately in relation to static analysis on trees with data values.

First-order logic.

One such formalisms is $\mathrm{FO}^2(<_h, succ_h, <_v, succ_v, \sim)$, first order logic with two variables, and binary relations to navigate the tree: the descendant $<_v$, child $succ_v$, next sibling $succ_h$ and following sibling $<_h$ (*i.e.*, the transitive closure of $succ_h$); and an equivalence relation $\sim$ to express that two nodes of the trees have the same data value. Although the decidability status for the satisfiability problem of this logic is unknown, it is known to be as hard as the reachability problem for BVASS (Branching Vector Addition System with States) [4]. If the signature has only the child and next sibling relation—$\mathrm{FO}^2(succ_h, succ_v, \sim)$—the logic is decidable in 3NEXPTIME as shown in [4].

Automata.

There have also been works on automata models for trees with data. Tree automata with registers to store and compare data values were studied in [20] as an extension to a similar model on words [19, 22]. A decidable alternating version of these automata called ATRA was studied in [18], and it was extended in [9, 12] to show decidability of the satisfiability problem for forward-XPath. The work [3] introduces a simple yet powerful automata model called *Class Automata* on data trees that can capture $FO^2(<_h, succ_h, <_v, succ_v, \sim)$, XPath, ATRA, and other models. Although its emptiness problem is undecidable, classes of data trees for which it is decidable are studied in [1]. Other formalisms include tree automata with set and linear constraints on cardinalities of sets of data values [6, 23].

XPath.

Here we concentrate on XPath, which is incomparable in terms of expressiveness with all the previously mentioned formalisms (except for Class Automata).

XPath is arguably the most widely used XML query language. It is implemented in XSLT and XQuery and it is used as a constituent part of several specification and update languages. XPath is fundamentally a general purpose language for addressing, searching, and matching pieces of an XML document. It is an open standard and constitutes a World Wide Web Consortium (W3C) Recommendation [5].

Query containment and query equivalence are important static analysis problems, which are useful to, for example, query optimization tasks. In logics closed under boolean operators—as the one treated here—, these problems reduce to checking for *satisfiability*: Is there a document on which a given query has a non-empty result? By answering this question we can decide at compile time whether the query contains a contradiction and thus the computation of the query (or subquery) on the document can be avoided. Or, by answering the query equivalence problem, one can test if a query can be safely replaced by another one which is more optimized in some sense (*e.g.*, in the use of some resource). Moreover, the satisfiability problem is crucial for applications on security [7], type checking transformations [21], and consistency of XML specifications.

Core-XPath (term coined in [17]) is the fragment of XPath 1.0 that captures all the navigational behavior of XPath. It has been well studied and its satisfiability problem is known to be decidable even in the presence of DTDs. The extension of this language with the possibility to make equality and inequality tests between attributes of elements in the XML document is named Core-Data-XPath in [4].

In an nutshell, the important formulas of Core-Data-XPath (henceforth *XPath*) are of the form

$$\langle \alpha @_i = \beta @_j \rangle,$$

where α, β are *path expressions*, that navigate the tree using *axes*: descendant, child, ancestor, next-sibling, etc. and can make tests in intermediary nodes. Such a formula is true at a node x of a multi-attribute data tree if there are two nodes y, z in the tree that can be reached with the relations denoted by α, β respectively, so that the ith attribute of y carries the *same* datum as the jth attribute of z.

Unfortunately, the satisfiability problem for XPath is undecidable [16]. How can we regain decidability for satisfiability of XPath then? We can restrict the models, or restrict the logic. The first possibility is to restrict the classes of documents in which one is interested, which is the approach taken in [1]. Another, more studied, approach is to restrict the syntax, which is the one taken here. One way to regain decidability is to syntactically restrict the amount of nodes that the XPath properties can talk about. In this vein, there have been studies on fragments without negation or without transitive axes [2, 16]. These fragments enjoy a small model property and are decidable. However, they cannot state global properties, involving all the nodes in an XML document. Ideally, we seek fragments with the following desirable features

- closed under boolean operators,
- having as much freedom as possible to navigate the tree in many directions: up, down, left, right,
- having the possibility to reach any node of the tree, with transitive axes, like descendant, following sibling (the transitive closure of the next sibling axis), etc.

However, decidability results are scarce, and most fragments with the characteristics just described are undecidable. There are, however, some exceptions ([10]).

- The *downward* fragment of XPath, containing the child and descendant axes, is decidable, ExpTime-complete [8, 13].
- The *forward* fragment of XPath, extending the downward fragment with the next sibling and the following sibling axes, is decidable with non-primitive recursive complexity [9, 12].
- The *vertical* fragment of XPath, extending the downward fragment with the parent and ancestor axes, is decidable with non-primitive recursive complexity [15].
- A last example is the present work: XPath with the reflexive transitive closure of the child, next-sibling and previous-sibling relations is decidable.

All the non-primitive recursive (NPR) upper bounds of the forward and vertical fragments are also matched with NPR lower bounds. That is, there is no primitive recursive function that bounds the time or space needed by any algorithm that computes the satisfiability for any of these two logics. Moreover, it is known that any fragment of XPath containing a transitive rightward, leftward or upward axis has a satisfiability problem which is either undecidable or decidable with a NPR lower bound [14].[1] Further, as soon as we have both the rightward and leftward transitive axes, the satisfiability becomes undecidable [14]. (Indeed, the downward fragment of XPath seemed to be the only one with elementary complexity up to now.)

The aforementioned hardness results make use of non-reflexive transitive relations. Surprisingly, the reductions do not seem to work when the relations are also reflexive. What is then the decidability status of the fragments of XPath with reflexive-transitive relations? This was a question raised in [14].

A partial answer to this question was given in [11]. There, it was shown that XPath restricted to data words is decidable even when we have both a reflexive-transitive future and past relations. (One can think of data words as XML documents of height 1, with only one attribute per node.) This result may seem surprising taking into account that if one of these relations is non-reflexive it is no longer decidable; and if we have only one non-reflexive transitive relation it is decidable with non-primitive recursive complexity. In [11] it was shown that the satisfiability problem is in 2ExpSpace (or ExpSpace if we adopt a certain normal form of

[1] These are the axes that are called preceding-sibling, following-sibling and ancestor in the XPath jargon.

the formulas). This was a first step in our study of the computational behavior of XPath with reflexive-transitive axes. The present work corresponds to the second part, in which we study XPath on XML documents (*i.e.*, trees) instead of words.

Contribution

We show decidability of the satisfiability for XPath with data equality tests between attributes, where navigation can be done going downwards, rightwards or leftwards in the XML document. The navigation can only be done by reflexive-transitive relations. These correspond to the XPath axes: preceding-sibling-or-self, following-sibling-or-self, and descendant-or-self axes.[2] Here we denote these axes with $^*\!\!\leftarrow$, $\rightarrow^*$ and $\downarrow_*$ respectively. As already mentioned, the fact that the relations are reflexive-transitive (as opposed to just transitive) is an essential feature to achieve decidability. Given the known complexity results on XPath, this fragment seems to be in balance between navigation and complexity. This work then argues in favor of studying XPath-like logics for trees with data with reflexive-transitive relations, since they may behave computationally much better than the non-reflexive counterpart, as evidenced here.

The extension of the prior work [11] on data words to work with trees with a descendant axis is highly non-trivial, requiring an altogether different formalism and algorithm strategy. Whereas in [11] the main object of study is a transition system—which comes naturally when working with words—this does not adapt well to working with trees. Instead, here we work with an algebra operating on abstractions of *forests* of multi-attribute data trees. Over this algebra, we prove some monotonicity properties, which are necessarily more involved than those used in [11] to account for the interplay between horizontal and vertical navigation of the logic.

Our algorithm yields a 3EXPSPACE upper bound for the satisfiability problem of this XPath fragment. We also show that this can be lowered to 2EXPSPACE if we work with an expressive-equivalent normal form, called *direct normal form*. Since XPath with just one reflexive-transitive relation is already EXPSPACE-hard (even when the formula is in direct normal form) by [11], we cannot aim for much better complexities.

2. PRELIMINARIES

Basic notation.

Let $\mathbb{N}_0 \stackrel{def}{=} \{0, 1, 2, \dots\}$, $\mathbb{N} \stackrel{def}{=} \{1, 2, 3, \dots\}$, and let $[n] \stackrel{def}{=} \{1, \dots, n\}$ for any $n \in \mathbb{N}$. We fix once and for all $\mathbb{D}$ to be any infinite domain of data values; for simplicity in our examples we will consider $\mathbb{D} = \mathbb{N}_0$. In general we use the symbols $\mathbb{A}$, $\mathbb{B}$ for finite alphabets, and the symbols $\mathbb{E}$ and $\mathbb{F}$ for any kind of alphabet. By $\mathbb{E}^*$ we denote the set of finite sequences over $\mathbb{E}$, by $\mathbb{E}^+$ the set of finite sequences with at least one element over $\mathbb{E}$. We write 'ϵ' for the empty sequence and '$\cdot$' as the concatenation operator between sequences. By $|S|$ we denote the length of S (if S is a finite sequence), or its cardinality (if S is a set). We use $(a_i)_{i\in\{j,\dots,j+n\}}$ as short for $a_j a_{j+1} \cdots a_{j+n}$.

[2]Strictly speaking, these axes do not exist in XPath [5]. They must be interpreted as the reflexive version of the preceding-sibling, following-sibling and descendant axes respectively.

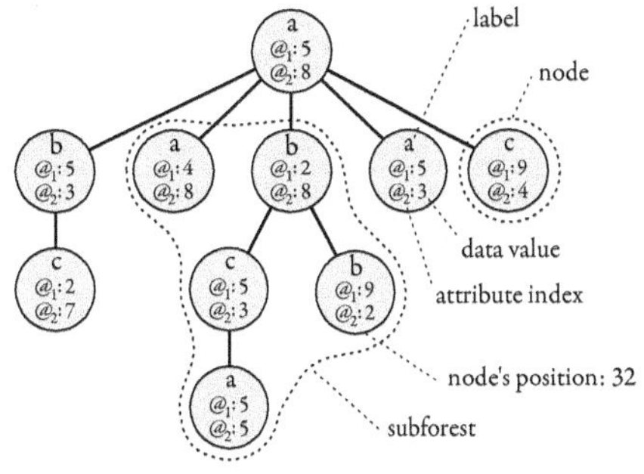

Figure 1: A multi-attribute data tree, where $\mathbb{A} = \{a, b, c\}$ and $\mathbf{k} = 2$.

Unranked finite trees with data.

By *Trees*($\mathbb{E}$) we denote the set of finite ordered and unranked trees over an alphabet $\mathbb{E}$. We view each **position** in a tree as an element of $\mathbb{N}^*$. Formally, we define $\mathsf{POS} \subseteq 2^{\mathbb{N}^*}$ as the set of sets of finite tree positions, such that: $X \in \mathsf{POS}$ iff (a) $X \subseteq \mathbb{N}^*, |X| < \infty$; (b) X is prefix-closed; and (c) if $n{\cdot}(i+1) \in X$ for $i \in \mathbb{N}$, then $n{\cdot}i \in X$. A tree is then a mapping from a set of positions to labels of the alphabet $\mathit{Trees}(\mathbb{E}) \stackrel{def}{=} \{\mathbf{t} : P \to \mathbb{E} \mid P \in \mathsf{POS}\}$. The root's position is the empty string ϵ. The position of any other node in the tree is the concatenation of the position of its parent and the node's index in the ordered list of siblings.

Given a tree $\mathbf{t} \in \mathit{Trees}(\mathbb{E})$, $pos(\mathbf{t})$ denotes the domain of $\mathbf{t}$, which consists of the set of positions of the tree, and $\mathsf{alph}(\mathbf{t}) = \mathbb{E}$ denotes the alphabet of the tree. From now on, we informally refer by 'node' to a position x together with the value $\mathbf{t}(x)$.

Given two trees $\mathbf{t}_1 \in \mathit{Trees}(\mathbb{E})$, $\mathbf{t}_2 \in \mathit{Trees}(\mathbb{F})$ such that $pos(\mathbf{t}_1) = pos(\mathbf{t}_2) = P$, we define $\mathbf{t}_1 \otimes \mathbf{t}_2 : P \to (\mathbb{E}\times\mathbb{F})$ as $(\mathbf{t}_1 \otimes \mathbf{t}_2)(x) \stackrel{def}{=} (\mathbf{t}_1(x), \mathbf{t}_2(x))$.

The set of **multi-attribute data trees** over a finite alphabet $\mathbb{A}$ of labels, $\mathbf{k}$ different attributes, and an infinite domain $\mathbb{D}$ is defined as $\mathit{Trees}(\mathbb{A}\times\mathbb{D}^{\mathbf{k}})$. Note that every tree $\mathbf{t} \in \mathit{Trees}(\mathbb{A}\times\mathbb{D}^{\mathbf{k}})$ can be decomposed into two trees $\mathbf{a} \in \mathit{Trees}(\mathbb{A})$ and $\mathbf{d} \in \mathit{Trees}(\mathbb{D}^{\mathbf{k}})$ such that $\mathbf{t} = \mathbf{a} \otimes \mathbf{d}$. Figure 1 shows an example of a multi-attribute data tree. The notation for the set of data values used in a data tree is $data(\mathbf{a} \otimes \mathbf{d}) \stackrel{def}{=} \{\mathbf{d}(x)(i) \mid x \in pos(\mathbf{d}), i \in [\mathbf{k}]\}$. With an abuse of notation we write $data(X)$ to denote all the elements of $\mathbb{D}$ contained in X, for whatever object X may be.

A **forest** is a sequence of trees, and the set of **multi-attribute data forests** over $\mathbb{A}$ and $\mathbf{k}$ is $(\mathit{Trees}(\mathbb{A}\times\mathbb{D}^{\mathbf{k}}))^*$. We will normally use the symbol $\bar{\mathbf{t}}$ for a forest of multi-attribute data trees. That is, $\bar{\mathbf{t}} \in (\mathit{Trees}(\mathbb{A}\times\mathbb{D}^{\mathbf{k}}))^*$. (Note that in particular $\bar{\mathbf{t}}$ can be an *empty* forest.) For any $(a, \bar{d}) \in \mathbb{A} \times \mathbb{D}^{\mathbf{k}}$, let us write $(a, \bar{d})\bar{\mathbf{t}}$ for the multi-attribute data tree that results from adding $(a, \bar{d})$ as a root of $\bar{\mathbf{t}}$. We call this operation **rooting**. We will usually write $\mathbf{t}$ (resp. $\bar{\mathbf{t}}$) to denote multi-attribute data trees (resp. forests) and t (resp. $\bar{t}$) to denote trees (resp. forests) over a finite alphabet.

XPath.

Next we define transitive XPath, the fragment of XPath where all axes are reflexive and transitive.

Transitive XPath is a two-sorted language, with *path* ex-

$$
\begin{array}{llr}
\alpha, \beta ::= o \mid \alpha[\varphi] \mid [\varphi]\alpha \mid \alpha\beta & & o \in \{\varepsilon, \downarrow_*, \uparrow^*, \rightarrow^*, {}^*\!\leftarrow\}\ , \\
\varphi, \psi ::= a \mid \neg\varphi \mid \varphi \wedge \psi \mid \varphi \vee \psi \mid \langle\alpha\rangle \mid \langle \alpha @_i = \beta @_j \rangle \mid \langle \alpha @_i \neq \beta @_j \rangle & & a \in \mathbb{A}, i, j \in [\mathbf{k}]\ .
\end{array}
$$

$$
\begin{array}{rlrl}
[\![\downarrow_*]\!]^{\mathbf{t}} &= \{(x, x{\cdot}i) \mid x{\cdot}i \in pos(\mathbf{t})\}^* & [\![\uparrow^*]\!]^{\mathbf{t}} &= \{(x{\cdot}i, x) \mid x{\cdot}i \in pos(\mathbf{t})\}^* \\
[\![\rightarrow^*]\!]^{\mathbf{t}} &= \{(x{\cdot}i, x{\cdot}(i+1)) \mid x{\cdot}i, x{\cdot}(i+1) \in pos(\mathbf{t})\}^* & [\![{}^*\!\leftarrow]\!]^{\mathbf{t}} &= \{(x{\cdot}(i+1), x{\cdot}i) \mid x{\cdot}i, x{\cdot}(i+1) \in pos(\mathbf{t})\}^* \\
[\![\varepsilon]\!]^{\mathbf{t}} &= \{(x, x) \mid x \in pos(\mathbf{t})\} & [\![\alpha\beta]\!]^{\mathbf{t}} &= \{(x, z) \mid \text{ there exists } y \text{ such that} \\
& & & \quad (x, y) \in [\![\alpha]\!]^{\mathbf{t}}, (y, z) \in [\![\beta]\!]^{\mathbf{t}}\} \\
[\![[\varphi]]\!]^{\mathbf{t}} &= \{(x, x) \in \mid x \in pos(\mathbf{t}), x \in [\![\varphi]\!]^{\mathbf{t}}\} & [\![\langle\alpha\rangle]\!]^{\mathbf{t}} &= \{x \in pos(\mathbf{t}) \mid \exists y.(x, y) \in [\![\alpha]\!]^{\mathbf{t}}\} \\
[\![a]\!]^{\mathbf{t}} &= \{x \in pos(\mathbf{t}) \mid \mathbf{a}(x) = a\} & [\![\varphi \wedge \psi]\!]^{\mathbf{t}} &= [\![\varphi]\!]^{\mathbf{t}} \cap [\![\psi]\!]^{\mathbf{t}} \\
[\![\neg\varphi]\!]^{\mathbf{t}} &= pos(\mathbf{t}) \setminus [\![\varphi]\!]^{\mathbf{t}} & & \\
[\![\langle \alpha @_i = \beta @_j \rangle]\!]^{\mathbf{t}} &= \{x \in pos(\mathbf{t}) \mid \exists y, z\ (x, y) \in [\![\alpha]\!]^{\mathbf{t}}, & [\![\langle \alpha @_i \neq \beta @_j \rangle]\!]^{\mathbf{t}} &= \{x \in pos(\mathbf{t}) \mid \exists y, z\ (x, y) \in [\![\alpha]\!]^{\mathbf{t}}, \\
& \quad (x, z) \in [\![\beta]\!]^{\mathbf{t}}, \mathbf{d}(y)(i) = \mathbf{d}(z)(j)\} & & \quad (x, z) \in [\![\beta]\!]^{\mathbf{t}}, \mathbf{d}(y)(i) \neq \mathbf{d}(z)(j)\}
\end{array}
$$

Figure 2: The syntax of transitive XPath; and its semantics for a multi-attribute data tree $\mathbf{t} = \mathbf{a} \otimes \mathbf{d}$.

pressions (that we write $\alpha, \beta, \gamma, \delta$) and *node* expressions (that we write φ, ψ, η). Path expressions denote binary relations, resulting from composing the descendant, ancestor, preceding sibling and following sibling relations (which are denoted respectively by $\downarrow_*$, $\uparrow^*$, ${}^*\!\leftarrow$, $\rightarrow^*$ respectively), and node expressions. Node expressions are boolean formulas that test a property of a node like, for example, that is has a certain label, or that it has a descendant labeled a with the same data value in attribute i as the attribute j of an ancestor labeled b, which is expressed by $\langle \downarrow_*[a]@_i = \uparrow^*[b]@_j \rangle$. We write XPath($\downarrow_*, \uparrow^*, \rightarrow^*, {}^*\!\leftarrow, =$) to denote this logic, and we write XPath($\mathcal{O}, =$) for some $\mathcal{O} \subseteq \{\downarrow_*, \uparrow^*, \rightarrow^*, {}^*\!\leftarrow\}$, to denote the logic containing only the axes in $\mathcal{O}$. A *formula* of XPath($\downarrow_*, \uparrow^*, \rightarrow^*, {}^*\!\leftarrow, =$) is either a node expression or a path expression of the logic. Its syntax and semantics are defined in Figure 2. As another example, we can select the nodes that have a sibling labeled a to the left whose first attribute is the same as the second attribute of some descendant of a right sibling by the formula $\varphi = \langle {}^*\!\leftarrow[a]@_1 = \rightarrow^*\downarrow_*@_2 \rangle$. Given a tree $\mathbf{t}$ as in Figure 1, we have $[\![\varphi]\!]^{\mathbf{t}} = \{\epsilon, 2, 3, 4, 5, 311\}$.

We write $\mathbf{t}, x \models \varphi$ (resp. $\mathbf{t}, (x, y) \models \alpha$) for $x \in pos(\mathbf{t})$ (resp. $x, y \in pos(\mathbf{t})$) as short for $x \in [\![\varphi]\!]^{\mathbf{t}}$ (resp. $(x, y) \in [\![\alpha]\!]^{\mathbf{t}}$). We write $\mathbf{t} \models \varphi$ as short for $\epsilon \in [\![\varphi]\!]^{\mathbf{t}}$.

In the case of XPath(${}^*\!\leftarrow, \downarrow_*, \rightarrow^*, =$), we also extend the evaluation to multi-attribute data forests. Let $(a, \bar{d})$ be an arbitrary fix element of $\mathbb{A} \times \mathbb{D}^{\mathbf{k}}$. Given a forest $\bar{\mathbf{t}}$ and $x, y \in pos((a, \bar{d})\bar{\mathbf{t}})$, $x, y \neq \epsilon$, we define the satisfaction relation $\models$, as $\bar{\mathbf{t}}, x \models \varphi$ (resp. $\bar{\mathbf{t}}, (x, y) \models \alpha$) if $(a, \bar{d})\bar{\mathbf{t}}, x \models \varphi$ (resp. $(a, \bar{d})\bar{\mathbf{t}}, (x, y) \models \alpha$). (Note that since XPath(${}^*\!\leftarrow, \downarrow_*, \rightarrow^*, =$) has no ascending axes, whether $\bar{\mathbf{t}}, x \models \varphi$ or not does not depend on $(a, \bar{d})$, we use it as a simple way of defining its semantics.)

The **satisfiability problem** for XPath($\mathcal{O}, =$) (henceforth noted SAT-XPath($\mathcal{O}, =$)) is the problem of, given a formula φ of XPath($\mathcal{O}, =$), wether there exists a multi-attribute data tree $\mathbf{t}$ such that $\mathbf{t} \models \varphi$.

3. PROOF SKETCH

The main contribution of this paper is the following.

THEOREM 3.1. *SAT-*XPath(${}^*\!\leftarrow, \downarrow_*, \rightarrow^*, =$) *is decidable in 3*EXPSPACE.

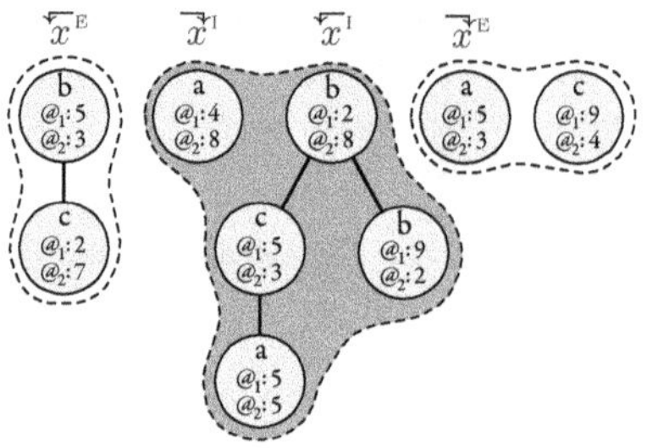

Figure 3: A multi-attribute data forest, with its left and right forests.

We reduce the problem of whether a formula φ of our logic XPath(${}^*\!\leftarrow, \downarrow_*, \rightarrow^*, =$) is satisfiable, to the problem of whether one can obtain an element with a certain property by repeated applications of operations in some algebra, starting from a basic set of elements. We call it the *derivation problem.* First we introduce the algebra (Section 4), we then solve the derivation problem (Section 5) and finally we show the reduction from the logic into the derivation problem (Section 6).

We first introduce *forest profiles* in Section 4, which constitute the algebra domain. A forest profile is an abstraction of a multi-attribute data forest inside a context, where the context consists of the two (possibly empty) forests that are to the left and to the right. Figure 3 depicts one such possible forest, together with the left and right context forests. A forest profile contains, for each data value d and each path expression, the information of whether d can be reached by the path expression, and *where* it can be reached, either

- inside the main forest, starting from the leftmost root (the node $\overrightarrow{x}^{\mathrm{I}}$ in Figure 3),
- inside the main forest but starting with the rightmost root (the node $\overleftarrow{x}^{\mathrm{I}}$ in Figure 3),
- in the left context forest (starting from the node $\overleftarrow{x}^{\mathrm{E}}$ in Figure 3), or
- in the right context forest (starting from the node $\overrightarrow{x}^{\mathrm{E}}$ in Figure 3).

In this setting, path expressions are called *patterns* and their navigation is greatly simplified. Patterns can go first to the left, and then down, or first to the right and then down, or only down. They correspond to path expressions like, for example, $\rightarrow^*[a]\rightarrow^*[b]\downarrow_*[c]\downarrow_*[a \vee b]@_1$, or $^*\!\leftarrow[\neg a]\downarrow_*[a]@_2$. Further, node expressions contained in patterns are simple boolean combinations of tests for labels.

A forest profile also keeps track of a set of important data values called the *rigid values.* These are data values that play a determined function in the forest containing the abstracted forest (*i.e.*, in the concatenation of the left, main and right forests). Intuitively, a data value is rigid in a forest if it can be pinpointed by a path expression, in the sense that it is the *only* data value that can be reached with some path expression $\alpha@_i$. At this level of detail, we just mention that some special care must be taken for these rigid data values.

We equip the set of forest profiles with two operations, one that corresponds to concatenating two of the forests being abstracted, and another operation that corresponds to adding a root to the forest, converting it into a tree. This algebra is introduced in Section 4.2. In particular, the root operation is restricted to work only with forest profiles that are from certain set of *consistent* profiles. Consistent profiles will play an important role in the reduction from the logic to the algebra. The idea is that they are those profiles that are not in contradiction with the formula φ to test for satisfiability, that is, that could abstract subforests of a model of φ.

A *root profile*, is a profile that comes from the application of the root operation with a certain label of a certain alphabet $\mathbb{A}_{root}$ of root labels. An *empty profile* is the profile corresponding to the empty forest with an empty context. In Section 5 we define the *derivation problem* for forest profiles as the problem of whether there is a way of obtaining a root profile from the empty profile by repeated applications of the algebra operations.

We show that the derivation problem is decidable in 2EXPSPACE in Section 5. We first define a partial ordering on profiles in Section 5.2, this ordering will be of chief importance in our decidability result. We show a series of monotonicity properties that show that the set of derivable profiles is upward-closed. The purpose of the partial ordering is to reduce the derivation problem on the infinite set of forest profiles into a problem on a *finite* set of minimal profiles. The fact that the derivable profiles is upward-closed is indeed a key ingredient for this reduction to work.

However, one problem we need to face is that the ordering has infinite antichains: every two profiles with different set of rigid values are incomparable. We tackle this in Section 5.4, where we show that we can bound the set of rigid values, obtaining an equivalent derivation problem on profiles with a small set of rigid values. Once we obtain this bound, the set of minimal profiles becomes finite, doubly exponential. Next, in Section 5.5 we show that, thanks to the monotonicity properties enjoyed by the algebra, we can work only with minimal elements. Finally, in Section 5.6 we give the concrete saturation-style algorithm that solves the derivation problem using doubly exponential space.

In Section 6 we show that the satisfiability problem for XPath($^*\!\leftarrow, \downarrow_*, \rightarrow^*, =$) can be reduced to the derivation problem in EXPSPACE. In Section 6.1 we show a normal form, called *direct unnested normal form*, where direct unnested path expressions correspond, precisely, to the pattern expressions used in the forest profiles (basically all path expressions are of the form already described). We then show in Section 6.2 that one can reduce, in EXPSPACE, the satisfiability problem for formulas in this normal form into the derivation problem, obtaining a 3EXPSPACE decidability procedure for SAT-XPath($^*\!\leftarrow, \downarrow_*, \rightarrow^*, =$), obtaining Theorem 3.1.

4. FOREST PROFILES

We define abstractions of forests of multi-attribute data trees. These are called *forest profiles.* They are the main construct in our solution. One must think of a forest profile as the description, for every data value $d \in \mathbb{D}$, of all the possible ways of reaching the data value d via path expressions of XPath($^*\!\leftarrow, \downarrow_*, \rightarrow^*, =$). Some ways of reaching the data value may lie inside the forest being abstracted, and some outside the forest. Take for instance the forest in the middle of Figure 3. For every forest there we identify 4 nodes: the leftmost root, the rightmost root, the node to the left of the leftmost root (if any), and the node to the right of the rightmost root (if any). These are the nodes identified by $\overleftarrow{x}^{\mathrm{I}}, \overrightarrow{x}^{\mathrm{I}}, \overleftarrow{x}^{\mathrm{E}}, \overrightarrow{x}^{\mathrm{E}}$ respectively in the figure. The profile of this forest is represented by all the paths that can reach the data value 4, all those that can reach 2, etc. Take as an example the data value 5; this data value can be reached by

(i) $\rightarrow^*[a]@_1$ from $\overleftarrow{x}^{\mathrm{E}}$,

(ii) $^*\!\leftarrow[b]\downarrow_*[a]@_1$ from $\overleftarrow{x}^{\mathrm{I}}$,

(iii) $\rightarrow^*[a]\rightarrow^*[b]\downarrow_*[c]@_1$ from $\overrightarrow{x}^{\mathrm{I}}$, etc.

Remember that expressions are evaluated in a forest and, for example, an expression starting with $\rightarrow^*$ denotes the possibility to move forward in the sequence of tree roots of the forest. The idea is that we limit ourselves that whenever there are paths departing from $\overrightarrow{x}^{\mathrm{I}}$ or $\overleftarrow{x}^{\mathrm{I}}$ they must be *internal* to the forest (*i.e.*, internal to the gray forest in Figure 3), whenever there are paths from $\overrightarrow{x}^{\mathrm{E}}$ or $\overleftarrow{x}^{\mathrm{E}}$ they must be *external* to the forest (*i.e.*, either in the forest depicted to the left or to the right of the gray forest in Figure 3).

Let $\mathbb{A}$ be a finite alphabet of **labels**, let $\mathbb{A}_{root} \subseteq \mathbb{A}$ be the set of **root labels**, and let $\mathbb{D}$ be an infinite domain of **data values**. The set $\mathcal{B}(\mathbb{A})$ is the boolean closure of tests for labels from $\mathbb{A}$. For any $a \in \mathbb{A}$ and $\psi \in \mathcal{B}(\mathbb{A})$, we write $a \models \psi$ if the interpretation assigning *true* to a, and *false* to every other $b \in \mathbb{A}$, satisfies ψ. Let $\mathbf{k} \in \mathbb{N}$ be a fixed natural number, corresponding to the number of **attributes** at each node. We say that $i \in [\mathbf{k}]$ is an **attribute index**. We define the set of **patterns**, as any finite, subword-closed, subset of $(\mathcal{B}(\mathbb{A}))^*$, and we denote it by $\mathcal{P}$. We generally use the symbols $\alpha, \beta, \gamma, \delta \in \mathcal{P}$ to denote patterns. For every label $a \in \mathbb{A}$ we define the following set of patterns $\boldsymbol{\sigma}_a \subseteq \mathcal{P}$

$$\boldsymbol{\sigma}_a \stackrel{def}{=} \{\psi_1 \cdots \psi_k \in \mathcal{P} \mid a \models \psi_1 \wedge \cdots \wedge \psi_k\}.$$

Note that $\epsilon \in \boldsymbol{\sigma}_a$. The set of **composed patterns** is

$$\Pi \stackrel{def}{=} (\mathcal{P} \setminus \{\epsilon\}) \times \mathcal{P} \times [\mathbf{k}].$$

The intended meaning is that the first component operates on the siblings, the second on a downward path, and the third retrieves a data value from an attribute index. We will sometimes use the symbol $\bar{\alpha}$ to represent elements from

Π, or (α, β, i) if we need to explicit the components of the composed pattern.

A **forest profile** $\mathfrak{f}$ is a tuple

$$\mathfrak{f} = (\overleftarrow{\chi}^{\mathrm{E}}, \overrightarrow{\chi}^{\mathrm{I}}, \overleftarrow{\chi}^{\mathrm{I}}, \overrightarrow{\chi}^{\mathrm{E}}, R)$$

where $R \subseteq \mathbb{D}$, and we call it the set of **rigid values** of $\mathfrak{f}$, and $\overleftarrow{\chi}^{\mathrm{E}}, \overrightarrow{\chi}^{\mathrm{I}}, \overleftarrow{\chi}^{\mathrm{I}}, \overrightarrow{\chi}^{\mathrm{E}} \subseteq \mathbb{D} \times \Pi$, and we call them the set of left/right external/internal **descriptions** respectively. In the example before, one shall interpret (i) as $(5, a, \epsilon, 1) \in \overrightarrow{\chi}^{\mathrm{E}}$, (ii) as $(5, b, a, 1) \in \overleftarrow{\chi}^{\mathrm{I}}$ and (iii) as $(5, a{\cdot}b, c, 1) \in \overrightarrow{\chi}^{\mathrm{I}}$. We use χ to denote a subset of $\mathbb{D} \times \Pi$; and we write $\bar{\chi}$ (resp. $\bar{\chi}_i$) to denote the 4-uple $(\overleftarrow{\chi}^{\mathrm{E}}, \overrightarrow{\chi}^{\mathrm{I}}, \overleftarrow{\chi}^{\mathrm{I}}, \overrightarrow{\chi}^{\mathrm{E}})$ (resp. $(\overleftarrow{\chi}_i^{\mathrm{E}}, \overrightarrow{\chi}_i^{\mathrm{I}}, \overleftarrow{\chi}_i^{\mathrm{I}}, \overrightarrow{\chi}_i^{\mathrm{E}})$). Likewise, we use $\mathfrak{f}$ (resp. $\mathfrak{f}_i$) to denote $(\bar{\chi}, R)$ (resp. $(\bar{\chi}_i, R_i)$).

We define, for every $\chi \subseteq \mathbb{D} \times \Pi$,

$$\chi(d) \stackrel{def}{=} \{(\alpha, \beta, i) \in \Pi \mid (d, \alpha, \beta, i) \in \chi\},$$

$$\chi(\alpha, \beta, i) \stackrel{def}{=} \{d \in \mathbb{D} \mid (d, \alpha, \beta, i) \in \chi\}, \text{ and}$$

$$\bar{\chi}(d) \stackrel{def}{=} (\overleftarrow{\chi}^{\mathrm{E}}(d), \overrightarrow{\chi}^{\mathrm{I}}(d), \overleftarrow{\chi}^{\mathrm{I}}(d), \overrightarrow{\chi}^{\mathrm{E}}(d)).$$

We define $data(\mathfrak{f}) \stackrel{def}{=} R \cup \{d \in \mathbb{D} \mid \bar{\chi}(d) \neq (\emptyset, \emptyset, \emptyset, \emptyset)\}$. We call $data(\mathfrak{f}) \setminus R$ the set of **flexible values** of $\mathfrak{f}$. We use the symbol $\bar{\pi}$ to denote $(\overleftarrow{\pi}^{\mathrm{E}}, \overrightarrow{\pi}^{\mathrm{I}}, \overleftarrow{\pi}^{\mathrm{I}}, \overrightarrow{\pi}^{\mathrm{E}})$ where $\overleftarrow{\pi}^{\mathrm{E}}, \overrightarrow{\pi}^{\mathrm{I}}, \overleftarrow{\pi}^{\mathrm{I}}, \overrightarrow{\pi}^{\mathrm{E}} \subseteq \Pi$. We further say that $\bar{\pi}$ is **the description of** $d \in \mathbb{D}$ **in** $\mathfrak{f}$ if $\bar{\chi}(d) = \bar{\pi}$.

4.1 Rigid and flexible values

In a forest satisfying some XPath formula, different data values have different roles. We distinguish here two categories of data values: rigid and flexible. Rigid data values are important for the satisfaction of the formula and special care is needed to treat these, whereas flexible values are not crucial, and they can be sometimes removed from the tree. Let us give some more precise intuition. We use the logic XPath to make this intuition clear, but we will then state the definitions in terms of forest profiles.

Given a multi-attribute data forest $\bar{\mathbf{t}}$ where $\bar{\mathbf{t}}, i \models \varphi$, suppose there is a data value d such that: there is some position $1 \leq j \leq |\bar{\mathbf{t}}|$ and some path expression α of φ of the form $\alpha = \rightarrow^* \beta@_k$ or $\alpha = {}^*\!\!\leftarrow \beta@_k$ so that d is the *only* data value that can be reached through α from j. When there is such a d we call it a **rigid value** for j, since the logic can identify it and pinpoint it from the rest of the data values. If d is rigid for at least one position $j \in \{1, \dots, |\bar{\mathbf{t}}|\}$ we say that d is rigid for $\bar{\mathbf{t}}$. All the remaining data values of $\bar{\mathbf{t}}$ (which are the **flexible values**) play the role of assuring that "there are at least two data values reachable through α from position j" for some α and j. As such, its importance is only relative. In particular, if $\bar{\mathbf{t}}$ is a forest satisfying φ and containing d as a flexible value, consider $\bar{\mathbf{t}}'$ as the result of replacing, for some fresh data value d', every tree $\mathbf{t}''$ of $\bar{\mathbf{t}}$ with the forest $\mathbf{t}''{\cdot}(\mathbf{t}''[d \mapsto d'])$, where $\mathbf{t}''[d \mapsto d']$ is the result of replacing the data value d with d' in $\mathbf{t}''$, and leaving all the structures and labels as they were. Indeed, $\bar{\mathbf{t}}'$ will continue to satisfy φ; but this is not necessarily true if d was a rigid value. The same notions hold for our algebra on forest profiles. This is a key property that we need to exploit and hence the need to make explicit the set of rigid values of any given profile. We formalize this by defining an ordering on profiles corresponding to the operation just described, so that the forest profile abstracting $\bar{\mathbf{t}}'$ is bigger than the profile abstracting $\bar{\mathbf{t}}$. We make explicit (in Lemma 5.1) the aforementioned argument as a monotonicity property of the algebra.

We say that a forest profile $\mathfrak{f} = (\bar{\chi}, R)$ is **valid** if every $d \in \mathbb{D}$ so that $\overrightarrow{\chi}^{\mathrm{E}}(\alpha, \beta, i) = \{d\}$ or $\overleftarrow{\chi}^{\mathrm{E}}(\alpha, \beta, i) = \{d\}$ for some $(\alpha, \beta, i) \in \Pi$, is in R. We define $\mathfrak{F}$ as the set of all valid profiles.

4.2 Algebra

We equip $\mathfrak{F}$ with two operations. The idea is that these operations correspond to the *concatenation* of two forests, and to the addition of a root to a forest (called *rooting*), turning it into a tree.

Preliminaries

The set of **root patterns** of a forest profile $\mathfrak{f}$, denoted by $[\mathfrak{f}]\!\!\rightarrow, \leftarrow\!\![\mathfrak{f}] \subseteq \mathcal{P}$ is defined as follows

$$[\mathfrak{f}]\!\!\rightarrow \stackrel{def}{=} \{\alpha \mid (d, \alpha, \beta, i) \in \overrightarrow{\chi}^{\mathrm{I}} \text{ for some } d, \beta, i\},$$

$$\leftarrow\!\![\mathfrak{f}] \stackrel{def}{=} \{\alpha \mid (d, \alpha, \beta, i) \in \overleftarrow{\chi}^{\mathrm{I}} \text{ for some } d, \beta, i\}.$$

Given $P \subseteq \mathcal{P}$ and $\chi \subseteq \mathbb{D} \times \Pi$, we define the **extension of** χ **by** P, denoted by $P{\cdot}\chi$, as the set

$$P{\cdot}\chi \stackrel{def}{=} \chi \cup \{(d, \alpha' \cdot \alpha, \beta, i) \in \mathbb{D} \times \Pi \mid (d, \alpha, \beta, i) \in \chi, \alpha' \in P\}.$$

It is easy to see that the extension operation distributes over union (*i.e.*, $P{\cdot}(\chi \cup \chi') = P{\cdot}\chi \cup P{\cdot}\chi'$ and $(P \cup P'){\cdot}\chi = P{\cdot}\chi \cup P'{\cdot}\chi$).

Fingerprints

We now define the *fingerprint* of a forest profile. It contains a summary information, sufficient to decide whether the tree abstracted by the profile satisfies a formula of XPath—as we show in Section 6.

Let $\mathcal{A} = \{\overleftarrow{\circ}, \overrightarrow{\circ}, \circ^{\downarrow}, \circ\}$. Given a profile $\mathfrak{f} \in \mathfrak{F}$ and $a \in \mathcal{A}$, we define the set $\mathfrak{f}.\chi_a$ as

- $\overleftarrow{\chi}^{\mathrm{I}} \cup \leftarrow\!\![\mathfrak{f}]{\cdot}\overleftarrow{\chi}^{\mathrm{E}}$ if $a = \overleftarrow{\circ}$,
- $\overrightarrow{\chi}^{\mathrm{I}} \cup [\mathfrak{f}]\!\!\rightarrow{\cdot}\overrightarrow{\chi}^{\mathrm{E}}$ if $a = \overrightarrow{\circ}$,
- $\{(d, \alpha', \beta, i) \in \mathbb{D} \times \Pi \mid \exists \alpha.(d, \alpha, \beta, i) \in \overleftarrow{\chi}^{\mathrm{I}} \cup \overrightarrow{\chi}^{\mathrm{I}}\}$ if $a = \circ^{\downarrow}$, or
- $\{(d, \alpha, \beta, i) \in \overrightarrow{\chi}^{\mathrm{I}} \cup \overleftarrow{\chi}^{\mathrm{I}} \mid \beta = \epsilon\}$ if $a = \circ$.

Note that $\mathfrak{f}.\chi_a(\alpha, \beta, i)$ is independent of α when $a = \circ^{\downarrow}$, but it takes an element of Π as argument for the sake of uniformity of notation. The **fingerprint** of a profile $\mathfrak{f}$, noted $\xi(\mathfrak{f})$, is an element of

$$\mathcal{F} \stackrel{def}{=} \Pi \times \mathcal{A} \to \{0, 1, 2+\} \quad \cup \quad \Pi \times \mathcal{A} \times \Pi \times \mathcal{A} \to \{0, 1+\},$$

where for $\bar{\alpha}, \bar{\alpha}' \in \Pi$, $a, a' \in \mathcal{A}$, we define $\xi(\mathfrak{f})(\bar{\alpha}, a, \bar{\alpha}', a')$ as 0 or 1+ depending on whether $|\mathfrak{f}.\chi_a(\bar{\alpha}) \cap \mathfrak{f}.\chi_{a'}(\bar{\alpha}')| = 0$ or not; and we define $\xi(\mathfrak{f})(\bar{\alpha}, a)$ as 0, 1, or 2+ depending on $|\mathfrak{f}.\chi_a(\bar{\alpha})|$ being 0, 1 or greater than 1 respectively.

We fix the set of **consistent fingerprints**, as a set of fingerprints $\Gamma \subseteq \mathcal{F}$. The usefulness of this set will become apparent in the reduction from XPath to the derivation problem of forest profiles in Section 6.2, but we can anticipate that this set will represent all the profiles abstracting multi-attribute data trees that do not contradict the formula we are trying to satisfy. For the moment, however, the reader may simply consider Γ as a given arbitrary set of fingerprints.

Concatenation

For every two $\mathfrak{f}_1, \mathfrak{f}_2 \in \mathfrak{F}$ so that

(a) $R_1 = R_2$,

(b) $\overrightarrow{\chi}_1^{\mathrm{E}} = \overrightarrow{\chi}_2^{\mathrm{I}} \cup [\mathfrak{f}_2\rangle \cdot \overrightarrow{\chi}_2^{\mathrm{E}}$, and

(c) $\overleftarrow{\chi}_2^{\mathrm{E}} = \overleftarrow{\chi}_1^{\mathrm{I}} \cup \langle\mathfrak{f}_1] \cdot \overleftarrow{\chi}_1^{\mathrm{E}}$;

we define the **concatenation** of $\mathfrak{f}_1$ and $\mathfrak{f}_2$, denoted as $\mathfrak{f}_1 + \mathfrak{f}_2$ as $\mathfrak{f}_3$, where

$$R_3 = R_1 = R_2 \qquad (+1)$$

$$\overrightarrow{\chi}_3^{\mathrm{E}} = \overrightarrow{\chi}_2^{\mathrm{E}} \qquad (+2)$$

$$\overleftarrow{\chi}_3^{\mathrm{E}} = \overleftarrow{\chi}_1^{\mathrm{E}} \qquad (+3)$$

$$\overrightarrow{\chi}_3^{\mathrm{I}} = \overrightarrow{\chi}_1^{\mathrm{I}} \cup [\mathfrak{f}_1\rangle \cdot \overrightarrow{\chi}_2^{\mathrm{I}} \qquad (+4)$$

$$\overleftarrow{\chi}_3^{\mathrm{I}} = \overrightarrow{\chi}_2^{\mathrm{I}} \cup \langle\mathfrak{f}_2] \cdot \overleftarrow{\chi}_1^{\mathrm{I}}. \qquad (+5)$$

Notice that

- the concatenation is associative ($(\mathfrak{f}_1 + \mathfrak{f}_2) + \mathfrak{f}_3 = \mathfrak{f}_1 + (\mathfrak{f}_2 + \mathfrak{f}_3)$),
- the extension operation $\cdot$ distributes over the concatenation operation $+$ ($[\mathfrak{f}_1 + \mathfrak{f}_2\rangle \cdot \chi = [\mathfrak{f}_1\rangle \cdot ([\mathfrak{f}_2\rangle \cdot \chi)$),
- if $\mathfrak{f}_1 + \mathfrak{f}_2 = \mathfrak{f}_3$ and $\mathfrak{f}_1, \mathfrak{f}_2 \in \mathfrak{F}$, then $\mathfrak{f}_3 \in \mathfrak{F}$.

Rooting

Given $a \in \mathbb{A}$, and $\bar{d} \in \mathbb{D}^{\mathbf{k}}$, we define $(a, \bar{d})\mathfrak{f}_1 \subseteq \mathfrak{F}$, where $\mathfrak{f}_2 \in (a, \bar{d})\mathfrak{f}_1$ if

(a) $\xi(\mathfrak{f}_2) \in \Gamma$,

(b) $\overrightarrow{\chi}_1^{\mathrm{E}} = \overleftarrow{\chi}_1^{\mathrm{E}} = \emptyset$,

(c) $\overrightarrow{\chi}_2^{\mathrm{I}} = \overleftarrow{\chi}_2^{\mathrm{I}} = \{(d, \alpha, \beta \cdot \gamma, i) \in \mathbb{D} \times \Pi \mid \exists \alpha'.(d, \alpha', \gamma, i) \in \overrightarrow{\chi}_1^{\mathrm{I}} \cup \overleftarrow{\chi}_1^{\mathrm{I}}, \alpha, \beta \in \boldsymbol{\sigma}_a\} \cup \bigcup_{i \in [\mathbf{k}]} (\{\bar{d}(i)\} \times (\boldsymbol{\sigma}_a \setminus \{\epsilon\}) \times \boldsymbol{\sigma}_a \times \{i\})$

We say that $\mathfrak{f}_2$ is a **rooting of $\mathfrak{f}_1$ with** $(a, \bar{d})$.

Notice that since the root pattern of any pair of profiles $\mathfrak{f}_1, \mathfrak{f}_2 \in (a, \bar{d})\mathfrak{f}_3$ is the same, it is idempotent and absorbing ($[\mathfrak{f}_1\rangle \cdot [\mathfrak{f}_2\rangle \cdot \chi = [\mathfrak{f}_1\rangle \cdot \chi = [\mathfrak{f}_2\rangle \cdot \chi$, $[\mathfrak{f}_1\rangle \cdot \overrightarrow{\chi}_1^{\mathrm{I}} = \overrightarrow{\chi}_1^{\mathrm{I}}$).

4.3 The derivation problem

We define the **empty profile** as $\mathfrak{f}_\emptyset \stackrel{def}{=} (\emptyset, \emptyset, \emptyset, \emptyset, \emptyset)$. Note that $\mathfrak{f}_\emptyset \in \mathfrak{F}$. The set of profiles that can be obtained from empty profiles by applying the rooting and concatenation operations is called the set of **derivable profiles**, and noted $\mathfrak{D}$. We say that $\mathfrak{f}$ is a **derivable root profile** if $\overrightarrow{\chi}^{\mathrm{E}} = \overleftarrow{\chi}^{\mathrm{E}} = \emptyset$ and $\mathfrak{f} \in (a, \bar{d})\mathfrak{f}'$ for some $\mathfrak{f}' \in \mathfrak{D}$, $a \in \mathbb{A}_{root}$ and $\bar{d} \in \mathbb{D}^{\mathbf{k}}$. Let a **derivation tree** for $\mathfrak{f}$ be a tree t whose every node is labeled by a forest profile and an element from $\mathbb{A} \times \mathbb{D}^{\mathbf{k}}$, except the leaves that are labeled only by the forest profile $\mathfrak{f}_\emptyset$ and

- the root is labeled with $\mathfrak{f}$,
- every internal node x of t labeled with a forest profile $\mathfrak{f}'$ and $(a, \bar{d})$ is so that $\mathfrak{f}' \in (a, \bar{d})(\mathfrak{f}_1 + \cdots + \mathfrak{f}_n)$, where $\mathfrak{f}_1, \ldots, \mathfrak{f}_n$ are the labels of the children of x.

Similarly, a **derivation forest** $\bar{t}$ for $\mathfrak{f}$ is a forest of derivation trees $\bar{t} = t_1 \cdots t_n$ for some profiles $\mathfrak{f}_1, \ldots, \mathfrak{f}_n$ so that $\mathfrak{f} = \mathfrak{f}_1 + \cdots + \mathfrak{f}_n$. Therefore, a profile $\mathfrak{f}$ is derivable if, and only if, there is a derivation forest for $\mathfrak{f}$.

We can now state the *derivation problem*, that is, whether there exists a derivable root profile, given $\mathbb{A}$, $\mathbb{A}_{root}$, $\mathcal{P}$ and Γ.

PROBLEM:	**The derivation problem**
INPUT:	A finite alphabet $\mathbb{A}$, $\mathbb{A}_{root} \subseteq \mathbb{A}$, a set of patterns $\mathcal{P}$, a set of fingerprints $\Gamma \subseteq \mathcal{F}$.
QUESTION:	Is there a derivable root profile?

In the next section we show that this problem is decidable. Later, in Section 6, we show that this problem is reducible from SAT-XPath($^*\!\!\leftarrow, \downarrow_*, \rightarrow^*, =$).

5. COMPUTING DERIVABLE PROFILES

In this section we solve the derivation problem, showing that it is decidable in 2EXPSPACE. To show this problem we work with some partial ordering on forest profiles (Section 5.2) that has some good monotonicity closure properties with our forest profile algebra (Section 5.3). This allows us to reduce the problem to a restricted derivation problem in which solutions can be found by only inspecting profiles with a bounded number of rigid values (Section 5.4), that are minimal elements of the ordering (Section 5.5). These are bounded and computable, allowing us to produce an algorithm solving the problem (Section 5.6).

5.1 Preliminaries

Given $\mathfrak{f}_1, \mathfrak{f}_2 \in \mathfrak{F}$ we define that $\mathfrak{f}_1$ and $\mathfrak{f}_2$ are **equivalent**, and we note it $\mathfrak{f}_1 \sim \mathfrak{f}_2$, if there is some bijection $g : \mathbb{D} \to \mathbb{D}$ so that $\mathfrak{f}_2$ is the result of replacing d by $g(d)$ in $\mathfrak{f}_1$; in this case we write $g(\mathfrak{f}_1) = \mathfrak{f}_2$. For a set $C \subseteq \mathfrak{F}$, we write $\mathfrak{f} \in_{\sim} C$ if there is $\mathfrak{f}' \sim \mathfrak{f}$ so that $\mathfrak{f}' \in C$. Given a forest profile $\mathfrak{f}$ and two data values $d \in data(\mathfrak{f})$, $d' \notin data(\mathfrak{f})$, we define $\mathfrak{f}[d \mapsto d']$ as the result of replacing d by d' in $\mathfrak{f}$. Note that $\mathfrak{f}[d \mapsto d'] \sim \mathfrak{f}$. Given two data values d, d' we write $\mathfrak{f}[d \mapsto d, d']$ to denote $\mathfrak{f}'$ where $R' = R$, $\bar{\chi}'(d') = \bar{\chi}(d)$ and $\bar{\chi}'(e) = \bar{\chi}(e)$ for every other $e \neq d'$. Note that if $d \in data(\mathfrak{f}) \setminus R$ and $d' \notin data(\mathfrak{f})$, we have that if $\mathfrak{f} \in \mathfrak{F}$ then $\mathfrak{f}[d \mapsto d, d'] \in \mathfrak{F}$.

We say that a data value $d \in \mathbb{D}$ is an **external data value** of $\mathfrak{f}$ if $\overleftarrow{\chi}^{\mathrm{E}}(d) \cup \overrightarrow{\chi}^{\mathrm{E}}(d) \neq \emptyset$. If further $\overrightarrow{\chi}^{\mathrm{I}}(d) \cap \overleftarrow{\chi}^{\mathrm{I}}(d) = \emptyset$, we say that d is a **strict external data value** of $\mathfrak{f}$. If $d \in data(\mathfrak{f})$ is not a strict external data value, it is then an **internal data value**, and if it is not en external data value, it is then a **strict internal data value**.

5.2 Ordering on profiles

We define a partial order $\preceq$ on forest profiles, that follows from our discussion of Section 4 on the role of flexible and rigid data values. It is the order in which we can make a profile bigger by adding a fresh data value to it, with the same description as that of a flexible data value already contained in it.

Given $\mathfrak{f}_1, \mathfrak{f}_2 \in \mathfrak{F}$, we define $\mathfrak{f}_1 \preceq \mathfrak{f}_2$ if either $\mathfrak{f}_1 = \mathfrak{f}_2$, or there is a flexible datum d of $\mathfrak{f}_1$ so that $\mathfrak{f}_1[d \mapsto d, d'] \preceq \mathfrak{f}_2$ for some $d' \notin data(\mathfrak{f}_1)$. Note that $\preceq$ is recursive, reflexive and transitive, and it is hence a partial order.

Note that if $\mathfrak{f}_1 \preceq \mathfrak{f}_2$ then $\langle\mathfrak{f}_1] = \langle\mathfrak{f}_2]$ and $[\mathfrak{f}_1\rangle = [\mathfrak{f}_2\rangle$. Note also that if $\mathfrak{f} \preceq \mathfrak{f}'$ then $\xi(\mathfrak{f}) = \xi(\mathfrak{f}')$.

We write $\mathfrak{f} \precsim \mathfrak{f}'$ if $\mathfrak{f} \preceq \mathfrak{f}''$ for some $\mathfrak{f}'' \sim \mathfrak{f}'$. We say that a set of forest profiles $G \subseteq \mathfrak{F}$ is **upward closed** (resp. **downward closed**) with respect to $\precsim$, if for every $\mathfrak{f} \in G$ and $\mathfrak{f}' \succsim \mathfrak{f}$ (resp. $\mathfrak{f} \succsim \mathfrak{f}'$), we have $\mathfrak{f}' \in G$. We write

$$\uparrow G \stackrel{def}{=} \{\mathfrak{f} \in \mathfrak{F} \mid \mathfrak{f} \succsim \mathfrak{f}' \text{ for some } \mathfrak{f}' \in G\}$$

$$\downarrow G \stackrel{def}{=} \{\mathfrak{f} \in \mathfrak{F} \mid \mathfrak{f}' \succsim \mathfrak{f} \text{ for some } \mathfrak{f}' \in G\}$$

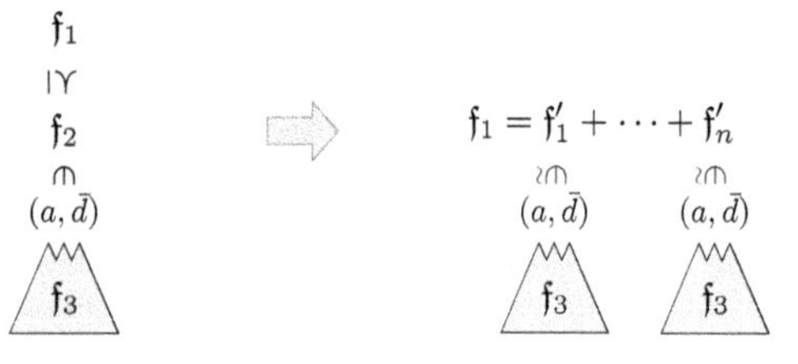

Figure 4: Statement of Lemma 5.1.

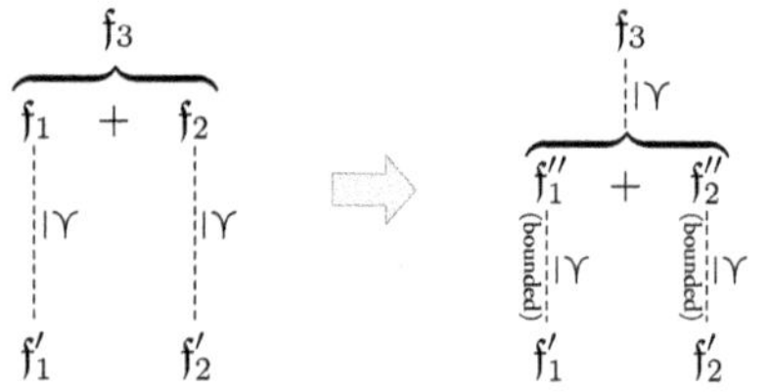

Figure 5: Statement of Lemma 5.3.

for the upward and downward closure of G with respect to $\precsim$. We say that G is $\uparrow\downarrow$-closed, if it is both upward and downward closed, that is, $G = \uparrow\downarrow G$.

5.3 Monotonicity properties

In order to devise an algorithm that tests the existence of a derivable root profile, we will need some monotonicity lemmas evidencing the relationship between $\preceq$ and the rooting and concatenation operations on profiles. The ultimate goal of these lemmas is to restrict the derivation problem to profiles that are *minimal* with respect to $\precsim$.

The next Lemma 5.1 states that for any two profiles $\mathfrak{f}_1 \succeq \mathfrak{f}_2$, $\mathfrak{f}_1$ can be seen as a concatenation of profiles that share the same descriptions of internal values as $\mathfrak{f}_1$, under certain restrictions, as it is shown next. This is a crucial property that follows from our discussion in Section 4.1.

LEMMA 5.1 (FIGURE 4). *For every $\mathfrak{f}_1 \succeq \mathfrak{f}_2 \in (a,\bar{d})\mathfrak{f}_3$, there is $n \in \mathbb{N}$, and $\mathfrak{f}'_i \Subset (a,\bar{d})\mathfrak{f}_3$ for every $i \in [n]$ so that*

$$\mathfrak{f}_1 = \mathfrak{f}'_1 + \cdots + \mathfrak{f}'_n.$$

The lemma above implies that the set of derivable profiles is upward closed.

LEMMA 5.2. *$\mathfrak{D} = \uparrow\mathfrak{D}$.*

We finally state two other monotonicity properties that will be required to reduce the derivation problem into a similar problem that works only with minimal profiles in Section 5.5.

We say that a profile $\mathfrak{f}'$ is a **bounded extension** of a profile $\mathfrak{f}$ if $\mathfrak{f} \preceq \mathfrak{f}'$ and $|data(\mathfrak{f}')| \leq |data(\mathfrak{f})| + 3|\Pi|^4$. The following lemma tells us that for any $G \subseteq \mathfrak{F}$ and any profiles $\mathfrak{f}_1, \mathfrak{f}_2 \in \uparrow G$, there are bounded extensions $\mathfrak{f}''_1, \mathfrak{f}''_2$ of profiles of G so that $\mathfrak{f}''_1 + \mathfrak{f}''_2 \precsim \mathfrak{f}_1 + \mathfrak{f}_2$, as in Figure 5.

LEMMA 5.3 (FIGURE 5). *If $\mathfrak{f}_1 + \mathfrak{f}_2 = \mathfrak{f}_3$ and $\mathfrak{f}'_1 \preceq \mathfrak{f}_1$, $\mathfrak{f}'_2 \preceq \mathfrak{f}_2$, then $\mathfrak{f}''_1 + \mathfrak{f}''_2 \preceq \mathfrak{f}_3$, for some $\mathfrak{f}''_1, \mathfrak{f}''_2 \in \mathfrak{F}$ so that $\mathfrak{f}''_i$ is a bounded extension of $\mathfrak{f}'_i$, for all $i \in \{1,2\}$.*

A similar lemma holds for the rooting operation.

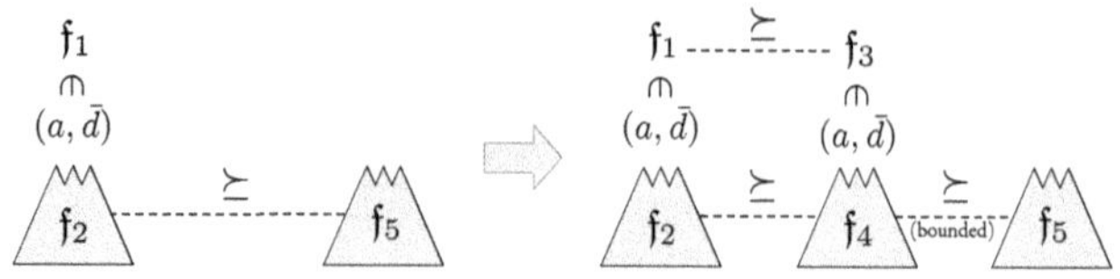

Figure 6: Statement of Lemma 5.4.

LEMMA 5.4 (FIGURE 6). *For every $\mathfrak{f}_1 \in (a,\bar{d})\mathfrak{f}_2$ and $\mathfrak{f}_2 \succeq \mathfrak{f}_5$, there is $\mathfrak{f}_4 \succeq \mathfrak{f}_5$ and $\mathfrak{f}_3 \Subset (a,\bar{d})\mathfrak{f}_4$ so that $|data(\mathfrak{f}_4)| \leq |data(\mathfrak{f}_5)| + |\Pi|^4 + |R_1|$ and $\mathfrak{f}_3 \preceq \mathfrak{f}_1$, $\mathfrak{f}_4 \preceq \mathfrak{f}_2$.*

5.4 Bounding the rigid values

In this section we show that we can reduce the derivation problem into a similar problem where all the profiles have boundedly many rigid values. This will be combined with the result of the next sections, stating that the derivation problem restricted to profiles with boundedly many rigid values is decidable in 2EXPSPACE, to solve the derivation problem.

LEMMA 5.5. *If there is a derivable root profile, then there is a derivation tree for a root profile so that all the profiles in the forest have no more than $2|\Pi|$ rigid values.*

Let $\mathfrak{F}_b$ be the set of all $\mathfrak{f} \in \mathfrak{F}$ that have no more than $2|\Pi|$ rigid values. Let $\mathfrak{D}_b$ be the set of derivable profiles restricted to $\mathfrak{F}_b$.

REMARK 5.6. *By Lemma 5.5 and in light of the definition of bounded extension, it follows that Lemma 5.4, when applied to profiles of $\mathfrak{F}_b$, yields a profile $\mathfrak{f}_4$ that is a* bounded extension *of $\mathfrak{f}_5$.*

By the Lemma just shown, we have the following

LEMMA 5.7. *There is a derivable root profile in $\mathfrak{D}$ if and only if there is a derivable root profile in $\mathfrak{D}_b$.*

We have then reduced the derivation problem into a simpler problem, the **bounded derivation problem**: testing whether there is a derivable root profile in $\mathfrak{D}_b$.

REMARK 5.8. *We have that $\mathfrak{D}_b$ is upward closed since $\mathfrak{D}$ is upward closed. That is, $\mathfrak{D}_b = \uparrow\mathfrak{D}_b$.*

Note that $\mathfrak{F}_b$ has boundedly many $\precsim$-minimal elements. In the next section we show how to restrict the problem to a problem that uses only these $\precsim$-minimal profiles. We will show how this yields a 2EXPSPACE algorithm in Section 5.6.

5.5 Restricting to minimal elements

Thanks to the result from the previous section stating that $\mathfrak{D}_b$ is upward closed, we can now show that we can work only with the minimal elements of $\mathfrak{F}_b$. The main necessary property concerns all those profiles $\mathfrak{f}' \in \mathfrak{F}_b$ that are '$\precsim$-related' to a profile $\mathfrak{f}'' \in \mathfrak{D}_b$, in the sense that $\mathfrak{f}' \succsim \mathfrak{f} \precsim \mathfrak{f}'' \in \mathfrak{D}_b$ for some $\mathfrak{f}$. (Note that this set of profiles is precisely $\uparrow\downarrow\mathfrak{D}_b$.) The property states that the forest profiles algebra preserves the $\precsim$-relatedness.

Given $G \subseteq \mathfrak{F}_b$, let

$$\boldsymbol{R}^{(a,\bar{d})}_{up}(G) \stackrel{def}{=} \{\mathfrak{f} \in \mathfrak{F}_b \mid \mathfrak{f} \in (a,\bar{d})\mathfrak{f}', \mathfrak{f}' \in G\}$$

for $(a,\bar{d}) \in \mathbb{A} \times \mathbb{D}^{\mathsf{k}}$,

$$R_{up}(G) \stackrel{def}{=} \bigcup_{(a,\bar{d})\in\mathbb{A}\times\mathbb{D}^{\mathbf{k}}} R_{up}^{(a,\bar{d})}(G),$$

$$R_{+}(G) \stackrel{def}{=} \{\mathfrak{f} \in \mathfrak{F}_b \mid \mathfrak{f} = \mathfrak{f}_1 + \mathfrak{f}_2 \text{ where } \mathfrak{f}_1, \mathfrak{f}_2 \in G\},$$

$$R(G) \stackrel{def}{=} R_{up}(G) \cup R_{+}(G).$$

LEMMA 5.9. $R(\uparrow\downarrow\mathfrak{D}_b) \subseteq \downarrow\mathfrak{D}_b$.

5.6 The algorithm

In this section we show how to compute, in 2EXPSPACE, whether there exists a derivable root profile in $\mathfrak{D}_b$, solving thus the derivation problem.

For $G \subseteq \mathfrak{F}_b$, we define $G^{\sim} \stackrel{def}{=} \{\mathfrak{f} \mid \mathfrak{f} \sim \mathfrak{f}' \text{ for some } \mathfrak{f}' \in G\}$. We define $G/{\sim}$ as the set containing one representative profile of G for each $\sim$-equivalence class. We define MIN(G) as the set of $\precsim$-minimal elements of G,

$$\text{MIN}(G) \stackrel{def}{=} \{\mathfrak{f} \in G \mid \text{for all } \mathfrak{f}' \in G \text{ so that } \mathfrak{f}' \precsim \mathfrak{f} \text{ we have } \mathfrak{f} \sim \mathfrak{f}'\}.$$

For any $\mathfrak{f} \in \mathfrak{F}$, we write $|\mathfrak{f}|$—the **size** of $\mathfrak{f}$—, as the size needed to write $\mathfrak{f}$. Note that for all $\mathfrak{f} \in \text{MIN}(\mathfrak{F}_b)$, $|\mathfrak{f}|$ is at most exponential in $|\mathcal{P}|$. For any $G \subseteq \mathfrak{F}$, we write $|G|$ to denote $\sum_{\mathfrak{f}\in G} |\mathfrak{f}|$.

Let us define C_i for every $i \in \mathbb{N}_0$ as

$$C_0 \stackrel{def}{=} \{\mathfrak{f}_\emptyset\},$$

$$C_{i+1} \stackrel{def}{=} C_i \cup \text{MIN}(\downarrow R(\uparrow\downarrow C_i))/{\sim}.$$

Let $k_0 \in \mathbb{N}_0$ be the first index so that $C_{k_0}^{\sim} = C_{k_0+1}^{\sim}$.

REMARK 5.10. *For every $i \in \mathbb{N}_0$, $C_i \subseteq \text{MIN}(\mathfrak{F}_b)$.*

As a consequence of the property of the preceding section, we have that this algorithm computes MIN($\downarrow\mathfrak{D}_b$).

LEMMA 5.11. $C_{k_0}^{\sim} = \text{MIN}(\downarrow\mathfrak{D}_b)$.

We further have that this computation is in 2EXPSPACE since $|\text{MIN}(\mathfrak{F}_b)/{\sim}|$ is doubly exponential in $|\mathcal{P}|$, hence we obtain the following.

PROPOSITION 5.12. *The derivation problem is decidable in 2EXPSPACE.*

6. FROM XPATH TO FOREST PROFILES

In this section we reduce the satisfiability problem for XPath($^*\!\leftarrow, \downarrow_*, \rightarrow^*, =$) into the derivation problem for forest profiles.

In Section 6.1 we define a normal form for XPath($^*\!\leftarrow, \downarrow_*, \rightarrow^*, =$), called *direct unnested normal form*, and in Section 6.2 we show the reduction from the satisfiability problem of direct unnested XPath($^*\!\leftarrow, \downarrow_*, \rightarrow^*, =$) formulas into the derivation problem for forest profiles.

6.1 Normal forms

We will assume a certain normal form of the formula $\varphi \in$ XPath($^*\!\leftarrow, \downarrow_*, \rightarrow^*, =$) to test for satisfiability. This will simplify the reduction into the derivation problem for forest profiles.

The normal form has two main properties. Firstly, it contains only path expressions that are *direct*, in the sense that the navigation consists in going left and then down, or going right and then down. And secondly, path expressions do not contain data tests as node expressions, in other words the formula is *unnested.* Next, we explain in detail these properties.

Preliminaries

Let $\alpha = a_1 \cdots a_n$ with $n > 0$ be a XPath($^*\!\leftarrow, \downarrow_*, \rightarrow^*, =$) path expression, where for every i, $a_i = [\psi]$ for some node expression ψ, or $a_i \in \{\varepsilon, {}^*\!\leftarrow, \downarrow_*, \rightarrow^*\}$. We say that α is in **alternating path normal form** if either $\alpha = \varepsilon$, or n is even and for all $1 \leq i \leq n$

- if i is even, $a_i = [\psi]$ for some node expression ψ,
- if i is odd, $a_i \in \{{}^*\!\leftarrow, \downarrow_*, \rightarrow^*\}$.

In other words, the path alternates between axes and tests for node expressions. We say that a formula is in alternating path normal form if all its path expressions are in alternating path normal form. Note that one can turn any formula $\varphi \in$ XPath($^*\!\leftarrow, \downarrow_*, \rightarrow^*, =$) into an equivalent formula φ' in alternating path normal form in polynomial time, using the equivalences

$$\begin{aligned}
&\langle [\psi]\alpha@_i \odot \beta@_j \rangle \equiv \psi \wedge \langle \alpha@_i \odot \beta@_j \rangle \text{ for } \odot \in \{=, \neq\},\\
&\langle \alpha@_i \odot [\psi]\beta@_j \rangle \equiv \psi \wedge \langle \alpha@_i \odot \beta@_j \rangle \text{ for } \odot \in \{=, \neq\},\\
&\alpha[\psi_1][\psi_2]\beta \equiv \alpha[\psi_1 \wedge \psi_2]\beta, \text{ and},\\
&\text{if } \alpha\beta \neq \epsilon,\ \alpha\beta \equiv \alpha[\top]\beta \text{ and } \alpha\varepsilon\beta \equiv \alpha\beta.
\end{aligned} \tag{$\triangle$}$$

For simplicity and without any loss of generality we can further assume that all our formulas do not contain formulas of the type $\langle\alpha\rangle$, since it is equivalent to $\langle \alpha@_1 = \alpha@_1 \rangle$. We will henceforth assume that all the formulas we work with are in this form.

We say that a path expression in alternating path normal form is a **rightward path expression**, if it starts with $\rightarrow^*$ and all the axes in it are $\rightarrow^*$ (similarly with **leftward**, **downward** and $^*\!\leftarrow$, $\downarrow_*$). Notice that, for example, a leftward expression may contain node tests using rightward or downward axes. For example, $^*\!\leftarrow[\langle\downarrow_*[a]\rangle]^*\!\leftarrow[b]$ is a leftward expression while $^*\!\leftarrow[a]\downarrow_*[\langle^*\!\leftarrow[a]\rangle]$ is not.

Direct normal form

The object of the direct normal form is to avoid having unnecessary mixed directions in path formulas, that use perhaps $\rightarrow^*$ and $^*\!\leftarrow$ in the same expression, or that contain a $^*\!\leftarrow$ (or $\rightarrow^*$) axis after a $\downarrow_*$ axis. That is, we avoid having formulas like

$$\langle \rightarrow^*[a]^*\!\leftarrow@_1 = \downarrow_*[b]\rightarrow^*@_2 \rangle$$

in favor of equivalent formulas with a more *direct* navigation, like

$$\begin{aligned}
&\langle \rightarrow^*[\langle\rightarrow^*[a]\rangle]@_1 = \downarrow_*[\langle^*\!\leftarrow[b]\rangle]@_2 \rangle \vee\\
&\langle [\langle\rightarrow^*[a]\rangle]^*\!\leftarrow@_1 = \downarrow_*[\langle^*\!\leftarrow[b]\rangle]@_2 \rangle.
\end{aligned} \tag{$\ddagger$}$$

In the formula above we factor the loops that may be in the navigation of the path expression to obtain a simple navigation that goes in only one horizontal direction.

We say that a formula $\varphi \in$ XPath($^*\!\leftarrow, \downarrow_*, \rightarrow^*, =$) is in **direct normal form**, if every path expression is ε, or of the form $\alpha{\cdot}\beta$, where $\alpha{\cdot}\beta \neq \epsilon$ (*i.e.*, it is not the empty string), α is leftward, rightward or empty, and β is downward or empty. Note that, strictly speaking, the formula ($\ddagger$) is not in direct normal form since its second disjunct is not in alternating path normal form, but the equivalent alternating path expression—using ($\triangle$)—is in direct normal form.

LEMMA 6.1 (DIRECT NORMAL FORM). *There exists an exponential time translation that for every node expression*

$\varphi \in \text{XPath}({}^*\!\!\leftarrow, \downarrow_*, \rightarrow^*, =)$ *returns an equivalent node expression* ψ *in direct normal form.*

Unnested normal form

The second normal form consists in having formulas without nesting of data tests. That is, we avoid treating formulas like, for example

$$\langle\ \downarrow_* \underbrace{[\langle\ {}^*\!\!\leftarrow[a]@_1 = \rightarrow^*[b]@_1\ \rangle]}_{\text{nested data test}}@_1 \ = \ \rightarrow^*[c]@_2\ \rangle\ .$$

If a formula is such that all its path expressions α contain only (boolean combinations of) tests for labels we call it a **non-recursive** formula.

We say that φ is in unnested normal form if $\varphi = \varphi_1 \wedge \varphi_2$ where $\varphi_1 \in \mathcal{B}(\mathbb{A})$ and φ_2 is a conjunction of tests of the form "if a node has some of the labels $\{a_1, \dots, a_n\}$ then it satisfies ψ" for some non-recursive formula ψ and labels $a_1, \dots, a_n \in \mathbb{A}$. Formally, φ_2 contains a conjunction of tests of the form

$$\neg\langle\ \downarrow_*[\tau \wedge \neg\psi]\ \rangle$$

for τ a disjunction of labels and ψ a non-recursive formula. Given $\varphi = \varphi_1 \wedge \varphi_2$ in unnested normal form, we write $\gamma_\varphi(a)$ for $a \in \mathbb{A}$ to denote the function where $\gamma_\varphi(a)$ is the conjunction of all the formulas ψ such that φ_2 contains $\neg\langle\rightarrow^*[\tau\wedge\neg\psi]\rangle$ as a subformula, for some disjunctive formula τ containing the label a.

Then, we obtain the following.

LEMMA 6.2 (UNNESTED NORMAL FORM). *There exists an exponential time translation that for every formula* $\eta \in \text{XPath}({}^*\!\!\leftarrow, \downarrow_*, \rightarrow^*, =)$ *returns a formula* φ *in unnested normal form such that* η *is satisfiable iff* φ *is satisfiable. Further, the translation of a formula in direct normal form is in direct normal form.*

COROLLARY 6.3. *About the translation of Lemma 6.2:*

1. *The set of path subformulas resulting from the translation has cardinality polynomial in* η.
2. *Every path subformula resulting from the translation can be written using polynomial space.*

6.2 Reduction to the derivation problem

In this section we show how we can reduce the satisfiability problem of direct unnested $\text{XPath}({}^*\!\!\leftarrow, \downarrow_*, \rightarrow^*, =)$ formulas into the derivation problem for forest profiles.

Let us fix $\phi = \phi_1 \wedge \phi_2$ in direct unnested normal form, where $\mathbb{A}$ as the finite alphabet, $\mathbf{k}$ as the number of attributes, $\mathbb{D}$ as any infinite domain, and $\mathbb{A}_{root}$ is the set of all $a \in \mathbb{A}$ that make ϕ_1 true.

Given a pattern $\alpha = \psi_1 \cdots \psi_k \in \mathcal{P}$, and an axis $o \in \{{}^*\!\!\leftarrow, \downarrow_*, \rightarrow^*\}$, we can convert α into a path expression as follows:

$$\mathrm{P}_o(\epsilon) \stackrel{def}{=} \varepsilon \qquad \text{if } k = 0,$$

$$\mathrm{P}_o(\psi_1 \cdots \psi_k) \stackrel{def}{=} o[\psi_1]\, o \cdots o[\psi_k] \qquad \text{if } k > 0.$$

Note that P_o is injective.

Let us define $\mathcal{P}_\phi$ as the set of patterns consisting of

- the constant $\top$ and the empty string ϵ,
- ψ, for every $\psi \in \mathcal{B}(\mathbb{A})$ that is a subformula of ϕ,
- every $\alpha \in (\mathcal{B}(\mathbb{A}))^*$ so that $\mathrm{P}_{\rightarrow^*}(\alpha)$, $\mathrm{P}_{{}^*\!\leftarrow}(\alpha)$, or $\mathrm{P}_{\downarrow_*}(\alpha)$ is a substring of ϕ.

It follows that $\mathcal{P}_\phi$ is finite and subword-closed.

For any direct non-recursive formula ψ that is a boolean combination of subformulas of ϕ and forest profile $\mathfrak{f}$, we define $\mathfrak{f} \vdash \psi$ as follows. If $\psi \in \mathbb{A}$, then $\mathfrak{f} \vdash \psi$ if and only if there is some $d \in \mathbb{D}$ and $i \in [\mathbf{k}]$ so that $(\psi, \epsilon, i) \in \overrightarrow{\chi}^{\mathrm{I}}(d)$. For all the boolean cases $\vdash$ is homomorphic. Suppose now that $\psi = \langle \alpha{\cdot}\beta@_i \neq \gamma{\cdot}\delta@_j \rangle$ where α is leftward, ε or empty, γ is rightward, ε or empty, and β, δ are downward or empty. We define $\mathfrak{f} \vdash \psi$ if there are some $d, d' \in \mathbb{D}$ so that $d \neq d'$ and

- if $\alpha = \epsilon$ or $\alpha = \varepsilon$, $(\top, \mathrm{P}^{-1}_{\downarrow_*}(\beta), i) \in \overleftarrow{\chi}^{\mathrm{I}}(d)$,
- if $\alpha \neq \epsilon$, $\alpha \neq \varepsilon$, $(\mathrm{P}^{-1}_{{}^*\!\leftarrow}(\alpha), \mathrm{P}^{-1}_{\downarrow_*}(\beta), i) \in (\leftarrow\!\![\mathfrak{f}]{\cdot}\overleftarrow{\chi}^{\mathrm{E}} \cup \overleftarrow{\chi}^{\mathrm{I}})(d)$,
- if $\gamma = \epsilon$ or $\gamma = \varepsilon$, $(\top, \mathrm{P}^{-1}_{\downarrow_*}(\delta), j) \in \overrightarrow{\chi}^{\mathrm{I}}(d')$,
- if $\gamma \neq \epsilon$, $\gamma \neq \varepsilon$, $(\mathrm{P}^{-1}_{\rightarrow^*}(\gamma), \mathrm{P}^{-1}_{\downarrow_*}(\delta), j) \in ([\mathfrak{f}]\!\!\rightarrow{\cdot}\overrightarrow{\chi}^{\mathrm{E}} \cup \overrightarrow{\chi}^{\mathrm{I}})(d')$.

Note that if $\alpha = \varepsilon$ then $\beta = \epsilon$ (resp. with γ and δ). If both α and γ are rightwards or leftwards it is defined in an analogous way. The case for $=$ is also analogous, where $d = d'$. The idea is that $\mathfrak{f} \vdash \psi$ makes only sense when the derivation forest for $\mathfrak{f}$ is a tree, and the multi-attribute data tree $\mathbf{t}$ associated to the derivation tree is so that $\mathbf{t} \models \psi$.

For example, testing ψ is the same as testing if there is some pattern $(\psi, \_, \_)$ in $\overleftarrow{\chi}^{\mathrm{I}}$ or $\overrightarrow{\chi}^{\mathrm{I}}$. In a similar way, checking a formula like

$$\langle \rightarrow^*[a]\downarrow_*[b]@_1 = \downarrow_*[c]@_2 \rangle$$

reduces to checking if there is a data value $d \in \mathbb{D}$ that can be reached with $(\top, c, 2)$ in the main forest (*i.e.*, in $\overleftarrow{\chi}^{\mathrm{I}}$ or $\overrightarrow{\chi}^{\mathrm{I}}$), and either

- d can be reached by $(a, b, 1)$ in the main forest, that is, $(a, b, 1) \in \overrightarrow{\chi}^{\mathrm{I}}$ (or equivalently $\overleftarrow{\chi}^{\mathrm{I}}$), or
- d can be reached in the right forest by $(a, b, 1)$, where a could be tested in the main forest (*i.e.*, $a \in [\mathfrak{f}]\!\!\rightarrow$), that is, $(a, b, 1) \in [\mathfrak{f}]\!\!\rightarrow{\cdot}\overrightarrow{\chi}^{\mathrm{E}}$.

Note that checking $\mathfrak{f} \vdash \psi$ takes polynomial time in the size of $\mathfrak{f}$ and ψ. Also, whether $\mathfrak{f} \vdash \bigwedge_{a\in\mathbb{A}}(a \Rightarrow \gamma_\varphi(a))$ holds or not depends only on $\xi(\mathfrak{f})$.

LEMMA 6.4. *Given a direct non-recursive formula* ψ *that is a boolean combination of subformulas of* ϕ*, and two forest profiles* $\mathfrak{f}, \mathfrak{f}' \in \mathfrak{F}$ *so that* $\xi(\mathfrak{f}) = \xi(\mathfrak{f}')$ *then* $\mathfrak{f} \vdash \psi$ *if, and only if,* $\mathfrak{f}' \vdash \psi$.

We can then write $\xi \models \psi$ for $\xi \in \mathcal{F}$ instead of $\mathfrak{f} \models \psi$ for any $\mathfrak{f}$ so that $\xi(\mathfrak{f}) = \xi$. We define the set of consistent profiles Γ_ϕ as all $\xi \in \mathcal{F}$ so that $\xi \vdash \bigwedge_{a\in\mathbb{A}}(a \Rightarrow \gamma_\varphi(a))$. The following lemma follows straight from the above definition of $\vdash$.

LEMMA 6.5. $\mathfrak{f} \vdash \bigwedge_{a\in\mathbb{A}}(a \Rightarrow \gamma_\varphi(a))$ *iff* $\xi(\mathfrak{f}) \in \Gamma_\phi$.

Abstractions.

Given multi-attribute data forests $\bar{\mathbf{t}}_l, \bar{\mathbf{t}}, \bar{\mathbf{t}}_r$, we define

$$abs(\bar{\mathbf{t}}_l, \bar{\mathbf{t}}, \bar{\mathbf{t}}_r)$$

as the forest profile that abstracts the forest $\bar{\mathbf{t}}$ in the context of the forests $\bar{\mathbf{t}}_l$ to the left and $\bar{\mathbf{t}}_r$ to the right. We have already discussed the idea of this abstraction in Section 4. For example, for the forest of Figure 3, assuming $\mathcal{P} = \{\top, b{\cdot}c, b, c, \epsilon\}$, we would obtain an abstraction where

$$\overleftarrow{\chi}^{\text{E}} = \{(5, b, b, 1), (5, b, \epsilon, 1), (3, b, \epsilon, 2), (2, b, c, 1), \dots\}.$$

We have that *abs* is basically an algebra morphism between multi-attribute data forests with rooting and concatenation and forest profiles with profile rooting and profile concatenation. Further, the profile $abs(\epsilon, \mathbf{t}, \epsilon)$ is a derivable root profile whenever $\mathbf{t} \models \phi$; and every derivable root profile is the abstraction of some tree $\mathbf{t}$ so that $\mathbf{t} \models \phi$.As a corollary from these properties, we have the following.

COROLLARY 6.6. *There is a derivable root forest profile if, and only if, ϕ is satisfiable.*

By the above Corollary 6.6 and Proposition 5.12, we can check in 2EXPSPACE if there is a derivable root profile. This is 2EXPSPACE in the size of $\mathcal{P}_\phi$. Although bringing a formula φ into direct unnested normal form may result in a doubly exponential formula, by Corollary 6.3 it can be stored in exponential space, and $\mathcal{P}_\phi$ is then singly exponential. Hence, the procedure is 3EXPSPACE in the original formula φ. Thus, the decision procedure is in 3EXPSPACE and Theorem 3.1 follows.

Note that if the input formula is in direct normal form then we save one exponential in the reduction and we hence obtain a 2EXPSPACE decision procedure.

THEOREM 6.7. *The satisfiability problem for formulas of XPath($^*\!\!\leftarrow, \downarrow_*, \rightarrow^*, =$) in direct normal form is decidable in 2EXPSPACE.*

7. DISCUSSION

We have shown that XPath with downward, rightward and leftward reflexive-transitive axes is decidable. To show this, we devised an algebra with good monotonicity properties. This seems to be the right kind of approach to work with transitive relations, and it generalizes and simplifies, in some aspects, the work of [11].

Upward axes

One natural question that stems from the result presented here is whether it can be extended to work with an *upward* axis as well. However, we claim (without a proof) that already SAT-XPath($\uparrow^*, \rightarrow^*, =$) has a non-primitive recursive lower bound. Indeed, this can be proved by reusing the results on lower bounds of [14]. The cited work shows that XPath with one non-reflexive transitive axis is enough to prove non-primitive recursiveness provided that the axis is functional (*i.e.*, the transitive closure of an axis like $\rightarrow$, $\leftarrow$, $\uparrow$ but unlike $\downarrow$). Here, however, we feature *reflexive*-transitive axes instead of only transitive. Therefore, in principle we cannot use this result. However, one can somehow code $\uparrow^+$ with $\rightarrow^*[a]\uparrow^*[\neg a]$ for some label a. We leave the proof of this claim for the journal version of the present work.

By the previous claim, although it could be that full transitive XPath is decidable, it would have a non-primitive recursive lower bound. We can then answer negatively to the conjecture proposed in [11, Conjecture 2], stating that XPath($^*\!\!\leftarrow, \downarrow_*, \uparrow^*, \rightarrow^*, =$) be decidable in elementary time.

Future work

- The present work can be seen as a step forward in answering [11, Conjecture 1], suggesting that the extension of XPath($^*\!\!\leftarrow, \downarrow_*, \rightarrow^*, =$) with the *child* axis is decidable with elementary complexity. Our approach may perhaps be extended to handle the child relation.
- We suspect that XPath($^*\!\!\leftarrow, \downarrow_*, \rightarrow^*, =$) is in fact hard for 2EXPSPACE, even when the formulas are in direct normal form, and hence that SAT-direct-XPath($^*\!\!\leftarrow, \downarrow_*, \rightarrow^*, =$) is 2EXPSPACE-complete.
- We would also like to investigate further the approach taken in this paper to attempt to generalize it to work with the class of reflexive-transitive closures of regular languages.

8. REFERENCES

[1] Vince Bárány, Mikołaj Bojańczyk, Diego Figueira, and Paweł Parys. Decidable classes of documents for XPath. In *IARCS Annual Conference on Foundations of Software Technology and Theoretical Computer Science (FSTTCS'12)*, Leibniz International Proceedings in Informatics (LIPIcs), Hyderabad, India, 2012. Leibniz-Zentrum für Informatik.

[2] Michael Benedikt, Wenfei Fan, and Floris Geerts. XPath satisfiability in the presence of DTDs. *Journal of the ACM*, 55(2):1–79, 2008.

[3] Mikołaj Bojańczyk and Sławomir Lasota. An extension of data automata that captures XPath. In *Annual IEEE Symposium on Logic in Computer Science (LICS '10)*, 2010.

[4] Mikołaj Bojańczyk, Anca Muscholl, Thomas Schwentick, and Luc Segoufin. Two-variable logic on data trees and XML reasoning. *Journal of the ACM*, 56(3):1–48, 2009.

[5] James Clark and Steve DeRose. XML path language (XPath). Website, 1999. W3C Recommendation. `http://www.w3.org/TR/xpath`.

[6] Claire David, Leonid Libkin, and Tony Tan. Efficient reasoning about data trees via integer linear programming. *ACM Transactions on Database Systems*, 37(3):19, 2012.

[7] Wenfei Fan, Chee Yong Chan, and Minos N. Garofalakis. Secure XML querying with security views. In *ACM SIGACT-SIGMOD-SIGART International Conference on Management of Data (SIGMOD'04)*, pages 587–598. ACM Press, 2004.

[8] Diego Figueira. Satisfiability of downward XPath with data equality tests. In *ACM SIGACT-SIGMOD-SIGART Symposium on Principles of Database Systems (PODS'09)*, pages 197–206. ACM Press, 2009.

[9] Diego Figueira. Forward-XPath and extended register automata on data-trees. In *International Conference on Database Theory (ICDT'10)*. ACM Press, 2010.

[10] Diego Figueira. *Reasoning on Words and Trees with Data*. Phd thesis, Laboratoire Spécification et Vérification, ENS Cachan, France, December 2010.

[11] Diego Figueira. A decidable two-way logic on data words. In *Annual IEEE Symposium on Logic in Computer Science (LICS'11)*, pages 365–374, Toronto, Canada, 2011. IEEE Computer Society Press.

[12] Diego Figueira. Alternating register automata on finite data words and trees. *Logical Methods in Computer Science*, 8(1), 2012.

[13] Diego Figueira. Decidability of downward XPath. *ACM Trans. Comput. Log.*, 13(4), 2012.

[14] Diego Figueira and Luc Segoufin. Future-looking logics on data words and trees. In *Int. Symp. on Mathematical Foundations of Comp. Sci. (MFCS'09)*, volume 5734 of *LNCS*, pages 331–343. Springer, 2009.

[15] Diego Figueira and Luc Segoufin. Bottom-up automata on data trees and vertical XPath. In *International Symposium on Theoretical Aspects of Computer Science (STACS'11)*, Leibniz International Proceedings in Informatics (LIPIcs). Leibniz-Zentrum für Informatik, 2011.

[16] Floris Geerts and Wenfei Fan. Satisfiability of XPath queries with sibling axes. In *International Symposium on Database Programming Languages (DBPL'05)*, volume 3774 of *Lecture Notes in Computer Science*, pages 122–137. Springer, 2005.

[17] Georg Gottlob, Christoph Koch, and Reinhard Pichler. Efficient algorithms for processing XPath queries. *ACM Transactions on Database Systems*, 30(2):444–491, 2005.

[18] Marcin Jurdziński and Ranko Lazić. Alternating automata on data trees and xpath satisfiability. *ACM Trans. Comput. Log.*, 12(3):19, 2011.

[19] Michael Kaminski and Nissim Francez. Finite-memory automata. *Theoretical Computer Science*, 134(2):329–363, 1994.

[20] Michael Kaminski and Tony Tan. Tree automata over infinite alphabets. In *Pillars of Computer Science*, volume 4800 of *Lecture Notes in Computer Science*, pages 386–423. Springer, 2008.

[21] Wim Martens and Frank Neven. Frontiers of tractability for typechecking simple xml transformations. *J. Comput. Syst. Sci.*, 73(3):362–390, 2007.

[22] Frank Neven, Thomas Schwentick, and Victor Vianu. Finite state machines for strings over infinite alphabets. *ACM Trans. Comput. Log.*, 5(3):403–435, 2004.

[23] Tony Tan. An automata model for trees with ordered data values. In *Annual IEEE Symposium on Logic in Computer Science (LICS'12)*, pages 586–595. IEEE Computer Society Press, 2012.

A Trichotomy for Regular Simple Path Queries on Graphs

Guillaume Bagan
INRIA, France
guillaume.bagan@inria.fr

Angela Bonifati
Lille 1 University & INRIA, France
angela.bonifati@inria.fr

Benoit Groz
Tel-Aviv University, Israel
benoit.groz@crans.org

ABSTRACT

Regular path queries (RPQs) select vertices connected by some path in a graph. The edge labels of such a path have to form a word that matches a given regular expression. We investigate the evaluation of RPQs with an additional constraint that prevents multiple traversals of the same vertices. Those regular simple path queries (RSPQs) quickly become intractable, even for basic languages such as $(aa)^*$ or a^*ba^*.

In this paper, we establish a comprehensive classification of regular languages with respect to the complexity of the corresponding regular simple path query problem. More precisely, we identify for which languages RSPQs can be evaluated in polynomial time, and show that evaluation is NP-complete for languages outside this fragment. We thus fully characterize the frontier between tractability and intractability for RSPQs, and we refine our results to show the following trichotomy: evaluation of RSPQs is either AC^0, NL-complete or NP-complete in data complexity, depending on the language L. The fragment identified also admits a simple characterization in terms of regular expressions.

Finally, we also discuss the complexity of deciding whether a language L belongs to the fragment above. We consider several alternative representations of L: DFAs, NFAs or regular expressions, and prove that this problem is NL-complete for the first representation and PSPACE-complete for the other two. As a conclusion we extend our results from edge-labeled graphs to vertex-labeled graphs.

Categories and Subject Descriptors: G.2.2, F.2.0

General Terms: Algorithms, Languages, Theory

Keywords: Graphs, Paths, Regular Simple Paths, Complexity, Regular Languages, Automata.

1. INTRODUCTION

The reachability problem for graphs (finding a path between two vertices) has been heavily investigated in computer science, and admits very efficient algorithms. However, for many real-world problems, constraints on the path need to be considered and, as a consequence, the reachability problem can become computationally hard. Constrained path problems on regular paths are of particular interest. For graph databases, such problems have been examined in the context of regular path queries (RPQs). Given a language L and two vertices in a database graph, a regular path query selects pairs of vertices connected by a path whose edge labels form a word in L. Graph databases and RPQs have been investigated starting from the late 80s [1, 6, 9, 10, 11, 14, 15, 19, 28, 30], and are now again in vogue due to their wide application scenarios, e.g. in social networks [36], biological and scientific databases [27, 33], and the Semantic Web [18]. Regular path queries allow to traverse the same vertices multiple times, whereas regular simple path queries (RSPQs) permit to traverse each vertex only once. From a theoretical viewpoint, the former notion has overridden the latter, mainly for complexity reasons. Indeed, RPQs are computable in time polynomial in both query and data complexity (combined complexity), while the evaluation of RSPQs is NP-complete even for fixed basic languages such as $(aa)^*$ or a^*ba^* [30]. RSPQs, however, are desired in many application scenarios [27, 33, 7, 25, 23, 41], such as transportation problems, VLSI design, metabolic networks, DNA matching and routing in wireless networks. As a further example, the problem of finding subgraphs matching a graph pattern can be generalized to use regular expressions on pattern edges [15]. Such queries may also enforce the condition that their matched vertices are distinct. Additionally, regular simple paths have been recently considered in SPARQL 1.1 queries exhibiting property paths. In particular, recent studies on the complexity of property paths in SPARQL [3, 29] have highlighted the hardness of the semantics proposed by W3C to evaluate such paths in RDF graphs. Roughly speaking, according to the semantics considered in [29], the evaluation of expressions under Kleene-star closure imposes that the involved path is simple, whereas the evaluation of the remaining expressions allows to traverse the same vertex multiple times. As such, the semantics studied in [29] is an hybrid between regular paths and regular simple paths semantics.

Contributions. In this paper, we address the long standing open question [30, 7] of exactly characterizing the maximal class of regular languages for which RSPQs are tractable. By "tractable" we mean computable in time polynomial in the size of the database. Precisely, we establish a comprehensive classification of the complexity of RSPQs for a fixed regular language L: given an edge-labeled graph G and two vertices x and y, is there a simple path from x to y whose edge labels

PODS'13, June 22–27, 2013, New York, New York, USA.

form a word of L? A first step towards this important issue has been made in [30]. They exhibit a tractable fragment: the class of languages closed by subword. However, their fragment is not maximal.

Our contributions can be detailed as follows. We introduce a class of languages, named $\mathcal{C}_{tract}$, for which RSPQs are computable in polynomial time, and even in NL. We then show that this fragment is maximal as the RSPQ problem is NP-complete for every regular language that does not belong to $\mathcal{C}_{tract}$. Consequently, we characterize the frontier between tractability and intractability for this problem, under the hypothesis NL $\neq$ NP that is actually weaker than PTIME $\neq$ NP. Additionally, $\mathcal{C}_{tract}$ also represents the maximal class for which finding a shortest path that satisfies a RSPQ is tractable. We note that we focus on data complexity as we assume that the language L is fixed. At this point, the chart of the classification of the languages is not yet complete. Therefore, we refine our results to show the following trichotomy: the RSPQ problem is either AC^0, NL-complete or NP-complete.

We discuss the complexity to decide, given a language L, whether the RSPQ problem for L is tractable. We consider several alternative representations of L: DFAs, NFAs or regular expressions. We prove that this problem is NL-complete for the first representation and PSPACE-complete for the two others.

Next, we give a characterization of the tractable fragment $\mathcal{C}_{tract}$ for edge-labeled graphs in term of regular expressions. Moreover, $\mathcal{C}_{tract}$ is closed by union and intersection and languages in $\mathcal{C}_{tract}$ are aperiodic i.e. can be expressed by first-order formulas [39].

The above results hold for the usual definition of database graphs, i.e. edge-labeled graphs. However, it seems natural to take into consideration both queries on top of vertices labels and queries on top of vertices and edges labels. As an example, a Google Maps user may be interested to specify as a condition a regular expression that enforces a stop over in a given city and avoids another city while preferring certain types of roads. For such a reason, we focus on another model: vertex-labeled graphs. Surprisingly, for some languages, the RSPQ problem is simpler on vertex-labeled graphs than on edge-labeled graphs. With $L = (ab)^*$ for instance, RSPQ is polynomial for vertex-labeled graphs and NP-complete for edge-labeled graphs. Furthermore, we can adapt our results to prove, for this model, a classification of the same kind as the one shown for vertex-labeled graphs: the RSPQ problem is either AC^0, NL-complete or NP-complete.

As a final contribution, we have obtained two minor results. First, we have attempted to study the parametrized complexity of tractable RSPQs queries when the parameter is the size of the query. However, we obtained a partial result: we prove that the problem is FPT for the class of finite languages. Moreover, we prove that the problem is also FPT for the class of all regular languages when the parameter is the size of the path. As a second result, we prove that the problem RSPQ is polynomial w.r.t. combined complexity on graphs of bounded directed treewidth. This is actually a straightforward generalization of a result of [24].

Related Work. Regular path queries express ways to evaluate regular expressions on database graph models [1, 6, 9, 10, 11, 14, 15, 19, 28, 30] or tree-structured models, such as XML [12]. While the regular path problem has been extensively studied in the literature, the regular simple path problem has received less attention in both the database and graph communities. Besides the works on regular paths, there have been studies on finding paths with some constraints. In particular, Lapaugh et al. [26] prove that finding simple paths of even length is polynomial for non directed graphs and NP-complete for directed graphs. This study has been extended in [4] by considering paths of length i mod k. Similarly, finding k disjoint paths with extremities given as input is polynomial for non directed graphs [35] and NP-complete for directed graphs [17]. Mendelzon and Wood [30] show that the regular simple path problem is NP-complete in the general case. However, they show that the problem can be decided in polynomial time for subword-closed languages. They also show that the problem becomes polynomial under some restrictions on the size of cycles of both graph and automaton. A subsequent paper [32] proves the polynomiality for the class of outerplanar graphs. Barrett et al. [7] extend this result, proving that the regular simple path problem is polynomial w.r.t. combined complexity for graphs of bounded treewidth. Let us also observe that the existence of a regular simple path between two vertices is MSO-definable, and therefore a well-known result of Courcelle [13] already implies the same result but w.r.t. data complexity only. Barrett et al. [7] also show that the problem is NP-complete for the class of grid graphs even when the language is fixed. Practical algorithms for regular simple paths on large graphs have been proposed in [23, 25].

Regular simple paths have been also investigated in the context of SPARQL property paths with the semantics proposed in a working draft of SPARQL 1.1. Notice that such semantics of SPARQL property paths doesn't exactly correspond to regular simple paths queries. Losemann and Martens [29] and Arenas et al. [3] investigate the complexity of evaluating such property paths. They show that the evaluation is NP-complete in several cases, along with exhibiting cases in which it is polynomial. More precisely, Losemann and Martens consider different fragments of regular expressions and classify them with respect to the complexity of evaluating SPARQL property paths. Both papers also show that counting the number of paths that match a regular expression (which is permitted by the working draft) is hard in many cases.

2. PRELIMINARIES

For the rest of the paper, Σ always denotes a finite alphabet. We use the notation $[n]$ to denote the set of integers $\{1, \ldots, n\}$. Given a word w and a language L, $w^{-1}L = \{w' : ww' \in L\}$.

Complexity: NL, P, NP, PSPACE refer to the classical classes of complexity [34]. The reductions we consider are many-to-one logspace reductions [34] and completeness of problems are under this type of reductions. For some proofs, we consider non deterministic algorithms (Turing machines) using oracles. We use the Ruzzo-Simon-Tompa model [37]. In this model, the Turing machine needs to be deterministic while it makes queries to the oracle. The class AC^0 refers to uniform AC^0 that is equivalent to $FO(+, \times)$ or $FO(BIT, <)$ [22]. For definition of FPT, see [16].

Graphs: In our paper, we essentially consider db-graphs even if we also consider vertex-labeled graphs. A db-graph is a tuple $G = (V, \Sigma, E)$ where V is a set of vertices, Σ is a set of labels and $E \subseteq V \times \Sigma \times V$ is a set of edges labeled by symbols of Σ. A path p of a db-graph G from x to y is a sequence $(v_1 = x, a_1, \ldots, v_m, a_m, v_{m+1} = y)$ such that for each $i \in [m+1]$, v_i is a vertex in G and for each $i \in [m]$, (v_i, a_i, v_{i+1}) is an edge in G. A path p is simple if all vertices v_i in p are distinct. Given a language $L \subseteq \Sigma^*$, p is L-labeled if $a_1 \ldots a_m \in L$. Given a subset $S \subseteq V$, p is S-restricted if every intermediate vertex of p belongs to S. Given a simple path p and two vertices x and y in p, $p[x, y]$ denotes the subpath of p from x to y.

Languages and automata: Let L be a regular language. We denote by $A_L = (Q_L, i_L, F_L, \Delta_L)$ the minimal DFA for L, and by M_L the number of states $M_L = |Q_L|$ in A_L. Whenever the language is obvious from context, we drop the subscript and write M instead of M_L. We assume that A_L is complete i.e. Δ_L is a total function, so that in general A_L may have a sink state. For any $q \in Q, w \in \Sigma^*$, $\Delta_L(q, w)$ denotes the state obtained when reading w from q. Finally, $\mathscr{L}_q$ denotes the set of all words accepted from q. For every state q we denote by $Loop(q)$ the set of all non empty words that allow to loop on q: $Loop(q) = \{w \in \Sigma^+ \mid \Delta_L(q, w) = q\}$. Strongly connected components of (the graph of) A_L are simply called components. The run of L (or A_L) over a p be a path $p = (v_1, a_1, \ldots, a_m, v_{m+1})$ is the mapping $\rho : \{v_1, \ldots, v_{m+1}\} \mapsto Q_L$ such that: $\rho(v_1) = i_L$ and $\rho(v_{i+1}) = \Delta_L(i_L, a_1 \ldots a_i)$ for every $i \in [m]$. There are many characterisations of aperiodic languages [39]. A language L is aperiodic if and only if it satisfies $\Delta_L(q, w^{M+1}) = \Delta_L(q, w^M)$ for every state q and word w.

RSPQ: Given a class $\mathcal{L}$ of regular languages and a class $\mathcal{G}$ of db-graphs, we define the following problem:

RSPQ$(\mathcal{L}, \mathcal{G})$

Input: a language $L \in \mathcal{L}$,
a db-graph $G = (V, \Sigma, E) \in \mathcal{G}$,
and two vertices $x, y \in V$
Question: is there a simple L-labeled path from x to y?

The encoding of the language L will be specified when required. We denote by "All" the class of db-graphs, RSPQ$(\mathcal{L})$ means RSPQ$(\mathcal{L}, \text{All})$. For any single language L, we use RSPQ$(L, \mathcal{G})$ to denote RSPQ$(\{L\}, \mathcal{G})$. Since L is fixed, we focus on data complexity. Notice that the representation of L does not matter here. Although we consider the boolean version of the problem, namely deciding the existence of a path, our algorithms actually also return a simple L-labeled path.

Given a regular language L, our main question is to give a criterion to decide whether RSPQ(L) is tractable (i.e. decidable in polynomial time) or not (i.e. NP-complete). We address this question in the next and following sections.

EXAMPLE 1. *As an introductory example, consider the language $L = a^*(bb^+ + \epsilon)c^*$. We wish to decide whether there exists a simple path from x to y labeled by L, given two vertices x, y of a db-graph G. It is not absolutely trivial that this problem can be solved efficiently: the problem has indeed been proved NP-complete for the language a^*bc^*. Yet we can give a polynomial algorithm for L.*

We distinguish two cases: there is a simple L-labeled path from x to y if and only if one of the following cases holds:

1. *there exists a simple $a^*b^kc^*$-labeled path from x to y for some $k \in \{0, 2, 3\}$*

2. *case 1 does not hold and there exists a simple $a^*b^4b^*c^*$-labeled path from x to y.*

The first case is the easiest to check. We essentially enumerate all possible combinations for the k b-labeled edges, for increasing values of k. For each such combination one only needs to check the following conditions: (1) there is an a^*-labeled path leading from x to the first b-edge (without crossing the other b-edges) (2) there is a c^*-labeled path leading from the last b-edge to y (without crossing the other b-edges). For details about why these verifications suffice to check case 1, we refer the reader to the long version [5].

Let us now assume w.l.o.g. that there is no $a^*b^kc^*$-labeled path from x to y for $k \in \{0, 2, 3\}$. We can show that in this second case there exists a simple L-labeled path from x to y if and only if there exist six vertices $v_1, v_2, v_3, v_4, v_5, v_6$, all distinct except that v_3 may equal v_4, two integers l_a, l_b and two sets S_a, S_b satisfying all following conditions:

- *there is a b-labeled edge from v_1 to v_2, from v_2 to v_3, from v_4 to v_5, and from v_5 to v_6.*

- *there is an a^*-labeled path from x to v_1 avoiding all other v_is $(i > 1)$. The shortest possible such path has length l_a.*

- *S_a is the set of all vertices reachable from x through an a^*-labeled path of length at most l_a that avoids all other v_is $(i > 1)$.*

- *there is a b^*-labeled path from v_3 to v_4 of which all vertices (but the first and last) avoid S_a and the v_is. The shortest possible such path has length l_b.*

- *S_b is the set of all vertices reachable from v_3 through any b^*-labeled path of length at most l_b that avoids S_a and all other v_is $(i \neq 4)$.*

- *a c^*-labeled path from v_6 to y of which all vertices (but the first) avoid S_a and S_b and all other v_is $(i < 6)$.*

The figure below summarizes all these conditions.

$$x \xrightarrow{a^*} v_1 \xrightarrow{b} v_2 \xrightarrow{b} v_3 \xrightarrow{b^*} v_4 \xrightarrow{b} v_5 \xrightarrow{b} v_6 \xrightarrow{c^*} y$$
$$S_a \qquad\qquad S_b \subseteq V \setminus S_a \qquad \subseteq V \setminus (S_a \cup S_b)$$

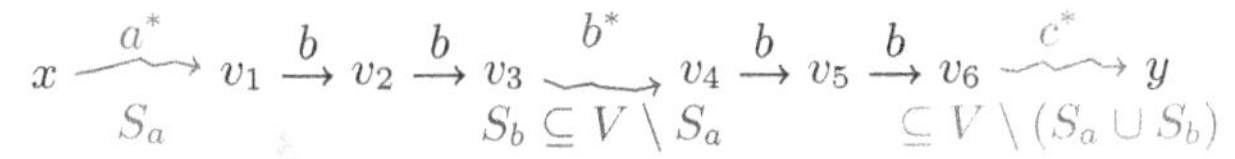

These conditions can clearly be verified in time polynomial in G. It is relatively clear also that the path constructed above is a simple L-labeled path from x to y, so the conditions are sufficient to obtain an L-labeled simple path. Proving that they are necessary requires a little more attention: why should we indeed avoid all vertices from S_a when building the path from v_3 to v_4? The reason why we choose to avoid a superset of the subpath from x to v_1 instead of the subpath itself is obvious: we want our algorithm to be "memoryless" in the sense that the a^* and b^* subpaths should be constructed independently, lest we enumerate exponentially many paths. But how can we ascertain that we do not overlook a simple L-labeled path when do not find any? For the present, we only claim that every shortest L-labeled simple path from x to y yields vertices $v_1, \ldots, v_6$ satisfying the conditions above. A sketch of proof is given in the long version for this specific example, and we develop in this paper the general idea underlying this argument to elaborate an algorithm for tractable instances.

3. A TRICHOTOMY FOR RSPQ

Here and henceforth, M refers to the size of Q_L. We next define a class of languages. We will prove that it is exactly the class of regular languages for which RSPQ(L) is tractable.

DEFINITION 1. *We define $\mathcal{C}_{tract}$ as the class of regular languages L that satisfy $w^M \mathcal{L}_{q_2} \subseteq \mathcal{L}_{q_1}$ for all pairs of states $q_1, q_2 \in Q_L$ and word w such that $Loop(q_1) \neq \emptyset$, $Loop(q_2) \neq \emptyset$, $q_2 \in \Delta_L(q_1, \Sigma^*)$ and $w \in Loop(q_2)$.*

This definition is merely a technical definition for the $\mathcal{C}_{tract}$, but Theorem 4 provides more intuitive characterizations of the class.

3.1 Hard languages for RSPQ

This section is devoted to the proof of a hardness result: RSPQ(L) is NP-hard for every regular language L that does not belong to $\mathcal{C}_{tract}$.

The first step toward that proof lies in the following characterization of $\mathcal{C}_{tract}$. We call *witness for hardness* a tuple (q, w_m, w_r, w_1, w_2) where $q \in Q_L$, $w_r \in \Sigma^*$, $w_1 \in Loop(q)$ and $w_2, w_m \in \Sigma^+$ satisfying

- $w_m w_2^* w_r \subseteq \mathcal{L}_q$
- $(w_1 + w_2)^* w_r \cap \mathcal{L}_q = \emptyset$.

LEMMA 1. *Let L be a regular language that does not belong to $\mathcal{C}_{tract}$. Then, L admits a witness for hardness.*

PROOF. Let L be a regular language that does not belong to $\mathcal{C}_{tract}$. For commodity, we distinguish two cases, depending on whether L satisfies or not the following property: $\mathcal{L}_{q_2} \subseteq \mathcal{L}_{q_1}$ for every $q_1, q_2 \in Q_L$ such that $q_2 \in \Delta_L(q_1, \Sigma^*)$ and $Loop(q_1) \cap Loop(q_2) \neq \emptyset$ (Property $\mathcal{P}$) .

We first prove that every language satisfying property $\mathcal{P}$ is aperiodic. Let L be a language satisfying property $\mathcal{P}$, $q \in Q_L$ and w a word. Let also q' denote the state $q' = \Delta_L(q, w^M)$. We denote by q'' the state $\Delta_L(q', w)$. We want to prove that $q' = q''$. It is trivial when $w = \epsilon$. Thus, we assume that $w \neq \epsilon$. According to the pumping lemma, there exists some k such that $\Delta_L(q', w^k) = q'$. Then q' and q'' both loop on w^k, so that $\mathcal{L}_{q'} = \mathcal{L}_{q''}$ by definition of $\mathcal{P}$, hence $q' = q''$ by minimality. Consequently, L is aperiodic.

If L does not satisfy Property $\mathcal{P}$, there exist q, q_2, w_m, w, w_r such that $\Delta_L(q, w_m) = q_2$, $w \in Loop(q) \cap Loop(q_2)$, and $w_r \in \mathcal{L}_{q_2} \setminus \mathcal{L}_q$. Then $q, w_m, w_r, w_1 = w_2 = w$ is a witness for hardness.

Assume now that L still does not belong to $\mathcal{C}_{tract}$, but satisfies Property $\mathcal{P}$, and so in particular is aperiodic. By definition of $\mathcal{C}_{tract}$ there exist states q, q_2 and words w_1, w_2, w_m, w_r' such that $w_1 \in Loop(q)$, $w_2 \in Loop(q_2)$, $\Delta_L(q, w_m) = q_2$, $w_r' \in \mathcal{L}_{q_2}$ and $w_2^M w_r' \notin \mathcal{L}_q$. W.l.o.g. we can suppose that $w_1 = (w_1')^M$ for some word w_1'. We then claim that $\mathcal{L}_{q'} \subseteq \mathcal{L}_q$ for every q' in $\Delta_L(q, \Sigma^* w_1)$. Indeed, every $q' \in \Delta_L(q, \Sigma^* w_1)$ loops over w_1 by the pumping lemma and aperiodicity of L, hence $w_1 \in Loop(q) \cap Loop(q')$ and therefore $\mathcal{L}_{q'} \subseteq \mathcal{L}_q$ due to Property $\mathcal{P}$.

Let $w_r = w_2^M w_r'$. By definition, $w_m w_2^* w_r \subseteq \mathcal{L}_q$ because $w_r \in \mathcal{L}_{q_2}$. We now prove that $(w_1 + w_2)^* w_r \cap \mathcal{L}_q = \emptyset$, because any word in $(w_1 + w_2)^* w_r$ can be decomposed into uv with $u \in \epsilon + (w_1 + w_2)^* w_1$ and $v \in (w_2)^* w_r$. We recall that $w_r = w_2^M w_r' \notin \mathcal{L}_q$ and L is aperiodic, so that $v \notin \mathcal{L}_q$. Furthermore, we have just proved that $q' = \Delta_L(q, u)$ satisfies $\mathcal{L}_{q'} \subseteq \mathcal{L}_q$. Consequently, $v \notin \mathcal{L}_{q'}$ and $uv \notin \mathcal{L}_q$. Thus, q, w_m, w_r, w_1, and w_2 provide a witness for hardness, which concludes the proof of Lemma 1. □

We can now prove our hardness result, by reduction from Vertex-Disjoint-Path, a problem also used in [30] to prove hardness in the particular case of a^*ba^*.

Vertex-Disjoint-Path
Input: A directed graph $G = (V, E)$, four vertices $x_1, y_1, x_2, y_2 \in V$
Question: are there two disjoint paths, one from x_1 to y_1 and the other from x_2 to y_2?

LEMMA 2. *Let L be a regular language that does not belong to $\mathcal{C}_{tract}$. Then, RSPQ(L) is* NP*-hard.*

PROOF. Let $L \notin \mathcal{C}_{tract}$. We exhibit a reduction from the Vertex-Disjoint-Path problem to RSPQ(L). According to Lemma 1, L admits a witness for hardness q, w_m, w_r, w_1, w_2. Let w_l be a word such that $\Delta(i_L, w_l) = q$. By definition we get $w_l(w_1 + w_2)^* w_r \cap L = \emptyset$ and $w_l w_1^* w_m w_2^* w_r \subseteq L$.

We build from G a db-graph G' whose edges are labeled by non empty words. This is actually a generalization of db-graphs. Nevertheless, by adding intermediate vertices, an edge labeled by a word w can be replaced with a path whose edges form the word w.

G' is constructed as follows. The vertices of G' are the same as the vertices of G. For each edge (v_1, v_2) in G, we add two edges (v_1, w_1, v_2) and (v_1, w_2, v_2). Moreover, we add two new vertices x, y and three edges (x, w_l, x_1), (y_1, w_m, x_2) and (y_2, w_r, y).

By construction, for every simple path p from x to y in G' that contains the edge (y_1, w_m, x_2), we can obtain a similar path that matches a word in $w_l w_1^* w_m w_2^* w_r$ by switching w_1 and w_2 edges, keeping the same vertices. Every simple path p from x to y in G' that does not contain the edge (y_1, w_m, x_2) matches a word in $w_l(w_1 + w_2)^* w_r$. By definition of q, w_m, w_r, w_1, w_2, no path of that form $w_l(w_1 + w_2)^* w_r$ is L-labeled, whereas every path matching $w_l w_1^* w_m w_2^* w_r$ is L-labeled. Thus, RSPQ(L) returns True for (G', x, y) iff there is a simple path from x to y in G' that contains the edge (y_1, w_m, x_2) that is, iff Vertex-Disjoint-Path returns True for (G, x_1, y_1, x_2, y_2). We illustrate below the reduction for $L = a^*b(cc)^*d$, on an instance (G, x_1, y_1, x_2, y_2), choosing $w_l = w_1 = a$, $w_m = b$, $w_2 = cc$, and $w_r = d$. □

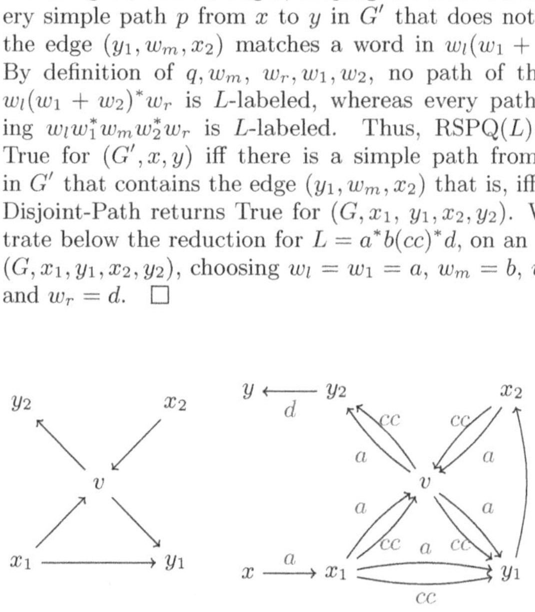

Input instance G RSPQ instance: graph G'

Figure 1: Reduction for $L = a^*b(cc)^*d$.

3.2 Tractable languages for RSPQ

The main result of this section is that for every $L \in \mathcal{C}_{tract}$, RSPQ($L$) $\in$ NL. The general idea is to exploit a particular kind of pumping argument between strongly connected components of the automaton to prove that if we build carefully a path using the usual reachability algorithm inside the strongly connected components, then we need not care about possible intersections between subpaths corresponding to different components. For this purpose, we first prove several lemmas on the structure of automata that recognize $\mathcal{C}_{tract}$ languages. To begin with, we prove that every language from $\mathcal{C}_{tract}$ is aperiodic and deduce an alternative characterization of $\mathcal{C}_{tract}$.

3.2.1 Alternative characterization of $\mathcal{C}_{tract}$.

LEMMA 3. *Let L be a regular language in $\mathcal{C}_{tract}$. Then L is aperiodic.*

PROOF. In the proof of Lemma 1 we defined a property $\mathcal{P}$ and showed that languages satisfying property $\mathcal{P}$ are aperiodic. We show that every $L \in \mathcal{C}_{tract}$ satisfies property $\mathcal{P}$. Let $L \in \mathcal{C}_{tract}$, $q_1, q_2 \in Q_L$ and w satisfy $q_2 \in \Delta_L(q_1, \Sigma^*)$ and $w \in Loop(q_1) \cap Loop(q_2)$. By definition of $\mathcal{C}_{tract}$, $w^M \mathscr{L}_{q_2} \subseteq \mathscr{L}_{q_1}$, hence $\mathscr{L}_{q_2} \subseteq \mathscr{L}_{q_1}$ because $w \in Loop(q_1)$. □

We then exploit this aperiodicity property to establish the following characterization of $\mathcal{C}_{tract}$, which strengthens the requirements from Definition 1 on the loops of A_L.

LEMMA 4. *Let L be a regular language. Then, L belongs to $\mathcal{C}_{tract}$ iff for all pair of states $q_1, q_2 \in Q_L$ such that $Loop(q_1) \neq \emptyset$, $Loop(q_2) \neq \emptyset$ and $q_2 \in \Delta_L(q_1, \Sigma^*)$, the following statement holds: $(Loop(q_2))^M \mathscr{L}_{q_2} \subseteq \mathscr{L}_{q_1}$.*

PROOF. The (if) implication is immediate by Definition 1. Let us now prove the (only if) implication. Assume $L \in \mathcal{C}_{tract}$. Let $q_1', q_2' \in Q_L$ satisfy $Loop(q_1') \neq \emptyset$, $Loop(q_2') \neq \emptyset$, $q_2' \in \Delta_L(q_1', \Sigma^*)$, and let $w \in Loop(q_2')$. Let also q_3 denote the state $\Delta_L(q_1', w^M)$. Then Definition 1 implies $w^M \mathscr{L}_{q_2'} \subseteq \mathscr{L}_{q_1'}$. Thus, $\mathscr{L}_{q_2'} \subseteq \mathscr{L}_{q_3}$. The crux of the proof is to choose carefully q_1', q_2' and w to exploit the constraints on $\mathscr{L}_{q_3}$.

Let q_1, q_2 be two states such that $Loop(q_1) \neq \emptyset$, $Loop(q_2) \neq \emptyset$ and $q_2 \in \Delta_L(q_1, \Sigma^*)$. Let $v_1 \ldots v_M \in (Loop(q_2))^M$ and $q_3 = \Delta_L(q_1, v_1 \ldots v_M)$. We wish to prove $\mathscr{L}_{q_2} \subseteq \mathscr{L}_{q_3}$.

For some i, j, $1 \leq i < j \leq M$, we get $\Delta_L(q_1, v_1 \ldots v_i) = \Delta_L(q_1, v_1 \ldots v_j)$, using the convention $\Delta_L(q_1, v_1 \ldots v_i) = q_1$ for $i = 0$. Let $u_1 = v_1 \ldots v_i$, $u_2 = v_{i+1} \ldots v_j$ and $u_3 = v_{j+1} \ldots v_k$. Let $q_4 = \Delta_L(q_1, u_1)$. We claim that $\mathscr{L}_{q_2} \subseteq \mathscr{L}_{q_4}$. The result then follows from $\mathscr{L}_{q_2} = u_3^{-1} \mathscr{L}_{q_2} \subseteq u_3^{-1} \mathscr{L}_{q_4} = \mathscr{L}_{q_3}$. To prove the claim, let $w = u_1 u_2^M$ and $q_5 = \Delta_L(q_1, w^M)$. As $\Delta_L(q_1, w^M) = q_5$ and $w \in Loop(q_2)$, we get $\mathscr{L}_{q_2} \subseteq \mathscr{L}_{q_5}$ through Definition 1 with q_1, q_2 and w. Furthermore, u_2 belongs to $Loop(q_5)$ because L is aperiodic. To conclude the proof, we observe that $\mathscr{L}_{q_5} \subseteq \mathscr{L}_{q_4}$, by Definition 1 with q_5, q_4 and u_2, and because $\Delta_L(q_4, u_2^M) = q_4$ and $u_2 \in Loop(q_5)$.[1] □

3.2.2 Technical lemmas on the components of A_L

From now on, and until the end of the section, we fix a language $L \in \mathcal{C}_{tract}$. We introduce in Lemmas 7 and 9 the pumping argument that we exploit in the algorithm to compute a simple path. In the other lemmas we prove auxiliary results, based on the decomposition of the automaton in strongly connected components. We prove that components of languages in $\mathcal{C}_{tract}$ are very particular, in the sense that every word staying long enough in the component is synchronizing. A preliminary lemma shows that that two distinct states q_1 and q_2 in the same component cannot loop on the same word.

LEMMA 5. *Let q_1 and q_2 be two states belonging to the same component of A_L. If $Loop(q_1) \cap Loop(q_2) \neq \emptyset$, then $q_1 = q_2$.*

PROOF. Let q_1, q_2 as above, and let w a word in $Loop(q_1) \cap Loop(q_2)$. According to Definition 1, $w^M \mathscr{L}_{q_2} \subseteq \mathscr{L}_{q_1}$, hence $\mathscr{L}_{q_2} \subseteq \mathscr{L}_{q_1}$ since $w \in Loop(q_1)$. By symmetry, $\mathscr{L}_{q_2} = \mathscr{L}_{q_1}$, which implies $q_2 = q_1$. □

The next two lemmas characterize the internal language of a component.

LEMMA 6. *Let C be a component of A_L, $q_1, q_2 \in C$ and $a \in \Sigma$. Then $\Delta_L(q_1, a) \in C$ iff $\Delta_L(q_2, a) \in C$.*

PROOF. Let $q_1 \neq q_2$ two states in the same component C. Let a satisfy $\Delta_L(q_1, a) \in C$. Let also $w \in Loop(q_1) \cap a\Sigma^*$ and $q_3 = \Delta_L(q_2, w^M)$. We will prove that q_3 belongs to C and consequently $\Delta_L(q_2, a) \in C$. As L is aperiodic, $w \in Loop(q_3)$, and consequently, $w^M \mathscr{L}_{q_3} \subseteq \mathscr{L}_{q_1}$ by Definition 1. Furthermore, $w^M \mathscr{L}_{q_1} \subseteq \mathscr{L}_{q_2}$ also by Definition 1. Hence $\mathscr{L}_{q_3} \subseteq \mathscr{L}_{q_1}$ and $\mathscr{L}_{q_1} \subseteq (w^M)^{-1} \mathscr{L}_{q_2} = \mathscr{L}_{q_3}$. Thus, $\mathscr{L}_{q_1} = \mathscr{L}_{q_3}$ and, by minimality of A_L, $q_1 = q_3$, so that $q_3 \in C$. □

NOTATION 1. *We denote the internal alphabet of a component C of A_L by $\Sigma_C = \{a \in \Sigma : \exists q_1, q_2 \in C. \Delta_L(q_1, a) = q_2\}$.*

As a direct consequence of Lemma 6 we get:

LEMMA 7. *Let C be a component of A_L, $q \in C$ and $w \in \Sigma^*$. Then $\Delta_L(q, w) \in C$ iff $w \in (\Sigma_C)^*$.*

Finally, we prove that inside a component, every word with length at least M^2 is synchronizing. This result is the core of our pumping argument between strongly connected components as exposed in Lemma 9.

LEMMA 8. *Let C be a component of A_L, Σ_C be the internal alphabet of C, q_1, q_2 be two states of C and $w \in (\Sigma_C)^{M^2}$. Then, $\Delta_L(q_1, w) = \Delta_L(q_2, w)$.*

PROOF. Assume that $w = a_1 \ldots a_{M^2}$. For each i from 0 to M^2 and $\alpha = 1, 2$, let $q_{\alpha,i} = \Delta_L(q_\alpha, a_1 \ldots a_i)$. Since there are at most M^2 distinct pairs $(q_{1,i}, q_{2,i})$, there exist i, j, with $i < j$ such that $q_{1,i} = q_{1,j}$ and $q_{2,i} = q_{2,j}$. By Lemma 7, $q_{1,i}, q_{2,i} \in C$. Let $w' = a_{i+1} \ldots a_j$. We have $w' \in Loop(q_{1,i}) \cap Loop(q_{2,i})$, hence $q_{1,i} = q_{2,i}$ by Lemma 5. As a consequence, $\Delta_L(q_1, w) = \Delta_L(q_2, w)$. □

Here and thereafter, we fix the constant $N = 2M^2$.

LEMMA 9. *Let q_1, q_2 be two states such that $Loop(q_1) \neq \emptyset$, $Loop(q_2) \neq \emptyset$, and $q_2 \in \Delta_L(q_1, \Sigma^*)$. Let C be the component that contains q_2 and Σ_C be the internal alphabet of C. Then, $\mathscr{L}_{q_2} \cap (\Sigma_C)^N \Sigma^* \subseteq \mathscr{L}_{q_1}$.*

[1]This last application of Definition 1 corresponds actually to observing that every language in $\mathcal{C}_{tract}$ satisfies property $\mathcal{P}$ from Lemma 1.

PROOF. Let $w \in \mathscr{L}_{q_2} \cap (\Sigma_C)^N \Sigma^*$. There are some words $u, v \in (\Sigma_C)^{M^2}$, $w' \in \Sigma^*$ such that $w = uvw'$. By Lemma 7 and the Pigeonhole Principle, there exist a state $q_3 \in C$ and $M + 1$ non-empty words $v_1, \ldots, v_{M+1}$ such that $v = v_1 \ldots v_{M+1}$ and $\Delta_L(q_2, uv_1 \ldots v_i) = q_3$ for every $i \in [M]$. Therefore, $w \in uv_1(Loop(q_3))^{M-1}v_{M+1}w'$. By Lemma 8, $\Delta_L(q_3, uv_1) = \Delta_L(q_2, uv_1) = q_3$. Thus, w belongs to both $(Loop(q_3))^M v_{M+1}w'$ and $\mathscr{L}_{q_3}$. By Lemma 4, $w \in \mathscr{L}_{q_1}$. □

3.2.3 Computing RSPQ(L) for L in $\mathcal{C}_{tract}$

In the following, we describe a polynomial algorithm that computes RSPQ(L) when L belongs to $\mathcal{C}_{tract}$. Observe that a dynamic programming approach can be used to obtain a non necessarily simple regular path with label L between two points. This is because such paths can be built incrementally by storing only the last vertex in the (partial) path together with the corresponding state. This approach is not adequate to build a *simple* path, as we need to memorize all the vertices in the path to check the absence of loops. In such a case, we would need to consider an exponential number of paths.

Nevertheless, we will show that in the case where L belongs to $\mathcal{C}_{tract}$, we can identify a finite number of vertices that suffice to check if the path is (or can be transformed into) a simple path labeled with L. These "critical" vertices shall be stored in a path summary, as presented in the following. Unlike paths, summaries can be enumerated in logarithmic space, and we shall explain how one can use the summaries to check whether there exists a simple path between the input vertices. Roughly speaking, the idea of a summary is to keep only a bounded number of vertices of p, that depends only on L. Using Lemma 9, we actually show that it is enough to record the first vertex and the N last vertices having their state in C, for each component C of A_L. Additionally, if the number of such vertices is greater than $N+1$, we replace the path between the first vertex and the N last ones by a cut symbol cut_C. This symbol intuitively represents a Σ_C^*-labeled path that has been cut from the path. More formally, a summary is defined as follows.

DEFINITION 2 (LONG RUN COMPONENTS OF A PATH p). *Let $p = (v_1, a_1, \ldots, a_m, v_{m+1})$ be a path and let ρ be the run of L over p. A long run component of p is a component C of A_L such that there are at least $N+2 = 2M^2+2$ vertices v in p such that $\rho(v) \in C$. We denote by $C_1, \ldots, C_l$ the long run components of p (the sequence is sorted by order of appearance in p). For each integer $i \in [l]$, Σ_{C_i} is the internal alphabet of C_i, $left_i$ is the first vertex v_j of p such that $\rho(v_j) \in C_i$ and $right_i$ is the last vertex v_j of p such that $\rho(v_j), \ldots, \rho(v_{j+N}) \in C_i$.*

DEFINITION 3 (CUT SYMBOLS AND SUMMARY). *We introduce a new "cut" symbol cut_C for each component C of A_L. The set of all cut symbols is denoted by $Cuts$. Let $p = (v_1, a_1, \ldots, a_m, v_{m+1})$ with run ρ. Let $(C_i, \Sigma_{C_i}, left_i, right_i)_{i \in [l]}$ be as defined in Definition 2. The summary S of the path p (w.r.t. A_L) is the sequence obtained from p by replacing, for each $i \in [l]$ the subpath $p[left_i, right_i]$ by the sequence $(left_i, cut_{C_i}, right_i)$ where cut_{C_i} is the cut symbol of component C_i.*

A summary contains at most $NM = 2M^3$ elements (vertices, labels and cut symbols), which is constant if L is fixed. Actually, we chose this large constant to simplify the presentation of the proofs and because we focus on data-complexity, considering L to be fixed. But the bound can easily be improved without even changing the structure of the proofs: in Lemma 8, $|C|^2$ is clearly an upper bound (not even tight) on the minimal length of synchronizing words. This allows to replace $N = 2M^2$ with $2M|C|$ in Lemma 9. This in turn allows to lower the size of a summary to $2M^2$.

As a consequence of this constant bound on the number of elements in a summary (for fixed L), each summary can be represented with a logarithmic number of bits.

We also observe that in a summary, all cut symbols are clearly distinct by definition of strongly connected components. A summary depends on a path p. However, we would like a notion of summary S that is independent of any path p. We thus define a candidate summary as an alternative sequence of vertices and symbols or cut symbols of the form above. Consequently, a summary is always a candidate summary but the converse is not true.

DEFINITION 4 (CANDIDATE SUMMARY). *We define as a candidate summary S any sequence of vertices and labels of the form above; $S = (v_1, \alpha_1, \ldots, \alpha_m, v_{m+1})$ where $\alpha_i \in \Sigma \cup Cuts$ for every $i \in [m]$, all cut symbols are distinct, and $m \leq NM$. Similarly to Definition 2, we denote by $cut_{C_1}, \ldots, cut_{C_l}$ the sequence of cut symbols appearing in S. Furthermore we define, for each $i \in [l]$, $left_i$ (resp. $right_i$) as the vertex at left (resp. right) of cut_{C_i} in p.*

A path p obtained by replacing each subsequence $(left_i, cut_{C_i}, right_i)$ with a simple $\Sigma_{C_i}^*$-labeled path from $left_i$ to $right_i$ is called a *completion* of the candidate summary S.

LEMMA 10. *Let S be the summary of an L-labeled path p and let p' be a completion of S. Then, p' is an L-labeled path with summary S.*

EXAMPLE 2. *Figure 2 represents the minimal DFA for $L = a(c^{\geq 2} + \epsilon)(a+b)^*(ac)?a^*$ (we did not represent the sink state). This automaton can loop in three strongly connected components: $C_1 = \{q_4\}$, $C_2 = \{q_5, q_6\}$, and $C_3 = \{q_7\}$. The accepting states are q_2, q_4, q_5, q_6, and q_7. We shall pretend that $N = 3$ for our example as this value is sufficient for our algorithm, although the correct value for N should be $2M^2$ according to our rough bounds. Let us consider the path p_1 illustrated in Figure 3 with thick edges. The table below details this path and the corresponding run.*

v_1	v_2	v_3	v_4	v_5	v_7	v_8	v_9	v_{10}	v_{11}	v_{12}	v_{13}	v_{14}	v_{15}
q_1	q_2	q_3	q_4	q_4	q_4	q_4	q_4	q_5	q_6	q_5	q_5	q_5	q_5
			run in C_1					*run in C_2*					

We observe that p_1 is a simple L-labeled path. The summary S of p_1 is obtained by removing the second (resp. second and third) vertex with state in C_1 (resp. C_2): only the highlighted vertices are preserved. The components of eliminated vertices are represented by cut symbols cut_{C_1} and cut_{C_2}.

$$S = (v_1, a, v_2, c, v_3, c, v_4, cut_{C_1}, v_7, c, v_8, c, v_9, a, v_{10}, cut_{C_2}, v_{13}, a, v_{14}, a, v_{15}).$$

Lemma 10 provides us with an NL algorithm to obtain an L-labeled path from a summary S. However, such a path is not necessarily simple, even if S is the summary

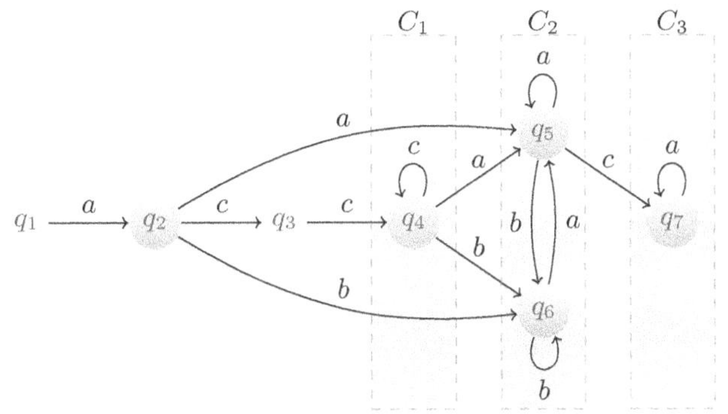

Figure 2: Minimal DFA for $a(c^{\geq 2} + \epsilon)(a+b)^*(ac)?a^*$

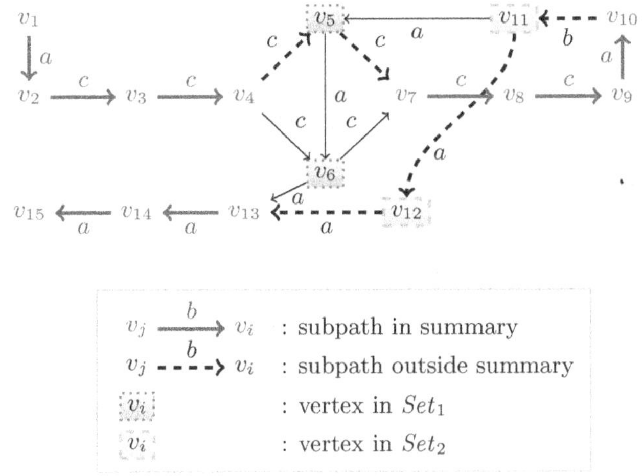

Figure 3: Admissible simple path, and its summary.

of a simple path. The reason is that the paths $(p_i)_{i\in[l]}$ we have built between each $left_i$ and $right_i$ are not necessarily disjoint. To overcome this problem, we will define *local domains* $Set_1, \ldots, Set_l$ which are disjoint sets of vertices from G. For each $i \in [l]$, we require the path p_i between $left_i$ and $right_i$ to be Set_i-restricted. Consequently, these paths will be disjoint. On the other hand, we do not want that the local domains are too restrictive because we must preserve the existence of at least one solution that satisfies these conditions for every positive instance (G, x, y) of RSPQ(L). In order to avoid oversized local domains, we limit Set_i to the set of vertices that might occur on a *shortest* $\Sigma^*_{C_i}$-labeled path from $left_i$ to $right_i$ that avoids all Set_j $(j < i)$. The following definition specifies more formally the local domains.

DEFINITION 5 (LOCAL DOMAINS). *Let S be a candidate summary. Let $(C_i, left_i, right_i)_{i\in[l]}$ be as stated in Definition 4 and $V(S)$ be the set of vertices appearing in S. We define the local domains Set_i recursively for each i from 1 to l. The set Set_i will be defined as a particular subset of $V_i = V \setminus (V(S) \cup \bigcup_{j<i} Set_j)$. If there is no V_i-restricted $\Sigma^*_{C_i}$-labeled simple path p from $left_i$ to $right_i$, then $Set_i = \emptyset$. Otherwise, we denote by k_i the length of the shortest such path and define Set_i as the set of vertices y in V_i that can be reached from $left_i$ by a V_i-restricted $\Sigma^*_{C_i}$-labeled path p of length at most $k_i - 1$.*

The following lemma is a direct consequence of Definition 5.

LEMMA 11. *Let S be a candidate summary. Then all sets $V(S), (Set_i)_{i\in[l]}$ from Definition 5 are disjoint.*

DEFINITION 6 (ADMISSIBLE PATH). *Let p be a path with label in L, run ρ and summary S. We qualify p as* admissible *if the following two conditions are satisfied: (a) all vertices appearing in S are distinct and (b) for every $i \in [l]$, the path $p[left_i, right_i]$ is simple and Set_i-restricted.*

By the definition and Lemma 11, an admissible path is necessarily simple.

LEMMA 12. *Let p be an admissible L-labeled path from x to y. Then p is simple.*

EXAMPLE 3. *The path p_1 defined in Example 2 is admissible, since $Set_1 = \{v_5, v_6\}$ and $Set_2 = \{v_{11}, v_{12}\}$, as illustrated in Figure 3. The definition of admissible paths guarantees the paths replacing cut_{C_1} and cut_{C_2} are disjoint. Indeed we can check that $\{v_5\} \cap \{v_{11}, v_{12}\} = \emptyset$.*

Being an admissible path is clearly more restrictive than being a simple path. However, it turns out that shortest simple paths are admissible, as shown below. That means that the existence of a simple path is equivalent to the existence of an admissible path.

LEMMA 13. *Let (G, x, y) be a RSPQ(L) instance. Every shortest simple L-labeled path from x to y is admissible.*

PROOF. Let $p = (v_1, a_1, \ldots, a_m, v_{m+1})$ be a shortest simple L-labeled path from x to y. Assume that p is not admissible. That means there is some i and vertex v between $left_i$ and $right_i$ such that $v \notin Set_i$. We choose i minimal such that (1) there is $j > i$ and a vertex v between $left_j$ and $right_j$ such that $v \in Set_i$ or (2) there is a vertex v between $left_i$ and $right_i$ such that $v \notin Set_i$. For each of the two cases, we will construct a path p' shorter than p from x to y. We then prove that in both cases p' is an L-labeled simple path, which contradicts our assumption that p is the shortest such path.

case (1): Let us say that a vertex v satisfies property $\mathcal{P}_1$ if there exists $j > i$ such that $v \in Set_i$ and v appears in p between $left_j$ and $right_j$. Let v be a vertex satisfying property $\mathcal{P}_1$. Then, by definition of Set_i, there is a Set_i-restricted $\Sigma^*_{C_i}$-labeled simple path sp from $left_i$ to v that is shorter than the subpath $p[left_i, right_i]$ and, consequently, shorter than $p[left_i, v]$. Let p' be the path obtained from p by replacing $p[left_i, v]$ with sp. This path p' is shorter than p. For the remainder of the proof we assume that v is the last vertex in p satisfying property $\mathcal{P}_1$ and define p' accordingly.

case (2): we assume additionally that no vertex satisfies property $\mathcal{P}_1$. That means there is a vertex v' that does not belong to Set_i but belongs to $V \setminus (V(S) \cup \bigcup_{j<i} Set_j)$. Consequently, there is a Set_i-restricted L-labeled simple path sp between $left_i$ and $right_i$ that is no longer than $p[left_i, v']$ and, consequently, shorter than $p[left_i, right_i]$. We choose p' as the path obtained from p by replacing $p[left_i, right_i]$ with sp. Furthermore, for homogeneity of the proof, we define $v = right_i$.

The remainder of the proof is common to the two cases. We need to prove that p' is a simple L-labeled path. We first prove that p' is an L-labeled path. Let ρ' be the run of L over p'. Let w be the word formed by the labels of the subpath $p[v, y]$. We know that $w \in \mathscr{L}_{\rho(v)}$ since p is an L-labeled path. We will show using Lemma 9 that $w \in \mathscr{L}_{\rho'(v)}$. By definition, $\rho'(\mathit{left}_i)$ belongs to the component C_i and the path $s = p'[\mathit{left}_i, v]$ is $\Sigma^*_{C_i}$-labeled, hence $\rho'(v) \in C_i$ by Lemma 7. Furthermore $\rho(v) \in C_j$ and C_j is reachable from C_i. In addition, by definition of a summary, there are at least $N+1$ vertices v'' of p after v such that $\rho'(v'') = \rho(v'') \in C_j$, and therefore the N labels following vertex v in p belong to Σ_{C_j} by Lemma 7 again. We have proved that $q_1 = \rho'(v)$ and $q_2 = \rho(v)$ meet all requirements for Lemma 9, which implies $w \in \mathscr{L}_{\rho'(v)}$. Consequently, p' is an L-labeled path.

We now prove that p' is simple. Since p is simple, it suffices to prove that the vertices in sp (between left_i and v) are disjoint with other vertices in p'. Notice that all intermediate vertices of sp belong to Set_i. By minimality of i, for all $i' < i$, the vertices between $\mathit{left}_{i'}$ and $\mathit{right}_{i'}$ belong to $Set_{i'}$ and, since $Set_{i'}$ and Set_i are disjoint (Lemma 11), do not belong to Set_i. Consequently, there is no vertex v' before left_i such that v' belong to Set_i. By construction, in the two cases (1) and (2), there is no vertex v' after v such that v' belongs to Set_i. That concludes the proof. □

We next show how an admissible summary can be completed in logarithmic space into a simple path. We first prove that local domains Set_i can be computed in logarithmic space.

LEMMA 14. *Let L be a fixed language in $\mathcal{C}_{tract}$. The following problem P_{Set} is in* NL. *Given an instance (G, x, y) of RSPQ(L), a candidate summary S, a vertex z and an integer i, decide whether $z \in Set_i$.*

PROOF. The proof is based on the following result due to Immerman [21]: $\mathrm{NL}^{\mathrm{NL}} = \mathrm{NL}$. In other words, if a decision problem P can be solved by an NL-algorithm using an oracle in NL, then this problem P belongs to NL [2]. Consider, for each $k \geq 0$, P^k_{Set} be the decision problem P_{Set} with the restriction $i \leq k$ i.e. (G, x, y, S, z, i) is a positive instance of P^k_{Set} iff (G, x, y, S, z, i) is a positive instance of P^k_{Set} and $i \leq k$. Notice that i belongs to the input of P^k_{Set} while this is not the case for k. Clearly, the number l of cuts in a summary S as in Definition 3, is bounded by the number K of strongly connected components of L. Consequently, $P_{Set} = P^K_{Set}$. Let us prove, that $P^k_{Set} \in \mathrm{NL}$ for each $k \geq 0$. If $k = 0$, P^0_{Set} always returns False because Set_i is not defined for $i = 0$. So P^0_{Set} is trivially in NL. Assume, by induction, that $P^k_{Set} \in \mathrm{NL}$. It suffices to show that there is an NL-algorithm for P^{k+1}_{Set} using P^k_{Set} as oracle. Since $\mathrm{NL}^{\mathrm{NL}} = \mathrm{NL}$, that implies that $P^{k+1}_{Set} \in \mathrm{NL}$. Let (G, x, y, S, z, i) be an instance of P^{k+1}_{Set}. If $i \leq k$, we return the same answer as the oracle P^k_{Set}. If $i = k+1$, using the definition and notations of Set_{k+1}, the problem essentially boils down to computing the distances between the vertices left_{k+1} and z on one side, left_{k+1} and right_{k+1} on the other side in the graph $G' = (V', E')$ where $V' = V_{k+1} \cup \{\mathit{left}_{k+1}, \mathit{right}_{k+1}\}$ and E' is the set of $\Sigma_{C_{k+1}}$-labeled edges of G. It is easily seen that this can be done in non deterministic log-space using the oracle P^k_{Set}. □

LEMMA 15. *Let L be a fixed language in $\mathcal{C}_{tract}$. There exists a non deterministic log-space algorithm that given an instance (G, x, y) of RSPQ(L) and a candidate summary S tests whether there is an admissible L-labeled path p from x to y with summary S.*

[2]This result is true with the Ruzzo-Simon-Tompa model [37] but $\mathrm{NL}^{\mathrm{NL}} = \mathrm{NP}$ with others models of oracles.

PROOF. We propose the following algorithm. It returns "Yes" if all the following tests succeed and "No" otherwise.

1. Check that all vertices of S are distinct;
2. Compute a path p from S by replacing, for each $i \in [l]$, the sequence $(\mathit{left}_i, \mathit{cut}_{C_i}, \mathit{right}_i)$ by a simple Set_i-restricted $\Sigma^*_{C_i}$-labeled path from left_i to right_i. The test fails if it is not possible;
3. Check that p is an L-labeled path;
4. Check that S is the summary of p.

Let us prove that the algorithm is correct. First, we assume that there is an admissible (simple) L-labeled path with summary S from x to y. Then, by definition of an admissible path, test 1 and test 2 both succeed. Since p is a completion of S, Lemma 10 implies that p is an L-labeled path with summary S. Thus, tests 3 and 4 succeed too and the algorithm returns "Yes". Reciprocally, assume now that the algorithm returns "Yes". Tests 3 and 4 guarantee that p is an L-labeled path with summary S. Tests 1 and 2 guarantee that p is admissible. Consequently, p is an admissible L-labeled from x to y.

We still have to check the complexity. Notice that the sets Set_i are not stored in memory: we only need to check on-the-fly if a given vertex belongs those sets, which only requires logarithmic space according to Lemma 14. The same remark applies to the path p that is generated on the fly for the tests of tests 3 and 4. Taking these remarks into consideration, the algorithm can easily be implemented in NL. □

We eventually show the main Lemma of this section, proving that RSPQ(L) is tractable for every language in $\mathcal{C}_{tract}$.

LEMMA 16. *Let $L \in \mathcal{C}_{tract}$. Then, RSPQ($L$) $\in$ NL.*

PROOF. We simply enumerate all possible candidate summaries S w.r.t. (L, G, x, y), and apply on each summary the algorithm of Lemma 15. We return "Yes" if this algorithm returns "Yes" for at least one candidate summary S. Otherwise, we return "No". Therefore, our algorithm returns "Yes" if and only if there exists an admissible path from x to y, and consequently, if and only if there is a simple path from x to y (Lemmas 12 and 13). Since L is fixed, there is a polynomial number of candidate summaries, each of logarithmic size. Consequently, they can be enumerated within logarithmic space. □

Notice that we can easily adapt our algorithm so that it outputs a shortest path for positive instances. This computation of a shortest simple path generalizes to db-graphs weighted by a function $E \to \mathbb{R}^+$. The main theorem summarizes our results, combining Lemma 2 with Lemma 16.

THEOREM 1. *Let L be a regular language. Then, RSPQ(L) is in* NL *if $L \in trC$ and is* NP*-complete otherwise.*

3.3 Towards a complete classification

Actually, the classification can be made more precise. We have partitioned the RSPQ(L) problems into NL and NP-complete problems. To refine the partition, we now can envisage a classification within the class of NL problems.

LEMMA 17. *For every regular language L, RSPQ(L) $\in$ AC^0 if L is finite, otherwise RSPQ(L) is NL-hard.*

The proof is based on a reduction from the following NL-complete problem [34].

Reachability
Input: A directed graph G and two vertices x, y in G
Question: Is there a path from x to y?

PROOF. (Membership) Immerman [22] proves that AC^0 exactly corresponds to structures definable in FO (first order logic). Thus, we will prove that RSPQ(L) is definable in FO if L is finite. Given an alphabet Σ, we consider the signature $\tau = (R_a)_{a\in\Sigma}$ of binary predicates. We can view a db-graph (V, Σ, E) as a τ-structure $\mathcal{M} = (V, (R_a)_{a\in\Sigma})$ of domain V and such that for every $v_1, v_2 \in V$ and $a \in \Sigma$, $(v_1, v_2) \in R_a$ iff $(v_1, a, v_2) \in E$. Let $w = a_1 \dots a_k$ be a word. Let us define the predicate $\text{path}_w(x, y)$ that checks the existence of a simple w-labeled path between x and y. We let the reader verify that predicate $\text{path}_w(x, y)$ is expressible in FO.

(Hardness) We exhibit a reduction from Reachability. Let L be an infinite regular language. By the Pumping Lemma, there exist non empty words u, v, w such that $uv^*w \subseteq L$. We build a db-graph G' from G by first relabeling every edge of G with v, and then adding two vertices x' and y' with edges (x', u, x) and (y, w, y'). There is a (not necessarily simple) path from x to y in G iff there is an L-labeled simple path from x' to y' in G'. Consequently, RSPQ(L) is NL-hard. □

Our results so far can be summarized in the following trichotomy which refines Theorem 1.

THEOREM 2. *Let L be a regular language. The complexity of RSPQ(L) can be determined as follows.*

1. *L is finite: RSPQ(L) $\in AC^0$;*
2. *$L \in \mathcal{C}_{tract}$ and L is infinite: RSPQ(L) is NL-complete;*
3. *$L \notin \mathcal{C}_{tract}$: RSPQ($L$) is NP-complete.*

3.4 Recognition of tractable languages

The following theorem establishes the complexity of deciding if RSPQ(L) is tractable (i.e. deciding if RSPQ(L) can be computed in polynomial time). We consider different representations of L (DFAs, NFAs and regular expressions).

THEOREM 3. *Testing whether a regular language L belongs to $\mathcal{C}_{tract}$ is:*

1. *NL-complete if L is given by a DFA;*
2. *PSPACE-complete if L is given by an NFA (resp. a regular expression).*

The proofs of hardness for DFAs and NFAs rely on reductions from the following two problems.

Emptiness
Input: A DFA $A_L = (Q_L, \Sigma, i_L, F_L, \Delta_L)$ that recognizes a language L
Question: is $L = \emptyset$?

Universality
Input: An NFA (or a regular expression) that recognizes a language $L \subseteq \{0,1\}^*$
Question: $L = \{0,1\}^*$?

The NL-completeness of Emptiness can easily be deduced from the NL-completeness of Reachability [34]. Stockmeyer and Meyer [40] proved that Universality is PSPACE-complete.

3.5 Characterization by regular expressions

In this section, we propose two characterizations of $\mathcal{C}_{tract}$ languages. The first in terms of regular expressions and the second in terms of a pumping property. Unlike the other properties discussed before on the minimal DFA of L, the pumping property is expressed directly on the language L. The languages in $\mathcal{C}_{tract}$ are exactly those that can be expressed with an expression in the fragment Ψ_{tr} defined below. This fragment essentially enforces restrictions on the concatenation of subexpressions: except at the highest level, only expressions of the form $e + \epsilon$ can be concatenated.

Ψ_{tr}-terms are defined as follows:

$$\Psi_{tr}\text{-term} \quad ::= \quad w + \epsilon \mid A^{\geq k} + \epsilon$$

where w is a word, A is a subset of Σ and $A^{\geq k}$ is a shortcut for $A^k A^*$. A Ψ_{tr}-sequence is a concatenation of terms $w\varphi_1 \dots \varphi_l w'$ where w and w' are words and $\varphi_1 \dots \varphi_l$ are Ψ_{tr}-terms. Finally, the fragment Ψ_{tr} is the set of disjunctions of Ψ_{tr}-sequences.

EXAMPLE 4. *For instance, the expression $a^*(b^{\geq 2} + \epsilon)c^*$ investigated in Example 1 belongs to the fragment Ψ_{tr} (using notation $c^* = c^{\geq 0}$). Expression $a^*ba^* + (a + b)^*$, on the opposite, does not, but is clearly equivalent to $(a + b)^{\geq 0}$, which does. The following theorem, however, implies that a^*ba^* is not equivalent to any expression from Ψ_{tr}.*

THEOREM 4. *Let L be a regular language. The three following statements are equivalent:*

1. *A language L belongs to $\mathcal{C}_{tract}$*
2. *L is recognized by a regular expression in Ψ_{tr}.*
3. *There is an integer $i \geq 0$ such that for every word $w_l, w_m, w_r \in \Sigma^*$ and every non empty words $w_1, w_2 \in \Sigma^+$, $w_l w_1^i w_m w_2^i w_r \in L$ implies $w_l w_1^i w_2^i w_r \in L$.*

COROLLARY 1. *$\mathcal{C}_{tract}$ is closed by intersection, union and word reversing.*

We observe that adapting the notion of summaries allows for a proof of Lemma 16 that directly considers regular expressions in Ψ_{tr}. Since $\mathcal{C}_{tract}$ is closed by union, we can restrict ourselves to Ψ_{tr}-sequences $\varphi_1 \dots \varphi_l$ where φ_1, φ_l are words and $\varphi_2, \dots, \varphi_{l-1}$ are Ψ_{tr}-terms. Let p be an L-path. We decompose p into subpaths $p_1, \dots p_l$ such that p_i matches the expression φ_i for every $i \in [l]$. The summary of p is built as follows:

- if φ_i is a word or an expression of the form $w + \epsilon$, we keep all vertices of p_i in the summary;
- if φ_i is an expression of the form $A^{\geq k} + \epsilon$, we keep the k first and k last vertices and replace the rest of the path by the special symbol cut_A.

4. OTHER RESULTS

This section investigates three further issues. First, we consider RSPQs over vertex-labeled graphs. Then, we give minor results on the parametrized complexity of the RSPQ problem. Finally, we discusses the complexity of RSPQs over graphs of bounded directed treewidth. These are straightforward applications of standard techniques, yet the results may be of practical interest.

4.1 Other models of database graphs

The goal of this section is to adapt our classification to another model of graphs: vl-graphs i.e. vertex-labeled graphs. We denote by vlg the class of vl-graphs.

For simplicity, we will consider vl-graphs as special db-graphs. We can put the label of a vertex into edges. Consequently, we see vls-graphs as db-graphs that respect the following restriction: there exists no pair of edges $e = (x, a, y)$ and $e' = (x', a', y)$ such that $a \neq a'$.

Clearly, given a language L, RSPQ(L, vlg) is at most as difficult as RSPQ(L). However, for some languages, the problem is easier. For example, RSPQ(L, vlg) $\in$ PTIME while RSPQ(L, vlg) is NP-complete for $L = a^*bc^*$. The key is that a vertex cannot have two different labels, and, consequently, a path that matches a^* is always disjoint from a path that matches c^*. By contrast, for $L = a^*ba^*$ or $L = (aa)^*$, the problem remains NP-complete.

By generalizing this, we can obtain the following result:

THEOREM 5. *Let $\mathcal{C}^{vlg}_{tract}$ be the class of regular languages L that satisfy $(aw_2)^M \mathscr{L}_{q_2} \subseteq \mathscr{L}_{q_1}$ for every pair of states $q_1, q_2 \in Q_L$, label a and pair of words w_1, w_2 such that $aw_1 \in Loop(q_1)$, $aw_2 \in Loop(q_2) \neq \emptyset$ and $q_2 \in \Delta_L(q_1, \Sigma^*)$.*

Let L be a regular language. Then, RSPQ(L, vlg) is in NL *if $L \in \mathcal{C}^{vlg}_{tract}$ and is* NP*-complete otherwise.*

4.2 Parametrized complexity

The next section focuses on the parametrized complexity of the RSPQ problem.

> **para-RSPQ($\mathcal{L}$)**
> **Input:** a db-graph graph $G = (V, \Sigma, E)$,
> a regular language $L \in \mathcal{L}$ given by an NFA $A_L = (Q_L, i_L, F_L, \Delta_L)$
> two vertices x and y
> **Parameter:** $k = |Q_L|$
> **Question:** Is there a simple L-path from x to y in G?

Our initial goal was to determine the parametrized complexity para-RSPQ($\mathcal{C}_{tract}$). Unfortunately, we could only partially reach this goal. We first address the parametrized complexity of RSPQs when the parameter is the size of the path.

> **k-RSPQ**
> **Input:** a db-graph graph $G = (V, \Sigma, E)$,
> a regular language L given by an NFA $A_L = (Q_L, i_L, F_L, \Delta_L)$,
> two vertices x and y
> an integer $k \geq 0$
> **Parameter:** k
> **Question:** Is there a simple L-labeled path of size at most k from x to y in G?

THEOREM 6. *k-RSPQ is* FPT. *More precisely, the problem is solvable in time $O(2^{O(k)}|A_L| \cdot |G| \cdot \log |G|)$.*

The proof is based on the Color Coding method [2]. As a consequence of this theorem we get:

COROLLARY 2. *Let $\mathcal{L}$ denote the class of finite languages. Then para-RSPQ($\mathcal{L}$) $\in$* FPT.

The finite language can be given by an acyclic NFA or a star-free regular expression.

4.3 Directed treewidth

Directed treewidth is a notion introduced in [24]. It generalizes many other measures such as treewidth, dag-width or Kelly-width [8, 20]. Directed treewidth measures in some sense how close a digraph is to a DAG. Johnson et al. [24] present a general method to design polynomial algorithms on graphs of bounded directed treewidth. Like most algorithms exploiting treewidth, this method leverages a dynamic programming approach on the decomposition tree. They apply this method to show that testing the existence of a Hamiltonian path is polynomial on such classes of graphs. Here, we extend this result to show that the regular simple path problem is also computable in polynomial time for the same classes.

It has been observed in the literature that RSPQ has polynomial combined complexity on two interesting classes of graphs: graphs of bounded treewidth [7], and DAGs [30]. The result for DAGs is immediate indeed, as every path in a DAG is simple. The next theorem generalizes both these two results.

THEOREM 7. *Let $k \geq 0$ and $\mathcal{G}$ be a class of db-graphs with directed treewidth at most k. Then, RSPQ($Reg, \mathcal{G}$) is polynomial, where Reg denotes the regular languages.*

5. CONCLUSION

We now pinpoint some directions for future work.

- As an extension of our work, we can consider context-free languages. It seems to be difficult to obtain useful results, since we can easily prove that distinguishing polynomial and NP-hard instances is undecidable if P $\neq$ NP (cf the long version [5]).
- We have studied the regular simple path problem from the data complexity perspective. An interesting continuation of our work is to include the language in the input (combined complexity). The question is to decide given a class of language $\mathcal{L}$ whether RSPQ($\mathcal{L}$) is in P or NP-complete.
- What becomes tractable under restrictions to the graph such as planar digraphs or undirected graphs? Notice that both disjoint paths and even path problems are polynomial in these cases [26, 31, 35, 38].
- From the parametrized complexity perspective, what is the complexity of para-RSPQ($\mathcal{C}_{tract}$)? We conjecture that it is in FPT.

We would like to thank Thomas Schwentick, Slawomir Staworko, Sophie Tison and the anonymous referees for their thoughtful comments that let us improve the paper.

6. REFERENCES

[1] S. Abiteboul and V. Vianu. Regular path queries with constraints. *J. Comput. Syst. Sci.*, 58(3):428–452, 1999.

[2] N. Alon, R. Yuster, and U. Zwick. Color-Coding. *J. ACM*, 42(4):844–856, 1995.

[3] M. Arenas, S. Conca, and J. Pérez. Counting beyond a yottabyte, or how sparql 1.1 property paths will prevent adoption of the standard. In *WWW*, pages 629–638, 2012.

[4] E. M. Arkin, C. H. Papadimitriou, and M. Yannakakis. Modularity of Cycles and Paths in Graphs. *J. ACM*, 38(2):255–274, 1991.

[5] G. Bagan, A. Bonifati, and B. Groz. A trichotomy for regular simple path queries on graphs. *CoRR*, abs/1212.6857, 2012.

[6] P. Barceló, L. Libkin, and J. L. Reutter. Querying graph patterns. In *PODS*, pages 199–210. ACM, 2011.

[7] C. L. Barrett, R. Jacob, and M. V. Marathe. Formal-language-constrained path problems. *SIAM Journal on Computing*, 30(3):809–837, 2000.

[8] D. Berwanger, A. Dawar, P. Hunter, S. Kreutzer, and J. Obdrzálek. The dag-width of directed graphs. *J. Comb. Theory, Ser. B*, 102(4):900–923, 2012.

[9] D. Calvanese, G. D. Giacomo, M. Lenzerini, and M. Y. Vardi. Answering regular path queries using views. In *ICDE*, pages 389–398, 2000.

[10] D. Calvanese, G. D. Giacomo, M. Lenzerini, and M. Y. Vardi. Rewriting of regular expressions and regular path queries. *J. Comput. Syst. Sci.*, 64(3):443–465, 2002.

[11] D. Calvanese, G. D. Giacomo, M. Lenzerini, and M. Y. Vardi. Reasoning on regular path queries. *SIGMOD Record*, 32(4):83–92, 2003.

[12] D. Calvanese, G. D. Giacomo, M. Lenzerini, and M. Y. Vardi. An automata-theoretic approach to regular xpath. In *DBPL*, pages 18–35, 2009.

[13] B. Courcelle. Graph rewriting: An algebraic and logic approach. In *Handbook of Theoretical Computer Science, Volume B: Formal Models and Sematics (B)*, pages 193–242. 1990.

[14] I. F. Cruz, A. O. Mendelzon, and P. T. Wood. A graphical query language supporting recursion. In *SIGMOD Conference*, pages 323–330, 1987.

[15] W. Fan, J. Li, S. Ma, N. Tang, and Y. Wu. Adding regular expressions to graph reachability and pattern queries. In *ICDE*, pages 39–50. IEEE Computer Society, 2011.

[16] J. Flum and M. Grohe. *Parameterized Complexity Theory (Texts in Theoretical Computer Science. An EATCS Series)*. 2006.

[17] M. R. Garey and D. S. Johnson. *Computers and Intractability: A Guide to the Theory of NP-Completeness*. W. H. Freeman, 1979.

[18] C. Gutierrez, C. A. Hurtado, A. O. Mendelzon, and J. Pérez. Foundations of semantic web databases. *J. Comput. Syst. Sci.*, 77(3):520–541, 2011.

[19] R. H. Güting. GraphDB: A Data Model and Query Language for Graphs in Databases. In *Proc. 20th Int. Conf. on Very Large Data Bases*, pages 297–308, 1994.

[20] P. Hunter and S. Kreutzer. Digraph measures: Kelly decompositions, games, and orderings. *Theor. Comput. Sci.*, 399(3):206–219, 2008.

[21] N. Immerman. Nondeterministic space is closed under complementation. *SIAM J. Comput.*, 17(5):935–938, 1988.

[22] N. Immerman. *Descriptive complexity*. Springer, 1999.

[23] R. Jin, H. Hong, H. Wang, N. Ruan, and Y. Xiang. Computing label-constraint reachability in graph databases. In *SIGMOD Conference*, pages 123–134, 2010.

[24] T. Johnson, N. Robertson, P. D. Seymour, and R. Thomas. Directed tree-width. *J. Comb. Theory, Ser. B*, 82(1):138–154, 2001.

[25] A. Koschmieder and U. Leser. Regular path queries on large graphs. In *SSDBM*, pages 177–194, 2012.

[26] A. S. Lapaugh and C. H. Papadimitriou. The even-path problem for graphs and digraphs. *Networks*, 14(4):507–513, 1984.

[27] U. Leser. A query language for biological networks. In *ECCB/JBI*, page 39, 2005.

[28] L. Libkin and D. Vrgoc. Regular Path Queries on Graphs with Data. In *ICDT 2012*, pages 74–85, 2012.

[29] K. Losemann and W. Martens. The complexity of evaluating path expressions in sparql. In *PODS*, pages 101–112. ACM, 2012.

[30] A. O. Mendelzon and P. T. Wood. Finding Regular Simple Paths in Graph Databases. *SIAM J. Comput.*, 24(6):1235–1258, 1995.

[31] Z. P. Nedev. Finding an Even Simple Path in a Directed Planar Graph. *SIAM J. Comput.*, 29:685–695, 1999.

[32] Z. P. Nedev and P. T. Wood. A polynomial-time algorithm for finding regular simple paths in outerplanar graphs. *J. Algorithms*, 35(2):235–259, 2000.

[33] F. Olken. Graph data management for molecular biology. *OMICS*, 7(1):75–78, 2003.

[34] C. H. Papadimitriou. *Computational complexity*. Addison-Wesley, 1994.

[35] N. Robertson and P. D. Seymour. Graph Minors .XIII. The Disjoint Paths Problem. *J. Comb. Theory, Ser. B*, 63(1):65–110, 1995.

[36] R. Ronen and O. Shmueli. Soql: A language for querying and creating data in social networks. In *ICDE*, pages 1595–1602, 2009.

[37] W. L. Ruzzo, J. Simon, and M. Tompa. Space-bounded hierarchies and probabilistic computations. *J. Comput. Syst. Sci.*, 28(2):216–230, 1984.

[38] A. Schrijver. Finding k Disjoint Paths in a Directed Planar Graph. *SIAM J. Comput.*, 23(4):780–788, 1994.

[39] M. P. Schützenberger. On finite monoids having only trivial subgroups. *Information and Control*, 8(2):190–194, 1965.

[40] L. J. Stockmeyer and A. R. Meyer. Word problems requiring exponential time: Preliminary report. In *STOC*, pages 1–9, 1973.

[41] C. B. Ward and N. M. Wiegand. Complexity results on labeled shortest path problems from wireless routing metrics. *Computer Networks*, 54(2):208–217, 2010.

Communication Steps for Parallel Query Processing*

Paul Beame, Paraschos Koutris and Dan Suciu
University of Washington, Seattle, WA
{beame,pkoutris,suciu}@cs.washington.edu

ABSTRACT

We consider the problem of computing a relational query q on a large input database of size n, using a large number p of servers. The computation is performed in *rounds*, and each server can receive only $O(n/p^{1-\varepsilon})$ bits of data, where $\varepsilon \in [0,1]$ is a parameter that controls replication. We examine how many global communication steps are needed to compute q. We establish both lower and upper bounds, in two settings. For a single round of communication, we give lower bounds in the strongest possible model, where arbitrary bits may be exchanged; we show that any algorithm requires $\varepsilon \geq 1 - 1/\tau^*$, where τ^* is the fractional vertex cover of the hypergraph of q. We also give an algorithm that matches the lower bound for a specific class of databases. For multiple rounds of communication, we present lower bounds in a model where routing decisions for a tuple are tuple-based. We show that for the class of *tree-like* queries there exists a tradeoff between the number of rounds and the space exponent ε. The lower bounds for multiple rounds are the first of their kind. Our results also imply that transitive closure cannot be computed in $O(1)$ rounds of communication.

Categories and Subject Descriptors

H.2.4 [**Systems**]: Parallel Databases

Keywords

Parallel Computation, Lower Bounds

1. INTRODUCTION

Most of the time spent in big data analysis today is allocated in data processing tasks, such as identifying relevant data, cleaning, filtering, joining, grouping, transforming, extracting features, and evaluating results [5, 8]. These tasks form the main bottleneck in big data analysis, and a major challenge for the database community is improving the performance and usability of data processing tools. The motivation for this paper comes from the need to understand the complexity of query processing in big data management.

Query processing is typically performed on a shared-nothing parallel architecture. In this setting, the data is stored on a large number of independent servers interconnected by a fast network. The servers perform local computations, then exchange data in global data shuffling steps. This model of computation has been popularized by MapReduce [7] and Hadoop [15], and can be found in most big data processing systems, like PigLatin [21], Hive [23], Dremmel [19].

Unlike traditional query processing, the complexity is no longer dominated by the number of disk accesses. Typically, a query is evaluated by a sufficiently large number of servers such that the entire data can be kept in the main memory of these servers. The new complexity bottleneck is the communication. Typical network speeds in large clusters are 1Gb/s, which is significantly lower than main memory access. In addition, any data reshuffling requires a global synchronization of all servers, which also comes at significant cost; for example, everyone needs to wait for the slowest server, and, worse, in the case of a straggler, or a local node failure, everyone must wait for the full recovery. Thus, the dominating complexity parameters in big data query processing are the number of communication steps, and the amount of data being exchanged.

MapReduce-related models.

Several computation models have been proposed in order to understand the power of MapReduce and related massively parallel programming methods [9, 16, 17, 1]. These all identify the number of communication steps/rounds as a main complexity parameter, but differ in their treatment of the communication.

The first of these models was the MUD (Massive, Unordered, Distributed) model of Feldman et al. [9]. It takes as input a sequence of elements and applies a binary merge operation repeatedly, until obtaining a final result, similarly to a User Defined Aggregate in database systems. The paper compares MUD with streaming algorithms: a streaming algorithm can trivially simulate MUD, and the converse is also possible if the merge operators are computationally powerful (beyond PTIME).

Karloff et al. [16] define $\mathcal{MRC}$, a class of multi-round algorithms based on using the MapReduce primitive as the sole building block, and fixing specific parameters for balanced processing. The number of processors p is $\Theta(N^{1-\epsilon})$, and each can exchange MapReduce outputs expressible in $\Theta(N^{1-\epsilon})$ bits per step, resulting in $\Theta(N^{2-2\epsilon})$ total storage

*This work was partially supported by NSF IIS-1115188, IIS-0915054, IIS-1247469, CCF-0830626, and CCF-1217099.

PODS'13, June 22–27, 2013, New York, New York, USA.

among the processors on a problem of size N. Their focus was algorithmic, showing simulations of other parallel models by $\mathcal{MRC}$, as well as the power of two round algorithms for specific problems.

Lower bounds for the single round MapReduce model are first discussed by Afrati et al. [1], who derive an interesting tradeoff between reducer size and replication rate. This is nicely illustrated by Ullman's drug interaction example [25]. There are n ($= 6,500$) drugs, each consisting of about 1MB of data about patients who took that drug, and one has to find all drug interactions, by applying a user defined function (UDF) to all pairs of drugs. To see the tradeoffs, it helps to simplify the example, by assuming we are given *two* sets, each of size n, and we have to apply a UDF to every pair of items, one from each set, in effect computing their cartesian product. There are two extreme ways to solve this. One can use n^2 reducers, one for each pair of items; while each reducer has size 2, this approach is impractical because the entire data is replicated n times. At the other extreme one can use a single reducer that handles the entire data; the replication rate is 1, but the size of the reducer is $2n$, which is also impractical. As a tradeoff, partition each set into g groups of size n/g, and use one reducer for each of the g^2 pairs of groups: the size of a reducer is $2n/g$, while the replication rate is g. Thus, there is a tradeoff between the replication rate and the reducer size, which was also shown to hold for several other classes of problems [1].

Towards lower bound models.

There are two significant limitations of this prior work: (1) As powerful and as convenient as the MapReduce framework is, the operations it provides may not be able to take full advantage of the resource constraints of modern systems. The lower bounds say nothing about alternative ways of structuring the computation that send and receive the same amount data per step. (2) Even within the MapReduce framework, the only lower bounds apply to a single communication round, and say nothing about the limitations of multi-round MapReduce algorithms.

While it is convenient that MapReduce hides the number of servers from the programmer, when considering the most efficient way to use resources to solve problems it is natural to expose information about those resources to the programmer. In this paper, we take the view that the number of servers p should be an explicit parameter of the model, which allows us to focus on the tradeoff between the amount of communication and the number of rounds. For example, going back to our cartesian product problem, if the number of servers p is known, there is one optimal way to solve the problem: partition each of the two sets into $g = \sqrt{p}$ groups, and let each server handle one pair of groups.

A model with p as explicit parameter was proposed by Koutris and Suciu [17], who showed both lower and upper bounds for one round of communication. In this model only tuples are sent and they must be routed independent of each other. For example, [17] proves that multi-joins on the same attribute can be computed in one round, while multi-joins on different attributes, like $R(x), S(x,y), T(y)$ require strictly more than one round. The study was mostly focused on understanding data skew, the model was limited, and the results do not apply to more than one round.

In this paper we develop more general models, establish lower bounds that hold even in the absence of skew, and use a bit model, rather than a tuple model, to represent data.

Our lower bound models and results.

We define the *Massively Parallel Communication* (MPC) model, to analyze the tradeoff between the number of rounds and the amount of communication required in a massively parallel computing environment. We include the number of servers p as a parameter, and allow each server to be infinitely powerful, subject only to the data to which it has access. The model requires that each server receives only $O(N/p^{1-\varepsilon})$ bits of data at any step, where N is the problem size, and $\varepsilon \in [0,1]$ is a parameter of the model. This implies that the replication factor is $O(p^{\varepsilon})$ per round. A particularly natural case is $\varepsilon = 0$, which corresponds to a replication factor of $O(1)$, or $O(N/p)$ bits per server; $\varepsilon = 1$ is degenerate, since it allows the entire data to be sent to every server.

We establish both lower and upper bounds for computing a full conjunctive query q, in two settings. First, we restrict the computation to a single communication round and examine the minimum parameter ε for which it is possible to compute q with $O(N/p^{1-\varepsilon})$ bits per processor; we call this the *space exponent*. We show that the space exponent for connected queries is always at least $1 - 1/\tau^*(q)$, where $\tau^*(q)$ is the *fractional (vertex) covering number* of the hypergraph associated with q [6], which is the optimal value of the vertex cover linear program (LP) for that hypergraph. This lower bound applies to the strongest possible model in which servers can encode any information in their messages, and have access to a common source of randomness. This is stronger than the lower bounds in [1, 17], which assume that the units being exchanged are tuples.

Our one round lower bound holds even in the special case of *matching databases*, when all attributes are from the same domain $[n]$ and all input relations are (hypergraph) matchings, in other words, every relation has exactly n tuples, and every attribute contains every value $1, 2, \ldots, n$ exactly once. Thus, the lower bound holds even in a case in which there is no data skew. We describe a simple tuple-independent algorithm that is easily implementable in the MapReduce framework, which, in the special case of matching databases, matches our lower bound for any conjunctive query. The algorithm uses the optimal solution for the fractional vertex cover to find an optimal split of the input data to the servers. For example, the linear query $L_2 = S_1(x,y), S_2(y,z)$ has an optimal vertex cover $0, 1, 0$ (for the variables x, y, z), hence its space exponent is $\varepsilon = 0$, whereas the cycle query $C_3 = S_1(x,y), S_2(y,z), S_3(z,x)$ has optimal vertex cover $1/2, 1/2, 1/2$ and space exponent $\varepsilon = 1/3$. We note that recent work [13, 4, 20] gives upper bounds on the query size in terms of a fractional *edge cover*, while our results are in terms of the *vertex cover*. Thus, our first result is:

THEOREM 1.1. *For every connected conjunctive query q, any p-processor randomized MPC algorithm computing q in one round requires space exponent $\epsilon \geq 1 - 1/\tau^*(q)$. This lower bound holds even over matching databases, for which it is optimal.*

Second, we establish lower bounds for multiple communication steps, for a restricted version of the MPC model, called *tuple-based* MPC model. The messages sent in the first round are still unrestricted, but in subsequent rounds the servers can send only tuples, either base tuples in the input tables, or join tuples corresponding to a subquery; moreover, the destinations of each tuple may depend only on the tuple content, the message received in the first round, the server, and the round. We note that any multi-step MapReduce program is tuple-based, because in any map function the key of the intermediate value depends only on the input tuple to the map function. Here, we prove that the number of rounds required is, essentially, given by the depth of a query plan for the query, where each operator is a subquery that can be computed in one round for the given ε. For example, to compute a length k chain query L_k, if $\varepsilon = 0$, the optimal computation is a bushy join tree, where each operator is L_2 (a two-way join) and the optimal number of rounds is $\log_2 k$. If $\varepsilon = 1/2$, then we can use L_4 as operator (a four-way join), and the optimal number of rounds is $\log_4 k$. More generally, we can show nearly matching upper and lower bounds based on graph-theoretic properties of the query such as the following:

THEOREM 1.2. *For space exponent ε, the number of rounds required for any tuple-based MPC algorithm to compute any tree-like conjunctive query q is at least $\lceil \log_{k_\varepsilon}(diam(q)) \rceil$ where $k_\varepsilon = 2\lfloor 1/(1-\varepsilon) \rfloor$ and $diam(q)$ is the diameter of q. Moreover, for any connected conjunctive query q, this lower bound is nearly matched (up to a difference of essentially one round) by a tuple-based MPC algorithm with space exponent ε.*

These are the first lower bounds that apply to multiple rounds of MapReduce. Both lower bounds in Theorem 1.1 and Theorem 1.2 are stated in a strong form: we show that any algorithm on the MPC model retrieves only a $1/p^{\Omega(1)}$ fraction of the answers to the query in expectation, when the inputs are drawn uniformly at random (the exponent depends on the query and on ε); Yao's Lemma [26] immediately implies a lower bound for any randomized algorithm over worst-case inputs. Notice that the fraction of answers gets worse as the number of servers p increases. In other words, the more parallelism we want, the worse an algorithm performs, if the number of communication rounds is bounded.

Related work in communication complexity.

The results we show belong to the study of communication complexity, for which there is a very large body of existing research [18]. Communication complexity considers the number of bits that need to be communicated between cooperating agents in order to solve computational problems when the agents have unlimited computational power. Our model is related to the so-called number-in-hand multiparty communication complexity, in which there are multiple agents and no shared information at the start of communication. This has already been shown to be important to understanding the processing of massive data: Analysis of number-in-hand (NIH) communication complexity has been the main method for obtaining lower bounds on the space required for data stream algorithms (e.g. [3]).

However, there is something very different about the results that we prove here. In almost all prior lower bounds, there is at least one agent that has access to all communication between agents[1]. (Typically, this is either via a shared blackboard to which all agents have access or a referee who receives all communication.) In this case, no problem on N bits whose answer is M bits long can be shown to require more than $N + M$ bits of communication.

In our MPC model, all communication between servers is *private* and we restrict the communication per processor per step, rather than the total communication. Indeed, the privacy of communication is essential to our lower bounds, since we prove lower bounds that apply when the total communication is much larger than $N + M$. (Our lower bounds for some problems apply when the total communication is as large as $N^{1+\delta}$.)

2. PRELIMINARIES

2.1 Massively Parallel Communication

We fix a parameter $\varepsilon \in [0, 1]$, called the *space exponent*, and define the MPC(ε) model as follows. The computation is performed by p servers, called *workers*, connected by a complete network of private channels. The input data has size N bits, and is initially distributed evenly among the p workers. The computation proceeds in rounds, where each round consists of local computation at the workers interleaved with global communication. The complexity is measured in the number of communication rounds. The servers have unlimited computational power, but there is one important restriction: at each round, a worker may receive a total of only $O(N/p^{1-\varepsilon})$ bits of data from all other workers combined. Our goal is to find lower and upper bounds on the number of communication rounds.

The space exponent represents the degree of replication during communication; in each round, the total amount of data exchanged is $O(p^\varepsilon)$ times the size of the input data. When $\varepsilon = 0$, there is no replication, and we call this the basic MPC model. The case $\varepsilon = 1$ is degenerate because each server can receive the entire data, and any problem can be solved in a single round. Similarly, for any fixed ε, if we allow the computation to run for $\Theta(p^{1-\varepsilon})$ rounds, the entire data can be sent to every server and the model is again degenerate.

We denote M^r_{uv} the message sent by server u to server v during round r and denote $M^r_v = (M^{r-1}_v, (M^r_{1v}, \ldots, M^r_{pv}))$ the concatenation of all messages sent to v up to round r. Assuming $O(1)$ rounds, each message M^r_v holds $O(N/p^{1-\varepsilon})$ bits. For our multi-round lower bounds in Section 4, we will further restrict what the workers can encode in the messages M^r_{uv} during rounds $r \geq 2$.

2.2 Randomization

The MPC model allows randomization. The random bits are available to all servers, and are computed independently of the input data. The algorithm may fail to produce its output with a small probability $\eta > 0$, independent of the input. For example, we use randomization for load balancing, and

[1]Though private-messages models have been defined before, we are aware of only two lines of work where lower bounds make use of the fact that no single agent has access to all communication: (1) Results of [11, 14] use the assumption that communication is both private and (multi-pass) one-way, but unlike the bounds we prove here, their lower bounds are smaller than the total input size; (2) Tiwari [24] defined a distributed model of communication complexity in networks in which in input is given to two processors that communicate privately using other helper processors. However, this model is equivalent to ordinary public two-party communication when the network allows direct private communication between any two processors, as our model does.

abort the computation if the amount of data received during a communication would exceed the $O(N/p^{1-\varepsilon})$ limit, but this will only happen with exponentially small probability.

To prove lower bounds for randomized algorithms, we use Yao's Lemma [26]. We first prove bounds for *deterministic* algorithms, showing that any algorithm fails with probability at least η over inputs chosen randomly from a distribution μ. This implies, by Yao's Lemma, that every randomized algorithm with the same resource bounds will fail on some input (in the support of μ) with probability at least η over the algorithm's random choices.

2.3 Conjunctive Queries

In this paper we consider a particular class of problems for the MPC model, namely computing answers to conjunctive queries over an input database. We fix an input vocabulary $S_1, \ldots, S_\ell$, where each relation S_j has a fixed arity r_j; we denote $r = \sum_{j=1}^{\ell} r_j$. The input data consists of one relation instance for each symbol. We denote n the largest number of tuples in any relation S_j; then, the entire database instance can be encoded using $N = O(n \log n)$ bits, because $\ell = O(1)$ and $r_j = O(1)$ for $j = 1, \ldots, \ell$.

We consider full conjunctive queries (CQs) without self-joins, denoted as follows:

$$q(x_1, \ldots, x_k) = S_1(\bar{x}_1), \ldots, S_\ell(\bar{x}_\ell) \quad (1)$$

The query is *full*, meaning that every variable in the body appears the head (for example $q(x) = S(x, y)$ is not full), and *without self-joins*, meaning that each relation name S_j appears only once (for example $q(x, y, z) = S(x, y), S(y, z)$ has a self-join). The *hypergraph* of a query q is defined by introducing one node for each variable in the body and one hyperedge for each set of variables that occur in a single atom. We say that a conjunctive query is *connected* if the query hypergraph is connected (for example, $q(x, y) = R(x), S(y)$ is not connected). We use vars(S_j) to denote the set of variables in the atom S_j, and atoms(x_i) to denote the set of atoms where x_i occurs; k and ℓ denote the number of variables and atoms in q, as in (1). The *connected components* of q are the maximal connected subqueries of q. Table 1 illustrates example queries used throughout this paper.

We consider two query evaluation problems. In JOIN-REPORTING, we require that all tuples in the relation defined by q be produced. In JOIN-WITNESS, we require the production of at least one tuple in the relation defined by q, if one exists; JOIN-WITNESS is the verified version of the natural decision problem JOIN-NONEMPTINESS.

Characteristic of a Query.

The *characteristic* of a conjunctive query q as in (1) is defined as $\chi(q) = k + \ell - \sum_j r_j - c$, where k is the number of variables, ℓ is the number of atoms, r_j is the arity of atom S_j, and c is the number of connected components of q.

For a query q and a set of atoms $M \subseteq$ atoms(q), define q/M to be the query that results from contracting the edges in the hypergraph of q. As an example, for the query L_5 in Table 1, $L_5/\{S_2, S_4\} = S_1(x_1, x_2), S_3(x_2, x_4), S_5(x_4, x_6)$.

LEMMA 2.1. *The characteristic of a query q satisfies the following properties:*

(a) If $q_1, \ldots, q_c$ are the connected components of q, then $\chi(q) = \sum_{i=1}^{c} \chi(q_i)$.

(b) For any $M \subseteq$ atoms(q), $\chi(q/M) = \chi(q) - \chi(M)$.

(c) $\chi(q) \leq 0$.

(d) For any $M \subseteq$ atoms(q), $\chi(q) \leq \chi(q/M)$.

PROOF. Property (a) is immediate from the definition of χ, since the connected components of q are disjoint with respect to variables and atoms. Since q/M can be produced by contracting according to each connected component of M in turn, by property (a) and induction it suffices to show that property (b) holds in the case that M is connected. If a connected M has k_M variables, ℓ_M atoms, and total arity r_M, then the query after contraction, q/M, will have the same number of connected components, $k_M - 1$ fewer variables, and the terms for the number of atoms and total arity will be reduced by $\ell_M - r_M$ for a total reduction of $k_M + \ell_M - r_M - 1 = \chi(M)$. Thus, property (b) follows.

By property (a), it suffices to prove (c) when q is connected. If q is a single atom then $\chi(q) \leq 0$, since the number of variables is at most the arity of the atom in q. We reduce to this case by repeatedly contracting the atoms of q until only one remains and showing that $\chi(q) \leq \chi(q/S_j)$: Let $m \leq r_j$ be the number of distinct variables in atom S_j. Then, $\chi(q/S_j) = (\ell - 1) + (k - m + 1) - (r - r_j) - 1 = \chi(q) + (r_j - m) \geq \chi(q)$. Property (d) also follows by the combination of property (b) and property (c) applied to M. □

Finally, let us call a query q *tree-like* if q is connected and $\chi(q) = 0$. For example, the query L_k is tree-like, and so is any query over a binary vocabulary whose graph is a tree. Over non-binary vocabularies, any tree-like query is acyclic, but the converse does not hold: $q = S_1(x_0, x_1, x_2), S_2(x_1, x_2, x_3)$ is acyclic but not tree-like. An important property of tree-like queries is that every connected subquery will be also tree-like.

Vertex Cover and Edge Packing.

A *fractional vertex cover* of a query q is any feasible solution of the LP shown on the left of Fig. 1. The vertex cover associates a non-negative number u_i to each variable x_i s.t. every atom S_j is "covered", $\sum_{i:x_i \in \text{vars}(S_j)} v_i \geq 1$. The dual LP corresponds to a *fractional edge packing* problem (also known as a *fractional matching* problem), which associates non-negative numbers u_j to each atom S_j. The two LPs have the same optimal value of the objective function, known as the *fractional covering number* [6] of the hypergraph associated with q and denoted by $\tau^*(q)$. Thus, $\tau^*(q) = \min \sum_i v_i = \max \sum_j u_j$. Additionally, if all inequalities are satisfied as equalities by a solution to the LP, we say that the solution is *tight*.

For a simple example, a fractional vertex cover of the query[2] $L_3 = S_1(x_1, x_2), S_2(x_2, x_3), S_3(x_3, x_4)$ is any solu-

[2]We drop the head variables when clear from the context.

Vertex Covering LP	Edge Packing LP
$\forall j \in [\ell]:$ $\sum_{i:x_i \in \text{vars}(S_j)} v_i \geq 1$ (2) $\forall i \in [k]: v_i \geq 0$	$\forall i \in [k]:$ $\sum_{j:x_i \in \text{vars}(S_j)} u_j \leq 1$ (3) $\forall j \in [\ell]: u_j \geq 0$
minimize $\sum_{i=1}^{k} v_i$	maximize $\sum_{j=1}^{\ell} u_j$

Figure 1: The vertex covering LP of the hypergraph of a query q, and its dual edge packing LP.

tion to $v_1+v_2 \geq 1$, $v_2+v_3 \geq 1$ and $v_3+v_4 \geq 1$; the optimal is achieved by $(v_1, v_2, v_3, v_4) = (0, 1, 1, 0)$, which is not tight. An edge packing is a solution to $u_1 \leq 1$, $u_1 + u_2 \leq 1$, $u_2 + u_3 \leq 1$ and $u_3 \leq 1$, and the optimal is achieved by $(1, 0, 1)$, which is tight.

The fractional edge *packing* should not be confused with the fractional edge *cover*, which has been used recently in several papers to prove bounds on query size and the running time of a sequential algorithm for the query [4, 20]; for the results in this paper we need the fractional packing. The two notions coincide, however, when they are tight.

2.4 Input Servers

We assume that, at the beginning of the algorithm, each relation S_j is stored on a separate server, called an *input server*, which during the first round sends a message M^1_{ju} to every worker u. After the first round, the input servers are no longer used in the computation. All lower bounds in this paper assume that the relations S_j are given on separate input servers. All upper bounds hold for either model.

The lower bounds for the model with separate input servers carry over immediately to the standard MPC model, because any algorithm in the standard model can be simulated in the model with separate input servers. Indeed, the algorithm must compute the output correctly for any initial distribution of the input data on the p servers: we simply choose to distribute the input relations $S_1, \ldots, S_\ell$ such that the first p/ℓ servers receive S_1, the next p/ℓ servers receive S_2, etc., then simulate the algorithm in the model with separate input servers (see [17, proof of Proposition 3.5] for a detailed discussion). Thus, it suffices to prove our lower bounds assuming that each input relation is stored on a separate input server. In fact, this model is even more powerful, because an input server has now access to the entire relation S_j, and can therefore perform some global computation on S_j, for example compute statistics, find outliers, etc., which are common in practice.

2.5 Input Distribution

We find it useful to consider input databases of the following form that we call a *matching* database: The domain of the input database will be $[n]$, for $n > 0$. In such a database each relation S_j is an *r_j-dimensional matching*, where r_j is its arity. In other words, S_j has exactly n tuples and each of its columns contains exactly the values $1, 2, \ldots, n$; each attribute of S_j is a key. For example, if S_j is binary, then an instance of S_j is a permutation on $[n]$; if S_j is ternary then an instance consists of n node-disjoint triangles. Moreover, the answer to a connected conjunctive query q on a matching database is a table where each attribute is a key, because we have assumed that q is full; in particular, the output to q has at most n tuples. In our lower bounds we assume that a matching database is randomly chosen with uniform probability, for a fixed n.

Matching databases are database instances *without skew*. By stating our lower bounds on matching databases we make them even stronger, because they imply that a query cannot be computed even in the absence of skew; of course, the lower bounds also hold for arbitrary instances. Our upper bounds, however, hold only on matching databases. Data skew is a known problem in parallel processing, and requires dedicated techniques. Lower and upper bounds accounting for the presence of skew are discussed in [17].

2.6 Friedgut's Inequality

Friedgut [10] introduces the following class of inequalities. Each inequality is described by a hypergraph, which in our paper corresponds to a query, so we will describe the inequality using query terminology. Fix a query q as in (1), and let $n > 0$. For every atom $S_j(\bar{x}_j)$ of arity r_j, we introduce a set of n^{r_j} variables $w_j(\mathbf{a}_j) \geq 0$, where $\mathbf{a}_j \in [n]^{r_j}$. If $\mathbf{a} \in [n]^r$, we denote by $\mathbf{a}_j$ the vector of size r_j that results from projecting on the variables of the relation S_j. Let $\mathbf{u} = (u_1, \ldots, u_\ell)$ be a fractional *edge cover* for q. Then:

$$\sum_{\mathbf{a}\in[n]^k} \prod_{j=1}^{\ell} w_j(\mathbf{a}_j) \leq \prod_{j=1}^{\ell} \left(\sum_{\mathbf{a}_j \in [n]^{r_j}} w_j(\mathbf{a}_j)^{1/u_j} \right)^{u_j} \tag{4}$$

We illustrate Friedgut's inequality on C_3 and L_3:

$$\begin{aligned} C_3(x, y, z) &= S_1(x, y), S_2(y, z), S_3(z, x) \\ L_3(x, y, z, w) &= S_1(x, y), S_2(y, z), S_3(z, w) \end{aligned} \tag{5}$$

C_3 has cover $(1/2, 1/2, 1/2)$, and L_3 has cover $(1, 0, 1)$. Thus, we obtain the following inequalities, where a, b, c stand for w_1, w_2, w_3 respectively:

$$\sum_{x,y,z\in[n]} a_{xy} \cdot b_{yz} \cdot c_{zx} \leq \sqrt{\sum_{x,y\in[n]} a^2_{xy} \sum_{y,z\in[n]} b^2_{yz} \sum_{z,x\in[n]} c^2_{zx}}$$

$$\sum_{x,y,z,w\in[n]} a_{xy} \cdot b_{yz} \cdot c_{zw} \leq \sum_{x,y\in[n]} a_{xy} \cdot \max_{y,z\in[n]} b_{yz} \cdot \sum_{z,w\in[n]} c_{zw}$$

where we used the fact that $\lim_{u\to 0}(\sum b_{yz}^{\frac{1}{u}})^u = \max b_{yz}$.

Friedgut's inequalities immediately imply a well known result developed in a series of papers [13, 4, 20] that gives an upper bound on the size of a query answer as a function on the cardinality of the relations. For example in the case of C_3, consider an instance S_1, S_2, S_3, and set $a_{xy} = 1$ if $(x, y) \in S_1$, otherwise $a_{xy} = 0$ (and similarly for b_{yz}, c_{zx}). We obtain then $|C_3| \leq \sqrt{|S_1| \cdot |S_2| \cdot |S_3|}$. Note that all these results are expressed in terms of a fractional edge *cover*. When we apply Friedgut's inequality in Section 3.2 to a fractional edge *packing*, we ensure that the packing is tight.

3. ONE COMMUNICATION STEP

Let the *space exponent* of a query q be the smallest $\varepsilon \geq 0$ for which q can be computed using one communication step in the MPC(ε) model. In this section, we prove Theorem 1.1, which gives both a general lower bound on the space exponent for evaluating connected conjunctive queries and a precise characterization of the space exponent for evaluating them them over matching databases. The proof consists of two parts: we show the optimal algorithm in 3.1, and then present the matching lower bound in 3.2.

3.1 An Algorithm for One Round

We describe here an algorithm, which we call HYPERCUBE (HC), that computes a conjunctive query in one step. It uses ideas that can be traced back to Ganguly [12] for parallel processing of Datalog programs, and were also used by Afrati and Ullman [2] to optimize joins in MapReduce, and by Suri and Vassilvitskii [22] to count triangles.

Let q be a query as in (1). Associate to each variable x_i a real value $e_i \geq 0$, called the *share exponent* of x_i, such that $\sum_{i=1}^{k} e_i = 1$. If p is the number of servers, define $p_i = p^{e_i}$: these values are called *shares* [2]. We assume that

Conjunctive Query	Expected answer size	Minimum Vertex Cover	Variable Shares	Value $\tau^*(q)$	Space Exponent
$C_k(x_1, \dots, x_k) = \bigwedge_{j=1}^{k} S_j(x_j, x_{(j+1) \bmod k})$	1	$\frac{1}{2}, \dots, \frac{1}{2}$	$\frac{1}{k}, \dots, \frac{1}{k}$	$k/2$	$1 - 2/k$
$T_k(z, x_1, \dots, x_k) = \bigwedge_{j=1}^{k} S_j(z, x_j)$	n	$1, 0, \dots, 0$	$1, 0, \dots, 0$	1	0
$L_k(x_0, x_1, \dots, x_k) = \bigwedge_{j=1}^{k} S_j(x_{j-1}, x_j)$	n	$0, 1, 0, 1, \dots$	$0, \frac{1}{\lceil k/2 \rceil}, 0, \frac{1}{\lceil k/2 \rceil}, \dots$	$\lceil k/2 \rceil$	$1 - 1/\lceil k/2 \rceil$
$B_{k,m}(x_1, \dots, x_k) = \bigwedge_{I \subseteq [k], \lvert I \rvert = m} S_I(\bar{x}_I)$	$n^{k-(m-1)\binom{k}{m}}$	$\frac{1}{m}, \dots, \frac{1}{m}$	$\frac{1}{k}, \dots, \frac{1}{k}$	k/m	$1 - m/k$

Table 1: Running examples in this paper: C_k = cycle query, L_k = linear query, T_k = star query, and $B_{k,m}$ = query with $\binom{k}{m}$ relations, where each relation contains a distinct set of m out of the k head variables. Assuming the inputs are random permutation, the answer sizes represent exact values for L_k, T_k, and expected values for $C_k, B_{k,m}$.

the shares are integers. Thus, $p = \prod_{i=1}^{k} p_i$, and each server can be uniquely identified with a point in the k-dimensional hypercube $[p_1] \times \cdots \times [p_k]$.

The algorithm uses k independently chosen random hash functions $h_i : [n] \to [p_i]$, one for each variable x_i. During the communication step, the algorithm sends every tuple $S_j(\mathbf{a}_j) = S_j(a_{i_1}, \dots, a_{i_{r_j}})$ to all servers $\mathbf{y} \in [p_1] \times \cdots \times [p_k]$ such that $h_{i_m}(a_{i_m}) = \mathbf{y}_{i_m}$ for any $1 \leq m \leq r_j$. In other words, the tuple $S_j(\mathbf{a}_j)$ knows the server number along the dimensions $i_1, \dots, i_{r_j}$, but does not know the server number along the other dimensions, and there it needs to be replicated. After receiving the data, each server outputs all query answers derivable from the received data. The algorithm finds all answers, because each potential output tuple $(a_1, \dots, a_k)$ is known by the server $\mathbf{y} = (h_1(a_1), \dots, h_k(a_k))$.

EXAMPLE 3.1. *We illustrate how to compute the query* $C_3(x_1, x_2, x_3) = S_1(x_1, x_2), S_2(x_2, x_3), S_3(x_3, x_1)$. *Consider the share exponents* $e_1 = e_2 = e_3 = 1/3$. *Each of the* p *servers is uniquely identified by a triple* (y_1, y_2, y_3), *where* $y_1, y_2, y_3 \in [p^{1/3}]$. *In the first communication round, the input server storing* S_1 *sends each tuple* $S_1(a_1, a_2)$ *to all servers with index* $(h_1(a_1), h_2(a_2), y_3)$, *for all* $y_3 \in [p^{1/3}]$: *notice that each tuple is replicated* $p^{1/3}$ *times. The input servers holding* S_2 *and* S_3 *proceed similarly with their tuples. After round 1, any three tuples* $S_1(a_1, a_2)$, $S_2(a_2, a_3)$, $S_3(a_3, a_1)$ *that contribute to the output tuple* $C_3(a_1, a_2, a_3)$ *will be seen by the server* $\mathbf{y} = (h_1(a_1), h_2(a_2), h_3(a_3))$: *any server that detects three matching tuples outputs them.*

PROPOSITION 3.2. *Fix a fractional vertex cover* $\mathbf{v} = (v_1, \dots, v_k)$ *for a connected conjunctive query* q, *and let* $\tau = \sum_i v_i$. *The HC algorithm with share exponents* $e_i = v_i/\tau$ *computes* q *on any matching database in one round in* $MPC(\varepsilon)$, *where* $\varepsilon = 1 - 1/\tau$, *with probability of failure* $\eta \leq exp(-O(n/p^{\varepsilon}))$.

This proves the optimality claim of Theorem 1.1: choose a vertex cover with value $\tau^*(q)$, the fractional covering number of q. Proposition 3.2 shows that q can be computed in one round in $MPC(\varepsilon)$, with $\varepsilon = 1 - 1/\tau^*$.

PROOF. Since $\mathbf{v}$ forms a fractional vertex cover, for every relation symbol S_j we have $\sum_{i:x_i \in \text{vars}(S_j)} e_i \geq 1/\tau$. Therefore, $\sum_{i:x_i \notin \text{vars}(S_j)} e_i \leq 1 - 1/\tau$. Every tuple $S_j(\mathbf{a}_j)$ is replicated $\prod_{i:x_i \notin \text{vars}(S_j)} p_i \leq p^{1-1/\tau}$ times. Thus, the total number of tuples that are received by all servers is $O(n \cdot p^{1-1/\tau})$. We claim that these tuples are uniformly distributed among the p servers: this proves the theorem, since then each server receives $O(n/p^{1/\tau})$ tuples.

To prove the claim, we note that for each tuple $t \in S_j$, the probability over the random choices of the hash functions $h_1, \dots, h_k$ that the tuple is sent to server s is precisely $\prod_{i:x_i \in \text{vars}(S_j)} p_i^{-1}$. Thus, the expected number of tuples from S_j sent to s is $n/\prod_{i:x_i \in S_j} p_i \leq n/p^{1-\varepsilon}$. Since S_j is an r_j-matching, different tuples are sent by the random hash functions to independent destinations, since any two tuples differ in every attribute. Using standard Chernoff bounds, we derive that the probability that the actual number of tuples per server deviates more than a constant factor from the expected number is $\eta \leq \exp(-O(n/p^{1-\varepsilon}))$. □

3.2 A Lower Bound for One Round

For a fixed n, consider a probability distribution where the input I is chosen randomly, with uniform probability from all matching database instances. Let $\mathbf{E}[|q(I)|]$ denote the expected number of answers to the query q. We prove in this section:

THEOREM 3.3. *Let* q *be a connected conjunctive query, let* τ^* *be the fractional covering number of* q, *and* $\varepsilon < 1 - 1/\tau^*$. *Then, any deterministic MPC(ε) algorithm that runs in one communication round on* p *servers reports* $O(\mathbf{E}[|q(I)|]/p^{\tau^*(1-\varepsilon)-1})$ *answers in expectation.*

In particular, the theorem implies that the space exponent of q is at least $1 - 1/\tau^*$. Before we prove the theorem, we show how to extend it to randomized algorithms using Yao's principle. For this, we show a lemma that we also need later.

LEMMA 3.4. *The expected number of answers to connected query* q *is* $\mathbf{E}[|q(I)|] = n^{1+\chi(q)}$, *where the expectation is over a uniformly chosen matching database* I.

PROOF. For any relation S_j, and any tuple $\mathbf{a}_j \in [n]^{r_j}$, the probability that S_j contains $\mathbf{a}_j$ is $\mathbf{P}(\mathbf{a_j} \in S_j) = n^{1-r_j}$. Given a tuple $\mathbf{a} \in [n]^k$ of the same arity as the query answer, let $\mathbf{a}_j$ denote its projection on the variables in S_j. Then:

$$\mathbf{E}[|q(I)|] = \sum_{\mathbf{a} \in [n]^k} \mathbf{P}(\bigwedge_{j=1}^{\ell} (\mathbf{a}_j \in S_j))$$

$$= \sum_{\mathbf{a} \in [n]^k} \prod_{j=1}^{\ell} \mathbf{P}(\mathbf{a}_j \in S_j) = \sum_{\mathbf{a} \in [n]^k} \prod_{j=1}^{\ell} n^{1-r_j} = n^{k+\ell-r}$$

Since query q is connected, $k + \ell - r = 1 + \chi(q)$ and hence $\mathbf{E}[|q(I)|] = n^{1+\chi(q)}$. □

Theorem 3.3 and Lemma 3.4, together with Yao's lemma, imply the following lower bound for randomized algorithms.

COROLLARY 3.5. *Let* q *be any connected conjunctive query. Any one round randomized* $MPC(\varepsilon)$ *algorithm with* $p = \omega(1)$ *and* $\varepsilon < 1 - 1/\tau^*(q)$ *fails to compute* q *with probability* $\eta = \Omega(n^{\chi(q)}) = n^{-O(1)}$.

PROOF. Choose a matching database I input to q uniformly at random. Let $a(I)$ denote the set of correct answers returned by the algorithm on I: $a(I) \subseteq q(I)$. Observe that the algorithm fails on I iff $|q(I) - a(I)| > 0$.

Let $\gamma = 1/p^{\tau^*(q)(1-\varepsilon)-1}$. Since $p = \omega(1)$ and $\varepsilon < 1 - 1/\tau^*(q)$, it follows that $\gamma = o(1)$. By Theorem 3.3, for any deterministic one round MPC(ε) algorithm we have $\mathbf{E}[|a(I)|] = O(\gamma)\mathbf{E}[|q(I)|]$ and hence, by Lemma 3.4,

$$\mathbf{E}[|q(I) - a(I)|] = (1 - o(1))\mathbf{E}[|q(I)|] = (1 - o(1))n^{1+\chi(q)}$$

However, we also have that

$$\mathbf{E}[|q(I) - a(I)|] \leq \mathbf{P}[|q(I) - a(I)| > 0] \cdot \max_I |q(I) - a(I)|.$$

Since $|q(I) - a(I)| \leq |q(I)| \leq n$ for all I, we see that the failure probability of the algorithm for randomly chosen I, $\mathbf{P}[|q(I) - a(I)| > 0]$, is at least $\eta = (1 - o(1))n^{\chi(q)}$ which is $n^{-O(1)}$ for any q. Yao's lemma implies that every one round randomized MPC(ε) algorithm will fail to compute q with probability at least η on some matching database input. □

In the rest of the section we prove Theorem 3.3, which deals with one-round deterministic algorithms and random matching databases I. Let us fix some server and let $m(I)$ denote the function specifying the message the server receives on input I. Intuitively, this server can only report those tuples that it knows are in the input based on the value of $m(I)$. To make this notion precise, for any fixed value m of $m(I)$, define the set of tuples of a relation R of arity r *known* by the server given message m as

$$K_m(R) = \{t \in [n]^r \mid \text{for all matching databases } I, \; m(I) = m \Rightarrow t \in R(I)\}$$

We will particularly apply this definition with $R = S_j$ and $R = q$. Clearly, an output tuple $\mathbf{a} \in K_m(q)$ iff for every j, $\mathbf{a}_j \in K_m(S_j)$, where $\mathbf{a}_j$ denotes the projection of $\mathbf{a}$ on the variables in the atom S_j.

We will first prove an upper bound for each $|K_m(S_j)|$ in Section 3.2.1. Then in Section 3.2.2 we use this bound, along with Friedgut's inequality, to establish an upper bound for $|K_m(q)|$ and hence prove Theorem 3.3.

3.2.1 Bounding the Knowledge of Each Relation

Fix a server, and an input relation S_j. We prove here:

LEMMA 3.6. *$\mathbf{E}[|K_{m(I)}(S_j)|] = O(n/p^{1-\varepsilon})$ for random I.*

Since S_j has exactly n tuples, the lemma says that any server knows, in expectation, only a fraction $f = O(1/p^{1-\varepsilon})$ of tuples from S_j. While $m = m(I)$ is the concatenation of ℓ messages, one for each input relation, $K_m(S_j)$ depends only on the part of the message corresponding to S_j, so we can assume w.l.o.g. that m is a function only of S_j, denoted by m_j. For convenience, we also drop the index j and write $S = S_j, r = r_j$, $m = m_j$; $m(S)$ is now a function computed on the single r-dimensional matching relation S.

Observe that for a randomly chosen matching database I, S is a uniformly chosen r-dimensional matching. There are precisely $(n!)^{r-1}$ different r-dimensional matchings on $[n]$ and, since q is of fixed total arity, the number of bits N necessary to represent the entire input I is $\Theta(\log(n!)) = \Theta(n \log n)$. Therefore, $m(S)$ is at most $O((n \log n)/p^{1-\varepsilon})$ bits long for all S.

LEMMA 3.7. *Suppose that for all r-dimensional matchings S, $m(S)$ is at most $f \cdot (r-1)\log(n!)$ bits long. Then $\mathbf{E}[|K_{m(S)}(S)|] \leq f \cdot n$, where the expectation is taken over random choices of the matching S.*

We observe that Lemma 3.6 is an immediate corollary of Lemma 3.7 by setting f to be $O(1/p^{1-\varepsilon})$.

PROOF. Let m be a possible value for $m(S)$. Since m fixes precisely $|K_m(S)|$ tuples of S,

$$\begin{aligned}\log|\{S \mid m(S) = m\}| &\leq (r-1)\textstyle\sum_{i=1}^{n-|K_m(S)|} \log i \\ &\leq (1 - |K_m(S)|/n)(r-1)\textstyle\sum_{i=1}^{n} \log i \\ &= (1 - |K_m(S)|/n)\log(n!)^{r-1}. \end{aligned} \quad (6)$$

We can bound the value we want by considering the binary entropy of the distribution S, $H(S) = \log(n!)^{r-1}$. By applying the chain rule for entropy, we have

$$\begin{aligned} H(S) &= H(m(S)) + \textstyle\sum_m \mathbf{P}(m(S) = m) \cdot H(S|m(S) = m) \\ &\leq f \cdot H(S) + \textstyle\sum_m \mathbf{P}(m(S) = m) \cdot H(S|m(S) = m) \\ &\leq f \cdot H(S) + \textstyle\sum_m \mathbf{P}(m(S) = m) \cdot (1 - |K_m(S)|/n)H(S) \\ &= f \cdot H(S) + (1 - \textstyle\sum_m \mathbf{P}(m(S) = m)\; |K_m(S)|/n)H(S) \\ &= f \cdot H(S) + (1 - \mathbf{E}[|K_{m(S)}(S)|]/n)H(S) \end{aligned} \quad (7)$$

where the first inequality follows from the assumed upper bound on $|m(S)|$, the second inequality follows by (6), and the last two lines follow by definition. Dividing both sides of (7) by $H(S)$ and rearranging we obtain that $\mathbf{E}[|K_{m(S)}(S)|] \leq f \cdot n$, as required. □

3.2.2 Bounding the Knowledge of the Query

Here we conclude the proof of Theorem 3.3 using the results in the previous section. Let us fix some server. Lemma 3.6 implies that, for $f = c/p^{1-\varepsilon}$ for some constant c and randomly chosen matching database I, $\mathbf{E}[|K_{m_j(I)}(S_j)|] = \mathbf{E}[|K_{m_j(S_j)}(S_j)|] \leq f \cdot n$ for all $j \in [\ell]$. We prove:

LEMMA 3.8. *$\mathbf{E}[|K_{m(I)}(q)|] \leq f^{\tau^*(q)} n^{1+\chi(q)}$ for randomly chosen matching database I.*

This proves Theorem 3.3, since the total number of tuples known by all p servers is bounded by:

$$\begin{aligned} p \cdot \mathbf{E}[|K_{m(I)}(q)|] &\leq p \cdot f^{\tau^*(q)} \mathbf{E}[|q(I)|] \\ &= p \cdot c^{\tau^*(q)} \cdot \mathbf{E}[|q(I)|]/p^{(1-\varepsilon)\tau^*(q)} \end{aligned}$$

which is the upper bound in Theorem 3.3 since c and $\tau^*(q)$ are constants. In the rest of the section we prove Lemma 3.8.

We start with some notation. For $\mathbf{a}_j \in [n]^{r_j}$, let $w_j(\mathbf{a}_j)$ denote the probability that the server knows the tuple $\mathbf{a}_j$. In other words $w_j(\mathbf{a}_j) = \mathbf{P}(\mathbf{a}_j \in K_{m_j(S_j)}(S_j))$, where the probability is over the random choices of S_j.

LEMMA 3.9. *For any relation S_j:*

(a) $\forall \mathbf{a}_j \in [n]^{r_j} : w_j(\mathbf{a}_j) \leq n^{1-r_j}$, and

(b) $\sum_{\mathbf{a}_j \in [n]^{r_j}} w_j(\mathbf{a}_j) \leq fn$.

PROOF. To show (a), notice that $w_j(\mathbf{a}_j) \leq \mathbf{P}(\mathbf{a}_j \in S_j) = n^{1-r_j}$, while (b) follows from the fact $\sum_{\mathbf{a}_j \in [n]^{r_j}} w_j(\mathbf{a}_j) = \mathbf{E}[|K_{m_j(S_j)}(S_j)|] \leq fn$. □

Since the server receives a separate message for each relation S_j, from a distinct input server, the events $\mathbf{a}_1 \in K_{m_1}(S_1), \ldots, \mathbf{a}_\ell \in K_{m_\ell}(S_\ell)$ are independent, hence:

$$\mathbf{E}[|K_{m(I)}(q)|] = \sum_{\mathbf{a}\in[n]^k} \mathbf{P}(\mathbf{a} \in K_{m(I)}(q)) = \sum_{\mathbf{a}\in[n]^k} \prod_{j=1}^{\ell} w_j(\mathbf{a}_j)$$

We now prove Lemma 3.8 using Friedgut's inequality. Recall that in order to apply the inequality, we need to find a fractional edge cover. Fix an optimal fractional edge packing $\mathbf{u} = (u_1, \ldots, u_\ell)$ as in Fig. 1. By duality, we have that $\sum_j u_j = \tau^*$, where τ^* is the fractional covering number (which is the value of the optimal *fractional vertex cover*, and equal to the value of the optimal *fractional edge packing*). Given q, defined as in (1), consider the *extended query*, which has a new unary atom for each variable x_i:

$$q'(x_1, \ldots, x_k) = S_1(\bar{x}_1), \ldots, S_\ell(\bar{x}_\ell), T_1(x_1), \ldots, T_k(x_k)$$

For each new symbol T_i, define $u'_i = 1 - \sum_{j:x_i\in\text{vars}(S_j)} u_j$. Since $\mathbf{u}$ is a packing, $u'_i \geq 0$. Let us define $\mathbf{u}' = (u'_1, \ldots, u'_k)$.

LEMMA 3.10. *(a) The assignment $(\mathbf{u}, \mathbf{u}')$ is both a tight fractional edge packing and a tight fractional edge cover for q'. (b) $\sum_{j=1}^{\ell} r_j u_j + \sum_{i=1}^{k} u'_i = k$*

PROOF. (a) is straightforward, since for every variable x_i we have $u'_i + \sum_{j:x_i\in\text{vars}(S_j)} u_j = 1$. Summing up:

$$k = \sum_{i=1}^{k}(u'_i + \sum_{j:x_i\in\text{vars}(S_j)} u_j) = \sum_{i=1}^{k} u'_i + \sum_{j=1}^{\ell} r_j u_j$$

which proves (b). □

We will apply Friedgut's inequality to the extended query q' to prove Lemma 3.8. Set the variables $w(-)$ used in Friedgut's inequality as follows:

$$w_j(\mathbf{a}_j) = \mathbf{P}(\mathbf{a}_j \in K_{m_j(S_j)}(S_j)) \quad \text{for } S_j\text{, tuple } \mathbf{a}_j \in [n]^{r_j}$$
$$w'_i(a) = 1 \quad \text{for } T_i\text{, value } a \in [n]$$

Recall that, for a tuple $\mathbf{a} \in [n]^k$ we use $\mathbf{a}_j \in [n]^{r_j}$ for its projection on the variables in S_j; with some abuse, we write $\mathbf{a}_i \in [n]$ for the projection on the variable x_i. Then, interpreting $(\sum_{\mathbf{a}} b_{\mathbf{a}}^{1/u})^u$ as $\max_{\mathbf{a}} b_{\mathbf{a}}$ for $u = 0$:

$$\mathbf{E}[|K_m(q)|] = \sum_{\mathbf{a}\in[n]^k} \prod_{j=1}^{\ell} w_j(\mathbf{a}_j) = \sum_{\mathbf{a}\in[n]^k} \prod_{j=1}^{\ell} w_j(\mathbf{a}_j) \prod_{i=1}^{k} w'_i(\mathbf{a}_i)$$

$$\leq \prod_{j=1}^{\ell}\left(\sum_{\mathbf{a}\in[n]^{r_j}} w_j(\mathbf{a})^{1/u_j}\right)^{u_j} \prod_{i=1}^{k}\left(\sum_{a\in[n]} w'_i(a)^{1/u'_i}\right)^{u'_i}$$
$$= \prod_{j=1}^{\ell}\left(\sum_{\mathbf{a}\in[n]^{r_j}} w_j(\mathbf{a})^{1/u_j}\right)^{u_j} \prod_{i=1}^{k} n^{u'_i}$$

Assume first that all $u_j > 0$. By Lemma 3.9, we obtain:

$$\sum_{\mathbf{a}\in[n]^{r_j}} w_j(\mathbf{a})^{1/u_j} \leq (n^{1-r_j})^{1/u_j - 1} \sum_{\mathbf{a}\in[n]^{r_j}} w_j(\mathbf{a})$$
$$\leq n^{(1-r_j)(1/u_j-1)} fn = fn^{(r_j - r_j/u_j + 1/u_j)}$$

Plugging this in the bound, we have shown that:

$$\mathbf{E}[|K_m(q)|] \leq \prod_{j=1}^{\ell}(fn^{(r_j-r_j/u_j+1/u_j)})^{u_j} \prod_{i=1}^{k} n^{u'_i}$$
$$= f^{\sum_{j=1}^{\ell} u_j} n^{(\sum_{j=1}^{\ell} r_j u_j - r + \ell)} n^{\sum_{i=1}^{k} u'_i}$$
$$= n^{(\ell-r)} f^{\sum_{j=1}^{\ell} u_j} n^{(\sum_{j=1}^{\ell} r_j u_j + \sum_{i=1}^{k} u'_i)}$$
$$= n^{\ell+k-r} f^{\tau^*(q)} = n^{1+\chi(q)} f^{\tau^*(q)} \quad (8)$$

If some $u_j = 0$, then replace each u_j with $u_j + \delta$ (still an edge cover). Now we have $\sum_j r_j u_j + \sum_i u'_i = k + r\delta$, hence an extra factor $n^{r\delta}$ in (8), which $\to 1$ when $\delta \to 0$. Lemma 3.8 follows from (8) and $\mathbf{E}[|q(I)|] = n^{1+\chi(q)}$.

3.3 Extensions

Proposition 3.2 and Theorem 3.3 imply that, over matching databases, the space exponent of a query q is $1 - 1/\tau^*$, where τ^* is its fractional covering number. Table 1 illustrates the space exponent for various families of conjunctive queries. We now discuss a few extensions and corollaries whose proofs are given in the full paper: As a corollary of Theorem 3.3 we can characterize the queries with space exponent zero, i.e. those that can be computed in a single round without any replication.

COROLLARY 3.11. *A query q has covering number $\tau^*(q) = 1$ iff there exists a variable shared by all atoms.*

Thus, a query can be computed in one round on MPC(0) iff it has a variable occurring in all atoms. The corollary should be contrasted with the results in [17], which proved that a query is computable in one round iff it is *tall-flat*. Any connected tall-flat query has a variable occurring in all atoms, but the converse is not true in general. The algorithm in [17] works for *any* input data, including skewed inputs, while here we restrict to matching databases. For example, $S_1(x, y), S_2(x, y), S_3(x, z)$ can be computed in one round if all inputs are permutations, but it is not tall-flat, and hence it cannot be computed in one round on general input data.

Theorem 3.3 tells us that a query q can report at most a $1/p^{\tau^*(q)(1-\varepsilon)-1}$ fraction of answers. We show that there is an algorithm achieving this for matching databases:

PROPOSITION 3.12. *Given q and $\varepsilon < 1 - 1/\tau^*(q)$, there exists an algorithm that reports $\Theta(\mathbf{E}[|q(I)|]/p^{\tau^*(q)(1-\varepsilon)-1})$ answers in expectation using one round in the MPC(ε) model.*

Note that the algorithm is forced to run in one round, in an MPC(ε) model strictly weaker than its space exponent, hence it cannot find all the answers: the proposition says that the algorithm can find an expected number of answers that matches Theorem 3.3.

So far, our lower bounds were for the JOIN-REPORTING problem. We can extend the lower bounds to the JOIN-WITNESS problem. For this, we choose unary relations $R(w)$ and $T(z)$ to include each element from $[n]$ independently with probability $1/\sqrt{n}$, and derive:

PROPOSITION 3.13. *For $\varepsilon < 1/2$, there exists no one-round MPC(ε) algorithm that solves JOIN-WITNESS for the query $q(w, x, y, z) = R(w), S_1(w, x), S_2(x, y), S_3(y, z), T(z)$.*

4. MULTIPLE COMMUNICATION STEPS

In this section we consider a restricted version of the MPC(ε) model, called the *tuple-based* MPC(ε) model, which can simulate multi-round MapReduce for database queries. We will establish both upper and lower bounds on the number of rounds needed to compute any connected query q in this tuple-based MPC(ε) model, proving Theorem 1.2.

4.1 An Algorithm for Multiple Rounds

Given an $\varepsilon \geq 0$, let Γ^1_ε denote the class of connected queries q for which $\tau^*(q) \leq 1/(1-\varepsilon)$; these are precisely the queries that can be computed in one round in the MPC(ε) model on matching databases. We extend this definition inductively to larger numbers of rounds: Given Γ_ε^r for some $r \geq 1$, define Γ_ε^{r+1} to be the set of all connected queries q constructed as follows. Let $q_1, \dots, q_m \in \Gamma_\varepsilon^r$ be m queries, and let $q_0 \in \Gamma_\varepsilon^1$ be a query over a different vocabulary $V_1, \dots, V_m$, such that $|\text{vars}(q_j)| = \text{arity}(V_j)$ for all $j \in [m]$. Then, the query $q = q_0[q_1/V_1, \dots, q_m/V_m]$, obtained by substituting each view V_j in q_0 with its definition q_j, is in Γ_ε^{r+1}. In other words, Γ_ε^r consists of queries that have a *query plan* of depth r, where each operator is a query computable in one step. The following proposition is straightforward.

PROPOSITION 4.1. *Every query in Γ_ε^r can be computed by an MPC(ε) algorithm in r rounds on any matching database.*

EXAMPLE 4.2. *Let $\varepsilon = 1/2$. The query L_k in Table 1 for $k = 16$ has a query plan of depth $r = 2$. The first step computes in parallel four queries, $v_1 = S_1, S_2, S_3, S_4, \dots, v_4 = S_{13}, S_{14}, S_{15}, S_{16}$. Each is isomorphic to L_4, therefore $\tau^*(q_1) = \dots = \tau^*(q_4) = 2$ and each can be computed in one step. The second step computes the query $q_0 = V_1, V_2, V_3, V_4$, which is also isomorphic to L_4. We can generalize this approach for any L_k: for any $\varepsilon \geq 0$, let k_ε be the largest integer such that $\tau^*(L_{k_\varepsilon}) \leq 1/(1-\varepsilon)$: $k_\varepsilon = 2\lfloor 1/(1-\varepsilon) \rfloor$. Then, for any $k \geq k_\varepsilon$, L_k can be computed using L_{k_ε} as a building block at each round: the plan will have a depth of $\lceil \log k / \log k_\varepsilon \rceil$.*

We also consider the query $SP_k = \bigwedge_{i=1}^{k} R_i(z, x_i), S_i(x_i, y_i)$. Since $\tau^*(SP_k) = k$, the space exponent for one round is $1 - 1/k$. However, SP_k has a query plan of depth 2 for MPC(0), by computing the joins $q_i = R_i(z, x_i), S_i(x_i, y_i)$ in the first round and in the second round joining all q_i on the common variable z. Thus, if we insist in answering SP_k in one round, we need a huge replication $O(p^{1-1/k})$, but we can compute it in two rounds with replication $O(1)$.

We next present an upper bound on the number of rounds needed to compute any query. Let $\text{rad}(q) = \min_u \max_v d(u, v)$ denote the *radius* of a query q, where $d(u, v)$ denotes the distance between two nodes in the hypergraph. For example, $\text{rad}(L_k) = \lceil k/2 \rceil$ and $\text{rad}(C_k) = \lfloor k/2 \rfloor$.

LEMMA 4.3. *Fix $\varepsilon \geq 0$, let $k_\varepsilon = 2\lfloor 1/(1-\varepsilon) \rfloor$, and let q be any connected query. Let $r(q) = \lceil \log(rad(q))/\log k_\varepsilon \rceil + 1$ if q is tree-like, and let $r(q) = \lceil \log(rad(q) + 1)/\log k_\varepsilon \rceil + 1$ otherwise. Then, q can be computed in $r(q)$ rounds on any matching database input by repeated application of the HC algorithm in the MPC(ε) model.*

PROOF. By definition of $\text{rad}(q)$, there exists some node $v \in \text{vars}(q)$, such that the maximum distance of v to any other node in the hypergraph of q is at most $\text{rad}(q)$. If q is tree-like then we can decompose q into a set of at most $|\text{atoms}(q)|^{\text{rad}(q)}$ (possibly overlapping) paths $\mathcal{P}$ of length $\leq \text{rad}(q)$, each having v as one endpoint. Since it is essentially isomorphic to L_ℓ, a path of length $\ell \leq \text{rad}(q)$ can be computed in at most $\lceil \log(\text{rad}(q))/\log k_\varepsilon \rceil$ rounds using the query plan from Proposition 4.1 together with repeated use of the one-round HC algorithm for paths of length k_ε as shown in Proposition 3.2 for $\tau = 1/(1-\varepsilon)$. Moreover, all the paths in $\mathcal{P}$ can be computed in parallel, because $|\mathcal{P}|$ is a constant depending only on q. Since every path will contain variable v, we can compute the join of all the paths in one final round without any replication. The only difference for general connected queries is that q may also contain atoms that join vertices at distance $\text{rad}(q)$ from v that are not on any of the paths of length $\text{rad}(q)$ from v: these can be covered using paths of length $\text{rad}(q) + 1$ from v. □

q query	ε space exponent	r rounds for $\varepsilon = 0$	$r = f(\varepsilon)$ raounds/space tradeoff
C_k	$1 - 2/k$	$\lceil \log k \rceil$	$\sim \frac{\log k}{\log(2/(1-\varepsilon))}$
L_k	$1 - \frac{1}{\lceil k/2 \rceil}$	$\lceil \log k \rceil$	$\sim \frac{\log k}{\log(2/(1-\varepsilon))}$
T_k	0	1	NA
SP_k	$1 - 1/k$	2	NA

Table 2: The tradeoff between space and communication rounds for several queries.

As an application of this proposition, Table 2 shows the number of rounds required by different types of queries.

4.2 Lower Bounds for Multiple Rounds

Our lower bound results for multiple rounds are restricted in two ways: they apply only to an MPC model where communication at rounds ≥ 2 is of a restricted form, and they match the upper bounds only for a restricted class of queries.

4.2.1 Tuple-Based MPC

Recall that $M_u^1 = (M_{1u}^1, \dots, M_{\ell u}^1)$, where M_{ju}^1 denotes the message sent during round 1 by the input server for S_j to the worker u. Let I be the input database instance, and q be the query we want to compute. A *join tuple* is any tuple in $q'(I)$, where q' is any connected subquery of q.

The *tuple-based* MPC(ε) model imposes the following two restrictions during rounds $r \geq 2$, for every worker u: (a) the message M_{uv}^r sent to v is a set of join tuples, and (b) for every join tuple t, the worker u decides whether to include t in M_{uv}^r based only on t, u, v, r and M_{ju}^1, for all j s.t. t contains a base tuple in S_j.

The restricted model still allows unrestricted communication during the first round; the information M_u^1 received by server u in the first round is available throughout the computation. However, during the following rounds, server u can only send messages consisting of join tuples, and, moreover, the destination of these join tuples can depend only on the tuple itself and on M_u^1. Since a join tuple is represented using $\Theta(\log n)$ bits, each server receives $O(n/p^{1-\varepsilon})$ join tuples at each round. We now describe the lower bound for multiple rounds in the tuple-based MPC model.

4.2.2 A Lower Bound

We give here a general lower bound for connected, conjunctive queries, and show how to apply it to L_k, to tree-like queries, and to C_k; these results prove Theorem 1.2. We postpone the proof to the next subsection.

DEFINITION 4.4. *Let q be a connected, conjunctive query. A set $M \subseteq atoms(q)$ is ε-good for q if it satisfies:*

1. *Every subquery of q that is in Γ_ε^1 contains at most one atom in M. (Γ_ε^1 defined in Sec. 4.2.1)*
2. *$\chi(\overline{M}) = 0$, where $\overline{M} = atoms(q) - M$. (Hence by Lemma 2.1, $\chi(q/\overline{M}) = \chi(q)$. This condition is equivalent to each connected component of $\overline{M}$ being tree-like.)*

An (ε, r)-plan $\mathcal{M}$ is a sequence $M_1, \dots, M_r$, with $M_0 = atoms(q) \supset M_1 \supset \cdots M_r$ such that (a) for all $j \in [r]$, M_{j+1} is ε-good for $q/\overline{M}_j$ where $\overline{M}_j = atoms(q) - M_j$, and (b) $q/\overline{M}_r \notin \Gamma_\varepsilon^1$.

THEOREM 4.5. *If q has a (ε, r)-plan then every randomized algorithm running in $r+1$ rounds on the tuple-based MPC(ε) model with $p = \omega(1)$ processors fails to compute q with probability $\Omega(n^{\chi(q)})$.*

We prove the theorem in the next section. Here, we show how to apply it to three cases. Assume $p = \omega(1)$, and recall that $k_\varepsilon = 2\lfloor 1/(1-\varepsilon)\rfloor$ (Example 4.2). First, consider L_k.

LEMMA 4.6. *Any tuple-based MPC(ε) algorithm that computes L_k needs at least $\lceil \log k/\log k_\varepsilon\rceil$ rounds.*

PROOF. We show inductively how to produce an (ε, r)-plan for L_k with $r = \lceil \log k/\log k_\varepsilon\rceil - 1$. The subqueries that are in Γ^1_ε are precisely L_{k_0} for $k_0 \le k_\varepsilon$, hence any set of atoms M that consists of every k_ε-th atom in L_ℓ is ε-good for L_ℓ for any $\ell \ge k_\varepsilon$. Let M_1 be such a set starting with the first atom. Then $L_k/\overline{M}_1$ is isomorphic to $L_{\lceil k/k_\varepsilon\rceil}$. For $j = 2, .., r$, choose M_j to consist of every k_ε-th atom starting at the first atom in $L_k/\overline{M}_{j-1}$. Finally, $L_k/\overline{M}_{j-1}$ will be isomorphic to a path query of length L_ℓ for some $\ell \ge k_\varepsilon + 1$ and hence is not in Γ^1_ε. Thus $M_1, \ldots, M_r$ is the desired (ε, r)-plan and the lower bound follows from Theorem 4.5. □

Combined with Example 4.2, it implies that L_k requires precisely $\lceil \log k/\log k_\varepsilon\rceil$ rounds on the tuple-based MPC(ε).

Second, we give a lower bound for tree-like queries, and for that we use a simple observation:

PROPOSITION 4.7. *If q is a tree-like query, and q' is any connected subquery of q, q' needs at least as many rounds as q in the tuple-based MPC(ε) model.*

PROOF. Given any tuple-based MPC(ε) algorithm A for computing q in r rounds we construct a tuple-based MPC(ε) algorithm A' that computes q' in r rounds. A' will interpret each instance over q' as part of an instance for q by using the relations in q' and using the identity permutation ($S_j = \{(1,1,\ldots),(2,2,\ldots),\ldots\}$) for each relation in $q \setminus q'$. Then, A' runs exactly as A for r rounds; after the final round, A' projects out for every tuple all the variables not in q'. The correctness of A' follows from the fact that q is tree-like. □

Define diam(q), the *diameter* of a query q, to be the longest distance between any two nodes in the hypergraph of q. In general, $\text{rad}(q) \le \text{diam}(q) \le 2\,\text{rad}(q)$. For example, $\text{rad}(L_k) = \lfloor k/2\rfloor$, $\text{diam}(L_k) = k$ and $\text{rad}(C_k) = \text{diam}(C_k) = \lfloor k/2\rfloor$. Lemma 4.6 and Proposition 4.7 imply:

COROLLARY 4.8. *Any tuple-based MPC(ε) algorithm that computes a tree-like query q needs at least $\lceil \log_{k_\varepsilon}(diam(q))\rceil$ rounds.*

Let us compare the lower bound $r_{\text{low}} = \lceil \log_{k_\varepsilon}(\text{diam}(q))\rceil$ and the upper bound $r_{\text{up}} = \lceil \log_{k_\varepsilon}(\text{rad}(q))\rceil + 1$ (Lemma 4.3): $\text{diam}(q) \le 2\text{rad}(q)$ implies $r_{\text{low}} \le r_{\text{up}}$, while $\text{rad}(q) \le \text{diam}(q)$ implies $r_{\text{up}} \le r_{\text{low}} + 1$. The gap between the lower bound and the upper bound is at most 1, proving Theorem 1.2. When $\varepsilon < 1/2$, these bounds are matching, since $k_\varepsilon = 2$ and $2\text{rad}(q) - 1 \le \text{diam}(q)$ for tree-like queries. The tradeoff between the space exponent ε and the number of rounds r for tree-like queries is $r \cdot \log \frac{2}{1-\varepsilon} \approx \log(\text{rad}(q))$.

Third, we study one instance of a non tree-like query:

LEMMA 4.9. *Any tuple-based MPC(ε) algorithm that computes C_k needs at least $\lceil \log(k/(m_\varepsilon+1))/\log k_\varepsilon\rceil + 1$ rounds, where $m_\varepsilon = \lfloor 2/(1-\varepsilon)\rfloor$.*

PROOF. Observe that any set M of atoms that are (at least) k_ε apart along any cycle C_ℓ is ϵ-good for C_ℓ and $C_\ell/\overline{M}$ is isomorphic to $C_{\lfloor \ell/k_\varepsilon\rfloor}$. If $k \ge k_\varepsilon^r(m_\varepsilon + 1)$, we can repeatedly choose such ε-good sets to construct an (ε, r)-plan $M_1, \ldots, M_r$ such that the final contracted query $C_k/\overline{M}_r$ contains a cycle $C_{\ell'}$ with $\ell' \ge m_\varepsilon + 1$ (and therefore cannot be computed in 1 round by any MPC(ε) algorithm). The result now follows from Theorem 4.5. □

Here, too, we have a gap of 1 between this lower bound and the upper bound in Lemma 4.3. Consider C_5 and $\varepsilon = 0$; $\text{rad}(C_5) = \text{diam}(C_5) = 2$, $k_\varepsilon = m_\varepsilon = 2$. The lower bound is $\lfloor \log 5/3\rfloor + 1 = 2$ rounds, the upper bound is $\lceil \log 3\rceil + 1 = 3$ round. The exact number of rounds for C_5 is open.

As a final application, we show how to apply Lemma 4.6 to show that transitive closure requires many rounds (the proof is included in the full version of the paper).

COROLLARY 4.10. *For any fixed $\varepsilon < 1$, there is no p-server algorithm in the tuple-based MPC(ε) model that uses $o(\log p)$ rounds and computes the transitive closure of an arbitrary input graph.*

4.2.3 Proof of Theorem 4.5

Given an (ε, r)-plan $\mathcal{M}$ (Definition 4.4) for a query q, define $\tau^*(\mathcal{M})$ to be the minimum of $\tau^*(q/\overline{M}_r)$, and the minimum of $\tau^*(q')$, where q' ranges over all connected subqueries of $q/\overline{M}_{j-1}$, $j \in [r]$, such that $q' \notin \Gamma^1_\varepsilon$. Since every q' satisfies $\tau^*(q')(1-\varepsilon) > 1$ (by $q' \notin \Gamma^1_\varepsilon$), and $\tau^*(q/\overline{M}_r)(1-\varepsilon) > 1$ (by the definition of goodness), we have $\tau^*(\mathcal{M})(1-\varepsilon) > 1$.

THEOREM 4.11. *If q has an (ε, r)-plan $\mathcal{M}$ then any deterministic tuple-based MPC(ε) algorithm running in $r+1$ rounds reports $O(\mathbf{E}(|q(I)|)/p^{\tau^*(\mathcal{M})(1-\varepsilon)-1})$ correct answers in expectation over uniformly chosen matching database I.*

The argument in Corollary 3.5 extends immediately to this case, implying that every randomized tuple-based MPC(ε) algorithm with $p = \omega(1)$ and $r+1$ rounds will fail to compute q with probability $\Omega(n^{\gamma(q)})$. This proves Theorem 4.5.

The rest of this section gives the proof of this theorem. The intuition is this. Consider a ε-good set M; then any matching database i consists of two parts, $i = (i_M, i_{\overline{M}})$, where i_M are the relations for atoms in M, and $i_{\overline{M}}$ are the other relations. We show that, for a fixed instance $i_{\overline{M}}$, the algorithm A can be used to compute $q/\overline{M}(i_M)$ in $r+1$ rounds; however, the first round is almost useless, because the algorithm can discover only a tiny number of join tuples with two or more atoms $S_j \in M$, since every subquery q' of q that has two M-atoms is not in Γ^1_ε. This shows that the algorithm computes $q/\overline{M}(i_M)$ in only r rounds, and we repeat the argument until a one-round algorithm remains.

First, we need some notation. For a connected subquery q' of q, $q'(I)$ denotes as usual the answer to q' on an instance I. Whenever $\text{atoms}(q') \subseteq \text{atoms}(q'')$, then we say that a tuple $t'' \in q''(I)$ *contains* a tuple $t' \in q'(I)$, if t' is equal to the projection of t'' on the variables of q'; if $A \subseteq q''(I), B \subseteq q'(I)$, then $A \ltimes B$, called the *semijoin*, denotes the subset of tuples $t'' \in A$ that contain some tuple $t' \in B$.

Let A be a deterministic algorithm with $r+1$ rounds, $k \in [r+1]$ a round number, u a server, and q' a subquery of q. For a matching database input i, define $m_{A,u,k}(i)$ to be the vector of messages received by server u during the first k rounds of the execution of A on input i. Define $m_{A,k}(i) = (m_1, \ldots, m_p)$, where $m_u = m_{A,u,k}(i)$ for all $u \in [p]$, and:

$$K_m^{A,u,k}(q') = \{t' \in [n]^{\text{vars}(q')} \mid \text{ for all matching databases } i, \; m_{A,u,k}(i) = m \Rightarrow t' \in q'(i)\}$$

$$K_m^{A,k}(q') = \bigcup_u K_{m_u}^{A,u,k}(q') \qquad A(i) = K_{m_{A,r+1}(i)}^{A,r+1}(q).$$

$K_{m_{A,u,k}(i)}^{A,u,k}(q')$ and $K_{m_{A,k}(i)}^{A,k}(q')$ denote the set of join tuples from q' known at round k by server u, and by all servers, respectively, on input i. $A(i)$ is w.l.o.g. the final answer of A on input i. Define

$$J^{A,q}(i) = \bigcup\{K_{m_{A,1}(i)}^{A,1}(q') \mid q' \text{ connected subquery of } q\}$$

$$J_\varepsilon^{A,q}(i) = \bigcup\{K_{m_{A,1}(i)}^{A,1}(q') \mid q' \notin \Gamma_\varepsilon^1 \text{ connected subquery of } q\}$$

$J_\varepsilon^{A,q}(i)$ is precisely the set of join tuples known after the first round, but which correspond to subqueries that are themselves not computable in one round; thus, the number of tuples in $J_\varepsilon^{A,q}(i)$ will be small. Next, we need two lemmas.

LEMMA 4.12. *Let q be a query, and M be any ε-good set for q. If A is an algorithm with $r+1$ rounds for q, then for any matching database $i_{\overline{M}}$ over the atoms of $\overline{M}$, there exists an algorithm A' with r rounds for $q/\overline{M}$ such that, for every matching database i_M defined over the atoms of M:*

$$|A(i_M, i_{\overline{M}})| \le |q(i_M, i_{\overline{M}}) \ltimes J_\varepsilon^{A,q}(i_M, i_{\overline{M}})| + |A'(i_M)|.$$

In other words, the algorithm returns no more answers than the (very few) tuples in J, plus what another algorithm A' (to be defined) computes for $q/\overline{M}$ in *one less* rounds.

PROOF. The proof requires two constructions.

1. Contraction. Call $q/\overline{M}$ the *contracted* query. While the original query q takes as input the complete database $i = (i_M, i_{\overline{M}})$, the input to the contracted query is only i_M. We show how to use the algorithm A for q to derive an algorithm, denoted A_M, for $q/\overline{M}$.

For each connected component C of $\overline{M}$, choose a representative variable $z_c \in \text{vars}(C)$; also denote S_C the result of applying the query C to $i_{\overline{M}}$; S_c is a matching, because C is tree-like. Denote $\bar\sigma = \{\sigma_x \mid x \in \text{vars}(q)\}$, where, for every variable $x \in \text{vars}(q)$, σ_x is the following permutation on $[n]$: if $x \notin \text{vars}(\overline{M})$ then $\sigma_x =$ the identity; otherwise $\sigma_x = \Pi_{xz_c}(S_C)$, for the unique connected component s.t. $x \in \text{vars}(C)$. We think of $\bar\sigma$ as permuting the domain of each attribute $x \in \text{vars}(q)$. Then $\bar\sigma(q(i)) = q(\bar\sigma(i))$, and $\bar\sigma(i_{\overline{M}}) = \mathbf{id}_{\overline{M}}$ the identity matching database (where each relation in $\overline{M}$ is $\{(1,1,\ldots),(2,2,\ldots),\ldots\}$), and therefore:

$$q/\overline{M}(i_M) = \bar\sigma^{-1}(\Pi_{\text{vars}(q/\overline{M})}(q(\bar\sigma(i_M), \mathbf{id}_{\overline{M}})))$$

(We assume $\text{vars}(q/\overline{M}) \subseteq \text{vars}(q)$; for that, when we contract a set of nodes of the hypergraph, we replace them with one of the nodes in the set.)

The algorithm A_M for $q/\overline{M}(i_M)$ is this. First, each input server for $S_j \in M$ replaces S_j with $\bar\sigma(S_j)$ (since $i_{\overline{M}}$ is fixed, it is known to all servers, hence, so is $\bar\sigma$); next, run A unchanged, substituting all relations $S_j \in \overline{M}$ with the identity; finally, apply $\bar\sigma^{-1}$ to the answers and return them. We have:

$$A_M(i_M) = \bar\sigma^{-1}(\Pi_{\text{vars}(q/\overline{M})}(A(\bar\sigma(i_M), \mathbf{id}_{\overline{M}}))) \qquad (9)$$

2. Retraction. Next, we transform A_M into a new algorithm R_{A_M} called the *retraction* of A_M, as follows:

(a) During round 1 of R_{A_M}, each input server for S_j sends (in addition to the messages sent by A_M) every tuple in $t \in S_j$ to all servers u that eventually receive t. In other words, the input server sends t to every u for which there exists $k \in [r+1]$ such that $t \in K_{m_{A_M,u,k}(I_M)}^{A_M,u,k}(S_j)$. This is possible because of the restrictions in the tuple-based MPC(ε) model: all destinations of t depend only on S_j, and hence can be computed by the input server. Note that this may increase the total number of bits received in the first round by a factor of r, which is $O(1)$ in our setting. R_{A_M} will not send any atomic tuples during rounds $k \ge 2$. (b) In round 2, R_{A_M} sends *no* tuples. (c) In rounds $k \ge 3$, R_{A_M} sends a tuple t from u to v if server u knows t at round k, and algorithm A_M sends t from u to v at round k.

It follows that, for each round k, and for each subquery q' of $q/\overline{M}$ with at least two atoms, $K_{m(i)}^{R_{A_M},u,k}(q') \subseteq K_{m(i)}^{A_M,u,k}(q')$: in other words, R_{A_M} knows a subset of the non-atomic tuples known by A_M. Moreover, let $J_+^{A_M}(i_M)$ be the set of non-atomic tuples known by A_M after round 1, $J_+^{A_M}(i_M) = \bigcup\{K_{m(i)}^{R_{A_M},u,1}(q') \mid q' \text{ has at least two atoms}\}$: these are the tuples that we refused to sent in round 2. Then:

$$A_M(i_M) \subseteq (q/\overline{M}(i_M) \ltimes J_+^{A_M}) \cup R_{A_M}(i_M) \qquad (10)$$

Since R_{A_M} wastes one round, we can compress it to an algorithm A' with only r rounds. To prove the lemma, we convert (10) into a statement about A. (9) already showed that $A_M(i_M)$ is related to $A(i_M, i_{\overline{M}})$. Now we show how $J_+^{A_M}$ is related to $J_\varepsilon^{A,q}(i)$: $J_+^{A_M}(i_M) \subseteq \sigma^{-1}(\Pi_{\text{vars}(q/\overline{M})}(J_\varepsilon^{A,q}(\bar\sigma(i))))$ because, by the definition of ε-goodness, if a subquery q' of q has two atoms in M, then $q' \notin \Gamma_\varepsilon^1$. (10) becomes:

$$A_M(i_M) \subseteq (q/\overline{M}(i_M) \ltimes \Pi_{\text{vars}(q/\overline{M})}(J_\varepsilon^{A,q}(i))) \cup \bar\sigma^{-1}(A'(i_M))$$

The lemma follows from $q/\overline{M}(i_M) \ltimes \Pi_{\text{vars}(q/\overline{M})}(J_\varepsilon^{A,q}(i)) \subseteq \Pi_{\text{vars}(q/\overline{M})}(q(i) \ltimes J_\varepsilon^{A,q}(i))$ and $|A_M(i_M)| = |A(i_M, i_{\overline{M}})|$, by (9). $\square$

LEMMA 4.13. *Let q be a conjunctive query, and q' a subquery; if i is a database instance for q, we write i' for its restriction to the relations occurring in q'. Let B be any algorithm for q' (meaning that, for every matching database i', $B(i') \subseteq q'(i')$), and assume that $\mathbf{E}[|B(I')|] \le \gamma \cdot \mathbf{E}[|q'(I')|]$. Then, $\mathbf{E}[|q(I) \ltimes B(I')|] \le \gamma \mathbf{E}[|q(I)|]$ where I is a uniformly chosen matching database.*

While, in general, q' may return many more answers than q, the lemma says that, if B returns only a fraction of q', then $q \ltimes B$ returns only the same fraction of q.

PROOF. Let $\bar y = (y_1, \ldots, y_k)$ be the variables occurring in q'. For any $\bar a \in [n]^k$, let $\sigma_{\bar y = \bar a}(q(i))$ denote the subset of tuples $t \in q(i)$ whose projection on $\bar y$ equals $\bar a$. By symmetry, the quantity $\mathbf{E}[|\sigma_{\bar y=\bar a}(q(I))|]$ is independent of $\bar a$, and therefore equals $\mathbf{E}[|q(I)|]/n^k$. Notice that $\sigma_{\bar y=\bar a}(B(i'))$ is either $\emptyset$ or $\{\bar a\}$. We have:

$$\mathbf{E}[|q(I) \ltimes B(I')|] = \textstyle\sum_{\bar a \in [n]^k} \mathbf{E}[|\sigma_{\bar y=\bar a}(q(I)) \ltimes \sigma_{\bar y=\bar a}(B(I'))|]$$
$$= \textstyle\sum_{\bar a \in [n]^k} \mathbf{E}[|\sigma_{\bar y=\bar a}(q(I))|] \cdot \mathbf{P}(\bar a \in B(I'))$$
$$= \mathbf{E}[|q(I)|] \cdot \textstyle\sum_{\bar a \in [n]^k} \mathbf{P}(\bar a \in B(I'))/n^k = \mathbf{E}[|q(I)|] \cdot \mathbf{E}[|B(I')|]/n^k$$

Repeating the same calculations for q' instead of B,

$$\mathbf{E}[|q(I) \ltimes q'(I')|] = \mathbf{E}[|q(I)|]\mathbf{E}[|q'(I')|]/n^k$$

The lemma follows immediately, by using the fact that, by definition, $q(i) \ltimes q'(i') = q(i)$. $\square$

Finally, we prove Theorem 4.11.

Proof of Theorem 4.11. Given the (ε, r)-plan atoms(q) $= M_0 \supset \ldots \supset M_r$, define $\hat{M}_k = \overline{M}_k - \overline{M}_{k-1}$, for $k \geq 1$. We build up $i_{\overline{M}_r}$ by iteratively choosing matching databases $i_{\hat{M}_k} = \overline{M}_k - \overline{M}_{k-1}$ for $k = 1, \ldots, r$ and applying Lemma 4.12 with q replaced by $q/\overline{M}_{k-1}$ and M replaced by M_k to obtain algorithms $A^k = A^k_{(i_{\hat{M}_1}, \ldots, i_{\hat{M}_k})}$ for $q/\hat{M}_1 \cdots \hat{M}_k$ such that the following inequality holds for every choice of matching databases given by i_{M_r} and $i_{\overline{M}_r} = (i_{\hat{M}_1}, \ldots, i_{\hat{M}_r})$:

$$\begin{aligned} |A(i_{M_r}, i_{\overline{M}_r})| &= |A(i_{M_r}, i_{\hat{M}_1}, \ldots, i_{\hat{M}_r})| \\ &\leq |q(i_{M_r}, i_{\overline{M}_r}) \ltimes J_\varepsilon^{A,q}(i_{M_r}, i_{\hat{M}_1}, \ldots, i_{\hat{M}_r})| \\ &+ |q(i_{M_r}, i_{\overline{M}_r}) \ltimes J_\varepsilon^{A^1, q/\hat{M}_1}(i_{M_r}, i_{\hat{M}_2}, \ldots, i_{\hat{M}_r})| \\ &+ \ldots + |q(i_{M_r}, i_{\overline{M}_r}) \ltimes J_\varepsilon^{A^{r-1}, q/\hat{M}_1 \cdots \hat{M}_{r-1}}(i_{M_r}, i_{\hat{M}_r})| \\ &+ |A^r(i_{M_r})| \end{aligned} \quad (11)$$

We now average (11) over a uniformly chosen matching database I and upper bound each of the resulting terms: For all $k \in [r]$ we have $\chi(q/\overline{M}_k) = \chi(q)$ (see Definition 4.4), and hence, by Lemma 3.4, we have $\mathbf{E}[|q(I)|] = \mathbf{E}[|(q/\overline{M}_k)(I_{M_k})|]$. By definition, we have $\tau^*(q/\overline{M}_r) \geq \tau^*(\mathcal{M})$ and hence by Theorem 3.3,

$$\begin{aligned} \mathbf{E}[|A^r(I_{M_r})|] &= O(\mathbf{E}[|(q/\overline{M}_r)(I_{M_r})|]/p^{\tau^*(\mathcal{M})(1-\varepsilon)-1}) \\ &= O(\mathbf{E}[|q(I)|]/p^{\tau^*(\mathcal{M})(1-\varepsilon)-1}) \end{aligned}$$

Note that $I_{M_{k-1}} = (I_{M_r}, I_{\hat{M}_k}, \ldots, I_{\hat{M}_r})$ and consider the expected number of tuples in $J = J_\varepsilon^{A^{k-1}, q/\hat{M}_1 \cdots \hat{M}_{k-1}}(I_{M_{k-1}})$. The algorithm $A^{k-1} = A^{k-1}_{I_{\overline{M}_{k-1}}}$ itself depends on the choice of $I_{\overline{M}_{k-1}}$; still, we show that J has a small number of tuples. Every subquery q' of $q/\hat{M}_1 \cdots \hat{M}_{k-1}$ that is not in Γ^1_ε (hence contributes to J) has $\tau^*(q') \geq \tau^*(\mathcal{M})$. By Theorem 3.3, for each fixing $I_{\overline{M}_{k-1}} = i_{\overline{M}_{k-1}}$, the expected number of tuples produced for subquery q' by $B_{q'}$, where $B_{q'}$ is the portion of the first round of $A^{k-1}_{i_{\overline{M}_{k-1}}}$ that produces tuples for q', satisfies $\mathbf{E}[|B_{q'}(I_{M_{k-1}})|] = O(\mathbf{E}[|q'(I_{M_{k-1}})|]/p^{\tau^*(\mathcal{M})(1-\varepsilon)-1})$. We now apply Lemma 4.13 to derive

$$\begin{aligned} \mathbf{E}[|q(I) \ltimes B_{q'}(I_{M_{k-1}})|] &= \mathbf{E}[|(q/\overline{M}_{k-1})(I_{M_{k-1}}) \ltimes B_{q'}(I_{M_{k-1}})|] \\ &= O(\mathbf{E}[|(q/\overline{M}_{k-1})(I_{M_{k-1}})|]/p^{\tau^*(\mathcal{M})(1-\varepsilon)-1}) \\ &= O(\mathbf{E}[|q(I)|]/p^{\tau^*(\mathcal{M})(1-\varepsilon)-1}). \end{aligned}$$

Averaging over all choices of $I_{\overline{M}_{k-1}} = i_{\overline{M}_{k-1}}$ and summing over the constant number of different queries q' we obtain

$$\begin{aligned} \mathbf{E}[|q(I) \ltimes J_\varepsilon^{A^{k-1}, q/\hat{M}_1 \cdots \hat{M}_{k-1}}(I_{M_{k-1}})|] \\ = O(\mathbf{E}[|q(I)|]/p^{\tau^*(\mathcal{M})(1-\varepsilon)-1}). \end{aligned}$$

Combining the bounds for the $r+1$ terms in (11) we obtain that $\mathbf{E}[|A(I)|] = O(r\mathbf{E}[|q(I)|]/p^{\tau^*(\mathcal{M})(1-\varepsilon)-1})$. □

5. CONCLUSION

We have introduced powerful models for capturing tradeoffs between rounds and amount of communication required for parallel computation of relational queries. For one round on the most general model we have shown that queries are characterized by τ^* which determines the space exponent $\varepsilon = 1 - 1/\tau^*$ that governs the replication rate as a function of the number of processors. For multiple rounds we derived a strong lower bound tradeoff between the number of rounds r and the replication rate of $r \cdot \log 2/(1-\varepsilon) \approx \log(\text{rad}(q))$ for more restricted tuple-based communication. For both, we showed matching or nearly matching upper bounds given by simple and natural algorithms.

6. REFERENCES

[1] F. N. Afrati, A. D. Sarma, S. Salihoglu, and J. D. Ullman. Upper and lower bounds on the cost of a map-reduce computation. *CoRR*, abs/1206.4377, 2012.

[2] F. N. Afrati and J. D. Ullman. Optimizing joins in a map-reduce environment. In *EDBT*, pages 99–110, 2010.

[3] N. Alon, Y. Matias, and M. Szegedy. The space complexity of approximating the frequency moments. *JCSS*, 58(1):137–147, 1999.

[4] A. Atserias, M. Grohe, and D. Marx. Size bounds and query plans for relational joins. In *FOCS*, pages 739–748, 2008.

[5] S. Chaudhuri. What next?: a half-dozen data management research goals for big data and the cloud. In *PODS*, pages 1–4, 2012.

[6] F. R. K. Chung, Z. Füredi, M. R. Garey, and R. L. Graham. On the fractional covering number of hypergraphs. *SIAM J. Discrete Math.*, 1(1):45–49, 1988.

[7] J. Dean and S. Ghemawat. Mapreduce: Simplified data processing on large clusters. In *OSDI*, pages 137–150, 2004.

[8] EMC Corporation. Data science revealed: A data-driven glimpse into the burgeoning new field. `http://www.emc.com/collateral/about/news/emc-data-science-study-wp.pdf`.

[9] J. Feldman, S. Muthukrishnan, A. Sidiropoulos, C. Stein, and Z. Svitkina. On distributing symmetric streaming computations. *ACM Transactions on Algorithms*, 6(4), 2010.

[10] E. Friedgut. Hypergraphs, entropy, and inequalities. *American Mathematical Monthly*, pages 749–760, 2004.

[11] A. Gál and P. Gopalan. Lower bounds on streaming algorithms for approximating the length of the longest increasing subsequence. In *FOCS*, pages 294–304, 2007.

[12] S. Ganguly, A. Silberschatz, and S. Tsur. Parallel bottom-up processing of datalog queries. *J. Log. Program.*, 14(1&2):101–126, 1992.

[13] M. Grohe and D. Marx. Constraint solving via fractional edge covers. In *SODA*, pages 289–298, 2006.

[14] S. Guha and Z. Huang. Revisiting the direct sum theorem and space lower bounds in random order streams. In *ICALP*, volume 5555 of *LNCS*, pages 513–524. Springer, 2009.

[15] Hadoop. `http://hadoop.apache.org/`.

[16] H. J. Karloff, S. Suri, and S. Vassilvitskii. A model of computation for mapreduce. In *SODA*, pages 938–948, 2010.

[17] P. Koutris and D. Suciu. Parallel evaluation of conjunctive queries. In *PODS*, pages 223–234, 2011.

[18] E. Kushilevitz and N. Nisan. *Communication Complexity*. Cambridge University Press, Cambridge, England ; New York, 1997.

[19] S. Melnik, A. Gubarev, J. J. Long, G. Romer, S. Shivakumar, M. Tolton, and T. Vassilakis. Dremel: Interactive analysis of web-scale datasets. *PVLDB*, 3(1):330–339, 2010.

[20] H. Q. Ngo, E. Porat, C. Ré, and A. Rudra. Worst-case optimal join algorithms: [extended abstract]. In *PODS*, pages 37–48, 2012.

[21] C. Olston, B. Reed, U. Srivastava, R. Kumar, and A. Tomkins. Pig latin: a not-so-foreign language for data processing. In *SIGMOD Conference*, pages 1099–1110, 2008.

[22] S. Suri and S. Vassilvitskii. Counting triangles and the curse of the last reducer. In *WWW*, pages 607–614, 2011.

[23] A. Thusoo, J. S. Sarma, N. Jain, Z. Shao, P. Chakka, S. Anthony, H. Liu, P. Wyckoff, and R. Murthy. Hive - a warehousing solution over a map-reduce framework. *PVLDB*, 2(2):1626–1629, 2009.

[24] P. Tiwari. Lower bounds on communication complexity in distributed computer networks. *JACM*, 34(4):921–938, Oct. 1987.

[25] J. D. Ullman. Designing good mapreduce algorithms. *ACM Crossroads*, 19(1):30–34, 2012.

[26] A. C. Yao. Lower bounds by probabilistic arguments. In *FOCS*, pages 420–428, Tucson, AZ, 1983.

A Dichotomy in the Intensional Expressive Power of Nested Relational Calculi augmented with Aggregate Functions and a Powerset Operator

Limsoon Wong
School of Computing
National University of Singapore
13 Computing Drive, Singapore 117417
wongls@comp.nus.edu.sg

ABSTRACT

The extensional aspect of expressive power—i.e., what queries can or cannot be expressed—has been the subject of many studies of query languages. Paradoxically, although efficiency is of primary concern in computer science, the intensional aspect of expressive power—i.e., what queries can or cannot be implemented efficiently—has been much neglected. Here, we discuss the intensional expressive power of $\mathcal{NRC}(Q, +, \cdot, -, \div, \sum, \mathit{powerset})$, a nested relational calculus augmented with aggregate functions and a powerset operation. We show that queries on structures such as long chains, deep trees, etc. have a dichotomous behaviour: Either they are already expressible in the calculus without using the powerset operation or they require at least exponential space. This result generalizes in three significant ways several old dichotomy-like results, such as that of Suciu and Paredaens that the complex object algebra of Abiteboul and Beeri needs exponential space to implement the transitive closure of a long chain. Firstly, a more expressive query language—in particular, one that captures SQL—is considered here. Secondly, queries on a more general class of structures than a long chain are considered here. Lastly, our proof is more general and holds for all query languages exhibiting a certain normal form and possessing a locality property.

Categories and Subject Descriptors

H.2.3 [**Languages**]: Query languages; F.4.1 [**Mathematical logic**]: Model theory

Keywords

Intensional expressive power; normal form; conservative extension property; locality property; dichotomy; nested relational calculus; SQL.

1. INTRODUCTION

A function f that is expressible[1] in a query language can be implemented or executed in many different ways, each corresponding to a different algorithm. These algorithms may have different complexity. Some of these algorithms for f may be expressible in the given query language, while some of them may not be expressible in it. Even though efficiency is a key issue in computer science, we seldom see results that study the power of query languages from this "intensional" perspective.

This lack of attention may be attributable to the logical vs physical separation, where a database system may use different execution plans for the same query depending on optimization factors such as what indices are available. Nevertheless, the syntax of a query naturally suggests an (unoptimized and possibly naive) implementation. Thus, as argued by Suciu, Paredeans, and Wong [14, 15], there is a so-called "natural operational semantics" for a query language; and intensional expressive power can be studied with respect to it. Yet it is significantly more difficult to study intensional expressive power and, in particular, there is a very limited repertoire of general techniques that can be applied.

Some of the papers that are in the spirit of intensional expressive power, with respect to the respective natural operational semantics of various query languages, include the followings:

- Colson [7] shows that while the function which computes the minimum of two integers in unary representation can be expressed using primitive recursion, all such expressions have higher than $O(min(m,n))$ complexity.
- Abiteboul and Vianu [2] show that while the parity query can be expressed by a generic machine, all such expressions have higher than PTIME complexity.
- Suciu and Wong [15] show that while sequential iteration queries (called *sri* queries in their paper) can be uniformly translated into data-parallel iteration queries (called *sru* queries in their paper), all such uniform translations must map some PTIME queries into exponential space ones.

[1]Throughout this paper, when we use the term "expressive power" without explicitly indicating whether it is the extensional aspect or the intensional aspect, we mean the extensional aspect.

- Suciu and Paredaens [14] show that while the transitive closure of a long chain can be expressed in the complex object algebra of Abiteboul and Beeri, all such expressions must use exponential space.

- Van den Bussche [6] shows that, when retricted to unary database schemas (i.e., when the input relations all have exactly one column), every query in the complex object algebra of Abiteboul and Beeri is either already expressible without using the powerset operator or must use exponential space.

- Biskup et al. [3] show that while the parity query can be expressed in what they called the equation algebra, all such expressions must use exponential space.

These are impressive results and their proofs are tour de force undertakings. Unfortunately, they are also query specific; and the proofs are complex and not easily "portable" to other queries. Therefore, more light ought to be shed on the structure of the query languages concerned or the structure of inefficient queries in these query languages that make the cause of the inefficiency clear.

In this paper, we study the intensional expressive power of $\mathcal{NRC}(Q, +, \cdot, -, \div, \sum, \mathit{powerset})$, a nested relational calculus endowed with aggregate functions and a powerset operation. This calculus can express all the usual SQL queries such as group-by, count, average, etc. So it is a query language that is considerably more expressive than the complex object algebra of Abiteboul and Beeri [1]. Moreover, we study the intensional expressive power of $\mathcal{NRC}(Q, +, \cdot, -, \div, \sum, \mathit{powerset})$ in a non-query-specific setting.

Our main result is a Dichotomy Theorem that, all queries on a general class of structures—which includes deep trees, long chains, etc.—are either already expressible in $\mathcal{NRC}(Q, +, \cdot, -, \div, \sum, \mathit{powerset})$ without using its powerset operation or must use an exponential amount of space. Since $\mathcal{NRC}(Q, +, \cdot, -, \div, \sum, \mathit{powerset})$ is more general than the complex object algebra of Abiteboul and Beeri and the class of structures includes long chains, this result is a powerful generalization of the old result of Suciu and Paredaens [14] and also that of Van den Bussche [6]. Furthermore, our proof of this Dichotomy Theorem factors through a locality property [9] and the normal form induced by the conservative extension property [16]. Thus it holds also for any query language exhibiting a similar normal form and the locality property, offering a high potential for generalization to many other query languages. We demonstrate this last aspect on the equation algebra of Biskup and colleagues [3].

The organization of this paper is as follows. Section 2 presents the query language $\mathcal{NRC}(Q, +, \cdot, -, \div, \sum, \mathit{powerset})$. Section 3 presents the conservative extension property, its associated rewrite rules, and the locality property. Section 4 proves our main result, the Dichotomy Theorem. Section 5 concludes the paper with an extensive discussion on how the Dichotomy Theorem generalizes the results of Suciu and Paredeans [14], Van den Bussche [6], and Biskup and colleagues [3].

2. $\mathcal{NRC}$, AGGREGATES, AND POWERSET

The ambient language for our study is $\mathcal{NRC}(Q, +, \cdot, -, \div, \sum, \mathit{powerset})$. This query language is built upon the nested relational calculus $\mathcal{NRC}$ from Buneman et al. [5], by augmenting it with arithmetic operations, a summation operation, and a powerset operation. The base language $\mathcal{NRC}$ is equivalent to the usual nested relational algebra [5]. The extension of $\mathcal{NRC}$ by arithmetic operations and the summation operation makes it into $\mathcal{NRC}(Q, +, \cdot, -, \div, \sum)$, which is able to express group-by and aggregate functions, and captures the expressive power of SQL [13].

The types and expressions in $\mathcal{NRC}$ are given in Figure 1. The type superscripts in the figure are conventionally omitted because they can be inferred. The semantics of a type is just a set of complex objects—i.e., a set of objects built up by nesting sets and records of base type objects:

- There are some base types b, as well as the usual base types *bool* (i.e., Booleans) and Q (i.e., numbers).

- An object of type $s_1 \times \cdots \times s_n$ is a tuple (i.e., a record) whose ith component is an object of type s_i, for $1 \leq i \leq n$.

- An object of type $\{s\}$ is a finite set whose elements are objects of type s. An object of type $\{s\}$ is called a "relation". Moreover, if $s = b \times \cdots \times b$, then an object of type $\{s\}$ (or s) is called a "flat relation". However, if s contains some set brackets, then an object of type $\{s\}$ is called a "nested relation". More generally, a type s containing n levels of nested set brackets is said to be of height n; e.g., $b \times b$ has height 0, $\{b \times b\}$ has height 1, and $\{b \times \{b\}\}$ has height 2.

The meaning of the expression constructs are described below:

- The expression c denotes constants of a base type, i.e., the atomic objects.

- The expressions *true*, *false*, and *if* e_1 *then* e_2 *else* e_3 have their usual meaning.

- The expression $(e_1, \ldots, e_n)$ forms a tuple whose ith component is the object denoted by e_i, for $1 \leq i \leq n$.

- The expression $\pi_i\ e$ extracts the ith component of the tuple e.

- The expressions $\{\}$, $\{e\}$, and $e_1 \cup e_2$ have their usual meaning as set operations.

- The expression $\bigcup\{e_1 \mid x \in e_2\}$ forms the set obtained by first applying the function $f(x) = e_1$ to each object in the set e_2 and then taking their union. That is, $\bigcup\{e_1 \mid x \in e_2\} = f(C_1) \cup \ldots \cup f(C_n)$, where $f(x) = e_1$ and $\{C_1, \ldots, C_n\}$ is the set denoted by e_2. This construct is the sole means in $\mathcal{NRC}$ for iterating over a set.

- The expression $e_1 = e_2$ denotes an equality test between e_1 and e_2. Here, e_1 and e_2 denote objects of the same base type. With this construct, it is straightforward to define in $\mathcal{NRC}$ equality tests for all types.

- The expression *isempty* e tests whether a set e is empty. Here, e denote a set of tuples of objects of base types. With this construct, it is straightforward to define in $\mathcal{NRC}$ emptiness tests for all set types.

TYPES IN $\mathcal{NRC}$

$$B ::= b \mid bool \mid Q \qquad s ::= B \mid s_1 \times \cdots \times s_n \mid \{s\}$$

EXPRESSIONS IN $\mathcal{NRC}$

$$\frac{}{c : B} \qquad \frac{}{x^s : s} \qquad \frac{e_1 : s_1 \quad \ldots \quad e_n : s_n}{(e_1, \ldots, e_n) : s_1 \times \cdots \times s_n} \qquad \frac{e : s_1 \times \cdots \times s_n}{\pi_i\ e : s_i} 1 \le i \le n$$

$$\frac{}{\{\}^s : \{s\}} \qquad \frac{e : s}{\{e\} : \{s\}} \qquad \frac{e_1 : \{s\} \quad e_2 : \{s\}}{e_1 \cup e_2 : \{s\}} \qquad \frac{e_1 : \{s\} \quad e_2 : \{t\}}{\bigcup\{e_1 \mid x^t \in e_2\} : \{s\}}$$

$$\frac{}{true : bool} \qquad \frac{}{false : bool} \qquad \frac{e_1 : bool \quad e_2 : s \quad e_3 : s}{if\ e_1\ then\ e_2\ else\ e_3 : s}$$

$$\frac{e_1 : B \quad e_2 : B}{e_1 = e_2 : bool} \qquad \frac{e : \{B_1 \times \cdots \times B_n\}}{isempty\ e : bool}$$

ARITHMETICS AND AGGREGATE FUNCTIONS IN $\mathcal{NRC}(Q,\ +,\ \cdot,\ -,\ \div,\ \sum)$

$$\frac{e_1 : Q \quad e_2 : Q}{e_1 + e_2 : Q} \qquad \frac{e_1 : Q \quad e_2 : Q}{e_1 - e_2 : Q} \qquad \frac{e_1 : Q \quad e_2 : Q}{e_1 \cdot e_2 : Q} \qquad \frac{e_1 : Q \quad e_2 : Q}{e_1 \div e_2 : Q} \qquad \frac{e_1 : Q \quad e_2 : \{s\}}{\sum\{\!|e_1 \mid x^s \in e_2|\!\} : Q}$$

POWERSET OPERATOR IN $\mathcal{NRC}(Q,\ +,\ \cdot,\ -,\ \div,\ \sum,\ powerset)$

$$\frac{e : \{b \times \cdots \times b\}}{powerset\ e : \{\{b \times \cdots \times b\}\}}$$

Figure 1: $\mathcal{NRC}$ and its extensions $\mathcal{NRC}(Q,\ +,\ \cdot,\ -,\ \div,\ \sum)$ and $\mathcal{NRC}(Q,\ +,\ \cdot,\ -,\ \div,\ \sum,\ powerset)$.

There is a straightforward translation between this syntax and the comprehension syntax [4] of the form $\{e \mid \delta_1, \ldots, \delta_n\}$ where each δ_i either has the form $x_i \in e_i$ or the form e_i. The translation is given by:

- $\{e \mid x_1 \in e_1, \Delta\} =_{df} \bigcup\{\{e \mid \Delta\} \mid x_1 \in e_1\}$;
- $\{e \mid e_1, \Delta\} =_{df}$ *if* e_1 *then* $\{e \mid \Delta\}$ *else* $\{\}$; and
- $\{e \mid \} =_{df} \{e\}$.

We use the comprehension syntax to write examples, but the reader should understand these examples as syntactic sugars of the actual $\mathcal{NRC}$ expressions.

Example 1. Let $X : \{employee \times salary \times dept\}$ be a relation that records the annual salary of employees in a company. Let $Y : \{employee \times \{employee\}\}$ be a relation that records the set of immediate reportees of each manager.

- The managers in the company can be expressed in $\mathcal{NRC}$ as $\Pi_1(Y) =_{df} \{\pi_1\ y \mid y \in Y\}$.
- A flat version of the manager-reportee relation can be expressed as $unnest(Y) =_{df} \{(\pi_1\ y,\ x) \mid y \in Y, x \in \pi_2\ y\}$.
- The annual salary of managers in the company can be expressed as $join(X,Y) =_{df} \{(y, \pi_2\ x) \mid y \in \Pi_1(Y), x \in X, y = \pi_1\ x\}$.
- A nested version of the salary relation where employees are grouped by department is $nest(X) =_{df} \{(\pi_3\ x, \{(\pi_1\ y, \pi_2\ y) \mid y \in X, \pi_3\ y = \pi_3\ x\}) \mid x \in X\}$.

While all the operations of the usual nested relational algebra can be expressed in $\mathcal{NRC}$ [5], aggregate functions usually encountered in SQL queries are not expressible in $\mathcal{NRC}$. So we augment $\mathcal{NRC}$ with the usual arithmetic operations $+$, $-$, $\cdot$ and $\div$ and a summation construct $\sum\{\!|e_1 \mid x \in e_2|\!\}$ to give the query language $\mathcal{NRC}(Q,\ +,\ \cdot,\ -,\ \div,\ \sum)$. The summation construct $\sum\{\!|e_1 \mid x \in e_2|\!\}$ first applies the function $f(x) = e_1$ to each object in the set e_2 and sums the resulting numbers; that is, $\sum\{\!|e_1 \mid x \in e_2|\!\} = f(C_1) + \cdots + f(C_n)$, where $f(x) = e_1$ and $\{C_1, \ldots, C_n\}$ is the set denoted by e_2. Here are some illustrative examples showing how this construct captures the usual group-by and aggregate functions in SQL queries.

Example 2. As before, let $X : \{employee \times salary \times dept\}$ be a relation that records the annual salary of employees in a company.

- The number of employees in the company can be expressed in $\mathcal{NRC}(Q,\ +,\ \cdot,\ -,\ \div,\ \sum)$ as $count(X) =_{df} \sum\{\!|1 \mid x \in X|\!\}$.
- The annual EOM budget of the company can be expressed as $sum(X) =_{df} \sum\{\!|\pi_2\ x \mid x \in X|\!\}$.
- The mean annual salary of employees of the company can be expressed as $ave(X) =_{df} sum(X) \div count(X)$.
- Finally, the mean annual salary of each department can be produced by $dept\_ave(X) =_{df} \{(\pi_1\ x, ave(\pi_2\ x)) \mid x \in nest(X)\}$.

Let us use the notation $e[\vec{R}]$ to mean the an expression e with free variables $\vec{R}$. However, when it is not important to explicitly list the free variables, we write it simply as e. For a list of objects $\vec{O}$ that conform to the types of $\vec{R}$, we use the notation $e[\vec{O}/\vec{R}]$ for the expression obtained by substituting $\vec{O}$ for $\vec{R}$. We think of the expression $e[\vec{R}]$ as a "query" where $\vec{R}$ are its input; equivalently, we can think of it as a function $f(\vec{R}) = e[\vec{R}]$. The expression $e[\vec{R}]$ is said to be a "flat relational query" if each R in $\vec{R}$ is a flat relation and $e[\vec{R}] : \{b \times \cdots \times b\}$. Recall that a flat relation can have type $\{b \times \cdots \times b\}$ or type $b \times \cdots \times b$. So, we use the notation $e[\vec{R}, \vec{x}]$ when it is important to explicitly separate the two kinds of variables in a flat relational query.

Below are some well-known results [5, 16, 13, 8, 10].

PROPOSITION 1. *1. $\mathcal{NRC}$ is in PTIME.*

2. $\mathcal{NRC}$ is equivalent to the classical nested relational algebra.

3. $\mathcal{NRC}$ restricted to flat relational queries is equivalent to the classical relational algebra.

4. $\mathcal{NRC}(Q,\ +,\ \cdot,\ -,\ \div,\ \sum)$ is in PTIME.

5. $\mathcal{NRC}(Q,\ +,\ \cdot,\ -,\ \div,\ \sum)$ restricted to flat relational queries is equivalent to the aggregate logic $L_{aggr}(Q,\ +,\ \cdot,\ -,\ \div,\ \sum)$.

6. $\mathcal{NRC}(Q,\ +,\ \cdot,\ -,\ \div,\ \sum)$ cannot express recursive queries such as transitive closure.

Due to the equivalence of $\mathcal{NRC}(Q,\ +,\ \cdot,\ -,\ \div,\ \sum)$ and $L_{aggr}(Q,\ +,\ \cdot,\ -,\ \div,\ \sum)$ on flat relational queries, every flat relational query $e[\vec{R}, \vec{x}]$ in $\mathcal{NRC}(Q,\ +,\ \cdot,\ -,\ \div,\ \sum)$ can be translated to a logic formula $\varphi_e^{\vec{R}}(\vec{x}, y)$ in $L_{aggr}(Q,\ +,\ \cdot,\ -,\ \div,\ \sum)$. So, for any objects $\vec{O}$, $\vec{o}$, $\{o'\}$ conforming to the types of $\vec{R}$, $\vec{x}$, and e, it is the case that $o' \in e[\vec{O}/\vec{R}, \vec{o}/\vec{x}]$ if and only if $[\vec{O}/\vec{R}, \vec{o}/\vec{x}, o'/y] \models \varphi_e^{\vec{R}}(\vec{x}, y)$.

The formula $\varphi_e^{\vec{R}}(\vec{x}, y)$ in $L_{aggr}(Q,\ +,\ \cdot,\ -,\ \div,\ \sum)$ actually only has variables on atomic objects. For ease of understanding and cross-referencing:

- We use the convention of treating each variable x_i in $\mathcal{NRC}(Q,\ +,\ \cdot,\ -,\ \div,\ \sum)$ as a tuple of variables $x_{i,1}$, ..., $x_{i,n}$ in $L_{aggr}(Q,\ +,\ \cdot,\ -,\ \div,\ \sum)$, where each $x_{i,j}$ is to take on the value of the jth component of the value taken on by x_i.
- We adopt the convention of using R_1, R_2, ... to name the input relations in both $\mathcal{NRC}(Q,\ +,\ \cdot,\ -,\ \div,\ \sum)$ and $L_{aggr}(Q,\ +,\ \cdot,\ -,\ \div,\ \sum)$.
- We use x_1, x_2, ... to name the free variables in a query in $\mathcal{NRC}(Q,\ +,\ \cdot,\ -,\ \div,\ \sum)$, which represent the input variables of the query.
- We use y (actually, $y_{,1}$, $y_{,2}$, ...) to name the free variables in a translated logic formula $\varphi_e^{\vec{R}}(\vec{x}, y)$ that corresponds to the outputs of the original query $e[\vec{R}, \vec{x}]$.
- We write φ_e and even φ instead of $\varphi_e^{\vec{R}}(\vec{x}, y)$ when there is no confusion.

As noted in Proposition 1, recursive queries such as transitive closure are inexpressible in $\mathcal{NRC}(Q,\ +,\ \cdot,\ -,\ \div,\ \sum)$. In an influential paper [1], Abiteboul and Beeri suggest augmenting $\mathcal{NRC}$ with a powerset operation, resulting in the query language $\mathcal{NRC}(\mathit{powerset})$, to enable such queries to be expressed without resorting to explicit recursion. So we also augment $\mathcal{NRC}(Q,\ +,\ \cdot,\ -,\ \div,\ \sum)$ with a powerset operation on flat relations to obtain the query language $\mathcal{NRC}(Q,\ +,\ \cdot,\ -,\ \div,\ \sum,\ \mathit{powerset})$, as shown in Figure 1. Here, *powerset* e produces a set containing all the subsets of the set denoted by e, provided e is a flat relation. $\mathcal{NRC}(Q,\ +,\ \cdot,\ -,\ \div,\ \sum,\ \mathit{powerset})$ can express recursive queries such as transitive closure, as illustrated in the following example.

Example 3. Let $Y : \{\mathit{employee} \times \mathit{employee}\}$ be a relation that the direct reportees of each employee. The direct and indirect reportees of each employee can be expressed in $\mathcal{NRC}(Q,\ +,\ \cdot,\ -,\ \div,\ \sum,\ \mathit{powerset})$ as

$$tc(Y) =_{df} \bigcap\{X \mid X \in \mathit{powerset}\ cp(dom(Y)),\ subset(Y, X),\ closed(X)\},$$

where

- $dom(Y) =_{df} \{\pi_1\ y \mid y \in Y\} \cup \{\pi_2\ y \mid y \in Y\}$,
- $cp(Z) =_{df} \{(u, v) \mid u \in Z,\ v \in Z\}$,
- $subset(Y, X) =_{df} \mathit{isempty}\ \{y \mid y \in Y,\ \mathit{isempty}\ \{y \mid x \in X, y = x\}\}$,
- $closed(Z) =_{df} subset(\{\pi_1\ u,\ \pi_2\ v) \mid u \in Z,\ v \in Z,\ \pi_2\ u = \pi_1\ v\},\ Z)$, and
- $\bigcap(Z) = \{u \mid u \in Z,\ subset(\{subset(u, v) \mid v \in Z\},\ \{true\})\}$.

As our interest is in the intensional aspect of expressive power, we need to know how each expression in $\mathcal{NRC}(Q,\ +,\ \cdot,\ -,\ \div,\ \sum,\ \mathit{powerset})$ is executed. We specify this explicitly in Figure 2, as a call-by-value operational semantics. A call-by-value operational semantics is widely adopted in programming languages and has also been used for several variations of $\mathcal{NRC}$ in earlier works [14, 15] on intensional expressive power.

In Figure 2, the notation $e \Downarrow C$ means the closed expression e is evaluated to the object C. The notation $C_1 \cup \cdots \cup C_n$ means the set of objects obtained by the union of the sets $C_1, \ldots, C_n$. The notations $C_1 + C_2$, $C_1 - C_2$, $C_1 \cdot C_2$, $C_1 \div C_2$ mean the objects obtained as the sum, difference, product, and division of C_1 and C_2 respectively. This evaluation is sound in the sense that, when $e : s$ and $e \Downarrow C$, then C is an object of type s and $e = C$. Hence each $e : s$ evaluates to a unique C. We use the notation $e \Downarrow$ to refer to the unique evaluation tree of e.

Here, we do not define the space complexity $\mathit{sizeof}(e \Downarrow)$ of an evaluation in terms of the size of the evaluation tree. Instead, we define it in terms of the size of the largest object in the evaluation tree—viz., $\mathit{sizeof}(e \Downarrow) = \max\{\mathit{sizeof}(C) \mid$ the object C occurs in the evaluation tree $e \Downarrow\}$. The size of an object is the number of atomic objects (i.e., objects of base type b) that it contains. This way of defining the complexity of evaluation has also been used in earlier works on intensional expressive power [14, 15].

Analogously, we define the time complexity $\mathit{timeof}(e \Downarrow)$ of an evaluation in terms of time complexity of the largest node

$$\frac{}{c \Downarrow c} \qquad \frac{e_1 \Downarrow C_1 \quad \ldots \quad e_n \Downarrow C_n}{(e_1, \ldots, e_n) \Downarrow (C_1, \ldots, C_n)} \qquad \frac{e \Downarrow (C_1, \ldots, C_n)}{\pi_i\ e \Downarrow C_i}\, 1 \leq i \leq n$$

$$\frac{}{\{\} \Downarrow \{\}} \qquad \frac{e \Downarrow C}{\{e\} \Downarrow \{C\}} \qquad \frac{e_1 \Downarrow C_1 \quad e_2 \Downarrow C_2}{e_1 \cup e_2 \Downarrow C_1 \cup C_2}$$

$$\frac{e_2 \Downarrow \{C_1, \ldots, C_n\} \quad e_1[C_1/x] \Downarrow C'_1 \quad \cdots \quad e_1[C_n/x] \Downarrow C'_n}{\bigcup\{e_1 \mid x \in e_2\} \Downarrow C'_1 \cup \cdots \cup C'_n}$$

$$\frac{}{\mathit{true} \Downarrow \mathit{true}} \qquad \frac{}{\mathit{false} \Downarrow \mathit{false}} \qquad \frac{e_1 \Downarrow \mathit{true} \quad e_2 \Downarrow C}{\mathit{if}\ e_1\ \mathit{then}\ e_2\ \mathit{else}\ e_3 \Downarrow C} \qquad \frac{e_1 \Downarrow \mathit{false} \quad e_3 \Downarrow C}{\mathit{if}\ e_1\ \mathit{then}\ e_2\ \mathit{else}\ e_3 \Downarrow C}$$

$$\frac{e_1 \Downarrow C_1 \quad e_2 \Downarrow C_2}{e_1 = e_2 \Downarrow \mathit{true}}\, C_1 = C_2 \qquad \frac{e_1 \Downarrow C_1 \quad e_2 \Downarrow C_2}{e_1 = e_2 \Downarrow \mathit{false}}\, C_1 \neq C_2$$

$$\frac{e \Downarrow C}{\mathit{isempty}\ e \Downarrow \mathit{true}}\, C = \{\} \qquad \frac{e \Downarrow C}{\mathit{isempty}\ e \Downarrow \mathit{false}}\, C \neq \{\}$$

$$\frac{e_1 \Downarrow C_1 \quad e_2 \Downarrow C_2}{e_1 + e_2 \Downarrow C_1 + C_2} \qquad \frac{e_1 \Downarrow C_1 \quad e_2 \Downarrow C_2}{e_1 - e_2 \Downarrow C_1 - C_2} \qquad \frac{e_1 \Downarrow C_1 \quad e_2 \Downarrow C_2}{e_1 \cdot e_2 \Downarrow C_1 \cdot C_2} \qquad \frac{e_1 \Downarrow C_1 \quad e_2 \Downarrow C_2}{e_1 \div e_2 \Downarrow C_1 \div C_2}$$

$$\frac{e_2 \Downarrow \{C_1, \ldots, C_n\} \quad e_1[C_1/x] \Downarrow C'_1 \quad \cdots \quad e_1[C_n/x] \Downarrow C'_n}{\sum\{\!|e_1 \mid x \in e_2|\!\} \Downarrow C'_1 + \cdots + C'_n}$$

$$\frac{e \Downarrow \{C_1, \ldots, C_n\}}{\mathit{powerset}\ e \Downarrow \{C'_1, \ldots, C'_{2^n}\}}$$
where $C'_1, \ldots, C'_{2^n}$ are the subsets of $\{C_1, \ldots, C_n\}$

Figure 2: A call-by-value operational semantics of $\mathcal{NRC}(Q,\ +,\ \cdot,\ -,\ \div,\ \sum,\ \mathit{powerset})$.

in the evaluation tree—viz., $\mathit{timeof}(e \Downarrow) = \max\{\mathit{timeof}(e' \Downarrow C') \mid$ the node $e' \Downarrow C'$ occurs in the evaluation tree of $e \Downarrow \}$. Here, the time complexity $\mathit{timeof}(e' \Downarrow C')$ of a node is defined in general as the number of branches that the node has. For example, in Figure 2, $\mathit{timeof}(e_1 + e_2 \Downarrow C_1 + C_2) = 2$ and $\mathit{timeof}(\bigcup\{e_1 \mid x \in e_2\} \Downarrow C_1 \cup \cdots \cup C'_n) = n+1$. However, for primitive operations, we assign them their expected time complexity. For example, $\mathit{timeof}(\mathit{powerset}\ e \Downarrow C) = 2^n$, where n is the cardinality of e.

The deep result below is due to Suciu and Paredaens [14].

PROPOSITION 2. *Let $e[R]$ be a query that implements the transitive closure of an input flat relation $R : \{b \times b\}$ in $\mathcal{NRC}(\mathit{powerset})$. Let O be a sufficiently long chain of type $\{b \times b\}$. Then $\mathit{sizeof}(e[O/R] \Downarrow)$ is $\Omega(2^{|O|})$. Thus every implementation of transitive closure in $\mathcal{NRC}(\mathit{powerset})$ requires exponential space.*

One may say that, since transitive closure is inexpressible in $\mathcal{NRC}$, any implementation of it in $\mathcal{NRC}(\mathit{powerset})$ must use the powerset operation and therefore must take exponential space. This is naive because there may exist a clever implementation that uses the powerset operation only on small intermediate data and, thus, achieves an overall PTIME complexity. Proposition 2 rules this out.

The proof of this result by Suciu and Paredaens also contains an implicit proof of another result, which Van den Bussche [6] proves explicitly in a later paper, that queries in $\mathcal{NRC}(\mathit{powerset})$ on unary database schemas are either already expressible in $\mathcal{NRC}$ (i.e., do not use the powerset operation) or must use exponential space (i.e., must use the powerset operation in a non-trivial way). It is known from Biskup et al. [3] that the parity query, which tests whether an input set has even cardinality, must use exponential space in a so-called equation algebra. The equation algebra is equivalent to $\mathcal{NRC}(\mathit{powerset})$, and every expression in $\mathcal{NRC}(\mathit{powerset})$ can be translated to an expression in the equation algebra having the same space complexity [3]. Thus every query can be implemented in the equation algebra with equal or better space complexity than in $\mathcal{NRC}(\mathit{powerset})$. Combining these two results of Van den Bussche and Biskup et al., we have the following result.

PROPOSITION 3. *1. Every flat relational query on unary database schemas in $\mathcal{NRC}(\mathit{powerset})$ is either already expressible in $\mathcal{NRC}$ or requires exponential space.*

2. In particular, every implementation of the parity query in $\mathcal{NRC}(\mathit{powerset})$ requires exponential space.

In the rest of this paper, we aim to generalize these two results to a Dichotomy Theorem on a large class of flat relational queries expressible in $\mathcal{NRC}(Q,\ +,\ \cdot,\ -,\ \div,\ \sum,\ \mathit{powerset})$. In particular, these flat relational queries expressible in $\mathcal{NRC}(Q,\ +,\ \cdot,\ -,\ \div,\ \sum,\ \mathit{powerset})$ are shown here to be dichotomous in the sense that either they are already expressible in $\mathcal{NRC}(Q,\ +,\ \cdot,\ -,\ \div,\ \sum)$ or they require at least exponential space. Hence, the extra expressive power that the powerset operation buys for $\mathcal{NRC}(Q,\ +,\ \cdot,\ -,\ \div,\ \sum,\ \mathit{powerset})$ comes strictly with an exponential cost.

3. TWO POWERFUL PROPERTIES

We need the conservative extension property and the locality property to prove our main results.

3.1 Conservative Extension

The conservative extension property and its system of rewrite rules, in Figure 3, were introduced by Wong [16] and generalized by Libkin and Wong [12, 13]. The last rule deserves a special mention. Consider the incorrect equation: $\sum\{\!|e \mid x \in \bigcup\{e_1 \mid y \in e_2\}|\!\} = \sum\{\!|\sum\{\!|e \mid x \in e_1|\!\} \mid y \in e_2|\!\}$. Suppose e_2 evaluates to a set of two distinct objects $\{o_1, o_2\}$; $e_1[o_1/y]$ and $e_1[o_2/y]$ both evaluate to $\{o_3\}$; and $e[o_3/x]$ evaluates to 1. Then the left-hand-side of the "equation" returns 1 but the right-hand-side yields 2. The division operation in the last rule in Figure 3 is used to handle duplicates properly. The following properties of this system of rewrite rules are well known [16, 12, 13].

PROPOSITION 4 (CONSERVATIVE EXTENSION).

1. *This system of rewrite rules is sound.*
2. *This system of rewrite rules is strongly normalizing.*
3. *Let e be an expression in $\mathcal{NRC}(Q, +, \cdot, -, \div, \sum$, powerset) that is in normal form with respect to this system of rewrite rules. That is, no rule can be applied to further rewrite e. Let $e'[\vec{R}] : s$ be a subexpression in e. Suppose $\vec{R}$ have types whose height is at most h, and the type s has height h'. Then all the types appearing in the type derivation of $e'[\vec{R}] : s$ have height at most $\max(h, h')$, if the powerset operation does not appear in $e'[\vec{R}]$; or, they have height at most $\max(h, h', 2)$, if the powerset operation appears in $e'[\vec{R}]$.*

This system of rewrite rules does not increase the complexity of evaluation.

PROPOSITION 5. *Let $e[\vec{R}] \mapsto e'[\vec{R}]$. Let $\vec{O}$ be a list of objects conforming to the types of $\vec{R}$. Then*

1. *$sizeof(e[\vec{O}/\vec{R}] \Downarrow) \geq sizeof(e'[\vec{O}/\vec{R}] \Downarrow)$.*
2. *$timeof(e[\vec{O}/\vec{R}] \Downarrow) \geq timeof(e'[\vec{O}/\vec{R}] \Downarrow)$.*

3.2 Locality

The second powerful machinery needed to prove our dichotomy result is the locality property. We need some understanding of "τ structure", "Gaifman graph", "r-sphere", and "r-neighbourhood", before we can explain the locality property [11].

A signature τ is a list of symbols $\vec{R}$, where $\vec{R}$ is to be regarded as input for a query. Each symbol R_i in $\vec{R}$ has type of the form $\{b \times \cdots \times b\}$. A τ structure $\mathcal{A} = \langle A, \vec{O}\rangle$ has a universe A (which is a finite nonempty set of objects of type b) and a list of objects $\vec{O}$ (and each object O_i in $\vec{O}$ has the type of R_i and is the interpretation of R_i). Each O_i in $\vec{O}$ is a set of tuples, and each element $o_{i,j}$ in a tuple $o_i \in O_i$ is in the universe A. Each object in the universe is required to be in some O_i. We use STRUCT[τ] to denote the class of τ structures, and the symbol $\simeq$ to denote the isomorphism of τ structures. Also, we use the symbol τ_m to denote the signature obtained by extending the signature τ with m new constant symbols.

The Gaifman graph $\mathcal{G}(\mathcal{A})$ of a τ structure $\mathcal{A} = \langle A, \vec{O}\rangle$ is a graph whose edges are pairs (a, b) where there is a tuple $o_i \in O_i$, for some O_i in $\vec{O}$, such that both a and b are elements in o_i. The distance $d^{\mathcal{A}}(a, b)$ is the length of the shortest path from a to b in $\mathcal{G}(\mathcal{A})$. Given a tuple $\vec{a} = (a_1, \ldots, a_m)$ of objects in A, and some $r \geq 0$, the r-sphere of $\vec{a}$ is defined as $S_r^{\mathcal{A}}(\vec{a}) = \bigcup_{1 \leq i \leq m} S_r^{\mathcal{A}}(a_i)$, where $S_r^{\mathcal{A}}(a_i) = \{b \in A \mid d^{\mathcal{A}}(a_i, b) \leq r\}$. The r-neighbourhood of $\vec{a}$ is the τ_m structure $N_r^{\mathcal{A}}(\vec{a}) = \langle S_r^{\mathcal{A}}(\vec{a}), \vec{O}|_{S_r^{\mathcal{A}}(\vec{a})}, a_1, \ldots, a_m\rangle$, meaning that $N_r^{\mathcal{A}}(\vec{a})$ is obtained by restricting $\mathcal{A}$ to the universe $S_r^{\mathcal{A}}(\vec{a})$ and adding some extra constants which are the elements of $\vec{a}$.

As shown by Gaifman [9], the result of any first-order query can be determined by considering "small neighbourhoods" of its input—the locality property. As shown by Dong et al. [8], flat relational queries expressible in $\mathcal{NRC}(Q, +, \cdot, -, \div, \sum)$ also enjoy this kind of locality property, modulo a mild restriction on input relations. It is also shown by Hella et al. [10] and Libkin [11] that flat relational queries in $L_{aggr}(Q, +, \cdot, -, \div, \sum)$ enjoy the locality property even when it is further augmented with any collection Ω of functions on numbers[2] and any collection Θ of aggregate functions.[3] Since $\mathcal{NRC}(Q, +, \cdot, -, \div, \sum)$ and $L_{aggr}(Q, +, \cdot, -, \div, \sum)$ have equivalent expressive power in terms of flat relational queries, see Proposition 1, this means that flat relational queries in $\mathcal{NRC}(Q, +, \cdot, -, \div, \sum)$ actually enjoy the locality property without any restriction, even when the query language is further augmented with any collection Ω of functions on numbers and any collection Θ of aggregate functions.

PROPOSITION 6 (LOCALITY). *Every flat relational query $e[\vec{R}]$ in $\mathcal{NRC}(Q, +, \cdot, -, \div, \sum)$ has the locality property. That is, there is a finite natural number r such that, for every $\mathcal{A} = \langle A, \vec{O}\rangle \in STRUCT[\vec{R}]$, for every two m-ary vectors $\vec{a}$ and $\vec{b}$ of elements of A, it is the case that $N_r^{\mathcal{A}}(\vec{a}) \simeq N_r^{\mathcal{A}}(\vec{b})$ implies $\vec{a} \in e[\vec{O}/\vec{R}]$ if and only if $\vec{b} \in e[\vec{O}/\vec{R}]$.*

So for every flat relational query expressible in $\mathcal{NRC}(Q, +, \cdot, -, \div, \sum)$, there is some number r such that, for every pair $(\vec{a}, \vec{b})$ whose neighbourhoods are isomorphic up to radius r, they must either be both in the result of the query or both not in the result of the query. We call the smallest such number r the "locality index" of the query.

An equivalence relation $\vec{a} \approx_r^{\mathcal{A}} \vec{b}$ is induced by $N_r^{\mathcal{A}}(\vec{a}) \simeq N_r^{\mathcal{A}}(\vec{b})$. Each resulting isomorphism type, also called a neighbourhood type, induced by this equivalence relation is definable by a first-order formula $\xi(\vec{u})$ such that $\vec{a} \approx_r^{\mathcal{A}} \vec{b}$ if and only if $\mathcal{A}, [\vec{b}/\vec{u}] \models \xi(\vec{u})$. This formula can be thought of as a "diagram" showing how objects in this neighbourhood type are "connected" to each other and to the reference objects (i.e., $\vec{u}$). If a restriction is imposed so that $\mathcal{G}(\mathcal{A})$ has degree at most k, the number of resulting isomorphism types realised for each $r > 0$ is finite. This restriction, together with the locality property, implies that the result of any flat relational query $e[\vec{R}]$ in $\mathcal{NRC}(Q, +, \cdot, -, \div, \sum)$ is completely characterized by a finite number of neighbourhood types.

[2]A function $f \in \Omega$ has type of the form $Q \times \cdots \times Q \rightarrow Q$.
[3]An aggregate function $g \in \Theta$ has type of the form $\{\!|Q|\!\} \rightarrow Q$, where $\{\!|Q|\!\}$ denotes the type of multiset of numbers.

$$
\begin{array}{rcl}
\bigcup\{e \mid x \in \{\}\} & \mapsto & \{\} \\
\bigcup\{e_1 \mid x \in \{e_2\}\} & \mapsto & e_1[e_2/x] \\
\bigcup\{e \mid x \in (e_1 \cup e_2)\} & \mapsto & \bigcup\{e \mid x \in e_1\} \cup \bigcup\{e \mid x \in e_2\} \\
\bigcup\{e_1 \mid x \in \bigcup\{e_2 \mid y \in e_3\}\} & \mapsto & \bigcup\{\bigcup\{e_1 \mid x \in e_2\} \mid y \in e_3\} \\
\bigcup\{e \mid x \in (\textit{if } e_1 \textit{ then } e_2 \textit{ else } e_3)\} & \mapsto & \textit{if } e_1 \textit{ then } \bigcup\{e \mid x \in e_2\} \textit{ else } \bigcup\{e \mid x \in e_3\} \\
\pi_i(e_1, \ldots, e_2) & \mapsto & e_i \\
\pi_i\ (\textit{if } e_1 \textit{ then } e_2 \textit{ else } e_3) & \mapsto & \textit{if } e_1 \textit{ then } \pi_i\ e_2 \textit{ else } \pi_i\ e_3 \\
\textit{if true then } e_2 \textit{ else } e_3 & \mapsto & e_2 \\
\textit{if false then } e_2 \textit{ else } e_3 & \mapsto & e_3 \\
\sum\{\!|e \mid x \in \{\}|\!\} & \mapsto & 0 \\
\sum\{\!|e \mid x \in \{e'\}|\!\} & \mapsto & e[e'/x] \\
\sum\{\!|e \mid x \in \textit{if } e_1 \textit{ then } e_2 \textit{ else } e_3|\!\} & \mapsto & \textit{if } e_1 \textit{ then } \sum\{\!|e \mid x \in e_2|\!\} \textit{ else } \sum\{\!|e \mid x \in e_3|\!\} \\
\sum\{\!|e \mid x \in e_1 \cup e_2|\!\} & \mapsto & \sum\{\!|e \mid x \in e_1|\!\} + \sum\{\!|\textit{if } x \in e_1 \textit{ then } 0 \textit{ else } e \mid x \in e_2|\!\} \\
\sum\{\!|e \mid x \in \bigcup\{e_1 \mid y \in e_2\}|\!\} & \mapsto & \sum\{\!|\sum\{\!|(e \div \sum\{\!|\sum\{\!|\textit{if } x = v \textit{ then } 1 \textit{ else } 0 \mid v \in e_1|\!\} \\
& & \mid y \in e_2|\!\})| \, x \in e_1|\!\} \mid y \in e_2|\!\}
\end{array}
$$

Figure 3: A system of rewrite rules for $\mathcal{NRC}(Q,\ +,\ \cdot,\ -,\ \div,\ \sum,\ \textit{powerset})$.

The following proposition on objects that are connected in a neighbourhood type is easily proved.

PROPOSITION 7. *Given a neighbourhood type $\xi(u_1, \ldots, u_m)$ induced by some r-neighbourhood. Suppose u_i and u_j are connected to each other in $\xi(u_1, \ldots, u_m)$. Then for any τ_m structure $\mathcal{A} = \langle A, \vec{O}, o_1, \ldots, o_m\rangle$ realizing $\xi(u_1, \ldots, u_m)$, it is the case that $d^{\mathcal{A}}(o_i, o_j) \leq 2mr + 1$.*

4. COMPLEXITY OF QUERIES ON SEVERELY DICHOTOMOUS STRUCTURES

Given a signature τ. A "motif" of radius r is a first-order formula $\rho(u)$ with a single free variable u and has locality index r on all τ structures. We say a τ structure $\mathcal{A}$ is "bounded" at threshold g by a motif $\rho(u)$ of radius r if there are at most rg elements in the universe of $\mathcal{A}$ that make $\rho(u)$ true—i.e., $|\{a \in A \mid \mathcal{A}, [a/u] \models \rho(u)\}| \leq rg$. We say a class $\mathcal{C}$ of τ structures is "bounded" at threshold g by a motif $\rho(u)$ if $\rho(u)$ bounds all structures in $\mathcal{C}$ at threshold g. On the other hand, we say $\mathcal{C}$ is "unbounded" by $\rho(u)$ if for every $g > 0$, there is $\mathcal{A} \in \mathcal{C}$ that is not bounded at threshold g by $\rho(u)$.

Now we define the class of dichotomous structures.

Definition 1.

1. A class $\mathcal{C}$ of τ structures is called "dichotomous" at threshold g if and only if (i) $\mathcal{C}$ is unbounded by some motifs, and (ii) $\mathcal{C}$ is bounded by all other motifs at threshold g.
2. A dichotomous class $\mathcal{C}$ is "deep" if it is unbounded by some motifs of radius r at every r.
3. A dichotomous class $\mathcal{C}$ has "severity" ℓ if for every motif $\rho(u)$ that unbounds $\mathcal{C}$, there is a sequence of structures $\mathcal{A}_1, \mathcal{A}_2, \ldots$, in $\mathcal{C}$ having universe of increasing size, and the ratio $|\{a \in A_i \mid \mathcal{A}_i, [a/u] \models \rho(u)\}|/|A_i|$ tends to ℓ as i tends to infinity.
4. A dichotomous class is "severely dichotomous" if it has severity 1.

Given a τ structure $\mathcal{A} = \langle A, \vec{O}\rangle$, we define its size as the size of its universe: $|\mathcal{A}| = |A|$. We can now state and prove our Dichotomy Theorem for $\mathcal{NRC}(Q,\ +,\ \cdot,\ -,\ \div,\ \sum,\ \textit{powerset})$.

THEOREM 1 (DICHOTOMY). *Let $e[\vec{R}] : \{b \times \cdots \times b\}$ be a flat relational query in $\mathcal{NRC}(Q,\ +,\ \cdot,\ -,\ \div,\ \sum,\ \textit{powerset})$ and the input $\vec{R}$ comes from a class $\mathcal{C}$ where (i) $\mathcal{C}$ is severely dichotomous, and (ii) the Gaifman graphs of its structures have degree at most k. Then either $e[\vec{R}]$ is expressible in $\mathcal{NRC}(Q,\ +,\ \cdot,\ -,\ \div,\ \sum)$; or there is a sequence of structures $\mathcal{A}_i = \langle A_i, \vec{O}_i\rangle \in \mathcal{C}$ of increasing size, such that $\textit{sizeof}(e[\vec{O}_i/\vec{R}] \Downarrow)$ is $\Omega(2^{|A_i|})$.*

PROOF. Let $\mathcal{C}$ be severely dichotomous at threshold g, and the Gaifman graphs of structures in it have degree at most k. Let $\mathcal{A} = \langle A, \vec{O}\rangle \in \mathcal{C}$ be the input to the query $e[\vec{R}]$.

By Proposition 5, the system of rewrite rules in Figure 3 does not increase complexity. By Proposition 4, it is sound and strongly normalizing. Thus we assume $e[\vec{R}]$ is an expression in normal form with respect to this system of rewrite rules.

If the powerset operation does not appear in $e[\vec{R}]$, then the theorem trivially holds. So, let it contain some occurrences of the powerset operation. Suppose $\textit{powerset}\ e'[\vec{R}, \vec{x}]$ is the earliest occurrence of the powerset operation to be evaluated when $e[\vec{R}]$ is evaluated according to the operational semantics given in Figure 2.

There are only two ways to introduce a new variable in $\mathcal{NRC}(Q,\ +,\ \cdot,\ -,\ \div,\ \sum,\ \textit{powerset})$, namely the $\bigcup\{e_1 \mid x \in e_2\}$ construct and the $\sum\{\!|e_1 \mid x \in e_2|\!\}$ construct. So, each new free variable x_i in $\vec{x}$ must have been introduced in an enclosing expression of the form $\bigcup\{\cdots \textit{powerset}\ e'[\vec{R}, \vec{x}] \cdots \mid x_i \in E\}$ or the form $\sum\{\!|\cdots \textit{powerset}\ e'[\vec{R}, \vec{x}] \cdots \mid x_i \in E|\!\}$. As the entire expression $e[\vec{R}]$ is in normal form, and $e'[\vec{R}, \vec{x}]$ is the earliest instance of the powerset operation to be evaluated, E must be one of the R_i in $\vec{R}$, which is a flat relation. Hence, x_i must have height 0 and has a type of the form $b \times \cdots \times b$. As the powerset operation requires its input to be a flat relation, we know $e'[\vec{R}, \vec{x}]$ has type of the form $\{b \times \cdots \times b\}$. Therefore, $e'[\vec{R}, \vec{x}]$ is a flat relational query in $\mathcal{NRC}(Q,\ +,\ \cdot,\ -,\ \div,\ \sum)$.

We need to inspect the entire expression $e[\vec{R}]$ to extract all the conditions $\psi(\vec{x})$ that must hold on $\vec{x}$ before $e'[\vec{R}, \vec{x}]$ is evaluated. Let the notation $\odot$ represents a subexpression that contains the occurrence of the expression $e'[\vec{R}, \vec{x}]$, and recall that φ_E denotes the formula in $L_{aggr}(Q, +, \cdot, -, \div, \sum)$ that the expression E in $\mathcal{NRC}(Q, +, \cdot, -, \div, \sum)$ translates to. We define the extraction function $\overrightarrow{e[\vec{R}]}$ by induction below.

- $\overrightarrow{\bigcup\{\textit{if } E \textit{ then } \odot \textit{ else } F \mid x \in R\}} = (x, \vec{x}' : R, \vec{R}' : \varphi_E \wedge \psi)$, where $\overrightarrow{\odot} = (\vec{x}' : \vec{R}' : \psi)$.
- $\overrightarrow{\bigcup\{\textit{if } E \textit{ then } F \textit{ else } \odot \mid x \in R\}} = (x, \vec{x}' : R, \vec{R}' : \neg\varphi_E \wedge \psi)$, where $\overrightarrow{\odot} = (\vec{x}' : \vec{R}' : \psi)$.
- $\overrightarrow{\bigcup\{\textit{if } \odot \textit{ then } E \textit{ else } F \mid x \in R\}} = (x, \vec{x}' : R, \vec{R}' : \psi)$, where $\overrightarrow{\odot} = (\vec{x}' : \vec{R}' : \psi)$.
- $\overrightarrow{\odot \cup E} = \overrightarrow{\odot}$,
- $\overrightarrow{E \cup \odot} = \overrightarrow{\odot}$,
- the remaining rules are analogous; we omit them to avoid tedium.

By the conservative extension property (Proposition 4), all the types that appear in the typing derivation of $e'[\vec{R}, \vec{x}]$ have height at most 1 (i.e., must be flat). We note that, by Proposition 1, $e'[\vec{R}, \vec{x}]$ is equivalent to a formula $\varphi(\vec{x}, y)$ in $L_{aggr}(Q, +, \cdot, -, \div, \sum)$. We extract all the conditions $\psi(\vec{x})$ that must hold on $\vec{x}$ before $e'[\vec{R}, \vec{x}]$ is evaluated—i.e., $\overrightarrow{e[\vec{R}]} = (\vec{x} : \vec{R} : \psi(\vec{x}))$. Let $C[\vec{x}]$ be the expression in $\mathcal{NRC}(Q, +, \cdot, -, \div, \sum)$ that is equivalent to the formula $\psi(\vec{x})$ in $L_{aggr}(Q, +, \cdot, -, \div, \sum)$. Now we define $\phi(\vec{x}, y) =_{df} \bigwedge_i R_i(x_i) \wedge \psi(\vec{x}) \wedge \varphi(\vec{x}, y)$, which is a formula in $L_{aggr}(Q, +, \cdot, -, \div, \sum)$ and corresponds to the query $\{(\vec{x}, y) \mid x_1 \in R_1, ..., x_n \in R_n, C[\vec{x}], y \in e'[\vec{R}, \vec{x}]\}$ in $\mathcal{NRC}(Q, +, \cdot, -, \div, \sum)$.

By the locality property (Proposition 6) of $\mathcal{NRC}(Q, +, \cdot, -, \div, \sum)$, let $\phi(\vec{x}, y)$'s locality index be r. Since the Gaifman graph of our input structure has degree at most k, there is a finite number of r-neighbourhood types $\xi_h(\vec{x}, y)$ such that $\neg(\xi_h(\vec{x}, y) \Rightarrow \neg\phi(\vec{x}, y))$. Thus $\bigvee_h \xi_h(\vec{x}, y)$ if and only if $\phi(\vec{x}, y)$. For convenience, let us refer to these neighbourhood types as the "qualifying neighbourhood types".

Let $x_{i,j}$ be the jth component of x_i in $\vec{x}$, $y_{,l}$ be the lth component of y, and $\pi_l o'$ the lth component of a tuple o' of objects in $\mathcal{A}$. Suppose for each $y_{,l}$ and qualifying neighbourhood type $\xi_h(\vec{x}, y)$, we are able to determine a number $H_{h,l}$ in a manner that is independent of $\mathcal{A}$, such that given any $\vec{o}$ of the appropriate types, it is the case that $|\{\pi_l o' \mid \mathcal{A}, [\vec{o}/\vec{x}, o'/y] \models \xi_h(\vec{x}, y)\}| < H_{h,l}$. Then we can make the following conclusions. There are at most $H_{h,l}$ distinct instantiations of $y_{,l}$ that make $\xi_h(\vec{x}, y)$ true. Thus, there are at most $H_h^* = \prod_l H_{h,l}$ distinct instantiations of y that make $\xi_h(\vec{x}, y)$ true. Thus, there are at most $H^* = \sum_h \prod_l H_{h,l}$ distinct instantiations of y that make $\phi(\vec{x}, y)$ true. By definition of $\phi(\vec{x}, y)$, there are at most H^* tuples in the result of evaluating $e'[\vec{O}'/\vec{R}, \vec{o}/\vec{x}]$ in the context of $e[\vec{R}]$. In this case, this powerset operation can be eliminated by replacing it with an expression $\textit{powerset}_{H^*}\ e'[\vec{R}, \vec{x}]$. Here, $\textit{powerset}_{H^*}$ is a function for producing subsets of size at most H^* and is expressible in $\mathcal{NRC}(Q, +, \cdot, -, \div, \sum)$. We repeat the entire process above as many times as necessary. If all occurrences of the powerset operation are eliminated, then the original query $e[\vec{R}]$ must already be expressible in $\mathcal{NRC}(Q, +, \cdot, -, \div, \sum)$.

Now, let us show how to determine the crucial number $H_{h,l}$. We only need to consider three situations when we compute $H_{h,l}$. The first situation is when $y_{,l}$ is connected to some $x_{i,j}$ in $\xi_h(\vec{x}, y)$. Since $\xi_h(\vec{x}, y)$ describes a r-neighbourhood, by Proposition 7, the distance between $x_{i,j}$ and $y_{,l}$ is at most $2mr + 1$, where m is the length of the tuple of variables denoted by $\vec{x}, y$. Since the Gaifman graph of our input structure has degree at most k, for any instantiation $\vec{o}$ for $\vec{x}$, there are at most k^{2mr+1} distinct instantiations for $y_{,l}$. So we can set $H_{h,l} = k^{2mr+1}$ for this first situation.

On the other hand, $y_{,l}$ may not be connected to any $x_{i,j}$ in $\xi_h(\vec{x}, y)$. Let $\xi'_h(y_{,l}) =_{df} \exists \vec{x}, y_{,1}, \ldots y_{,l-1}, y_{,l+1}, \ldots y_{,m}.\xi_h(\vec{x}, y)$. By the locality property (Proposition 6), let the locality index of ξ'_h be r'. Since the Gaifman graph has degree at most k, there is a finite number of r'-neighbourhood types $\rho_{h,d}(y_{,l})$ such that $\neg(\rho_{h,d}(y_{,l}) \Rightarrow \neg\xi'_h(y_{,l}))$. Thus $\bigvee_d \rho_{h,d}(y_{,l})$ if and only if $\xi'_h(y_{,l})$. Suppose we are able to determine a number $H'_{h,l,d}$, in a manner that is independent of $\mathcal{A}$, such that $|\{a \mid \mathcal{A}, [a/y_{,l}] \models \rho_{h,d}(y_{,l})\}| < H'_{h,l,d}$. Then we can set $H_{h,l} = \sum_d H'_{h,l,d}$.

How do we determine $H'_{h,l,d}$? Each $\rho_{h,d}(y_{,l})$ is a motif that either bounds $\mathcal{C}$ at threshold g or unbounds $\mathcal{C}$. This brings us into the second and the third situation respectively.

The second situation is when $\rho_{h,d}(y_{,l})$ bounds $\mathcal{C}$ at threshold g. Recall that the locality index of ξ'_h is r'. So the locality index of $\rho_{h,d}(y_{,l})$ is also r'. Then, by definition of bounding motifs, there are at most $r'g$ number of instantiations for $y_{,l}$ that make $\rho_{h,d}(y_{,l})$ true. So we can set $H_{h,l,d} = r'g$.

The third and last situation is when $\rho_{h,d}(y_{,l})$ unbounds $\mathcal{C}$. As $\mathcal{C}$ is severely dichotomous, there is a sequence of structures $\mathcal{A}_1 = \langle A_1, \vec{O}_1 \rangle$, $\mathcal{A}_2 = \langle A_2, \vec{O}_2 \rangle$, ... in $\mathcal{C}$ having universe of increasing size, such that the ratio $|\{a \in A_i \mid \mathcal{A}_i, [a/y_{,l}] \models \rho_{h,d}(y_{,l})\}|/|A_i|$ tends to 1. Note that all of the objects a in $\{a \in A_i \mid \mathcal{A}_i, [a/y_{,l}] \models \rho_{h,d}(y_{,l})\}$ must be used to instantiate $y_{,l}$ as required by the locality property, because $\rho_{h,d}(y_{,l})$ is a neighbourhood type. That is, the number of instantions for $y_{,l}$ is essentially $|A_i|$. In this case, we cannot set $H_{h,l,d}$ (and thus $H_{h,l}$) to a finite value in a manner that is independent of the input structure to our query $e[\vec{R}]$. Therefore, the powerset operation in $\textit{powerset}\ e'[\vec{R}, \vec{x}]$ cannot be eliminated in this situation. On the other hand, the number of instantiations for y is $\Omega(|A_i|)$ since one of its components, $y_{,l}$, has $|A_i|$ instantiations. So, $e'[\vec{R}, \vec{x}]$ has $\Omega(|A_i|)$ elements. Thus, $\textit{sizeof}(e[\vec{O}_i/\vec{R}] \Downarrow)$ is $\Omega(2^{|A_i|})$ as desired.

By the way, if $\mathcal{C}$'s severity level was some $\ell < 1$, the number of instantiations for $y_{,l}$ would be $\ell|A_i|$. In this case, $\textit{sizeof}(e[\vec{O}_i/\vec{R}] \Downarrow)$ would be $\Omega(2^{\ell|A_i|})$. □

5. REMARKS

Let us close this paper by discussing how the Dichotomy Theorem generalizes the old results of Suciu, Paredaens, Van den Bussche, Biskup, and others [14, 6, 3].

5.1 On the result of Suciu and Paredaens

Suciu and Paredaens [14] have shown earlier that all implementations of the transitive closure of a single long chain in the nested relational algebra of Abiteboul and Beeri [1], which is equivalent to $\mathcal{NRC}(\textit{powerset})$, require exponential space. In this paper, we have improved on this result in several significant ways.

Firstly, our Dichotomy Theorem is not limited to a single specific query such as the transitive closure of a chain. It works equally well for all flat relational queries (on severely dichotomous structures) that are inexpressible in $\mathcal{NRC}(Q, +, \cdot, -, \div, \sum)$ but expressible in $\mathcal{NRC}(Q, +, \cdot, -, \div, \sum, \mathit{powerset})$, such as the transitive closure of a set of k single long chains, a set of k long circles, a deep full binary tree, and many more.

COROLLARY 1. *For any flat relational query on any severely dichotomous class of structures whose Gaifman graphs have degree at most* k*, if it is inexpressible in* $\mathcal{NRC}(Q, +, \cdot, -, \div, \sum)$ *but is expressible in* $\mathcal{NRC}(Q, +, \cdot, -, \div, \sum, \mathit{powerset})$*, then all of its implementations in* $\mathcal{NRC}(Q, +, \cdot, -, \div, \sum, \mathit{powerset})$ *need exponential space.*

Secondly, our Dichotomy Theorem is not limited to $\mathcal{NRC}(\mathit{powerset})$. We have already shown it for a more powerful query language, $\mathcal{NRC}(Q, +, \cdot, -, \div, \sum, \mathit{powerset})$, which has aggregate functions and better captures queries in SQL.

Thirdly, our proof technique is more general. So long as the query language has the locality property before the *powerset* operation is added to it and, after the *powerset* operation is added to it, has a normal form induced by the conversative extension property, our proof works. For example, let Ω comprise the functions $\otimes$, ι, and $\oslash$; and Θ comprise the aggregate function Π as defined below:

- $\otimes : Q \times Q \to Q$ is a commutative associative function;
- $\iota : Q$ is its identity;
- $\oslash : Q \times Q \to Q$ is a "duplicate compensator" function satisfying

$$\overbrace{(a \oslash n) \otimes \cdots \otimes (a \oslash n)}^{n \text{ times}} = a;$$

- $\Pi\{\!|e_2 \mid x \in e_1|\!\}$ is an aggregate function that applies the function $f(x) = e_2$ to every object in the set e_1 and aggregate the results using $\otimes$, and so satisfying $\Pi\{\!|e_2 \mid x \in e_1|\!\} = f(o_1) \otimes \cdots \otimes f(o_m) \otimes \iota$ where e_1 is the set $\{o_1, \ldots, o_m\}$.

Then we can prove the following more general Dichotomy Theorem.

THEOREM 2. *For any flat relational query on any severely dichotomous class of structures whose Gaifman graphs have degree at most* k*, if it is inexpressible in* $\mathcal{NRC}(\Omega, \Theta, Q, +, \cdot, -, \div, \sum)$ *but is expressible in* $\mathcal{NRC}(\Omega, \Theta, Q, +, \cdot, -, \div, \sum, \mathit{powerset})$*, then all of its implementations in* $\mathcal{NRC}(\Omega, \Theta, Q, +, \cdot, -, \div, \sum, \mathit{powerset})$ *need exponential space.*

PROOF. (Sketch) It is easy to show that $\mathcal{NRC}(\Omega, \Theta, Q, +, \cdot, -, \div, \sum, \mathit{powerset})$ has the conservative extension property by adding the following rules to the rewrite system:

- $\Pi\{\!|e \mid x \in \bigcup\{e_1 \mid y \in e_2\}|\!\} \mapsto \Pi\{\!|\Pi\{\!|(e \oslash \sum\{\!|\sum\{\!|\mathit{if}\ x = v\ \mathit{then}\ 1\ \mathit{else}\ 0 \mid v \in e_1|\!\} \mid y \in e_2|\!\})| x \in e_1|\!\} \mid y \in e_2|\!\}$,
- the other rules are analogous to those for $\sum$ and are omitted.

The result of Hella et al. [10] also implies $\mathcal{NRC}(\Omega, \Theta, Q, +, \cdot, -, \div, \sum)$ has the locality property. So the proof of our Dichotomy Theorem can be applied verbatim to conclude this proposition. □

We have also gained some further insights on the use of *powerset* operation. If a function f on a severely dichotomous class of structures of degree $\leq k$ is expressible in $\mathcal{NRC}(Q, +, \cdot, -, \div, \sum)$, but an implementation e of it in $\mathcal{NRC}(Q, +, \cdot, -, \div, \sum, \mathit{powerset})$ uses the *powerset* operation, our Dichotomy Theorem actually does not guarantee the removal of *powerset* operation in the implementation e. It is perfectly reasonable for f to have an inefficient implementation in $\mathcal{NRC}(Q, +, \cdot, -, \div, \sum, \mathit{powerset})$; i.e., the Dichotomy Theorem is not a clever optimizer. On the other hand, the Dichotomy Theorem is sufficient for us to conclude that, if f is inexpressible in $\mathcal{NRC}(Q, +, \cdot, -, \div, \sum)$, then all of its implementation in $\mathcal{NRC}(Q, +, \cdot, -, \div, \sum, \mathit{powerset})$ have to use the *powerset* operation at least once in a non-trivial way.

5.2 On the result of Van den Bussche

Definition 1 divides the severely dichotomous class of structures into two subclasses: the class of structures that are deep and the class of structures that are not deep. The deep class has motifs of increasingly large radius that unbounds the class, while in the non-deep class, all motifs that unbound the class have small radius. Structures in the non-deep class are basically things like an arbitrarily large set of short chains—the class is unbounded by the number of short chains rather than the length of these chains.

We have so far encountered examples of deep severely dichotomous classes of structures. Let us now give an example of non-deep severely dichotomous classes of structures, viz., the class of sets of type $\{b\}$ having an arbitrarily large number of elements! The following result is a simple consequence of Corollary 1.

COROLLARY 2. 1. *For any flat relational query on unary database schemas, if it is inexpressible in* $\mathcal{NRC}(Q, +, \cdot, -, \div, \sum)$*, but is expressible in* $\mathcal{NRC}(Q, +, \cdot, -, \div, \sum, \mathit{powerset})$*, then all of its implementations in* $\mathcal{NRC}(Q, +, \cdot, -, \div, \sum, \mathit{powerset})$ *need exponential space.*

2. *In particular, all implementations of the parity query in* $\mathcal{NRC}(Q, +, \cdot, -, \div, \sum, \mathit{powerset})$ *need exponential space.*

PROOF. The first part follows immediately from Corollary 1 and the fact that the class of sets of type $\{b\}$ having a large number elements is severely dichotomous.

For the second part, we observe that if the parity query is expressible in $\mathcal{NRC}(Q, +, \cdot, -, \div, \sum)$, then it is also possible to express a query in $\mathcal{NRC}(Q, +, \cdot, -, \div, \sum)$ to test whether a single long chain has an even number of nodes. By the finite-cofiniteness property of $\mathcal{NRC}(Q, +, \cdot, -, \div, \sum)$ established by Libkin and Wong [13], the latter query is inexpressible in $\mathcal{NRC}(Q, +, \cdot, -, \div, \sum)$. Thus, the parity query is inexpressible in $\mathcal{NRC}(Q, +, \cdot, -, \div, \sum)$. Since the simplest instance of the parity query is an example of a query on unary database schemas, it follows from the first part that exponential space is needed to implement the parity query in $\mathcal{NRC}(Q, +, \cdot, -, \div, \sum, \mathit{powerset})$. □

This corollary straightforwardly generalizes the old result of Van den Bussche (i.e., Proposition 3) to a more powerful query language.

5.3 On the result of Biskup et al.

It is possible to capture the key feature of the equation algebra of Biskup et al. [3] by augmenting $\mathcal{NRC}$ with the following construct:

$$\frac{e_1 : \{\{b \times \cdots \times b\}\} \quad e_2 : \{b \times \cdots \times b\}}{\bigcup\{e_1 \mid x^{\{b\times\cdots\times b\}} \subseteq e_2\} : \{\{b \times \cdots \times b\}\}}$$

with the following call-by-value operational semantics:

$$\frac{\begin{array}{c} e_2 \Downarrow \{C_1, \ldots, C_n\} \\ e_1[C'_1/x] \Downarrow C''_1 \quad \ldots \quad e_1[C'_{2^n}/x] \Downarrow C''_{2^n} \end{array}}{\begin{array}{c}\bigcup\{e_1 \mid x \subseteq e_2\} \Downarrow C''_1 \cup \cdots \cup C''_{2^n} \\ \text{where } C'_1, \ldots, C'_{2^n} \text{ are the subsets of } \{C_1, \ldots, C_n\}\end{array}}$$

The meaning of the construct $\bigcup\{e_1 \mid x \subseteq e_2\}$ is the set $f(C'_1) \cup \cdots \cup f(C'_{2^n})$, where $f(x) = e_1$ and C'_1, ..., C'_{2^n} are all the subsets of e_2. Operationally, as in Biskup et al. [3], this construct is executed by enumerating each subset C'_i of e_2 and inserting $f(C_i)'$ into the result set one by one. If most of the $f(C_i)'$ are empty or identical, the evaluation of this construct should take only polynomial space even though the time complexity is exponential.

We denote the extensions of $\mathcal{NRC}$ and $\mathcal{NRC}(Q, +, \cdot, -, \div, \sum)$ with this contruct by $\mathcal{NRC}(eqn)$ and $\mathcal{NRC}(Q, +, \cdot, -, \div, \sum, eqn)$ respectively.

It is easy to see $\bigcup\{e_1 \mid x \subseteq e_2\} = \bigcup\{e_1 \mid x \in \mathit{powerset}\ e_2\}$ and $\mathit{powerset}\ e = \bigcup\{\{x\} \mid x \subseteq e\}$. Thus, $\mathcal{NRC}(\mathit{powerset})$ and $\mathcal{NRC}(eqn)$ have the same expressive power and, similarly, $\mathcal{NRC}(Q, +, \cdot, -, \div, \sum, \mathit{powerset})$ and $\mathcal{NRC}(Q, +, \cdot, -, \div, \sum, eqn)$ have the same expressive power.

If an upperbound n on the cardinality of e_2 is known in advance, we can replace $\bigcup\{e_1 \mid x \subseteq e_2\}$ by an expression $\bigcup\{e_1 \mid x \in \mathit{powerset}_n\ e_2\}$. Here, $\mathit{powerset}_n\ e_2$ is an expression that enumerates all subsets of e_2 upto size k, which is obviously definable in $\mathcal{NRC}$.

It follows easily from the work of Biskup et al. [3] that the transitive closure query can be implemented in $\mathcal{NRC}(eqn)$ using polynomial space. Therefore, the Dichotomy Theorem in terms of space complexity does not hold in $\mathcal{NRC}(eqn)$ and $\mathcal{NRC}(Q, +, \cdot, -, \div, \sum, eqn)$.

PROPOSITION 8. *1. There is a flat relational query on a severely dichotomous class of structures of degree at most k that cannot be implemented in $\mathcal{NRC}(Q, +, \cdot, -, \div, \sum)$, but can be implemented in $\mathcal{NRC}(eqn)$ using polynomial space.*

2. In particular, transitive closure is such a query.

Nevertheless, it is possible to prove a general Dichotomy Theorem in terms of time complexity for $\mathcal{NRC}(eqn)$ and $\mathcal{NRC}(Q, +, \cdot, -, \div, \sum, eqn)$. We sketch a proof for the latter.

THEOREM 3. *Let $e[\vec{R}] : \{b \times \cdots \times b\}$ be a flat relational query in $\mathcal{NRC}(Q, +, \cdot, -, \div, \sum, eqn)$ and the input $\vec{R}$ comes from a class $\mathcal{C}$ where (i) $\mathcal{C}$ is severely dichotomous, and (ii) the Gaifman graphs of its structures have degree at most k. Then either $e[\vec{R}]$ is expressible in $\mathcal{NRC}(Q, +, \cdot, -, \div, \sum)$; or there is a sequence of structures $\mathcal{A}_i = \langle A_i, \vec{O}_i\rangle \in \mathcal{C}$ of increasing size such that $\mathit{timeof}(e[\vec{O}_i/\vec{R}_i] \Downarrow)$ is $\Omega(2^{|\mathcal{A}_i|})$.*

PROOF. (Sketch) It can be shown that $\mathcal{NRC}(Q, +, \cdot, -, \div, \sum, eqn)$ has the conservative extension property. Moreover, the associated rewrite rules do not increase time complexity; see Proposition 5. So $e[\vec{R}]$ is assumed to be in normal form. Now, we look for the first expression of the form $\bigcup\{e_1 \mid x \subseteq e_2\}$ in $e[\vec{R}]$ that is to be executed. Then, by an argument similar to that in Theorem 4, we know e_2 is a flat relational query in $\mathcal{NRC}(Q, +, \cdot, -, \div, \sum)$. Since $\mathcal{NRC}(Q, +, \cdot, -, \div, \sum)$ has the locality property, again by an argument similar to that in Theorem 4, we can either determine an upper bound n on the size of e_2 independent of the universe of the input structure or show that its size is as large as the universe of the input structure. In the first situation, the expression can be replaced by $\bigcup\{e_1 \mid x \in \mathit{powerset}_n\ e_2\}$, which is expressible in $\mathcal{NRC}(Q, +, \cdot, -, \div, \sum)$; so we make the replacement and repeat the whole process. In the second situation, we know that this occurrence of $\bigcup\{e_2 \mid x \subseteq e_2\}$ takes exponential time to evaluate. ☐

Since parity, transitive closure, etc. are inexpressible in $\mathcal{NRC}(Q, +, \cdot, -, \div, \sum)$, and their input can be easily restricted to severely dichotomous classes of structures having degree at most k, all their implementations in $\mathcal{NRC}(Q, +, \cdot, -, \div, \sum, eqn)$ require exponential time.

COROLLARY 3. *1. All implementations of the parity query in $\mathcal{NRC}(Q, +, \cdot, -, \div, \sum, eqn)$ need exponential time.*

2. All implementations of the transitive closure query in $\mathcal{NRC}(Q, +, \cdot, -, \div, \sum, eqn)$ need exponential time.

6. ACKNOWLEDGEMENTS

I have not done work on query language theory for more than a decade. I re-started on the subject when Val Tannen asked me to contribute a book chapter to a festschrift for Peter Buneman last year. I am grateful to both of them for their mentorship when I was a student at UPenn and for re-triggering my interest in query language theory. I dedicate this paper to Peter Buneman.

I am also thankful to an anonymous referee who pointed out the relevant works of Van den Bussche and Biskup et al. This led me to expand this paper to include new results on the parity query and the equation algebra. These inclusions help provide a more complete appreciation of the Dichotomy Theorem.

This work was supported in part by a Singapore Ministry of Education grant MOE-T1-251RES1206.

7. REFERENCES

[1] S. Abiteboul and C. Beeri. The power of languages for the manipulation of complex values. *VLDB Journal*, 4(4):727–794, 1995.

[2] S. Abiteboul and V. Vianu. Generic computation and its complexity. In *Proc. 23rd ACM Symp. Theory of Computing*, pages 209–219, 1991.

[3] J. Biskup, J. Paredaens, T. Schwentick, and J. Van den Bussche. Solving equations in the relational algebra. *SIAM Journal on Computing*, 33(5):1052–1055, 2004.

[4] P. Buneman, L. Libkin, D. Suciu, V. Tannen, and L. Wong. Comprehension syntax. *SIGMOD Record*, 23(1):87–96, 1994.

[5] P. Buneman, S. Naqvi, V. Tannen, and L. Wong. Principles of programming with complex objects and collection types. *Theoretical Computer Science*, 149(1):3–48, 1995.

[6] J. Van den Bussche. Simulation of the nested relational algebra by the flat relational algebra, with an application to the complexity of evaluating powerset algebra expressions. *Theoretical Computer Science*. 254(1–2):363–377, 2001.

[7] L. Colson. About primitive recursive algorithms. *Theoretical Computer Science*, 83:57–69, 1991.

[8] G. Dong, L. Libkin, and L. Wong. Local properties of query languages. *Theoretical Computer Science*, 239:277–308, 2000.

[9] H. Gaifman. On local and non-local properties. In *Proc. Herbrand Symp., Logic Colloq. '81*, pages 105–135, 1982.

[10] L. Hella, L. Libkin, J. Nurmonen, and L. Wong. Logics with aggregate operators. *Journal of the ACM*, 48(4):880–907, 2001.

[11] L. Libkin. On forms of locality over finite models. In *Proc. 12th IEEE Symp. Logic in Computer Science*, pages 204–215, 1997.

[12] L. Libkin and L. Wong. Conservativity of nested relational calculi with internal generic functions. *Information Processing Letters*, 49(6):273–280, 1994.

[13] L. Libkin and L. Wong. Query languages for bags and aggregate functions. *Journal of Computer and System Sciences*, 55(2):241–272, 1997.

[14] D. Suciu and J. Paredaens. The complexity of the evaluation of complex algebra expressions. *Journal of Computer and Systems Sciences*, 55(2):322–343, 1997.

[15] D. Suciu and L. Wong. On two forms of structural recursion. In *Proc. of 5th Intl. Conf. on Database Theory*, pages 111–124, 1995.

[16] L. Wong. Normal forms and conservative extension properties for query languages over collection types. *Journal of Computer and System Sciences*, 52(3):495–505, 1996.

Enumeration of First-Order Queries on Classes of Structures With Bounded Expansion

Wojciech Kazana[*]
INRIA and ENS Cachan
kazana@lsv.ens-cachan.fr

Luc Segoufin
INRIA and ENS Cachan
http://pages.saclay.inria.fr/luc.segoufin/

ABSTRACT

We consider the evaluation of first-order queries over classes of databases with *bounded expansion*. The notion of bounded expansion is fairly broad and generalizes bounded degree, bounded treewidth and exclusion of at least one minor. It was known that over a class of databases with bounded expansion, first-order sentences could be evaluated in time linear in the size of the database. We first give a different proof of this result. Moreover, we show that answers to first-order queries can be enumerated with constant delay after a linear time preprocessing. We also show that counting the number of answers to a query can be done in time linear in the size of the database.

Categories and Subject Descriptors

F.4.1 [**Mathematical Logic and Formal Languages**]: Mathematical Logic; F.1.3 [**Computation by Abstract Devices**]: Complexity Measures and Classes

General Terms

Logic, algorithmic

Keywords

First-Order, bounded expansion, enumeration

1. INTRODUCTION

Query evaluation is certainly the most important problem in databases. Given a query q and a database $\mathbf{D}$ it is to compute the set $q(\mathbf{D})$ of all tuples in the output of q on $\mathbf{D}$. However, the set $q(\mathbf{D})$ may be larger than the database itself as it can have a size of the form n^l where n is the size of the database and l the arity of the query. It can therefore require too many of the available resources to compute it entirely.

[*]This work has been partially funded by the European Research Council under the European Community's Seventh Framework Programme (FP7/2007-2013) / ERC grant Webdam, agreement 226513. http://webdam.inria.fr/

PODS'13, June 22–27, 2013, New York, New York, USA.

There are many solutions to overcome this problem. For instance one could imagine that a small subset of $q(\mathbf{D})$ can be quickly computed and that this subset will be enough for the user needs. Typically one could imagine computing the top-ℓ most relevant answers relative to some ranking function or to provide a sampling of $q(\mathbf{D})$ relative to some distribution. One could also imagine computing only the number of solutions $|q(\mathbf{D})|$ or providing an efficient test for whether a given tuple belongs to $q(\mathbf{D})$ or not.

In this paper we consider a scenario consisting in enumerating $q(\mathbf{D})$ with constant delay. Intuitively, this means that there is a two-phase algorithm working as follows: a preprocessing phase that works in time linear in the size of the database, followed by an enumeration phase outputting one by one all the elements of $q(\mathbf{D})$ with a constant delay between any two consecutive outputs. In particular, the first answer is output after a time linear in the size of the database and once the enumeration starts a new answer is being output regularly at a speed independent from the size of the database. Altogether, the set $q(\mathbf{D})$ is entirely computed in time $f(q)(n+|q(\mathbf{D})|)$ for some function f depending only on q and not on $\mathbf{D}$.

One could also view a constant delay enumeration algorithm as follows. The preprocessing phase computes in linear time an index structure representing the set $q(\mathbf{D})$ in a compact way (of size linear in n). The enumeration algorithm is then a streaming decompression algorithm.

One could also require that the enumeration phase outputs the answers in some given order. Here we will consider the lexicographical order based on a linear order on the domain of the database.

There are many problems related to enumeration. The main one is the model checking problem. This is the case when the query is boolean, i.e. outputs only 0 or 1. In this case a constant delay enumeration algorithm is a Fixed Parameter Linear (FPL) algorithm for the model checking problem of q, i.e. it works in time $f(q)n$. This is a rather strong constraint as even the model checking problem for conjunctive queries is not FPL (modulo some hypothesis in parametrized complexity) [19]. Hence, in order to obtain constant delay enumeration algorithms, we need to make restrictions on the queries and/or on the databases. Here we consider first-order (FO) queries over classes of structures having "bounded expansion".

The notion of class of graphs with bounded expansion was introduced by Nešetřil and Ossona de Mendez in [16]. Its precise definition can be found in Section 2.2. At this point it suffices to know that it contains the class of graphs of bounded degree, the class of graphs of bounded treewidth, the class of planar graphs, and any class of graphs excluding at least one minor. This notion is generalized to classes of structures via their Gaifman graphs or adjacency graphs.

For the class of structures with bounded degree and FO queries the model checking is in FPL [20] and there also are constant delay enumeration algorithms [9, 13]. In the case of structures of bounded treewidth and FO queries (actually even MSO queries with first-order free variables) the model checking is also in FPL [8] and there are constant delay enumeration algorithms [4, 14]. For classes of structures with bounded expansion the model checking problem for FO queries was recently shown to be in FPL [10, 12].

Our results can be summarized as follows. For FO queries and any class of structures with bounded expansion:

- we provide a new proof that the model checking problem can be solved in FPL,
- we show that the set of solutions to a query can be enumerated with constant delay,
- we show that computing the number of solutions can be done in FPL,
- we show that, after a preprocessing in time linear in the size of the database, one can test on input $\bar{a}$ whether $\bar{a} \in q(\mathbf{D})$ in constant time.

Concerning model checking, our method uses a different technique than the previous ones. There are several characterizations of classes having bounded expansion [16]. Among them we find the "low tree depth coloring" and the "transitive fraternal augmentations". The previous methods were based on the low tree depth coloring characterization while ours is based on transitive fraternal augmentations. We argue that the use of transitive fraternal augmentations gives a simpler proof. The reason is that it gives a useful normal form on quantifier-free formulas that will be the core of our algorithms for constant delay enumeration and for counting the number of solutions. As for the previous proofs, we exhibit a quantifier elimination method, also based on our normal form. Our quantifier elimination method results in a quantifier-free formula but over a recoloring of a functional representation of a "fraternal and transitive augmentation" of the initial structure.

Our other algorithms (constant delay enumeration, counting the number of solution or testing whether a tuple is a solution or not) start by eliminating the quantifiers as for the model checking algorithm. Note that for all these problems, the quantifier-free case is already non trivial and require the design and the computation of new index structures. For instance consider the simple query $R(x, y)$. Given a pair (a, b) we would like to test whether (a, b) is a tuple of the database in constant time. In general, index structures can do this with $\log n$ time. We will see that we can do constant time, assuming bounded expansion.

In the presence of a linear order on the domain of the database, our constant delay algorithm can output the answers in the corresponding lexicographical order.

Related work.

We make use of a functional representation of the initial structures. Without this functional representations we would not be able to eliminate first-order quantifiers. Indeed, with this functional representation we can talk of a node at distance 2 from x using the quantifier-free term $f(f(x))$, avoiding the existential quantification of the middle point. This idea was already taken in [9] for eliminating first-order quantifiers over structures of bounded degree. Our approach differs from theirs in the fact that in the bounded degree case the functions can be assumed to be permutations (in particular they are invertible) while this is no longer true in our setting, complicating significantly the combinatorics.

Once we have a quantifier-free formula, constant delay enumeration could also be obtained using the characterization of bounded expansion based on low tree depth colorings. Indeed, using this characterization one can easily show that enumerating a quantifier-free formula over structures of bounded expansion amounts in enumerating an MSO query over structures of bounded tree-width and for those known algorithms exist [4, 14]. However, the known enumeration algorithms of MSO over structures of bounded treewidth are rather complicated while our direct approach is fairly simple. Actually, our proof shows that constant delay enumeration of FO queries over structures of bounded treewidth can be done using simpler algorithms than for MSO queries. Moreover, it gives a constant delay algorithm outputting the solutions in lexicographical order. No such algorithms were known for FO queries over structures of bounded treewidth. In the bounded degree case, both enumeration algorithms of [9, 13] output their solutions in lexicographical order.

Similarly, counting the number of solutions of a quantifier-free formula over structures of bounded expansion reduces to counting the number of solutions of a MSO formula over structures of bounded treewidth. This latter problem is known to be in FPL [3]. We give here a direct and simple proof of this fact for FO queries over structures of bounded expansion.

2. PRELIMINARIES

In this paper a database is a finite relational structure. A *relational signature* is a tuple $\sigma = (R_1, \ldots, R_l)$, each R_i being a relation symbol of arity r_i. A *relational structure* over σ is a tuple $\mathbf{D} = \left(D, R_1^{\mathbf{D}}, \ldots, R_l^{\mathbf{D}}\right)$, where D is *the domain* of $\mathbf{D}$ and $R_i^{\mathbf{D}}$ is a subset of D^{r_i}. We fix a reasonable encoding of structures by words over some finite alphabet, as in [1] for instance. The *size* of $\mathbf{D}$ is denoted by $\|\mathbf{D}\|$ and is the length of the encoding of $\mathbf{D}$.

By *query* we mean a formula written in the first-order logic, FO, built from atomic formulas of the form $x = y$ or $R_i(x_1, \ldots, x_{r_i})$ for some relation R_i, and closed under the usual Boolean connectives $(\neg, \vee, \wedge)$ and existential and universal quantifications $(\exists, \forall)$. We write $\phi(\bar{x})$ to denote a query whose free variables are $\bar{x}$, and the number of free variables is called the *arity of the query*. A *sentence* is a query of arity 0. Given a structure $\mathbf{D}$ and a query ϕ, an *answer* to q in $\mathbf{D}$ is a tuple $\bar{a}$ of elements of $\mathbf{D}$ such that $\mathbf{D} \models \phi(\bar{a})$. We write $\phi(\mathbf{D})$ for the set of answers to q in $\mathbf{D}$, i.e. $\phi(\mathbf{D}) = \{\bar{a} \mid \mathbf{D} \models \phi(\bar{a})\}$. By $|\phi(\mathbf{D})|$ we denote the cardinality of the set $\phi(\mathbf{D})$. As usual, $|\phi|$ denotes the size of ϕ.

Let $\mathcal{C}$ be a class of structures. The model checking problem of FO over $\mathcal{C}$ is the computational problem of given a **sentence** $q \in$ FO and a database

We now introduce our running examples.

EXAMPLE A-1. *The first query has arity 2 and returns pairs of nodes at distance at most two in a graph. We use the classical notion of distance that ignores the possible orientation of the edges. The query is of the form $\exists z E(x, z) \wedge E(z, y)$, where E is the symmetric closure of the input relation.*

Testing the existence of a solution to this query can be easily done in time linear in the size of the database. For instance one can go trough all nodes of the database and check whether it has degree two. The degree of each node can be computed in linear time by going through all edges of the database and incrementing the degree counters associated with its endpoints.

EXAMPLE B-1. *The second query has arity 3 and returns triples (x, y, z) such that y is connected to x and z via an edge but x is not connected to z. The query is of the form $E(x, y) \wedge E(y, z) \wedge \neg E(x, z)$, where E is the symmetric closure of the input relation.*

It is not clear at all how to test the existence of a solution to this query in time linear in the size of the database. The problem is

similar to the one of finding a triangle in a graph, for which the best known algorithm has complexity even slightly worse than matrix multiplication [2]. If the degree of the input structure is bounded by a constant d, we can test the existence of a solution in linear time by the following algorithm. We first go through all edges (x, y) of the database and add y to a list associated with x and x to a list associated with y. It remains now to go through all nodes y of the database, consider all pairs (x, z) of nodes in the associated list (the number of such pairs is bounded by d^2) and then test whether there is an edge between x and z (by testing whether x is in the list associated with z).

We aim at generalizing this kind of reasoning to structures with bounded expansion.

Given a query q, we care about "enumerating" $q(\mathbf{D})$ efficiently. Let $\mathcal{C}$ be a class of structures. For a query $q(\bar{x})$, *the enumeration problem of q over $\mathcal{C}$* is, given a database $\mathbf{D} \in \mathcal{C}$, to output the elements of $q(\mathbf{D})$ one by one with no repetition. The maximal time between any two consecutive outputs of elements of $q(\mathbf{D})$ is called *the delay*. The definition below requires a constant time between any two consecutive outputs. We formalize these notions in the forthcoming sections.

2.1 Model of computation and enumeration

We use Random Access Machines (RAM) with addition and uniform cost measure as a model of computation. For further details on this model and its use in logic see [9]. In the sequel we assume without loss of generality that the input relational structure comes with a linear order on its domain (if not, we use the one induced by the encoding of the database as a word). Whenever we iterate through all nodes of the domain, the iteration is with respect to the initial linear order.

We say that the enumeration problem of q over a class $\mathcal{C}$ of structures is in the class CONSTANT-DELAY$_{lin}$, or equivalently that we can enumerate q over $\mathcal{C}$ with constant delay[1], if it can be solved by a RAM algorithm which, on input $\mathbf{D} \in \mathcal{C}$, can be decomposed into two phases:

- a precomputation phase that is performed in time $O(\|\mathbf{D}\|)$,
- an enumeration phase that outputs $q(\mathbf{D})$ with no repetition and a constant delay between two consecutive outputs. The enumeration phase has full access to the output of the precomputation phase but can use only a constant total amount of extra memory.

Notice that if we can enumerate q with constant delay, then all answers can be output in time $O(\|\mathbf{D}\| + |q(\mathbf{D})|)$ and the first output is computed in time linear in $\|\mathbf{D}\|$. In the particular case of boolean queries, the associated model checking problem must be solvable in time linear in $\|\mathbf{D}\|$.

We may in addition require that the enumeration phase outputs the answers to q using the lexicographical order. We then say that we can enumerate q over $\mathcal{C}$ with constant delay in lexicographical order.

EXAMPLE A-2. *Over the class of all graphs, we cannot enumerate pairs of nodes at distance 2 with constant delay unless the Boolean Matrix Multiplication problem can be solved in quadratic time [6]. However, over the class of graphs of degree d, there is a simple constant delay enumeration algorithm. During the preprocessing phase, we associate with each node the list of all its neighbors at distance 2. This can be done in time linear in the database as in Example B-1. We then color in blue all nodes having a non empty list and make sure each blue node points to the next blue node (according to the linear order on the domain). This also can be done in time linear in the database and concludes the preprocessing phase. The enumeration phase now goes through all blue nodes x using the pointer structure and, for each of them, outputs all pairs (x, y) where y is in the list associated with x.*

[1]For readability we use the term "enumerate with constant delay", but technically speaking it should read "enumerate with constant delay after linear preprocessing". The reader should keep in mind that the linear preprocessing, although not explicitly mentioned, always precedes the enumeration process.

EXAMPLE B-2. *Over the class of all graphs, the query of this example cannot be enumerated in constant delay because, as mentioned in Example B-1, testing whether there is one solution is already non linear. Over the class of graphs of bounded degree, there is a simple constant delay enumeration algorithm, similar to the one from Example A-2.*

Note that in general constant delay enumeration algorithms are not closed under any boolean operations. For instance it is not because we can enumerate q and q' with constant delay, that we can enumerate $q \vee q'$ with constant delay as enumerating one query after the other would break the "no repetition" requirement. However, if we can enumerate with constant delay in the lexicographical order, then a simple argument that resembles the problem of merging two sorted lists shows closure under union:

LEMMA 1. *If both queries $q(\bar{x})$ and $q'(\bar{x})$ can be enumerated in lexicographical order with constant delay then the same is true for $q(\bar{x}) \vee q'(\bar{x})$.*

It will follow from our results that the enumeration problem of FO over the class of structures with "bounded expansion" is in CONSTANT-DELAY$_{lin}$. The notion of bounded expansion was defined in [16] for graphs and then it was generalized to structures via their Gaifman or Adjacency graphs. We start with defining it for graphs.

2.2 Graphs with bounded expansion and augmentation

In this paper a graph is a directed graph with colors on vertices. We can then view a graph as a relational structure $\mathbf{G} = (V, E, P_1, \ldots, P_l)$, where V is the set of nodes, $E \subseteq V^2$ is the set of oriented edges and, for each $1 \leq i \leq l$, P_i is a predicate of arity 1. A pair $(u, v) \in E$ represents an edge from node u to node v. The *in-degree* of a node v is the number of nodes u such that $(u, v) \in E$. By $\Delta^-(\mathbf{G})$ we mean the maximal in-degree of a node of $\mathbf{G}$.

In [16] several equivalent definitions of bounded expansion were shown. We will not use here the initial definition but the one exploiting the notion of "augmentations". The interested reader should refer to [16] for more information.

Let $\mathbf{G}$ be a graph. A *1-transitive fraternal augmentation of* $\mathbf{G}$ is any graph $\mathbf{H}$ with the same vertex set as $\mathbf{G}$ and the same colors of vertices, including all edges of $\mathbf{G}$ (with their orientation) and such that for any three vertices x, y, z of $\mathbf{G}$ we have the following:

(transitivity) if (x, y) and (y, z) are edges in $\mathbf{G}$, then (x, z) is an edge in $\mathbf{H}$,

(fraternity) if (x, z) and (y, z) are edges in $\mathbf{G}$, then at least one of the edges: (x, y), (y, x) is in $\mathbf{H}$,

(strictness) moreover, if $\mathbf{H}$ contains an edge that was not present in $\mathbf{G}$, then it must have been added by one of the previous two rules.

Note that the notion of 1-transitive fraternal augmentation is not a deterministic operation. Although transitivity induces precise edges, fraternity implies nondeterminism and thus there can possibly be many different 1-transitive fraternal augmentations. We care here about choosing the orientations of the edges resulting from the fraternity rule in order to minimize the maximal in-degree.

Following [17] we fix a deterministic algorithm computing a "good" choice of orientations of the edges induced by the fraternity property. The precise definition of the algorithm is not important for us, it only matters here that the algorithm runs in time linear in the size of the input graph (see Lemma 2 below). With this algorithm fixed, we can now speak of **the** 1-transitive fraternal augmentation of $\mathbf{G}$.

Let $\mathbf{G}$ be a graph. The *transitive fraternal augmentation* of $\mathbf{G}$ is the sequence $\mathbf{G} = \mathbf{G}_0 \subseteq \mathbf{G}_1 \subseteq \mathbf{G}_2 \subseteq \ldots$ such that for each $i \geq 1$ the graph $\mathbf{G}_{i+1}$ is the 1-transitive fraternal augmentation of $\mathbf{G}_i$. We will say that $\mathbf{G}_i$ is the i-th augmentation of $\mathbf{G}$.

DEFINITION 1. *[16] Let $\mathcal{C}$ be a class of graphs. $\mathcal{C}$ has bounded expansion if there exists a function $\Gamma_\mathcal{C} : \mathbb{N} \to \mathbb{R}$ such that for each graph $\mathbf{G} \in \mathcal{C}$ the transitive fraternal augmentation $\mathbf{G} = \mathbf{G}_0 \subseteq \mathbf{G}_1 \subseteq \mathbf{G}_2 \subseteq \ldots$ of $\mathbf{G}$ is such that for each $i \geq 0$ we have $\Delta^-(\mathbf{G}_i) \leq \Gamma_\mathcal{C}(i)$.*

Consider for instance a graph of degree d. Notice that the 1-transitive fraternal augmentation introduces an edge between nodes that were at distance at most 2 in the initial graph. Hence, when starting with a graph of degree d, we end up with a graph of degree at most d^2. This observation shows that the class of graphs of degree d has bounded expansion as witnessed by the function $\Gamma(i) = d^{2^i}$. Exhibiting the function Γ for the other examples of classes with bounded expansion mentioned in the introduction: bounded treewidth, planar graphs, graphs excluding at least one minor, requires more work [16].

The following lemma shows that within a class $\mathcal{C}$ of bounded expansion the i-th augmentation of $\mathbf{G} \in \mathcal{C}$ can be computed in linear time.

LEMMA 2. *[17] Let $\mathcal{C}$ be a class of bounded expansion. For each $\mathbf{G} \in \mathcal{C}$ and each i, $\mathbf{G}_i$ is computable from $\mathbf{G}_{i-1}$ in time $O(\|\mathbf{G}_{i-1}\|)$.*

In particular Lemma 2 implies that for each i, given $\mathbf{G} \in \mathcal{C}$, $\mathbf{G}_i$ is computable from $\mathbf{G}$ in time $O(\|\mathbf{G}\|)$.

2.3 Graphs of bounded in-degree as functional structures

For the rest of this section we fix a class $\mathcal{C}$ of graphs with bounded expansion and let $\Gamma_\mathcal{C}$ be the function given by Definition 1. For any graph $\mathbf{G} \in \mathcal{C}$ its transitive fraternal augmentation $\mathbf{G} = \mathbf{G}_0 \subseteq \mathbf{G}_1 \subseteq \mathbf{G}_2 \subseteq \ldots$ is such that for all i, $\mathbf{G}_i$ has in-degree bounded by $\Gamma_\mathcal{C}(i)$. From the definition of bounded expansion it follows that the maximal in-degree of the graphs we will manipulate is always bounded by a number independent of the graph. We will use this property by constantly referring to the $1^{st}, 2^{nd} \ldots$ predecessor of a node. It will therefore be convenient for us to represent the graphs $\mathbf{G}_i$ as functional structures where this predecessors are images of the current node via some suitable functions. As mentioned in the introduction, this functional representation is also useful for eliminating some quantifiers.

A *functional signature* is a tuple $\sigma = (f_1, \ldots, f_l, P_1, \ldots, P_m)$, each f_i being a functional symbol of arity 1 and each P_i being an unary predicate. A *functional structure* over σ is then defined as for relational structures. FO is defined as usual over the functional signature. In particular, it can use atoms of the form $f(f(f(x)))$, which is crucial for the quantifier elimination step of Section 3 as the usual relational representation would require existential quantification for denoting the same element. A graph $\mathbf{G}$ of in-degree l and colored with m colors can be represented as a functional structure $\vec{\mathbf{G}}$, where the unary predicates encode the various colors and $v = f_i(u)$ if v is the ith element (according to some arbitrary order that will not be relevant in the sequel) such that (v, u) is an edge of $\mathbf{G}$. We call such node v the ith *predecessor* of u (where "i^{th} predecessor" should really be viewed as an abbreviation for "the node v such that $f_i(u) = v$" and not as a reference to the chosen order). If we do not care about i and we only want to say that v is the image of u under some function, we call it a *predecessor* of u. Given $\mathbf{G} \in \mathcal{C}$ we define $\vec{\mathbf{G}}$ to be the functional representation of $\mathbf{G}$ as described above. Note that $\vec{\mathbf{G}}$ is computable in time linear in $\|\mathbf{G}\|$ and that for each first order query $\phi(\bar{x})$ one can easily compute a first order query $\psi(\bar{x})$ such that $\phi(\mathbf{G}) = \psi(\vec{\mathbf{G}})$.

EXAMPLE A-3. *With the functional point of view, the query computing nodes at distance at most two is of the form:*

$$\bigvee_{f,g\in\sigma} \begin{array}{r} f(g(x)) = y \vee g(f(y)) = x \vee f(x) = g(y) \vee \\ \exists z \; f(z) = x \wedge g(z) = y \end{array}$$

where there is one disjunct per possible orientation of the edges on the path from x to y. We have removed the inner node z whenever this was possible.

EXAMPLE B-3. *Similarly, the query of Example B-1 is equivalent to:*

$$\bigvee_{f,g\in\sigma} \begin{array}{l} \bigwedge_{h\in\sigma} (h(x) \neq z \wedge h(z) \neq x) \\ \wedge \; [(f(x) = y \wedge g(y) = z) \\ \quad \vee (x = f(y) \wedge g(y) = z) \\ \quad \vee (f(x) = y \wedge y = g(z)) \\ \quad \vee (x = f(y) \wedge y = g(z))]. \end{array}$$

Recall that the augmentation steps only introduce new edges and do not affect the vertex set. It will be convenient for us to be able to recover $\mathbf{G}_i$ from $\mathbf{G}_{i+1}$. For this we use extra function symbols denoting the edges resulting from an augmentation step. The definition of bounded expansion guarantees that the number of required new symbols is bounded by $\Gamma_\mathcal{C}(i+1)$ and does not depend on the graph.

From this it follows that we have functional signatures $\sigma_\mathcal{C}(0) \subseteq \sigma_\mathcal{C}(1) \subseteq \sigma_\mathcal{C}(2) \subseteq \ldots$, where $\sigma_\mathcal{C}(0)$ is the initial signature and $\sigma_\mathcal{C}(i+1)$ is $\sigma_\mathcal{C}(i)$ plus the $\Gamma_\mathcal{C}(i+1)$ extra symbols needed for the extra augmentation step, such that for any graph $\mathbf{G} \in \mathcal{C}$ and for all i:

1. $\vec{\mathbf{G}}_i$ is a functional structure over $\sigma_\mathcal{C}(i)$,
2. $\vec{\mathbf{G}}_i \subseteq \vec{\mathbf{G}}_{i+1}$ and $\vec{\mathbf{G}}_{i+1}$ is computable in linear time from $\vec{\mathbf{G}}_i$,
3. for every FO query $\phi(\bar{x})$ over $\sigma_\mathcal{C}(i)$ and every $j \geq i$ we have that $\phi(\vec{\mathbf{G}}_i) = \phi(\vec{\mathbf{G}}_j)$.

We denote by $\alpha_\mathcal{C}(i)$ the number of function symbols of $\sigma_\mathcal{C}(i)$. It follows from the discussion above that $\alpha_\mathcal{C}(i) = \Sigma_{j\leq i}\Gamma_\mathcal{C}(j)$. It would be tempting to reduce this number by reusing function symbols, but that would then be problematic to enforce 3.

We say that a functional signature σ' is a *recoloring* of σ if it extends σ with some extra unary predicates (colors), while the functional part remains unchanged. Similarly, a functional structure $\vec{\mathbf{G}}'$

over σ' is a *recoloring* of $\vec{\mathbf{G}}$ over σ if σ' is a recoloring of σ and $\vec{\mathbf{G}}'$ is a σ'-expansion of $\vec{\mathbf{G}}$ (i.e. it does not differ from $\vec{\mathbf{G}}$ on the predicates in σ). We write ϕ *is over a recoloring of* σ if ϕ is over σ' and σ' is a recoloring of σ.

For each $p \geq 0$ we define $\mathcal{C}_p$ to be the class of all recolorings $\vec{\mathbf{G}}'_p$ of $\vec{\mathbf{G}}_p$ for some $\mathbf{G} \in \mathcal{C}$. In other words $\mathcal{C}_p$ is the class of functional representations of all recolorings of all p-th augmentations of graphs from $\mathcal{C}$. Note that all graphs from $\mathcal{C}_p$ are recolorings of a structure in $\sigma_\mathcal{C}(p)$, hence they use at most $\alpha_\mathcal{C}(p)$ function symbols.

From now on we assume that all graphs from $\mathcal{C}$ and all queries are in their functional representation. It follows from the discussion above that this is without loss of generality.

2.4 From structures to graphs

The *adjacency graph* of a relational structure $\mathbf{D}$, denoted by Adjacency($\mathbf{D}$), is a functional graph defined as follows. The set of vertices of Adjacency($\mathbf{D}$) is $D \cup T$ where T is the set of tuples occurring in some relation of $\mathbf{D}$. For each relation R_i in the schema of $\mathbf{D}$, there is a unary symbol P_{R_i} coloring the elements of T belonging to R_i. For each tuple $t = (a_1, \cdots, a_{r_i})$ such that $\mathbf{D} \models R_i(t)$ for some relation R_i of arity r_i, we have an edge $f_j(t) = a_j$ for all $j \leq r_i$.

OBSERVATION 1. *It is immediate to see that for every relational structure* $\mathbf{D}$ *we can compute Adjacency*($\mathbf{D}$) *in time* $O(\|\mathbf{D}\|)$.

Let $\mathcal{C}$ be a class of relational structures. We say that $\mathcal{C}$ has *bounded expansion* if the class $\mathcal{C}$' of adjacency graphs of structures from $\mathcal{C}$ has bounded expansion.

REMARK 1. *In the literature, for instance [10, 12], a class $\mathcal{C}$ of relational structures is said to have bounded expansion if the class of their Gaifman graphs has bounded expansion. Our definition can be shown to be equivalent to the usual one. As it gives directly an oriented graph, it is more convenient for us.*

Let $\Gamma_{\mathcal{C}'}$ be the function given by Definition 1 for $\mathcal{C}$'. The following lemma is immediate.

LEMMA 3. *Let $\mathcal{C}$ be a class of relational structures with bounded expansion and let $\mathcal{C}$' be the underlying class of adjacency graphs. Let $\phi(\bar{x}) \in$ FO. In time linear in the size of ϕ we can find a query $\psi(\bar{x})$ over $\sigma_{\mathcal{C}'}(0)$ such that for all $\mathbf{D} \in \mathcal{C}$ we have $\phi(\mathbf{D}) = \psi(Adjacency(\mathbf{D}))$.*

As a consequence of Lemma 3 it follows that model checking, enumeration and counting of first-order queries over relational structures reduce to the graph case. Therefore in the rest of the paper we will only concentrate on the graph case (viewed as a functional structure), but the reader should keep in mind that all the results stated over graphs extend to relational structures via this lemma.

2.5 Normal form for quantifier-free first-order queries

We conclude this section by proving a normal form on quantifier-free FO formulas. This normal form will be the ground for all our algorithms later on. It basically says that, modulo performing some extra augmentation steps, a quantifier-free formula has a very simple form.

Fix class $\mathcal{C}$ of graphs with bounded expansion. Recall that we are now implicitly assuming that graphs are represented as functional structures.

A formula is *simple* if it does not contain atoms of the form $f(g(x))$, i.e. it does not contain any compositions of functions. Observe that, modulo augmentations, any formula can be transformed into a simple one.

LEMMA 4. *Let $\psi(\bar{x})$ be a formula over a recoloring of $\sigma_\mathcal{C}(p)$. Then, for $q = p + |\psi|$, there is a simple formula $\psi'(\bar{x})$ over a recoloring of $\sigma_\mathcal{C}(q)$ such that:*

for all $\vec{\mathbf{G}} \in \mathcal{C}_p$ there is a $\vec{\mathbf{G}}' \in \mathcal{C}_q$ computable in time linear in $\|\vec{\mathbf{G}}\|$ such that $\psi(\vec{\mathbf{G}}) = \psi'(\vec{\mathbf{G}}')$.

PROOF. This is a simple consequence of transitivity. Any composition of two functions in $\vec{\mathbf{G}}$ represents a transitive pair of edges and becomes a single edge in the 1-augmentation $\vec{\mathbf{H}}$ of $\vec{\mathbf{G}}$. Then $f(g(x))$ over $\vec{\mathbf{G}}$ is equivalent to $h(x) \wedge P_{f,g,h}(x)$ over $\vec{\mathbf{H}}$, where the newly introduced color $P_{f,g,h}$ holds for those nodes v, for which the $f(g(v)) = h(v)$. As the nesting of compositions of functions is at most $|\psi|$, the result follows. The linear time computability is immediate from Lemma 2. □

We make one more observation before proving the normal form:

LEMMA 5. *Let $\vec{\mathbf{G}} \in \mathcal{C}_p$. Let u be a node of $\vec{\mathbf{G}}$. Let S be all the predecessors of u in $\vec{\mathbf{G}}$ and set $q = p + \Gamma_\mathcal{C}(p)$. Let $\vec{\mathbf{G}}' \in \mathcal{C}_q$ be the $(q-p)$-th augmentation of $\vec{\mathbf{G}}$. There exists a linear order $<$ induced on S by $\vec{\mathbf{G}}'$, such that for all $v, v' \in S$, $v < v'$ implies $v' = f(v)$ is an edge of $\vec{\mathbf{G}}'$ for some function f from $\sigma_\mathcal{C}(q)$.*

PROOF. This is because all nodes of S are fraternal and the size of S is at most $\Gamma_\mathcal{C}(p)$. Hence, after one step of augmentation, all nodes of S are pairwise connected and, after at most $\Gamma_\mathcal{C}(p) - 1$ further augmentation steps, if there is a directed path from one node u of S to another node v of S, then there is also a directed edge from u to v. By induction on $|S|$ we show that there exists a node $u \in S$ such that for all $v \in S$ there is an edge from v to u. If $|S| = 1$ there is nothing to prove. Otherwise fix $v \in S$ and let $S' = S \setminus \{v\}$. By induction we get a u in S' satisfying the properties. If there is an edge from v to u, u also works for S and we are done. Otherwise there must be an edge from u to v. But then there is a path of length 2 from any node of S' to v. By transitivity this means that there is an edge from any node of S' to v and v is the node we are looking for.

We then set u as the minimal element of our order on S and we repeat this argument with $S \setminus \{u\}$. □

Lemma 5 justifies the following definition.

DEFINITION 2. *A p-type $\tau_p(x)$ is a quantifier-free conjunctive formula expressing all the relations between predecessors of a node x in some graph $\vec{\mathbf{G}} \in \mathcal{C}_p$ in the $(q-p)$-th augmentation $\vec{\mathbf{G}}'$ of $\vec{\mathbf{G}}$, where q is given by Lemma 5. More precisely, for every functions $f_i, f_j \in \sigma_\mathcal{C}(p)$, $\tau_p(x)$ contains at least one of the conjuncts $h_{i,j}(f_i(x)) = f_j(x)$ or $h_{j,i}(f_j(x)) = f_i(x)$, where $h_{i,j}$ and $h_{j,i}$ are function symbols from $\sigma_\mathcal{C}(q)$.*

In particular, a p-type τ induces a linear order on the predecessors of x as described by Lemma 5 ($f_i(x) < f_j(x)$ whenever $h_{i,j}(f_i(x)) = f_j(x)$ is a conjunct of τ) and moreover specifies all the relations between these predecessors in $\vec{\mathbf{G}}'$. Note that for a given p there are only finitely many possible p-types and that each of them can be specified with a conjunctive formula over $\sigma_\mathcal{C}(q)$.

We now state the normal form result.

PROPOSITION 1. *Let $\phi(\bar{x}y)$ be a simple quantifier-free query over a recoloring of $\sigma_\mathcal{C}(p)$. There exists q that depends only on p and ϕ and a quantifier-free query ψ over a recoloring of $\sigma_\mathcal{C}(q)$ that is a disjunction of formulas:*

$$\psi_1(\bar{x}) \wedge \tau(y) \wedge \Delta^{=}(\bar{x}y) \wedge \Delta^{\neq}(\bar{x}y), \qquad (1)$$

where $\tau(y)$ contains a p-type of y; $\Delta^=(\bar{x}y)$ is either empty or contains one clause of the form $y = f(x_i)$ or one clause of the form $f(y) = g(x_i)$ for some suitable i, f and g; and $\Delta^{\neq}(\bar{x}y)$ contains arbitrarily many clauses of the form $y \neq f(x_i)$ or $f(y) \neq g(x_j)$. Moreover, ψ is such that:

for all $\vec{\mathbf{G}} \in \mathcal{C}_p$ there is a $\vec{\mathbf{G}}' \in \mathcal{C}_q$ computable in time linear in $\|\vec{\mathbf{G}}\|$ with $\phi(\vec{\mathbf{G}}) = \psi(\vec{\mathbf{G}}')$.

PROOF. Set q as given by Lemma 5. We first put ϕ into a disjunctive normal form (DNF) and in front of each such disjunct we add a big disjunction over all possible p-types of y (recall that a type can be specified as a conjunctive formula). Let ϕ' be the resulting formula.

We deal with each disjunct of ϕ' separately.

Note that each disjunct is a query over $\sigma_\mathcal{C}(q)$ of the form:

$$\psi_1(\bar{x}) \wedge \tau(y) \wedge \Delta^=(\bar{x}y) \wedge \Delta^{\neq}(\bar{x}y),$$

where all sub-formulas except for $\Delta^=$ are as desired. Moreover, $\psi_1(\bar{x})$, $\Delta^=(\bar{x}y)$ and $\Delta^{\neq}(\bar{x}y)$ are in fact queries over $\sigma_\mathcal{C}(p)$. At this point $\Delta^=$ contains arbitrarily many clauses of the form $y = f(x_i)$ or $f(y) = g(x_i)$. If it contains at least one clause of the form $y = f(x_i)$, we can replace each other occurrence of y by $f(x_i)$ and we are done.

Assume now that $\Delta^=$ contains several conjuncts of the form $f_i(y) = g(x_k)$. Assume wlog that τ is such that $f_1(y) < f_2(y) < \cdots$, where $f_1(y), f_2(y), \cdots$ are all the predecessors of y from $\sigma_\mathcal{C}(p)$. Let i_0 be the smallest index i such that a clause of the form $f_i(y) = g(x_k)$ belongs to $\Delta^=$. We have $f_{i_0}(y) = g(x_k)$ in $\Delta^=$ and observe that τ specifies for $i < j$ a function $h_{i,j}$ in $\sigma_\mathcal{C}(q)$ such that $h_{i,j}(f_i(y)) = f_j(y)$. Then, as y is of type τ, a clause of the form $f_j(y) = h(x_{k'})$ with $i_0 < j$ is equivalent to $h_{i_0,j}(g(x_k)) = h(x_{k'})$.

Let ψ be the result of performing this operation on each disjunct of ϕ'.

Now, given $\vec{\mathbf{G}} \in \mathcal{C}_p$, let $\vec{\mathbf{G}}' \in \mathcal{C}_q$ be the $(q-p)$-th augementation of $\vec{\mathbf{G}}$. It is computable in time linear in $\vec{\mathbf{G}}$ by Lemma 2. By Lemma 5 we have $\phi(\vec{\mathbf{G}}) = \phi'(\vec{\mathbf{G}}')$. By construction we have $\psi(\vec{\mathbf{G}}') = \phi'(\vec{\mathbf{G}}')$ and the result follows. □

EXAMPLE A-4. *Let us see what Lemma 4 and the normalization algorithm do for $p = 0$ and some of the disjuncts of the query of Example A-3:*

In the case of $f(g(x)) = y$ note that by transitivity, in the augmented graph, this clause is equivalent to one of the form $y = h(x) \wedge P_{f,g,h}(x)$ (this case is handled by Lemma 4).

Consider now $\exists z \;\; f(z) = x \wedge g(z) = y$. It will be convenient to view this query when z plays the role of y in Proposition 1. Notice that in this case it is not in normal form as $\Delta^=$ contains two elements. However, the two edges $f(z) = x$ and $g(z) = y$ are fraternal. Hence, after one augmentation step, a new edge is added between x and y and we either have $y = h(x)$ or $x = h(y)$ for some h in the new signature.

Let $\tau_{h,f,g}(z)$ be a 0-type stating that $h(f(z)) = g(z)$ and $\tau_{h,g,f}(z)$ be a 0-type stating that $h(g(z)) = f(z)$. It is now easy to see that the query $\exists z \;\; f(z) = x \wedge g(z) = y$ is equivalent, in the augmented graph, to

$$\exists z \bigvee_h \; y = h(x) \wedge \tau_{h,f,g}(z) \wedge f(z) = x \;\; \vee$$
$$x = h(y) \wedge \tau_{h,g,f}(z) \wedge f(z) = x$$

3. MODEL CHECKING

In this section we show that the model checking problem of FO over a class of structures with bounded expansion can be done in time linear in the size of the structure. This gives a new proof of the result of [10]. Recall that by Lemma 3 it is enough to consider oriented graphs viewed as functional structures.

THEOREM 1. *[10] Let $\mathcal{C}$ be a class of graphs with bounded expansion and let ψ be a sentence of* FO. *Then, for all $\vec{\mathbf{G}} \in \mathcal{C}$, testing whether $\vec{\mathbf{G}} \models \psi$ can be done in time $O(\|\vec{\mathbf{G}}\|)$.*

The proof of Theorem 1 is done using a quantifier elimination procedure: given a query $\psi(\bar{x}y)$ with at least one free variable we can compute a quantifier-free query $\phi(\bar{x})$ that is "equivalent" to $\exists y \psi(\bar{x}y)$. Again, the equivalence should be understood modulo some augmentation steps for a number of augmentation steps depending only on $\mathcal{C}$ and $|\psi|$. When starting with a sentence ψ we end-up with ϕ being a boolean combination of formulas with one variable. Those can be easily tested in linear time in the size of the augmented structure, which in turns can be computed in time linear from the initial structure by Lemma 2. The result follows. We now state precisely the quantifier elimination step:

PROPOSITION 2. *Let $\mathcal{C}$ be a class of graphs with bounded expansion witnessed by the function $\Gamma_\mathcal{C}$. Let $\psi(\bar{x}y)$ be a quantifier-free formula over a recoloring of $\sigma_\mathcal{C}(p)$. Then one can compute a q and a quantifier-free formula $\phi(\bar{x})$ over a recoloring of $\sigma_\mathcal{C}(q)$ such that:*

for all $\vec{\mathbf{G}} \in \mathcal{C}_p$ there is a $\vec{\mathbf{G}}' \in \mathcal{C}_q$ such that:

$$\phi(\vec{\mathbf{G}}') = (\exists y \psi)(\vec{\mathbf{G}})$$

Moreover, $\vec{\mathbf{G}}'$ is computable in time $O(\|\vec{\mathbf{G}}\|)$.

Before going into details, we start with an outline of the proof. The reasoning is going to be as follows:

• Using Lemma 4 and Proposition 1 we argue that it suffices to show the quantifier elimination procedure only for $\psi(\bar{x}y)$ being of the special form given by (1), that is:

$$\psi_1(\bar{x}) \wedge \tau(y) \wedge \Delta^=(\bar{x}y) \wedge \Delta^{\neq}(\bar{x}y).$$

• In order to eliminate the existentially quantified variable y we somehow need to encode its existence in terms of properties of $\bar{x}$.

• In the easy case when ψ contains conjunct of the form $f(x_i) = y$, we can replace each occurrence of y with $f(x_i)$ and we are done.

• The most interesting case is when ψ contains conjunct of the form $f(y) = g(x_i)$. Then the algorithm proceeds as follows:

∘ it iterates through all nodes v of the graph (think of v as of a candidate for substituting the existentially quantified variable y) and in a sense "registers" its existence to node $f(v)$,

∘ given tuple $\bar{u}$ to be substituted for for $\bar{x}$ it is enough to only check nodes from the "list of registrants" of $g(u_i)$ as the possible candidates for y,

∘ unfortunately the above procedure could produce "lists of registrants" of arbitrary lengths, so we have to be more careful,

∘ therefore we limit the "registration" process and allow new nodes to register only if they are "different enough" (in terms of the sets of their predecessors) from the nodes that already registered,

∘ this way we define so called WITNESS sets that are of constant (i.e. independent from the size of $\vec{\mathbf{G}}$) sizes and such that if there exists a valid node for y, there also exists such a node inside WITNESS$(g(u_i))$,

∘ the rest of the argument is a way of encoding WITNESS sets by only recoloring the structure and not altering its functional part.

We now formalize the above approach:

PROOF OF PROPOSITION 2. Wlog (modulo augmentations, see Lemma 4 for details) we assume that ψ is simple.

We apply Proposition 1 to ψ and p and obtain a q and an equivalent formula in DNF, where each disjunct has the special form given by (1). As disjunction and existential quantification commute, it is enough to treat each part of the disjunction separately.

We thus assume that $\psi(\bar{x}y)$ is a quantifier-free conjunctive formula over a recoloring of $\sigma_C(q)$ of the form (1):

$$\psi_1(\bar{x}) \wedge \tau(y) \wedge \Delta^{=}(\bar{x}y) \wedge \Delta^{\neq}(\bar{x}y).$$

We assume wlog that τ contains a p-type enforcing $f_1(y) < f_2(y) < \cdots$, where $f_1(y), f_2(y), \cdots$ are all the images of y by a function from $\sigma_C(p)$. Moreover, for each $i < j$, τ contains an atom of the form $h_{i,j}(f_i(y)) = f_j(y)$ for some function $h_{i,j} \in \sigma_C(q)$.

If $\Delta^{=}$ is $y = g(x_k)$ for some function g and some k, then we replace y with $g(x_k)$ everywhere in $\psi(\bar{x}y)$ resulting in a formula $\phi(\bar{x})$ having obviously the desired properties.

Assume now that $\Delta^{=}$ is $f(y) = g(x_i)$. Wlog assume that f is f_{i_0} in the order specified by the p-type τ and that $i = 1$. Hence we have $f_{i_0}(y) = g(x_1)$ in $\Delta^{=}$.

We will introduce extra colors in order to simulate all interactions between y and $\bar{x}$.

Let $\vec{\mathbf{G}}''$ be the $(q-p)$-th augmentation of $\vec{\mathbf{G}}$. We construct in time linear in $\|\vec{\mathbf{G}}''\|$ a set WITNESS(v) for each v of $\vec{\mathbf{G}}'$ such that for all tuples $\bar{v}$ of $\vec{\mathbf{G}}''$, if $\vec{\mathbf{G}}'' \models \psi(\bar{v}u)$ for some node u, then there is a node $u' \in$ WITNESS$(g(v_1))$ such that $\vec{\mathbf{G}}' \models \psi(\bar{v}u')$. Moreover, for all v, $|$WITNESS$(v)| \leq N$ where N is a number depending only on p. We then encode these witness sets using suitable extra colors.

Computation of the Witness function.

We start by initializing WITNESS$(v) = \emptyset$ for all v.

We then successively investigate all nodes u of $\vec{\mathbf{G}}''$ and do the following. If $\vec{\mathbf{G}}'' \models \neg\tau(u)$ then we move on to the next u. If $\vec{\mathbf{G}}'' \models \tau(u)$ then let $u_1, \cdots, u_l$ be the current value of WITNESS$(f_{i_0}(u))$.

Let β_p be $\alpha_C(p)(\alpha_C(p)+1)|\bar{x}|+1$.

Let i be minimal such that there exists j with $f_i(u_j) = f_i(u)$ and set $i = \alpha_C(p)+1$ if such an i does not exists. Let $S_i = \{f_{i-1}(u_j) \mid f_i(u_j) = f_i(u)\}$, where $f_0(u_j)$ is u_j in the case where $i = 1$. If $|S_i| \leq \beta_p$ then we add u to WITNESS$(f_{i_0}(u))$.

The algorithm is linear time and the size of WITNESS$(v) \leq (\beta_p+1)^{\beta_p+1}$. It remains to show that it has the desired properties.

Analysis of the Witness function.

Assume $\vec{\mathbf{G}}'' \models \psi(\bar{v}u)$. If $u \in$ WITNESS$(g(v_1))$ we are done. Otherwise note that $f_{i_0}(u) = g(v_1)$ and that $\vec{\mathbf{G}}'' \models \tau(u)$. Let i and S_i be as described in the algorithm when investigating u. As u was not added to WITNESS$(f_{i_0}(u))$, we must have $|S_i| > \beta_p$. Let $S_i = \{u_{i_1}, \cdots, u_{\beta_p}, \cdots\}$ be the corresponding elements of WITNESS$(g(v_1))$. Among these data values, for each j at most $\alpha_C(p)$ of them may be a predecessor of v_j. Similarly, for each $i' \leq i$ and each j, at most $\alpha_C(p)$ of them may be such that their image by $f_{i'}$ is a predecessor of v_j. For each $i' > i$ their image is exactly $f_{i'}(u)$ and it does not falsify any inequality conjuncts of ψ. Hence, at most $\alpha_C(p)(\alpha_C(p)+1)|\bar{v}|$ of them may falsify at least one of the inequality conjuncts of ψ. We can therefore find in WITNESS$(g(v_1))$ at least one element satisfying the formula, as $|S_i| > \alpha_C(p)(\alpha_C(p)+1)|\bar{v}|$.

Recoloring of $\vec{\mathbf{G}}''$.

Based on WITNESS we recolor $\vec{\mathbf{G}}''$ as follows. Let $\gamma_p = (\beta_p+1)^{\beta_p+1}$. For each $v \in \vec{\mathbf{G}}''$ we order WITNESS(v). We can now speak of the ith witness of v.

For each $i \leq \gamma_p$ we introduce a new unary predicate P_i and for each $u \in \vec{\mathbf{G}}''$ we set $P_i(u)$ if WITNESS(u) contains at least i elements.

For each $i \leq \gamma_p$ and each $h, h' \in \alpha_C(q)$ we introduce a new unary predicate $P_{i,h,h'}$ and for each $v \in \vec{\mathbf{G}}''$ we set $P_{i,h,h'}(v)$ if the ith witness of $h(v)$ is an element u with $h'(u) = v$.

For each $i \leq \gamma_p$, $h \in \alpha_C(q)$ we introduce a new unary predicate $Q_{i,h}$ and for each $v \in \vec{\mathbf{G}}''$ we set $Q_{i,h}(v)$ if the ith witness of $h(v)$ is v.

We denote by $\vec{\mathbf{G}}'$ the resulting graph and notice that it can be computed in linear time from $\vec{\mathbf{G}}$.

Finally, note that if y is the ith witness of $g(x_1)$, the equality $f_j(y) = h(x_k)$ with $j < i_0$ is equivalent over $\vec{\mathbf{G}}'$ to $h_{j,i_0}(h(x_k)) = g(x_1) \wedge P_{i,h_{j,i_0},f_j}(h(x_k))$ and the equality $y = h(x_k)$ is equivalent over $\vec{\mathbf{G}}'$ to $f_{i_0}(h(x_k)) = g(x_1) \wedge Q_{i,f_{i_0}}(h(x_k))$. From the definition of p-type, the equality $f_j(y) = h(x_k)$ with $j > i_0$ is equivalent to $h_{i_0,j}(g(x_1)) = h(x_k)$.

Computation of ϕ.

In view of the analysis above, $\psi(\bar{x}y)$ is equivalent to a formula:

$$\bigvee_{i \leq \gamma_p} \psi_1(\bar{x}) \wedge \psi^i(\bar{x})$$

where $\psi^i(\bar{x})$ checks that the ith witness of $g(x_1)$ makes the initial formula true. In view of the above, this formula $\psi^i(\bar{x})$ is defined by

$$\begin{aligned} P_i(g(x_1)) \quad \wedge & \bigwedge_{\substack{f_j(y) \neq h(x_k) \in \Delta^{\neq} \\ j < i_0}} \neg(h_{j,i_0}(h(x_k)) = g(x_1) \wedge P_{i,h_{j,i_0},f_j}(h(x_k))) \\ \wedge & \bigwedge_{\substack{f_j(y) \neq h(x_k) \in \Delta^{\neq} \\ j \geq i_0}} h_{i_0,j}(g(x_1)) \neq h(x_k) \\ \wedge & \bigwedge_{y \neq h(x_k) \in \Delta^{\neq}} \neg(f_{i_0}(h(x_k)) = g(x_1) \wedge Q_{i,f_{i_0}}(h(x_k))) \end{aligned}$$

The special case when $\Delta^{=}$ is empty is a simpler version of the previous case, only this time it is enough to construct a set WITNESS which does not depend on v. The details are omitted in this conference version. □

EXAMPLE A-5. *Consider one of the quantified formulas as derived by Example A-4:*

$$\exists z \;\; y = h(x) \wedge \tau_{h,f,g}(z) \wedge f(z) = x$$

The resulting quantifier-free query has the form:

$$P(x) \wedge h(x) = y$$

where $P(x)$ is a newly introduced color saying "$\exists z \;\; \tau_{h,f,g}(z) \wedge f(z) = x$". The key point is that this new predicate can be computed in linear time by iterating through all nodes z, testing whether $\tau_{h,f,g}(z)$ is true and, if this is the case, coloring $f(z)$ with color P.

Applying the quantifier elimination process from inside out using Proposition 2 for each step and then applying Lemma 4 to the result yields:

THEOREM 2. *Let $\mathcal{C}$ be a class of graphs with bounded expansion. Let $\psi(\bar{x})$ be a query of* FO *over a recoloring of $\sigma_{\mathcal{C}}(0)$ with at least one free variable. Then one can compute a p and a simple quantifier-free formula $\phi(\bar{x})$ over a recoloring of $\sigma_{\mathcal{C}}(p)$ such that:*

for all $\vec{\mathbf{G}} \in \mathcal{C}$, we can construct in time $O(\|\vec{\mathbf{G}}\|)$ a graph $\vec{\mathbf{G}}' \in \mathcal{C}_p$ such that

$$\phi(\vec{\mathbf{G}}') = \psi(\vec{\mathbf{G}})$$

We will make use of the following useful consequence of Theorem 2:

COROLLARY 1. *Let $\mathcal{C}$ be a class of graphs with bounded expansion and let $\psi(\bar{x})$ be a formula of* FO *with at least one free variable. Then, for all $\vec{\mathbf{G}} \in \mathcal{C}$, after a preprocessing in time $O(\|\vec{\mathbf{G}}\|)$, we can test, given $\bar{u}$ as input, whether $\vec{\mathbf{G}} \models \psi(\bar{u})$ in constant time.*

PROOF. By Theorem 2 it is enough to consider quantifier-free simple queries. Hence it is enough to consider a query consisting of a single atom of either $P(x)$ or $P(f(x))$ or $x = f(y)$ or $f(x) = g(y)$.

During the preprocessing phase we associate with each node v of the input graph a list $L(v)$ containing all the predicates satisfied by v and all the images of v by a function symbol from the signature. This can be computed in linear time by enumerating all relations of the database and updating the appropriate lists with the corresponding predicate or the corresponding image.

Now, because we use the RAM model, given u we can in constant time recover the list $L(u)$. Using those lists it is immediate to check all atoms of the formula in constant time. □

Theorem 1 is a direct consequence of Theorem 2 and Corollary 1: Starting with a sentence, and applying Theorem 2 for eliminating quantifiers from inside out we end up with a Boolean combination of formulas with one variable. Each such formula can be tested in $O(\|\vec{\mathbf{G}}\|)$ by iterating through all nodes v of $\vec{\mathbf{G}}$ and in constant time (using Corollary 1) checking if v can be substituted for the sole existentially quantified variable.

On top of Theorem 1 the following corollary is immediate from Theorem 2 and Corollary 1:

COROLLARY 2. *Let $\mathcal{C}$ be a class of graphs with bounded expansion and let $\psi(x)$ be a formula of* FO *with one free variable. Then, for all $\vec{\mathbf{G}} \in \mathcal{C}$, computing the set $\psi(\vec{\mathbf{G}})$ can be done in time $O(\|\vec{\mathbf{G}}\|)$.*

4. ENUMERATION

In this section we consider first-order formulas with free variables and show that we can enumerate their answers over any class with bounded expansion with constant delay. Moreover, assuming a linear order on the domain of the input structure, we will see that the answers can be output in the lexicographical order. As before we only state the result for graphs, but it immediately extends to arbitrary structures by Lemma 3. Recall that we assumed (without loss of generality) the presence of a linear order of the domain.

THEOREM 3. *Let $\mathcal{C}$ be a class of graphs with bounded expansion and let $\phi(\bar{x})$ be a first-order query over $\sigma_{\mathcal{C}}(0)$. Then the enumeration problem of ϕ over $\mathcal{C}$ is in* CONSTANT-DELAY$_{lin}$.
Moreover the answers to ϕ can be output in lexicographical order.

Before going into details, we start with an outline of the proof. The reasoning is going to be as follows:

- The proof is by induction on the number of free variables.
- The case $k = 1$ is done by Corollary 2.
- For $k > 1$, using the normalization and quantification procedures of the previous sections, it is enough to consider quantifier-free queries $\psi(\bar{x}y)$ of the form:

$$\psi_1(\bar{x}) \wedge \tau(y) \wedge \Delta^{=}(\bar{x}y) \wedge \Delta^{\neq}(\bar{x}y).$$

We further set $\psi''(\bar{x})$ the formula $\exists y \psi(\bar{x}y)$.

- In the easy case when ψ contains conjunct of the form $f(x_i) = y$, we enumerate $\psi''(\bar{x})$ by induction and append $f(x_i)$ to each resulting tuple.
- The most interesting case is when ψ contains conjunct of the form $f(y) = g(x_i)$. Then the algorithm proceeds as follows:
  - ◦ It enumerates all the solutions of $\psi''(\bar{x})$ by induction and appends to it all the relevant y.
  - ◦ For this it computes, during the preprocessing phase, several successor functions among nodes, such that for each $\bar{x}$, at least one of them will enumerate the associated y.
  - ◦ The key point is that only finitely many successor functions need to be precomputed and that the suitable one can be found by looking only at $\bar{x}$.

We now formalize the above approach:

PROOF. Fix a class $\mathcal{C}$ of graphs with bounded expansion and a query $\phi(\bar{x})$ with k free variables. Let $\vec{\mathbf{G}}$ be the input graph and V be its set of vertices.

The proof is by induction on the number of free variables. The case $k = 1$ is done by Corollary 2.

Assume now that $k > 1$ and that $\bar{x}$ and y are the free variables of ϕ, where $|\bar{x}| = k - 1$.

We apply Theorem 2 to get a simple quantifier-free query $\varphi(\bar{x}y)$ and a structure $\vec{\mathbf{G}}' \in \mathcal{C}_p$, for some p that does not depend on $\vec{\mathbf{G}}$, such that $\varphi(\vec{\mathbf{G}}') = \phi(\vec{\mathbf{G}})$ and $\vec{\mathbf{G}}'$ can be computed in linear time from $\vec{\mathbf{G}}$.

We normalize the resulting simple quantifier-free query using Proposition 1, and obtain an equivalent quantifier-free formula ψ and a structure $\vec{\mathbf{G}}'' \in \mathcal{C}_q$, where q depends only on p and φ, $\vec{\mathbf{G}}''$ can be computed in linear time from $\vec{\mathbf{G}}'$, $\varphi(\vec{\mathbf{G}}') = \psi(\vec{\mathbf{G}}'')$ and ψ is a disjunction of formulas of the form (1):

$$\psi_1(\bar{x}) \wedge \tau(y) \wedge \Delta^{=}(\bar{x}y) \wedge \Delta^{\neq}(\bar{x}y),$$

where $\Delta^{=}(\bar{x}y)$ is either empty or contains one clause of the form $y = f(x_i)$ or one clause of the form $f(y) = g(x_i)$ for some suitable i, f and g; and $\Delta^{\neq}(\bar{x}y)$ contains arbitrarily many clauses of the form $y \neq f(x_i)$ or $f(y) \neq g(x_j)$.

By Lemma 1 it is enough to show that we can enumerate each disjunct separately. In the sequel we then assume that ψ has the form described in (1). We let $\psi'(y)$ be the formula $\exists \bar{x} \psi(\bar{x}y)$ and $\psi''(\bar{x})$ the formula $\exists y \psi(\bar{x}y)$.

If $\Delta^{=}$ contains an equality of the form $y = f(x_i)$ then we replace y by $f(x_i)$ in τ and $\Delta^{\neq}$, enumerate by induction the formula ψ'' and replace each of its output $\bar{a}$ with $(\bar{a}f(a_i))$ in order to obtain the desired constant delay enumeration algorithm. We therefore now assume that $\Delta^{=}$ does not contain such equality.

We now define two functions $L : V \to 2^V$ and $W : V^{k-1} \to V$ depending on whether $\Delta^{=}$ is empty or consists of a single clause of the form $f(y) = g(x_i)$. If $\Delta^{=}$ is empty we pick an arbitrary node w in $\vec{\mathbf{G}}''$ and set $L(w) = \psi'(\vec{\mathbf{G}}'')$, $L(v) = \emptyset$ for $v \neq w$, and $W(\bar{v}) = w$ for all tuples $\bar{v}$. If $\Delta^{=} = \{f(y) = g(x_i)\}$ we set $W(\bar{v}) = g(v_i)$ for all tuples $\bar{v}$ and define L using the following procedure. We initialize $L(v)$ to $\emptyset$ for each $v \in V$. Then, for each $v \in \psi'(\vec{\mathbf{G}}'')$, we add v to the set $L(f(v))$.

Notice that L can be computed in time linear in $\|\vec{\mathbf{G}}''\|$ (using Corollary 2), that each list $L(v)$ is sorted with respect to the linear order on the domain and that, given $\bar{v}$, $W(\bar{v})$ can be computed in constant time. Moreover, for each $\bar{v}u$, $\vec{\mathbf{G}}'' \models \psi(\bar{v}u)$ implies $u \in L(W(\bar{v}))$ and if $u \in L(W(\bar{v}))$ then $\Delta^=(\bar{v}u)$ is true.

By induction we can enumerate $\psi''(\bar{x})$ with constant delay.

On top of the linear time preprocessing necessary for enumerating ψ'' we do the following extra preprocessing. We first compute $L(v)$ for all $v \in V$. Then, for each $v \in V$, we perform the following procedure on $L(v)$. Each procedure will work in time linear in the size of $L(v)$, hence the total preprocessing will take time $O(|V|)$.

Fix v and set $L = L(v)$. We denote by $<$ the order on L. (Recall that this order is consistent with the initial order on the domain.)

For $S_1, \ldots, S_{\alpha_C(q)} \subseteq V$ we define $\text{NEXT}_{f_1,S_1,\ldots,f_{\alpha_C(q)},S_{\alpha_C(q)}}(u)$ to be the first element $w \geq u$ of L such that $f_1(w) \notin S_1, \ldots,$ and $f_{\alpha_C(q)}(w) \notin S_{\alpha_C(q)}$. If such w does not exist, the value of $\text{NEXT}_{f_1,S_1,\ldots,f_{\alpha_C(q)},S_{\alpha_C(q)}}(u)$ is NULL. When all S_i are empty, we write $\text{next}_\emptyset(u)$ and by the above definitions we always have $\text{next}_\emptyset(u) = u$. We denote such functions as *shortcut pointers of* u. We write $\text{NEXT}_{f_1,S'_1,\ldots,f_{\alpha_C(q)},S'_{\alpha_C(q)}}(u) \preceq \text{NEXT}_{f_1,S_1,\ldots,f_{\alpha_C(q)},S_{\alpha_C(q)}}(u)$ if for each $1 \leq i \leq \alpha_C(q)$ we have $S'_i \subseteq S_i$. Note that for a given u the $\preceq$ relation is a partial order on the set of shortcut pointers of u. A trivial observation is that if $\text{NEXT}_{f_1,S'_1,\ldots,f_{\alpha_C(q)},S'_{\alpha_C(q)}}(u) \preceq \text{NEXT}_{f_1,S_1,\ldots,f_{\alpha_C(q)},S_{\alpha_C(q)}}(u)$, then $\text{NEXT}_{f_1,S'_1,\ldots,f_{\alpha_C(q)},S'_{\alpha_C(q)}}(u) \leq \text{NEXT}_{f_1,S_1,\ldots,f_{\alpha_C(q)},S_{\alpha_C(q)}}(u)$. The *size* of a shortcut pointer $\text{NEXT}_{f_1,S_1,\ldots,f_{\alpha_C(q)},S_{\alpha_C(q)}}(u)$ is the sum of sizes of the sets S_i.

In order to avoid writing too long expressions containing shortcut pointers, we introduce the following abbreviations:

- $\text{NEXT}_{f_1,S_1,\ldots,f_{\alpha_C(q)},S_{\alpha_C(q)}}(u)$ is denoted with $\text{NEXT}_{\vec{S}}(u)$,
- $\text{NEXT}_{f_1,S_1,\ldots,f_i,S_i\cup\{u_i\},\ldots,f_{\alpha_C(q)},S_{\alpha_C(q)}}(u)$ is denoted with $\text{NEXT}_{\vec{S}[S_i+=\{u_i\}]}(u)$.

Set $\beta_q = (k-1) \cdot \alpha_C(q)^2$.

Computing all shortcut pointers of size β_q would take more than linear time. We therefore compute a subset of those, denoted SC_L, that will be sufficient for our needs. SC_L is defined in an inductive manner. For all u, $\text{next}_\emptyset(u) \in \text{SC}_L$. Moreover, if the shortcut pointer NULL $\neq \text{NEXT}_{\vec{S}}(u) \in \text{SC}_L$ and has a size smaller than β_q, then, for each i, $\text{NEXT}_{\vec{S}[S_i+=\{u_i\}]}(u) \in \text{SC}_L$, where $u_i = f_i(\text{NEXT}_{\vec{S}}(u))$. We then say that $\text{NEXT}_{\vec{S}}(u)$ is the *origin* of $\text{NEXT}_{\vec{S}[S_i+=\{u_i\}]}(u)$. Note that SC_L contains all the shortcut pointers of the form $\text{NEXT}_{f_i,\{f_i(u)\}}(u)$ for $u \in L$ and these are exactly the shortcut pointers of u of size 1. By $\text{SC}_L(u) \subseteq \text{SC}_L$ we denote the shortcut pointers of u that are in SC_L.

The set SC_L has the following properties:

CLAIM 1. *Let* $\text{NEXT}_{\vec{S}}(u)$ *be a shortcut pointer of size not greater than* β_q. *Then there exists* $\text{NEXT}_{\vec{S'}}(u) \in \text{SC}_L$ *such that* $\text{NEXT}_{\vec{S}}(u) = \text{NEXT}_{\vec{S'}}(u)$. *Moreover, such* $\text{NEXT}_{\vec{S'}}(u)$ *can be found in constant time.*

PROOF SKETCH. The desired shortcut pointer is $\text{NEXT}_{\vec{S'}}(u) \in \text{SC}_L$ that is maximal in terms of size shortcut pointer of u such that $\text{NEXT}_{\vec{S'}}(u) \preceq \text{NEXT}_{\vec{S}}(u)$. □

CLAIM 2. *There exists a constant* $\zeta(q,k)$ *such that for every node* u *we have* $|\text{SC}_L(u)| \leq \zeta(q,k)$.

PROOF SKETCH. This is a direct consequence of the recursive definition of $\text{SC}_L(u)$. □

The following claim guarantees that SC_L can be computed in linear time and has therefore a linear size.

CLAIM 3. SC_L *can be computed in time linear in* $|L|$.

PROOF SKETCH. SC_L can be constructed in an inductive manner starting from the last node on the list L and moving backward. Claim 1 plays the key role in constructing each shortcut pointer in constant time, while Claim 2 guarantees that the total size of SC_L is linear in $|L|$. □

The computation of SC_L concludes the preprocessing phase and it follows from Claim 3 that it can be done in linear time. We now turn to the enumeration phase.

We enumerate one by one the solutions to $\psi''(\bar{x})$ by simulating the enumeration algorithm obtained from the induction.

Having a solution $\bar{v}$ to ψ'' by construction we know that all nodes u such that $\vec{\mathbf{G}}'' \models \psi(\bar{v}u)$ are in $L = L(W(\bar{v}))$. Recall also that all elements $u \in L$ make $\tau(u) \wedge \Delta^=(\bar{v}u)$ true. For $1 \leq i \leq \alpha_C(q)$ we set $S_i = \{g(v_j) : g(x_j) \neq f_i(y)$ is a conjunct of $\Delta^{\neq}\}$. Starting with u the first node of the sorted list L, we apply the following procedure:

1. If $u =$ NULL, finish the nested enumeration procedure for $\bar{v}$. If not, let $\text{NEXT}_{\vec{S'}}(u)$ be the shortcut pointer from the application of Claim 1 to $\text{NEXT}_{\vec{S}}(u)$. Set $u' = \text{NEXT}_{\vec{S'}}(u)$. If $u' =$ NULL, finish the nested enumeration procedure for $\bar{v}$.
2. If $\vec{\mathbf{G}}'' \models \psi(\bar{v}u')$, output $(\bar{v}u')$.
3. Reinitialize u to the successor of u' in L and continue with Step 1.

We now show that the algorithm is correct, i.e. that it outputs all $\psi(\vec{\mathbf{G}}'')$ with no repetition.

The algorithm clearly outputs a subset of $\psi(\vec{\mathbf{G}}'')$ as it tests whether $\vec{\mathbf{G}}'' \models \psi(\bar{v}u')$ before outputting tuple $(\bar{v}u')$.

By the definition, list L contains no duplicates and as the algorithm moves only forward on that list, there are no repetitions during the output process.

By the definition of sets S_i and $\text{NEXT}_{\vec{S}}(u)$, for each $u \leq w < u'$ there is a suitable i and j such that $g(v_j) = f_i(w)$ and $g(x_j) \neq f_i(y)$ is a conjunct of $\Delta^{\neq}$. This way the algorithm does not skip any solutions at Step 1 and so it outputs exactly $\psi(\vec{\mathbf{G}}'')$.

It remain to show that there is a constant time between any two outputs.

By construction, for each $\bar{v}$, $L = L(W(\bar{v}))$ contains an element u such that $(\bar{v}u)$ is a solution. We therefore need to show that there is a constant time between any two outputs involving an element in L. Step 1 takes constant time due to Claim 1. From there the algorithm either immediately outputs a solution at Step 2 or jumps to Step 3. This means that $\vec{\mathbf{G}}'' \not\models \psi(\bar{v}u')$, but from the definitions of list L, sets S_i and shortcut pointers $\text{NEXT}_{\vec{S}}(u)$ it is only the $\Delta^{\neq}$ that is falsified and it is because of an inequality of the form $y \neq g(x_j)$ for some suitable g and j (where g may possibly be identity). This implies that $u' = g(v_j)$. As all the elements on L are distinct, the algorithm can skip over Step 2 up to $(k-1) \cdot (\alpha_C(q)+1)$ times for each tuple $\bar{v}$ (there are up to that many different images of nodes from $\bar{v}$ under $\alpha_C(q)$ different functions and the initial values of $\bar{v}$). This way the delay is bounded by up to $k \cdot (\alpha_C(q)+1)$ consecutive applications of Claim 1 and is in fact constant.

As the list L was sorted with respect to the linear order on the domain, it is clear that the enumeration procedure outputs the set of solutions in lexicographical order.

This concludes the proof of the theorem. $\Box$

5. COUNTING

In this section we investigate the problem of counting the number of solutions to a query, i.e. computing $|q(\mathbf{D})|$. As usual we only state and prove our results over graphs but they generalize to arbitrary relational structures via Lemma 3. The proof goes by induction on the number of free variables and follows the same outline as for enumeration. It only replaces the step of enumeration pre-computing several successor functions by a combinatorial argument counting their number.

THEOREM 4. *Let $\mathcal{C}$ be class of graphs with bounded expansion and let $\phi(\bar{x})$ be a first-order formula. Then, for all $\vec{\mathbf{G}} \in \mathcal{C}$, we can compute $|\phi(\vec{\mathbf{G}})|$ in time $O(\|\vec{\mathbf{G}}\|)$.*

PROOF. The key idea is to prove a weighted version of the desired result. Assume $\phi(\bar{x})$ has exactly k free variables and for $1 \leq i \leq k$ we have functions $\#_i : V \to \mathbb{N}$. We will compute in time linear in $\|\vec{\mathbf{G}}\|$ the following number:

$$|\phi(\vec{\mathbf{G}})|_{\#} := \sum_{\bar{u} \in \phi(\vec{\mathbf{G}})} \prod_{1 \leq i \leq k} \#_i(u_i).$$

By setting all $\#_i$ to be constant functions with value 1 we get the regular counting problem. Hence Theorem 4 is an immediate consequence of the next lemma.

LEMMA 6. *Let $\mathcal{C}$ be class of graphs with bounded expansion and let $\phi(\bar{x})$ be a first-order formula with exactly k free variables. For $1 \leq i \leq k$ let $\#_i : V \to \mathbb{N}$ be functions such that for each v the value of $\#_i(v)$ can be computed in constant time. Then, for all $\vec{\mathbf{G}} \in \mathcal{C}$, we can compute $|\phi(\vec{\mathbf{G}})|_{\#}$ in time $O(\|\vec{\mathbf{G}}\|)$.*

PROOF. The proof is by induction on the number of free variables.

The case $k = 1$ is trivial: in time linear in $\|\vec{\mathbf{G}}\|$ we compute $\phi(\vec{\mathbf{G}})$ using Corollary 2. By hypothesis, for each $v \in \phi(\vec{\mathbf{G}})$, we can compute the value of $\#_1(v)$ in constant time. Therefore the value

$$|\phi(\vec{\mathbf{G}})|_{\#} = \sum_{v \in \phi(\vec{\mathbf{G}})} \#_1(v)$$

can be computed in linear time as desired.

Assume now that $k > 1$ and that $\bar{x}$ and y are the free variables of ϕ, where $|\bar{x}| = k - 1$.

We apply Theorem 2 to get a simple quantifier-free query $\varphi(\bar{x}y)$ and a structure $\vec{\mathbf{G}}' \in \mathcal{C}_p$, for some p that does not depend on $\vec{\mathbf{G}}$, such that $\varphi(\vec{\mathbf{G}}') = \phi(\vec{\mathbf{G}})$ and $\vec{\mathbf{G}}'$ can be computed in linear time from $\vec{\mathbf{G}}$. Note that $|\phi(\vec{\mathbf{G}})|_{\#} = |\varphi(\vec{\mathbf{G}}')|_{\#}$, so it is enough to compute the latter value.

We normalize the resulting simple quantifier-free query using Proposition 1, and obtain an equivalent quantifier-free formula ψ and a structure $\vec{\mathbf{G}}'' \in \mathcal{C}_q$, where q depends only on p and φ, $\vec{\mathbf{G}}''$ can be computed in linear time from $\vec{\mathbf{G}}'$, $\varphi(\vec{\mathbf{G}}') = \psi(\vec{\mathbf{G}}'')$ and ψ is a disjunction of formulas of the form (1):

$$\psi_1(\bar{x}) \wedge \tau(y) \wedge \Delta^{=}(\bar{x}y) \wedge \Delta^{\neq}(\bar{x}y),$$

where $\Delta^{=}(\bar{x}y)$ is either empty or contains one clause of the form $y = f(x_i)$ or one clause of the form $f(y) = g(x_i)$ for some suitable i, f and g; and $\Delta^{\neq}(\bar{x}y)$ contains arbitrarily many clauses of the form $y \neq f(x_i)$ or $f(y) \neq g(x_j)$. Note that $|\varphi(\vec{\mathbf{G}}')|_{\#} = |\psi(\vec{\mathbf{G}}'')|_{\#}$, so it is enough to compute the latter value.

Observe that it is enough to solve the weighted counting problem for each disjunct separately, as we can then combine the results using a simple inclusion-exclusion reasoning. In the sequel we then assume that ψ has the form described in (1).

The proof now goes by induction on the number of inequalities in $\Delta^{\neq}$. While the inductive step turns out to be fairly easy, the difficult part is the base step of the induction.

We start with proving the inductive step. Let $g(y) \neq f(x_i)$ be an arbitrary inequality from $\Delta^{\neq}$ (where g might possibly be the identity). Let ψ^- be ψ with this inequality removed and $\psi^+ = \psi^- \wedge g(y) = f(x_i)$. Of course ψ and ψ^+ have disjoint sets of solutions and we have:

$$|\psi(\vec{\mathbf{G}}'')|_{\#} = |\psi^-(\vec{\mathbf{G}}'')|_{\#} - |\psi^+(\vec{\mathbf{G}}'')|_{\#}.$$

Note that ψ^- and ψ^+ have one less conjunct in $\Delta^{\neq}$. The problem is that ψ^+ is not of the form (1) as it may now contain two elements in $\Delta^{=}$. However it can be seen that the removal of the extra equality in $\Delta^{=}$ as described in the proof of Proposition 1 does not introduce any new elements in $\Delta^{\neq}$. (the details are omitted in this conference version.) We can therefore remove the extra element in Δ^+ and assume that ψ^+ has the desired form. We can now use the inductive hypothesis on the size of $\Delta^{\neq}$ to both ψ^- and ψ^+ in order to compute both $|\psi^-(\vec{\mathbf{G}}'')|_{\#}$ and $|\psi^+(\vec{\mathbf{G}}'')|_{\#}$ and derive $|\psi(\vec{\mathbf{G}}'')|_{\#}$.

It remains to show the base of the inner induction. In the following we assume that $\Delta^{\neq}$ is empty. The rest of the proof is a case analysis on the content of $\Delta^{=}$. Due to space limitations we analyze in full details only the situation when $\Delta^{=}$ consists of an atom of the form $y = f(x_1)$. Although this case is not the most difficult, we find it the most explanatory and still generic enough.

Assume then that $\Delta^{=}$ consists of an atom of the form $y = f(x_1)$. Note that the solutions to ψ are of the form $(\bar{a}f(a_1))$. We have:

$$\begin{aligned}
|\psi(\vec{\mathbf{G}}'')|_{\#} &= \sum_{(\bar{u}v) \in \psi(\vec{\mathbf{G}}'')} \left(\#_k(v) \prod_{1 \leq i \leq k-1} \#_i(u_i) \right) \\
&= \sum_{(\bar{u}f(u_1)) \in \psi(\vec{\mathbf{G}}'')} \left(\#_k(f(u_1)) \prod_{1 \leq i \leq k-1} \#_i(u_i) \right) \\
&= \sum_{(\bar{u}f(u_1)) \in \psi(\vec{\mathbf{G}}'')} \left(\#_1(u_1)\#_k(f(u_1)) \prod_{2 \leq i \leq k-1} \#_i(u_i) \right)
\end{aligned}$$

In linear time we now iterate through all nodes u in $\vec{\mathbf{G}}''$ and set

$$\begin{aligned}
\#'_1(u) &:= \#_1(u) \cdot \#_k(f(u)) \\
\#'_i(u) &:= \#_i(u) \qquad \text{for } 2 \leq i \leq k-1.
\end{aligned}$$

Let $\vartheta(\bar{x})$ be ψ with all occurrences of y replaced with $f(x_1)$. We then have:

$$\begin{aligned}
|\psi(\vec{\mathbf{G}}'')|_{\#} &= \sum_{(\bar{u}f(u_1)) \in \psi(\vec{\mathbf{G}}'')} \left(\#'_1(u_1) \prod_{2 \leq i \leq k-1} \#'_i(u_i) \right) \\
&= \sum_{\bar{u} \in \vartheta(\vec{\mathbf{G}}'')} \prod_{1 \leq i \leq k-1} \#'_i(u_i) \\
&= |\vartheta(\vec{\mathbf{G}}'')|_{\#'}
\end{aligned}$$

By induction on the number of free variables, as $\#'_i(u)$ can be computed in constant time for each i and u, we can compute $|\vartheta(\vec{\mathbf{G}}'')|_{\#'}$ in time linear in $\|\vec{\mathbf{G}}''\|$ and we are done.

For the case when $\Delta^=$ consists of an atom $g(y) = f(x_1)$ we use the same approach, only this time we set:

$$\#'_1(u) := \#_1(u) \cdot \sum_{\substack{\{v \in (\exists \bar{x}\psi(\bar{x}y))(\vec{\mathbf{G}}'') \\ g(v)=u\}}} \#_k(v)$$

$$\#'_i(u) := \#_i(u) \qquad \text{for } 2 \leq i \leq k-1$$

and conclude with $|(\exists y\psi(\bar{x}y))(\vec{\mathbf{G}}'')|_{\#'} = |\psi(\vec{\mathbf{G}}'')|_{\#}$. The details for this case and the case when $\Delta^=$ is empty are omitted in this conference version. □

As we said earlier, Theorem 4 is an immediate consequence of Lemma 6. □

6. CONCLUSIONS

Queries written in first-order logic can be efficiently processed over the class of structures having bounded expansion. We have seen that over this class the problems investigated in this paper can be computed in time linear in the size of the input structure. The constant factor however is not very good. The approach taken here, as well as the ones of [10, 12], yields a constant factor that is a tower of exponentials whose height depends on the size of the query. This nonelementary constant factor is unavoidable already on the class of unranked trees, assuming FPT≠AW[*] [11]. In comparison, this factor can be triply exponential in the size of the query in the bounded degree case [20, 13].

It is possible that the results presented here can be generalized to a larger class of structures. In [18] the class of nowhere dense graphs was introduced and it generalizes the notion of bounded expansion. It seems that nowhere dense graphs do enjoy good algorithmic properties. However, we do not know yet whether the model checking problem of first-order logic can be done in linear time over nowhere dense structures. Actually, we do not even know whether the model checking problem is Fixed Parameter Tractable (FPT) over nowhere dense graphs.

The class of nowhere dense structures seems to be the limit for having good algorithmic properties for first-order logic. Indeed, it is known that the model checking problem of first-order logic over a class of structures that is not nowhere dense cannot be FPT [15] (modulo some complexity assumptions and closure of the class under substructures).

For structures of bounded expansion, an interesting open question is whether a sampling of the solutions can be performed in linear time. For instance: can we compute the j-th solution in constant time after a linear preprocessing? This can be done in the bounded degree case [7] and in the bounded treewidth case [5]. We leave the bounded expansion case for future research.

7. REFERENCES

[1] S. Abiteboul, R. Hull, and V. Vianu. *Foundations of Databases*. Addison Wesley, 1995.

[2] Noga Alon, Raphael Yuster, and Uri Zwick. Color-Coding. *J. ACM*, 42(4):844–856, 1995.

[3] Stefan Arnborg, Jens Lagergren, and Detlef Seese. Easy Problems for Tree-Decomposable Graphs. *J. of Algorithms*, 12(2):308–340, 1991.

[4] Guillaume Bagan. MSO Queries on Tree Decomposable Structures Are Computable with Linear Delay. In *Conf. on Computer Science Logic (CSL)*, pages 167–181, 2006.

[5] Guillaume Bagan. *Algorithmes et complexité des problèmes d'énumération pour l'évaluation de requêtes logiques*. PhD thesis, Université de Caen, 2009.

[6] Guillaume Bagan, Arnaud Durand, and Etienne Grandjean. On Acyclic Conjunctive Queries and Constant Delay Enumeration. In *Conf. on Computer Science Logic (CSL)*, pages 208–222, 2007.

[7] Guillaume Bagan, Arnaud Durand, Etienne Grandjean, and Frédéric Olive. Computing the jth solution of a first-order query. *RAIRO Theoretical Informatics and Applications*, 42(1):147–164, 2008.

[8] Bruno Courcelle. Graph Rewriting: An Algebraic and Logic Approach. In *Handbook of Theoretical Computer Science, Volume B: Formal Models and Sematics (B)*, pages 193–242. 1990.

[9] Arnaud Durand and Etienne Grandjean. First-order queries on structures of bounded degree are computable with constant delay. *ACM Trans. on Computational Logic (ToCL)*, 8(4), 2007.

[10] Zdeněk Dvořák, Daniel Král, and Robin Thomas. Deciding First-Order Properties for Sparse Graphs. In *Symp. on Foundations of Computer Science (FOCS)*, pages 133–142, 2010.

[11] Markus Frick and Martin Grohe. The complexity of first-order and monadic second-order logic revisited. *Ann. Pure Appl. Logic*, 130(1-3):3–31, 2004.

[12] Martin Grohe and Stephan Kreutzer. *Model Theoretic Methods in Finite Combinatorics*, chapter Methods for Algorithmic Meta Theorems. American Mathematical Society, 2011.

[13] Wojciech Kazana and Luc Segoufin. First-order query evaluation on structures of bounded degree. *Logical Methods in Computer Science (LMCS)*, 7(2), 2011.

[14] Wojciech Kazana and Luc Segoufin. Enumeration of monadic second-order queries on trees. *ACM Trans. on Computational Logic (ToCL)*, to appear.

[15] Stephan Kreutzer and Anuj Dawar. Parameterized complexity of first-order logic. *Electronic Colloquium on Computational Complexity (ECCC)*, 16:131, 2009.

[16] Jaroslav Nešetřil and Patrice Ossona de Mendez. Grad and classes with bounded expansion I. Decompositions. *Eur. J. Comb.*, 29(3):760–776, 2008.

[17] Jaroslav Nešetřil and Patrice Ossona de Mendez. Grad and classes with bounded expansion II. Algorithmic aspects. *Eur. J. Comb.*, 29(3):777–791, 2008.

[18] Jaroslav Nešetřil and Patrice Ossona de Mendez. On nowhere dense graphs. *European J. of Combinatorics*, 32(4):600–617, 2011.

[19] Christos H. Papadimitriou and Mihalis Yannakakis. On the Complexity of Database Queries. *J. on Computer and System Sciences (JCSS)*, 58(3):407–427, 1999.

[20] Detlef Seese. Linear Time Computable Problems and First-Order Descriptions. *Mathematical Structures in Computer Science*, 6(6):505–526, 1996.

The Fine Classification of Conjunctive Queries and Parameterized Logarithmic Space Complexity

Hubie Chen
Departamento LSI, Facultad de Informática
Universidad del País Vasco
E-20018 San Sebastián, Spain
hubie.chen@ehu.es
and
IKERBASQUE, Basque Foundation for Science
E-48011 Bilbao, Spain

Moritz Müller
Kurt Gödel Research Center
Währinger Straße 25
1090 Wien, Austria
moritz.mueller@univie.ac.at

ABSTRACT

We perform a fundamental investigation of the complexity of conjunctive query evaluation from the perspective of parameterized complexity. We classify sets of boolean conjunctive queries according to the complexity of this problem. Previous work showed that a set of conjunctive queries is fixed-parameter tractable precisely when the set is equivalent to a set of queries having bounded treewidth. We present a fine classification of query sets up to parameterized logarithmic space reduction. We show that, in the bounded treewidth regime, there are three complexity degrees and that the properties that determine the degree of a query set are bounded pathwidth and bounded tree depth. We also engage in a study of the two higher degrees via logarithmic space machine characterizations and complete problems. Our work yields a significantly richer perspective on the complexity of conjunctive queries and, at the same time, suggests new avenues of research in parameterized complexity.

Categories and Subject Descriptors

F.1.3 [**Complexity Measures and Classes**]: [Reducibility and completeness, Relations among complexity classes]; F.4.1 [**Mathematical Logic**]: [Logic and constraint programming]; H.2.3 [**Languages**]: [Query languages]

Keywords

Conjunctive queries, parameterized complexity, graph minors, logarithmic space

1. INTRODUCTION

Conjunctive queries are the most basic and most heavily studied database queries, and can be formalized logically as formulas consisting of a sequence of existentially quantified variables, followed by a conjunction of atomic formulas. Ever since the landmark 1977 article of Chandra and Merlin [4], complexity-theoretic aspects of conjunctive queries have been a research subject of persistent and enduring interest which continues to the present day (as a sampling, we point to the works [1, 21, 25, 17, 18, 19, 8, 26, 23]; see the discussions and references therein for more information). The problem of evaluating a conjunctive query on a relational database is equivalent to a number of well-known problems, including conjunctive query containment, the homomorphism problem on relational structures, and the constraint satisfaction problem [4, 21]. That this evaluation problem appears in many equivalent guises attests to the fundamental and primal nature of this problem, and it has correspondingly been approached and studied from a wide variety of perspectives and motivations. The resulting literature has not only been fruitful in terms of continually providing insights into and notions for understanding conjunctive queries themselves, but has also meaningfully fed back into a richer understanding of computational complexity theory at large, and of common complexity classes in particular. This is witnessed by the observation that various flavors of conjunctive query evaluation are used as prototypical complete problems for complexity classes such as NP and W[1] (refer, for example, to the books by Creignou, Khanna, and Sudan [7] and by Flum and Grohe [16], respectively). Another example of this phenomenon is the work showing LOGCFL-completeness of evaluating acyclic conjunctive queries (as well as of many related problems) due to Gottlob, Leone, and Scarcello [17].

As has been eloquently articulated in the literature [25], the employment of classical complexity notions such as polynomial-time tractability to grade the complexity of conjunctive query evaluation is not totally satisfactory. For in the context of databases, the typical scenario is the evaluation of a relatively short query on a relatively large database; this suggests a notion of time complexity wherein a non-polynomial dependence on the query may be tolerated, so long as the dependence on the database is polynomial. Computational complexity theory has developed and studied precisely such a relaxation of polynomial-time tractability, called *fixed-parameter tractability*, in which arbitrary dependence in a *parameter* is permitted; in our query evaluation setting, the query size is normally taken as the parameter. The class of such tractable problems is denoted by FPT. Fixed-parameter tractability is the base tractability notion of *parameterized complexity theory*, a comprehensive theory for studying problems where each instance has an associated parameter. As a parameterized problem, conjunctive query evaluation is complete for the parameterized complexity class W[1] [25, 16]; the property of W[1]-hardness plays, in the parameterized set-

PODS'13, June 22–27, 2013, New York, New York, USA.

ting, a role similar to that played by NP-hardness in the classical setting.

Due to the general intractability of conjunctive query evaluation, a recurring theme in the study of conjunctive queries is the identification of structural properties that provide tractability; such properties include *acyclicity* and *bounded treewidth* [17, 21]. A natural research issue is to obtain a systematic understanding of what properties ensure tractability, by classifying all sets of queries according to the complexity of the evaluation problem. We focus on boolean conjunctive queries, which, in logical parlance, are queries without free variables. Formally, let Φ be a set of boolean conjunctive queries, and define $\mathrm{EVAL}(\Phi)$ to be the problem of deciding, given a query $\phi \in \Phi$ and a relational structure $\mathbf{B}$, whether or not ϕ evaluates to true on $\mathbf{B}$. One can then inquire for which sets Φ the problem $\mathrm{EVAL}(\Phi)$ is tractable. For mathematical convenience, we use an equivalent formulation of this problem. It is known that each boolean conjunctive query ϕ can be bijectively represented as a relational structure $\mathbf{A}$ in such a way that, for any relational structure $\mathbf{B}$, it holds that ϕ is true on $\mathbf{B}$ if and only if there exists a homomorphism from $\mathbf{A}$ to $\mathbf{B}$. Hence, the following family of problems is equivalent to the family of problems $\mathrm{EVAL}(\Phi)$. Let $\mathcal{A}$ be a set of structures, and denote by $\mathrm{HOM}(\mathcal{A})$ the problem of deciding, given a structure $\mathbf{A} \in \mathcal{A}$ and a second structure $\mathbf{B}$, whether or not there is a homomorphism from $\mathbf{A}$ to $\mathbf{B}$. Use $p\text{-}\mathrm{HOM}(\mathcal{A})$ to denote the parameterized version of this problem, where the size of $\mathbf{A}$ is taken as the parameter.

Under the assumption that the structures in $\mathcal{A}$ have bounded arity, Grohe [19] presented a classification of the tractable problems of this form: if the *cores* of $\mathcal{A}$ have bounded treewidth, then the problem $p\text{-}\mathrm{HOM}(\mathcal{A})$ is fixed-parameter tractable; otherwise, the problem $p\text{-}\mathrm{HOM}(\mathcal{A})$ is W[1]-hard. The *core* of a structure can be intuitively thought of as a smallest equivalent structure. Grohe's classification thus shows that, in the studied setting, the condition of bounded treewidth is the *only* property guaranteeing tractability (assuming $\mathrm{FPT} \neq \mathrm{W}[1]$). Recall that treewidth is a graph measure which, intuitively speaking, measures the similitude of a graph to a tree, with a lower measure indicating a higher degree of similarity. The assumption of bounded arity provides robustness in that translating between two reasonable representations of structures can be done efficiently; this is in contrast to the case of unbounded arity, where the choice of representation can dramatically affect complexity [5].

The present article was motivated by the following fundamental research question: *What algorithmic/complexity behaviors of conjunctive queries are possible, within the regime of fixed-parameter tractability?* That is, we endeavored to obtain a finer perspective on the parameterized complexity of conjunctive queries, and in particular, on the possible sources of tractability thereof, by presenting a classification result akin to Grohe's, but for queries that are fixed-parameter tractable. As is usual in computational complexity, we make use of a weak notion of reduction in order to be able to make fine distinctions within the tractable zone. Logarithmic space computation is a common machine-based mode of computation that is often used to make distinctions within polynomial time; correspondingly, we adopt *parameterized logarithmic space computation*, which is obtained by relaxing logarithmic space computation much in the way that fixed-parameter tractability is obtained by relaxing polynomial time, as the base complexity class and as the reduction notion used in our investigation.

We present a classification theorem that comprehensively describes, for each set $\mathcal{A}$ of structures having bounded arity and bounded treewidth, the complexity of the problem $p\text{-}\mathrm{HOM}(\mathcal{A})$, up to parameterized logarithmic space reducibility (Section 3). Let $\mathcal{T}$ denote the set of all graphs that are trees, $\mathcal{P}$ denote the set of all graphs that are paths, and, for a set of structures $\mathcal{A}$, let $\mathcal{A}^*$ denote the set of structures obtainable by taking a structure $\mathbf{A} \in \mathcal{A}$ and adding each element of $\mathbf{A}$ as a relation. Our theorem shows that precisely three degrees of behavior are possible: such a problem $p\text{-}\mathrm{HOM}(\mathcal{A})$ is either equivalent to $p\text{-}\mathrm{HOM}(\mathcal{T}^*)$, equivalent to $p\text{-}\mathrm{HOM}(\mathcal{P}^*)$, or is solvable in parameterized logarithmic space (Theorem 3.1). Essentially speaking, bounded pathwidth and bounded tree depth are the properties that determine which of the three cases hold; as with treewidth, both pathwidth and tree depth are graph measures that associate a natural number with each graph. A key component of our classification theorem's proof is a reduction that, in effect, allows us to prove hardness results on a problem $p\text{-}\mathrm{HOM}(\mathcal{A})$ based on the hardness of $p\text{-}\mathrm{HOM}(\mathcal{M}^*)$ where $\mathcal{M}$ consists of certain graph minors derived from $\mathcal{A}$ (Lemma 3.6). The proof of our classification theorem utilizes this reduction in conjunction with excluded minor characterizations of graphs of bounded pathwidth and of bounded tree depth. We remark that, in combination with the *excluded grid theorem* from graph minor theory, the discussed reduction can be employed to readily derive Grohe's classification from the hardness of the *colored grid homomorphism problem*; this hardness result was presented by Grohe, Schwentick, and Segoufin [20]. A fascinating aspect of our classification theorem, which is shared with that of Grohe, is that natural graph-theoretic conditions–in our case, those of bounded pathwidth and bounded tree depth–arise naturally as the relevant properties that are needed to present our classification. This theorem also widens the interface among conjunctive queries, graph minor theory, and parameterized complexity that is present in the discussed work [20, 19].

Given that the problems $p\text{-}\mathrm{HOM}(\mathcal{P}^*)$ and $p\text{-}\mathrm{HOM}(\mathcal{T}^*)$ are the *only* problems (up to equivalence) above parameterized logarithmic space that emerge from our classification, we then seek a richer understanding of these problems. In particular, we engage in a study of the complexity classes that these problems define: we study the class of problems that reduce to $p\text{-}\mathrm{HOM}(\mathcal{P}^*)$, and likewise for $p\text{-}\mathrm{HOM}(\mathcal{T}^*)$ (Sections 4 and 5). Following a time-honored tradition in complexity theory, we present machine-based definitions of these classes, which classes we call PATH and TREE, respectively. The machine definition of PATH comes from recent work of Elberfeld, Stockhusen, and Tantau [11] and is based on nondeterministic Turing machines satisfying two simultaneous restrictions: first, that only parameterized logarithmic space is consumed; second, that the number of nondeterministic bits used is bounded, namely, by the product of the logarithm of the input size and a constant depending on the parameter. The machine characterization of TREE is similar, but it is based on alternating Turing machines where, in addition to the nondeterministic bits permitted previously, a parameter-dependent number of conondeterministic bits may also be used. In addition to proving that the problems $p\text{-}\mathrm{HOM}(\mathcal{P}^*)$ and $p\text{-}\mathrm{HOM}(\mathcal{T}^*)$ are complete for the machine-defined classes, we also prove that for any set of structures $\mathcal{A}$ having bounded pathwidth, the parameterized *embedding* problem $p\text{-}\mathrm{EMB}(\mathcal{A})$ is in PATH, and prove an analogous result for structures of bounded treewidth and the class TREE.

In the final section of the paper, we present a fine classification for the problem of counting homomorphisms which is analogous to our classification for the homomorphism problem (Section 6).

Our work shows that the complexity classes PATH and TREE are heavily populated with complete problems, and, along with the recent work [11], suggests the further development of the study of space-bounded parameterized complexity [14, 6] and, speaking more broadly, the study of complexity classes within FPT, which may include classes based on circuit or parallel models of computation. We can mention the following natural structural questions. Are either of the classes PATH or TREE closed under complement? Can any evidence be given either in favor of or against such closure? Even if the classes PATH and TREE are not closed under complement, could it be that co-PATH $\subseteq$ TREE? Another avenue for future research is to develop the theory of the degrees of counting problems identified by our counting classification.

2. PRELIMINARIES

For $n \in \mathbb{N}$ we define $[n] := \{1, \ldots, n\}$ if $n > 0$ and $[0] := \emptyset$.

2.1 Structures, homomorphisms and cores

Structures

A *vocabulary* τ is a finite set of relation symbols, where each $R \in \tau$ has an associated *arity* $\mathsf{ar}(R) \in \mathbb{N}$. A *$\tau$-structure* $\mathbf{A}$ consists of a nonempty finite set A, its *universe*, together with an *interpretation* $R^{\mathbf{A}} \subseteq A^{\mathsf{ar}(R)}$ of every $R \in \tau$. Let us emphasize that, in this article, we consider only finite structures. A *substructure (weak substructure)* of $\mathbf{A}$ is a structure *induced* by a nonempty subset X of A, i.e. the structure $\langle X \rangle^{\mathbf{A}}$ with universe X that interprets every $R \in \tau$ by (respectively, a subset of) $X^{\mathsf{ar}(R)} \cap R^{\mathbf{A}}$. A *restriction* of a structure is obtained by forgetting the interpretations of some symbols, and an *expansion* of a structure is obtained by adding interpretations of some symbols. We view *directed graphs* as $\{E\}$-structures $\mathbf{G} := (G, E^{\mathbf{G}})$ for binary E; $\mathbf{G}$ is a *graph* if $E^{\mathbf{G}}$ is irreflexive and symmetric. Note that a weak substructure of a graph is a subgraph. The graph *underlying* a directed graph $\mathbf{G}$ without loops (i.e. with irreflexive $E^{\mathbf{G}}$) is obtained by replacing $E^{\mathbf{G}}$ with its symmetric closure. We shall be concerned with the following classes of structures.

- For $k \geq 2$, the structure $\overrightarrow{\mathbf{P}_k}$ has universe $[k]$ and edge relation $\{(i, i+1) \mid i \in [k-1]\}$. The class $\overrightarrow{\mathcal{P}}$ of *directed paths* consists of the structures that are isomorphic to a structure of this form. Let $\mathbf{P}_k$ be the graph underlying $\overrightarrow{\mathbf{P}_k}$. The class $\mathcal{P}$ of *paths* consists of the structures that are isomorphic to a structure of this form.
- For $k \geq 2$, the structure $\overrightarrow{\mathbf{C}_k}$ has universe $[k]$ and edge relation $\{(i, i+1) \mid i \in [k-1]\} \cup \{(k, 1)\}$. The class $\overrightarrow{\mathcal{C}}$ of *directed cycles* consists of the structures that are isomorphic to a structure of this form. Let $\mathbf{C}_k$ be the graph underlying $\overrightarrow{\mathbf{C}_k}$. The class $\mathcal{C}$ of *cycles* consists of the structures that are isomorphic to a structure of this form.
- Finally, $\mathcal{T}$ is the class of *trees*, that is, the class of connected, acyclic graphs.

A class of structures $\mathcal{A}$ has *bounded arity* if there exists a $r \in \mathbb{N}$ such that any relation symbol interpreted in any structure $\mathbf{A} \in \mathcal{A}$ has arity at most r.

Homomorphisms

Let $\mathbf{A}$, $\mathbf{B}$ be structures. A *homomorphism* from $\mathbf{A}$ to $\mathbf{B}$ is a function $h : A \to B$ such that for all $R \in \tau$ and for all $\bar{a} = (a_1, \ldots, a_{\mathsf{ar}(R)}) \in R^{\mathbf{A}}$ it holds that $h(\bar{a}) \in R^{\mathbf{B}}$ where we write $h(\bar{a}) = (h(a_1), \ldots, h(a_{\mathsf{ar}(R)}))$. A *partial* homomorphism from $\mathbf{A}$ to $\mathbf{B}$ is the empty set or a homomorphism from a substructure of $\mathbf{A}$ to $\mathbf{B}$; equivalently, this is a partial function h from A to B that is a homomorphism from $\langle \mathsf{dom}(h) \rangle^{\mathbf{A}}$ to $\mathbf{B}$ if the domain $\mathsf{dom}(h)$ of h is not empty. As has become usual in our context, by an *embedding* we mean an injective homomorphism.

A structure $\mathbf{A}$ is a *core* if all homomorphisms from $\mathbf{A}$ to $\mathbf{A}$ are embeddings. Every structure $\mathbf{A}$ maps homomorphically to a weak substructure of itself which is a core. This weak substructure is unique up to isomorphism and called the core *of* $\mathbf{A}$ (cf. [12]). For a set of structures $\mathcal{A}$ we let $\mathsf{core}(\mathcal{A})$ denote the set of cores of structures in $\mathcal{A}$. It is not hard to see that two structures $\mathbf{A}, \mathbf{B}$ are homomorphically equivalent (that is, there are homomorphisms in both directions) if and only if they have the same core.

When $\mathbf{A}$ is a structure, we use $\mathbf{A}^*$ to denote its expansion that interprets for every $a \in A$ a fresh unary relation symbol C_a by $C_a^{\mathbf{A}^*} = \{a\}$. For a class of structures $\mathcal{A}$ we let

$$\mathcal{A}^* := \{\mathbf{A}^* \mid \mathbf{A} \in \mathcal{A}\}.$$

EXAMPLE 2.1. The following facts are straightforward to verify. Trees with at least two vertices and cycles of even length have a single edge as core, and so do cycles of even length. Cycles of odd length are cores, and so are directed paths. Structures of the form $\mathbf{A}^*$ are cores.

2.2 Notions of width

We rely on Bodlaender's survey [3] as a general reference for the notions of treewidth and pathwidth. Tree depth was introduced in [24].

A *tree-decomposition* of a graph $\mathbf{G} = (G, E^{\mathbf{G}})$ is a pair of a tree $\mathbf{T}$ and a family of *bags* $X_t \subseteq G$ for $t \in T$ such that $G = \bigcup_{t \in T} X_t$, $E^{\mathbf{G}} \subseteq \bigcup_{t \in T} X_t^2$ and $X_t \cap X_{t'} \subseteq X_{t''}$ whenever t'' lies on the simple path from t to t'; it is called a *path-decomposition* if $\mathbf{T}$ is a path; its *width* is $\max_{t \in T} |X_t| - 1$.

The *treewidth* $\mathsf{tw}(\mathbf{G})$ of $\mathbf{G}$ is the minimum width of a tree-decomposition of $\mathbf{G}$. The *pathwidth* $\mathsf{pw}(\mathbf{G})$ of $\mathbf{G}$ is the minimum width of a path-decomposition of $\mathbf{G}$.

By a *rooted tree* $\mathbf{T}$ we mean an expansion $(T, E^{\mathbf{T}}, \mathit{root}^{\mathbf{T}})$ of a tree $(T, E^{\mathbf{T}})$ by a unary relation symbol *root* interpreted by a singleton containing the *root*. The *tree depth* $\mathsf{td}(\mathbf{G})$ of $\mathbf{G}$ is the minimum $h \in \mathbb{N}$ such that every connected component of $\mathbf{G}$ is a subgraph of the closure of some rooted tree of height h. Here, the *closure* of a rooted tree is obtained by adding an edge from t to t' whenever t lies on the simple path from the root to t'.

The tree depth $\mathsf{td}(\mathbf{A})$ of an arbitrary structure $\mathbf{A}$ is the tree depth of its *Gaifman graph*: it has vertices A and an edge between a and a' if and only if a and a' are different and occur together in some tuple in some relation in $\mathbf{A}$. The notions $\mathsf{pw}(\mathbf{A})$ and $\mathsf{tw}(\mathbf{A})$ are similarly defined.

A class $\mathcal{A}$ of structures has *bounded tree depth* if there is $w \in \mathbb{N}$ such that $\mathsf{td}(\mathbf{A}) \leq w$ for all $\mathbf{A} \in \mathcal{A}$. Having bounded pathwidth or treewidth is similarly explained. It is not hard to see that bounded pathwidth is implied by bounded tree depth, and, trivially, bounded treewidth is implied by bounded pathwidth. Such classes are characterized as those excluding certain minors as follows. The first two statements are well-known from Robertson and Seymour's graph minor series (cf. [3, Theorems 12,13]) and the third is from [2, Theorem 4.8].

THEOREM 2.2. *Let $\mathcal{C}$ be a class of graphs.*

1. (Excluded Grid Theorem) *$\mathcal{C}$ has bounded treewidth if and only if $\mathcal{C}$ excludes some grid as a minor.*
2. (Excluded Tree Theorem) *$\mathcal{C}$ has bounded pathwidth if and only if $\mathcal{C}$ excludes some tree as a minor.*
3. (Excluded Path Theorem) *$\mathcal{C}$ has bounded tree depth if and only if $\mathcal{C}$ excludes some path as a minor.*

A class of graphs $\mathcal{C}$ *excludes* a graph $\mathbf{M}$ *as a minor* if $\mathbf{M}$ is not a minor of any graph in $\mathcal{C}$. Recall, $\mathbf{M}$ is a *minor* of a graph $\mathbf{G}$ if there exists a *minor map* μ from $\mathbf{M}$ to $\mathbf{G}$, that is, a family $(\mu(m))_{m\in M}$ of pairwise disjoint, non-empty, connected subsets of G such that for all $(m, m') \in E^{\mathbf{M}}$ there are $v \in \mu(m)$ and $v' \in \mu(m')$ with $(v, v') \in E^{\mathbf{G}}$.

2.3 Parameterized complexity

Turing machines

We identify (classical) problems with sets $Q \subseteq \{0,1\}^*$ of finite binary strings. We use Turing machines with a (read-only) input tape and several worktapes as our basic model of computation. We will consider nondeterministic and alternating Turing machines with binary nondeterminism and co-nondeterminism. For concreteness, let us agree that a nondeterministic machine has a special *(existential) guess state*; a configuration with the guess state has two successor configurations obtained by changing the guess state to one out of two further distinguished states s_0, s_1. An alternating machine may additionally have a *universal guess state* that follows a similar convention. For a function $f : \{0,1\}^* \to \mathbb{N}$ we say that $\mathbb{A}$ *uses f (co-)nondeterministic bits* if for every input $x \in \{0,1\}^*$ every run of $\mathbb{A}$ on x contains at most $f(x)$ many configurations with the existential (respectively, universal) guess state.

Fixed-parameter (in)tractability

A *parameterized problem* (Q, κ) is a pair of a classical problem $Q \subseteq \{0,1\}^*$ and a logarithmic space computable *parameterization* $\kappa : \{0,1\}^* \to \mathbb{N}$ associating with any instance $x \in \{0,1\}^*$ its *parameter* $\kappa(x) \in \mathbb{N}$.[1] A Turing machine is *fpt-time bounded (with respect to κ)* if on input $x \in \{0,1\}^*$ it runs in time $f(\kappa(x)) \cdot |x|^{O(1)}$ where $f : \mathbb{N} \to \mathbb{N}$ is a computable function. The class FPT (para-NP) contains the parameterized problems (Q, κ) such that Q is decided (accepted) by an fpt-time bounded deterministic (nondeterministic) Turing machine. An *fpt-reduction* from (Q, κ) to (Q', κ') is a reduction $R : \{0,1\}^* \to \{0,1\}^*$ from Q to Q' that is computable by a fpt-time bounded (with respect to κ) Turing machine and such that $\kappa' \circ R \leq f \circ \kappa$ for some computable f.

We are concerned with homomorphism and embedding problems associated with classes of structures $\mathcal{A}$.

p-HOM($\mathcal{A}$)	
Instance:	A pair of structures $(\mathbf{A}, \mathbf{B})$ where $\mathbf{A} \in \mathcal{A}$.
Parameter:	$\lvert\mathbf{A}\rvert$.
Problem:	Is there a homomorphism from $\mathbf{A}$ into $\mathbf{B}$?

p-EMB($\mathcal{A}$)	
Instance:	A pair of structures $(\mathbf{A}, \mathbf{B})$ where $\mathbf{A} \in \mathcal{A}$.
Parameter:	$\lvert\mathbf{A}\rvert$.
Problem:	Is there an embedding from $\mathbf{A}$ into $\mathbf{B}$?

These problem definitions exemplify how we present parameterized problems. More formally, the parameterization indicated is the function that maps a string encoding a pair of structures $(\mathbf{A}, \mathbf{B})$ to $|\mathbf{A}|$, and any other string to, say, 0. Here, $|\mathbf{A}| := |\tau| + |A| + \sum_{R\in\tau} |R^A| \cdot \mathsf{ar}(R)$ is the *size* of $\mathbf{A}$; note that the length of a reasonable binary encoding of $\mathbf{A}$ is $O(|\mathbf{A}| \cdot \log |A|)$ (cf. [13]).

The theory of parameterized intractability is centered around the W-hierarchy, which consists of the classes $W[1] \subseteq W[2] \subseteq \cdots \subseteq W[P]$. The class W[P] contains the parameterized problems (Q, κ) that are accepted by nondeterministic Turing machines that are fpt-time bounded with respect to κ and use $f(\kappa(x)) \cdot \log |x|$ many nondeterministic bits. We refer to the monographs [16, 10] for more information about the W-hierarchy. It is well-known that the problems p-HOM($\mathcal{A}$) and p-EMB($\mathcal{A}$) are contained in W[1], and e.g. when $\mathcal{A}$ is the class of cliques, these problems are W[1]-hard and hence W[1]-complete under fpt-reductions.

[1]Usually polynomial time is allowed to compute κ but as we are interested in parameterized logarithmic space we adopt a more restrictive notion as [11]. Natural parameterizations are often simply projections.

Parameterized logarithmic space

A Turing machine is *parameterized logarithmic space bounded (with respect to κ)*, in short, *pl-space bounded (with respect to κ)* if on input $x \in \{0,1\}^*$ it runs in space $O(f(\kappa(x)) + \log n)$, where $f : \mathbb{N} \to \mathbb{N}$ is some computable function. The class para-L (para-NL) contains the parameterized problems (Q, κ) such that Q is decided (accepted) by a (non)deterministic Turing machine that is pl-space bounded with respect to κ. Obviously,

$$\text{para-L} \subseteq \text{para-NL} \subseteq \text{FPT} \subseteq \text{W[P]} \subseteq \text{para-NP}.$$

Let κ be a parameterization. A function $F : \{0,1\}^* \to \{0,1\}^*$ is *implicitly pl-computable (with respect to κ)* if the parameterized problem

BITGRAPH(F)	
Instance:	A triple (x, i, b) where $x \in \{0,1\}^*$, $i \geq 1$, and $b \in \{0,1\}$.
Parameter:	$\kappa(x)$.
Problem:	Does $F(x)$ have length $\lvert F(x)\rvert \geq i$ and ith bit equal to b?

is in para-L. The following is straightforwardly verified as in the classical setting of logarithmic space computability.

LEMMA 2.3. *Let κ, κ' be parameterizations and let $F, F' : \{0,1\}^* \to \{0,1\}^*$ be implicitly pl-computable with respect to κ and κ' respectively. Then $F' \circ F$ is implicitly pl-computable with respect to κ.*

Let $(Q, \kappa), (Q', \kappa')$ be parameterized problems. A *pl-reduction* from (Q, κ) to (Q', κ') is a reduction $R : \{0,1\}^* \to \{0,1\}^*$ from Q to Q' that is implicitly pl-computable[2] with respect to κ and such that there exists a computable function $f : \mathbb{N} \to \mathbb{N}$ such that $\kappa' \circ R \leq f \circ \kappa$. We write $(Q, \kappa) \leq_{\text{pl}} (Q', \kappa')$ to indicate that such a reduction exists. We write $(Q, \kappa) \equiv_{\text{pl}} (Q', \kappa')$ if both $(Q, \kappa) \leq_{\text{pl}} (Q', \kappa')$ and $(Q', \kappa') \leq_{\text{pl}} (Q, \kappa)$.

3. CLASSIFICATION

THEOREM 3.1 (CLASSIFICATION THEOREM). *Let $\mathcal{A}$ be a decidable class of structures of bounded arity such that* $\mathsf{core}(\mathcal{A})$ *has bounded treewidth.*

1. *If* $\mathsf{core}(\mathcal{A})$ *has unbounded pathwidth, then p-HOM($\mathcal{A}$) $\equiv_{\text{pl}}$ p-HOM($\mathcal{T}^*$).*
2. *If* $\mathsf{core}(\mathcal{A})$ *has bounded pathwidth and unbounded tree depth, then p-HOM($\mathcal{A}$) $\equiv_{\text{pl}}$ p-HOM($\mathcal{P}^*$).*
3. *If* $\mathsf{core}(\mathcal{A})$ *has bounded tree depth, then p-HOM($\mathcal{A}$) is in* para-L.

[2]It is routine to verify that F is implicitly pl-computable if and only if it is computable by a pl-space bounded Turing machine with a write-only output tape. Our definition is equivalent to the ones in [14, 6, 11].

REMARK 3.2. If $\mathcal{A}$ is assumed to be only computably enumerable instead of decidable, then the theorem stays true understanding all mentioned problems in a suitable way as promise problems. If no computability assumption is placed on $\mathcal{A}$, then the theorem stays true in the non-uniform setting of parameterized complexity theory (cf. [10]).

We break the proof into several lemmas.

To prove statement (3) of Theorem 3.1 we show that the canonical query of a structure of *tree depth* w is equivalent to an existential first-order sentence of *quantifier rank* $w+1$, and that model-checking such sentences can be done in parameterized logarithmic space. A proof can be found in Section 3.2.

LEMMA 3.3. *Assume $\mathcal{A}$ is a decidable class of structures of bounded arity such that* $\mathsf{core}(\mathcal{A})$ *has bounded tree depth. Then* p-HOM$(\mathcal{A}) \in$ para-L.

To prove statements (1) and (2) of Theorem 3.1 we need to deal with homomorphism problems for classes $\mathcal{A}$ that are not necessarily decidable. Slightly abusing notation, we say p-HOM$(\mathcal{A}) \leq_{\mathrm{pl}}$ p-HOM$(\mathcal{A}')$ for arbitrary classes of structures $\mathcal{A}, \mathcal{A}'$ if there is a implicitly pl-computable *partial* function F that is defined on those instances $(\mathbf{A}, \mathbf{B})$ of p-HOM$(\mathcal{A})$ with $\mathbf{A} \in \mathcal{A}$ and maps them to equivalent instances $(\mathbf{A}', \mathbf{B}')$ of p-HOM$(\mathcal{A}')$ with $\mathbf{A}' \in \mathcal{A}'$ such that $|\mathbf{A}'|$ is effectively bounded in $|\mathbf{A}|$. By saying that a partial function F is implicitly pl-computable with respect to a parameterization κ we mean that there are a computable $f : \mathbb{N} \to \mathbb{N}$ and a Turing machine that on those instances (x, i, b) of BITGRAPH(F) such that F is defined on x, runs in space $O(f(\kappa(x)) + \log |x|)$ and answers $(x, b, i) \overset{?}{\in}$ BITGRAPH(F); on other instances the machine may do whatever it wants.

The following lemma takes care of the reductions from left to right in statements (1) and (2) of Theorem 3.1.

LEMMA 3.4. *Let $\mathcal{A}$ be a class of structures and $\mathcal{R} \subseteq \mathcal{T}$ be a computably enumerable class of trees. Assume there is $w \in \mathbb{N}$ such that every structure in $\mathcal{A}$ has a tree decomposition of width at most w whose tree is contained in $\mathcal{R}$. Then,*

$$p\text{-HOM}(\mathcal{A}) \leq_{\mathrm{pl}} p\text{-HOM}(\mathcal{R}^*).$$

PROOF. Let $(\mathbf{A}, \mathbf{B})$ with $\mathbf{A} \in \mathcal{A}$ be an instance of p-HOM$(\mathcal{A})$. Enumerating $\mathcal{R}$, test successively for $\mathbf{T} \in \mathcal{R}$ whether there exists a width $\leq w$ tree-decomposition $(\mathbf{T}, (X_t)_{t \in T})$ of $\mathbf{A}$. Since $\mathbf{A} \in \mathcal{A}$ this test eventually succeeds, and the time needed is effectively bounded in the parameter $|\mathbf{A}|$. With such a tree-decomposition at hand produce the instance $(\mathbf{T}^*, \mathbf{B}')$ of the problem p-HOM$(\mathcal{R}^*)$ where the structure $\mathbf{B}'$ is defined as follows. Write $\mathsf{dom}(f)$ for the domain of a partial function f; two partial functions f and g are *compatible* if they agree on arguments where they are both defined.

$$\begin{aligned} B' &:= \{f \mid f \text{ is a partial homomorphism from } \mathbf{A} \text{ to } \mathbf{B} \\ &\qquad \text{and } |\mathsf{dom}(f)| \leq w\}; \\ E^{\mathbf{B}'} &:= \{(f, g) \in B' \times B' \mid f \text{ and } g \text{ are compatible}\}; \\ C_t^{\mathbf{B}'} &:= \{f \in B' \mid \mathsf{dom}(f) = X_t\}, \quad \text{for every } t \in T. \end{aligned}$$

Suppose that h is a homomorphism from $\mathbf{A}$ to $\mathbf{B}$. Then the mapping $h' : T \to B'$ defined by $h'(t) = h \restriction X_t$ is straightforwardly verified to be a homomorphism from $\mathbf{T}^*$ to $\mathbf{B}'$.

Conversely, let h' be a homomorphism from $\mathbf{T}^*$ to $\mathbf{B}'$. Then, $h'(t)$ is a partial homomorphism from $\mathbf{A}$ to $\mathbf{B}$ with domain X_t. Since $\mathbf{T}$ is connected the values of h' are pairwise compatible. Hence $h := \bigcup_{t \in T} h'(t)$ is a function from $\bigcup_{t \in T} X_t = A$ to B. To see h is a homomorphism, consider a tuple $(a_1, \ldots, a_r) \in R^{\mathbf{A}}$ for some r-ary relation R in the vocabulary of $\mathbf{A}$. Then $\{a_1, \ldots, a_r\}$ is contained in some bag X_t since it is a clique in the Gaifman graph of $\mathbf{A}$ (cf. [3, Lemma 4]). But $h'(t)$ maps this tuple to a tuple in $R^{\mathbf{B}}$, so the mapping h does as well. $\square$

For later use we make the following remark concerning the above proof.

REMARK 3.5. The previous proof associates with a homomorphism h from $\mathbf{A}$ to $\mathbf{B}$ the homomorphism h' from $\mathbf{T}^*$ to $\mathbf{B}'$ that maps t to $h \restriction X_t$. This association $h \mapsto h'$ is injective because every $a \in A$ appears in some bag X_t. It is also surjective: a homomorphism h' from $\mathbf{T}^*$ to $\mathbf{B}'$, is associated with $h := \bigcup_{t \in T} h'(t)$; the previous proof argued that h is a homomorphism from $\mathbf{A}$ to $\mathbf{B}$. Hence, there is a bijection between the set of homomorphisms from $\mathbf{A}$ to $\mathbf{B}$ and the set of homomorphisms from $\mathbf{T}^*$ to $\mathbf{B}'$.

At the heart of the proof of Theorem 3.1 is the following sequence of reductions, proved in the following subsection. The appropriately informed reader will recognize elements from Grohe's proof [19].

LEMMA 3.6 (REDUCTION LEMMA). *Let $\mathcal{A}$ be a computably enumerable class of structures of bounded arity, let $\mathcal{G}$ be the class of Gaifman graphs of* $\mathsf{core}(\mathcal{A})$, *and let $\mathcal{M}$ be the class of minors of graphs in $\mathcal{G}$. Then*

$$\begin{aligned} p\text{-HOM}(\mathcal{M}^*) &\leq_{\mathrm{pl}} p\text{-HOM}(\mathcal{G}^*) \\ &\leq_{\mathrm{pl}} p\text{-HOM}(\mathsf{core}(\mathcal{A})^*) \\ &\leq_{\mathrm{pl}} p\text{-HOM}(\mathsf{core}(\mathcal{A})) \\ &\leq_{\mathrm{pl}} p\text{-HOM}(\mathcal{A}). \end{aligned}$$

With the Reduction Lemma, we can give the proof of the Classification Theorem.

PROOF. (Theorem 3.1) The reduction from left to right in statements (1) and (2) follow from Lemma 3.4. The reductions from right to left follow from the Reduction Lemma 3.6 via the Excluded Tree Theorem 2.2 (2) and the Excluded Path Theorem 2.2 (3). Statement (3) is proved as Lemma 3.3. $\square$

3.1 Proof of the Reduction Lemma

As a consequence of the assumption that $\mathcal{A}$ is computably enumerable, each of the sets $\mathcal{M}^*$, $\mathcal{G}^*$, $\mathsf{core}(\mathcal{A})^*$, and $\mathsf{core}(\mathcal{A})$ are computably enumerable. The statement of the theorem claims the existence of four reductions. The last one from p-HOM$(\mathsf{core}(\mathcal{A}))$ to p-HOM$(\mathcal{A})$ is easy to see. We construct the first three in sequence.

LEMMA 3.7. *Let $\mathcal{G}$ be a class of graphs which is computable enumerable, and let $\mathcal{M}$ be the class of minors of graphs in $\mathcal{G}$. Then*

$$p\text{-HOM}(\mathcal{M}^*) \leq_{\mathrm{pl}} p\text{-HOM}(\mathcal{G}^*).$$

PROOF. Let $(\mathbf{M}^*, \mathbf{B})$ with $\mathbf{M}^* \in \mathcal{M}^*$ be an instance of the problem p-HOM$(\mathcal{M}^*)$. Enumerating $\mathcal{G}$, test successively for $\mathbf{G} \in \mathcal{G}$ whether $\mathbf{M}$ is a minor of $\mathbf{G}$. Since $\mathbf{M} \in \mathcal{M}$ this test eventually succeeds, and then compute a minor map μ from $\mathbf{M}$ to $\mathbf{G}$. The time needed is effectively bounded in the parameter $|\mathbf{M}^*|$. The reduction then produces the instance $(\mathbf{G}^*, \mathbf{B}')$ of p-HOM$(\mathcal{G}^*)$, where

$\mathbf{B}'$ is defined as follows. Let I denote the set $\bigcup_{m\in M}\mu(m)$.

$$\begin{aligned} B' &:= (M\times B)\dot\cup\{\bot\};\\ E^{\mathbf{B}'} &:= \{((m_1,b_1),(m_2,b_2)) \mid [m_1=m_2 \Rightarrow b_1=b_2] \text{ and }\\ &\qquad [(m_1,m_2)\in E^{\mathbf{M}} \Rightarrow (b_1,b_2)\in E^{\mathbf{B}}]\}\\ &\quad \cup\{(\bot,b') \mid b'\in B'\}\cup\{(b',\bot)\mid b'\in B'\};\\ C_v^{\mathbf{B}'} &:= \{(m,b)\mid b\in C_m^{\mathbf{B}}\}, \quad \text{if } m\in M \text{ and } v\in\mu(m);\\ C_v^{\mathbf{B}'} &:= \{\bot\}, \quad \text{if } v\notin I. \end{aligned}$$

Suppose that h is a homomorphism from $\mathbf{M}^*$ to $\mathbf{B}$. Let $h' : G\to B'$ be the map that sends, for each $m\in M$, the elements in $\mu(m)$ to $(m,h(m))$ and that sends all elements $v\notin I$ to $\bot$. Then h' is a homomorphism from $\mathbf{G}^*$ to $\mathbf{B}'$.

Suppose that g is a homomorphism from $\mathbf{G}^*$ to $\mathbf{B}'$. We show that g is of the form h' for a homomorphism h from $\mathbf{M}^*$ to $\mathbf{B}$. First, by definition of the $C_v^{\mathbf{B}'}$, it holds that $g(v)=\bot$ for all $v\notin I$. Next, let v,w be elements of a set $\mu(m)$, with $m\in M$. The definition of the $C_v^{\mathbf{B}'}$ ensures that $g(v)$ and $g(w)$ have the form $(m,\cdot)$. Since $\mu(m)$ is connected, the definition of $E^{\mathbf{B}'}$ ensures that $g(v)=g(w)$. Finally, suppose that $(m_1,m_2)\in E^{\mathbf{M}}$, let (m_1,b_1) be the image of $\mu(m_1)$ under g, and let (m_2,b_2) be the image of $\mu(m_2)$ under g. We claim that $(b_1,b_2)\in E^{\mathbf{B}}$. But there exist $v_1\in\mu(m_1)$ and $v_2\in\mu(m_2)$ such that $(v_1,v_2)\in E^{\mathbf{G}}$. We then have $(g(v_1),g(v_2))\in E^{\mathbf{B}'}$ and the definition of $E^{\mathbf{B}'}$ ensures that $(b_1,b_2)\in E^{\mathbf{B}}$. □

LEMMA 3.8. *Let $\mathcal{A}$ be a computably enumerable class of structures of bounded arity, and let $\mathcal{G}$ be the class of Gaifman graphs of $\mathcal{A}$. Then p-HOM$(\mathcal{G}^*)\le_{\mathrm{pl}} p$-HOM$(\mathcal{A}^*)$.*

PROOF. Let the pair $(\mathbf{G}^*,\mathbf{B})$ with $\mathbf{G}\in\mathcal{G}$ be an instance of p-HOM$(\mathcal{G}^*)$. Similarly as seen in the previous proof, one can compute from $\mathbf{G}$ a structure $\mathbf{A}\in\mathcal{A}$ whose Gaifman graph is $\mathbf{G}$. The reduction produces the instance $(\mathbf{A}^*,\mathbf{B}')$ of p-HOM$(\mathcal{A}^*)$, where $\mathbf{B}'$ is defined as follows.

$$\begin{aligned} B' &:= B;\\ C_a^{\mathbf{B}'} &:= C_a^{\mathbf{B}}, \quad \text{for every } a\in A;\\ R^{\mathbf{B}'} &:= \{(b_1,\dots,b_r)\mid \{b_1\dots,b_r\} \text{ is a clique in } (B,E^{\mathbf{B}})\}, \end{aligned}$$

for every r-ary symbol R from the vocabulary of $\mathbf{A}$. It is straightforward to verify that a function $h: A\to B$ is a homomorphism from $\mathbf{G}$ to $\mathbf{B}$ if and only if it is a homomorphism from $\mathbf{A}$ to $\mathbf{B}'$. □

Recall that the *direct product* $\mathbf{A}\times\mathbf{B}$ of two τ-structures $\mathbf{A}$ and $\mathbf{B}$ has universe $A\times B$ and interprets a relation symbol $R\in\tau$ by $\{((a_1,b_1),\dots,(a_{\mathsf{ar}(R)},b_{\mathsf{ar}(R)}))\mid \bar a\in R^{\mathbf{A}},\bar b\in R^{\mathbf{B}}\}$.

LEMMA 3.9. *Let $\mathcal{A}$ be a class of structures. Then*

$$p\text{-HOM}(\mathsf{core}(\mathcal{A})^*)\le_{\mathrm{pl}} p\text{-HOM}(\mathsf{core}(\mathcal{A})).$$

PROOF. Let $(\mathbf{D}^*,\mathbf{B})$ with $\mathbf{D}\in\mathsf{core}(\mathcal{A})$ be an instance of p-HOM$(\mathsf{core}(\mathcal{A})^*)$. Let $\mathbf{B}_*$ be the restriction of $\mathbf{B}$ to the vocabulary of $\mathbf{D}$. The reduction produces the instance $(\mathbf{D},\mathbf{B}')$ of the problem p-HOM$(\mathsf{core}(\mathcal{A}))$, where

$$\mathbf{B}' := \langle\{(d,b)\in D\times B\mid b\in C_d^{\mathbf{B}}\}\rangle^{\mathbf{D}\times\mathbf{B}_*}.$$

Suppose that h is a homomorphism from $\mathbf{D}^*$ to $\mathbf{B}$. Then, the mapping $h': D\to B'$ defined by $h'(d)=(d,h(d))$ is straightforwardly verified to be a homomorphism from $\mathbf{D}$ to $\mathbf{B}'$.

Suppose that g is a homomorphism from $\mathbf{D}$ to $\mathbf{B}'$. Write π_1 and π_2 for the projections that map a pair to its first and second component respectively. The composition $(\pi_1\circ g)$ is a homomorphism from $\mathbf{D}$ to itself; since $\mathbf{D}$ is a core, $(\pi_1\circ g)$ is bijective. Hence, there exists a natural $m\ge 1$ such that $(\pi_1\circ g)^m$ is the identity on D. Define h as $g\circ(\pi_1\circ g)^{m-1}$. Clearly, h is a homomorphism from $\mathbf{D}$ to $\mathbf{B}'$, so $\pi_2\circ h$ is a homomorphism from $\mathbf{D}$ to $\mathbf{B}_*$. We claim that $\pi_2\circ h$ is also a homomorphism from $\mathbf{D}^*$ to $\mathbf{B}$. Observe that $\pi_1\circ h$ is the identity on D. In other words, for every $d\in D$ there is $b_d\in B$ such that $h(d)=(d,b_d)$. By definition of $\mathbf{B}'$ we get $b_d\in C_d^{\mathbf{B}}$, establishing the claim. □

Observe that the map h' constructed in the above proof is an embedding. Hence we have the following corollary that we note explicitly for later use.

COROLLARY 3.10. *Let $\mathcal{A}$ be a class of structures. Then*

$$p\text{-HOM}(\mathsf{core}(\mathcal{A})^*)\le_{\mathrm{pl}} p\text{-EMB}(\mathsf{core}(\mathcal{A})).$$

3.2 Proof of Lemma 3.3

Let τ be a vocabulary. *First-order τ-formulas* are built from *atoms* $R\bar x, x=x$ by Boolean combinations and existential and universal quantification. Here, $\bar x$ is a tuple of variables of length matching the arity of R. We write $\varphi(\bar x)$ for a (first-order) τ-formula φ to indicate that the free variables in φ are among the components of $\bar x$. The *quantifier rank* $\mathsf{qr}(\varphi)$ of a formula φ is defined as follows: $\mathsf{qr}(\varphi)=0$ for atoms φ; $\mathsf{qr}(\neg\varphi)=\mathsf{qr}(\varphi)$; $\mathsf{qr}(\varphi\wedge\psi)=\mathsf{qr}(\varphi\vee\psi)=\max\{\mathsf{qr}(\varphi),\mathsf{qr}(\psi)\}$; $\mathsf{qr}(\exists x\varphi)=\mathsf{qr}(\forall x\varphi)=1+\mathsf{qr}(\varphi)$.

Given a structure $\mathbf{A}$, its *canonical query* is a quantifier-free conjunction in the variables x_a for $a\in A$; namely, for every relation symbol R of $\mathbf{A}$ and every $(a_1,\dots,a_{\mathsf{ar}(R)})\in R^{\mathbf{A}}$ it contains the conjunct $Rx_{a_1}\cdots x_{a_{\mathsf{ar}(R)}}$. It is easy to see that the canoncial query of $\mathbf{A}$ is satisfiable in a structure $\mathbf{B}$ if and only if there is an homomorphism from $\mathbf{A}$ to $\mathbf{B}$.

LEMMA 3.11. *The parameterized problem*

p-MC(FO)	
Instance:	a structure $\mathbf{A}$, a first-order sentence φ.
Parameter:	$\lvert\varphi\rvert$.
Problem:	$\mathbf{A}\models\varphi$?

can be decided in space $O(|\varphi|\cdot\log|\varphi|+(\mathsf{qr}(\varphi)+\mathsf{ar}(\varphi))\cdot\log|A|)$, where $\mathsf{qr}(\varphi)$ is the quantifier rank of φ and $\mathsf{ar}(\varphi)$ is the maximal arity over all relation symbols in φ

PROOF. We give an algorithm expecting inputs $(\mathbf{A},\varphi,\alpha)$ where φ is a formula and α is an assignment for φ in $\mathbf{A}$, that is, a map from a superset of the free variables of φ into A. The algorithm determines whether α satisfies φ in $\mathbf{A}$. It executes a depth-first recursion as follows.

If φ is an atom $R\bar y$ the algorithm writes the tuple $\alpha(\bar y)\in A^{\mathsf{ar}(R)}$ on the worktape and checks whether it is contained in $R^{\mathbf{A}}$ by scanning the input; it then erases the tuple and returns the bit corresponding to the answer obtained.

If $\varphi=(\psi\wedge\chi)$, the algorithm recurses on ψ (with the same assignment); upon completing the recursion it erases all space used in it, stores a bit for the answer obtained, and then recurses on χ; upon completion it erases the space used in it and returns the minimum of the bit obtained and the stored bit. The cases $\varphi=(\psi\vee\chi)$ and $\varphi=\neg\psi$ are similar.

If $\varphi(\bar x)=\exists y\psi(\bar x,y)$ the algorithm loops through $b\in A$ and recurses on ψ with assignment α extended by mapping y to b; it maintains a bit which is intially 0 and updates it after each loop to the maximum of the bit obtained in the loop; after each loop it erases the space used in in it. Upon completing the loop it returns this bit, and restricts the assignment back to its old domain without y. The case $\varphi(\bar{x}) = \forall y \psi(\bar{x}, y)$ is similar.

Each recursive step adds space $O(\log|\varphi|)$ to remember the (position of) the subformula ψ plus one bit plus $O(\log|A|)$ for the loop on $b \in A$ in the quantifier case and plus $O(\mathsf{ar}(\varphi) \cdot \log|A|)$ in the atomic case. The assignments α occuring in the recursion all have cardinality $w \leq \mathsf{qr}(\varphi)$, so need space $O(w(\log|\varphi| + \log|A|))$ to be stored. □

PROOF. (Lemma 3.3) Choose $w \in \mathbb{N}$ such that $\mathsf{td}(\mathsf{core}(\mathbf{A})) \leq w$ for all $\mathbf{A} \in \mathcal{A}$. Given a structure $\mathbf{A}$ we compute a sentence $\varphi_{\mathbf{A}}$ of quantifier rank at most $w+1$ such that for all structures $\mathbf{B}$, the sentence $\varphi_{\mathbf{A}}$ is true in $\mathbf{B}$ if and only if there is a homomorphism from $\mathbf{A}$ to $\mathbf{B}$. This is enough by Lemma 3.11.

Given $\mathbf{A}$ we check $\mathbf{A} \in \mathcal{A}$ running some decision procedure for $\mathcal{A}$. If $\mathbf{A} \notin \mathcal{A}$ we let $\varphi_{\mathbf{A}} := \exists x \neg x = x$. If $\mathbf{A} \in \mathcal{A}$, compute the core $\mathbf{A}_0$ of $\mathbf{A}$ and compute for every connected component C of the Gaifman graph of $\mathbf{A}_0$ some rooted tree $\mathbf{T}$ with vertices $T = C$ and height at most w such that every edge of the Gaifman graph of $\langle C \rangle^{\mathbf{A}_0}$ is in the closure of $\mathbf{T}$.

Consider a component C and let $\mathbf{T}$ be the rooted tree computed for C. For $c \in C = T$ we compute the following first-order formula φ_c. We use variables x_c for $c \in C = T$. If c is a leaf of $\mathbf{T}$, let φ_c be the canonical query of $\langle P_c \rangle^{\mathbf{A}_0}$ where P_c is the path in $\mathbf{T}$ leading from the root r of $\mathbf{T}$ to c. For an inner vertex c define

$$\varphi_c := \textstyle\bigwedge_d \exists x_d\, \varphi_d,$$

where d ranges over the successors of c. The following claims are straightforwardly verified by induction along the recursive definition of the φ_cs.

Claims. For every $c \in C$:

1. the quantifier rank of φ_c equals the height of the subtree of $\mathbf{T}$ rooted at c;
2. the free variables of φ_c are $\{x_d \mid d \in P_c\}$;
3. φ_c is satisfiable in $\mathbf{B}$ if and only if so is the canonical query of $\langle C(c) \rangle^{\mathbf{A}_0}$ where $C(c)$ contains P_c and the vertices in the subtree rooted at c.

Letting r range over the roots of the trees $\mathbf{T}$ chosen for the connected components C of $\mathbf{A}_0$, we set

$$\varphi_{\mathbf{A}} := \textstyle\bigwedge_r \exists x_r \varphi_r.$$

By Claim 2 this is a sentence and by Claim 1 it has quantifier rank at most $w+1$. It is true in $\mathbf{B}$ if and only if every $\exists x_r \varphi_r$ is true in $\mathbf{B}$, and by Claim 3 this holds if and only if the canonical query of $\langle C(r) \rangle^{\mathbf{A}_0}$ is satisfiable in $\mathbf{B}$ for every connected component C. Noting $C(r) = C$, this means that every $\langle C \rangle^{\mathbf{A}_0}$ maps homomorphically to $\mathbf{B}$, and this means that $\mathbf{A}_0$ maps homomorphically to $\mathbf{B}$. Recalling that $\mathbf{A}_0$ is the core of $\mathbf{A}$, we see that this is equivalent to $\mathbf{A}$ mapping homomorphically to $\mathbf{B}$. □

4. THE CLASS PATH

We present the complexity class PATH to capture the complexity of p-HOM($\mathcal{P}^*$). This class was discovered very recently by Elberfeld et al. [11] with a different angle of motivation; they refer to this class as para-NL[f log]. Among other results, they show that the following problem is complete for this class: check if a digraph contains a path from a distinguished vertex s to another distinguished vertex t of length at most k; here, k is the parameter. We use p-st-PATH to denote the corresponding problem for (undirected) graphs.

p-st-PATH	
Instance:	A graph $\mathbf{G}$, $s, t \in G$ and $k \in \mathbb{N}$.
Parameter:	k.
Problem:	Is there a path in $\mathbf{G}$ from s to t of length at most k ?

DEFINITION 4.1. The class PATH contains a parameterized problem (Q, κ) if there are a computable function $f : \mathbb{N} \to \mathbb{N}$ and a nondeterministic Turing machine that accepts Q, is pl-space bounded with respect to κ, and uses $f(\kappa(x)) \cdot \log|x|$ many nondeterministic bits.

It follows immediately from the definitions that

$$\text{para-L} \subseteq \text{PATH} \subseteq \text{para-NL}.$$

Recall that, using the notation in [14], one has

$$\text{FPT} = \text{para-P} \subseteq \text{W[P]} \subseteq \text{para-NP}.$$

Observe that PATH is a natural class in that it has a natural machine characterization that is analogous to the one of W[P]. We shall see that it captures the complexity of many natural problems.

PROPOSITION 4.2. *The complexity class* PATH *is closed under pl-reductions.*

THEOREM 4.3. p-HOM($\mathcal{P}^*$) *is complete for* PATH *under pl-reductions.*

That p-HOM($\mathcal{P}^*$) is contained in PATH can be seen by the guess-and-check paradigm. We find it informative to present algorithms in a computational model tailored specifically for this kind of nondeterminism.

DEFINITION 4.4. A *jump machine* is a Turing machine with an input tape and a special *jump state*. When the machine enters the jump state the head on the input tape is set nondeterministically on one of the cells carrying an input bit; we say that the machine *jumps to* the cell. When this occurs, no other head moves or writes and the state is changed to the starting state. Acceptance is defined as usual, that is, such a machine accepts an input if there exists a sequence of nondeterministic jump choices under which the machine accepts. An *injective jump machine* is defined similarly to a jump machine, but never jumps to a cell that has already been jumped to.

For a function $j : \{0,1\}^* \to \mathbb{N}$, we say that a jump machine (an injective jump machine) uses j *many* (injective) jumps if for every input x and every run on x, it enters the jump state at most $j(x)$ many times.

The idea is that a jump corresponds to a guess of a number in $[n]$ where n is the length of the input. Observe that one can compute in logarithmic space the number $m \in [n]$ of the cell it jumps to by moving the head to the left and stepwise increasing a counter.

LEMMA 4.5. *Let* (Q, κ) *be a parameterized problem. The following are equivalent.*

1. $(Q, \kappa) \in$ PATH.
2. *There exists a computable* $f : \mathbb{N} \to \mathbb{N}$ *and a jump machine* $\mathbb{A}$ *using* $(f \circ \kappa)$ *many jumps that accepts* Q *and is pl-space bounded with respect to* κ.

3. *There exists a computable $f : \mathbb{N} \to \mathbb{N}$ and an injective jump machine $\mathbb{A}$ using $(f \circ \kappa)$ many injective jumps that accepts Q and is pl-space bounded with respect to κ.*

The crucial implication here is the one from (3) to (1). It is proved by colour coding methods, more precisely, it relies on the following lemma (see [16, p.349]).

LEMMA 4.6. *For every sufficiently large n, it holds that for all $k \in \mathbb{N}$ and for every k-element subset X of $[n]$, there exists a prime $p < k^2 \log n$ and $q < p$ such that the function*

$$h_{p,q} : [n] \to \{0, \dots, k^2 - 1\} : h_{p,q}(m) := (q \cdot m \bmod p) \bmod k^2$$

is injective on X.

PROOF. (Lemma 4.5) (1) implies (2): assume (1) and choose $\mathbb{A}$ and f according Definition 4.1. Given an input x we simulate $\mathbb{A}$ by a jump machine $\mathbb{B}$ that makes use of an extra worktape. When $\mathbb{A}$ enters its guess state $\mathbb{B}$ moves its head on the extra worktape right and continues the simulation of $\mathbb{A}$ in state s_b where $b \in \{0, 1\}$ is the bit scanned by this head. In case the head scans a blank cell, $\mathbb{B}$ stores the number j of the cell its input head is scanning and then performs a jump, say to cell $m \in [|x|]$. It computes the binary code of m of length $\lceil \log(|x| + 1) \rceil$. It overwrites the content of the extra worktape by this code and sets its head on the first bit b of the code, moves the input head back to cell j and continues the simulation of $\mathbb{A}$ in state s_b. Then $\mathbb{B}$ makes at most $f(\kappa(x))$ many jumps.

(2) implies (3): let $\mathbb{A}$ and f accord (2). To get a machine according to (3) we intend to simply simulate $\mathbb{A}$ on an injective jump machine. This works provided $\mathbb{A}$ does not have accepting runs with two jumps to the same cell. To ensure this condition we replace $\mathbb{A}$ by the following machine $\mathbb{A}'$. Intuitively, if $\mathbb{A}$ jumps k times then $\mathbb{A}'$ jumps $2k$ times and accepts only if these $2k$ jumps encode pairs $(1, m_1), \dots, (2k, m_{2k})$; the simulation of the ith jump of $\mathbb{A}$ is done by jumping to the (m_{2i}, m_{2i+1})th cell. Details follow.

The machine $\mathbb{A}'$ on x first computes $k := f(\kappa(x))$: note $\kappa(x)$ can be computed in space $O(\log |x|)$ by our convention on parameterizations; then k can be computed from $\kappa(x)$ running some machine computing f on $\kappa(x)$ – this needs additional space which is effectively bounded in the parameter $\kappa(x)$.

Then $\mathbb{A}'$ checks that $2k \cdot \lceil \sqrt{n} \rceil \leq n$ where $n := |x|$. If this check fails, $\mathbb{A}'$ simulates some fixed decision procedure for Q (note that (2) implies that Q is decidable). Observe that in this case $k \geq \Omega(\sqrt{n})$, so the decision procedure runs in space effectively bounded in k and hence in the parameter. Otherwise $2k \cdot \lceil \sqrt{n} \rceil \leq n$ and $\mathbb{A}'$ simulates $\mathbb{A}$ as follows. Throughout the simulation it maintains a counter for jumps that initially is set to 0. It will be clear that this counter always stores a number $\leq 2k$.

When $\mathbb{A}$ jumps, $\mathbb{A}'$ jumps twice and computes the two numbers a, b of the cells it jumped to. It interprets a, b as encoding pairs $(i_a, m_a), (i_b, m_b) \in [2k] \times [\lceil \sqrt{n} \rceil]$. More precisely, $i_a := \lceil a / \lceil \sqrt{n} \rceil \rceil$ is the least i such that $i \cdot \lceil \sqrt{n} \rceil \geq a$ and $m_a := 1 + a - (i_a - 1) \cdot \lceil \sqrt{n} \rceil$; similarly for (i_b, m_b). If (i_a, m_a) or (i_b, m_b) is not in $[2k] \times [\lceil \sqrt{n} \rceil]$, then $\mathbb{A}'$ halts and rejects.

For i the value of the jump counter, $\mathbb{A}'$ checks that $i + 1 = i_a$ and that $i + 2 = i_b$. Then it computes $m := m_a \cdot \lceil \sqrt{n} \rceil + m_b$ and checks that $m \in [n]$. Then $\mathbb{A}'$ increases the jump counter by two, moves the input head to cell m, changes to the starting state and resumes the simulation of $\mathbb{A}$.

(3) implies (1): choose a machine $\mathbb{A}$ and a function f according (3) and define a machine $\mathbb{B}$ as follows. On x it first computes $k := f(\kappa(x))$ (within allowed space as seen above) and $n := |x|$. If $k \geq \log n$ it runs some fixed machine $\mathbb{Q}$ deciding Q and answers accordingly. Since $k \geq \log n$ this needs space effectively bounded in k and thus in the parameter. If otherwise $k < \log n$, then $\mathbb{B}$ simulates $\mathbb{A}$ as follows. During the simulation it maintains a set X containing at most k natural numbers all smaller k^2 – intuitively, this set contains fingerprints of the jumps sofar. Initially, $X = \emptyset$.

To begin, $\mathbb{B}$ guesses a pair (p, q) with $q < p < k^2 \log n$ and stores it. Note that this requires only $O(\log k + \log\log n) \leq O(\log\log n)$ nondeterministic bits and space. Then $\mathbb{B}$ starts simulating $\mathbb{A}$. When $\mathbb{A}$ jumps, $\mathbb{B}$ guesses $\lceil \log(n + 1) \rceil$ many bits encoding a number $m \in [n]$. It computes $f := h_{p,q}(m)$ and checks that $f \notin X$. Then it adds f to X, moves the input head to the mth input bit, changes to the starting state and continues the simulation of $\mathbb{A}$.

Obviously, if $\mathbb{A}$ jumps at most ℓ times, then $\mathbb{B}$ uses at most $O(\log\log n + \ell \log n)$ nondeterministic bits. To see that $\mathbb{B}$ runs in allowed space, observe that the "fingerprint" f can be computed in space $O(\log n)$: first $b := qm \bmod p$ can trivially be computed in space polynomial in $\log p$ and this is space $(\log\log n)^{O(1)} \leq O(\log n)$; second, $f = b \mod k^2$ can trivially be computed in space polynomial in $(\log k + \log b)$ and the space usage her is $(\log\log n)^{O(1)}$.

We show that $\mathbb{B}$ accepts x if and only if $x \in Q$. If $\mathbb{B}$ accepts x then either because $\mathbb{Q}$ accepts x (and then trivially $x \in Q$) or because $\mathbb{A}$ reaches an accepting state when it jumps to cells numbered $m_1, \dots, m_\ell$; note that the fingerprints of these cell numbers are pairwise different, and hence so are the numbers. This implies $x \in Q$. Conversely, if $x \in Q$, then there is an accepting run of $\mathbb{A}$ on x with $\ell \leq k$ jumps to pairwise different cells $m_1, \dots, m_\ell$. By Lemma 4.6 there exist $q < p < k^2 \log n$ such that $h_{p,q}$ is injective on $\{m_1, \dots, m_\ell\}$. Then $\mathbb{B}$ accepts when first guessing some such pair (p, q) and then strings encoding $m_1, \dots, m_\ell$. □

THEOREM 4.7. *Let $\mathcal{A}$ be a decidable class of structures of bounded arity and of bounded pathwidth. Then p-EMB$(\mathcal{A}) \in$* PATH.

PROOF. Choose a constant $w \in \mathbb{N}$ bounding the pathwidth of $\mathcal{A}$. We use a machine $\mathbb{A}$ with injective jumps to solve p-EMB$(\mathcal{A})$. The result will then follow from Lemma 4.5.

Given an instance $(\mathbf{A}, \mathbf{B})$ of p-EMB$(\mathcal{A})$ the machine first computes a width $\leq w$ path-decomposition $(\mathbf{P}_k, (X_i)_{i \in [k]})$ of $\mathbf{A}$ such that $X_i \subsetneq X_{i+1}$ or $X_{i+1} \subsetneq X_i$ for all $i \in [k-1]$; we further assume that no X_i is empty. This is done in space effectively bounded in the parameter $|\mathbf{A}|$ and, in particular, k is effectively bounded in $|\mathbf{A}|$.

It then computes inductively for each $i \in [k]$ a map h_i from X_i into B that is a partial homomorphism from $\mathbf{A}$ into $\mathbf{B}$. To start, the machine $\mathbb{A}$ jumps $|X_1|$ times to guess elements $b_1, \dots b_{|X_1|} \in B$. It checks that the function $h_1 : X_1 \to B$ that maps the ith element of X_1 to b_i defines a partial homomorphism from $\mathbf{A}$ into $\mathbf{B}$. Having computed h_i the machine computes h_{i+1} as follows. If $X_{i+1} \subsetneq X_i$, then $h_{i+1} := h_i \upharpoonright X_{i+1}$ is the restriction of h_i to X_{i+1}. Otherwise $X_{i+1} \supsetneq X_i$, say $X_{i+1} = X_i \cup \{a_1, \dots, a_d\}$; then $\mathbb{A}$ jumps d times to guess $b_1, \dots b_d \in B$ and checks that $h_{i+1} := (h_i \upharpoonright X_i) \cup \{(a_j, b_j) \mid j \in [d]\}$ is a partial homomorphism from $\mathbf{A}$ into $\mathbf{B}$. In the end, if no check fails, $\mathbb{A}$ halts accepting.

This procedure can be implemented in pl-space: the space to store the path decomposition is bounded in the parameter, and storing one h_i needs space roughly $w \cdot (\log |A| + \log |B|)$.

It is routine to check that $\mathbb{A}$ makes exactly $|A|$ many jumps, and that it accepts only if $\bigcup_i h_i$ is a homomorphism from $\mathbf{A}$ to $\mathbf{B}$. Since the machine has injective jumps it accepts in fact only if this homomorphism is an embedding. Conversely, it is obvious that the machine accepts if an embedding from $\mathbf{A}$ into $\mathbf{B}$ exists. □

PROOF. (Theorem 4.3) To see p-HOM$(\mathcal{P}^*) \in$ PATH, just consider the machine $\mathbb{A}$ described in the proof of Theorem 4.7 as a machine with jumps instead of as a machine with injective jumps.

To see that p-HOM$(\mathcal{P}^*)$ is hard for PATH under pl-reductions, let $(Q, \kappa) \in$ PATH and choose a Turing machine $\mathbb{A}$ with jumps according Lemma 4.5 (2) that accepts Q. We can assume that there are computable $f, g : \mathbb{N} \to \mathbb{N}$ such that $\mathbb{A}$ on $x \in \{0,1\}^*$ runs in space $O(g(\kappa(x)) + \log|x|)$ and makes on every run exactly $f(\kappa(x))$ many jumps.

Fix $x \in \{0,1\}^*$ and set $k := \kappa(x)$ and $n := |x|$. Let $\mathbb{A}_{det}$ be the deterministic Turing machine defined as $\mathbb{A}$ but with the jump state interpreted as a rejecting halting state. Observe that $\mathbb{A}_{det}$ (and $\mathbb{A}$) has at most $m := 2^{g(k)} \cdot n^c$ configurations where $c \in \mathbb{N}$ is a suitable constant. Let $c_1, \ldots, c_m$ be a list (possibly with repetitions) of all configurations of $\mathbb{A}_{det}$ on x whose state is the starting state. Assume that c_1 is the starting configuration of $\mathbb{A}_{det}$. For $i, j \in [m]$, say i *reaches* j if the computation of $\mathbb{A}_{det}$ started on c_i (with x on the input tape) reaches in at most m steps a configuration c with the jump state, and c_j is obtained from c by changing the jump state to the starting state and changing the position of the input head to some arbitrary cell storing an input bit. Further, call $i \in [m]$ *accepting* if $\mathbb{A}_{det}$ started on c_i accepts within at most m steps.

Consider the structure $\mathbf{B}_x$ given by

$$\begin{aligned} B_x &:= [f(k)+1] \times [m], \\ E^{\mathbf{B}_x} &:= \text{the symmetric closure of} \\ &\quad\ \{((i,j),(i+1,j')) \mid i \in [f(k)], j \text{ reaches } j'\}, \\ C_1^{\mathbf{B}_x} &:= \{(1,1)\}, \\ C_i^{\mathbf{B}_x} &:= \{i\} \times [m] \text{ for } 2 \le i \le f(k), \\ C_{f(k)+1}^{\mathbf{B}_x} &:= \{(f(k)+1, j) \mid j \text{ is accepting}\}. \end{aligned}$$

It is clear that there exists a homomorphism from $\mathbf{P}^*_{f(k)+1}$ to $\mathbf{B}_x$ if and only if $\mathbb{A}$ accepts x, that is, the map $x \mapsto (\mathbf{P}^*_{f(\kappa(x))+1}, \mathbf{B}_x)$ is a reduction from (Q, κ) to p-HOM$(\mathcal{P}^*)$. The new parameter $|\mathbf{P}^*_{f(\kappa(x))+1}|$ depends only on $\kappa(x)$. The reduction is implicitly pl-computable: first observe that the numbers $f(k)$ and m can be computed from x in pl-space. A counter for numbers up to m needs only space $O(g(k) + \log n)$. Hence one can tell whether or not i reaches j in pl-space simply by simulating $\mathbb{A}_{det}$ for at most m many steps. Similarly, this space is sufficient to tell whether or not a given $j \in [m]$ is accepting. □

The following result gives information about fundamental problems: the problems p-EMB$(\overrightarrow{\mathcal{P}})$, p-EMB$(\mathcal{C})$, and p-EMB$(\overrightarrow{\mathcal{C}})$ are the parameterized problems of determining if an input graph contains a simple directed k-path, a simple undirected k-cycle, and a simple directed k-cycle, respectively; these problems are denoted respectively by p-DIRPATH, p-CYCLE, and p-DIRCYCLE by Flum and Grohe [15].

THEOREM 4.8. *The following parameterized problems are complete for* PATH *under pl-reductions:*

p-st-PATH,
p-HOM$(\overrightarrow{\mathcal{P}})$, p-EMB$(\overrightarrow{\mathcal{P}})$,
p-HOM$(\mathcal{C})$, p-EMB$(\mathcal{C})$,
p-HOM$(\overrightarrow{\mathcal{C}})$, p-EMB$(\overrightarrow{\mathcal{C}})$.

PROOF. By Theorem 4.7 all embedding problems are contained in PATH. For the homomorphism problems and p-st-PATH the same argument works (see the proof of Theorem 4.3). We are thus left to prove hardness.

Recall Example 2.1. Corollary 3.10 implies that

$$p\text{-HOM}(\overrightarrow{\mathcal{P}}^*) \le_{\text{pl}} p\text{-EMB}(\overrightarrow{\mathcal{P}})$$

and also that

$$p\text{-HOM}(\overrightarrow{\mathcal{C}}^*) \le_{\text{pl}} p\text{-EMB}(\overrightarrow{\mathcal{C}}).$$

Since we trivially have p-HOM$(\mathcal{A}) \le_{\text{pl}} p$-HOM$(\mathcal{A}^*)$ for all classes $\mathcal{A}$, we conclude that p-HOM$(\overrightarrow{\mathcal{P}}) \le_{\text{pl}} p$-EMB$(\overrightarrow{\mathcal{P}})$ and also that p-HOM$(\overrightarrow{\mathcal{C}}) \le_{\text{pl}} p$-EMB$(\overrightarrow{\mathcal{C}})$. For $\mathcal{C}$ we similarly get

$$p\text{-HOM}(\mathcal{C}_{\text{odd}}) \le_{\text{pl}} p\text{-EMB}(\mathcal{C}_{\text{odd}})$$

where $\mathcal{C}_{\text{odd}}$ is the class of odd length cycles. By $\overrightarrow{\mathcal{C}}_{\text{odd}}$ we denote the class of odd length directed cycles.

It thus suffices to show that the problems

$$p\text{-HOM}(\overrightarrow{\mathcal{P}}), p\text{-HOM}(\overrightarrow{\mathcal{C}}), p\text{-HOM}(\mathcal{C}_{\text{odd}}), p\text{-}st\text{-PATH}$$

are PATH-hard. By Theorem 4.3, we know that p-HOM$(\mathcal{P}^*)$ is hard for PATH. We give the sequence of reductions

$$p\text{-HOM}(\mathcal{P}^*) \le_{\text{pl}} p\text{-HOM}(\overrightarrow{\mathcal{P}}) \le_{\text{pl}} p\text{-}st\text{-PATH} \le_{\text{pl}} p\text{-HOM}(\overrightarrow{\mathcal{C}}_{\text{odd}})$$

and then show the hardness of p-HOM$(\mathcal{C}_{\text{odd}})$.

p-HOM$(\mathcal{P}^*) \le_{\text{pl}} p$-HOM$(\overrightarrow{\mathcal{P}})$. Let $(\mathbf{P}^*_k, \mathbf{B})$ be an instance of p-HOM$(\mathcal{P}^*)$. The reduction produces the instance $(\overrightarrow{\mathbf{P}}_k, \mathbf{B}')$ where $\mathbf{B}'$ is the directed graph with vertices $B' := [k] \times B$ and edges

$$E^{\mathbf{B}'} := \{((i,b),(i+1,b')) \mid i \in [k-1], b \in C_i^{\mathbf{B}}, b' \in C_{i+1}^{\mathbf{B}}\}.$$

p-HOM$(\overrightarrow{\mathcal{P}}) \le_{\text{pl}} p$-$st$-PATH. Let $(\overrightarrow{\mathbf{P}}_k, \mathbf{G})$ be an instance of p-HOM$(\overrightarrow{\mathcal{P}})$. The reduction produces the instance $(\mathbf{G}', s, t, k+2)$ where $\mathbf{G}'$ has vertices $G' := \{s,t\} \cup ([k] \times G)$ and as edges the symmetric closure of

$$\begin{aligned} &\{((i,u),(i+1,v)) \mid i \in [k-1], (u,v) \in E^{\mathbf{G}}\} \\ &\cup (\{s\} \times ([1] \times G)) \cup (\{t\} \times ([k] \times G)). \end{aligned}$$

p-st-PATH $\le_{\text{pl}} p$-HOM$(\overrightarrow{\mathcal{C}}_{\text{odd}})$. Let $(\mathbf{G}, s, t, k)$ be an instance of the former problem; by the previous reduction, we may assume that it is a yes instance if and only if there is an s-t path of length exactly k. We can assume that k is odd (otherwise we take a new neighbor of the given s as our new s). Define the graph $\mathbf{G}'$ with vertices $([k] \times G)$ and edges as follows. When $i \in [k-1]$ and $(u,v) \in E^G$, there is an edge from (i,u) to $(i+1,v)$; also, there is an edge from (k,t) to $(1,s)$. Then $(\mathbf{G}, s, t, k) \mapsto (\overrightarrow{\mathbf{C}}_k, \mathbf{G}')$ is a reduction as desired.

Finally, we show the hardness of p-HOM$(\mathcal{C}_{\text{odd}})$. By appeal to Lemma 3.9, it suffices to demonstrate a reduction p-st-PATH $\le_{\text{pl}}$ p-HOM$(\mathcal{C}^*_{\text{odd}})$. Given an instance $(\mathbf{G}, s, t, k)$ of the former problem of the above form, we define $\mathbf{G}'$ as in the previous reduction. The produced instance is $(\mathbf{C}^*_k, \mathbf{G}'')$, where $\mathbf{G}''$ is the expansion of the symmetric closure of $\mathbf{G}'$ with $C_i^{\mathbf{G}''} = \{i\} \times G$. □

5. THE CLASS TREE

We give a machine characterization of the class of parameterized problems that are pl-reducible to p-HOM$(\mathcal{T}^*)$.

DEFINITION 5.1. The class TREE contains a parameterized problem (Q, κ) if there are a computable function $f : \mathbb{N} \to \mathbb{N}$ and an alternating Turing machine that accepts Q, is pl-space bounded with respect to κ, and uses $f(\kappa(x)) \cdot \log|x|$ nondeterministic bits and $f(\kappa(x))$ co-nondeterministic bits.

The following proposition is straightforward to verify.

PROPOSITION 5.2. *The complexity class* TREE *is closed under pl-reductions.*

DEFINITION 5.3. An *alternating Turing machine with jumps* is a Turing machine $\mathbb{A}$ using nondeterministic jumps and a universal guess state (see Preliminaries). It *accepts* an input $x \in \{0,1\}^*$ if its starting configuration on x is *accepting*: it is already explained what an accepting halting configuration is, and a non-halting configuration which is not in the universal guess state (resp. is in the universal guess state) is accepting if at least one (resp. both) of its successor configurations are accepting.

LEMMA 5.4. *Let (Q,κ) be a parameterized problem. The following are equivalent.*

1. $(Q,\kappa) \in$ TREE
2. *There exists a computable $f : \mathbb{N} \to \mathbb{N}$ and an alternating Turing machine $\mathbb{A}$ with $f \circ \kappa$ many jumps and $f \circ \kappa$ many co-nondeterministic bits that accepts Q and is pl-space bounded with respect to κ.*

PROOF. The implication from (1) to (2) can be seen analoguously to the corresponding implication in Lemma 4.5.

Conversely, let $\mathbb{A}$ and f accord (2). A machine $\mathbb{B}$ according (1) can be obtained by simulating a jump of $\mathbb{A}$ by existentially guessing a binary string encoding a number $m \in [n]$ and moving the input head to cell m. □

THEOREM 5.5. *p-*HOM*$(\mathcal{T}^*)$ is complete for* TREE *under pl-reductions.*

PROOF. (Theorem 5.5) We show that p-HOM$(\mathcal{T}^*) \in$ TREE. Consider the following alternating Turing machine. Given an instance $(\mathbf{T},\mathbf{B})$ of p-HOM$(\mathcal{T}^*)$, the machine chooses some $t \in T$ as a "root" and computes the directed "tree" $\mathbf{T}'$ with edges directed away from t. It existentially guesses ($O(\log|B|)$ bits encoding) a $b \in C_t^B$ and writes (t,b) on some tape. While the pair (t,b) written on the tape is such that t has children in $\mathbf{T}'$ the machine does the following: universally guess ($O(\log|T|)$ bits encoding) a child t' of t; existentially guess $b' \in B$; check that $(b,b') \in E^B$ and $b' \in C_{t'}^B$. The while loop is left rejecting if this check fails. If the machine leaves the while loop otherwise, it accepts.

The number of universal guesses is bounded by $O(|T| \cdot \log|T|)$. The number of existential guesses is bounded by $|T| \cdot \log|B|$. The machine uses space to store $\mathbf{T}'$ and at most two pairs in $T \times B$, so it is pl-space bounded.

To show p-HOM$(\mathcal{T}^*)$ is TREE-hard under pl-reductions, let the parameterized problem (Q,κ) be in TREE. Choose an alternating machine $\mathbb{A}$ with jumps according to Lemma 5.4 for (Q,κ). By adding some dummy jumps and dummy universal guesses we can assume that $\mathbb{A}$ on every x and every run on x first makes one universal guess, then one jump, then one universal guess and so on. We can further assume that $\mathbb{A}$ on x on every run on x makes exactly $f(\kappa(x))$ many jumps and exactly $f(\kappa(x))$ many universal guesses. Let $\mathbb{A}^0$ ($\mathbb{A}^1$) be the machine obtained from $\mathbb{A}$ by fixing the transition from a configuration with universal guess state to the first (second) successor configuration. Note $\mathbb{A}^0$ and $\mathbb{A}^1$ are Turing machines with jumps.

Let $x \in \{0,1\}^*, k := \kappa(x), n := |x|$. Recall the proof of Theorem 4.3. As there, let $c_1,\dots,c_m$ enumerate all configurations of $\mathbb{A}$ on x with the starting state; assume c_1 is the starting configuration. Let $\mathbb{A}^0_{det}$ and $\mathbb{A}^1_{det}$ be the deterministic machines obtained form $\mathbb{A}^0$ and $\mathbb{A}^1$ by interpreting the jump state as a rejecting halting state. For $i,j \in [m], b \in \{0,1\}$ we define what it means that i *b-reaches* j as in the proof of Theorem 4.3 with $\mathbb{A}^b_{det}$ in place of $\mathbb{A}_{det}$ there; call i *accepting* if $\mathbb{A}^0_{det}$ (equivalently $\mathbb{A}^1_{det}$) started on c_i accepts in at most m steps without entering the universal guess state.

Let $\mathbf{B}_k$ denote the full binary tree of height k with universe $\{0,1\}^{\leq k}$, the set of binary strings of length at most k; it has edges between x and $x0$ and between x and $x1$ for all $\{0,1\}^{\leq k-1}$. The reduction outputs $(\mathbf{B}^*_{f(k)+1},\mathbf{B})$ where $\mathbf{B}$ is defined as follows.

$$B := \{0,1\}^{\leq f(k)+1} \times [m],$$
$$E^{\mathbf{B}} := \text{the symmetric closure of}$$
$$\{((\sigma,j),(\sigma b,j')) \mid b \in \{0,1\}, \sigma \in \{0,1\}^{\leq f(k)}, j \text{ } b\text{-reaches } j'\},$$
$$C^{\mathbf{B}}_\lambda := \{(\lambda,1)\}, \text{ where } \lambda \text{ is the empty string},$$
$$C^{\mathbf{B}}_\sigma := \{\sigma\} \times [m], \text{ for } 1 \leq |\sigma| \leq f(k),$$
$$C^{\mathbf{B}}_\sigma := \{(\sigma,j) \mid j \text{ is accepting}\}, \text{ for } |\sigma| = f(k)+1.$$

It is not hard to see that $(\mathbf{B}^*_{f(k)+1},\mathbf{B})$ can be computed in pl-space (cf. Proof of Theorem 4.3). To see this indeed defines a reduction, first assume h is a homomorphism from $\mathbf{B}^*_{f(k)+1}$ to $\mathbf{B}$. As h preserves the unary relations C_σ, for every σ there is an $i_\sigma \in [m]$ such that $h(\sigma) = (\sigma, i_\sigma)$. It follows by induction on ℓ that for every $\sigma \in \{0,1\}^{f(k)+1-\ell}$ the configuration c_{i_σ} is accepting (Definition 5.3). But $i_\lambda = 1$, so $c_{i_\lambda} = c_1$ is the starting configuration and $\mathbb{A}$ accepts x.

Conversely, assume $\mathbb{A}$ accepts x. We define an accepting configuration c_σ for every $\sigma \in \{0,1\}^{\leq f(k)+1}$: c_λ is the starting configuration c_1. All other c_σs are going to be the result of a jump (are a successor of a configuration in the jump state). Assume c_σ is already defined. Then c_σ is the starting configuration or results from a jump. In both cases the machine $\mathbb{A}$ reaches from c_σ deterministically a universal guess state with two accepting successors c'_0, c'_1. For every $b \in \{0,1\}$, $\mathbb{A}$ reaches deterministically from c'_b either an accepting halting configuration or a configuration in the jump state. In the first case let $c_{\sigma b}$ be this accepting halting configuration and in the second let it be some accepting successor of the jump. For every σ choose $i_\sigma \in [m]$ such that $c_\sigma = c_{i_\sigma}$. Then $\sigma \mapsto (\sigma, i_\sigma)$ defines a homomorphism from $\mathbf{B}^*_{f(k)+1}$ to $\mathbf{B}$. □

THEOREM 5.6. *Let $\mathcal{A}$ be a decidable class of structures of bounded arity and bounded treewidth. Then p-*EMB*$(\mathcal{A}) \in$* TREE.

PROOF. Call a structure connected if its Gaifman graph is connected.

Claim 1. For every decidable class of structures $\mathcal{A}$ of bounded treewidth there exists a decidable class of connected structures $\mathcal{A}'$ of bounded treewidth such that p-EMB$(\mathcal{A}) \leq_{\text{pl}} p$-EMB$(\mathcal{A}')$.

Proof of Claim 1. Assume $\mathcal{A}$ has treewidth at most c. Fix a computable function that maps every $\mathbf{A} \in \mathcal{A}$ to a width $\leq c+1$ tree decomposition $(\mathbf{T},(X_t)_{t\in T})$ of $\mathbf{A}$ such that $|X_t| \geq 2$ for all $t \in T$, and $X_s \cap X_t \neq \emptyset$ for all $(s,t) \in E^{\mathbf{T}}$. Let $\mathbf{A}'$ be the expansion of $\mathbf{A}$ by interpreting a new binary relation symbol R by $\bigcup_{t\in T} X_t^2$. Then $(\mathbf{T},(X_t)_{t\in T})$ is also a tree decomposition of $\mathbf{A}'$ and $\mathbf{A}'$ is connected. Clearly, $\mathcal{A}' := \{\mathbf{A}' \mid \mathbf{A} \in \mathcal{A}\}$ is decidable. The map $(\mathbf{A},\mathbf{B}) \mapsto (\mathbf{A}',\mathbf{B}')$, where $\mathbf{B}'$ is the expansion of $\mathbf{B}$ interpreting R by B^2, is a pl-reduction from p-EMB$(\mathcal{A})$ to p-EMB$(\mathcal{A}')$. ⊣

Claim 2. p-EMB$(\mathcal{A}) \leq_{\text{pl}} p$-HOM$(\mathcal{A}^*)$ for every decidable class of connected structures $\mathcal{A}$.

Proof of Claim 2. Map an instance $(\mathbf{A},\mathbf{B})$ to $(\mathbf{A}^*,\mathbf{B}_*)$ where $\mathbf{B}_*$ is defined as follows. We assume that $B = [|B|]$ and $A = [|A|]$.

Let F be the set

$$\{g \circ h_{p,q} \mid g : \{0, \ldots, |A|^2 - 1\} \to A \text{ and } q < p < |A|^2 \log |B|\}.$$

Here, $h_{p,q} : [|B|] \to \{0, \ldots, |A|^2 - 1\}$ is the function from Lemma 4.6 (for $n := |B|$ and $k := |A|$). For $f \in F$, let $\mathbf{B}_f$ be the expansion of $\mathbf{B}$ that interprets every $C_a, a \in A$, by $f^{-1}(a) \subseteq B$ and define $\mathbf{B}_*$ as the disjoint union of the structures $\mathbf{B}_f$. We verify

$$(\mathbf{A}, \mathbf{B}) \in p\text{-EMB}(\mathcal{A}) \iff (\mathbf{A}^*, \mathbf{B}_*) \in p\text{-HOM}(\mathcal{A}^*).$$

Note that the sets $C_a^{\mathbf{B}_*}, a \in A$, are pairwise disjoint, so every homomorphism from $\mathbf{A}^*$ to $\mathbf{B}_*$ is an embedding. And because $\mathbf{A}^*$ is connected, it is an embedding into (the copy of) some $\mathbf{B}_f$, so it corresponds to an embedding from $\mathbf{A}$ into $\mathbf{B}$. Conversely, assume e is an embedding of $\mathbf{A}$ into $\mathbf{B}$. By Lemma 4.6 there are p, q with $q < p < |A|^2 \log |B|$ such that $h_{p,q}$ is injective on the image of e. Then there exists $g : \{0, \ldots, |A|^2 - 1\} \to A$ such that $g \circ h_{p,q} \circ e$ is the identity on A. Then $f := g \circ h_{p,q} \in F$ and e is an embedding of $\mathbf{A}^*$ into $\mathbf{B}_f$ and hence into $\mathbf{B}_*$. ⊣

To prove the theorem, let $\mathcal{A}$ be a decidable class of structures of bounded arity that has bounded treewidth. Choose $\mathcal{A}'$ according Claim 1. With Claim 2, then $p\text{-EMB}(\mathcal{A}) \leq_{\text{pl}} p\text{-HOM}((\mathcal{A}')^*)$. By the Classification Theorem, the latter problem pl-reduces to $p\text{-HOM}(\mathcal{T}^*)$, so is contained in TREE by Theorem 5.5. □

6. COUNTING CLASSIFICATION

In this section we present a classification of the counting problems corresponding to the problems $p\text{-HOM}(\mathcal{A})$.

Preliminaries on parameterized counting complexity

A machine with oracle $O \subseteq \{0,1\}^*$ has an extra write-only *oracle tape*; such a machine has a *query state* and the word y written on the oracle tape is the *query* of a configuration with this state; the successor state is obtained by erasing the oracle tape and moving to one of two distinguished states depending of whether the query is contained in the oracle O or not. The oracle tape is not accounted for in space bounds (as in [22]).

A *parameterized counting problem* is a pair (F, κ) of a function $F : \{0,1\}^* \to \mathbb{N}$ and a parameterization κ. To say it is in para-L, means that F is implicitly pl-computable with respect to κ. Equivalently one could say that there is a Turing machine with a write-only output tape that computes F and is pl-space bounded with respect to κ.

A *parsimonius fpt-reduction* from (F, κ) to another parameterized counting problem (F', κ') is a function $R : \{0,1\}^* \to \{0,1\}^*$ that is computable by an fpt-time bounded (with respect to κ) Turing machine such that $F = F' \circ R$ and $\kappa' \circ R \leq f \circ \kappa$ for some computable $f : \mathbb{N} \to \mathbb{N}$. In the logspace setting we define a *parsimonious pl-reduction* similarly demanding that the reduction is implicitly pl-computable instead of computable by a fpt-time bounded machine. We again write $(F, \kappa) \leq_{\text{pl}} (F', \kappa')$ if such a reduction exists. We say (F, κ) is *pl-Turing reducible* to (F', κ') and write $(F, \kappa) \leq_{\text{pl}}^T (F', \kappa')$ if there are a pl-space bounded (with respect to κ) Turing machine $\mathbb{A}$ with oracle to $\text{BITGRAPH}(F')$ that decides $\text{BITGRAPH}(F)$, and a computable f such that on every input $x \in \{0,1\}^*$ all queries $y \overset{?}{\in} \text{BITGRAPH}(F')$ of $\mathbb{A}$ on x have parameter $\kappa'(y) \leq f(\kappa(x))$. Here, we denote the parameterizations of $\text{BITGRAPH}(F)$ and $\text{BITGRAPH}(F')$ again by κ and κ' respectively.

Classification theorem

For a class of structures $\mathcal{A}$ consider the parameterized counting problem.

p-#HOM($\mathcal{A}$)	
Instance:	A pair of structures $(\mathbf{A}, \mathbf{B})$ where $\mathbf{A} \in \mathcal{A}$.
Parameter:	$\lvert\mathbf{A}\rvert$.
Problem:	Compute the number of homomorphisms from $\mathbf{A}$ to $\mathbf{B}$.

Dalmau and Jonsson [9] gave a classification of counting problems of this form, showing that for a class of structures $\mathcal{A}$ of bounded arity, the problem $p\text{-\#HOM}(\mathcal{A})$ is in FPT if $\mathcal{A}$ has bounded treewidth, and is #W[1]-complete otherwise. We give a fine classification of the case where $\mathcal{A}$ has bounded treewidth, analogous to our fine classification for the problem $p\text{-HOM}(\mathcal{A})$.

THEOREM 6.1 (COUNTING CLASSIFICATION). *Let $\mathcal{A}$ be a decidable class of structures having bounded arity and bounded treewidth.*

1. *If $\mathcal{A}$ has unbounded pathwidth, then*
$$p\text{-\#HOM}(\mathcal{A}) \leq_{\text{pl}} p\text{-\#HOM}(\mathcal{T}^*) \leq_{\text{pl}}^T p\text{-\#HOM}(\mathcal{A}).$$
2. *If $\mathcal{A}$ has bounded pathwidth and unbounded tree depth, then*
$$p\text{-\#HOM}(\mathcal{A}) \leq_{\text{pl}} p\text{-\#HOM}(\mathcal{P}^*) \leq_{\text{pl}}^T p\text{-\#HOM}(\mathcal{A}).$$
3. *If $\mathcal{A}$ has bounded tree depth, then $p\text{-\#HOM}(\mathcal{A})$ is in* para-L.

7. ACKNOWLEDGEMENTS

The first author was supported by the Spanish Project FORMALISM (TIN2007-66523), by the Basque Government Project S-PE12UN050(SAI12/219), and by the University of the Basque Country under grant UFI11/45.

The second author thanks the FWF (Austrian Science Fund) for its support through Project P 24654 N25.

8. REFERENCES

[1] S. Abiteboul, R. Hull, and V. Vianu. *Foundations of Databases*. Addison-Wesley, 1995.

[2] A. Blumensath and B. Courcelle. On the monadic second-order transduction hierarchy. *Logical Methods in Computer Science*, 6(2), 2010.

[3] H. Bodlaender. A partial k-arboretum of graphs with bounded treewidth. *Theoretical Computer Science*, 209:1–45, 1998.

[4] A. K. Chandra and P. M. Merlin. Optimal implementation of conjunctive queries in relational data bases. In *Proceddings of STOC'77*, pages 77–90, 1977.

[5] H. Chen and M. Grohe. Constraint satisfaction with succinctly specified relations. *Journal of Computer and System Sciences*, 76(8):847–860, 2010.

[6] Y. Chen, J. Flum, and M. Grohe. Bounded nondeterminism and alternation in parameterized complexity theory. *18th IEEE Conference on Computational Complexity*, pages 13–29, 2003.

[7] N. Creignou, S. Khanna, and M. Sudan. *Complexity Classification of Boolean Constraint Satisfaction Problems*. SIAM Monographs on Discrete Mathematics and Applications. Society for Industrial and Applied Mathematics, 2001.

[8] N. Creignou, P. G. Kolaitis, and H. Vollmer, editors. *Complexity of Constraints - An Overview of Current Research Themes*, volume 5250 of *Lecture Notes in Computer Science*. Springer, 2008.

[9] V. Dalmau and P. Jonsson. The complexity of counting homomorphisms seen from the other side. *Theoretical Computer Science*, 329:315–323, 2004.

[10] R. G. Downey and M. R. Fellows. *Parameterized Complexity*. Springer, 1999.

[11] M. Elberfeld, C. Stockhusen, and T. Tantau. On the space complexity of parameterized problems. *7th International Symposium of Parameterized and Exact Computation, Springer LNCS*, 7535:206–217, 2012.

[12] T. Feder and M. Y. Vardi. The computational structure of monotone monadic snp and constraint satisfaction: A study through datalog and group theory. *SIAM Journal on Computing*, 28(1):57–104, 1999.

[13] J. Flum, M. Frick, and Grohe. Query evaluation via tree-decompositions. *Journal of the ACM*, 49(6):716–752, 2002.

[14] J. Flum and M. Grohe. Describing parameterized complexity classes. *Information and Computation*, 187:291–319, 2003.

[15] J. Flum and M. Grohe. The parameterized complexity of counting problems. *SIAM Journal on Computing*, 33:892–922, 2006.

[16] J. Flum and M. Grohe. *Parameterized Complexity Theory*. Springer, 2006.

[17] G. Gottlob, N. Leone, and F. Scarcello. The complexity of acyclic conjunctive queries. *Journal of the ACM*, 48(3):431–498, 2001.

[18] G. Gottlob, N. Leone, and F. Scarcello. Hypertree decompositions and tractable queries. *J. Comput. Syst. Sci.*, 64(3):579–627, 2002.

[19] M. Grohe. The complexity of homomorphism and constraint satisfaction problems seen from the other side. *Journal of the ACM*, 54(1), 2007.

[20] M. Grohe, T. Schwentick, and L. Segoufin. When is the evaluation of conjunctive queries tractable? In *STOC 2001*, 2001.

[21] P. Kolaitis and M. Y. Vardi. Conjunctive-query containment and constraint satisfaction. *17th ACM Symposium on Principles of Database Systems*, 10:205–213, 1998, full version at: `http://www.cs.rice.edu/~vardi/papers`.

[22] R. E. Ladner and N. A. Lynch. Relativization of questions about log space computability. *Mathematical Systems Theory*, 10:19–32, 1976.

[23] D. Marx. Tractable hypergraph properties for constraint satisfaction and conjunctive queries. In *Proceedings of the 42nd ACM Symposium on Theory of Computing*, pages 735–744, 2010.

[24] J. Nešetřil and P. O. de Mendez. Tree depth, subgraph coloring, and homomorphism bounds. *European Journal of Combinatorics*, 27(6):1022–1041, 2006.

[25] C. Papadimitriou and M. Yannakakis. On the Complexity of Database Queries. *Journal of Computer and System Sciences*, 58(3):407–427, 1999.

[26] N. Schweikardt, T. Schwentick, and L. Segoufin. Database theory: Query languages. In M. J. Atallah and M. Blanton, editors, *Algorithms and Theory of Computation Handbook*, volume 2: Special Topics and Techniques, chapter 19. CRC Press, second edition, Nov 2009.

Authors Index